BENSON** and **HEDGES

Fifteenth Edition

September 1995 to September 1996

Editor **David Lemmon**

Foreword by **David Lloyd**

B L O O M S B U R Y

Editor's note

The aim of *Benson and Hedges Cricket Year* is to give the cricket enthusiast an opportunity to read through the happenings in the world of cricket from each October until the following September (the end of the England season). The structure of the book, as ever, offers a three-dimensional look at the year – in words, pictures and statistics. This year's foreword is written by England coach David Lloyd, and we are delighted, too, to include contributions from umpire Dickie Bird and from John Woodcock, former cricket correspondent of *The Times*, former editor of *Wisden Cricketers' Almanack* and President of the Cricket Writers' Club.

Form charts are included for first-class matches in England and Australia, and first-class averages are provided for cricketing nations throughout the world.

The symbol * indicates not out or wicket-keeper according to context.

Once more I would like to give thanks to those friend without whose work this book would not have been possibl The assistance and encouragement of Brian Croudy, ever source of comfort, are deeply appreciated. Les Hatto remains king of the Sunday League and the information an statistics he provides are invaluable. Sudhir Vaidya's splendid work on Indian cricket is indispensable to this publication and is a source of joy. The same must be said o Anthony Lalley's meticulous work on Australia and of th loving care that Ian Smith provides in supplying statistic from New Zealand. My thanks are due, too, to Charlie Wat o Australia, Andrew Samson of South Africa and Qama Ahmed of Pakistan. Victor Isaacs and Jo King, statistician supreme, are ever-ready to assist, and I am eternally grateful to county secretaries who are always willing and able t answer queries. The world of cricket has a wonderful bon of friendship.

David Lemmo

First published in 1996 by
Bloomsbury Publishing Plc
38 Soho Square
London W1V 5DF

A copy of the CIP entry for this book is available from the British Library

ISBN 0 7475 2761 X

10 9 8 7 6 5 4 3 2 1

Edited, designed and typeset by Book Creation Services, London

Printed by Bath Press, Great Britain

Contents

Sponsor's Message

Once again we have 'done the impossible' and brought you a complete record of the events of the summer within weeks of the final matches. All credit to David Lemmon who has worked so hard to ensure that *The Benson and Hedges Cricket Year* remains the first publication to do this and continues to be a 'must have' for all cricket enthusiasts. Of course, the English cricket season is only part of it – the book is first and foremost a record of world cricket and contains accounts of both international and national cricket competitions throughout the last 12 months. I am sure one of our contributors, David Lloyd, will be scanning the Zimbabwe and New Zealand sections to see which players have been successful in these countries this year.

I would like to offer a special welcome to the book's new publishers Bloomsbury. Not only have they kept the tradition of publishing so quickly after the end of the season, but they have added a few new touches to help us in our quest to keep *The Benson and Hedges Cricket Year* a lively, interesting and most importantly accurate account of cricket played throughout the world over the past 12 months. Bloomsbury have been instrumental in the new design of the book with its lighter, airier feel. The sheer volume of information means that the layout is vital to the book and with changes to the design and greater emphasis on photography we hope we have made the book still easier to use.

We have been fortunate this year that David Lloyd had agreed to write the foreword and share with us his view of his first season as Coach of the England team. While one man starts a new career another reaches the twilight of his. This season saw the last international cricket match to be umpired by Dickie Bird and he looks back on his last Test, played at his beloved Lord's, and talks to Rob Mills of the Yorkshire Post about his experiences over the years. Finally, one of the world's greatest cricket writers, John Woodcock, gives us his views on the current state of world cricket. Three great names indeed and we are grateful to them for their contributions.

I hope you will find the fifteenth edition of *The Benson and Hedges Cricket Year* an enjoyable and informative read and a stimulating way to relive some of the highlights of the summer.

Phil Tritton
Marketing Manager
Benson and Hedges

Comment

by David Lemmon

To trace cricket through the past twelve months is to discover a year of romance, although some followers of the game in England may find this hard to accept. It began, of course, in Pakistan where Sri Lanka, a young nation bleeding from internal conflict, beat one of the world's strongest cricketing countries in both a Test and one-day series. Not content with that, they won a tournament in Sharjah, reached the Benson and Hedges World Series Final in Australia and triumphed in the World Cup. Cinderella had come to the ball, and she seemed determined to stay there.

It was not just Sri Lanka's success that was refreshing, but the manner of that success. Their batting was a wonder, thrilling strokes, beautifully executed. Executed, if we are to believe what we read, as once executed by those ancients of the golden age which is always just out of sight.

People were excited by the Sri Lankan success, for it was attended by joy, and all said it was good for the game. But we could be forgiven if we doubted the sincerity of the applause that came from some quarters. There are first and second divisions in world cricket, and the fact remains that, although Sri Lanka have had Test status for 15 years, they have been granted only five Test matches against England during that that time and never a series. The reasons, we are led to believe, are commercial – better to play West Indies and Australia at every opportunity – but if finance becomes the only guiding force, then romance dies. To take the romance from cricket is to kill the game itself.

There was not much romance for England in South Africa and what there was was provided by Atherton and Russell in a brave rearguard action in Johannesburg. For the most part, South Africa was fraught with disaster and error as far as England were concerned, and the side that went to the World Cup was both ill-chosen and ill-prepared.

On the Indian sub-continent, the romance and honour belonged entirely to Sri Lanka who swept aside all opposition as easily as they had brushed aside the snubs offered them by Australia and West Indies. For England, there was humiliation rather than defeat and they exited the competition without grace or dignity, their going bemoaned by none. Jayasuriya

and his colleagues took their spectacular batting to other parts of the world; England returned home to another enquiry.

The enquiry, of course, did not seek the views of those who actually pay to watch the game, and its main conclusion was that England's Test players should be rested from county matches when selectors so desired. What perhaps should have been considered is a cutback in the number of international matches. There were 103 limited-over internationals played in 1995–96, and, even without the World Cup, 1996–97 promises more.

A pyramid is built from the bottom. To continue to gnaw away at the County Championship will destroy the very fabric on which the game is built. Promising players will only become good players if they are tested against the best at county level.

There is, too, another factor which is so often overlooked and that is that England is the only country in which the first-class game is totally professional, the only country which pays more than 360 men to play cricket. This is why England is able to attract and import cricketers like Caddick, Mullally, Hick and Curran, all of whom learned the game elsewhere. There is, of course, a responsibility in being paid to do a job – you have to turn up to work.

Most of the problems that have plagued English cricket over the past few years have been self-inflicted, and the 1996 season began with the knowledge that, for reasons off the field, the selectors would call upon neither the fastest bowler nor the best spinner available to them for the series against India and Pakistan. Off the field incidents seemed to dominate – books revealing all and a tedious and unnecessary court case. How refreshing then to turn to Christopher Martin-Jenkins' *World Cricketers* (OUP) which is a huge collection of biographies of cricketers and is full of wit, wisdom and charm, and how refreshing to learn of NBC Cricket Scholarships. The scheme, masterminded by Neil Burns, the former Somerset wicket-keeper, will take 18 county cricketers to South Africa for the winter.

The philosophy behind the scheme is that England does not have an adequate *off-season* structure to improve playing standards. The scholarships will help the English professional in the areas of competitive match play, personal fitness, skill and tactical awareness, training in vision and bio-mechanics and nutritional analysis among other things. It is an intense programme and it should be looked at seriously, for it has been well thought out and has much to offer.

Refreshing, too, was the appointment of David Lloyd as England coach. His methods do not please everyone – many feel that Elgar and Parry are best in the concert hall – but he is an optimist, one who believes that cricket should be enjoyed, and he has much to contribute to English cricket. Success in the Texaco Trophy series and in the Test series against India was some comfort after the gloom of what had gone before.

Defeats at the hands of Pakistan were disturbing in that they both involved dreadful batting collapses, but even in these defeats there was some comfort. Pakistan had begun the year in disarray, and they were the first to suffer at the hands of Sri Lanka. They underwent disappointment in the World Cup, but by the time they arrived in England they were an exciting unified side with a passionate desire to win. In twelve months they had been transformed from beast to beauty. They had their share of romance.

England still look for their share. Patience, commitment, an acceptance of the game as it is with all its demands, an end of whingeing, an approach to cricket which combines passion and joy: these could offer a way back to a leading place among the cricket nations of the world, but there are no easy opponents any more.

There were many glimmers of hope in 1996. There was Hussain's solidity, character and style in the hitherto troublesome number three spot. There was the exuberence of Irani and Ealham at international level, and the batting of Chris Adams of Derbyshire in the county game. Silverwood of Yorkshire is emerging as a bowler of talent, and Rollins of Essex is an outstanding wicket-keeper. Robert Croft of Glamorgan looked totally at ease in the England side, and John Crawley's century in The Oval Test was radiant, a confirmation that here was a batsman of rare quality. Knight hit two centuries in the Texaco matches against Pakistan, exciting affairs which were full of self-belief and sound temperament.

And in the county championship, there was a lad named Botham who took five wickets on the occasion of his first-class debut. His father was quite a good player. Perhaps English cricket's share of romance is not too far away.

Foreword

by David Lloyd

England in South Africa was always going to be tough and so it turned out to be. Centurion Park promised so much for England and then, typically, the rains came. South Africa would have had to play very well on that pitch to stay in the game. Come Johannesburg in December and everyone back home was proud to be British. What a wonderful achievement by Michael Atherton and Jack Russell to bat for seven hours together and save the game. Atherton's epic effort spanning nearly eleven hours at the crease plumbed the bowels of endurance, concentration and sheer bloody-mindedness for the cause. What a strong character he is and such a fighter in adversity. Anyone with any criticism of the lad are just anonymous outsiders who cannot possibly know him. It must have been dreadfully disappointing to lose the final Test after staying with the opposition on their own soil for so long.

Whether England suffered mentally from their exertions in the Test series no-one will ever know, but to lose so badly in the one-day matches really knocked the stuffing out of the team and we did appear to be at sixes and sevens. Seven One-Day Internationals in ten days is simply too much for our players and from a distance one could tell that we were suffering. It has to be remembered that England went to South Africa after a full domestic season *and* a Test series against West Indies. South Africa had their feet up throughout this period and planned specifically how to take on and beat England.

The World Cup gave England little comfort or satisfaction, but what a joy for Sri Lanka. They beat the lot and lifted the Trophy and succeeded in shutting up one or two of the big 'I ams' in world cricket.

Inevitably, our new season started under a cloud with yet another new structure. I was asked to be Coach of the England Team and accepted the position on a bench in Montego Bay, Jamaica. Not bad, I thought, for a start. The water was very still but if I was to be totally honest I knew there would be some turbulence ahead. My first priority, I thought, was to calm everything down and work out a plan that would take us forward.

India were our first opponents and whether they were cold or not doesn't really matter. We won the Texaco One-day Series in style with a team specific to the disciplines of one-day cricket – athletic players who can improvise and play with flair with the bat and bowl with guile and imagination. In the Cornhill Test Series England got on top in the first Test at Edgbaston and went one up in the three match series. India then had to play catch up and although Sachin Tendulkar played beautifully at times and Saurav Ganguly emerged as a class batsman, the captain, Mohammad Azharuddin, had a miserable time and has since relinquished the captaincy.

Enter Pakistan with a swagger. Everyone (English) was telling me it will be different against Pakistan; much stronger. Actually, I did not need telling. With world class bowlers in Wasim Akram, Waqar Younis and Mushtaq Ahmed we were going to have a severe examination. We lost the series 2–0 after squandering an opportunity in the second Test at Headingley through some indifferent bowling on the first morning. I know I run the risk of being accused of wingeing, so I will quote Pakistan's players, "Why do you always play us on pitches that we are suited to?" Enough said.

Balls were talked often. Regulations say that if you have more than one major manufacturer of cricket balls you must offer the choice to the opposition and if you disagree you toss up. 'Athers', bless him, lost every toss and therefore Pakistan used the Reader ball which is actually the one they would use in a home series. Doom and gloom set in and we braced ourselves for severe criticism. Our challenge is quite simply to find a bowling attack that will bowl the opposition out twice and, I personally, will treat this as a priority. It may take time and I would much prefer to get on with it minus the hysterical rhetoric that some are prone to indulge in. I hope it is not too much to ask.

We finished off the international season in great style and I was so pleased we came back strongly in the Texaco Series against Pakistan after the disappointment of losing the Cornhill Test Series. Again, the team was selected specifically with an eye to one-day cricket and included five players making their debuts: Nick Knight, Adam Hollioake, Graham Lloyd, Robert Croft and Dean Headley. The outfielding was excellent, Nick Knight played superbly at Edgbaston and Trent Bridge and Robert Croft never conceded more than 40 runs in any of the matches. I was thrilled to win the series 2–1 against a very classy, experienced Pakistan team.

In the Benson and Hedges Cup, Lancashire prospered again after nail biting of elbow length proportion in the knock-out rounds. I hear that smelling salts are the order of the day now at Old Trafford. The NatWest Trophy also went to Lancashire to give the Red Rose County a memorable one-day double. One or two myths were exploded in the final – win the toss, win the game by batting second and England bowlers cannot swing the ball. It's all balls you know!

Great relief at The Foster's Oval with Surrey taking the AXA Equity and Law Sunday League. Maybe they just need that one to trigger them off.

Leicestershire won the Britannic Assurance County Championship with a terrific team effort. James Whitaker was a superb leader. Phil Simmons was what every overseas player should be, an inspiration and an example, but those two would be quick to point out the contribution of the whole squad. Jack Birkenshaw is the coach and if commitment could be bottled he would be a millionaire.

What else took my fancy during the season? Well, the team gave it everything. Alan Mullally took 21 wickets in his first season in international cricket and we won one Test series and lost one. Our challenge has been identified and every player who has represented England this season will know this quote from Christopher Martin-Jenkins very well, England will need "sharply honed, dedicated and committed players; an aggressive approach; attacking bowling; superlative fielding; and flexible orthodox batting with an emphasis on the psychological and physical." The message is that you all need to be tough and ruthless just like the team who visit here next summer.

One last thought: can every county, hand on heart, say that their Championship pitches are suitable for Test match cricket and the preparation of Test match cricketers? As Alan Mullally would say, "I'll leave that one with you!"

An Interview with Dickie Bird, M.B.E.

Dickie Bird in Conversation with Rob Mills, Chief Sports Writer of the Yorkshire Post

It seemed somehow appropriate that Harold 'Dickie' Bird's last Test match should start with rain and poor light and, when the sun did shine, move on to a Mexican wave among the Lord's crowd which threatened to hold up play. After all, they have been blaming him for holding up cricket matches for years.

Less fitting, to some anyway, that his first and last acts to do with the cricket should be to raise the finger to signal lbw dismissals, one of them astonishingly in the first over to send Michael Atherton on his way. Bowlers throughout the world have been driven to distraction by Bird's belief in the basic truth that not many deliveries are actually hitting the stumps.

The second Cornhill Test between England and India was unusual in that it started in tears and ended in stalemate. Bird knew full well that he would cry but even he was surprised by the strength of the emotion expressed from the stands. By comparison some of the greatest players ever to have graced the game have departed with merely a whimper. It showed how beautifully daft we English can be when it comes to saying goodbye to figures regarded as national institutions.

He was in tears long before he set foot on green grass and as he made his way to the middle used one hand to deliver Harold Wilson-like waves to the assembled throng while using the other to mop away the waves of tears.

It was typical of Bird that, despite all the fuss, he should turn down the offer from his umpiring colleague to take the first over. He has been accused by some of being the archetypal 'professional Yorkshireman' whose northern roots and upbringing have accentuated his foibles and by others (like Ian Botham) of being plain 'barking mad' but he has never been one to shirk responsibility and has over the years earned the sometimes grudging but lasting respect of the finest players in the world.

There are two Dickie Birds. Off the cricket field he is a throwback to an age when men were expected to be hopeless around the house. In his cottage he has a new cooker and if the day should ever dawn when he ups sticks and moves to one of those flash pads just outside Lord's (not likely) he will still be able to advertise it as unused.

When at home he relies on his sister to do his washing, including his cricket gear, and if that devoted lady should turn up at his front door with his umpire's coats looking anything less than Persil-white she is likely to be asked to go away and try again.

When on duty he prefers where possible to avoid hotels and lodge with nice elderly ladies who over the years have come to know his habits, likes and dislikes and do not mind if he occasionally goes into a re-run of a run-out incident that has happened during that day's play.

On the field he is the absolute professional and although temperamentally he is not the embodiment of calm authority he is, in his own fussy and demonstrative way, in control.

It all started at his beloved Headingley in 1973 for the England-New Zealand match. "I had only been umpiring for three years then, so it was a fairly rapid rise to that level for me.

"I was there very early – always am – at about 7 a.m. and sat on my own at the back of the football stand surveying the scene and wondering what was in store. There was not another soul about. I might be wrong about this but I think the fee for an umpire then was £25; now we get £2,300. I have made a lot of money and travelled the world. Cricket has been very good to me.

"I have the 1997 season to do in county cricket and my marks are still good but there's no doubt in my mind that it was the right time to go as far as Tests are concerned. The pressures have increased but I have always thought you create your own pressure. The trick is to keep enjoying it.

"But I must admit that in recent years I have not found it so easy. It has become a young man's game and honestly feel that they will have to think about lowering the retirement age. Even for umpires there is no substitute for experience and we have to bring in younger men so that they can gain that vital know-how.

"Times have changed. I wrote off to become an umpire in 1969 and got straight on the list. That was because not many people wanted to be umpires then. It was regarded as a duff job with not much money in it.

"I have made some mistakes in the last 12 months or so and I find that hard to accept. I have set myself high standards and it disturbs me when I cannot maintain them, so I thought it was time to go."

The ease with which his eyes water at the very mention of the term MBE suggest that Bird is a real softie but throughout his career he has been a stern disciplinarian.

"I have never had any problems with players. I did an Australia-Pakistan series recently which everyone said might be troublesome but it was played in a great spirit. I want to tell you that Australia's captain, Mark Taylor, is a real credit to his profession. He will not tolerate dissent among his players and that makes life much easier.

"Then again in the early seventies the likes of the Chappells, Thomson and Walters for Australia had a bad press because they were reckoned to be big sledgers but I never had a moment's bother with them.

"My rule has always been to treat them as professional and they will accept your decisions. The one big change I have noticed is that the more money coming into the game the more you get mass appealing and you have to be strong enough to stand up to it and have the strength of your convictions. There is nothing in the laws to stop it.

"It's a source of great pride to me that players like Imran Khan, Ian Chappell, Sir Richard Hadlee and Allan Border have all said that there have been times when all hell was about to break out but I would come up with a funny story or something daft to say and the Test match would roll on peacefully.

"The key to it is to treat them as gentlemen and professional cricketers. When I played for Leicestershire at Old Trafford I recall sitting with the soccer playing Denis Law in the hotel and we got moaning on about officials. He said that he could not bring himself to respect a referee who treated him as a schoolboy and that has stuck with me.

"Mind you, I am not a soft touch and the players know that. I have never run away from the issue of intimidatory bowling. I won't have it. You still have to have authority but it's the way you get the message across that matters.

"When I am in the middle I develop a sort of tunnel vision. The identity of the bowler and the batsman does not matter at all. It could be anyone. I have seen some spectacular performances but it is only a while later that I realise that a particular batsman has been playing out of his skin."

Bird is, you will not be surprised to know, a firm traditionalist. The huge increase in the amount of one-day cricket has of course enhanced his earning power enormously but he remains convinced that we play too much of it and that there is nothing like Test match cricket.

He has, however, moved with the times in coming to welcome the advent of the third umpire and he believes that its scope will be increased to decide on whether slip catches have been taken.

"They want perfect decisions these days and no human being on his own can deliver. Run-out decisions were always my big strength and I take pride in the fact that I was getting the narrow ones right before the third umpire came in. But to be honest I am now going to the camera when I don't need to, because I have been told to do so.

"In England's last series in South Africa there was a controversy over a Graham Thorpe run-out. The umpire made a mistake in my view by allowing himself to be persuaded to go to camera after he had made his decision. He may have been wrong but he should have stuck to it."

He rates as the most exciting Test match in which he has stood the Pakistan-Australia clash in Karachi in 1995 when Mustaq Ahmed and Inzaman-ul-Haq figured in a huge last-wicket stand to give the home side an astonishing win.

"The 1975 World Cup final between Australia and the West Indies was memorable for some thrilling fielding at cover and mid-wicket by Viv Richards, who ran three of them out.

"The best Test innings? It was not even a 50, but John Edrich played the best one I have seen at Edgbaston in 1975 after Mike Denness had made the fatal mistake of putting the Aussies in. On the second day there was a thunderstorm. I think we got started at 3.45 and England were nine down at the close.

"That was a great knock on a rain-affected track but I believe that players should learn their trade on the best pitches possible, not on uncovered ones.

"My best world side would be: Barry Richards, Sunil Gavaskar, Viv Richards, Greg Chappell, Graeme Pollock, Garry Sobers, Alan Knott, Richard Hadlee, Dennis Lillee, Michael Holding and Derek Underwood with Lance Gibbs in reserve. But if I had to pick someone to bat for my life it would be Geoff Boycott – the best self-made player in history."

Prize for the top prankster goes to Allan Lamb. Bird did not find it all that funny at the time but at the end of one season, after a match at Old Trafford, Lamb had taken all four wheels off his car, jacked it up on bricks and left a note on the windscreen saying "All the best Dickie, have a nice journey". It has been.

John Woodcock, O.B.E.

The reasons why England are no longer a force to be reckoned with in Test cricket are not hard to find. They all have to do with bowling; but goodness knows how to change things round. To blame the county system is altogether too simplistic, while to maintain that the decline is cyclical, and that all will come right with time, becomes increasingly less convincing.

Except on palpably dodgy pitches, such as are found occasionally at Port of Spain and more often at Edgbaston, or on others that are specially tailored to suit the home side, the Test matches that matter most are won today, with any consistency, only by great fast bowling or wrist spin of the highest class, two departments in which England are ill-equipped. The days are gone, sadly, when we could rule the roost with finger spin and seam; they came to an end in the early 1980s with the advent of full and unconditional covering.

Australia have batted and fielded as keenly and well in the last three or four years as they are ever likely to, and no side is more uncompromisingly committed. Yet without Shane Warne, I doubt they would have won many more Test matches than England have. They might have lost fewer, but I am now talking about *winning* matches – not one-day internationals but Test matches, in which it is necessary to bowl sides out.

Pakistan beat Australia at Sydney, New Zealand at Christchurch and England at Lord's and The Oval between December 1995 and August 1996, because, in Wasim Akram, Waqar Younis and Mushtaq Ahmed, they own three modern-day match-winners. South Africa have made steady progress up the field since their return to Test cricket because Allan Donald, Brett Schultz (in Sri Lanka) and Shaun Pollock have provided the speed and hostility that spell victory.

West Indies, on the other hand, are not the power they were because their supply of awesomely fast bowlers has suddenly dried up. However many Brian Laras they may find, their great days will only return when the shoes of Michael Holding, Malcolm Marshall, Joel Garner, Andy Roberts, and of the ageing Courtney Walsh and Curtly Ambrose, are adequately filled. Without 'pace like fire' West Indies will remain a shadow of what we know they can be. For them it is speed or nothing; spin in the Caribbean has gone right out of fashion.

So far as England are concerned, it seems to me that unless we try doctoring our pitches or leaving them uncovered again, we are going to have to find some authentic fast bowlers or world-class leg spinners. And there is about as much chance of that as of the next half-dozen Christmases all being white. With due respect to B.J.T. Bosanquet and Rockley Wilson and 'Tich' Freeman and Ian Peebles and Greville Stevens and Tommy Mitchell and Walter Robins and Doug Wright and Eric Hollies and 'Dusty' Rhodes and Robin Hobbs and Tommy Greenough and Ian Salisbury and anyone else you care to mention, England never have had a Shane Warne or a Mushtaq Ahmed, a full-time, on-the-ball Test match conjuror; nor, on the pitches in this country and with all the one-day cricket that is played here, are they ever going to.

It is not quite the same story with the fast men. There was, after all, the bodyline tour of 1932–33, when Australia were battered to defeat by four fast bowlers, and in the 1950s Fred Trueman, Brian Statham, Frank Tyson and Peter Loader formed a quartet who would have been a force at any time. The fact remains, though, that in the last 30 years only John Snow and Bob Willis have fallen into the relevant category – plus, of course, the slower but famously irrepressible Ian Botham.

Remember, too, that India and Pakistan provide a vastly stiffer opposition today than they used to, anyway in England, and that Sri Lanka are no sort of a pushover. Until the 1960s Ceylon, as Sri Lanka then was, had to be content with a one-day picnic match against English and Australian touring sides putting in at Colombo, and very one-sided affairs they were. Today they would be profoundly disappointed not to make 400 against England at Lord's or The Oval.

So what can England do to revive their fortunes? It was never any good thinking that four-day county cricket would provide the panacea. It would have been far better to have kept the championship structure as it was but with the four-day game played on covered pitches and the three-day games with the covers off. The Academy when it comes, as no doubt it will, should tighten up the batting, but it is unlikely to do much for the bowling. Australia's, situated in Adelaide and considered a model of its kind, has yet to turn out an outstanding bowler (Warne failed to the last course), and it is bowlers that England so desperately need.

The Academy I would go for would not be at Shenley or Lord's; it would take the form of a winter school in South Africa, perhaps at Kimberley or Bloemfontein, where there would be fewer distractions than down at the Cape, and our young bowlers would have the sun on their backs, and the ball would bounce as it seldom does in England and the value of the pound would make it financially viable. In short, the conditions would be there to fire the imagination.

We are being held back by our climate to an extent that never happened when the pitches were uncovered. In one fell swoop, full covering took away the historical advantage that our environment gave us over visiting sides. As the Pakistanis said this year, they were delighted to be allowed to play on pitches at Kennington and Headingley that could just as well have been at Karachi or Hyderabad.

Finally, to the schools. It should be compulsory for every school in the country to have an artificial pitch, where it would be possible to stage an instant game of cricket in which the young could be introduced to the joys of batting and essentials of bowling. It would be the gallows, too, for the next council official found selling off a school playing field for some other purpose. If I sound an apostle of gloom, I am sorry. But we are in a bad way – and it all started when the covers went on. All our greatest cricketers – bowlers no less than batsmen – became the players they were not in spite of uncovered pitches but just as much because of them.

International Rankings

Last year we introduced a statistical assessment of countries' achievements at international level during the period covered by this book. The method employed is simple – two points are given for a win and one for a draw or abandonment. Points obtained are divided by points possible to arrive at a percentage.

One does not offer these rankings as an official verdict on country's standing in the cricket world. West Indies, for example, played only two Test matches, against New Zealand in the Caribbean in 1995–96, while Pakistan entertained Sri Lanka and visited Australia, New Zealand and England. Nevertheless, as one said last year, the figures offer some interesting comparisons.

There were 29 Test matches played in the period covered by this book as opposed to 38 last year. Last year 87 one-day internationals were played; this year there have been 103. Even as I write, *Cricket Year 1996–97* is beginning with a four-nation limited-over competition in Sri Lanka, and similar tournaments in Kenya and Sharjah will follow hot on its heels. There could be a danger of indigestion.

David Lemmon

Test Rankings

	P	W	L	D	Pts won	Pts poss	%
Australia	6	5	1	–	10	12	83.33
West Indies	2	1	–	4	3	4	75.00
South Africa	6	2	–	4	8	12	66.66
Pakistan	10	5	4	1	11	20	55.00
India	6	1	1	4	6	12	50.00
England	11	1	3	7	9	22	40.90
Sri Lanka	6	2	4	–	4	12	33.33
Zimbabwe	3	–	1	2	2	6	33.33
New Zealand	8	–	3	5	5	16	31.25

Limited-Over International Rankings

	P	W	L	Ab	Pts won	Pts poss	%
South Africa	20	18	2	–	36	40	90.00
Australia	17	12	5	–	24	34	70.58
Sri Lanka	28	17	11	–	34	56	60.71
Pakistan	27	13	14	–	26	54	48.14
New Zealand	23	11	12	–	22	46	47.82
West Indies	25	11	14	–	22	50	44.00
India	22	9	12	1	19	44	43.18
England	19	7	11	1	15	38	39.47
Zimbabwe	10	2	8	–	4	20	20.00
Kenya	5	1	4	–	2	10	20.00
United Arab Emirates	5	1	4	–	2	10	20.00
Holland	5	–	5	–	0	10	0.00

The matches between Sri Lanka and Australia, and Sri Lanka and West Indies which were awarded to Sri Lanka by default are not included in this analysis.

Benson and Hedges Cricket Year World XI 1996

Choosing a World XI to play Mars or Venus has long been a fascinating diversion. Such selections are invariably based on personal likes and dislikes and emotional responses. Some years ago, for example, I was taken to task by Mark Nicholas, then captain of Hampshire, for suggesting that any World XI could take the field without Malcolm Marshall among its number. Certainly, most followers of the game at that time would have seen Marshall as an automatic choice in any select eleven, but *Benson and Hedges Cricket Year* World XI is determined by certain criteria. The selections reflect performances during the period covered by this book. It ranges from Sri Lanka's visit to Pakistan in 1995 to the Texaco Trophy matches between England and Pakistan, and it takes into account achievements in Test and one-day international cricket as well as in domestic competitions.

The most notable omission from the World XI for 1996 is Brian Lara, and it is an omission that will cause raised eyebrows and, in some quarters, even consternation, yet Lara's form in 1995–96 does not warrant his inclusion. He played in only two Test matches during the period in which his highest score was 74. He appeared in only one other first-class game in the Caribbean, and he declined to play for West Indies in the World Series in Australia. He scored a century and a fifty in the World Cup, but he was no more successful in that competition than Hick, Aamir Sohail, Hudson and Ranatunga among others. One does not doubt his greatness, but, at the last, one can only judge by performance.

Michael Slater and Anil Kumble, members of last year's eleven, lost form towards the end of the year, while Wasim Akram, injured for much of the period, only found his best form in the later stages of the series in Australia and in England. Ijaz Ahmed, Saurav Ganguly and Saeed Anwar were three brilliant late-comers of whom, surely,

Above: Nathan Astle (Ross Kinnaird/Allsport)
Below: Sachin Tendulkar (Graham Chadwick/Allsport)
Left: Gary Kirsten (Graham Chadwick/Allsport)

Top left: Aravinda de Silva (Chris Cole/Allsport)
Top right: Steve Waugh (Joe Mann/Allsport)
Above: Mark Waugh (Joe Mann/Allsport)

more will be heard at the very highest level. Michael Atherton played one of the very greatest match-saving innings that Test cricket has known when he hit 185 not out in Johannesburg, and he played some equally courageous and defiant knocks of lesser stature against Pakistan, but his overall form during the year does not gain him recognition. McMillan and Inzamam-ul-Haq are unlucky and must be considered as excellent reserves.

The final choice was between Waqar Younis and Curtly Ambrose as the second fast bowler. Ambrose gains selection for his consistency over the year in all forms of cricket. Waqar recovered from serious injury and came to something like his full flowering on the tour of England. Having seen all the great fast bowlers since the Second World War, from Lindwall and Miller to West Indian quartets, I still assert that Waqar has no superior in the past half-century.

If one could make a tip for the future: John Crawley, whose century in The Oval Test was a boost for England supporters; and Stuart Law, captain of Queensland, a powerful force for Essex and a man destined to score many runs for Australia.

Gary Kirsten (South Africa)
The most consistent opening batsman in the world over the past twelve months. He averaged over 50 in the Test series against England and hit a century in the one-day series which followed. In the World Cup, he created a record with an innings of 188 not out, and his aggregate of 391 runs, average 78.20, was bettered by only three other batsmen in the tournament – Mark Waugh, Tendulkar and de Silva. Kirsten maintained his form as one of the world's outstanding fielders.

Nathan Astle (New Zealand)
This is the selection that will cause most surprise and debate, but Astle's record over the past twelve months demands that he be included. Chosen to play in the limited-over internationals in India, he hit 59 out of New Zealand's 145 in his second match. On returning to New Zealand, he became the first batsman to hit a century in a Shell Cup Final. He played in the one-day series against Pakistan and took 2 for 34 in the first game and 3 for 42 in the third; all his victims were prime batsmen. He made his Test debut against Zimbabwe and hit a century against that country in the first one-day international. A century against England in the World Cup (pictured here) followed. In the Caribbean, he hit centuries in each of the two Test matches against West Indies. Few batsmen have equalled that feat. England should take note of him for their forthcoming tour.

Top: Ian Healy (Adrian Murrell/Allsport)
Below: Shane Warne (Ben Radford/Allsport)

Sachin Tendulkar (India)
By his standards Sachin Tendulkar enjoyed only a moderate season in Indian domestic cricket. He averaged only 51.25. His 523 runs made him the most prolific scorer in the World, and he hit centuries in the one-day tournaments in Singapore and Sharjah. Two centuries in three Test matches in England confirmed the belief that he is the finest right-handed batsman in world cricket. Named as captain of India after that tour, he began 1996–97 with a century in a one-day international in Sri Lanka. He is 23 years old and has already scaled the cricketing heights. One can only surmise what the future holds.

Mark Waugh (Australia)
Mark Waugh hit centuries in the Test series against both Pakistan and Sri Lanka, scored a hundred in the World Series and was promoted to open the Australian innings in the World Cup. He established a record for the finals of that competition by hitting three centuries, and only Tendulkar bettered his aggregate of 484 runs. He was also capable of taking useful wickets with is medium pace or off-spin and is a magnificent fielder. The one criticism that could be levelled at him is that he has such talent, is so beautiful to watch that he frustrates one by giving his wicket away unnecessarily on occasions.

Aravinda de Silva (Sri Lanka)
Aravinda de Silva's century in the Benson and Hedges Cup Final of 1995 will for ever burn bright in the memory as will some of the spectacular innings he played for Kent during that season. He helped them win the Sunday League and then flew to Pakistan where he hit a century in the second Test match and played a significant part in Sri Lanka's historic series victory. He was also instrumental in helping his country to carry off the Champions' Trophy in Sharjah and in reaching the World Series Finals in Australia. His crowning glory came in the World Cup where he scored 448 runs, average 89.60, and hit two centuries, one of which, vitally, came in the final. In six matches, he was named Man of the Match on four occasions. He also took valuable wickets and was ever a joy to watch.

Steve Waugh (Australia)
Steve Waugh's batting exploits in Test cricket in the past twelve months have lifted him to number in the Coopers and Lybrand computer ratings. He hit three centuries in the series against Pakistan and Sri Lanka, and his record against Sri Lanka was 362 runs in three innings for once out. His bowling also met with considerable success, and he was an invaluable all-rounder in the World Cup. Once believed to be suspect against short-pitched fast bowling, he has eradicated technical problems and has now 11 Test centuries and more than 5000 Test runs to his credit.

Ian Healy (Australia)
Ian Healy has held a permanent place in the World XI since he was first included in 1991. His consistency over the past six years in keeping wicket to all types of bowling has been remarkable, and he and Richardson of South Africa have been the only keepers in recent years to be automatic choices for their respective countries. Healy has scored nearly 3000 runs in Test cricket and more than 1500 runs in limited-over internationals. He is now vice-captain of Australia and led the side to Sri Lanka when Taylor was injured.

Top left: Curtly Ambrose
Top right: Allan Donald (Graham Chadwick/Allsport)
Above: Mushtaq Ahmed (David Munden/Allsport)

Shane Warne (Australia)
Arguably the greatest bowler in world cricket with 207 wickets in 44 Tests, Shane Warne continued to dominate in 1995-96. He took 19 wickets at 10.42 runs each in three Tests against Pakistan and 12 wickets in three Tests against Sri Lanka, failing to shine in only the last match of that series. Carrying an injury, he was believed to be below his best in the World Cup but still took 12 wickets. Only Kumble and Waqar Younis took more. Warne is a bowler who wins matches, as Australia will testify.

Mushtaq Ahmed (Pakistan)
The rise and rise of Mushtaq Ahmed was one of the most pleasing and remarkable events of 1996. Mushtaq had been out of favour with the Pakistan selectors for some time but was recalled for the tour of Australia. He was brought into the Test side for the second match of the series and took five wickets in a Test innings for the first time. He captured four in the second innings, and this was followed by nine wickets in the third Test in which he bowled Pakistan to victory. He did even better in New Zealand where he claimed 10 wickets in the Test. In England, he was Man of the Series and bowled magnificently at Lord's and The Oval, where he was instrumental in bringing about two astonishing victories.

Curtly Ambrose (West Indies)
One cannot help but feel that Curtly Ambrose's great career is nearing its close, yet he still maintains high standards. He was West Indies' leading bowler in the two-Test series against New Zealand, and he was behind only Donald and Strang in the World Cup bowling averages. Returning to Northamptonshire, he helped the county to the Benson and Hedges Cup Final and remained among the most feared and successful of bowlers in first-class cricket.

Allan Donald (South Africa)
For long recognised as one of the world's great fast bowlers, Donald became a Test-match winner in 1995–96. He savaged Zimbabwe in Harare with 11 wickets in the match and proceeded to devastate England with 19 wickets in the series. His haul included 5 for 46 and 2 for 49 in the final Test which South Africa won to clinch the series. He was equally effective in the one-day series, and he finished top of the bowling averages in the World Cup.

South Africa

South Africa's triumphs in the Rugby World Cup and in the African Nations' Soccer Cup seemed to suggest to the romantics that the South African cricketers would complete a hat-trick by lifting the World Cup on the Indian sub-continent in March. Certainly no side prepared more assiduously, nor had more experience of limited-over cricket, which is by far the most popular form of the game in the Republic.

Jacques Kallis was recalled from Australia where he was touring with Western Province in order to play for South Africa 'A' against Zimbabwe 'A'. Kallis is a player of immense talent and won his first Test cap during the series with England. (David Munden/Sportsline)

The 1995–96 season began with a short visit from a Zimbabwe 'A' side, a tour that was treated seriously enough for Jacques Kallis to be recalled from Australia where he was on tour with Western Province to play for South Africa 'A' against the Zimbabweans. The South African national side would follow Zimbabwe back to Harare where they would play one Test match and two one-day internationals, preparing them for the five-match Test series and seven limited-over internationals against England. This, it was believed, would put them in top form for the World Cup, for that, above all else, was their priority.

Under the guidance of Bob Woolmer and his team of advisers and assistants, South Africa are a formidable combination. Cronje has proved an inspiring and intelligent leader, and as a fielding side South Africa has no superior. If the batting still lacks the flair and excitement that a McEwan or a Procter would have brought, it is not alone in the world in that. The batting is now reliable, and is not without attraction. Players are batting to their full potential, and they are aware of what they are capable, and what they are not capable, of doing, but, like all good cricketers, they are for ever learning.

In Richardson, South Africa have a most efficient wicket-keeper and a more than useful batsman who is able to fill any place in the order. The fast bowling is strong with Donald, de Villiers and Schultz proven at the highest level. Only in the spin department could the side said to be weak, but as they were to be confronted by an England side with, arguably, the weakest spin attack in living memory, this issue was not likely to decide the series – or so it was thought.

Every season brings surprises, and South African cricket was bubbling with excitement and expectation – England were on their way.

Zimbabwe 'A' Tour

21, 22, 23 and 24 September 1995
at Wanderers, Johannesburg
Zimbabwe 'A' 264 (A.H. Omarshah 85, G.K. Bruk-Jackson 65, G.C. Yates 5 for 69) and 312 (M.H. Dekker 162 not out, C.E. Eksteen 4 for 107)
Transvaal 509 (N.D. McKenzie 120, G.A Pollock 95, N. Pothas 78, C.E. Eksteen 58, P.A. Strang 5 for 109) and 70 for 1
Transvaal won by 9 wickets

A Zimbabwe side rich in experience was crushed by a much less experienced Transvaal eleven. Led by Ken Rutherford, the former New Zealand skipper, the Castle Cup team owed much to 'Bertie' McKenzie, who hit a maiden first-class century, and Graeme Pollock, left-handed son of a famous left-handed father, who shared a fifth wicket stand of 202. Mark Dekker faced 351 balls and carried his bat throughout Zimbabwe's second innings for what was by far the highest score of his career, but he received little support.

26 September 1995
at PAM Brink Stadium, Springs
Zimbabwe 'A' 225 for 9 (G.C. Martin 64 not out)
Easterns 169 for 9 (W.R. Radford 73)
Zimbabwe 'A' won by 56 runs

Former Eastern Transvaal, now the Eastern Cricket Union, entertained the tourists in a 45-over day/night game and fell to the hitting of Gary Martin at number eight.

28, 29 and 30 September 1995
at St George's Park, Port Elizabeth
Zimbabwe 'A' 112 (B.N. Schultz 5 for 35, D. Rossouw 4 for 35) and 144 (S. Abrahams 5 for 49)
Eastern Province 313 (K.C. Wessels 110, D.J. Callaghan 78, H.R. Olonga 4 for 57)
Eastern Province won by an innings and 57 runs

Anxious to prove his fitness before the arrival of the England party, Brett Schultz devastated Zimbabwe with match figures of 8 for 66. Shafiek Abrahams' off-breaks brought him the first five-wicket haul of his career, and Kepler Wessels hit the 59th hundred of his career in a totally one-sided match.

3 October 1995
at St George's Park, Port Elizabeth
Invitation XI 166 for 7 (C.C. Bradfield 66)
Zimbabwe 'A' 167 for 9
Zimbabwe 'A' won by 1 wicket

Zimbabwe won this 45-over match off the penultimate ball.

6, 7, 8 and 9 October 1995
At Kingsmead, Durban
Zimbabwe 'A' 221 (G.J. Whittall 62, S.M. Pollock 5 for 65) and 256 for 8 (C.N. Evans 74, W.R. James 64)
South Africa 'A' 310 (S.M. Pollock 74 not out, J.H. Kallis 57, S.D. Jack 55, N.C. Johnson 55, P.A. Strang 5 for 69)
Match drawn

Zimbabwe's tour culminated in the match against South Africa 'A'. They were saved at the last by Evans and James who added 139 after five second innings wickets had gone for 60. Most impressive in a smart looking South African side was Shaun Pollock who shared an eighth wicket stand of 108 with Jack and had match figures of 8 for 113. The leg-spinner Paul Strang was again the best of the Zimbabwe bowlers and is maturing rapidly into a cricketer of high quality.

The England Tour

With Ray Illingworth in supreme command, and with coaches John Edrich and Peter Lever initially accompanying the party, England arrived in South Africa for their first official tour for 31 years. The reception was enthusiastic and characteristically cordial. The hospitality was warm, but, unquestionably, South Africa were determined to win and to continue the encouragement and development of cricket in the country. England began the playing side of the trip in a leisurely manner, but storm clouds were soon to threaten.

24 October 1995
at Randjesfontein
England XI 242 for 5 dec. (A.J. Stewart 74)
Nicky Oppenheimer's XI 130 (R.K. Illingworth 5 for 48)
England XI won by 112 runs

In what has become the traditional setting for the first match of a tour of South Africa, the Republic's answer to Arundel, England enjoyed a pleasant work-out. The batsmen all scored a few runs, and once Malcolm had bowled Mandy Yachad, now retired from first-class cricket, the spinners took over to give the tourists a comfortable win.

25 October 1995
at PAM Brink Stadium, Springs
Easterns 261 for 5 (W.R. Radford 92, C. Grainger 58 not out)
England XI 264 for 5 (M.R. Ramprakash 89 not out)
England XI won by 5 wickets

England had a somewhat difficult time in this 50-over encounter. Wayne Radford and his opening partner Mitchley put on 115, and Chad Grainger maintained the momentum. England were 165 for 5 before Ramprakash and Cork took them to victory off the last ball of the 49th over. Ramprakash's 89 came off 93 balls.

The England tour begins, and Wayne Radford hits 92 and shares an opening partnership of 115 with Mitchley for Easterns at Springs. (Paul Sturgess/ Sportsline)

27, 28, 29 and 30 October 1995
at Soweto Oval
England XI 332 (A.J. Stewart 94, J.P. Crawley 85, M.A. Atherton 59, M.J.G. Davis 4 for 68) and 282 for 5 dec. (A.J. Stewart 101 not out, G.A. Hick 55)
South African Invitation XI 210 (W.J. Cronje 56, R.K. Illingworth 6 for 76) and 25 for 1
Match drawn

The first first-class match to be played at the new Soweto Oval or, indeed, the first to be played in any black township, attracted great attention. President Nelson Mandela arrived on the first morning and greeted the players. This was not the only significant event on the opening day. Atherton and Stewart shared an opening stand of 163 in 50 overs, and Meyrick Pringle, one of four Test players in the Invitation XI, dismissed Russell, Watkinson and Ilott with successive deliveries to complete the first hat-trick of his career and to put the seal on an historic and memorable day.

Crawley batted with great patience in an attempt to confirm a place in the Test side, but he was out on the second morning when a century was looming. Once again it was the spinners who did most damage for England as the Invitation XI's middle order collapsed, but it must be admitted that the pitch was below standard.

When England batted a second time Atherton retired with a hamstring injury, Robin Smith was caught behind for 0 and Alec Stewart hit the first century of the tour.

The first first-class match to be played in Soweto was attended by President Nelson Mandela. He greets Devon Malcolm who began the tour as a hero and ended in dispute with the management. (Graham Chadwick/Allsport)

The surprise of the season, 'a frog in a blender', Paul Adams troubled England when they first met him in Kimberley and was to torment them later in the fourth and fifth Test matches. Adams enjoyed outstanding success in his first season in first-class cricket. (Graham Chadwick/Allsport)

Overnight rain prevented any play on the fourth day, but that did not stop England from creating news. Devon Malcolm had been taken from the match in Soweto for special net practice. The following day, there was an explosion in the press when Malcolm was strongly criticised by both Ray Illingworth and bowling coach Peter Lever. Lever was quoted as saying that Malcolm had just one asset – pace – and that apart from this he was a 'nonentity in cricketing terms'.

Ray Illingworth's tendency towards public executions is one of the blights on the game, and that Malcolm should have been subjected to such humiliation was both unforgivable and disgraceful. If those whose job it was to select the England party were concerned about the attitude, action or any other facet of Malcolm's game, then why was he chosen? Malcolm is fast, wild and often erratic, but once a series he is capable of winning a Test match as he proved at The Oval in 1994 and as he nearly proved in Trinidad in 1990 when he took three prime wickets in four balls.

England's problems had begun early. Whatever the players were to prove, the administration had given strong evidence that it was weak in man-management.

2, 3, 4 and 5 November 1995
at Buffalo Park, East London
England XI 351 (J.P. Crawley 108, M.R. Ramprakash 70, R.C. Russell 64, B.C. Fourie 4 for 75)
Border 166 (P.N. Kirsten 53, D.G. Cork 5 for 48) and 132 (D.J. Cullinan 55, M.C. Ilott 5 for 36)
England XI won by an innings and 53 runs

While the amount of practice before the first Test was limited and every minute in the middle had to be grabbed, England had also to cultivate the habit of winning, and this they did in East London. Another patient innings from Crawley brought a century, but the competition for the number three spot remained heated as Ramprakash hit an attractive 70. Worryingly, Robin Smith again failed to score. The second day was lost to rain, and extensions were made to the last two days in compensation, but the local people showed little interest and attendances were very poor. Cork, 8 for 81 in the match, Gough and Ilott all bowled well, but Malcolm was sidelined with a knee problem.

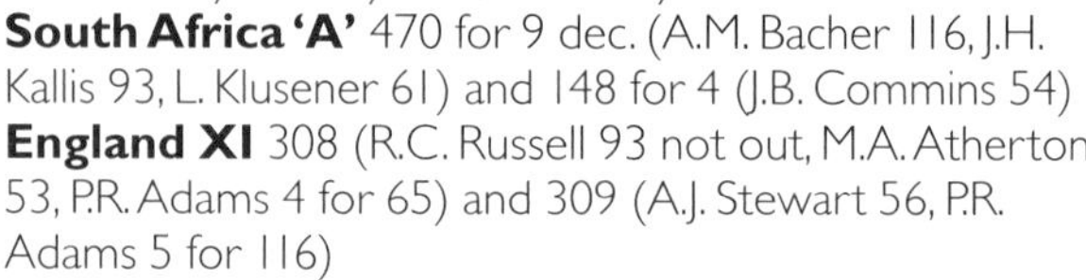

9, 10, 11 and 12 November 1995
at Kimberley Country Club, Kimberley
South Africa 'A' 470 for 9 dec. (A.M. Bacher 116, J.H. Kallis 93, L. Klusener 61) and 148 for 4 (J.B. Commins 54)
England XI 308 (R.C. Russell 93 not out, M.A. Atherton 53, P.R. Adams 4 for 65) and 309 (A.J. Stewart 56, P.R. Adams 5 for 116)
South Africa 'A' won by 6 wickets

England's final match before the first Test was a disaster for them, but not for the South Africans. On the first day, the home side scored 325 for 5, with Jacques Kallis, on the verge of the national side, and Adam Bacher, nephew of the managing director of the Union Cricket Board of South Africa, scoring 181 for the second wicket. Malcolm was wasteful, Watkinson ineffective, and Fraser and Gough the pick of the bowlers. With the South African tail giving further substance to the innings, England went in to bat on the second day against a total of 470, which was hardly surprising on a flat pitch of even bounce. The surprise was to come on the second evening when Paul Adams, an unorthodox left-arm spinner, was brought on to bowl. Having played his first senior first-class cricket only a week earlier, Adams, a Cape-Coloured teenager, demonstrated why he had been pitched into this important match by having Stewart bowled as he pushed forward to a ball which turned sharply, having Thorpe taken at silly point and enticing Hick to offer a return catch. Adams bowls the left-arm googly as his stock ball, but he uses the chinaman to good effect. His action sees him either looking at the sky or the ground, and he has memorably been likened to 'a frog in a blender'. Suddenly, England were posed with an unexpected and potent threat.

In spite of Russell's rearguard action, England had to follow on, and Adams took five wickets in the second innings to complement his four in the first. Robin Smith showed resilience, but the omens on the eve of the Test series pointed very much in favour of South Africa.

Above: Adam Bacher, nephew of the managing director of the UCB of South Africa, raises his bat to acknowledge the applause for his century for South Africa 'A' against the England tourists at Kinberley. (Graham Chadwick/Allsport)

Below: Ramprakash is caught by Richardson off Donald in the first Test match, the beginning of a wretched time for the Middlesex batsman. (Patrick Eagar)

First Test Match

South Africa v. England *at Verwoerdburg*

Ramprakash claimed the number three spot, Robin Smith held his place and Shaun Pollock, son of Peter, the former Test bowler and now chairman of selectors, made his international debut for South Africa. Cronje won the toss and asked England to bat. South Africa had resisted the temptation to call up Adams after his success in the South African shadow eleven.

Although the conditions did not justify Cronje's decision to bowl first, the capture of three early wickets did. Stewart pulled lazily at Schultz and was spectacularly caught by Matthews at square-leg leaping high to his right. Ramprakash again found Test cricket a chilling contrast to the county game. He froze and speared at a ball outside the off stump which he could have ignored and gave Richardson a straightforward catch. Thorpe's dismissal followed the same pattern although he was victim of Pollock's admirable line and movement. Atherton, typically, had shored up one end, and he now found a resolute partner in Hick who played with confidence, calm and total command. The pair added 142 and survived much hostility with equable temperament before Atherton, just before the close, lobbed to gully off the top edge. There was still time for Hick to complete a very fine century, and England closed on 221 for 4.

Graeme Hick pulls a ball to the boundary during his magnificent 141 in the rain-ruined first Test match.
(Clive Mason/Allsport)

Hick was finally out for 141, an innings which remarkably included 25 fours. He faced 278 balls and was at the crease for more than six and a half hours. Smith and Russell both supported him splendidly, and Russell's early batting form on the tour was heartening for England.

England were even dreaming of victory, so high had their spirits been lifted, but the rains came. A violent storm halted play on the second afternoon, and it never restarted.

23, 24 and 25 November 1995
at Springbok Park, Bloemfontein
England XI 316 for 4 dec. (G.P. Thorpe 131 not out, A.J. Stewart 110) and 239 for 4 dec. (J.P. Crawley 90, D.G. Cork 67 not out)
Orange Free State 245 for 9 dec. (D. Jordaan 52) and 110 for 3 (G.F. Craven 60 not out)
Match Drawn

16 November 1995
at Springbok Park, Bloemfontein
Orange Free State 201 for 8 (D. Jordaan 54)
England XI 202 for 3 (A.J. Stewart 81, M.A. Atherton 60)
England XI won by 7 wickets

England played two matches in between the first and second Tests, the first a three-day game that ended in lethargic fashion, and a 50-over match that they won with nine overs to spare. The Surrey pair, Thorpe and Stewart, hit centuries and shared a stand of 141 after two wickets had gone for 45 on the first day, but the game never came alive although Crawley again batted with much patience in trying to win a place in the Test side

First Test Match – South Africa v. England

16, 17, 18, 19 and 20 November 1995 at Centurion Park, Verwoerdburg

England

	First Innings	
M.A. Atherton (Capt)	c Donald, b Polloack	78
A.J. Stewart	c Matthews, b Schultz	6
M.R. Ramprakash	c Richardson, b Donald	9
G.P. Thorpe	c Richardson, b Pollock	13
G.A. Hick	lbw, b Pollock	141
R.A. Smith	b McMillan	43
*R.C. Russell	not out	50
D.G. Cork	c Matthews, b McMillan	13
D. Gough	b McMillan	0
R.K. Illingworth	b Donald	0
A.R.C. Fraser	not out	4
	lb 16, w 1, nb 7	24
	(for 9 wickets)	381

	O	M	R	W
Donald	33	10	92	2
Schultz	16	5	47	1
Matthews	30	13	63	–
Pollock	29	7	98	3
McMillan	25	10	50	3
Cronje	8	5	14	–
Kirsten	2	1	1	–

Fall of Wickets
1–**14**, 2–**36**, 3–**64**, 4–**206**, 5–**290**, 6–**320**, 7–**350**, 8–**358**, 9–**359**

South Africa

A.C. Hudson
G. Kirsten
W.J. Cronje (Capt)
D.J. Cullinan
J.N. Rhodes
B.M. McMillan
*D.J. Richardson
S.M. Pollock
C.R. Matthews
A.A. Donald
B.N. Schultz

Umpires: C.J. Mitchley & S. Venkataraghavan

Match drawn

Second Test Match

South Africa *v.* England *at Johannesburg*

South Africa made two changes from the side that had played in the first Test match. Schultz, whose lack of fitness had been the subject of much debate after the first game, was replaced by Pringle, while left-arm spinner Eksteen came in for Matthews to give the attack a more balanced look. England made one change, Malcolm regaining his place at the expense of the injured Illingworth so that the England attack had a less-balanced look.

Atherton won the toss and followed the example set in the first Test by asking the opposition to bat. In spite of the fact that Hudson was caught in the gully off bat and pad in Cork's fourth over, Atherton's decision was hard to understand. Cronje batted freely until he followed a good outswinger from Cork, but, in the afternoon session, Kirsten and Cullinan scored 110 runs without looking as if they would be parted. They were separated half an hour after tea when Cullinan pushed forward rather limply at a Hick floater and was caught behind.

Gary Kirsten reached a maiden Test century, with an innings of great determination in which he offered no chance nor any hint of human weakness. He lost Rhodes quickly, however, caught at the wicket off the admirable Cork, and then he himself succumbed to Malcolm who took two wickets in four balls with the second new ball, Richardson offering Russell the easiest of his five catches of the day. This spell by Malcolm brought about a dramatic change in the game, and when Cork trapped McMillan leg before in the last over of the day England had tilted the match away from South Africa, who were 278 for 7.

If South Africa had their hero in Kirsten, who batted for 353 minutes, faced 241 balls and hit 16 fours, England had a hero to match in Dominic Cork. He bowled five spells during the day and captured four richly deserved wickets. He never flagged, bowled his outswinger splendidly and maintained both accuracy and aggression over a gruelling day.

One of the great match-saving innings in Test history – Mike Atherton 185 not out in Johannesburg. (Clive Mason/Allsport)

Twice in the second Test match, Gary Kirsten was caught behind off Devon Malcolm. In the first innings he made 110; in the second, here, he was out for 1. Russell created a Test record with 11 catches in the match. (Patrick Eagar)

On the second day, Pollock displayed an ease and energy with the bat that extended the South African innings beyond a point which England had hoped for and expected. Cork deservedly finished with five wickets, and Russell claimed his sixth catch of the innings. The game, nevertheless, moved most firmly in favour of South Africa.

In the third over of England's innings, Atherton shouldered arms to a ball from Donald which clipped his off stump, and, it is now recognised, the early dismissal of Atherton is the worst of omens for England. Ramprakash spent close to an hour of agony at the crease before Donald thankfully ended his ordeal by knocking over his middle stump. Thorpe, somewhat fortunate to escape an appeal for leg before, was less fortunate when given out caught at short-leg to Eksteen's first ball. Stewart had batted rather unconvincingly before clipping Pringle to short mid-wicket just before tea, and Hick and Russell both perished to poor shots off Eksteen. Ironically, it was the spinner, a species scorned by England, who undermined the England innings.

Cork was caught low down at slip, and Fraser and Gough were victims of Pollock's pace. Robin Smith, another to receive public admonishment from the England supremo, batted doggedly for 141 minutes in an effort to salvage something from the wreckage and was last out when he gave McMillan a return catch off a leading edge. England, all out in 68.3 overs for 200 runs, had been destroyed by some fine attacking cricket and by their own decision to ask South Africa to bat first on a pitch that was showing signs of deterioration.

South Africa began the third day with five runs on the board and another 132 in credit from the first innings. By the end of the day, their overall lead was 428, and the game was totally beyond England's reach. This was not the pattern in the morning when both openers fell to catches by Russell, but Cronje and Cullinan restored supremacy in a stand of 87 which was ended when Cullinan hit a long hop to mid-on. Eight overs later, Cronje edged an outswinger to give Russell

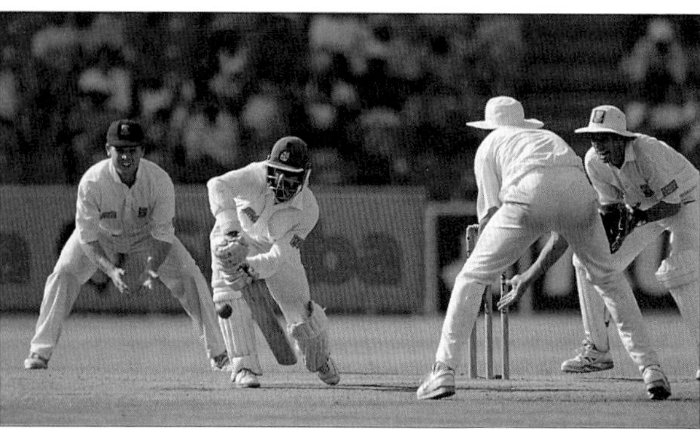

They shall not pass. 'Jack' Russell in defiant mood in the second Test match. (Graham Chadwick/Allsport)

his ninth catch of the game, and the wicket-keeper equalled the world record when he took a fine one-handed catch to his right to account for Rhodes who had, by then, rehabilitated himself with an innings of 57. McMillan and Richardson clouted tired bowling, and England slept uneasily.

The early stages of the fourth day were significant for two reasons. Firstly, Brian McMillan reached the second Test century of his career, his runs coming off 168 balls and including three sixes and nine fours, and 'Jack' Russell established a world record when he caught Eksteen off Cork. It was his eleventh victim of the match and so surpassed the mark set by Bob Taylor against India in 1980. It was a triumph for Russell who has battled his way back into the Test side after being discarded in favour of Rhodes and Stewart, and he deserves every congratulation, yet it would be true to say that he is not now as good a keeper as he was when he first won a place in the England team.

The pitch had not worn as much as expected, and Atherton and Stewart batted through the half hour before lunch that Cronje had left them with no alarms. They had scored 75 in 88 minutes when Stewart played a loose drive at a ball of full length from McMillan and was bowled. Ramprakash was hit on the pad first ball and bowled between bat and pad second ball. His abysmal record at Test level is as sad as it is inexplicable. Thorpe, too, remains something of a mystery in a different way. He began by swatting at anything and everything, was then becalmed and finally leg before as he appeared to lose balance. Hick provided Donald with his hundredth wicket in Test cricket. Smith stayed with the defiant and courageous Atherton, 82 not out in 11 minutes under five hours, until the end of the day, but England, 167 for 4, were in the shadows of defeat.

Smith survived a tumultuous appeal for a catch behind in Donald's second over of the final day. In fact, Smith survived until lunch was approaching. He batted with rugged determination until he chanced his deliberate upper-cut over slips once too often and was caught at third man. South Africa could now have delivered the knock-out blow. Pringle turned Russell square, and the batsman popped up a straightforward return catch which the bowler dropped. It was not until four hours later that the real

Second Test Match – South Africa *v.* England

30 November, 1, 2, 3 and 4 December 1995 at Wanderers, Johannesburg

South Africa

	First Innings		Second Innings	
A.C. Hudson	c Stewart, **b** Cork	**0**	c Russell, **b** Fraser	**17**
G. Kirsten	c Russell, **b** Malcolm	**110**	c Russell, **b** Malcolm	**1**
W.J. Cronje (Capt)	c Russell, **b** Cork	**35**	c Russell, **b** Cork	**48**
D.J. Cullinan	c Russell, **b** Hick	**69**	c Gough, **b** Cork	**61**
J.N. Rhodes	c Russell, **b** Cork	**5**	c Russell, **b** Fraser	**57**
B.M. McMillan	lbw, **b** Cork	**35**	not out	**100**
*D.J. Richardson	c Russell, **b** Malcolm	**0**	c Ramprakash, **b** Malcolm	**23**
S.M. Pollock	c Smith, **b** Malcolm	**33**	lbw, **b** Cork	**5**
C.E. Eksteen	c Russell, **b** Cork	**13**	c Russell, **b** Cork	**2**
M.W. Pringle	not out	**10**	c Hick, **b** Fraser	**2**
A.A. Donald	**b** Malcolm	**0**	not out	**9**
	b **1**, lb **14**, w **2**, nb **5**	**22**	b **5**, lb **12**, w **1**, nb **3**	**21**
		332	(for 9 wickets, dec.)	**346**

	O	M	R	W	O	M	R	W
Cork	32	7	84	**5**	31.3	6	78	**4**
Malcolm	22	5	62	**4**	13	2	65	**2**
Fraser	20	5	69	**–**	29	6	84	**3**
Gough	15	2	64	**–**	12	2	48	**–**
Hick	15	1	38	**1**	15	3	35	**–**
Ramprakash					4	–	19	**–**

Fall of Wickets
1–**3**, 2–**74**, 3–**211**, 4–**221**, 5–**260**, 6–**260**, 7–**278**, 8–**314**, 9–**331**
1–**7**, 2–**29**, 3–**116**, 4–**145**, 5–**244**, 6–**296**, 7–**304**, 8–**311**, 9–**314**

England

	First Innings		Second Innings	
M.A. Atherton (Capt)	**b** Donald	**9**	not out	**185**
A.J. Stewart	c Kirsten, **b** Pringle	**45**	**b** McMillan	**38**
M.R. Ramprakash	**b** Donald	**4**	**b** McMillan	**0**
G.P. Thorpe	c Kirsten, **b** Eksteen	**34**	lbw, **b** Pringle	**17**
G.A. Hick	c and **b** Eksteen	**6**	c Richardson, **b** Donald	**4**
R.A. Smith	c and **b** McMillan	**52**	c Pollock, **b** Donald	**44**
*R.C. Russell	c Rhodes, **b** Eksteen	**12**	not out	**29**
D.G. Cork	c Cullinan, **b** Pollock	**8**		
D. Gough	c and **b** Pollock	**2**		
A.R.C. Fraser	lbw, **b** Pollock	**0**		
D.E. Malcolm	not out	**0**		
	b **6**, lb **1**, nb **21**	**28**	b **4**, lb **7**, nb **23**	**34**
		200	(for 5 wickets)	**351**

	O	M	R	W	O	M	R	W
Donald	15	3	49	**2**	35	9	95	**2**
Pringle	17	4	46	**1**	23	5	52	**1**
Pollock	15	2	44	**3**	29	11	65	**–**
McMillan	10.3	–	42	**1**	21	–	50	**2**
Eksteen	11	5	12	**3**	52	20	76	**–**
Cronje					3	1	2	**–**
Kirsten					2	2	0	**–**

Fall of Wickets
1–**10**, 2–**45**, 3–**109**, 4–**116**, 5–**125**, 6–**147**, 7–**178**, 8–**193**, 9–**200**
1–**75**, 2–**75**, 3–**134**, 4–**145**, 5–**232**

Umpires: D.B. Hair & K.E. Liebenberg

Match drawn

The beautiful ground at Paarl, venue for Boland v. England XI. (Paul Sturgess/Sportsline)

significance of this miss was revealed. A catch of even greater significance had been missed before Smith's departure. Atherton was on 99 when he turned a ball from Donald straight into the hands of Kirsten at short-leg. The ball went in, and out, of the fielder's hands, and next ball Atherton reached a century of high calibre.

From 35 overs in the afternoon session only 55 runs were scored, and there was a creeping awareness in the South African camp that they were going to be denied victory. Seven minutes from the scheduled close, Cronje accepted this as a fact and led his side from the field. His opposite number, Mike Atherton, had played one of the monumental match-saving innings in Test history. He was at the wicket for ten hours 45 minutes, faced 492 balls and hit 28 fours in his 185. It was a triumph of technique, tenacity and temperament. Even so, Atherton would not have succeeded in his task but for the extraordinary application of 'Jack' Russell who faced 235 balls in his 277-minute stay and hit just three fours. At one time, he went 70 minutes without scoring, but he helped save the day, and, deservedly, was voted joint Man of the Match with his skipper.

South Africa could only ponder what might have been and contemplate their own shortcomings in a match which they had dominated for four days.

Crawley is stumped by Germishuys off the bowling of Drew in the match at Paarl. (Paul Sturgess/Sportsline)

7, 8 and 9 December 1995
at Paarl CC, Paarl
England XI 402 for 8 dec. (R.C. Russell 129 not out, R.K. Illingworth 57 not out, G.P. Thorpe 56) and 33 for 2
Boland 288 (P.A.J. DeFreitas 54)
Match drawn

10 December 1995
at Paarl CC, Paarl
England XI 244 (M.A. Atherton 77)
Boland 170 (A.P. Kuiper 54, P.J. Martin 4 for 35)
England XI won by 74 runs

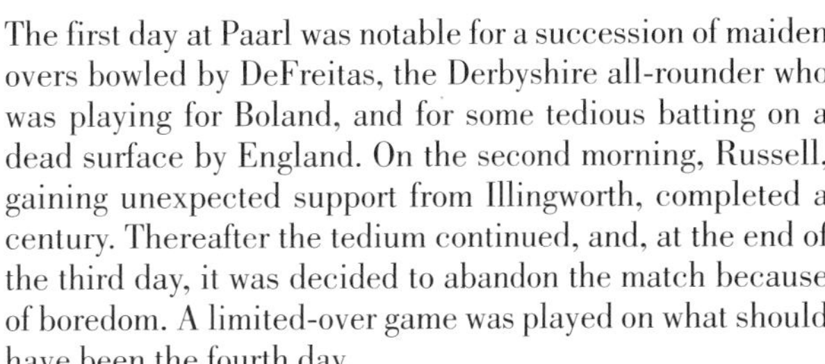

The first day at Paarl was notable for a succession of maiden overs bowled by DeFreitas, the Derbyshire all-rounder who was playing for Boland, and for some tedious batting on a dead surface by England. On the second morning, Russell, gaining unexpected support from Illingworth, completed a century. Thereafter the tedium continued, and, at the end of the third day, it was decided to abandon the match because of boredom. A limited-over game was played on what should have been the fourth day.

In a tour studded by errors on and off the field, this was an unforgivable surrender of principles and created a precedent which many county members who have had four-day cricket forced upon them may wish to follow.

Third Test Match

South Africa v. England *at Durban*

Jacques Kallis of Western Province, a highly talented cricketer, won his first Test cap. He and Matthews replaced Eksteen and Pringle in the South African side, while England brought in Crawley, Martin, Ilott and Illingworth for Ramprakash, Malcolm, Gough and Fraser. Cronje won the toss, and South Africa batted.

Two hours were lost to bad light on the first day, but England's attack, limited in experience, did well. Hudson launched an assault on the bowling which brought him nine fours, but Kirsten was becalmed before cutting recklessly to be caught high at second slip. Two runs later, Hudson offered no shot at a ball from Illingworth and was adjudged caught pad and glove at silly point. In attempting to hit Illingworth over the in-field, Cronje was caught at mid-on, and South Africa lunched at 76 for 3.

In the afternoon, Cullinan was caught at cover and Kallis was the victim of a very fine outswinger from Martin. Rhodes and McMillan now offered the first real substance of the day and took the score to 139 when play ended just after tea.

McMillan was caught low to his right by Russell early on the second morning, and Ilott then took three wickets in six balls to put England in total command. Rhodes was given leg before on the front pad, and Richardson was caught behind off a speculative shot. Matthews was leg before to the first ball of Ilott's next over, and South Africa were 153 for 9. A last wicket stand of 72 between Donald and Pollock revived a sick South Africa, and the loss of Crawley with an injured left hamstring gave England added problems. It transpired that Crawley's part in the tour was over.

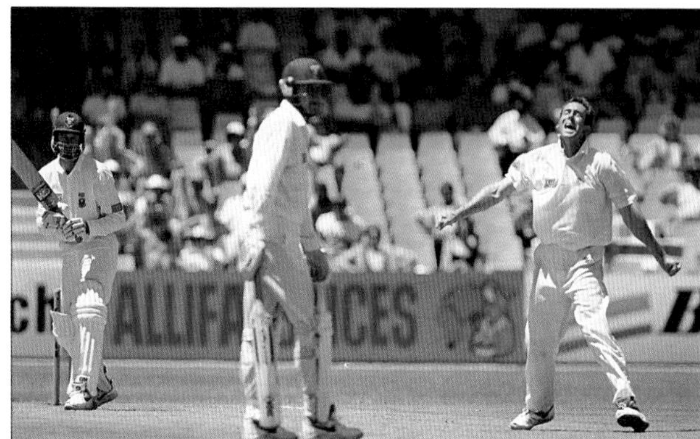

Mark Ilott traps Matthews leg before first ball in the third Test. Ilott bowled well on the tour, but injury during the fourth Test meant an early return to England. (Mike Hewitt/Allsport)

Having frustrated England with the bat, Donald now tormented them with the ball. With the last ball of the opening over, he had Atherton caught low in the gully, the first of five excellent catches. The second accounted for Thorpe,

Third Test Match – South Africa v. England

14, 15, 16, 17 and 18 December 1995 at Kingsmead, Durban

South Africa

	First Innings	
G. Kirsten	c Hick, b Martin	8
A.C. Hudson	c Crawley, b Illingworth	45
W.J. Cronje (Capt)	c Martin, b Illingworth	8
D.J. Cullinan	c Smith, b Martin	10
J.N. Rhodes	lbw, b Ilott	38
J.H. Kallis	c Russell, b Martin	1
B.M. McMillan	c Russell, b Martin	28
*D.J. Richardson	c Russell, b Ilott	7
S.M. Pollock	not out	36
C.R. Matthews	lbw, b Ilott	0
A.A. Donald	b Illingworth	32
	lb 11, nb 1	12
		225

	O	M	R	W
Cork	27	12	64	–
Ilott	15	3	48	3
Martin	27	9	60	4
Illingworth	29	12	37	3
Hick	2	–	5	–

Fall of Wickets
1–54, 2–56, 3–73, 4–85, 5–89, 6–141, 7–152, 8–153, 9–153

England

	First Innings	
M.A. Atherton (Capt)	c Hudson, b Donald	2
A.J. Stewart	c Hudson, b Matthews	41
G.P. Thorpe	c Cullinan, b Donald	2
R.A. Smith	c McMillan, b Matthews	34
G.A. Hick	not out	31
*R.C. Russell	c Rhodes, b Matthews	8
D.G. Cork	not out	23
J.P. Crawley		
P.J. Martin		
R.K. Illingworth		
M.C. Ilott		
	lb 4, nb 7	11
	(for 5 wickets)	152

	O	M	R	W
Donald	12.1	1	57	2
Pollock	15	2	39	–
Matthews	12	5	31	3
McMillan	9	3	21	–

Fall of Wickets
1–2, 2–13, 3–83, 4–93, 5–109

Umpires: S.A. Bucknor & D.L. Orchard

Match drawn

Hudson is caught at silly point by Crawley off Illingworth at the beginning of the rain-affected third Test match.
(Mike Hewitt/Allsport)

Cullinan again taking the ball low at first slip. Smith began nervously, but he and Stewart recovered equanimity to add 70. Both fell to Matthews, who added the scalp of Russell to his collection before bad light brought an early close and relief to England.

The third day's play was restricted to 32 minutes in which 29 runs were scored. Then the rains came, and the match was at an end with no play possible on the fourth or fifth days. England created another off-field surprise by sending for Gallian as replacement for the injured Crawley. Logic had suggested that Hussain, enjoying an inspiring tour with England 'A' – a natural number three which England lacked, and a brilliant fielder which England much needed – would be Crawley's replacement, but a glorious opportunity to strengthen the side was missed.

20, 21 and 22 December 1995
at Pietermaritzburg
Combined Tertiary Institutions 269 for 8 dec.
(N. Pothas 147, N. Boje 51, M.C. Ilott 6 for 89)
England XI 186 for 2 (A.J. Stewart 89 not out, M.A. Atherton 50)
Match drawn

A fine spell of new-ball bowling by Mark Ilott, a spell in which he took 4 for 23, was followed by a most impressive maiden first-class century from Nic Pothas, the 22-year-old Transvaal wicket-keeper. He and Boje added 157 for the seventh wicket. Gallian, in his first game of the tour, scored 3 as England reached a solid 186 in four hours ten minutes. Stewart was in sight of a century when the rains came again.

Fourth Test Match

South Africa *v.* England *at Port Elizabeth*

South Africa gave a first Test cap to the discovery of the season, Paul Adams, the Cape-Coloured left-arm wrist spinner. The match was played in a friendly atmosphere before a multi-racial crowd, but the cricket did not match a holiday feeling. It was played on a slow pitch, and there was a general lack of imagination and enterprise. This time the weather could not be blamed for the draw.

South Africa won the toss and batted. By the end of a 90-over day, they were 230 for 4. England had made only one change, Gallian accepting the poison chalice of number three instead of Crawley who was injured and out.

The start was unexceptional as Hudson and Kirsten scored 57. The partnership was ended when the persevering Cork found the edge of Hudson's bat for Russell to take a simple catch. England now enjoyed a fruitful period. Cronje batted for 49 minutes during which he hit a boundary, his

Cullinan, stumped Russell, bowled Illingworth for 14 in the second innings of the fourth Test. Russell established a record for an England wicket-keeper with 27 dismissals in the series.
(Patrick Eagar)

only scoring shot. Sensing the opposing captain's growing frustration, Atherton placed himself at short-extra cover and held a fine catch high to his left when Cronje attempted to drive Martin. Three overs later, Ilott found the edge of Kirsten's bat and Thorpe took a low catch at slip. At tea, after two full sessions, South Africa had moved to 135 for 3 from 59 overs, but Cullinan and Rhodes increased the tempo as best they could in the last session until Cork, inevitably, made a vital breakthrough with the second new ball, having Rhodes caught at square-leg off a full-blooded pull.

England had a bad second day. Nine short of his century, Cullinan chased a widish ball from Cork to give Russell a tumbling catch, but this was the only wicket to fall before lunch. Richardson seemed more at home on the dreary pitch than any other batsman and dominated a stand of 75 with McMillan, who became the first of Illingworth's three victims. The slow left-arm bowler was a disappointment, content to concentrate on containment and lacking spin and inventiveness. In spite of this, he had three catches put down in one over. He was guilty of one lapse himself, but the over said much about England's out-cricket.

There was a further handicap for England when Ilott injured his side. His part in England's plans was over at least until the summer.

Richardson, aided by Pollock, took South Africa to a position of impregnability, but, like Cullinan, he was denied a century. He swept at Illingworth, but touched the ball onto his pad from where it lobbed gently into the air. By now England were decidedly ragged, and they were thankful that a stumping and a senseless run out of the debutant Adams brought the South African innings to a close.

Fourth Test Match – South Africa v. England

26, 27, 28, 29 and 30 December 1995 at St George's Park, Port Elizabeth

South Africa

	First Innings		Second Innings	
A.C. Hudson	c Russell, b Cork	31	c Russell, b Martin	4
G. Kirsten	c Thorpe, b Ilott	51	c Illingworth, b Martin	69
W.J. Cronje (Capt)	c Atherton, b Martin	4	c Russell, b Martin	6
D.J. Cullinan	c Russell, b Cork	91	st Russell, b Illingworth	14
J.N. Rhodes	c Smith, b Cork	49	lbw, b Cork	0
B.M. McMillan	c Russell, b Illingworth	49	c Hick, b Cork	1
*D.J. Richardson	c Russell, b Illingworth	84	c Russell, b Cork	0
S.M. Pollock	lbw, b Cork	23	c Cork, b Illingworth	32
C.R. Matthews	st Russell, b Illingworth	15	c and b Illingworth	5
A.A. Donald	not out	12	not out	12
P.R. Adams	run out	0	not out	0
	lb 11, nb 8	19	b 8, lb 7, w 1, nb 3	19
		428	(for 9 wickets, dec.)	162

	O	M	R	W	O	M	R	W
Cork	43.2	12	113	4	26.3	5	63	3
Martin	33	9	79	1	17	8	39	3
Ilott	29.4	8	82	1				
Illingworth	39.5	8	105	3	22	7	45	3
Hick	12	2	32	–				
Gallian	2	–	6	–				

Fall of Wickets
1–**57**, 2–**85**, 3–**89**, 4–**207**, 5–**251**, 6–**326**, 7–**379**, 8–**408**, 9–**426**
1–**6**, 2–**18**, 3–**60**, 4–**65**, 5–**69**, 6–**69**, 7–**135**, 8–**146**, 9–**160**

England

	First Innings		Second Innings	
M.A. Atherton (Capt)	c Richardson, b Adams	72	lbw, b Matthews	34
A.J. Stewart	c Richardson, b Pollock	4	c Hudson, b Donald	81
J.E.R. Gallian	c Cullinan, b Pollock	14	lbw, b Adams	28
G.P. Thorpe	c Rhodes, b Adams	27	not out	12
G.A. Hick	lbw, b Donald	62	not out	11
R.A. Smith	lbw, b McMillan	2		
*R.C. Russell	c Cullinan, b Donald	30		
D.G. Cork	c Richardson, b Pollock	1		
R.K. Illingworth	c Hudson, b Donald	28		
P.J. Martin	b Adams	4		
M.C. Ilott	not out	0		
	lb 9, w 1, nb 9	19	b 9, lb 8, w 1, nb 5	23
		263	(for 3 wickets)	189

	O	M	R	W	O	M	R	W
Donald	25.4	7	49	3	19	4	60	1
Pollock	22	8	58	3	10	4	15	–
Adams	37	13	75	3	28	13	51	1
Matthews	20	7	42	–	19	10	29	1
McMillan	15	6	30	1	14	6	16	–
Cronje	1	1	0	–				
Kirsten					2	1	1	–

Fall of Wickets
1–**7**, 2–**50**, 3–**88**, 4–**163**, 5–**168**, 6–**199**, 7–**200**, 8–**258**, 9–**263**
1–**84**, 2–**157**, 3–**167**

Umpires: S.A. Bucknor & C.J. Mitchley

Match drawn

Shaun Pollock has Gallian caught by a tumbling Cullinan in the fourth Test. Pollock took 16 wickets in his first Test series and his contribution to South Africa's success was immeasurable.
(Clive Mason/Allsport)

The thanks were short-lived, for Stewart was out second ball as he thrust firm-footed outside the off stump, and Gallian lived dangerously. England were 40 for 1 from 20 overs when play ended for the day.

The gloom deepened for England on the third day, and they did not enjoy good fortune. Gallian did not add to his overnight score. He pushed at a ball from Pollock and was caught behind. Thorpe bustled busily until he pulled a long-hop into the hands of mid-wicket, and England were tentative until lunch which came at 109 for 3.

Not for the first time, Atherton was holding one end and giving England substance. He had been in for 297 minutes when a ball from Adams brushed his pad and was caught by Richardson. There was a noise and the fielders behind the bat appealed. Umpire Mitchley raised his finger. It was by no means his first error of judgement in Test cricket, and one fears that it will not be his last. McMillan almost immediately claimed Smith who offered no stroke, and when Cronje took the new ball in the final session Hick, who had batted with composure for 190 minutes, and Cork were out in rapid succession. Russell and Illingworth ground to the close at 250 for 7. It had been a hard day's viewing.

Kallis is leg before to Martin, and England's hopes are still alive in the fifth Test.
(David Munden/Sportsline)

The last three England wickets produced little on the fourth morning, but they were just three of the nine wickets that fell in the first two sessions of the day. With the comfort of a first innings lead of 165, South Africa batted a second time, but in just over half an hour they were 18 for 2. Both Hudson and Cronje were victims of Martin's outswinger, and the England attack, without Ilott, was very much on top.

At lunch, South Africa were 34 for 2, and it seemed that any crisis had been averted as the patient Kirsten and a restrained Cullinan brought them past 50. The stand was ended when Cullinan moved outside leg stump in an attempt to destroy Illingworth's line, but he swung wildly and was stumped. Now Dominic Cork gained reward for a sustained and inspired spell of quick bowling. In the space of 17 balls, he captured three wickets at no personal cost. Rhodes pushed half forward and was leg before. McMillan played indecisively at a lifting ball and was caught at leg slip while Richardson was caught behind. Suddenly, South Africa were 69 for 6, and a result seemed possible.

Kirsten and Pollock nearly doubled the score in a 95-minute stand that really made it impossible for England to win, and when Cronje declared, he was secure in the knowledge that England would have to make 328 in a minimum of 100 overs, a scoring rate that neither side had remotely approached on the first four days.

England ended the fourth day on 20, and Atherton and Stewart withstood Donald's fire on the fifth morning, and the opening pair were not separated until after lunch when Atherton was leg before to Matthews. He had batted for 172 minutes, and Gallian now occupied the crease for 145 minutes. At tea, England were 134 for 1 from 68 overs. Gallian fell to Adams, and when Stewart was finally caught off Donald he had been at the wicket for 338 minutes, faced 262 balls and hit 13 fours. He had also made completely sure that England entered the last Test on level terms.

Fifth Test Match

South Africa *v.* England *at Cape Town*

South Africa brought back Kallis in place of Matthews for the final Test while England had Watkinson, Fraser and Malcolm instead of Gallian, Illingworth and Ilott. Atherton won the toss, and England batted. The fact that Atherton called right was the only good thing that happened for England for three days.

Twenty-five minutes, six overs at the start of the match, and neither Atherton nor Stewart could score a run. The third ball of the seventh over saw Atherton go back to Donald and angle the ball low to third slip. Pollock was unable to follow Donald in accuracy or fire, but McMillan found bounce and swing, and Stewart, becalmed and frustrated, was bowled off the inside edge as he pushed at a ball away from his body. England lunched at 54 for 2.

With his first ball of the afternoon session, Donald tempted Thorpe to drive at a delivery that was slanted across his body and McMillan accepted the catch at second slip. Three balls later, McMillan took another catch as Hick played back fatally. Russell attempted to revive the innings in his usual busy manner, and he stayed for 79 minutes while 43 runs were scored, but he had managed only nine of them before he hung out his bat to Pollock for McMillan to take a third catch. In his next over, Pollock claimed Watkinson with a ball of full length. At tea, England were 125 for 6 and sinking fast.

The unexpected resistance that turned the course of the fifth Test – Paul Adams flicks Dominic Cork to the boundary during a last wicket stand with Richardson which realised 73.
(Clive Mason/Allsport)

Refreshed by his tea, Donald scattered Cork's stumps and gave Martin an uncomfortably brief time before having him caught at slip off his glove. Smith had batted for over four hours with much courage and determination but never suggesting an ability to deal with Adams to whom he finally played on. Malcolm flayed and missed, and England were all out for 153 in 68.1 overs.

Fifth Test Match – South Africa v. England

2, 3 and 4 January 1996 at Newlands, Cape Town

England

	First Innings		Second Innings	
M.A. Atherton (Capt)	c Hudson, b Donald	0	c Richardson, b Donald	10
A.J. Stewart	b McMillan	13	c Cullinan, b Pollock	7
R.A. Smith	b Adams	66	(4) c Richardson, b Adams	13
G.P. Thorpe	c McMillan, b Donald	20	(5) run out	59
G.A. Hick	c McMillan, b Donald	2	(6) lbw, Pollock	36
*R.C. Russell	c McMillan, b Pollock	9	(7) c Hudson, b Pollock	2
M. Watkinson	lbw, b Pollock	11	(8) lbw, b Adams	0
D.G. Cork	b Donald	16	(9) c Kallis, b Pollock	8
P.J. Martin	c Hudson, b Donald	0	(10) c Adams, b Pollock	9
A.R.C. Fraser	not out	5	(3) c Adams, b Donald	1
D.E. Malcolm	b Adams	1	not out	0
	b 4, lb 1, w 1, nb 4	10	b 2, lb 5, nb 5	12
		153		157

	O	M	R	W	O	M	R	W
Donald	16	5	46	5	18	6	49	2
Pollock	14	6	26	2	15.5	4	32	5
McMillan	10	2	22	1	7	3	16	–
Adams	20.1	5	52	2	22	6	53	2
Kallis	4	2	2	–				
Cronje	4	4	0	–				

Fall of Wickets
1–**0**, 2–**24**, 3–**58**, 4–**60**, 5–**103**, 6–**115**, 7–**141**, 8–**147**, 9–**151**
1–**16**, 2–**22**, 3–**22**, 4–**66**, 5–**138**, 6–**140**, 7–**140**, 8–**140**, 9–**150**

South Africa

	First Innings		Second Innings	
G. Kirsten	c Atherton, b Watkinson	23	not out	41
A.C. Hudson	lbw, b Cork	0	not out	27
W.J. Cronje (Capt)	c Russell, b Cork	12		
D.J. Cullinan	c Russell, b Martin	62		
J.N. Rhodes	c Russell, b Fraser	16		
B.M. McMillan	run out	11		
J.H. Kallis	lbw, b Martin	7		
*D.J. Richardson	not out	54		
S.M. Pollock	c Smith, b Watkinson	4		
A.A. Donald	c Russell, b Cork	3		
P.R. Adams	c Hick, b Martin	29		
	lb 22, nb 1	23	lb 1, nb 1	2
		244	(for no wicket)	70

	O	M	R	W	O	M	R	W
Cork	25	6	60	3	4	–	23	–
Malcolm	20	6	56	–	2	–	12	–
Martin	24	9	37	3	4	2	3	–
Fraser	17	10	34	1				
Watkinson	15	3	35	2	4	–	24	–
Hick					1.4	–	7	–

Fall of Wickets
1–**1**, 2–**19**, 3–**79**, 4–**125**, 5–**125**, 6–**144**, 7–**154**, 8–**163**, 9–**171**

Umpires: S.G. Randell & D.L. Orchard

South Africa won by 10 wickets

South Africa appeal for run out against Thorpe who was on 59. Umpire Orchard said 'not out', but was persuaded to consult the third umpire who ruled that Thorpe was well short of his ground. (Clive Mason/Allsport)

South Africa had two significant batting failures in the series, and neither redeemed himself at Newlands. Cork, whose capacity never to admit defeat is one of his great assets, trapped Hudson leg before fifth ball and then had Cronje caught behind after 35 minutes of uncertainty. South Africa closed on 44 for 2, and England still breathed.

For much of the second day they continued to breathe. South Africa were looking as if they would impose total dominance on the game when Kirsten lost his admirable self-discipline for the first time and pulled a short ball from Watkinson into the hands of mid-wicket. This was South Africa's only morning mishap and they reached lunch at 109 for 3.

In the afternoon, when only 25 overs were bowled and 38 runs were scored England captured three more wickets. Cullinan and Rhodes fell to catches behind which meant that Russell had established a new record for England in the number of wicket-keeping dismissals in a series. Cork then ran out McMillan with a direct hit on the bowler's stumps from cover, and almost immediately after tea Kallis was leg before to Martin, who bowled well. Pollock was brilliantly caught at short-leg by Smith, and, with South Africa 163 for 8, England were very much alive.

Atherton took the second new ball, and Cork and Russell disposed of Donald. It was Russell's 27th dismissal in six innings. The last man Adams entered with a first-class career record of four runs off 16 balls. Presumably, Malcolm took pity on him. The Derbyshire pace man had found neither rhythm nor rhyme throughout the match, and now he became positively wasteful. Adams' first run came off a Malcolm full toss, and Cork's wild throw turned it into five. Adams also hit three fours, and as Richardson played with customary intelligence, the last wicket realised 73 runs in 67 minutes. Those 67 minutes left England's tour in ruins.

Hick ended the stand with a spectacular catch at second slip, but South Africa led by 91, and when Atherton offered a faint edge to a short ball total despair had descended on England.

An overnight 17 for 1 became 22 for 3 in the first half hour of the third day. Stewart waved his bat outside the off stump to give a simple catch to first slip, and Fraser fended a lifting ball to backward short-leg. Smith and Thorpe seemed to be repairing damage when Smith pushed forward to an Adams googly and appeared to withdraw his bat. The ball turned and was caught by Richardson who appealed, and umpire Orchard immediately raised his finger – a rather impetuous decision.

Hick was initially unimpressive, but after lunch he was positive in all he did. He took England into the lead and hit Adams for consecutive sixes. He was in full flow when Pollock returned to trap him leg before with a ball which kept low. Four balls later, Russell steered Pollock to gully. Without addition to the score, Thorpe was needlessly run out. He took a single to short-fine leg where Hudson gathered and threw to the bowler, Adams, in one movement. Thorpe was well short of his ground, but umpire Orchard gave him 'not out'. Cronje showed obvious dissent and badgered the umpire into consulting the third arbitrator, the television monitor. Orchard gave way, and Liebenberg, with the aid of the photograph, confirmed that Thorpe was out. It was a sad, sour blemish on a series played in good spirits.

A third wicket fell at 140 as Watkinson was leg before to Adams, and Pollock accounted for Cork and Martin to give himself five wickets in a Test innings for the first time. England's last six wickets had gone down for 19 runs. Hudson and Kirsten needed only 15.4 overs in which to score the runs needed for victory as England suffered their third Test defeat inside three days in just over a year, and South Africa deservedly won the series.

Test Match Averages – South Africa v. England

South Africa Batting

	M	Inns	NO	Runs	HS	Av	100s	50s
D.J. Cullinan	5	6	–	307	91	51.16		4
G. Kirsten	5	7	1	303	110	50.50	1	2
B.M. McMillan	5	6	1	224	100*	44.80	1	
D.J. Richardson	5	6	1	168	84	33.60		2
J.N. Rhodes	5	6	–	165	57	27.50		1
S.M. Pollock	5	6	1	133	36*	26.60		
A.A. Donald	5	6	3	68	32	22.66		
A.C. Hudson	5	7	1	124	45	20.66		
W.J. Cronje	5	6	–	113	48	18.83		
P.R. Adams	2	3	1	29	29	14.50		
C.R. Matthews	3	3	–	20	15	6.66		
J.H. Kallis	2	2	–	8	7	4.00		

Played in one Test: C.E. Eksteen 13 & 2; M.W. Pringle 10* & 2; B.N. Schultz did not bat

England Batting

	M	Inns	NO	Runs	HS	Av	100s	50s
M.A. Atherton	5	8	1	390	185*	55.71	1	2
G.A. Hick	5	8	2	293	141	48.83	1	1
R.A. Smith	5	7	–	254	66	36.28		2
A.J. Stewart	5	8	–	235	81	29.37		1
R.C. Russell	5	7	2	140	50*	28.00		1
G.P. Thorpe	5	8	1	184	59	26.28		1
R.K. Illingworth	3	2	–	28	28	14.00		
D.G. Cork	5	6	1	69	23*	13.80		
A.R.C. Fraser	3	4	2	10	5*	5.00		
P.J. Martin	3	3	–	13	9	4.33		
M.R. Ramprakash	2	3	–	13	9	4.33		
D. Gough	2	2	–	2	2	1.00		
D.E. Malcolm	2	3	2	1	1	1.00		

Played in two Tests: M.C. Ilott 0*
Played in one Test: M. Watkinson 11 & 0; J.E.R. Gallian 14 & 28; J.P. Crawley did not bat

South Africa Bowling

	Overs	Mds	Runs	Wks	Av	Best	5/inn
S.M. Pollock	149.5	44	377	16	23.56	5/32	1
A.A. Donald	173.4	45	497	19	26.15	5/46	1
P.R. Adams	107.1	37	231	8	28.87	3/75	
C.E. Eksteen	63	25	88	3	29.33	3/12	
B.M. McMillan	111.3	30	247	8	30.87	3/50	
C.R. Matthews	81	35	165	4	41.25	3/31	
M.W. Pringle	40	9	98	2	29.00	1/46	
G. Kirsten	6	4	2	–	–		
W.J. Cronje	16	11	16	–	–		

Bowled in one innings: B.N. Schultz 16–5–47–1; J.H. Kallis 4–2–2–0

England Bowling

	Overs	Mds	Runs	Wks	Av	Best	5/inn
P.J. Martin	105	37	218	11	19.81	4/60	
R.K. Illingworth	90.5	27	187	9	20.77	3/37	
D.G. Cork	189.2	48	485	19	25.52	5/84	1
M. Watkinson	19	3	59	2	29.50	2/35	
M.C. Ilott	44.4	10	130	4	32.50	3/48	
D.E. Malcolm	57	13	195	6	32.50	4/62	
A.R.C. Fraser	66	21	187	4	46.75	3/84	
G.A. Hick	45.4	6	117	1	117.00	1/38	
D. Gough	27	4	112	–	–		

Bowled in one innings: M.R. Ramprakash 4–0–19–0; J.E.R. Gallian 2–0–6–0

South Africa Fielding Figures

8 – D.J. Richardson; 7 – A.C. Hudson; 5 – D.J. Cullinan and B.M. McMillan; 3 – J.N. Rhodes; 2 – G. Kirsten, S.M. Pollock, P.R. Adams and C.R. Matthews; 1 – A.A. Donald, C.E. Eksteen and J.H. Kallis

England Fielding Figures

27 – R.C. Russell (ct 25 / st 2); 4 – G.A. Hick and R.A. Smith; 2– M.A. Atherton and R.K. Illingworth; 1 – A.J. Stewart, G.P. Thorpe, D.G. Cork, P.J. Martin, M.R. Ramprakash, D. Gough and J.P. Crawley

One-day International Series

South Africa in complete control as England are humiliated.

6 January, 1996
at Newlands, Cape Town
England XI 195 (M.W. Pringle 4 for 34)
Western Province 200 for 7 (F. Davids 55 not out)
Western Province won by 3 wickets

This match was hastily arranged after England had been beaten in three days in the fifth Test. A weakened Western Province side won with an over to spare. Fayeh Davids and Paul Kirsten hit 68 for the eighth wicket. Fraser, Ilott and Malcolm were now back in England, where Malcolm reacted angrily to the treatment he had received at the hands of supremo Illingworth. Fairbrother, Reeve, Neil Smith, White, inexplicably, and DeFreitas, bewilderingly, now joined the party as bits and pieces players. Poor Ramprakash was out for 0.

Shaun Pollock bowls Gough and South Africa win the first one-day international by six runs. In his first limited-over international, Pollock took the Man of the Match award. (Mike Hewitt/Allsport)

The One-day Matches

If the Test series had been disappointing for England, the one-day series was a nightmare that ended in total disaster. When the seven matches were over England were prepared neither mentally nor physically for the World Cup and no technical plan or policy was discernible.

It all began under the lights of Newlands where South Africa won a thrilling victory which gave scant indication of what was to come. England started well. Gary Kirsten was an early Cork victim, and Stewart, back behind the stumps, held four good catches in succession as profligate batsmen drove or cut extravagantly at the swinging ball.

Cronje and Kallis, a batsman of regal potential who was making his debut in one-day internationals, added 30 in seven overs for the sixth wicket. They were parted in the 31st over by Thorpe's magnificent dive, stop and throw from the boundary which left Cronje short of his line as he went for a third run.

Pollock now joined Kallis to whom he first played a supporting role. Once Kallis had gone, Pollock struck hard and often. He batted intelligently, and of the 104 runs scored from the last 19 overs, he was responsible for 66 off 66 deliveries.

Allan Donalds bowls Hick in the third match of the series. (Mike Hewitt/Allsport)

In spite of this, South Africa's 211 did not look to be a winning score, and this was emphasised when England reached 155 for 3 in the 37th over. Atherton, enjoying good fortune, and Stewart started with a stand of 59 before Donald, coming on as first change, removed both openers and Hick in his first three overs. Hick faced only 18 balls, but his aggression helped drive Adams from the attack.

It was the return of Pollock which undermined England. Fairbrother was caught at mid-on, and White and Reeve made only brief appearances. Cork ran himself out, and Neil Smith, making his debut, was caught at first slip. Thorpe fell to a fine running catch, and Gough was bowled by Pollock. The last seven England wickets had gone down in 14 overs for 50 runs. Pollock added 4 for 34 to his 66 and took the individual award of the occasion of his debut in one-day international cricket.

Raymond Illingworth offered the criticism that the presence of families and friends had blurred the focus of the England players.

For the second match, England replaced Gough and Reeve by DeFreitas and Ramprakash, and South Africa had Boje, Hudson and Snell in for Adams, Cullinan and Matthews. Snell, for long a candidate to share the new ball with Donald in Test cricket, was used as an opening batsman, and he and Hudson had 116 on the board in 23 overs. They were separated by Fairbrother's excellent catch on the long-on boundary. McMillan and Kallis maintained the momentum, but, from 164 for 1 in the 34th over South Africa fell away as Cork took three wickets in nine balls towards the end of the innings.

England caused a surprise by sending in DeFreitas with Atherton, a move that was only partly successful. Hick, however, was at his mightiest. He hit a six and nine fours as he made 55 off 43 balls, and with Atherton following solidity with belligerence, England prospered. Atherton was brilliantly caught by Cronje, and although Ramprakash, the voodoo sign surely upon him, was run out and Fairbrother

First One-day International – South Africa v. England

9 January 1996 at Newlands, Cape Town

South Africa

G. Kirsten	lbw, **b** Cork	8
*D.J. Richardson	**c** Stewart, **b** Martin	11
B.M. McMillan	**c** Stewart, **b** Martin	4
D.J. Cullinan	**c** Stewart, **b** Reeve	17
J.N. Rhodes	**c** Stewart, **b** White	16
W.J. Cronje (Capt)	run out	24
J.H. Kallis	**c** Thorpe, **b** White	38
S.M. Pollock	not out	66
C.R. Matthews	**c** Reeve, **b** Cork	10
A.A. Donald		
P.R. Adams		
	b **1**, lb **6**, w **4**, nb **6**	17
	50 overs (for 8 wickets)	211

	O	M	R	W
Cork	10	–	51	2
Martin	10	1	34	2
Gough	9	–	39	–
Reeve	9	1	40	1
White	10	1	31	2
N.M.K. Smith	2	–	9	–

Fall of Wickets
1–**12**, 2–**20**, 3–**44**, 4–**57**, 5–**77**, 6–**102**, 7–**152**, 8–**211**

England

M.A. Atherton (Capt)	**b** Donald	35
*A.J. Stewart	lbw, **b** Donald	23
G.A. Hick	lbw, **b** Donald	21
G.P. Thorpe	**c** Matthews, **b** McMillan	62
N.H. Fairbrother	**c** Adams, **b** Pollock	28
C. White	**c** and **b** Pollock	5
D.A. Reeve	**c** Richardson, **b** Matthews	2
D.G. Cork	run out	7
N.M.K. Smith	**c** McMillan, **b** Pollock	3
D. Gough	**b** Pollock	3
P.J. Martin	not out	4
	lb **6**, w **4**, nb **2**	12
	49.5 overs	205

	O	M	R	W
Matthews	10	1	39	1
Pollock	9.5	–	34	4
Donald	10	–	38	3
McMillan	10	–	38	1
Adams	2	–	18	–
Cronje	5	–	18	–
Kallis	3	–	14	–

Fall of Wickets
1–**59**, 2–**64**, 3–**95**, 4–**155**, 5–**161**, 6–**166**, 7–**177**, 8–**189**, 9–**199**

Umpires: K.E. Liebenberg & D.L. Orchard *Man of the Match:* S.M. Pollock

South Africa won by 6 runs

caught, Thorpe, again at his best, and Stewart took England to victory with ten balls to spare. That was the last of the winter joy.

England decided to shuffle their pack for the third encounter and suffered defeat with 11 balls unused. Atherton chose to bat first in conditions in which the ball was swinging, and he himself was caught at slip first ball, which has ever been an ill omen for England. Robin Smith, playing his first game of the series, offered no shot and was leg before, and when De Freitas slogged to mid-off Pollock had destroyed the top of the England batting with 3 for 8 in six overs.

Hick had narrow escapes before chopping a ball from Donald into his stumps, and England were 53 for 4. Ramprakash was relieved to score runs and help in a mild recovery which was carried on by Fairbrother and White, but 199 never looked like being a daunting target.

It looked even less daunting when Gough sprayed the ball in all directions in his opening over. Thankfully he recovered to return decent figures, but it was DeFreitas who made the early inroads. At 73 for 4, South Africa were in some trouble, but Rhodes and McMillan batted sensibly, and the good sense continued to the end. The victory was

An outstanding member of the South Africa side throughout the season, Dave Richardson's injury in the one-day series was a grievous blow and had an adverse effect upon South Africa's chances in the World Cup. (David Munden/Sportsline)

Second One-day International – South Africa v. England

11 January 1996 at Springbok Park, Bloemfontein

South Africa

A.C. Hudson	c Stewart, b Hick	64
R.P. Snell	c Fairbrother, b Hick	63
B.M. McMillan	b Martin	44
J.H. Kallis	c Hick, b Smith	29
W.J. Cronje (Capt)	b Cork	19
J.N. Rhodes	b Cork	4
G. Kirsten	c Fairbrother, b Cork	2
S.M. Pollock	c Ramprakash, b Smith	5
*D.J. Richardson	not out	13
N. Boje	not out	2
A.A. Donald		
	b 6, lb 4, w 7	17
	50 overs (for 8 wickets)	262

	O	M	R	W
Cork	10	–	44	3
DeFreitas	6	–	30	–
White	6	–	37	–
Martin	6	–	43	1
Smith	10	–	46	2
Hick	10	–	38	2
Ramprakash	2	–	14	–

Fall of Wickets
1–116, 2–164, 3–197, 4–226, 5–228, 6–236, 7–237, 8–248

England

P.A.J. DeFreitas	c Rhodes, b Pollock	17
M.A. Atherton (Capt)	c Cronje, b Pollock	85
G.A. Hick	lbw, b Cronje	55
G.P. Thorpe	not out	72
M.R. Ramprakash	run out	1
N.H. Fairbrother	c Rhodes, b McMillan	12
*A.J. Stewart	not out	13
C. White		
D.G. Cork		
N.M.K. Smith		
P.J. Martin		
	lb 4, w 5, nb 1	10
	48.2 overs (for 5 wickets)	265

	O	M	R	W
Pollock	9.2	–	48	2
Snell	6	–	39	–
McMillan	7	–	46	1
Donald	10	1	44	–
Cronje	7	–	32	1
Kallis	5	–	27	–
Boje	4	–	25	–

Fall of Wickets
1–37, 2–108, 3–198, 4–201, 5–223

Umpires: R.E. Koertzen & W. Diedricks *Man of the Match:* M.A. Atherton

England won by 5 wickets

Third One-day International – South Africa v. England

13 January 1996 at Wanderers, Johannesburg

England

P.A.J. DeFreitas	c Donald, b Pollock	13
M.A. Atherton (Capt)	c McMillan, b Pollock	0
R.A. Smith	lbw, b Pollock	9
G.A. Hick	b Donald	14
M.R. Ramprakash	c Richardson, b Cronje	27
N.H. Fairbrother	not out	57
C. White	c Cronje, b McMillan	34
D.A. Reeve	c Richardson, b Donald	10
*R.C. Russell	c Cronje, b Snell	18
M. Watkinson		
D. Gough		
	lb 7, w 7, nb 2	16
	50 overs (for 8 wickets)	198

	O	M	R	W
Pollock	10	2	31	3
Matthews	8	–	34	–
Donald	10	–	53	2
McMillan	10	–	27	1
Snell	6	1	29	1
Cronje	6	–	17	1

Fall of Wickets
1–**1**, 2–**23**, 3–**25**, 4–**53**, 5–**88**, 6–**139**, 7–**168**, 8–**198**

South Africa

A.C. Hudson	b Gough	17
R.P. Snell	c Fairbrother, b DeFreitas	8
W.J. Cronje (Capt)	c Russell, b DeFreitas	7
D.J. Cullinan	c Russell, b Gough	25
J.H. Kallis	run out	16
J.N. Rhodes	c Russell, b Gough	44
B.M. McMillan	c Smith, b White	35
S.M. Pollock	not out	18
*D.J. Richardson	not out	10
C.R. Matthews		
A.A. Donald		
	b 1, lb 7, w 8, nb 3	19
	48.1 overs (for 7 wickets)	199

	O	M	R	W
Gough	10	2	31	3
DeFreitas	8	–	35	2
Reeve	10	1	43	–
Hick	3	–	13	–
Watkinson	9	–	43	–
White	8.1	1	26	1

Fall of Wickets
1–**19**, 2–**29**, 3–**63**, 4–**73**, 5–**114**, 6–**157**, 7–**180**

Umpires: D.L. Orchard & R.E. Koertzen *Man of the Match:* S.M. Pollock

South Africa won by 3 wickets

Fourth One-day International – South Africa v. England

14 January 1996 at Centurion Park, Verwoerdburg

England

A.J. Stewart (Capt)	c Cullinan, b Symcox	64
R.A. Smith	c Symcox, b Donald	63
G.A. Hick	b Cronje	21
G.P. Thorpe	c Pollock, b Symcox	15
M.R. Ramprakash	c Kallis, b Donald	32
C. White	c Donald, b Cronje	19
*R.C. Russell	not out	39
D.G. Cork	c Richardson, b Matthews	0
P.A.J. DeFreitas	c Cullinan, b Donald	2
D. Gough	not out	1
R.K. Illingworth		
	lb 5, w 10, nb 1	16
	50 overs (for 8 wickets)	272

	O	M	R	W
Matthews	10	–	48	1
Pollock	10	1	36	–
Cronje	10	–	57	2
Donald	9	–	72	3
Symcox	10	1	48	2
Kirsten	1	–	6	–

Fall of Wickets
1–**103**, 2–**139**, 3–**168**, 4–**174**, 5–**216**, 6–**245**, 7–**249**, 8–**260**

South Africa

A.C. Hudson	lbw, b Gough	72
G. Kirsten	b Cork	116
W.J. Cronje (Capt)	c Thorpe, b Illingworth	47
D.J. Cullinan	not out	25
J.H. Kallis	not out	14
J.N. Rhodes		
*D.J. Richardson		
S.M. Pollock		
C.R. Matthews		
P.L. Symcox		
A.A. Donald		
	w 2	2
	48 overs (for 3 wickets)	276

	O	M	R	W
Cork	10	–	65	1
DeFreitas	10	–	46	–
Gough	10	1	41	1
Hick	3	–	17	–
Illingworth	9	–	65	1
White	6	1	42	–

Fall of Wickets
1–**156**, 2–**223**, 3–**247**

Umpires: W. Diedricks & K.E. Liebenberg *Man of the Match:* G. Kirsten

South Africa won by 7 wickets

Craig White makes a vain attempt to lift England's batting hopes in the final match of the series. (Mike Hewitt/Allsport)

more emphatic and comfortable than the score would suggest.

Atherton stood down for the fourth match of the series, and Stewart, leading England, won the toss. He and Robin Smith scored 103 in 23 overs, and although Hick and Thorpe fell to loose shots, Ramprakash and Russell effected a recovery. A total of 272 looked highly satisfactory.

South Africa made it look ridiculously inadequate. Hudson, two sixes and seven fours in his 72 off 85 balls, and Kirsten, 11 fours in his scintillating 116 off 125 balls, made 156 in 29 overs. Cronje found form with two sixes and three fours in his 47 off 46 deliveries, and the pounding of the England attack was unabated. Cronje was caught on the boundary by Thorpe off Illingworth, but the wicket cost the slow left-arm bowler 65 runs from nine overs. A South African victory had become a rout.

England surrendered the series when they were soundly beaten in the fifth match. The game followed a familiar pattern. Atherton and Stewart put on 51 for the first wicket, and Donald then tore the heart out of the batting with four wickets in 27 balls. Thorpe, inevitably, brought some dignity to the innings, putting on 54 in 14 overs with White and 32 in seven overs with Russell. He was bowled after scoring 63 off 74 deliveries after which England surrendered feebly, the last five wickets falling for 20 runs.

Cork dismissed Hudson and Kirsten in his first nine balls before Cronje and Kallis added 118, a South African third wicket record for a one-day international. England put down four catches. Stewart split the webbing on his left hand in missing one of them, and if three of the catches were sharp chances, the one which DeFreitas put down to reprieve Cronje was a sitter.

South Africa duly won with ten balls to spare, and England were outplayed in every department of the game.

Thorpe surveys the wreckage having been bowled by Matthews for 63 in the fifth match of the series. (Mike Hewitt/Allsport)

Fifth One-day International – South Africa v. England

17 January 1996 at Kingsmead, Durban

England

M.A. Atherton (Capt)	c Richardson, b Donald	17
A.J. Stewart	b Donald	31
R.A. Smith	c Richardson, b Donald	8
G.A. Hick	c Richardson, b Donald	6
G.P. Thorpe	b Matthews	63
C. White	b Pollock	16
*R.C. Russell	run out	21
D.G. Cork	b Matthews	1
P.A.J. DeFreitas	b Pollock	3
D. Gough	b de Villiers	3
P.J. Martin	not out	2
	b 1, lb 6, w 6	13
	49.5 overs	184

	O	M	R	W
Pollock	10	1	31	2
Matthews	10	1	37	2
de Villiers	9.5	–	35	1
Donald	10	–	41	4
McMillan	8	–	25	–
Cronje	2	–	8	–

Fall of Wickets
1–51, 2–52, 3–61, 4–78, 5–132, 6–164, 7–170, 8–177, 9–178

South Africa

A.C. Hudson	lbw, b Cork	5
G. Kirsten	c Russell, b Cork	0
W.J. Cronje (Capt)	b White	78
J.H. Kallis	c Hick, b DeFreitas	67
B.M. McMillan	c Hick, b DeFreitas	13
J.N. Rhodes	not out	12
S.M. Pollock	not out	1
*D.J. Richardson		
P.S. de Villiers		
C.R. Matthews		
A.A. Donald		
	lb 2, w 3, nb 4	9
	48.2 overs (for 5 wickets)	185

	O	M	R	W
Martin	10	2	34	–
Cork	9.2	3	29	2
DeFreitas	9	–	41	2
Gough	10	–	32	–
White	8	1	39	1
Hick	2	–	8	–

Fall of Wickets
1–1, 2–9, 3–127, 4–150, 5–183

Umpires: W. Diedricks & D.L. Orchard *Man of the Match:* A.A. Donald

South Africa won by 5 wickets

Sixth One-day International – South Africa v. England

19 January 1996 at Buffalo Park, East London

South Africa

G. Kirsten	c R.A. Smith, b Cork	17
R.P. Snell	c Atherton, b Martin	8
W.J. Cronje (Capt)	b White	13
J.H. Kallis	lbw, b Martin	0
B.M. McMillan	not out	45
J.N. Rhodes	c Gough, b Illingworth	10
L. Klusener	lbw, b Gough	0
S.M. Pollock	b Gough	6
*D.J. Richardson	lbw, b Gough	0
P.S. de Villiers	b White	15
P.R. Adams	b Cork	0
	b 1, lb 11, w 1, nb 2	15
	41.4 overs	129

	O	M	R	W
Cork	8.4	1	22	2
Martin	7	–	23	2
Gough	10	1	25	3
White	7	1	18	2
Illingworth	9	1	29	1

Fall of Wickets
1–25, 2–29, 3–29, 4–54, 5–89, 6–89, 7–98, 8–98, 9–128

England

M.A. Atherton (Capt)	c Richardson, b de Villiers	6
C. White	c Richardson, b de Villiers	6
R.A. Smith	b Pollock	0
G.A. Hick	c Kirsten, b Adams	39
*R.C. Russell	run out	12
G.P. Thorpe	b Adams	0
N.H. Fairbrother	b Snell	13
D.G. Cork	b Adams	2
R.K. Illingworth	run out	1
D. Gough	lbw, b Snell	4
P.J. Martin	not out	5
	b 1, lb 13, w 12, nb 1	27
	43.4 overs	115

	O	M	R	W
Pollock	10	3	15	1
de Villiers	8	1	10	2
Klusener	4	–	19	–
Snell	9.4	2	22	2
Kallis	3	–	9	–
Adams	9	1	26	3

Fall of Wickets
1–10, 2–11, 3–19, 4–75, 5–76, 6–78, 7–88, 8–95, 9–104

Umpires: C.J. Mitchley & D.L. Orchard *Man of the Match:* P.R. Adams

South Africa won by 14 runs

In reaching his first fifty in international cricket, Kallis gave further evidence of his quality. One also realised that the season had seen South Africa bring to the fore three cricketers of international standing, Adams, Pollock and Kallis, while England stumbled blindly in search of a formula.

If one felt that things could not get worse for England, events in East London proved otherwise. The pitch was not good, but South Africa decided to bat first when they won the toss. They included Lance Klusener, the Natal all-rounder, for the first time and brought back Adams. Only McMillan found a way to survive and score on a pitch that quickly displayed its vagaries, and South Africa were bowled out in 41.4 overs for 129, their lowest score in a limited-over international in South Africa.

England were soon 19 for 3 as de Villiers showed a complete return to fitness after injury. Hick and Russell combined in the only fifty partnership in the match, and, after 28 overs, England were 75 for 3. Cronje brought on Adams who had not bowled since the first match of the series at Cape Town where he was severely punished by Hick in the only two overs he bowled. With the first ball of his second over, Adams had Hick caught behind, and with his next ball he bowled Thorpe through his legs. That was the signal for collapse. Russell and Illingworth were run out on suicidal missions, and no-one could take control as England plunged to defeat as they fell 14 runs short of South Africa's meagre score.

In winning the series, South Africa had suffered a grievous loss, for an injury to Richardson was to keep him out of the World Cup. He was replaced by Palframan who made his debut in the seventh and last match of the series against England.

England were well served by Gough who cut back South Africa who had reached 167 for 3 in the 40th over following another cracking innings by Cronje. To restrict South Africa to 51 from the last ten overs was a fine effort by England, but once again the batting failed miserably. White was used as the 'pinch hitter' for the second time, but he looked no happier in this position than he has done in any other role in international cricket. England reached 70 for 2 and then lost Robin Smith and Fairbrother to successive deliveries. Thorpe and Hick added 43, but thereafter all was doom and gloom.

Adrian Kuiper, who damaged a hamstring and batted for the most part with a runner, hit 61 off 66 balls and was named Man of the Match. Pollock was Man of the Series. Although saddened and weakened by the loss of Richardson with a broken finger, South Africa were well prepared and in good heart for the World Cup. For England's ill-chosen party, it was a case of 'Where do we go from here?'. There seemed neither rhyme nor reason in much of what had happened since the side landed in South Africa in October.

Seventh One-day International – South Africa v. England

21 January 1996 at St George's Park, Port Elizabeth

South Africa

A.C. Hudson	c Thorpe, **b** White	44
*S.J. Palframan	c Russell, **b** Martin	10
G. Kirsten	c Russell, **b** Gough	17
W.J. Cronje (Capt)	c Hick, **b** Martin	60
A.P. Kuiper	not out	61
J.H. Kallis	run out	2
B.M. McMillan	**b** White	4
S.M. Pollock	c Thorpe, **b** Gough	0
P.L. Symcox	**b** Gough	7
P.S. de Villiers	**b** Gough	0
P.R. Adams	not out	0
	b 1, lb 7, w 5	13
	50 overs (for 9 wickets)	218

	O	M	R	W
Cork	10	–	53	–
Martin	9	–	47	2
Gough	10	–	33	4
Illingworth	10	1	31	–
Hick	4	–	19	–
White	7	–	27	2

Fall of Wickets
1–30, 2–61, 3–123, 4–167, 5–172, 6–195, 7–196, 8–206, 9–206

England

M.A. Atherton (Capt)	c McMillan, **b** Pollock	3
C. White	c sub (Donald), **b** de Villiers	20
R.A. Smith	c Palframan, **b** McMillan	21
G.A. Hick	**b** Symcox	43
N.H. Fairbrother	**b** McMillan	0
G.P. Thorpe	**b** Adams	21
*R.C. Russell	c McMillan, **b** Symcox	3
D.G. Cork	lbw, **b** de Villiers	21
P.J. Martin	c Symcox, **b** de Villiers	6
D. Gough	**b** de Villiers	4
R.K. Illingworth	not out	2
	b 1, lb 5, w 2, nb 2	10
	46.1 overs	154

	O	M	R	W
de Villiers	9.1	1	32	4
Pollock	6	1	17	1
Cronje	4	–	17	–
McMillan	8	–	29	2
Symcox	10	–	31	2
Adams	9	1	22	1

Fall of Wickets
1–5, 2–35, 3–70, 4–70, 5–113, 6–118, 7–124, 8–147, 9–151

Umpires: R.E. Koertzen & C.J. Mitchley *Man of the Match:* A.P. Kuiper

South Africa won by 64 runs

England in South Africa 1995–96 First-class Matches Batting

	v. S.A. Invitation XI (Soweto) 27–30 October 1995		v. Border (East London) 2–5 November 1995		v. South Africa 'A' (Kimberley) 9–12 November 1995		First Test Match (Pretoria) 16–20 November 1995		v. Orange Free State (Bloemfontein) 23–25 November 1995		Second Test Match (Johannesberg) 30 November –4 December 1995		v. Boland (Paarl) 7–9 December 1995		Third Test Match (Durban) 14–18 December 1995		v. S.A. Students XI (Pietermaritzburg) 20–22 December 1995		Fourth Test Match (Port Elizabeth) 26–30 December 1995		Fifth Test Match (Cape Town) 2–4 January 1996		M	Inns	NO	Runs	HS	Av
M.A. Atherton	59	22*			53	0	78	–	0	13	9	185*			2	–	50	–	72	34	0	10	9	15	2	587	185*	45.15
A.J. Stewart	94	101*	11	–	34	56	6	–	110	–	45	38	39	–	41	–	89*	–	4	81	13	7	11	16	2	769	110	54.92
J.P. Crawley	85	1	108	–					28*	90			6	18*	–	–							5	7	2	336	108	67.20
R.A. Smith	4	0	0	–	48	28	43	–	27	0	52	44	39	1	34	–	–	–	2	–	66	13	11	16	–	401	66	25.06
G.A. Hick	15	55	18	–	0	43	141	–			6	4	32	–	31*	–	–	–	62	11*	2	36	10	14	2	456	141	38.00
R.C. Russell	11	43	64	–	93*	40	50*	–			12	29*	129*	–	8	–	–	–	30	–	9	2	10	13	4	520	129*	57.77
M. Watkinson	0	26			2	2							24	–			–	–			11	0	5	7	–	65	26	9.28
M.C. Ilott	0	6*	1*	–					–	–			–	8	–	–	–	–	0*	–			7	5	3	15	8	7.50
R.K. Illingworth	19	–	3	–			0	–	–	5*			57*	–	–	–	–	–	28	–			8	6	2	112	57*	28.00
A.R.C. Fraser	6	–			5	15	4*	–			0	–									5*	1	5	7	2	36	15	7.20
D.E. Malcolm	0*	–			13	48*			–	–	0*	–									1	0*	5	6	4	62	48*	31.00
M.R. Ramprakash			70	–	1	42	9	–	15	42	4	0											5	8	–	183	70	22.87
D.G. Cork			43	–			13	–	–	67*	8	–			23*	–			1	–	16	8	7	8	2	179	67*	29.83
D. Gough			7	–	26	4	0	–			2	–	3	–									5	6	–	42	26	7.00
P.J. Martin			5	–					–	13*			3	–	–	–	–	–	4	–	0	9	7	6	1	34	13*	6.80
G.P. Thorpe					1	3	13	–	131*	–	34	17	56	3*	2	–	37*	–	27	12*	20	59	9	14	4	415	131*	41.50
J.E.R. Gallian																	3	–	14	28			2	3	–	45	28	15.00
Byes	9	9	1		14	10				3	6	4					4			9	4	2						
Leg-byes	14	5	6		9	7	16		2	2	1	7	8		4				9	8	1	5						
Wides		1	2		9	9	1		2	1			3	3			1		1	1	1							
No-balls	16	13	12			2	7		1	3	21	23	3		7		2		9	5	4	5						
Total	332	282	351		308	309	381		316	239	200	351	402	33	152		186		263	189	153	157						
Wickets	10	5	10		10	10	9		4	4	10	5	8	2	5		2		10	3	10	10						
Result	D		W		L		Ab		D		D		D		D		D		D		L							

Fielding Figures

44 – R.C. Russell (ct 39 / st 5)
10 – R.A. Smith
8 – G.A. Hick
6 – J.P. Crawley
5 – A.J. Stewart
3 – M.A. Atherton, R.K. Illingworth and G.P. Thorpe
2 – M. Watkinson and D.G. Cork
1 – A.R.C. Fraser, D. Gough, P.J. Martin and M.R. Ramprakash

Bowling

	D.E. Malcolm	M.C. Ilott	A.R.C. Fraser	R.K. Illingworth	M. Watkinson	D.G. Cork	D. Gough	P.J. Martin	G.P. Thorpe	G.A. Hick	M.R. Ramprakash	J.E.R. Gallian	Byes	Leg-byes	Wides	No-balls	Total	Wkts
v. South African Invitation XI	14–4–32–0	14–6–41–1	9–2–14–0	25.1–10–76–6	16–5–38–3									9		3	210	10
(Soweto) 27–30 October 1995	5–1–18–0		2–2–0–0	2–2–0–0	3–1–4–1								1	2			25	1
v. Border (East London)		14–4–34–1		9–4–17–0		16.3–2–48–5	12–4–30–3	7–2–23–0					8	6	1	9	166	10
2–5 November 1995		13.5–3–36–5		12–1–33–0		12–0–33–3	9–3–9–2	5–2–11–0						10		1	132	10
v. South Africa 'A' (Kimberley)	22–3–88–1		25–3–78–1		42–8–137–2		29–6–85–3		4–1–15–0	14–3–34–2	6–1–11–0		16	6	2	11	470	9
9–12 November 1995	7–0–27–0		15–4–49–3		7.5–0–32–0		8–0–33–1			1–0–7–0					1	3	148	4
First Test Match (Pretoria)																		Ab
16–20 November 1995																		
v. Orange Free State (Bloemfontein)	15–2–59–1	10–1–37–1		19–6–50–3		13–2–40–2		12–3–45–2			3–1–7–0			7	1	3	245	9
23–25 November 1995	9–1–32–1	7–3–12–1		7–2–7–0		7–2–21–0		6–0–29–0			3–1–7–1			2		2	110	3
Second Test Match (Johannesberg)	22–5–62–4		20–5–69–0			32–7–84–5	15–2–64–0			15–1–38–1			1	14	2	5	332	10
30 November–2 December	13–2–65–2		29–6–84–3			31.3–6–78–4	12–2–48–0			15–3–35–0	4–0–19–0		5	12	1	3	346	9
v. Boland (Paarl)		22–8–48–3		50–16–89–2	38–17–82–2		3.4–1–14–0	21.2–6–48–2					5	2		1	288	10
7–9 December 1995																		
Third Test Match (Durban)		15–3–48–3		29–12–37–3		27–12–64–0		27–9–60–4		2–0–5–0				11		1	225	10
14–18 December 1995																		
v. S.A. Students XI (Pietermaritzburg)		24–6–89–6		24–3–65–0	17.1–4–54–1			11–5–33–1		5–0–7–0		5–0–19–0		2	1	3	269	8
20–22 December 1995																		
Fourth Test Match (Port Elizabeth)		29.4–7–82–1		39.5–8–105–3		42.2–2–113–4		33–9–79–1		12–2–32–0		2–0–6–0		11		8	428	10
26–30 December 1995				22–7–45–3		26.3–5–63–3		17–8–39–3					8	7	1	3	162	9
Fifth Test Match (Cape Town)	20–6–56–0		17–10–34–1		15–3–35–2	25–6–60–3		24–9–37–3						22		1	244	10
2–4 January 1996	2–0–12–0				4–0–24–0	4–0–23–0		4–2–3–0		1.4–0–7–0				1		1	70	0
Bowler's average	129–24– 451–9 50.11	149.3–41– 427–22 19.40	117–32– 328–8 41.00	239–71– 524–21 24.95	143–38– 406–11 36.90	236.5–54– 627–29 21.62	88.4–18– 283–9 31.44	167.2–55– 407–16 25.43	4–1– 15–0 –	65.4–9– 165–3 55.00	16–3– 44–1 44.00	7–0– 25–0 –						

Castle Cup

Transvaal pay dearly for a sub-standard pitch.

27, 28, 29 and 30 October 1995
at Newlands, Cape Town
Transvaal 375 (K.R. Rutherford 134, D.R. Laing 72, N.D. McKenzie 67, C.R. Matthews 4 for 72) and 266 (M.W. Rushmere 83, N. Pothas 66, G.A. Pollock 52, C.R. Matthews 5 for 43)
Western Province 304 (J.H. Kallis 146, G. Kirsten 53) and 258 (B.M. McMillan 60, D.L. Haynes 52, S.D. Jack 4 for 55)
Transvaal won by 79 runs
Transvaal 19 pts, Western Province 7 pts

at Centurion Park, Verwoerdburg
Northern Transvaal 365 (M.J.R. Rindel 67, I. Pistorius 63 not out, D.J. van Zyl 56, B.N. Schultz 6 for 84) and 263 for 8 dec. (C.B. Lambert 108, A.J. Seymore 72, T.G. Shaw 5 for 98)
Eastern Province 331 for 4 dec. (G.C. Victor 88, L.J. Koen 82, D.J. Callaghan 73 not out) and 150 for 7 (K.C. Wessels 66 not out)
Match drawn
Eastern Province 6 pts, Northern Transvaal 4 pts

at Springbok Park, Bloemfontein
Orange Free State 451 for 9 dec. (L.J. Wilkinson 226 not out, H.C. Bakkes 68, R. Telemachus 5 for 152)
Boland 215 (T.N. Lazard 63) and 226 for 7 (K.C. Jackson 57, P.A.J. DeFreitas 53)
Match drawn
Orange Free State 9 pts, Boland 5 pts

at Buffalo Park, East London
Natal 448 (D.N. Crookes 83, P.J.R. Steyn 79, M.L. Bruyns 62, N.C. Johnson 55, S.M. Pollock 53 not out, P.A.N. Emslie 4 for 83)
Border 91 (S.M. Pollock 7 for 33) and 277 (P.N. Kirsten 147, P.J. Botha 81, D.N. Crookes 5 for 59, M.D. Marshall 4 for 48)
Natal won by an innings and 80 runs
Natal 17 pts, Border 2 pts

South Africa's premier first-class competition began a week after England had arrived in the country, and the tournament opened with what is always seen as one of the most decisive matches, Western Province against Transvaal. Transvaal were led by Ken Rutherford, the former New Zealand captain. Having been dropped by New Zealand, Rutherford chose to play for Transvaal, and, in his first match, hit 134 off 201 balls with three sixes and 21 fours. This was a remarkable performance as, having been put in, Transvaal lost their first three wickets for 29. The splendid Kallis responded with a century for Western Province, and Matthews bowled well, but Steven Jack, match figures of 7 for 108, turned the game in favour of the visitors.

Acting-skipper of Free State, Louis Wilkinson hit the first double century of his career in the match against Boland at Springbok Park. (Paul Sturgess/Sportsline)

Brett Schultz gave the South African selectors a reminder that he was back to full fitness, but Northern Transvaal still had the edge over Eastern Province, who were ultimately indebted to a three-hour innings from skipper Kepler Wessels for their survival.

Free State had lost batsmen through retirement and movement, but skipper Louis Wilkinson filled the breach with the first double century of his career. He hit a six and 22 fours and remained unbeaten after 308 balls. He was at the crease for 446 minutes. Boland were forced to follow on, but Stelling and Henderson held out for over an hour to save the game.

Malcolm Marshall's ambition to lead Natal to the Castle Cup began well. Consistent scoring took Natal to a good score, and an outstanding spell of fast bowling by Shaun Pollock saw Border bowled out on the second day. They batted with great determination when they followed on, and Peter Kirsten, now 41 years old, hit 147 in six-and-a-quarter hours, but the match was over early on the fourth day.

3, 4, 5 and 6 November 1995
at Kingsmead, Durban
Natal 297 (J.N. Rhodes 82, D.N. Crookes 81, R.P. Snell 5 for 67, S.D. Jack 4 for 83) and 253 (A.C. Hudson 93, M.L. Bruyns 52, C.E. Eksteen 4 for 64)
Transvaal 259 (D.R. Laing 56, K.R. Rutherford 51, R.E. Veenstra 5 for 77) and 124 (A.N. Bacher 53)
Natal won by 167 runs
Natal 17 pts, Transvaal 7 pts

at St George's Park, Port Elizabeth
Eastern Province 218 (P.G. Amm 89, A.A. Donald 5 for 44) and 458 (K.C. Wessels 173, D.J. Richardson 122, G.C. Victor 58, C.F. Craven 4 for 62)
Orange Free State 517 for 9 dec. (F.D. Stephenson 166, J.F. Venter 91, D. Jordaan 88, H.C. Bakkes 54 not out) and 136 for 5 (W.J. Cronje 70 not out)
Match drawn
Orange Free State 8 pts, Eastern Province 4 pts

4, 5, 6 and 7 November 1995
at Centurion Park, Verwoerdburg
Northern Transvaal 344 (A.J. Seymore 124, G.J. Smith 68) and 231 (P.R. Adams 6 for 101)
Western Province 451 (B.M. McMillan 116, J.B. Commins 94, D.L. Haynes 71, E.O. Simons 54) and 126 for 2 (J.H. Kallis 55 not out)
Western Province won by 8 wickets
Western Province 17 pts, Northern Transvaal 5 pts

Natal made it two wins in two matches with victory over Transvaal. They recovered well from a horrendous start that saw them at 45 for 5. Rhodes and Crookes added 132, and the tail wagged hard. Transvaal were handicapped when Snell retired hurt and took no further part in the match. They slipped to 50 for 6 in their second innings, and there was no way back.

Stephenson and Venter added 125 for Free State's fifth wicket against Eastern Province, and the much travelled Stephenson added another 125 with Bakkes for the ninth. Stephenson was finally run out for 166 made off 279 balls with three sixes and 17 fours. Free State seemed well set for victory, but they were thwarted by Wessels and Richardson who scored 229 for the fifth wicket. Eventually, Free State needed 160 off 18 overs, and, with Cronje hitting 70 off 56 balls, they made a brave, but unsuccessful effort.

Left-arm spinner Paul Adams, playing in his first Castle Cup game, destroyed Northern Transvaal with match figures of 8 for 190. The unorthodox Adams took Western Province to a comfortable victory and was immediately recognised by the South African selectors.

10, 11, 12 and 13 November 1995
at Newlands, Cape Town
Eastern Province 234 (D.J. Callaghan 59, E.O. Simons 4 for 38, A. Martyn 4 for 68) and 109 (M.W. Pringle 6 for 32)
Western Province 121 (A. Badenhorst 5 for 49, D.J. Callaghan 4 for 17) and 224 for 3 (G. Kirsten 104 not out, H.D. Ackerman 50 not out)
Western Province won by 7 wickets
Western Province 14 pts, Eastern Province 6 pts

at Springbok Park, Bloemfontein
Northern Transvaal 259 (M.J.G. Davis 71, F.D. Stephenson 4 for 58) and 368 (M.J.R. Rindel 174, D.J. van Zyl 57 not out, F.D. Stephenson 5 for 63)
Orange Free State 239 (W.J. Cronje 54) and 389 for 6 (W.J. Cronje 158, J.F. Venter 95, F.D. Stephenson 51)
Orange Free State won by 4 wickets
Orange Free State 16 pts, Northern Transvaal 7 pts

at Wanderers, Johannesburg
Transvaal 431 (M.W. Rushmere 133, B.M. White 85, K.R. Rutherford 51) and 77 for 1 (N. Pothas 54 not out)
Border 180 (P.N. Kirsten 62, S. Jacobs 5 for 30) and 324 (P.J. Botha 94, P.N. Kirsten 85, S. Jacobs 4 for 45, T.C. Webster 4 for 113)
Transvaal won by 9 wickets
Transvaal 19 pts, Border 4 pts

at Boland Bank Park, Paarl
Boland 255 (A.P. Kuiper 87, K.C. Jackson 69, S.M. Pollock 4 for 57) and 128 (R.E. Veenstra 6 for 38)
Natal 363 (E.L.R. Stewart 119, A.C. Hudson 67, J.N. Rhodes 52, D.N. Crookes 51) and 22 for 1
Natal won by 9 wickets
Natal 13 pts, Boland 3 pts

Western Province trailed Eastern Province by 113 runs on the first innings but still won in three days. Medium-pacer Meyrick Pringle turned the match for them with an outstanding second innings bowling performance which brought him 6 for 32 in 12.4 overs. Needing 223 to win, Western Province were 17 for 2 at the end of the second day, but a blazing hundred from Gary Kirsten took them to victory.

In spite of Mike Rindel's career-best 174 off 266 balls, Northern Transvaal lost to Free State, who were again wonderfully served by skipper Hansie Cronje who hit 158 off 216 balls with 22 fours. He and Venter shared a third wicket stand of 215.

Transvaal disposed of Border early on the fourth day. Border had been forced to follow on, but Botha and Peter Kirsten showed great resilience in a third wicket stand of 138 in 195 minutes which helped avoid an innings defeat

Natal crushed Boland to go top of the table, two points ahead of Transvaal. Stewart took the individual award for his 119 off 316 deliveries, but Natal's wicket-keeper Mark Bruyns equalled the association's record with nine dismissals in the match, all catches. Dennis Gamsy performed the feat three times in the sixties, but he never managed nine catches.

24, 25, 26 and 27 November 1995

at Buffalo Park, East London
Northern Transvaal 183 (M.J.R. Rindel 82) and 118 (F.J.C. Cronje 4 for 16)
Border 427 (P.J. Botha 71, S.Tikolo 64, P.N. Kirsten 63)
Border won by an innings and 126 runs
Border 16 pts, Northern Transvaal 2 pts

at Boland Bank Park, Paarl
Boland 199 (A.P. Kuiper 52, S.D. Jack 4 for 54) and 361 (A.P. Kuiper 155, L.D. Ferreira 50, S.D. Jack 5 for 69)
Transvaal 310 (A.M. Bacher 91, M.W. Rushmere 83, D.R. Laing 71) and 251 for 7 (D.R. Laing 107, K.R. Rutherford 50)
Transvaal won by 3 wickets
Transvaal 17 pts, Boland 5 pts

at Kingsmead, Durban
Eastern Province 71 (S.M. Pollock 5 for 19) and 219 (K.C. Wessels 77, D.J. Callaghan 65 not out, S.M. Pollock 5 for 40)
Natal 449 for 5 dec. (A.C. Hudson 153, P.J.R. Steyn 108, D.N. Crookes 64)
Natal won by an innings and 159 runs
Natal 19 pts, Eastern Province 1 pt

Border beat Northern Transvaal in three days, and the Man of the Match award went to Steve Tikolo who was to perform nobly for Kenya in the World Cup.

Transvaal maintained their challenge for the title with a win over Boland. Steve Jack, genuinely quick, bowled very well, but Adrian Kuiper, now captain of Boland, almost transformed the match with an innings of 155 off 195 balls. He hit four sixes and 12 fours, and with Boland's tail proving stubborn, Transvaal suddenly had a fight on their hands. They ended the third day with three wickets down and only one run on the board. Revival, and ultimately victory, came through the efforts of Dean Laing who hit the second and higher century of his career.

Natal moved to their fourth win in as many matches as they routed Eastern Province before lunch on the final day. Shaun Pollock was again in devastating form with 10 for 59 in the match. Hudson and Steyn began Natal's innings with a partnership of 270.

1, 2, 3 and 4 December 1995

at St George's Park, Port Elizabeth
Eastern Province 452 for 3 dec. (L.J. Koen 202 not out, P.G. Amm 157, K.C. Wessels 57) and 139 for 8 dec. (K.C. Wessels 51, C.W. Henderson 4 for 71)
Boland 326 (T.N. Lazard 77, E.A.E. Baptiste 4 for 58) and 110 for 4
Match drawn
Eastern Province 7 pts, Boland 2 pts

Consistently fine bowling by Boland's medium-pacer Roger Telemachus earned him a place in the South African 'A' side to tour England. (Paul Sturgess/Sportsline)

8, 9, 10 and 11 December 1995

at Springbok Park, Bloemfontein
Orange Free State 532 for 7 dec. (G.F.J. Liebenberg 229, W.J. Cronje 116, L.J. Wilkinson 61, D.N. Crookes 5 for 119) and 113 for 2
Natal 167 (N.C. Johnson 75 not out, N.W. Pretorius 4 for 28) and 474 (E.L.R. Stewart 131, M.D. Marshall 99 not out, D.N. Crookes 63, J.F. Venter 4 for 52, N. Boje 4 for 128)
Orange Free State won by 8 wickets
Orange Free State 18 pts, Natal 1 pt

at Buffalo Park, East London
Border 173 (M.W. Pringle 4 for 30, C.R. Matthews 4 for 46) and 306 (P.N. Kirsten 104, D.J. Cullinan 56, S.Tikolo 55, P.R. Adams 5 for 128, A.C. Dawson 4 for 25)
Western Province 500 for 5 dec. (G. Kirsten 244, H.D. Ackerman 83 not out, J.H. Kallis 53, D.L. Haynes 52)
Western Province won by an innings and 21 runs
Western Province 18 pts, Border 1 pt

Making his debut for Eastern Province, Prince was bowled by DeFreitas without a run scored, but in the next 418 minutes, Amm and Koen scored 338, a second wicket record by a South African pair. Louis Koen's double century was the first of his career. Consistent batting enabled Boland to avoid the follow-on, and the match was drawn.

Natal's winning run came crashing to an end when Hansie Cronje and Gerhadus Liebenberg scored 225 in 220 minutes for Free State's second wicket. Liebenberg reached the first double century of his career. Forced to follow on, Natal avoided an innings defeat thanks to Stewart's 131 off 142 balls and to Malcolm Marshall's unbeaten 99. Marshall and Veenstra added 74 for the last wicket before Veenstra was bowled by Venter. Free State hit off the required runs at four an over.

Paul Adams struck again and Gary Kirsten recorded his highest score as Western Province demolished Border for whom skipper Peter Kirsten hit a brave but unavailing century.

15, 16, 17 and 18 December 1995
at Boland Bank Park, Paarl
Boland 209 (T.N. Lazard 89 not out, B.C. Fourie 5 for 46) and 185 (P.J. Botha 4 for 31)
Border 177 (C.W. Henderson 4 for 41) and 221 for 8 (P.J. Botha 93, P.C. Strydom 69, R. Telemachus 5 for 72)
Border won by 2 wickets
Border 15 pts, Boland 6 pts

at Newlands, Cape Town
Orange Free State 247 (M.W. Pringle 5 for 89) and 252 (F.D. Stephenson 104, M.W. Pringle 4 for 76)
Western Province 257 (S.G. Koenig 65, J.B. Commins 55, N.W. Pretorius 5 for 79, J.F. Venter 4 for 52) and 162 for 4 (N. Boje 4 for 39)
Match drawn
Western Province 7 pts, Orange Free State 6 pts

at Wanderers, Johannesburg
Northern Transvaal 131 (S.D. Jack 4 for 24) and 191 (C.B. Lambert 69, R.P. Snell 4 for 43)
Transvaal 130 (R.E. Bryson 4 for 16) and 83 (G.J. Smith 5 for 32)
Northern Transvaal won by 109 runs
Northern Transvaal 14 pts, Transvaal 0 pts

Border gained their second win of the season early on the fourth day in Paarl while Free State and Western Province played a rather dour draw at Newlands. Meyrick Pringle continued with his inspired bowling form and Franklyn Stephenson was again in good form with the bat.

The centre of attention was on the Wanderers where Northern Transvaal broke their barren spell with victory in two days. Even though they made two scores of under two hundred, they won by a margin of more than 100 runs. West Indian Clayton Lambert threw caution to the wind and hit 69 off 67 balls with a six and ten fours. All others had perished on a treacherous pitch. The result was that Transvaal were fined and deducted four points – the four bowling bonus points that they had earned in the match – for a sub-standard pitch. It was to prove a costly penalty.

26, 27, 28 and 29 December 1995
at Boland Bank Park, Paarl
Boland 231 (K.C. Jackson 56, M.W. Pringle 5 for 67) and 123 (M.W. Pringle 6 for 41)
Western Province 422 for 9 dec. (H.H. Gibbs 112, H.D. Ackerman 84, J.B. Commins 57, D.R. Rundle 50, M. Erasmus 5 for 87, C.W. Henderson 4 for 147)
Western Province won by an innings and 68 runs
Western Province 18 pts, Boland 1 pt

at Buffalo Park, East London
Orange Free State 188 and 167 (S.C. Pope 7 for 62)
Border 301 (P.C. Strydom 58, J.F. Venter 4 for 65) and 55 for 0
Border won by 10 wickets
Border 17 pts, Orange Free State 3 pts

1, 2, 3 and 4 January 1996
at Kingsmead, Durban
Northern Transvaal 161 (M.J.R. Rindel 51, L. Klusener 5 for 57) and 191 (C.B. Lambert 95 not out)
Natal 369 (E.L.R. Stewart 75, N.C. Johnson 55)
Natal won by an innings and 17 runs
Natal 19 pts, Northern Transvaal 5 pts

4, 5, 6 and 7 January 1996
at St George's Park, Port Elizabeth
Eastern Province 390 for 6 dec. (D.J. Callaghan 133 not out, K.C. Wessels 94, T.G. Shaw 74 not out) and 241 for 7 dec. (L.J. Koen 84)
Transvaal 331 for 7 dec. (N.D. McKenzie 150 not out) and 281 (K.R. Rutherford 109, N.D. McKenzie 60)
Eastern Province won by 19 runs
Eastern Province 14 pts, Transvaal 5 pts

Ever the telling period in South African cricket, the Christmas/New Year matches saw Western Province, deprived of their Test players, continue their challenge for the cup. They owed much to the astonishing form of Meyrick Pringle who captured 11 for 108 in the match against Boland. There was also a sparkling hundred from Herschelle Gibbs.

The surprise of the season was the humiliation of Free State by Border inside three days. Steve Pope, an occasional medium-pacer and nephew of the great Ken McEwan, had moved to Border from Eastern Province and returned the best bowling performance of his career, a match-winning achievement.

Natal came back to winning ways with a three-day victory over Northern Transvaal, while Transvaal lost more ground when they were narrowly beaten by Eastern Province. Neil McKenzie, in his first full season, hit a maiden first-class hundred but still finished on the losing side.

No man contributed more to Western Province's success in the Castle Cup than Meyrick Pringle with his fast medium-pace bowling. (Paul Sturgess/Sportsline)

26, 27, 28 and 29 January 1996
at St George's Park, Port Elizabeth
Border 263 (P.C. Strydom 50, T.G. Shaw 6 for 45) and 181
Eastern Province 409 (L.J. Koen 154, P.G. Amm 83, D.J. Callaghan 66, B.C. Fourie 6 for 76) and 39 for 0
Eastern Province won by 10 wickets
Eastern Province 16 pts, Border 3 pts

at Centurion Park, Verwoerdburg
Boland 256 (K.C. Jackson 100, A. Wessels 65, P.S. de Villiers 4 for 53)
Northern Transvaal 95 (R. Telemachus 4 for 25, C.W. Henderson 4 for 33) and 335 for 8 (M.J.R. Rindel 81, M.J.G. Davis 65, R.F. Pienaar 50, H.S. Williams 4 for 48)
Match drawn
Boland 7 pts, Northern Transvaal 4 pts

at Kingsmead, Durban
Natal 277 (D.N. Crookes 111 not out)
Western Province 85 (L. Klusener 8 for 34) and 271 for 7 (G. Kirsten 76 not out, H.D. Ackerman 50)
Match drawn
Natal 7 pts, Western Province 4 pts

at Wanderers, Johannesburg
Transvaal 214 (M.W. Rushmere 62) and 294 for 8 (R.P. Snell 105, N.D. McKenzie 88)
Orange Free State 203 for 7 dec. (J.F. Venter 56 not out) and 301 (C.F. Craven 90, L.J. Wilkinson 66)
Transvaal won by 4 runs
Transvaal 15 pts, Orange Free State 6 pts

Eastern Province, finishing strongly, beat Border with plenty of time to spare on the last day. There was another strong partnership from Koen, and some fine left-arm spin bowling from Tim Shaw, who has failed to establish himself in the South African side to the surprise of many.

Little more than an hour's play was possible on the second day at Centurion Park, which virtually doomed the match to a draw, and there was no play at all possible on the second day in Durban and very little on the third. Derek Crookes hit an aggressive hundred on the first day, but the honours went to Lance Klusener, medium-pace, who produced one of the best-ever bowling performances seen at Kingsmead. Twenty-four-year-old Klusener, who bats left and bowls right, is an all-rounder destined, one feels, for the highest honours. Gary Kirsten who, like Simons, was forced to retire hurt at one time, thwarted Natal when Western Province were forced to follow on. This defiance meant much, for it restricted Natal's lead at the top of the table to eight points with one round of matches remaining.

Rain also restricted play in Johannesburg, but the positive captaincy of Rutherford and Hansie Cronje brought a fine match. Richard Snell, disappointingly omitted from South Africa's World Cup squad, hit 105 off 129 balls after six Transvaal second innings wickets had fallen for 64. This enabled Rutherford to set a target of 306 in 82 overs. There was some spectacular play from Venter, Wilkinson, Bakkes and Boje, but Free State were bowled out for 301 with seven balls remaining.

9, 10, 11 and 12 February 1996
at Newlands, Cape Town
Western Province 266 (H.D. Ackerman 106 not out, E.O. Simons 71) and 230 (S.G. Koening 56, B.P. Horan 4 for 43)
Border 206 (A. Martyn 5 for 63, M.W. Pringle 4 for 73) and 198 (P.C. Strydom 69, M.W. Pringle 5 for 67)
Western Province won by 92 runs
Western Province 17 pts, Border 6 pts

at Wanderers, Johannesburg
Boland 206 (R.P. Snell 5 for 64) and 182 (A.P. Kuiper 51, W. Kidwell 4 for 36)
Transvaal 365 (B.M. White 159 not out, K.R. Rutherford 54, R.P. Snell 52, C.M. Willoughby 4 for 86) and 27 for 1
Transvaal won by 9 wickets
Transvaal 18 pts, Boland 5 pts

Lance Klusener produced the outstanding bowling performance of the season in the Castle Cup when he took 8 for 34 for Natal against Western Province in Durban. (Paul Sturgess/Sportsline)

at Springbok Park, Bloemfontein
Eastern Province 391 (D.J. Callaghan 105, L.J. Koen 93, P.G. Amm 90) and 275 for 8 dec. (P.G. Amm 76, D.J. Callaghan 55, M.G. Beamish 52)
Orange Free State 317 (C.F. Craven 86, N. Boje 69, G.F.J. Liebenberg 63, B.N. Schultz 6 for 90) and 172 for 4 (G.F.J. Liebenberg 65)
Match drawn
Orange Free State 7 pts, Eastern Province 7 pts

at Centurion Park, Verwoerdburg
Northern Transvaal 213 (S. Elworthy 51 not out)
Natal 169 for 6 (D.N. Crookes 74, G.J. Smith 4 for 49)
Match drawn
Natal 5 pts, Northern Transvaal 4 pts

Cricket can be a very cruel game. In beating Border at Newlands, Western Province won the Castle Cup. They owed much to Ackerman and, inevitably, to Pringle, but they also owed much to the weather. In Durban, no play was possible on the third and fourth days so that Natal were denied the points that would have given them the title. In Johannesburg, Snell gave more proof that he should have been in the World Cup squad, as did Callaghan and Schultz in Bloemfontein, and Transvaal won with ease. The left-handed Brad White batted through the 104.5 overs of the innings for the highest score of his career, and the points that Transvaal gained took them to second place, two points behind Western Province. Transvaal, it will be remembered, were deducted four points for a sub-standard pitch. Cricket can be a very cruel game.

Castle Cup Final Table

	P	W	L	D	Pts
Western Province	8	5	1	2	102
Transvaal	8	5	3	–	100
Natal	8	5	1	2	98
Orange Free State	8	2	2	4	73
Border	8	3	5	–	64
Eastern Province	8	2	2	4	61
Northern Transvaal	8	1	4	3	45
Boland	8	–	5	3	34

UCB Bowl

Rain thwarts Natal for a second time.

Group A

27, 28 and 29 October 1995
at St George's Park, Port Elizabeth
Griqualand West 392 for 9 dec. (M.I. Gidley 106, W.M. Dry 99) and 133 for 7
Eastern Province 'B' 256 (M.G. Beamish 101, V.A. Walsh 6 for 52)
Match drawn
Griqualand West 5 pts, Eastern Province 'B' 4 pts

at Wanderers, Johannesburg
Transvaal 'B' 320 for 6 dec. (M. Benfield 96, H.A. Manack 94) and 225 for 3 dec. (B.M. White 102 not out, M. Benfield 52)
Northern Transvaal 'B' 301 for 9 dec. (L.P. Vorster 88, G. Dros 56, M.J. Vandrau 4 for 93) and 180 for 5 (L.P. Vorster 90 not out, M. van Jaarsveld 64)
Match drawn
Transvaal 'B' 7 pts, Northern Transvaal 'B' 6 pts

at Boland Bank Park, Paarl
Boland 'B' 238 (M.S. Nackerdien 117, A.K. Volsteedt 61, S.G. Peall 9 for 76) and 226 for 6 dec. (B.C. Baguley 50)
Zimbabwe Board XI 229 for 9 dec. (A.D.R. Campbell 64, S.G. Davies 50 not out, C.M. Willoughby 4 for 43) and 176 for 7
Match drawn
Boland 'B' 6 pts, Zimbabwe Board XI 6 pts

24, 25 and 26 November 1995
at St George's Park, Port Elizabeth
Transvaal 'B' 316 for 6 dec. (B.M. White 180 not out) and 214 for 4 dec. (B.M. White 60, M. Benfield 59, G.A. Pollock 50 not out)
Eastern Province 'B' 248 for 9 dec. (M.G. Beamish 86, S. Abrahams 52, W. Kidwell 4 for 54) and 172 for 3 (M.C. Venter 70 not out)
Match drawn
Transvaal 'B' 7 pts, Eastern Province 'B' 5 pts

at Centurion Park, Verwoerdburg
Northern Transvaal 'B' 339 (G. Dros 83 not out, M. van Jaarsveld 81, L.P. Vorster 66, B.C. Strang 5 for 69) and 244 for 8 dec. (M. van Jaarsveld 93, D.J.J. de Vos 77, E.A. Brandes 4 for 46)
Zimbabwe Board XI 334 for 9 dec. (G.J. Whittall 85, A.D.R. Campbell 53) and 131 for 7 (D.J.J. de Vos 4 for 34)
Match drawn
Northern Transvaal 'B' 6 pts, Zimbabwe Board XI 6 pts

at Kimberley County Club, Kimberley
Boland 'B' 215 (A.T. Holdstock 81, J.M. Villet 51, J.E. Johnson 4 for 54, V.A. Walsh 4 for 65) and 196 (A.T. Holdstock 55)
Griqualand West 283 (C.V. English 67 not out) and 132 for 9 (F.C. Brooker 50, B.J. Drew 5 for 79)
Griqualand West won by 1 wicket
Griqualand West 17 pts, Boland 'B' 7 pts

9, 10 and 11 December 1995
at NFO Ground, Randjesfontein
Boland 'B' 108 (W. Kidwell 6 for 23) and 215 (A.K. Volsteedt 92, W. Kidwell 6 for 65)
Transvaal 'B' 297 (Z. de Bruyn 78, G.C. Yates 50, M. Erasmus 5 for 70) and 30 for 0
Transvaal 'B' won by 10 wickets
Transvaal 'B' 18 pts, Boland 'B' 5 pts

15, 16 and 17 December, 1995
at Harare South Country Club
Griqualand West 290 for 9 dec. (M.I. Gidley 105, W.M. Dry 93, H.K. Olonga 4 for 94) and 183 for 9 dec. (F.C. Brooker 53)
Zimbabwe Board XI 153 (V.A. Walsh 4 for 37, C.V. English 4 for 47) and 258 for 9 (A.C. Waller 74, S.V. Carlisle 54)
Match drawn
Griqualand West 8 pts, Zimbabwe Board XI 5 pts

at Harlequins, Pretoria
Eastern Province 'B' 150 (G.C. Victor 73, G.J. Kruis 5 for 36) and 190 for 4 (M.C. Venter 107 not out)
Northern Transvaal 'B' 296 (L.P. Vorster 77, D.J. van Zyl 69, D. Rossouw 5 for 57)
Match drawn
Northern Transvaal 'B' 8 pts, Eastern Province 'B' 5 pts

25, 26 and 27 January 1996
at Boland Bank Park, Paarl
Northern Transvaal 'B' 277 for 9 dec. (B.J. Somerville 138, N. Martin 56, Z. Ebrahim 4 for 49) and 203 for 5 dec. (N. Martin 89 not out)
Boland 'B' 201 and 136 (P. de Bruyn 6 for 38)
Northern Transvaal 'B' won by 143 runs
Northern Transvaal 'B' 17 pts, Boland 'B' 5 pts

at Alexandra Sports Club
Eastern Province 'B' 297 for 6 (G.C. Victor 100)
v. **Zimbabwe Board XI**
Match drawn
no points

26, 27 and 28 January 1996
at Kimberley Country Club
Transvaal 'B' 157 for 6 dec. (Z. de Bruyn 126 not out, N.R. Rhodes 98, H.A. Manack 51) and 74 for 2
Griqualand West 421 for 8 dec. (J.M. Arthur 109, P.H. Barnard 108, M.I. Gidley 91, M.J. Vandrau 4 for 97)
Match drawn
Griqualand West 4 pts, Transvaal 'B' 3 pts

8, 9 and 10 February 1996
at Boland Bank Park, Paarl
Boland 'B' 217 for 9 dec. (E. Liebenberg 62, A.R. Wylie 50) and 263 for 5 (A.R. Wylie 108 not out)
Eastern Province 'B' 148 for 6 dec. (M.C. Venter 119, C.C. Wait 78, C.C. Bradfield 61, A.G. Prince 50)
Match drawn
Eastern Province 'B' 5 pts, Boland 'B' 2 pts

at Bulawayo Athletic Club
Transvaal 'B' 119 for 4 dec. (Z. de Bruyn 60 not out) and 67 for 2
Zimbabwe Board XI 0 for 0 dec.
Match drawn
no points

9, 10 and 11 February 1996
at Kimberley Country Club, Kimberley
Northern Transvaal 'B' 131 (N. Martin 64, A.J. Swanepoel 5 for 35, V.A. Walsh 4 for 61) and 156 (A.J. Swanepoel 5 for 29, V.A. Walsh 4 for 44)
Griqualand West 345 (M.I. Gidley 85, W.E. Schonegevel 55, P. de Bruyn 4 for 96)
Griqualand West won by an innings and 58 runs
Griqualand West 17 pts, Northern Transvaal 'B' 3 pts

The energetic and enthusiastic reconstruction of cricket in South Africa has yet to touch the UCB Bowl, a competition which includes eight second elevens and yet, perversely, is still recognised as first-class. The 1995-96 tournament offered the opportunity for several young players to prove themselves and to win places in the Castle Cup sides, which were weakened by international calls. None did better than Brad White, an opening batsman, and Ridwell, an opening bowler, both of whom won promotion with Transvaal. Former Leicestershire batsman, the left-handed Martyn Gidley scored consistently, and the Derbyshire all-rounder Matthew Vandrau had a good season.

Wicket-keepers had an outstanding time in Group 'A'. Mark Johnston of Transvaal 'B' held nine catches in the match against Boland 'B', and Bradley Robinson from Zimbabwe, new to the competition, had eight dismissals in the game against Griqualand West, seven catches and a stumping, six dismissals in the second innings. In the final match in the group, Jaco Burger of Griqualand West equalled the South African record with ten catches against Northern Transvaal 'B'.

Zimbabwe were again invited to enter a side, and the Board XI contained several players rich in Test experience, but, plagued by bad weather, they did not fare well. The exception was Stephen Peall, the off-spinner, who produced the season's outstanding bowling performance with 9 for 75 against Boland 'B'.

Group A Final Table

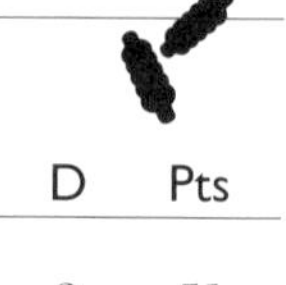

	P	W	L	D	Pts
Griqualand West	5	2	–	3	51
Northern Transvaal 'B'	5	1	1	3	40
Transvaal 'B'	5	1	–	4	35
Boland 'B'	5	–	3	2	25
Eastern Province 'B'	5	–	–	5	19
Zimbabwe Board XI	5	–	–	5	17

Chad Grainger, 199 for Easterns against Western Province 'B' at Springs. (Paul Sturgess/Sportsline)

Group B

27, 28 and 29 October 1995
at Witrand Stadium, Potchefstroom
Western Transvaal 202 and 298 (H.M. de Vos 115, B.T. Player 4 for 73, S.C. Cronje 4 for 87)
Orange Free State 'B' 273 (F.P. Schoeman 103, C.C. van der Merwe 64, G. Radford 5 for 51) and 159 for 3 (H. Wessels 80 not out)
Match drawn
Orange Free State 'B' 7 pts, Western Transvaal 6 pts

at PAM Brink Stadium, Springs
Easterns 391 for 9 dec. (C. Grainger 119, M.J. Mitchley 92, C.R. Norris 59) and 207 for 6 (M.J. Mitchley 58)
Western Province 'B' 360 for 6 dec. (F.B. Touzel 102, S.C. Koenig 89)
Match drawn
Easterns 7 pts, Western Province 'B' 6 pts

at Kingsmead, Durban
Border 'B' 86 (K.G. Storey 5 for 26) and 210 (D.O. Nosworthy 94, K.G. Storey 5 for 38, R.K. McGlashan 4 for 83)
Natal 'B' 468 for 7 dec. (E.L.R. Stewart 207 not out, K.A. Forde 122, R.E. Veenstra 57, S.E. Fourie 4 for 117)
Natal 'B' won by an innings and 172 runs
Natal 'B' 22 pts, Border 'B' 2 pts

16, 17 and 18 November, 1995
at Newlands, Cape Town
Natal 'B' 243 (D.M. Benkenstein 98, R.K. McGlashan 64, A. Martyn 6 for 67) and 417 (U.H. Goedeke 137, A.G. Small 72)
Western Province 'B' 350 (D.B. Rundle 103, M.T. Solomons 67, D.J. Pryke 5 for 92, K.G. Storey 4 for 78) and 7 for 0
Match Drawn
Western Province 'B' 8 pts, Natal 'B' 6 pts

26, 27 and 28 November, 1995
at Newlands, Cape Town
Orange Free State 'B' 206 (F. Davids 4 for 24) and 124 (A.C. Dawson 6 for 18)
Western Province 'B' 289 (G.F. Gillett 65, A.C. Dawson 55, F. Davids 52) and 41 for 1
Western Province 'B' won by 9 wickets
Western Province 'B' 18 pts, Orange Free State 'B' 6 pts

at PAM Brink Stadium, Springs
Easterns 228 (C. Grainger 71, B.P. Horan 4 for 48, S.C. Pope 4 for 54) and 307 for 7 dec. (C. Grainger 65, S.M. Skeete 61 not out)
Border 'B' 289 for 9 dec. (D.O. Nosworthy 141) and 91 for 2
Match drawn
Easterns 7 pts, Border 'B' 7 pts

1, 2 and 3 December 1995
at Kingsmead, Durban
Natal 'B' 401 for 7 dec. (K.A. Forde 121, C.B. Sugden 91, P.L. Symcox 65)
Western Transvaal 59 (D.J. Pryke 6 for 27, K.G. Storey 4 for 20) and 259 (M. Strydom 58, R.K. McGlashan 5 for 94, P.L. Symcox 4 for 61)
Natal 'B' won by an innings and 83 runs
Natal 'B' 20 pts, Western Transvaal 3 pts

15, 16 and 17 December 1995
at Sandringham Ground, Queenstown
Border 'B' 86 for 4
v. **Western Transvaal**
Match drawn
no points

at Springbok Park, Bloemfontein
Orange Free State 'B' 199
Easterns 317 for 6 dec. (C.R. Norris 132, C. Grainger 73)
Match drawn
Easterns 9 pts, Orange Free State 'B' 5 pts

25, 26 and 27 January 1996
at Fanie du Toit Stadium, Potchefstroom
Western Transvaal 97 (A. Martyn 6 for 22)
Western Province 'B' 229 for 9 (F.B. Touzel 90, G. Radford 6 for 70)
Match drawn
Western Province 'B' 7 pts, Western Transvaal 4 pts

at PAM Brink Stadium, Springs
Easterns *v.* **Natal 'B'**
Match abandoned

26, 27 and 28 January 1996
at Springbok Park, Bloemfontein
Border 'B' 301 for 5 dec. (W. Wiblin 160) and 91 for 0 dec.
Orange Free State 'B' 100 for 5 dec. and 291 for 6 (A. Moreby 79, C.C. van der Merwe 67)
Orange Free State 'B' won by 4 wickets
Orange Free State 'B' 13 pts, Border 'B' 7 pts

8, 9 and 10 February 1996
at Kingsmead, Durban
Orange Free State 'B' 201 (H. Wessels 58, G.M. Gilder 5 for 40) and 115 (G.M. Gilder 5 for 20)
Natal 'B' 246 (D.J. Watson 103 not out, H. Botha 4 for 31) and 71 for 5
Natal 'B' won by 5 wickets
Natal 'B' 17 pts, Orange Free State 'B' 7 pts

at Buffalo Park, East London
Border 'B' 242 (P.B. du Plessis 101, A. van Reenen 5 for 47) and 285 for 5 dec. (P.B. du Plessis 104 not out, S.C. Pope 71)
Western Province 'B' 275 for 6 dec. (M.C. de Villiers 88, D.B. Rundle 69 not out) and 256 for 4 (M.C. de Villiers 86, F.B. Touzel 75, T.J. Mitchell 50 not out)
Western Province 'B' won by 6 wickets
Western Province 'B' 18 pts, Border 'B' 6 pts

at Fanie du Toit Stadium, Potchesfstroom
Western Transvaal 240 (J.S. Oliver 101) and 352 for 5 dec. (S. Nicolson 117 not out, A.J. van Deventer 57, S. Kip 50)
Easterns 334 (B. Randall 68 not out, J.S. Lerm 56, C. Grainger 51) and 123 for 4 (C.T. Enslin 4 for 46)
Match drawn
Easterns 7 pts, Western Transvaal 6 pts

As in Group 'A', Group 'B' provided matches for veterans and rising stars. At 27, Errol Stewart is hardly a veteran. He toured Australia with South Africa and played in one-day internationals. For Natal 'B' in the opening round of matches in the UCB Bowl, he hit 207 off 245 balls with 18 fours and three sixes. He and Keith Forde added 191 in 115 minutes after three wickets had fallen for 59 runs. Forde's 122 came off only 93 balls with 13 fours and three sixes. This was against Border 'B', and Forde repeated his aggression against Western Transvaal when he hit 121 off 125 balls with four sixes and 13 fours. Among the bowlers, Gary Gilder, left-arm fast medium, took ten wickets in a match for the first time, and Martyn's rehabilitation after injury progressed well.

Group B Final Table

	P	W	L	D	Ab	Pts
Natal 'B'	5	3	–	1	1	65
Western Province 'B'	5	2	–	3		57
Orange Free State 'B'	5	1	2	2		38
Easterns	5	–	–	4	1	30
Border 'B'	5	–	3	2		22
Western Transvaal	5	–	1	4		19

UCB Bowl Final

8, 9 and 10 March 1996
at Kingsmead, Durban
Griqualand West 406 for 7 dec. (M.I. Gidley 160, P.H. Barnard 146) and 161 for 2 (M.I. Gidley 79, J.M. Arthur 66 not out)
Natal 'B' 398 (K.A. Forde 129, D.J. Watson 86, C.B. Sugden 70, M.L. Bruyns 55)
Match drawn

Put in to bat, Griqualand West lost two wickets for nine runs before the left-handed Martyn Gidley and the right-handed Pieter Barnard combined to add 256, a record for Griqualand West's third wicket. Both batsmen made the highest score of their careers. Natal 'B' responded consistently with Forde again providing the panache, 129 off 158 balls with two sixes and 19 fours. As Natal 'B' still had five wickets standing at the end of the second day, a draw was inevitable.

Craig Norris hit the highest score of his career, 132 for Easterns against Orange Free State 'B' in Bloemfontein.
(Paul Sturgess/Sportsline)

Friendly Match

1, 2 and 3 April 1996
at Centurion Park, Verwoerdburg
Glamorgan 243 (H. Morris 77, P.A. Cottey 65, P. de Bruyn 4 for 44) and 140 (M.P. Maynard 65, R.E. Bryson 4 for 33)
Northern Transvaal 201 (M. van Jaarsveld 69, S.D. Thomas 4 for 46) and 187 for 3 (A.J. Seymore 77)
Northern Transvaal won by 7 wickets

Glamorgan engaged in one first-class match on their tour of Southern Africa.

Benson and Hedges Night Series

The 45-over night series remains by far the most popular form of cricket in South Africa. The 1995-96 series produced some spectacular cricket. Brett Schultz did the hat-trick, and there were centuries for Hudson, Gibbs, Desmond Haynes, Kallis and Gary Kirsten. Schultz's hat-trick was part of his 6 for 22 for Eastern Province against Transvaal who were 7 for 5. Dean Laing and Nic Pothas then added 158 in 151 minutes, and Pothas was run out for 101 off 106 balls. For Boland against Griqualand West, Jackson and Kuiper both hit centuries and added 198 in 114 minutes. Then it rained. Tikolo, the Kenyan, hit 104 off 95 balls for Border against Northern Transvaal, and Jordaan and Stephenson began Free State's innings against Easterns with 187 in 108 minutes of which Franklyn Stephenson scored 108 off 80 balls. Free State went on to reach the final where they trounced Transvaal. Player hit 83 off 50 balls with 11 fours and four sixes. He and Jordaan added 125 in 65 minutes after Stephenson had been bowled at seven.

Final

29 March, 1996
at Wanderers, Johannesburg
Orange Free State 290 for 6 (B.T. Player 73, G.F.J. Liebenberg 70, D. Jordaan 51)
Transvaal 148
Orange Free State won by 142 runs

Leading wicket-keeper of the year with 43 dismissals, Pauls Kirsten of Western Province, one of three brothers to appear in first-class cricket in South Africa in 1995–96. (David Munden/Sportsline)

First-Class Averages

Batting

	M	Inns	NO	Runs	HS	Av	100s	50s
Z. de Bruyn	5	9	5	390	126*	97.50	1	2
E.L.R. Stewart	7	8	2	568	207*	94.66	3	1
M.I. Gidley	5	7	–	637	160	91.00	3	3
K.A. Forde	5	6	1	444	129	88.80	3	
M.C. Venter	5	7	2	341	119	68.20	2	1
D.N. Crookes	7	9	1	537	111*	67.12	1	6
B.M. White	8	16	4	787	180*	65.58	3	2
G. Kirsten	10	16	3	812	244	62.46	3	4
D.J. Callaghan	9	16	4	739	133*	61.58	2	6
C. Grainger	4	7	–	420	119	60.00	1	4
F.B. Touzel	5	7	1	349	102	58.16	1	2
D.B. Rundle	7	9	3	324	103	54.00	1	2
L.J. Koen	9	16	1	804	202*	53.60	2	3
K.C. Wessels	9	16	1	803	173	53.53	2	5
H.C. Bakkes	9	13	6	359	68	51.28		3
H.D. Ackerman	8	13	3	504	106*	50.40	1	4
L.J. Wilkinson	9	17	4	605	226*	46.53	1	2
W.J. Cronje	11	16	2	650	158	46.42	2	3
N. Martin	6	10	3	318	89*	45.42		3
S.G. Koening	6	10	1	401	89	44.55		3

Batting

	M	Inns	NO	Runs	HS	Av	100s	50s
L.P. Vorster	5	9	1	354	90*	44.25		4
P.N. Kirsten	9	16	–	699	147	43.68	2	4
S.M. Pollock	10	11	3	348	74*	43.50		2
P.G. Amm	9	17	2	646	157	43.06	1	4
T.N. Lazard	8	14	2	508	89*	42.33		3
B.M. McMillan	9	12	1	465	116	42.27	2	1
J.H. Kallis	8	12	–	506	146	42.16	1	4
W.M. Dry	6	9	–	374	99	41.55		2
P.H. Barnard	6	10	1	364	146	40.44	2	
G.F.J. Liebenberg	9	15	–	599	229	39.93	1	2
N.D. McKenzie	9	15	1	559	150*	39.92	2	3
M.J.R. Rindel	8	15	–	598	174	39.86	1	4
P.J. Botha	9	17	1	636	94	39.75		4
M. van Jaarsveld	7	11	–	435	93	39.54		4
C.B. Lambert	8	15	1	550	108	39.28	1	2
M.G. Beamish	6	11	1	382	101	38.20	1	2
J.B. Commins	8	14	2	457	94	38.08		4
G.A. Pollock	7	11	2	340	95	37.77		3
N.C. Johnson	10	13	3	365	75*	36.50		4
D.J. Cullinan	10	15	–	547	91	36.46		6

First-Class Averages (continued)

Batting

	M	Inns	NO	Runs	HS	Av	100s	50s
A.C. Hudson	11	16	2	508	153	36.28	1	2
K.R. Rutherford	9	15	–	544	134	36.26	2	4
N. Pothas	10	17	1	575	147	35.93	1	3
F.D. Stephenson	8	13	–	462	166	35.53	2	1
M.W. Rushmere	8	16	2	478	133	34.14	1	3
G.C. Victor	6	11	–	372	100	33.81	1	3
H.H. Gibbs	7	10	1	303	112	33.66	1	
C.F. Craven	8	14	3	370	90	33.63		3
A.P. Kuiper	8	14	–	470	155	33.57	1	3
D.J. Richardson	10	15	3	402	122	33.50	1	2
D.J. van Zyl	6	11	1	332	69	33.20		3
P.J.R. Steyn	8	11	–	348	108	31.63	1	1
K.C. Jackson	9	16	–	499	100	31.18	1	3
D.L. Haynes	8	14	1	403	71	31.00		3
D.R. Laing	8	14	1	402	107	30.92	1	3
D.M. Benkenstein	10	13	2	325	98	29.54		1
A.M. Bacher	10	19	2	498	116	29.29	1	2
J.N. Rhodes	10	13	1	347	82*	28.91		3
J.F. Venter	9	16	2	395	95	28.21		3
P.C. Strydom	10	16	–	429	69	26.81		4
D. Jordaan	9	17	1	425	88	26.56		2
M.L. Bruyns	10	13	–	333	62	25.61		3
A.J. Seymore	9	17	–	417	124	24.52	1	2
R.F. Pienaar	8	15	–	346	50	23.06		1
F.J.C. Cronje	9	16	1	302	48	20.13		

(Qualification – 300 runs)

Bowling

	Overs	Mds	Runs	Wks	Av	Best	10/m	5/inn
A.J. Swanepoel	77	19	165	15	11.00	5/29	1	2
D.J. Pryke	76	22	189	14	13.50	6/27		2
S.G. Peall	102.5	30	220	16	13.75	9/76	1	1
G.M. Gilder	54	15	153	11	13.90	5/20	1	2
W. Kidwell	174.3	39	477	31	15.38	6/23	1	2
S.M. Pollock	340.1	94	798	51	15.64	7/33	1	5
K.G. Storey	172	42	462	25	18.48	5/26	1	2
V.A. Walsh	209	56	583	31	18.80	6/52		1
M.W. Pringle	300.4	53	887	47	18.87	6/32	1	5
G. Radford	116.4	29	361	19	19.00	6/70		2
A. Martyn	252.1	54	685	35	19.57	6/22		3
G.C. Yates	108.4	26	314	16	19.62	5/69		1
S. Jacobs	277.3	83	639	32	19.96	5/30		1
J. Albanie	81	22	226	11	20.54	3/18		
R.P. Snell	194.5	41	589	28	21.03	5/64		2
R.E. Veenstra	196.3	52	529	25	21.16	6/38		2
P.A. Strang	119	29	365	17	21.47	5/69		2
G.J. Kruis	168	44	410	19	21.57	5/36		1
M. Erasmus	157.3	43	411	19	21.63	5/70		2
P. de Bruyn	131	34	350	16	21.87	6/38		1
C.R. Matthews	235.3	85	508	23	22.08	5/43		1
H. Botha	76.2	12	243	11	22.09	4/31		
A.C. Dawson	187.3	50	469	21	22.33	6/18		1
B.C. Fourie	316.5	88	739	33	22.39	6/76		2
S.D. Jack	273.2	65	878	39	22.51	5/69		1
E.O. Simons	105	33	233	10	23.30	4/38		
G.J. Smith	212.5	54	616	26	23.69	5/32		1
B.N. Schultz	302.1	65	854	36	23.72	6/84		3
J.F. Venter	119.1	52	504	21	24.00	4/52		

Bowling

	Overs	Mds	Runs	Wks	Av	Best	10/m	5/inn
L. Klusener	191.5	30	653	27	24.18	8/34	1	2
A.A. Donald	309.5	85	823	34	24.20	5/44		2
D.B. Rundle	186.2	59	438	18	24.33	3/26		
D.N. Crookes	144.1	22	392	16	24.50	5/59		2
P.R. Adams	415	116	1065	43	24.76	6/101		3
P.A.J. DeFreitas	163.3	43	354	14	25.28	3/42		
B.P. Horan	125.5	21	398	15	26.53	4/43		
S. Elworthy	173	26	572	21	27.23	3/19		
C.F. Craven	138	41	327	12	27.25	4/62		
D. Rossouw	105	24	301	11	27.36	5/57		1
S.C. Pope	109.2	13	438	16	27.37	7/62		1
S.A. Cilliers	121.3	15	441	16	27.56	3/26		
N.C. Johnson	141.5	37	387	14	27.64	3/25		
R.E. Bryson	191.3	41	583	21	27.76	4/16		
R. Telemachus	272.5	50	780	28	27.85	5/72		1
P. Joubert	98.2	24	279	10	27.90	3/73		
H.R. Olonga	84.5	7	314	11	28.54	4/57		
M.D. Marshall	176.3	50	403	14	28.78	4/48		
E.A.E. Baptiste	164	49	377	13	29.00	4/58		
B.M. McMillan	193.3	51	444	15	29.60	3/46		
C.W. Henderson	405	91	1075	36	29.86	4/33		
B.C. Strang	143.1	46	391	13	30.07	5/69		1
F.J.C. Cronje	137.5	33	378	12	31.50	4/16		
D.J.J. de Vos	132	42	347	11	31.54	4/34		
F.D. Stephenson	249.5	56	727	23	31.60	5/63		1
C.V. English	168	28	506	16	31.62	4/47		
C.M. Willoughby	173	33	517	16	32.31	4/43		
J.H. Kallis	131	38	363	11	33.00	3/32		
B.T. Player	107	22	334	10	33.40	4/73		
A. Badenhorst	189.4	48	554	16	34.62	5/49		1
E.A. Brandes	115.2	24	382	11	34.72	4/46		
S. Abrahams	183	50	455	13	35.00	5/49		1
L.C.R. Jordaan	143	25	420	12	35.00	3/25		
C.E. Eksteen	490.3	146	1201	34	35.32	4/64		
M.J. Vandrau	106.5	16	355	10	35.50	4/93		
C. van Noordwyk	119	27	355	10	35.50	2/15		
P.J. Botha	153	47	358	10	35.80	4/31		
T.G. Shaw	404.1	125	970	27	35.92	6/45		2
N. Boje	406.5	113	973	27	36.03	4/39		
G.A. Roe	152.5	44	368	10	36.80	3/34		
I.L. Howell	317.4	77	777	21	37.00	3/52		
M. Ntini	190	34	630	17	37.05	3/49		
S.G. Cronje	158	45	454	12	37.83	4/87		
N.W. Pretorius	251	51	857	21	40.80	5/79		1
W.F. Stelling	186.3	62	455	11	41.36	2/8		
A. Cilliers	154.2	32	499	12	41.58	3/53		
M.J.G. Davis	245.5	61	636	15	42.40	4/68		
H.C. Bakkes	238.3	54	708	16	44.25	3/50		
A.G. Huckle	236.4	39	716	15	47.73	3/130		
T.C. Webster	137.2	23	483	10	48.30	4/113		
M.C. Krug	250.5	76	583	12	48.58	3/32		
B.J. Drew	261.2	58	728	14	52.00	5/79		1

(Qualification – 10 wickets)

Leading Fielders

43 – P. Kirsten (ct 42 / st 1); 41 – N. Pothas (ct 36 / st 5); 27 – M.L. Bruyns, D.J. Richardson (ct 25 / st 2) and L.M. Germishuys (ct 22 / st 5); 24 – S.J. Palframan (ct 21 / st 3); 23 – J. Burger; 21 – P.J.L. Radley (ct 18 / st 3); 19 – A.M. Bacher; 18 – L.J. Koen; 17 – I. Pistorius (ct 16 / st 1); 16 – G. Morgan (ct 13 / st 3); 15 – M.M. Brick (ct 14 / st 1); 14 – N.C. Johnson, L. Masikazana (ct 11 / st 3) and M.O. Johnston (ct 12 / st 2); 13 – D.J. Smith (ct 12 / st 1)

Pakistan

Pakistan cricket seems to be perpetually shrouded in suspicion, crisis and dispute. There is a constant power struggle as to who should control the game, and former Test players are for ever levelling criticism at their contemporaries and present Test cricketers and administrators. Within the administration rival factions war to such an extent as to make observers believe that the eleven best available players are rarely chosen to represent Pakistan.

Pakistan's latest recruit to Test cricket, Saqlain Mushtaq, an 18-year-old off-spinner who took nine wickets in his first two Tests.
(Shaun Botterill/Allsport)

Pakistan v. Sri Lanka,
Test and one-day international series
England 'A' tour
BCCP Patron's Trophy
Quaid-e-Azam Trophy
Pentagular Trophy
First-class averages

Pakistan cricket has learned to live with the burden of disputes, but, more recently, troubles have multiplied with allegations of ball-tampering and, more seriously, with accusations of bribery and match-fixing. These accusations, made primarily by members of the Australian Test side, had led to the suspension of Salim Malik pending investigations.

Salim, the latest in a long line of Pakistan Test captains, had led the side against Australia and in Zimbabwe and South Africa. The tours in these last two countries had been marked by dissension and defeat. Internal strife reached the point where Basit Ali and Rashid Latif, the vice-captain, had announced their immediate retirements from Test cricket. In the wake of Salim's suspension, Rashid and Basit had reversed their decisions to retire and made themselves available for the series against Sri Lanka.

Rashid's temporary absence, however, had given Moin Khan the opportunity to re-establish himself as Pakistan's first-choice wicket-keeper. He was appointed captain of the side that unsuccessfully contested the Asia Cup in Sharjah. Unfortunately, he was forced to return home with injury after the second match. His improved and consistent batting made it likely that he would resist the return of Rashid and hold his place. Moin's injury had been a slight one – more serious were the injuries that affected Javed Miandad and Waqar Younis. In spite of the advance of Inzamam-ul-Haq, Pakistan's batting had appeared distinctly vulnerable in recent series, and, with Salim Malik under suspension, maturity and steadiness were desperately required. Javed had been one of the world's great batsmen, but a knee injury had failed to respond to treatment and still troubled him. He was beyond his 38th birthday, and there seemed little possibility that he would play Test cricket again.

Waqar Younis had been out of cricket for six months with a back injury. Without him, Pakistan were a much weakened force, for he is, in the opinion of many, the best fast bowler in the world and one of the greatest in the history of the game. His return to fitness was eagerly anticipated, but the first indications were that he was overweight and that a spark had gone from his bowling.

These were troubled times for Pakistan whose authorities were also being criticised for their tardiness in preparations for the World Cup, of which they were co-hosts. Their first task, however, was to appoint a captain for the series against Sri Lanka, and for this they turned to Rameez Raja.

Thirty-three years old and an experienced Test cricketer, Rameez had been jettisoned after the disastrous tour of West Indies in 1993. Now he was recalled to lead a side that lacked temperament, commitment and technique. It was not an enviable task, and Pakistan looked to Basit Ali to rediscover his appetite for the game, to Aamir Sohail to wed his skill and mental strength to a discipline that had so far escaped him, and to the selectors to field a side that was chosen on merit and balance rather than on a variety of political intrigues.

The Sri Lankan Tour

30, 31 August, 1 September 1995
at Defence Stadium, Karachi
Sri Lankans 286 for 8 dec. (S. Ranatunga 58, S.T. Jayasuriya 55) and 148 for 4 (A.P. Gurusinha 82)
Pakistan Cricket Board XI 244 for 8 dec. (Aamir Sohail 80)
Match drawn

4 and 5 September 1994
at Pindi Cricket Stadium, Rawalpindi
Sri Lankans 104 and 171 (Saqlain Mushtaq 4 for 67)
Pakistan Cricket Board Patron's XI 281 for 9 dec. (Saeed Azad 81, Shoaib Mohammad 73)
Pakistan Cricket Board Patron's XI won by an innings and 6 runs

Long gone are the days when a tour was a leisurely affair incorporating a variety of matches outside a Test series. As is now the custom, the Sri Lankans played two warm-up matches before the start of the first Test. They gained little comfort from either game, but Pakistan were well pleased with the showing of the young off-spinner Saqlain Mushtaq, and he earned a place in the squad for the first Test match.

Test Series

Sri Lanka become the fourth side in Test history to come from behind to win a three-match series as Pakistan suffer defeat in a home series for the first time in 15 years.

Wasim Akram had returned from England and his successes with Lancashire in time to play in the first Test match, and he was to take the individual award for a splendid all-round performance. Pakistan gave first Test caps to Ijaz Ahmed junior and to the19-year-old Saqlain Mushtaq.

Sri Lanka were without Aravinda de Silva who was unable to join the party until the second Test match because of his commitment to Kent.

Leading Pakistan for the first time, Rameez Raja won the toss, and Pakistan batted. Saeed and Aamir gave the home side a solid start, and Pakistan reached 118 for 2 at lunch. A patient 78 in 281 minutes from skipper Rameez gave the innings real substance and enabled Inzamam to play with more freedom later in a day which was shortened by 12.3 overs because of bad light.

There had been other stoppages, caused by what seemed to be inevitable crowd disturbances. Pakistan ended the day on 235 for 3, with Inzamam unbeaten on 65.

He looked set for a century, but was leg before to Vaas for 95. He and Shoaib had added 51, and Shoaib went on to make 57 before becoming another Vaas victim. Shoaib had been recalled after a 21-month absence to give stability to the mid-order, and he did his job well.

Moin Khan was Pakistan's outstanding batsman in both the Test and one-day series against Sri Lanka, but the wicket-keeper later lost his place to Rashid Latif. (Shaun Botterill/Allsport)

Moin Khan and Wasim Akram were able to bat with the freedom and panache that the situation needed, and their seventh wicket stand of 82 came in as many minutes. The last three wickets before the declaration went down for three runs, but Pakistan were already in an unassailable position.

The nine Pakistani wickets were shared by Vaas and Muralitharan. Vaas, the left-arm fast medium-pacer, continued to impress as he had done in New Zealand, but Pushpakumara, who had promised so much a year earlier in the series in Zimbabwe, was a great disappointment.

Sri Lanka ended a shortened second day on 23 for 0. They were soon in trouble on the third morning when Waqar had Mahanama caught behind. It proved to be Waqar's only wicket in the match, and he looked far below Test fitness. Saqlain celebrated his Test debut by dismissing Hathurusinghe with the first ball of his second over, and he later had Gurusinha taken at long-off. Arjuna Ranatunga was leg before to Aqib, and Sri Lanka lunched at 102 for 4.

In the afternoon, they were wrecked by Wasim Akram. Bowling at a lively pace, he cut and swung the old ball to such a degree as to be practically unplayable, although he was aided by a certain lack of application on the part of the Sri Lankan batsmen. He had Sanjeewa Ranatunga leg before with a full toss and trapped Dunusinghe plum in front. Vaas and Wickremasinghe both had their stumps uprooted in the same over.

Tillekeratne hit Saqlain for three fours in succession, and he and Muralitharan put on 41 for the ninth wicket before Wasim struck for the fifth time. Inevitably Sri Lanka followed on and lost Mahanama and Gurusinha for 86 before the close. Hathurusinghe was defiant with 53 not out.

Sadly, Hathurusinghe did not add to his overnight score, and his departure was soon followed by that of Sanjeewa Ranatunga. Arjuna Ranatunga and Hashan Tillekeratne batted with an authority that might well have been copied by their colleagues and added 125 in 154 minutes. This was Sri Lanka's highest fifth wicket stand against Pakistan. Ranatunga hit 12 fours, and Tillekeratne six. Ranatunga was taken at slip, and Tillekeratne fell to Wasim after lunch. The last six wickets went down for 19 runs, and the match was over before tea on the fourth day. Aamir Sohail finished with his best bowling figures in Test cricket, and young Saqlain again bowled impressively.

This was the first Test to be played at the Arbab Niaz Stadium, and Rameez became the first Pakistani captain to lead his side to an innings victory in his debut Test as skipper.

Sri Lanka made two changes for the second Test match. They welcomed Aravinda de Silva after his joyous season with Kent – he replaced Sanjeewa Ranatunga – and Dharmasena came in for Pushpakumara. Pakistan made one change. Mohammad Akram played his first Test match at the expense of Waqar Younis who had shown that he was palpably short of match-fitness.

Put in to bat, Sri Lanka made the worst of starts. Mahanama was leg before to Wasim on the fifth ball of the opening over. Wasim also caught Gurusinha off Aqib, and when Saqlain dismissed de Silva, driving uppishly, and Ranatunga, sweeping too soon to be caught bat and pad, with successive deliveries, Sri Lanka were 33 for 4. Hathurusinghe and Tillekeratne steadied the innings with a stand of 84, which was ended when Mohammad Akram deceived Hathurusinghe with a change of pace to capture his first Test wicket.

Tillekeratne batted with the utmost concentration and application, hitting 20 fours in an innings that lasted 226 minutes. He was ninth out, becoming Saqlain's third victim. The young off-spinner again bowled with intelligence and maturity.

Pakistan faced 18 overs before the close and lost Aamir Sohail with 43 scored. Night-watchman Saqlain proved obdurate, and Rameez Raja hit 11 fours in another useful innings. Inzamam-ul-Haq adopted a positive approach, and although Pakistan lost three wickets for three runs towards the end of the day, they finished with a lead of 71 and two wickets standing.

Those last two wickets were quite productive, and Pakistan's first innings lead grew to a formidable 110. Muralitharan, the off-spinner, again finished with commendable figures.

Pakistan were handicapped in that Wasim Akram was unable to bowl because of a sprained left shoulder, but they seemed in command when Mohammad Akram gained an early breakthrough when Sri Lanka batted again. Gurusinha fell to Aqib Javed, and the visitors were still 86 runs in arrears with two wickets down. Hathurusinghe was then joined by de Silva, and the pair proceeded to transform the game. As they gained in assurance, so Pakistan in the field lapsed into customary faults. Catches were dropped and

First Test Match – Pakistan v. Sri Lanka

8, 9, 10 and 11 September 1995 at Arbab Niaz Stadium, Peshawar

Pakistan

	First Innings	
Saeed Anwar	c A. Ranatunga, b Muralitharan	50
Aamir Sohail	c Dunusinghe, b Vaas	28
Rameez Raja (Capt)	c Pushpakumara, b Vaas	78
Inzamam-ul-Haq	lbw, b Vaas	95
Shoaib Mohammad	c A. Ranatunga, b Vaas	57
Ijaz Ahmed jnr	c Gurusinha, b Muralitharan	5
Wasim Akram	c and b Muralitharan	36
*Moin Khan	c Hathurusinghe, b Vaas	51
Waqar Younis	c Mahanama, b Muralitharan	0
Aqib Javed	not out	28
Saqlain Mushtaq	not out	8
	b 1, lb 4, w 1, nb 17	23
	(for 9 wickets, dec.)	459

	O	M	R	W
Wickremasinghe	32	5	98	–
Vaas	29	3	99	5
Pushpakumara	17	2	89	–
Muralitharan	50	9	134	4
Hathurusinghe	18	10	29	–
Gurusinha	3	1	5	–

Fall of Wickets
1–**59**, 2–**102**, 3–**234**, 4–**285**, 5–**318**, 6–**340**, 7–**422**, 8–**422**, 9–**425**

Sri Lanka

	First Innings		Second Innings	
R.S. Mahanama	c Moin, b Waqar	29	lbw, b Aqib Javed	2
U.C. Hathurusinghe	c Inzamam, b Saqlain	23	c Saeed, b Wasim Akram	53
A.P. Gurusinha	c Wasim, b Saqlain	24	c Saeed, b Aamir Sohail	10
S. Ranatunga	lbw, b Wasim Akram	33	c Moin, b Aqib Javed	18
A. Ranatunga (Capt)	lbw, b Aqib Javed	8	c Inzamam, b Aamir	76
H.P. Tillekeratne	not out	44	c Rameez, b Wasim Akram	48
*C.I. Dunusinghe	lbw, b Wasim Akram	0	c Rameez, b Aamir Sohail	0
W.P.U.J.C. Vaas	b Wasim Akram	4	c Rameez, b Saqlain	4
G.P. Wickremasinghe	b Wasim Akram	0	c Rameez, b Saqlain	6
M. Muralitharan	c Saqlain, b Wasim	8	st Moin, b Aamir Sohail	0
K.R. Pushpakumara	run out	1	not out	0
	b 1, lb 6, nb 5	12	b 1, lb 6, nb 9	16
		186		233

	O	M	R	W	O	M	R	W
Wasim Akram	20	3	55	5	10	3	24	2
Waqar Younis	11	2	47	1	9	1	39	–
Saqlain Mushtaq	18	4	49	2	26	10	58	2
Aqib Javed	11.1	2	27	1	13	1	50	2
Aamir Sohail	2	1	1	–	21	4	54	4
Ijaz Ahmed jnr					1	–	1	–

Fall of Wickets
1–**39**, 2–**76**, 3–**83**, 4–**102**, 5–**132**, 6–**134**, 7–**142**, 8–**143**, 9–**184**
1–**8**, 2–**36**, 3–**86**, 4–**89**, 5–**214**, 6–**222**, 7–**222**, 8–**232**, 9–**233**

Umpires: Mahboob Shah & B.L. Aldridge

Pakistan won by an innings and 40 runs

Second Test Match – Pakistan v. Sri Lanka

15, 16, 17, 18 and 19 September 1995 at Iqbal Stadium, Faisalabad

Sri Lanka

	First Innings		Second Innings	
R.S. Mahanama	lbw, b Wasim Akram	0	lbw, b Mohammad Akram	10
U.C. Hathurusinghe	c Saeed, b Mohammad	47	c Ijaz jnr, b Aqib	83
A.P. Gurusinha	c Wasim, b Aqib Javed	9	lbw, b Aqib Javed	12
P.A. de Silva	c and b Saqlain	0	lbw, b Saqlain	105
A. Ranatunga (Capt)	c Ijaz jnr, b Saqlain	0	(6) c and b Aamir	2
H.P. Tillekeratne	c Moin, b Saqlain	115	(5) lbw, b Aqib Javed	0
H.D.P.K. Dharmasena	run out	0	c Moin, b Mohammad Akram	49
*C.I. Dunusinghe	lbw, b Wasim Akram	12	c Mohammad, b Saqlain	27
W.P.U.J.C. Vaas	c Ijaz jnr, b Aqib	21	b Aqib Javed	40
G.P. Wickremasinghe	c Ijaz jnr, b Aqib	1	(11) b Aqib Javed	2
M. Muralitharan	not out	8	(10) not out	10
	b 3, lb 1, nb 6	10	b 4, lb 10, nb 7	21
		223		361

	O	M	R	W	O	M	R	W
Wasim Akram	13	6	31	2				
Mohammad Akram	14	4	42	1	27	5	78	2
Aqib Javed	13	5	34	3	23.3	6	84	5
Saqlain Mushtaq	20	3	74	3	36	12	84	2
Aamir Sohail	7	2	28	–	44	12	87	1
Shoaib Mohammad	3	2	10	–	4	2	9	–
Ijaz Ahmed jnr					3	–	5	–

Fall of Wickets
1–**0**, 2–**23**, 3–**33**, 4–**33**, 5–**117**, 6–**117**, 7–**149**, 8–**213**, 9–**213**
1–**11**, 2–**24**, 3–**200**, 4–**212**, 5–**225**, 6–**240**, 7–**279**, 8–**346**, 9–**354**

Pakistan

	First Innings		Second Innings	
Saeed Anwar	c de Silva, b Muralitharan	53	b Dharmasena	50
Aamir Sohail	b Muralitharan	20	lbw, b Vaas	0
Saqlain Mushtaq	c Mahanama, b Muralitharan	34	(9) c Ranatunga, b Vaas	7
Rameez Raja (Capt)	c sub (Samaraweera), b de Silva	75	(3) c Tillekeratne, b Muralitharan	25
Inzamam-ul-Haq	b Gurusinha	50	(4) c and b Muralitharan	26
Shoaib Mohammad	run out	12	(5) lbw, b Wickremasinghe	5
Ijaz Ahmed jnr	c Dunusinghe, b Wickremasinghe	16	(6) c Dharmasena, b Vaas	8
Wasim Akram	c Mahanama, b Gurusinha	2	(8) b Dharmasena	26
*Moin Khan	st Dunusinghe, b Muralitharan	30	(7) c Muralitharan, b Vaas	50
Aqib Javed	b Muralitharan	8	not out	1
Mohammad Akram	not out	0	c Mahanama, b Dharmasena	0
	b 4, lb 15, nb 13	32	nb 11	11
		333		209

	O	M	R	W	O	M	R	W
Wickremasinghe	23	6	53	1	11	1	23	1
Vaas	14	4	35	–	15	2	45	4
Gurusinha	8	1	30	2				
Dharmasena	30	4	79	–	22.1	6	43	3
Muralitharan	23.3	6	68	5	20	2	83	2
Hathurusinghe	6	1	10	–				
de Silva	13.3	3	39	1	4	–	15	–

Fall of Wickets
1–**42**, 2–**109**, 3–**168**, 4–**214**, 5–**248**, 6–**288**, 7–**288**, 8–**291**, 9–**324**
1–**6**, 2–**58**, 3–**99**, 4–**108**, 5–**119**, 6–**129**, 7–**175**, 8–**206**, 9–**207**

Umpires: Khizar Hayat & N.T. Plews

Sr Lanka won by 42 runs

Chaminda Vaas played a vital role in Sri Lanka's victories in the second an third Test matches.
(Stephen Laffer/Allsport)

heads went down. Rameez failed to utilise either Mohammad Akram or Saqlain Mushtaq to good effect. He set defensive fields and showed little trust in Mohammad who had looked both lively and promising. Sri Lanka closed on 174 for 2.

The partnership between de Silva and Hathurusinghe was finally broken when Aqib had Hathurusinghe caught at second slip for 83, his highest Test score. He had shared a third wicket stand of 176 with de Silva, a Sri Lankan record in Test cricket. Aravinda de Silva went on to complete a serene and majestic century. He hit 11 fours and batted for 352 minutes to reach three figures. It was an innings that made a Sri Lankan victory possible – something that had looked out of the question on the third morning.

There were mid-order tremors as four wickets fell for 67 runs, but Dharmasena and Vaas added 67 for the eighth wicket, and, eventually, Pakistan were left to make 252 to win, not an easy task.

Aqib finished with five wickets in a Test innings for the first time and shouldered responsibility well in the absence of Wasim, but Aamir Sohail was grossly over-bowled. He was then asked to open and responded with a volley of abuse when adjudged leg before for nought. He received only a verbal reprimand from his own

Third Test Match – Pakistan v. Sri Lanka

22, 23, 24, 25 and 26 September 1995 at Jinnah Stadium, Sialkot

Sri Lanka

	First Innings		Second Innings	
R.S. Mahanama	c Mohammad, b Aqib	21	lbw, b Aqib	20
U.C. Hathurusinghe	c Inzamam, b Aamer	12	c Moin, b Aqib	73
A.P. Gurusinha	run out	45	c Rameez, b Ata	18
P.A. de Silva	c Shoaib, b Ata	0	lbw, b Aamer Nazir	8
A. Ranatunga (Capt)	b Aamir Sohail	24	c Inzamam, b Mohammad	87
H.P. Tillekeratne	c Inzamam, b Mohammad	24	(7) b Aamir Sohail	50
H.D.P.K. Dharmasena	not out	62	(8) c Inzamam, b Mohammad	7
*C.I. Dunusinghe	lbw, b Aqib	1	(6) b Mohammad Akram	7
W.P.U.J.C. Vaas	b Aqib	16	run out	27
M. Muralitharan	c Aamir, b Aamer Nazir	4	not out	0
G.P. Wickremasinghe	run out	1		
	b 1, lb 12, nb 9	22	b 23, lb 10, nb 8	41
		232	(for 9 wickets, dec)	338

	O	M	R	W	O	M	R	W
Aqib Javed	19.3	6	47	3	24	2	71	2
Mohammad Akram	17	4	37	1	20	5	39	3
Aamer Nazir	19	6	46	2	17	2	55	1
Ata-ur-Rehman	19	4	42	1	23	5	66	1
Aamir Sohail	17	4	45	1	25.3	7	55	1
Shoaib Mohammad	1	–	2	–	11	3	19	–

Fall of Wickets
1–**32**, 2–**36**, 3–**41**, 4–**108**, 5–**118**, 6–**158**, 7–**171**, 8–**216**, 9–**225**
1–**37**, 2–**71**, 3–**97**, 4–**175**, 5–**206**, 6–**265**, 7–**279**, 8–**338**, 9–**338**

Pakistan

	First Innings		Second Innings	
Aamir Sohail	b Dharmasena	48	c Hathurusinghe, b Wickremasinghe	5
Shoaib Mohammad	lbw, b Muralitharan	8	c and b Vaas	1
Rameez Raja (Capt)	lbw, b Muralitharan	26	c Mahanama, b Wickremasinghe	4
Inzamam-ul-Haq	b Wickremasinghe	21	c Mahanama, b Vaas	0
Basit Ali	lbw, b Muralitharan	4	c Dharmasena, b Vaas	27
Zahid Fazal	st Dunusinghe, b de Silva	23	c Gurusinha, b Vaas	1
*Moin Khan	c Dunusinghe, b Wickremasinghe	26	not out	117
Aqib Javed	c Dunusinghe, b Dharmasena	19	run out	6
Ata-ur-Rehman	c Mahanama, b de Silva	9	c Dunusinghe, b Wickremasinghe	4
Mohammad Akram	b Muralitharan	5	b Wickremasinghe	2
Aamer Nazir	not out	5	c Tillekeratne, b de Silva	11
	b 3, lb 4, nb 13	20	b 13, lb 10, nb 11	34
		214		212

	O	M	R	W	O	M	R	W
Wickremasinghe	13	2	29	2	18	4	55	4
Vaas	14	–	39	–	24	9	37	4
Gurusinha	3	–	6	–	3	–	16	–
Muralitharan	27.1	6	72	4	17	3	53	–
de Silva	10	1	29	2	4	2	5	1
Dharmasena	16	5	33	2	10	2	23	–

Fall of Wickets
1–**39**, 2–**72**, 3–**111**, 4–**119**, 5–**122**, 6–**173**, 7–**173**, 8–**196**, 9–**204**
1–**7**, 2–**7**, 3–**7**, 4–**13**, 5–**15**, 6–**79**, 7–**106**, 8–**132**, 9–**147**

Umpires: Shakeel Khan & B.L. Aldridge

Sri Lanka won by 144 runs

management. In the last over of the day, Rameez Raja was caught, and Pakistan were 58 for 2.

Saeed Anwar, unbeaten on 30 overnight, was bowled by the brisk off-spin of Dharmasena as soon as he had completed his fifty, and Inzamam was caught and bowled by Muralitharan who took seven wickets in the match and won the individual award. He also became Sri Lanka's leading wicket-taker in Test cricket, passing Ramesh Ratnayake's record of 73 wickets.

Shoaib and Ijaz junior went quickly, and Sri Lanka seemed on the brink of victory, but Moin and Wasim, batting in spite of his injured shoulder, raised Pakistan's hopes with a partnership of 46. When Moin was caught at point off a ball from Vaas which lifted sharply, however, hopes vanished. Moin's 50 had come off 90 balls. After tea, the last three wickets fell in 25 minutes for three runs. Vaas, who put on another impressive bowling performance, and Dharmasena were the decisive bowlers, but this historic victory was essentially a result of a fine team performance. Tillekeratne and de Silva both had the unusual experience of hitting centuries of exceptional quality in one innings and being dismissed without scoring in the other.

Not surprisingly, Sri Lanka remained unchanged for the deciding Test, but Pakistan made several changes. Aamer Nazir, Ata-ur-Rehman, Zahid Fazal and Basit Ali replaced Wasim Akram, Saqlain Mushtaq, Saeed Anwar and Ijaz Ahmed junior. The first three were unfit, and the last had disappointed in his two Test appearances. Ranatunga won the toss and Sri Lanka batted.

The wicket was on the slow side, and the ball tended to keep low. The Pakistan attack exploited the conditions well, and, with de Silva caught in the gully without scoring, Sri Lanka were struggling on 41 for 3. Ranatunga and Gurusinha set about rebuilding the innings, but both were dismissed in the afternoon session. Ranatunga swung wildly at Aamir Sohail and was bowled while Gurusinha, who made 45 in 173 minutes, was run out when Basit Ali's throw hit the stumps. At 118 for 5, Sri Lankan prospects looked bleak, but Dharmasena, a very useful cricketer, batted most sensibly. He ended the day unbeaten on 52, with Sri Lanka 216 for 7.

Vaas was bowled without addition the next morning, and only 16 runs were added as the last three wickets fell. Dharmasena remained unbeaten on 62, his highest Test score.

Pakistan were soon in trouble on a pitch of uneven bounce. They lost Shoaib before lunch, and by tea they were 130 for 5. Aamir Sohail batted with some resolution, and Moin and Zahid put on 51 for the sixth wicket before de Silva struck with two wickets. Pakistan closed on 199 for 8, and they added only 15 on the third morning, the innings ending when Muralitharan bowled Mohammad Akram with his first delivery.

Batting for a second time with an unexpected lead of 18, Sri Lanka reached 37 before Mahanama was leg before to Aqib. Gurusinha and de Silva went cheaply, but Hathurusinghe and Ranatunga added 78. Hathurusinghe reached his third half-century of the series and was looking most accomplished until he edged Aqib to the wicket-keeper shortly before the close. He had batted for 353 minutes, hit seven fours and faced 224 balls. Above all, he had helped take Sri Lanka to a position where they could begin to dream of victory.

Resuming on 177 for 4, Sri Lanka showed no inclination to loosen their grip on the match. Nightwatchman Dunusinghe was out at 206, but Tillekeratne and Ranatunga added 59. Both men played admirably, and it was apparent that Ranatunga was determined to steer his side to a position from which defeat would be impossible. He played with the utmost sense but was denied the century he deserved and looked certain to get. There was a flourish from Vaas, and the declaration came 15 minutes before tea. Pakistan were set a target of 357 to win.

Soon their innings was in shreds. Aamir Sohail fell to Wickremasinghe in the fifth over, and, in the next over, Vaas caught and bowled Shoaib with his first delivery and had Inzamam taken at slip off his third. Six runs later, Rameez was gone, and Zahid became Vaas' third victim to make Pakistan 15 for 5. Moin Khan and Basit Ali stopped the rot with a partnership of 64. Then Basit aimed a hook at Vaas, mistimed it and was caught at short fine-leg. Vaas ended the day with figures of 4 for 16 in 12 overs, and Pakistan were on the brink of defeat at 99 for 6. Moin Khan had scored 46 of their runs.

Moin reached his fifty early on the last morning, but he soon lost Aqib who was run out by de Silva. Moin kept the strike to reach his second and higher Test century. He batted for 233 minutes and hit two sixes, off Muralitharan, and 11 fours. It was a brave, purposeful innings, but it could only delay the inevitable, and the match was over 48 minutes after lunch.

So Sri Lanka won their second Test series on foreign soil within a few months. It was an outstanding achievement, and, in taking the series, Ranatunga emulated W.G. Grace, Hansie Cronje and Salim Malik in leading his side to victory in a three-match series after losing the first Test. For Sri Lanka, the victory had immense significance, and it sent shock waves through the cricket world.

The defeat gave Pakistan cause to ponder, and those in power could well muse upon the advice given in *The Cricketer Pakistan* – 'The deed has been done, what is now required is for all concerned to carry out a constructive post mortem, instead of calling for the heads to roll and ex-players and administrators settling scores behind the humiliation of a home series defeat.'

Test Match Averages – Pakistan v. Sri Lanka

Pakistan Batting

	M	Inns	NO	Runs	HS	Av	100s	50s
Moin Khan	3	5	1	274	117*	68.50	1	2
Saeed Anwar	2	3	–	154	54	51.33		3
Rameez Raja	3	5	–	208	78	41.60		2
Inzamam-ul-Haq	3	5	–	192	95	38.40		2
Saqlain Mushtaq	2	3	1	49	34	24.50		
Wasim Akram	2	3	–	64	36	21.33		
Aqib Javed	3	5	2	62	28*	20.66		
Aamir Sohail	3	5	–	101	48	20.20		
Shoaib Mohammad	3	5	–	83	57	16.60		1
Ijaz Ahmed jnr	2	3	–	29	16	9.66		
Mohammad Akram	2	4	1	7	5	2.33		

Played in one Test: Basit Ali 4 & 27; Zahid Fazal 23 & 1; Ata-ur-Rehman 9 & 4; Aamer Nazir 5* & 11; Waqar Younis 0

Sri Lanka Batting

	M	Inns	NO	Runs	HS	Av	100s	50s
H.P. Tillekeratne	3	6	1	281	115	56.20	1	1
U.C. Hathurusinghe	3	6	–	291	83	48.50		3
H.D.P.K. Dharmasena	2	4	1	118	62*	39.33		1
A. Ranatunga	3	6	–	197	87	32.83		1
P.A. de Silva	2	4	–	113	105	28.25	1	
A.P. Gurusinha	3	6	–	118	45	19.66		
W.P.U.J.C. Vaas	3	6	–	112	40	18.66		
R.S. Mahanama	3	6	–	82	29	13.66		
M. Muralitharan	3	6	3	30	10*	10.00		
C.I. Dunusinghe	3	6	–	47	27	7.83		
G.P. Wickremasinghe	3	5	–	10	6	2.00		

Played in one Test: S. Ranatunga 33 & 18; K.R. Pushpakumara 1* & 0*

Pakistan Bowling

	Overs	Mds	Runs	Wks	Av	Best	5/inn
Wasim Akram	43	12	110	9	12.22	5/55	1
Aqib Javed	104	22	313	16	19.56	5/84	1
Mohammad Akram	78	15	196	7	28.00	3/39	
Saqlain Mushtaq	100	29	265	9	29.44	3/74	
Aamer Nazir	36	8	101	3	33.66	2/46	
Aamir Sohail	116.2	30	270	7	38.57	4/54	
Ata-ur-Rehman	42	9	108	2	54.00	1/42	
Waqar Younis	20	3	86	1	86.00	1/47	
Ijaz Ahmed jnr	4	–	6	–	–		
Shoaib Mohammad	19	7	40	–	–		

Sri Lanka Bowling

	Overs	Mds	Runs	Wks	Av	Best	5/inn
W.P.U.J.C. Vaas	96	20	254	13	19.53	5/99	1
P.A. de Silva	31.3	6	88	4	22.00	2/29	
M. Muralitharan	137.4	26	410	15	27.33	5/68	1
A.P. Gurusinha	17	2	57	2	28.50	2/30	
G.P. Wickremasinghe	97	18	258	8	32.25	4/55	
H.D.P.K. Dharmasena	78.1	17	178	5	35.60	3/43	
U.C. Hathurusinghe	24	11	39	–	–		

Bowled in one innings: K.R. Pushpakumara 17–2–89–0

Pakistan Fielding Figures

6 – Inzamam-ul-Haq and Moin Khan (ct 5 / st 1); 5 – Rameez Raja; 4 – Ijaz Ahmed jnr; 3 – Saeed Anwar; 2 – Aamir Sohail, Mohammad Akram, Saqlain Mushtaq and Wasim Akram; 1 – Shoaib Mohammad

Sri Lanka Fielding Figures

7 – R.S. Mahanama and C.I. Dunusinghe (ct 5 / st 2); 3 – M. Muralitharan and A. Ranatunga; 2 – U.C. Hathurusinghe, A.P. Gurusinha, H.P. Tillekeratne and H.D.P.K. Dharmasena; P.A. de Silva, K.R. Pushpakumara, W.P.U.J.C. Vaas and sub (D.P. Samaraweera)

One-day Series

Sri Lanka become the first side since Clive Lloyd's West Indians in 1980–81 to win both the Test and limited-over series in Pakistan. Once again they recovered after losing the first match.

Pakistan took the first match with such ease that one wondered why they had ever struggled in the Test series. Put in to bat, Sri Lanka trembled at 48 for 3 in the 13th over, but Gurusinha and Ranatunga added 137. Ranatunga hit his second century in one-day internationals, his runs coming off 112 balls with nine fours.

Saeed Anwar had reported unfit for Pakistan, and he was replaced by Salim Elahi, the 19-year-old brother of Manzoor Elahi and a cricketer with very limited experience. One would not have known it. He and Aamir Sohail put on 156 in 201 balls, and Salim Elahi went on to become the first Pakistani batsman to score a century on his one-day international debut. He joined an elite band – Dennis Amiss, Desmond Haynes and Andy Flower. He reached his century by hitting Wickremasinghe for six back over the bowler's head, and his innings included seven fours. He faced 133 balls and hit with great power. Pakistan won with six overs to spare. Unfortunately, there were again disruptions due to crowd trouble and the throwing of missiles.

Rameez Raja won the toss for the second time and again asked Sri Lanka to bat when the two sides met in Faisalabad. On this occasion, the Sri Lankans batted with consistency and purpose. Mahanama and Jayasuriya, who took advantage of lapses in the field to hit 51 off 72 deliveries, began with a stand of 75 in 18 overs.

A century in the second Test and a match-winning innings in the third, Hashan Tillekeratne was also named as Sri Lanka's Man of the Series in the one-day matches. (Chris Cole/Allsport)

First One-day International – Pakistan v. Sri Lanka

29 September 1995 at Jinnah Stadium, Gujranwala

Sri Lanka

R.S. Mahanama	run out	**12**
S.T. Jayasuriya	**c** Basit Ali, **b** Ata-ur-Rehman	**25**
A.P. Gurusinha	**c** Saqlain, **b** Mohammad	**57**
P.A. de Silva	**c** Saqlain, **b** Ata-ur-Rehman	**1**
A. Ranatunga (Capt)	not out	**102**
*R.S. Kaluwitharana	run out	**6**
H.P. Tillekeratne	not out	**11**
R.A. Kalpage		
H.D.P.K. Dharmasena		
G.P. Wickremasinghe		
K.R. Pushpakumara		
	b **1**, lb **8**, w **6**, nb **4**	**19**
	50 overs (for 5 wickets)	**233**

	O	M	R	W
Aqib Javed	9	1	43	–
Mohammad Akram	10	1	43	1
Ata-ur-Rehman	10	–	46	2
Aamer Hanif	10	–	38	–
Saqlain Mushtaq	5	–	27	–
Aamir Sohail	6	–	27	–

Fall of Wickets
1–**32**, 2–**39**, 3–**48**, 4–**185**, 5–**206**

Pakistan

Aamir Sohail	**c** sub (Muralitharan), **b** Jayasuriya	**77**
Salim Elahi	not out	**102**
Rameez Raja (Capt)	not out	**44**
Inzamam-ul-Haq		
Basit Ali		
*Moin Khan		
Aamer Hanif		
Saqlain Mushtaq		
Aqib Javed		
Mohammad Akram		
Ata-ur-Rehman		
	b **1**, lb **1**, w **7**, nb **2**	**11**
	44 overs (for 1 wicket)	**234**

	O	M	R	W
Wickremasinghe	7	–	41	–
Pushpakumara	7	–	47	–
Dharmasena	7	1	35	–
Ranatunga	2	–	14	–
Kalpage	6	–	32	–
Jayasuriya	10	–	43	1
de Silva	5	–	20	–

Fall of Wickets
1–**156**

Umpires: Mian Mohammad Aslam & Ikram Rabani *Man of the Match:* Salim Elahi

Pakistan won by 9 wickets

Second One-day International – Pakistan v. Sri Lanka

1 October 1995 at Iqbal Stadium, Faisalabad

Sri Lanka

R.S. Mahanama	lbw, **b** Ata-ur-Rehman	**30**
S.T. Jayasuriya	**c** Aqib Javed, **b** Ata-ur-Rehman	**51**
A.P. Gurusinha	**st** Moin Khan, **b** Arshad Khan	**66**
P.A. de Silva	run out	**47**
A. Ranatunga (Capt)	**b** Mohammad Akram	**15**
H.P. Tillekeratne	**b** Mohammad Akram	**14**
*R.S. Kaluwitharana	run out	**11**
W.P.U.J.C. Vaas	not out	**0**
H.D.P.K. Dharmasena	not out	**1**
G.P. Wickremasinghe		
M. Muralitharan		
	lb **14**, w **5**, nb **3**	**22**
	50 overs (for 7 wickets)	**257**

	O	M	R	W
Aqib Javed	8	1	34	–
Mohammad Akram	10	–	48	2
Ata-ur-Rehman	10	–	46	2
Aamer Hanif	2	–	21	–
Arshad Khan	10	–	32	1
Aamir Sohail	10	–	62	–

Fall of Wickets
1–**75**, 2–**100**, 3–**209**, 4–**222**, 5–**232**, 6–**256**, 7–**256**

Pakistan

Aamir Sohail	**c** Muralitharan, **b** Vaas	**9**
Salim Elahi	run out	**47**
Rameez Raja (Capt)	**c** Jayasuriya, **b** Dharmasena	**33**
Inzamam-ul-Haq	**c** Gurusinha, **b** Jayasuriya	**14**
*Moin Khan	**c** sub (Kalpage), **b** Muralitharan	**31**
Basit Ali	**b** Jayasuriya	**16**
Aamer Hanif	**b** de Silva	**19**
Aqib Javed	**b** de Silva	**21**
Ata-ur-Rehman	not out	**6**
Arshad Khan	not out	**4**
Mohammad Akram		
	lb **5**, w **1**, nb **2**	**8**
	50 overs (for 8 wickets)	**208**

	O	M	R	W
Wickremasinghe	7	–	36	–
Vaas	2	–	17	1
de Silva	10	–	33	2
Dharmasena	10	–	38	1
Muralitharan	10	2	37	1
Jayasuriya	10	–	38	2
Ranatunga	1	–	4	–

Fall of Wickets
1–**10**, 2–**89**, 3–**92**, 4–**116**, 5–**154**, 6–**160**, 7–**195**, 8–**200**

Umpires: Saleem Badar & Siddiq Khan *Man of the Match:* S.T. Jayasuriya

Sri Lanka won by 49 runs

The first Pakistani batsman to score a century on his one-day international debut, Salim Elahi, 19-year old brother of Manzoor Elahi. (Shaun Botterill/Allsport)

This provided the ideal platform, and Gurusinha and de Silva gave the innings real substance with a third wicket partnership that realised 109 off 106 balls. Gurusinha hit a six and five fours, and his 66 came from 73 deliveries. He passed 3000 runs in one-day international cricket.

Pakistan lost Aamir Sohail in the second over, but Salim Elahi and Rameez Raja scored 79 in 107 balls, and victory looked probable. Salim again batted well, but he was left stranded when he attempted to take a second run in the 19th over. Rameez was caught at deep mid-wicket two overs later, and Pakistan began to lose their way. They needed 97 from the last ten overs with four wickets standing, but Jayasuriya and de Silva, in particular, bowled tightly, and the task proved well beyond the home side.

Overnight rain delayed the start of the deciding match by three hours, and the game had to be reduced to 38 overs per innings. Put in to bat, Pakistan were given a useful start by Aamir Sohail and Salim Elahi, but thereafter the batting was disappointing. There was no partnership of note, and only Aamer Hanif showed real defiance. Inzamam did reach 3000 runs in one-day internationals, but the honours were with the Sri Lankan bowlers.

Sri Lanka were 63 for 3 in 15 overs before de Silva and Ranatunga rallied them with a stand of 75. From the last five overs, Sri Lanka needed 32 runs, but this was brought down to two from the last over, a task which was easily accomplished.

Tillekeratne and Moin Khan were named Men of the Series. Sri Lanka, in a euphoric state after their magnificent achievements, looked to Sharjah and Australia with confidence. Pakistan contemplated the debris. Wasim Akram announced that he was unavailable for the Sharjah tournament, but Waqar Younis and leg-spinner Mushtaq Ahmed were recalled. Rameez Raja retained the captaincy. These were troubled times for Pakistan.

Third One-day International – Pakistan v. Sri Lanka

3 October 1995 at Pindi Stadium, Rawalpindi

Pakistan

Aamir Sohail	**st** Kaluwitharana, **b** Dharmasena	**26**
Salim Elahi	**c** Kalpage, **b** Dharmasena	**30**
Rameez Raja (Capt)	**st** Kaluwitharana, **b** Dharmasena	**4**
Inzamam-ul-Haq	**c** Jayasuriya, **b** de Silva	**25**
Saeed Azad	**c** Wickremasinghe, **b** de Silva	**19**
Aamer Hanif	not out	**36**
*Moin Khan	**c** Kaluwitharana, **b** de Silva	**0**
Zafar Iqbal	run out	**13**
Aqib Javed	**c** Gurusinha, **b** Kalpage	**11**
Arshad Khan	run out	**2**
Mohammad Akram	not out	**0**
	lb **7**, w **6**, nb **4**	**17**
	38 overs (for 9 wickets)	**183**

	O	M	R	W
Wickremasinghe	5	–	11	**–**
Upashantha	5	–	36	**–**
Dharmasena	8	–	30	**3**
Gurusinha	1	–	6	**–**
Kalpage	4	–	26	**1**
Jayasuriya	8	–	31	**–**
de Silva	7	–	36	**3**

Fall of Wickets
1–**55**, 2–**65**, 3–**80**, 4–**104**, 5–**134**, 6–**134**, 7–**158**, 8–**176**, 9–**180**

Sri Lanka

R.S. Mahanama	**b** Zafar Iqbal	**23**
S.T. Jayasuriya	**c** Inzamam-ul-Haq, **b** Aqib	**19**
A.P. Gurusinha	**b** Zafar Iqbal	**10**
P.A. de Silva	lbw, **b** Aamer Hanif	**32**
A. Ranatunga (Capt)	lbw, **b** Aamer Hanif	**42**
*R.S. Kaluwitharana	**c** Saeed Azad, **b** Aamer Hanif	**12**
H.P. Tillekeratne	not out	**13**
R.S. Kalpage	not out	**10**
H.D.P.K. Dharmasena		
E. Upashantha		
G.P. Wickremasinghe		
	lb **12**, w **11**	**23**
	37.4 overs (for 6 wickets)	**184**

	O	M	R	W
Aqib Javed	7.4	–	28	**1**
Mohammad Akram	8	–	38	**–**
Zafar Iqbal	8	–	37	**2**
Arshad Khan	7	1	26	**–**
Aamer Hanif	6	–	36	**3**
Aamir Sohail	1	–	7	**–**

Fall of Wickets
1–**42**, 2–**60**, 3–**63**, 4–**138**, 5–**151**, 6–**165**

Umpires: Shakeel Khan & Islam Khan *Man of the Match:* A. Ranatunga

Sri Lanka won by 4 wickets

England 'A' Tour

For the seventh time an England 'A' team was sent on tour, and for the second time it went to Pakistan. The first projected 'A' tour of Pakistan had been an ill-fated one: only two limited-over matches had been played before the outbreak of the Gulf War caused the England side to abandon Pakistan for Sri Lanka. The 1995 tour suffered no such intrusions and was a complete success in every way. The side was managed by John Emburey, already spoken of as Ray Illingworth's successor, and was captained by Nasser Hussain of Essex. Hussain was a surprise selection as skipper, but it proved to be an inspired choice although most felt that Hussain should have been with the premier side in South Africa

Hussain had with him four players who had appeared in Test cricket, Gallian, Knight, Salisbury and White, while Udal had appeared in ten one-day internationals. Giddins, Headley, Irani, McGrath, Ostler, Piper, Pooley and Mike Smith made up the party. Martin had originally been chosen, but he had joined the premier side when Johnson of Middlesex had withdrawn through injury. Pooley had replaced Symonds, an original selection, who declined the invitation to tour and played for Queensland in the Sheffield Shield. The side was to play 11 matches, including three 'Tests' and three representative limited-over internationals, in the space of seven weeks.

1 November 1995

at Defence Stadium, Karachi

Pakistan Cricket Board XI 191 for 9 (Shahid Anwar 84 not out)
England 'A' 192 for 4 (N.V. Knight 78, N. Hussain 60)
England 'A' won by 6 wickets

England 'A' began their tour with a win off the last ball in a match that was originally scheduled for the National Stadium. Shahid Anwar carried his bat through the 50 overs of the Board XI's innings which featured some tight bowling and eager fielding. Knight and Hussain added 112 in 29.2 overs for the second England 'A' wicket, but victory was not easily attained. Pooley and Piper needed to score five from the last four balls, which they just managed.

3 November 1995

at Makli Cricket Ground, Thatta

England 'A' 168 (N. Hussain 64, Kabir Khan 4 for 20)
Pakistan Cricket Board XI 161
England 'A' won by 7 runs

The ground at Thatta, 60 miles from Karachi, had not staged a first-class match and this was the first game of any importance to be staged there. Put in on a moist, green pitch, England 'A' lost Pooley in the fourth over, but Hussain and McGrath added 71. White was unable to play because of a hairline fracture of the thumb sustained in the opening match, but the visiting bowlers, well marshalled by Hussain, kept the batsmen in control. Nevertheless, at 101 for 3, the home side looked likely winners. They were restricted by brilliant fielding and fine bowling, and 13 runs were needed from the last two overs. In desperation, losing patience, Kabir Khan swung at Giddins and was caught by Irani with eight balls of the 45-over quota remaining.

5, 6, 7 and 8 November 1995

at Defence Stadium, Karachi

Karachi Combined XI 204 (Azam Khan 55, I.D.K. Salisbury 4 for 72) and 223 (Mohammad Ramzan 121 not out, R.C. Irani 5 for 19, I.D.K. Salisbury 4 for 74)
England 'A' 312 (N. Hussain 89, S.D. Udal 50, Shahid Khan Afridi 4 for 72) and 116 for 4 (N.V. Knight 71 not out)
England 'A' won by 6 wickets

The first first-class match was a tough assignment for the England 'A' who were faced by a side led by Shoaib Mohammad and who were handicapped when Smith suffered a recurrence of a rib injury. Hussain handled his depleted attack splendidly, and Salisbury and Giddins, backed by bright fielding, bowled out the Combined XI on the opening day. Knight and McGrath scored 47 before the close and extended their partnership to 70 before being separated. On a blistering hot day, against some taxing spin bowling from Nadeed Khan, slow left arm, and Shahid Khan Afridi, leg-breaks, Hussain batted magnificently for 216 minutes to hold his side together and to take them into a good lead. The lead was extended on the third morning when Udal and Giddins scored another 33 runs to make their last wicket partnership worth 36.

When the Combined XI batted a second time their middle order was ripped apart by Ronnie Irani who took four wickets in 24 balls and finished with the best bowling figures of his career. Mohammad Ramzan carried his bat through the innings for a fine century, but Salisbury took eight wickets in the match, and England 'A' won with time to spare on the last day when Hussain shuffled his batting order to give players practice.

11, 12, 13 and 14 November 1995

at Bagh-e-Jinnah Ground, Lahore

Pakistan Cricket Board Combined XI 301 (Saeed Azad 117, Shadab Kabir 61, Adil Nisar 57, D.W. Headley 5 for 68) and 153 (R.D. Stemp 4 for 46)
England 'A' 355 (A. McGrath 103, N. Hussain 83, J.E.R. Gallian 67, Mubashir Nazir 4 for 51) and 100 for 2 (R.C. Irani 53 not out)
England 'A' won by 8 wickets

Batting first on a good pitch, the Board XI reached 259 for 4 on the first day. White was back in the England 'A' side, but

England 'A' struggle to save the third 'Test' and win the series. Keith Piper is caught behind by Wasim Yousufi off Salman Fazal.
(Ben Radford/Allsport)

he was wayward, and it was Dean Headley who took the honours with controlled and intelligently varied bowling. Saeed Azad, 96 overnight, completed his hundred on the second morning. His was an innings of violent drives and wild swings. He should have been given out on the first day when he edged Stemp to Piper, but his innings had much to commend it and was deservedly warmly applauded.

With White finding rhythm and Headley in an aggressive mood, the home side could add only 42 on the second morning. England 'A' quickly lost Knight, but Gallian and, inevitably, Hussain added 117. The rest faltered and the visitors closed on 199 for 5.

That England 'A' took a first innings lead of 54 was due primarily to Anthony McGrath, the youngest member of the party, who reached a maiden first-class century on the third day after five and a half hours batting. McGrath revealed an exemplary temperament and an admirably compact defence. Stemp helped him to reach his century as the pair added 64 for the last wicket. The Combined XI were 67 for 4 at the close, and they never made an effective recovery as Stemp and Salisbury mopped up the tail. Irani then flayed a quick fifty and England 'A' had won four out of four.

17, 18, 19, 20 and 21 November 1995
at Qasim Bagh Stadium, Multan
Pakistan 'A' 137 (Shahid Anwar 50, I.D.K. Salisbury 6 for 39) and 147 (Asif Mujtaba 57, D.W. Headley 5 for 34, R.D. Stemp 5 for 64)
England 'A' 327 (J.E.R. Gallian 62, R.C. Irani 58, N. Hussain 52, Mohammad Zahid 4 for 67)
England 'A' won by an innings and 43 runs

The fifth day of the first 'Test' match was not required, for England 'A' gained an innings victory over their hosts on the fourth afternoon. Confident, assured, totally professional in application, England 'A' led from start to finish on a pitch that favoured the bowlers but which provided a sound enough surface for batsmen willing to apply themselves. Led by Asif Mujtaba, who had three other Test cricketers in his side, Pakistan 'A', a blend of youth and experience, batted first when they won the toss. Confronted by consistently accurate bowling and dynamic fielding, they committed many errors and were punished accordingly. Ian Salisbury claimed six wickets, including that of Shahid Anwar who batted for four hours as those around him fell. Giddins started the rout by dismissing Mohammad Ramzan and Shadab Kabir with successive deliveries, but all the England bowlers did well, and Headley was particularly impressive.

Night-watchman Ian Salisbury, Sussex and England 'A', battles his way to a career-best 86 in the second 'Test' match in Rawalpindi. Wasim Yousufi is the wicket-keeper.
(Ben Radford/Allsport)

Knight and Gallian put England 'A' in a strong position with an opening stand of 117 in 27 overs, and when they and McGrath fell in quick succession Hussain and Irani added 92. Hussain's fifth fifty of the tour included five fours and a six while Irani's 58 contained eight fours and two sixes. By the third day, England 'A' had a total hold on the match. Piper's 46 had boosted the score and taken his side to a first innings lead of 190, and Pakistan 'A' had lost five wickets and still trailed by 75 runs when bad light ended play early for the third day running.

There was no reprieve for the home side as Headley, Man of the Match, and Stemp completed the rout on the fourth day.

25, 26 and 27 November 1995
at Bagh-e-Jinnah Ground, Lahore
England 'A' 298 for 6 dec. (N.V. Knight 107, J.C. Pooley 100 not out) and 130 for 4 dec.
Pakistan Board Patron's XI 187 for 9 dec. (Azhar Mahmood 63 not out, T.A. Munton 5 for 54) and 88 for 3
Match drawn

Hussain failed to reach fifty and England 'A' failed to win for the first time, but once again they had much to enthuse about. Knight made what was only his second first-class century since leaving Essex, and Pooley hit a fierce hundred off 138 balls. Tim Munton, newly arrived as cover for the injured Mike Smith, tore the heart out of the home side's batting on the second day, taking four wickets in 13 balls. The Patron's XI were 48 for 6 before Azhar Mahmood brought some respectability. Bad light and rain settled the issue on the third day, and it was decided that Mike Smith should return to England because of his injury.

30 November, 1, 2, 3 and 4 December 1995
at KLR Ground, Rawalpindi
Pakistan 'A' 214 (Shakeel Ahmed 62, D.W. Headley 6 for 73) and 154 for 4 (Shakeel Ahmed 73)
England 'A' 332 for 6 dec. (J.E.R. Gallian 153, I.D.K. Salisbury 86)
Match drawn

The second 'Test' was ruined by the weather. No play was possible on the first day, and only 34 overs were bowled on the second, during which Pakistan 'A', having been put in, scored 73 for 1. A second five-wicket haul by the mightily impressive Dean Headley was the highlight of the third day. He was ably supported by Ian Salisbury, who bowled his leg-breaks with confidence and accuracy, and then, coming in as night-watchman, helped Gallian to add 197 after Knight had gone for 0. Salisbury's 86 was the highest score of his career while Gallian went on to make 153, the highest score of the tour. England 'A' could not make up for the lost time, however, and the match was drawn. Richard Stemp was cautioned by manager John Emburey when he was accused of using verbal abuse on the pitch.

8, 9, 10, 11 and 12 December 1995
at Arbab Niaz Stadium, Peshawar
England 'A' 199 (D.P. Ostler 68, N.V. Knight 55, Shahid Nazir 6 for 64) and 191 for 8 (J.E.R. Gallian 58)
Pakistan 'A' 300 (Asif Mujtaba 147 not out, E.S.H. Giddins 5 for 104, D.W. Headley 5 for 109)
Match drawn

Dampness, gloom and the fact the groundsman had not handed over his pitch delayed the start of the third and final 'Test', and England 'A' struggled to reach 102 for 4 on the first day. There was some impressive medium-pace bowling by Shahid Nazir, 18 years old, but Dominic Ostler held the lower order together in determined fashion to take his side to 199. This looked a massive score when, with his third and fourth deliveries, Headley bowled Shahid Anwar and Babar Zaman. The hat-trick ball found the edge of Asif Mujtaba's bat, but Knight failed to hold the catch at slip. He did catch Shakeel Ahmed off Giddins in the next over, and Pakistan 'A' were 1 for 3, but the dropping of Asif proved very costly. The third day began 100 minutes late, but by the end of it, the Pakistan 'A' captain had completed his century. He was unbeaten on 147 when the innings ended on the fourth day. Leading by 101, Pakistan 'A' captured Knight and night-watchman Salisbury before the close when England 'A' had reached 62. There was more delay on the last morning before Hussain began hitting the ball sweetly until he ran himself out. This brought about a worrying collapse, which was ended by good sense and technically accomplished batting from Pooley and Headley who shared an unbroken ninth wicket stand of 49.

The draw in this thoroughly unsatisfactory match gave England 'A' the series, most deservedly.

One-day International Series

15 December 1995
at Arbab Niaz Stadium, Peshawar
England 'A' 225 for 5 (N. Hussain 100 not out)
Pakistan 'A' 224 for 6 (Shahid Anwar 100 not out)
England 'A' won by one run

18 December 1995
at Iqbal Stadium Faisalabad
Pakistan 'A' 186 for 6 (Shahid Anwar 87 not out)
England 'A' 190 for 3 (N.V. Knight 90 not out, N. Hussain 50)
England 'A' won by 7 wickets

20 December 1995
at Sheikhupra Stadium, Sheikhupra
Pakistan 'A' 248 for 5 (Shakeel Ahmed 69, Asif Mujtaba 62)
England 'A' 115 (Sajid Shah 6 for 43)
Pakistan 'A' won by 133 runs.

The England 'A' tour ended with three one-day matches against Pakistan 'A'. In the first match, Hussain, coming to the wicket when Gallian was out at 18, reached a century off 109 balls. It was a splendid effort, full of majestic cover drives, and it took England 'A' to a good score on a slow pitch on which the ball tended to keep low. Unfortunately, the England bowlers were below form and the fielding was not of the standard that had been set throughout the tour. Shahid Anwar looked certain to win the match for the home side, particularly after Headley had dropped a skier. The Kent all-rounder restored sanity with an excellent 39th over that left Pakistan 'A' needing five from the final over. White restricted them to two singles off his first five deliveries, and the sixth was sliced to Gallian in the covers, leaving England 'A' winners by one run.

With Gallian departed to join the premier side in South Africa, a surprising choice considering the achievements of Hussain, Ostler moved up the order to open in the second 40-over match. Giddins, who came in for Gallian, and Stemp, who replaced the out-of-form Udal, bowled well to take wickets and stem runs. Shahid Anwar batted throughout the innings, but he was never able to accelerate at the close. Knight was dropped second ball, but he and Ostler scored 48 for the first wicket before Hussain, 50 off 67 balls, joined Knight in a stand worth 110 in 21 overs. The inevitable victory came with nine balls to spare, and England 'A' added triumph in the one-day series to their success in the 'Test' series.

The third and final match of the series and of the tour was a disappointment for England 'A' in that they surrendered their unbeaten record. Put in to bat, Pakistan 'A' were 53 for 2, but Shakeel Ahmed and Asif Mujtaba added 118 against bowling that looked rather weary. Facing a target that demanded that they score at more than six runs an over, the tourists lost Knight for 0, and pace bowler Sajid Shah tore the top order to shreds as England 'A' were bowled out in 23.4 overs.

An outstanding success of the England 'A' tour, Dean Headley returned to Kent and injury which kept him out of the opening weeks of the England season. (Ben Radford/Allsport)

The disappointment at this defeat could not detract from the fact that this had been a highly successful tour. Admirably managed by Mike Vockins and John Emburey, the team had played consistently well, displaying vigour, purpose and commitment. Hussain had an outstanding tour as captain and batsman while Gallian and Knight, who enjoyed some fortune, also did well. Dean Headley showed considerable advance as a bowler, and Ian Salisbury kept alive his flickering hopes of regaining a Test place. Irani, too, showed that he was a player of class and energy, and the tour could point to few failures.

Patron's Trophy

9, 10, 11 and 12 September 1995
at Defence Stadium, Karachi
Habib Bank 348 (Anwar Miandad 121, Asadullah Butt 61, Salman Fazal 6 for 110) and 112 for 3 (Shakeel Ahmed 58 not out)
National Bank 258 (Saeed Azad 94, Asadullah Butt 4 for 75, Nadeem Ghauri 4 for 89)
Match drawn
Habib Bank 2 pts, National Bank 0 pts

at Montgomery Ground, Sahiwal
ADBP 284 (Javed Hayat 79, Mohammad Ali 60 not out, Mohammad Zahid 6 for 103) and 291 for 6 dec. (Zahoor Elahi 117, Ghaffar Kazmi 69, Mohammad Zahid 4 for 102)
Allied Bank 192 (Aalay Haider 81, Javed Hayat 5 for 44, Mohammad Asif 4 for 82) and 165 for 3 (Iqbal Saleem 59, Wajatullah 50 not out)
Match drawn
ADBP 2 pts, Allied Bank 0 pts

at KRL Ground, Rawalpindi
PIA 411 for 8 dec. (Wasim Haider 184, Javed Qadir 66 not out, Aamer Wasim 4 for 111)
Railways 192 (Mohammad Nawaz jnr 79, Nadeem Khan 5 for 78) and 27 for 2
Match drawn
PIA 2 pts, Railways 0 pts

at Pindi Cricket Stadium, Rawalpindi
PNSC 210 (Sajjad Akbar 70, Tahir Mahmood 50) and 188 (Sajjad Akbar 95 not out, Ali Gohar 6 for 83)
United Bank 294 (Aamer Bashir 93, Mohammad Hussain 58 not out, Basit Ali 56) and 108 for 1 (Javed Sami 55 not out)
United Bank won by 9 wickets
United Bank 12 pts, PNSC 0 pts

The first of Pakistan's domestic competitions was, inevitably, dwarfed by the national side's meetings with Sri Lanka and by the England 'A' tour and Pakistan's tour of Australia. United Bank emerged as the only outright winners in the first round of matches. For ADBP, Mohammad Ali, batting at number 11 against Allied Bank, hit 60 off 80 balls in a last wicket stand of 81. Wasim Haider's 184 off 295 balls for PIA was the highlight of the round and a career-best score.

15, 16, 17 and 18 September 1995
at Montgomery Ground, Sahiwal
PIA 409 (Rizwan-uz-Zaman 83, Mahmood Hamid 65, Zahid Ahmed 58, Sagheer Abbas 51, Shahid Mahmood 4 for 196)
Habib Bank 205 (Shahid Nawaz 75, Tahir Rasheed 66, Mohammad Zahid 5 for 44) and 196
PIA won by an innings and 8 runs
PIA 12 pts, Habib Bank 0 pts

at Zafar Ali Stadium, Sahiwal
ADBP 458 (Atif Rauf 163, Mansoor Rana 71, Zahoor Elahi 54)
National Bank 303 (Zafar Iqbal 99, Athar Laeeq 51, Manzoor Elahi 5 for 58) and 265 for 3 (Sajid Ali 106, Ameer Akbar 51 not out, Wasim Arif 50)
Match drawn
ADBP 2 pts, National Bank 0 pts

at KRL Ground, Rawalpindi
PNSC 272 (Mazhar Qayyum 72, Nasir Wasti 70, Sajjad Akbar 58 not out, Bilal Rana 4 for 44) and 128 (Sher Ali 51, Ata-ur-Rehman 8 for 56)
Allied Bank 244 (Mohammad Nawaz 69, Bilal Rana 62 not out, Mohsin Kamal 4 for 80) and 111 (Mohsin Kamal 5 for 46, Sajjad Ali 5 for 47)
PNSC won by 45 runs
PNSC 12 pts, Allied Bank 0 pts

at LCCA Ground, Lahore
Railways 155 (Ali Gohar 6 for 56) and 99 (Ali Gohar 6 for 28)
United Bank 418 for 6 dec. (Mansoor Akhtar 202, Mohammad Ramzan 80, Umar Rasheed 57 not out, Aamer Wasim 4 for 149)
United Bank won by an innings and 164 runs
United Bank 12 pts, Railways 0 pts

Consistent scoring was the basis of PIA's victory over Habib Bank while Atif Rauf hit the 13th century of his career and shared a third wicket stand of 190 with Mansoor Rana as ADBP forced National Bank to follow on. Sajid Ali's three-hour century helped stave off defeat.

Ata-ur-Rehman won a recall to the Test side with the best bowling performance of his career, 8 for 56 against PNSC, but his side – Allied Bank – were surprisingly defeated. Waqar Younis returned to strengthen United Bank and took six wickets in the victory over Railways, but it was his new-ball partner Ali Gohar who took the honours with match figures of 12 for 84.

21, 22, 23 and 24 September 1995
at Qasim Bagh Stadium, Multan
PNSC 447 (Azam Khan 138, Mazhar Qayyum 119 not out, Sohail Jaffer 58, Aamer Wasim 7 for 169)
Railways 165 (Murtaza Hussain 4 for 22) and 195 (Majid Saeed 90, Tariq Hussain 4 for 27, Murtaza Hussain 4 for 68)
PNSC won by an innings and 87 runs
PNSC 12 pts, Railways 0 pts

at Defence Stadium, Karachi
PIA 277 (Ayaz Jilani 77, Zahid Ahmed 57) and 111 for 1 (Mahmood 66 not out)
United Bank 355 (Mohammad Ramzan 127 not out, Ayaz Jilani 4 for 90)
Match drawn
United Bank 2 pts, PIA 0 pts

at Arbab Niaz Stadium, Peshawar
ADBP 354 (Mansoor Rana 75, Javed Hayat 75, Sabih Azhar 51 not out, Asif Malik 4 for 106)
Habib Bank 112 (Manzoor Elahi 6 for 38, Mohammad Ali 4 for 60) and 214 (Mohammad Ali 5 for 68)
ADBP won by an innings and 28 runs
ADBP 12 pts, Habib Bank 0 pts

at Montgomery Ground, Sahiwal
National Bank 307 (Ameer Akbar 128, Shahid Mahboob 4 for 63) and 246 (Sajid Ali 98, Bilal Rana 5 for 58)
Allied Bank 588 for 7 dec. (Aamer Hanif 179, Manzoor Akhtar 145, Raj Hans 110)
Allied Bank won by an innings and 35 runs
Allied Bank 12 pts, National Bank 0 pts

Pakistan National Shipping Corporation gained their second victory in succession and came within two points of United Bank, who were unfortunate in that there was no play on the first day of their match in Karachi due to a strike. ADBP won convincingly over Habib Bank, using only three bowlers to twice dismiss their opponents. Allied Bank crushed National Bank in their first win of the season. They lost Kamran Khan at seven, but their later batsmen savaged the Allied bowling.

27, 28, 29 and 30 September 1995
at LCCA Ground, Lahore
Allied Bank 156 (Nadeem Ghauri 4 for 48) and 255 (Kamran 124, Mohammad Nawaz 51)
Habib Bank 163 (Shahid Mahboob 6 for 80) and 132 (Bilal Rana 4 for 40, Hamayun Fida Hussain 4 for 43)
Allied Bank won by 116 runs
Allied Bank 12 pts, Habib Bank 0 pts

at Arbab Niaz Stadium, Peshawar
National Bank 247 (Tahir Shah 55, Saeed Azad 50, Azhar Abbas 4 for 96) and 66 for 0
Railways 94 (Athar Laeeq 5 for 27) and 218 (Majid Saeed 89, Zafar Iqbal 5 for 49)
National Bank won by 10 wickets
National Bank 12 pts, Railways 0 pts

A fine all-round season for Shakeel Ahmed.
(Ben Radford/Allsport)

at Montgomery Ground, Sahiwal
PIA 498 for 6 dec. (Asif Mujtaba 170, Rizwan-uz-Zaman 105, Wasim Haider 69 not out, Sagheer Abbas 50)
PNSC 502 for 7 (Azam Khan 92, Sohail Jaffer 90, Tahir Mahmood 82 not out, Aamer Ishaq 60, Mazhar Qayyum 58)
Match drawn
PNSC 2 pts, PIA 0 pts

at KRL Ground, Rawalpindi
ADBP 83 (Mohammad Hussain 6 for 35) and 129 (Manzoor Elahi 50, Tauseef Ahmed 4 for 50)
United Bank 97 (Javed Hayat 6 for 41, Mohammad Asif 4 for 23) and 93
ADBP won by 22 runs
ADBP 12 pts, United Bank 0 pts

A second innings second wicket stand of 118 between Kamran Khan and Mohammad Nawaz turned the course of the game in Lahore where Allied Bank won after trailing on the first innings. Railways remained pointless after four matches when they suffered their third defeat in succession in Peshawar, while the pitch in Sahiwal was of such a nature as to produce a stalemate. A third wicket stand of 128 between two seasoned batsmen, Rizwan-uz-Zaman and Asif

Mujtaba, set up PIA's big score. Rizwan hit a six and 11 fours in his 264-ball innings while Asif Mujtaba faced 319 balls and hit a six and 15 fours. Wasim Haider hit 69 off 45 deliveries with five sixes, and Asif declared late on the second day. With consistent application – only Sher Ali failed to reach 20 – PNSC batted nearly 200 overs and took first-innings points.

The condition of the KRL Ground drew much criticism, and United Bank were beaten on the third day without reaching a hundred in either innings and without managing to score at two an over. ADBP found it equally hard to score runs, but Manzoor Elahi's two-hour fifty proved decisive.

3, 4, 5 and 6 October 1995
at Jinnah Stadium, Sialkot
PIA 478 (Rizwan-uz-Zaman 155, Asif Mujtaba 121, Wasim Haider 54, Mohammad Asif 4 for 100) and 57 for 3
ADBP 235 (Mohammad Zahid 5 for 76) and 293 (Zahoor Elahi 100, Javed Hayat 60, Nadeem Khan 4 for 90)
PIA won by 7 wickets
PIA 12 pts, ADBP 0 pts

at Iqbal Stadium, Faisalabad
Allied Bank 194 (Aamer Wasim 6 for 74, Mohammad Nawaz jnr 4 for 56) and 127 (Aamer Wasim 5 for 56, Mohammad Nawaz jnr 4 for 37)
Railways 166 (Bilal Rana 6 for 64) and 108 (Bilal Rana 5 for 32)
Allied Bank won by 47 runs
Allied Bank 12 pts, Railways 0 pts

at Jinnah Stadium, Gujranwala
Habib Bank 144 (Mushtaq Ahmed 6 for 56) and 199 (Shakeel Ahmed 96, Mushtaq Ahmed 4 for 78)
United Bank 392 for 7 dec. (Iqbal Imam 100, Javed Sami 63, Mohammad Hussain 58 not out, Asadullah Butt 4 for 102)
United Bank won by an innings and 49 runs
United Bank 12 pts, Habib Bank 0 pts

at LCCA Ground, Lahore
PNSC 594 (Azam Khan 122, Sajjad Ali 100, Sohail Jaffer 98, Nasir Wasti 84, Mohammad Javed 5 for 119)
National Bank 508 (Shahid Anwar 195, Sajid Ali 139, Mohammad Javed 51)
Match drawn
PNSC 2 pts, National Bank 0 pts

Rizwan-uz-Zaman and Asif Mujtaba again shared a third wicket partnership, which this time realised 233 runs, set up victory over ADBP and gave PIA the chance of a place in the semi-finals. Allied Bank were virtually assured of their place when they beat the luckless Railways in a low-scoring encounter. They owed much to the slow left-arm bowling of Bilal Rana who took ten or more wickets in a match for the second time in his career. Babar Javed of Railways caught five of the first six Allied batsmen. United Bank, able to call upon Rashid Latif, Waqar Younis and Mushtaq Ahmed, were too strong for Habib Bank and won before tea on the third day. Iqbal Imam's 100 was scored off 169 balls in 218 minutes.

In Lahore, PNSC's innings was over late on the second day and was again marked by its consistency. There were centuries of contrasting styles from Azam Khan and Sajjad Ali whose 100 came off 146 balls, and the approach was always brisk. National Bank countered with an opening stand of 301 between Shahid Anwar and Sajid Ali. Thereafter, no batsmen stayed long enough to bring National Bank close enough to PNSC's score. Shahid Anwar batted eight and a quarter hours for the highest score of his career.

9, 10, 11 and 12 October 1995
at Qasim Bagh Stadium, Multan
Railways 193 (Mohammad Nawaz jnr 54, Raja Afaq 5 for 40) and 386 for 9 dec. (Rana Qayyum 150 not out, Intikhab Alam 127, Mohammad Asif 4 for 105)
ADBP 203 (Aamer Wasim 5 for 80) and 345 for 8 (Zahoor Elahi 178, Nadeem Hussain 105, Aamer Wasim 4 for 149)
Match drawn
ADBP 2 pts, Railways 0 pts

at Zafar Ali Stadium, Sahiwal
Habib Bank 389 (Sohail Fazal 87 not out, Moin-ul-Atiq 81, Shaukat Mirza 78, Shahid Javed 73, Sajjad Akbar 7 for 103) and 230 (Shakeel Ahmed 50, Tariq Hussain 4 for 80)
PNSC 405 (Mazhar Qayyum 129, Sohail Jaffer 122) and 217 for 7 (Nasir Wasti 68, Aamer Ishaq 57)
PNSC won by 3 wickets
PNSC 12 pts, Habib Bank 0 pts

at Bagh-e-Jinnah Ground, Lahore
Allied Bank 333 (Manzoor Akhtar 97, Rafaqat Ali 62, Ali Gohar 5 for 86, Shahzad Butt 4 for 109) and 11 for 1
United Bank 141 (Humayun Fida Hussain 5 for 64, Shahid Mahboob 4 for 60) and 202 (Javed Sami 67, Mohammad Ramzan 52, Shahid Mahboob 5 for 72)
Allied Bank won by 9 wickets
Allied Bank 12 pts, United Bank 0 pts

at Jinnah Stadium, Gujranwala
PIA 323 (Asif Mujtaba 118, Shoaib Mohammad 60, Mohammad Javed 5 for 88, Athar Laeeq 4 for 87) and 204 for 2 (Shoaib Mohammad 102 not out, Rizwan-uz-Zaman 65)
National Bank 387 (Shahid Anwar 85, Saeed Azad 57, Ameer Akbar 56)
Match drawn
National Bank 2 pts, PIA 0 pts

Trailing by ten runs on the first innings, Railways made a brave attempt to win their first points of the season. Intikhab

Captain of Pakistan 'A' and the season's leading batsman with 1367 runs and eight centuries, Asif Mujtaba.
(Ben Radford/Allsport)

Alam and Rana Qayyum shared a fifth wicket stand of 245 in 280 minutes, and Kifayat Hussain was able to declare and set ADBP a target of 377 in 76 overs. A second wicket partnership of 264 in 242 minutes between Zahoor Elahi and Nadeem Hussain brought a glimpse of a great victory, but the next highest scorer was Javed Hayat with 18, and ADBP failed to reach their target by 32 runs. Zahoor Elahi's 178 off 199 balls was the highest score of his career.

A stand of 209 between Mazhar Qayyum and Sohail Jaffer helped take PNSC to a first innings lead over Habib Bank, but their final target of 215 in 40 overs was a daunting one. Aamer Ishaq began with 57 off 50 balls, and Nasir Wasti hit 68 off 85 balls to see PNSC home with nine balls to spare. The win confirmed their place in the semi-finals.

Allied Bank, too, confirmed their place with a resounding victory over a United Bank side minus most of their star players. Asif Mujtaba's third century in successive matches could not bring his side a point against National Bank, and PIA looked unlikely to qualify for the last four.

15, 16, 17 and 18 October 1995
at Arbab Niaz Stadium, Peshawar
Allied Bank 154 (Ijaz Ahmed jnr 60, Nadeem Khan 6 for 42)
PIA 157 for 1 (Shoaib Mohammad 71 not out)
Match drawn
PIA 2 pts, Allied Bank 0 pts

at Jinnah Stadium, Sialkot
Railways 267 (Mohammad Nawaz jnr 71, Intikhab Alam 64, Kabir Khan 4 for 85) and 267 (Rana Qayyum 86, Kifayat Hussain 50, Kabir Khan 4 for 84, Abdul Qadir 4 for 104)
Habib Bank 377 (Shakeel Ahmed 101, Shaukat Mirza 96 not out, Moin-ul-Atiq 50, Aamer Wasim 6 for 80) and 126 for 7 (Moin-ul-Atiq 58)
Match drawn
Habib Bank 2 pts, Railways 0 pts

at Pindi Cricket Stadium, Rawalpindi
National Bank 133 (Shahzad Butt 4 for 34)
United Bank 134 for 8 (Mohammad Javed 4 for 40)
Match drawn
United Bank 2 pts, National Bank 0 pts

at LCCA Ground, Lahore
ADBP 483 for 9 dec. (Nadeem Younis 135, Mansoor Rana 113 not out, Mohammad Nadeem 68)
PNSC 308 (Sohail Jaffer 78, Aamir Ishaq 54, Mohammad Asif 5 for 69) and 222 for 4 (Sohail Jaffer 108 not out)
Match drawn
ADBP 2 pts, PNSC 0 pts

The last round of matches had no effect on the final placings. No play was possible on the first two days in Peshawar and only 23 overs were bowled on the third day. There was a similar situation in Rawalpindi. In Sialkot, the veteran Abdul Qadir had his best return of the competition, but his side, Habib Bank, fell just short of scoring 158 in 19 overs which would have brought them their first win of the season. A high-scoring game in Lahore saw PNSC fail to get a point for the first time since the opening match of the season, but they batted well to stave off defeat in the second innings.

Patron's Trophy – Final Qualifying Table

	P	W	L	D	Pts
Allied Bank	7	4	1	2	48
Pakistan National Shipping Corporation	7	3	1	3	40
United Bank	7	3	2	2	40
Agricultural Development Bank of Pakistan	7	2	1	4	32
Pakistan International Airlines	7	2	–	5	28
National Bank of Pakistan	7	1	1	5	14
Habib Bank	7	–	5	2	4
Pakistan Railways	7	–	4	3	0

Semi-Finals

21, 22, 23 and 24 October 1995
at Bagh-e-Jinnah Ground, Lahore
Allied Bank 437 (Aamer Hanif 117, Bilal Rana 116, Mohammad Nawaz 100, Shahzad Butt 5 for 127, Ali Gohar 4 for 132) and 136 for 3 (Mohammad Nawaz 72 not out)
United Bank 251 (Javed Sami 83, Shahid Mahboob 7 for 101)
Match drawn

23, 24, 25 and 26 October 1995
at Pindi Cricket Stadium, Rawalpindi
PNSC 68 (Manzoor Elahi 6 for 32, Mohammad Ali 4 for 34) and 239 (Sohail Jaffer 83, Mohammad Ali 6 for 103)
ADBP 570 (Mansoor Rana 188, Nadeem Younis 91, Sabih Azhar 91 not out, Javed Hayat 55)
ADBP won by an innings and 263 runs

Three centurions, a second wicket stand of 191 between Mohammad Nawaz and Aamer Hanif, and careful batting in the lower order took Allied Bank to a formidable score and assured them of a place in the final by virtue of their first innings lead.

Put in to bat in Rawalpindi, PNSC were bowled out in under 30 overs by Manzoor Elahi and Mohammad Ali. Mansoor Rana, the ADBP skipper, then led the relentless and complete destruction of the PNSC attack. A ninth wicket stand between Mansoor and Sabih Azhar realised 184. PNSC had appeared to run out of steam towards the end of the competition.

Final

29, 30, 31 October, 1 and 2 November 1995
at Arbab Niaz Stadium, Peshawar
ADBP 295 (Nadeem Younis 107, Atif Rauf 84, Hamayun Fida Hussain 5 for 76) and 273 (Raja Afaq 56, Hamayun Fida Hussain 4 for 71, Shahid Mahboob 4 for 120)
Allied Bank 212 (Manzoor Elahi 6 for 68) and 144 (Mohammad Ali 6 for 63)
ADBP won by 212 runs

The Agricultural Development Bank of Pakistan, put in to bat, responded by reaching 278 for 8 on the first day. They owed much to Nadeem Younis who played aggressively for his 107, and to Atif Rauf who was unbeaten at the close after a more circumspect innings. Atif added only eight to his overnight score before falling to Hamayun Fida Hussain, but Manzoor Elahi produced a magnificent spell that reduced Allied Bank, the holders, to 65 for 6. There was a recovery of sorts, but ADBP now had a grip on the game which they never lost. They scored purposefully in their second innings with Mohammad Asif and Raja Afaq adding a match-winning 105 for the eighth wicket. From that point on, the trophy was always going to ADBP.

Wasim Yousufi, United Bank and Pakistan 'A' wicket-keeper, held 37 catches in the season.
(Ben Radford/Allsport)

Quaid-e-Azam Trophy

2, 3, 4 and 5 November 1995
at Asghar Ali Shah Stadium, Karachi
Karachi Whites 323 for 6 dec. (Faisal Qureshi 105, Sohail Jaffer 85) and 199 for 5 (Saeed Azad 106 not out, Iqbal Imam 60)
Karachi Blues 168 (Munir-ul-Haq 57, Iqbal Imam 4 for 42) and 353 for 8 dec. (Manzoor Akhtar 114, Munir-ul-Haq 77, Irfanullah 56, Wasim Arif 53, Wasim-ur-Rehman 4 for 113)
Karachi Whites won by 5 wickets
Karachi Whites 12 pts, Karachi Blues 0 pts

at Mahmood Stadium, Rahim Yar Khan
Bahawalpur 309 (Saifullah 77, Majid Saeed 59, Sohail Qureshi 4 for 79)
Hyderabad 101 (Murtaza Hussain 4 for 22, Mohammad Altaf 4 for 25) and 197 (Abdul Waheed Rashid 75 not out, Mohammad Altaf 5 for 82)
Bahawalpur won by an innings and 11 runs
Bahawalpur 12 pts, Hyderabad 0 pts

at Boharnwali Ground, Faisalabad
Lahore 398 (Zahid Umar 93, Shahid Nawaz 91, Masood Anwar 5 for 100)
Faisalabad 218 (Mohammad Ashraf 56) and 116 (Akram Raza 5 for 43)
Lahore won by an innings and 64 runs
Lahore 12 pts, Faisalabad 0 pts

at KRL Ground, Rawalpindi
Rawalpindi 'B' 177 (Shakeel Ahmed 5 for 58) and 192 (Pervez Iqbal 76, Shakeel Ahmed 4 for 41)
Rawalpindi 'A' 303 (Nadeem Younis 132, Nadeem Hussain 65, Naeem Akhtar 6 for 80) and 68 for 2 (Naseer Ahmed 50 not out)
Rawalpindi 'A' won by 8 wickets
Rawalpindi 'A' 12 pts, Rawalpindi 'B' 0 pts

3, 4, 5 and 6 November 1995
at Arbab Niaz Stadium, Peshawar
Peshawar 101 (Bilal Rana 4 for 11, Fahad Khan 4 for 14) and 76 (Bilal Rana 4 for 10)
Islamabad 362 (Ahsan Butt 136, Raj Hans 83, Arshad Khan 4 for 84)
Islamabad won by an innings and 185 runs
Islamabad 12 pts, Peshawar 0 pts

Pakistan's senior domestic competition, the Quaid-e-Azam Trophy, followed hot upon the heels of the Patron's Trophy and consisted of ten teams. Newcomers were Hyderabad who replaced Sargodha, expelled for failing to arrive for two of their matches in 1994–95. The first round of matches generally saw the slaughter of the innocents by stronger opposition, although Karachi Whites forced the Blues, the senior Karachi side, to follow on and beat them by five wickets.

8, 9, 10 and 11 November 1995
at Karachi CCA Stadium, Karachi
Karachi Whites 185 (Mohammad Javed 58, Tauqeer Hussain 5 for 68) and 349 for 8 dec. (Javed Sami 92, Saeed Azad 68, Iqbal Imam 54)
Rawalpindi 'B' 214 (Tassawar Hussain 61, Naeem Tayyab 7 for 66) and 168 (Shakeel Ahmed 75, Naeem Tayyab 5 for 67)
Karachi Whites won by 152 runs
Karachi Whites 12 pts, Rawalpindi 'B' 0 pts

at Makli Cricket Ground, Thatta
Hyderabad 172 (Ghulam Abbas 5 for 43) and 190
Karachi Blues 331 (Moin-ul-Atiq 84, Sajid Ali 64, Ghulam Ali 57, Shahid Iqbal 4 for 75, Aamer Ali 4 for 99) and 33 for 2
Karachi Blues won by 8 wickets
Karachi Blues 12 pts, Hyderabad 0 pts

at Arbab Niaz Stadium, Peshawar
Lahore 293 (Manzoor Elahi 72, Kabir Khan 4 for 94) and 201 (Shahid Hussain 5 for 55)
Peshawar 168 (Sher Ali 63, Mohammad Hussain 4 for 28) and 292 (Aamer Bashir 76, Taimur Khan 57)
Lahore won by 34 runs
Lahore 12 pts, Peshawar 0 pts

at Boharnwali Ground, Faisalabad
Bahawalpur 289 (Pervez Shah 87, Azhar Shafiq 77, Masood Anwar 4 for 52) and 157 (Majid Saeed 59)
Faisalabad 256 (Hamayun Fida Hussain 83, Saadat Gul 62) and 179 (Murtaza Hussain 5 for 56)
Bahawalpur won by 12 runs
Bahawalpur 12 pts, Faisalabad 0 pts

at KRL Ground, Rawalpindi
Islamabad 213 (Raj Hans 93, Alay Haider 72) and 261 for 9 dec. (Alay Haider 69, Shoaib Akhtar 5 for 97)
Rawalpindi 'A' 263 (Shahid Javed 69, Mohammad Ali 54 not out, Raj Hans 5 for 46) and 91 (Azhar Mahmood 6 for 40)
Islamabad won by 120 runs
Islamabad 12 pts, Rawalpindi 'A' 0 pts

The competition soon looked as if it would be dominated by five teams with five others making up the numbers. Both Karachi sides triumphed, and Hyderabad confirmed that they were finding Grade One cricket difficult as they crashed to the Blues inside three days. Peshawar struggled bravely against Lahore, but they were still beaten for the second time, as were Faisalabad who ran Bahawalpur close. Rawalpindi 'A' were not helped by the fact that, having taken 7 for 178 in the match against Islamabad, Shoaib

Akhtar was called up to join the Pakistan 'A' side to play England 'A' and could not bat in the second innings of the match at the KRL Ground.

14, 15, 16 and 17 November 1995

at Asghar Ali Stadium, Karachi
Rawalpindi 'B' 288 (Tassawar Hussain 87, Manzoor Akhtar 5 for 38) and 215 (Manzoor Akhtar 6 for 72)
Karachi Blues 427 for 7 dec. (Mahmood Hamid 162, Moin-ul-Atiq 120) and 77 for 2
Karachi Blues won by 8 wickets
Karachi Blues 12 pts, Rawalpindi 'B' 0 pts.

at Arbab Niaz Stadium, Peshawar
Hyderabad 184 (Tahir Mahmood 52, Farrukh Zaman 4 for 59) and 72 (Sajid Shah 6 for 29)
Peshawar 91 (Shahid Iqbal 4 for 48) and 166 for 3 (Sher Ali 88)
Peshawar won by 7 wickets
Peshawar 12 pts, Hyderabad 0 pts

at LCCA Ground, Lahore
Karachi Whites 488 (Azam Khan 215 not out, Sohail Jaffer 58, Mohammad Hussain 4 for 131) and 78 for 1
Lahore 272 (Tahir Shah 77, Idrees Baig 68, Aamer Malik 61, Naeem Tayyab 8 for 112) and 290 (Shahid Nawaz 105, Naeem Tayyab 5 for 128)
Karachi Whites won by 9 wickets
Karachi Whites 12 pts, Lahore 0 pts

at KRL Ground, Rawalpindi
Rawalpindi 'A' 167 (Mohammad Wasim 57, Shahid Nazir 5 for 49) and 269 (Shahid Javed 104)
Faisalabad 288 (Shahid Nazir 60 not out, Mohammad Nawaz 55) and 149 for 6 (Sami-ul-Haq 63)
Faisalabad won by 4 wickets
Faisalabad 12 pts, Rawalpindi 'A' 0 pts

at Bahawalpur Stadium, Bahawalpur
Islamabad 155 (Murtaza Hussain 9 for 54) and 189 (Mohammad Zahid 6 for 49)
Bahawalpur 142 (Bilal Rana 6 for 51, Raj Hans 4 for 72) and 200 (Raj Hans 6 for 90, Bilal Rana 4 for 56)
Islamabad won by 2 runs
Islamabad 12 pts, Bahawalpur 0 pts

Karachi Blues showed their strength with some impressive all-round cricket in conquering Rawalpindi 'B', while Hyderabad surprised themselves by leading Peshawar on the first innings only to lose in three days. Azam Khan hit 215 off 286 balls to dominate Karachi Whites' triumph over Lahore, but the Whites had another hero in Naeem Tayyab who had 13 wickets in the match. Faisalabad claimed their first win when they beat Rawalpindi 'A', and Islamabad maintained their one hundred per cent record by beating Bahawalpur by the narrowest of margins. Off-break bowler Murtaza Hussain produced the best bowling performance of his career as Islamabad were bowled out for 155. Slow left-arm Bilal Rana, enjoying a fine season, and off-break bowler Raj Hans struck back for Islamabad who grabbed a first innings lead of 13. It proved vital. Needing 203 to win, Bahawalpur reached 160 for 8, but the ninth wicket pair added 37 before Raj Hans took the last two wickets to bring victory.

20, 21, 22 and 23 November 1995

at Defence Stadium, Karachi
Karachi Blues 296 (Sajid Ali 98, Munir-ul-Haq 57, Mohammad Hussain 5 for 115)
Lahore 141 (Aamer Hanif 4 for 49) and 193 for 4 (Babar Zaman 65)
Lahore conceded the match
Karachi Blues 12 pts, Lahore 0 pts

at Choudray Rahmat Ali Ground, Islamabad
Hyderabad 161 (Abdul Waheed Rashid 80) and 242 (Abdul Waheed Rashid 70, Bilal Rana 4 for 37)
Islamabad 460 for 9 dec. (Alay Haider 105, Raj Hans 102, Bilal Rana 68, Ahsan Butt 50, Montesham Rasheed 4 for 85)
Islamabad won by an innings and 57 runs
Islamabad 12 pts, Hyderabad 0 pts

at Bahawalpur Stadium, Bahawalpur
Rawalpindi 'B' 135 (Shakeel Ahmed 81 not out, Murtaza Hussain 5 for 34) and 189 (Mohammad Zahid 4 for 60, Murtaza Hussain 4 for 65)
Bahawalpur 281 (Rana Qayyum 102, Majid Saeed 64, Tauqeer Hussain 6 for 87) and 47 for 3
Bahawalpur won by 7 wickets
Bahawalpur 12 pts, Rawalpindi 'B' 0 pts

at Boharnwali Ground, Faisalabad
Faisalabad 177 (Saadat Gul 58 not out, Shahid Hussain 5 for 67, Arshad Khan 4 for 69) and 157 (Arshad Khan 6 for 54)
Peshawar 127 (Masood Anwar 5 for 24) and 210 for 2 (Sher Ali 113 not out, Jahangir Khan 87)
Peshawar won by 8 wickets
Peshawar 12 pts, Faisalabad 0 pts

at KRL Ground, Rawalpindi
Rawalpindi 'A' 257 (Shahid Javed 64, Salman Shah 53, Salman Fazal 5 for 94, Naeem Tayyab 4 for 116) and 265 for 6 dec. (Masroor 96, Naseer Ahmed 92)
Karachi Whites 201 (Kashif Ahmed 111 not out, Raja Afaq 5 for 76)
Match drawn
Rawalpindi 'A' 2 pts, Karachi Whites 0 pts

Lahore conceded the match against Karachi Blues at the end of the third day, and Islamabad gained their fourth victory in succession. Shakeel Ahmed carried his bat through Rawalpindi 'B's innings against Bahawalpur, but finished on the losing side. Peshawar trailed by 50 runs on the first innings against Faisalabad, but gained a resounding victory when Sher Ali and Jahangir Khan scored 193 in 197 minutes for their first wicket as they chased a target of 208. The game in Rawalpindi became the first to be drawn.

26, 27, 28 and 29 November 1995
at Defence Stadium, Karachi
Faisalabad 121 and 232 (Ali Hassan Rizvi 6 for 77)
Karachi Blues 355 (Mahmood Hamid 106, Mohammad Wasim 4 for 103)
Karachi Blues won by an innings and 2 runs
Karachi Blues 12 pts, Faisalabad 0 pts

at Choudray Rahmat Ali Ground, Islamabad
Islamabad 176 (Ahsan Butt 58, Lal Faraz 4 for 33)
Karachi Whites 354 for 3 (Javed Sami 141 not out, Sohail Jaffer 125)
Match drawn
Karachi Whites 2 pts, Islamabad 0 pts

at Bahawalpur Stadium, Bahawalpur
Lahore 152 and 173 (Inamullah 67 not out, Murtaza Hussain 4 for 57)
Bahawalpur 117 (Mohammad Asif 5 for 29, Mohammad Hussain 4 for 50) and 169 (Mohammad Asif 7 for 49)
Lahore won by 39 runs
Lahore 12 pts, Bahawalpur 0 pts

at Pindi Cricket Stadium
Rawalpindi 'B' 184 (Mohammad Naved 86, Shahid Iqbal 4 for 60) and 42 for 2
Hyderabad 118 (Sabih Azhar 5 for 30)
Match drawn
Rawalpindi 'B' 2 pts, Hyderabad 0 pts

at KRL Ground, Rawalpindi
Peshawar 106 (Mohammad Riaz 7 for 27)
Rawalpindi 'A' 299 for 7 (Masroor Hussain 125 not out)
Match drawn
Rawalpindi 'A' 2 pts, Peshawar 0 pts

Karachi Blues moved inexorably towards the semi-finals with another comfortable victory while three other matches were abandoned because of rain. Lahore were victorious in Bahawalpur, the match ending in three days.

2, 3, 4 and 5 December 1995
at LCCA Ground, Lahore
Lahore 372 (Mujahid Jamshed 134, Shahid Nawaz 116, Shahid Iqbal 6 for 77)
Hyderabad 144 (Mohammad Asif 5 for 29) and 126 (Maumanullah 50, Ali Kamran 5 for 63)
Lahore won by an innings and 102 runs
Lahore 12 pts, Hyderabad 0 pts

at Army Cricket Ground, Rawalpindi
Rawalpindi 'A' 216 (Naseer Ahmed 100 not out, Murtaza Hussain 5 for 79) and 150 (Mohammad Altaf 5 for 34)
Bahawalpur 76 (Shakeel Ahmed 4 for 7, Raja Afaq 4 for 41) and 94 (Raja Afaq 5 for 42)
Rawalpindi 'A' won by 196 runs
Rawalpindi 'A' 12 pts, Bahawalpur 0 pts

at Arbab Niaz Stadium, Peshawar
Rawalpindi 'B' 230 (Mohammad Naved 76, Iqbal Saleem 50, Ijaz Elahi 4 for 40) and 132
Peshawar 92 (Naeem Akhtar 10 for 28) and 149 (Jahangir Khan 67, Sabih Azhar 5 for 50)
Rawalpindi 'B' won by 122 runs
Rawalpindi 'B' 12 pts, Peshawar 0 pts

at Choudray Rahmat Ali Ground, Islamabad
Karachi Blues 162 (Stephen John 7 for 51)
Islamabad 164 for 4 (Zaheer Abbasi 93 not out)
Match drawn
Islamabad 2 pts, Karachi Blues 0 pts

3, 4, 5 and 6 December 1995
at Defence Stadium, Karachi
Karachi Whites 263 (Tahir Rasheed 85 not out, Azam Khan 53, Mohammad Wasim 4 for 87) and 237 for 7 (Azam Khan 62, Mohammad Javed 60 not out, Mohammad Wasim 5 for 63)
Faisalabad 326 (Mohammad Ramzan 141, Shahid Afridi 5 for 93)
Match drawn
Faisalabad 2 pts, Karachi Whites 0 pts

When Lahore conceded their fourth round match to Karachi Blues they ruled themselves out of the tournament. Both the umpires and the match referee rejected the claim of Aamir Malik and his team that Karachi had changed the ball. Aamir took the unprecedented action of conceding the match, refusing to play on the fourth day. He was banned for the rest of the season, and Lahore, who won their fourth match when they beat Hyderabad, were excluded from the semi-finals.

The outstanding performance in the sixth round of matches was by the medium-pacer Naeem Akhtar who, beginning on his 28th birthday, took all ten Peshawar wickets in 21.3 overs for 28 runs. He also took three wickets in the second innings as Rawalpindi 'B' won by 122 runs.

8, 9, 10 and 11 December 1995
at Bahawalpur Stadium, Bahawalpur
Karachi Whites 101 (Murtaza Hussain 6 for 27) and 162 (Murtaza Hussain 4 for 73)
Bahawalpur 307 (Saifullah 62, Nasir Jam 53)
Bahawalpur won by an innings and 44 runs
Bahawalpur 12 pts, Karachi Whites 0 pts

at LCCA Ground, Lahore
Lahore 267 (Mujahid Jamshed 79, Manzoor Elahi 70, Shahid Nawaz 60, Mohammad Riaz 4 for 50) and 211 (Mujahid Jamshed 79, Shakeel Ahmed 6 for 77)
Rawalpindi 'A' 261 (Abdul Basit 128, Mohammad Asif 6 for 105, Mohammad Hussain 4 for 84) and 26 for 1
Match drawn
Lahore 2 pts, Rawalpindi 'A' 0 pts

at Boharnwali Ground, Faisalabad
Hyderabad 234 (Abdul Waheed Rashid 71 not out, Hamid Iqbal 4 for 83) and 354 for 7 (Ijaz Shah 90, Maumanullah 86, Hanif-ur-Rehman 76)
Faisalabad 487 for 9 dec. (Mohammad Nawaz snr 171, Naseer Shaukat 62 not out, Amjad Ali 57)
Match drawn
Faisalabad 2 pts, Hyderabad 0 pts

at KRL Ground, Rawalpindi
Rawalpindi 'B' *v.* **Islamabad**
Match abandoned
No points

at Gymkhana Club Ground, Peshawar
Karachi Blues 191 (Mahmood Hussain 85 not out, Sajid Shah 7 for 63) and 48 for 2
Peshawar 124 (Nadeem Khan 5 for 36)
Match drawn
Karachi Blues 2 pts, Peshawar 0 pts

Rain washed out the match in Rawalpindi and badly affected the game in Peshawar. Hyderabad gave one of their most spirited performances. Trailing by 253 on the first innings against Faisalabad, they wiped off the arrears for the loss of only two wickets, but they still remained pointless.

14, 15, 16 and 17 December 1995
at National Stadium, Karachi
Rawalpindi 'A' 84 (Imranullah 5 for 32, Aamer Hanif 4 for 15) and 135 (Imranullah 5 for 45)
Karachi Blues 173 (Hamuyan Fida Hussain 4 for 44, Yasir Ashfaq 4 for 63) and 47 for 2
Karachi Blues won by 8 wickets
Karachi Blues 12 pts, Rawalpindi 'A' 0 pts

at Mahmood Stadium, Rahim Yar Khan
Hyderabad 207 (Iqbal Sheikh 84) and 224 (Naeem Tayyab 6 for 82)
Karachi Whites 425 for 5 dec. (Azam Khan 174 not out, Sohail Jaffer 117, Abdul Wahid Rasheed 4 for 182) and 7 for 0
Karachi Whites won by 10 wickets
Karachi Whites 12 pts, Hyderabad 0 pts

at Bahawalpur Stadium, Bahawalpur
Peshawar 106 (Murtaza Hussain 5 for 35) and 242 (Akhtar Sarfraz 134 not out, Mohammad Altaf 5 for 46)
Bahawalpur 224 (Saifullah 66, Shahid Hussain 6 for 77) and 125 for 3
Bahawalpur won by 7 wickets
Bahawalpur 12 pts, Peshawar 0 pts

at LCCA Ground, Lahore
Rawalpindi 'B' 212 (Sabih Azhar 71, Naeem Akhtar 51, Manzoor Elahi 5 for 40) and 221 (Mohammad Hussain 7 for 80)
Lahore 419 (Kamran Khan 152, Aamer Manzoor 127, Mohammad Asif 70, Naeem Akhtar 5 for 111) and 17 for 0
Lahore won by 10 wickets
Lahore 12 pts, Rawalpindi 'B' 0 pts

at Boharnwali Ground, Faisalabad
Islamabad 275 (Zaheer Abbasi 84, Alay Haider 76, Mohammad Wasim 4 for 48) and 309 for 7 dec. (Zaheer Abbasi 62, Mohammad Wasim 4 for 88)
Faisalabad 237 (Mohammad Nawaz jnr 94, Raj Hans 5 for 86) and 118 for 8 (Rizwan Bhatti 4 for 7)
Match drawn
Islamabad 2 pts, Faisalabad 0 pts

Karachi Blues won inside two days, and the Whites, with Azam Khan and Sohail Jaffer sharing a fourth wicket stand of 255, also triumphed to move closer to the semi-finals. Bahawalpur's win strengthened their position considerably, while Aamer Manzoor and Kamran Khan shared a fourth wicket stand of 205 in 185 minutes for Lahore.

20, 21, 22 and 23 December 1995
at KCCA Stadium, Karachi
Peshawar 260 (Akhtar Sarfraz 162, Naeem Tayyab 4 for 83) and 181 (Asmatullah 50, Wasim-ur-Rehman 5 for 41, Naeem Tayyab 4 for 66)
Karachi Whites 225 (Faisal Qureshi 89) and 220 for 4 (Mohammad Javed 60 not out, Kashif Ahmed 59)
Karachi Whites won by 6 wickets
Karachi Whites 12 pts, Peshawar 0 pts

at Mahmood Stadium, Rahim Yar Khan
Hyderabad 117 (Irfan Bhatti 4 for 16) and 100 (Shakeel Ahmed 4 for 37)
Rawalpindi 'A' 406 (Naseer Ahmed 161, Basit Niazi 69, Iqbal Sikander 5 for 86)
Rawalpindi 'A' won by an innings and 189 runs
Rawalpindi 'A' 12 pts, Hyderabad 0 pts

at Makli Cricket Ground, Thatta
Karachi Blues 101 (Azhar Shafiq 6 for 37) and 224 (Ishtaq Ahmed 64 not out, Ameer-ud-din 59, Azhar Shafiq 7 for 93)

Bahawalpur 144 (Aamir Sohail jnr 52, Aamer Hanif 6 for 56) and 151 (Azhar Shafiq 63, Aamer Hanif 6 for 55, Mohammad Hasnain 4 for 62)
Karachi Blues won by 30 runs
Karachi Blues 12 pts, Bahawalpur 0 pts

at LCCA Ground, Lahore
Lahore 513 for 9 dec. (Shahid Nawaz 130, Mujahid Jamshed 125, Aamir Malik 117 not out)
Islamabad 150 (Atif Dar 5 for 85) and 221 for 3 (Shahid Naqi 108, Ahsan Butt 51)
Match drawn
Lahore 2 pts, Islamabad 0 pts

at KRL Ground, Rawalpindi
Rawalpindi 'B' 252 (Arif Butt 111, Nadeem Ashraf 5 for 48, Mohammad Wasim 4 for 92) and 278 (Arif Butt 74, Sabih Azhar 62, Nadeem Ashraf 5 for 81)
Faisalabad 270 (Javed Iqbal 101, Raja Sarfraz 4 for 55) and 99 for 4
Match drawn
Faisalabad 2 pts, Rawalpindi 'B' 0 pts

With his suspension lifted, Aamir Malik returned to captain Lahore and to hit 117 off 116 deliveries.

The league programme completed, the semi-finals were delayed until after the conclusion of the World Cup.

Final League Positions

	P	W	L	D	Pts
Karachi Blues	9	6	1	2	74
Lahore	9	5	2	2	64
Karachi Whites	9	5	1	3	62
Bahawalpur	9	5	4	–	60
Islamabad	9	4	–	5	52
Rawalpindi 'A'	9	3	3	3	40
Peshawar	9	2	6	1	24
Faisalabad	9	1	4	4	18
Rawalpindi 'B'	9	1	4	4	14
Hyderabad	9	–	7	2	0

Semi-Finals

29, 30, 31 March and 1 April 1996
at National Stadium, Karachi
Islamabad 215 (Kamran Siddiqui 54, Athar Laeeq 4 for 44) and 197 (Asif Ali 72, Aamer Hanif 5 for 58)
Karachi Blues 627 for 9 dec. (Asif Mujtaba 139 not out, Manzoor Akhtar 105, Sajid Ali 100, Athar Laeeq 99, Shadab Kabir 88, Mahmood Hamid 59, Shahid Mahboob 4 for 151)
Karachi Blues won by an innings and 215 runs

1, 2, 3 and 4 April 1996
at Makli Cricket Ground, Thatta
Bahawalpur 240 (Pervez Shah 50, Mohammad Javed 5 for 48) and 198 (Lal Faraz 4 for 66)
Karachi Whites 267 (Naeem Tayyab 71, Jahangir Bux 51, Azhir Shafiq 5 for 82) and 172 for 3 (Sohail Jaffer 76 not out)
Karachi Whites won by 7 wickets

Karachi Blues totally outplayed Islamabad at the National Stadium. They dismissed their opponents for 215 and Sajid Ali began the Karachi innings with 100 off 116 balls. Athar Laeeq hit the highest score of his career and shared a ninth wicket stand of 185 with Asif Mujtaba, who had returned to captain the side.

The Whites had a closer game at Thatta where there was some off-field drama. Match referee Taslim Arif fined Bahawalpur for delaying the toss because they were short of players and fined the secretary of Bahawalpur for 'misbehaving' on the opening day. One of the umpires, Feroze Butt, deserted the semi-final on the third day to catch a flight to Bangladesh, yet he signed the match report for all four days. The matter is under investigation.

Quaid-e-Azam Final

6, 7, 8 and 9 April 1996
at National Stadium, Karachi
Karachi Blues 181 (Lal Faraz 5 for 66, Mohammad Javed 4 for 63) and 425 (Asif Mujtaba 114, Zafar Iqbal 79, Mahmood Hamid 54, Mohammad Javed 4 for 125)
Karachi Whites 297 (Faisal Qureshi 85, Iqbal Imam 66, Zafar Iqbal 5 for 94) and 250 (Saeed Azad 76, Athar Laeeq 4 for 59)
Karachi Blues won by 59 runs

Put in to bat, Karachi Blues were bowled out on the opening day, but the Whites failed to build a big enough lead. Faisal Qureshi batted 290 minutes to hold the innings together, and skipper Iqbal Imam chose aggression with 66 off 112 balls. Tahir Rasheed hit 48 off 45 balls, but there was a lack of consistent application. Whites still held the balance when Blues were 144 for 4 in their second innings, but Asif Mujtaba, batsman of the season, dropped anchor for five hours and ten minutes to reach his sixth hundred of the season. Zafar Iqbal, Man of the Match, played a controlled innings of 79 off 150 balls, and he followed this with another good bowling display, which brought him match figures of 8 for 164. Athar Laeeq took four wickets to add to the three he had in the first innings, and the Whites lost their last five wickets for 52 runs.

Pentagular Trophy

12, 13, 14 and 15 April 1996
at Pindi Cricket Ground, Rawalpindi
Allied Bank 144 (Mohammad Nawaz snr 57, Tauseef Ahmed 4 for 22) and 160 (Azhar Mahmood 6 for 45)
United Bank 109 (Aamer Nazir 7 for 54) and 111 (Shahid Mahboob 5 for 51)
Allied Bank won by 84 runs
Allied Bank 12 pts, United Bank 0 pts

at KRL Ground, Rawalpindi
PNSC 417 for 9 dec. (Kamran Khan 114, Sajjad Akbar 100 not out, Sher Ali 75, Aamir Sohail 4 for 64)
Bahawalpur 209 (Azher Shafiq 70) and 204 (Bilal Moin 71, Tahir Mahmood 4 for 45)
PNSC won by an innings and 4 runs
PNSC 12 pts, Bahawalpur 0 pts

In a seeming desire for overkill, the Pakistan Board decided that a Test series, a World Cup, visits by the national side to four countries and two domestic first-class competitions was not enough and the season was to end with the once defunct Pentagular Tournament. Three business houses and two associations were to compete, and, for the first time, there was to be a final.

With an average of 102.33 from five matches, Wasim Haider of Pakistan International Airlines topped the first-class batting. (Ben Radford/Allsport)

17, 18, 19 and 20 April 1996
at KRL Ground, Rawalpindi
Allied Bank 294 (Ijaz Ahmed jnr 127 not out, Murtaza Hussain 5 for 92) and 302 for 6 dec. (Ijaz Ahmed jnr 106, Bilal Rana 68)
PNSC 280 (Zeeshan Siddiqui 91, Shahid Mahboob 4 for 69)
Match drawn
Allied Bank 2 pts, PNSC 0 pts

at Pindi Cricket Ground, Rawalpindi
Karachi 414 (Mahmood Hamid 118, Saeed Azad 99, Mohammad Javed 75, Azhar Shafiq 5 for 97)
Bahawalpur 153 (Mohammad Javed 6 for 62) and 120 (Mohammad Javed 5 for 44)
Karachi won by an innings and 141 runs
Karachi 12 pts, Bahawalpur 0 pts

Ijaz Ahmed jnr, out of favour with the selectors, hit a century in each innings, and Bahawalpur were beaten in three days and looked out of their class in this competition.

22, 23, 24 and 25 April 1996
at Pindi Cricket Ground, Rawalpindi
Karachi 193 (Mahmood Hamid 66 not out) and 335 (Asif Mujtaba 115, Saeed Azad 56, Sajjad Akbar 4 for 75)
PNSC 319 (Azam Khan 100, Lal Faraz 4 for 68) and 213 for 9 (Sohail Jaffer 70, Naeem Tayyab 4 for 58)
PNSC won by 1 wicket
PNSC 12 pts, Karachi 0 pts

at KRL Ground, Rawalpindi
Bahawalpur 190 (Azhar Shafiq 86) and 127 (Mohammad Hussain 5 for 44, Tauseef Ahmed 4 for 33)
United Bank 403 (Aamer Bashir 95, Mohammed Ramzan 67, Mohammad Hussain 63, Wahid Baksh 5 for 101)
United Bank won by an innings and 86 runs
United Bank 12 pts, Bahawalpur 0 pts

Asif Mujtaba hit his seventh century of the season to revive his side, but Karachi were thwarted at the last. Needing 210 to win, PNSC lost their eighth wicket at 206 and their ninth a run later as off-spinner Naeem Tayyab, enjoying an outstanding season, threatened to snatch victory for Karachi. Sajid Shah and Pervez-ul-Hussan kept their heads, and Pervez struck the winning boundary off Lal Faraz.

2, 3, 4 and 5 May 1996
at National Stadium, Karachi
Bahawalpur 103 (Bilal Khilji 50, Aqib Javed 5 for 13) and 193 (Bilal Khilji 72, Aqib Javed 4 for 59)
Allied Bank 476 for 2 dec. (Aamer Hanif 225, Mohammad Nawaz snr 200)
Allied Bank won by an innings and 180 runs
Allied Bank 12 pts, Bahawalpur 0 pts

at United Sports Complex, Karachi
United Bank 237 (Saleem Elahi 78, Athar Laeeq 5 for 61) and 255 (Basit Ali 55)
Karachi 209 (Moin Khan 65, Hasnain Kazim 4 for 37, Shahzed Butt 4 for 41) and 151 (Saeed Azad 52, Tauseef Ahmed 4 for 23)
United Bank won by 132 runs
United Bank 12 pts, Karachi 0 pts

With the first three rounds having been played in Rawalpindi, the teams moved to Karachi for the last two rounds and the final. The move certainly suited Allied Bank who massacred Bahawalpur in three days. Mohammad Nawaz snr and Aamer Hanif, who hit the highest score of his career, scored 380 in 324 minutes for Allied Bank's first wicket. Allied's 476 runs were scored in less than 100 overs while Aqib Javed, dropped from the Pakistan side for the tour of England, disposed of Bahawalpur in quick time.

7, 8, 9 and 10 May 1996
at United Bank Sports Complex, Karachi
Karachi 295 (Asif Mujtaba 107, Aqib Javed 4 for 57) and 172 for 3 (Saeed Azad 103 not out)
Allied Bank 110 (Athar Laeeq 5 for 36) and 355 (Aamir Sohail 104, Alay Haider 90, Mohammad Nawaz snr 51, Lal Faraz 5 for 105)
Karachi won by 7 wickets
Karachi 12 pts, Allied Bank 0 pts

at National Stadium, Karachi
PNSC 144 (Kamran Haider 69 not out) and 164 (Tauseef Ahmed 5 for 56)
United Bank 208 (Basit Ali 64, Aamir Bashir 53, Murtaza Hussain 4 for 46) and 101 for 3 (Javed Sami 55 not out)
United Bank won by 7 wickets
United Bank 12 pts, PNSC 0 pts

Asif Mujtaba hit his eighth century of the season and led his side to victory over Allied Bank, but he could not take Karachi into the final. Allied Bank were already assured of a place, and United Bank's victory over PNSC confirmed them as the other finalists. Veteran off-spinner Tauseef Ahmed again bowled admirably with match figures of 7 for 70.

Pentagular Trophy – Final League Positions

	P	W	L	D	Pts
United Bank	4	3	1	–	36
Allied Bank	4	2	1	1	26
Karachi	4	2	2	–	24
Pakistan National Shipping Corporation	4	2	1	1	24
Bahawalpur	4	–	4	–	0

Final

13, 14, 15 and 16 May 1996
at National Stadium, Karachi
Allied Bank 233 (Ijaz Ahmed jnr 52, Tauseef Ahmed 5 for 47) and 227 (Manzoor Akhtar 104)
United Bank 353 (Basit Ali 155, Inzamam-ul-Haq 56, Azhar Mahmood 55, Aamir Sohail 4 for 49) and 110 for 5
United Bank won by 5 wickets

Basit Ali at last found form to hit a dashing 155 in the Pentagular final which United Bank won with time to spare. Their victory brought to an end a season which had begun in August. 'For this relief much thanks.'

Ata-ur-Rehman – a good season and a place in the side to tour England as a pace bowler.
(Mark Thompson/Allsport)

First-Class Averages

Batting

	M	Inns	NO	Runs	HS	Av	100s	50s
Wasim Haider	5	4	1	307	184	102.33	1	2
Asif Mujtaba	16	22	2	1367	170	68.35	8	1
Rizwan-uz-Zaman	6	8	–	497	155	62.12	2	2
Mahmood Hamid	20	28	7	1151	162	54.80	3	6
Sajid Ali	14	18	1	897	139	52.76	3	3
Munir-ul-Haq	5	6	–	309	77	51.50		3
Saeed Azad	16	26	2	1189	117	49.54	3	9
Mansoor Rana	8	12	1	542	188	49.27	2	2
A.W. Rasheed	7	13	5	389	80	48.62		4
Naseer Ahmed	9	15	2	612	161	47.07	2	2
Aamer Hanif	11	16	1	699	225	46.60	3	
Mohammad Nawaz snr	16	27	1	1205	200	46.34	3	7
Mujahid Jamshed	7	11	–	508	134	46.18	2	2
Ameer Akbar	7	9	2	315	128*	45.00	1	2
Shahid Anwar	8	11	–	490	195	44.54	1	2
Sohail Jaffer	23	35	2	1465	125	44.39	4	9
Basit Ali	6	9	–	396	155	44.00	1	3
Azam Khan	20	31	2	1242	215*	42.82	5	4
Shoaib Mohammad	10	16	3	551	102*	42.38	1	4
Sajjad Akbar	10	15	3	502	100*	41.83	1	3
Zahoor Elahi	10	16	–	668	178	41.75	3	1
Mohammad Ramzan	16	23	2	867	141	41.28	3	4
Inzamam-ul-Haq	5	8	–	325	95	40.62		3
Akhtar Sarfraz	5	9	1	311	162	38.87	2	
Manzoor Akhtar	19	27	4	891	145	38.73	4	1
Masroor Hussain	6	11	2	346	125*	38.44	1	1
Shakeel Ahmed	13	25	2	875	101	38.04	1	7
Zaheer Abbasi	8	12	1	417	93*	37.90		3
Javed Sami	16	25	4	794	141*	37.80	1	6
Aamir Malik	11	14	2	436	117*	36.33	1	1
Shahid Nawaz	14	23	1	791	130	35.95	3	3
Aamir Sohail	6	10	–	346	104	34.60	1	1
Moin Khan	9	14	1	444	118*	34.15	1	3
Nadeem Younis	14	23	–	774	135	33.65	3	1
Moin-ul-Atiq	14	25	3	726	120	33.00	1	4
Mazhar Qayyum	17	27	3	781	129	32.54	2	2
Ahsan Butt	11	18	2	516	136	32.25	1	3
Raj Hans	15	22	3	612	110*	32.21	2	2
Ijaz Ahmed jnr	14	22	2	644	127*	32.20	2	2
Sher Ali	13	22	1	673	113*	32.04	1	4
Majid Saeed	12	22	1	659	90	31.38		6
Faisal Qureshi	9	16	2	438	105	31.28	1	2
Atif Rauf	7	10	–	311	163	31.10	1	1
Mansoor Akhtar	12	17	1	495	202	30.93	1	
Arif Butt	7	14	–	428	111	30.57	1	1
Shahid Javed	11	19	–	575	104	30.26	1	3
Intikhab Alam jnr	7	13	2	329	127	29.90	1	1
Mohammad Naveed	6	12	1	324	86	29.45		2
Kamran Khan	13	21	1	586	152	29.30	2	
Mohammad Javed	17	26	5	615	75	29.28		5
Iqbal Imam	16	22	–	622	100	28.27	1	3
Aalay Haider	22	33	–	922	105	27.93	1	5
Qayyum-ul-Hassan	14	24	2	612	150*	27.81	2	1
Kashif Ahmed	12	21	3	498	111*	27.66	1	1
Mohammad Nadeem	11	18	–	496	105	27.55	1	2
Tahir Shah	9	11	–	303	77	27.54		2
Jahangir Khan	9	16	–	433	87	27.06		2
Azhar Mahmood	11	18	4	369	63*	26.35		2
Bilal Rana	15	23	2	553	116	26.33	1	3
Javed Hayat	12	18	1	445	79	26.17		4
Pervez Shah	7	13	–	332	87	25.53		2
Athar Laeeq	15	19	2	427	99	25.11		2
Tahir Rasheed	15	23	2	516	85*	24.57		2
Mohammad Hussain	20	29	4	572	63	22.88		4
Wasim Arif	10	14	–	319	53	22.78		2
Saifullah	12	20	1	432	77	22.73		3
Sabih Azhar	16	28	2	589	91*	22.65		4
Manzoor Elahi	16	25	1	531	72	22.12		3
Aamer Bashir	19	28	1	586	95	21.70		4
Azhar Shafiq	14	26	–	560	86	21.53		4
Mohammad Nawaz jnr	13	26	–	543	94	20.88		4
Tassawar Hussain	8	16	1	307	87	20.46		2
Shadab Kabir	12	19	1	362	88	20.11		2
Aamer Sohail	13	24	1	441	52	19.17		1
Wajahatullah	10	18	1	312	50*	18.35		1
Sajjad Ali	11	19	1	325	100	18.05	1	
Mohammad Asif	16	23	4	341	70	17.94		1

(Qualification: 300 runs, average 10.00)

Bowling

	Overs	Mds	Runs	Wks	Av	Best	10/m	5/inn
Mohammad Riaz	92.1	23	181	18	10.05	7/27		1
Mohammad Altaf	246.3	77	408	35	11.65	5/34		3
Bilal Rana	464.4	164	929	63	14.74	6/51	2	4
Shakeel Ahmed	251.4	58	597	39	15.30	6/77		2
Tauseef Ahmed	286	69	594	38	15.63	5/47		2
Aamer Hanif	217.3	51	617	36	17.13	6/55	1	3
Hasnain Kazim	116.4	25	326	19	17.15	4/37		
Masood Anwar	165.4	54	365	21	17.38	5/24		2
Naeem Akhtar	202.3	42	596	34	17.52	10/28	1	3
Sabih Azhar	139	33	352	20	17.60	5/30		2
Aqib Javed	189.1	34	572	32	17.87	5/13		2
Murtaza Hussain	851	277	1882	105	17.92	9/54	2	7
Humayun Fida Hussain	232.2	48	646	35	18.45	5/64		2
Raja Afaq	198.2	36	464	25	18.56	5/40		3
Mohammad Hussain	671.4	206	1500	78	19.23	7/80	1	4
Mohammad Asif	659.5	165	1392	72	19.33	7/49	1	5
Shahid Nazir	137.5	30	388	20	19.40	6/64		2
Manzoor Elahi	339.5	68	1001	51	19.62	6/32		5
Shahid Hussain	332.5	88	753	38	19.81	6/77		3
Imranullah	123.3	23	420	21	20.00	5/32	1	2
Naeem Tayyab	522.3	102	1401	69	20.30	8/112	2	5
Wasim-ur-Rehman	290	80	675	33	20.45	5/41		1
Raj Hans	297.1	60	782	37	21.13	6/90	1	3
Saqlain Mushtaq	123.1	32	342	16	21.37	4/67		
Ali Hussain Rizvi	186.3	49	451	21	21.47	6/77		1
Ata-ur-Rehman	155	32	433	20	21.65	8/56	1	1
Athar Laeeq	413.3	84	1170	54	21.66	5/27		2
Mohammad Javed	416	69	1338	61	21.93	6/62	1	5
Shahid Mahboob	402.4	79	1232	56	22.00	7/101		4
Azhar Mahmood	307	78	839	38	22.07	6/40		2
Shahzad Butt	211	27	752	34	22.11	5/127		1
Aamer Wasim	464.3	92	1175	53	22.16	7/169	1	5
Ali Gohar	279.4	41	905	40	22.62	6/28	1	4
Nadeem Khan	376.5	96	953	42	22.69	6/42		3
Mohammad Zahid (Bahawalpur)	386	126	778	34	22.88	6/49	1	2
Mohammad Zahid (Pakistan 'A')	143.2	20	508	22	23.09	5/44		2
Sajid Shah	309	42	1104	47	23.48	7/63		3
Azhar Shafiq	244.1	41	854	36	23.72	7/93	1	4
Zafar Iqbal	169	19	654	27	24.22	5/49		2
Wasim Hussain	245.3	45	784	32	24.50	5/63		1
Lal Faraz	361	59	1159	46	25.19	5/66		2
Javed Hayat	192.5	32	479	19	25.21	6/41		2
Umar Rasheed	211	60	487	19	25.63	3/19		
Shahid Iqbal	209.1	46	668	26	25.69	6/77		1
Aamer Sohail	154	37	437	17	25.70	4/64		
Asrhad Khan	483.4	124	1131	44	25.70	6/54	1	1
Sajjad Akbar	291	64	740	28	26.42	7/103		1
Aamer Nazir	190.3	34	661	25	26.44	7/54		1
Tauqeer Hussain	182.4	21	610	22	27.72	6/87		2
Mohammad Nawaz jnr	159.2	19	447	16	27.93	4/37		
Aamir Sohail	166.1	39	421	15	28.06	4/49		
Shoaib Akhtar	106	8	471	16	29.43	5/97		1
Stephen John	156	29	514	17	30.23	7/51		1
Kabir Khan	207.3	29	670	21	31.90	4/84		
Mohammad Ali	372.4	67	1265	39	32.43	6/63	1	3
Salman Fazal	377.3	108	911	28	32.53	6/110		2
Tariq Hussain	226.3	55	587	18	32.61	4/27		
Manzoor Akhtar	223.2	31	738	22	33.54	6/72	1	2
Sajjad Ali	292	35	1143	32	35.71	5/47		1
Fahad Khan	172.3	20	650	18	36.11	4/14		
Mohsin Kamal	219.4	31	835	22	37.95	5/46		1
Naved Nazir	350.5	93	791	20	39.55	3/41		

(Qualification: 15 wickets)

Leading Fielders

56 – Tahir Rasheed (ct 48 / st 8); 46 – Rafiq Ali (ct 44 / st 2); 37 – Wasim Yousufi;
35 – Mohammad Nadeem (ct 28 / st 7); 30 – Wasim Arif (ct 26 / st 4); 29 – Moin Khan (ct 26 / st 3);
26 – Pervez-ul-Hassan (ct 22 / st 4); 24 – Rashid Latif (ct 21 / st 3); 23 – Saifullah (ct 19 / st 4) and Iqbal Saleem (ct 19 / st 4); 22 Javed Qayyum (ct 19 / st 3); 19 – Asif Mujtaba;
18 – Javed Qadir (ct 17 / st 1), Javed Sami and Aamir Malik (ct 17 / st 1);
17 – Qayyum-ul-Hassan, Mohammad Ramzan, Mohammad Arif and Jahangir Khan jnr (ct 15 / st 2);
16 – Faisal Qureshi and Mohammad Nawaz snr

Sharjah

The tournaments in Sharjah, in which England have made only the briefest of appearances, are among the most lucrative in the world. However, the Champions Trophy at the end of 1995 had more than money to offer. Sri Lanka arrived bubbling with confidence after their Test and one-day triumphs in Pakistan. Pakistan themselves arrived more subdued, while West Indies surprised many by making major changes to their squad.

Rohan Mahanama – Man of the Series as Sri Lanka win the Champions Trophy, their first success in an overseas tournament involving more than two teams.
(Paul Sturgess/Sportsline)

The Champions Trophy
Sharjah Cup

Pakistan had resisted making wholesale changes following their recent humiliations, and Rameez Raja had retained the captaincy. Waqar Younis, palpably unfit at the start of the Test series against Sri Lanka, was recalled after showing signs of regaining form in domestic cricket, as was the leg-spinner Mushtaq Ahmed, who had been out of favour for some time. Wasim Akram, however, declared that he was unavailable and did not elaborate the point.

The news regarding the Pakistan squad was, for the most part, predictable, but the squad chosen by West Indies took most by surprise. It had been apparent that all was not well within the party that had toured England in 1995. There were constant murmurings against the captaincy of Richie Richardson, and factions formed within the side. Ambrose, Kenny and Winston Benjamin, Hooper and Lara were among those whose names were cited as being malcontents, and Winston Benjamin was expelled from the party. The rumours of unrest were confirmed when West Indies named their side for the Champions Trophy. Only nine members of the party that had toured England were chosen.

Walsh and Ambrose were rested while Arthurton, Drakes, Kenny Benjamin, Dhanraj, Hooper and Junior Murray were omitted. Adams was chosen but decided not to risk playing so soon after fracturing a cheekbone in England. While the omission of Murray and Dhanraj could be explained on the basis of form, the absence of Kenny Benjamin and Carl Hooper fuelled speculation that these two were seen as leading dissidents. The attitude of Drakes, too, had been questioned by many when he was drafted into the party as a replacement for Winston Benjamin.

It all made an interesting backdrop to the Champions Trophy, which was sponsored by Singer.

Champions Trophy

Sri Lanka, West Indies and Pakistan triangular tournament

Sri Lanka were favourites to reach the final, and this was endorsed with a dramatic victory over West Indies in the opening match. They began uncertainly, but Mahanama hit his fourth limited-over international hundred off 148 balls, and with Ranatunga striking three sixes and two fours in his 54-ball innings, Sri Lanka reached a higher total than anticipated at the outset. Phil Simmons became the eighth fielder to hold four catches in a one-day international.

Campbell hit 86 off 119 balls, and with Richardson hitting his 42nd fifty in one-day internationals, West Indies seemed to be cruising to victory at 192 for 3. Astonishingly, they lost their way, particularly against the brisk off-spin of Dharmasena and finished six runs adrift. Browne and Anthony made their debuts in this form of cricket.

Pakistan showed a welcome return to form by crushing Sri Lanka in the second match of the tournament. An opening stand of 107 between Aamir Sohail and Salim Elahi provided the ideal platform for Pakistan to reach a commanding score, and Inzamam played just the innings that was needed with 69 off 59 balls. Sri Lanka were never in contention as the Pakistani spinners dominated, and the offerings of Kalpage and Dharmasena came long after the game had been decided. Aamir Sohail returned his best figures in a one-day international.

The Pakistan revival seemed complete as they gained their second victory in two days, this time against West Indies. They began shakily, losing three wickets for 49 runs before Basit Ali and Rameez Raja shared a stand of 141. Moin Khan hit 27 off ten balls, and the innings ended in a ferocious manner as he and Rameez plundered 27 off Bishop's final over, so equalling the one-day international record. Rameez hooked a four to complete his century and then took a single. Moin Khan finished the over with six, four, six, six.

West Indies batted recklessly, and no-one provided the substance needed to reach a target in the region of 250.

Two days later, West Indies claimed their revenge, and problems were beginning to surface in the Pakistan camp. Saeed Anwar had returned to Pakistan reportedly suffering from typhoid fever, and Aamir Sohail was injured. More depressingly, internal bickerings were festering. It seemed that the managers, Mushtaq Mohammad and Majid Khan, were unable to set things right in the dressing room and to motivate players. It was rumoured that Aamir Sohail was threatening to fly home after a dispute with Rameez and Majid. These dissensions showed on the field, where Pakistan batted lamely after Salim Elahi hit 66 off 109 balls.

Williams hit 57 off 63 balls and Lara 52 off 58 balls, and West Indies won with 10.5 overs to spare, in spite of another impressive bowling performance by the off-spinner Saqlain.

The second encounter between West Indies and Sri Lanka was the outstanding match of the tournament. Brian Lara hit his sixth, and highest, century in one-day internationals. It was an astonishing innings which included four sixes and 15 fours, and his 169 came off only 129 balls. He dominated a stand of 96 with Richardson and shared a fifth wicket stand of 89 with Chanderpaul.

In spite of another good innings from Mahanama, Sri Lanka slipped to 103 for 5 and looked well beaten in the face of a massive target of 334. Tillekeratne thought otherwise, and he and Mahanama added 68. He then joined in an 86-run stand with Hathurusinghe. Dharmasena also batted until being run out, and the last over arrived with eight runs needed for victory and one wicket standing. Three runs were scored from Cummins' first two deliveries. The third, Tillekeratne hit to mid-wicket where Williams took the catch.

Ironically, it was in defeat that Sri Lanka revealed their new found strength. To their undoubted experienced batting ability has been added a toughness and a self-belief. They are now formidable opponents.

The sixth match was to be the decider as to who would meet West Indies in the final. Sri Lanka had been boosted by their massive, though inadequate, score in the fifth game. Pakistan now appeared in disarray. Inzamam-ul-Haq had joined the ranks of the unfit so that, in effect, Rameez had with him only two other front-line batsmen, and Aamer Hanif and Moin Khan were promoted to numbers four and five. As it transpired, the match was as one-sided as might have been expected. Pakistan were bowled out for 143 with only Mushtaq Ahmed and Saqlain Mushtaq offering token resistance in a seventh wicket stand of 52. Sri Lanka strolled to victory and into the final with 23.1 overs to spare. To compound Pakistan's worries, it was obvious that Waqar Younis was far from being the force of old.

League Final Positions

	P	W	L	Pts	R/R
West Indies	4	2	2	4	5.71
Sri Lanka	4	2	2	4	5.05
Pakistan	4	2	2	4	4.21

Final

Put in to bat, Sri Lanka batted with consistent aggression on a placid pitch. Mahanama, named Man of the Series, again gave the Sri Lankan innings a sound basis with 66 off 103 balls as he and Jayasuriya shared an opening stand of 111. Jayasuriya's knock included three sixes and five fours and occupied only 82 balls. Aravinda de Silva maintained the momentum with an exciting 50 off 35 balls. He hit two sixes and four fours. There were valuable contributions all down the order, and Sri Lanka, bowled out with one ball of their quota remaining, reached a challenging 273.

West Indies were never in touch with the required run rate. Lara was out of form, and spent 25 balls making eight before giving Upashantha a return catch. The batting cracked under the pressure imposed by accurate bowling supported by crisp fielding. One of the features of Sri Lanka's cricket, evident both in Pakistan and in Sharjah, was the standard to which their fielding had been raised. They are an exhilarating side, and this famous and thoroughly deserved triumph was achieved without the aid of their main strike bowler, Vaas. The Champions Cup was Sri Lanka's first success in an overseas tournament involving more than two teams.

Like Pakistan, West Indies revealed that they had problems. Without Walsh and Ambrose, their attack was threadbare, and Bishop, like Waqar Younis, was a pale carbon copy of a once-great bowler. Lara played one magnificent innings but he appeared jaded, and the batting as a whole had an air of uncertainty and a lack of self-belief which was also evident in the field. The debate on leadership remained unresolved.

Champions Trophy – Match One – Sri Lanka v. West Indies

11 October 1995 at Sharjah C.A. Stadium

Sri Lanka

R.S. Mahanama	c Simmons, b Bishop	101
S.T. Jayasuriya	c Simmons, b Bishop	1
A.P. Gurusinha	c Harper, b Simmons	18
P.A. de Silva	c Simmons, b Chanderpaul	9
A. Ranatunga (Capt)	c Browne, b Gibson	58
*R.S. Kaluwitharana	run out	11
H.P. Tillekeratne	c Simmons, b Bishop	7
R.S. Kalpage	not out	1
H.D.P.K. Dharmasena	not out	1
M. Muralitharan		
G.P. Wickremasinghe		
	lb 7, w 20	27
	50 overs (for 7 wickets)	234

	O	M	R	W
Bishop	10	1	42	3
Gibson	10	1	40	1
Anthony	8	–	49	–
Simmons	8	1	29	1
Harper	10	–	49	–
Chanderpaul	4	–	18	1

Fall of Wickets
1–8, 2–59, 3–84, 4–210, 5–222, 6–228, 7–233

West Indies

P.V. Simmons	c de Silva, b Wickremasinghe	5
S.L. Campbell	c Dharmasena, b Muralitharan	86
B.C. Lara	run out	19
R.C. Richardson (Capt)	st Kaluwitharana, b Jayasuriya	67
R.I.C. Holder	not out	26
R.A. Harper	c and b Jayasuriya	1
S. Chanderpaul	c de Silva, b Dharmasena	11
O.D. Gibson	lbw, b Dharmasena	0
H.A.G. Anthony	c Muralitharan, b de Silva	2
*C.O. Browne	st Kaluwitharana, b Dharmasena	2
I.R. Bishop	not out	1
	lb 6, w 1, nb 1	8
	50 overs (for 9 wickets)	228

	O	M	R	W
Wickremasinghe	7	–	27	1
de Silva	10	–	38	1
Dharmasena	9	–	49	3
Muralitharan	10	1	35	1
Jayasuriya	10	–	48	2
Kalpage	4	–	25	–

Fall of Wickets
1–13, 2–69, 3–165, 4–192, 5–194, 6–211, 7–211, 8–218, 9–226

Umpires: D.B. Hair & R.S. Dunne *Man of the Match:* R.S. Mahanama

Sri Lanka won by 6 runs

Champions Trophy – Match Two – Pakistan v. Sri Lanka

12 October 1995 at Sharjah C.A. Stadium

Pakistan

Aamir Sohail	c Kaluwitharana, b Muralitharan	85
Salim Elahi	c Wickremasinghe, b de Silva	50
Rameez Raja (Capt)	c Hathurusinghe, b Muralitharan	12
Inzamam-ul-Haq	c Jayasuriya, b Dharmasena	69
Saeed Anwar	st Kaluwitharana, b Jayasuriya	14
*Moin Khan	c Ranatunga, b Wickremasinghe	5
Zafar Iqbal	c Gurusinha, b Dharmasena	2
Mushtaq Ahmed	not out	9
Waqar Younis	not out	9
Aqib Javed		
Saqlain Mushtaq		
	b 2, lb 1, w 6	9
	50 overs (for 7 wickets)	264

	O	M	R	W
Wickremasinghe	7	1	54	1
Hathurusinghe	10	–	39	–
Dharmasena	10	–	43	2
Muralitharan	10	–	51	2
Jayasuriya	8	–	51	1
de Silva	5	–	23	1

Fall of Wickets
1–**107**, 2–**138**, 3–**162**, 4–**213**, 5–**232**, 6–**244**, 7–**246**

Sri Lanka

U.C. Hathurusinghe	lbw, b Aqib Javed	11
S.T. Jayasuriya	c sub (Basit Ali), b Saqlain	24
A.P. Gurusinha	b Aamir Sohail	19
P.A. de Silva	c and b Saqlain Mushtaq	3
A. Ranatunga (Capt)	c Rameez Raja, b Aamir Sohail	14
H.P. Tillekeratne	c Moin Khan, b Aamir Sohail	15
*R.S. Kaluwitharana	b Aamir Sohail	19
R.S. Kalpage	b Saeed Anwar	22
H.D.P.K. Dharmasena	not out	30
M. Muralitharan	not out	7
G.P. Wickremasinghe		
	lb 10, w 3, nb 5	18
	50 overs (for 8 wickets)	182

	O	M	R	W
Waqar Younis	7	–	29	–
Aqib Javed	8	1	31	1
Zafar Iqbal	5	1	12	–
Saqlain Mushtaq	10	1	30	2
Aamir Sohail	8	–	22	4
Mushtaq Ahmed	10	–	39	–
Saeed Anwar	2	1	9	1

Fall of Wickets
1–**33**, 2–**44**, 3–**51**, 4–**67**, 5–**82**, 6–**107**, 7–**114**, 8–**174**

Umpires: R.S. Dunne & N.T. Plews *Man of the Match:* Aamir Sohail

Pakistan won by 82 runs

Champions Trophy – Match Three – Pakistan v. West Indies

13 October 1995 at Sharjah C.A. Stadium

Pakistan

Aamir Sohail	c Browne, b Bishop	10
Salim Elahi	c Harper, b Cummins	9
Rameez Raja (Capt)	not out	104
Saeed Anwar	c Browne, b Anthony	18
Basit Ali	c Harper, b Cummins	64
*Moin Khan	not out	27
Zafar Iqbal		
Waqar Younis		
Mushtaq Ahmed		
Saqlain Mushtaq		
Aqib Javed		
	lb 1, w 8, nb 1	10
	50 overs (for 4 wickets)	242

	O	M	R	W
Bishop	10	–	78	1
Cummins	10	–	31	2
Anthony	10	–	47	1
Simmons	9	–	40	–
Harper	10	–	38	–
Chanderpaul	1	–	7	–

Fall of Wickets
1–**16**, 2–**24**, 3–**49**, 4–**190**

West Indies

P.V. Simmons	lbw, b Waqar Younis	4
S.L. Campbell	lbw, b Aamir Sohail	42
B.C. Lara	c Aqib Javed, b Saqlain	21
R.B. Richardson (Capt)	b Aqib Javed	34
S. Chanderpaul	c Salim Elahi, b Waqar Younis	36
R.I.C. Holder	st Moin Khan, b Saqlain	11
R.A. Harper	not out	43
*C.O. Browne	st Moin Khan, b Saqlain	12
A.C. Cummins	c Moin Khan, b Saqlain	4
H.A.G. Anthony	run out	0
I.R. Bishop	st Moin Khan, b Mushtaq Ahmed	7
	lb 8, w 3, nb 2	13
	49 overs	227

	O	M	R	W
Aqib Javed	9	–	30	1
Waqar Younis	9	–	51	2
Zafar Iqbal	1	–	13	–
Saqlain Mushtaq	10	1	47	4
Aamir Sohail	10	1	40	1
Mushtaq Ahmed	10	1	38	1

Fall of Wickets
1–**5**, 2–**21**, 3–**74**, 4–**124**, 5–**154**, 6–**156**, 7–**189**, 8–**197**, 9–**198**

Umpires: R.S. Dunne & N.T. Plews *Man of the Match:* Rameez Raja

Pakistan won by 15 runs

Champions Trophy – Match Four – Pakistan v. West Indies

15 October 1995 at Sharjah C.A. Stadium

Pakistan

Salim Elahi	run out	**66**
Rameez Raja (Capt)	**b** Simmons	**20**
Inzamam-ul-Haq	**c** sub (Holder), **b** Harper	**34**
Basit Ali	**c** Lara, **b** Bishop	**25**
*Moin Khan	run out	**1**
Zafar Iqbal	run out	**0**
Mushtaq Ahmed	**c** Browne, **b** Gibson	**4**
Waqar Younis	lbw, **b** Gibson	**6**
Aqib Javed	not out	**8**
Saqlain Mushtaq	run out	**0**
Mohammad Akram	not out	**7**
	lb **5**, w **17**, nb **1**	**23**
	50 overs (for 9 wickets)	**194**

	O	M	R	W
Bishop	8	–	29	**1**
Cummins	9	–	31	**–**
Gibson	9	1	47	**2**
Simmons	10	1	31	**1**
Chanderpaul	5	–	25	**–**
Harper	9	1	26	**1**

Fall of Wickets
1–**74**, 2–**139**, 3–**148**, 4–**150**, 5–**150**, 6–**168**, 7–**177**, 8–**180**, 9–**181**

West Indies

S.C. Williams	**c** Zafar Iqbal, **b** Saqlain	**57**
S.L. Campbell	**c** Basit Ali, **b** Mohammad	**20**
B.C. Lara	**c** Basit Ali, **b** Mushtaq Ahmed	**52**
R.B. Richardson (Capt)	**b** Saqlain Mushtaq	**34**
P.V. Simmons	lbw, **b** Mohammad Akram	**1**
S. Chanderpaul	**c** Moin Khan, **b** Aqib Javed	**11**
R.A. Harper	not out	**5**
*C.O. Browne	not out	**2**
A.C. Cummins		
O.D. Gibson		
I.R. Bishop		
	lb **3**, w **9**, nb **1**	**13**
	39.1 overs (for 6 wickets)	**195**

	O	M	R	W
Aqib Javed	8.1	–	41	**–**
Waqar Younis	4	–	30	**–**
Mushtaq Ahmed	10	1	43	**1**
Mohammad Akram	7	–	36	**2**
Saqlain Mushtaq	10	1	42	**2**

Fall of Wickets
1–**44**, 2–**109**, 3–**147**, 4–**151**, 5–**183**, 6–**189**

Umpires: R.S. Dunne & D.B. Hair *Man of the Match:* S.C. Williams

West Indies won by 4 wickets

Champions Trophy – Match Five – West Indies v. Sri Lanka

16 October 1995 at Sharjah C.A. Stadium

West Indies

S.C. Williams	lbw, **b** Wickremasinghe	**2**
S.L. Campbell	**c** de Silva, **b** Wickremasinghe	**10**
B.C. Lara	**b** Dharmasena	**169**
R.B. Richardson (Capt)	**b** Muralitharan	**29**
P.V. Simmons	**b** Hathurusinghe	**30**
S. Chanderpaul	not out	**62**
O.D. Gibson	**c** Mahanama, **b** Hathurusinghe	**10**
R.A. Harper	run out	**1**
A.C. Cummins	not out	**0**
*C.O. Browne		
I.R. Bishop		
	lb **3**, w **12**, nb **5**	**20**
	50 overs (for 7 wickets)	**333**

	O	M	R	W
Wickremasinghe	10	–	58	**2**
Hathurusinghe	10	–	67	**2**
de Silva	6	–	51	**–**
Dharmasena	10	–	72	**1**
Muralitharan	10	–	52	**1**
Jayasuriya	4	–	30	**–**

Fall of Wickets
1–**6**, 2–**37**, 3–**133**, 4–**193**, 5–**282**, 6–**315**, 7–**319**

Sri Lanka

R.S. Mahanama	**c** and **b** Simmons	**76**
S.T. Jayasuriya	**c** Richardson, **b** Gibson	**5**
P.A. de Silva	lbw, **b** Bishop	**20**
*R.S. Kaluwitharana	**c** Simmons, **b** Cummins	**31**
A.P. Gurusinha	**b** Harper	**1**
A. Ranatunga (Capt)	run out	**0**
H.P. Tillekeratne	**c** Williams, **b** Cummins	**100**
U.C. Hathurusinghe	**c** Chanderpaul, **b** Gibson	**45**
H.D.P.K. Dharmasena	run out	**24**
M. Muralitharan	run out	**2**
G.P. Wickremasinghe	not out	**5**
	lb **4**, w **15**, nb **1**	**20**
	49.3 overs	**329**

	O	M	R	W
Cummins	9.3	–	61	**2**
Gibson	8	–	74	**2**
Bishop	8	–	63	**1**
Harper	10	–	38	**1**
Simmons	10	–	53	**1**
Chanderpaul	4	–	36	**–**

Fall of Wickets
1–**21**, 2–**46**, 3–**101**, 4–**103**, 5–**103**, 6–**171**, 7–**257**, 8–**306**, 9–**316**

Umpires: R.S. Dunne & N.T. Plews *Man of the Match:* B.C. Lara

West Indies won by 4 runs

Champions Trophy – Match Six – Pakistan v. Sri Lanka

17 October 1995 at Sharjah C.A. Stadium

Pakistan

Salim Elahi	c Kaluwitharana, b Hathurusinghe	0
Rameez Raja (Capt)	c Kaluwitharana, b Wickremasinghe	9
Basit Ali	c Mahanama, b Ranatunga	21
Aamer Hanif	run out	17
*Moin Khan	c and b Dharmasena	16
Zafar Iqbal	c Mahanama, b Ranatunga	2
Mushtaq Ahmed	b Jayasuriya	26
Saqlain Mushtaq	c Wickremasinghe, b Dharmasena	30
Waqar Younis	lbw, b Dharmasena	3
Aqib Javed	not out	3
Mohammad Akram	c Ranatunga, b Jayasuriya	1
	lb 1, w 11, nb 3	15
	48.3 overs	143

	O	M	R	W
Wickremasinghe	7	1	19	1
Hathurusinghe	10	1	33	1
Muralitharan	9	–	43	–
Ranatunga	10	1	21	2
Dharmasena	10	3	16	3
Jayasuriya	2.3	–	10	2

Fall of Wickets
1–11, 2–25, 3–52, 4–63, 5–68, 6–82, 7–134, 8–137, 9–140

Sri Lanka

R.S. Mahanama	not out	45
S.T. Jayasuriya	c Moin Khan, b Mohammad Akram	25
A.P. Gurusinha	c Salim Elahi, b Mushtaq Ahmed	31
P.A. de Silva	not out	35
A. Ranatunga (Capt)		
H.P. Tillekeratne		
*R.S. Kaluwitharana		
U.C. Hathurusinghe		
H.D.P.K. Dharmasena		
M. Muralitharan		
G.P. Wickremasinghe		
	lb 7, w 2, nb 4	13
	26.5 overs (for 2 wickets)	149

	O	M	R	W
Aqib Javed	5	–	25	–
Mohammad Akram	5	–	24	1
Saqlain Mushtaq	4.5	–	27	–
Mushtaq Ahmed	8	–	35	1
Zafar Iqbal	1	–	8	–
Waqar Younis	3	–	23	–

Fall of Wickets
1–35, 2–94

Umpires: N.T. Plews & R.S. Dunne *Man of the Match:* A. Ranatunga

Sri Lanka won by 8 wickets

Champions Trophy Final – Sri Lanka v. West Indies

20 October 1995 at Sharjah C.A. Stadium

Sri Lanka

R.S. Mahanama	b Cummins	66
S.T. Jayasuriya	c Gibson, b Simmons	57
P.A. de Silva	c Chanderpaul, b Anthony	50
A. Ranatunga (Capt)	c Cummins, b Anthony	17
H.P. Tillekeratne	c Browne, b Gibson	32
*R.S. Kaluwitharana	b Cummins	15
A.P. Gurusinha	c Browne, b Gibson	12
U.C. Hathurusinghe	b Gibson	0
H.D.P.K. Dharmasena	c Campbell, b Gibson	4
E. Upashantha	run out	3
M. Muralitharan	not out	0
	lb 8, w 7, nb 2	17
	49.5 overs	273

	O	M	R	W
Cummins	9	1	50	2
Gibson	5.5	–	35	4
Anthony	8	–	47	2
Simmons	7	1	44	1
Harper	10	1	36	–
Chanderpaul	10	–	53	–

Fall of Wickets
1–111, 2–157, 3–196, 4–215, 5–234, 6–259, 7–259, 8–269, 9–273

West Indies

S.C. Williams	c Muralitharan, b Upashantha	5
S.L. Campbell	b Muralitharan	38
B.C. Lara	c and b Upashantha	8
R.B. Richardson (Capt)	run out	10
P.V. Simmons	run out	7
S. Chanderpaul	c Muralitharan, b Dharmasena	27
R.A. Harper	c sub (Kalpage), b Muralitharan	31
*C.O. Browne	c and b Jayasuriya	18
A.C. Cummins	c Ranatunga, b Muralitharan	0
O.D. Gibson	not out	33
H.G. Anthony	c de Silva, b Dharmasena	21
	lb 15, w 7, nb 3	25
	47.5 overs	223

	O	M	R	W
Upashantha	8	1	24	2
Hathurusinghe	8	–	30	–
Muralitharan	10	–	31	3
Ranatunga	7	–	25	–
Dharmasena	8.3	1	58	2
Jayasuriya	6	–	40	1

Fall of Wickets
1–28, 2–41, 3–59, 4–74, 5–88, 6–141, 7–156, 8–157, 9–177

Umpires: R.S. Dunne & D.B. Hair *Man of the Match:* P.A. de Silva

Sri Lanka won by 50 runs

Sharjah Cup

Pakistan, India and South Africa triangular tournament

The Sharjah Cup closely followed the World Cup and the Singer Cup. Sponsored by Pepsi Cola, it was condensed into a week in mid-April. Pakistan and India came straight from the tournament in Singapore and were joined in the United Arab Emirate by South Africa. For both India and Pakistan, the Sharjah Cup was important in that both countries were attempting to finalise their parties for the coming England tour. Pakistan were still without Wasim Akram and were led by Aamir Sohail, while India gave opportunities to Rathore and Dravid. Prabhakar had retired from international cricket following his omission from the Singer Cup. South Africa rested Donald, but their side was basically the same as that which had operated so successfully in the World Cup, and they were strengthened by the return of Richardson after injury. South Africa were to dominate the Sharjah Cup.

The start of the tournament was put back for twenty-four hours because of the death of Sheikh Mohammed bin Khalid al-Qassimi, chairman of the Sharjah Department of Culture and Information. The revised itinerary brought Pakistan and India together in the first match. Aamir Sohail hit his fifth century in one-day internationals to put his side in a commanding position. He and Saeed Anwar scored 77 in the first 13.4 overs, and runs came easily thereafter with Aamir reaching his hundred in the 44th over. His innings included eight fours. With Tendulkar caught at cover when slashing at Aqib Javed, India were soon in trouble, but Jadeja and Sidhu added 68. Four wickets went down for 19 runs before Manjrekar and Mongia added 116 in splendid style, but the required rate rose to ten an over, and this proved beyond the later batsmen.

Pakistan were brought down to earth the following day when they were overwhelmed by South Africa. A maiden century in limited-over international cricket by Daryll Cullinan, 110 off 109 balls, put South Africa in an impregnable position after Kirsten and Hudson began the match with a stand of 115. Cullinan hit three sixes and six fours and played fiercely towards the end of his innings. Cronje and Rhodes gave excellent support. Inside 16 overs, Pakistan had subsided to 62 for 6. Salim Malik, 64 off 115 balls, and Aqib Javed, 45 off 70 balls, put on 81, but the result of the match had long since been decided.

South Africa's victory over India was almost as convincing as their trouncing of Pakistan. They lost Hudson for nought and were 56 for 3 after ten overs, but Kirsten and Cronje added 154 from 155 balls. Kirsten stayed until the 43rd over, but the real blast was provided by Cronje who hit 90 off 82 balls. After 14 overs, India were 62 for 4, and, although Manjrekar and Azharuddin put on 81, victory never seemed possible. This was the 100th one-day international to be played at the Sharjah Stadium and, to mark the occasion, the captains Cronje and Azharuddin were presented with a gold coin each.

Vitally, India beat Pakistan in the second meeting of the two sides. The success was founded on a second wicket stand of 231, a record for India in one-day cricket, between Tendulkar and Sidhu. The Indian total of 305 for 5 was also a record. Pakistan batted consistently in reply, but lost too many wickets in maintaining the required run rate.

South Africa made sure of a place in the final when they trounced Pakistan for a second time. With Matthews, de Villiers and Kallis taking three wickets apiece, Pakistan were bowled out in 45 overs for a modest 188. Kirsten and Hudson scored 73 in 13 overs, and Hudson finished on 94 not out off 85 balls. He hit two sixes and 11 fours as South Africa won with nearly 17 overs to spare.

South Africa maintained a one hundred per cent record when they beat India by five wickets. On his first appearance in the competition, Paul Adams took three wickets and claimed the individual award. India never looked like setting a big target when they lost five wickets for 100 runs in 28.3 overs, but Jadeja hit 71 off 69 balls, including 17 off the last over, bowled by Crookes, to lift them to respectability. This final burst also meant that their run rate was sufficient to put them into the final ahead of Pakistan.

A maiden century in limited-over internationals for Daryll Cullinan of South Africa, 110 off 109 balls, with three sixes and six fours, as the Sharjah Cup winners trounce Pakistan. (David Munden/Sportsline)

Sharjah Cup – Match One – Pakistan v. India

12 April 1996 at Sharjah C.A. Stadium

Pakistan

Aamir Sohail (Capt)	c and b Kumble	105
Saeed Anwar	b Vaidya	44
Rameez Raja	run out	17
Salim Malik	run out	22
Inzamam-ul-haq	c Mongia, b Tendulkar	9
Ijaz Ahmed	not out	43
*Rashid Latif	not out	21
Mushtaq Ahmed		
Waqar Younis		
Saqlain Mushtaq		
Aqib Javed		
	lb 6, w 4	10
	50 overs (for 5 wickets)	271

	O	M	R	W
Srinath	10	1	46	–
Vaidya	10	–	55	1
Kumble	10	–	50	1
Venkatapathy Raju	8	–	57	–
Tendulkar	10	–	46	1
Azharuddin	2	–	11	–

Fall of Wickets
1–**77**, 2–**115**, 3–**156**, 4–**167**, 5–**235**

India

A.D. Jadeja	c Saeed Anwar, b Saqlain	43
S.R. Tendulkar	c Saeed Anwar, b Aqib Javed	1
N.S. Sidhu	c and b Saqlain Mushtaq	31
M. Azharuddin (Capt)	c Aqib Javed, b Mushtaq Ahmed	7
R.S. Dravid	c Rashid, b Mushtaq Ahmed	3
S.V. Manjrekar	c Saeed Anwar, b Waqar	59
*N.R. Mongia	b Mushtaq Ahmed	69
J. Srinath	run out	0
A.R. Kumble	c sub, b Mushtaq Ahmed	3
P.S. Vaidya	b Waqar Younis	3
Venkatapathy Raju	not out	0
	lb 4, nb 10	14
	47.2 overs	233

	O	M	R	W
Waqar Younis	9	1	44	2
Aqib Javed	7	–	33	1
Saqlain Mushtaq	9	–	42	2
Mushtaq Ahmed	9.2	–	47	4
Aamir Sohail	6	–	28	–
Salim Malik	7	–	35	–

Fall of Wickets
1–**8**, 2–**76**, 3–**89**, 4–**91**, 5–**95**, 6–**211**, 7–**212**, 8–**219**, 9–**229**

Umpires: M.J. Kitchen & D.B. Cowie *Man of the Match:* Aamir Sohail

Pakistan won by 38 runs

Sharjah Cup – Match Two – Pakistan v. South Africa

13 April 1996 at Sharjah C.A. Stadium

South Africa

A.C. Hudson	c Aqib Javed, b Waqar Younis	57
G. Kirsten	b Aqib Javed	64
D.J. Cullinan	not out	110
W.J. Cronje (Capt)	c Inzamam-ul-Haq, b Mushtaq	26
J.N. Rhodes	not out	47
B.M. McMillan		
*D.J. Richardson		
C.R. Matthews		
S.M. Pollock		
P.L. Symcox		
P.S. de Villiers		
	lb 7, w 3	10
	50 overs (for 3 wickets)	314

	O	M	R	W
Waqar Younis	10	1	56	1
Aqib Javed	9	–	59	1
Mushtaq Ahmed	10	–	63	1
Saqlain Mushtaq	9	1	55	–
Aamir Sohail	10	–	56	–
Salim Malik	2	–	18	–

Fall of Wickets
1–**115**, 2–**157**, 3–**222**

Pakistan

Aamir Sohail (Capt)	c Hudson, b de Villiers	11
Saeed Anwar	c Cronje, b de Villiers	33
Rameez Raja	c McMillan, b Pollock	1
Salim Malik	not out	64
Inzamam-ul-Haq	run out	1
Ijaz Ahmed	c Richardson, b McMillan	1
*Rashid Latif	c McMillan, b Matthews	2
Saqlain Mushtaq	lbw, b Cronje	7
Aqib Javed	not out	45
Mushtaq Ahmed		
Waqar Younis		
	b 1, lb 1, w 3, nb 1	6
	50 overs (for 7 wickets)	171

	O	M	R	W
Pollock	10	1	44	1
de Villiers	10	–	40	2
McMillan	7	1	20	1
Matthews	8	1	21	1
Symcox	10	1	21	–
Cronje	5	–	23	1

Fall of Wickets
1–**24**, 2–**45**, 3–**49**, 4–**50**, 5–**58**, 6–**62**, 7–**90**

Umpires: B.C. Cooray & D.B. Cowie *Man of the Match:* D.J. Cullinan

South Africa won by 143 runs

Sharjah Cup – Match Three – India v. South Africa

14 April 1996 at Sharjah C.A. Stadium

South Africa

Batsman	Dismissal	Runs
G. Kirsten	**b** Venkatapathy Raju	**106**
A.C. Hudson	**c** Tendulkar, **b** Srinath	**0**
D.J. Cullinan	**c** Dravid, **b** Kumble	**28**
P.L. Symcox	**b** Kumble	**0**
W.J. Cronje (Capt)	run out	**90**
J.N. Rhodes	**c** Dravid, **b** Venkatapathy Raju	**23**
B.M. McMillan	not out	**14**
S.M. Pollock	not out	**15**
*D.J. Richardson		
C.R. Matthews		
P.S. de Villiers		
	lb **7**, w **4**, nb **1**	**12**
	50 overs (for 6 wickets)	**288**

	O	M	R	W
Srinath	9	–	43	**1**
Vaidya	6	–	42	**–**
Kumble	10	–	45	**2**
Venkatapathy Raju	10	–	67	**2**
Tendulkar	7	–	40	**–**
Jadeja	8	–	44	**–**

Fall of Wickets
1–**1**, 2–**56**, 3–**56**, 4–**210**, 5–**249**, 6–**266**

India

Batsman	Dismissal	Runs
A.D. Jadeja	**c** Richardson, **b** Matthews	**42**
S.R. Tendulkar	**c** Kirsten, **b** de Villiers	**2**
P.S. Vaidya	lbw, **b** Pollock	**12**
N.S. Sidhu	**c** Kirsten, **b** Pollock	**1**
S.V. Manjrekar	**c** Cronje, **b** Symcox	**53**
M. Azharuddin (Capt)	**c** Hudson, **b** Symcox	**28**
J. Srinath	**b** de Villiers	**35**
R.S.Dravid	**c** Rhodes, **b** Pollock	**11**
*N.R. Mongia	not out	**9**
A.R. Kumble	not out	**9**
Venkatapathy Raju		
	b **1**, lb **1**, w **3**, nb **1**	**6**
	50 overs (for 8 wickets)	**208**

	O	M	R	W
Pollock	10	–	42	**3**
de Villiers	10	–	54	**2**
McMillan	7	–	18	**–**
Matthews	10	–	26	**1**
Symcox	7	–	43	**2**
Cronje	6	–	23	**–**

Fall of Wickets
1–**20**, 2–**41**, 3–**45**, 4–**62**, 5–**143**, 6–**147**, 7–**187**, 8–**195**

Umpires: M.J. Kitchen & B.C. Cooray *Man of the Match:* W.J. Cronje

South Africa won by 80 runs

Sharjah Cup – Match Four – India v. Pakistan

15 April 1996 at Sharjah C.A. Stadium

India

Batsman	Dismissal	Runs
V.S. Rathore	**c** Inzamam-ul-Haq, **b** Waqar	**2**
S.R. Tendulkar	**c** Aamir Sohail, **b** Waqar	**118**
N.S. Sidhu	run out	**101**
A.D. Jadeja	**c** Rashid Latif, **b** Waqar	**17**
J. Srinath	**c** Aamir, **b** Ata-ur-Rehman	**16**
M. Azharuddin (Capt)	not out	**29**
S.V. Manjrekar	not out	**0**
*N.R. Mongia		
A.R. Kumble		
A.R. Kapoor		
Venkatesh Prasad		
	b **2**, lb **7**, w **12**, nb **1**	**22**
	50 overs (for 5 wickets)	**305**

	O	M	R	W
Waqar Younis	10	2	44	**3**
Aqib Javed	10	–	58	**–**
Ata-ur-Rehman	10	–	85	**1**
Saqlain Mushtaq	10	1	60	**–**
Aamir Sohail	10	–	49	**–**

Fall of Wickets
1–**9**, 2–**240**, 3–**245**, 4–**264**, 5–**281**

Pakistan

Batsman	Dismissal	Runs
Aamir Sohail (Capt)	run out	**78**
Saeed Anwar	**c** Mongia, **b** Venkatesh Prasad	**2**
*Rashid Latif	**c** Azharuddin, **b** Kumble	**50**
Ijaz Ahmed	**b** Srinath	**42**
Salim Malik	**c** Kapoor, **b** Kumble	**42**
Inzamam-ul-Haq	**c** Azharuddin, **b** Venkatesh	**6**
Basit Ali	**c** Rathore, **b** Tendulkar	**32**
Aqib Javed	**c** Rathore, **b** Srinath	**5**
Waqar Younis	not out	**8**
Ata-ur-Rehman	**c** sub (Dravid), **b** Srinath	**4**
Saqlain Mushtaq	lbw, **b** Tendulkar	**0**
	lb **4**, w **4**	**8**
	46.1 overs	**277**

	O	M	R	W
Srinath	10	–	65	**3**
Venkatesh Prasad	9	–	64	**2**
Kumble	9	1	38	**2**
Kapoor	9	–	52	**–**
Tendulkar	7.1	–	40	**2**
Jadeja	2	–	14	**–**

Fall of Wickets
1–**16**, 2–**88**, 3–**172**, 4–**190**, 5–**199**, 6–**248**, 7–**260**, 8–**271**, 9–**277**

Umpires: M.J. Kitchen & D.B. Cowie *Man of the Match:* S.R. Tendulkar

India won by 28 runs

Sharjah Cup – Match Five – Pakistan v. South Africa

16 April 1996 at Sharjah C.A. Stadium

Pakistan

Aamir Sohail (Capt)	c Cronje, b Matthews	46
Saeed Anwar	c Kirsten, b Pollock	10
Rameez Raja	c Matthews, b de Villiers	40
Inzamam-ul-Haq	c Richardson, b Kallis	41
*Rashid Latif	lbw, b de Villiers	7
Salim Malik	c Crookes, b Matthews	10
Basit Ali	c Crookes, b Kallis	8
Aqib Javed	c Richardson, b Matthews	6
Waqar Younis	not out	8
Mushtaq Ahmed	c Richardson, b Kallis	0
Mohammad Akram	lbw, b de Villiers	0
	b 2, lb 4, w 6	12
	45 overs	188

	O	M	R	W
de Villiers	10	1	28	3
Pollock	8	1	34	1
Matthews	8	1	19	3
Cronje	1	–	4	–
Symcox	7	–	38	–
Crookes	5	–	38	–
Kallis	6	1	21	3

Fall of Wickets
1–22, 2–84, 3–145, 4–151, 5–162, 6–169, 7–177, 8–185, 9–185

South Africa

A.C. Hudson	not out	94
G. Kirsten	c Mohammad Akram, b Waqar	32
P.L. Symcox	lbw, b Mohammad Akram	35
J.H. Kallis	not out	24
W.J. Cronje (Capt)		
J.N. Rhodes		
D.N. Crookes		
S.M. Pollock		
*D.J. Richardson		
C.R. Matthews		
P.S. de Villiers		
	w 4	4
	33.1 overs (for 2 wickets)	189

	O	M	R	W
Mohammad Akram	10	–	52	1
Aqib Javed	4	–	27	–
Mushtaq Ahmed	10	1	50	–
Aamir Sohail	1	–	12	–
Waqar Younis	7	–	44	1
Salim Malik	1.1	–	4	–

Fall of Wickets
1–73, 2–132

Umpires: D.B. Cowie & B.C. Cooray *Man of the Match:* C.R. Matthews

South Africa won by 8 wickets

Sharjah Cup – Match Six – India v. South Africa

17 April 1996 at Sharjah C.A. Stadium

India

V.S. Rathore	c Cronje, b Adams	50
S.R. Tendulkar	c Kirsten, b de Villiers	17
N.S. Sidhu	lbw, b de Villiers	1
S.V. Manjrekar	c Kirsten, b Kallis	14
M. Azharuddin (Capt)	st Richardson, b Adams	4
A.D. Jadeja	not out	71
*N.R. Mongia	c Kirsten, b Adams	13
A.R. Kumble	run out	16
J. Srinath	c sub (Matthews), b Pollock	15
Venkatesh Prasad	not out	1
Venkatapathy Raju		
	lb 4, w 7, nb 2	13
	50 overs (for 8 wickets)	215

	O	M	R	W
Pollock	8	–	39	1
de Villiers	10	2	28	2
McMillan	5	–	25	–
Kallis	7	–	34	1
Adams	10	–	30	3
Crookes	10	–	55	–

Fall of Wickets
1–23, 2–26, 3–72, 4–89, 5–100, 6–140, 7–177, 8–199

South Africa

G. Kirsten	c Mongia, b Kumble	39
J.H. Kallis	run out	22
D.J. Cullinan	c Prasad, b Venkatapathy Raju	64
W.J. Cronje (Capt)	b Venkatapathy Raju	1
D.N. Crookes	b Venkatapathy Raju	54
S.M. Pollock	not out	11
J.N. Rhodes	not out	12
B.M. McMillan		
*D.J. Richardson		
P.S. de Villiers		
P.R. Adams		
	b 3, lb 2, w 8	13
	47.1 overs (for 5 wickets)	216

	O	M	R	W
Srinath	10	–	55	–
Venkatesh Prasad	10	–	43	–
Kumble	10	–	37	1
Venkatapathy Raju	10	–	38	3
Jadeja	7	–	37	–
Sidhu	0.1	–	1	–

Fall of Wickets
1–53, 2–85, 3–98, 4–192, 5–193

Umpires: B.C. Cooray & M.J. Kitchen *Man of the Match:* P.R. Adams

South Africa won by 5 wickets

Sharjah Cup Final – South Africa v. India

19 April 1996 at Sharjah C.A. Stadium

South Africa

G. Kirsten	not out	**115**
A.C. Hudson	**c** Azharuddin, **b** Srinath	**0**
D.J. Cullinan	**b** Venkatesh Prasad	**2**
P.L. Symcox	**c** Jadeja, **b** Venkatapathy Raju	**61**
W.J. Cronje (Capt)	**c** Rathore, **b** Kumble	**25**
D.N. Crookes	**c** Rathore, **b** Kumble	**26**
B.M. McMillan	not out	**37**
C.R. Matthews		
*D.J. Richardson		
S.M. Pollock		
P.S. de Villiers		
	lb **5**, w **16**	**21**
	50 overs (for 5 wickets)	**287**

	O	M	R	W
Srinath	10	1	51	**1**
Venkatesh Prasad	10	–	50	**1**
Tendulkar	7	–	51	**–**
Kumble	10	1	42	**2**
Venkatapathy Raju	9	–	70	**1**
Jadeja	4	–	18	**–**

Fall of Wickets
1–**5**, 2–**20**, 3–**115**, 4–**175**, 5–**227**

India

V.S. Rathore	**c** Richardson, **b** Matthews	**23**
S.R. Tendulkar	run out	**57**
A.R. Kumble	run out	**10**
N.S. Sidhu	**c** Matthews, **b** Cronje	**26**
S.V. Manjrekar	run out	**41**
M. Azharuddin (Capt)	run out	**39**
A.D. Jadeja	**c** Cullinan, **b** McMillan	**2**
J. Srinath	**c** Richardson, **b** de Villiers	**10**
*N.R. Mongia	**c** and **b** Pollock	**23**
Venkatesh Prasad	not out	**5**
Venkatapathy Raju	not out	**0**
	lb **10**, w **1**, nb **2**	**13**
	50 overs (for 9 wickets)	**249**

	O	M	R	W
de Villiers	10	–	42	**1**
Pollock	10	–	57	**1**
McMillan	10	–	48	**1**
Matthews	10	1	46	**1**
Symcox	6	–	23	**–**
Cronje	4	–	23	**1**

Fall of Wickets
1–**59**, 2–**78**, 3–**112**, 4–**130**, 5–**204**, 6–**208**, 7–**209**, 8–**243**, 9–**249**

Umpires: B.C. Cooray & M.J. Kitchen *Man of the Match:* G. Kirsten

South Africa won by 38 runs

Kirsten and Kallis began South Africa's reply with a stand of 53, but it was the belligerence of Cullinan and Crookes, who added 94 off 117 balls for the fourth wicket before both falling to Venkatapathy Raju in the same over which saw South Africa romp to victory. Crookes' 54 came from 61 deliveries with two sixes.

League Final Positions

	P	W	L	Pts	R/R
South Africa	4	4	–	8	5.58
India	4	1	3	2	4.80
Pakistan	4	1	3	2	4.53

Final

The dominance that South Africa had shown throughout the tournament continued into the final where they gained their third victory over India in five days. South Africa recovered from the early loss of Hudson and Cullinan through a stand of 95 runs from 91 balls between Kirsten and Symcox whose promotion in the order proved highly successful. Kirsten held the innings together, batting through the 50 overs to score his second century against India and to be named Man of the Tournament. McMillan, who hit three sixes, made a positive contribution towards the end of the innings.

India were given a sound start by Rathore and Tendulkar, but Tendulkar was forced to play more circumspectly as his colleagues displayed lack of judgement. There were four batsmen run out in the Indian innings, and they slipped from 204 for 4 to 243 for 8 as the target became out of reach. South Africa deservedly gained some consolation for their disappointment in the World Cup.

Man of the Series in the Sharjah Cup was Gary Kirsten, who hit two centuries against India. (David Munden/Sportsline)

Australia

The 1995–96 season in Australia had a special international flavour. A tour by Western Province heralded the year; then came Test series against Sri Lanka and Pakistan, and West Indies joined Australia and Sri Lanka for the Benson and Hedges World Series. The domestic competition promised to be as keen as ever, with Queensland anxious to hold on to the Sheffield Shield, which they won for the first time in 1994–95.

Michael Kasprowicz was the leading wicket-taker in the season with 64 first-class wickets. The Queensland and former Essex pace bowler won international recognition when he was chosen for the Australian side in the World Series. (Stephen Laffer/Sportsline)

Tour by Western Province
Pakistan tour and Test series
Sri Lanka tour and Test series
West Indies tour
Benson and Hedges World Series
Mercantile Mutual Cup
Sheffield Shield
First-class averages
Form charts

Australia entered cricket year 1995–96 on top of the world. They had proved to be supreme among Test nations, and their famous victory in the Caribbean in April, 1995, had shown that they possessed strength in depth. If McDermott, troubled by injury, could be said to be nearing the end of his career, other quick bowlers like McGrath, Fleming, Reiffel and Julian were jostling to be recognised as Australia's leading strike bowler. If Boon, too, was close to the end of an illustrious career, Ponting, Bevan, Law and DiVenuto were among a host of batsmen anxious to claim his spot in the national side. Australia had an abundance of riches and were favourites to win the World Cup, for no country has more experience of the limited-over game.

Western Province Tour

The power of Australian cricket is apparent in a lightning tour.

18, 19 and 20 September 1995
at Beenleigh
Queensland XI 299 for 6 dec. (P. Skuse 96, T.J. Barsby 71, T.J. Dixon 70) and 288 (B. Spanner 92, M. Hayward 60)
Western Province 354 for 6 dec. (G. Kirsten 140, J.B. Commins 112, H.D. Ackerman 55 not out, M.S. Kasprowicz 4 for 57) and 62 for 3
Match drawn

26, 27 and 28 September 1995
at Woolloongabba, Brisbane
Western Province 112 (J.H. Kallis 58, M.S. Kasprowicz 6 for 17) and 478 for 3 dec. (J.H. Kallis 186 not out, G. Kirsten 130, J.B. Commins 120)
Queensland 275 for 9 dec. (T.J. Barsby 65) and 316 for 4 (T.J. Dixon 122, S.G. Law 73, M.L. Love 60)
Queensland won by 6 wickets

29 September 1995

at Woolloongabba, Brisbane
Queensland 283 (A. Symonds 87, S.A. Prestwidge 55, C.R. Matthews 4 for 51)
Western Province 162 (G. Kirsten 64)
Queensland won by 121 runs

The game at Beenleigh was not accorded first-class status, but it did reveal that Western Province would find strong opposition on their short tour of Eastern Australia. This was confirmed when they were resoundingly beaten in the first-class match at The Gabba. Michael Kasprowicz gave an early indication of outstanding form with his best figures in Australian cricket, but Western Province had a second innings revival when Jacques Kallis shared a stand of 210 with Gary Kirsten and 183 with John Commins. Kallis' 186 not out was the first first-class century of his career. Needing 316 to win, Queensland romped to victory by six wickets. Troy Dixon, playing in his second first-class match, hit a maiden century, but the fact that he did not appear again in the season says much about the strength of Australian cricket.

Queensland also won the day/night match with great ease. Batting at number nine, Andrew Symonds hit 87.

3, 4 and 5 October 1995
at Hurstville Oval, Sydney
New South Wales 244 for 6 dec. (S. Lee 84, C.R. Matthews 4 for 64) and 202 for 3 dec. (M.G. Bevan 119 not out, S. Lee 67 not out)
Western Province 128 and 192 (S.G. Koening 57, D.A. Freedman 5 for 75)
New South Wales won by 126 runs

Kallis was recalled to South Africa before the match against New South Wales so that he could play for South Africa 'A' against Zimbabwe 'A'. Western Province were also without Commins who had returned home to be with his sick father. The South African provincial side could ill afford to lose such cricketers, and were no match for New South Wales who won with consummate ease.

Pakistan Tour

The Pakistanis arrived in Perth at the end of October in an atmosphere of controversy, apprehension and eager anticipation. The controversy concerned the publication of Judge Fakhruddin Ebrahim's findings in the Salim Malik affair. Salim had been accused of offering bribes in an attempt to determine the outcome of matches by persuading Australian bowlers to bowl badly during the Test series between Pakistan and Australia in 1994. May, Warne and Mark Waugh had given sworn statements to this effect, but the Australian players had refused to go to Pakistan to give testimony. Judge Ebrahim's findings exonerated Salim, and he was selected for the party to tour Australia – hence the controversy.

Apprehension came with controversy, for there were misgivings as to how the Pakistanis, and Salim in particular, would be received in Australia and in what spirit the series would be played. Nevertheless, the series was eagerly anticipated for Pakistan had been the last nation to defeat Australia in a Test series, and revenge was keenly desired.

Inevitably, Pakistan had their own domestic problems which involved administrators, selectors and managers. Defeat in Sharjah had led to the reinstatement of Wasim Akram as captain although he had once been ousted by a players' revolt. Wasim replaced Rameez Raja who was never likely to survive as leader after the home defeat by Sri Lanka and the dreadful performance in Sharjah.

Aamir Sohail was vice-captain. This appointment could well have been made in an attempt to give Aamir responsibility which would lead to stricter self-discipline. Rashid Latif, having made an 'unconditional apology' for certain criticisms he had made of other players, was recalled to the squad.

With Trevor Hohns now chairman of selectors and Geoff Marsh a new member of the panel, Australia were confident to face all comers.

26 October 1995
at Lilac Hill
Pakistanis 210 (Rameez Raja 106, Aamir Sohail 74, J. Angel 5 for 40)
Australian Cricket Board Chairman's XI 207 (J.L. Langer 85)
Pakistanis won by 3 runs

Mike Hussey of Western Australia hit a maiden first-class century against the Pakistan tourists. Hussey is one of the young batsmen who assures Australia of a bright future.
(Stephen Laffer/Sportsline)

28, 29, 30 and 31 October 1995
at WACA Ground, Perth
Western Australia 402 for 5 dec. (M.E. Hussey 146, G.B. Hogg 101 not out, A.C. Gilchrist 58 not out) and 189 for 7 dec. (Saqlain Mushtaq 5 for 39)
Pakistanis 164 (Moin Khan 56, Salim Elahi 54) and 226 for 8 (Rameez Raja 84, Basit Ali 69 not out)
Match drawn

The tourists gained little comfort from the warm-up matches played in Western Australia. They won the fifty-over match at Lilac Hill, but they were confronted by an attack which included veterans Lillee and Hughes. Aamir Sohail and Rameez Raja added 147 for the second wicket, but no other batsman reached double figures.

In the first-class match, Hussey and Hogg scored maiden centuries, and Moin Khan batted for 232 minutes to ward off defeat. The cheering news for Pakistan was the bowling of off-spinner Saqlain Mushtaq.

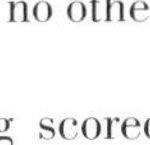

2, 3, 4 and 5 November 1995
at Adelaide Oval
South Australia 392 for 8 dec. (D.S. Lehmann 138, T.J. Nielsen 57, B.A. Johnson 54) and 249 for 5 dec. (J.D. Siddons 125, G.S. Blewett 103 not out, Wasim Akram 4 for 43
Pakistanis 276 (Basit Ali 137, J.N. Gillespie 4 for 82, M.A. Harrity 4 for 90) and 298 for 5 (Basit Ali 101 not out, Inzamam-ul-Haq 96)
Match drawn

A century in each innings by the enigmatic Basit Ali and a good knock by Inzamam-ul-Haq was reassuring for Pakistan on the eve of the first Test, but their bowlers still suffered at the hands of the state batsmen. Siddons and Blewett shared a fifth wicket stand of 101 in South Australia's second innings.

24, 25 and 26 November 1995
at MCG, Melbourne
Pakistanis 154 and 279 (Inzamam-ul-Haq 132, D.W. Fleming 4 for 64)
Victoria 362 (D.M. Jones 127, Saqlain Mushtaq 5 for 107) and 72 for 2
Victoria won by 8 wickets

Pakistan's only other match outside the Test series took place against Victoria between the second and third Tests. Without both Wasim Akram and Waqar Younis, their attack was anaemic, and Victoria were in control from the start. Jones established a record with his 27th hundred for Victoria while Berry created a record by claiming 11 victims, a feat never before accomplished by any wicket-keeper against a touring team in Australia. All of Berry's victims were caught.

Test Series

Australia v. Pakistan

Australia fielded the same eleven in all three Tests against Pakistan, with Julian acting as twelfth man on each occasion. In the opening match, Pakistan, with their fourth captain inside a year, gave a Test debut to Salim Elahi, and played Moin Khan instead of Rashid Latif and Saqlain Mushtaq instead of Mushtaq Ahmed. They brought Salim Malik back to Test cricket and chose Mohammad Akram as the third seamer. Taylor won the toss, and Australia batted.

Slater was dropped three times before lunch as Australia batted with determination rather that flair. Taylor and Slater completed their eighth century stand in Test cricket before Taylor pulled Saqlain into the hands of Salim Malik, who took the catch but split the webbing by his left thumb in the process and effectively put himself out of the match. Slater soon followed his captain, but David Boon and Mark Waugh then added 94 in 106 minutes. They both fell in the last hour of the day. Mark Waugh was caught bat and pad, and Boon edged the second new ball to slip. Steve Waugh might also have gone had Wasim Akram held on to a return catch, but Australia ended the day on 262 for 4.

The solidity continued into the second morning as Steve Waugh and Blewett negotiated a difficult and hostile pre-lunch period. The batting was gritty rather than pretty, but the stand of 135, which was ended by a Waqar yorker, gave a substance to the Australian innings, which formed a platform for victory. It must be admitted that – not for the first time – Pakistan were poor in the field. Catches were missed, and Moin Khan's wicket-keeping was far below Test standard.

Steve Waugh reached his ninth Test century as the Australian tail tumbled in a flurry of hit or miss. Pakistan faced a daunting 463, and they were soon in desperate trouble. Both Salim Elahi and Rameez Raja were taken at slip, and night-watchman Saqlain Mushtaq was leg before to the last ball of the day. At 40 for 3, Pakistan faced a worrying evening.

Matters did not improve for Pakistan. With Salim Malik unable to bat, they were all out before lunch on the third day, and the last six wickets to fall went to the remarkable Shane Warne. Aamir Sohail swatted and missed. Inzamam-ul-Haq scooped to mid-wicket, and Moin Khan slashed to mid-on. Basit Ali was caught at slip after remaining becalmed for over an hour. Wasim Akram was taken at short-leg and Mohammad Akram at cover, and Pakistan were following on 366 runs in arrears.

Salim Elahi and Rameez Raja soon became victims of McGrath, but Aamir Sohail played a gem of an innings. He displayed a variety of elegant shots on his way to 99 off 155 balls. His innings included 15 exquisite fours and was ended by a McGrath yorker. Inzamam-ul-Haq and Basit Ali took the score to 197 for 3 by the end of the day, but they fell in quick succession on the fourth morning. Wasim Akram

First Test Match – Australia v. Pakistan

9, 10, 11 and 13 November 1995 at Woolloongabba, Brisbane

Australia

	First Innings	
M.A. Taylor (Capt)	c Salim Malik, b Saqlain	69
M.J. Slater	c Mohammad, b Wasim Akram	42
D.C. Boon	c Inzamam-ul-Haq, b Wasim	54
M.E. Waugh	c Salim Elahi, b Saqlain	59
S.R. Waugh	not out	112
G.S. Blewett	lbw, b Waqar Younis	57
*I.A. Healy	c sub (Mushtaq), b Mohammad	18
P.R. Reiffel	lbw, b Waqar Younis	9
S.K. Warne	c Moin Khan, b Aamir Sohail	5
C.J. McDermott	b Waqar Younis	8
G.D. McGrath	st Moin Khan, b Aamir Sohail	5
	b 2, lb 6, w 4, nb 13	25
		463

	O	M	R	W
Wasim Akram	38	9	84	2
Waqar Younis	29.5	7	101	3
Mohammad Akram	33.1	4	97	1
Saqlain Mushtaq	44	12	130	2
Aamir Sohail	16.5	2	43	2

Fall of Wickets
1–**107**, 2–**119**, 3–**213**, 4–**250**, 5–**385**, 6–**411**, 7–**434**, 8–**441**, 9–**452**

Pakistan

	First Innings		Second Innings	
Aamir Sohail	st Healy, b Warne	32	b McGrath	99
Salim Elahi	c Taylor, b McDermott	11	c Healy, b McGrath	2
Rameez Raja	c Taylor, b Warne	8	c Healy, b McGrath	16
Saqlain Mushtaq	lbw, b McGrath	0	(9) not out	2
Inzamam-ul-Haq	c S.R. Waugh, b Warne	5	(4) c McDermott, b M.E. Waugh	62
Basit Ali	c Taylor, b Warne	1	(5) lbw, b McGrath	26
*Moin Khan	c McDermott, b Warne	4	(6) c Healy, b Reiffel	9
Wasim Akram (Capt)	c Boon, b Warne	1	(7) c Slater, b Warne	6
Waqar Younis	not out	19	(10) lbw, b Warne	0
Mohammad Akram	c Blewett, b Warne	1	(11) lbw, b Warne	0
Salim Malik	absent injured	–	(8) c McDermott, b Warne	0
	b 4, lb 5, nb 6	15	b 7, nb 11	18
		97		240

	O	M	R	W	O	M	R	W
McDermott	11	4	32	1	11	–	47	–
McGrath	14	3	33	1	25	7	76	4
Warne	16.1	9	23	7	27.5	10	54	4
Reiffel					15	4	47	1
S.R. Waugh					2	1	3	–
M.E. Waugh					5	2	6	1

Fall of Wickets
1–**20**, 2–**37**, 3–**40**, 4–**62**, 5–**66**, 6–**70**, 7–**70**, 8–**80**, 9–**97**
1–**30**, 2–**88**, 3–**167**, 4–**217**, 5–**218**, 6–**233**, 7–**233**, 8–**239**, 9–**240**

Umpires: S.G. Randell & K.E Liebenberg

Australia won by an innings and 126 runs

Wasim Akram bowls Mark Taylor for 40 in the first innings of the second Test, Australia v. Pakistan. Taylor took his revenge with a second-innings century. (Stephen Laffer/Sportsline)

and Salim Malik fell in the same over from Warne. Reiffel took the edge of Moin's bat, and Warne quickly disposed of the last two batsmen to finish with match figures of 11 for 77, the best performance by an Australian bowler against Pakistan. Australia won by an innings and 126 runs.

For the second Test, Pakistan brought in Ijaz Ahmed for the injured Salim Malik and Mushtaq Ahmed for Saqlain Mushtaq. Australia again won the toss and batted.

This time there was no fruitful beginning as Slater fell to Wasim Akram's in-swinger without a run scored. Boon helped Taylor to add 68 but was run out when sent back by his captain, and Taylor himself edged Wasim into his stumps on 111. Mark Waugh batted fluently, but Steve Waugh, having survived a barrage of bouncers, was caught behind as he attempted to cut at Mushtaq Ahmed. Blewett was bowled by Mushtaq's googly without addition, and Australia were struggling at 156 for 5. Healy played some powerful shots before becoming Mushtaq's third victim, and Mark Waugh was eighth out when he drove Mushtaq to long-on. This dismissal gave Mushtaq Ahmed five wickets in a Test innings for the first time.

Warne clouted Mushtaq for three sixes, but the great Australian leg-spinner was hit on the toe by a yorker from Waqar and was unable to bowl in the match, nor did he bat in the second innings. Australia finished with a disappointing 267, but Pakistan were soon in trouble once more. Salim Elahi, a premature choice for Test cricket, was bowled by McGrath, and Mushtaq, sent in as night-watchman after a hard stint of bowling, was leg before first ball. Pakistan tottered at 33 for 2 when stumps were drawn.

Rain interrupted the second day, but Pakistan, not threatened by Warne, looked at ease with Aamir and Rameez playing confidently. At lunch, they were 78 for 2, but Aamir Sohail was adjudged caught behind immediately after the break, and when Rameez pushed a return catch to Reiffel Australia sensed a breakthrough.

Inzamam-ul-Haq fatally leg-glanced Steve Waugh into the hands of Healy, and Basit Ali, highly talented but still searching for credibility at the top level, quickly fell to McGrath. Moin Khan, whose wicket-keeping had again been embarrassing, swung madly at McDermott, and it was left to Ijaz Ahmed, newly arrived from Pakistan to bolster the middle order, to procure what crumbs he could as those about him succumbed to Reiffel. Australia were grateful for a lead of 69, and this was rapidly extended. In the 24 overs remaining at the end of an extended damp day, Taylor and Slater scored 107, and Australia were in total command.

Australia lost three wickets before lunch on the third day. Slater, having hit 73 off 90 balls with a six and eight fours, was leg before to Mushtaq's top-spinner, and Boon was caught at point off the same bowler. Mark Waugh failed for once, and Pakistan had clawed back some advantage by reducing Australia to 132 for 3.

Mark Taylor and Steve Waugh added 57 valuable runs before Waugh was caught behind. Blewett was out of touch, but Taylor confidently and solidly reached his third Test century against Pakistan, his 14th in all. He was finally yorked by Waqar Younis. He had batted for 356 minutes, faced 243 balls and hit 13 fours. Healy and McDermott made useful contributions, and Pakistan faced a target of 376. They scored 15 without loss before the close although Aamir Sohail had retired hurt with a painful knee. He was to return at the fall of the first wicket.

Salim Elahi was caught off McGrath, and Reiffel had Rameez Raja adjudged leg before. Aamir Sohail suggested elegance and dominance and hit six fours before presenting Blewett with his first Test wicket, a catch at square-leg. Ijaz Ahmed was not the first Pakistani batsman to suffer a harsh decision when he was given out leg before as he padded up to Blewett. Pakistan were now in terminal decline as wickets fell regularly. Wasim Akram hit a defiant 33 off 53 balls, but the cause had long since been lost. McGrath finished with his third five-wicket haul

Mushtaq Ahmed traps Slater leg before to end an opening stand of 120. The inclusion of Mushtaq strengthened the Pakistan side enormously. (Shaun Botterill/Allsport)

Second Test Match – Australia v. Pakistan

17, 18, 19, 20 and 21 November 1995 at Bellerive Oval, Hobart

Australia

	First Innings		Second Innings	
M.J. Slater	lbw, **b** Wasim Akram	**0**	(2) lbw, **b** Mushtaq	**73**
M.A. Taylor (Capt)	**b** Wasim Akram	**40**	(1) **b** Waqar Younis	**123**
D.C. Boon	run out	**34**	**c** Waqar, **b** Mushtaq	**0**
M.E. Waugh	**c** Rameez, **b** Mushtaq	**88**	**b** Wasim Akram	**3**
S.R. Waugh	**c** Moin, **b** Mushtaq	**7**	**c** Moin, **b** Mohammad	**29**
G.S. Blewett	**b** Mushtaq Ahmed	**0**	**c** Basit, **b** Wasim	**11**
*I.A. Healy	**c** Basit, **b** Mushtaq	**37**	**c** Inzamam, **b** Wasim	**24**
P.R. Reiffel	**c** Mohammad, **b** Mushtaq	**14**	**b** Mushtaq Ahmed	**0**
S.K. Warne	not out	**27**	absent injured	**–**
C.J. McDermott	**b** Waqar Younis	**0**	(9) **c** Wasim, **b** Mushtaq	**20**
G.D. McGrath	**b** Wasim Akram	**3**	(10) not out	**2**
	b **3**, lb **9**, nb **5**	**17**	b **6**, lb **5**, w **1**, nb **9**	**21**
		267		**306**

	O	M	R	W	O	M	R	W
Wasim Akram	18.3	7	42	**3**	26.1	7	72	**3**
Waqar Younis	17	3	54	**1**	20	4	67	**1**
Mohammad Akram	10	1	41	**–**	10	1	58	**1**
Mushtaq Ahmed	30	5	115	**5**	38	8	83	**4**
Aamir Sohail	3	1	3	**–**	8	2	15	**–**

Fall of Wickets
1–**0**, 2–**68**, 3–**111**, 4–**156**, 5–**156**, 6–**209**, 7–**235**, 8–**238**, 9–**244**
1–**120**, 2–**125**, 3–**132**, 4–**189**, 5–**233**, 6–**255**, 7–**256**, 8–**296**, 9–**306**

Pakistan

	First Innings		Second Innings	
Aamir Sohail	**c** Healy, **b** Reiffel	**32**	**c** sub (Julian), **b** Blewett	**57**
Salim Elahi	**b** McGrath	**13**	**c** Boon, **b** McGrath	**17**
Mushtaq Ahmed	lbw, **b** McGrath	**0**	(9) **b** McGrath	**8**
Rameez Raja	**c** and **b** Reiffel	**59**	(3) lbw, **b** Reiffel	**25**
Inzamam-ul-Haq	**c** Healy, **b** S.R. Waugh	**27**	(4) lbw, **b** Reiffel	**40**
Ijaz Ahmed	not out	**34**	(5) lbw, **b** Blewett	**4**
Basit Ali	lbw, **b** McGrath	**2**	(6) **b** Reiffel	**5**
*Moin Khan	**b** McDermott	**12**	(7) **c** M.E. Waugh, **b** McGrath	**16**
Wasim Akram (Capt)	**c** Taylor, **b** McDermott	**2**	(8) **c** Blewett, **b** McGrath	**33**
Waqar Younis	**c** sub (Julian), **b** Reiffel	**10**	**c** Blewett, **b** McGrath	**4**
Mohammad Akram	lbw, **b** Reiffel	**0**	not out	**0**
	lb **1**, nb **6**	**7**	lb **11**	**11**
		198		**220**

	O	M	R	W	O	M	R	W
McDermott	18	2	72	**2**	16	7	38	**–**
McGrath	19	4	46	**3**	24.3	7	61	**5**
Reiffel	15.5	3	38	**4**	14	6	42	**3**
M.E. Waugh	8	–	23	**–**	12	2	24	**–**
S.R. Waugh	6	–	18	**1**	8	1	19	**–**
Blewett					10	4	25	**2**

Fall of Wickets
1–**24**, 2–**24**, 3–**79**, 4–**126**, 5–**150**, 6–**155**, 7–**173**, 8–**183**, 9–**198**
1–**27**, 2–**62**, 3–**132**, 4–**142**, 5–**152**, 6–**157**, 7–**205**, 8–**210**, 9–**220**

Umpires: H.D. Bird & D.B. Hair

Australia won by 155 runs

Third Test Match – Australia v. Pakistan

30 November, 1, 2, 3 and 4 December at SCG, Sydney

Pakistan

	First Innings		Second Innings	
Aamir Sohail	**c** M.E. Waugh, **b** McDermott	**4**	**c** Boon, **b** McDermott	**9**
Rameez Raja	**c** Slater, **b** Warne	**33**	**c** M.E. Waugh, **b** Warne	**39**
Ijaz Ahmed	**c** McGrath, **b** Warne	**137**	lbw, **b** Warne	**15**
Inzamam-ul-Haq	**c** Healy, **b** Warne	**39**	(6) **c** Taylor, **b** McDermott	**59**
Salim Malik	lbw, **b** McGrath	**36**	(4) lbw, **b** M.E. Waugh	**45**
Basit Ali	**c** Slater, **b** McDermott	**17**	(5) **b** Warne	**14**
*Rashid Latif	**c** Healy, **b** McDermott	**1**	(8) lbw, **b** Warne	**3**
Wasim Akram (Capt)	**c** and **b** McGrath	**21**	(7) lbw, **b** McDermott	**5**
Saqlain Mushtaq	run out	**0**	**c** M.E. Waugh, **b** McDermott	**2**
Mushtaq Ahmed	**c** McDermott, **b** Warne	**0**	lbw, **b** McDermott	**2**
Waqar Younis	not out	**0**	not out	**1**
	lb **3**, w **3**, nb **5**	**11**	b **1**, lb **5**, nb **4**	**10**
		299		**204**

	O	M	R	W	O	M	R	W
McDermott	21	6	62	**3**	15.3	–	49	**5**
McGrath	22.2	1	79	**2**	17	3	47	**–**
Reiffel	22	4	71	**–**	8.3	2	15	**–**
Warne	34	20	55	**4**	27	13	66	**4**
M.E. Waugh	10	4	23	**–**	14	4	21	**1**
Blewett	4	2	6	**–**	2	2	0	**–**

Fall of Wickets
1–**4**, 2–**64**, 3–**141**, 4–**210**, 5–**263**, 6–**269**, 7–**297**, 8–**299**, 9–**299**
1–**18**, 2–**58**, 3–**82**, 4–**101**, 5–**163**, 6–**185**, 7–**188**, 8–**198**, 9–**203**

Australia

	First Innings		Second Innings	
M.J. Slater	**b** Wasim Akram	**1**	(2) lbw, **b** Mushtaq	**23**
M.A. Taylor (Capt)	**c** Rashid, **b** Saqlain	**47**	(1) **st** Rashid, **b** Mushtaq	**59**
D.C. Boon	**c** Rashid, **b** Mushtaq	**16**	**c** sub (Moin Khan), **b** Saqlain	**6**
M.E. Waugh	**c** Mushtaq, **b** Wasim	**116**	**c** Rashid, **b** Wasim Akram	**34**
S.R. Waugh	**st** Rashid, **b** Mushtaq	**38**	(6) **b** Mushtaq Ahmed	**14**
G.S. Blewett	**b** Mushtaq Ahmed	**5**	(7) **b** Waqar Younis	**14**
*I.A. Healy	**c** Rashid, **b** Mushtaq	**6**	(5) **c** Rashid, **b** Wasim	**7**
P.R. Reiffel	not out	**10**	(10) not out	**2**
S.K. Warne	**c** Rashid, **b** Wasim	**2**	(8) **c** Saqlain, **b** Mushtaq	**5**
C.J. McDermott	**b** Wasim Akram	**0**	(9) **b** Waqar Younis	**0**
G.D. McGrath	**c** Wasim, **b** Mushtaq	**0**	**b** Waqar Younis	**0**
	lb **6**, nb **10**	**16**	lb **5**, nb **3**	**8**
		257		**172**

	O	M	R	W	O	M	R	W
Wasim Akram	24	4	50	**4**	16	5	25	**2**
Waqar Younis	11	4	26	**–**	6.1	2	15	**3**
Mushtaq Ahmed	36.2	7	95	**5**	30	6	91	**4**
Saqlain Mushtaq	22	2	62	**1**	13	5	35	**1**
Aamir Sohail	5	–	18	**–**	1	–	1	**–**

Fall of Wickets
1–**2**, 2–**44**, 3–**91**, 4–**174**, 5–**182**, 6–**226**, 7–**240**, 8–**249**, 9–**249**
1–**42**, 2–**69**, 3–**117**, 4–**126**, 5–**146**, 6–**152**, 7–**170**, 8–**170**, 9–**172**

Umpires: S.G. Randell & H.D. Bird

Pakistan won by 74 runs

in Test cricket, and Australia took the match by 155 runs with a day to spare. With this victory came victory in the series.

For the third Test, Pakistan brought back Salim Malik for Salim Elahi, with Rameez moving up to open the innings. Rashid Latif and Saqlain Mushtaq replaced Moin Khan and Mohammad Akram. With eight dismissals in the match, Rashid Latif gave evidence of how important a part he might have played in the first two matches of the series had he been selected ahead of Moin. Pakistan won the toss and batted.

Aamir Sohail hit a boundary and was out to the third ball of the match as he slashed at McDermott. Rameez was the only other pre-lunch victim, taken at mid-on off Warne who found the conditions to his liking. Ijaz Ahmed played with total assurance, and he and Inzamam-ul-Haq added 77 in 96 minutes before Inzamam essayed a cut at Warne and presented Healy with his 500th first-class dismissal.

Salim Malik also played well and drove McGrath to the cover boundary three times in one over, but the tall fast bowler had his revenge. Ijaz Ahmed reached the third Test century of his career, a splendid effort that left observers bewildered as to why this batsman of charm and application had been jettisoned by the Pakistan Board for the best part of a year. Pakistan closed on 231 for 4.

Basit Ali added just nine to his overnight score before being caught at cover off McDermott who also had Rashid Latif caught behind. Ijaz's 422-minute innings, his highest in Test cricket, came to an end when he swept at Warne. He had faced 332 balls and hit two sixes and 17 fours. His dismissal brought an abrupt end to the innings, the last four wickets falling for two runs.

Wasim Akram bowled Slater before lunch, and Boon floundered for 79 minutes before edging Mushtaq Ahmed to the wicket-keeper. Taylor, too, was a victim of Rashid's, and this brought the Waugh twins together. By the end of the day, they had taken the score to 151 amid gathering gloom. Eventually, their stand was worth 83 in 126 minutes, and took Australia to a point where the advantage could have been seized, but thereafter Mark Waugh fought a lone battle. He hit a six and eight fours in his ninth Test century

Taylor is stumped by Rashid Latif off Mushtaq for 59, and Pakistan sense victory. (Shaun Botterill/Allsport)

Ijaz Ahmed hit a brilliant 137 which set up Pakistan's victory in the third Test. (Shaun Botterill/Allsport)

before being seventh out at 240 as Australia's last five wickets went down for 31 runs. Mushtaq Ahmed again bowled well and thoroughly deserved his second five-wicket haul in Test cricket.

Pakistan led by 42 runs, but they soon lost the impetuous Aamir Sohail who pulled McGrath for six, was dropped at slip and caught at point in his 19 minutes at the crease. Ijaz Ahmed was beaten by Warne's top-spinner, and the same bowler had Rameez taken bat and pad at silly mid-off. The great leg-spinner, Man of the Series, was not finished yet. With the last ball of the day he bowled Basit Ali round his legs with a delivery that spun in from well wide of the stumps. Pakistan were 101 for 4.

Salim Malik batted with a charm that is not recognised by the Australians, and he and Inzamam added a significant 62 before Salim was adjudged leg before. Inzamam went on to reach a calm, impressive fifty, but he could not stem the flood of wickets, the last five going down for 19 runs. Needing 247 to win, Australia ended the fourth day on 121 for the loss of Slater, Mark Waugh and Boon whose Test career was clearly in its twilight period.

Australia, it seemed, clearly held the edge, with 126 runs needed and seven wickets in hand, but events proved otherwise. Healy edged to the 'keeper, and Steve Waugh misread Mushtaq's googly. Taylor, who had batted fitfully and dangerously for 218 minutes, charged wildly at Mushtaq and was stumped by the highly efficient Rashid. With eight victims, Rashid equalled the record for an Australia–Pakistan series.

Waqar found the pace and energy that he had lacked in the earlier innings to help bring about a quick demise of the Australian innings, and the game was over ten minutes before lunch on the fifth day. Mushtaq Ahmed took nine wickets for the second Test in succession, and Pakistan had shown a determination and pleasing 'togetherness' which gave heart for the future.

Cracks had begun to appear in the Australian armour, but there was plenty of talent in reserve.

Test Match Averages – Australia v. Pakistan

Australia Batting

	M	Inns	NO	Runs	HS	Av	100s	50s
M. A. Taylor	3	5	–	338	123	67.60	1	2
M.E. Waugh	3	5	–	300	116	60.00	1	2
S.R. Waugh	3	5	1	200	112*	50.00	1	
M.J. Slater	3	5	–	139	73	27.80		1
D.C. Boon	3	5	–	110	54	22.00		1
I.A. Healy	3	5	–	92	37	18.40		
G.S. Blewett	3	5	–	87	57	17.40		1
S.K. Warne	3	4	1	39	27*	13.00		
P.R. Reiffel	3	5	2	35	14	11.66		
C.J. McDermott	3	5	–	28	20	5.60		
G.D. McGrath	3	5	1	10	3	2.50		

Pakistan Batting

	M	Inns	NO	Runs	HS	Av	100s	50s
Ijaz Ahmed	2	4	1	190	137*	63.33	1	
Aamir Sohail	3	6	–	233	99	38.83		2
Inzamam-ul-Haq	3	6	–	232	62	38.66		2
Rameez Raja	3	6	–	180	59	30.00		1
Salim Malik	2	3	–	81	45	27.00		
Wasim Akram	3	6	–	68	33	11.33		
Waqar Younis	3	6	3	34	19*	11.33		
Basit Ali	3	6	–	65	26	10.83		
Salim Elahi	2	4	–	43	17	10.75		
Moin Khan	2	4	–	41	16	10.25		
Mushtaq Ahmed	2	4	–	10	8	2.50		
Saqlain Mushtaq	2	4	1	4	2*	1.33		
Mohammad Akram	2	4	1	1	1	0.33		

Played in one Test: Rashid Latif 1&3

Australia Bowling

	Overs	Mds	Runs	Wks	Av	Best	10/m	5/inn
S.K. Warne	105	52	198	19	10.42	7/23	1	1
G.S. Blewett	16	8	31	2	15.50	2/25		
G.D. McGrath	121.4	25	342	15	22.80	5/61		1
P.R. Reiffel	75.2	19	213	8	26.62	4/38		
C.J. McDermott	92.3	19	300	11	27.27	5/49		1
S.R. Waugh	16	2	40	1	40.00	1/18		
M.E. Waugh	49	12	97	2	48.50	1/6		

Pakistan Bowling

	Overs	Mds	Runs	Wks	Av	Best	10/m	5/inn
Wasim Akram	122.4	32	273	14	19.50	4/50		
Mushtaq Ahmed	134.2	26	384	18	21.33	5/95		1
Waqar Younis	84	20	263	8	32.87	3/15		
Aamir Sohail	33.5	5	80	2	40.00	2/43		
Saqlain Mushtaq	79	19	227	4	56.75	2/130		
Mohammad Akram	53.1	6	196	2	98.00	1/58		

Australia Fielding Figures

8 – I.A. Healy (ct 7 / st 1); 5 – M.A. Taylor; 4 – M.E. Waugh and C.J. McDermott; 3 – M.J. Slater, D.C. Boon and G.S. Blewett; 2 – G.D. McGrath and sub (B.P. Julian); 1 – S.R. Waugh and P.R. Reiffel

Pakistan Fielding Figures

8 – Rashid Latif (ct 6 / st 2); 4 – Moin Khan (ct 3 / st 1) (plus one as sub); 2 – Inzamam-ul-Haq, Mohammad Akram, Basit Ali and Wasim Akram; 1 – Mushtaq Ahmed (plus one as sub), Rameez Raja, Salim Malik, Waqar Younis, Salim Elahi and Saqlain Mushtaq

Sri Lanka Tour

Allegations of ball-tampering and Muralitharan no-balled for throwing. Australia triumph in a series tinged with acrimony and controversy.

19 November 1995

at Cairns
Queensland 208 (M.L. Hayden 53)
Sri Lankans 162 (R.S. Mahanama 58, A.P. Gurusinha 50, S.G. Law 5 for 26)
Queensland won by 46 runs

22, 23, 24 and 25 November 1995

at Harrup Park, Mackay
Queensland 305 (A. Symonds 73, J.P. Maher 50, G.P. Wickremasinghe 4 for 49) and 255 (T.J. Barsby 51, M. Muralitharan 5 for 87, K.J. Silva 5 for 96)
Sri Lankans 178 (A. Ranatunga 77, M.S. Kasprowicz 7 for 64) and 109 (M.S. Kasprowicz 5 for 31)
Queensland won by 273 runs

Sri Lanka played two fifty-over matches and two first-class matches in preparation for the Test series, and the performances in Queensland did not bode well. In Cairns, Sri Lanka lost their last nine wickets for 38 runs and were bowled out in 45.1 overs. In Mackay, they bowled tidily and batted dreadfully. In their first innings, a fifth wicket stand of 81 between Arjuna Ranatunga and Romesh Kaluwitharana was the only source of substance, while in the second innings they lost their last seven wickets for 22 runs. The match was a triumph for Michael Kasprowicz who captured ten wickets for the first time. His 7 for 64 was also his career-best performance in Australia or England.

29 November 1995

at Devonport Oval
Tasmania 230 for 5 (R.T. Ponting 99, S. Young 76)
Sri Lankans 220 for 5 (P.A. de Silva 67)
Sri Lankans won on faster run rate

1, 2, 3 and 4 December 1995

at Launceston
Tasmania 335 for 4 dec. (R.T. Ponting 131 not out, A.J. Daly 70, R.J. Tucker 54 not out) and 273 for 5 dec. (A.J. Daly 62 not out, R.J. Tucker 60 not out)
Sri Lankans 369 (A. Ranatunga 145, U.C. Hathurusinghe 73) and 160 for 2 (U.C. Hathurusinge 61 not out, R.S. Kaluwitharana 53)
Match drawn

Sri Lanka's ventures in Tasmania were more fruitful than those in Queensland. They were subjected to some brilliant batting from Ponting in both matches against the island side, but they were cheered by victory in the first game and by a fine innings of 145 off 158 balls from skipper Arjuna Ranatunga in the second. He hit 20 fours and a six and played some spectacular cricket.

Test Series

Australia v. Sri Lanka

With Steve Waugh not deemed fully fit, Australia gave a first Test cap to the Queensland captain Stuart Law. Ricky Ponting, whose exceptional talent as a batsman could be denied no longer, also made a debut for Australia. Blewett made way for him. Julian replaced Reiffel from the side that had played against Pakistan, which meant that Kasprowicz was the twelfth man. He deserved more. Ranatunga won the toss and Sri Lanka batted.

On a gusty day, the visitors promised more than they achieved. McGrath again bowled well, and McDermott showed better form than he had done at the start of the series against Pakistan. Warne was as threatening as ever. Gurusinha attempted to hold the innings together for Sri Lanka for nearly three hours while Ranatunga hit a belligerent 32. Kaluwitharana made 50 off 74 balls, and both Dharmasena and Wickremasinghe, who made his highest Test score, were positive, but the innings lacked backbone. Disappointingly, Sri Lanka were all out for 251 on the first day, and the advantage of winning the toss on a good pitch had been lost.

That advantage was firmly in the hands of the Australians by the end of the second day. Slater and Taylor quickly posted a century partnership: when Taylor was leg before to Aravinda de Silva four short of his century the pair had scored 228 in 224 minutes. Boon was given out caught at slip, but that was the only other success Sri Lanka had on an unhappy second day on which Australia reached 358 for 2. Slater had batted with assurance and had hit five sixes, four of them off Muralitharan, in reaching 189, but Mark Waugh had been dropped by wicket-keeper Kaluwitharana before he had scored and was far from certain.

On the third morning, Slater completed the first double century of his Test career. When he was third out, caught and bowled by the persevering Muralitharan, he had hit 219 off 321 balls in 460 minutes. His innings included five sixes and 15 fours. He and Mark Waugh had added 156, and Waugh went on to complete his tenth Test hundred.

Ponting played a delightful first Test innings. He survived a stumping chance, but he seemed certain to glide to a century before he was harshly adjudged leg before to Vaas. He and Law had added 121 in a debut partnership. Ponting's dismissal brought the declaration and an uneasy four overs for Sri Lanka in which 13 runs were scored and Hathurusinghe was dropped off Warne.

The umpiring in the series with Pakistan had been criticised as being of a poor standard, and that criticism continued into this series. On the second day, the umpires alleged that the Sri Lankans were guilty of ball-tampering. This charge was passionately and emphatically rejected by team manager Duleep Mendis, but the damage had been done, and the series was soured. One can only observe that, as Australia scored 617 for 5 from 174 overs, if the Sri Lankans were guilty of ball-tampering, they had not been very effective in their efforts.

Sri Lanka batted with considerable flair on the fourth day. If they were to lose, it would be in style. Ranatunga made a rapid 46, and Hashan Tillekeratne batted with majesty to reach his fourth Test century. His driving was powerful and elegant, and his runs came off 206 deliveries with 12 fours. It was his third Test hundred of the year and showed, perhaps, a growing maturity in the Sri Lankan side. Kaluwitharana played another whirlwind innings, 40 off 42 balls, but these knocks could only be gestures in the face of inevitable defeat.

For the second Test match, Steve Waugh and Paul Reiffel, both deemed fit again, returned in place of Law and Julian. Sri Lanka made one change from the side heavily defeated in the first match, slow left-arm bowler Jayantha Silva making his Test debut at the expense of Dharmasena. Australia won the toss and batted.

The ICC had cleared Sri Lanka of ball-tampering in the first Test, but the tourists were now to be subjected to

Michael Slater on his way to a double century against Sri Lanka in the first Test. Thereafter, Slater's season began to fall apart. (Shaun Botterill/Allsport)

Shane Warne once again enjoying outstanding success at international level. He celebrates the capture of Aravinda de Silva. (Shaun Botterill/Allsport)

another indignity. They enjoyed early success when Wickremasinghe dismissed Taylor. Then came the blight: umpire Darrell Hair no-balled off-spinner Muralitharan for 'throwing' seven times in the space of three overs.

Muralitharan, Sri Lanka's leading wicket-taker, was playing in his 23rd Test, and, although his action had been carefully studied, he had escaped censure in the past. Most observers and critics thought that Muralitharan and Sri Lanka had been unfairly treated by umpire Hair who was standing well back from the popping crease and seemed to be concentrating only on Muralitharan's bowling action, for, from his position, he was unable to ascertain clearly the bowler's front foot placing. When Muralitharan later bowled with Hair at square-leg, the position usually associated with a 'throwing' call, the umpire did not no-ball him. Allan Border, Richie Richardson and Sri Lankan coach Dav Whatmore were among those who came to the bowler's defence, and the tourists produced a medical report which vindicated Muralitharan. This unhappy incident clouded the Test, and the remainder of the tour.

In another impressive batting display, Australia reached 234 for 3 at the end of the first day. Slater dominated a stand of 102 with Boon who then put on 103 with Mark Waugh. Boon, 93 not out overnight, reached his 21st Test hundred on the second morning. He took more than six hours to reach his century which was to be his last in Test cricket. Omitted from the limited-over side and from the party selected for the World Cup, Boon announced his retirement from international cricket. He has served his country nobly.

Boon's successor was already on display. Ricky Ponting gave another glittering performance, hitting 71 off 94 deliveries. Steve Waugh, using a runner for the last part of his innings, moved effortlessly to his tenth Test century, being at the crease for five and a half hours and hitting 11 fours.

First Test Match – Australia v. Sri Lanka

8, 9, 10 and 11 December 1995 at WACA Ground, Perth

Sri Lanka

	First Innings		Second Innings	
R.S. Mahanama	c Warne, **b** McDermott	**15**	**b** McGrath	**48**
U.C. Hathurusinghe	c Law, **b** McGrath	**14**	c Healy, **b** McGrath	**11**
A.P. Gurusinha	**b** McGrath	**46**	c Healy, **b** McDermott	**7**
P.A. de Silva	c and **b** Warne	**10**	c Ponting, **b** Warne	**20**
A. Ranatunga (Capt)	c Healy, **b** McGrath	**32**	**b** McGrath	**46**
H.P. Tillekeratne	lbw, **b** McDermott	**6**	c Ponting, **b** Warne	**119**
*R.S. Kaluwitharana	c Taylor, **b** Warne	**50**	c Ponting, **b** Julian	**40**
H.D.P.K. Dharmasena	**b** McDermott	**30**	lbw, **b** McDermott	**18**
W.P.U.J.C. Vaas	c Healy, **b** Warne	**4**	c Healy, **b** Warne	**4**
G.P. Wickremasinghe	c Julian, **b** McGrath	**28**	c Warne, **b** McDermott	**0**
M. Muralitharan	not out	**0**	not out	**3**
	b **4**, lb **9**, nb **3**,	**16**	lb **4**, nb **10**	**14**
		251		**330**

	O	M	R	W	O	M	R	W
McDermott	18.4	5	44	**3**	20	3	73	**3**
McGrath	24	3	81	**4**	24	7	86	**3**
Julian	17	8	32	**–**	13	4	40	**1**
Warne	27	7	75	**3**	29.4	6	96	**3**
M.E. Waugh	3	1	6	**–**	4	–	22	**–**
Law					3	1	9	**–**

Fall of Wickets
1–**25**, 2–**38**, 3–**54**, 4–**129**, 5–**132**, 6–**172**, 7–**193**, 8–**205**, 9–**251**
1–**35**, 2–**56**, 3–**87**, 4–**105**, 5–**193**, 6–**258**, 7–**310**, 8–**318**, 9–**319**

Australia

	First innings	
M.J. Slater	c and **b** Muralitharan	**219**
M.A. Taylor (Capt)	lbw, **b** de Silva	**96**
D.C. Boon	c Hathurusinghe, **b** Muralitharan	**13**
M.E. Waugh	c Kaluwitharana, **b** Vaas	**111**
R.T. Ponting	lbw, **b** Vaas	**96**
S.G. Law	not out	**54**
*I.A. Healy		
S.K. Warne		
B.P. Julian		
C.J. McDermott		
G.D. McGrath		
	b **4**, lb **6**, nb **18**	**28**
	(for 5 wickets, dec.)	**617**

	O	M	R	W
Wickremasinghe	31	3	123	**–**
Vaas	31	5	103	**2**
Muralitharan	54	3	224	**2**
Hathurusinghe	9	3	31	**–**
Dharmasena	31	5	84	**–**
de Silva	18	1	42	**1**

Fall of Wickets
1–**228**, 2–**266**, 3–**422**, 4–**496**, 5–**617**

Umpires: Khizar Hayat & P.D. Parker

Australia won by an innings and 36 runs

He and Healy quickly added 93, aided by some poor fielding, with catches and stumpings missed. Taylor declared at 500, giving Australia enough time to have Mahanama caught at slip. Sri Lanka ended the day on 29 for 1.

By the end of the third day, they were 33 for 1 in their second innings. There was no immediate collapse, but wickets fell at regular intervals, and it was McGrath, with five wickets in a Test innings for the fourth time, who did most of the damage. There were dashing innings again from Kaluwitharana and Ranatunga, who injured a finger, but there remained a lack of substance.

Mahanama was out cheaply for the second time in the match, but on the fourth day, Sri Lanka showed a disciplined approach which made certain that the match would go into the fifth day. Aravinda de Silva, who did not enjoy the best of tours, batted with sense, and Hathurusinghe suggested he might provide the innings with a sound basis, but too much was left to Asanka Gurusinha. He reached the seventh Test century of his career, hitting a six and 15 fours in a stay of 353 minutes. He faced 274 balls and was fifth out at 255. His 143 was his highest Test score.

Following his dismissal, the innings faded with Warne and McGrath wreaking havoc. Sri Lanka closed on 284 for 6 but soon succumbed the next morning. Left a target of 41 runs, Australia raced to their task in 7.4 overs and took the series.

The second and third Tests were separated by a month in which the World Series was played. Arjuna Ranatunga aggravated his finger injury and missed the last Test. He was replaced by his brother Sanjeeva. Mahanama gave way to Jayasuriya, and Dharmasena and Pushpakumara came in for Muralitharan and Silva. Australia fielded the side that had won in Melbourne, and they won the toss and batted.

Arjuna Ranatunga is bowled by McGrath for 46 in the second innings of the first Test between Australia and Sri Lanka. McGrath had memorable series against both Sri Lanka and Pakistan capturing 36 wickets in six Tests. (Shaun Botterill/Allsport)

Second Test Match – Australia v. Sri Lanka

26, 27, 28, 29 and 30 December 1995 at MCG, Melbourne

Australia

	First Innings		Second Innings	
M.J. Slater	**c** Wickremasinghe, **b** Vaas	**62**	(2) not out	**13**
M.A. Taylor (Capt)	**b** Wickremasinghe	**7**	(1) not out	**25**
D.C. Boon	**c** Muralitharan, **b** Wickremasinghe	**110**		
M.E. Waugh	**b** Muralitharan	**61**		
S.R. Waugh	not out	**131**		
R.T. Ponting	**c** Gurusinha, **b** Silva	**71**		
*I.A. Healy	**c** Muralitharan, **b** de Silva	**41**		
P.R. Reiffel	not out	**4**		
S.K. Warne				
C.J. McDermott				
G.D. McGrath				
	lb **8**, w **2**, nb **3**	**13**	lb **1**, nb **2**	**3**
	(for 6 wickets, dec.)	**500**	(for no wicket)	**41**

	O	M	R	W	O	M	R	W
Wickremasinghe	30.2	9	77	**2**				
Vaas	40.4	11	93	**1**	3	–	25	**–**
Hathurusinghe	9	–	23	**–**				
Gurusinha	2	–	8	**–**	3	1	6	**–**
Muralitharan	38	7	124	**1**				
Silva	35	5	120	**1**				
de Silva	10	–	47	**1**	1	–	4	**–**
Tillekeratne					0.4	–	5	**–**

Fall of Wickets
1–**14**, 2–**116**, 3–**219**, 4–**280**, 5–**395**, 6–**488**

Sri Lanka

	First Innings		Second Innings	
R.S. Mahanama	**c** Taylor, **b** McGrath	**3**	**c** Warne, **b** Reiffel	**3**
U.C. Hathurusinghe	lbw, **b** McGrath	**23**	lbw, **b** Warne	**39**
A.P. Gurusinha	**c** Healy, **b** Ponting	**27**	lbw, **b** Reiffel	**143**
P.A. de Silva	**c** Reiffel, **b** McGrath	**18**	**c** Healy, **b** McDermott	**28**
A. Ranatunga (Capt)	**c** Warne, **b** McDermott	**51**	(7) not out	**11**
H.P. Tillekeratne	**c** Taylor, **b** Warne	**14**	**c** Ponting, **b** M.E. Waugh	**38**
*R.S. Kaluwitharana	**c** Boon, **b** McDermott	**50**	(5) **st** Healy, **b** Warne	**2**
W.P.U.J.C. Vaas	**c** Healy, **b** Reiffel	**0**	**c** Boon, **b** McGrath	**6**
G.P. Wickremasinghe	**c** Healy, **b** McGrath	**10**	**st** Healy, **b** Warne	**17**
M. Muralitharan	**c** Slater, **b** McGrath	**11**	**c** Taylor, **b** Warne	**0**
K.J. Silva	not out	**6**	**b** McGrath	**0**
	b **6**, lb **7**, nb **7**	**20**	b **7**, lb **5**, nb **8**	**20**
		233		**307**

	O	M	R	W	O	M	R	W
McDermott	23	8	63	**2**	17	1	54	**1**
McGrath	23.4	9	40	**5**	33.5	6	92	**2**
Reiffel	20	5	60	**1**	20	7	59	**2**
Ponting	4	2	8	**1**				
Warne	18	5	49	**1**	37	10	71	**4**
M.E. Waugh					9	1	19	**1**

Fall of Wickets
1–**3**, 2–**64**, 3–**68**, 4–**128**, 5–**140**, 6–**182**, 7–**183**, 8–**213**, 9–**221**
1–**11**, 2–**97**, 3–**168**, 4–**172**, 5–**255**, 6–**273**, 7–**285**, 8–**306**, 9–**306**

Umpires: R.S. Dunne & D.B. Hair

Australia won by 10 wickets

The centre of controversy – Sri Lankan off-spinner Muralitharan, no-balled for 'throwing' by umpire Hair in the second Test. (Shaun Botterill/Allsport)

The Sri Lankans were still resentful of the way in which they had been treated, and, with some justification, they were aggrieved by the standard of umpiring, which they saw as biased. They were to gain no compensation in this match, but began joyously enough when Slater was given out caught behind in the first over of the game. This brought in David Boon who received a standing ovation in his last Test. He was adjudged not out first ball although the appeal had more justification than the one that had sent Slater on his way. Taylor was caught behind on 36 and Boon played on to Pushpakumara when the score was 96. Mark Waugh was busy and purposeful until he slashed the ball into the hands of gully, and Ponting encountered Test match failure for the first time when he gave Kaluwitharana his third catch of the day. Australia were 196 for five, and Sri Lanka had the edge. From that point on, however, the game moved increasingly in favour of the home side. Steve Waugh and Healy took the score to 239 by the close, and eventually their stand became worth 130 in 161 minutes.

Reiffel made his highest Test score and helped Steve Waugh to add 117, and when Taylor finally called a halt Steve Waugh was unbeaten on 170 which had come off 316 balls in 421 minutes. The last four Australian wickets had realised 306 runs, and Steve Waugh had nursed his colleagues through this period with ruthless and calm authority as he registered his 11th Test hundred.

For once, Sri Lanka survived the last overs of the day and scored 80. The opening stand was broken early next

Third Test Match – Australia v. Sri Lanka

25, 26, 27, 28 and 29 January 1996 at Adelaide Oval

Australia

	First Innings		Second Innings	
M.A. Taylor (Capt)	c Kaluwitharana, b Vaas	21	(2) b Pushpakumara	10
M.J. Slater	c Kaluwitharana, b Vaas	0	(1) b Wickremasinghe	15
D.C. Boon	b Pushpakumara	43	c Kaluwitharana, b Vaas	35
M.E. Waugh	c Pushpakumara, b Wickremasinghe	71	c Tillekeratne, b Vaas	12
S.R. Waugh	b Pushpakumara	170	not out	61
R.T. Ponting	c Kaluwitharana, b Vaas	6	c Kaluwitharana, b Vaas	20
*I.A. Healy	c Pushpakumara, b Dharmasena	70	c Hathurusinghe, b Pushpakumara	43
P.R. Reiffel	c Gurusinha, b Wickremasinghe	56	not out	14
S.K. Warne	c Pushpakumara, b Wickremasinghe	33		
C.J. McDermott	not out	15		
G.D. McGrath				
	b 5, lb 9, w 1, nb 2	17	b 1, lb 1, nb 3	5
	(for 9 wickets, dec.)	502	(for 6 wickets, dec)	215

	O	M	R	W	O	M	R	W
Vaas	42	11	106	3	21	6	44	3
Pushpakumara	34	4	126	2	17	2	63	2
Wickremasinghe	39.3	7	120	3	13	1	39	1
Hathurusinghe	4	–	15	–				
Dharmasena	25	3	80	1	22	1	67	–
Jayasuriya	13	2	41	–				

Fall of Wickets
1–1, 2–36, 3–96, 4–181, 5–196, 6–326, 7–443, 8–467, 9–502
1–22, 2–36, 3–70, 4–75, 5–122, 6–186

Sri Lanka

	First Innings		Second Innings	
U.C. Hathurusinghe	c M.E. Waugh, b Reiffel	28	c Healy, b McGrath	14
S.T. Jayasuriya	c Healy, b Reiffel	48	c Healy, b S.R. Waugh	112
A.P. Gurusinha	c Reiffel, b McGrath	17	b Reiffel	2
S. Ranatunga	c S.R. Waugh, b McDermott	60	c Healy, b S.R. Waugh	65
*R.S. Kaluwitharana	lbw, b Reiffel	31	b S.R. Waugh	0
H.P. Tillekeratne	c Healy, b McGrath	65	c Healy b McGrath	3
P.A. de Silva (Capt)	c Taylor, b McGrath	19	c Taylor, b M.E. Waugh	3
H.P.D.K. Dharmasena	c Healy, b McGrath	0	c Taylor, b S.R. Waugh	2
W.P.U.J.C. Vaas	c M.E. Waugh, b Reiffel	8	c Healy, b McGrath	26
G.P. Wickremasinghe	b Reiffel	10	b Warne	6
K.R. Pushpakumara	not out	2	not out	3
	b 8, lb 13, w 1, nb 7	29	b 1, lb 6, nb 9	16
		317		252

	O	M	R	W	O	M	R	W
McDermott	20	5	81	1	9	3	20	–
McGrath	27	4	91	4	22.2	6	48	3
Warne	26	4	74	–	27	11	68	1
Reiffel	19.1	4	39	5	15	–	60	1
M.E. Waugh	5	2	11	–	4	1	15	1
S.R. Waugh					19	8	34	4

Fall of Wickets
1–86, 2–89, 3–129, 4–171, 5–237, 6–290, 7–290, 8–299, 9–309
1–51, 2–70, 3–195, 4–195, 5–199, 6–208, 7–216, 8–225, 9–232

Umpires: L.H. Barker & S.G. Randell

Australia won by 148 runs

Test Match Averages – Australia v. Sri Lanka

Australia Batting

	M	Inns	NO	Runs	HS	Av	100s	50s
S.R. Waugh	2	3	2	362	170*	362.00	2	1
M.J. Slater	3	5	1	309	219	77.25	1	1
P.R. Reiffel	2	3	2	74	56	74.00		1
M.E. Waugh	3	4	–	255	111	63.75	1	2
I.A. Healy	3	3	–	154	70	51.33		1
D.C. Boon	3	4	–	201	110	50.25	1	
R.T. Ponting	3	4	–	193	96	48.25		2
M.A. Taylor	3	5	1	159	96	39.75		1

Played in three Tests: S.K. Warne 33; C.J. McDermott 15*; G.D. McGrath did not bat
Played in one Test: S.G. Law 54*; B.P. Julian did not bat

Sri Lanka Batting

	M	Inns	NO	Runs	HS	Av	100s	50s
A. Ranatunga	2	4	1	140	51	46.66		2
H.P. Tillekeratne	3	6	–	245	119	40.83	1	1
A.P. Gurusinha	3	6	–	242	143	40.33	1	
R.S. Kaluwitharana	3	6	–	173	50	28.33		2
U.C. Hathurusinghe	3	6	–	129	39	21.50		
R.S. Mahanama	2	4	–	69	48	17.25		
P.A. de Silva	3	6	–	98	28	16.33		
H.D.P.K. Dharmasena	2	4	–	50	30	12.50		
G.P. Wickremasinghe	3	6	–	71	28	11.83		
W.P.U.J.C. Vaas	3	6	–	48	26	8.00		
M. Muralitharan	2	4	2	14	11	7.00		

Played in one Test: S.T. Jayasuriya 112 & 48; S. Ranatunga 60 & 65; K.J. Silva 6* & 0; K.R. Pushpakumara 2* & 3*

Australia Bowling

	Overs	Mds	Runs	Wks	Av	Best	10/m	5/inn
G.D. McGrath	154.5	35	438	21	20.85	5/40		1
P.R. Reiffel	74.1	16	218	9	24.22	5/39		1
C.J. McDermott	107.4	25	335	10	33.50	3/44		
S.K. Warne	164.4	43	433	12	36.08	4/71		
M.E. Waugh	25	5	73	2	36.50	1/15		
B.P. Julian	30	12	72	1	72.00	1/40		

Bowled in one innings: R.T. Ponting 4–2–8–1; S.R. Waugh 19–8–34–4; S.G. Law 3–1–9–0

Sri Lanka Bowling

	Overs	Mds	Runs	Wks	Av	Best	10/m	5/inn
W.P.U.J.C. Vaas	137.4	33	371	9	41.22	3/44		
P.A. de Silva	29	1	93	2	46.50	1/42		
K.R. Pushpakumara	51	6	189	4	47.25	2/63		
G.P. Wickremasinghe	113.5	20	359	6	59.83	3/120		
M. Muralitharan	92	10	348	3	116.00	2/224		
H.D.P.K. Dharmasena	78	9	231	1	231.00	1/80		
A.P. Gurusinha	5	1	14	–	–			
U.C. Hathurusinghe	22	3	69	–	–			

Bowled in one innings: K.J. Silva 35–5–120–1; H.P. Tillekeratne 0.4–0–5–0; S.T. Jayasuriya 13–2–41–0

Australia Fielding Figures

19 – I.A. Healy (ct 17 / st 2); 7 – M.A. Taylor; 5 – S.K. Warne; 4 – R.T. Ponting; 2 – P.R. Reiffel, M.E. Waugh and D.C Boon; 1 – S.R. Waugh, M.J. Slater, S.G. Law and B.P. Julian

Sri Lanka Fielding Figures

6 – R.S. Kaluwitharana; 3 – M. Muralitharan and K.R. Pushpakumara; 2 – A.P. Gurusinha and U.C. Hathurusinghe; 1 – H.P. Tillekeratne and G.P. Wickremasinghe

morning, but the 86 runs had come in 82 minutes with Jayasuriya indicating the shape of things to come with 48 off 57 balls. He hit a six and seven fours. Unfortunately, he and Hathurusinghe fell to Reiffel within three runs of each other, and the impetus of the innings was lost. Sanjeeva Ranatunga, newly arrived to bolster the party, batted 203 minutes for his 60, and Tillekeratne batted four minutes longer for his 65. Kaluwitharana played with his usual hurry – his innings included a six and four fours – but Sri Lanka saved the follow-on with two wickets standing. There was another impressive bowling performance by McGrath, but the major honours went to Reiffel who captured five wickets in a Test innings for the third time.

Australia ended the third day on 16 without loss, but the Sri Lankan pace bowlers struck back on the fourth morning. Taylor was bowled by Pushpakumara, and Slater fell to Wickremasinghe. The New South Wales' right-hander had finished the season poorly after some glorious displays earlier. Mark Waugh, too, had an unaccustomed failure, and when Boon, who hit five fours in his 66-ball farewell to Test cricket, was caught behind for an aggressive 35, Australia were 75 for 4. Steve Waugh again came to the rescue, and he was given admirable support by Ian Healy who ran and scampered as quickly as ever. Taylor declared, and Sri Lanka had seven hours in which to score 412 to win.

Jayasuriya went off in whirlwind fashion, but he lost Hathurusinghe on 51. Eighteen more runs came before the close, and there were no further mishaps, but Gurusinha was out first thing on the last morning. Sanjeeva Ranatunga and Jayasuriya gave Sri Lanka renewed hope with a partnership of 125. McDermott was palpably unfit and bowled only nine overs, while Warne was tamed. In desperation, or with genius, Taylor turned to Steve Waugh who had bowled little in the season. Taylor's move brought instant reward, for Steve Waugh had Jayasuriya caught behind after making a memorable maiden Test hundred. The young left-hander had bristled with positive intent and hit two sixes and 14 fours in his 188-ball innings. In this match, and on this tour, he had announced his arrival at international level. Here is a shining star, one who, hopefully, will lighten the gloom and dazzle the eyes for many seasons to come.

Steve Waugh bowled Kaluwitharana second ball, heralding a collapse as the last eight wickets fell for 57 runs to leave Australia clear winners. For Sri Lanka, this was a bitter disappointment. They had hoped for more after their successes in Pakistan and Sharjah, but even though they were beaten three – nil and suffered unhappy decisions and allegations, there was more than promise in their performance. There were signs that they had nearly come of age.

West Indies Tour

7, 8, 9 and 10 December 1995
at Newcastle
West Indians 246 (C.L. Hooper 63, S.L. Campbell 53, D.A. Freedman 8 for 49) and 160 (G.R.J. Matthews 5 for 43)
New South Wales 308 (R. Chee Quee 105, K.J. Roberts 86, C.A. Walsh 4 for 61) and 69 for 2
Match drawn

In preparation for the World Series, West Indies played two first-class matches and four one-day games. They arrived in some disarray. Lara had declined to play in the tournament, and the Benjamins were not considered for disciplinary reasons. There was a sense of unease about the Caribbean contingent, and it was apparent that the underlying divisions within the party and the criticisms regarding leadership still existed. The West Indians were fortunate to avoid defeat in their first match. Needing 90 to win, New South Wales were 69 for 2 when a thunderstorm ended the game. Two days earlier, the match against The Prime Minister's XI at Manuka Oval had been abandoned without a ball being bowled because of a downpour.

The match at Newcastle was a triumph for the New South Wales' slow left-arm bowler David Freedman who took a career-best 8 for 49.

12 December 1995
at Dalton Park, Woollongong
West Indians 92
Australian Cricket Academy 96 for 2
Australian Cricket Academy won by 8 wickets

22, 23 and 24 December 1995
at Woolloongabba, Brisbane
Australian XI 323 for 7 dec. (G.S. Blewett 115, M.T.G. Elliott 76) and 17 for 0
West Indians 325 (G.S. Blewett 4 for 59)
Match drawn

The West Indians suffered the same fate that England had suffered a year earlier when they were humiliated by the Academy side. Rain ruined the match in Brisbane, but Grey Blewett and Matthew Elliott gave the Australian selectors timely reminders.

26 December 1995
at Woolloongabba, Brisbane
West Indians 206 for 8
Queensland 207 for 6 (S.G. Law 70)
Queensland won by 4 wickets

29 December 1995
at Toowoomba
Queensland 237 for 8 (T.J. Dixon 51, C.L. Hooper 4 for 28)
West Indians 241 for 3 (P.V. Simmons 91, R.B. Richardson 75 not out)
West Indians won by 7 wickets

10 January 1996
at SCG, Sydney
West Indians 243 for 5 (R.I.C. Holder 80 not out, S.C. Williams 57)
Australia 'A' 245 for 4 (G.S. Blewett 85, S.R. Waugh 56)
Australia 'A' won by 6 wickets

Victory over a Queensland XI, which contained four players with no first-class experience, was all the West Indians had to show from their warm-up matches. In Sydney, Australia 'A' reached a target of 244 with more than nine overs to spare.

David Freedman took a career-best 8 for 49 for New South Wales against the West Indian tourists.
(Stephen Laffer/Sportsline)

Benson and Hedges World Series

Sri Lanka's success in the limited over game continues as Lara-less West Indies show further signs of decline. Australia remain on top of the world – for the time being.

One does not have to be a cricket expert to understand that West Indies were invited to play in the World Series in the expectation that they would reach the final where they would meet Australia. Sri Lanka were looked upon as a side to make the numbers up. They had other ideas from the outset. In the opening match, they bowled and fielded well, survived the early loss of Mahanama, a loss which once would have undermined them totally, and romped to victory over West Indies with five overs to spare. Not least among their qualities was Arjuna Ranatunga's shrewd captaincy.

Two days later, West Indies met Australia at Adelaide Oval and suffered another humiliation. A typically pugnacious and consistent Australian batting performance brought 242 runs in a match which had been reduced to 47 overs by rain. This set West Indies a daunting target that became out of their reach by the ninth over, by which time they were 17 for 4. Chanderpaul, Adams and Harper strove manfully, but resuscitation was impossible, and West Indies could manage only half Australia's total.

Australia inflicted another defeat on West Indies when the teams moved to Melbourne. Australia, who brought in Kasprowicz for his first international, began uncertainly and were 46 for 3 before Taylor and Law added 118. Law was particularly commanding and fluent, hitting 74 off 86 balls, but it was Bevan who destroyed the West Indian attack with a violent 44 off 41 deliveries. He and Healy added a match-winning 68. West Indies moved smoothly to 84 for 1 in 21 overs, but thereafter they lost their way. Bevan's left-arm spin brought him the wickets of Chanderpaul and Hooper, and when Warne had the dangerous Hooper stumped West Indies were doomed.

Australia maintained their one hundred per cent record when they beat Sri Lanka in Sydney, but they had to break a record to win, and they found Sri Lanka stiffer opponents than West Indies. Again Sri Lanka showed growing maturity when they refused to be upset by the early loss of a wicket. Aravinda de Silva found his touch with 75 from 94 balls while earlier Jayasuriya had set the pattern with 24 off 26 balls, including 14 off one Kasprowicz over. Undeterred by a fall of wickets, Tillekeratne hit 62 from 67 balls. The Sri Lankans were over-enthusiastic in their running between the wickets: four men were run out, and twice they were penalised for running short. No side had reached a target as high as 256 in a limited-over international at Sydney, but Taylor gave his side a sparkling example with 90 off 115 balls, and Mark Waugh and Ponting maintained the run rate. The game reached a dramatic climax when Bevan hit the fourth ball of the final over to the boundary to clinch victory.

Following a break for the second Test against Sri Lanka, Australia returned to the fray, and once again Bevan

Benson and Hedges World Series – Match One – Sri Lanka v. West Indies

15 December 1995 at Adelaide Oval

West Indies

P.V. Simmons	c Mahanama, b Ranatunga	18
R.B. Richardson (Capt)	c Kaluwitharana, b Ranatunga	5
S.L. Campbell	lbw, b Muralitharan	47
S. Chanderpaul	run out	1
C.L. Hooper	c Tillekeratne, b Muralitharan	23
J.C. Adams	c Muralitharan, b Dharmasena	11
R.A. Harper	c Jayasuriya, b Vaas	23
*C.O. Browne	run out	6
I.R. Bishop	not out	8
C.E.L. Ambrose	not out	0
C.A. Walsh		
	lb 10, w 6, nb 2	18
	50 overs (for 8 wickets)	160

	O	M	R	W
Wickremasinghe	7	–	22	–
Vaas	7	1	17	1
Gurusinha	8	–	25	–
Ranatunga	10	1	24	2
Muralitharan	10	–	35	2
Dharmasena	8	–	27	1

Fall of Wickets
1–40, 2–50, 3–56, 4–101, 5–122, 6–122, 7–136, 8–160

Sri Lanka

R.S. Mahanama	c Campbell, b Ambrose	0
S.T. Jayasuriya	c Bishop, b Walsh	28
A.P. Gurusinha	b Bishop	15
P.A. de Silva	c Browne, b Hooper	46
A. Ranatunga (Capt)	c Campbell, b Bishop	27
H.P. Tillekeratne	not out	17
*R.S. Kaluwitharana	c Browne, b Bishop	8
H.D.P.K. Dharmasena	not out	5
W.P.U.J.C. Vaas		
G.P. Wickremasinghe		
M. Muralitharan		
	b 1, lb 5, w 2, nb 7	15
	45 overs (for 6 wickets)	161

	O	M	R	W
Ambrose	7	–	29	1
Walsh	10	5	23	1
Bishop	10	1	38	3
Simmons	3	–	17	–
Harper	5	–	25	–
Hooper	10	1	23	1

Fall of Wickets
1–0, 2–24, 3–54, 4–113, 5–130, 6–152

Umpires: T.A. Prue & D.J. Harper *Man of the Match:* A. Ranatunga

Sri Lanka won by 4 wickets

Benson and Hedges World Series – Match Two – Australia v. West Indies

17 December 1995 at Adelaide Oval

Australia

M.A. Taylor (Capt)	**b** Harper	**47**
M.J. Slater	**b** Bishop	**32**
M.E. Waugh	**c** Hooper, **b** Harper	**53**
R.T. Ponting	**st** Browne, **b** Harper	**11**
S.G. Law	**c** Hooper, **b** Harper	**13**
M.G. Bevan	not out	**32**
S. Lee	**st** Browne, **b** Hooper	**39**
*I.A. Healy	not out	**0**
S.K. Warne		
C.J. McDermott		
G.D. McGrath		
	b **1**, lb **7**, w **7**	**15**
	47 overs (for 6 wickets)	**242**

	O	M	R	W
Ambrose	9	–	43	**–**
Walsh	10	1	46	**–**
Bishop	8	–	33	**1**
Simmons	2	–	17	**–**
Hooper	8	–	49	**1**
Harper	10	–	46	**4**

Fall of Wickets
1–**60**, 2–**108**, 3–**142**, 4–**166**, 5–**169**, 6–**232**

West Indies

P.V. Simmons	**c** M.E. Waugh, **b** McGrath	**7**
S.L. Campbell	run out	**4**
R.B. Richardson	**c** Healy, **b** McDermott	**4**
C.L. Hooper	lbw, **b** McDermott	**0**
S. Chanderpaul	**c** Taylor, **b** M.E. Waugh	**39**
J.C. Adams	**c** Law, **b** Lee	**20**
R.A. Harper	not out	**31**
*C.O. Browne	not out	**11**
I.R. Bishop		
C.E.L. Ambrose		
C.A. Walsh		
	lb **2**, w **3**	**5**
	47 overs (for 6 wickets)	**121**

	O	M	R	W
McDermott	7	2	8	**2**
McGrath	5	1	13	**1**
Law	7	1	23	**–**
Lee	7	–	20	**1**
M.E. Waugh	10	–	26	**1**
Warne	7	1	22	**–**
Bevan	3	–	7	**–**
Slater	1	1	0	**–**

Fall of Wickets
1–**8**, 2–**16**, 3–**16**, 4–**17**, 5–**54**, 6–**97**

Umpires: T.A. Prue & A.J. McQuillan *Man of the Match:* M.E. Waugh

Australia won by 121 runs

Benson and Hedges World Series – Match Three – Australia v. West Indies

19 December 1995 at MCG, Melbourne

Australia

M.J. Slater	**c** Richardson, **b** Ambrose	**2**
M.A. Taylor (Capt)	**c** Hooper, **b** Simmons	**63**
M.E. Waugh	run out	**15**
R.T. Ponting	**c** Browne, **b** Walsh	**6**
S.G. Law	**c** Browne, **b** Hooper	**74**
M.G. Bevan	not out	**44**
S. Lee	**c** Chanderpaul, **b** Ambrose	**3**
*I.A. Healy	not out	**34**
S.K. Warne		
C.J. McDermott		
M.S. Kasprowicz		
	lb **4**, w **2**, nb **2**	**8**
	50 overs (for 6 wickets)	**249**

	O	M	R	W
Ambrose	10	1	36	**2**
Walsh	9	–	32	**1**
Cummins	6	–	40	**–**
Harper	10	1	46	**–**
Hooper	9	–	60	**1**
Simmons	6	–	31	**1**

Fall of Wickets
1–**6**, 2–**39**, 3–**46**, 4–**164**, 5–**172**, 6–**181**

West Indies

S.C. Williams	lbw, **b** Lee	**44**
S.L. Campbell	**c** Ponting, **b** Kasprowicz	**2**
S. Chanderpaul	**c** and **b** Bevan	**73**
P.V. Simmons	**c** McDermott, **b** M.E. Waugh	**24**
C.L. Hooper	**c** Healy, **b** Bevan	**10**
R.B. Richardson (Capt)	**c** Law, **b** McDermott	**15**
R.A. Harper	**st** Healy, **b** Warne	**15**
A.C. Cummins	not out	**26**
*C.O. Browne	run out	**2**
C.E.L. Ambrose	**b** McDermott	**1**
C.A. Walsh	**c** Healy, **b** Warne	**1**
	lb **9**, w **1**, nb **2**	**12**
	49.1 overs	**225**

	O	M	R	W
McDermott	10	–	40	**2**
Kasprowicz	6	–	32	**1**
Lee	10	1	40	**1**
Warne	9.1	1	41	**2**
M.E. Waugh	6	–	32	**1**
Bevan	8	–	31	**2**

Fall of Wickets
1–**5**, 2–**84**, 3–**125**, 4–**147**, 5–**166**, 6–**177**, 7–**209**, 8–**213**, 9–**224**

Umpires: S.G. Randell & P.D. Parker *Man of the Match:* M.G. Bevan

Australia won by 24 runs

Benson and Hedges World Series – Match Four – Australia *v.* Sri Lanka

21 December 1995 at SCG, Sydney

Sri Lanka

R.S. Mahanama	run out	5
S.T. Jayasuriya	c Healy, b McGrath	24
A.P. Gurusinha	c M.E. Waugh, b Bevan	38
P.A. de Silva	c and b Lee	75
A. Ranatunga (Capt)	run out	7
H.P. Tillekeratne	c Lee, b McGrath	62
*R.S. Kaluwitharana	b Kasprowicz	0
H.D.P.K. Dharmasena	run out	7
W.P.U.J.C. Vaas	run out	14
G.P. Wickremasinghe	not out	4
M. Muralitharan	not out	0
	b 2, lb 11, w 5, nb 1	19
	50 overs (for 9 wickets)	255

	O	M	R	W
McGrath	10	1	47	2
Kasprowicz	10	–	51	1
Lee	10	–	40	1
Warne	10	1	53	–
M.E. Waugh	6	–	31	–
Bevan	4	–	20	1

Fall of Wickets
1–7, 2–32, 3–111, 4–134, 5–173, 6–175, 7–203, 8–239, 9–253

Australia

M.A. Taylor (Capt)	run out	90
M.J. Slater	c Kaluwitharana, b Vaas	10
M.E. Waugh	run out	55
R.T. Ponting	c Muralitharan, b Dharmasena	56
S.G. Law	run out	7
M.G. Bevan	not out	18
S. Lee	not out	4
*I.A. Healy		
S.K. Warne		
M.S. Kasprowicz		
G.D. McGrath		
	lb 13, w 4	17
	49.4 overs (for 5 wickets)	257

	O	M	R	W
Wickremasinghe	7	–	24	–
Vaas	9	–	50	1
Gurusinha	2	–	12	–
Ranatunga	1	–	12	–
Muralitharan	10	–	52	–
Dharmasena	8.4	–	41	1
Jayasuriya	8	–	35	–
de Silva	4	–	18	–

Fall of Wickets
1–23, 2–131, 3–192, 4–212, 5–239

Umpires: D.B. Hair & D.J. Harper *Man of the Match:* M.A. Taylor

Australia won by 5 wickets

Benson and Hedges World Series – Match Five – Australia *v.* West Indies

1 January 1996 at SCG, Sydney

West Indies

S.C. Williams	c Healy, b Reiffel	5
S.L. Campbell	lbw, b Warne	15
P.V. Simmons	c Warne, b Reiffel	4
S. Chanderpaul	c Taylor, b Reiffel	3
C.L. Hooper	not out	93
J.C. Adams	c M.E. Waugh, b Warne	0
R.A. Harper	run out	28
O.D. Gibson	b McGrath	4
*C.O. Browne	c Warne, b Reiffel	2
C.E.L. Ambrose	b Warne	0
C.A. Walsh (Capt)	not out	3
	lb 6, w 7, nb 2	15
	43 overs (for 9 wickets)	172

	O	M	R	W
McGrath	9	2	22	1
Reiffel	9	2	29	4
Law	6	–	34	–
Lee	6	–	20	–
Warne	9	2	30	3
Bevan	4	–	31	–

Fall of Wickets
1–13, 2–21, 3–28, 4–54, 5–54, 6–135, 7–150, 8–164, 9–168

Australia

M.J. Slater	c Simmons, b Ambrose	5
M.A. Taylor (Capt)	run out	1
M.E. Waugh	c Harper, b Gibson	16
R.T. Ponting	b Ambrose	0
S.G. Law	c Browne, b Ambrose	10
M.G. Bevan	not out	78
S. Lee	c Browne, b Gibson	0
*I.A. Healy	b Harper	16
P.R. Reiffel	c Hooper, b Simmons	34
S.K. Warne	run out	3
G.D. McGrath	not out	1
	lb 2, w 3, nb 4	9
	43 overs (for 9 wickets)	173

	O	M	R	W
Ambrose	9	3	20	3
Walsh	9	2	22	–
Gibson	9	2	40	2
Harper	8	–	38	1
Simmons	5	–	31	1
Hooper	3	–	20	–

Fall of Wickets
1–4, 2–15, 3–15, 4–32, 5–38, 6–38, 7–74, 8–157, 9–167

Umpires: P.D. Parker & A.J. McQuillan *Man of the Match:* M.G. Bevan

Australia won by 1 wicket

provided the dramatic climax to a day-night match reduced to 43 overs by rain. He struck the last ball of the contest, bowled by Roger Harper, for four to give Australia their fourth win in as many matches. This was the sixth boundary of Bevan's 89-ball innings, and he and Reiffel had brought Australia from the jaws of defeat with an eighth wicket stand of 83. At one time, Australia had been 38 for 6. Credit must go to McGrath who scampered the single which gave Bevan the strike for the last two balls of the match. West Indies, too, had their rescuer. They were 54 for 5 before Carl Hooper hit 93 off 99 balls.

West Indies gained their first victory in the competition when Sri Lanka surrendered with remarkable ease in Hobart. Muralitharan bowled for the first time since the second Test match in which he had been no-balled by umpire Hair. He was closely scrutinised by umpires Davis and Prue who saw nothing illegal in his action. West Indies, propped up by Chanderpaul's 77, were bowled out for 194, but Sri Lanka batted dreadfully in reply. Gibson took five wickets, and Sri Lanka lost with 12.2 overs of their quota unused.

Sri Lanka gave an even worse performance three days later when they were routed by West Indies who won by seven wickets with 23.5 overs to spare. Still smarting from the Muralitharan incident in the second Test, Sri Lankan officials engaged in lengthy discussions with ICC and decided to call up Kalpage as cover for the off-spinner. Muralitharan did not play in the third Test, nor did he appear again in the World Series. He was to return with a vengeance in the World Cup.

West Indies made it three wins in a row when they beat Australia in the eighth match of the series. Richie Richardson showed a return to form with his first fifty in seven World Series innings, and Ottis Gibson revived West Indies' chances when he hit two sixes and four fours in his 52 off 40 balls. Gibson's knock highlighted an undisciplined approach by some of the top order batsmen. Australia began badly, but Ponting and Law added 115 before Ponting fell to a rash pull shot and Law to a brilliant caught and bowled by Simmons. Australia still seemed most likely to win when they reached 216 for 7, but Reiffel was run out, and Gibson dismissed Healy and McDermott with successive deliveries.

Michael Slater's sixth failure in the series – he was caught behind for two – was to cost him his place in the team for the rest of the tournament, and, as it proved, in the World Cup eleven itself. Against Sri Lanka, at Melbourne, Australia descended to 54 for 4 before Bevan joined Ponting in a stand of 159, a fifth wicket record for all limited-over international cricket. Ponting reached his first hundred for Australia. His delightful 123 came off 142 balls. Sri Lanka changed their batting order with Kaluwitharana opening alongside Jayasuriya. This was a move that was to have profound significance in the coming weeks, and Kaluwitharana justified his promotion with a blistering 77 off 79 deliveries. This belligerence allowed the more contemplative Mahanama to steer Sri Lanka to the point of victory, which came with 15 balls to spare.

Australia had their revenge in the tenth match of the series three days later when they scored a resounding victory by 83 runs. Mark Waugh, who opened the innings in place of Slater, made his highest score in a one-day international, 130. He dominated an opening stand of 189, an Australian record, with Mark Taylor. The runs came off 216 balls. The partnership put Australia in a very strong position; in spite of a brisk opening stand between Jayasuriya and Kaluwitharana, Sri Lanka's response was weak. Vitally, they lost de Silva for nought as three wickets went down on 56. Gurusinha was reprimanded following an exchange of words with Steve Waugh who had just delivered a wide.

Sri Lanka showed their new found iron and determination in beating West Indies in the penultimate game of the qualifying competition. Their 202 hardly seemed adequate, but they bowled tidily and fielded tigerishly to thwart West Indies who batted poorly. Sri Lanka had filed an official request that the controversial umpire Darrell Hair should not stand again in the series. He did, in fact, stand in the last qualifying match and in the first final, and the rejection of Sri Lanka's request, and the manner in which it was rejected, did little to ease the tension between the tourists and their hosts.

Sri Lanka shattered preconceived ideas by beating Australia in the last match of the qualifying tournament and so qualified for a place in the final ahead of West Indies. Australia had seemed well on top when Steve Waugh made his first century in his 187th one-day international. His 102 not out came off 116 balls, and he shared a stand of 102 with Law and an unbroken partnership of 86 with Bevan. Australia had been 54 for 3 in the 17th over, but Steve Waugh's effort took them to 242, a total which looked large enough to win the game.

Romesh Kaluwitharana of Sri Lanka was named as the outstanding player of the preliminary matches in the Benson and Hedges World Series.
(Chris Cole/Allsport)

Benson and Hedges World Series – Match Six – Sri Lanka *v.* West Indies

3 January 1996 at Bellerive Oval, Hobart

West Indies

P.V. Simmons	c Kaluwitharana, b Vaas	0
S.L. Campbell	c Kaluwitharana, b Hathurusinghe	38
S. Chanderpaul	c Vaas, b Muralitharan	77
R.B. Richardson (Capt)	c Gurusinha, b Dharmasena	18
C.L. Hooper	c de Silva, b Vaas	36
R.A. Harper	b Muralitharan	1
O.D. Gibson	c de Silva, b Hathurusinghe	6
*C.O. Browne	not out	4
I.R. Bishop	run out	3
C.E.L. Ambrose	c Tillekeratne, b Vaas	0
C.A. Walsh	b Munasinghe	1
	lb 3, w 7	10
	48.2 overs	194

	O	M	R	W
Vaas	9	2	21	3
Munasinghe	8.2	1	21	1
Hathurusinghe	10	1	50	2
Gurusinha	3	–	14	–
Muralitharan	10	–	46	2
Dharmasena	6	–	30	1
Jayasuriya	2	–	9	–

Fall of Wickets
1–**0**, 2–**83**, 3–**125**, 4–**161**, 5–**168**, 6–**179**, 7–**187**, 8–**193**, 9–**193**

Sri Lanka

R.S. Mahanama	c Campbell, b Gibson	10
S.T. Jayasuriya	c Ambrose, b Walsh	3
A.P. Gurusinha	run out	48
P. A. de Silva (Capt)	c Campbell, b Gibson	6
H.P. Tillekeratne	c Browne, b Gibson	5
*R.S. Kaluwitharana	run out	8
U.C. Hathurusinghe	c Richardson, b Bishop	3
H.D.P.K. Dharmasena	c Browne, b Gibson	12
W.P.U.J.C. Vaas	c Campbell, b Harper	10
M. Munasinghe	c Simmons, b Gibson	0
M. Muralitharan	not out	2
	lb 2, w 5, nb 10	17
	37.4 overs	124

	O	M	R	W
Ambrose	6	–	13	–
Walsh	8	1	22	1
Bishop	8	1	28	1
Gibson	8.4	–	42	5
Harper	7	–	17	1

Fall of Wickets
1–**4**, 2–**39**, 3–**47**, 4–**74**, 5–**89**, 6–**94**, 7–**100**, 8–**121**, 9–**121**

Umpires: S.J. Davis & T.A. Prue *Man of the Match:* S. Chanderpaul

West Indies won by 70 runs

Benson and Hedges World Series – Match Seven – Sri Lanka *v.* West Indies

5 January 1996 at Woolloongabba, Brisbane

Sri Lanka

U.C. Hathurusinghe	c Browne, b Ambrose	0
S.T. Jayasuriya	c Browne, b Walsh	3
A.P. Gurusinha	c Hooper, b Ambrose	3
P.A. de Silva (Capt)	c Gibson, b Bishop	10
R.S. Mahanama	c Browne, b Ambrose	0
H.P. Tillekeratne	not out	37
*R.S. Kaluwitharana	run out	0
W.P.U.J.C. Vaas	c Browne, b Gibson	14
M. Munasinghe	c Browne, b Simmons	8
G.P. Wickremasinghe	c Harper, b Walsh	2
M. Muralitharan	b Gibson	0
	lb 2, w 18, nb 5	25
	45.2 overs	102

	O	M	R	W
Ambrose	10	3	20	3
Walsh	9	2	19	2
Gibson	8.2	2	15	2
Bishop	7	1	18	1
Simmons	9	2	19	1
Harper	2	–	9	–

Fall of Wickets
1–**0**, 2–**12**, 3–**17**, 4–**19**, 5–**33**, 6–**34**, 7–**77**, 8–**95**, 9–**98**

West Indies

P.V. Simmons	lbw, b Vaas	6
S.L. Campbell	c Muralitharan, b Vaas	34
S. Chanderpaul	run out	10
R.B. Richardson (Capt)	not out	19
C.L. Hooper	not out	18
R.A. Harper		
O.D. Gibson		
*C.O. Browne		
C.E.L. Ambrose		
I.R. Bishop		
C.A. Walsh		
	lb 2, w 8, nb 7	17
	26.1 overs (for 3 wickets)	104

	O	R	M	W
Vaas	10	2	24	2
Munasinghe	7	1	34	–
Wickremasinghe	6	–	24	–
Muralitharan	3	–	16	–
Tillekeratne	0.1	–	4	–

Fall of Wickets
1–**6**, 2–**46**, 3–**68**

Umpires: A.J. McQuillan & R. Emerson *Man of the Match:* C.E.L. Ambrose

West Indies won by 7 wickets

Benson and Hedges World Series – Match Eight – Australia v. West Indies

7 January 1996 at Woolloongabba, Brisbane

West Indies

S.C. Williams	c Healy, b McGrath	0
S.L. Campbell	b McGrath	5
P.V. Simmons	c Lee, b M.E. Waugh	42
R.B. Richardson (Capt)	c Bevan, b Law	81
C.L. Hooper	c Slater, b Reiffel	18
R.A. Harper	b M.E. Waugh	10
*C.O. Browne	run out	1
O.D. Gibson	b Lee	52
I.R. Bishop	run out	5
C.E.L. Ambrose	not out	3
C.A. Walsh	b McGrath	0
	lb 3, w 6, nb 5	14
	49.3 overs	231

	O	M	R	W
McGrath	9.3	1	47	3
Reiffel	7	1	50	1
McDermott	8	–	43	–
M.E. Waugh	10	–	30	2
Bevan	3	–	16	–
Lee	8	1	30	1
Law	4	1	12	1

Fall of Wickets
1–2, 2–27, 3–103, 4–133, 5–167, 6–169, 7–173, 8–220, 9–230

Australia

M.A. Taylor (Capt)	c Browne, b Bishop	14
M.J. Slater	c Campbell, b Ambrose	0
M.E. Waugh	c Browne, b Walsh	5
R.T. Ponting	c Harper, b Bishop	61
S.G. Law	c and b Simmons	62
M.G. Bevan	run out	17
S. Lee	c Simmons, b Walsh	6
*I.A. Healy	c Walsh, b Gibson	15
P.R. Reiffel	run out	14
C.J. McDermott	b Gibson	1
G.D. McGrath	not out	0
	lb 6, w 7, nb 9	22
	47.4 overs	217

	O	M	R	W
Ambrose	9	2	20	1
Walsh	9	–	56	2
Bishop	10	–	49	2
Gibson	5.4	–	38	2
Harper	4	1	9	–
Simmons	10	–	39	1

Fall of Wickets
1–1, 2–10, 3–27, 4–142, 5–179, 6–180, 7–187, 8–216, 9–217

Umpires: D.B. Hair & P.D. Parker *Man of the Match:* O.D. Gibson

West Indies won by 14 runs

Benson and Hedges World Series – Match Nine – Australia v. Sri Lanka

9 January 1996 at MCG, Melbourne

Australia

M.J. Slater	c Kaluwitharana, b Munasinghe	2
M.A. Taylor (Capt)	c Kaluwitharana, b Munasinghe	9
M.E. Waugh	b Munasinghe	0
R.T. Ponting	run out	123
S.G. Law	c Tillekeratne, b Wickremasinghe	8
M.G. Bevan	not out	65
S. Lee		
*I.A. Healy		
P.R. Reiffel		
S.K. Warne		
C.J. McDermott		
	lb 2, w 2, nb 2	6
	50 overs (for 5 wickets)	213

	O	M	R	W
Vaas	10	3	41	–
Munasinghe	10	1	30	3
Wickremasinghe	6	–	29	1
Dharmasena	10	–	31	–
Jayasuriya	10	–	56	–
Kalpage	4	–	24	–

Fall of Wickets
1–8, 2–10, 3–33, 4–54, 5–213

Sri Lanka

S.T. Jayasuriya	c Lee, b Reiffel	8
*R.S. Kaluwitharana	run out	77
A.P. Gurusinha	run out	0
P.A. de Silva (Capt)	lbw, b McDermott	35
R.S. Mahanama	lbw, b Bevan	51
H.P. Tillekeratne	lbw, b McDermott	0
R.S. Kalpage	b Warne	1
H.D.P.K. Dharmasena	not out	28
W.P.U.J.C. Vaas	not out	0
M. Munasinghe		
G.P. Wickremasinghe		
	lb 7, w 5, nb 2	14
	47.3 overs (for 7 wickets)	214

	O	M	R	W
McDermott	10	–	42	2
Reiffel	10	–	47	1
Lee	6	2	26	–
Warne	10	1	37	1
M.E. Waugh	6	–	31	–
Bevan	5.3	–	24	1

Fall of Wickets
1–17, 2–39, 3–127, 4–144, 5–144, 6–147, 7–209

Umpires: D.B. Hair & P.D. Parker *Man of the Match:* R.S. Kaluwitharana

Sri Lanka won by 3 wickets

Benson and Hedges World Series – Match Ten – Australia v. Sri Lanka

12 January 1996 at WACA Ground, Perth

Australia

M.A. Taylor (Capt)	c sub (Muralitharan), b Jayasuriya	85
M.E. Waugh	run out	130
R.T. Ponting	b Jayasuriya	11
S.R. Waugh	b Vaas	11
S.G. Law	run out	9
M.G. Bevan	not out	1
*I.A. Healy	c Jayasuriya, b Vaas	0
S.K. Warne		
P.R. Reiffel		
C.J. McDermott		
G.D. McGrath		
	lb 8, w 9, nb 2	19
	50 overs (for 6 wickets)	266

	O	M	R	W
Vaas	10	1	33	2
Pushpakumara	8	–	41	–
Wickremasinghe	9	–	60	–
Dharmasena	10	–	51	–
de Silva	1	–	7	–
Kalpage	2	–	18	–
Jayasuriya	10	–	48	2

Fall of Wickets
1–189, 2–209, 3–251, 4–258, 5–266, 6–266

Sri Lanka

*R.S. Kaluwitharana	c Ponting, b McGrath	20
S.T. Jayasuriya	c Healy, b Law	27
A.P. Gurusinha	b McDermott	45
P.A. de Silva (Capt)	lbw, b Law	0
R.S. Mahanama	c Healy, b Reiffel	3
H.P. Tillekeratne	not out	58
R.S. Kalpage	c Bevan, b McDermott	1
H.D.P.K. Dharmasena	run out	2
W.P.U.J.C. Vaas	st Healy, b Warne	10
G.P. Wickremasinghe	run out	2
K.R. Pushpakumara	not out	1
	lb 8, w 5, nb 1	14
	50 overs (for 9 wickets)	183

	O	M	R	W
McDermott	10	–	39	2
McGrath	8	1	22	1
Law	10	–	30	2
Reiffel	9	2	25	1
Warne	10	–	45	1
S.R. Waugh	3	–	14	–

Fall of Wickets
1–56, 2–56, 3–56, 4–67, 5–138, 6–142, 7–151, 8–172, 9–175

Umpires: D.B. Hair & P.D. Parker *Man of the Match:* M.E. Waugh

Australia won by 83 runs

Benson and Hedges World Series – Match Eleven – Sri Lanka v. West Indies

14 January 1996 at WACA Ground, Perth

Sri Lanka

S.T. Jayasuriya	lbw, b Gibson	28
*R.S. Kaluwitharana	b Gibson	50
A.P. Gurusinha	c Browne, b Gibson	5
P.A. de Silva (Capt)	run out	1
H.P. Tillekeratne	c Browne, b Gibson	0
R.S. Mahanama	b Bishop	50
S. Ranatunga	b Hooper	5
H.D.P.K. Dharmasena	hit wkt, b Walsh	16
W.P.U.J.C. Vaas	c Ambrose, b Gibson	21
E. Upashantha	not out	8
K.R. Pushpakumara	run out	5
	lb 4, w 4, nb 5	13
	50 overs	202

	O	M	R	W
Ambrose	8	2	32	–
Walsh	9	–	34	1
Bishop	10	2	46	1
Gibson	10	1	40	5
Hooper	10	–	33	1
Simmons	3	–	13	–

Fall of Wickets
1–80, 2–89, 3–90, 4–91, 5–92, 6–121, 7–161, 8–176, 9–193

West Indies

P.V. Simmons	b Upashantha	5
S.L. Campbell	c Vaas, b de Silva	20
S. Chanderpaul	c Gurusinha, b de Silva	44
R.B. Richardson (Capt)	run out	7
C.L. Hooper	c Gurusinha, b Dharmasena	1
R.I.C. Holder	c Kaluwitharana, b Jayasuriya	38
*C.O. Browne	c Pushpakumara, b Vaas	22
O.D. Gibson	st Kaluwitharana, b de Silva	19
I.R. Bishop	run out	4
C.E.L. Ambrose	not out	8
C.A. Walsh	not out	3
	lb 3, w 4, nb 8	15
	50 overs (for 9 wickets)	186

	O	M	R	W
Vaas	9	–	27	1
Pushpakumara	8	2	21	–
Upashantha	6	–	31	1
Dharmasena	7	2	22	1
de Silva	10	–	43	3
Jayasuriya	10	1	39	1

Fall of Wickets
1–18, 2–51, 3–65, 4–67, 5–114, 6–131, 7–160, 8–171, 9–176

Umpires: T.A. Prue & D.J. Harper *Man of the Match:* R.S. Kaluwitharana

Sri Lanka won by 16 runs

Kaluwitharana had other notions. He attacked from the start and raced to 50 in 32 balls. He was finally out for 74 from 69 deliveries. Undaunted by a rash of falling wickets, Sri Lanka were kept in the hunt by de Silva and Mahanama, and, ultimately, by Dharmasena and Vaas. Victory came with two balls to spare when Dharmasena edged McGrath to the boundary.

Qualifying Table

	P	W	L	Pts	NRR
Australia	8	5	3	10	0.52
Sri Lanka	8	4	4	8	–0.53
West Indies	8	3	5	6	–0.1

Benson and Hedges World Series Finals

Australia *v.* Sri Lanka

An inspired spell of left-arm fast medium-pace bowling from Vaas, who dismissed both Australian openers in his first three overs, gave Sri Lanka an immediate advantage in the first final. When Steve Waugh and Stuart Law went cheaply Australia were 39 for 4 and sinking fast. Ponting and Bevan brought calm with a stand of 61. Ponting again proved himself at home in international cricket with 51 off 74 balls, and Bevan further consolidated his place in the side with a bright innings that was ended by a diving catch at long-on. Ian Healy played another of his vital late-order innings, and Australia were thankful to reach 201. This appeared to hold few fears for Sri Lanka who reached 107 for 2 in the 24th over, but Shane Warne then struck. He had slowed the run rate and now he accounted for de Silva and Tillekeratne in quick succession. With the required rate of scoring rising over by over, Gurusinha fell to a rash shot, and Dharmasena and Vaas perished in the chase. Arjuna Ranatunga battled bravely to the end, and he and Pushpakumara shared a last wicket stand of 31 which raised hopes of a famous victory. With 11 balls remaining, Ranatunga was bowled by McGrath.

Two days later, the sides met in Sydney where Australia reached a formidable 273 which was founded on an opening stand of 135 between Taylor and Mark Waugh. A thunderstorm interrupted play, and Sri Lanka faced a revised target of 168 from 25 overs; a required run rate of 6.72 an over. With five overs remaining, Sri Lanka were 135 for 5 so that 33 from five overs was within their grasp. The return of Warne brought the end of Ranatunga and Dharmasena while Mark Waugh ran out Tillekeratne to leave Sri Lanka nine short of their target.

Taylor and Warne were jointly named as Players of the Final while Kaluwitharana won the Player of the Preliminary Series award. Australia took the trophy, but one felt that Sri Lanka had learned much. They had shaped a side and tactics for the World Cup, and, feeling that they had been unfairly and unjustly treated in Australia, they had hardened their resolve. Revenge was to be very sweet.

Benson and Hedges World Series – Match Twelve – Australia *v.* Sri Lanka

16 January 1996 at MCG, Melbourne

Australia

M.E. Waugh	c Mahanama, b Vaas	6
M.A. Taylor (Capt)	c Kaluwitharana, b Wickremasinghe	32
R.T. Ponting	c Kaluwitharana, b Wickremasinghe	5
S.R. Waugh	not out	102
S.G. Law	c Ranatunga, b Pushpakumara	47
M.G. Bevan	not out	43
*I.A. Healy		
P.R. Reiffel		
S.K. Warne		
C.J. McDermott		
G.D. McGrath		
	lb 3, w 2, nb 2	7
	50 overs (for 4 wickets)	242

	O	M	R	W
Vaas	10	2	43	1
Pushpakumara	10	–	47	1
Wickremasinghe	8	–	33	2
Dharmasena	8	–	42	–
de Silva	6	–	30	–
Jayasuriya	8	–	44	–

Fall of Wickets
1–**12**, 2–**28**, 3–**54**, 4–**156**

Sri Lanka

S.T. Jayasuriya	c Healy, b McGrath	3
*R.S. Kaluwitharana	c M.E. Waugh, b Warne	74
A.P. Gurusinha	c Healy, b Reiffel	17
H.P. Tillekeratne	c Healy, b Warne	0
P.A. de Silva	lbw, b Bevan	45
R.S. Mahanama	b Warne	31
A. Ranatunga (Capt)	run out	18
H.D.P.K. Dharmasena	not out	24
W.P.U.J.C. Vaas	not out	13
G.P. Wickremasinghe		
K.R. Pushpakumara		
	b 1, lb 18, w 2	21
	49.4 overs (for 7 wickets)	246

	O	M	R	W
McDermott	10	3	27	–
McGrath	9.4	–	76	1
Reiffel	10	1	36	1
Warne	10	–	40	3
Law	6	–	28	–
M.E. Waugh	2	–	11	–
Bevan	2	–	9	1

Fall of Wickets
1–**35**, 2–**96**, 3–**107**, 4–**108**, 5–**180**, 6–**196**, 7–**222**

Umpires: D.B. Hair & S.G. Randell *Man of the Match:* R.S. Kaluwitharana

Sri Lanka won by 3 wickets

Benson and Hedges World Series – First Final – Australia *v.* Sri Lanka

18 January 1996 at MCG, Melbourne

Australia

M.A. Taylor (Capt)	c Kaluwitharana, b Vaas	0
M.E. Waugh	b Vaas	4
R.T. Ponting	run out	51
S.R. Waugh	c Gurusinha, b Wickremasinghe	13
S.G. Law	c Kaluwitharana, b Pushpakumara	0
M.G. Bevan	c Mahanama, b Pushpakumara	59
*I.A. Healy	not out	50
P.R. Reiffel	b Vaas	15
S.K. Warne	not out	3
C.J. McDermott		
G.D. McGrath		
	lb 3, w 2, nb 1	6
	50 overs (for 7 wickets)	201

	O	M	R	W
Vaas	10	1	42	3
Pushpakumara	10	1	34	2
Wickremasinghe	8	–	30	1
Dharmasena	10	1	31	–
de Silva	5	–	24	–
Jayasuriya	7	–	37	–

Fall of Wickets
1–**0**, 2–**9**, 3–**39**, 4–**39**, 5–**100**, 6–**155**, 7–**192**

Sri Lanka

S.T. Jayasuriya	c S.R. Waugh, b McGrath	19
*R.S. Kaluwitharana	lbw, b McGrath	13
A.P. Gurusinha	c Bevan, b McDermott	47
P.A. de Silva	c Taylor, b Warne	34
H.P. Tillekeratne	c Healy, b Warne	1
R.S. Mahanama	b M.E. Waugh	16
A. Ranatunga (Capt)	b McGrath	31
H.D.P.K. Dharmasena	b McDermott	4
W.P.U.J.C. Vaas	c Healy, b McDermott	2
G.P. Wickremasinghe	c Taylor, b Reiffel	0
K.R. Pushpakumara	not out	8
	lb 5, w 2, nb 1	8
	48.1 overs	183

	O	M	R	W
McGrath	9.1	–	28	3
Reiffel	10	2	44	1
M.E. Waugh	6	–	23	1
McDermott	10	1	41	3
Warne	10	1	29	2
Law	3	–	13	–

Fall of Wickets
1–**17**, 2–**46**, 3–**107**, 4–**110**, 5–**120**, 6–**129**, 7–**131**, 8–**132**, 9–**152**

Umpires: S.G. Randell & D.B. Hair

Australia won by 18 runs

Benson and Hedges World Series – Second Final – Australia *v.* Sri Lanka

20 January 1996 at SCG, Sydney

Australia

M.E. Waugh	c and b Kalpage	73
M.A. Taylor (Capt)	c Kaluwitharana, b Kalpage	82
R.T. Ponting	c Vaas, b Dharmasena	17
S.R. Waugh	c Kalpage, b Dharmasena	2
S.G. Law	b Vaas	21
M.G. Bevan	not out	32
*I.A. Healy	not out	40
P.R. Reiffel		
S.K. Warne		
C.J. McDermott		
G.D. McGrath		
	lb 5, w 1	6
	50 overs (for 5 wickets)	273

	O	M	R	W
Vaas	10	1	47	1
Pushpakumara	8	1	39	–
Munasinghe	4	–	33	–
Dharmasena	10	–	45	2
Kalpage	10	–	47	2
Jayasuriya	8	–	57	–

Fall of Wickets
1–**135**, 2–**170**, 3–**176**, 4–**184**, 5–**210**

Sri Lanka

S.T. Jayasuriya	c McGrath, b Warne	30
*R.S. Kaluwitharana	lbw, b McGrath	0
P.A. de Silva	c Reiffel, b M.E. Waugh	6
A.P. Gurusinha	c Warne, b Reiffel	24
A. Ranatunga (Capt)	c Law, b Warne	41
R.S. Kalpage	c Taylor, b McDermott	9
H.P. Tillekeratne	run out	25
H.D.P.K. Dharmasena	c S.R. Waugh, b Warne	7
M. Munasinghe	not out	3
W.P.U.J.C. Vaas	not out	8
K.R. Pushpakumara		
	lb 3, w 3	6
	25 overs (for 8 wickets)	159

	O	M	R	W
McGrath	5	–	36	1
M.E. Waugh	5	–	31	1
Warne	5	–	20	3
S.R. Waugh	1	–	14	–
Reiffel	4	–	22	1
McDermott	5	–	33	1

Fall of Wickets
1–**1**, 2–**22**, 3–**49**, 4–**66**, 5–**87**, 6–**135**, 7–**146**, 8–**146**

Umpires: S.G. Randell & P.D. Parker

Australia won on a faster scoring rate

Mercantile Mutual Cup

Australia's limited over competition assumed a new format that did not please all. Each state was to play the other, and the top four teams would qualify for the semi-finals. The system was deemed unfair by many, and the dramatic impact of the tournament was certainly reduced.

8 October 1995
at Woolloongabba, Brisbane
Queensland 173 for 4 (S.G. Law 77, M.L. Hayden 62 not out)
Victoria
Match abandoned
Queensland 1 pt, Victoria 1 pt

Rain caused the abandonment after 32.2 overs of the Queensland innings. Hayden and Law had added 135 for the second wicket.

15 October 1995
at North Sydney Oval
New South Wales 273 for 8 (M.J. Slater 77, S.A. Prestwidge 4 for 56)
Queensland 262 (A.R. Border 50)
New South Wales (2 pts) won by 11 runs

at WACA Ground, Perth
Tasmania 204 for 7 (M.J. DiVenuto 59, D.C. Boon 54)
Western Australia 207 for 7 (J.L. Langer 93 not out)
Western Australia (2 pts) won by 3 wickets

21 October 1995
at Adelaide Oval
South Australia 176
Tasmania 177 for 2 (R.T. Ponting 87 not out, D.C. Boon 54 not out)
Tasmania (2 pts) won by 8 wickets

22 October 1995
at WACA Ground, Perth
Western Australia 200 for 8 (M.P. Lavender 65, A.C. Gilchrist 64)
New South Wales 201 for 3 (S.R. Waugh 90, M.A. Taylor 70)
New South Wales (2 pts) won by 7 wickets

29 October 1995
at Woolloongabba, Brisbane
Queensland 274 for 7 (S.G. Law 109, M.L. Hayden 51)
South Australia 213 (J.D. Siddons 61, A.J. Bichel 4 for 45)
Queensland (2 pts) won by 61 runs

By the end of October, only New South Wales and Western Australia were unbeaten. Stuart Law hit the first century of the season, but after he had been run out umpire Peter Parker inadvertently allowed Queensland the chance to stretch their score by extending Ben Johnson's fourth over to 11 balls. The home side scored seven runs from the extra five deliveries. Match referee Mel Johnson confirmed that the runs scored should be counted.

5 November 1995
at MCG, Melbourne
Victoria 106 (N.D. Maxwell 4 for 15)
New South Wales 91 for 3
New South Wales (2 pts) won on faster scoring rate

10 December 1995
at Bellerive Oval, Hobart
Victoria 218 for 4 (D.M. Jones 121 not out, M.T.G. Elliott 64)
Tasmania 175 for 8
Victoria (2 pts) won by 43 runs

at Adelaide Oval
Western Australia 160 for 7 (R.M. Baker 55)
South Australia 163 for 4 (D.S. Lehmann 52)
South Australia (2 pts) won by 6 wickets

Jason Gillespie, the young, pony-tailed South Australian fast bowler, had a highly successful season and was chosen ahead of several contenders to fly to Asia as replacement for the injured Craig McDermott in Australia's World Cup Side.
(Stephen Laffer/Sportsline)

With three victories in three matches, the third coming on a faster run-rate when the match against Victoria was abandoned after 26.2 overs of their innings, New South Wales took a clear lead into the New Year.

2 February 1996
at MCG, Melbourne
Victoria 180
Western Australia 181 for 5 (M.P. Lavender 72, J.L. Langer 58)
Western Australia (2 pts) won by 5 wickets

3 February 1996
at Bellerive Oval, Hobart
Tasmania 175 (M.S. Kasprowicz 4 for 21)
Queensland 158 (J.P. Marquet 5 for 23)
Tasmania (2 pts) won by 17 runs

4 February 1996
at SCG, Sydney
New South Wales 248 for 7 (K.J. Roberts 101, R. Chee Quee 80, J.N. Gillespie 4 for 46)
South Australia 249 for 7 (D.S. Lehmann 67, J.D. Siddons 58, J.C. Scuderi 55 not out)
South Australia (2 pts) won by 3 wickets

Joshua Marquet of Tasmania produced the best one-day performance of his career, and in the process became the only bowler to take five wickets in a Mercantile Mutual Cup match during the season. Roberts and Chee Quee added 156 for New South Wales' fifth wicket against South Australia but still finished on the losing side.

17 February 1996
at Bellerive Oval, Hobart
New South Wales 207 for 9 (M.T. Haywood 57)
Tasmania 151
New South Wales (2 pts) won by 56 runs

18 February 1996
at MCG, Melbourne
Victoria 186
South Australia 187 for 3 (G.S. Blewett 59 not out)
South Australia (2 pts) won by 7 wickets

at WACA Ground, Perth
Queensland 237 (A. Symonds 85, B.P. Julian 4 for 43)
Western Australia 229 (D.R. Martyn 79, A.C. Gilchrist 59)
Queensland (2 pts) won by 8 runs

In spite of losing to Queensland, Western Australia claimed a place in the semi-finals by virtue of a superior run-rate.

Qualifying Table

	P	W	L	Ab	Pts
New South Wales	5	4	1	–	8
South Australia	5	3	2	–	6
Queensland	5	2	2	1	5
Western Australia	5	2	3	–	4
Tasmania	5	2	3	–	4
Victoria	5	1	1	1	3

Semi-Finals

24 February 1996
at Adelaide Oval
Queensland 230 for 5 (J.P. Maher 62)
South Australia 139 (G.I. Foley 4 for 34)
Queensland won by 81 runs

25 February 1996
at SCG, Sydney
New South Wales 210 (M.T. Haywood 60)
Western Australia 211 for 7 (A.C. Gilchrist 76 not out)
Western Australia won by 3 wickets

Queensland entered the final with a crushing victory over South Australia who were bowled out in 42.2 overs. Geoff Foley and Michael Kasprowicz shared seven wickets between them, while Maher and Barsby put on 113 for the Bulls' first wicket. In Sydney, Adam Gilchrist, heir-apparent to Healy's place in the national side, held three catches and made a stumping. He followed this by sharing a record eighth wicket partnership of 106 in 75 balls with Brendon Julian, which gave Western Australia victory with 16 balls to spare.

Final

3 March 1996
at Woolloongabba, Brisbane
Western Australia 166
Queensland 167 for 6 (T.J. Barsby 50)
Queensland won by 4 wickets

Queensland won their first one-day domestic title since 1989 in a rather disappointing final. Foley and Prestwidge took three wickets each as Western Australia were bowled out for 166 in 49.1 overs. Barsby, Man of the Finals, hit 50 off 81 balls, Symonds hit 25 off 21 balls with five fours, and Foley and Prestwidge shared a vital sixth wicket partnership of 36 as Queensland stumbled to victory with 5.1 overs to spare.

21 March 1996
at MCG, Melbourne
World XI 210 for 9 (D.M. Jones 103)
Australia 211 for 5 (M.A. Taylor 78, M.E. Waugh 56 not out)
Australia won by 5 wickets

A post World Cup celebratory game saw Dean Jones, omitted from the Australian squad, hit a century against his countrymen. He arrived at the crease in the fourth over and reached his hundred by hitting the second ball of the last over for six. Sadly, Michael Slater, who had not appeared in the World Cup although a member of the squad, sustained a broken thumb when hit by a delivery from Heath Streak.

Adam Gilchrist of Western Australia gained official recognition as understudy to Ian Healy as Australia's wicket-keeper. Gilchrist had an outstanding run of success in the Mercantile Mutual Cup and hit a career-best 189 not out in the Sheffield Shield final. (Stephen Laffer/Sportsline)

Sheffield Shield

Australia's most prized domestic trophy was held by Queensland, who had taken the Shield for the first time in their history in 1995. They began the 1995–96 season as favourites to retain the trophy.

In effect, the demands of the national side were such that no state could be confident of fielding full-strength elevens for much of the campaign. New South Wales had long been considered the most powerful side in the competition, but they were certain to lose Taylor, McGrath, Slater and the Waugh twins to international cricket, and they would most probably be deprived of the services of Bevan and Lee as well. Other states faced similar problems.

18, 19, 20 and 21 October 1995
at WACA Ground, Perth
Western Australia 351 for 3 dec. (M.P. Lavender 173 not out, T.M. Moody 57 not out) and 206 for 4 dec. (M.E. Hussey 81)
New South Wales 211 for 9 dec. and 243 for 4 (M.J. Slater 96)
Match drawn
Western Australia 2 pts, New South Wales 0 pts

at Woolloongabba, Brisbane
Queensland 361 for 8 dec. (S.G. Law 89, J.P. Maher 88, M.L. Hayden 64, W.A. Seccombe 54 not out) and 246 for 6 (A.R. Border 70 not out, S.G. Law 53)
Victoria 482 (D.M. Jones 145, M.T.G. Elliott 138, D.S. Berry 74, P.W. Jackson 4 for 158)
Match drawn
Victoria 2 pts, Queensland 0 pts

The two sides in Perth were both playing under new coaches. Wayne Clark had taken over Western Australia while Geoff Lawson was in charge of New South Wales. No play was possible on the first day because of rain, and the home state plundered runs on the second and captured the wicket of Slater before the close. Mark Lavender hit his sixth and highest first-class hundred and shared an opening stand of 111 with the left-handed Mike Hussey. Bruce Reid bowled well and hoped to be recalled to the Australian side if he could maintain fitness. Western Australia gave a debut to Oldroyd. In New South Wales' second innings, Slater hit 96 off 109 balls.

Queensland were victims of a second wicket partnership of 234 between Elliott and Jones, but the game was marred by rain. Border and Rackemann took their places in the Queensland side, but Rackemann was to fade from the scene after a few weeks. Border retired at the end of the season. Victoria gave a debut to Broster, but he failed to give the middle order a much needed boost.

25, 26, 27 and 28 October 1995
at Woolloongabba, Brisbane
South Australia 276 (J.D. Siddons 130, M.S. Kasprowicz 6 for 48) and 243 (G.S. Blewett 126, J.A. Brayshaw 64, C.J. McDermott 5 for 58)
Queensland 356 (J.P. Maher 108, M.L. Love 62, A.R. Border 59, J.N. Gillespie 4 for 62) and 164 for 2 (T.J. Barsby 69)
Queensland won by 8 wickets
Queensland 6 pts, South Australia 0 pts

26, 27, 28 and 29 October 1995
at SCG, Sydney
New South Wales 457 for 4 dec. (S.R. Waugh 107, M.G. Bevan 103 not out, S. Lee 101 not out) and 188 for 2 dec. (M.J. Slater 100 not out, S.R. Waugh 54)
Tasmania 262 (J. Cox 62) and 165 (D.C. Boon 57, S.H. Cook 4 for 20, S. Lee 4 for 20)
New South Wales won by 218 runs
New South Wales 6 pts, Tasmania 0 pts

The reigning champions, without Healy but otherwise at full strength, claimed the season's first outright victory when they thrashed South Australia. Siddons hit a hundred on the opening day, but the chief honours went to Michael Kasprowicz who began an outstanding season with match figures of 9 for 126. McDermott was also in fine form with seven wickets in the match. Medium-pacer Paul Wilson, who had not appeared in the Shield before, soon disposed of

Dene Hills reached the first double century of his career as Tasmania drew with Queensland in Hobart in the beginning of November. (Stephen Laffer/Sportsline)

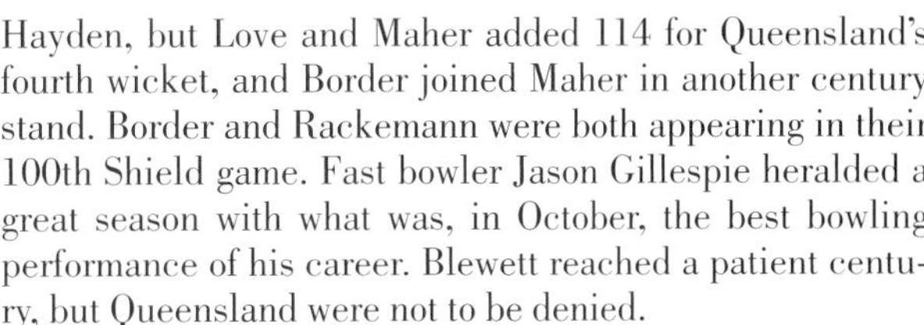

Hayden, but Love and Maher added 114 for Queensland's fourth wicket, and Border joined Maher in another century stand. Border and Rackemann were both appearing in their 100th Shield game. Fast bowler Jason Gillespie heralded a great season with what was, in October, the best bowling performance of his career. Blewett reached a patient century, but Queensland were not to be denied.

With Matthews retired and Mills of Leicestershire not returning to Australia, Tasmania's attack looked woefully weak, and they were cruelly savaged by New South Wales who were 363 for 3 at the end of the first day. In all, New South Wales produced four centuries, and Cook, who had transferred from Victoria, and Lee both produced their best bowling figures for New South Wales.

1, 2 and 3 November 1995
at MCG, Melbourne
Victoria 158 (M.T.G. Elliott 53, G.R.J. Matthews 4 for 52) and 241
New South Wales 344 (M.A. Taylor 126, S.R. Waugh 80, S.K. Warne 5 for 122) and 56 for 4
New South Wales won by 6 wickets
New South Wales 6 pts, Victoria 0 pts

2, 3, 4 and 5 November 1995
at Bellerive Oval, Hobart
Tasmania 458 for 2 dec. (D.F. Hills 220 not out, R.T. Ponting 118 not out, D.C. Boon 88) and 290 for 3 dec. (R.T. Ponting 100 not out, S. Young 62 not out, D.C. Boon 56)
Queensland 377 for 1 dec. (M.L. Love 185 not out, M.L. Hayden 152 not out) and 260 for 5 (S.G. Law 107 not out, T.J. Barsby 74)
Match drawn
Tasmania 2 pts, Queensland 0 pts

New South Wales won their second match in succession and moved to the top of the table. They took command of the game in Melbourne on the opening day when spinners Matthews and Freedman took seven wickets between them. Freedman brought an end to the Victoria innings by taking three wickets in four balls. Earlier, New South Wales had lost Cook in the second over of the day when he retired with a stress fracture of the leg after bowling four balls. Victoria were equally handicapped when Fleming retired with hamstring problems after bowling nine balls. Taylor, who equalled the Shield record with seven catches in the match, and Steve Waugh added 152 for New South Wales' third wicket. With McGrath reaching double figures in a first-class match for the first time, the Blues took a first innings lead of 186. Victoria lost eight wickets before avoiding an innings defeat, and the match was over in three days.

Hobart confirmed its reputation as the bowler's graveyard when only three wickets fell on the first two days of the match between Tasmania and Queensland. Dene Hills reached his first double century, and Ricky Ponting scored

The left-handed Darren Lehmann scored consistently to play a major part in seeing South Australia to the Sheffield Shield final. (Stephen Laffer/Sportsline)

a century in each innings. He and Hills shared an unbroken third wicket stand of 245. Hayden and Love hit 368 in 255 minutes for Queensland's second wicket without being separated before Healy conceded first innings points in an attempt to bring a result. Law scored 107 off 104 balls, but the match was drawn after 1,385 runs had been scored for the loss of 11 wickets.

24, 25, 26 and 27 November 1995
at Bellerive Oval, Hobart
New South Wales 368 for 9 dec. (G.R.J. Matthews 73, S. Lee 63, M.J. Slater 55, S. Young 4 for 74) and 270 for 5 dec. (M.A. Taylor 73, K.J. Roberts 62, M.J. Slater 50)
Tasmania 263 (D.F. Hills 85, N.D. Maxwell 6 for 56) and 266 (S. Young 57, G.R.J. Matthews 4 for 31)
New South Wales won by 105 runs
New South Wales 6 pts, Tasmania 0 pts

at Adelaide Oval
Western Australia 309 (A.C. Gilchrist 99 not out, M.A. Harrity 4 for 75) and 376 for 9 dec. (J.L. Langer 153, A.C. Gilchrist 68)
South Australia 353 for 9 dec. (D.S. Lehmann 116, J.D. Siddons 96, B.P. Julian 5 for 70, B.A. Reid 4 for 53) and 186 (G.S. Blewett 66, B.A. Johnson 54, G.B. Hogg 5 for 59)
Western Australia won by 146 runs
Western Australia 6 pts, South Australia 2 pts

New South Wales completed an emphatic victory in Hobart to make it three wins in a row and a ten-point lead at the top of the table. They batted consistently, with Lee and Matthews adding 107 for the sixth wicket, and bowled well. Maxwell took six wickets in an innings for the first time as Tasmania lost their last eight wickets for 82 runs. Taylor and Slater began the Blues' second innings with a stand of 70, of which Slater hit 50 off 43 balls. As New South Wales celebrated victory, coach Geoff Lawson reminded them that it was now up to the younger players to complete what the seniors had started, for Taylor and company were now required by Australia.

Western Australia gained their first win of the season after trailing to South Australia on the first innings. Gilchrist, confirmed by the Australian Cricket Board as Healy's deputy, and Langer were the batting stars. However, it looked as if Lehmann and Siddons had given South Australia the platform for victory with a 188-run sixth wicket stand. Siddons' 96 came off only 111 balls, and he hit 17 fours and a six. In their second innings, South Australia lost their last nine wickets for 87 runs. Reid continued his comeback with match figures of 7 for 93 while Brad Hogg's left-arm wrist spin brought him a career-best 5 for 59.

30 November, 1, 2 and 3 December 1995
at Woolloongabba, Brisbane
Western Australia 110 (A.J. Bichel 5 for 31) and 241 (T.M. Moody 82, M.S. Kasprowicz 5 for 72)
Queensland 362 (T.J. Barsby 133, J.P. Maher 88, J. Angel 5 for 90)
Queensland won by an innings and 11 runs
Queensland 6 pts, Western Australia 0 pts

at Adelaide Oval
Victoria 297 (D.M. Jones 79, M.A. Harrity 4 for 84) and 237 (D.M. Jones 85, T.B.A. May 5 for 70)
South Australia 397 (J.A. Brayshaw 113, D.S. Lehmann 103, B.A. Johnson 61, B.A. Williams 6 for 98) and 141 for 4
South Australia won by 6 wickets
South Australia 6 pts, Victoria –0.3 pts

Western Australia gave a wretched performance against Queensland and were beaten in three days. Queensland bowled well but batted inconsistently. Barsby and Maher held their innings together with a fourth wicket stand of 124. This defeat for Western Australia was part of a crisis which saw Damien Martyn resign the captaincy in favour of Tom Moody.

Matthew Elliott, the Victorian opener, followed his double century against Tasmania with a century in each innings against Western Australia in Perth. Elliott finished the season top of the first class batting averages and won the Sheffield Shield Player of the Year. (Mike Hewitt/Allsport)

Dean Jones' captaincy was also under scrutiny as Victoria not only lost to South Australia but were deducted 0.3 points for a slow over-rate. Jones himself batted well enough, and there was some lively bowling from Brad Williams, but centuries from Lehmann and Brayshaw put South Australia firmly in control. When he had made his debut nine years earlier the left-handed Lehmann had been seen as another Bradman, but injury had badly affected his career. Nevertheless, his century against Victoria was the 21st of his career in which he is close to seven thousand runs and averages close to fifty.

13, 14, 15 and 16 December 1995

at MCG, Melbourne
Victoria 430 for 6 dec. (M.T.G. Elliott 203, G.R. Vimpani 71, P.J. Roach 62 not out) and 174 for 7 dec. (G.R. Vimpani 51, M.A. Hatton 4 for 48)
Tasmania 292 (J. Cox 99, D.F. Hills 54) and 313 for 6 (R.J. Tucker 95 not out, J. Cox 79, D.F. Hills 59)
Tasmania won by 4 wickets
Tasmania 6 pts, Victoria 1.9 pts

Despite a maiden double century from Matthew Elliott and a first innings lead of 138, Victoria were beaten by Tasmania and once again were penalised for a slow over-rate. Elliott faced 358 balls, hit a six and 17 fours, and shared century stands with Vimpani and Roach who had taken over as wicket-keeper from Berry. Hills and Cox scored 125 for Tasmania's first wicket, but the last nine wickets went down for 79 runs. Jones asked Tasmania to make 313 in 90 overs. Hills and Cox again scored 125 for the first wicket, but five wickets went down for 35 runs before Atkinson and Tucker added 81. Tucker's 95 off 110 balls won the match with 6.3 overs to spare.

29, 30, 31 December 1995 and 1 January 1996

at Adelaide Oval
South Australia 331 (P.C. Nobes 56, G.S. Blewett 51) and 252 for 9 dec. (D.S. Lehmann 71, A.J. Bichel 4 for 58)
Queensland 200 (A.R. Border 79, T.B.A. May 5 for 88) and 242 (A.R. Border 94, T.B.A. May 6 for 83, J.N. Gillespie 4 for 50)
South Australia won by 141 runs
South Australia 6 pts, Queensland 0 pts

at WACA Ground, Perth
Western Australia 413 for 7 dec. (J.L. Langer 161, A.C. Gilchrist 82) and 238 for 8 (T.M. Moody 59, J.L. Langer 56)
Victoria 215 (M.T.G. Elliott 104 not out, B.A. Reid 5 for 36) and 459 for 9 dec. (M.T.G. Elliott 135, P.J. Roach 84, D.M. Jones 70, I.J. Harvey 55, G.B. Hogg 5 for 126)
Match drawn
Western Australia 2 pts, Victoria 0 pts

A second victory of the season for South Australia was built around more consistent batting from their top six and on the spin of Tim May who took 11 wickets in the match. There was also another impressive performance by the twenty-year old pace bowler Jason Gillespie. The veteran Allan Border was the only Queensland batsman to offer serious resistance. His second innings' 94 proved to be his highest score in his farewell season.

Another big innings from Langer and an impressive knock from Gilchrist put Western Australia in a strong position against Victoria, who lost Brad Williams through injury for the rest of the season – a bitter blow. Matthew Elliott carried his bat through 84.5 overs, but Victoria were forced to follow on. Elliott, who hit his second century of the match, and Jones put on 163 for the first wicket. With Roach, controversially chosen ahead of Berry, making his highest score, Jones was able to set Western Australia a target of 262 in 40 overs. They went for the runs, but it nearly cost them the match.

For Queensland against Tasmania, at Brisbane at the end of January, Martin Love hit 186 and shared a record second wicket partnership of 365 with Matthew Hayden. (Stephen Laffer/Sportsline)

5, 6, 7 and 8 January 1996
at WACA Ground, Perth
South Australia 235 (D.S. Lehmann 62, J.A. Brayshaw 60) and 390 (D.S. Lehmann 161, G.S. Blewett 96, T.M. Moody 4 for 68)
Western Australia 377 (M.E. Hussey 96, G.B. Hogg 66, T.B.A. May 4 for 131) and 204 for 9 (M.P. Lavender 55, J.L. Langer 51, J.N. Gillespie 6 for 68)
Match drawn
Western Australia 2 pts, South Australia 0 pts

For the second match in succession, Western Australia surrendered a strong position and came close to defeat. They led by 142 on the first innings, but another fine innings from Lehmann, who shared a third wicket stand of 146 with Blewett, revived South Australia and meant that the home state had 54 overs in which to score 249. Gillespie confirmed his immense promise with six wickets in an innings for the first time, and Western Australia were fortunate to survive.

12, 13, 14 and 15 January 1996
at Adelaide Oval
South Australia 392 (P.C. Nobes 121, J.D. Siddons 110 not out) and 243 for 8 dec. (D.S. Webber 89, P.C. Nobes 55)
New South Wales 284 (P.A. Emery 60, G.R.J. Matthews 55, K.J. Roberts 50) and 229 (T.B.A. May 4 for 72)
South Australia won by 122 runs
South Australia 6 pts, New South Wales 0 pts

at Bellerive Oval, Hobart
Victoria 275 (I.J. Harvey 85, D.M. Jones 53, J.P. Marquet 4 for 63) and 206 (D.M. Jones 58)
Tasmania 455 for 8 dec. (D.C. Boon 108, S. Young 100 not out, D.F. Hills 66, M.J. DiVenuto 61) and 27 for 0
Tasmania won by 10 wickets
Tasmania 6 pts, Victoria 0 pts

South Australia lost four wickets for 54 runs before Siddons joined Nobes in a stand of 238 that set up a comfortable win over New South Wales. Gillespie and May, jettisoned by the Australian selectors, again bowled effectively.

Tasmania beat Victoria for the second time in a month. Joshua Marquet and Shaun Young were most instrumental in bowling out the visitors for 275, and Young followed with a fine century. Boon led from the front, and he and DiVenuto added 149 for the fourth wicket. Young was dropped on 97 on the last ball before tea. He was able to run three, and Boon declared.

26, 27, 28 and 29 January 1996
at SCG, Sydney
Western Australia 402 (G.B. Hogg 111 not out, M.E. Hussey 105) and 193 for 4 dec. (M.P. Lavender 73)
New South Wales 259 (S. Lee 69, B.P. Julian 5 for 58) and 220 for 5 (M.G. Bevan 109)
Match drawn
Western Australia 2 pts, New South Wales 0 pts

at Woolloongabba, Brisbane
Queensland 533 for 6 dec. (M.L. Hayden 234, M.L. Love 186, S.G. Law 53)
Tasmania 336 (M.J. DiVenuto 89, D.F. Hills 85, S. Young 56, S.G. Law 5 for 39, A.J. Bichel 4 for 87) and 330 for 8 (S. Young 175 not out)
Match drawn
Queensland 2 pts, Tasmania 0 pts

The most significant events at Sydney were maiden Shield centuries for Brad Hogg and Michael Hussey. Bevan's patient hundred saved the Blues from defeat.

At Brisbane, Matthew Hayden, troubled by a back injury, and Martin Love shared a second wicket stand of 365. This is a Queensland record for the second wicket, and the second highest for any wicket in the state's history. It is also the highest partnership recorded at Brisbane. Hayden's second double century advanced his previous best score by 33 runs. Tasmania could not avoid the follow-on, but Shaun Young's career-best 175 not out saved them from defeat after they had been 18 for 3.

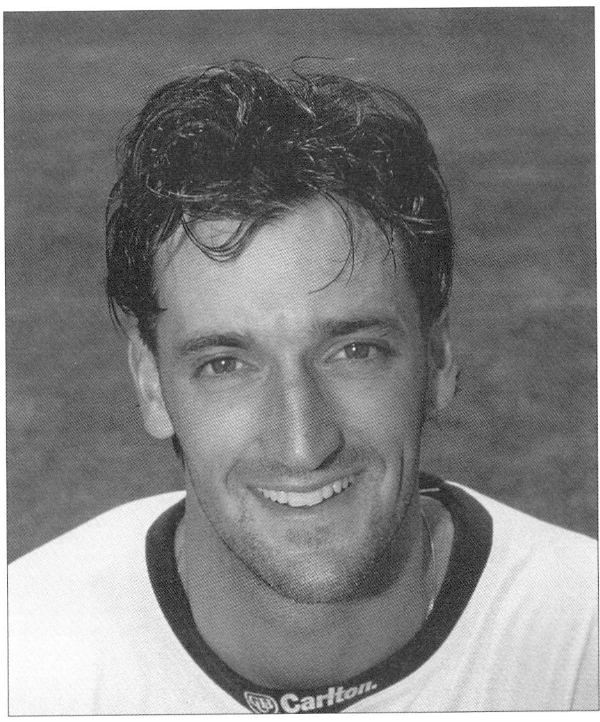

Michael DiVenuto played a leading role in Tasmania's thrilling victory over Western Australia in Perth. (Stephen Laffer/Sportsline)

7, 8, 9 and 10 February 1996
at Woolloongabba, Brisbane
Queensland 150 (A.M. Stuart 4 for 48) and 181 (A.M. Stuart 4 for 33, G.R.J. Matthews 4 for 34)
New South Wales 159 (D. Tazelaar 5 for 42) and 160 (D. Tazelaar 4 for 29)
Queensland won by 12 runs
Queensland 6 pts, New South Wales 2 pts

at Bellerive Oval, Hobart
Tasmania 258 for 8 dec. (M.N. Atkinson 59 not out, P. Wilson 4 for 50) and 21 for 1 dec.
South Australia 0 for 0 dec. and 280 for 4 (D.S. Lehmann 105, J.A. Brayshaw 80 not out)
South Australia won by 6 wickets
South Australia 6 pts, Tasmania 2 pts

A round of controversial matches saw 19 wickets fall on the first day at The Gabba. New South Wales recovered from 4 for 4 to take a first innings lead of nine, but left-arm pace bowler Dirk Tazelaar, briefly of Surrey, won the match for the Bulls, who were reluctantly captained by Border in the absence of Heal and Law.

There was more controversy in Hobart where Boon and Siddons arranged declarations to keep alive a match ruined by rain. South Australia forfeited their first innings, and Boon declared after three overs of Tasmania's second when Miller suffered a double fracture of a cheekbone. He was unable to bowl, and South Australia reached a target of 280 in 73 overs with 20 balls to spare. Lehmann and Brayshaw added 110 for the fourth wicket.

13, 14, 15 and 16 February 1996
at MCG, Melbourne
South Australia 309 (T.J. Nielsen 115, P.C. Nobes 86) and 229 (P.C. Nobes 74, D.S. Lehmann 64, A.I.C. Dodemaide 4 for 49)
Victoria 519 for 7 dec. (M.T.G. Elliott 200, I.J. Harvey 136, W.G. Ayres 73, D.M. Jones 56) and 20 for 0
Victoria won by 10 wickets
Victoria 6 pts, South Australia 0 pts

at WACA Ground, Perth
Queensland 154 and 237 (M.L. Love 89, J. Anger 5 for 45)
Western Australia 207 (T.M. Moody 59) and 185 for 3 (M.P. Lavender 77)
Western Australia won by 7 wickets
Western Australia 6 pts, Queensland 0 pts

South Australia's win in Hobart had taken them to the top of the table, but they suffered a set-back in Melbourne where Victoria gained their first win of the season. Nielsen hit his second and higher century before Elliott made his second double century of the season and became the first player to reach a thousand runs. There was a maiden century by Ian Harvey, and Victoria romped to victory. Tony Dodemaide returned to the Victorian side after making just one appearance in 1994–95 and bowled with considerable success.

Bruce Reid withdrew from the Western Australian side on the eve of the match in Perth and announced his retirement due to a series of chronic injuries. He possessed a rare talent, as 350 first-class wickets, 113 in 29 Tests, would indicate. Without him, Western Australia still beat Queensland with considerable ease to maintain their challenge for a place in the Shield final.

8, 9, 10 and 11 March 1996
at WACA Ground, Perth
Western Australia 224 (T.M. Moody 90) and 361 for 8 dec. (D.R. Martyn 203 not out, J.L. Langer 107, J.P. Marquet 5 for 94)
Tasmania 184 (M.J. DiVenuto 104, J. Angel 6 for 68) and 402 for 6 (D.C. Boon 152, J. Cox 96, M.J. DiVenuto 66)
Tasmania won by 4 wickets
Tasmania 6 pts, Western Australia 2 pts

at SCG, Sydney
New South Wales 319 for 5 dec. (M.T. Haywood 97, K.J. Roberts 72) and 99
Victoria 99 (G.R.J. Matthews 4 for 19, A.M. Stuart 4 for 22) and 338 for 8 (B.P. Ricci 55, G.R. Vimpani 54, A.M. Stuart 4 for 48)
Match drawn
New South Wales 2 pts, Victoria 0 pts

Warren Ayres made an impressive return to the Victoria side with 466 runs in four matches at the end of the season. (Stephen Laffer/Sportsline)

A young fast bowler of immense promise, Anthony Stuart of New South Wales – top of the averages with 25 wickets at 13.40 runs apiece. (Stephen Laffer/Sportsline)

With an astonishing victory at Perth, Tasmania kept alive their hopes of reaching the Shield final. The left-handed Michael DiVenuto had been the only batsman to pass 20 and to keep his side in touch with Western Australia, who were 30 for 4 in their second innings before Langer and Martyn added 236. Martyn went on to reach the first double hundred of his career, and Tasmania were left a target of 402. They lost Hills for 0, but Cox and DiVenuto added 113, and Cox and Boon 148. Boon was masterly and led his side to a memorable victory.

In Sydney, New South Wales, having bowled out Victoria for 99, were thwarted by a consistently defiant rear-guard action.

14, 15, 16 and 17 March 1996
at SCG, Sydney
Queensland 371 (T.J. Barsby 79, A.R. Border 78, M.L Love 69, D.A. Freedman 5 for 91, G.R.J. Matthews 5 for 134) and 1 for 0
New South Wales 193 (R. Chee Quee 59) and 178 (P.A. Emery 72, M.S. Kasprowicz 5 for 34)
Queensland won by 10 wickets
Queensland 6 pts, New South Wales 0 pts

at MCG, Melbourne
Victoria 182 (W.G. Ayres 79, B.P. Julian 5 for 41) and 456 for 6 dec. (W.G. Ayres 140, D.M. Jones 107, M.T.G. Elliott 98, I.J. Harvey 54)
Western Australia 223 (T.M. Moody 60, A.I.C. Dodemaide 6 for 67) and 309 (M.E. Hussey 85)
Victoria won by 76 runs
Victoria 6 pts, Western Australia 2 pts

at Adelaide Oval
South Australia 507 for 7 dec. (J.A. Brayshaw 141 not out, G.S. Blewett 135, D.S. Lehmann 89, M.W. Ridgway 4 for 166) and 182 for 9 dec. (J.A. Brayshaw 59, D.S. Lehmann 50, M.W. Ridgway 5 for 64)
Tasmania 320 (D.C. Boon 117, D.F. Hills 70, P.E. McIntyre 4 for 75) and 348 (M.J. DiVenuto 154, T.B.A. May 4 for 106)
South Australia won by 21 runs
South Australia 6 pts, Tasmania 0 pts

Queensland maintained their ambition of retaining the Sheffield Shield when they beat New South Wales with ease in three days in Sydney. Meanwhile, in Melbourne, Victoria survived a first innings deficit of 41 runs to overcome Western Australia. Warren Ayres, once of Woodford Wells, made the highest score of his career and shared stands of 165 with Elliott and 176 with Jones. There was another outstanding bowling performance from Tony Dodemaide who had match figures of 8 for 124.

Tasmania just failed to bring off another remarkable victory in a run chase against South Australia. Led by the reliable Brayshaw, South Australia had amassed a big score, but Boon's hundred had kept Tasmania in touch. Asked to make 370 at nearly four an over, Tasmania put up a brave fight, with DiVenuto, in excellent form at the end of the season, leading the challenge which narrowly failed.

When the last round of matches began only Victoria had no hope of reaching the final.

23, 24, 25 and 26 March 1996
at SCG, Sydney
South Australia 383 (G.S. Blewett 106, D.S. Lehmann 82, P.C. Nobes 70) and 234 (B.A. Johnson 90)
New South Wales 267 (M.G. Bevan 87, M.E. Waugh 57, J.N. Gillespie 4 for 50, P.E. McIntyre 4 for 94) and 323 for 9 (M.G. Bevan 57, D.A. Freedman 54 not out)
Match drawn
South Australia 2 pts, New South Wales 0 pts

at Bellerive Oval, Hobart
Tasmania 357 for 9 dec. (M.J. DiVenuto 93, D.C. Boon 91, J. Cox 54) and 183 (S. Young 51 not out, T.M. Moody 7 for 38)
Western Australia 357 (J.L. Langer 120, D.R. Martyn 65, M.W. Ridgway 4 for 89) and 184 for 5 (D.R. Martyn 62 not out)
Western Australia won by 5 wickets
Western Australia 6 pts, Tasmania 1 pt

at MCG, Melbourne
Queensland 142, (D.J. Saker 7 for 32) and 338 (M.L. Love 88, A.I.C. Dodemaide 5 for 70, D.J. Saker 4 for 88)
Victoria 255 (D.M. Jones 69, W.G. Ayres 68, M.S. Kasprowicz 5 for 74) and 226 for 5 (W.G. Ayres 100, M.T.G. Elliott 54, M.S. Kasprowicz 5 for 74)
Victoria won by 5 wickets
Victoria 5.8 pts, Queensland 0 pts

By finishing top of the Sheffield Shield table, South Australia confirmed that they would host the final. They took first innings points comfortably enough, and New South Wales were left 82 overs in which to score 351 to win or to hold out. At 294 for 9, they looked doomed, but, astonishingly, McGrath, the most noted of rabbits, made the highest score of his career, Freedman hit the second, and higher, fifty of his career, and New South Wales drew.

Western Australia qualified to meet South Australia in the final by beating Tasmania in Hobart. Westerns lost their last six first innings wickets for 52 runs, and the scores were tied on the first innings. Tasmania then collapsed against Tom Moody, who returned the best bowling figures of his career and took his side into the final.

Victoria ended on a winning note although they lost another fraction of a point for a slow over-rate. Queensland succumbed to David Saker who took five or more wickets in an innings for the first time in his career, and ten wickets in a match for the first time. He had fine support from Dodemaide whose return late in the season was a tonic to Victoria. The same could be said of Ayres who passed fifty for the fifth time in seven innings as he completed his second century. With Elliott named as Sheffield Shield Player of the Year, Victoria had much to comfort them, but the debate over Jones' captaincy continued.

Jamie Siddons holds aloft the Sheffield Shield after South Australia's brave rearguard action. (Stephen Laffer/Sportsline)

Sheffield Shield Final Table

	P	W	L	D	Pts
South Australia	10	5	3	2	34
Western Australia	10	3	3	4	30
Queensland	10	4	3	3	26
Tasmania	10	3	5	2	23
New South Wales	10	3	3	4	22
Victoria	10	3	4	3	21.4

Sheffield Shield Final

South Australia v. Western Australia

30, 31 March, 1, 2 and 3 April 1996
at Adelaide Oval
Western Australia 520 (A.C. Gilchrist 189 not out, R.M. Baker 83, T.M. Moody 68, G.B. Hogg 61) and 169 for 8 dec. (T.M. Moody 72, J.N. Gillespie 4 for 33)
South Australia 347 (P.C. Nobes 103, J.A. Brayshaw 87, B.P. Julian 5 for 95) and 208 for 9 (G.S. Blewett 72, J.A. Brayshaw 66, B.P. Julian 4 for 56)
Match drawn
South Australia won the Sheffield Shield by virtue of topping the league table

South Australia took the Shield for the first time in 14 years. The match ended in the most dramatic fashion as the last South Australian pair held out for 40 minutes to gain the draw that gave their side the title. All had seemed to go well for South Australia at first, with Lavender, Langer and Hussey being dismissed cheaply. Baker and Moody revived

matters, and Adam Gilchrist played a wonderful career-best innings of 189 not out.

South Australia were in trouble at 8 for 2 before Nobes and Lehmann added 123. Brayshaw held the late order together for South Australia to finish 173 in arrears.

Moody eventually set South Australia the task of scoring 343 to win in 129 overs. At 67 for 4, with Lehmann leg before to Julian for nought, the task looked hopeless, but Blewett and Brayshaw put on 102. When they were separated South Australia could only play for a draw. Siddons, in chronic pain with a hip injury, batted 166 minutes for four, and May held out for 64 minutes without scoring. The last session of the match brought only 15 runs, but every wicketless ball was cheered by an excited home crowd. George, 1 not out, and McIntyre, 6 not out, blocked out the final 9.5 overs to earn the draw and the Shield.

First-Class Averages

Batting

	M	Inns	NO	Runs	HS	Av	100s	50s
M.T.G. Elliott	11	21	3	1233	203	68.50	5	4
R.T. Ponting	8	13	3	681	131*	68.10	4	5
W.G. Ayres	4	7	–	466	140	66.57	2	3
M.G.Bevan	8	15	4	721	119*	65.54	3	3
S.R. Waugh	10	18	3	952	170*	63.46	4	3
S. Lee	8	14	6	494	101*	61.75	1	4
D.S. Lehmann	12	23	1	1237	161	56.22	5	6
D.F. Hills	10	19	2	914	220*	53.76	1	6
M.L. Hayden	10	17	3	752	234	53.71	2	1
S.G. Law	9	14	3	565	107*	51.36	1	5
D.M. Jones	11	19	–	974	145	51.26	3	6
A.C. Gilchrist	13	22	5	859	189*	50.52	1	5
S. Young	11	19	4	739	175*	49.26	2	4
M.A. Taylor	11	20	1	931	126	49.00	2	5
M.J. Slater	11	20	2	863	219	47.94	2	5
M.E. Waugh	11	19	2	805	116	47.35	2	5
J.A. Brayshaw	12	22	3	865	141*	45.52	2	6
D.C. Boon	15	25	–	1134	152	45.36	4	5
G.S. Blewett	15	27	1	1173	135	45.11	5	5
T.M. Moody	12	24	4	887	90	44.35		8
M.J. DiVenuto	11	19	1	791	154	43.94	2	4
M.L. Love	13	22	1	921	186	43.85	2	5
A.R. Border	11	17	1	669	94	41.81		5
J.D. Siddons	11	20	1	790	130	41.57	3	1
J.L. Langer	12	24	1	950	161	41.30	4	2
M.E. Hussey	12	24	1	945	146	41.08	2	3
P.C. Nobes	12	23	–	840	121	36.52	2	5
D.R. Martyn	12	24	3	757	203*	36.04	1	2
G.R. Vimpani	7	14	2	414	79	34.50		4
J.P. Maher	12	19	2	578	108	34.00	1	3
M.P. Lavender	13	26	2	797	173*	33.20	1	3
I.A. Healy	9	12	1	357	70	32.45		1
P.J. Roach	7	13	5	258	84	32.25		2
P.J. Berry	4	6	1	161	74	32.20		1
J. Cox	11	22	1	670	99	31.90		5
I.J. Harvey	7	13	–	414	136	31.84	1	3
W.A. Seccombe	9	13	3	316	54*	31.60		1
G.R.J. Matthews	12	19	5	442	73	31.57		2
A.J. Daly	4	8	2	187	70	31.16		2
T.J. Barsby	11	21	1	616	133	30.80	1	5
G.B. Hogg	13	20	5	456	111*	30.40	2	2
R.J. Tucker	11	18	4	420	95*	30.00		3
B.A. Johnson	5	10	–	296	90	29.60		4
R. Chee Quee	6	10	–	287	105	28.70	1	1
B.A. Williams	6	9	4	140	41*	28.00		
D.A. Freedman	12	11	5	166	54*	27.66		1
R.M. Baker	6	11	1	266	83	26.60		1
D.S. Webber	9	17	1	415	89	25.93		2
M.T. Haywood	3	5	–	123	97	24.60		1
M.N. Atkinson	11	17	3	335	59*	23.92		1
C.J. Peake	6	11	1	237	46	23.70		
K.J. Roberts	7	12	–	277	72	23.08		3
P.A. Emery	12	15	2	300	72	23.07		2
R.J. Davison	5	9	1	177	44	22.12		
B.J. Hodge	5	9	1	174	43	21.75		
T.J. Nielsen	12	21	1	431	115	21.55	1	1
S.M. Thompson	5	7	1	128	49*	21.33		
G.B. Gardiner	3	6	–	124	31	20.66		
A. Symonds	7	12	1	223	73	20.27		1
P.R. Reiffel	9	13	5	162	56	20.25		1
N.D. Maxwell	9	12	3	178	46*	19.77		
B.P. Julian	13	17	2	283	43	18.86		
S.K. Warne	9	9	2	132	36	18.85		
C.J. Richards	5	10	–	176	46	17.60		
C.R. Miller	6	11	1	174	34	17.40		
A.J. Bichel	7	9	–	151	36	16.77		
M.S. Kasprowicz	11	14	2	199	44	16.58		
J.L. Arnberger	4	7	–	116	47	16.57		
R.P. Larkin	4	7	–	113	49	16.14		
D.W. Fleming	7	10	–	131	30	13.10		
T.B.A. May	12	19	2	211	41	12.41		
J. Angel	12	15	3	123	23	10.25		

(Qualification – 100 runs, average 10.00)
(Played in one match – T.J. Dixon 25 & 122)

Bowling

	Overs	Mds	Runs	Wks	Av	Best	10/m	5/inn
A.M. Stuart	119.2	36	335	25	13.40	4/22		
A.I.C. Dodemaide	157.2	41	374	22	17.00	6/67		2
S.R. Waugh	81	21	200	10	20.00	4/34		
M.S. Kasprowicz	428.3	108	1310	64	20.46	7/64	2	8
J.N. Gillespie	366.3	93	1142	51	22.39	6/68		1
G.D. McGrath	445.4	115	1142	51	22.39	5/40		2
B.A. Reid	285.5	77	569	24	23.70	5/36		1
D. Tazelaar	237.5	66	571	24	23.79	5/42		1
A.J. Bichel	229.4	49	767	32	23.96	5/31		1
J. Angel	445	128	1225	49	25.00	6/68		2
S.K. Warne	449.5	131	1057	42	25.16	7/23	1	2
D.J. Saker	277.4	86	763	30	25.43	7/32	1	1
G.J. Rowell	104.3	19	296	11	26.90	3/31		
D.A. Freedman	384.3	88	1083	40	27.07	8/49	1	3
P.R. Reiffel	284	75	772	28	27.57	5/39		1
G.R.J. Matthews	499.4	140	1236	43	28.74	5/43		2
B.P. Julian	442.5	120	1327	46	28.84	5/41		4
I.J. Harvey	151.5	34	497	16	31.06	3/25		
C.J. McDermott	343.1	83	1083	34	31.85	5/49		2
N.D. Maxwell	255	59	706	22	32.09	6/56		1
S.R. Cary	200.5	70	500	15	33.33	3/35		
S. Lee	173.4	31	540	16	33.75	4/20		
T.B.A. May	561.5	115	1540	44	35.00	6/83	1	3
T.M. Moody	319	83	880	25	35.20	7/38		1
S.M. Thompson	143	25	528	15	35.20	3/59		
B.J. Oldroyd	147	50	389	11	35.36	3/41		
M.W. Ridgway	327.5	57	1152	32	36.00	5/64		1
S.G. Law	164	56	365	10	36.50	5/39		1
M.A. Harrity	261.4	37	1021	27	37.81	4/75		
B.A. Williams	219	38	720	20	38.50	6/98		1
P.E. McIntyre	476.1	84	1502	39	38.51	6/133	1	1
D.W. Fleming	235	49	703	18	39.05	4/64		
J.P. Marquet	336.3	70	1140	28	40.71	5/94		1
G.S. Blewett	202.3	54	614	14	43.85	4/59		
G.B. Hogg	340.5	103	942	21	44.85	5/59		2
C.R. Miller	191	29	696	14	49.71	3/47		
R.J. Tucker	145	21	502	10	50.20	3/33		
M.A. Hatton	161.2	29	639	12	53.25	4/48		
P.W. Jackson	303.5	93	828	15	55.20	4/158		
S. Young	254	52	813	14	58.07	4/74		

(Qualification – 10 wickets)

Leading Fielders

60 – A.C. Gilchrist (ct 56 / st 4); 59 – W.A. Seccombe (ct 57 / st 2); 47 – T.J. Nielsen (ct 38 / st 9); 46 – P.A. Emery (ct 35 / st 11); 32 – I.A. Healy (ct 29 / st 3); 27 – P.J. Roach; 24 – M.A. Taylor; 22 – J.D. Siddons; 20 – D.S. Berry (ct 18 / st 2) and M.N. Atkinson (ct 16 / st 4); 18 – T.M. Moody; 15 – M.T.G. Elliott and N.D. Maxwell; 14 – D.C. Boon, M.L. Love, J.P. Maher, J.L. Langer and B.P. Julian; 12 – A.R. Border and M.P. Lavender; 11 – D.M. Jones, G.R.J. Matthews, M.E. Waugh and D.S. Webber

New South Wales First-Class Matches

Batting

	v. Western Province (Sydney) 3–5 October 1995		v. Western Australia (Perth) 18–21 October 1995		v. Tasmania (Sydney) 26–29 October 1995		v. Victoria (Melbourne) 1–3 November 1995		v. Tasmania (Hobart) 24–27 November 1995		v. West Indies (Newcastle) 7–10 December 1995		v. South Australia (Adelaide) 12–15 January 1996		v. Western Australia (Sydney) 26–29 January 1996		v. Queensland (Brisbane) 7–9 February 1996		v. Victoria (Sydney) 8–11 March 1996		v. Queensland (Sydney) 14–16 March 1996		v. South Australia (Sydney) 23–26 March 1996		M	Inns	NO	Runs	HS	Av
J.L. Arnberger	17	6																	47	–	10	10	5	21	4	7	–	116	47	16.57
M.G. Bevan	45	119*	27	30*	103*	–	44*	2	4	2	86	4			2	109							87	57	8	15	4	721	119*	65.54
S.R. Waugh	47	0	0	31	107	54	80	5															25	41	5	10	–	390	107	39.00
K.J. Roberts	4	0							20	62	10	–	50	39	0	3	0	17	72	–					7	12	–	277	72	23.08
S. Lee	84	67*	6	10*	101*	–	20	–	63	33*	12	3*			69	22*							4	0	8	14	6	494	101*	61.75
G.R.J. Matthews	1	–	40	–	24	–	6	5*	73	40*	17	–	55	10	15	15*	5	0	40*	–	17*	18	45	16	12	19	5	442	73	31.57
P.A. Emery	36*	–	10	–	–	–	10	–	4	–	3	–	60	6	1	–	24	5	31*	–	1	72	1	36	12	15	2	300	72	23.07
N.D. Maxwell	1*	–							46*	–	1	–	4	26	30	–	20	21*	–	–	10	7	0	12	9	12	3	178	46*	19.77
S.H. Cook	–	–	13*	–	–	–	–	–																	4	1	1	13	13*	–
A.M. Stuart	–	–											0	7			8*	10	–	–	0	2*			5	6	2	27	10	6.75
D.A. Freedman	–	–	37	–	–	–	2	–	6*	–	2*	–	2	21*	4*	–			–	–	15	23	0	54*	11	11	5	166	54*	27.66
M.A. Taylor			21	38	53	14	126	10	29	73													38	32	5	10	–	434	126	43.40
M.J. Slater			1	96	5	100*	29	19	55	50			16	44											5	10	1	415	100*	46.11
M.E. Waugh			48	33	44	17*	1	10*	14	0													57	26	5	10	2	250	57	31.25
G.D. McGrath			–	–	–	–	10	–															0*	18*	4	3	2	28	18*	28.00
S.M. Thompson									40	–	10	–	49*	7	0	–	16	6							5	7	1	128	49*	21.33
C.J. Richards											29	25	1	0	28	46	0	2			22	23			5	10	–	176	46	17.60
R.J. Davison											11	30*	27	25	44	15	2	4	19	–					5	9	1	177	44	22.12
R. Chee Quee											105	–	5	29	21	0	32	32	0	–	59	4			6	10	–	287	105	28.70
M.T. Haywood																	0	7	97	–	17	2			3	5	–	123	97	24.60
B.E. McNamara																	28	36			0	0			2	4	–	64	36	16.00
W.J. Holdsworth																			–	–					1					–
D.P. Waugh																					19	3			1	2	–	22	19	11.00
Byes	7	1		4	5		4	1		2	2			5	5	1	1		3		2	5		2						
Leg-byes		1	3	1	11	3	7	4	7	4	14	3	10	5	16	5	7	9	8		5	3	5	5						
Wides		2	1				1		1				1	1			2	1	2					1						
No-balls	2	6	4		4		4		6	4	6	4	4	4	24	4	14	10			16	6		2						
Total	244	202	211	243	457	188	344	56	368	270	308	69	284	229	259	220	159	160	319		193	178	267	323						
Wickets	6	3	9	4	5	2	9	4	9	5	10	2	10	10	10	5	10	10	5		10	10	10	9						
Result	W		D		W		W		W		D		L		D		L		D		L		D							
Points	–		0		6		6		6		–		0		0		2		2		0		0							

Fielding Figures

46 – P.A. Emery (ct 35 / st 11)
15 – N.D. Maxwell
12 – M.A. Taylor
11 – G.R.J. Matthews
7 – K.J. Roberts
6 – S. Lee
5 – M.G. Bevan, M.E. Waugh, R.J. Davison and subs
4 – A.M. Stuart and S.M. Thompson
3 – J.L. Arnberger, S.R. Waugh, R. Chee Quee and M.T. Haywood
2 – C.J. Richards and B.E. McNamara
1 – S.H. Cook, D.A. Freedman, M.J. Slater, G.D. McGrath and D.P. Waugh

Bowling

	A.M. Stuart	S.H. Cork	N.D. Maxwell	S. Lee	G.R.J. Matthews	D.A. Freedman	G.D McGrath	M.E. Waugh	M.G. Bevan	S.R. Waugh	S.M. Thompson	R.J. Davison	B.E. McNamara	W.J. Holdsworth	M.T. Haywood	Byes	Leg-byes	Wides	No-balls	Total	Wkts
v. Western Province (Sydney)	11.2–6–31–3	8–0–23–2	9–1–29–1	7–3–5–2	9–3–30–0	2–1–2–1											8	1	11	128	10
3–5 October 1995	11–5–18–1	9–2–21–0	12–5–18–2	4–0–17–0	14–5–33–1	30.2–8–75–5											10	2	2	192	10
v. Western Australia (Perth)		20–7–53–0		12–1–52–0	19–4–77–0	15–4–51–0	23–8–61–1	2–0–5–0	1–1–0—0	12–2–41–1						10	1		8	351	3
18–21 October 1995		11–3–31–0		6–0–17–0	24–4–73–2	5–2–11–0	18–3–42–0			6–2–25–2							7		2	206	4
v. Tasmania (Sydney)		13.5–5–43–3		6–2–5–0	35–10–82–2	32–8–67–2	26–8–48–3	2–1–3–0	1–0–9–0								5			262	10
26–29 October 1995		9.3–2–20–4		11–2–20–4	21–2–55–1	16–3–38–0	13–5–27–1									1	4			165	10
v. Victoria (Melbourne)		0.4–0–0–0		12.2–2–42–1	22–5–52–4	8.1–1–19–3	17–9–16–1	6–2–8–0		7–2–13–0						4	4		2	158	10
1–3 November 1995				14–3–29–2	23–4–101–3	5.4–0–27–1	22–5–59–3	4–0–14–1									11	1		241	10
v. Tasmania (Hobart)			23.5–6–56–6	19–3–51–1	26–9–49–0	16–3–41–0					18–3–59–3					2	5		8	263	10
24–27 November 1995			18–3–64–1	8–0–48–0	23.4–9–31–4	16–2–46–2					18–2–65–3					3	9			266	10
v. West Indies (Newcastle)			12–3–34–1	13–2–49–0	16–5–52–0	28.4–14–49–8					13–1–56–1					4	2		12	246	10
7–10 December 1995			12–3–25–3	4–0–18–0	23–6–43–5	20.5–4–44–2					5–2–20–0					2	8		2	160	10
v. South Australia (Adelaide)	23–5–67–3		22–3–73–1		19–3–70–1	24.5–4–69–2					23–2–95–2					7	11	6	16	392	10
12–15 January 1996	10–2–43–2		8–0–19–0		17–4–57–0	18–3–73–2					9–1–34–1	5–1–15–2				1	1		12	243	8
v. Western Australia (Sydney)			29–5–75–3	28.2–9–75–2	33–9–65–2	19–1–75–0					24–5–94–2					3	15		6	402	10
26–29 January 1996			15–4–29–0	7–1–32–0		20–4–71–3			7–2–23–0		9–2–27–1					8	3			193	4
v. Queensland (Brisbane)	11–0–48–4		10.3–4–17–3								11–4–32–2		10–3–44–1			6	3	3	20	150	10
7–9 February 1996	16–5–33–4		13–2–38–0		32.3–17–34–4						13–3–46–0		11–4–28–2				2		4	181	10
v. Victoria (Sydney)	13–7–22–4		8–3–19–0		16.1–9–19–4	5–1–13–2								9–3–20–0		3	3		4	99	10
8–11 March 1996	17–5–48–4		13–2–56–0		36–13–75–3	22–6–62–1						2–1–4–0		14–1–92–0		1		4	14	338	8
v. Queensland (Sydney)	7–1–25–0		17–8–43–0		37.2–6–134–5	30–9–91–5							21–6–62–0		1–0–5–0	3	8		4	371	10
14–16 March 1996															0.5–0–1–0					1	0
v. South Australia (Sydney)			25–7–74–0	15–2–53–3	25–6–53–0	18–5–63–0	29–9–70–3		7–2–23–2	12–3–32–1						6	9	1	8	383	10
23–26 March 1996			7.4–0–37–1	7–1–27–1	28–7–51–2	8–2–26–0	21–8–39–3	7–1–19–2	4–0–19–0	9–4–15–1							1			234	10
	119.2–36–335–25	72–19–191–9	225–59–706–22	173.4–31–540–16	499.5–140–1236–43	360.3–85–1013–39	169–55–362–15	21–4–49–3	20–5–74–2	46–11–126–5	143–25–528–15	7–2–19–2	42–13–134–3	23–4–112–0	1.5–0–6–0						
Bowler's average	13.40	21.22	32.09	33.75	28.74	25.97	24.13	16.33	37.00	25.20	35.20	9.50	44.66	–	–						

Queensland First-Class Matches

Batting

	v. Western Province (Brisbane) 26–28 September 1995		*v.* Victoria (Brisbane) 19–22 October 1995		*v.* South Australia (Brisbane) 25–28 October 1995		*v.* Tasmania (Hobart) 2–5 November 1995		*v.* Sri Lankans (Mackay) 22–25 November 1995		*v.* Western Australia (Brisbane) 30 November–2 December 1995		*v.* South Australia (Adelaide) 29 December 1995–1 January 1996		*v.* Tasmania (Brisbane) 26–29 January 1996		*v.* New South Wales (Brisbane) 7–9 February 1996		*v.* Western Australia (Perth) 13–16 February 1996		*v.* New South Wales (Sydney) 14–16 March 1996		*v.* Victoria (Melbourne) 23–26 March 1996		M	Inns	NO	Runs	HS	Av
T.J. Barsby	65	3	0	0	18	69	5	74	15	51	133	–	28	6			0	43	4	4	79	0*	19	0	11	21	1	616	133	30.80
T.J. Dixon	25	122																							1	2	–	147	122	73.50
M.L. Love	10	60	18	40	62	3	185*	9	14	0	0	–	26	15	186	–	8	14	11	89	69	–	8	88	12	21	1	915	186	45.75
S.G. Law	6	73	89	53	16	38*	–	107*	27	15	6	–			53	–							0	28	8	13	2	511	107*	46.45
J.P. Maher	17	16*	88	23	108	–	–	27	50	22	88	–	2	7	12*	–	11	24	23	13	3	–	28	16	12	19	2	578	108	34.00
A. Symonds	28	31*							73	14	0	–	14	11	5	–	26	3	6	12					7	12	1	223	73	20.27
I.A. Healy	41	–					–	4*															21	45	3	4	1	111	45	37.00
A.J. Bichel	24	–							10	0	1	–	0	36	–	–					25	–	25	30	7	9	–	151	36	16.77
C.J. McDermott	0*	–	1	–	15	–	–	–																	4	3	1	16	15	8.00
M.S. Kasprowicz	33	–	9	17*	14	–	–	–	11	13	31	–			–	–	44	0	3	7	9*	–	0	8	11	14	2	199	44	16.58
P.W. Jackson	11*	–	6*	–	6*	–	–	–					22*	8			6	6	8	14*	1	–	4*	5	9	12	6	97	22*	16.16
M.L. Hayden			64	11	11	47*	152*	15	1	36	32	–	17	25	234	–					44	1*	16	33	9	16	3	739	234	56.84
A.R. Border			20	70*	59	–	–	20	48	31	8	–	79	94	20	–	5	29	25	45	78	–	4	34	11	17	1	669	94	41.81
W.A. Seccombe			54*	19	27	–			22	38*	48*	–	0	10	–	–	4	36	25	10	23	–			9	13	3	316	54	31.60
C.G. Rackemann			–	–	2*	–	–	–									0*	0*							3	3	3	2	2*	–
D. Tazelaar									0*	14	8	–	5	4*			1	4	0*	2	2	–	3	6*	7	12	4	49	14	6.12
G.J. Rowell													0	11	–	–			8	6					3	4	–	25	11	6.25
M.P. Mott															15	–	13	16	35	12					3	5	–	91	35	18.20
G.I. Foley																					23	–			1	1	–	23	23	23.00
Byes	2		2	1	2	1	1			7			1	2			6			2	3									
Leg-byes	1	1	8	4	9		6	2	3	5	7		6	9	7		3	2	2	7	8		2	11						
Wides			2		1					1					1		3							4						
No-balls	12	10		8	6	6	28	2	31	8				4			20	4	4	14	4		12	30						
Total	275	316	361	246	356	164	377	260	305	255	362		200	242	533		150	181	154	237	371	1	142	338						
Wickets	9	4	8	6	9	2	1	5	10	10	10		10	10	6		10	10	10	10	10	0	10	10						
Result	W		D		W		D		W		W		L		D		W		L		W		L							
Points	–		0		6		0		–		6		0		2		6		0		6		0							

Fielding Figures

59 – W.A. Seccombe (ct 57 / st 2)
14 – M.L. Love and J.P. Maher
12 – A.R. Border
6 – T.J. Barsby, A.J. Bichel and S.G. Law
5 – I.A. Healy, M.S. Kasprowicz, M.L. Hayden and D. Tazelaar
4 – M.P. Mott
3 – C.J. McDermott, A. Symonds and G.I. Foley
2 – T.J. Dixon
1 – C.G. Rackemann and sub

Bowling

	C.J. McDermott	A.J. Bichel	S.G. Law	M.S. Kasprowicz	P.W. Jackson	J.P. Maher	A. Symonds	C.G. Rackemann	A.R. Border	I.A. Healy	D. Tazelaar	G.J. Rowell	M.P. Mott	G.I. Foley	Byes	Leg-byes	Wides	No-balls	Total	Wkts
v. Western Province (Brisbane)	13–4–29–1	12–2–41–2	8–4–20–1	12.4–4–17–6												5	1		112	10
26–28 September 1995		27.2–5–90–2	9–3–26–0	27–2–116–0	31–9–79–0	10–1–32–0	23–4–125–1								6	4	1	2	478	3
v. Victoria (Brisbane)	37–15–93–2		11–2–52–0	26.1–4–94–3	42–5–158–4			27–6–71–1	1–1–0–0						4	10	2	14	482	10
19–22 October 1995																				
v. South Australia (Brisbane)	24–6–82–2		17–8–29–1	26.1–11–48–6	8–2–27–0			27–10–82–1								8		12	276	10
25–28 October 1995	25–9–58–5		7–3–17–0	24.3–4–78–3	15–4–38–1			13–2–49–1								3		8	243	10
v. Tasmania (Hobart)	26–4–121–1		17–4–50–0	23–3–102–0	19–0–77–0			23–5–74–1	7–0–22–0						5	7		10	458	2
2–5 November 1995	18–1–65–2			11–1–62–0	22–7–80–1			15–0–77–0		0.1–0–1–0						5		4	290	3
v. Sri Lankans (Mackay)		19–5–43–3	7–2–14–0	22.3–7–64–7			3–0–11–0		5–2–3–0		18–6–38–0					5	1	12	178	10
22–25 November 1995		11–1–40–2		8.3–2–31–5							15–5–36–3				1	1		10	109	10
v. Western Australia (Brisbane)		12–4–31–5	8–5–10–2	17.2–4–37–1							15–4–31–2					1		10	110	10
30 November–2 December 1995		23–9–51–0	16–7–22–1	19–4–72–5			14.3–5–34–2				25–10–51–2				4	7	1	12	241	10
v. South Australia (Adelaide)		22–1–97–1			32–11–71–1	11–5–21–2	7–2–19–1				23–5–69–2	22.1–5–50–3				4	1	27	331	10
29 December 1995–1 January 1996		10–2–58–4			18–5–60–0	5–0–25–1	11–2–45–1				8–2–27–0	12.2–3–31–3			4	2		15	252	9
v. Tasmania (Brisbane)		27.4–8–87–4	26–7–39–5	23–4–80–1		3–0–18–0	18–9–29–0		1–1–0–0			25–3–74–0				9	1	30	336	10
26–29 January 1996		15–3–46–2	17–6–33–0	21–5–61–2			21–7–51–0		20–5–65–1			18–1–53–3	3–0–13–0			8		24	330	8
v. New South Wales (Brisbane)				14–7–52–2	5–2–15–0	6–2–12–1		11.3–2–30–1			17–5–42–5				1	7	2	14	159	10
7–9 February 1996				25–8–57–3	8–2–25–0			12–3–40–3			14–4–29–4					9	1	10	160	10
v. Western Australia (Perth)				27–11–63–2	16–5–51–1	5–1–11–3					15.5–4–28–2	19–7–51–2				3		26	207	10
13–16 February 1996				22–5–45–2	16.1–5–32–1	9–3–14–0	2–0–11–0				22–5–41–0	8–0–37–0	1–0–1–0		1	3	1	20	185	3
v. New South Wales (Sydney)		11.4–2–34–3		14–4–49–1	39–24–39–3						15–5–28–2			12–1–36–1	2	5		16	193	10
14–16 March 1996		13–5–22–2		16–7–34–5	17.4–9–36–2						14–6–38–0			18–4–40–1	5	3		6	178	10
v. Victoria (Melbourne)		14–1–67–2	12–3–27–0	25.5–7–74–5	9–3–21–1	2–1–1–0					21–4–59–2				1	5		22	255	10
23–26 March 1996		12–1–60–0	6–1–17–0	22.5–4–74–5	6–0–19–0						15–1–54–0					2		14	226	5
	143–39– 448–13	229.4–49– 767–32	161–55– 356–10	428.3–108– 1310–64	303.5–93– 828–15	51–13– 134–7	99.3–29– 325–5	128.3–28– 423–8	34–9– 90–1	0.1–0– 1–0	237.5–66– 571–24	104.3–19– 296–11	4–0– 14–0	30–5– 76–2						
Bowler's average	34.46	23.96	35.60	20.46	55.20	19.14	65.00	52.87	90.00	–	23.79	26.90	–	38.00						

South Australia First-Class Matches

Batting

Batting	v. Queensland (Brisbane) 25–28 October 1995		v. Pakistanis (Adelaide) 2–5 November 1995		v. Western Australia (Adelaide) 24–27 November 1995		v. Victoria (Adelaide) 30 November–3 December 1995		v. Queensland (Adelaide) 29 December 1995–1 January 1996		v. Western Australia (Perth) 5–8 January 1996		v. New South Wales (Adelaide) 12–15 January 1996		v. Tasmania (Hobart) 7–10 February 1996		v. Victoria (Melbourne) 13–16 February 1996		v. Tasmania (Adelaide) 14–17 March 1996		v. New South Wales (Sydney) 23–26 March 1996		v. Western Australia (Adelaide) 30 March–3 April 1996		M	Inns	NO	Runs	HS	Av
B.A. Johnson	23	0	54	0	9	54	61	4													1	90			5	10	–	296	90	29.60
P.C. Nobes	6	13	0	0	48	8	43	27	56	18	17	1	121	55	–	8	86	74	17	7	70	38	103	24	12	23	–	840	121	36.52
G.S. Blewett	25	126	28	103*	44	66			51	24	8	96	2	13	–	0	5	22	135	28	106	12	5	72	11	21	1	971	135	48.55
D.S. Lehmann	0	4	138	0	116	0	103	44*	32	71	62	161	5	10	–	105	23	64	89	50	82	35	43	0	12	23	1	1237	161	56.22
J.A. Brayshaw	0	64	40*	3	11	12	113	–	25	47	60	13	15	0	–	80*	20	1	141*	59	8	0	87	66	12	22	3	865	141*	45.52
J.D. Siddons	130	8	20	125	96	9	26	–	24	22	18	40	110	20	–	27*	6	29	36	2			38	4	11	20	1	790	130	41.57
T.J. Nielsen	47	1	57	12*	10	2	12	–	26	6	0	2	27	23	–	–	115	4	0	8	32	16	27	4	12	21	1	431	115	21.55
T.B.A. May	13	11	0	–	0	0	4	–	30	0	22	5	15	–	–	–	8	8*	41	2*	33	14	5	0	12	19	2	211	41	12.41
J.N. Gillespie	5*	3	20	–	0	11	2	1	3	0	3	2	35	3*	–	–	4	13			12	1	10	5	11	19	2	133	35	7.82
P. Wilson	0	2*													–	–	5*	1							3	4	2	8	5*	4.00
M.A. Harrity	7	0	–	–	–	1	0*	–	2*	–	6	1*							–	–	4*	1*			8	9	5	22	7	5.50
P.E.McIntyre			–	–	0*	9*	1	0	0	1*	12*	3	0*	15*			10	1	–	0	1	12	0	6*	10	17	7	71	15*	7.10
D.S. Webber							6	45*	50	42	13	37	2	89	–	46	12	0	28	16	10	14	0	5	9	17	1	415	89	25.93
R.A. Swain													20	1											1	2	–	21	20	10.50
B.N. Wigney															–	–									1					–
S.P. George																			–	0			0*	1*	2	3	2	1	1*	1.00
Byes			3			2	7	12		4			7	1		2			5	3	6		3	7						
Leg-byes	8	3	8	2	5	6	8	1	4	2	5	7	11	1		4	7	6	8	5	9	1	1							
Wides							1	5	1		1		6			2	2		1		1		3	1						
No-balls	12	8	24	4	14	6	10	2	27	15	8	22	16	12		6	6	6	6	2	8		22	13						
Total	276	243	392	249	353	186	397	141	331	252	235	390	392	243	0	280	309	229	507	182	383	234	347	208						
Wickets	10	10	8	5	9	10	10	4	10	9	10	10	10	8	0	4	10	10	7	9	10	10	10	9						
Result	L		D		L		W		W		D		W		W		L		W		D		D							
Points	0		–		2		6		6		0		6		6		0		6		2		–							

Fielding Figures

47 – T.J. Nielsen (ct 38 / st 9)
22 – J.D. Siddons
11 – D.S. Webber
9 – J.A. Brayshaw
7 – D.S Lehmann
6 – P.C. Nobes
5 – B.A. Johnson, G.S. Blewett, J.N. Gillespie and P.E. McIntyre
4 – T.B.A. May
3 – subs
2 – M.A. Harrity
1 – S.P. George

Bowling

Bowling	M.A. Harrity	J.N. Gillespie	P. Wilson	G.S. Blewett	T.B.A. May	B.A. Johnson	P.E. McIntyre	J.A. Brayshaw	R.A. Swain	B.N. Wigney	P.C. Nobes	S.P. George	D.S. Lehmann	Byes	Leg-byes	Wides	No-balls	Total	Wkts
v. Queensland (Brisbane)	27–6–91–2	21–2–62–4	23–2–74–2	13–2–52–0	19–7–47–1	5–0–19–0								2	9	1	6	356	9
25–28 October 1995	12–0–50–2	8.4–1–34–0	8–4–26–0		17–4–53–0									1			6	164	2
v. Pakistanis (Adelaide)	24.2–4–90–4	21–6–82–4			18–6–34–0		27–9–67–2								3		2	276	10
2–5 November 1995	16–2–71–2	16–3–58–1		8–3–16–0	27–2–86–1	3–0–8–0	18–3–52–0							2	5		6	298	5
v. Western Australia (Adelaide)	19.4–2–75–4	16–3–58–1		12–3–36–1	22–4–83–3		17–1–51–1								6	2	12	309	10
24–27 November 1995	19–3–87–1	24–4–94–3		5–2–7–0	25.3–3–65–3	6–1–15–1	33–7–97–1							1	10	2	8	376	9
v. Victoria (Adelaide)	20–1–84–4	17.2–4–48–2			29–6–82–1		23–4–79–2							1	3	1	6	297	10
30 November–3 December 1995	19–4–62–1	10–3–22–1			26.1–4–70–5		18–4–73–2							3	7	2	4	237	10
v. Queensland (Adelaide)	5–2–15–0	15–5–38–1		3–1–6–0	36–8–88–5		27–7–46–3							1	6			200	10
29 December 1995–1 January 1996	11–2–34–0	23–9–50–4		3–0–13–0	39.4–14–83–6		21–4–51–0							2	9		4	242	10
v. Western Australia (Perth)	11.5–4–25–1	24.2–8–51–2		23.1–6–73–1	49–12–131–4		26–4–92–1							2	3	5	10	377	10
5–8 January 1996	4.5–0–23–1	19.1–3–68–6		7–2–22–0			20–0–70–2	3–0–15–0							6	1	6	204	9
v. New South Wales (Adelaide)		25–9–71–3		4–0–14–1	33–7–76–2		27.5–8–70–3		15–4–43–1						10	1	4	284	10
12–15 January 1996		17–5–39–3		5–0–16–0	34.5–7–72–4		26–9–59–3		7–0–33–0					5	5	1	4	229	10
v. Tasmania (Hobart)		21–5–69–2	22–10–50–4	4–1–15–0	29–4–66–0					20–6–51–2				1	6		18	258	8
7–10 February 1996		2–0–14–0								1–0–4–0				2	1	1	2	21	1
v. Victoria (Melbourne)		29–7–105–3	29–9–54–1	14–3–53–0	33–5–128–0		29.5–1–171–3							3	5	2	14	519	7
13–16 February 1996			4–0–9–0				3–0–10–0				0.5–0–1–0							20	0
v. Tasmania (Adelaide)	19–1–69–1			10–3–34–2	29–8–56–2		27.2–2–75–4					19–1–81–1		1	4		14	320	10
14–17 March 1996	13–1–63–2			8–0–21–0	29–2–106–4		35–9–85–2					15.1–2–57–2		2	14	5	14	348	10
v. New South Wales (Sydney)	13–0–72–0	18–5–50–4		15–6–46–2			31.1–7–94–4								5			267	10
23–26 March 1996	22–5–86–2			13–2–31–0		11–1–60–0	35–4–133–6						1–0–6–1	2	5	1	2	323	9
v. Western Australia (Adelaide)		30–10–96–3		15–4–53–1	47.4–9–157–2		23–0–105–0					30–4–102–2	1–0–3–0		4	1	14	520	9
30 March–3 April 1996		9–1–33–4		6–1–16–0	18–3–57–1		8–1–22–0					8.5–2–36–1			5		10	169	8
Bowler's average	256.4–37– 997–27 36.92	366.3–93– 1142–51 22.39	86–25– 213–7 30.42	168.1–39– 524–8 65.50	561.5–115– 1540–44 35.00	25–2– 102–1 102.00	476.1–84– 1502–39 38.51	3–0– 15–0 –	22–4– 76–1 76.00	21–6– 55–2 27.50	0.5–0– 1–0 –	73–9– 276–6 46.00	2–0– 9–1 9.00						

Tasmania First-Class Matches

Batting

Batting	v. New South Wales (Sydney) 26–29 October 1995		v. Queensland (Hobart) 2–5 November 1995		v. New South Wales (Hobart) 24–27 November 1995		v. Sri Lankans (Launceston) 1–4 December 1995		v. Victoria (Melbourne) 13–16 December 1995		v. Victoria (Hobart) 12–15 January 1996		v. Queensland (Brisbane) 26–29 January 1996		v. South Australia (Hobart) 7–10 February 1996		v. Western Australia (Perth) 8–11 March 1996		v. South Australia (Adelaide) 14–17 March 1996		v. Western Australia (Hobart) 23–26 March 1996		M	Inns	NO	Runs	HS	Av
D.F. Hills	43	29	220*	24	85	32			54	59	66	9*	85	0	47	–	0	0	70	30	43	18	10	19	2	914	220*	53.76
J. Cox	62	0	10	39	33	42	19	34	99	79	9	18*	3	21	0	5	4	96	5	4	54	34	11	22	1	670	99	31.90
D.C. Boon	26	57	88	56	6	17			45	6	108	–			31	–	18	152	117	4	91	1	9	16	–	823	152	51.43
R.T. Ponting	20	43	118*	100*	46	22	131*	–													8	0	5	9	3	488	131*	81.33
S. Young	35	9	–	62*	5	57	10	20	45	6	100*	–	56	175*	10	–	4	10	32	38	14	51*	11	19	4	739	175*	49.26
M.J. DiVenuto	27	0	–	–	7	46	19	26	0	0	61	–	89	23	26	5*	104	66	27	154	93	18	11	19	1	791	154	43.94
R.J. Tucker	19	0	–	–	40*	0	54*	60*	0	95*	19	–	21	42	6	–	0	37	1	5	4	17	11	18	4	420	95*	30.00
M.N. Atkinson	2	16	–	–	3	31*	–	42	2	40	37	–	18	4	59*	–	19	4*	12	22	9	15	11	17	3	335	59*	23.92
M.A. Hatton	10*	2					–	–	4	15*	35	–	0	0	23	–							6	8	2	89	35	14.83
C.R. Miller	13	0							5	–			13	30	31	5*			23	34	15	5	6	11	1	174	34	17.40
G.J. Denton	0	4*			14	0	–	–	0*	–													4	5	2	18	14	6.00
M.G. Farrell			–	–			–	14			12	–											3	2	–	26	14	13.00
M.W. Ridgway			–	–	9	7			5	–	1*	–	1	0*	0*	–	18*	–	14	2*	4*	9	9	12	6	70	18*	11.66
J.P. Marquet			–	–	0	0	–	–			–	–	0*	–	–	–	1	–	0*	0	–	0	9	7	2	1	1	0.20
A.J. Daly							70	62*					10	3			0	22*	0	20			4	8	2	187	70	31.16
J.M. Saint																	6	–					1	1	–	6	6	6.00
Byes		1	5		2	3	1	3	8		1					2	1	4	1	2								
Leg-byes	5	4	7	5	5	9	9	2	20	12	6		9	8	1	1	3	5	4	14	12	9						
Wides									1	1			1		6	1		2		5								
No-balls			10	4	8		22	10	4				30	24	18	2	6	4	14	14	10	6						
Total	262	165	458	290	263	266	335	273	292	313	455	27	336	330	258	21	184	402	320	348	357	183						
Wickets	10	10	2	3	10	10	4	5	10	6	8	0	10	8	8	1	10	6	10	10	9	10						
Result	L		D		L		D		W		W		D		L		W		L		L							
Points	0		2		0		–		6		6		0		2		6		0		1							

Fielding Figures

20 – M.N. Atkinson (ct 16 / st 4)
9 – D.C. Boon
8 – S. Young, M.J. DiVenuto and R.J. Tucker
7 – D.F. Hills
5 – J. Cox
4 – J.P. Marquet
3 – R.T. Ponting, M.G. Farrell, A.J. Daly and M.W. Ridgway
2 – J.M. Saint and subs
1 – M.A. Hatton and G.J. Denton

Bowling

Bowling	S. Young	C.R. Miller	G.J. Denton	M.A. Hatton	R.J. Tucker	D.C. Boon	J.P. Marquet	M.W. Ridgway	M.G. Farrell	R.T. Ponting	M.J. DiVenuto	J.M. Saint	Byes	Leg-byes	Wides	No-balls	Total	Wkts
v. New South Wales (Sydney)	29–6–102–0	31–3–96–1	26–4–105–0	25–3–110–2	8–2–28–1								5	11		4	457	5
26–29 October 1995	6–1–24–0	7–1–33–1	7–1–29–0	9–1–60–1	1.5–0–10–0	6–0–29–0								3			188	2
v. Queensland (Hobart)	16–3–55–0				13–2–47–0		17–5–69–1	18–0–112–0	18–2–67–0	5–1–20–0			1	6		28	377	1
2–5 November 1995	5–1–28–0				10–1–43–1		14–0–77–0	15–3–59–3	12–1–51–1					2		2	260	5
v. New South Wales (Hobart)	28–6–74–4		20–2–99–2		10–2–31–0		13–2–58–1	18–5–60–0		7–1–39–1				7	1	6	368	9
24–27 November 1995	17–5–38–2		12–5–46–0		12–4–23–1	2–0–13–0	14–1–68–0	21–4–68–1		1–0–8–0			2	4		4	270	5
v. Sri Lankans (Launceston)	21–5–66–2		9–2–40–0	32–11–87–3	7–1–29–1		22–3–82–1		16.3–5–47–2	1–0–1–0			6	11		8	369	10
1–4 December 1995			8–1–40–1	9–0–57–0			9–5–21–0		7–0–38–1					4			160	2
v. Victoria (Melbourne)	21–2–70–0	25–6–84–1	22–3–79–1	23–3–78–0	10.1–3–26–2	1–1–0–0		25–3–82–1					4	7	7	8	430	6
13–16 December 1995	3–0–24–0	6–2–20–1	9–4–25–0	11.2–2–48–4	3–0–16–1			16–3–39–1						2		2	174	7
v. Victoria (Hobart)	24–6–51–3			11–0–48–1	6–0–19–0		21.1–6–63–4	21–3–73–1	3–0–10–1					11		8	275	10
12–15 January 1996	5–1–19–1			17–3–54–0	18–4–33–3		20.5–5–45–2	22–8–37–3	2–0–7–0				6	5		2	206	10
v. Queensland (Brisbane)	16–4–53–0	37–6–141–2		18–4–67–0	7–1–42–0		35–5–128–2	28.5–6–94–1			1–0–1–0			7	1		533	6
26–29 January 1996																		
v. South Australia (Hobart)																	0	0
7–10 February 1996				6–2–30–1	14–0–60–0		22.4–5–84–1	18–3–71–2			9–1–29–0		2	4	2	6	280	4
v. Western Australia (Perth)	7–2–21–2				3–0–17–0	1.3–1–0–1	22–6–50–3	18–3–57–3				21–5–68–1	2	9	2		224	10
8–11 March 1996	23–7–69–0				14–0–48–0	7–1–17–0	32–11–94–5	10–0–24–2				22.5–5–105–1		4			361	8
v. South Australia (Adelaide)	13–2–37–0	38–6–151–2			8–1–30–0		36–8–110–1	43–3–166–4					5	8	1	6	507	7
14–17 March 1996		11–2–47–3					16–2–63–1	17.3–3–64–5					3	5		2	182	9
v. Western Australia (Hobart)	15–1–52–0	26–2–82–2				4–0–19–1	28.5–3–83–3	22–5–89–4		3–0–17–0			3	12		6	357	10
23–26 March 1996	5–0–30–0	10–1–42–1					13–3–45–3	14.3–5–57–1					6	4		2	184	5
Bowler's average	254–52–813–14 58.07	191–29–696–14 49.71	113–22–463–4 115.75	161.2–29–639–12 53.25	145–21–502–10 50.20	21.3–3–78–2 39.00	336.3–70–1140–28 40.71	327.5–57–1152–32 36.00	58.3–8–220–5 44.00	17–2–85–1 85.00	10–1–30–0 –	43.5–10–173–2 86.50						

Victoria First-Class Matches

Batting

	v. Queensland (Brisbane) 19–22 October 1995		v. New South Wales (Melbourne) 1–3 November 1995		v. Pakistanis (Melbourne) 24–26 November 1995		v. South Australia (Adelaide) 30 November–3 December 1995		v. Tasmania (Melbourne) 13–16 December 1995		v. Western Australia (Perth) 29 December 1995–1 January 1996		v. Tasmania (Hobart) 12–15 January 1996		v. South Australia (Melbourne) 13–16 February 1996		v. New South Wales (Sydney) 8–11 March 1996		v. Western Australia (Melbourne) 14–17 March 1996		v. Queensland (Melbourne) 23–26 March 1996		M	Inns	NO	Runs	HS	Av
M.T.G. Elliott	138	–	53	32	29	8	15	35	203	11	104*	135	3	21	200	3*			3	98	8	54	10	19	2	1153	203	67.82
R.P. Larkin	34	–	3	0	9	17	49	1															4	7	–	113	49	16.14
D.M. Jones	145	–	28	28	127	–	2	85	45	37	18	70	53	58	56	–	0	45	1	107	69	0	11	19	–	974	145	51.26
J.R. Bakker	2	–	31	3	31	–	1	11															4	6	–	79	31	13.16
B.J. Hodge	1	–	5	4													23	22	43	28	15	33*	5	9	1	174	43	21.75
P.A. Broster	8	–	5	22																			2	3	–	35	22	11.66
D.S. Berry	74	–	11*	48	5	–	16	7															4	6	1	161	74	32.20
P.R. Reiffel	24	–	0	11																	16	–	3	4	–	51	24	12.75
S.K. Warne	9	–	0	36																	15*	–	3	4	1	60	36	20.00
D.W. Fleming	15	–	0	30	4	–	29	0	–	–	0	19	13	21									7	10	–	131	30	13.10
B.A. Williams	2*	–	12	15*	35*	–	18	12	–	5	0	41*											6	9	4	140	41*	28.00
G.R. Vimpani					23	32*	79	8	71	51	6	10	3	46	8	17*	6	54					7	14	2	414	79	34.50
C.J. Peake					21	8*	46	43	10	22	34	5	36	12	0	–							6	11	1	237	46	23.70
D.J. Saker					9	–	19	0					15	4	–	–	0	–	1*	–	0	–	7	8	1	48	19	6.85
C. Howard					20	–	12*	19*															2	3	2	51	20	51.00
G.B. Gardiner									6	31	24	12	29	22									3	6	–	124	31	20.66
I.J. Harvey									7	3	6	55	85	4	136	–	1	46	0	54	6	11	7	13	–	414	136	31.84
P.J. Roach									62*	10*	4	84	12	1	15*	–	8	14	9	0*	29	10*	7	13	5	258	84	32.25
B.B.J. Doyle									–	–													1					–
T.F. Corbett									–	–	0	3*	0*	2*									3	4	3	5	3*	5.00
J.M. Davison											5	2	7	2	7	–	3	0					4	7	–	26	7	3.71
W.G. Ayres															73	–	6	0	79	140	68	100	4	7	–	466	140	66.57
A.I.C. Dodemaide															–	–	2	49*	0	–	0	–	4	4	1	51	49*	17.00
I.S.L. Hewett															–	–	4*	34*					2	2	2	38	34*	–
B.P. Ricci																	36	55	2	2	1	2	3	6	–	98	55	16.33
A.D. McGinty																			4	–			1	1	–	4	4	4.00
B.J. Stacey																			2	–			1	1	–	2	2	2.00
Byes	4		4		7		1	3	4		3			6	3		3			2	1							
Leg-byes	10		4	11	3		3	7	7	2	5	3	11	5	5		3	1	6	9	5	2						
Wides	2			1		1	1	2	7						2			4										
No-balls	14		2		39	6	6	4	8	2	6	20	8	2	14		4	14	2	16	22	14						
Total	482		158	241	362	72	297	237	430	174	215	459	275	206	519	20	99	338	152	456	255	226						
Wickets	10		10	10	10	2	10	10	6	7	10	9	10	10	7	0	10	8	10	6	10	5						
Result	D		L		W		L		L		D		L		W		D		W		W							
Points	2		0		–		-0.3		1.9		0		0		6		0		6		5.8							

Fielding Figures

27 – P.J. Roach
20 – D.S. Berry (ct 18 / st 2)
14 – M.T.G. Elliott
11 – D.M. Jones
5 – I.J. Harvey
4 – S.K. Warne and C.J. Peake
3 – D.W. Fleming and B.P. Ricci
2 – R.P. Larkin, J.R. Bakker, B.A. Williams, D.J. Saker, A.D. McGinty, subs and J.M. Davison
1 – G.R. Vimpani, P.A. Broster, P.R. Reiffel, B.B.J. Doyle, T.F. Corbett, W.G. Ayres, A.I.C. Dodemaide and I.S.L. Hewett

Bowling

	P.R. Reiffel	D.W. Fleming	B.A. Williams	J.R. Bakker	S.K. Warne	A.D. McGinty	D.J. Saker	C. Howard	D.M. Jones	C.J. Peake	T.F. Corbett	I.J. Harvey	B.J. Hodge	J.M. Davison	I.S.L. Hewett	A.I.C. Dodemaide	Byes	Leg-byes	Wides	No-balls	Total	Wkts
v. Queensland (Brisbane)	26–10–57–2	20–4–75–0	23–4–80–1	9–2–28–1	34–5–11–3												2	8	2		361	8
19–22 October 1995	15–3–43–1	9–0–40–1	21–4–69–2	6–0–27–0	27–4–62–1												1	4		8	246	6
v. New South Wales (Melbourne)	35–13–73–2	1.3–1–5–0	30.3–6–95–1	15–3–36–0	45–9–122–5												4	7	1	4	344	9A
1–3 November 1995	8–1–19–3		6–1–20–1		3.1–0–12–0												1	4			56	4
v. Pakistanis (Melbourne)		14–3–30–1	14–1–57–3	5–2–10–1			12.5–2–35–3	7–1–13–2									8	1		2	154	10
24–26 November 1995		23–4–64–4	23.4–6–83–2	11–4–12–1			17–5–49–1	14–4–47–0	1–1–0–0	5–0–20–1							2	2	2	2	279	
v. South Australia (Adelaide)		31–7–86–1	32–7–98–6	14–5–28–0			24.4–7–63–2	10–2–55–1	3–1–17–0	4–0–35–0							7	8	1	10	397	10
30 November–3 December 1995		12–6–29–2	9–0–44–1	4–1–12–0			8–3–23–0	3.3–0–20–0									12	1	5	2	141	4
v Tasmania (Melbourne)		21–4–54–1	24.5–5–76–2							1–0–3–0	24–8–53–2	23–10–46–3					8	20	1	4	292	10
13–16 December 1995		21.3–5–72–3	15–1–78–0								20–5–51–1	12–1–42–2						12	1		313	6B
v. Western Australia (Perth)		29–6–88–1	20–3–70–1							2–0–11–1	18–5–73–0	14.5–5–39–2		35–6–120–1				12	1	10	413	7
29 December 1995–1 January 1996		12–0–48–1							1–0–11–0		10–1–64–3	11–0–46–1		10–1–51–2			4	14	2	6	238	8
v. Tasmania (Hobart)		41–9–112–3					43–13–105–3				29–6–70–1	27–7–78–1		35–8–83–0			1	6			455	8
12–15 January 1996										1.1–0–2–0	4–0–14–0	3–1–11–0									27	0
v. South Australia (Melbourne)							27–11–82–3					18–4–78–2		12–1–26–0	23–9–72–2	20–6–44–2		7	2	6	309	10
13–16 February 1996							24–4–66–3					10.3–1–25–3		1–0–9–0	20–2–74–0	17–3–49–4		6		6	229	10
v. New South Wales (Sydney)							36–13–111–2					14.3–1–59–0		11–1–28–0	28–8–63–1	34–14–47–2	3	8	2		319	5
8–11 March 1996																						
v. Western Australia (Melbourne)						20.2–6–41–1	19–5–43–0					11–3–27–1				24–7–67–6	4	7			223	10
14–17 March 1996						15–6–38–1	20–9–66–2					7–1–46–1	1–1–0–0			19.5–2–57–2	1	12			309	10C
v. Queensland (Melbourne)	10–2–43–0				15–5–25–2		18.2–8–32–7									13–1–40–1		2		12	142	10
23–26 March 1996	23.3–4–75–1				46–13–94–0		27.5–6–88–4						1–1–0–0			29.3–8–70–5		11	4	30	338	10
	117.3–33–	235–49–	219–38–	64–17–	170.1–36–	35.2–12–	277.4–86–	34.3–7–	5–2–	13.1–0–	105–25–	151.5–34–	2–2–	104–17–	71–19–	157.2–41–						
	310–9	703–18	770–20	153–3	426–11	79–2	763–30	135–3	28–0	71–2	325–7	497–16	0–0	317–3	209–3	374–22						
Bowler's average	34.44	39.05.	38.50	51.00	38.72	39.50	25.43	45.00	–	35.50	46.42	31.06	–	105.66	69.66	17.00						

A. P.A. Broster 3–1–2–0
B. B.B.J. Doyle 19–8–32–2; 12–1–58–0
C. B.J. Stacey 11–4–34–5; 19–3–89–2

Western Australia First-Class Matches

Batting

Batting	v. New South Wales (Perth) 18–21 October 1995		v. Pakistanis (Perth) 28–31 October 1995		v. South Australia (Adelaide) 24–27 November 1995		v. Queensland (Brisbane) 30 November–2 December 1995		v. Victoria (Perth) 29 December 1995–1 January 1996		v. South Australia (Perth) 5–8 January 1996		v. New South Wales (Sydney) 26–29 January 1996		v. Queensland (Perth) 13–16 February 1996		v. Tasmania (Perth) 8–11 March 1996		v. Victoria (Melbourne) 14–17 March 1996		v. Tasmania (Hobart) 23–26 March 1996		v. South Australia (Adelaide) 30 March–3 April 1996		M	Inns	NO	Runs	HS	Av
M.P. Lavender	173*	46	21	49	27	32	27	12	26	9	34	55	15	73	8	77	2	1	10	8	25	18	18	6	12	24	1	772	173*	33.56
M.E. Hussey	42	81	146	17	48	5	7	5	37	25*	96	38	105	49	4	31	10	7	13	85	47	4	11	32	12	24	1	945	146	41.08
J.L. Langer	15	13	5	40	3	153	10	14	161	56	44	51*	9	5	26	32	22	107	0	0	120	6	30	28	12	24	1	950	161	41.30
D.R. Martyn	45	9	1	15	27	43	29	37	14	30	19	17	41	37	6	13*	15	203*	8	10	65	62*	9	2	12	24	3	757	203*	36.04
T.M. Moody	57*	30*	42	26	31	18	7	82	27	59	15	4	16	15*	59	7*	90	8	60	37	29	28	68	72	12	24	4	887	90	44.35
A.C. Gilchrist	–	18*	58*	20	99*	68	3	47	82	9	8	22	26	–	35	–	2	19	21	59	9	41*	189*	0	12	21	5	835	189*	52.18
G.B. Hogg	–	–	101*	7*	0	0	4	0	31	0	66	0	111*	–	4*	–	4	10	14	25	5	–	61	1*	12	19	5	444	111*	31.71
B.P. Julian	–	–	–	6	42	14			12*	21	5	1	43	–	0	–	23	0	19	31	4	–	25	2	11	16	1	248	43	16.53
J. Angel	–	–	–	–	1	15	4	8		2	23	3	10	–	7	–	10*	2*	21	10*	0	–	7	–	12	15	3	123	23	10.25
B.J. Oldroyd	–	–	–	–	11	7*	2	12*	–	1*	47	0													6	7	3	80	47	20.00
B.A. Reid	–	–	–	–	0	–	2*	0	–	–	0*	0*	1	–											7	6	3	3	2*	1.00
C.E. Coulson							4	0																	1	2	–	4	4	2.00
R.M. Baker													1	3*	27	–	21	0	46	29	32	13	83	11	6	11	1	266	83	26.60
S.R. Cary															2	–	12	–	0*	2	0*	–	–	–	5	5	2	16	12	5.33
Byes	10					1		4		4	2		3	8		1	2		4	1	3	6								
Leg-byes	1	7	5	1	6	10	1	7	12	14	3	6	15	3	3	3	9	4	7	12	12	4	4	5						
Wides			1		2	2		1	1	2	5	1				1	2						1							
No-balls	8	2	22	8	12	8	10	12	10	6	10	6	6		26	20					6	2	14	10						
Total	351	206	402	189	309	376	110	241	413	238	377	204	402	193	207	185	224	361	223	309	357	184	520	169						
Wickets	3	4	5	7	10	9	10	10	7	8	10	9	10	4	10	3	10	8	10	10	10	5	9	8						
Result	D		D		W		L		D		D		D		W		L		L		W		D							
Points	2		–		6		0		2		2		2		6		2		2		6		–							

Fielding Figures

60 – A.C. Gilchrist (ct 56 / st 4)
18 – T.M. Moody
14 – J.L. Langer
13 – B.P. Julian
12 – M.P. Lavender
9 – M.E. Hussey and G.B. Hogg
7 – D.R. Martyn
5 – R.M. Baker
4 – J. Angel
2 – B.A. Reid
1 – B.J. Olroyd, C.E. Coulson and S.R. Cary

Bowling

Bowling	B.A. Reid	J. Angel	B.P. Julian	T.M. Moody	B.J. Oldroyd	G.B. Hogg	D.R. Martyn	C.E. Coulson	R.M. Baker	S.R. Cary	J.L. Langer	Byes	Leg-byes	Wides	No-balls	Total	Wkts
v. New South Wales (Perth)	25–8–44–2	26.1–11–55–2	15–5–47–2	7–1–20–1	7–3–15–1	13–6–27–1							3	1	4	211	9
18–21 October 1995	11–2–24–1	9–1–30–0	6–3–17–0		21–2–82–3	15–0–85–0						4	1			243	4
v. Pakistanis (Perth)	13–5–27–0	11.2–3–42–3	16–9–32–3	1–0–3–0	19–11–45–3	2–1–12–0							3			164	10
28–31 October 1995	18–6–36–1	26–7–61–3	16–3–58–0	3–1–16–0	24–13–33–1	24–15–22–2								1	4	226	8
v. South Australia (Adelaide)	25.3–7–53–4	20–2–74–0	16–3–70–5	16–2–66–0	10–3–45–0	4–0–31–0	1–0–9–0						5		14	353	9
24–27 November 1995	20–6–40–3	8.2–2–19–1	4–0–23–0	7–2–13–1	11–3–24–0	26–8–59–5						2	6		6	186	10
v. Queensland (Brisbane)	27–5–56–0	24–4–90–5		17–1–60–0	17–3–41–3	1–0–8–0		29–7–100–2					7			362	10
30 November–2 December 1995																	
v. Victoria (Perth)	22.5–12–36–5	19–7–45–2	11–2–26–0	10–2–22–2	12–3–42–0	10–1–36–0						3	5		6	215	10
29 December 1995–1 January 1996	23–8–53–1	19–8–62–0	18–4–69–0	25–1–98–2	13–3–38–0	35–6–126–5	2–0–10–0						3		20	459	9
v. South Australia (Perth)	22.5–6–54–3	17–2–53–3	12–2–39–2	18–8–57–1		9–2–27–1							5	1	8	235	10
5–8 January 1996	18–2–66–1	22–7–82–2	23–5–81–3	19.1–7–68–4	13–6–24–0	16–4–62–0							7		22	390	10
v. New South Wales (Sydney)	18.4–3–59–3	15–4–50–1	19–3–58–5	16–6–37–0		17–5–30–1	5–2–4–0					5	16		24	259	10
26–29 January 1996	14–7–21–0	16–5–29–0	23–7–58–1	10–1–33–2		17–3–41–0	3–2–6–0		15–4–26–2			1	5		4	220	5
v. Queensland (Perth)		15–9–20–2	15–4–36–1	13.1–3–37–2		3–1–10–2				18–4–49–3			2		4	154	10
13–16 February 1996		23–7–45–5	19–5–44–1	16–3–40–1		23.5–7–40–1				24–10–59–2		2	7		14	237	10
v. Tasmania (Perth)		23–5–68–6	19–9–42–3	10–4–24–0		3–0–14–0				16–7–32–1		1	3		6	184	10
8–11 March 1996		29–9–64–3	25–5–80–2	21–3–80–0		16–0–58–0	1–0–8–0		4–0–13–0	27.5–6–90–1		4	5	2	4	402	6
v. Victoria (Melbourne)		22–11–41–3	15.3–3–41–5	15–6–22–1		3–1–7–0				18–11–35–1			6		2	152	10
14–17 March 1996		26.1–8–107–1	22–3–86–0	16–5–44–1		7–1–32–0	3–0–14–0		32–7–93–2	28–9–69–1		2	9		16	456	6
v. Tasmania (Hobart)		28.1–8–79–3	29–5–80–2	11–2–33–0			4–3–6–0		21–5–63–0	30–8–82–3	1–0–2–0		12		10	357	9
23–26 March 1996		9–2–26–0	7–0–40–0	21.4–6–38–7		12–5–30–0	3–1–5–0		2–2–0–0	15–5–35–3			9		6	183	10
v. South Australia (Adelaide)		17.5–4–56–3	30.2–7–95–5	27–10–45–0		34–10–89–0	4–1–12–1		8–5–9–0	16–6–29–0	5–2–8–0	3	1	3	22	347	10
30 March–3 April 1996		19–7–27–1	29–13–56–4	19–9–24–0		36–25–42–3	7–5–6–0		11–3–26–1	8–4–20–0		7		1	13	208	9
	258.5–77–569–24	445–128–1225–49	389.5–100–1178–44	319–83–880–25	147–50–389–11	326.5–101–888–21	33–14–80–1	29–7–100–2	93–26–230–5	200.5–70–500–15	6–2–10–0						
Bowler's average	23.70	25.00	26.77	35.20	35.36	42.28	80.00	50.00	46.00	33.33	–						

India

As one of the hosts for the World Cup, India showed a customary emphasis on one-day internationals in the programme that they arranged prior to the competition. New Zealand visited India for three Tests and double that number of limited-over internationals. Such a menu has now become a staple diet for Indian cricket at international level. One feels that if this pattern continues, it can only have an adverse effect on cricket in India.

Anil Kumble, destroyer of New Zealand in the first Test and captain of Karnataka as they triumphed in the Ranji Trophy.
(David Munden/Sportsline)

Irani Cup
New Zealand tour, Test and one-day international series
Duleep Trophy
Ranji Trophy
First-class averages

In 1994–95, for example, India played three Test matches, against West Indies at home, and 21 one-day internationals. Although they were to tour England after the World Cup and to play three Test matches, the number of one-day games in which they appeared in 1995–96 would again be far in excess of their Test schedule.

Indian officials would argue that, together with Australia and South Africa, India had the most stable of national sides, and that their results in one-day internationals made them favourites to win the World Cup, especially as it was being played on the Indian sub-continent. Azharuddin was now one of the longest serving of Test captains, and he led a side that was strong and exciting in batting. There were no doubts as to the quality of the spin bowling, and Kumble's outstanding feats for Northamptonshire had been well documented. More significant for India, however, was the splendid season that Srinath had enjoyed with Gloucestershire in 1995. His advance as a new-ball bowler brought to the Indian attack a cutting edge which some believed had been lacking.

There were early season rumours that Kapil Dev was to come out of retirement and would play in the World Cup, but this idea was later discounted. Maninder Singh, the left-arm spinner who had prospered in Kapil Dev's time, announced his retirement from international cricket.

Irani Cup

2, 3 and 4 October 1995
at Wankhede Stadium, Bombay
Rest of India 99 (P.L. Mhambrey 5 for 20) and 186
Bombay 266 (V.G. Kambli 112, Venkatesh Prasad 4 for 75) and 20 for 1
Bombay won by 9 wickets

The Irani Cup match is recognised as a Test trial: the selectors traditionally choose the national side after this game between the reigning Ranji Trophy holders and the Rest of India. The encounter, which heralded the start of the 1995–96 season, offered the selectors little guidance, and the match, scheduled for five days, was over in just three. Medium-pacer Paras Mhambrey destroyed the Rest on the opening day and Bombay already had a lead of 35 by the end of the day.

Bombay boast a formidable batting line-up with Manjrekar, Tendulkar, Kambli and Muzumdar in the top six. The left-handed Kambli dominated on this occasion, hitting three sixes and 13 fours in his 244-minute innings. He finally became one of Venkatapathy Raju's three victims, the left-arm spinner having him caught on the boundary.

Mhambrey brought his match figures to 8 for 55 as the Rest of India collapsed for a second time, and the game was over before lunch on the third day.

New Zealand Tour

7, 8 and 9 October 1995
at Municipal Ground, Rajkot
New Zealanders 366 for 5 dec. (M.J. Greatbatch 138, A.C. Parore 79, B.A. Young 52) and 251 for 5 dec. (M.D. Crowe 101 not out, S.P. Fleming 72)
BCCI President's XI 399 for 6 dec. (R.S. Dravid 145 not out, M. Azharuddin 100, Robin Singh 50) and 69 for 1
Match drawn

Following their recent disasters, New Zealand boldly embarked on a period of reconstruction. Lee Germon, captain and wicket-keeper of Canterbury, was appointed captain of the national side for an eight-month span although his international experience was limited to one one-day match which had been abandoned because of rain. Germon had long been canvassed as New Zealand's best prospect as captain, having led Canterbury since the age of 22. The deposed skipper, Rutherford, chose to accept an

Paras Mhambrey was successful in the Irani Cup and also won a place in the party to tour England. (Ben Radford/Allsport)

invitation to play in South Africa. New to the Kiwis' party was Roger Twose, the Warwickshire all-rounder, who has settled in New Zealand, but there were disappointments in that Greg Loveridge, a most promising leg-spinner, and Dipak Patel, the veteran off-spinner, were injured and could not make the trip. Mark Haslam, a slow left-arm spinner who had played against Zimbabwe, came in as replacement, and New Zealand were happy to welcome a fit Chris Cairns. Glenn Turner was the new coach of the national side.

The first day's play in India was most encouraging. Mark Greatbatch hit three sixes and 18 fours in a four-hour innings in which he was twice dropped. He shared an opening partnership of 128 with Bryan Young and a second wicket partnership of 149 with Adam Parore, who was to relinquish his wicket-keeping duties and concentrate on batting during the tour. The Indian skipper Mohammad Azharuddin countered for the President's XI on the second day, but Martin Crowe's century gave the tourists great heart.

13, 14 and 15 October 1995
at Wankhede Stadium, Bombay
New Zealanders 217 for 8 dec. (M.J. Greatbatch 100, P.L. Mhambrey 4 for 79) and 192 for 3 (S.P. Fleming 79 not out, A.C. Parore 64)
Bombay 360 (V.G. Kambli 104, S.V. Manjrekar 79, A.A. Muzumdar 53)
Match drawn

The tourists' second and last match before the first Test was interrupted by rain. The New Zealanders began poorly, but Greatbatch reached another century to take them to respectability. On his dismissal, the visitors collapsed. Bombay found runs easy with Kambli again in fine form, and the New Zealanders were handicapped when Germon had to go to hospital after being struck on the cheek while keeping wicket. The tourists were happy to draw.

Test Series

India show their dominance over the reshaped New Zealand side, but rain destroys the series.

From the 14 players that had been selected for the first Test, India omitted Rathore, the only newcomer, Hirwani and Prasad. Sidhu was unfit and was not in the squad. Lee Germon's Test debut came as captain of New Zealand. He won the toss, and New Zealand batted.

Germon was at the crease sooner than he would have liked or could have anticipated. He came to the wicket four overs after lunch with his side 71 for 6 and sinking fast. Srinath had started the decline when he bowled Greatbatch who played a loose shot. The pitch had been very damp from the copious rain sweeping the country, and it had looked a good surface on which to bat, but it was drying quickly, presenting problems for the New Zealand batsmen which they found difficult to cope with.

First Test Match – India v. New Zealand

18, 19 and 20 October 1995 at M. Chinnaswamy Stadium, Bangalore

New Zealand

	First Innings		Second Innings	
B.A. Young	c Tendulkar, b Raju	14	(2) lbw, b Prabhakar	8
M.J. Greatbatch	b Srinath	10	(1) b Prabhakar	16
A.C. Parore	lbw, b Srinath	2	lbw, b Srinath	3
M.D. Crowe	c Tendulkar, b Kumble	11	lbw, b Kumble	24
S.P. Fleming	c Mongia, b Srinath	16	c and b Kumble	41
S.A. Thomson	c Mongia, b Chauhan	17	c Mongia, b Kumble	6
C.L. Cairns	c Manjrekar, b Raju	15	b Srinath	23
*L.K. Germon (Capt)	c Tendulkar, b Kumble	48	lbw, b Kumble	41
D.J. Nash	lbw, b Kumble	0	c Kumble, b Raju	17
M.N. Hart	c Prabhakar, b Kumble	1	not out	27
D.K. Morrison	not out	1	c Azharuddin, b Kumble	9
	b 4, lb 5, nb 1	10	b 8, lb 10	18
		145		233

	O	M	R	W	O	M	R	W
Prabhakar	6	–	15	–	8	3	23	2
Srinath	14	5	24	3	15	6	41	2
Venkatapathy Raju	16	6	47	2	14	2	43	1
Kumble	18	5	39	4	27.2	4	81	5
Chauhan	11	7	11	1	9	1	27	–

Fall of Wickets
1–**14**, 2–**22**, 3–**30**, 4–**44**, 5–**71**, 6–**71**, 7–**116**, 8–**116**, 9–**144**,
1–**19**, 2–**32**, 3–**36**, 4–**58**, 5–**80**, 6–**130**, 7–**134**, 8–**173**, 9–**210**

India

	First Innings		Second Innings	
M. Prabhakar	c Germon, b Morrison	4	c Greatbatch, b Hart	43
A.D. Jadeja	c Young, b Morrison	59	c Parore, b Hart	73
S.V. Manjrekar	lbw, b Nash	15	not out	29
S.R. Tendulkar	c Young, b Nash	4	not out	0
M. Azharuddin (Capt)	b Cairns	87		
V.G. Kambli	c Parore, b Nash	27		
*N.R. Mongia	lbw, b Cairns	1		
A.R. Kumble	not out	6		
J. Srinath	b Cairns	0		
R.K. Chauhan	c Young, b Morrison	1		
Venkatapathy Raju	c Hart, b Cairns	0		
	lb 8, w 4, nb 12	24	lb 3, nb 3	6
		228	(for 2 wickets)	151

	O	M	R	W	O	M	R	W
Morrison	18	5	61	3	7	1	34	–
Cairns	17.4	5	44	4	6	1	13	–
Nash	16	3	50	3	7	1	26	–
Hart	7	1	28	–	9.5	3	34	2
Thomson	12	3	37	–	11	3	41	–

Fall of Wickets
1–**11**, 2–**45**, 3–**54**, 4–**149**, 5–**211**, 6–**214**, 7–**220**, 8–**220**, 9–**227**,
1–**101**, 2–**145**

Umpires: M.J. Kitchen & S.K. Bansai

India won by 8 wickets

Second Test Match – India v. New Zealand

25, 26, 27, 28 and 29 October 1995 at M.A. Chidambaram Stadium, Madras

India

	First Innings	
M. Prabhakar	not out	**41**
A.D. Jadeja	**b** Nash	**3**
N.S. Sidhu	**c** Twose, **b** Cairns	**33**
S.R. Tendulkar	not out	**52**
M. Azharuddin (Capt)		
V.G. Kambli		
*N.R. Mongia		
A.R. Kumble		
J. Srinath		
R.K. Chauhan		
Venkatapathy Raju		
	lb **1**, w **1**, nb **13**	**15**
	(for 2 wickets)	**144**

	O	M	R	W
Morrison	14	4	34	–
Cairns	16	7	18	**1**
Nash	15	3	22	**1**
Haslam	17.1	4	50	–
Thomson	9	–	19	–

Fall of Wickets
1–**18**, 2–**73**

New Zealand

M.J. Greatbatch
R.G. Twose
A.C. Parore
M.D. Crowe
S.P. Fleming
C.L. Cairns
S.A. Thomson
*L.K. Germon (Capt)
D.J. Nash
D.K. Morrison
M.J. Haslam

Umpires: K.T. Francis & S. Venkataraghavan

Match drawn

Third Test Match – India v. New Zealand

8, 9, 10, 11 and 12 November, 1995 at Barabati Stadium, Cuttack

India

	First Innings	
M. Prabhakar	**c** Crowe, **b** Nash	**22**
A.D. Jadeja	**c** Hart, **b** Cairns	**45**
N.S. Sidhu	**c** Fleming, **b** Nash	**41**
S.R. Tendulkar	**b** Cairns	**2**
M. Azharuddin (Capt)	lbw, **b** Cairns	**35**
V.G. Kambli	**c** Germon, **b** Nash	**28**
*N.R. Mongia	not out	**45**
A.R. Kapoor	**st** Germon, **b** Haslam	**42**
A.R. Kumble	**c** Greatbatch, **b** Nash	**2**
J. Srinath	not out	**21**
N.D. Hirwani		
	lb **10**, nb **3**	**13**
	for 8 wickets, dec.	**296**

	O	M	R	W
Morrison	13	–	52	–
Cairns	26.5	4	95	**3**
Nash	29	4	62	**4**
Twose	1	–	5	–
Haslam	15	1	42	**1**
Hart	5	–	30	–

Fall of Wickets
1–**69**, 2–**75**, 3–**77**, 4–**143**, 5–**172**, 6–**188**, 7–**254**, 8–**267**

New Zealand

	First Innings	
M.J. Greatbatch	**c** Jadeja, **b** Hirwani	**50**
R.G. Twose	lbw, **b** Hirwani	**36**
A.C. Parore	**c** Mongia, **b** Hirwani	**12**
M.D. Crowe	**c** Kambli, **b** Hirwani	**15**
C.L. Cairns	**c** Jadeja, **b** Hirwani	**13**
*L.K. Germon (Capt)	run out	**2**
M.N. Hart	**c** Srinath, **b** Hirwani	**8**
D.J. Nash	not out	**10**
D.K. Morrison	lbw, **b** Kumble	**0**
M.J. Haslam	not out	**1**
S.P. Fleming		
	b **7**, lb **19**, nb **2**	**28**
	(for 8 wickets, dec.)	**175**

	O	M	R	W
Prabhakar	5	2	10	–
Srinath	8	3	16	–
Kapoor	17	3	32	–
Kumble	27	12	32	**1**
Hirwani	31	12	59	**6**

Fall of Wickets
1–**86**, 2–**109**, 3–**130**, 4–**139**, 5–**151**, 6–**155**, 7–**166**, 8–**166**

Umpires: V.K. Ramaswamy & I.D. Robinson

Match drawn

Srinath trapped Parore, and Venkatapathy Raju accounted for Young who passed a thousand runs in Test cricket, but the prize scalp went to Kumble. He made a ball rear sharply at Martin Crowe who gloved it to slip. It was the leg-spinner's 100th Test wicket.

Germon used his feet sensibly against the spinners. He has both the technique and the desire to succeed at the top level. He hit nine fours and was by far the most impressive of the New Zealand batsmen.

Morrison, Cairns and Nash proved to be a lively trio with the new ball, and Germon took a fine catch to get rid of Prabhakar. Nash had Manjrekar leg before and, most importantly, had Tendulkar taken at slip to leave India on 54 for 3. Jadeja and Azharuddin added 27 more untroubled runs before the close.

Jadeja reached his highest Test score, and he and Azharuddin shared a stand of 95 before the opener, playing his first Test for three years, was caught at slip. Azharuddin batted magnificently. He alone seemed untroubled by the vagaries of the pitch and showed total mastery until he was deceived by what was, in effect, a brisk off-break from Cairns. It was the rejuvenated Cairns who was primarily responsible for the last six Indian wickets falling for 17 runs. Trailing by 83 runs, New Zealand had clawed their way back into the game, but their position was still precarious.

It became even more precarious as they lost five wickets in clearing the arrears. Fleming and Cairns stood firm, and New Zealand closed on 126 for 5.

Cairns was bowled by Srinath on the third morning without adding to his overnight score, and Fleming was out seven runs later, caught and bowled by Kumble who exploited the uncertainties of the pitch gleefully to claim five wickets in a Test innings for the sixth time. Germon again batted well and was mainly responsible for 99 being added for the last three wickets. This meant that India needed 151, which was probably a few more than they would have liked.

They need have had no worries. Prabhakar and Jadeja began with a partnership of 101. Both fell to Hart, the left-arm spinner, with Jadeja brilliantly caught by Parore diving at cover. By then, however, Jadeja had bettered the Test score he had hit in the first innings. His blazing display brought him 12 fours in his 73 off 92 balls. Victory came with an hour of the third day to spare. Azharuddin was named Man of the Match, but he himself played special tribute to Jadeja.

For the second Test match, Sidhu returned to the Indian side in place of Manjrekar. Roger Twose, making his Test debut, and Haslam replaced Young and Hart in the New Zealand team.

The changes mattered little. Azharuddin won the toss, and India batted when the match finally got under way after tea. Jadeja was becalmed before playing back to a full length ball from Nash and being bowled off his boot. Bad light ended play early, with India 54 for 1 from 35.3 overs.

No play was possible on the second or third days, and on the fourth, play was brought to an early end by another downpour. Tendulkar hit 50 in 88 minutes off 76 balls, and Sidhu was out when he flicked at a ball from Cairns, who bowled very well, and was splendidly caught at backward square-leg by Twose.

There was no play on the fifth day.

The New Zealanders played one match against the Indian Colts XI before the final Test match.

For the third Test match, Hart was recalled in place of Thomson while India included Kapoor in place of Chauhan, and Hirwani played his first Test in five years in place of Venkatapathy Raju. India won the toss and batted.

Jadeja and Prabhakar started briskly with 58 coming from 14 overs in the first hour. Both fell to fine slip catches. Prabhakar was taken high at second slip by Martin Crowe, and Jadeja, having hit six fours, was caught low at third slip by Hart. Tendulkar was bowled by an outstanding delivery by Cairns who straightened an in-swinger to hit off stump as the batsman attempted to turn the ball to leg. Lunch was taken at 84 for 3, and a drizzle prevented an immediate resumption. Sidhu and Azharuddin played with confidence when play restarted, but, at 120 for 3, a storm ended the day's cricket, and no play was possible on the second and third days. That there was no play on the third day was due to leaking covers on the pitch, a disgrace for a Test ground.

Leg-spinner Narendra Hirwani was recalled to the Test side for the third match against New Zealand and took 6 for 59. (Graham Chadwick/Allsport)

On the fourth day, India collapsed to 188 for 6 against New Zealand's pace attack before Mongia and Kapoor added 66. India declared at their overnight score, and New Zealand batted on a painfully slow pitch on the final day to reach 175 for 8 from 88 overs.

Roger Twose at last batted in a Test match, 20 days after first being selected, and was in for three-and-a-half hours for his 36. Greatbatch and Twose scored 86 for the first wicket before Greatbatch became the first of Hirwani's six victims, caught bat and pad.

The leg-spinner made a remarkable return to Test cricket, taking six of the first seven wickets to fall. He and Kumble bowled in tandem, masters of a difficult art and contrasting in style. It was the most fascinating aspect of a match ruined by rain.

2, 3 and 4 November 1995
at Hyderabad
New Zealanders 454 (R.G. Twose 119 retired, C.L. Cairns 75 not out, S.P. Fleming 65) and 276 for 4 (S.P. Fleming 100 not out, A.C. Parore 96)
Indian Colts XI 180 (M.N. Hart 6 for 73)
Match drawn

New Zealand had one match between the second and third Test, in which they indulged in batting practice against weak opposition.

One-day International Series

New Zealand beat India on Indian soil in a one-day international for the first time, but the home side still comes out on top as rain again interferes.

The six-match series began with New Zealand's first win over India in a limited-over match outside New Zealand. Germon won the toss and asked India to bat. Tendulkar began with an aggressive 30, and by the 32nd over, India were 159 for 2 with Prabhakar in control. There came a collapse as the last eight Indian wickets went down for 77 runs. Astle, who, like Larsen, had joined the New Zealand squad for the one-day games, was soon out and Greatbatch fell at 66, but Crowe and Fleming took New Zealand to victory with three overs to spare as they shared an unbroken partnership of 171. Crowe hit his fourth century in one-day internationals, but he was dropped three times. Tendulkar was twice the unlucky bowler as Prabhakar put down a catch at short mid-wicket when Crowe was 29, and when he was 34 Crowe was dropped at cover by Jadeja. Shortly after he reached his fifty he was missed by Chatterjee who failed to accept an easy chance off his own bowling. Crowe hit eight fours and two sixes in what transpired to be his last century in international cricket.

India drew level by winning the second match, at Amritsar. Put in to bat on a pitch that was lively and on which the occasional delivery kept low, New Zealand were wrecked by the swing bowling of Manoj Prabhakar who

First One-day International – India *v.* New Zealand

15 November 1995 at Keenan Stadium, Jamshedpur

India

M. Prabhakar	c Astle, **b** Larsen	**83**
S.R. Tendulkar	c Greatbatch, **b** Morrison	**30**
N.S. Sidhu	c Nash, **b** Larsen	**12**
M. Azharuddin (Capt)	**b** Cairns	**32**
V.G. Kambli	**b** Nash	**15**
A.D. Jadeja	**c** and **b** Thomson	**0**
*N.R. Mongia	**b** Morrison	**26**
A.R. Kumble	**b** Nash	**4**
J. Srinath	not out	**17**
U. Chatterjee	run out	**3**
Venkatesh Prasad	**b** Cairns	**1**
	lb **6**, w **7**	**13**
	49.1 overs	**236**

	O	M	R	W
Morrison	9	–	49	**2**
Nash	10	–	56	**2**
Cairns	9.1	1	33	**2**
Larsen	10	–	40	**2**
Astle	3	–	17	**–**
Thomson	8	–	35	**1**

Fall of Wickets
1–**45**, 2–**94**, 3–**159**, 4–**177**, 5–**178**, 6–**194**, 7–**204**, 8–**222**, 9–**234**

New Zealand

M.J. Greatbatch	**b** Venkatesh Prasad	**31**
N.J. Astle	lbw, **b** Prabhakar	**7**
M.D. Crowe	not out	**107**
S.P. Fleming	not out	**78**
R.G. Twose		
S.A. Thomson		
C.L. Cairns		
*L.K. Germon (Capt)		
G.R. Larsen		
D.K. Morrison		
D.J. Nash		
	lb **9**, w **3**, nb **2**	**14**
	47 overs (for 2 wickets)	**237**

	O	M	R	W
Prabhakar	7	–	36	**1**
Srinath	8	1	30	**–**
Venkatesh Prasad	10	1	50	**1**
Kumble	10	–	40	**–**
Chatterjee	9	–	54	**–**
Tendulkar	3	–	18	**–**

Fall of Wickets
1–**18**, 2–**66**

Umpires: O.K. Sathe & Gire'Dhan *Man of the Match:* M.D. Crowe

New Zealand won by 8 wickets

Second One-day International – India v. New Zealand
18 November 1995 at Gandhi Ground, Amritsar

New Zealand

M.J. Greatbatch	c Tendulkar, b Prabhakar	2
N.J. Astle	lbw, b Tendulkar	59
M.D. Crowe	lbw, b Prabhakar	2
S.P. Fleming	c Mongia, b Srinath	3
R.G. Twose	b Venkatesh Prasad	5
C.L. Cairns	b Kumble	4
S.A. Thomson	c Srinath, b Prabhakar	14
*L.K. Germon (Capt)	c Mongia, b Prabhakar	9
G.R. Larsen	c Mongia, b Srinath	20
D.J. Nash	lbw, b Prabhakar	0
D.K. Morrison	not out	2
	b 2, lb 12, w 8, nb 3	25
	44.1 overs	145

	O	M	R	W
Prabhakar	10	–	33	5
Srinath	8	1	26	2
Venkatesh Prasad	6	–	14	1
Kumble	6	–	16	1
Kapoor	10	1	27	–
Tendulkar	4	–	15	1

Fall of Wickets
1–12, 2–22, 3–37, 4–57, 5–69, 6–96, 7–112, 8–123, 9–123

India

M. Prabhakar	lbw, b Nash	1
S.R. Tendulkar	c Germon, b Thomson	39
N.S. Sidhu	c Fleming, b Cairns	8
M. Azharuddin (Capt)	run out	17
S.V. Manjrekar	not out	44
A.D. Jadeja	not out	26
*N.R. Mongia		
J. Srinath		
A.R. Kumble		
A.R. Kapoor		
Venkatesh Prasad		
	b 2, lb 1, w 4, nb 4	11
	43.4 overs (for 4 wickets)	146

	O	M	R	W
Morrison	6	–	20	–
Nash	6	1	17	1
Cairns	7	–	33	1
Larsen	10	3	23	–
Thomson	10	1	38	1
Astle	4	–	9	–
Twose	0.4	–	3	–

Fall of Wickets
1–2, 2–25, 3–65, 4–72

Umpires: S.K. Porel & S.K. Sharma *Man of the Match:* M. Prabhakar

India won by 6 wickets

Fourth One-day International – India v. New Zealand
24 November 1995 at Nehru Stadium, Pune

New Zealand

M.J. Greatbatch	c Mongia, b Srinath	13
N.J Astle	run out	11
M.D. Crowe	lbw, b Kapoor	15
S.P. Fleming	c and b Tendulkar	26
R.G. Twose	c Mongia, b Venkatesh Prasad	46
C.L. Cairns	st Mongia, b Tendulkar	103
S.A. Thomson	not out	7
*L.K. Germon (Capt)		
G.R. Larsen		
D.J. Nash		
D.K. Morrison		
	lb 7, w 5, nb 2	14
	50 overs (for 6 wickets)	235

	O	M	R	W
Prabhakar	8	–	31	–
Srinath	10	1	42	1
Venkatesh Prasad	8	1	45	1
Kumble	8	–	35	–
Kapoor	7	–	26	1
Tendulkar	9	–	49	2

Fall of Wickets
1–27, 2–31, 3–68, 4–75, 5–222, 6–235

India

M. Prabhakar	c Twose, b Cairns	20
S.R. Tendulkar	c Larsen, b Morrison	7
V.G. Kambli	run out	42
M. Azharuddin (Capt)	lbw, b Cairns	58
S.V. Manjrekar	not out	47
A.D. Jadeja	b Cairns	12
*N.R. Mongia	not out	36
A.R. Kumble		
J. Srinath		
A.R. Kapoor		
Venkatesh Prasad		
	lb 3, w 8, nb 3	14
	45.5 overs (for 5 wickets)	236

	O	M	R	W
Morrison	9	–	62	1
Nash	8	–	48	–
Cairns	10	1	37	3
Larsen	8.5	–	42	–
Thomson	4	–	17	–
Twose	3	–	16	–
Astle	3	–	11	–

Fall of Wickets
1–20, 2–56, 3–127, 4–158, 5–179

Umpires: S. Chowdhary & K. Pathasarathi *Man of the Match:* C.L. Cairns

India won by 5 wickets

Fifth One-day International – India v. New Zealand

26 November 1995 at Vidarbha C.A. Stadium, Nagpur

New Zealand

M.J. Greatbatch	b Kapoor	38
N.J. Astle	c Azharuddin, b Prasad	114
M.D. Crowe	st Mongia, b Kapoor	63
S.P. Fleming	c Azharuddin, b Prasad	60
C.L. Cairns	c Manjrekar, b Kumble	14
R.G. Twose	run out	9
S.A. Thomson	lbw, b Kumble	15
*L.K. Germon (Capt)	b Srinath	1
G.R. Larsen	not out	5
D.J. Nash	not out	4
D.K. Morrison		
	lb 20, w 3, nb 2	25
	50 overs (for 8 wickets)	348

	O	M	R	W
Prabhakar	8	–	55	–
Srinath	9	–	42	1
Kapoor	7	–	48	2
Kumble	10	–	49	2
Venkatesh Prasad	8	–	61	2
Tendulkar	6	–	54	–
Jadeja	2	–	19	–

Fall of Wickets
1–62, 2–190, 3–288, 4–306, 5–317, 6–323, 7–337, 8–343

India

M. Prabhakar	run out	9
S.R. Tendulkar	run out	65
V.G. Kambli	c Crowe, b Cairns	16
M. Azharuddin (Capt)	c and b Cairns	1
S.V. Manjrekar	c sub (Young), b Astle	44
A.D. Jadeja	st Germon, b Larsen	61
*N.R. Mongia	c sub (Young), b Thomson	20
J. Srinath	c Nash, b Thomson	6
A.R. Kapoor	lbw, b Larsen	6
A.R. Kumble	c sub (Young), b Thomson	12
Venkatesh Prasad	not out	0
	lb 5, nb 4	9
	39.3 overs	249

	O	M	R	W
Morrison	4	–	25	–
Nash	5	–	35	–
Cairns	7	–	32	2
Larsen	9	–	58	2
Astle	5	–	31	1
Thomson	9.3	–	63	3

Fall of Wickets
1–23, 2–71, 3–77, 4–123, 5–150, 6–202, 7–211, 8–218, 9–241

Umpires: M. Menon & S. Shastri *Man of the Match:* N.J. Astle

New Zealand won by 99 runs

Manoj Prabhakar was India's leading all-rounder in the one-day series against New Zealand, but he later lost favour with the Indian selectors and retired from international cricket after the World Cup. (David Munden/Sportsline)

returned his best figures in a one-day international. He had Greatbatch caught at slip by Tendulkar and then trapped Crowe leg before with a ball that kept low and moved in from off-stump. Nathan Astle hit 59 off 86 balls before being sixth out, but when Germon and Nash fell to successive deliveries from Prabhakar, New Zealand were doomed. There were some early mishaps for India, but Manjrekar and Jadeja combined in an unbroken stand of 74 which brought victory with 38 balls to spare.

The third match, scheduled to be played in Margoa, was abandoned without a single ball bowled because of heavy rain. The fourth game produced some fine cricket. Electing to bat, New Zealand stuttered to 75 for 4, at which point Chris Cairns joined Roger Twose. Cairns dominated a stand worth 147 and was out to the final ball of the innings having hit 103 off 87 balls. His innings included four sixes and ten fours, and his century was his first in international cricket. Cairns' appetite for cricket at the highest level seemed to have been revived under Germon's influence. India lost Tendulkar early in their innings, and Cairns bowled particularly well, but Kambli, Azharuddin, Manjrekar and Mongia all batted with authority and victory came with surprising ease.

The fifth match of the series was a tragic and fiery encounter. The tragedy occurred at the lunch interval when a wall collapsed on the second level of the eastern stand of the Vidarbha Stadium. Eight people were killed, and 69 others were injured. The match continued, and many were unaware of the disaster.

Sixth One-day International – India v. New Zealand

29 November 1995 at Brabourne Stadium, Bombay

New Zealand

M.J. Greatbatch	c Manjrekar, b Srinath	4
N.J. Astle	c Prasad, b Prabhakar	9
S.P. Fleming	c and b Srinath	8
A.C. Parore	run out	14
R.G. Twose	st Mongia, b Kapoor	14
S.A. Thomson	run out	20
*L.K. Germon (Capt)	b Kumble	29
G.R. Larsen	c Srinath, b Kapoor	6
D.J. Nash	c Venkatesh Prasad, b Kumble	11
S.B. Doull	c Venkatesh Prasad, b Kumble	2
D.K. Morrison	not out	1
	lb 3, w 2, nb 3	8
	35 overs	126

	O	M	R	W
Prabhakar	5	–	29	1
Srinath	6	–	22	2
Venkatesh Prasad	6	–	22	–
Kapoor	10	–	33	2
Kumble	8	–	17	3

Fall of Wickets
1–7, 2–20, 3–38, 4–38, 5–64, 6–69, 7–97, 8–113, 9–123

India

M. Prabhakar	not out	32
S.R. Tendulkar	b Morrison	1
V.G. Kambli	c Greatbatch, b Doull	48
M. Azharuddin (Capt)	c Germon, b Doull	4
S.V. Manjrekar	c Thomson, b Doull	0
A.D. Jadeja	not out	35
*N.R. Mongia		
A.R. Kapoor		
A.R. Kumble		
J. Arinath		
Venkatesh Prasad		
	lb 2, w 6	8
	32 overs (for 4 wickets)	128

	O	M	R	W
Morrison	9	2	32	1
Nash	8	1	25	–
Doull	6	–	42	3
Larsen	9	1	27	–

Fall of Wickets
1–7, 2–71, 3–75, 4–75

Umpires: I. Shivram & A.V. Jayaprakash *Man of the Match:* J. Srinath

India won by 6 wickets

Put in to bat, New Zealand were splendidly served by Nathan Astle who hit his maiden century in international cricket. This was the first occasion on which three New Zealanders have scored centuries in the same series. All the top order batted well, and New Zealand's 348 was their highest score in a limited-over international, and the third highest ever recorded. There was some controversy when Manjrekar claimed to have caught Cairns on the boundary, and Twose, the non-striker, abused the Indian fielders, insisting that Manjrekar had put his foot on the boundary rope. Twose was later fined half his match fee for using abusive language, and India were fined five per cent of their match fees for failing to bowl 50 overs in three and a half hours. Referee Burge also reduced their quota of overs to 49. They scored very rapidly, but the task was always beyond them.

Having made their highest score in a one-day international, New Zealand made their lowest in the deciding encounter,' which was a very disappointing affair. Srinath's early burst undermined the New Zealand innings, and there was no effective recovery. Tendulkar, who had not enjoyed a good series, was soon out when India batted, and there were problems when Simon Doull, in his first representative match of the tour, took three wickets while only four runs were scored. However, Jadeja's exuberance matched the steadiness of Prabhakar, Man of the Series, and victory came with 18 overs to spare.

Venkatesh Prasad, India's most promising newcomer as a seam bowler. (David Munden/Sportsline)

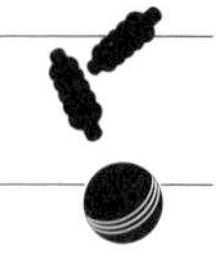

Duleep Trophy

11, 12, 13, 14 and 15 October 1995
at Vidarbha C.A. Stadium, Nagpur
North Zone 200 (Bhupinder Singh jnr 51) and 123 (A.R. Kumble 4 for 35)
South Zone 424 (A.R. Kumble 111 not out, W.V. Raman 103, R.S. Dravid 75, A.R. Kapoor 7 for 144)
South Zone won by an innings and 101 runs
South Zone 6 pts, North Zone 0 pts

at Indira Gandhi Stadium, Alwar
Central Zone 356 (P.K. Amre 152, C.S. Pandit 85, Avinash Kumar 6 for 94) and 32 for 0
East Zone 154 (N.D. Hirwani 5 for 41) and 231 (D. Gandhi 54, R.K. Chauhan 4 for 35)
Central Zone won by 10 wickets
Central Zone 6 pts, East Zone 0 pts

The Duleep Trophy found itself competing with the New Zealand tour and the Test series for much of the time, so congested has the international programme become.

The tournament began in a surprising manner with the strong North Zone side crumbling to the varied South Zone attack at Nagpur. Ajay Sharma had chosen to bat when he won the toss, but by the end of the first day his side was in deep trouble as Srinath, Kumble, Robin Singh and Venkatapathy Raju never allowed them to settle on a pitch that did not assist the bowlers. South Zone quickly lost Vaidya, but on the second day Raman's patient century, which included 12 fours and three sixes, gave the South a firm grip on the match. The South Zone skipper added 144 for the third wicket with Dravid, and on the third day, Anil Kumble reached 111 off 167 balls, his first century in the Duleep Trophy. He then became the arch destroyer as the reigning champions were beaten in four days. Venkatapathy Raju took 3 for 3 in eight overs as the last five wickets went down for 21 runs.

Central Zone enjoyed an equally emphatic victory. Pravin Amre won the toss and batted, and, after two wickets had fallen for 15, he and Pandit added 233 for the third wicket. Amre seems to have been forgotten by the Indian selectors, yet only three years ago he stood alongside Tendulkar and Kambli as India's hopes for a glorious future. Now he hit 152 off 169 balls to evoke memories of things past and rekindle hope for seasons to come. On the second day, East Zone collapsed before the spin of Chauhan and Hirwani, and the match was over nine minutes before tea on the third day.

20, 21, 22, 23 and 24 October 1995
at Vidarbha C.A. Stadium, Nagpur
West Zone 197 (S.S. Bhave 98) and 176 (S.V. Bahutule 61)
East Zone 551 for 8 dec. (S.S. Karim 200 not out, Saurav Ganguly 171, S.S. Das 62)
East Zone won by an innings and 78 runs
East Zone 6 pts, West Zone 0 pts

at Jayanti Stadium, Bhilai
Central Zone 373 for 6 dec. (G.K. Khoda 100, C.S. Pandit 90, A.R. Khurasia 89)
South Zone 234 for 4 (R.S. Dravid 69 not out, M.V. Sridhar 53)
Match drawn
Central Zone 2 pts, South Zone 2 pts

Surendra Bhave stood alone among the ruins as West Zone were bowled out for 197 on a moist pitch following a blank first day. East Zone took a vice-like grip on the match when Saurav Ganguly and skipper Syed Karim added 250 for the fourth wicket. Karim hit 16 fours and six sixes in his double century. West Zone collapsed a second time against a varied attack to leave East Zone comfortable winners.

No play was possible on the first three days in Bhilai, and the start was delayed 55 minutes on the fifth day because of the solar eclipse. Khoda's century occupied 275 minutes and included a six and 11 fours.

10, 11, 12, 13 and 14 November 1995
at Sukhadia Stadium, Bhilwara
Central Zone 404 (Y.T. Ghare 122, Abhay Sharma 63, Rizwan Shamshad 63, B. Vij 4 for 121) and 67 (B. Vij 6 for 19)
North Zone 259 (V. Rathore 64, Ajay Sharma 51) and 112 (Mohammad Aslam 5 for 42, R.K. Chauhan 4 for 41)
Central Zone won by 100 runs
Central Zone 6 pts, North Zone 0 pts

at Indira Gandhi Stadium, Alwar
South Zone 313 (S. Sharath 51) and 293 for 3 dec. (V.V.S. Laxman 121, R.S. Dravid 101 not out)
West Zone 181 and 282 (S.S. Sugwekar 83 not out, S.S. Bhave 65, D. Vasu 4 for 36)
South Zone won by 143 runs
South Zone 6 pts, West Zone 0 pts

Beaten by Central Zone, North Zone virtually relinquished their hold on the Duleep Trophy. Yogesh Ghare, a last minute replacement in the Central side, hit a sparkling century on the opening day. Central finished the day on 349 for 6, and, on a slow turning wicket, Chauhan and Mohammad Aslam destroyed the top of the North Zone batting on the second day. North closed at 251 for 9, but no one was prepared for what happened on an astonishing third day when 21 wickets fell and the match was over 29 minutes after tea. Left-arm spinner Vij took 6 for 19 in seven overs as Central were shot out in 111 minutes, but North could not cope with the conditions and again crumbled before the spinners. Mohammad Aslam had match figures of 8 for 85.

A consistent batting performance took South Zone to a good position against West Zone who again failed miserably with the bat. South's second innings was marked by a 199-run third wicket stand between Laxman and Dravid. Laxman, a few days beyond his 21st birthday, played with confidence and aggression while the 22-year old Dravid confirmed why he has already won a place in the national squad. West Zone, initially undermined by medium pacer David Johnson, fell eventually to the left-arm medium pace of Divakar Vasu and remained pointless after three matches.

19, 20, 21, 22 and 23 November 1995
at K.D. Singh 'Babu' Stadium, Lucknow
South Zone 165 (P.S. Vaidya 5 for 50) and 360 (V.V.S. Laxman 137, R.S. Dravid 59, P.S. Vaidya 5 for 76)
East Zone 159 and 147 (S.B. Joshi 5 for 26)
South Zone won by 219 runs
South Zone 6 pts, East Zone 0 pts

at Nehru Stadium, Indore
West Zone 526 (A.A. Muzumdar 209, A.V. Kale 144, F. Ghayas 4 for 103) and 298 (M.V. Jogekar 79, S.S. Bhave 57, B. Vij 6 for 87)
North Zone 371 (Ajay Sharma 188, V. Rathore 53, V. Yadav 53, S.A. Ankola 5 for 90, V. Buch 4 for 72) and 206
West Zone on by 247 runs
West Zone 6 pts, North Zone 0 pts

South Zone recovered from a disastrous first day to beat East Zone and assure themselves of at least a share of the Duleep Trophy. The swing bowling of Prashant Vaidya undermined the South's batting, and a last wicket stand of 37 between Venkatapahty Raju and Kanwaljit Singh saved the South from total ignominy. East Zone floundered on the second day and conceded a six-run lead. Laxman then proceeded to play another innings of great maturity, and the South Zone swept to victory on the fourth day.

The precocious talent of Amol Muzumdar was again in evidence as West Zone gained their first points of the competition. He hit the third double century of his youthful career and shared a fifth wicket stand of 285 with Abhijit Kale who reached his first Duleep Trophy century. Skipper Ajay Sharma made a wonderfully aggressive response for the North, but the West were always on top and were victorious just after lunch on the fifth day.

28, 29, 30 November, 1 and 2 December 1995
at K.D. Singh 'Babu' Stadium, Lucknow
East Zone 184 (F. Ghayas 4 for 35, B. Vij 4 for 64) and 184 (D. Ganhi 81, Saurav Ganguly 55, B. Vij 4 for 95)
North Zone 381 (Bhupinder Singh jnr 100, V. Yadav 66, P. Dharmani 65, Ajay Sharma 65) and 92 for 2 (P. Dharmani 56 not out)
North Zone won by 8 wickets
North Zone 6 pts, East Zone 0 pts

A forgotten hero of Indian cricket, Pravin Amre of Rajasthan. (Mike Hewitt/Allsport)

at Railways Stadium, Bikaner
Central Zone 127 (G.K. Khoda 58, V. Buch 4 for 5) and 180 (G. Pande 71, V. Buch 5 for 55, S.A. Ankola 4 for 52)
West Zone 352 (J.J. Martin 115, M.V. Joglekar 55, R.K. Chauhan 5 for 120, Iqbal Thakur 4 for 89)
West Zone won by an innings and 45 runs
West Zone 6 pts, Central Zone 0 pts

North Zone claimed victory on the fourth day at Lucknow and so recorded their first points of the tournament. At Bikaner, West Zone won in three days, and South Zone were confirmed as winners of the Duleep Trophy. Left-arm spinner Valimiki Buch was the architect of the West's victory, taking 4 for 5 in six overs in the first innings and finishing with match figures of 9 for 60. Jacob Martin's 115 came off 147 deliveries.

Duleep Trophy Final Table

	P	W	L	D	Pts
South Zone	4	3	–	1	19
Central Zone	4	2	1	1	13
West Zone	4	2	2	–	12
North Zone	4	1	3	–	6
East Zone	4	1	3	–	6

Ranji Trophy

India's premier first-class competition witnesses the eclipse of mighty Bombay and Delhi.

Central Zone

10, 11, 12 and 13 December 1995
at Green Park, Kanpur
Uttar Pradesh 442 for 6 dec. (R.V. Sapru 200 not out, G.K. Pande 71, R. Shamshad 61) and 113 for 3
Vidarbha 349 (Y.T. Ghare 108, P.K. Hedaoo 66)
Match drawn
Uttar Pradesh 2 pts, Vidarbha 0 pts

at Roop Singh Stadium, Gwalior
Railways 247 (A. Kapoor 68, H.S. Sodhi 6 for 55) and 299 for 6 (K. Yeregoud 79 not out, K. Bharatan 58 not out)
Madhya Pradesh 380 (J.P. Yadav 125, K.K. Patel 79, K. Bharatan 5 for 99, M. Suresh Kumar 5 for 125)
Match drawn
Madhya Pradesh 2 pts, Railways 0 pts

Uttar Pradesh lost four wickets for 147 runs before Rahul Sapru hit the first double century of his career, sharing a fifth wicket stand of 157 with Gayanendrakumar Pande. Sapru hit a six and 18 fours and faced 388 balls. Ghare's century saved Vidarbha from the depths of 78 for 4, and the tail wagged strongly to help avoid the follow-on.

Railways, too, were grateful to their tail. Arvind Kapoor hit the first fifty of his career after six wickets had fallen for 108. Jai Yadav hit the highest score of his career and shared an opening stand of 206 with Kirti Patel which assured Madhya Pradesh of first innings points. Yeregoud and Bharatan shared an unbroken seventh wicket partnership of 127 which saved Railways from defeat.

18, 19, 20 and 21 December 1995
at Vidarbha C.A. Stadium, Nagpur
Railways 246 (P.S. Rawat 140 not out, P.B. Hingnikar 5 for 62) and 275 for 1 dec. (S.B. Bangar 148, Vijendra Yadav 100 not out)
Vidarbha 341 (S.V. Wankhede 76, M.S. Doshi 52) and 97 for 4
Match drawn
Vidarbha 2 pts, Railways 0 pts

at M.B. College Ground, Udaipur
Madhya Pradesh 516 (J.P. Yadav 135, A.R. Khurasia 131, D.K. Nilosey 81) and 30 for 1
Rajasthan 228 (N.D. Hirwani 4 for 75) and 317 (G.K. Khoda 115, P. Krishna Kumar 69)
Madhya Pradesh won by 9 wickets
Madhya Pradesh 6 pts, Rajasthan 0 pts

A maiden first-class hundred by Prahlad Rawat could not give Railways first innings points against Vidarbha. When Railways batted again, Sanjay Bangar hit the first century of his career and shared an opening stand of 251 with Vijendra Yadav.

Madhya Pradesh completed the first outright win of the season in the Central Zone when Jai Yadav hit his second century in successive matches, bettering his score in the opening match and sharing a second wicket stand of 225 with Khurasia. Madhya Pradesh's strong spin attack twice accounted for Rajasthan in spite of a brave century from Khoda.

5, 6, 7 and 8 January 1996
at Karnail Singh Stadium, Delhi
Uttar Pradesh 261 (R.V. Sapru 68) and 164 (Satyendra Yadav 50, M. Suresh Kumar 6 for 34)
Railways 377 for 7 dec. (S.B. Bangar 161, P.S. Rawat 64, G.K. Pande 5 for 74) and 49 for 4
Railways won by 6 wickets
Railways 6 pts, Uttar Pradesh 0 pts

at Mansarovar Cricket Ground, Jaipur
Rajasthan 244 (A.D. Sinha 111, P.B. Hingnikar 4 for 74) and 188 (G.K. Khoda 90, A.S. Parma 50, M.S. Doshi 6 for 42, P.B. Hingnikar 4 for 38)
Vidarbha 278 and 134 (Mohammad Aslam 4 for 29)
Rajasthan won by 20 runs
Rajasthan 6 pts, Vidarbha 2 pts

Two surprising results threw the Central Zone competition completely open. Consistent batting took Uttar Pradesh to a reasonable score in Delhi, but Sanjay Bangar followed his maiden first-class century against Vidarbha with a patient 161 to give Railways a first innings lead of 116. Batting a second time, Uttar Pradesh ran into trouble against the left-arm spin of Mani Suresh Kumar, who returned the best bowling figures of his career. Needing 49 in 15 overs, Railways panicked, three batsmen being stumped by Mudgal, but won.

Anil Sinha hit the second and higher century of his career, but Vidarbha took first innings points. Khoda and Parmar shared a second wicket stand of 141 when Rajasthan batted a second time, but the last nine wickets went down for 35 runs as the pitch crumbled. Manish Doshi returned career-best bowling figures. Vidarbha needed only 155 to win, but they failed against the spinners.

13, 14, 15 and 16 January 1996

at Jayanti Stadium, Bhilai

Madhya Pradesh 536 for 7 dec. (A. Pande 209 not out, C.S. Pandit 202)
Uttar Pradesh 292 (J.P. Yadav 80, R. Shamshad 68, S.S. Lahore 5 for 75, H.S. Sodhi 4 for 102) and 240 for 4 (R. Shamshad 75, M.S. Mudgal 62, J.P. Yadav 51)

Match drawn
Madhya Pradesh 2 pts, Uttar Pradesh 0 pts

at Karnail Singh Stadium, Delhi
Railways 256 (D. Pal Singh 6 for 58) and 149 for 6 dec.
Rajasthan 107 (P.K. Amre 52, Javed Alam 4 for 29) and 60 for 3
Match drawn
Railways 2 pts, Rajasthan 0 pts

Aunshuman Pande batted for 676 minutes, faced 545 balls and hit 20 fours as he carried his bat for 209 on the occasion of his first-class debut. He and Pandit, who faced only 332 balls, put on 328 after three wickets had fallen for 113 runs. Uttar Pradesh were forced to follow on, but saved the match. Madhya Pradesh took two points to be assured of a place in the knock-out stage of the competition.

Railways, too, took two points in the rain-affected match in Delhi. Left-arm spinner Pal Singh had the best bowling performance of his career.

22, 23, 24 and 25 January 1996

at K.D. Singh 'Babu' Stadium, Lucknow
Uttar Pradesh 564 for 4 dec. (R. Shamshad 156, J.P. Yadav 146, R.V. Sapru 101 not out, Satyendra Yadav 79) and 50 for 2 dec.
Rajasthan 439 (P.K. Amre 161, A.S. Parmar 50, Jasbir Singh 6 for 122) and 95 for 8
Match drawn
Uttar Pradesh 2 pts, Rajasthan 0 pts

at Vidarbha C.A. Stadium, Nagpur
Vidarbha 240 (U.V. Gandhe 64 not out) and 144 (M. Majithia 4 for 29)
Madhya Pradesh 163 (M. Majithia 51, P.V. Gandhe 7 for 62) and 222 for 6 (K.K. Patel 71)
Madhya Pradesh 6 pts, Vidarbha 2 pts

Uttar Pradesh scored heavily against Rajasthan, but they were denied victory by Parmar and Pal Singh who held out after eight wickets had fallen for 64.

Vidarbha were beaten by Madhya Pradesh, but, vitally, took first innings points to clinch a place in the final stages of the competition. In his second first-class match, Aunshuman Pande 'bagged a pair'.

Central Zone Final Table

	P	W	L	D	Pts
Madhya Pradesh	4	2	–	2	16
Railways	4	1	–	3	8
Vidarbha	4	–	2	2	6
Rajasthan	4	1	1	2	6
Uttar Pradesh	4	–	1	3	4

East Zone

11, 12, 13 and 14 December 1995

at Baripada
Orissa 402 (P.R. Mohapatra 100, S.S. Das 95, A. Khatua 89 not out, U. Chatterjee 4 for 91)
Bengal 299 (D. Gandhi 147, R. Biswal 5 for 82)
Match drawn
Orissa 2 pts, Bengal 0 pts

at Polytechnic Ground, Agarta
Bihar 247 (V. Khullar 50, S. Chowdhary 5 for 64)
Tripura 70 and 132 (Deepak Kumar 4 for 30, Avinash Kumar 4 for 31)
Bihar won by an innings and 45 runs
Bihar 6 pts, Tripura 0 pts

Two very patient centuries were the main points of the game in Baripada, while Bihar were bowled out for 247 by Tripura yet still won by an innings. The outstanding feature of the match in Agarta was the bowling of Subal Chowdhary of Tripura who took five wickets on his debut in the Ranji Trophy.

20, 21, 22 and 23 December 1995

at Railway Stadium, Maligaon
Tripura 111 and 105 (S.V. Limaye 6 for 35)
Assam 405 for 9 dec. (S. Sawant 121, V. Sawant 75, Rajinder Singh 55, S.V. Limaye 50, C. Dey 5 for 87)
Assam won by an innings and 188 runs
Assam 6 pts, Tripura 0 pts

at Moinul Haque Stadium, Patna
Bihar 144 (U. Chatterjee 5 for 23, A. Sarkar 4 for 63) and 134 (V. Khullar 54, P.S. Vaidya 5 for 22)
Bengal 468 for 6 dec. (S.S. Karim 199, S.J. Kalyani 117 not out, A. Lahiri 58)
Bengal won by an innings and 190 runs
Bengal 6 pts, Bihar 0 pts

Tripura suffered their second innings defeat and in doing so emphasised the gap which exists between the top sides and the bottom sides in Indian cricket. Sunil Limaye, Assam's leg-break and googly bowler, returned the best figures of his career.

Bengal found form after their disappointing performance against Orissa and overwhelmed Bihar. Syed Karim and Shrikant Kalyani added 283 for Bengal's sixth wicket. Wicket-keeper Karim averages over 50 in first-class cricket, and has now hit 16 centuries in his career, which began in 1982 at the age of 15.

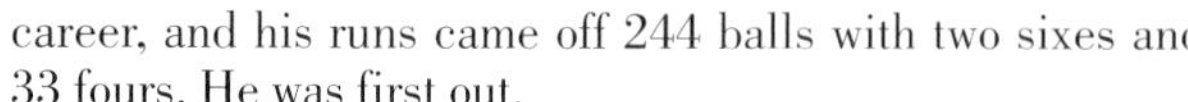

6, 7, 8 and 9 January 1996
at Keenan Stadium, Jamshedpur
Bihar 284 (Tariq-ur-Rehman 122, S. Banerjee 58)
and 133 (S. Kumar 74 not out, V. Sawant 4 for 55)
Assam 205 (S. Saikia 56, S.V. Limaye 51,
Avinash Kumar 5 for 44, Anil Kumar 5 for 74)
and 103 for 5
Match drawn
Bihar 2 pts, Assam 0 pts

at Barabatti Stadium, Cuttack
Tripura 141 (S. Khan 5 for 42, R. Biswal 5 for 54)
and 171
Orissa 521 for 6 dec. (S.S. Das 178, P.R. Mohapatra
105, S. Raul 71, M. Bhatt 68)
Orissa won by an innings and 209 runs
Orissa 6 pts, Tripura 0 pts

A maiden first-class century by Tariq-ur-Rehman brought substance to Bihar's first innings. This was followed by Anil Kumar taking five wickets on the occasion of his debut. He and Avinash Kumar assured Bihar of first innings points, but the home side fared badly in their second innings. Sunil Kumar carried his bat through the 60 overs to score 74 out of 133.

Once again Tripura were crushed as Orissa scored at more than five runs an over in Cuttack. Khan had claimed five wickets on his debut – he finished with match figures of 8 for 77 – and Shiv Sunder Das hit the highest score of his career.

14, 15, 16 and 17 January 1996
at Barabatti Stadium, Cuttack
Orissa 411 (S.S. Das 74, P.R. Mohapatra 72, R. Biswal
69 not out, S. Raul 60)
Assam 112 (Sushil Kumar 5 for 9, R. Biswal 4 for 29)
and 206 (R. Biswal 5 for 73)
Orissa won by an innings and 93 runs
Orissa 6 pts, Assam 0 pts

at Polytechnic Ground, Agartala
Bengal 446 for 4 dec. (D. Gandhi 213, A. Verma 141,
M. Sen Gupta 65)
Tripura 53 (P. Acharjee 7 for 6) and 42 (S.P. Mukherjee
5 for 18, P. Acharjee 4 for 10)
Bengal won by an innings and 351 runs
Bengal 6 pts, Tripura 0 pts

Orissa and Bengal assured themselves of a place in the final stages of the competition with crushing victories in the fourth round of matches. Orissa batted consistently, bowled well and claimed victory on the third day. Bengal scored at more than four an over and won in two days. Ajoy Verma and Devang Gandhi began the match with a partnership of 327 in 314 minutes. Gandhi hit the first double century of his career, and his runs came off 244 balls with two sixes and 33 fours. He was first out.

Prabir Acharjee made a remarkable debut for Bengal, taking seven wickets for six runs in nine overs as Tripura were bowled out in 87 minutes. They lasted 101 minutes, 29.3 overs, in their second innings with Acharjee again to the fore.

22, 23, 24 and 25 January 1996
at Permit Ground, Balasore
Orissa 471 (S. Raul 125, R. Biswal 73, P.R. Mohapatra 64,
Avinash Kumar 7 for 111) and 62 for 2
Bihar 293 (Tarun Kumar 100, Sunil Kumar 55, R. Biswal 5
for 114, Sushil Kumar 4 for 90) and 237 (Tariq-ur-Rehman
105, R. Biswal 5 for 44)
Orissa won by 8 wickets
Orissa 6 pts, Bihar 0 pts

at Krishnagar
Assam 301 (G. Dutta 87, D. Chakraborty 72,
N. Bordoloi 59, S.C. Ganguly 4 for 67) and 219 for 7 dec.
(S. Saikia 127)
Bengal 258 (S.P. Mukherjee 58, A. Bhagwat 6 for 49) and
266 for 1 (A. Verma 106 not out, D. Gandhi 76,
S.C. Ganguly 65 not out)
Bengal won by 9 wickets
Bengal 6 pts, Assam 2 pts

Orissa claimed the Mona Mitter Challenge Cup when they beat Bihar. Bihar were forced to follow on in spite of a spectacular maiden century from Tarun Kumar who reached 100 off 81 balls with eight fours and seven sixes in his 103-minute stay. Tariq-ur-Rehman hit his second century in successive matches, but Orissa hit 62 in 6.3 overs to win the match. Once again they were nobly served by skipper Ranjib Biswal who took 30 wickets with his off-breaks in four matches in the East Zone.

Assam strove hard to qualify for the knock-out stage of the competition and set Bengal a target of 263, but Bengal romped to victory with skipper Saurav Ganguly enjoying a fine match and Ajoy Verma hitting his second century in succession. The all-round cricket of Saurav Ganguly was one of the features of Bengali's season, and he won a place in India's party to tour England.

East Zone Final Table

	P	W	L	D	Pts
Orissa	4	3	–	1	20
Bengal	4	3	–	1	18
Bihar	4	1	2	1	8
Assam	4	1	2	1	8
Tripura	4	–	4	–	0

North Zone

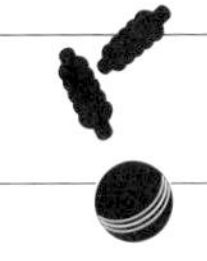

10, 11, 12 and 13 December 1995
at Palam Sports Club, Delhi
Delhi 262 (M. Prabhakar 111) and 160 (S. Dogra 74, V. Jain 5 for 34)
Haryana 153 (Robin Singh 7 for 53) and 124 (Shakti Singh 5 for 24)
Delhi won by 145 runs
Delhi 6 pts, Haryana 0 pts

at PCA Stadium, Mohali, Chandigarh
Punjab 360 for 5 dec. (N.S. Sidhu 137, P. Dharmani 113 not out, J.N. Pandey 4 for 96) and 18 for 1
Services 246 (Chinmoy Sharma 123 not out, Sandeep Sbarma 4 for 26)
Match drawn
Punjab 2 pts, Services 0 pts

Manoj Prabhakar's 236-ball innings on the opening day proved to be decisive in the match at Delhi. On the second day, Robin Singh devastated Haryana with a career-best bowling performance, and Delhi took a first innings lead of 109, a considerable advantage on a pitch that was becoming increasingly erratic. They themselves slumped to 91 for 6 by the end of the second day, but Dogra batted splendidly on the third morning, hitting 74 off 91 balls. Needing 270 to win, Haryana fell to the medium pace of Shakti Singh and were beaten inside three days.

Only 80 minutes of play was possible on the first day in Chandigarh, but on the second Sidhu and Dharmani added 228 for Punjab's fifth wicket. Sidhu declared at the overnight score, and on a dour third day Services scored 192 for 7 in 90 overs. It looked at one time as if they would have to follow on, but skipper Chinmoy Sharma played a lone hand to save his side the indignity. He completed his sixth century on a truncated fourth day, and the match was drawn. The match heralded a season of struggle for Services.

17, 18, 19 and 20 December 1995
at Burlton Park, Jalandhar
Punjab 507 for 4 dec. (N.S. Sidhu 259 not out, V. Rathore 156, A. Mehra 65)
Himachal Pradesh 149 (N. Gaur 56, B. Vij 5 for 29) and 100 (B. Vij 5 for 31, A.R. Kapoor 4 for 50)
Punjab won by an innings and 258 runs
Punjab 6 pts, Himachal Pradesh 0 pts

at Palam Sports Complex, Delhi
Delhi 519 for 5 dec. (S. Dogra 201 not out, A. Malhotra 197)
Services 135 (Sarabjit Singh 50, R. Sanghvi 7 for 42) and 176 (N. Chopra 6 for 91, R. Sanghvi 4 for 64)
Delhi won by an innings and 208 runs
Delhi 6 pts, Services 0 pts

Both Punjab and Delhi were successful inside three days. Sidhu and Rathore established a first wicket record for Punjab with a stand of 301 in 313 minutes. Thereafter it was merely a question of how long it would take Punjab to win.

There was a record, too, at Delhi where Akash Malhotra and Sumeet Dogra put on 391 for Delhi's fifth wicket. This was the highest partnership for the fifth wicket ever recorded in the Ranji Trophy. Both batsmen hit the highest scores of their careers. Another career-best followed when Rahul Sanghvi took 7 for 42 with his left-arm spin. Chopra's off-spin was potent when Services followed on, and Sanghvi finished with match figures of 11 for 106.

3, 4, 5 and 6 January 1996
at Gandhi Ground, Amritsar
Delhi 341 (Ajay Sharma 147, A. Malhotra 72, Sandeep Sharma 4 for 86) and 286 for 5 (A. Dani 141, Bantoo Singh 54, Ajay Sharma 51, B. Vij 4 for 75)
Punjab 415 (P. Dharmani 223 not out, N.S. Sidhu 63, R. Sanghvi 4 for 157)
Match drawn
Punjab 2 pt, Delhi 0 pts

An exciting season for Saurav Ganguly who scored heavily for East Zone in the Duleep Trophy and for Bengal in the Ranji Trophy.
(David Munden/Sportsline)

at Paddal Stadium, Mandi
Himachal Pradesh 172 (Virender Sharma 63, Arun Sharma 5 for 28) and 250 (R. Nayyar 134 not out)
Services 391 for 7 dec. (R. Mehta 103 not out, Chinmoy Sharma 95) and 32 for 0
Services won by 10 wickets
Services 6 pts, Himachal Pradesh 0 pts

Delhi reached 285 for 5 on the first day against Punjab, a score that owed much to Ajay Sharma's 19th Ranji Trophy century and his fifth wicket stand of 215 with Malhotra. Delhi faded on the second morning, and Dharmani and Sidhu put Punjab in a sound position when they scored 151 for the third wicket. Pankaj Dharmani became the hero when he carried his bat through Punjab's innings for the highest score of his career. He faced 446 balls, was at the crease for nearly nine-and-a-half hours and hit two sixes and 25 fours. Ashu Dani hit a hundred on the last day, but by then the match was dead.

In spite of a brave century from skipper Rajiv Nayyar, Himachal Pradesh were well beaten by Services and seemed destined for the wooden spoon.

9, 10, 11 and 12 January 1996
at Indira Stadium, Una
Himachal Pradesh 125 (R. Sanghvi 6 for 49) and 307 (R. Nayyar 125, Virender Sharma 73, N. Gaur 66, R. Sanghvi 5 for 137)
Delhi 483 for 6 dec. (M. Prabhakar 125, R. Chopra 95, A. Dani 83, A. Malhotra 65)
Delhi won by an innings and 51 runs
Delhi 6 pts, Himachal Pradesh 0 pts

11, 12, 13 and 14 January 1996
at Nahar Singh Stadium, Faridabad
Haryana 471 (A.D. Jadeja 189, Armajit Kaypee 110, R. Puri 73)
Services 209 (P. Jain 4 for 49) and 208 (K.M. Roshan 58, P. Thakur 5 for 66, P. Jain 4 for 39)
Haryana won by an innings and 64 runs
Haryana 6 pts, Services 0 pts

Bowled out for 125 in 47 overs on the first day, Himachal Pradesh suffered another innings defeat inside three days. They were wonderfully served by skipper Nayyar who hit his second century in successive matches, but the might of Delhi overwhelmed them. Dani and Rajneesh Chopra began with a stand of 160, and Prabhakar's 125 off 148 balls compounded the misery of the home side.

A third wicket stand of 229 between Jadeja and Armajit Kaypee took Haryana to a commanding total against Services who then succumbed to the off-spin of Thakur and the left-arm spin of Jain.

Delhi's victory over Himachal Pradesh assured them of the Devraj Puri Trophy as winners of the North Zone.

16, 17, 18 and 19 January 1996
at Vishwakarma School Ground, Rohtak
Himachal Pradesh 263 (R. Nayyar 114, Raj Kumar 52)
Haryana 264 for 6 (R. Puri 71, V. Yadav 58)
Match drawn
Haryana 2 pts, Himachal Pradesh 0 pts

No play was possible on the first day and only 84 minutes of cricket was played on the second day, but on the third, Rajeev Nayyar hit his third century in successive matches. He became the first Himachal Pradesh batsman to score 3000 runs in the Ranji Trophy and he eventually became Pradeep Jain's 200th Ranji Trophy victim. Haryana became sure of a place in the knock-out stages of the trophy when they won first innings points on the last day.

23, 24, 25 and 26 January 1996
at Nehru Stadium, Gurgaon
Haryana 233 and 241 (Dhanraj Singh 56, Avtar Singh 53, G. Doel 4 for 67)
Punjab 231 (Amit Sharma 69, P. Thakur 4 for 38) and 244 for 6 (V. Rathore 91)
Punjab won by 4 wickets
Punjab 6 pts, Haryana 2 pts

Dismissed for a meagre 233, Haryana fought back to capture first innings points as the last five Punjab wickets went down for 38 runs. Harayana stumbled in their second innings when they lost their last four wickets for seven runs, but Punjab were set the daunting task of scoring 244 to win at more than six runs an over. Vikram Rathore led a blistering attack on the bowling, and Punjab were 100 for 1 in 11 overs. Rathore hit 91 off 56 balls before skying a catch to the bowler. He hit three sixes and nine fours and was at the wicket for 77 minutes. He passed 3000 runs in his 40th Ranji Trophy match. Bhupinder Singh junior finished the job, and Punjab won with seven balls to spare, reaching their target in 34.5 overs.

North Zone Final Table

	P	W	L	D	Pts
Delhi	4	3	–	1	18
Punjab	4	2	–	2	16
Haryana	4	1	2	1	10
Services	4	1	2	1	6
Himachal Pradesh	4	–	3	1	0

Jammu and Kashmir did not arrive for any of their scheduled matches because of political unrest.

South Zone

10, 11, 12 and 13 December 1995
at M.A. Chidambaram Stadium, Madras
Tamil Nadu 245 (S. Ramesh 59, R. Sridhar 5 for 48) and 241 for 3 dec. (S. Ramesh 132, D. Vasu 53)
Hyderabad 292 (M.V. Sridhar 104, V. Pratap 66 not out, A. Nandakishore 56) and 57 for 2
Match drawn
Hyderabad 2 pts, Tamil Nadu 0 pts

at Alluri Seetharamaraju Stadium, Eluru
Karnataka 247 (A.R. Kumble 63, J. Aron Kumar 58, H. Ram Kishen 6 for 75)
Andhra 41 (Venkatesh Prasad 6 for 23, D. Ganesh 4 for 12) and 97
Karnataka won by an innings and 109 runs
Karnataka 6 pts, Andhra 0 pts

at Gymkhana Ground, Kampal, Panaji
Kerala 166 (S.V. Kamat 4 for 32) and 307 for 7 (A. Kudva 162 not out, S. Oasis 61, S.V. Mudkavi 4 for 78)
Goa 384 (V.B. Chandrasekhar 237 not out, M. Senthilnathan 60, K.N.A. Padmanabhan 7 for 113)
Match drawn
Goa 2 pts, Kerala 0 pts

There was movement in the South Zone. K. Srinath left Karnataka for Tamil Nadu, and Hyderabad gained Iqbal Siddiqui from Maharashtra. Siddiqui took the wickets of Ramesh and Sharath on his debut for his new side, but it was a career-best bowling performance from slow left-arm bowler Ramakrishnan Sridhar which put Tamil Nadu under pressure. Maruti Venkat Sridhar's 15th Ranji Trophy century took Hyderabad into the lead in spite of Robin Singh's 3 for 21. The Tamil Nadu skipper brought himself into the attack too late, for Hyderabad were 226 for 4 in 112 overs when he came on. It was a dour struggle, but left-handed debutant 20-year old Ramesh brightened the last day with a century.

Karnataka crushed Andhra in two days. Left-arm medium-pacer Ram Kishen produced the best bowling performance of his career, but Andhra were bowled out in 24.4 overs by Venkatesh Prasad and Ganesh, no Andhra batsman reaching double figures. They fared little better in their second innings.

Vakkadai Chandrasekhar and M. Senthilnathan moved from Tamil Nadu to Goa, and Chandrasekar celebrated his first game for Goa by carrying his bat through the innings for the first double century of his career. He faced 534 balls, batted for 12 hours and seven minutes and hit two sixes and 16 fours. Ajay Kudva's maiden first-class hundred thwarted Goa's bid for victory.

19, 20, 21 and 22 December 1995
at M. Chinnaswamy Stadium, Bangalore
Goa 132 and 97 (A.R. Kumble 6 for 20, S.B. Joshi 4 for 48)
Karnataka 466 (S. Somasunder 114, R.S. Dravid 108, A.R. Kumble 51 not out, S.V. Mudkavi 8 for 182)
Karnataka won by an innings and 237 runs
Karnataka 6 pts, Goa 0 pts

at Vizzy Stadium, Vishakhapatnam
Andhra 277 (A. Pathak 132, S. Subramaniam 7 for 85) and 219 (R.V. Prasad 61, M. Venkatramana 5 for 65, W.D. Balaji Rao 4 for 57)
Tamil Nadu 209 (S. Ramesh 75, H. Ram Kishen 6 for 89) and 288 for 8 (Robin Singh 71 not out, T. Karunamurthy 57, S. Sharath 54)
Tamil Nadu won by 2 wickets
Tamil Nadu 6 pts, Andhra 2 pts

at Vellayani Agriculture College Ground, Thiruvananthapauram
Hyderabad 283 (M.V. Sridhar 105, M. Azharuddin 91, B. Ramprakash 5 for 103, K.N.A. Padmanabhan 4 for 86) and 259 for 6 dec. (M.V. Sridhar 123, M. Azharuddin 105)
Kerala 234 (Venkatapathy Raju 5 for 89) and 183 (S. Shankar 54, K.N.A. Padmanabhan 51, Venkatapathy Raju 7 for 82)
Hyderabad won by 125 runs
Hyderabad 6 pts, Kerala 0 pts

Karnataka beat Goa after 79 minutes play on the third day. Sunil Joshi and Anil Kumble destroyed Goa for whom skipper Mudkavi bowled manfully for 54.2 overs.

Amit Pathak hit an elegant century to take Andhra to a surprising first innings lead over Tamil Nadu, but Robin Singh led his side to an exciting victory with seven balls to spare.

Maruti Sridhar hit a century in each innings for the second year running and shared third wicket standards of 173 and 189 with Azharuddin as Hyderabad crushed Kerala.

7, 8, 9 and 10 January 1996
at Vellayani Agriculture College Ground, Thiruvanthapauram
Andhra 206 (A. Pathak 73, K.N.A. Padmanabhan 5 for 73) and 105 (K.N.A. Padmanabhan 6 for 39)
Kerala 227 (S. Oasis 58, Chakradhar Rao 5 for 57) and 85 for 0 (K.N. Balasubramaniam 52 not out)
Kerala won by 8 wickets
Kerala 6 pts, Andhra 0 pts

at Arlem Ground, Margoa
Hyderabad 576 for 5 dec. (M.V. Sridhar 137, A. Nandkishore 132, M. Azharuddin 118, V. Pratap 58 not out)
Goa 182 (S. Kamath 53, Kanwaljit Singh 5 for 53) and 212 (S.V. Mudkavi 63, R. Sridhar 4 for 62)
Hyderabad won by an innings and 182 runs
Hyderabad 6 pts, Goa 0 pts

The leg-breaks and googlies of Padmanabhan brought Kerala victory over Andhra inside three days.

In Margoa, Maruti Sridhar hit his 18th Ranji Trophy century to establish a record for Hyderabad. It was his fourth hundred in five innings in the season, and his second innings against Tamil Nadu in the opening match had brought him 12 not out. There were also centuries for Nandkishore, a maiden one, and Azharuddin. Sridhar and Nandkishore added 223 for the second wicket.

16, 17, 18 and 19 January 1996
at Gymkhana Ground, Secunderabad
Hyderabad 223 (N. David 55, M.V. Sridhar 54, N. Madhukar 5 for 43) and 139 (H. Ram Kishen 4 for 68)
Andhra 332 (A. Pathak 116, M.S.K. Prasad 50, R. Sridhar 6 for 91) and 34 for 1
Andhra won by 9 wickets
Andhra 6 pts, Hyderabad 0 pts

18, 19, 20 and 21 January 1996
at RSI Stadium, Bangalore
Kerala 151 (D. Johnson 6 for 63) and 346 (S. Oasis 69, S. Shankar 57, D. Johnson 4 for 89)
Karnataka 244 (P.V. Shashikanth 103, B. Ramprakash 4 for 73) and 254 (S.B. Joshi 59 not out, K.A. Jeshwanth 59, S. Somasunder 51, B. Ramprakash 5 for 102)
Karnataka won by 3 wickets
Karnataka 6 pts, Kerala 0 pts

at Guru Nanak College Ground, Madras
Goa 312 (V.B. Chandrasekhar 168, Robin Singh 4 for 27) and 315 (B.K.P. Misquin 107, S. Mahadevan 57)
Tamil Nadu 509 for 6 dec. (S. Sharath 204 not out, R. Paul 100 not out, W.V. Raman 88, K. Srinath 52, Y. Barde 4 for 133) and 121 for 2 (W.V. Raman 86 not out)
Tamil Nadu won by 8 wickets
Tamil Nadu 6 pts, Goa 0 pts

Hostile bowling by Ram Kishen and Madhukar restricted Hyderabad on the opening day in Secunderabad. A century by opener Amit Pathak then helped Andhra to take the lead against some slack fielding and sparkless bowling. Hyderabad's batting wilted for a second time, and Andhra gained a surprise victory 45 minutes into the fourth day.

Karnataka laboured against Kerala, who were shot out by the medium pace of David Johnson on the first day. Karnataka lost seven wickets in taking first innings points, and they were much indebted to Shashikanth's 103 off 142 balls. He hit two sixes and 11 fours. Kerala batted with great determination in their second innings, and Karnataka only achieved victory shortly before tea on the final day.

Chandrasekhar exposed the limitations of the Tamil Nadu attack when he batted throughout the first day to register a century against his former side. The left-handed Sridaran Sharath hit the first double century of his career and shared a third wicket stand of 193 with Raman and an unfinished seventh wicket partnership of 145 with wicket-keeper Reuben Paul who was making his debut. Paul's remarkable 100 came off 60 balls in 62 minutes and included seven fours and seven sixes. Goa played an heroic rearguard action, with Balakrishna Misquin and Suresh Mahadevan adding 89 for the ninth wicket. Misquin's hundred was his first, but Tamil Nadu won with ease as Raman again batted fluently.

28, 29, 30 and 31 January 1996
at Gymkhana Ground, Secunderabad
Karnataka 398 (S.B. Joshi 118, P.V. Shashikanth 75, A. Vaidya 69, V. Pratap 5 for 100) and 19 for 1
Hyderabad 191 (V. Pratap 69, S.B. Joshi 7 for 60) and 222 (V.V.S. Laxman 79, Yuvaraj Singh 50, S.B. Joshi 4 for 66)
Karnataka won by 9 wickets
Karnataka 6 pts, Hyderabad 0 pts

at District Sports Stadium, Kakinada
Andhra 275 (A. Pathak 114, S.V. Mudkavi 8 for 83) and 271 for 6 dec. (M.S.K. Prasad 100 not out, B.S. Naik 64)
Goa 195 (V.B. Chandrasekhar 55, H. Ram Kishen 4 for 57) and 272 (V.B. Chandrasekhar 95, K. Chakradhar Rao 4 for 80, H. Ram Kishen 4 for 87)
Andhra won by 79 runs
Andhra 6 pts, Goa 0 pts

at Sankarnagar Ground, Tirunlveli
Tamil Nadu 541 for 5 dec. (K. Srinath 159, S. Ramesh 158, S. Sharath 101 not out, Robin Singh 57, K. Rejith Kumar 4 for 133)
Kerala 184 and 192 (K.N. Balasubramaniam 52, S. Shankar 50, S. Subramaniam 6 for 73, M. Venkatramana 4 for 66)
Tamil Nadu won by an innings and 165 runs
Tamil Nadu 6 pts, Kerala 0 pts

Karnataka made it four wins in four matches when an outstanding all-round performance from Sunil Joshi took them to a comfortable win over Hyderabad. The left-handed Joshi equalled his highest score and returned the best bowling figures of his career for innings and match.

Andhra's victory over Goa brought them level on points with Hyderabad but could not earn them a place in the pre-quarter-finals.

An opening stand of 329, a record for Tamil Nadu, between Srinath and Ramesh set up a massive win over Kerala. Sunil Subramaniam, slow left-arm, reached 200 wickets in the Ranji Trophy.

4, 5, 6 and 7 February 1996
at VISL Stadium, Bhadravathi
Karnataka 716 (K. Sriram 174, S. Somasunder 166, R. Vijay 122, K.A. Jeshwanth 91, S.B. Joshi 61 not out,

S. Subramaniam 4 for 174) and 172 for 3 (S. Somasunder 62)
Tamil Nadu 366 (W.V. Raman 89, Robin Singh 68, S. Ramesh 54, S.B. Joshi 4 for 93)
Match drawn
Karnataka 2 pts, Tamil Nadu 0 pts

Karnataka batted into the third day and equalled the highest score they had ever made against Tamil Nadu. There were three centurions, one of whom, K. Sriram, was making his debut. He hit three sixes and 15 fours in his 299-ball innings. In taking first innings points, Karnataka regained the M.D. Sounderrajan Trophy as South Zone champions.

South Zone Final Table

	P	W	L	D	Pts
Karnataka	5	4	–	1	26
Tamil Nadu	5	3	–	2	18
Hyderabad	5	2	2	1	14
Andhra	5	2	3	–	14
Kerala	5	1	3	1	6
Goa	5	–	4	1	2

West Zone

13, 14, 15 and 16 December 1995

at Nehru Stadium, Pune
Baroda 550 (N.R. Mongia 152, T.B. Arothe 142, K.S. More 71, M.S. Narula 60, J.J. Martin 56, M.S. Kulkarni 5 for 89)
Maharashtra 562 for 7 (S.S. Bhave 227, H.H. Kanitkar 142, V. Buch 4 for 185)
Match drawn
Maharashtra 2 pts, Baroda 0 pts

at Sardar Patel Stadium, Valsad
Gujarat 215 (B. Mehta 71, A. Dani 5 for 40) and 105 (A. Kuruvilla 5 for 44, S.V. Bahutule 4 for 15)
Bombay 430 for 8 dec. (V.G. Kambli 138, A. Dani 88, S.S. More 53, B. Mehta 4 for 119)
Bombay won by an innings and 110 runs
Bombay 6 pts, Gujarat 0 pts

With centuries from Mongia and Arothe, Baroda reached 494 for 6 at the end of the second day, but a third wicket stand of 270 between Bhave and Kanitkar took Maharashtra to a position where they could gain first innings points. Bhave claimed his sixth double century while Hrishikesh Kanitkar reached his second Ranji Trophy century.

Predictably, Bombay overwhelmed Gujarat in three days. Vinod Kambli made 138 off 172 balls, but Bombay unearthed a new star in Amit Dani, a seam bowler from the Union Bank of India, who took 5 for 40 and hit a violent 88 on his debut.

Woorkeri Raman, a constant inspiration to Tamil Nadu, finalists in the Ranji Trophy. (David Munden/Sportsline)

21, 22, 23 and 24 December 1995

at GSFC Ground, Fertilizer Nagar, Vadodara
Baroda 112 (N.M. Kulkarni 6 for 37) and 211 (V. Buch 53, T.B. Arothe 50, N.M. Kulkarni 4 for 87)
Bombay 238 (S.V. Bahutule 71, R.A. Swaroop 4 for 52) and 87 for 5
Bombay won by 5 wickets
Bombay 6 pts, Baroda 0 pts

at Municipal Corporation Ground, Rajkot
Gujarat 319 (M.H. Parmar 174) and 241 for 9 dec. (M.H. Parmar 101)
Saurashtra 252 (B. Jadeja 107 not out) and 140 for 5 (S.S. Tanna 74, B. Mehta 5 for 28)
Match drawn
Gujarat 2 pts, Saurashtra 0 pts

Career-best bowling performances by Nilesh Kulkarni set Bombay on the way to victory over Baroda on a wicket that always encouraged the bowler.

In Rajkot, Mukund Parmar set up a record by becoming the first batsman to score a century in each innings in the Ranji Trophy on three occasions. Off-spinner Bhavin Mehta caused Saurashtra embarrassment on the final day when the match looked to be petering out. Four wickets fell for eight runs to cause alarms.

10, 11, 12 and 13 January 1996
at Dadoji Konddeo Stadium, Thane
Bombay 427 (A.A. Muzumdar 165, S.S. Kulkarni 96, S.R. Tendulkar 81, S. Imamdar 4 for 82, M. Sane 4 for 119) and 361 for 3 (S.R. Tendulkar 151, S.S. More 110, A.A. Muzumdar 55)
Maharashtra 318 (S.S. Bhave 90, A.V. Kale 90, S.S. Sugwekar 85, S.V. Bahutule 6 for 90)
Match drawn
Bombay 2 pts, Maharashtra 0 pts

at Municipal Corporation Ground, Rajkot
Saurashtra 258 (S.S. Tanna 78) and 214 (S.S. Tanna 57, S.S. Hazare 5 for 81, R.A. Swaroop 4 for 42)
Baroda 239 (J.J. Martin 83, N.R. Mongia 70, H.J. Parsana 5 for 86) and 214 for 8 (R. Pandit 4 for 75)
Match drawn
Saurashtra 2 pts, Baroda 0 pts

Put in to bat, Bombay lost both openers for four, but Muzumdar and Tendulkar added 114. Muzumdar played a subdued but invaluable role and his 165 came off 363 balls, batting into the second day and adding 191 for the fifth wicket with Sulkashan Kulkarni. Sairaj Bahutule returned the best figures of his career with his leg-breaks as only three Maharashtra batsmen reached double figures, but all three passed 80. With no chance of a result, Tendulkar batted gloriously, hitting 151 off 105 balls with nine sixes and 12 fours. He and the more patient More added 124 for the third wicket.

Saurashtra claimed first innings points against Baroda, who were saved from ignominy by Mongia and Martin.

17, 18, 19 and 20 January 1996
at Dadoji Konddeo Stadium, Thane
Saurashtra 244 (N.R. Odedra 68, A. Kuruvilla 6 for 83) and 264 for 6 (B.M. Jadeja 88, N.R. Odedra 58)
Bombay 495 for 6 dec. (S.S. More 184, S.K. Kulkarni 161, S.S. Dighe 53)
Match drawn
Bombay 2 pts, Saurashtra 0 pts

at Sardar Oatel Stadium, Motera, Ahmedabad
Gujarat 640 (M.H. Parmar 283, Pathik Patel 68)
Maharashtra 449 for 7 (A.V. Kale 209, S.M. Kondhalkar 121)
Match drawn
Gujarat 1 pt, Maharashtra 1 pt

Saurashtra were asked to bat first in Thane and fell victim to Abey Kuruvilla's medium pace. Sulkashan Kulkarni and Sunil More added 295 for Bombay's fourth wicket with More making the highest score of his career. The points assured Bombay of the Talim Trophy as West Zone champions.

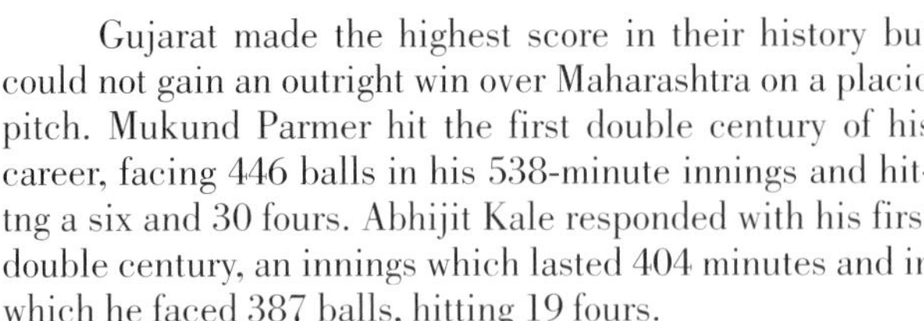
Gujarat made the highest score in their history but could not gain an outright win over Maharashtra on a placid pitch. Mukund Parmer hit the first double century of his career, facing 446 balls in his 538-minute innings and hittng a six and 30 fours. Abhijit Kale responded with his first double century, an innings which lasted 404 minutes and in which he faced 387 balls, hitting 19 fours.

25, 26, 27 and 28 January 1996
at Nehru Stadium, Pune
Maharashtra 388 (R. Kanade 122, A.V. Kale 77, S.S. Sugwekar 73, C.C. Mankad 4 for 117) and 373 for 5 (A.V. Kale 119, S.S. Bhave 103, H.H. Kanitkar 97)
Saurashtra 274 (N.R. Pana 61, S.S. Tanna 53)
Match drawn
Maharashtra 2 pts, Saurashtra 0 pts

at Motibaug Palace Ground, Baroda
Gujarat 146 (R.A. Swaroop 5 for 40) and 127 (R.A. Swaroop 5 for 51)
Baroda 298 (T.B. Arother 85, B. Mehta 5 for 107, Hiren Patel 4 for 94)
Baroda won by an innings and 25 runs
Baroda 6 pts, Gujarat 0 pts

Rahul Kanade made a century on his debut for Maharashtra and helped to bring his side the two points they needed to qualify for the knock-out stage.

They were joined there by Baroda who entered their last game pointless, but who had qualified by beating Gujarat inside three days. They were indebted to the off-breaks of Rayapet Swaroop who returned the best bowling figures of his career and claimed ten wickets in a match for the first time.

West Zone Final Table

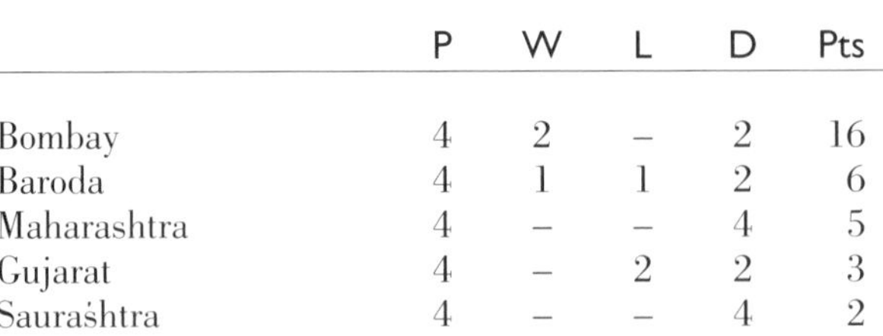

	P	W	L	D	Pts
Bombay	4	2	–	2	16
Baroda	4	1	1	2	6
Maharashtra	4	–	–	4	5
Gujarat	4	–	2	2	3
Saurashtra	4	–	–	4	2

Pre-Quarter-Finals

12, 13, 14, 15 and 16 February 1996
at Palam Sports Complex, Delhi
Maharashtra 345 (H.H. Kanitkar 104, A.V. Kale 63, S.S. Sugwekar 51, A.S. Wassan 5 for 92) and 284 (A.V. Kale 131, S.S. Bhave 52)
Delhi 454 (Ajay Sharma 187, R. Lamba 110, A. Malhotra 50, U. Gotkhindikar 4 for 86) and 123 for 2
Delhi won on first innings

at Karnail Singh Stadium, Delhi
Orissa 178 (P. Mohapatra 59) and 92 (K. Bharathan 6 for 36)
Railways 214 (S. Bangar 65, Sushil Kumar 4 for 28, R. Biswal 4 for 67) and 59 for 1
Railways won by 9 wickets

at PCA Stadium, Mohali, Chandigarh
Baroda 393 (K.S. More 112, T.B. Arothe 75, C. Williams 69, H. Indulkar 50) and 429 for 7 (C. Williams 109, V. Buch 94, J.J. Martin 81, H. Jadhav 58)
Punjab 314 (A. Mehra 95, V. Buch 4 for 65)
Baroda won on first innings

at Nehru Stadium, Indore
Tamil Nadu 325 (W.V. Raman 85, K. Srinath 53, N.D. Hirwani 5 for 88)
Madhya Pradesh 134 (S. Subramaniam 4 for 52) and 200 (P.K. Dwivedi 82, D. Vasu 5 for 36, Balaji Rao 5 for 53)
Tamil Nadu won by an innings and 11 runs

at VCA Ground, Nagpur
Vidarbha 414 (U. Ghani 94, Mohammad Sabir 87, P.V. Gandhe 81, U.V. Gandhe 50) and 269 for 7 dec. (M.S. Doshi 89, U. Ghani 66)
Haryana 355 (V. Yadav 111, Jitender Singh 79, R. Puri 55) and 64 for 2
Vidarbha won on first innings

at Gymkhana Ground, Secunderabad
Assam 112 (N.P. Singh 6 for 69) and 296 (S. Sawanth 55)
Hyderabad 294 (V.V.S. Laxman 130, N. David 56, Gautam Dutta 4 for 44) and 115 for 0 (M.V. Sridhar 69 not out)
Hyderabad won by 10 wickets

at RSI Ground, Bangalore
Bengal 153 (C.M. Sharma 59, D. Johnson 4 for 49) and 148 (S.B. Joshi 6 for 47)
Karnataka 330 (K.A. Jeshwanth 70, S. Somasunder 57)
Karnataka won by an innings and 29 runs

Atul Wassan recovered from a leg injury to take his place in the Delhi side to bring about a collapse in the Maharashtra batting. The last five wickets fell for 38 runs. By the end of the third day, with Raman Lamba and Ajay Sharma hitting centuries, Delhi were within three runs of Maharashtra's score with seven wickets standing. Thereafter, it was a case of what we have we hold.

In the quarter-final, Delhi would meet Railways who beat Orissa just 43 minutes into the third day.

Baroda had sneaked into the pre-quarter-finals on the strength of winning their final match in the West Zone, and they advanced into the quarter-finals at the expense of Punjab who suffered from losing Rathore run out early on. Kiran More's 200-ball innings put Baroda in a good position on the second day.

Batting consistently, Tamil Nadu beat Madhya Pradesh in three days. Vidarbha's batting was not so consistent. They were 158 for 6 before Ghani and Ulhas Gandhe added 101, but the partnership that really destroyed Haryana was the ninth wicket stand of 111 between Ghani and Pritam Gandhe who, batting at number ten, hit the highest score of his career. Former Test wicket-keeper Vijay Yadav hit 111 off 159 balls and shared a fifth wicket partnership of 167 with Rajesh Puri, but Haryana's last six wickets went down for 64 runs, and Vidarbha qualified for the quarter-finals for the first time in their history.

Hyderabad beat Assam in four days while Karnataka took only three days to dispose of Bengal.

Quarter-Finals

26, 27, 28, 29 February and 1 March 1996
at Palam Sports Complex, Delhi
Delhi 431 (Ajay Sharma 136, A. Malhotra 102, S. Dogra 86, Suresh Kumar 5 for 86, Iqbal Thakur 4 for 101) and 561 for 9 dec. (Ajay Sharma 182, Bantoo Singh 106, A. Malhotra 77, A. Dani 64, Shakti Singh 52 not out)
Railways 223 (Vijayendra Yadav 75, A.S. Wassan 6 for 75, R. Sanghvi 4 for 62)
Delhi won on first innings

Vinod Kambli – runs for Bombay in the Ranji Trophy and for India, but no place in the party to tour England for disciplinary reasons. (David Munden/Sportsline)

Rahul Dravid enjoyed an exceptional season with the bat for Karnataka, Ranji Trophy winners. (Graham Chadwick/Allsport)

at Gymkhana Ground, Secunderabad
Vidarbha 409 (U.S. Phate 115, U.V. Gandhe 97, P.V. Gandhe 60, N.P. Singh 4 for 120) and 32 for 1
Hyderabad 620 (V.V.S. Laxman 196, M.V. Sridhar 101, A. Nandakishore 90, N. David 64)
Hyderabad won on first innings

at RSI Ground, Bangalore
Karnataka 480 (K.A. Jeshwanth 138, R. Vijay 106, S.B. Joshi 56, R.A. Swaroop 4 for 84)
Baroda 213 (D. Johnson 5 for 91) and 188 (R. Ananth 4 for 57)
Karnataka won by an innings and 79 runs

at India Cement Ground, Sankarnagar, Tirunelveli
Tamil Nadu 246 (S. Sharath 86, S. Ramesh 52, S.V. Bahutule 5 for 91) and 250 (S. Sharath 90, D. Vasu 80)
Bombay 196 (S.K. Kulkarni 84 not out, A.A. Muzumdar 54, Balaji Rao 4 for 46) and 147 (A.A. Muzumdar 58 not out, Robin Singh 7 for 54)
Tamil Nadu won by 153 runs

Choosing to bat when they won the toss, Delhi lost three wickets for 47 before skipper Ajay Sharma, who was to hit a century in each innings, and Akash Malhotra put on 205. Sumeet Dogra also batted well, and Delhi moved to a strong position. Railways had no answer to Wassan and Sanghvi, and when Delhi batted a second time they were content to indulge in fruitful practice.

In spite of Phate's 344-ball century, Vidarbha struggled at 167 for 6. Once again Ulhas Gandhe came to their rescue with a career-best innings and a seventh wicket stand of 119 with Phate. Then Pritam Gandhe added 89 for the last wicket with Kanhere. These heroics proved to be all in vain as Laxman continued his outstanding form. He, Nandakishore and Sridhar saw Hyderabad into a first innings lead for the loss of only four wickets.

Karnataka destroyed Baroda in three days. They lost three wickets for 91 runs after they were put in, but Vijay and Jeshwanth added 156. From that point on, Karnataka were in total control.

The mighty Bombay, bereft of their leading players, were beaten by Tamil Nadu. Initially, all had gone well for Bombay. Leg-spinner Bahutule had Srinath caught behind and bowled Raman round his legs. Nilesh Kulkarni accounted for Robin Singh and Tanveer Jabbar, Ramesh was run out, and Tamil Nadu were 100 for 5. Sharath and Vasu countered by adding 116, but the last five wickets fell for 30 runs. Bombay still seemed set fair when they ended the second day on 141 for 4, but disaster struck on the third morning when Vasu broke through and the last six wickets went down for 28 runs. From that point on, the game belonged to Tamil Nadu. Sharath and Vasu added 107 after five wickets had fallen for 77, and Robin Singh bowled his side to victory on the last day. Needing 229 to win in 90 overs, Bombay were bowled out for 147 with Robin Singh taking seven wickets in an innings for the first time, including a spell of three in eight balls. It was Tamil Nadu's first win over Bombay in 14 meetings.

Semi-Finals

14, 15, 16, 17 and 18 March 1996
at M. Chinnaswamy Stadium, Bangalore
Karnataka 423 (R.S. Dravid 153, D. Ganesh 75 not out, S. Somasunder 74) and 312 (K.A. Jeshwanth 85, R. Vijay 57)
Hyderabad 188 (N. David 57, V.V.S. Laxman 51, S.B. Joshi 4 for 58) and 363 for 7 (V.V.S. Laxman 203 not out, S.B. Joshi 5 for 126)
Karnataka won on first innings

at M.A. Chidambaram Stadium, Madras
Delhi 256 (A. Malhotra 117, D. Vasu 5 for 71) and 232 (S. Dogra 97)
Tamil Nadu 272 (W.V. Raman 85, D. Vasu 57, N. Chopra 4 for 122) and 220 for 2 (W.V. Raman 110 not out, S. Sharath 76 not out)
Tamil Nadu won by 8 wickets

A century on the opening day by Rahul Dravid put Karnataka in a strong position against Hyderabad. The position became even stronger on the second day when Doddanarasish Ganesh hit a swashbuckling unbeaten 75 at number nine and four Hyderabad wickets fell for 114 before the close. There was no reprieve on the third day as Karnataka moved into an impregnable position. Ultimately, Hyderabad required 548 to win, an impossible task in spite of Laxman completing his first double century to end for him wahat had been an outstanding season.

In Madras, Delhi closed the first day in peril at 146 for 7. That they effected any sort of recovery was due to

Sunil Joshi, all-rounder of the season and a member of Karnataka's Trophy-winning side.
(Graham Chadwick/Allsport)

Malhotra and Sanghvi, but Raman quickly led his side to a good position. Delhi fought back on the third day as Tamil Nadu lost their last seven wickets for 62 runs. Trailing by a mere 16 runs, Delhi were back in the contest, but two brilliant slip catches by Robin Singh helped to reduce them to 96 for 5 when they batted a second time. At 140 for 8, they looked well beaten but Wassan helped Dogra to add 85. Eventually, Tamil Nadu needed 217 to win. Two wickets fell for 31 runs before Sharath joined Raman who hit a splendid century. His innings occupied 188 balls and contained six sixes and seven fours and took Tamil Nadu into the final.

Final

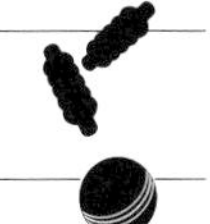

27, 28, 29, 30 and 31 March 1996
at M. Chidambaram Stadium, Madras
Karnataka 620 for 8 dec. (R. Vijay 146, R.S. Dravid 114, S. Somasunder 99, S.B. Joshi 86) and 277 for 6 dec. (A. Vaidya 61, S. Somasunder 53)
Tamil Nadu 370 (K. Srinath 85, W.V. Raman 61, A.R. Kumble 5 for 95) and 31 for 3
Karnataka won on first innings

As has often been the case, the Ranji Trophy was won by the side who batted first and occupied the crease for two-and-a-half days. A stand of 262 for the third wicket between Vijay and Dravid virtually assured Karnataka of the match, for they had lost only four wickets by the end of the second day. Joshi hit well and cleanly, and Kumble, returning from international duty to lead Karnataka in the final, declared. A spirited innings from Raman saw Tamil Nadu reach 172 for 2 by the close and gave glimpses of a miracle, but was not to be. They batted bravely but Kumble cast his spell on the fourth day, and Karnataka took a first innings lead of 250 with one day remaining. They had won the Ranji Trophy for the first time in 13 years.

First-Class Averages

Batting

	M	Inns	NO	Runs	HS	Av	100s	50s
R.V. Sapru	4	7	4	431	200*	143.66	2	1
N.S. Sidhu	5	5	1	533	259*	133.25	2	1
A.V. Kale	8	12	1	1006	209	91.45	4	3
A. Azharuddin	6	6	–	536	118	89.33	3	2
M.H. Parmar	4	7	–	595	283	85.00	3	
A.R. Kumble	7	7	4	255	111*	85.00	1	2
A. Verma	3	5	1	332	141	83.00	2	
R.S. Dravid	11	16	4	968	153	80.66	5	3
S.K. Kulkarni	4	6	1	392	161	78.40	1	2
V.V.S. Laxman	11	17	2	1170	203*	78.00	5	2
B.M. Jadeja	3	4	1	228	107*	76.00	1	1
V.B. Chandrasekhar	5	9	1	601	237*	75.12	2	2
S. Sharath	14	22	9	917	204*	70.53	2	5
A.K. Sharma	11	19	1	1217	188	67.61	5	3
S. Dogra	7	11	3	515	201*	64.37	1	3
W.V. Raman	11	15	2	835	116*	64.23	2	6
V.G. Kambli	7	7	–	449	138	64.14	3	
P. Dharmani	9	13	3	641	223*	64.10	2	2
S.S. Karim	8	11	2	569	200*	63.22	2	
S.B. Somasunder	9	13	–	803	166	61.76	2	6
P.R. Mphapatra	5	8	1	423	105	60.42	2	3
S.S. Brave	10	16	1	894	227	59.60	2	5
M.V. Sridhar	11	19	2	991	137	58.29	5	3
H.H. Kanitkar	5	7	–	401	142	57.28	2	1
R. Kanade	2	4	–	220	122	55.00	1	
A.D. Pandey	3	5	1	219	209*	54.75	1	
S.B. Joshi	12	15	4	600	118	54.54	1	4
A. Malhotra	10	17	2	815	197	54.33	3	4

Batting

	M	Inns	NO	Runs	HS	Av	100s	50s
A.S. Pathak	5	10	–	540	132	54.00	3	1
Chinmoy Sharma	4	6	1	269	123*	53.80	1	1
A.R. Khurasiya	5	6	–	322	131	53.66	1	1
A. Dani	3	2	–	107	88	53.50		1
R. Nayyar	5	9	1	423	134*	52.87	3	
A.A. Muzumdar	10	16	1	788	209	52.53	2	4
K. Sriram	5	7	–	367	174	52.42	1	
S.B. Banger	6	11	1	523	161	52.30	2	1
M. Prabhakar	7	10	1	468	125	52.00	2	
C.S. Pandit	8	12	1	567	202	51.54	1	2
D. Gandhi	9	14	–	718	213	51.28	2	3
S.R. Tendulkar	8	11	3	410	151	51.25	1	2
J.P. Yadav	5	8	–	409	135	51.12	2	
S.S. More	6	9	1	408	184	51.00	2	1
Jyotiprasa Yadav	5	8	–	407	146	50.87	1	3
R. Vijay	9	14	2	602	146	50.16	3	1
P.S. Rawat	5	7	2	250	140*	50.00	1	1
A.D. Jadeja	7	11	1	493	189	49.30	1	2
T.B. Arothe	6	9	–	442	142	49.11	1	3
U.V. Gandhe	6	10	4	291	97	49.50		3
P.K. Amre	7	12	1	530	161	48.18	2	1
S. Ramesh	9	15	–	710	158	47.33	2	4
Ashu Dani	5	9	–	424	141	47.11	1	2
Tariq-ur-Rehman	4	7	–	326	122	46.57	2	
R. Shamshed	8	14	1	599	156	46.07	1	4
S.S. Sugwekar	7	10	1	411	85	45.66		4
B.K.P. Misquin	2	4	–	180	107	45.00	1	
Rohit Mehta	3	5	1	178	103*	44.50	1	

First-Class Averages (continued)

Batting

	M	Inns	NO	Runs	HS	Av	100s	50s
S. Sawant	5	8	–	354	121	44.25	1	1
R. Puri	5	7	–	308	73	44.00		3
A.N. Kudua	5	9	1	349	162*	43.62	1	
K.A. Jeshwant	9	13	–	559	138	43.00	1	4
R.B. Biswal	6	7	2	214	73	42.80		2
U.I. Ghani	6	9	–	385	94	42.77		2
N.R. Mongia	7	9	1	341	152	42.62	1	1
S.S. Das	10	15	1	591	178	42.21	1	3
C. Williams	3	5	–	205	109	41.00	1	1
N.A. David	6	9	1	323	64	40.37		4
Sunil Kumar	4	7	1	242	74*	40.33		2
V.Z. Yadav	6	10	1	358	100*	39.77	1	1
S.S. Tanna	4	7	–	278	78	39.71		4
K. Srinath	8	11	–	432	159	39.27	1	3
Y. Gowda	6	9	3	325	79*	39.16		1
V. Rathore	9	15	–	580	156	38.66	1	3
K.S. More	6	9	–	337	112	37.44	1	1
G.K. Khoda	8	13	1	445	115	37.08	2	2
B. Subremaniam	3	6	1	184	52*	36.80		2
A.N. Kishore	8	14	1	478	132	36.76	1	2
J. Arun Kumar	4	5	–	175	58	35.00		1
S.J. Kalyani	7	9	2	244	117*	34.85	1	
S.C. Ganguly	9	14	1	451	171	34.69	1	2
S.V. Manjrekar	5	8	2	206	79	34.33		1
Avtar Singh	3	5	2	102	53	34.00		1
S.S. Raul	10	14	1	441	125	33.92	1	2
J.J. Martin	8	13	–	441	115	33.92	1	3
S.B. Saikia	5	9	–	305	127	33.88	1	1
S.V. Limaye	4	7	1	202	51	33.66		2
D. Vasu	10	11	–	368	80	33.45		3
Vijay Yadev	9	14	–	467	111	33.35	1	3
A.S. Kaypee	5	7	–	229	110	32.71	1	
S.M. Kondhalkar	5	7	1	196	121	32.66	1	
P.K. Dwevedi	5	8	1	225	82	32.14		1
A.S. Parmar	4	8	1	224	50	32.00		2
H. Indulkar	3	5	–	160	50	32.00		1
G.K. Pandey	7	11	3	255	71	31.87		2
Chetan Sharma	2	4	–	126	59	31.50		1
A. Vaidya	11	12	–	376	69	31.33		2
M. Sabir	3	5	–	156	87	31.20		1
H. Patel	4	7	1	186	81	31.00		1
D. Chakraborty	3	5	–	154	72	30.80		1
M.S. Dosi	7	10	2	246	89	30.75		2
V. Pratap	8	12	2	305	69	30.50		3
M.S. Narula	6	10	3	213	60	30.42		1

(Qualification: 100 runs, average 30.00)
(Played in one match: U.S. Phate 115; Tarun Kumar 100 & 2)

Bowling

	Overs	Mds	Runs	Wks	Av	Best	10/m	5/inn
P. Acharya	48.1	21	111	13	8.53	7/6	1	1
A.R. Kumble	163.2	47	378	32	11.81	6/20		3
Syed Khan	61.3	18	147	11	13.36	5/42		1
R.B. Biswal	228.2	82	535	35	15.28	5/44	1	5
Venkatapathy Raju	174	56	393	24	16.37	7/82	1	2
K.A. Jeshwant	66.5	13	181	11	16.45	3/40		
S.S. Hazare	108	35	217	13	16.69	5/81		1
N. Madhukar	94.3	27	241	14	17.21	5/43		1
P.L. Mhambrey	78.1	16	241	14	17.21	5/20		1
M. Suresh Kumar	292.2	95	571	33	17.30	6/34		3
R.A. Swarup	194.2	57	446	25	17.84	5/40	1	2
K. Bharatan	151	50	305	17	17.94	6/36		2
S.B. Joshi	529.1	174	1169	65	17.98	7/60	1	4
K. Chakradhar Rao	165.4	53	364	20	18.20	5/57		1
Venkatesh Prasad	114.5	37	299	16	18.68	6/23		1
Sushil Kumar	158.4	39	416	22	18.90	5/9		1
Abinash Kumar	360.4	115	739	39	18.94	7/111		3
H. Ramkishen	253.3	68	673	33	20.39	6/75		2
R.R. Sanghi	220	44	718	35	20.51	7/42	2	3
N.D. Hirwani	229.4	49	608	29	20.96	6/59		3
J. Srinath	107	28	296	14	21.14	3/24		
S.A. Ankola	18[illegible]	47	509	24	21.20	5/90		1
Robin Singh	82.1	19	255	12	21.25	7/53		1

Bowling

	Overs	Mds	Runs	Wks	Av	Best	10/m	5/inn
P.B. Hinhanikar	222.2	75	514	23	22.34	5/62		1
R. Sridhar	353.2	121	716	32	22.37	6/91		2
P.S. Vaidya	213	49	628	28	22.42	5/22	1	3
G. Dutta	135.3	40	320	14	22.85	4/44		
K.N.A. Padmanabhan	269.3	50	617	27	22.85	7/113	1	3
B. Vij	441	94	1125	49	22.95	6/19	2	4
Sandeep Sharma	187.2	55	462	20	23.10	4/26		
Robin R. Singhe	242.4	39	672	29	23.17	7/54		1
V.N. Buch	273	51	733	31	23.64	5/55		1
A. Kuruvilla	244.5	59	664	28	23.71	6/83		2
D.J. Johnson	205.1	27	720	30	24.00	6/63	1	2
Dhanraj Singh	102.4	28	271	11	24.63	3/54		
S.V. Limaye	83.2	18	249	10	24.90	6/35		1
S. Sawant	152	32	326	13	25.07	4/55		
D. Vasu	415.2	110	886	35	25.31	5/36		2
D. Ganesh	137.1	23	431	17	25.35	4/12		
J.P. Pandey	116.2	19	355	14	25.35	4/96		
R.K. Chauhan	328	92	788	31	25.41	5/120		1
V.B. Jain	136.1	26	407	16	25.43	5/34		1
S.S. Lahore	234.3	70	509	20	25.45	5/75		1
P. Jain	211.1	51	535	21	25.47	4/39		
S. Oasis	121.2	33	281	11	25.54	3/24		
B.N. Mehta	161.4	53	451	17	26.52	5/28		2
N. Chopra	139.3	23	411	15	27.40	6/91		1
A.R. Kapoor	161.1	25	526	19	27.68	7/144		1
Shakti Singh	137.3	29	363	13	27.92	5/24		1
R. Ananth	221.3	55	560	20	28.00	4/57		
G.K. Pandey	188	59	365	13	28.07	2/17		
S.V. Mudkavi	274.1	45	792	28	28.28	8/83	1	2
A.S. Wassan	196.5	37	594	21	28.28	6/75		2
Mohammad Aslam	231.3	50	681	24	28.37	5/42		1
N.M. Kulkarni	319.4	96	743	26	28.57	6/37	1	1
U. Chatterjee	230.3	61	603	21	28.71	5/23		1
P.K. Krishna Kumar	170.1	29	518	18	28.87	3/90		
F.K. Ghayas	157	28	504	17	29.64	4/35		
R.V. Pandit	213.2	62	517	17	30.41	4/75		
P. Munnuswamy	110.1	26	307	10	30.70	3/74		
S. Subramanian	424.5	117	1047	34	30.79	7/85		2
P. Thakur	225.5	54	560	18	31.11	5/66		1
S.V. Bahutule	453.5	111	1128	36	31.33	6/90		2
R.P. Singh	113	25	348	11	31.63	3/48		
T.B. Arothe	129.3	29	317	10	31.70	3/9		
Kanwaljit Singh	408.2	99	923	29	31.82	5/53		1
I.A. Thakur	134.2	23	446	14	31.85	4/89		
H.S. Sodhi	131.5	17	415	13	31.92	6/55		1
N.P. Singh	200	37	621	19	32.68	6/69		1
B. Ramprakash	287.2	55	706	21	33.61	5/102		2
W.D. Balaji Rao	305.3	53	890	26	34.23	5/53		1
Javed Alam Khan	170.3	36	514	15	34.26	4/29		
M.S. Dosi	231.2	49	492	14	35.14	6/42		1
C.C. Mankad	130	31	362	10	36.20	4/117		
U. Gotikhindikar	180.1	45	407	11	37.00	4/86		
S.T. Banerjee	118	15	450	12	37.50	3/41		
Iqbal Siddiqui	128	27	376	10	37.60	2/26		
A. Sarkar	164	31	455	12	37.91	4/63		
Harvinder Singh	156.1	37	470	12	39.16	3/33		
M.S. Kulkarni	275.5	67	707	18	39.27	5/89		1
P.V. Gandhe	306.2	59	780	19	41.05	7/62	1	1
M. Venkataramana	189.3	34	632	15	42.13	5/65		1
S. Mahesh	169.1	32	464	11	42.18	2/57		
H.J. Parsana	310	46	919	20	46.45	5/88		1
S. Subramaniya	195.2	25	644	10	64.40	3/117		
M. Sane	200.4	35	681	10	68.10	4/119		

(Qualification: 10 wickets)

Leading Fielders

40 – S.S. Dinghe (ct 33 / st 7); 31 – A. Vaidya (ct 27 / st 4); 28 – S.S. Karim (ct 23 / st 5); 27 – V. Yadav (ct 23 / st 4); 23 – Yuvraj Singh (ct 21 / st 2); 20 – S.V. Wankhede (ct 16 / st 4); 18 – M.S.K. Prasad (ct 14 / st 4), P. Dharmani (ct 12 / st 6) and Robin Singh; 16 – C.S. Pandit (ct 14/ st 2); 15 – V.V.S. Laxman (ct 14 / st 1), N.R. Mongia; (ct 10 / st 5), R. Paul (ct 13 / st 2), V.Z. Yadav and W.V. Raman; 14 – S.B. Joshi and K.J. Patel (ct 10 / st 4); 13 – R.S. Dravid, S. Ramesh, S.S. Raul and R. Vijay; 12 – S.S. Das, A.A. Muzumdar, V. Samant, P.V. Shashikant and S.R. Tendulkar

Zimbabwe

The nature of the international fixture list meant that Zimbabwe's preparation for the World Cup was more leisurely than most. The luxury of six Test matches and six one-day internationals in 1994–5 was not repeated, and the Zimbabwe public had to make do with a brief tour by Tasmania and a Test match and two one-day internationals against South Africa in 1995–6. There was a promise of a series against England in the not too distant future.

Andrew Hudson is finally bowled by Bryan Strang for 135, and an innings of high quality is at an end. Hudson's century was the basis of South Africa's victory over Zimbabwe, for the visitors lost their first four wickets for 85.
(Clive Mason/Allsport)

Tasmania tour
South Africa tour
Logan Cup
First-class averages

An 'A' side was sent to South Africa before the start of the season. Led by Wayne James, it was a blend of youth and experience, but its composition did emphasise Zimbabwe's crucial problem, a lack of strength in depth. The side struggled in the first-class matches but showed to better advantage in the limited-over games.

What the Zimbabwe selectors looked for from the matches against Tasmania and South Africa and from the domestic competition, the Logan Cup, was the development of Olonga as a quality fast bowler, the emergence of Whittall as an all-rounder of substance, and the full flowering of Campbell, as batsman of immense promise, still only 23 years old and yet to do himself full justice. If these three could fulfil their undoubted potential and their talents could be allied to the proven worth of the Flower brothers, Streak and the incomparable Houghton, Zimbabwe could field a side which would make a mark at international level and offer a positive challenge in the World Cup.

Tasmanian Tour

Stalemate in matches played in a holiday spirit, but Zimbabwe discover a seam bowler of Test potential.

3, 4 and 5 October 1995
at Harare Sports Club
Mashonaland 293 (C.B. Wishart 60, S. Young 5 for 68) and 296 for 7 dec. (D.L. Houghton 77 not out, G.A. Briant 61, A. Flower 57)
Tasmania 311 for 6 dec. (D.C. Boon 81, D.F. Hills 73, S. Young 59 not out) and 162 for 3 (D.F. Hills 70, J. Cox 54)
Match drawn

9, 10 and 11 October 1995
at Bulawayo Athletic Club
Tasmania 196 (A.C.I. Lock 6 for 59) and 309 for 4 (J. Cox 130, D.F. Hills 94)
Zimbabwe Cricket Union President's XI 403 for 9 dec. (D.L. Houghton 112, A. Flower 82, G.W. Flower 79, A.D.R. Campbell 68, M.A. Hatton 5 for 113, G.J. Denton 4 for 39)
Match drawn

Tasmania had much the better of the first of the two first-class matches, and Mashonaland were indebted to a second innings seventh wicket stand of 111 between Houghton and Briant which enabled them to escape defeat.

National coach Jackie Hampshire took charge of the President's XI in the second match, which went very much in favour of the home side until the last day. Medium-pacer Charlie Lock bowled superbly on the opening day, and his career-best bowling performance of 6 for 59 earned him a place in the side for the Test match against South Africa. The President's XI batted consistently well, and Houghton played brilliantly to hit 112 off 108 balls with two sixes and 20 fours. In the circumstances, Denton bowled remarkably well to take 4 for 39 from 28 overs. Hatton also bowled commendably. On the last day, Hills and Cox made the game safe for Tasmania with an opening stand of 194.

Andy Flower in lively form behind the stumps as he unsuccessfully attempts a run out in the first one-day international against South Africa.
(Clive Mason/Allsport)

South African Tour

Zimbabwe's courage is insufficient against the power of South Africa and the pace of Donald. South Africa dominate in the Test and one-day internationals.

Test Match

Zimbabwe gave first Test caps to Charlie Lock and Craig Wishart, a right-handed batsman and medium-pace bowler respectively. With de Villiers suffering from a hamstring problem, South Africa recalled Brett Schultz, the left-arm fast bowler, whose knee injury had kept him out of the game for almost two years. Andy Flower won the toss, and Zimbabwe batted.

The home side were soon in trouble. In the third over, Donald turned Dekker square with a lifting delivery that caught the shoulder of the bat and flew to slip. In a five-over spell, Schultz then destroyed the Zimbabwe top order. He forced Andy Flower to play on and had Houghton caught behind. The same fate befell Campbell one run later, and Zimbabwe were 23 for 4. Unfortunately, Schultz marred a fine display with an aggression which transmitted itself into verbal abuse and threatening gestures. He was severely reprimanded by umpires Shepherd and Tiffin, and by match referee Barry Jarman.

Grant Flower batted for 147 minutes for his 24 and added 48 with Whittall, but when Paul Strang was out first ball Zimbabwe were 84 for 7. Wishart had batted sensibly, but Heath Streak was the hero. He was last out, having hit a maiden Test fifty, 53 off 66 balls with a six and nine fours.

Streak then immediately accounted for Kirsten and Cronje, and with Lock claiming his first Test wicket before the close, South Africa ended the day on 74 for 3, and Zimbabwe had forced their way back into contention.

Left-arm seamer Bryan Strang soon trapped night-watchman Matthews leg before the next morning, but Hudson batted admirably and finally found an able partner in McMillan. In two hours, the pair added 101 for the sixth wicket. Hudson reached his third Test hundred, and, in all, faced 236 balls and hit two sixes and 18 fours in his 311-minute innings, during which he did not offer a chance. McMillan hit a six and 12 fours, and he and Donald, who made his highest Test score, put on 79 for the ninth wicket. McMillan looked sure to reach a hundred, but Schultz fell to Bryan Strang without scoring. The left-arm seamer ended with 5 for 101, his best Test figures, and Lock, 33 years old and returning to Zimbabwe after several years in England, bowled well on his Test debut.

Facing a deficit of 176, Zimbabwe were 13 for 0 at the close. They lost Grant Flower without addition the next morning, and although they displayed much more determination than they had done in the first innings, they were undermined by the pace and aggression of Allan Donald. Andy Flower and Guy Whittall added 97 in three hours for the fifth wicket, but, with the second new ball, Donald took four wickets for eight runs in the space of six overs.

Zimbabwe ended the third day on 272 for 8, but they added only 11 on the fourth morning. Donald claimed the last two wickets to give him 8 for 71, his best performance in Test cricket. His match figures were 11 for 113. Dave Richardson held six catches in the match to bring his total to 99 in 23 Tests.

Needing 108 to win, South Africa lost both openers to Lock who ended his maiden Test with a highly commendable 5 for 105. The out-of-form Rhodes was bowled by Streak, and the visitors tottered at 48 for 3 before Cronje and McMillan cast away any doubts.

The warning to England was loud and clear. Zimbabwe now had two one-day internationals and two Tests and a one-day series in New Zealand in which to regroup their forces for the World Cup.

19 October 1995
at Harare South Country Club
South Africans 354 for 6 (B.M. McMillan 135, P.J.R. Steyn 98, W.J. Cronje 51 not out)
Zimbabwe Country Districts 203 for 9 (A.C. Waller 77, B.N. Schultz 4 for 35)
South Africans won by 151 runs

The tourists played one 50-over match outside the international programme, but the opposition was far from strong. Brian McMillan hit 135 off 115 balls, and he and Steyn added 230 in 99 minutes for the second wicket.

Charlie Lock made a great impression for Mashonaland County Districts as a medium-pace bowler and won his first Test cap a month after his 33rd birthday. (Graham Chadwick/Allsport)

Test Match – Zimbabwe v. South Africa

13, 14, 15 and 16 October 1995 at Harare Sports Club, Harare

Zimbabwe

	First Innings		Second Innings	
M.H. Dekker	c Hudson, b Donald	1	c Hudson, b Schultz	24
G.W. Flower	c Richardson, b Donald	24	c McMillan, b Donald	5
*A. Flower (Capt)	b Schultz	7	(5) c Richardson, b Donald	63
D.L. Houghton	c Richardson, b Schultz	5	c Matthews, b Donald	30
A.D.R. Campbell	c Richardson, b Schultz	0	(3) c Schultz, b Matthews	28
G.J. Whittall	c Richardson, b Matthews	29	lbw, b Donald	38
C.B. Wishart	c Kirsten, b Symcox	24	b Donald	13
P.A. Strang	b Matthews	0	c Richardson, b Donald	37
H.H. Streak	c McMillan, b Donald	53	c Cronje, b Donald	0
B.C. Strang	lbw, b Schultz	0	not out	25
A.C.I. Lock	not out	8	b Donald	0
	b 10, w 5, nb 4	19	lb 10, w 1, nb 9	20
		170		283

	O	M	R	W	O	M	R	W
Donald	17.1	3	42	3	33	12	71	8
Schultz	21	7	54	4	24	7	72	1
Matthews	13	5	30	2	20	7	52	–
McMillan	3	–	13	–	15	3	53	1
Symcox	11	5	21	1	11	3	22	–
Cronje					1	–	3	–

Fall of Wickets
1–3, 2–12, 3–22, 4–23, 5–71, 6–84, 7–84, 8–127, 9–128
1–13, 2–64, 3–70, 4–102, 5–199, 6–206, 7–231, 8–231, 9–279

South Africa

	First Innings		Second Innings	
A.C. Hudson	b B.C. Strang	135	(2) c B.C. Strang, b Lock	4
G. Kirsten	lbw, b Streak	1	(1) c A. Flower, b Lock	13
W.J. Cronje (Capt)	c Houghton, b Streak	5	not out	56
D.J. Cullinan	c Whittall, b Lock	11		
C.R. Matthews	c G. Flower, b B. Strang	10		
J.N. Rhodes	c A. Flower, b B. Strang	15	(4) b Streak	6
B.M. McMillan	not out	98	(5) not out	25
*D.J. Richardson	c B.C. Strang, b Lock	13		
P.L. Symcox	c Houghton, b Lock	4		
A.A. Donald	b B.C. Strang	33		
B.N. Schultz	lbw, b B.C. Strang	0		
	b 9, lb 6, w 3, nb 3	21	lb 2, w 2	4
		346	(for 3 wickets)	108

	O	M	R	W	O	M	R	W
Streak	26	6	79	2	9	2	24	1
Lock	17	4	68	3	13	1	37	2
B.C. Strang	32	4	101	5	12	6	18	–
P.A. Strang	23	2	58	–	4	–	27	–
Whittall	2	–	11	–				
G.W. Flower	3	1	14	–				

Fall of Wickets
1–1, 2–24, 3–59, 4–85, 5–145, 6–246, 7–261, 8–265, 9–344
1–6, 2–36, 3–48

Umpires: D.R. Shepherd & R.B. Tiffin

South Africa won by 7 wickets

First One-day International – Zimbabwe v. South Africa

21 October 1995 at Harare Sports Club, Harare

South Africa

A.C. Hudson	run out	36
*D.J. Richardson	c A. Flower, b Olonga	5
B.M. McMillan	c A. Flower, b Streak	127
W.J. Cronje (Capt)	c Campbell, b P.A. Strang	33
J.N. Rhodes	c A. Flower, b Streak	25
G. Kirsten	not out	36
A.P. Kuiper	not out	14
N. Boje		
C.R. Matthews		
A.A. Donald		
P.S. de Villiers		
	b 4, lb 15, w 6, nb 2	27
	50 overs (for 5 wickets)	303

	O	M	R	W
Streak	10	2	54	2
Olonga	10	1	59	1
B.C. Strang	9	–	51	–
Whittall	7	–	48	–
P.A. Strang	10	–	51	1
G.W. Flower	4	–	21	–

Fall of Wickets
1–7, 2–66, 3–152, 4–192, 5–284

Zimbabwe

*A. Flower (Capt)	c Richardson, b Matthews	2
G.W. Flower	c Richardson, b McMillan	19
A.C. Waller	run out	0
D.L. Houghton	c Cronje, b Matthews	9
A.D.R. Cambell	not out	68
G.J. Whittall	c Richardson, b McMillan	6
C.N. Evans	c Richardson, b Donald	8
P.A. Strang	c Richardson, b Cronje	24
H.H. Streak	not out	23
B.C. Strang		
H.R. Olonga		
	lb 6, w 4	10
	50 overs (for 7 wickets)	169

	O	M	R	W
de Villiers	10	2	34	–
Matthews	10	1	42	–
McMillan	5	–	13	2
Donald	10	2	28	1
Boje	10	1	29	–
Cronje	5	–	17	1

Fall of Wickets
1–11, 2–14, 3–30, 4–30, 5–44, 6–68, 7–119

Umpires: I.D. Robinson & Q.J. Goosen *Man of the Match:* B.M. McMIllan

South Africa won by 134 runs

One-day Internationals

South African dominance continues, and they return home with a one hundred per cent record. The all-round strength of McMillan and the expertise of Richardson are again in evidence.

An innings of 127 off 120 balls with three sixes and 14 fours from Brian McMillan totally dominated the first one-day international. This was McMillan's first century in a limited-over international, and he followed it by taking two wickets for 13 runs. Olonga, who was making his debut in a one-day international, as was Boje, began the match by having Richardson caught behind, but thereafter Zimbabwe were outclassed.

McMillan was rested for the second match in which South Africa recovered from 29 for 3 to reach 239. Adrian Kuiper hit 50 off 72 balls, and Jonty Rhodes 53 off 47 balls. Cronje excelled as a bowler but Zimbabwe gave a miserable batting display. Streak took the individual award for his early bowling performance which had so rattled South Africa.

Dave Richardson confirmed his worth to his side with nine catches in the two games.

Pace bowler supreme and two first-class centuries in the season for Heath Streak.
(Graham Chadwick/Allsport)

Second One-day International – Zimbabwe v. South Africa

22 October 1995 at Harare Sports Club, Harare

South Africa

*D.J. Richardson	hit wkt, **b** Streak	0
G.F.J. Liebenberg	**c** A. Flower, **b** Streak	12
P.J.R. Steyn	**c** A. Flower, **b** Streak	4
A.P. Kuiper	lbw, **b** Campbell	50
G. Kirsten	run out	38
J.N. Rhodes	**c** Houghton, **b** Campbell	53
W.J. Cronje (Capt)	**c** A. Flower, **b** Whittall	7
P.L. Symcox	**c** Houghton, **b** Brandes	35
C.R. Matthews	**c** A. Flower, **b** Streak	6
P.S. de Villiers	**c** A. Flower, **b** Whittall	5
A.A. Donald	not out	5
	lb **7**, w **14**, nb **3**	24
	49.2 overs	239

	O	M	R	W
Streak	10	1	25	4
Olonga	4	–	32	–
Brain	5	1	28	–
Brandes	4.2	–	23	1
P.A. Strang	5	–	30	–
G.W. Flower	5	–	25	–
Whittalll	10	–	47	2
Campbell	6	1	22	2

Fall of Wickets
1–**1**, 2–**18**, 3–**29**, 4–**87**, 5–**171**, 6–**180**, 7–**184**, 8–**203**, 9–**217**

Zimbabwe

*A. Flower (Capt)	**c** Richardson, **b** Matthews	2
G.W. Flower	**c** Richardson, **b** Donald	21
A.C. Waller	**c** Richardson, **b** Cronje	15
D.L. Houghton	**c** de Villiers, **b** Symcox	25
A.D.R. Campbell	**c** Matthews, **b** Cronje	5
G.J. Whittall	run out	0
P.A. Strang	**b** Matthews	15
H.H. Streak	**c** Richardson, **b** Cronje	13
D.H. Brain	not out	12
E.A. Brandes	**c** Matthews, **b** Cronje	5
H.R. Olonga	**c** Symcox, **b** de Villiers	6
	lb **6**, w **1**, nb **1**	8
	42.5 overs	127

	O	M	R	W
de Villiers	8.5	2	30	1
Matthews	8	2	19	2
Cronje	10	–	33	4
Donald	8	–	21	1
Symcox	8	1	18	1

Fall of Wickets
1–**3**, 2–**35**, 3–**48**, 4–**53**, 5–**55**, 6–**82**, 7–**92**, 8–**113**, 9–**119**

Umpires: I.D. Robinson & R.B. Tiffin *Man of the Match:* H.H. Streak

South Africa won by 112 runs

Logan Cup

15, 16 and 17 September 1995
at Harare Sports Club
Matabeleland 305 (G.J. Whittall 99, M.D. Abrams 71, H.A. Price 53, S.A. Reid 4 for 52) and 300 for 7 dec. (W.R. James 66, G.J. Whittall 64)
Mashonaland 219 (S.G. Davies 71, G.C. Martin 50, H.R. Olonga 4 for 50) and 227 (S.G. Davies 63, J.A. Rennie 4 for 43)
Matabeleland won by 159 runs

at Alexandra Sports Club, Harare
Mashonaland Country Districts 309 (E.A. Brandes 65, P.A. Strang 63) and 264 for 2 dec. (A.D.R. Campbell 114 not out, C.N. Evans 66 not out, T.G. Bartlett 52)
Young Mashonaland 182 and 168 (A.C.I. Lock 4 for 23)
Mashonaland Country Districts won by 223 runs

Both Mashonaland sides were soundly beaten in the first round of matches in the Logan Cup, but both could claim that they were without their skippers, the Flower brothers, who were completing fine seasons in the Birmingham League. Outstanding for Matabeleland was Guy Whittall who scored 163 runs in the match, took five wickets and held three catches. There was also some fine bowling from the 19-year old Henry Olonga who has had his action remodelled by Dennis Lillee.

Young Mashonaland, formerly Mashonaland Under-24, were trounced by Mashonaland Country Districts for whom Alistair Campbell hit 114 not out from 124 balls. His innings included 17 fours and two sixes. Charlie Lock had match figures of 6 for 54.

3, 4 and 5 November 1995
at Bulawayo Athletic Club
Matabeleland 221 (H.H. Streak 70, M.H. Dekker 56, G.B. Brent 4 for 51) and 370 for 5 dec. (G.J. Whittall 139 not out, J.S. Laney 67, W.R. James 61, K. Newell 52)
Young Mashonaland 203 (G.J. Rennie 63, G.J. Whittall 4 for 63) and 202 for 2 (G.W. Flower 103 not out, C.B. Wishart 55 not out)
Match drawn.

Matabeleland had the better of a draw against Young Mashonaland for whom Grant Flower and Craig Wishart shared a match-saving unbroken stand of 128 after Streak had dismissed Rennie and Bennett. Guy Whittall enjoyed another magnificent all-round match.

17, 18 and 19 November 1995
at Harare Sports Club
Young Mashonaland 262 (G.W. Flower 66, D.H. Brain 6 for 61) and 250 (G.W. Flower 92)
Mashonaland 457 for 6 dec. (S.V. Carlisle 147, D.L. Houghton 127, S.G. Davies 117) and 59 for 0
Mashonaland won by 10 wickets

at Bulawayo Athletic Club
Matabeleland 152 (M.H. Dekker 50, B.C. Strang 5 for 41, E.A. Brandes 4 for 45) and 344 (H.H. Streak 131, M.H. Dekker 73, E.A. Brandes 6 for 98)
Mashonaland Country Districts 209 (H.R. Olonga 5 for 80, G.J. Whittall 4 for 39) and 283 (A.D.R. Campbell 78, C.N. Evans 73, H.H. Streak 7 for 69)
Matabeleland won by 4 runs

Stuart Carlisle hit a century for Mashonaland on his return from university in South Africa. There were also centuries from Sean Davies and David Houghton. Davies' maiden hundred came off 140 balls while Houghton lashed 127 off 116 balls in 123 minutes. His innings included 13 fours and six sixes. David Brain gave the selectors a reminder with match figures of 8 for 126.

In Bulawayo, Matabeleland won a thrilling and narrow victory in a match that was dominated by Heath Streak. In spite of some more good bowling from Olonga and Whittall, Matabeleland trailed by 57 on the first innings and lost three wickets in clearing the arrears. Streak then batted over four hours to hit the first century of his career, and he followed this with his career-best bowling performance which snatched victory for his side.

World record breaker Wayne James claimed 13 dismissals behind the stumps in the Logan Cup Final and scored 99 and 99 not out as he led his side to victory.
(Patrick Eagar)

8, 9 and 10 December 1995
at Harare South Country Club
Mashonaland 133 (D.L. Houghton 61) and 352 (D.L. Houghton 160, G.C. Martin 113, B.C. Strang 6 for 96)
Mashonaland Country Districts 279 (P.A. Strang 61, R.D. Brown 53) and 207 for 8 (P.A. Strang 56 not out, B.W.S. Pswarayi 5 for 72)
Mashonaland Country Districts won by 2 wickets

Country Districts took a firm grip on the game on the first day when Lock, Bryan Strang and Campbell bowled out Mashonaland for 133. Each of these bowlers took three wickets, and Campbell had 3 for 0 off 15 balls. Brisk scoring took Country Districts to 217 for 7 by the close, and a first innings lead of 146 seemed to have put them in an unassailable position. Mashonaland lost four wickets for 97 runs when they batted again, but Gary Martin then joined David Houghton in a stand worth 196. Houghton was again in masterly form with five sixes and 16 fours, but equal credit must go to Martin who hit the second century of his career, which included a six and 15 fours. Needing 207 to win, Country Districts were 151 for 8 before Paul Strang was joined by brother Bryan, who had already claimed 9 for 141 in the match. In 57 minutes, the brothers scored the 56 runs needed for victory. The win took Mashonaland Country Districts into the Logan Cup Final for the first time. There, they would meet Matabeleland, but it was decided that the final would be played after the World Cup in March.

Zimbabwe now set their eyes on New Zealand and the Indian sub-continent.

Logan Cup Final

19, 20 and 21 April 1996
at Bulawayo Athletic Club
Mashonaland Country Districts 265 (J. Oates 115, B.C. Strang 66, D. Vaghmaria 4 for 108) and 128 (J.A. Rennie 6 for 42)
Matabeleland 220 (W.R. James 99, B.C. Strang 4 for 69) and 176 for 4 (W.R. James 99 not out, M.H. Dekker 57 not out)
Matabeleland won by 6 wickets

There were disappointments for Zimbabwe in the World Cup. They had lost the services of their finest batsman, David Houghton, through injury in New Zealand, and they had not performed as well as expected, but they returned home to a Logan Cup Final that was to become part of cricket history. The hero of the match was 30-year-old wicket-keeper/batsman Wayne James, who did not take part in the World Cup although he had played in four Test matches for Zimbabwe.

Batting first, Mashonaland Country Districts owed much to a century by Oates and to a late flourish from Bryan Strang. The feature of the innings, however, was the performance of Wayne James who held seven catches and made two stumpings to equal Tahir Rasheed's world record.

James then came to the rescue of his side after their first three batsmen had scored just two between them. He hit 99 before falling to off-spinner Peall. Leading by 45 on the first innings, Mashonaland Country Districts were wrecked by medium-pacer John Rennie when they batted a second time. None of their first five batsmen reached double figures, and three fell to catches by James. When, later, the Matabeleland captain took his fourth catch of the innings to dispose of Bryan Strang, he established a new world record for a wicket-keeper of 13 dismissals in a match.

Yet another record awaited James. Needing 174 to win, Matabeleland began badly, with the first four batsmen falling in single figures. Wayne James joined Mark Dekker in a match-winning stand. He had reached his second 99 of the match when four byes gave Matabeleland victory. It is thought that James is only the second batsman to make two 99's in a first-class match.

Friendly Matches

1, 2 and 3 April 1996
at Harare Sports Club
Yorkshire 267 for 7 dec. (D. Byas 143 not out) and 215 for 7 dec.
Mashonaland 273 for 9 dec. (C.B. Wishart 75, A.D.R. Campbell 51) and 156 (I.D. Fisher 5 for 35, P.M. Hutchison 4 for 23)
Yorkshire won by 53 runs

11, 12 and 13 April 1996
at Bulawayo Athletic Club
Yorkshire 329 for 5 dec. (M.D. Moxon 134, M.P. Vaughan 106)
Matabeleland 84 and 234 (H.H. Streak 101, J.A. Rennie 52, P.J. Hartley 4 for 54)
Yorkshire won by an innings and 11 runs

14 April 1996
at Bulawayo Athletic Club
Matabeleland 196 for 9
Yorkshire 198 for 3 (A. McGrath 78, R.J. Blakey 53 not out)
Yorkshire won by 7 wickets

Yorkshire won all three matches on their short pre-England season tour of Zimbabwe. Left-arm pace bowler Paul Hutchison took six wickets on his first-class debut, against Mashonaland, and Moxon and Vaughan scored 203 for Yorkshire's first wicket in the second match.

First-Class Averages

Batting

	M	Inns	NO	Runs	HS	Av	100s	50s
D.L. Houghton	5	8	1	599	160	85.57	3	2
S.V. Carlisle	2	4	1	201	147	67.00	1	
J. Oates	1	2	–	115	115	57.50	1	
H.H. Streak	6	9	1	426	131	53.25	2	2
G.W. Flower	6	11	1	499	103*	49.90	1	3
S.G. Davies	5	9	1	362	117	45.25	1	2
W.R. James	5	10	1	391	99*	43.44		4
G.J. Whittall	5	10	1	381	139*	42.33	1	2
P.A. Strang	4	7	1	244	63	40.66		3
G.C. Martin	4	7	–	273	113	39.00	1	1
A.D.R. Campbell	8	15	1	514	114*	36.71	1	3
A. Flower	5	9	1	284	82	35.50		3
M.H. Dekker	6	12	1	344	73	31.27		4
C.B. Wishart	7	13	1	366	75	30.50		3
C.N. Evans	5	10	1	265	73	29.44		2
R.D. Brown	2	4	–	108	53	27.00		1
J.S. Laney	2	4	–	103	67	25.75		1
G.J. Rennie	4	8	–	201	63	25.12		1
M.D. Abrams	5	9	1	175	71	21.87		1
B.C. Strang	6	11	3	169	66	21.12		1
J.A. Rennie	4	7	1	114	52	19.00		1
G. Peck	6	10	3	124	41*	17.71		
S.G. Peall	5	9	1	131	38	16.37		
G.K. Bruk-Jackson	4	7	–	111	45	15.85		

(Qualification: 100 runs, average 10.00)

Bowling

	Overs	Mds	Runs	Wks	Av	Best	10/m	5/inn
E.A. Brandes	54.2	15	159	11	14.45	6/98	1	1
A.C.I. Lock	121.3	31	360	22	16.36	6/59		1
J.A. Rennie	81.4	22	238	14	17.00	6/42		1
H.R. Olonga	77	16	245	13	18.84	5/80		1
D.H. Brain	81.2	20	202	10	20.20	6/61		1
B.C. Strang	216.4	49	643	30	21.43	6/96		3
H.H. Streak	190	46	511	20	25.55	7/69		1
G.J. Whittall	98.5	11	387	13	29.76	4/39		
C.B. Wishart	92.4	19	376	10	37.60	3/86		
G.C. Martin	159.2	44	439	11	39.90	3/65		
M. Mbangwa	154	37	480	12	40.00	2/42		

(Qualification: 10 wickets)

Leading Fielders

27 – W.R. James (ct 25 / st 2); 21 – D.J.R. Campbell; 13 – A.R.G. Gilmour (ct 12 / st 1); 9 – C.B. Wishart; 8 – A. Flower (ct 7 / st 1) and G.J. Whittall; 7 – A.D.R. Campbell

Harare Sports Club, Harare. (David Munden)

New Zealand

For New Zealand, the centenary season of 1994–95 had been an utter disaster, ruined by a series of dreadful results both home and away. The authorities reacted boldly: Ken Rutherford was dismissed as captain, and went to play in South Africa, and Lee Germon was appointed in his stead. Germon would take the team to India, captain them in a home series against Zimbabwe, lead them into the World Cup and then be in charge on a short tour of West Indies.

The man entrusted with the post of reviving New Zealand's cricketing fortunes – Lee Germon, the Canterbury captain and wicket-keeper.
(Mike Hewitt/Allsport)

The selection of Lee Germon, whose international career was limited to one abandoned one-day international, surprised some. Germon was generally regarded as the best captain in New Zealand and had led Canterbury since 1990, being appointed when he was 20 years old. He had the reputation of being a strong disciplinarian, but his open criticism of administrators had, it was believed, cost him any chance of playing for New Zealand, let alone captaining the country. That he was appointed along with new coach and selector Glenn Turner showed that New Zealand were determined to establish their cricket on a more professional and positive basis. Undoubtedly, Lee Germon is committed to success.

Germon's side were badly hit by the weather in India where Roger Twose, formerly of Warwickshire and nephew of Roger Tolchard, the England and Leicestershire wicket-keeper of the 1970s, made his Test debut.

Sadly, the India tour saw the end of the international career of Martin Crowe, the greatest of New Zealand Test batsmen. Crowe had struggled against a knee injury for several years, and it became apparent that his brave fight to continue playing had at last met with defeat. He was given an opportunity to prove his fitness before the one-off Test match with Pakistan, but he was unable to satisfy either himself or the selectors.

As ever, the New Zealand season was neatly arranged, with the Shell Cup, the domestic one-day competition, occupying the last week in November and going through to 10 January, after which the Shell Trophy took place, and there were brief tours by Pakistan and Zimbabwe prior to the World Cup.

Lee Germon's determination to succeed was certainly reflected in the Shell Cup, in which each association played the other on a home and away basis. Led by Germon, Canterbury won every one of their ten fixtures in the qualifying league. In the semi-final, they crushed Northern Districts by 131 runs as Nathan Astle hit 96 off 101 balls. In the other semi-final, Wellington overcame Auckland, but were no match for Northern Districts whom they had to meet for the right to play Canterbury in the final.

A record Shell Cup crowd of 18,249 were at Lancaster Park for the final. Germon won the toss and decided to bat. Hartland and Astle hit 45 off the first 58 balls of the match, but this was nothing compared to what was to come. Astle went on to hit 129 off 126 balls with three sixes and 13 fours. It was his second hundred of the competition, and he was the first man ever to score a century in a Shell Cup final. Fleming became the second with his 102 off 96 balls. He and Astle shared a third wicket stand of 150 off 151 balls, and with Germon hitting the three balls he received for one, six and four, Canterbury finished their 50 overs with 329 for 5, a Shell Cup record to which Northern Districts had no answer.

By winning 12 matches in succession, Canterbury established another record while Astle's 687 runs (average 62.45) surpassed Bruce Edgar's previous record. Astle also captured ten wickets, but the leading wicket-taker in the competition was Justin Vaughan of Auckland with 25 wickets at 13.76 runs apiece.

Pakistan Tour

Pakistan arrived from Australia, where they had just recovered some pride by winning the third Test, in order to play one Test match and four one-day internationals before going into their final phase of training for the World Cup.

Test Match

New Zealand v. Pakistan

New Zealand gave a first Test cap to Craig Spearman, the Auckland opener, and Lee Germon created something of a surprise when he asked Pakistan to bat when he won the toss. The Pakistan openers appeared to relish the chance to bat first and scored 135 in 106 minutes, but a collapse followed. Four wickets fell for 14 runs as Pakistan's middle order again suggested a dreadful inadequacy. Aamir Sohail had hit 88 off 94 balls before becoming the second of Cairns' pre-lunch victims. Cairns took 3 for 3 in 21 balls in the morning session.

Martin Crowe – arguably the greatest of New Zealand Test batsmen was forced to retire through injury. (David Munden/Sportsline)

Basit Ali stood firm for more than half an hour while 28 were added, but four wickets then went down for seven runs, and when Pakistan were finally bowled out for 208 Germon was vindicated. All ten Pakistan wickets had fallen for 73 runs, and Germon had handled his bowling admirably.

Spearman impressed on his Test debut, hitting a six and five fours as he made 40 off 69 balls. Unfortunately, he and Parore, who was played exclusively as a batsman, were out in quick succession, and New Zealand closed on 98 for 3.

Fleming added only nine to his overnight score before being stumped by Rashid Latif off the bowling of Mushtaq Ahmed. Rashid was again in outstanding form behind the stumps, and Mushtaq was destined to be Man of the Match. For the moment, however, the advantage was with New Zealand as Twose and Cairns put on 102 for the fifth wicket and took their side into the lead. They both became victims of the Pakistan captain Wasim Akram, who produced a spell that brought him five wickets for 12 runs. Germon batted aggressively, but New Zealand's lead of 78 was not as great as they might have expected. By the end of the second day, it had been obliterated. Rameez Raja was hit on the forearm by a ball from Morrison and retired hurt with the score on two, and Aamir Sohail was bowled by Patel at 55, but Ijaz Ahmed and Inzamam-ul-Haq were in commanding form and by the end of the day Pakistan were 138 for 1 and very much in charge.

They batted steadily on the third day, content to build a substantial lead and with time on their side. Ijaz Ahmed completed his second Test century in 11 days. His arrival in Australia had done much to improve Pakistan's fortunes, and in New Zealand his 103 off 213 balls with two sixes and 13 fours did much to help win the Test. Inzamam-ul-Haq also batted well, his 80 coming off 141 balls with 13 fours. At the fall of the third wicket, Rameez Raja returned to play another innings that was stubborn and effective, and took Pakistan closer to a commanding lead in the match. They ended the day on 369 for 7, and New Zealand faced a daunting target.

The loss of Wasim Akram early on the fourth morning brought little relief to the hosts. Waqar Younis clouted seven fours in an innings that brought 34 runs off 55 balls. He was finally leg before to Larsen who bowled with admirable economy, but by then New Zealand had been left to score 357 to win. They began confidently enough with 50 in 59 minutes, and Spearman again justified his selection, but the advent of Mushtaq Ahmed with his leg-spin brought a dramatic change as New Zealand slipped to 75 for 5 within the next hour. Twose and Germon offered momentary respite, but the New Zealand captain was run out by Ijaz Ahmed, and Patel was bowled round his legs by a huge Mushtaq leg-break as he tried to sweep. The close came with the home side on 158 for 7 and with no hope of escape.

Only five runs were added on the last morning before Larsen became Mushtaq's sixth victim, and, after Nash had thrashed for 40 minutes, Morrison became his seventh – so improving his Test best bowling figures for the third Test in succession. Twose remained undefeated for his second fifty of the match, but the honours were firmly with Pakistan.

Test Match – New Zealand v. Pakistan

8, 9, 10, 11 and 12 December 1995 at Lancaster Park, Christchurch

Pakistan

	First Innings		Second Innings	
Aamir Sohail	hit wkt, **b** Cairns	**88**	**b** Patel	**30**
Rameez Raja	lbw, **b** Cairns	**54**	lbw, **b** Morrison	**62**
Ijaz Ahmed	**c** Morrison, **b** Larsen	**30**	**c** Germon, **b** Nash	**103**
Inzamam-ul-Haq	lbw, **b** Cairns	**0**	**c** Fleming, **b** Nash	**82**
Salim Malik	**c** Germon, **b** Nash	**0**	**c** Germon, **b** Morrison	**21**
Basit Ali	**c** Germon, **b** Larsen	**5**	lbw, **b** Cairns	**0**
*Rashid Latif	**c** Spearman, **b** Morrison	**2**	**c** Germon, **b** Cairns	**39**
Wasim Akram (Capt)	**c** Young, **b** Morrison	**2**	**c** Fleming, **b** Cairns	**19**
Mushtaq Ahmed	lbw, **b** Nash	**5**	**c** Germon, **b** Larsen	**24**
Waqar Younis	not out	**12**	lbw, **b** Larsen	**34**
Ata-ur-Rehman	**c** and **b** Cairns	**5**	not out	**0**
	lb **1**, w **1**, nb **3**	**5**	b **5**, lb **6**, w **4**, nb **5**	**20**
		208		**434**

	O	M	R	W	O	M	R	W
Morrison	14	–	57	**2**	27	5	99	**2**
Cairns	11.1	2	51	**4**	35	6	114	**3**
Larsen	15	2	44	**2**	29	10	58	**2**
Nash	11	3	43	**2**	30	6	91	**2**
Patel	3	1	12	**–**	24	8	61	**1**

Fall of Wickets

1–**135**, 2–**146**, 3–**148**, 4–**149**, 5–**177**, 6–**184**, 7–**184**, 8–**197**, 9–**203**
1–**55**, 2–**195**, 3–**224**, 4–**260**, 5–**265**, 6–**339**, 7–**363**, 8–**384**, 9–**425**

New Zealand

	First Innings		Second Innings	
B.A. Young	**c** Rashid, **b** Ata	**16**	**c** Rashid, **b** Mushtaq	**18**
C.M. Spearman	**b** Mushtaq Ahmed	**40**	**c** Aamir, **b** Mushtaq	**33**
A.C. Parore	**c** Rashid, **b** Ata	**9**	lbw, **b** Mushtaq Ahmed	**5**
S.P. Fleming	**st** Rashid, **b** Mushtaq	**25**	lbw, **b** Ata-ur-Rehman	**0**
R.G. Twose	lbw, **b** Wasim Akram	**59**	not out	**51**
C.L. Cairns	**b** Wasim Akram	**76**	**c** Salim, **b** Mushtaq	**8**
*L.K. Germon (Capt)	**c** Rashid, **b** Wasim	**21**	run out	**12**
D.N. Patel	**c** Aamir, **b** Wasim	**3**	**b** Mushtaq Ahmed	**15**
G.R. Larsen	not out	**5**	**c** Aamir, **b** Mushtaq	**13**
D.J. Nash	**c** Rashid, **b** Wasim	**11**	**b** Waqar Younis	**22**
D.K. Morrison	**b** Mushtaq Ahmed	**0**	**c** Salim, **b** Mushtaq	**1**
	lb **4**, nb **17**	**21**	b **3**, lb **9**, w **1**, nb **4**	**17**
		286		**195**

	O	M	R	W	O	M	R	W
Wasim Akram	24.5	4	53	**5**	11	3	31	**–**
Waqar Younis	16	2	60	**–**	26	6	73	**1**
Ata-ur-Rehman	17.1	4	47	**2**	9	1	23	**1**
Mushtaq Ahmed	30.4	4	115	**3**	34.4	13	56	**7**
Aamir Sohail	3	–	7	**–**				

Fall of Wickets

1–**48**, 2–**65**, 3–**73**, 4–**119**, 5–**221**, 6–**262**, 7–**265**, 8–**269**, 9–**283**
1–**50**, 2–**57**, 3–**60**, 4–**60**, 5–**75**, 6–**101**, 7–**131**, 8–**163**, 9–**192**

Umpires: B.C. Cooray & R.S. Dunne

Pakistan won by 161 runs

One-day Series

New Zealand v. Pakistan

There was some comfort for both sides as New Zealand displayed their power of recovery and resilience under Germon's leadership.

Confident from their recent successes in Sydney and Christchurch, Pakistan won the first of the four limited-over matches by 20 runs. Runs were not easy to come by, but Pakistan applied themselves consistently after Aamir Sohail had begun in his usual spectacular manner by hitting a six and two fours in his 20-ball innings. Perhaps the crucial contribution came from Rashid Latif, who came in with six wickets down for 138 and hit 26 off 33 balls without the help of a boundary.

New Zealand quickly lost Spearman, the only player to make his limited-over international debut during the series, and, at 94 for 7, they looked well beaten. That they avoided indignity was due to another fifty from Twose, his third in succession, and a brave rearguard action from Larsen, who is a very useful one-day cricketer. Waqar Younis turned the game in favour of Pakistan with a suggestion of past glories and former speed when he tore the middle out of the New Zealand innings.

Waqar might well have won the second match for Pakistan, but fate decreed otherwise. Choosing to bat once more when they won the toss, Pakistan scored 232 for nine, thanks mainly to a fourth wicket stand of 114 between Inzamam-ul-Haq and Salim Malik. Inzamam, in particular, was in brilliant form, hitting a six and six fours in his 80 off 95 balls. Basit Ali and Rashid Latif also made useful late contributions, and when Aqib Javed dismissed both New Zealand openers with just 21 scored Pakistan seemed to have taken a grip on the match. Young and Fleming steadied matters with a partnership of 77, and Parore and Cairns, who hit 54 off 63 balls, brought impetus before they were both removed by Wasim. Waqar Younis then brought Pakistan to the brink of victory with three wickets in one over. He dismissed Germon and Patel with successive deliveries and should have had Morrison caught by Mushtaq to give him the hat-trick, but the chance was dropped. This proved to be the only ball that Morrison faced, for Larsen took over and won the match in brave fashion.

Inzamam took the Man of the Match award, but credit should go to Morrison whose five wickets for 46 runs in ten overs represented his best performance in a one-day international and were outstanding figures in the conditions.

Asked to bat when Germon won the toss, Pakistan batted with consistent aggression in the third match to reach 261, and they went on to win with considerable ease. Having hit two sixes and three fours as he hit 36 off 15 balls, Wasim Akram then dismissed Spearman and Young with successive deliveries. In spite of Germon's late rally, New Zealand were never in sight of their target.

The final encounter saw Wasim win the toss and ask New Zealand to bat first in a game reduced to 45 overs. Spearman and Fleming established a brisk scoring rate in a second wicket stand worth 60, and Twose and Astle, in particular, made certain that Pakistan would face a big target at a challenging rate. They were especially severe on Waqar Younis whose nine overs cost 70 runs.

Aamir Sohail, 37 off 43 balls, and Rameez Raja, 46 off 54, gave Pakistan a bright start, but thereafter only Salim Malik kept hopes alive. He hit three sixes and four fours in his 58 off 52 balls, but Pakistan were well short of their target.

New Zealand showed great character to level the series, and it was apparent that a side was shaping that would do well in the World Cup. Pakistan, too, were comforted by the generally improved form of Waqar Younis and by the greater amount of substance being shown by the middle-order that, in the World Cup, would be boosted by the veteran Javed Miandad.

Mushtaq Ahmed, the Pakistan leg-spinner, enjoyed an outstanding run of success in two Tests in Australia and against New Zealand. He bettered his previous best Test bowling performance on each occasion, and his 7 for 56 in the Test at Christchurch won the game for his side. (Paul Sturgess/Sportsline)

First One-day International – New Zealand v. Pakistan

15 December 1995 at Carisbrook, Dunedin

Pakistan

Rameez Raja	**b** Cairns	**35**
Aamir Sohail	**c** Spearman, **b** Patel	**17**
Ijaz Ahmed	lbw, **b** Larsen	**9**
Inzamam-ul-Haq	**c** Patel, **b** Astle	**32**
Salim Malik	**c** Twose, **b** Astle	**13**
Basit Ali	run out	**19**
Wasim Akram (Capt)	run out	**16**
*Rashid Latif	not out	**26**
Mushtaq Ahmed	**c** Twose, **b** Cairns	**5**
Waqar Younis	**b** Morrison	**0**
Aqib Javed	not out	**8**
	lb **6**, w **3**	**9**
	50 overs (for 9 wickets)	**189**

	O	M	R	W
Patel	7	–	21	**1**
Morrison	9	–	39	**1**
Larsen	10	–	29	**1**
Cairns	9	1	42	**2**
Astle	10	–	34	**2**
Twose	5	–	18	**–**

Fall of Wickets
1–**31**, 2–**52**, 3–**82**, 4–**101**, 5–**123**, 6–**138**, 7–**158**, 8–**173**, 9–**175**

New Zealand

C.M. Spearman	**c** Ijaz Ahmed, **b** Aqib Javed	**5**
N.J. Astle	**c** and **b** Wasim Akram	**5**
B.A. Young	**b** Waqar Younis	**17**
S.P. Fleming	lbw, **b** Waqar Younis	**15**
A.C. Parore	**b** Waqar Younis	**2**
R.G. Twose	**b** Wasim Akram	**59**
C.L. Cairns	**c** Rashid, **b** Mushtaq Ahmed	**18**
*L.K. Germon (Capt)	**c** Wasim, **b** Mushtaq Ahmed	**1**
D.N. Patel	**c** Basit Ali, **b** Salim Malik	**9**
G.R. Larsen	**c** Ijaz Ahmed, **b** Wasim Akram	**23**
D.K. Morrison	not out	**0**
	lb **9**, w **5**, nb **1**	**15**
	47.4 overs	**169**

	O	M	R	W
Wasim Akram	9.4	1	18	**3**
Aqib Javed	9	–	38	**1**
Waqar Younis	9	–	38	**3**
Mushtaq Ahmed	10	1	31	**2**
Aamir Sohail	9	–	30	**–**
Salim Malik	1	–	5	**1**

Fall of Wickets
1–**5**, 2–**16**, 3–**43**, 4–**46**, 5–**50**, 6–**92**, 7–**94**, 8–**114**, 9–**164**

Umpires: R.S. Dunne & C.E. King *Man of the Match:* Waqar Younis

Pakistan won by 20 runs

Second One-day International – New Zealand v. Pakistan

17 December 1995 at Lancaster Park, Christchurch

Pakistan

Rameez Raja	**b** Morrison	**14**
Aamir Sohail	**c** Spearman, **b** Patel	**10**
Ijaz Ahmed	lbw, **b** Cairns	**14**
Inzamam-ul-Haq	**b** Larsen	**80**
Salim Malik	**c** sub (Loveridge), **b** Twose	**58**
Wasim Akram (Capt)	**b** Morrison	**10**
Basit Ali	**b** Morrison	**23**
*Rashid Latif	**c** Astle, **b** Morrison	**11**
Waqar Younis	**b** Morrison	**0**
Mushtaq Ahmed	not out	**0**
Aqib Javed		
	b **5**, lb **5**, w **2**	**12**
	(50 overs) for 9 wickets	**232**

	O	M	R	W
Patel	10	–	41	**1**
Morrison	10	–	46	**5**
Cairns	10	1	42	**1**
Larsen	10	–	49	**1**
Astle	8	–	32	**–**
Twose	2	–	12	**1**

Fall of Wickets
1–**25**, 2–**27**, 3–**61**, 4–**175**, 5–**185**, 6–**202**, 7–**230**, 8–**231**, 9–**232**

New Zealand

C.M. Spearman	**c** Rashid Latif, **b** Aqib Javed	**8**
N.J. Astle	**c** Rashid Latif, **b** Aqib Javed	**5**
B.A. Young	**c** Wasim, **b** Aamir Sohail	**34**
S.P. Fleming	**b** Aamir Sohail	**48**
A.C. Parore	**c** Basit Ali, **b** Wasim Akram	**45**
C.L. Cairns	**c** Rameez Raja, **b** Wasim	**54**
R.G. Twose	**c** Mushtaq Ahmed, **b** Waqar	**10**
*L.K. Germon (Capt)	**c** Basit Ali, **b** Waqar Younis	**5**
D.N. Patel	**c** Ijaz Ahmed, **b** Waqar Younis	**0**
G.R. Larsen	not out	**14**
D.K. Morrison	not out	**0**
	lb **5**, w **5**, nb **3**	**13**
	49.5 overs (for 9 wickets)	**236**

	O	M	R	W
Aqib Javed	10	–	53	**2**
Wasim Akram	9.5	–	41	**2**
Waqar Younis	10	–	55	**3**
Mushtaq Ahmed	6	–	30	**–**
Aamir Sohail	10	–	39	**2**
Salim Malik	4	–	13	**–**

Fall of Wickets
1–**13**, 2–**21**, 3–**98**, 4–**107**, 5–**204**, 6–**214**, 7–**220**, 8–**221**, 9–**221**

Umpires: C.E. King & D.M. Quested *Man of the Match:* Inzamam-ul-Haq

New Zealand won by 1 wicket

Third One-day International – New Zealand v. Pakistan

20 December 1995 at Basin Reserve, Wellington

Pakistan

Aamir Sohail	b Larsen	58
Rameez Raja	run out	21
Ijaz Ahmed	c Cairns, b Twose	42
Inzamam-ul-Haq	b Twose	54
Salim Malik	not out	42
Wasim Akram (Capt)	not out	36
Basit Ali		
*Rashid Latif		
Waqar Younis		
Mushtaq Ahmed		
Aqib Javed		
	b 2, lb 5, w 1	8
	50 overs (for 4 wickets)	261

	O	M	R	W
Morrison	10	–	59	–
Patel	10	2	43	–
Cairns	10	1	62	–
Larsen	10	–	37	1
Twose	7	–	31	2
Astle	3	–	22	–

Fall of Wickets
1–51, 2–107, 3–138, 4–217

New Zealand

C.M. Spearman	c Aamir Sohail, b Wasim	33
N.J. Astle	c Rameez Raja, b Aqib Javed	9
B.A. Young	lbw, b Wasim Akram	0
S.P. Fleming	c Basit Ali, b Mushtaq Ahmed	35
A.C. Parore	lbw, b Aqib Javed	4
R.G. Twose	b Aamir Sohail	37
C.L. Cairns	run out	7
*L.K. Germon (Capt)	b Wasim Akram	40
D.N. Patel	run out	13
G.R. Larsen	c sub (Moin Khan), b Aqib	2
D.K. Morrison	not out	11
	lb 13, w 3	16
	44.5 overs	207

	O	M	R	W
Aqib Javed	10	1	51	3
Wasim Akram	7.5	–	31	3
Waqar Younis	4	–	22	–
Mushtaq Ahmed	10	2	26	1
Salim Malik	3	–	17	–
Aamir Sohail	10	–	47	1

Fall of Wickets
1–48, 2–48, 3–48, 4–60, 5–107, 6–119, 7–143, 8–166, 9–174

Umpires: R.S. Dunne & E.A. Watkin *Man of the Match:* Wasim Akram

Pakistan won by 54 runs

Fourth One-day International – New Zealand v. Pakistan

23 December 1995 at Eden Park, Auckland

New Zealand

C.M. Spearman	c Basit Ali, b Mushtaq Ahmed	48
B.A. Young	c Rashid Latif, b Aqib Javed	15
S.P. Fleming	c Wasim, b Aamir Sohail	38
A.C. Parore	b Waqar Younis	42
C.L. Cairns	c Wasim, b Aamir Sohail	11
R.G. Twose	b Waqar Younis	41
N.J. Astle	not out	20
*L.K. Germon (Capt)	b Wasim Akram	5
D.N. Patel	lbw, b Waqar Younis	1
G.R. Larsen	not out	3
D.K. Morrison		
	lb 11, w 6, nb 3	20
	45 overs (for 8 wickets)	244

	O	M	R	W
Wasim Akram	9	–	27	1
Aqib Javed	6	–	28	1
Waqar Younis	9	–	70	3
Mushtaq Ahmed	7	–	39	1
Aamir Sohail	9	–	42	2
Salim Malik	5	–	27	–

Fall of Wickets
1–28, 2–88, 3–132, 4–148, 5–207, 6–214, 7–222, 8–223

Pakistan

Aamir Sohail	c Patel, b Cairns	37
Rameez Raja	c Cairns, b Astle	46
Salim Elahi	run out	7
Inzamam-ul-Haq	c sub (Loveridge), b Astle	17
Salim Malik	lbw, b Astle	58
Basit Ali	run out	0
Wasim Akram (Capt)	c Astle, b Morrison	4
*Rashid Latif	b Larsen	3
Mushtaq Ahmed	b Larsen	16
Waqar Younis	c Young, b Twose	5
Aqib Javed	not out	12
	lb 5, w 2	7
	41.4 overs	212

	O	M	R	W
Morrison	6	–	22	1
Patel	4	–	26	–
Cairns	7	–	38	1
Larsen	9	–	42	2
Twose	7.4	–	37	1
Astle	8	–	42	3

Fall of Wickets
1–56, 2–89, 3–109, 4–117, 5–118, 6–125, 7–146, 8–188, 9–196

Umpires: B.F. Bowden & D.B. Cowie *Man of the Match:* N.J. Astle

New Zealand won by 32 runs

First Test Match – New Zealand v. Zimbabwe

13, 14, 15, 16 and 17 January 1996 at Trust Bank Park, Hamilton

New Zealand

	First Innings		Second Innings	
C.M. Spearman	c A. Flower, b Streak	0	lbw, b Streak	27
R.G. Twose	b Brandes	42	run out	8
S.P. Fleming	run out	49	c A. Flower, b P.A. Strang	21
A.C. Parore	c A. Flower, b Streak	16	not out	84
N.J. Astle	lbw, b Streak	18	c Olonga, b B.C. Strang	32
C.L. Cairns	c A. Flower, b Streak	7	c Olonga, b Brandes	7
*L.K. Germon (Capt)	c Carlisle, b Olonga	24	not out	22
D.N. Patel	c Olonga, b P.A. Strang	31		
G.R. Loveridge	retired hurt	4		
R.J. Kennedy	not out	2		
G.I. Allott	not out	0		
	b 4, lb 11, w 1, nb 21	37	b 4, lb 7, w 4, nb 6	21
	(for 8 wickets, dec.)	230	(for 5 wickets, dec.)	222

	O	M	R	W	O	M	R	W
Streak	25	7	52	4	22	4	56	1
B.C. Strang	24	11	51	–	5	1	19	1
Olonga	14	2	65	1	3	1	20	–
Brandes	15	3	46	1	18	4	52	1
P.A. Strang	2	1	1	1	24	7	57	1
G.W. Flower					3	1	7	–

Fall of Wickets
1–**0**, 2–**67**, 3–**115**, 4–**143**, 5–**160**, 6–**164**, 7–**216**, 8–**226**
1–**36**, 2–**63**, 3–**64**, 4–**121**, 5–**140**

Zimbabwe

	First Innings		Second Innings	
G.W. Flower	b Cairns	5	c Germon, b Cairns	59
S.V. Carlisle	c Germon, b Cairns	4	c Fleming, b Patel	19
A.D.R. Campbell	c Astle, b Allott	5	(6) c Germon, b Patel	3
D.L. Houghton	lbw, b Cairns	31	lbw, b Twose	31
*A. Flower (Capt)	c Spearman, b Kennedy	6	not out	58
G.J. Whittall	c Germon, b Kennedy	54	(3) c Kennedy, b Twose	20
H.H. Streak	c Spearman, b Cairns	24	lbw, b Cairns	6
P.A. Strang	b Patel	49	not out	0
H.R. Olonga	c Germon, b Kennedy	0		
E.A. Brandes	not out	3		
B.C. Strang	c Astle, b Patel	4		
	lb 3, w 2, nb 6	11	lb 4, w 1, nb 7	12
		196	(for 6 wickets)	208

	O	M	R	W	O	M	R	W
Cairns	24	7	56	4	15	4	43	2
Allott	17	5	51	1	7	–	49	–
Kennedy	12	4	28	3	5	–	19	–
Twose	5	1	14	–	13	–	36	2
Patel	16.5	4	44	2	21	6	57	2

Fall of Wickets
1–**8**, 2–**13**, 3–**21**, 4–**41**, 5–**56**, 6–**98**, 7–**189**, 8–**189**, 9–**191**
1–**56**, 2–**99**, 3–**125**, 4–**143**, 5–**151**, 6–**177**

Umpires: L.H. Barker & D.M. Quested

Match drawn

Second Test Match – New Zealand v. Zimbabwe

20, 21, 22, 23 and 24 January 1996 at Eden Park, Auckland

New Zealand

	First Innings		Second Innings	
C.M. Spearman	c G.W. Flower, b B.C. Strang	42	c Carlisle, b Streak	112
R.G. Twose	c A. Flower, b Brandes	18	c and b Streak	94
S.P. Fleming	c Carlisle, b Whittall	84	c Wishart, b Streak	3
A.C. Parore	c A. Flower, b B.C. Strang	0	not out	76
N.J. Astle	c and b Brandes	14	c A. Flower, b Brandes	13
C.L. Cairns	c and b P.A. Strang	57	b Streak	120
*L.K. Germon (Capt)	c A. Flower, b Streak	25	not out	1
D.N. Patel	not out	7		
G.R. Larsen	lbw, b Streak	0		
R.J. Kennedy	c Campbell, b Streak	0		
G.I. Allott	c and b B.C. Strang	0		
	lb 3, nb 1	4	b 6, lb 15, nb 1	22
		251	(for 5 wickets, dec.)	441

	O	M	R	W	O	M	R	W
Streak	22	9	50	3	30	7	110	4
Brandes	18	3	69	2	13	3	41	1
B.C. Strang	31.3	8	64	3	27	8	64	–
P.A. Strang	12	2	29	1	43	7	142	–
Whittall	12	4	36	1	13	4	40	–
Campbell					2	–	3	–
G.W. Flower					5	–	20	–

Fall of Wickets
1–**50**, 2–**78**, 3–**86**, 4–**117**, 5–**216**, 6–**232**, 7–**244**, 8–**246**, 9–**246**
1–**214**, 2–**217**, 3–**221**, 4–**261**, 5–**427**

Zimbabwe

	First Innings		Second Innings	
G.W. Flower	lbw, b Allott	5	c Kennedy, b Patel	71
S.V. Carlisle	c Astle, b Kennedy	12	c Fleming, b Kennedy	58
G.J. Whittall	c Germon, b Cairns	27	c Germon, b Patel	10
D.L. Houghton	retired hurt	104		
A. Flower (Capt)	lbw, b Allott	35	(4) not out	45
A.D.R. Campbell	lbw, b Allott	17	(5) c Germon, b Twose	34
C.B. Wishart	b Larsen	7	(6) not out	12
H.H. Streak	b Cairns	2		
P.A. Strang	c Parore, b Patel	44		
E.A. Brandes	c Astle, b Patel	39		
B.C. Strang	not out	14		
	b 1, lb 11, w 2, nb 6	20	lb 6, w 2, nb 8	16
		326	(for 4 wickets)	246

	O	M	R	W	O	M	R	W
Cairns	31	12	92	2	23	6	49	–
Allott	23	7	56	3	19	3	53	–
Kennedy	20	3	73	1	22	3	61	1
Larsen	21	8	30	1	5	3	8	–
Patel	12	–	60	2	27	6	60	2
Astle	3	1	3	–	1	–	4	–
Twose					3	1	5	1

Fall of Wickets
1–**5**, 2–**38**, 3–**50**, 4–**138**, 5–**196**, 6–**217**, 7–**222**, 8–**310**, 9–**326**
1–**120**, 2–**144**, 3–**145**, 4–**225**

Umpires: D.B. Cowie & Mahboob Shah

Match drawn

Zimbabwe Tour

2,3 and 4 January 1996
at Victoria Park, Wanganui
New Zealand XI 111 (B.C. Strang 6 for 20) and 212 (L.G. Howell 51, B.C. Strang 6 for 39)
Zimbabwe XI 172 (R.J. Kennedy 4 for 22) and 154 for 3 (G.W. Flower 89)
Zimbabwe XI won by 7 wickets

6, 7 and 8 January 1996
at Cobham Oval, Whangarei
Zimbabwe XI 274 for 7 dec. (D.L. Houghton 86, A. Flower 73, G.I. Allott 4 for 32) and 207 for 4 dec. (A.D.R. Campbell 59 not out, G.W. Flower 53)
New Zealand Academy XI 213 for 1 dec. (R.A. Lawson 113 not out, M.D. Bell 83) and 109 for 1 (J.M. Aiken 51 not out)
Match drawn

Zimbabwe arrived in New Zealand in a mood of confidence that was close to arrogance. They firmly believed that they would beat New Zealand in the two-Test series and that they would have the better of the three-match limited-over series. They were a happy and united side and were convinced that they were close to achieving both substance and balance. The opening overs of their first match against a New Zealand XI consisting of players on the verge of international recognition gave every indication that their confidence was not misplaced. With left-arm pace bowler Bryan Strang producing the best performance of his career, the Test aspirants were shot out for 111. The tourists slipped to 91 for 6 by the end of the day, but Strang, Olonga and Brandes gave them a first innings lead of 61 with some hard hitting. The New Zealand XI fared better in their second innings, but Bryan Strang was again in fine form, and Zimbabwe found a target of 152 well within their reach.

Zimbabwe were less happy in their second encounter. Put in to bat, they were 12 for 3 before Andy Flower joined Dave Houghton in a stand of 155. Robert Lawson, with a maiden first-class century, and Matthew Bell, with the highest score of his career, scored 213 in 285 minutes for the young New Zealanders, and when they were separated Howell declared. The game petered out to a draw, but, on the eve of the first Test, Zimbabwe could take no comfort from the fact that they had captured only two wickets in 438 minutes of bowling.

Zimbabwe's David Houghton hit a brave century in the second Test match, but a broken foot cost him his place in the World Cup squad, and there was conjecture that Houghton's century was his last Test innings.
(David Munden/Sportsline)

Test Series

New Zealand *v.* Zimbabwe

New Zealand unearthed fresh talent in an even series in which both sides suffered serious losses through injury.

New Zealand bravely plunged four newcomers into the first Test: Geoff Allott, left-arm fast medium-pace bowler from Canterbury; Greg Loveridge, a leg-spinner from Central Districts; Nathan Astle, the Canterbury all-rounder who had made his mark in one-day internationals; and Robert Kennedy, a medium-pace bowler from Otago. Allott and Astle were 24 years old, Kennedy 23, and Loveridge celebrated his 21st birthday on the third day of a most unlucky first Test. Zimbabwe won the toss and Andy Flower asked New Zealand to bat.

The rain clouds had already delayed the start, and only 21 overs were possible on the opening day. New Zealand lost Spearman caught behind to the third ball of the match, and Fleming, having hit an exciting 49, ran himself out when he attempted a ridiculous run to the athletic Henry Olonga. At the close, the home side were 68 for 2, and they lost two more wickets on the second day when rain was again the only winner. Twose had looked particularly comfortable in an innings that lasted 227 minutes, which ended when he was bowled by Brandes. Parore became the second victim of the Andy Flower/Streak combination.

New Zealand began the third day on 154 for 4, and Germon made a bold declaration at 230 for 8, but only a few minutes before the declaration he had lost the services of his leg-spinner Loveridge. The young man from Central Districts had just scored his first Test runs when he suffered a dislocated fracture of a knuckle joint. It was his third break of the year and, with a pin in the joint, he postponed all cricket until 1996–97.

Chris Cairns, one of the great enigmas of international cricket, compensated for the loss of Loveridge with a dynamic spell that was well supported by debutants Allott and Kennedy. When thunder and lightning brought a dramatic end to play in mid-afternoon Zimbabwe were 82 for 5. They fought back strongly on the fourth morning and reduced New Zealand's lead to a mere 34.

Germon sought quick runs. Spearman hit 27 off 42 balls, Fleming 21 off 28, and New Zealand closed on 129 for 4. Parore regained his form with 84 not out as Germon bravely set Zimbabwe a target of 257 at little more than four runs an over. Fifty-six came in 53 minutes, and, at 143 for 3, 114 were needed from 21 overs, an attainable target. At this point, however, Houghton was adjudged leg before, and when Campbell and Streak went cheaply Zimbabwe settled for a draw.

In spite of Nash and Morrison now declaring themselves fit, New Zealand made only one change for the second Test, Larsen coming in for the injured Loveridge. For Zimbabwe, Wishart replaced Olonga. Germon won the toss, and New Zealand batted first on a friendly pitch. They should have scored a mass of runs, but they were impatient against an accurate attack, and by lunch Spearman, Parore and Twose had gone with 90 scored. Astle went shortly after lunch, but Cairns joined Fleming in a stand that became worth 99. Fleming looked set for a maiden Test century before being caught low at mid-on, and Cairns soon followed, seduced by the leg-spin of Paul Strang. New Zealand ended the day on 246 for 8 and all out early on the second morning.

They seized an advantage when they captured the first three Zimbabwe wickets for 50. Houghton stood firm, determined to bat out the day, and he reached 53 in a composed and careful manner. He was then struck on the left foot by a ball from Kennedy and sustained a broken bone that was, ultimately, to bring his innings to an end and to deprive Zimbabwe of their best batsman for their forthcoming World Cup campaign. Batting in considerable pain, Houghton became more aggressive and adopted Grant Flower as a runner. By stumps, he had reached 104 off 204 balls with 12 fours. His runs had come in 306 minutes, but by next morning his leg was encased in plaster, and his part in the match, and in cricket, was over for several weeks.

Beginning the third day on 231 for 7, Zimbabwe did not spoil the courage that had been Houghton's. The tail plundered 95 runs, and Zimbabwe led by 75. Spearman and Twose batted through the second and third sessions of the day to reach 138, and when Twose was finally caught and bowled by Streak they had recorded an opening partnership of 214 in 326 minutes. Craig Spearman was out eight minutes later, but, in only his third Test match, he had scored 112 off 219 balls. He hit a six and nine fours and proved he had the ability and temperament to prosper at the highest level. With the great Martin Crowe passing from the scene, New Zealand cricket had needed such a boost. Fleming and Astle missed their opportunities, but New Zealand cricket was to receive another tremendous fillip as Parore and Cairns put on 166 in two hours. The honours went chiefly to Chris Cairns for one of the most amazing innings seen in Test cricket.

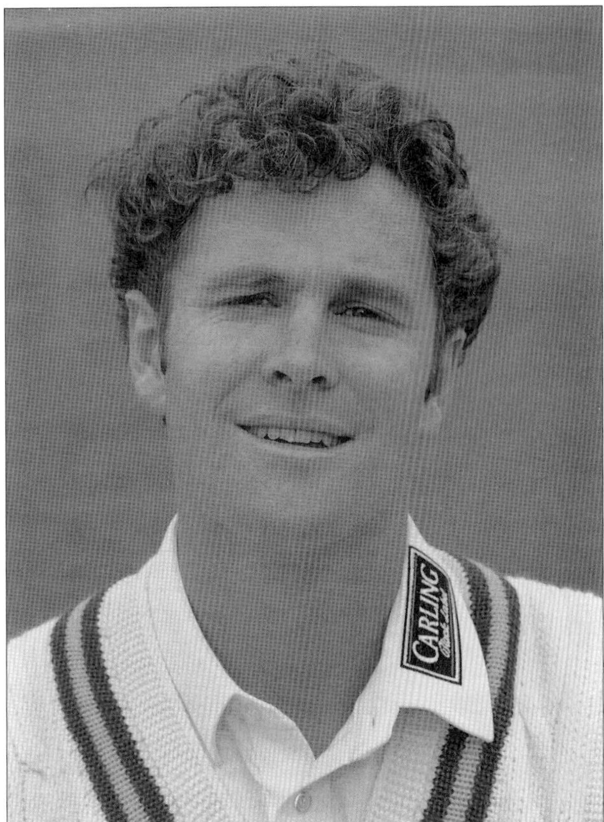

A spectacular maiden Test century for Chris Cairns at Auckland, yet the all-rounder ended the year with critics whispering doubts as to his commitment to New Zealand cricket.
(David Munden/Sportsline)

Cairns reached 50 off 47 balls and 100 off 86. By the time he was bowled by Streak he had made 120 off 96 balls with nine sixes and ten fours in his maiden Test hundred. Only Wally Hammond has hit more sixes in a Test innings, and his ten came in a knock of 336. Perhaps intoxicated by the brilliance of Cairns' innings, Lee Germon delayed his declaration, and the target he set, 366 in 109 overs, may have always seemed beyond the reach of Zimbabwe.

Grant Flower and Stuart Carlisle scored 39 before the end of the fourth day, and they were not separated until they had made 120, Carlisle notching up his first Test fifty. The New Zealand bowling was rather ragged, and it also lacked variety, but without Houghton Zimbabwe were happy to settle for a draw.

First One-day International – New Zealand v. Zimbabwe

28 January 1996 at Eden Park, Auckland

New Zealand

C.M. Spearman	c Whittall, b Streak	22
N.J. Astle	c Campbell, b Peall	120
S.P. Fleming	run out	2
R.G. Twose	c Brandes, b P.A. Strang	53
C.L. Cairns	run out	23
A.C. Parore	not out	26
S.A. Thomson	not out	11
*L.K. Germon (Capt)		
D.N. Patel		
G.R. Larsen		
D.K. Morrison		
	lb 6, w 14, nb 1	21
	50 overs (for 5 wickets)	278

	O	M	R	W
Streak	10	–	32	1
Brandes	6	–	58	–
B.C. Strang	7	–	34	–
Whittall	10	–	58	–
Peall	7	–	48	1
P.A. Strang	10	–	42	1

Fall of Wickets
1–**40**, 2–**61**, 3–**196**, 4–**232**, 5–**251**

Zimbabwe

G.W. Flower	c Parore, b Larsen	46
C.N. Evans	lbw, b Morrison	1
G.J. Whittall	run out	70
A. Flower (Capt)	c Larsen, b Thomson	21
A.D.R. Campbell	c sub (Nash), b Thomson	23
S.G. Davies	c Fleming, b Thomson	3
H.H. Streak	c Spearman, b Larsen	17
P.A. Strang	c Thomson, b Larsen	11
E.A. Brandes	b Morrison	1
S.G. Peall	c Patel, b Morrison	0
B.C. Strang	not out	0
	lb 2, w 4, nb 5	11
	43.5 overs	204

	O	M	R	W
Morrison	6.5	–	34	3
Patel	10	–	44	–
Larsen	8	–	42	3
Astle	5	–	28	–
Thomson	10	1	32	3
Twose	4	–	22	–

Fall of Wickets
1–**6**, 2–**91**, 3–**117**, 4–**158**, 5–**170**, 6–**171**, 7–**193**, 8–**200**, 9–**200**

Umpires: B.F. Bowden & R.S. Dunne *Man of the Match:* N.J. Astle

New Zealand won by 74 runs

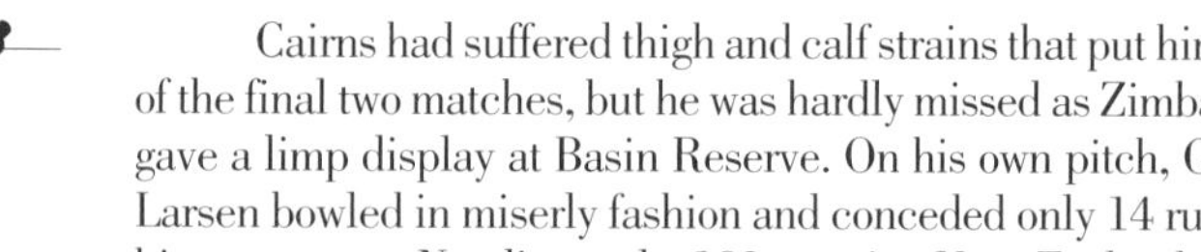

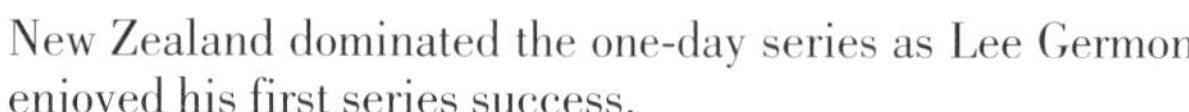

One-day Series

New Zealand v. Zimbabwe

New Zealand dominated the one-day series as Lee Germon enjoyed his first series success.

Germon won the toss in Auckland and New Zealand batted. Craig Spearman gave them an electric start with three fours and a six, but Nathan Astle was the hero of the match. He hit a six and 13 fours and made 120 off 137 balls to devastate the Zimbabwe bowling. He and Twose added 135 for the third wicket while the later batsmen scored at a run a ball. Grant Flower hit 46 off 48 balls, and he and Guy Whittall enjoyed a fruitful partnership that gave Zimbabwe every chance of winning. Grant Flower fell to a spectacular catch at point, and his brother Andy was brilliantly caught by Larsen. When Whittall was run out for 70, made off 73 balls with nine fours, Zimbabwe lost their way.

Cairns had suffered thigh and calf strains that put him out of the final two matches, but he was hardly missed as Zimbabwe gave a limp display at Basin Reserve. On his own pitch, Gavin Larsen bowled in miserly fashion and conceded only 14 runs in his ten overs. Needing only 182 to win, New Zealand were sparked to victory by Fleming's exhilarating 70 off 101 balls.

The third match was historic in that it was the first day/night match to be played in New Zealand. The lighting was not really up to standard, and there were further difficulties due to the fact that the ground authorities allowed overcrowding by almost a thousand. This led to angry exchanges and some ugly behaviour. Recovering from 38 for 3 after being put in, Zimbabwe batted consistently to reach 267. With Astle, Spearman, Fleming and Twose all scoring at a cracking pace, New Zealand looked set to win. They were 227 for 5, but, in the next 25 balls, they lost their last five wickets for 19 runs. Some of the batting was suicidal, but most of the credit must go to Charlie Lock who captured five wickets in 11 deliveries at a cost of two runs.

Second One-day International – New Zealand v. Zimbabwe

31 January 1996 at Basin Reserve, Wellington

Zimbabwe

G.W. Flower	run out	48
C.N. Evans	c Fleming, b Morrison	2
G.J. Whittall	run out	9
*A. Flower (Capt)	lbw, b Nash	10
A.D.R. Campbell	lbw, b Nash	2
S.G. Davies	b Larsen	10
S.V. Carlisle	run out	28
H.H. Streak	b Nash	15
P.A. Strang	not out	28
B.C. Strang	run out	3
A.C.I. Lock		
	b 1, lb 14, w 8, nb 3	26
	50 overs (for 9 wickets)	181

	O	M	R	W
Morrison	10	2	37	1
Kennedy	10	–	57	–
Nash	10	1	30	3
Larsen	10	5	14	1
Astle	10	–	28	–

Fall of Wickets
1–10, 2–33, 3–55, 4–65, 5–98, 6–98, 7–132, 8–171, 9–181

New Zealand

C.M. Spearman	c G.W. Flower, b Streak	1
N.J. Astle	b Whittall	18
S.P. Fleming	b Streak	70
R.G. Twose	c G.W. Flower, b Evans	41
A.C. Parore	not out	25
S.A. Thomson	not out	4
*L.K. Germon (Capt)		
G.R. Larsen		
D.J. Nash		
D.K. Morrison		
R.J. Kennedy		
	b 1, lb 7, w 15, nb 2	25
	39.3 overs (for 4 wickets)	184

	O	M	R	W
Streak	10	–	44	2
Lock	8	1	34	–
Whittall	5	–	22	1
B.C. Strang	9.3	–	50	–
P.A. Strang	5	–	20	–
Evans	2	1	6	1

Fall of Wickets
1–6, 2–56, 3–143, 4–169

Umpires: D.B. Cowie & C.E. King *Man of the Match:* S.P. Fleming

New Zealand won by 6 wickets

Third One-day International – New Zealand v. Zimbabwe

3 February 1996 at McLean Park, Napier

Zimbabwe

G.W. Flower	c Astle, b Morrison	7
C.N. Evans	c Fleming, b Morrison	0
G.J. Whittall	c Harris, b Morrison	12
*A.Flower (Capt)	lbw, b Patel	57
A.D.R. Campbell	c Germon, b Nash	26
S.G. Davies	run out	45
S.V. Carlisle	run out	25
H.H. Streak	not out	36
P.A. Strang	not out	24
E.A. Brandes		
A.C.I. Lock		
	b 1, lb 11, w 19, nb 4	35
	50 overs (for 7 wickets)	267

	O	M	R	W
Morrison	10	2	39	3
Kennedy	9	–	67	–
Patel	10	–	49	1
Nash	10	2	39	1
Astle	6	1	36	–
Harris	5	–	25	–

Fall of Wickets
1–6, 2–18, 3–38, 4–93, 5–133, 6–199, 7–213

New Zealand

C.M. Spearman	lbw, b Brandes	28
N.J. Astle	c A. Flower, b Brandes	30
S.P. Fleming	lbw, b P.A. Strang	50
R.G. Twose	lbw, b Lock	60
A.C. Parore	c Streak, b G.W. Flower	3
C.Z. Harris	c A. Flower, b P.A. Strang	22
*L.K. Germon (Capt)	b Lock	7
D.N. Patel	c and b Lock	4
D.J. Nash	b Lock	4
D.K. Morrison	lbw, b Lock	1
R.J. Kennedy	not out	8
	lb 11, w 14, nb 4	29
	48.1 overs	246

	O	M	R	W
Streak	9	–	45	–
Lock	8.1	–	44	5
Brandes	8	1	37	2
P.A. Strang	10	–	44	2
Whittall	9	–	49	–
G.W. Flower	4	–	16	1

Fall of Wickets
1–66, 2–72, 3–164, 4–169, 5–201, 6–228, 7–229, 8–233, 9–235

Umpires: R.S. Dunne & D.M. Quested *Man of the Match:* A.C.I. Lock

Zimbabwe won by 21 runs

Shell Trophy

17, 18, 19 and 20 January 1996
at Basin Reserve, Wellington
Wellington 282 (J.D. Wells 69) and 370 for 8 dec. (J.M. Aiken 170 not out)
Northern Districts 200 (D.R. Brown 4 for 35, R.G. Petrie 4 for 41) and 453 for 8 (M.N. Hart 87 not out, M.D. Bell 74, M.D. Bailey 72, S.B. Doull 67 not out, B.A. Pocock 50)
Northern Districts won by 2 wickets
Northern Districts 8 pts, Wellington 4 pts

at Lancaster Park, Christchurch
Canterbury 128 (A.J. Penn 4 for 53) and 199
Central Districts 475 for 9 dec. (L.G. Howell 181, M.J. Greatbatch 115, W.A. Wisneski 73)
Central Districts won by an innings and 148 runs
Central Districts 12 pts, Canterbury 0 pts

at Molyneux Park, Alexandra
Auckland 234 (S.B. O'Connor 4 for 62) and 394 for 6 dec. (A.C. Barnes 100 not out, R.A. Jones 75, J.M. Mills 73 not out)
Otago 127 (D.K. Morrison 5 for 43) and 353 (M.H. Richardson 146, M.J. Lamont 92, C. Pringle 4 for 54)
Auckland won by 148 runs
Auckland 12 pts, Otago 0 pts

New Zealand's senior domestic competition suffered under the weight of the Pakistan and Zimbabwe tours and the preparations for the World Cup. Each province played five rather than seven matches, and leading cricketers such as Germon and Astle were not able to represent their associations.

Gavin Larsen was unavailable for Wellington and Richard Petrie took over as captain. In spite of being able to call on Warwickshire's Dougie Brown, Wellington suffered a surprise defeat in their opening match. The left-handed John Aiken hit the highest score of his career, and Petrie was able to set Northern Districts a target of 453. They batted consistently, but, at 346 for 8, they looked beaten. Simon Doull joined Matthew Hart in an unbroken partnership of 107 in 88 minutes, which won the match. Hart hit the highest score of his career while Doull, who has a century to his credit, reached fifty for only the second time in his career.

Central Districts recovered from 18 for 3 to overwhelm the weakened Canterbury side. Llorne Howell and skipper Mark Greatbatch shared a fourth wicket stand of 193. Howell hit the highest score of his career, with four sixes and 14 fours, and Greatbatch made 115 off 127 balls with three sixes and 11 fours.

Auckland were always ahead against Otago. Internationals Morrison, eight wickets in the match, and Pringle bowled well while Barnes, who reached the first century of his career, and Mills shared an unbroken seventh wicket stand of 177.

22, 23, 24 and 25 January 1996
at Smallbone Park, Rotorua
Northern Districts 382 (B.A. Young 125, A.R. Tait 64, R.G. Hart 58, M.E. Parlane 54) and 128 for 1 (B.A. Young 71 not out)
Central Districts 456 (M.J. Greatbatch 202, L.G. Howell 92, A.R. Tait 5 for 109)
Match drawn
Central Districts 4 pts, Northern Districts 0 pts

at Dudley Park, Rangiora
Auckland 517 for 9 dec. (J.T.C. Vaughan 127, S.M. Lynch 65, S.J. Peterson 53, A.T. Reinholds 52, S.J. Roberts 4 for 113) and 46 for 0
Canterbury 216 (M.W. Priest 53) and 345 (R.M. Frew 125, M.E.L. Lane 52, M.J. Haslam 4 for 94)
Auckland won by 10 wickets
Auckland 12 pts, Canterbury 0 pts

at Carisbrook, Dunedin
Wellington 187 (J.W. Wilson 5 for 71, S.B. O'Connor 4 for 77) and 212 (J.M. Aiken 68, P.J. Wiseman 7 for 50)
Otago 169 (D.R. Brown 5 for 39) and 164 (J.W. Wilson 58, D.R. Brown 5 for 39, G.R. Jonas 4 for 40)
Wellington won by 67 runs
Wellington 12 pts, Otago 0 pts

Right-handed batsman and medium-pace bowler Alex Tait produced the best performances of his career with both bat and ball, and Bryan Young showed his best form in the rain-affected match in Rotorua. The honours, however, again went to Central Districts. Howell and Greatbatch shared another large fourth wicket partnership, with a score of 161. Greatbatch equalled the highest score of his career and hit a century in boundaries.

Justin Vaughan led Auckland to victory over Canterbury with the highest score of his career. Canterbury were forced to follow on, but they avoided an innings defeat thanks to an innings of 125 by Frew who hit 21 boundaries.

In a low-scoring match in Dunedin, Wellington were indebted to a second innings century opening partnership between Chandler and Aiken and to the bowling of Jonas and Brown. Otago's off-break bowler Paul Wiseman took five wickets in an innings for the first time, but still finished on the losing side.

4, 5, 6 and 7 February 1996
at Eden Park, Auckland
Central Districts 594 for 8 dec. (M.J. Greatbatch 162 not out, G.R. Sulzberger 142, M.D.J. Walker 63, S.W. Duff 57, A.H. Jones 55)
Auckland 161 (G.R. Sulzberger 4 for 19) and 343 (S.M. Lynch 63, J.T.C. Vaughan 62, S.W. Duff 4 for 41)
Central Districts won by an innings and 90 runs
Central Districts 12 pts, Auckland 0 pts

at Trust Bank Park, Hamilton
Otago 255 (R.A. King 64, M.J. Lamont 52) and 358 for 6 (M.H. Richardson 105 not out, M.J. Lamont 80, J.W. Wilson 59, C.B. Gaffaney 56)
Northern Districts 472 (B.A. Young 133, M.D. Bailey 98, R.G. Hart 58, B.A. Pocock 53, P.J. Wiseman 4 for 123)
Match drawn
Northern Districts 4 pts, Otago 0 pts

at Basin Reserve, Wellington
Canterbury 147 (R.G. Petrie 5 for 23) and 141 (H.T. Davis 5 for 32)
Wellington 190 (J.M. Aiken 55) and 101 for 2 (M.H. Austen 68 not out)
Wellington 12 pts, Canterbury 0 pts

Glen Sulzberger announced his arrival with a six and 19 fours in his 326-ball innings of 142 for Central Districts against Auckland. He shared an opening stand of 137 with Walker, but once more Mark Greatbatch stole most of the plaudits. He hit his third century in succession, 162 off 187 balls, with a six and 24 fours. Central Districts went on to win by an innings, with Sulzberger claiming a career best 4 for 19 in 18 overs with his spin.

Bryan Young gave further evidence of a return of form and confidence with his second century in successive matches, but Otago thwarted Northern Districts with a positive hundred from Mark Richardson.

Canterbury's sorry run continued with defeat in two days at Basin Reserve.

Mark Greatbatch hit 623 runs, average 155.75, but there was no recall to the New Zealand side. (Alan Cozzi)

9, 10, 11 and 12 February 1996
at Eden Park, Auckland
Auckland 189 (H.D. Barton 60 not out, S.B. Styris 4 for 43) and 173 (S.B. Styris 5 for 52)
Northern Districts 150 (M.D. Bailey 63, J.T.C. Vaughan 4 for 44) and 142
Auckland won by 70 runs
Auckland 12 pts, Northern Districts 0 pts

at Trafalgar Park, Nelson
Central Districts 65 (R.G. Petrie 4 for 10) and 247 (L.G. Howell 101, G.R. Jonas 4 for 39, S.W. Weenink 4 for 69)
Wellington 282 (W.A. Wisneski 5 for 88) and 31 for 0
Wellington won by 10 wickets
Wellington 12 pts, Central Districts 0 pts

at Lancaster Park, Christchurch
Otago 175 (S.A. Robinson 61) and 334 (S.A. Robinson 93, M.H. Richardson 66, G.I. Allott 6 for 93)
Canterbury 176 (B.R. Hartland 56, P.J. Wiseman 5 for 27, J.W. Wilson 4 for 51) and 335 for 5 (B.R. Hartland 95, G.R. Stead 66, B.J.K. Doody 61, C.D. McMillan 51 not out)
Canterbury won by 5 wickets
Canterbury 12 pts, Otago 0 pts

Auckland disposed of Northern Districts in three days and became strong favourites to reach the Shell Trophy final. They lost seven wickets for 107 runs, but young Hamish Barton batted with skill and maturity to hit a six and eight fours in his 60 off 104 balls – a decisive innings. Vaughan led by example as he and Haslam constantly exerted pressure on Northern with some attacking bowling. Medium-pacer Scott Styris had the best figures of his career for innings and match, but Vaughan, 7 for 84, and Haslam, 6 for 32, maintained the Auckland supremacy.

Wellington also won in three days and became virtually assured of a place in the final. Central Districts, who had made the highest score in their history in the previous match, were bowled out for 65, the fourth lowest total in their history. They were not helped by the fact that Greatbatch was run out for nought. Wellington batted with consistency to take a first innings lead of 217, and Llorne Howell's 101 off 131 balls with three sixes and ten fours could only delay the inevitable. Weenink had the best bowling performance of his brief career.

Otago and Canterbury both entered the game at Lancaster Park pointless. Canterbury took the narrowest of first innings' leads, and they were then bowled into a good position by Geoff Allott, New Zealand's new left-arm fast medium Test bowler. His 6 for 93 was a career-best.

Shane Robinson, returning to captain Otago after an absence of two years, held up Canterbury with the highest score of his career, and there were more scares for the home side when Cumming was out for 0. Hartland and Doody added 118, and Stead then joined Hartland in a partnership worth 95. McMillan and Priest finished the job and saved Canterbury from the wooden spoon.

15, 16, 17 and 18 February 1996
at Eden Park, Auckland
Wellington 157 (M.J. Haslam 4 for 60) and 230 (R.G. Petrie 65, I.S. Billcliff 59)
Auckland 143 (R.A. Jones 68, J.D. Wells 4 for 38) and 245 for 5 (M.A. Horne 113, M.H. Austen 4 for 43)
Auckland won by 5 wickets
Auckland 8 pts, Wellington 4 pts

at Trust Bank Park, Hamilton
Northern Districts 323 (M.E. Parlane 132 not out) and 109 for 1
Canterbury 98 (R.P. de Groen 7 for 58) and 331 (R.M. Frew 84 not out, B.R. Hartland 62, R.P. de Groen 4 for 71)
Northern Districts won by 9 wickets
Northern Districts 12 pts, Canterbury 0 pts

at McLean Park, Napier
Otago 280 (M.H. Richardson 104, P.J. Wiseman 77) and 571 for 8 (R.A. Lawson 200, R.T. King 117 not out, M.G. Croy 104)
Central Districts 526 (G.R. Sulzberger 128, M.J. Greatbatch 126, A.J. Penn 90)
Match drawn
Central Districts 4 pts, Otago 0 pts

The final round of matches saw Auckland and Wellington confirm their places in the final. Wellington led on the first innings, but a splendid 113 from Matt Horne and a blistering 43 from Andy Reinholds, in an innings which included a six and seven fours, set up Auckland's fourth win in five matches and gave them home advantage in the final.

Michael Parlane's maiden first-class hundred gave Northern Districts the edge over lowly Canterbury, but the hero of the match was Richard de Groen. The fast-medium pace bowler had announced his retirement from first-class cricket, and in this, his final match, he took 11 for 129, a record for a Northern Districts' bowler against Canterbury.

In Napier, Central Districts hit the second highest score in their history. Sulzberger hit his second hundred of the season; Greatbatch his fourth in five matches. There was also a career best 90 from Andy Penn. Wiseman, who enjoyed a good season with his off-breaks, was another to hit a career-best score, and when Otago batted a second time, Robert Lawson hit the first double century of his career and shared an opening stand of 305 with Martyn Croy, who scored a maiden first-class hundred. Richard King joined the party with his maiden century, and Otago finished the season on a note of hope.

Shell Trophy – Final Table

	P	W	L	D	Pts
Auckland	5	4	1	–	44
Wellington	5	3	2	–	44
Central Districts	5	2	1	2	32
Northern Districts	5	2	1	2	24
Canterbury	5	1	4	–	12
Otago	5	–	3	2	0

Shell Trophy Final

Auckland *v.* Wellington

29 February, 1, 2 and 3 March 1996
at Eden Park, Auckland
Auckland 416 (M.J. Horne 190, J.T.C. Vaughan 88, D.R. Brown 4 for 82) and 93 for 1 (A.T. Reinholds 52 not out)
Wellington 262 (C.J. Nevin 86, C. Pringle 4 for 46, C.M. Brown 4 for 80) and 247 (I.S. Billcliff 86, J.D. Wells 73, J.T.C. Vaughan 4 for 68)
Auckland won by 9 wickets

There was an element of controversy in the final in that Auckland were denied the services of Hamish Barton and Stephen Lynch, who were told that they must go to Australia with the national youth side. Auckland argued, correctly, that it would be more profitable for the two young players if they took part in the most important game in the domestic calendar. Authority thought otherwise, and one begins to wonder how much the administrators in any country value the domestic game, so obsessed have they become with any form of international cricket.

Put in to bat, Auckland lost Reinholds and Jones for 30, but Horne then dominated a stand of 124 in 95 minutes with Peterson. A stand of 153 with Vaughan followed. It was electrifying stuff. Matt Horne, another to return to the first-class game after a year's absence, made the highest score of his career, 190 off 192 balls with six sixes and 28 fours. Auckland scored at more than four an over, and by the end of the day they had captured two Wellington wickets.

At 137 for 8, Wellington were doomed to follow on, but Chris Nevin, who had an excellent first season as the Wellington 'keeper, and Heath Davis scored 116 and nearly saved the indignity. In their second innings, Wellington slipped to 19 for 4 before Wells and Billcliff added 148.

The match ended in rather bizarre fashion. Reinholds hit 52 off 36 balls, and, shortly after lunch on the final day, Heath Davis lost his stride and bowled a 12-ball over that cost 35 runs. Davis had bowled well in the first Auckland innings, but Reinholds and Richard Jones now scored the last 81 runs needed for victory off 56 balls in 40 minutes. Victory gave Auckland their second Shell Trophy in successive seasons, the first time that they had achieved this feat since 1940.

First-Class Averages

Batting

	M	Inns	NO	Runs	HS	Av	100s	50s
M.J. Greatbatch	5	6	2	623	202	155.75	4	
M.J. Horne	2	4	–	208	190	77.00	2	
L.G. Howell	7	9	1	550	181	68.75	2	2
M.H. Richardson	5	10	1	615	146	68.33	3	1
G.R. Sulzberger	5	6	–	328	142	54.66	2	
R.G. Twose	3	6	1	272	94	54.40		3
R.A. Lawson	5	9	1	414	200	51.75	2	
J.T.C. Vaughan	6	10	1	453	127	50.33	1	2
H.T. Davis	5	8	5	143	38*	47.66		
A.C. Parore	3	6	2	190	84*	47.50		2
M.D. Bailey	5	7	–	322	98	46.00		3
C.L. Cairns	3	6	–	275	120	45.33	1	2
B.A. Young	6	11	1	444	133	44.40	2	1
C.O. Findley	5	6	3	133	52	44.33		1
M.E. Parlane	5	8	2	261	132*	43.50	1	1
C.M. Spearman	3	6	–	254	112	42.33	1	
J.M. Aiken	8	15	3	501	170*	41.75	1	3
M.D. Bell	7	12	2	348	83	34.80		2
J.W. Wilson	5	10	1	312	59	34.66		2
A.T. Reinholds	6	12	2	345	52*	34.50		2
M.N. Hart	5	7	1	206	87*	34.33		1
C.J. Nevin	6	10	2	263	86	32.87		1
A.J. Penn	6	7	2	160	90	32.00		1
B.R. Hartland	5	10	–	319	95	31.90		3
R.T. King	5	10	1	275	117*	30.55	1	1
S.A. Robinson	5	10	1	274	93	30.44		2
S.P. Fleming	3	6	–	182	4	30.33		1
R.M. Frew	5	10	1	266	125	29.55	1	1
J.M. Mills	6	9	1	226	73*	28.25		1
A.C. Barnes	5	8	1	193	100*	27.57	1	
M.J. Lamont	5	10	–	275	92	27.50		3
B.J.K. Doody	2	4	–	110	61	27.50		1
S.M. Lynch	6	11	–	301	65	27.36		2
J.D. Wells	6	10	–	273	73	27.30		2
R.A. Jones	6	11	1	272	75	27.20		2
M.G. Croy	4	5	–	136	104	27.20	1	
R.G. Hart	6	9	–	237	58	26.33		2
L.K. Germon	3	6	2	105	25	26.25		
D.R. Brown	6	10	–	257	47	25.70		
S.J. Peterson	5	8	–	200	53	25.00		1
I.S. Billcliff	5	9	–	224	86	24.88		2
S.W. Duff	4	5	–	116	57	23.20		1
R.G. Petrie	6	10	–	227	65	22.70		1
B.A. Pocock	5	8	–	180	53	22.50		2
W.A. Wisneski	5	6	–	134	73	22.33		1
C.D. Cumming	5	10	–	220	43	22.00		
M.W. Priest	5	10	1	186	53	20.66		1
A.H. Jones	5	6	–	117	55	19.50		1
M.H. Austen	6	11	1	194	68*	19.40		1
C.D. McMillan	7	13	1	230	51*	19.16		1
P.J.B. Chandler	6	12	1	200	45	18.18		
C. Pringle	6	8	–	137	47	17.12		
S.R. Mather	5	9	1	128	25	16.00		
J.I. Pamment	5	9	1	126	30	15.75		
M.E.L. Lane	5	9	–	139	52	15.44		1
S.J. Roberts	5	9	–	138	34	15.33		
C.B. Gaffaney	4	8	–	119	56	14.87		1
P.J. Wiseman	5	9	–	124	77	13.77		1
G.R. Stead	5	10	–	133	66	13.30		1

(Qualification: 100 runs, average 10.00)

Bowling

	Overs	Mds	Runs	Wks	Av	Best	10/m	5/inn
S.B. Styris	54.4	19	132	10	13.20	5/52		1
D.R. Brown	166.1	50	440	28	15.71	5/39	1	2
R.G. Petrie	134.5	53	294	18	16.33	5/23		1
C.M. Brown	93	24	236	12	19.66	4/80		
R.P. de Groen	196.2	64	453	22	20.59	7/58	1	1
D.K. Morrison	116	27	376	18	20.88	5/43		1
G.R. Jonas	195.1	56	510	23	22.17	4/39		
C. Pringle	222.5	60	606	25	24.24	5/198		1
G.I. Allott	242.5	49	644	26	24.76	6/93		1
C.O. Findlay	110.3	34	301	12	25.08	2/19		
P.J. Wiseman	268.5	78	587	23	25.52	7/50		2
W.A. Wisneski	185.5	43	545	21	25.95	5/88		1
J.T.C. Vaughan	209.5	77	510	19	26.84	4/44		
C.L. Cairns	139.1	37	405	15	27.00	4/51		
R.J. Kennedy	101	23	281	10	28.10	4/22		
S.W. Duff	190.3	70	340	12	28.33	4/41		
M.J. Haslam	300.1	102	822	28	29.35	4/60		
H.T. Davis	127	26	482	16	30.12	5/32		1
R.L. Hayes	159.5	39	396	13	30.46	3/24		
A.J. Gale	121	36	313	10	31.30	3/58		
S.J. Roberts	170	41	523	16	32.68	4/113		
J.W. Wilson	194	49	529	15	35.26	5/71		1
S.B. O'Connor	183.2	47	529	15	35.26	4/62		
A.J. Penn	193	36	626	17	36.82	4/53		
M.N. Hart	189	50	466	11	42.36	3/15		

(Qualification: 10 wickets)

Leading Fielders

34 – C.J. Nevin (ct 33 / st 1); 19 – R.G. Hart (ct 16 / st 3); 18 – M.A. Sigley; 17 – M.E.L. Lane; 14 – L.K. Germon and J.M. Mills (ct 13 / st 1); 13 – B.A. Young; 12 – M.G. Croy (ct 11 / st 1); 9 – M.J. Greatbatch

Basin Reserve, Wellington (Ben Radford/Allsport)

The World Cup, 1996

The Sixth World Cup was played between the nine Test-playing countries in addition to the United Arab Emirates, Kenya and Holland. A total of thirty-seven matches were played over five weeks. The tournament had all the ingredients of a popular novel. It was touched by controversy, tinged with animosity, dramatised by twists of fate and fortune, offered the unexpected and the unwanted, saw David slay Goliath, and ended in romance.

The Opening Ceremony of the Sixth World Cup. (Mike Hewitt/Allsport)

The World Cup came into existence in 1975, some years after it was first proposed by Ben Brocklehurst, the former Somerset captain. Initially, it was a rather small and tentative affair involving six Test-playing countries supplemented by Sri Lanka and East Africa. It was blessed with good weather and an exciting final, and the tournament consisted of fifteen matches confined to a period of fifteen days.

Like Topsy in *Uncle Tom's Cabin*, the World Cup grew and grew, and the sixth gathering of nations, played in the Indian sub-continent in 1996, engaged the talents of the nine Test-playing countries and three qualifiers from the ICC Trophy competition – the United Arab Emirates, Holland and Kenya.

There were flaws in the structure of this year's competition in that the twelve teams were divided into two sections, the first of which included the youngest Test-playing country, Zimbabwe, and Kenya; and the second was the home for Holland and the United Arab Emirates. As four sides from each group qualified for the quarter-finals, this arrangement virtually assured that the leading Test nations would all be in the final stages of the competition and that the preliminary matches would, in a sense, be superfluous. As it transpired, these games were not without their surprises and thrills, but the end result was as expected.

Unfortunately, all else did not go according to plan. Sri Lanka were one of the three hosts of the tournament, and their matches against Australia, West Indies, Zimbabwe and Kenya were assigned to be played in Colombo and Kandy. Some weeks before the cup matches started, a Tamil Tiger suicide bomber caused many deaths and much destruction in the centre of Colombo. It followed that Australia and West Indies refused to play their matches in the Sri Lankan capital, their administrations announcing that they feared for the safety of their players, some of whom had expressed an unwillingness to travel to Sri Lanka.

While one can understand the reasoning, one wonders what would have happened had the World Cup been played in England as, at one time, it seemed likely to be. While the matches were in progress the IRA called off their cease-fire, and three bombs were exploded in London. Far fewer people were killed than had been killed in Colombo, but the threat remained. Would, one wonders, Australia and West Indies have refused to play at Lord's and The Oval?

Officials pleaded on behalf of Sri Lanka, but Australia and West Indies were adamant they would concede their matches. On 17 and 25 February, the Sri Lankan side arrived at the Premasda International Cricket Stadium. The opposition did not. Sri Lanka were awarded the two points on each occasion and found themselves top of Group One without playing a match. Thankfully, the rest was cricket.

Section A

In spite of the predictability of the four quarter-finalists, there was a shock for West Indies and a triumph for Sri Lanka.

Zimbabwe v. West Indies

Neither Zimbabwe nor West Indies arrived in India in a happy state of mind. West Indies had failed in both Sharjah and Australia and were still riven with internal strife. The withdrawal of Carl Hooper from the party had not been satisfactorily explained, particularly as the all-rounder accompanied his withdrawal with the news that he would definitely be returning to Kent for the England season. Zimbabwe had gone to New Zealand with high expectations, but had suffered a most grievous loss when their finest batsman, David Houghton, was injured and could not play in the World Cup. The extent to which he was missed was apparent in the opening encounter.

Andy Flower won the toss and batted. Ambrose began with a wild, nine-ball over, but he then found his rhythm and had the Zimbabwe captain caught behind off a vicious lifting ball in his second over. Grant Flower played two pleasing shots to the boundary before Gibson instinctively clung on to a return catch, and Campbell and Whittall were needlessly run out, the first by Lara's brilliance from square-leg, the second Bishop from mid-on. Waller, Evans and later Paul Strang worked hard, but the West Indian bowlers maintained a tight grip. The total of 151 was unlikely to be a challenge to any side in the tournament, least of all West Indies.

Streak bowled with hostility, but luck was not with him. West Indies were 78 in the 20th over when the leg-spin of Paul Strang accounted for Richardson who was caught at slip as he attempted to cut. Sherwin Campbell was bemused by the googly, and Chanderpaul, having hit his first two deliveries for four, fell to a high full toss. Arthurton was taken at slip off a googly to give Paul Strang his fourth wicket, a commendable performance. Unfortunately for Zimbabwe, Brian Lara was not to be disturbed, and he finished the match by hitting Strang over mid-off for six to give his side victory with more than twenty overs to spare. He had given much entertainment to an excited capacity crowd of 27,000.

India v. Kenya

The problem that faces a national hero is that his worshippers are so expectant that failure can break millions of hearts. No cricketer in the world is more worshipped than Sachin Tendulkar, and he began the World Cup with India's hopes of the prize resting decidedly upon him. Kenya exposed some weaknesses in the Indian bowling, and it was apparent that the home side's attack would rely heavily on Kumble and the left-arm spinner Venkatapathy Raju. None of the pace men impressed, and Steve Tikolo, who plays for Border in South Africa, hit an entertaining 65 off 80 balls,

Match One – Zimbabwe v. West Indies

16 February 1996 at Lal Bahadur Stadium, Hyderabad

Zimbabwe

*A. Flower (Capt)	c Browne, b Ambrose	3
G.W. Flower	c and b Gibson	31
G.J. Whittall	run out	14
A.D.R. Campbell	run out	0
A.C. Waller	st Browne, b Harper	21
C.N. Evans	c Browne, b Ambrose	21
S.G. Davies	run out	9
H.H. Streak	lbw, b Walsh	7
P.A. Strang	not out	22
E.A. Brandes	c Chanderpaul, b Ambrose	7
A.P.C. Lock	not out	1
	lb 10, w 4, nb 1	15
	50 overs (for 9 wickets)	151

	O	M	R	W
Ambrose	10	2	28	3
Walsh	10	3	27	1
Gibson	9	1	27	1
Bishop	10	3	18	–
Harper	10	1	30	1
Arthurton	1	–	11	–

Fall of Wickets
1–11, 2–53, 3–56, 4–58, 5–91, 6–103, 7–115, 8–125, 9–142

West Indies

S.L. Campbell	b P.A. Strang	47
R.B. Richardson (Capt)	c Campbell, b P.A. Strang	32
B.C. Lara	not out	43
S. Chanderpaul	b P.A. Strang	8
K.L.T. Arthurton	c Campbell, b P.A. Strang	1
R.A. Harper	not out	5
O.D. Gibson		
*C.O. Browne		
I.R. Bishop		
C.E.L. Ambrose		
C.A. Walsh		
	b 5, lb 3, w 10, nb 1	19
	29.3 overs (for 4 wickets)	155

	O	M	R	W
Streak	7	–	34	–
Lock	6	–	23	–
Brandes	7	–	42	–
Whittall	2	–	8	–
P.A. Strang	7.3	1	40	4

Fall of Wickets
1–78, 2–115, 3–123, 4–136

Umpires: S. Venkataraghavan & R.S. Dunne *Man of the Match:* C.E.L. Ambrose

West Indies won by 6 wickets

Match Two – India v. Kenya

18 February 1996 at Barabati Stadium, Cuttack

Kenya

D. Chudasama	c Mongia, b Venkatesh Prasad	29
*K. Otieno	c Mongia, b Venkatapathy Raju	27
S. Tikolo	c Kumble, b Venkatapathy Raju	65
M. Odumbe (Capt)	st Mongia, b Kumble	26
H. Modi	c Jadeja, b Kumble	2
T. Odoyo	c Prabhakar, b Kumble	8
E. Odumbe	not out	15
Asif Karim	not out	6
D. Tikolo		
M. Suji		
R. Ali		
	b 2, lb 11, w 7, nb 1	21
	50 overs (for 6 wickets)	199

	O	M	R	W
Prabhakar	5	1	19	–
Srinath	10	–	38	–
Venkatesh Prasad	10	–	41	1
Kumble	10	2	28	3
Venkatapathy Raju	10	2	34	2
Tendulkar	5	–	26	–

Fall of Wickets
1–41, 2–65, 3–161, 4–161, 5–165, 6–184

India

A.D. Jadeja	c Ali, b Asif Karim	53
S.R. Tendulkar	not out	127
N.S. Sidhu	c Suji, b S. Tikolo	1
V.G. Kambli	c D. Tikolo, b M. Odumbe	2
*N.R. Mongia	not out	8
M. Azharuddin (Capt)		
M. Prabhakar		
J. Srinath		
Venkatesh Prasad		
A.R. Kumble		
Venkatapathy Raju		
	b 3, w 7, nb 2	12
	41.5 overs (for 3 wickets)	203

	O	M	R	W
E. Odumbe	3	–	18	–
Suji	5	–	20	–
Asif Karim	10	1	27	1
Odoyo	3	–	22	–
Ali	5	–	25	–
S. Tikolo	3	–	26	1
M. Odumbe	9.5	1	41	1
D. Tikolo	3	–	21	–

Fall of Wickets
1–163, 2–167, 3–182

Umpires: D.R. Shepherd & K.T. Francis *Man of the Match:* S.R. Tendulkar

India won by 7 wickets

sharing a third wicket stand of 96 with skipper Maurice Odumbe. Kenya's batting was consistently cheerful, but a target of 200 presented few fears for India.

Jadeja and Tendulkar reached fifty inside ten overs, and the opening partnership was worth 163 in 33 overs. The game was won with 49 balls to spare, and Tendulkar finished with 15 fours and a six in his 127 off 134 balls. A capacity crowd of 23,000 had watched just what they came to see.

Sri Lanka *v.* Zimbabwe

Sri Lanka entered the fray in a resounding manner, crushing Zimbabwe by six wickets with 13 overs to spare. It was a performance that entranced a crowd of 15,000 and compensated in some measure for the refusal of Australia and West Indies to visit Colombo.

Zimbabwe again chose to bat when they won the toss, and they lost both of the Flower brothers to run outs: Andy, dubiously, when umpire Dunne declined to call on the third umpire; and Grant, crassly, when he responded to Whittall's insane call. Thereafter, Zimbabwe batted with some consistency, but with a lack of real conviction. Campbell played pleasingly, but one suspects that he is destined to be an under-achiever at international level.

The loss of both openers early on had no effect whatsoever on Sri Lanka's approach to the game. Gurusinha hit six sixes in his innings of 87, which ended more through fatigue than anything else, and he and de Silva added an astonishing 172 in 29 overs of thrilling batting. It was a record for any Sri Lankan wicket in a one-day international, and it made victory a formality. Aravinda de Silva's 91 was the highest score by a Sri Lankan in a World Cup match.

India *v.* West Indies

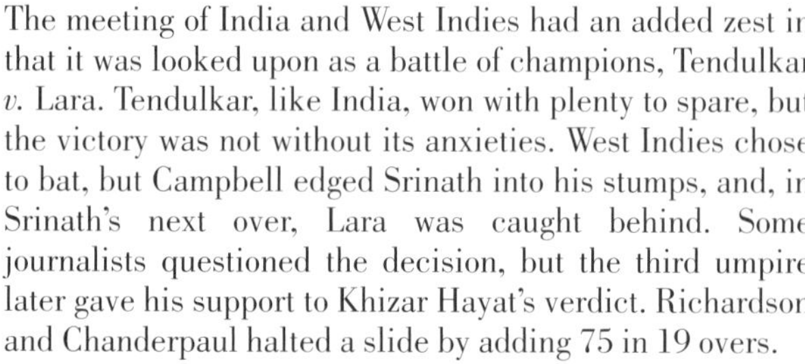

The meeting of India and West Indies had an added zest in that it was looked upon as a battle of champions, Tendulkar *v.* Lara. Tendulkar, like India, won with plenty to spare, but the victory was not without its anxieties. West Indies chose to bat, but Campbell edged Srinath into his stumps, and, in Srinath's next over, Lara was caught behind. Some journalists questioned the decision, but the third umpire later gave his support to Khizar Hayat's verdict. Richardson and Chanderpaul halted a slide by adding 75 in 19 overs.

Richardson had been watchful, but he fell to Prabhakar when he hooked uncertainly and was caught on the boundary. Chanderpaul, who hit six fours, was magnificently caught at mid-wicket, and Holder, yet to prove himself at the top level, was bowled as he tried to cut Kumble – an unwise ambition. Harper and Browne halted India's progress, but they could never increase momentum, and India were left with a simple task.

It looked less easy when Ambrose bowled both Jadeja and Sidhu in his first three overs. Had Tendulkar been held off a firm flick to square-leg when 12 – a difficult chance –

Match Three – Sri Lanka *v.* Zimbabwe

21 February 1996 at Sinhalese Sports Club, Colombo

Zimbabwe

Batsman	How out	Runs
*A. Flower (Capt)	run out	8
G.W. Flower	run out	15
G.J. Whittall	c Jayasuriya, b Muralitharan	35
A.D.R. Campbell	c Muralitharan, b Vaas	75
A.C. Waller	b Jayasuriya	19
C.N. Evans	not out	39
H.H. Streak	c de Silva, b Vaas	15
P.A. Strang	not out	0
E.A. Brandes		
A.P.C. Lock		
S.G. Peall		
	b 1, lb 16, w 4, nb 1	22
	50 overs (for 6 wickets)	228

Bowler	O	M	R	W
Vaas	10	–	30	2
Wickremasinghe	8	–	36	–
Ranatunga	2	–	14	–
Muralitharan	10	–	37	1
Dharmasena	10	–	50	–
Jayasuriya	10	–	44	1

Fall of Wickets
1–**19**, 2–**51**, 3–**92**, 4–**160**, 5–**194**, 6–**227**

Sri Lanka

Batsman	How out	Runs
S.T. Jayasuriya	b Streak	6
*R.S. Kaluwitharana	c Peall, b Streak	0
A.P. Gurusinha	run out	87
P.A. de Silva	lbw, b Streak	91
A. Ranatunga (Capt)	not out	13
H.P. Tillekeratne	not out	7
R.S. Mahanama		
W.P.U.J.C. Vaas		
H.D.P.K. Dharmasena		
G.P. Wickremasinghe		
M. Muralitharan		
	lb 5, w 17, nb 3	25
	37 overs (for 4 wickets)	229

Bowler	O	M	R	W
Streak	10	–	60	3
Lock	4	–	17	–
Peall	3	–	23	–
Brandes	8	–	35	–
P.A. Strang	5	–	43	–
Whittall	2	–	20	–
G.W. Flower	5	1	26	–

Fall of Wickets
1–**5**, 2–**23**, 3–**195**, 4–**209**

Umpires: R.S. Dunne & Mahboob Shah *Man of the Match:* P.A. de Silva

Sri Lanka won by 6 wickets

India would have been in dire straits. For West Indies, worse followed when, on 22, a straightforward offering from Tendulkar was put down by the wicket-keeper. Otherwise, Tendulkar played gloriously, hitting 70 off 91 balls with eight fours. He and Azharuddin added 79 before the captain was caught at long-on. Tendulkar ran himself out, but Kambli and Mongia batted with the utmost good sense to see India home with no more alarms.

Australia *v.* Kenya

Australia played their first match of the tournament and beat Kenya with the ease that had been expected. Kenya, ever keen and zestful in the field on a day of high temperature and humidity, captured the wickets of Ponting and Taylor with 26 scored, but they were then mercilessly savaged by the Waugh twins. The pair added 207 for the third wicket, establishing a new record for any wicket in the World Cup. Mark, relishing his opening role, hit 130 off 128 balls, and his innings included a six and 14 fours. It was a remarkable achievement in weather that left him struggling for breath towards the end of his 165-minute stay at the crease. Steve Waugh's 82 came off 88 balls and included a six and five fours.

Kenya responded bravely with Otieno and Maurice Odumbe scoring 102 in 18 overs after Chudasama and Steve Tikolo had gone for 30. To add to Australia's woes, McDermott limped off the field with a calf injury after

Glenn McGrath appeals for leg before in the match between Kenya and Australia. The batsman is Kennedy Otieno, the Kenyan wicket-keeper and opening batsman who scored 85 and impressed throughout the competition. (Shaun Botterill/Allsport)

Match Four – India *v.* West Indies

21 February 1996 at Roop Singh Stadium, Gwalior

West Indies

S.L. Campbell	**b** Srinath	**5**
R.B. Richardson (Capt)	**c** Kambli, **b** Prabhakar	**47**
B.C. Lara	**c** Mongia, **b** Srinath	**2**
S. Chanderpaul	**c** Azharuddin, **b** Kapoor	**38**
R.I.C. Holder	**b** Kumble	**0**
R.A. Harper	**b** Kumble	**23**
*C.O. Browne	**b** Prabhakar	**18**
O.D. Gibson	**b** Kumble	**6**
I.R. Bishop	run out	**9**
C.E.L. Ambrose	**c** Kumble, **b** Prabhakar	**8**
C.A. Walsh	not out	**9**
	lb **2**, w **5**, nb **1**	**8**
	50 overs	**173**

	O	M	R	W
Prabhakar	10	–	39	**3**
Srinath	10	–	22	**2**
Kumble	10	–	35	**3**
Venkatesh Prasad	10	–	34	**–**
Kapoor	10	2	41	**2**

Fall of Wickets
1–**16**, 2–**24**, 3–**91**, 4–**99**, 5–**99**, 6–**141**, 7–**141**, 8–**149**, 9–**162**

India

A.D. Jadeja	**b** Ambrose	**1**
S.R. Tendulkar	run out	**70**
N.S. Sidhu	**b** Ambrose	**1**
M. Azharuddin (Capt)	**c** Walsh, **b** Harper	**32**
V.G. Kambli	not out	**33**
M. Prabhakar	**c** and **b** Harper	**1**
*N.R. Mongia	not out	**24**
A.R. Kumble		
J. Srinath		
Venkatesh Prasad		
A.R. Kapoor		
	lb **3**, w **1**, nb **8**	**12**
	39.4 overs (for 5 wickets)	**174**

	O	M	R	W
Ambrose	8	1	41	**2**
Walsh	9	3	18	**–**
Bishop	5	–	28	**–**
Gibson	8.4	–	50	**–**
Harper	9	1	34	**2**

Fall of Wickets
1–**2**, 2–**15**, 3–**94**, 4–**125**, 5–**127**

Umpires: Khizar Hayat & I.D. Robinson *Man of the Match:* S.R. Tendulkar

India won by 5 wickets

Match Five – Australia v. Kenya

23 February 1996 at Municipal Stadium, Vishakhapatnam

Australia

M.A. Taylor (Capt)	c Modi, b Suji	6
M.E. Waugh	c Suji, b Ali	130
R.T. Ponting	c Otieno, b Ali	6
S.R. Waugh	c and b Suji	82
S.G. Law	run out	35
M.G. Bevan	b Ali	12
*I.A. Healy	c E. Odumbe, Asif Karim	17
P.R. Reiffel	not out	3
S.K. Warne	not out	0
C.J. McDermott		
G.D. McGrath		
	b 1, w 10, nb 2	13
	50 overs (for 7 wickets)	304

	O	M	R	W
Suji	10	1	55	2
Ali	10	–	45	3
Odoyo	8	–	58	–
E. Odumbe	4	–	21	–
Asif Karim	10	1	54	1
M. Odumbe	4	–	35	–
D. Tikolo	3	–	21	–
S. Tikolo	1	–	14	–

Fall of Wickets
1–**10**, 2–**26**, 3–**233**, 4–**237**, 5–**261**, 6–**301**, 7–**301**

Kenya

*K. Otieno	b McGrath	85
D. Chudasama	c Healy, b McDermott	5
S. Tikolo	c Ponting, b Reiffel	6
M. Odumbe (Capt)	c Reiffel, b Bevan	50
H. Modi	b Bevan	10
E. Odumbe	c Bevan, b Reiffel	14
D. Tikolo	not out	11
T. Odoyo	st Healy, b Warne	10
M. Suji	not out	1
Asif Karim		
R. Ali		
	lb 7, w 6, nb 2	15
	50 overs (for 7 wickets)	207

	O	M	R	W
McDermott	3	–	12	1
Reiffel	7	1	18	2
McGrath	10	–	44	1
S.R. Waugh	7	–	43	–
Warne	10	–	25	1
M.E. Waugh	5	–	23	–
Bevan	8	–	35	2

Fall of Wickets
1–**12**, 2–**30**, 3–**132**, 4–**167**, 5–**188**, 6–**195**, 7–**206**

Umpires: D.R. Shepherd & C.J. Mitchley *Man of the Match:* M.E. Waugh

Australia won by 97 runs

Match Six – Zimbabwe v. Kenya

27 February 1996 at Nehru Stadium, Pune

Kenya

D. Chudasama	run out	34
Tariq Iqbal	b Lock	1
*K. Otieno	b Peall	19
S. Tikolo	st A. Flower, b B. Strang	0
M. Odumbe (Capt)	c B. Strang, b P.A. Strang	30
H. Modi	b B. Strang	3
E. Odumbe	c Campbell, b P.A. Strang	20
T. Odoyo	c G.W. Flower, b P.A. Strang	0
Asif Karim	lbw, b P.A. Strang	0
M. Suji	c G.W. Flower, b P.A. Strang	15
R. Ali	not out	0
	lb 3, w 8, nb 1	12
	49.4 overs	134

	O	M	R	W
Streak	7	2	23	–
Lock	8	2	19	1
Whittall	5	–	21	–
Peall	10	1	23	1
B. Strang	10	–	24	2
P.A. Strang	9.4	1	21	5

Fall of Wickets
1–**7**, 2–**60**, 3–**61**, 4–**63**, 5–**67**, 6–**109**, 7–**109**, 8–**109**, 9–**134**

Zimbabwe

A.C. Waller	c S. Tikolo, b M. Odumbe	30
G.W. Flower	b Ali	45
A.D.R. Campbell	c S. Tikolo, b M. Odumbe	6
G.J. Whittall	c E. Odumbe, b Ali	6
*A. Flower (Capt)	b Ali	5
C.N. Evans	not out	8
H.H. Streak	not out	15
P.A. Strang		
S.G. Peall		
B. Strang		
A.P.C. Lock		
	b 3, lb 4, w 12, nb 3	22
	42.2 overs (for 5 wickets)	137

	O	M	R	W
Suji	9.2	–	37	–
Ali	8	1	22	3
E. Odumbe	2	–	14	–
Odoyo	2	–	7	–
Asif Karim	10	1	21	–
M. Odumbe	10	2	24	2
S. Tikolo	1	–	5	–

Fall of Wickets
1–**59**, 2–**79**, 3–**104**, 4–**108**, 5–**113**

Umpires: Khizar Hayat & C.J. Mitchley *Man of the Match:* P.A. Strang

Zimbabwe won by 5 wickets

bowling three overs. His contribution to the World Cup was over. South Australia's Jason Gillespie was named as replacement, but he was not selected for any of the matches.

Otieno batted splendidly and had scored 82 from 126 balls when he was forced to retire with a violent attack of cramp. When he returned he added just three off 11 balls.

Zimbabwe *v.* Kenya

Kenya could be considered to have been rather unlucky in their match against Zimbabwe. The match was scheduled for 26 February, and Kenya had reduced Zimbabwe to 45 for 3 in 15.5 overs when rain caused an abandonment. When the match restarted the following day, Kenya were put in to bat, and, having reached 60 for 2 in the 22nd over, they fell apart. Towards the end of the innings, leg-spinner Paul Strang took three wickets in four balls, and Zimbabwe faced an easy target.

Waller and Grant Flower raced to 59 at nearly five an over, but the loss of three wickets for nine runs when victory was in sight caused some concern until Evans and Streak calmed nerves and won the match with 7.4 overs to spare.

India *v.* Australia

Mark Waugh became the first batsman to score successive centuries in the World Cup and once again he confirmed that he is a batsman to rank alongside Tendulkar and Lara as the best in the world at the present time. Languid in approach, powerful in execution, he is, on occasions, profligate, but, as with Denis Compton of another age, the sense of vulnerability is part of the beauty. He and Mark Taylor posted 103 in 22 overs without ever slogging or taking unnecessary risks. Australia did not quite build on this fine opening as they should have done. Ponting was breathtakingly caught backward at cover, and Steve Waugh was run out when Venkatapathy Raju deflected a drive onto the stumps. It was the left-arm spinner who halted Australia's advance, and he and Kumble bowled most intelligently.

Mark Waugh was finally run out as he attempted to take a second run to deep square-leg, but by then he had hit a majestic 126 off 135 balls with three sixes and eight fours. His dismissal created a fashion trend as Australia lost their last seven wickets for 26 runs. Four wickets went down to the last four balls of the innings as Venkatesh Prasad conceded just one run in the final over.

Fleming, taking the new ball in the absence of McDermott, quickly dismissed Jadeja and Kambli, but Tendulkar was soon thrilling the capacity crowd. He reached 50 off 41 balls, and, after Azharuddin had edged a ball into his stumps, he and Manjrekar scored 73 in 16 overs. Tendulkar was stumped off a wide off-break from Mark Waugh, and if there was disappointment in his going, one could only give thanks for once again having savoured greatness.

Match Seven – India *v.* Australia

27 February 1996 at Wankhede Stadium, Bombay

Australia

M.E. Waugh	run out	**126**
M.A. Taylor (Capt)	**c** Srinath, **b** Venkatapathy	**59**
R.T. Ponting	**c** Manjrekar, **b** Venkatapathy	**12**
S.R. Waugh	run out	**7**
S.G. Law	**c** and **b** Kumble	**21**
M.G. Bevan	run out	**6**
S. Lee	run out	**9**
*I.A. Healy	**c** Kumble, **b** Venkatesh Prasad	**6**
S.K. Warne	**c** Azharuddin, **b** Venkatesh	**0**
D.W. Fleming	run out	**0**
G.D. McGrath	not out	**0**
	lb **8**, w **2**, nb **2**	**12**
	50 overs	**258**

	O	M	R	W
Prabhakar	10	–	54	**–**
Srinath	10	1	51	**–**
Venkatesh Prasad	10	–	50	**2**
Kumble	10	1	47	**1**
Venkatapathy Raju	10	–	48	**2**

Fall of Wickets
1–**103**, 2–**140**, 3–**157**, 4–**232**, 5–**237**, 6–**244**, 7–**258**, 8–**258**, 9–**258**

India

A.D. Jadeja	lbw, **b** Fleming	**1**
S.R. Tendulkar	**st** Healy, **b** M.E. Waugh	**90**
V.G. Kambli	**b** Fleming	**0**
M. Azharuddin (Capt)	**b** Fleming	**10**
S.V. Manjrekar	**c** Healy, **b** S.R. Waugh	**62**
M. Prabhakar	run out	**3**
*N.R. Mongia	**c** Taylor, **b** Warne	**27**
A.R. Kumble	**b** Fleming	**17**
J. Srinath	**c** Lee, **b** Fleming	**7**
Venkatesh Prasad	**c** Bevan, **b** S.R. Waugh	**0**
Venkatapathy Raju	not out	**3**
	b **5**, lb **8**, w **8**, nb **1**	**22**
	48 overs	**242**

	O	M	R	W
McGrath	8	3	48	**–**
Fleming	9	–	36	**5**
Warne	10	1	28	**1**
Lee	3	–	23	**–**
M.E. Waugh	10	–	44	**1**
Bevan	5	–	28	**–**
S.R. Waugh	3	–	22	**2**

Fall of Wickets
1–**7**, 2–**7**, 3–**70**, 4–**143**, 5–**147**, 6–**201**, 7–**205**, 8–**224**, 9–**231**

Umpires: D.R. Shepherd & R.S. Dunne *Man of the Match:* M.E. Waugh

Australia won by 16 runs

Match Eight – West Indies *v.* Kenya

29 February 1996 at Nehru Stadium, Pune

Kenya

D. Chudasama	c Lara, b Walsh	8
Tariq Iqbal	c Cuffy, b Walsh	16
*K. Otieno	c Ambrose, b Walsh	2
S. Tikolo	c Adams, b Harper	29
M. Odumbe (Capt)	hit wkt, b Bishop	6
H. Modi	c Adams, b Ambrose	26
M. Suji	c Lara, b Harper	0
T. Odoyo	st Adams, b Harper	24
E. Odumbe	b Cuffy	1
Asif Karim	c Adams, b Ambrose	11
R. Ali	not out	6
	lb 8, w 16, nb 13	37
	49.3 overs	166

	O	M	R	W
Ambrose	8.3	3	21	2
Walsh	9	–	46	3
Bishop	10	2	30	1
Cuffy	8	–	31	1
Harper	10	4	15	3
Arthurton	4	–	15	–

Fall of Wickets
1–15, 2–19, 3–45, 4–72, 5–77, 6–81, 7–125, 8–126, 9–155

West Indies

S.C. Campbell	b Suji	4
R.B. Richardson (Capt)	b Ali	5
B.C. Lara	c Tariq Iqbal, b Ali	8
S. Chanderpaul	c S. Tikolo, b M. Odumbe	19
K.L.T. Arthurton	run out	0
*J.C. Adams	c Modi, b M. Odumbe	9
R.A. Harper	c Tariq Iqbal, b M. Odumbe	17
I.R. Bishop	not out	6
C.E.L. Ambrose	run out	3
C.A. Walsh	c Chudasama, b Asif Karim	4
C.E. Cuffy	b Ali	1
	b 5, lb 6, w 4, nb 2	17
	35.2 overs	93

	O	M	R	W
Suji	7	2	16	1
Ali	7.2	2	17	3
Asif Karim	8	1	19	1
M. Odumbe	10	3	15	3
Odoyo	3	–	15	–

Fall of Wickets
1–18, 2–22, 3–33, 4–35, 5–56, 6–65, 7–78, 8–81, 9–89

Umpires: V.K. Ramaswamy & Khizar Hayat *Man of the Match:* M. Odumbe

Kenya won by 73 runs

Mark Waugh during his innings of 126 for Australia against India. Mongia is the wicket-keeper. Waugh hit three centuries during the competition to establish a new World Cup Final record. *(Shaun Botterill/Allsport)*

Mongia now gave hope that he and Manjrekar might steal the game for India, but Warne, having conceded ten in an unlucky first over, was now bowling in masterly fashion and had Mongia caught off a perfect leg-break. Outstanding out-cricket, shrewd captaincy, the accuracy of Steve Waugh and the aggression of Fleming were too much for the rest of the Indian batting, and a high-quality match ended in Australia's favour.

West Indies *v.* Kenya

The World Cup had been punctuated by some fine cricket and some quality matches, but until Kenya met West Indies it had provided no surprises. That changed in Pune. Put in to bat, Kenya lost half their wickets for 77 although West Indies did not bowl particularly well. Ambrose was hit for two fours in his first over while Walsh was hit for six by Steve Tikolo. Even so, West Indies, having gone through the motions in a desultory manner, dismissed Kenya for 166, thanks mainly to Harper.

If West Indies out-cricket was poor and sullen, their batting was a disgrace. In a spineless display, they were bowled out by a team of club cricketers whose honesty, effort, enthusiasm and transparent love of the game shamed

Andy Flower, the Zimbabwe captain, is stumped by Ian Healy off Shane Warne as his side crash to defeat against Australia. (Shaun Botterill/Allsport)

their mighty opponents. Led with passion and intelligence by Maurice Odumbe, Kenya bowled out West Indies for 93 as only Harper and Chanderpaul reached double figures, and both fell victim to the Kenyan captain who bowled his off-spinners with economy and purpose. By the time Odumbe destroyed the middle order, Lara was already back in the pavilion, having waved his bat once too often at Rajab Ali. Richardson apart, West Indies do not lose graciously.

Zimbabwe *v.* Australia

Australia moved comfortably into the quarter-finals with the easiest of wins over Zimbabwe, for Paul Strang once again bowled impressively. Andy Waller, who had joined the Zimbabwe party when Houghton was injured, played an excellent innings, hitting ten fours in his 67 off 101 balls. The rest were rather bemused by Shane Warne who turned his leg-breaks spitefully and experimented intelligently as befits a master craftsman.

Having hit centuries in his first two matches, Mark Waugh had to be content with 76 not out as Australia rattled off the required runs with 14 overs to spare.

India *v.* Sri Lanka

With disarming ease, Sri Lanka reached a challenging target with eight balls and six wickets to spare, silenced a large, partisan crowd and caused many to re-think their ideas as to who was the most accomplished side in the competition.

At the start of the day all had gone as the home crowd had expected. Tendulkar had hit his second century, another glorious innings which included five sixes, and he and Azharuddin scored a record 175 for the third wicket. India seemed secure in a total of 271, but this sense of security was shattered as soon as Sri Lanka began their innings. Jayasuriya hit 22 – four fours and a six – off Prabhakar's second over. This violent attack established the tone, and 82 runs came from the first ten overs while the hundred went up in the 14th.

Jayasuriya eased pressure on later batsmen, and when he was caught at long-on he had hit 79 off 76 balls. There were wickets in Kumble's next two overs as well, but, apart from the leg-spinner and some tidy overs of off-spin from Tendulkar, the rest of the Indian attack was savagely treated. Prabhakar returned to bowl two overs of off-spin, but Ranatunga blasted him out of the attack, and out of the Indian team. An unbroken stand of 131 between Tillekeratne and the Sri Lankan captain mocked the target that had been set and virtually ensured Sri Lanka of top place in Group A.

Match Nine – Zimbabwe v. Australia

1 March 1996 at Vidarbha C.A. Ground, Negpur

Zimbabwe

A.C. Waller	run out	67
G.W. Flower	**b** McGrath	4
G.J. Whittall	**c** and **b** S.R. Waugh	6
A.D.R. Campbell	**c** M.E. Waugh, **b** S.R. Waugh	5
*A. Flower (Capt)	**st** Healy, **b** Warne	7
C.N. Evans	**c** Healy, **b** Warne	18
H.H. Streak	**c** S.R. Waugh, **b** Fleming	13
P.A. Strang	not out	16
B. Strang	**b** Fleming	0
S.G. Peall	**c** Healy, **b** Warne	0
A.P.C. Lock	**b** Warne	5
	lb **8**, w **3**, nb **2**	13
	45.3 overs	154

	O	M	R	W
McGrath	8	2	12	1
Fleming	9	1	30	2
Lee	4	2	8	–
S.R. Waugh	7	2	22	2
Warne	9.3	1	34	4
M.E. Waugh	5	–	30	–
Law	3	–	10	–

Fall of Wickets
1–**21**, 2–**41**, 3–**55**, 4–**68**, 5–**106**, 6–**126**, 7–**140**, 8–**140**, 9–**145**

Australia

M.A. Taylor (Capt)	**c** B. Strang, **b** P.A. Strang	34
M.E. Waugh	not out	76
R.T. Ponting	**c** and **b** P.A. Strang	33
S.R. Waugh	not out	5
S.G. Law		
M.G. Bevan		
S. Lee		
*I.A. Healy		
S.K. Warne		
D.W. Fleming		
G.D. McGrath		
	b **6**, lb **2**, w **1**, nb **1**	10
	36 overs (for 2 wickets)	158

	O	M	R	W
Streak	10	3	29	–
Lock	4	–	25	–
B. Strang	3	–	20	–
Whittall	2	–	11	–
P.A. Strang	10	3	33	2
Peall	4	–	20	–
G.W. Flower	3	–	12	–

Fall of Wickets
1–**92**, 2–**150**

Umpires: R.S. Dunne & D.R. Shepherd *Man of the Match:* S.K. Warne

Australia won by 8 wickets

Match Ten – India v. Sri Lanka

2 March 1996 at Ferozeshah Kotla Stadium, Delhi

India

M. Prabhakar	**c** Gurusinha, **b** Pushpakumara	7
S.R. Tendulkar	run out	137
S.V. Manjrekar	**c** Kaluwitharana, **b** Dharmasena	32
M. Azharuddin (Capt)	not out	72
V.G. Kambli	not out	1
A.D. Jadeja		
*N.R. Mongia		
A.R. Kumble		
J. Srinath		
S.A. Ankola		
Venkatesh Prasad		
	b **4**, lb **7**, w **11**	22
	50 overs (for 3 wickets)	271

	O	M	R	W
Vaas	9	3	37	–
Pushpakumara	8	–	53	1
Muralitharan	10	1	42	–
Dharmasena	0	–	53	1
Jayasuriya	10	–	52	–
Ranatunga	4	–	23	–

Fall of Wickets
1–**27**, 2–**93**, 3–**268**

Sri Lanka

S.T. Jayasuriya	**c** Prabhakar, **b** Kumble	79
*R.S. Kaluwitharana	**c** Kumble, **b** Venkatesh Prasad	26
A.P. Gurusinha	run out	25
P.A. de Silva	**st** Mongia, **b** Kumble	8
A. Ranatunga (Capt)	not out	46
H.P. Tillekeratne	not out	70
R.S. Mahanama		
H.D.P.K. Dharmasena		
W.P.U.J.C. Vaas		
K.R. Pushpakumara		
M. Muralitharan		
	b **4**, lb **9**, w **3**, nb **2**	18
	48.4 overs (for 4 wickets)	272

	O	M	R	W
Prabhakar	4	–	47	–
Srinath	9.4	–	51	–
Venkatesh Prasad	10	1	53	1
Ankola	5	–	28	–
Kumble	10	1	39	2
Tendulkar	10	–	41	–

Fall of Wickets
1–**53**, 2–**129**, 3–**137**, 4–**141**

Umpires: C.J. Mitchley & I.D. Robinson *Man of the Match:* S.T. Jayasuriya

Sri Lanka won by 6 wickets

Match Eleven – Australia *v.* West Indies

4 March 1996 at Sawai Mansingh Stadium, Jaipur

Australia

M.E. Waugh	**st** Browne, **b** Harper	30
M.A. Taylor (Capt)	**c** Browne, **b** Walsh	9
R.T. Ponting	run out	102
S.R. Waugh	**b** Walsh	57
M.G. Bevan	run out	2
S.G. Law	not out	12
*I.A. Healy	run out	3
P.R. Reiffel	not out	4
S.K. Warne		
D.W. Fleming		
G.D. McGrath		
	lb **3**, w **6**, nb **1**	10
	50 overs (for 6 wickets)	229

	O	M	R	W
Ambrose	10	4	25	–
Walsh	9	2	35	2
Bishop	9	–	52	2
Harper	10	–	46	1
Arthurton	9	–	53	–
Adams	3	–	15	–

Fall of Wickets
1–**22**, 2–**84**, 3–**194**, 4–**200**, 5–**216**, 6–**224**

West Indies

S.L. Campbell	**c** Healy, **b** Fleming	1
*C.O. Browne	run out	10
B.C. Lara	**c** McGrath, **b** M.E. Waugh	60
R.B. Richardson (Capt)	not out	93
S. Chanderpaul	M.E. Waugh	10
R.A. Harper	lbw, **b** Reiffel	22
K.L.T. Arthurton	lbw, **b** M.E. Waugh	0
J.C. Adams	not out	17
I.R. Bishop		
C.E.L. Ambrose		
C.A. Walsh		
	lb **12**, w **5**, nb **2**	19
	48.5 overs (for 6 wickets)	232

	O	M	R	W
Reiffel	10	3	45	1
Fleming	7.5	1	44	1
McGrath	9	–	46	–
Warne	10	1	30	–
M.E. Waugh	10	1	38	3
Bevan	2	–	17	–

Fall of Wickets
1–**1**, 2–**26**, 3–**113**, 4–**146**, 5–**194**, 6–**196**

Umpires: Mahboob Shah & D.R. Shepherd *Man of the Match:* R.B. Richardson

West Indies won by 4 wickets

Australia *v.* West Indies

In the wake of West Indies' defeat at the hands of Kenya, Richie Richardson was to announce his retirement from international cicket and the West Indian Board were to replace both coach and manager, but, temporarily at least, some pride was restored and elimination from the World Cup averted when the sick giant of cricket beat Australia. Ambrose and Walsh, regaining self-discipline after the dreadful showing against Kenya, bowled tightly and restricted Australia in the opening stage. Although Mark Waugh 'failed' by the standards he had set himself in the competition, he defended solidly in a difficult period and helped provide a platform from which Ponting and Steve Waugh made 110 in 19 overs. It had taken Australia 22 overs to score a hundred and so this third wicket partnership gave necessary momentum to the innings. Steve Waugh's 57 came off 64 balls, but the real delight came from Ricky Ponting whose 102 off 111 balls was studded with beautiful shots to all parts of the ground.

With the pitch playing unevenly, Australia's 229 seemed a match-winning score, a view reinforced when Campbell and Browne were out with 26 scored. Lara made a rapid 60, but the real hero of West Indies' victory was Richie Richardson who batted faultlessly for his 93 and steered his side through mid-innings nerves. He is a man who has deserved better than the treatment he has received.

Ricky Ponting, the young Australian batsman, scored a brilliant century against West Indies, but still finished on the losing side. (Shaun Botterill/Allsport)

Match Twelve – Sri Lanka v. Kenya

6 March 1996 at Asgirya Stadium, Kandy

Sri Lanka

S.T. Jayasuriya	c D. Tikolo, b E. Odumbe	44
*R.S. Kaluwitharana	b E. Odumbe	33
A.P. Gurusinha	c Onayango, b Asif Karim	84
P.A. de Silva	c Modi, b Suji	145
A. Ranatunga (Capt)	not out	75
H.P. Tillekeratne	run out	0
R.S. Mahanama	not out	0
W.P.U.J.C. Vaas		
H.D.P.K. Dharmasena		
K.R. Pushpakumara		
M. Muralitharan		
	b 1, lb 5, w 11	17
	50 overs (for 5 wickets)	398

	O	M	R	W
Ali	6	–	67	–
Suji	9	–	85	1
Onayango	4	–	31	–
E. Odumbe	5	–	34	2
Asif Karim	10	–	50	1
D. Tikolo	2	–	13	–
M. Odumbe	9	–	74	–
S. Tikolo	5	–	38	–

Fall of Wickets
1–**83**, 2–**88**, 3–**271**, 4–**377**, 5–**383**

Kenya

D. Chudasama	b Muralitharan	27
*K. Otieno	b Vaas	14
S. Tikolo	b Dharmasena	96
M. Odumbe (Capt)	c Kaluwitharana, b Muralitharan	0
H. Modi	run out	41
D. Tikolo	not out	25
E Odumbe	c Muralitharan, b Ranatunga	4
L. Onayango	c sub, b Ranatunga	23
M. Suji	not out	2
Asif Karim		
R. Ali		
	b 1, lb 9, w 7, nb 5	22
	50 overs (for 7 wickets)	254

	O	M	R	W
Vaas	10	–	44	1
Muralitharan	10	1	40	2
Pushpakumara	7	–	46	–
Ranatunga	5	–	31	2
Dharmasena	10	–	45	1
Jayasuriya	7	–	34	–
Tillekeratne	1	–	4	–

Fall of Wickets
1–**47**, 2–**51**, 3–**51**, 4–**188**, 5–**196**, 6–**215**, 7–**246**

Umpires: R.S. Dunne & V.K. Ramaswamy *Man of the Match:* P.A. de Silva

Sri Lanka won by 144 runs

Match Thirteen – India v. Zimbabwe

6 March 1996 at Green Park, Kanpur

India

S.R. Tendulkar	b Streak	3
N.S. Sidhu	c Streak, b P.A. Strang	80
S.V. Manjrekar	c Campbell, b Lock	2
M. Azharuddin (Capt)	c Campbell, b B. Strang	2
V.G. Kambli	c G.W. Flower, b Lock	106
A.D. Jadeja	not out	44
*N.R. Mongia	not out	6
A.R. Kumble		
J. Srinath		
Venkatesh Prasad		
Venkatapathy Raju		
	lb 1, w 3	4
	50 overs (for 5 wickets)	247

	O	M	R	W
Streak	10	3	29	1
Lock	10	1	57	2
B. Strang	5	1	22	1
P.A. Strang	10	–	55	1
Peall	6	–	35	–
Whittall	3	–	19	–
G.W. Flower	3	–	16	–
Campbell	3	–	13	–

Fall of Wickets
1–**5**, 2–**25**, 3–**32**, 4–**174**, 5–**219**

Zimbabwe

A.C. Waller	c Tendulkar, b Kumble	22
G.W. Flower	c Azharuddin, b V. Raju	30
G.J. Whittall	run out	10
A.D.R. Campbell	c and b Jadeja	28
*A. Flower (Capt)	b Venkatapathy Raju	26
C.N. Evans	c Srinath, b Jadeja	6
H.H. Streak	lbw, b Venkatapathy Raju	30
P.A. Strang	b Srinath	14
B. Strang	lbw, b Srinath	3
S.G. Peall	c Venkatapathy Raju, b Kumble	9
A.P.C. Lock	not out	2
	b 4, lb 11, w 11, nb 1	27
	49.4 overs	207

	O	M	R	W
Srinath	10	1	36	2
Venkatesh Prasad	7	–	40	–
Kumble	9.4	1	32	2
Venkatapathy Raju	10	2	30	3
Tendulkar	6	–	23	–
Jadeja	7	–	31	2

Fall of Wickets
1–**59**, 2–**59**, 3–**96**, 4–**99**, 5–**106**, 6–**168**, 7–**173**, 8–**193**, 9–**195**

Umpires: S.A. Bucknor & C.J. Mitchley *Man of the Match:* A.D. Jadeja

India won by 40 runs

Leading from the front, Richie Richardson hit 93 not out to take West Indies to victory over Australia. Following the defeat at the hands of Kenya, West Indies needed to win this match to restore pride and to gain a place in the last eight. (Shaun Botterill/ Allsport)

Sri Lanka *v.* Kenya

If there were those who still harboured doubts as to the quality of Sri Lankan cricket, they were given further proof of that quality as Sri Lanka made the highest score ever attained in a one-day international. A capacity crowd of 20,000 saw them demolish the attack that had bowled out West Indies for 93. Jayasuriya and Kaluwitharana set the tempo with an opening stand of 83 off 39 balls, heady stuff, and this was followed by Aravinda de Silva becoming the first Sri Lankan to hit a century in the World Cup. His 145 included five sixes and 14 fours. Ranatunga contributed to the carnage.

To their credit, Kenya, who won many friends in the tournament, gave a spirited account of themselves when they batted, and Steve Tikolo gave more evidence of his ability with an innings of vigour. The aggregate match total of 652 for 12 wickets established another World Cup record.

India *v.* Zimbabwe

Zimbabwe sent shivers throughout the whole of India when, having asked the home country to bat first, they reduced them to 32 for 3 by the beginning of the 13th over. Streak bowled Tendulkar middle and off stump with a ball that came back sharply, and Manjrekar and Azharuddin both drove too early and were well caught. Zimbabwe now threw away a golden opportunity. Their bowling lost its edge, and chances were fumbled. Kambli enjoyed a charmed life on his way to a 110-ball century, and it was personal gratification for him after a poor start to the tournament. Sidhu played well, accumulating runs steadily, and Jadeja added the necessary panache towards the end of the innings.

A target of 248 was by no means impossible for Zimbabwe who batted with consistency, reached 50 off ten overs, but stuttered too often and could not find the man to play the substantial aggressive innings that could have turned the match. They left for home conscious that they had not done themselves justice in the tournament. India were set for the quarter-final against Pakistan.

Section A – Final Table

	P	W	L	Pts	R/R
Sri Lanka	5	5	–	10	1.64
Australia	5	3	2	6	0.88
India	5	3	2	6	0.47
West Indies	5	2	3	4	-0.12
Zimbabwe	5	1	4	2	-0.95
Kenya	5	1	4	2	-1.03

Australia and West Indies conceded their matches against Sri Lanka.

Section B

The four 'seeded' teams qualify, but the paucity of England's cricket is cruelly exposed, and South Africa show good organisation and a sense of purpose.

England v. New Zealand

An England side that had been ill-chosen and ill-prepared lost to lowly New Zealand in their opening match. Robin Smith was unfit to play, and there were doubts as to whether or not he would regain fitness before the qualifying round of the competition. New Zealand had had doubts about the pitch, which seemed damp, but these doubts disappeared once they had been put in. They were aided considerably by some wretched England fielding. Four catches were dropped, the most costly of them being when Thorpe put down Astle at slip when the batsman had scored one. Astle went on to record his third one-day hundred in recent months, hitting two sixes and eight fours in his 132-ball innings. He and Fleming added 96 in 19 overs of fluent batting. Fleming, dropped by Atherton, was caught sweeping at Hick, and Twose followed in the same manner. Cairns batted with considerable verve. He hit a six and four fours before clubbing Illingworth to point after facing 30 balls. Disappointingly, the last ten overs realised only 43 runs as three wickets fell, and the most enterprising play came from Lee Germon who pushed and ran intelligently.

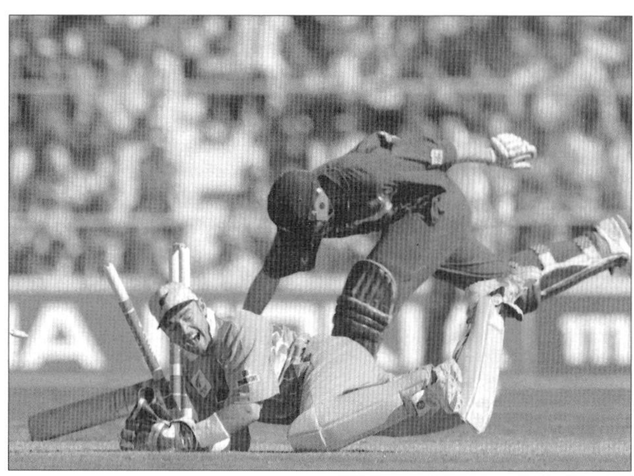

Mike Atherton, acting as runner for Graeme Hick, is run out by New Zealand skipper Lee Germon. Hick had made 85 at the time, and his dismissal signalled the collapse and defeat of England. (Ross Kinnaird/Allsport)

England lost Atherton in the second over, yorked by Nash, but Stewart and Hick suggested brisk assurance as they scored 99 for the second wicket. Stewart drove too early at the accurate Harris, and Thorpe was lost against Larsen and all else. The accuracy of Harris and Larsen began to tell on the England batsmen who went 13 overs without hitting a boundary. Hick was in fine form, but a hamstring injury forced him to use Atherton as a runner.

Match One – England v. New Zealand

14 February 1996 at Gujarat Stadium, Motera, Ahmedabad

New Zealand

Batsman	Dismissal	Runs
C.M. Spearman	c and **b** Cork	**5**
N.J. Astle	**c** Hick, **b** Martin	**101**
S.P. Fleming	**c** Thorpe, **b** Hick	**28**
R.G. Twose	**c** Thorpe, **b** Hick	**17**
C.L. Cairns	**c** Cork, **b** Illingworth	**36**
C.Z. Harris	run out	**10**
S.A. Thomson	not out	**17**
*L.K. Germon (Capt)	not out	**13**
D.J. Nash		
G.R. Larsen		
D.K. Morrison		
	b **4**, lb **2**, w **4**, nb **2**	**12**
	50 overs (for 6 wickets)	**239**

Bowler	O	M	R	W
Cork	10	1	36	**1**
Martin	6	–	37	**1**
Gough	10	–	63	**–**
Illingworth	10	1	31	**1**
Hick	9	–	45	**2**
White	5	–	21	**–**

Fall of Wickets
1–**12**, 2–**108**, 3–**131**, 4–**196**, 5–**204**, 6–**212**

England

Batsman	Dismissal	Runs
M.A. Atherton (Capt)	**b** Nash	**1**
A.J. Stewart	**c** and **b** Harris	**34**
G.A. Hick	run out	**85**
G.P. Thorpe	**b** Larsen	**9**
N.H. Fairbrother	**b** Morrison	**36**
*R.C. Russell	**c** Morrison, **b** Larsen	**2**
C. White	**c** Cairns, **b** Thomson	**13**
D.G. Cork	**c** Germon, **b** Nash	**19**
D. Gough	not out	**15**
P.J. Martin	**c** Cairns, **b** Nash	**3**
R.K. Illingworth	not out	**3**
	b **1**, lb **4**, w **1**, nb **2**	**8**
	50 overs (for 9 wickets)	**228**

Bowler	O	M	R	W
Morrison	8	–	38	**1**
Nash	7	1	26	**3**
Cairns	4	–	24	**–**
Larsen	10	1	33	**2**
Thomson	10	–	51	**1**
Harris	9	–	45	**1**
Astle	2	–	6	**–**

FALL OF WICKETS
1–**1**, 2–**100**, 3–**123**, 4–**144**, 5–**151**, 6–**180**, 7–**185**, 8–**210**, 9–**222**

Umpires: S.G. Randell & B.C. Cooray *Man of the Match:* N.J. Astle

New Zealand won by 11 runs

Fairbrother drove to cover, and both he and Atherton hesitated fatally. Twose dived, stopped the ball and returned quickly and accurately to leave Atherton short of his ground.

From that point on, England floundered against tight bowling, good fielding and astute captaincy, and New Zealand were always a length in front.

South Africa v. United Arab Emirates

The pairing of South Africa and United Arab Emirates was a no-contest. Gary Kirsten passed Viv Richards' previous World Cup record of 181 to reach 188 not out off 159 balls, hitting four sixes and 13 fours in the process. His third fifty came off only 29 balls, and he offered only one chance, on 118. The steadiest and by far the best of the UAE bowlers was the medium-paced Samarasekera who forced Hudson to play on.

The UAE batting looked marginally better than their bowling, but it was still scarcely club standard.

New Zealand v. Holland

Qualification for the World Cup Finals realised an ambition for Steve Lubbers, the 43-year old Dutch captain who has worked hard over the years to encourage cricket in his country. He had some gratification as his off-spin brought three wickets in Holland's first match in

Gary Kirsten established a new World Cup record with his innings of 188 not out against United Arab Emirates. He pulls a ball to the boundary as wicket-keeper Imtiaz Abbasi looks on. (Graham Chadwick/Allsport)

the tournament, but the game belonged totally to New Zealand. In spite of the early loss of Astle who responded hesitantly to Spearman's call, New Zealand scored briskly, 100 arriving in 16 overs. The middle-order sustained this brisk rate, and the 200 came up in the 36th over. Cairns hit 52 off 38 balls, with two sixes and four

Match Two – South Africa v. United Arab Emirates

16 February 1996 at Pindi Cricket Stadium, Rawalpindi

South Africa

Batsman	Dismissal	Runs
A.C. Hudson	**b** Samarasekera	27
G. Kirsten	not out	188
W.J. Cronje (Capt)	**st** Imtiaz Abbasi, **b** Zarawani	57
D.J. Cullinan	not out	41
J.H. Kallis		
J.N. Rhodes		
B.M. McMillan		
S.M. Pollock		
*S.J. Palframan		
C.R. Matthews		
A.A. Donald		
	b **1**, lb **1**, w **3**, nb **3**	8
	50 overs (for 2 wickets)	321

	O	M	R	W
Samarasekera	9	2	39	1
Shahzad Altaf	3	–	22	–
Arshad Laiq	6	–	52	–
Dukanwala	10	–	64	–
Azhar Saeed	7	–	41	–
Sultan Zarawani	10	–	69	1
Mazhar Hussain	5	–	32	–

Fall of Wickets
1–**60**, 2–**176**

United Arab Emirates

Batsman	Dismissal	Runs
Azhar Saeed	**c** McMillan, **b** Pollock	11
G. Mylvaganam	**c** Palframan, **b** Donald	23
Mazhar Hussain	**b** Donald	14
V. Mehra	run out	2
Mohammad Aslam	**b** McMillan	9
Arshad Laiq	not out	43
J.A. Samarasekera	**c** Hudson, **b** Donald	4
Sultan Zarawani (Capt)	**c** Cronje, **b** McMillan	0
*Imtiaz Abbasi	**c** Palframan, **b** McMillan	1
S. Dukanwala	not out	40
Shahzad Altaf		
	w **3**, nb **2**	5
	50 overs (for 8 wickets)	152

	O	M	R	W
Pollock	9	2	28	1
Matthews	10	–	39	–
Donald	10	–	21	3
Cronje	4	–	17	–
McMillan	8	1	11	3
Kallis	6	–	27	–
Kirsten	3	–	9	–

Fall of Wickets
1–**24**, 2–**42**, 3–**46**, 4–**60**, 5–**62**, 6–**68**, 7–**70**, 8–**82**

Umpires: S.A. Bucknor & V.K. Ramaswamy *Man of the Match:* G. Kirsten

South Africa won by 169 runs

Match Three – New Zealand v. Holland

17 February 1996 at IPCL Sports Complex, Baroda

New Zealand

C.M. Spearman	c Zuiderent, b Lubbers	68
N.J. Astle	run out	0
S.P. Fleming	c Zuiderent, b Lubbers	66
R.G. Twose	st Schewe, b Lubbers	25
C.L. Cairns	b Cantrell	52
A.C. Parore	c Clarke, b Aponso	55
C.Z. Harris	c Schewe, b Bakker	8
*L.K. Germon (Capt)	not out	14
D.N. Patel	c Schewe, b Bakker	11
D.K. Morrison	not out	0
R.J. Kennedy		
	lb 7, w 1	8
	50 overs (for 8 wickets)	307

	O	M	R	W
Lefebvre	10	–	47	–
Bakker	10	–	51	2
de Leede	7	–	58	–
Aponso	10	–	61	1
Lubbers	9	–	48	3
Cantrell	4	–	35	1

Fall of Wickets
1–1, 2–119, 3–155, 4–165, 5–253, 6–279, 7–292, 8–306

Holland

N.E. Clarke	b Kennedy	14
P.E. Cantrell	c Astle, b Harris	45
F. Aponso	c Astle, b Harris	11
S.W. Lubbers (Capt)	run out	5
R.P. Lefebvre	b Kennedy	45
T.B.M. de Leede	lbw, b Harris	1
K.J. van Noortwijk	not out	36
*M. Schewe	st Germon, b Fleming	12
B. Zuiderent	not out	1
E. Gouka		
P-J. Bakker		
	b 3, lb 5, w 8, nb 2	18
	50 overs (for 7 wickets)	188

	O	M	R	W
Morrison	4	1	11	–
Kennedy	10	2	36	2
Cairns	7	1	24	–
Harris	10	1	24	3
Patel	10	–	43	–
Astle	5	–	20	–
Fleming	2	–	8	1
Twose	2	–	14	–

Fall of Wickets
1–18, 2–52, 3–66, 4–100, 5–102, 6–147, 7–181

Umpires: Khizar Hayat & I.D. Robinson *Man of the Match:* C.M. Spearman

New Zealand won by 119 runs

fours, and Parore hit three sixes in an attractively belligerent innings. Before a crowd of 20,000, the Dutch did not wilt in the field and earned praise, but New Zealand's big total, their second highest in limited-over internationals, was well beyond their reach. New Zealand bowled tidily. Cantrell, once of Queensland, Lefebvre, of Glamorgan, and van Noortwijk, who had caught the eye in the Hong Kong 'sixes', all batted comfortably, but the result was as expected.

An inspiring captain, Hansie Cronje of South Africa hit 78 as his side crushed New Zealand. Rival skipper Lee Germon is the wicket-keeper. (Graham Chadwick/Allsport)

United Arab Emirates v. England

With DeFreitas providing a good opening spell and Neil Smith bowling tightly, England beat UAE with expected ease, but not without cost. Craig White retired from the fray after bowling nine balls, his side injury ending his part in the competition, and Dermot Reeve was summoned as replacement. While one had sympathy for White it was difficult to comprehend why he had been selected in the first place.

Smith followed his good spell of off-spin with four fours in his 27 off 31 balls. His innings ended when he was sick on the pitch, but he rightly took the individual award in a match which meant and proved little.

New Zealand v. South Africa

Few sides were hit as hard as South Africa on the eve of the World Cup. The loss of Richardson, ever present since his country's return to the international scene and a most accomplished wicket-keeper batsman, was a grievous blow. However, true to character, South Africa shrugged off the loss and pursued their disciplined and organised approach to the tournament. Their professionalism was apparent in the victory over New Zealand who, in contrast, gave a rather amateurish performance. Three run outs gave some testimony to this, although it must be conceded that Harris

Match Four – United Arab Emirates v. England

18 February 1996 at Arbab Niaz Stadium, Peshawar

United Arab Emirates

Azhar Saeed	lbw, **b** DeFreitas	**9**
G. Mylvaganam	**c** Fairbrother, **b** DeFreitas	**0**
Mazhar Hussain	**c** N.M.K. Smith	**33**
V. Mehra	**c** Russell, **b** N.M.K. Smith	**1**
Mohammad Aslam	**b** Gough	**23**
Arshad Laiq	**b** N.M.K. Smith	**0**
Salim Raza	**b** Cork	**10**
J.A. Samarasekera	run out	**29**
Sultan Zarawani (Capt)	**b** Cork	**2**
S. Dukanwala	lbw, **b** Ilingworth	**15**
*Imtiaz Abbasi	not out	**1**
	b **4**, lb **4**, w **4**, nb **1**	**13**
	48.3 overs	**136**

	O	M	R	W
Cork	10	1	33	**2**
DeFreitas	9.3	3	16	**2**
Gough	8	3	23	**1**
White	1.3	1	2	**–**
N.M.K. Smith	9.3	2	29	**3**
Illingworth	10	2	25	**1**

Fall of Wickets
1–**3**, 2–**32**, 3–**48**, 4–**49**, 5–**49**, 6–**80**, 7–**88**, 8–**100**, 9–**135**

England

A.J. Stewart	**c** Mylvaganam, **b** Arshad Laiq	**23**
N.M.K. Smith	retired ill	**27**
G.P. Thorpe	not out	**44**
M.A. Atherton (Capt)	**b** Azhar Saeed	**20**
N.H. Fairbrother	not out	**12**
*R.C. Russell		
C. White		
D.G. Cork		
P.A.J. DeFreitas		
D. Gough		
R.K. Illingworth		
	b **4**, lb **2**, w **2**, nb **6**	**14**
	35 overs (for 2 wickets)	**140**

	O	M	R	W
Samarasekera	7	1	35	**–**
Arshed Laiq	7	–	25	**1**
Salim Raza	5	1	20	**–**
Azhar Saeed	10	1	26	**1**
Zarawani	6	–	28	**–**

Fall of Wickets
1–**52**, 2–**109**

Umpires: V.K. Ramaswamy & B.C. Cooray *Man of the Match:* N.M.K. Smith

England won by 8 wickets

Match Five – New Zealand v. South Africa

20 February 1996 at Iqbal Stadium, Faisalabad

New Zealand

C.M. Spearman	**c** Palframan, **b** Matthews	**14**
N.J. Astle	run out	**1**
S.P. Fleming	**b** McMillan	**33**
R.G. Twose	**c** McMillan, **b** Pollock	**13**
C.L. Cairns	**b** Donald	**9**
A.C. Parore	run out	**27**
C.Z. Harris	run out	**8**
S.A. Thomson	**c** Cronje, **b** Donald	**28**
*L.K. Germon (Capt)	not out	**31**
G.R. Larsen	**c** Cullinan, **b** Donald	**1**
D.K. Morrison	not out	**5**
	lb **5**, nb **2**	**7**
	50 overs (for 9 wickets)	**177**

	O	M	R	W
Pollock	10	1	44	**1**
Matthews	10	2	30	**1**
Donald	10	–	34	**3**
Cronje	3	–	13	**–**
Symcox	10	1	25	**–**
McMillan	7	1	26	**1**

Fall of Wickets
1–**7**, 2–**17**, 3–**36**, 4–**54**, 5–**85**, 6–**103**, 7–**116**, 8–**158**, 9–**165**

South Africa

G. Kirsten	lbw, **b** Harris	**35**
*S.J. Palframan	**b** Morrison	**16**
W.J. Cronje (Capt)	**c** Fleming, **b** Astle	**78**
D.J. Cullinan	**c** Thomson, **b** Astle	**27**
J.H. Kallis	not out	**11**
J.N. Rhodes	**c** and **b** Larsen	**9**
B.M. McMillan	not out	**2**
S.M. Pollock		
C.R. Matthews		
P.L. Symcox		
A.A. Donald		
		0
	37.3 overs (for 5 wickets)	**178**

	O	M	R	W
Morrison	8	–	44	**1**
Cairns	6	–	24	**–**
Larsen	8	1	41	**1**
Harris	4	–	25	**1**
Thomson	8.3	–	34	**–**
Astle	3	1	10	**2**

Fall of Wickets
1–**41**, 2–**87**, 3–**146**, 4–**159**, 5–**170**

Umpires: S.G. Randell & S. Venkataraghavan *Man of the Match:* W.J. Cronje

South Africa won by 5 wickets

and Parore were victims of brilliant fielding, which is a strength of the South African side. New Zealand pushed for runs when steadiness would have served them better, and a late revival was cut short by the pace of Donald. Skipper Germon alone showed the blend of aggression, intelligence and application that was needed.

Where South Africa had provided stunning catches and breathtaking fielding, New Zealand missed three chances in the first eight overs. This gave Steve Palframan, an experimental opener, and Gary Kirsten the opportunity to give their side a rollicking start. Cronje responded to this encouragement by reaching 50 off 36 balls and bludgeoning 78 off 64 balls with three sixes and 11 fours. He battered the usually controlled and accurate Larsen out of the attack, and South Africa won with 63 balls to spare.

England v. Holland

By beating Holland, England virtually assured themselves of a place in the quarter-finals, but it was a victory that lacked conviction. Neil Smith again batted competently at the start of England's innings, but Stewart and Atherton gave more cause for anxiety with their total lack of form. Stewart was beaten several times by the portly veteran Bakker before he was bowled, and Atherton suffered a similar fate against Lubbers. The substance of the England innings came from a third wicket stand of 143 between Hick

Dutch batsmen Zuiderent (white helmet) and van Noortwijk gave England many alarms in their stand of 114 in the match in Peshawar. (Ross Kinnaird/Allsport)

Match Six – England v. Holland

22 February 1996 at Arbab Niaz Stadium, Peshawar

England

A.J. Stewart	**b** Bakker	**5**
N.M.K. Smith	**c** Clark, **b** Jansen	**31**
G.A. Hick	not out	**104**
G.P. Thorpe	lbw, **b** Lefebvre	**89**
M.A. Atherton (Capt)	**b** Lubbers	**10**
N.H. Fairbrother	not out	**24**
*R.C. Russell		
D.G. Cork		
D. Gough		
P.A.J. DeFreitas		
P.J. Martin		
	lb **12**, w **4**	**16**
	50 overs (for 4 wickets)	**279**

	O	M	R	W
Lefebvre	10	1	40	**1**
Bakker	8	–	46	**1**
Jansen	7	–	40	**1**
Aponso	8	–	55	**–**
Lubbers	10	–	51	**1**
de Leede	2	–	9	**–**
Cantrell	5	–	26	**–**

Fall of Wickets
1–**11**, 2–**42**, 3–**185**, 4–**212**

Holland

N.E. Clarke	lbw, **b** Cork	**0**
P.E. Cantrell	lbw, **b** DeFreitas	**28**
T.B.M. de Leede	lbw, **b** DeFreitas	**41**
S.W. Lubbers (Capt)	**c** Russell, **b** DeFreitas	**9**
K.J. van Noortwijk	**c** Gough, **b** Martin	**64**
B. Zuiderent	**c** Thorpe, **b** Martin	**54**
R.P. Lefebvre	not out	**11**
M. Schewe	not out	**11**
F. Aponso		
F. Jansen		
P-J. Bakker		
	lb **4**, w **6**, nb **2**	**12**
	50 overs (for 6 wickets)	**230**

	O	M	R	W
Cork	8	–	52	**1**
DeFreitas	10	3	31	**3**
N.M.K. Smith	8	–	27	**–**
Gough	3	–	23	**–**
Martin	10	1	42	**2**
Hick	5	–	23	**–**
Thorpe	6	–	28	**–**

Fall of Wickets
1–**1**, 2–**46**, 3–**70**, 4–**81**, 5–**195**, 6–**210**

Umpires: K.T. Francis & S.A. Bucknor *Man of the Match:* G.A. Hick

England won by 49 runs

and Thorpe. Hick reached his second hundred in limited-over internationals in the last over of the innings, and his 104 came off 133 balls with two sixes and six fours. He offered several half-chances, and although Hick won the individual award, Thorpe, one felt, played the more assertive innings, 89 off 82 balls, with a six, seven fours and a sense of total command.

Cork had Clarke leg before in his second over – the Dutch opener, once of Barbados, had a most disappointing World Cup – but thereafter the Derbyshire pace bowler lost his line. Gough never found his, and his three overs cost 23 runs. Tim de Leede scored 41 off 42 balls to give Holland the necessary scoring rate, but the loss of four wickets in the first 18 overs was a crippling blow. There were still alarms for England, however, as Klaas van Noortwijk and Baz Zuiderent played splendidly to add 114 in 27 overs, and Holland were well pleased with their efforts.

Pakistan *v.* United Arab Emirates

With Ramadan at an end, Pakistan had to endure a delayed entry into the World Cup, for bad weather cut 17 overs an innings off their match with UAE. It mattered little as the host country showed impressive form from the outset. Their bowling was hostile and varied; their batting positive to the extent that they scored at more than six runs an over to win the match. Pakistan's margin of victory, however, nine wickets with 15 overs to spare, did not flatter them.

England *v.* South Africa

The quality of England's challenge in the World Cup was put into true perspective when they were trounced yet again by South Africa. Cronje won the toss and decided to bat, and, for once, the England attack showed some control and aggression. Gary Kirsten and Steve Palframan scored 56 in 13 overs at the start of South Africa's innings. Palframan offered one chance to square-leg when he attempted a massive drive, and another such stroke saw him caught behind. Stewart ran out Kirsten, and when the dangerous Cronje fell to Gough's out-swinger South Africa were 88 for 3 and struggling. Cullinan looked in good form until a shower caused a twenty-minute break, and he did not recover his fluency on the return, succumbing to a slower ball from DeFreitas. Rhodes hit 37 off 32 balls, but no South African batsman played an innings of substance, and England could be well pleased with their work.

Their pleasure soon disappeared. Atherton had returned to his position of opener, but he hung out his bat to Pollock's fourth ball and was gone. Hick lasted until the eighth over when he clipped de Villiers into the hands of mid-wicket. Neil Smith, an honest worker but well short of international standard, was frustrated into submission, and England were 33 for 3. Stewart ambled insanely, failed to ground his bat and was run out. DeFreitas was later to be guilty of the same juvenile crime. Symcox spun his

Match Seven – Pakistan *v.* United Arab Emirates

24 February 1996 at Municipal Stadium, Gujranwala

United Arab Emirates

G. Mylvaganam	**b** Mushtaq Ahmed	**13**
Salim Raza	**c** Javed Miandad, **b** A. Javed	**22**
Azhar Saeed	run out	**1**
Mazhar Hussain	**c** Waqar Younis, **b** M. Ahmed	**7**
Mohammad Aslam	**b** Mushtaq Ahmed	**5**
Ishaq Mohammad	**b** Wasim Akram	**12**
Arshad Laiq	**c** Ijaz Ahmed, **b** Aqib Javed	**9**
J.A. Samarasekera	**b** Waqar Younis	**10**
S. Dukanwala	not out	**21**
Sultan Zarawani (Capt)	**b** Wasim Akram	**1**
*Imtiaz Abbasi	not out	**0**
	lb **1**, w **5**, nb **2**	**8**
	33 overs (for 9 wickets)	**109**

	O	M	R	W
Wasim Akram	7	1	25	**2**
Waqar Younis	7	–	33	**1**
Aqib Javed	6	–	18	**2**
Mushtaq Ahmed	7	–	16	**3**
Aamir Sohail	6	1	16	**–**

Fall of Wickets
1–**27**, 2–**40**, 3–**47**, 4–**53**, 5–**54**, 6–**70**, 7–**80**, 8–**108**, 9–**109**

Pakistan

Aamir Sohail	**b** Samarasekera	**5**
Saeed Anwar	not out	**40**
Ijaz Ahmed	not out	**50**
Inzamam-ul-Haq		
Javed Miandad		
Salim Malik		
*Rashid Latif		
Wasim Akram (Capt)		
Mushtaq Ahmed		
Waqar Younis		
Aqib Javed		
	lb **1**, w **12**, nb **4**	**17**
	18 overs (for 1 wicket)	**112**

	O	M	R	W
Samarasekera	3	–	17	**1**
Arshad Laiq	4	–	24	**–**
Dukanwala	3	1	14	**–**
Salim Raza	3	–	17	**–**
Sultan Zarawani	3	–	23	**–**
Azhar Saeed	2	–	16	**–**

Fall of Wickets
1–**7**

Umpires: D.C. Cooray & S.Venkataraghavan *Man of the Match:* Mushtaq Ahmed

Pakistan won by 9 wickets

Match Eight – England v. South Africa

25 February 1996 at Pindi Cricket Stadium, Rawalpindi

South Africa

G. Kirsten	run out	38
*S.J. Palframan	c Russell, b Martin	28
W.J. Cronje (Capt)	c Russell, b Gough	15
D.J. Cullinan	b DeFreitas	34
J.H. Kallis	c Russell, b Cork	26
J.N. Rhodes	b Martin	37
B.M. McMillan	b N.M.K. Smith	11
S.M. Pollock	c Fairbrother, b Cork	12
P.L. Symcox	c Thorpe, b Martin	1
C.R. Matthews	not out	9
P.S. de Villiers	c N.M.K. Smith, b Gough	12
	lb 1, w 5, nb 1	7
	50 overs	230

	O	M	R	W
Cork	10	–	36	2
DeFreitas	10	–	55	1
Gough	10	–	48	2
Martin	10	–	33	3
N.M.K. Smith	8	–	40	1
Thorpe	2	–	17	–

Fall of Wickets
1–56, 2–85, 3–88, 4–137, 5–163, 6–195, 7–199, 8–202, 9–213

England

M.A. Atherton (Capt)	c Palframan, b Pollock	0
N.M.K. Smith	b de Villiers	11
G.A. Hick	c McMillan, b de Villiers	14
G.P. Thorpe	c Palframan, b Symcox	46
A.J. Stewart	run out	7
N.H. Fairbrother	c Palframan, b Symcox	3
*R.C. Russell	c Rhodes, b Pollock	12
D.G. Cork	b Matthews	17
P.A.J. DeFreitas	run out	22
D. Gough	b Matthews	11
P.J. Martin	not out	1
	lb 7, w 1	8
	44.3 overs	152

	O	M	R	W
Pollock	8	1	16	2
de Villiers	7	1	27	2
Matthews	9.3	–	30	2
McMillan	6	–	17	–
Symcox	10	–	38	2
Cronje	4	–	17	–

Fall of Wickets
1–0, 2–22, 3–33, 4–52, 5–62, 6–97, 7–97, 8–139, 9–141

Umpires: I.D. Robinson & S.G. Randell *Man of the Match:* J.N. Rhodes

South Africa won by 78 runs

Match Nine – Pakistan v. Holland

26 February 1996 at Qaddafi Stadium, Lahore

Holland

N.E. Clarke	c Rashid Latif, b Aqib Javed	4
P.E. Cantrell	c Ijaz Ahmed, b Waqar Younis	17
T.B.M. de Leede	c Rashid Latif, b Waqar Younis	0
K.J. van Noortwijk	c Mushtaq Ahmed, b A. Javed	33
F. Aponso	b Waqar Younis	58
R.P. Lefebvre (Capt)	b Waqar Younis	10
B. Zuiderent	run out	6
E. Gouka	not out	0
F. Jansen		
*M. Schewe		
P-J. Bakker		
	lb 7, w 4, nb 6	17
	50 overs (for 7 wickets)	145

	O	M	R	W
Wasim Akram	10	1	30	–
Waqar Younis	10	1	26	4
Aqib Javed	9	2	25	2
Mushtaq Ahmed	10	2	27	–
Aamir Sohail	9	–	21	–
Salim Malik	2	–	9	–

Fall of Wickets
1–16, 2–28, 3–29, 4–102, 5–130, 6–143, 7–145

Pakistan

Aamir Sohail	c Jansen, b Lefebvre	9
Saeed Anwar	not out	83
Ijaz Ahmed	c Lefebvre, b Cantrell	39
Inzamam-ul-Haq	not out	18
Salim Malik		
Javed Miandad		
*Rashid Latif		
Wasim Akram (Capt)		
Mushtaq Ahmed		
Waqar Younis		
Aqib Javed		
	lb 1, w 1	2
	30.4 overs (for 2 wickets)	151

	O	M	R	W
Lefebvre	7	1	20	1
Bakker	7	1	13	–
Jansen	2	–	22	–
de Leede	4	–	20	–
Aponso	5	–	38	–
Cantrell	4	–	18	1
Gouka	1.4	–	19	–

Fall of Wickets
1–10, 2–104

Umpires: K.T. Francis & S.A. Bucknor *Man of the Match:* Waqar Younis

Pakistan won by 8 wickets

off-breaks appreciably and accounted for the left-handers Thorpe and Fairbrother. Russell cut Pollock to backward point. England were 97 for 7, the scoring rate needed was close to ten an over and only brave gestures were possible in inevitable defeat.

Frustrated by the accuracy of the South African bowling, England's Neil Smith is bowled by Fanie de Villiers. (Graham Chadwick/Allsport)

Pakistan v. Holland

Pakistan beat Holland as comfortably as they had beaten UAE. The most pleasing aspect of their victory was the form of Waqar Younis who dismissed Cantrell and de Leede in the space of three balls to leave Holland on 29 for 3. The left-handed Aponso hit a six and three fours before Waqar returned to knock back his leg stump. Needing 146 to win, Pakistan lost Aamir Sohail cheaply, but Saaed Anwar and Ijaz Ahmed hit 94 off 123 balls and victory came with nearly 20 overs to spare.

New Zealand v. United Arab Emirates

New Zealand claimed a place in the quarter-finals when they overwhelmed UAE. Their victory was founded upon the batting of Craig Spearman and Roger Twose. Spearman hit 78 off 77 balls, and Twose, whose innings included eight fours, made 92 from 112 balls. Mist had delayed the start of the match so that each side had three overs docked from their innings. New Zealand's 276 for 8 set a daunting target in these circumstances, and UAE never looked remotely as if they would approach it. Samarasekera hit seven fours in a valiant 47 off 59 balls.

Match Ten – New Zealand v. United Arab Emirates

27 February 1996 at Iqbal Stadium, Faisalabad

New Zealand

C.M. Spearman	b Salim Raza	78
N.J. Astle	b Samarasekera	2
S.P. Fleming	c and b Dukanwala	16
R.G. Twose	c Mazhar Hussain, b Azhar	92
C.L. Cairns	c Imtiaz Abbasi, b Zarawani	6
A.C. Parore	c Azhar Saeed, b Zarawani	15
S.A. Thomson	not out	31
*L.K. Germon (Capt)	b Azhar Saeed	3
D.J. Nash	lbw, b Azhar Saeed	8
D.K. Morrison	not out	10
R.J. Kennedy		
	b 2, lb 12, nb 1	15
	47 overs (for 8 wickets)	276

	O	M	R	W
Samarasekera	6	–	30	1
Arshad Laiq	2	–	16	–
Salim Raza	9	–	48	1
Dukanwala	10	–	46	1
Mazhar Hussain	3	–	28	–
Azhar Saeed	7	–	45	3
Sultan Zarawani	10	–	49	2

Fall of Wickets
1–**11**, 2–**42**, 3–**162**, 4–**173**, 5–**210**, 6–**228**, 7–**239**, 8–**266**

United Arab Emirates

Azhar Saeed	c Fleming, b Nash	5
Salim Raza	c Kennedy, b Morrison	21
Mazhar Hussain	c Cairns, b Thomson	29
V. Mehra	c Cairns, b Thomson	12
Mohammad Ishaq	c Cairns, b Kennedy	8
Mohammad Aslam	c Twose, b Thomson	1
S. Dukanwala	c and b Cairns	8
Arshad Laiq	run out	14
J.A. Samarasekera	not out	47
Sultan Zarawani (Capt)	c Thomson, b Nash	13
*Imtiaz Abbasi	not out	2
	lb 2, w 3, nb 2	7
	47 overs (for 9 wickets)	167

	O	M	R	W
Morrison	7	–	37	1
Nash	9	1	34	2
Cairns	10	2	31	1
Kennedy	6	–	20	1
Thomson	10	2	20	3
Astle	5	–	23	–

Fall of Wickets
1–**23**, 2–**29**, 3–**65**, 4–**70**, 5–**81**, 6–**88**, 7–**92**, 8–**124**, 9–**162**

Umpires: B.C. Cooray & S. Venkataraghavan *Man of the Match:* R.G. Twose

New Zealand won by 109 runs

Pakistan v. South Africa

In the most significant match to be played in Section B, South Africa overcame Pakistan and a partisan crowd of 33,000 who provided a constant barrage of noise. This was a most impressive performance by a splendidly organised side who were clear and purposeful in every aspect of the game.

Wasim Akram won the toss and Pakistan, strangely lacking Javed Miandad, batted. Aamir Sohail and Saeed Anwar took the score to 52 before Cronje brought himself on for the 12th over. Within his first four balls, he had Saeed taken at short extra-cover and Ijaz leg before. Aamir Sohail had begun uncertainly and was twice put down behind the stumps, but he stuck to his task and was the rock on which the Pakistan innings was founded. Cronje added to his laurels by running out Inzamam-ul-Haq with a direct hit on the stumps, and both Salim Malik and Aamir were puzzled by Adams who finally had Salim caught behind. Wasim, inevitably, played some lusty blows, and Aamir reached 111 before being out in the 49th over.

South Africa began at a furious rate, and the score was 105 for 2 in 15 overs. Fifty runs had come off the first seven overs, and Wasim quickly turned to his spinners. It was the policy of the South African batsmen to sweep the slow bowlers, and, although this policy cost Kirsten his wicket, it brought rich dividends, not the least of which was that it destroyed Mushtaq's control. Cullinan was in mighty form, and when he departed Cronje and Pollock continued the domination.

Holland v. United Arab Emirates

One of the surprises of the tournament was not only the fact that UAE beat Holland, but that they did so with such ease. With Clarke again disappointing, Holland were restricted to 216 for 9 in their 50 overs. Off-spinner Shaukat Dukanwala returned the impressive figures of 5 for 29.

Saleem Raza, playing in the city of his birth, soon gave indication that Holland's score was inadequate. He dominated an opening stand of 117 with Azhar Saeed as he hit 84 off 68 balls with seven fours and six sixes. He had now hit more sixes than anyone else in the competition. Mehra and Mohammed Ishaq shared an unbroken stand of 82 off 99 balls to take UAE to victory with 28 balls to spare.

Pakistan v. England

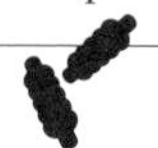

Robin Smith returned to the England side and shared an opening stand of 147 with skipper Mike Atherton who had entered the match with his captaincy under severe criticism. The stand was broken in the 29th over when Smith, who had batted with a runner because of cramp as he scored the last 20 runs of his innings, had driven Salim Malik to long-off. The openers had given England a splendid platform, and a

Match Eleven – Pakistan v. South Africa

29 February 1996 at National Stadium, Karachi

Pakistan

Aamir Sohail	c Cronje, b Pollock	111
Saeed Anwar	c McMillan, b Cronje	25
Ijaz Ahmed	lbw, b Cronje	0
Inzamam-ul-Haq	run out	23
Salim Malik	c Palframan, b Adams	40
Wasim Akram (Capt)	not out	32
*Rashid Latif	lbw, b Matthews	0
Rameez Raja	not out	2
Mushtaq Ahmed		
Waqar Younis		
Saqlain Mushtaq		
	b 1, lb 2, w 4, nb 2	9
	50 overs (for 6 wickets)	242

	O	M	R	W
Pollock	9	–	49	1
Matthews	10	–	47	1
Cronje	5	–	20	2
Donald	8	–	50	–
Adams	10	–	42	1
McMillan	8	–	31	–

Fall of Wickets
1–52, 2–52, 3–112, 4–189, 5–233, 6–235

South Africa

A.C. Hudson	b Waqar Younis	33
G. Kirsten	b Saqlain Mushtaq	44
B.M. McMillan	lbw, b Waqar Younis	1
D.J. Cullinan	b Waqar Younis	65
J.H. Kallis	c and b Saqlain Mushtaq	9
W.J. Cronje (Capt)	not out	45
S.M. Pollock	not out	20
*S.J. Palframan		
C.R. Matthews		
A.A. Donald		
P.R. Adams		
	b 8, lb 4, w 6, nb 8	26
	44.2 overs (for 5 wickets)	243

	O	M	R	W
Wasim Akram	9.2	–	49	–
Waqar Younis	8	–	50	3
Mushtaq Ahmed	10	–	54	–
Aamir Sohail	6	–	35	–
Saqlain Mushtaq	10	1	38	2
Salim Malik	1	–	5	–

Fall of Wickets
1–51, 2–53, 3–111, 4–125, 5–203

Umpires: S.A. Bucknor & K.T. Francis *Man of the Match:* W.J. Cronje

South Africa won by 5 wickets

Match Twelve – Holland v. United Arab Emirates

1 March 1996 at Qaddafi Stadium, Lahore

Holland

Batsman	How out	Runs
N.E. Clarke	c Mehra, b Shahzad Altaf	0
P.E. Cantrell	c Imtiaz Abbasi, b Azhar Saeed	47
F. Aponso	c and b Dukanwala	45
T.B.M. de Leede	c and b Azhar Saeed	36
K.J. van Noortwijk	c Zarawani, b Dukanwala	26
S.W. Lubbers (Capt)	c Saeed-al-Saffar, b Zarawani	8
R.P. Lefbevre	c sub, b Dukanwala	12
B. Zuiderent	st Imtiaz Abbasi, b Dukanwala	3
*M. Schewe	b Dukanwala	6
R.F. van Oosterom	not out	2
P-J. Bakker	not out	1
	b 4, lb 15, w 11	30
	50 overs (for 9 wickets)	216

	O	M	R	W
Shahzad Altaf	10	3	15	1
Samarasekera	9	1	36	–
Saeed-al-Saffar	3	–	25	–
Dukanwala	10	–	29	5
Sultan Zarawani	8	–	40	1
Saleem Raza	5	–	23	–
Azhar Saeed	5	–	29	2

Fall of Wickets
1–3, 2–77, 3–148, 4–153, 5–168, 6–200, 7–200, 8–209, 9–210

United Arab Emirates

Batsman	How out	Runs
Azhar Saeed	run out	32
Saleem Raza	c Zuiderent, b Lubbers	84
Mazhar Hussain	c Clarke, b Lefebvre	16
V. Mehra	not out	29
Mohammad Ishaq	not out	51
J.A. Samarasekera		
S. Dukanwala		
Sultan Zarawani (Capt)		
Saeed-al-Saffar		
*Imtiaz Abbasi		
Shahzad Altaf		
	lb 7, w 1	8
	44.2 overs (for 3 wickets)	220

	O	M	R	W
Lefebvre	8	–	24	1
Bakker	8	–	41	–
de Leede	4	–	33	–
Aponso	7.2	–	47	–
Lubbers	9	–	38	1
Cantrell	8	–	30	–

Fall of Wickets
1–117, 2–135, 3–138

Umpires: S.G. Randell & Mahboob Shah *Man of the Match:* S. Dukanwala & Saleem Raza

United Arab Emirates won by 7 wickets

Match Thirteen – Pakistan v. England

3 March 1996 at National Stadium, Karachi

England

Batsman	How out	Runs
R.A. Smith	c Waqar Younis, b Salim Malik	75
M.A. Atherton (Capt)	b Aamir Sohail	66
G.A. Hick	st Rashid Latif, b A. Sohail	1
G.P. Thorpe	not out	52
N.H. Fairbrother	c Wasim Akram, b M. Ahmed	13
*R.C. Russell	c and b Mushtaq Ahmed	4
D.A. Reeve	b Mushtaq Ahmed	3
D.G. Cork	lbw, b Waqar Younis	0
D. Gough	b Wasim Akram	14
P.J. Martin	run out	2
R.K. Illingworth	not out	1
	b 11, w 4, nb 3	18
	50 overs (for 9 wickets)	249

	O	M	R	W
Wasim Akram	7	1	31	1
Waqar Younis	10	1	45	1
Aqib Javed	7	–	34	–
Mushtaq Ahmed	10	–	53	3
Aamir Sohail	10	–	48	2
Salim Malik	6	1	27	1

Fall of Wickets
1–147, 2–151, 3–156, 4–194, 5–204, 6–212, 7–217, 8–241, 9–247

Pakistan

Batsman	How out	Runs
Aamir Sohail	c Thorpe, b Illingworth	42
Saeed Anwar	c Russell, b Cork	71
Ijaz Ahmed	c Russell, b Cork	70
Inzamam-ul-Haq	not out	53
Javed Mianded	not out	11
Salim Malik		
*Rashid Latif		
Wasim Akram (Capt)		
Mushtaq Ahmed		
Waqar Younis		
Aqib Javed		
	lb 1, w 2	3
	47.4 overs (for 3 wickets)	250

	O	M	R	W
Cork	10	–	59	2
Martin	9	–	45	–
Gough	10	–	45	–
Illingworth	10	–	46	1
Reeve	6.4	–	37	–
Hick	2	–	17	–

Fall of Wickets
1–81, 2–139, 3–214

Umpires: B.C. Cooray & S. Venkataraghavan *Man of the Match:* Aamir Sohail

Pakistan won by 7 wickets

Match Fourteen – South Africa v. Holland

5 March 1996 at Pindi Cricket Stadium, Rawalpindi

South Africa

G. Kirsten	c Zuiderent, b Aponso	83
A.C. Hudson	c Zuiderent, b Gouka	161
W.J. Cronje (Capt)	c Lubbers b Cantrell	41
D.J. Cullinan	not out	19
J.H. Kallis	not out	17
B.M. McMillan		
S.M. Pollock		
*S.J. Palframan		
P.L. Symcox		
C.R. Matthews		
A.A. Donald		
	lb 5, w 2	7
	50 overs (for 3 wickets)	328

	O	M	R	W
Bakker	10	1	64	–
Lubbers	8	–	50	–
de Leede	10	–	59	–
Aponso	10	–	57	1
Cantrell	10	–	61	1
Gouka	2	–	32	1

Fall of Wickets
1–**186**, 2–**274**, 3–**301**

Holland

N.E. Clarke	c Pollock, b Donald	32
P.E. Cantrell	c and b Matthews	23
T.B.M. de Leede	b Donald	12
K.J. van Noorwijk	c Palframan, b Symcox	9
F. Aponso	c Kirsten, b Symcox	6
B. Zuiderent	run out	27
*M. Schewe	b Matthews	20
E. Gouka	c Kallis, b Pollock	19
R.F. van Oosterom	not out	5
S.W. Lubbers (Capt)	not out	2
P-J. Bakker		
	lb 7, w 5, nb 1	13
	50 overs (for 8 wickets)	168

	O	M	R	W
Pollock	8	–	35	1
Matthews	10	–	38	2
Donald	6	–	21	2
Cronje	3	1	3	–
Symcox	10	1	22	2
McMillan	4	2	5	–
Kallis	7	1	30	–
Cullinan	2	–	7	–

Fall of Wickets
1–**56**, 2–**70**, 3–**81**, 4–**86**, 5–**97**, 6–**126**, 7–**158**, 8–**163**

Umpires: Khizar Hayat & S.G. Randell *Man of the Match:* A.C. Hudson

South Africa won by 160 runs

Match Fifteen – Pakistan v. New Zealand

6 March 1996 at Qaddafi Stadium, Lahore

Pakistan

Aamir Sohail	c Thomson, b Kennedy	50
Saeed Anwar	run out	62
Ijaz Ahmed	c Spearman, b Cairns	26
Inzamam-ul-Haq	run out	39
Javed Miandad	run out	5
Salim Malik	not out	55
Wasim Akram (Capt)	not out	28
*Rashid Latif		
Mushtaq Ahmed		
Waqar Younis		
Aqib Javed		
Extras	lb 5, w 5, nb 6	16
	50 overs (for 5 wickets)	281

	O	M	R	W
Morrison	2	–	17	–
Nash	10	1	49	–
Cairns	10	1	53	1
Kennedy	5	–	32	1
Astle	9	–	50	–
Thomson	6	–	35	–
Twose	8	–	40	–

Fall of Wickets
1–**70**, 2–**139**, 3–**155**, 4–**173**, 5–**200**

New Zealand

C.M. Spearman	c Rashid Latif, b Aqib Javed	14
N.J. Astle	c Rashid Latif, b Waqar Younis	6
*L.K. Germon (Capt)	c sub, b Mushtaq Ahmed	41
S.P. Fleming	st Rashid Latif, b Salim Malik	42
R.G. Twose	c Salim Malik, b M. Ahmed	24
C.L. Cairns	c Rashid Latif, b Aamir Sohail	32
A.C. Parore	c Mushtaq Ahmed, b S. Malik	36
S.A. Thomson	c Rashid Latif, b Waqar Younis	13
D.J. Nash	not out	5
R.J. Kennedy	b Aqib Javed	2
D.K. Morrison	absent injured	–
	b 4, lb 9, w 6, nb 1	20
	47.3 overs	235

	O	M	R	W
Waqar Younis	9	2	32	2
Aqib Javed	7.3	–	45	2
Mushtaq Ahmed	10	–	32	2
Salim Malik	7	–	41	2
Ijaz Ahmed	4	–	21	–
Aamir Sohail	10	–	51	1

Fall of Wickets
1–**23**, 2–**23**, 3–**83**, 4–**132**, 5–**132**, 6–**221**, 7–**228**, 8–**235**, 9–**235**

Umpires: K.T. Francis & I.D. Robinson *Man of the Match:* Salim Malik

Pakistan won by 46 runs

Rashid Latif is gleeful as Mike Atherton is bowled by Aamir Sohail in the game between Pakistan and England in Karachi. (Mike Hewitt/Allsport)

score in excess of 300 looked possible, but, not for the first time, the batting disintegrated. Hick was stumped second ball, and Atherton was bowled as he attempted to cut Aamir Sohail, who also claimed two valuable wickets after Mushtaq had been initially driven out of the attack. The leg-spinner returned to dismiss Fairbrother, Russell and Reeve in quick succession. Thorpe kept going, and Gough hit and ran, but 241 was a meagre return after so much promise. The last half of the England innings had produced 19 runs fewer than the first, and nine wickets had fallen.

Aamir Sohail and Saeed Anwar quickly announced themselves with a flurry of boundaries, mostly square of the wicket on either side. The partnership ended in the 16th over when Aamir hit Illingworth to mid-on, but there was no slowing of the scoring rate. Smith had retired from the field, and Fairbrother followed him after injuring a hamstring. This was the end of Fairbrother's competition, and Ramprakash was flown in to replace him. Hussain should have been in the side from the start, but by the time Fairbrother was injured it was apparent that it no longer mattered. England were down if not out.

Cork had both Saeed Anwar, 71 off 72 balls, and Ijaz Ahmed, 70 off 83 balls, caught by Russell, but this only served to bring in Javed Miandad, the local hero in his last big match in the National Stadium. He was there at the finish which came with 14 balls to spare, by which time Inzamam-ul-Haq had stroked 53 from 54 deliveries.

South Africa v. Holland

A World Cup first wicket record partnership between Andrew Hudson and Gary Kirsten decided the outcome of this match before it had reached the quarter stage. Hudson hit 161 off 131 deliveries, and his innings included four sixes and 13 fours. Clinical in approach, polite and graceful in bearing, South Africa maintained their usual batting order and chose not to resort to 'joke' bowling as they claimed their fifth win in as many matches in the tournament. They respected their opponents and their hosts, and they had become as popular a team as they were accomplished.

Pakistan v. New Zealand

The final match in Section B provided a comfortable win for Pakistan, but the loss of captain Wasim Akram with a pulled muscle that prevented him from bowling was a worry which clouded the victory. New Zealand, too, suffered a severe setback when Morrison was forced to retire after two overs with the recurrence of a groin injury. He had already conceded 17 runs in those two overs as Pakistan began scoring at a blistering pace against an attack which was bereft of the injured Larsen. Aamir Sohail was in astonishing form, entertaining an enthusiastic crowd with some magnificent off-side shots before being spectacularly caught left-handed, high above his head, by Thomson at square-leg. Others ran themselves out in a haste for runs, but Salim Malik, who played quite beautifully for his 55 from 47 balls, and Wasim Akram shared an unbroken stand of 80 in nine overs for the sixth wicket.

Astle, who had had a miserable run since his century against England, and Spearman were soon out when New Zealand batted. Germon, leading from the front as ever, and Fleming raised hopes, but the winning post always remained just out of sight. This was principally because Mushtaq Ahmed, who had bowled so well in the competition, bemused the middle order once again.

Section B Final Table

	P	W	L	Pts	R/R
South Africa	5	5	–	10	2.06
Pakistan	5	4	1	8	0.99
New Zealand	5	3	2	6	0.54
England	5	2	3	4	0.07
United Arab Emirates	5	1	4	2	-1.83
Holland	5	–	5	0	-9.5

Quarter-Finals

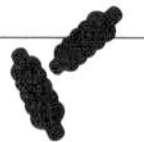

Exciting matches, brilliant individual performances, disappointment for South Africa, and the total eclipse of England.

England v. Sri Lanka

England's first piece of misfortune was that Cork was unable to play because of injury; their second was that they had to take on Sri Lanka, a team with enthusiasm and intelligence, passionately committed to the game. Atherton won the toss, and England batted. The England captain got off to a brisk start, and he had scored 22 out of 31 in the eighth over when he poked at Vaas in an attempt to steer the ball to third man and was caught behind. Hick, who finished the competition in unhappy form with bat and ball, fretted for seven overs before flicking Muralitharan to square-leg. Smith had been batting confidently before he turned a ball to short fine-leg only for Jayasuriya to hit the stumps at the bowler's end with his throw and Smith to be adjudged 'out' by the third umpire.

Thorpe hit across the line at Dharmasena and was bowled while Stewart was comprehensively beaten by an off-break. Russell, whose contribution in the World Cup had been less than anticipated, edged the ball into his stumps, and it was DeFreitas who was left to provide the fireworks with 67 off 64 balls. He hit two sixes and five fours in his

The destroyer of England in the quarter-final in Faisalabad. Sanath Jayasuriya, the most valuable cricketer in the tournament, swings a ball to the boundary as Sri Lanka rush to victory over England. Jayasuriya hit 82 off only 44 balls before being stumped by Russell who looks on in wonder. (Ross Kinnaird/Allsport)

Quarter-Final – England v. Sri Lanka

9 March 1996 at Iqbal Stadium, Faisalabad

England

R.A. Smith	run out	25
M.A. Atherton (Capt)	c Kaluwitharana, b Vaas	22
G.A. Hick	c Ranatunga, b Muralitharan	8
G.P. Thorpe	b Dharmasena	14
P.A.J. DeFreitas	lbw, b Jayasuriya	67
A.J. Stewart	b Muralitharan	17
*R.C. Russell	b Dharmasena	9
D.A. Reeve	b Jayasuriya	35
D. Gough	not out	26
P.J. Martin	not out	0
R.K. Illingworth		
	lb 8, w 4	12
	50 overs (for 8 wickets)	235

	O	M	R	W
Wickremasinghe	7	–	43	–
Vaas	8	1	29	1
Muralitharan	10	1	37	2
Dharmasena	10	–	30	2
Jayasuriya	9	–	46	2
de Silva	6	–	42	–

Fall of Wickets
1–31, 2–58, 3–66, 4–94, 5–145, 6–171, 7–173, 8–235

Sri Lanka

S.T. Jayasuriya	st Russell, b Reeve	82
*R.S. Kaluwitharana	b Illingworth	8
A.P. Gurusinha	run out	45
P.A. de Silva	c Smith, b Hick	31
A. Ranatunga (Capt)	lbw, b Gough	25
H.P. Tillekeratne	not out	19
R.S. Mahanama	not out	22
H.D.P.K. Dharmasena		
W.P.U.J.C. Vaas		
M. Muralitharan		
G.P. Wickremasinghe		
	lb 1, w 2, nb 1	4
	40.4 overs (for 5 wickets)	236

	O	M	R	W
Martin	9	1	41	–
Illingworth	10	1	72	1
Gough	10	1	36	1
DeFreitas	3.4	–	38	–
Reeve	4	1	14	1
Hick	4	–	34	1

Fall of Wickets
1–12, 2–113, 3–165, 4–194, 5–198

Umpires: Mahbood Shah & I.D. Robinson *Man of the Match:* S.T. Jayasuriya

Sri Lanka won by 5 wickets

first fifty in 101 one-day internationals. When he was leg before to Jayasuriya, the most valuable cricketer in the competition, England were 173 for 7 in the 41st over. Reeve and Gough now made the highest stand of the innings by pushing, running and slogging. They lifted England to 235 by the penultimate ball of the final over when Reeve slogged and missed. England's score looked some 60 short of a winning score. Once Jayasuriya started it looked about 160 short of a winning score.

Kaluwitharana hit two fours and was out in the second over to the third ball he faced. He was bowled round his legs by Richard Illingworth who had opened the bowling in an effort to counter Sri Lanka's customary blast off, but the Sri Lankans would not be still. Jayasuriya and Gurusinha gave an astonishing display of batting. Three consecutive balls from DeFreitas were hit over long-on, square driven to the boundary and hit on to the pavilion roof by Jayasuriya. Thirty-two runs came from DeFreitas' first 12 deliveries, and the first six overs bowled from the pavilion end, shared by Illingworth, Gough and DeFreitas, cost 76 runs.

Jayasuriya was brilliant in all aspects of that word – of outstanding ability and glittering. He hit 13 fours and three sixes, and his 82 occupied a mere 44 balls. When he was the victim of a leg-side stumping in the 13th over Sri Lanka had scored 113. If England believed there would now be a respite, they were cruelly mistaken. Aravinda de Silva drove majestically to long-on to announce his arrival, and stroked five fours in his 31 off 30 deliveries. He was splendidly caught at backward point, but this only brought in Arjuna Ranatunga who smote the first ball to the cover boundary, followed it with four more fours and when out, in the 26th over, had hit 25 off 17 balls, and Sri Lanka were just 42 runs short of victory with almost half their overs remaining.

Gurusinha was run out through tiredness, and Tillekeratne and Mahanama, both with Test centuries to their credit, were more sedate as they took their side to an emphatic win. For Sri Lanka, the highest possible praise. As for England, few, if any, were sorry to see them out of the competition. Lacking grace and charm, shabby in the field, ever complaining about conditions, facilities, decisions and the amount of cricket they play, they generally show a lack of manners to their hosts which sometimes borders on contempt, and many appear to have an inflated idea of their own limited ability.

India *v.* Pakistan

For most on the Indian sub-continent this was the final of the World Cup. Fate had decreed that India should meet Pakistan in the quarter-finals whereas the organisers had planned and hoped that they should meet in the final. India had not played as well as expected in the preliminary rounds, for many had expected them to sweep all before them. They redeemed themselves against Pakistan in a match of great passion.

Quarter-Final – India *v.* Pakistan

9 March 1996 at Chinnaswamy Stadium, Bangalore

India

N.S. Sidhu	**b** Mushtaq Ahmed	**93**
S.R. Tendulkar	**b** Ata-ur-Rehman	**31**
S.V. Manjrekar	**c** Javed Miandad, **b** A. Sohail	**20**
M. Azharuddin (Capt)	**c** Rashid Latif, **b** Waqar Younis	**27**
V.G. Kambli	**b** Mushtaq Ahmed	**24**
A.D. Jadeja	**c** Aamir Sohail, **b** Waqar Younis	**45**
*N.R. Mongia	run out	**3**
A.R. Kumble	**c** Javed Miandad, **b** Aqib Javed	**10**
J. Srinath	not out	**12**
Venkatesh Prasad	not out	**0**
Venkatapathy Raju		
	lb **3**, w **15**, nb **4**	**22**
	50 overs (for 8 wickets)	**287**

	O	M	R	W
Waqar Younis	10	1	67	**1**
Aqib Javed	10	–	67	**1**
Ata-ur-Rehman	10	–	40	**1**
Mushtaq Ahmed	10	–	56	**2**
Aamir Sohail	5	–	29	**1**
Salim Malik	5	–	25	**–**

Fall of Wickets
1–**90**, 2–**138**, 3–**168**, 4–**200**, 5–**226**, 6–**236**, 7–**260**, 8–**279**

Pakistan

Aamir Sohail (Capt)	**b** Venkatesh Prasad	**55**
Saeed Anwar	**c** Kumble, **b** Srinath	**48**
Ijaz Ahmed	**c** Srinath, **b** Venkatesh Prasad	**12**
Inzamam-ul-Haq	**c** Mongia, **b** Venkatesh Prasad	**12**
Salim Malik	lbw, **b** Kumble	**38**
Javed Miandad	run out	**38**
*Rashid Latif	**st** Mongia, **b** Venkatapathy Raju	**26**
Mushtaq Ahmed	**c** and **b** Kumble	**0**
Waqar Younis	not out	**4**
Ata-ur-Rehman	lbw, **b** Kumble	**0**
Aqib Javed	not out	**6**
	b **1**, lb **3**, w **5**	**9**
	49 overs (for 9 wickets)	**248**

	O	M	R	W
Srinath	9	–	61	**1**
Venkatesh Prasad	10	–	45	**3**
Kumble	10	–	48	**3**
Venkatapathy Raju	10	–	46	**1**
Tendulkar	5	–	25	**–**
Jadeja	5	–	19	**–**

Fall of Wickets
1–**84**, 2–**113**, 3–**122**, 4–**132**, 5–**184**, 6–**231**, 7–**232**, 8–**239**, 9–**239**

Umpires: S.U. Bucknor & D.R. Shepherd *Man of the Match:* N.S. Sidhu

India won by 39 runs

India v. Pakistan at Bangalore. Rashid Latif is stumped by Mongia, and India are on the verge of victory and a place in the semi-finals. (Shaun Botterill/Allsport)

Brian Lara ends South African dreams with an innings of 111 in the quarter-final in Karachi. Palframan is the wicket-keeper. (John Parkin/Allsport)

Batting first, they were given a sound base by Sidhu and Tendulkar who scored 90 in 21 overs. Sachin Tendulkar was more restrained than he had been in the earlier rounds, but a great responsibility was upon him. Aamir Sohail shouldered an even greater burden, for Wasim Akram had deemed himself unfit for the game, and Aamir was captain for the day. He was over-cautious, and India built steadily on their firm base. Manjrekar and Azharuddin played some delightful shots. Kambli was more eccentric, but briefly effective, and Sidhu, batting with a runner after injuring his leg, provided a most praiseworthy backbone to the innings. He batted with determination and vigour until he was deceived by Mushtaq's flipper.

If Pakistan had thought that this would bring relief, they were wrong. Ajay Jadeja led the assault in the closing overs by hitting 45 off 25 balls. Kumble hit Waqar Younis for consecutive fours, and the great fast bowler conceded 22 runs off the 48th over. He dismissed Jadeja in the final over, but that, too, cost 18 runs. From the last ten overs of the Indian innings came 96 runs, 62 of them from the last five overs.

Aamir Sohail and Saeed Anwar gave every hint of a Pakistan victory with 84 in ten overs, but the visitors were already batting with a liability, one over having been docked from their quota because of a slow over-rate in the Indian innings. There was a confrontation between Aamir and Venkatesh Prasad which was quickly defused by the admirable umpiring of Bucknor and Shepherd. The openers and Ijaz Ahmed surrendered their wickets impetuously, and

Quarter Final – West Indies *v.* South Africa

11 March 1996 at National Stadium, Karachi

West Indies

S. Chanderpaul	c Cullinan, b McMillan	56
*C.O. Browne	c Cullinan, b Matthews	26
B.C. Lara	c Pollock, b Symcox	111
R.B. Richardson (Capt)	c Kirsten, b Symcox	10
R.A. Harper	lbw, b McMillan	9
R.I.C. Holder	run out	5
K.L.T. Arthurton	c Hudson, b P.R. Adams	1
J.C. Adams	not out	13
I.R. Bishop	b P.R. Adams	17
C.E.L. Ambrose	not out	0
C.A. Walsh		
	b 2, lb 11, w 2, nb 1	16
	50 overs (for 8 wickets)	264

	O	M	R	W
Pollock	9	–	46	–
Matthews	10	–	42	1
Cronje	3	–	17	–
McMillan	10	1	37	2
Symcox	10	–	64	2
P.R. Adams	8	–	45	2

Fall of Wickets
1–**42**, 2–**180**, 3–**210**, 4–**214**, 5–**227**, 6–**230**, 7–**230**, 8–**254**

South Africa

A.C. Hudson	c Walsh, b J.C. Adams	54
G. Kirsten	hit wkt, b Ambrose	3
D.J. Cullinan	c Bishop, b J.C. Adams	69
W.J. Cronje (Capt)	c Arthurton, b J.C. Adams	40
J.N. Rhodes	c J.C. Adams, b Harper	13
B.M. McMillan	lbw, b Harper	6
S.M. Pollock	c J.C. Adams, b Harper	6
*S.J. Palframan	c and b Harper	1
P.L. Symcox	c Harper, b Arthurton	24
C.R. Matthews	not out	8
P.R. Adams	b Walsh	10
	b 1, lb 4, w 2, nb 4	11
	49.3 overs	245

	O	M	R	W
Ambrose	10	–	29	1
Walsh	8.3	–	51	1
Bishop	5	–	31	–
Harper	10	–	47	4
J.C. Adams	10	–	53	3
Arthurton	6	–	29	1

Fall of Wickets
1–**21**, 2–**118**, 3–**140**, 4–**186**, 5–**196**, 6–**196**, 7–**198**, 8–**227**, 9–**228**

Umpires: K.T. Francis & S.G. Randell *Man of the Match:* B.C. Lara

West Indies won by 19 runs

Pakistan began to slip behind the necessary run rate. The Indian spinners bowled with excellent control, and Venkatesh Prasad survived an early battering to play a vital part in his side's victory. There was some elegance from Salim Malik and a dashing little innings from Rashid Latif. Javed Miandad batted with restraint, endeavouring, perhaps, to hold things together, but when the red light shone to show that he had been run out after facing 64 balls Pakistan were beaten, and a great, if controversial, batsman exited the international stage. If Pakistan mourned at his going, 55,000 in Bangalore could not contain their joy.

West Indies *v.* South Africa

Brian Lara came out from under the shadows of Mark Waugh, Sachin Tendulkar and several Sri Lankans to hit 111 off 97 balls and play a vital role in steering West Indies into the semi-finals. For South Africa, who had won 12 one-day internationals in a row before this match, one must have sympathy, but, on the day, they were below their best, and they created a surprise by omitting Donald. Worst of all, they missed comfortable catches, an event totally out of character.

Choosing to bat first, West Indies lost Browne at 42, but Chanderpaul, opening the innings for the first time and encouraged by being dropped, shared a second wicket stand of 138 off 149 deliveries with Lara. Chanderpaul was out when he swept McMillan high in the air, but Lara was in ruthless form. He hit 16 boundaries, and he was particularly violent to the spinners, Adams and Symcox. Adams was hit for 19 in two overs, and six overs from Symcox round the wicket cost 45 runs. Eventually, South Africa faced a target of 265, which was not beyond their reach.

They were not helped by the early loss of Kirsten, and it was soon apparent that the West Indian bowling and fielding were much improved from the levels they had shown previously. Hudson and Cullinan added 97, and Cullinan looked in fiery form as he hit three sixes. Cronje, too, kept the innings going well until he was caught at deep mid-wicket off Jimmy Adams. Roger Harper then claimed four wickets in as many overs. Rhodes hoisted to leg, McMillan was trapped leg before, and Pollock fell to a fine catch. Symcox battled bravely, but the South African dream was over. If it was a consolation to them, they could return home in the knowledge that they had carried themselves with warmth and dignity, had played some splendidly entertaining and organised cricket and won many friends.

Australia *v.* New Zealand

When the New Zealanders were reduced to 44 for 3 by the Australian pace attack it seemed that this contest would be as one-sided as many had predicted it would be. The left-handed Chris Harris then joined skipper Lee Germon in a stand that was worth 168 in 27 overs. Germon raced to his fifty off 40 balls. Pace and spin alike were devastated as Harris hit four sixes. This was uninhibited batting from honest, joyful cricketers who, for two glorious hours, lit up the World Cup and were rapturously received by a crowd of 45,000 who had not really forgiven Australia for refusing to go to Sri Lanka.

Taylor persevered with his spinners, and, eventually, New Zealand fell a little short of the total they might have anticipated when Germon and Harris were in full flow. Nevertheless, 287 was a challenging target for Australia who soon lost Taylor to Germon's ploy of opening the attack with the off-spinner Patel. Harris bowled some mean overs, but the New Zealand attack lacked Morrison and the economic Larsen, and Cairns had been below par with his bowling throughout the competition.

Mark Waugh was completely unruffled, and Ponting made some brisk runs before falling to Thomson. Taylor sent in Warne at number four to lift the tempo, and, dropped at deep mid-wicket before he had scored, Warne responded with 24 off 14 balls. The twins added 86 which was ended when Mark Waugh was caught behind off Patel. By then, however, he had made 110 off 113 balls, his third century of the competition, and he had taken Australia to within sight of victory which was accomplished by his twin brother and Stuart Law with 13 balls remaining. Australia looked invincible; for New Zealand, nothing but praise in defeat.

Heroes in defeat. Chris Harris and Lee Germon who put on 168 for the fourth wicket after New Zealand had lost 3 for 44 against Australia. (Shaun Botterill/Allsport)

Quarter-Final – New Zealand *v.* Australia

11 March 1996 at Chidambaram Stadium, The Chepauk, Madras

New Zealand

Batsman	Dismissal	Runs
C.M. Spearman	c Healy, b Reiffel	13
N.J. Astle	c Healy, b D.W. Fleming	1
*L.K. Germon (Capt)	c D.W. Fleming, b McGrath	89
S.P. Fleming	c S.R. Waugh, b McGrath	8
C.Z. Harris	c Reiffel, b Warne	130
R.G. Twose	b Bevan	4
C.L. Cairns	c Reiffel, b M.E. Waugh	4
A.C. Parore	lbw, b Warne	11
S.A. Thomson	run out	11
D.N. Patel	not out	3
D.J. Nash		
	lb 6, w 3, nb 3	12
	50 overs (for 9 wickets)	286

	O	M	R	W
Reiffel	4	–	38	1
D.W. Fleming	5	1	20	1
McGrath	9	2	50	2
M.E. Waugh	8	–	43	1
Warne	10	–	52	2
Bevan	10	2	52	1
S.R. Waugh	4	–	25	–

Fall of Wickets
1–**15**, 2–**16**, 3–**44**, 4–**212**, 5–**227**, 6–**240**, 7–**259**, 8–**282**, 9–**286**

Australia

Batsman	Dismissal	Runs
M.A. Taylor (Capt)	c Germon, b Patel	10
M.E. Waugh	c Parore, b Nash	110
R.T. Ponting	c sub, b Thomson	31
S.K. Warne	lbw, b Astle	24
S.R. Waugh	not out	59
S.G. Law	not out	42
M.G. Bevan		
*I.A. Healy		
P.R. Reiffel		
D.W. Fleming		
G.D. McGrath		
	b 1, lb 6, w 3, nb 3	13
	47.5 overs (for 4 wickets)	289

	O	M	R	W
Nash	9	1	44	1
Patel	8	–	45	1
Cairns	6.5	–	51	–
Harris	10	1	41	–
Thomson	8	–	57	1
Astle	3	–	21	1
Twose	3	–	23	–

Fall of Wickets
1–**19**, 2–**84**, 3–**127**, 4–**213**

Umpires: S. Venkataraghavan & C.J. Mitchley *Man of the Match:* M.E. Waugh

Australia won by 6 wickets

Semi-Final – India *v.* Sri Lanka

13 March 1996 at Eden Gardens, Calcutta

Sri Lanka

S.T. Jayasuriya	c Venkatesh Prasad, **b** Srinath	**1**
*R.S. Kaluwitharana	**c** Manjrekar, **b** Srinath	**0**
A.P. Gurusinha	**c** Kumble, **b** Srinath	**1**
P.A. de Silva	**b** Kumble	**66**
R.S. Mahanama	retired hurt	**58**
A. Ranatunga (Capt)	lbw, **b** Tendulkar	**35**
H.P. Tillekeratne	**c** Tendulkar, **b** V. Prasad	**32**
H.D.P.K. Dharmasena	**b** Tendulkar	**9**
W.P.U.J.C. Vaas	run out	**23**
G.P. Wickremasinghe	not out	**4**
M. Muralitharan	not out	**5**
	b **1**, lb **10**, w **4**, nb **2**	**17**
	50 overs (for 8 wickets)	**251**

	O	M	R	W
Srinath	7	1	34	**3**
Kumble	10	–	51	**1**
Venkatesh Prasad	8	–	50	**1**
Kapoor	10	–	40	**–**
Jadeja	5	–	31	**–**
Tendulkar	10	1	34	**2**

Fall of Wickets
1–**1**, 2–**1**, 3–**35**, 4–**85**, 5–**168**, 6–**206**, 7–**236**, 8–**244**

India

S.R. Tendulkar	**st** Kaluwitharana, **b** Jayasuriya	**65**
N.S. Sidhu	**c** Jayasuriyam, **b** Vaas	**3**
S.V. Manjrekar	**b** Jayasuriya	**25**
M. Azharuddin (Capt)	**c** and **b** Dharmasena	**0**
V.G. Kambli	not out	**10**
J. Srinath	run out	**6**
A.D. Jadeja	**b** Jayasuriya	**0**
*N.R. Mongia	**c** Jayasuriya, **b** de Silva	**1**
A.R. Kapoor	**c** de Silva, **b** Muralitharan	**0**
A.R. Kumble		
Venkatesh Prasad		
	lb **5**, w **5**	**10**
	34.1 overs (for 8 wickets)	**120**

	O	M	R	W
Wickremasinghe	5	–	24	**–**
Vaas	6	1	23	**1**
Muralitharan	7.1	–	29	**1**
Dharmasena	7	–	24	**1**
Jayasuriya	7	1	12	**3**
de Silva	2	–	3	**1**

Fall of Wickets
1–**8**, 2–**98**, 3–**99**, 4–**101**, 5–**110**, 6–**115**, 7–**120**, 8–**120**

Umpires: C.J. Mitchley & R.S. Dunne *Man of the Match:* P.A. de Silva

Sri Lanka won by default

Semi-Finals

India go out in flames while Australia mount the great escape.

India *v.* Sri Lanka

The capacity crowd at Eden Gardens, destined to play a major part in the first semi-final, was ecstatic after four balls of the match had been bowled. The exciting openers, Jayasuriya and Kaluwitharana, had both perished to Srinath, caught at third man off sliced shots. Azharuddin's decision to ask Sri Lanka to bat first had been, it seemed, the right one, but later events were to suggest otherwise. In the past 12 months, Aravinda de Silva has claimed the international recognition that he has long richly deserved and now he proceeded to restore the Sri Lankan innings with another belligerent piece of magic. A batsman with steel wrists and silken shots, he hit 14 fours as he made 66 from 47 deliveries. Gurusinha had become Srinath's third victim at 35, but de Silva continued to steer the ball through gaps in the field, smooth and glorious in all he did. At 85, he was surprisingly bowled by Kumble off an inside edge, and one felt that his departure had come some ten overs or 60 runs before Sri Lanka would have felt comfortable. Ranatunga had shown intelligent captaincy, however, in promoting Mahanama to give solidity. In the first-class game, Mahanama is an opener, and he offered sober

The vital moment in the semi-final between India and Sri Lanka. Sachin Tendulkar falls to a fine leg side stumping by Romesh Kaluwitharana, and the Indian decline begins.
(Ross Kinnaird/ Allsport)

contrast to his flamboyant colleagues, but he, too, was soon scoring runs at an agreeable pace.

Ranatunga has a wonderfully assuring bulky presence, and he frustrated the Indian bowlers by nudging the ball past the wicket-keeper to the boundary as well as by his powerful drives. In fairness, the Indian bowlers did the job well, and Tendulkar's accuracy accounted for both Ranatunga and Dharmasena. Tillekeratne made an invaluable contribution, and Vaas smote lustily towards the close, but the real hero of the later stages had been Mahanama who was carried from the field with cramp and dehydration after he had scored 58, completing the salvation that de Silva had started.

Sidhu was caught at cover in the second over when India went in search of 252 to win. Tendulkar was masterly, as ever, but Manjrekar looked uncertain as the pitch now showed great encouragement to the spinners. Tendulkar lost his balance and was smartly stumped, Manjrekar was bowled by a ball which pitched in the rough outside his leg stump, and Azharuddin offered a simple return catch. There was panic in the air. Srinath was promoted and ran himself out indolently, Jadeja became another victim of a ball which turned viciously, and Mongia and Kapoor both hit high and wildly to leg. From 98 for 2 in the 23rd over, India had descended to 120 for 8 in the 35th. It was too much for certain elements in the crowd who abused their players, threw missiles and lit fires. The players left the field. An attempt to restart was aborted, and Sri Lanka were awarded a game which they had long since won. It was a sad and disgraceful end, but it could not diminish the glory that was Sri Lanka's.

Australia v. West Indies

If courage had been needed to survive the last stages of the first semi-final, nerves of steel were essential for surviving the climax of the game between West Indies and Australia, one of the most exciting and remarkable matches in World Cup history. Australia batted first and were soon in desperate trouble. Ambrose and a revitalised Bishop opened the West Indies' bowling. Ambrose's first delivery came back from well outside off-stump and had Browne moving way down the leg side to take it. The second trapped the prolific Mark Waugh leg before. With extras the main source of runs, Taylor cut at Bishop and chopped the ball into his stumps. Steve Waugh also played on, but by then Ponting had fallen leg before to Ambrose, and Australia were 15 for 4.

Law and Bevan had had little chance to show their worth in the competition, but they now joined in a stand of 138 which loosened West Indies' grip on the game, and the out-cricket deteriorated to a marked degree. The batting was intelligent and inventive. Law and Bevan hit the loose ball and ran purposefully although, eventually, unwisely as Law became a victim of his partner's eccentricity. Bevan himself was out 18 runs later, but Healy, hitting hard to leg and stealing runs at every point, saw Australia past 200. Even so, 207 looked a long way from being a winning total.

Mark Taylor showed a shrewd knowledge of his opponents when he quickly brought Warne into the attack to exploit Browne's known weakness to spin. Warne did all his captain wanted by having the West Indian 'keeper caught and bowled. Lara looked threateningly at ease. He hit five fours and had made 45 off 45 balls when Steve Waugh produced a magnificent delivery which drifted towards middle and leg before cutting away to beat the outside edge of the left-hander's bat and clipping off-stump.

Shane Warne holds on to a return catch from Courtney Browne, and Australia claim their first wicket in the semi-final. (Shaun Botterill/Allsport)

Semi-Final – Australia v. West Indies
14 March 1996 at Mohali Stadium, Chandigarh

Australia

M.E. Waugh	lbw, b Ambrose	0
M.A. Taylor (Capt)	b Bishop	1
R.T. Ponting	lbw, b Ambrose	0
S.R. Waugh	b Bishop	3
S.G. Law	run out	72
M.G. Bevan	c Richardson, b Harper	69
*I.A. Healy	run out	31
P.R. Reiffel	run out	7
S.K. Warne	not out	6
D.W. Fleming		
G.D. McGrath		
	lb 11, w 5, nb 2	18
	50 overs (for 8 wickets)	207

	O	M	R	W
Ambrose	10	1	26	2
Bishop	10	1	35	2
Walsh	10	1	33	–
Gibson	2	–	13	–
Harper	9	–	47	1
Adams	9	–	42	–

Fall of Wickets
1–0, 2–7, 3–8, 4–15, 5–153, 6–171, 7–186, 8–207

West Indies

S. Chanderpaul	c Fleming, b McGrath	80
*C.O. Browne	c and b Warne	10
B.C. Lara	b S.R. Waugh	45
R.B. Richardson (Capt)	not out	49
R.A. Harper	lbw, b McGrath	2
O.D. Gibson	c Healy, b Warne	1
J.C. Adams	lbw, b Warne	2
K.L.T. Arthurton	c Healy, b Fleming	0
I.R. Bishop	lbw, b Warne	3
C.E.L. Ambrose	run out	2
C.A. Walsh	b Fleming	0
	lb 4, w 2, nb 2	8
	49.3 overs	202

	O	M	R	W
McGrath	10	2	30	2
Fleming	8.3	–	48	2
Warne	9	–	36	4
M.E. Waugh	4	–	16	–
S.R. Waugh	7	–	30	1
Reiffel	5	–	13	–
Bevan	4	–	12	–
Law	2	–	13	–

Fall of Wickets
1–25, 2–93, 3–165, 4–173, 5–178, 6–183, 7–187, 8–194, 9–202

Umpires: B.C. Cooray & S.Venkataraghavan *Man of the Match:* S.K.Warne

Australia won by 5 runs

The dramatic end to a magnificent match. Healy leaps in the air as Fleming bowls Walsh to give Australia victory by five runs. Richardson, playing his last game in international cricket, looks on in despair. (John Parkin/Allsport)

There was still no cause for alarm on the part of West Indies, for Richardson joined Chanderpaul who was playing with calm and assurance. The run-rate slowed a little, but ten overs remained in which to score 47 runs, which was hardly a daunting task with eight wickets in hand. In the 41st over, the score was 165 for 2, but Chanderpaul became unnecessarily fretful, and he pulled McGrath to mid-on. That West Indies felt under pressure became apparent when Harper rather than Jimmy Adams was next to the crease. Harper fell quickly to McGrath, and Gibson, another slogger, was promoted and was caught behind off Warne as he swiped.

Warne was now spinning, twirling, flicking and bouncing with the enthusiasm of a bowler who knows he is on song. Adams and Bishop were his third and fourth victims in a wonderful spell, and Arthurton, who had a dreadful World Cup, flayed and was caught behind off Fleming. Fourteen had been needed off the last two overs, and ten were needed off the last although nine would have been sufficient to have tied the match and given West Indies a place in the final by virtue of their victory over Australia earlier in the competition. Richardson swung the first ball away for four and, incomprehensibly, tried to run a bye to the wicket-keeper off the second ball. Healy's throw narrowly beat Ambrose's lollop to the crease, and the red light shone in favour of Australia. The battle was now between Fleming and Walsh as five runs were needed from four balls for the match to be tied. Fleming bowled straight and true. Walsh swung in a thoughtless manner and his stumps went over. Australia's joy was unconfined. Richardson stood at the bowler's end, 49 not out, betrayed by the fallibilities of others for the last time in international cricket.

World Cup Final

Arjuna Ranatunga broke with tradition in that he asked Australia to bat first when he won the toss, for the side batting second had never been in the victors in the World Cup Final – but then Sri Lanka had broken with tradition by reaching the final. It pleased everybody, but it was not in the original script. The first blood went to Sri Lanka when Mark Waugh, so dominant until the semi-final stage, played loosely at Vaas' away-swinger. Taylor and Ponting seemed totally unaffected by this set-back and plundered runs with ease. They added 101, and Taylor scored 74 off 83 balls before he fell in de Silva's second over when he swept to backward square-leg.

Most of the runs came off the quick bowlers. Vaas and Wickremasinghe conceded 68 runs in 13 overs, but the spinners posed greater problems, and the scoring slowed. Aravinda de Silva followed his dismissal of Taylor by bowling Ponting as he tried to cut a ball too close to his body. When Australia had been 130 for 1 in 25 overs a total of 300 looked more than possible, but there was now a sense of concern in the Australian camp that the run rate was slipping badly. Warne again found himself at number four, but he was well stumped by Kaluwitharana after just five balls and five minutes at the crease. When Steve Waugh was caught at long-on off a leading edge Australia had lost four wickets in ten overs for 36 runs.

Bevan and Law worked hard. Law hit a six and pushed for runs, but the Sri Lankan fielding had gained in confidence since the dismissal of Taylor and was now of the highest standard. Jayasuriya was turning the ball from a good length, and Law was caught in the gully when he tried to attack the left-arm spinner. The return of de Silva saw Healy bowled third ball when he thrashed madly. Bevan and Reiffel played out the remaining overs content with what crumbs came their way.

A ploy fails. Warne, sent in at number five, is stumped off Muralitharan by Kaluwitharana, and Australia lose momentum. (Ross Kinnaird/Allsport)

Defending a total of 241 on a sound pitch with a short boundary on one side was never going to be a simple task, but what surprised Australia, and what Sri Lanka had learned from their practice under lights, was that the evening in Lahore brought a dew which would give bowlers problems in gripping the ball. This was not a consideration when Jayasuriya was beaten by McGrath's throw from third man and run out by millimetres, and when Kaluwitharana was late as he tried to pull Fleming.

Aravinda de Silva, Man of the Match, cracks a boundary in his innings of 107 not out. He played with beauty, control and aggression, and his batting in the 1996 World Cup will be long remembered. (Mike Hewitt/Allsport)

World Cup Final – Australia v. Sri Lanka

17 March 1996 at Qaddafi Stadium, Lahore

Australia

M.A. Taylor (Capt)	c Jayasuriya, **b** de Silva	**74**
M.E. Waugh	c Jayasuriya, **b** Vaas	**12**
R.T. Ponting	**b** de Silva	**45**
S.R. Waugh	c de Silva, **b** Dharmasena	**13**
S.K. Warne	**st** Kaluwitharana, **b** Muralitharan	**2**
S.G. Law	c de Silva, **b** Jayasuriya	**22**
M.G. Bevan	not out	**36**
*I.A. Healy	**b** de Silva	**2**
P.R. Reiffel	not out	**13**
D.W. Fleming		
G.D. McGrath		
	lb **10**, w **11**, nb **1**	**22**
	50 overs (for 7 wickets)	**241**

	O	M	R	W
Wickremasinghe	7	–	38	–
Vaas	6	1	30	1
Muralitharan	10	–	31	1
Dharmasena	10	–	47	1
Jayasuriya	8	–	43	1
de Silva	9	–	42	3

Fall of Wickets
1–**36**, 2–**137**, 3–**152**, 4–**156**, 5–**170**, 6–**202**, 7–**205**

Sri Lanka

S.T. Jaysuriya	run out	**9**
*R.S. Kaluwitharana	c Bevan, **b** Fleming	**6**
A.P. Gurusinha	**b** Reiffel	**65**
P.A. de Silva	not out	**107**
A. Ranatunga (Capt)	not out	**47**
H.P. Tillekeratne		
H.D.P.K. Dharmasena		
R.S. Mahanama		
W.P.U.J.C. Vaas		
G.P. Wickremasinghe		
M. Muralitharan		
	b **1**, lb **4**, w **5**, nb **1**	**11**
	46.2 overs (for 3 wickets)	**245**

	O	M	R	W
McGrath	8.2	1	28	–
Fleming	6	–	43	1
Warne	10	–	58	–
Reiffel	10	–	49	1
M.E. Waugh	6	–	35	–
S.R. Waugh	3	–	15	–
Bevan	3	–	12	–

Fall of Wickets
1–**12**, 2–**23**, 3–**148**

Umpires: D.R. Shepherd & S.A. Bucknor *Man of the Match:* P.A. de Silva **Sri Lanka won by 7 wickets**

Gurusinha had announced his arrival promptly with a fine off-drive, and de Silva, inevitably, was assured and looking for runs from the start. When Warne came into the attack Gurusinha bludgeoned him over long-off for six, and he also hit six fours in his 65 which came off 99 balls. First he calmed any nerves after the rapid loss of the two openers and then he attacked vigorously. As he did so, the Australian fielding wilted; catches were missed and balls were fumbled. When Gurusinha departed, bowled by Reiffel, Ranatunga joined de Silva who had driven the first ball he received back wide of the bowler. He and Gurusinha had reached fifty in the same over, and de Silva was on 60 when Gurusinha left. What majesty de Silva has, and on this, the greatest occasion of all, what temperament, control and judgement. Without a hint of rashness, he hit 13 fours as he reached 107 off 124 balls in under three hours at the wicket, and he knew he had won the World Cup for Sri Lanka. For the last 97 runs of the innings he had been in partnership with Arjuna Ranatunga, and there was general delight that the captain was at the wicket when victory was gained. He led his side with grace, charm and intelligence, particularly in the way in which he had manipulated his spinners. His 47 in his final innings of the tournament, in which he was dismissed only twice, came off 37 balls and contained a six and four fours. Warne had been battered, the Australians, like the other sides Sri Lanka had played, had been routed. This was the finest of hours for a small country whose cricketers have been treated harshly by Australia and West Indies and with arrogant contempt by England. Cinderella had arrived home from the ball and the glass slipper fitted perfectly.

Ranatunga held aloft the silver trophy. Now the senior nations would have to take notice, because, for three years at least, Sri Lanka were champions of the world.

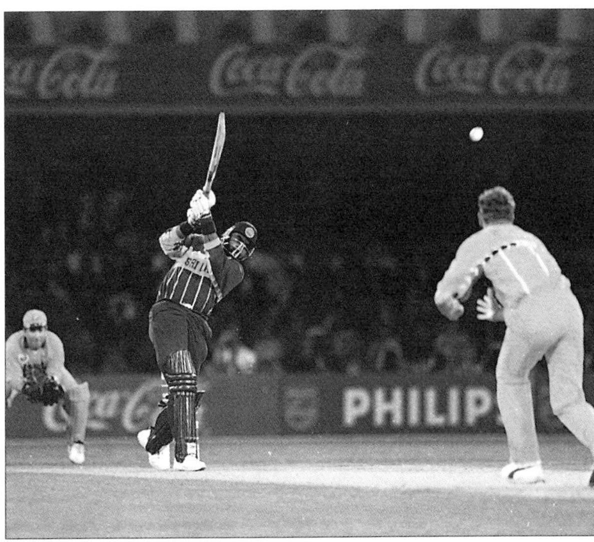

Gurusinha drives majestically during his partnership of 125 with de Silva. (Graham Chadwick/Allsport)

World Cup Averages

Batting

	M	Inns	NO	Runs	HS	Av	100s
A. Ranatunga	6	6	4	241	75*	120.50	
P.A. de Silva	6	6	1	448	145	89.60	2
S.R. Tendulkar	7	7	1	523	137	87.16	2
Saeed Anwar	6	6	2	329	83*	82.25	
M.E. Waugh	7	7	1	484	130	80.66	3
G. Kirsten	6	6	1	391	188*	78.20	1
A.C. Hudson	4	4	–	275	161	68.75	1
Salim Malik	6	3	1	133	55*	66.50	
H.P. Tillekeratne	6	5	3	128	70*	64.00	
D.J. Cullinan	6	6	2	255	69	63.75	
L.K. Germon	6	6	3	191	89	63.66	
G.P. Thorpe	6	6	2	254	89	63.50	
R.B. Richardson	6	6	2	236	93*	59.00	
W.J. Cronje	6	6	1	276	78	55.20	
B.C. Lara	6	6	1	269	111	53.80	1
G.A. Hick	5	5	1	212	104*	53.00	1
A.P. Gurusinha	6	6	–	307	87	51.16	
S.G. Law	7	6	2	204	72	51.00	
R.A. Smith	2	2	–	100	75	50.00	
Inzamam-ul-Haq	6	5	2	145	53*	48.33	
Aamir Sohail	6	6	–	272	111	45.33	1
S.R. Waugh	7	7	2	226	82	45.20	
P.A.J. DeFreitas	4	2	–	89	67	44.50	
V.G. Kambli	7	7	3	176	106	44.00	1

Bowling

	Overs	Mds	Runs	Wks	Av	Best	4/inn
A.A. Donald	34	–	126	8	15.75	3/21	
P.A. Strang	42.1	4	192	12	16.00	5/21	2
C.E.L. Ambrose	56.3	11	170	10	17.00	3/28	
R.A. Harper	58	6	219	12	18.25	4/47	1
D.W. Fleming	45.2	3	221	12	18.41	5/36	1
A.R. Kumble	69.4	5	280	15	18.66	3/28	
Waqar Younis	54	5	253	13	19.46	4/26	1
R. Ali	36.2	3	176	9	19.55	3/17	
Venkatapathy Raju	40	4	158	8	19.75	3/20	
B.M. McMillan	43	5	127	6	21.16	3/11	
P.A. de Silva	17	–	87	4	21.75	3/42	
S.K. Warne	68.3	3	263	12	21.91	4/34	2
R.J. Kennedy	21	2	88	4	22.00	2/36	
P.A.J. DeFreitas	33.1	6	140	6	23.33	3/31	
Mushtaq Ahmed	57	2	238	10	23.80	3/16	
N.M.K. Smith	25.3	2	96	4	24.00	3/29	
P.L. Symcox	40	2	148	6	24.66	2/22	
D.J. Nash	35	4	153	6	25.50	3/26	
S. Dukanwala	33	1	153	6	25.50	5/29	1
Azhar Saeed	31	1	157	6	26.16	3/45	
C.Z. Harris	33	2	135	5	27.00	3/24	
D.G. Cork	48	2	216	8	27.00	2/33	
Aqib Javed	39.3	2	189	7	27.00	2/18	

The greatest moment in the cricketing history of a small nation. Arjuna Ranatunga receives the World Cup from Pakistan's President Benazhir Bhutto. (Patrick Eagar)

Captain courageous, gracious and intelligent. Arjuna Ranatunga drives to the off as he and de Silva take Sri Lanka to victory with an unbroken partnership of 97. (Graham Chadwick/Allsport)

Singapore

Hot on the heels of the World Cup came the Singer Cup, a limited-over competition for the three Test-playing nations of Asia. Aamir Sohail led Pakistan in the absence of the injured Wasim Akram. India omitted Kambli and Prabhakar from their squad – a decision that prompted Prabhakar to retire from international cricket. Brief as the tournament was, it produced an astonishing world record and brought a set-back for Sri Lanka.

Aamir Sohail, deputising for Wasim Akram as captain, led Pakistan to victory in the Singer Cup. His 76 not out against India was instrumental in putting his side into the final. (Paul Sturgess/Sportsline)

The Singer Cup

Limited-over tournament between India, Sri Lanka and Pakistan

The tournament began sensationally, with a record 664 runs scored in the match between Pakistan and Sri Lanka. This first game was a personal triumph for Sanath Jayasuriya, the left-handed batsman who had been an outstanding success in the World Cup. He now surpassed his previous efforts by reaching 50 off 31 balls and moving to 100 off 48 balls. This established a new record for the fastest century in a one-day international, beating Azharuddin's previous record of 100 off 64 balls. When Jayasuriya was out to a 'wild' shot in the 21st over he had hit 134 from 65 balls. His innings included 11 sixes, three more than the previous record set by Gordon Greenidge, and 11 fours. Jayasuriya broke another record when he hit 29 off one over from Aamir Sohail, who also conceded a wide in the over.

Jayasuriya had first come to prominence with prolific scoring for Sri Lanka 'B' on their tour of Pakistan in

Sanath Jayasuriya of Sri Lanka established four world records for international limited-over cricket in the Singer Cup matches in Singapore. He hit the fastest fifty, off 17 balls, and the fastest century, off 48 balls; he took 29 runs off one over; and he hit 11 sixes in an innings. (Paul Sturgess/Sportsline)

Singer Cup – Match One – Pakistan *v.* Sri Lanka

2 April 1996 at The Padang, Singapore

Sri Lanka

Batsman	How out	Runs
S.T. Jayasuriya	c Mohammad, b Saqlain	134
*R.S. Kaluwitharana	c Saqlain Mushtaq, b Waqar	24
A.P. Gurusinha	c Aamir Sohail, b Saqlain	29
P.A. de Silva	c and b Salim Malik	7
A. Ranatunga (Capt)	c Inzamam-ul-Haq, b Waqar	14
H.P. Tillekeratne	b Mohammad Akram	25
R.S. Mahanama	c Waqar, b Mohammad Akram	35
H.D.P.K. Dharmasena	b Waqar Younis	51
W.P.U.J.C. Vaas	c Aamir Sohail, b Waqar Younis	6
G.P. Wickremasinghe	not out	7
M. Muralitharan	not out	2
	b 1, lb 3, w 9, nb 2	15
	50 overs (for 9 wickets)	349

	O	M	R	W
Waqar Younis	10	–	62	4
Mohammad Akram	7	–	66	2
Saqlain Mushtaq	10	–	45	2
Aqib Javed	10	–	65	–
Aamir Sohail	8	–	73	–
Salim Malik	5	–	34	1

Fall of Wickets
1–**40**, 2–**196**, 3–**197**, 4–**203**, 5–**238**, 6–**245**, 7–**318**, 8–**328**, 9–**348**

Pakistan

Batsman	How out	Runs
Aamir Sohail (Capt)	lbw, b Dharmasena	46
Saeed Anwar	c Kaluwitharana, b Vaas	32
Rameez Raja	c and b de Silva	27
Salim Malik	c Dharmasena, b Muralitharan	68
Inzamam-ul-Haq	b Vaas	67
Ijaz Ahmed	st Kaluwitharana, b Jayasuriya	32
Waqar Younis	c Muralitharan, b Dharmasena	1
*Rashid Latif	c Dharmasena, b Muralitharan	7
Saqlain Mushtaq	run out	0
Aqib Javed	c Muralitharan, b Tillekeratne	20
Mohammad Akram	not out	3
	b 3, lb 6, w 1, nb 2	12
	49.4 overs	315

	O	M	R	W
Wickremasinghe	4	–	46	–
Vaas	10	–	50	2
Muralitharan	10	–	59	2
Dharmasena	8	–	51	2
de Silva	4	–	22	1
Jayasuriya	10	–	45	1
Ranatunga	2	–	20	–
Tillekeratne	0.4	–	13	1

Fall of Wickets
1–**77**, 2–**96**, 3–**120**, 4–**247**, 5–**253**, 6–**257**, 7–**281**, 8–**291**, 9–**291**

Umpires: R. Tiffin & G. Sharp *Man of the Match:* S.T. Jayasuriya

Sri Lanka won by 34 runs

Singer Cup – Match Two – India v. Sri Lanka

3 April 1996 at The Padang, Singapore

India

S.R. Tendulkar	c Muralitharan, b Wickremasinghe	28
N.S. Sidhu	b Vaas	94
M. Azharuddin (Capt)	run out	9
R.S. Dravid	c Kaluwitharana, b Muralitharan	3
S.V. Manjrekar	lbw, b Muralitharan	7
A.D. Jadeja	c Chandana, b Jayasuriya	7
*N.R. Mongia	c and b de Silva	4
A.R. Kumble	c Atapattu, b de Silva	4
J. Srinath	not out	28
Venkatesh Prasad	c Jayasuriya, b Vaas	7
Venkatapathy Raju	b Vaas	0
	lb 2, w 2, nb 4	8
	45.4 overs	199

	O	M	R	W
Wickremasinghe	8	–	39	1
Vaas	7.4	–	35	3
Muralitharan	8	–	25	2
Chandana	10	–	52	–
Jayasuriya	8	–	31	1
de Silva	4	–	15	2

Fall of Wickets
1–**33**, 2–**58**, 3–**62**, 4–**82**, 5–**114**, 6–**130**, 7–**136**, 8–**191**, 9–**199**

Sri Lanka

S.T. Jayasuriya	c Manjrekar, b Srinath	7
*R.S. Kaluwitharana	c Azharuddin, b Srinath	4
M.S. Atapattu	lbw, b Srinath	10
P.A. de Silva	c Dravid, b Venkatesh Prasad	1
R.S. Mahanama	c Jadeja, b Venkatapathy Raju	59
A. Ranatunga (Capt)	c Azharuddin, b Venkatapathy	13
H.P. Tillekeratne	c Prasad, b Venkatapathy Raju	42
U.U. Chandana	run out	11
W.P.U.J.C. Vaas	b Srinath	6
M. Muralitharan	not out	7
G.P. Wickremasinghe	run out	11
	b 8, w 7, nb 1	16
	48.1 overs	187

	O	M	R	W
Srinath	10	–	35	4
Venkatesh Prasad	10	2	39	1
Kumble	10	1	46	–
Venkatapathy Raju	10	1	26	3
Tendulkar	5.1	–	19	–
Jadeja	3	–	14	–

Fall of Wickets
1–**5**, 2–**12**, 3–**13**, 4–**23**, 5–**53**, 6–**145**, 7–**163**, 8–**169**, 9–**169**

Umpires: G. Sharp & R. Tiffin *Man of the Match:* J. Srinath

India won by 12 runs

Singer Cup – Match Three – India v. Pakistan

5 April 1996 at The Padang, Singapore

India

N.S. Sidhu	c Rashid Latif, b Aqib Javed	14
S.R. Tendulkar	st Rashid Latif, b Saqlain	100
M. Azharuddin (Capt)	c Rashid Latif, b Aamir Sohail	29
R.S. Dravid	run out	4
S.V. Manjrekar	c Aqib Javed, b Saqlain	41
A.D. Jadeja	run out	5
*N.R. Mongia	run out	3
J. Srinath	st Rashid Latif, b Saqlain	0
A.R. Kumble	not out	14
Venkatesh Prasad	not out	1
Venkatapathy Raju		
	lb 3, w 9, nb 3	15
	47.1 overs (for 8 wickets)	226

	O	M	R	W
Waqar Younis	8	1	42	–
Aqib Javed	7.1	–	12	1
Inzamam-ul-Haq	1	–	10	–
Mushtaq Ahmed	9	–	58	–
Saqlain Mushtaq	10	–	38	3
Salim Malik	3	–	17	–
Aamir Sohail	9	–	46	1

Fall of Wickets
1–**44**, 2–**110**, 3–**127**, 4–**184**, 5–**195**, 6–**205**, 7–**223**, 8–**224**

Pakistan

Aamir Sohail (Capt)	not out	76
Saeed Anwar	c Dravid, b Venkatapathy Raju	74
Rameez Raja	lbw, b Kumble	5
Salim Malik	not out	25
Inzamam-ul-Haq		
Ijaz Ahmed		
*Rashid Latif		
Waqar Younis		
Mushtaq Ahmed		
Saqlain Mushtaq		
Aqib Javed		
	lb 3, w 4, nb 3	10
	28 overs (for 2 wickets)	190

	O	M	R	W
Srinath	7	–	34	–
Venkatesh Prasad	7	–	45	–
Kumble	7	1	39	1
Venkatapathy Raju	5	–	51	1
Tendulkar	2	–	18	–

Fall of Wickets
1–**144**, 2–**162**

Umpires: G. Sharp & R. Tiffin *Man of the Match:* Aamir Sohail

Pakistan won on a faster scoring rate

Singer Cup Final – Pakistan v. Sri Lanka

7 April 1996 at the Padang, Singapore

Pakistan

Aamir Sohail (Capt)	b Vaas	18
Saeed Anwar	c Muralitharan, b Wickremasinghe	17
Rameez Raja	run out	37
Salim Malik	c and b Muralitharan	27
Inzamam-ul-Haq	c Tillekeratne, b de Silva	24
Ijaz Ahmed	b Jayasuriya	51
*Rashid Latif	b Dharmasena	2
Aqib Javed	c Mahanama, b Muralitharan	11
Saqlain Mushtaq	c Tillekeratne, b Vaas	8
Waqar Younis	run out	0
Ata-ur-Rehman	not out	1
	b 6, lb 4, w 6, nb 3	19
	48.3 overs	215

	O	M	R	W
Wickremasinghe	8	1	30	1
Vaas	8	–	35	2
Muralitharan	10	–	42	2
Dharmasena	10	1	39	1
Jayasuriya	8.3	–	39	1
de Silva	4	–	20	1

Fall of Wickets
1–**29**, 2–**41**, 3–**102**, 4–**106**, 5–**140**, 6–**143**, 7–**175**, 8–**199**, 9–**199**

Sri Lanka

S.T. Jayasuriya	c Saeed Anwar, b Waqar	76
*R.S. Kaluwitharana	b Aqib Javed	0
A.P. Gurusinha	lbw, b Aqib Javed	20
P.A. de Silva	c Rashid, b Saqlain Mushtaq	4
A. Ranatunga (Capt)	c Rashid, b Saqlain Mushtaq	0
R.S. Mahanama	lbw, b Waqar Younis	14
H.P. Tillekeratne	lbw, b Ata-ur-Rehman	33
H.D.P.K. Dharmasena	c Inzamam-ul-Haq, b Saqlain	5
W.P.U.J.C. Vaas	not out	5
G.P. Wickremasinghe	b Ata-ur-Rehman	0
M. Muralitharan	c Rameez, b Ata-ur-Rehman	0
	lb 5, w 7, nb 3	15
	32.5 overs	172

	O	M	R	W
Waqar Younis	7	–	38	2
Aqib Javed	7	–	32	2
Ata-ur-Rehman	3.5	–	27	3
Saqlain Mushtaq	7	–	46	3
Aamir Sohail	6	–	21	–
Salim Malik	2	–	3	–

Fall of Wickets
1–**70**, 2–**96**, 3–**100**, 4–**106**, 5–**106**, 6–**146**, 7–**164**, 8–**172**, 9–**172**

Umpires: R. Tiffin & G. Sharp *Man of the Match:* Saqlain Mushtaq

Pakistan won by 43 runs

1988–89, but it was not until 1995–96, with a maiden Test century and a phenomenal record in one-day internationals, that he realised his potential as a cricketer of world class.

The second match was an unexpected anticlimax. Navjot Singh Sidhu hit 94 off 116 balls to hold together an Indian innings that produced a modest 199. Matters would have been far worse but for some late hitting from Srinath, who later undermined the Sri Lankan innings with three quick wickets. Sri Lanka gave an uncharacteristically inept batting display and fell short of a target that they had been expected to reach with ease. This was their first defeat since the World Series Final in Australia.

In the third game, Sachin Tendulkar hit a six and nine fours and was given good support by Azharuddin and Manjrekar as India reached 184 for 3, but they lost their way against the off-spin off Saqlain Mushtaq and slipped to 226 for 8 when rain intervened. A revised target left Pakistan 33 overs in which to score 187, and a sparkling opening partnership of 144 between Aamir Sohail and Saeed Anwar assured them of victory. Aamir hit Venkatapathy Raju for three sixes, and struck eight fours. Pakistan and Sri Lanka qualified for the final by virtue of faster run rates, 6.47 and 5.36 respectively, to India's 4.37.

The final saw Sri Lanka disappoint for a second time. Their bowlers performed admirably to bowl out Pakistan inside 49 overs for a moderate 215. Sanath Jayasuriya seemed to have set up victory when he claimed another world record of 50 off 17 deliveries. He was out at 96, having scored 76 off 27 balls with five sixes and eight fours. His dismissal brought about a collapse as four wickets fell for ten runs. Tillekeratne tried to restore order, but Sri Lanka were bowled out 44 runs short of their target with 17.1 overs unused.

Arjuna Ranatunga announced that he would stand down as Sri Lanka's captain. His achievements had been outstanding, and he handed a brilliantly entertaining and successful side to his successor, a fine platform for future triumphs, hopefully at Test level.

West Indies

Cricket Year 1995–96 is not a period that followers of the game in the Caribbean will remember with joy. It began badly when several players who had toured England in 1995 were subjected to fines and other forms of discipline on their return home. It was quickly apparent that all was not well within West Indian cricket. Factions were waging internal strife, and the leadership of Richie Richardson, a man of dignity and charm, was under attack.

A double century for Sherwin Campbell in the first Test match against New Zealand. It was Campbell's maiden Test hundred. (David Munden/Sportsline)

When the team to play in Sharjah was announced the depth of the divisions within West Indian cricket was revealed, and many believed that the international careers of the Benjamins were over. Defeat in Sharjah by Sri Lanka was the first of several indignities that the side was to suffer; the second was the failure to reach the final of the World Series in Australia. Two days before the party left for Australia, Brian Lara withdrew from the tour, giving further evidence to those who asserted that West Indies had in their midst a temperamental genius who was beyond discipline and who threatened to become bigger than the team and the game itself. Lara was certainly finding it increasingly difficult to come to terms with the demands that come with being a cricketer of world fame and outstanding ability. He later agreed to play in the World Cup, but then Carl Hooper, who had appeared before the same disciplinary committee in Barbados that Lara had faced, withdrew from the side for this most important of competitions.

West Indies failed to reach the final of the World Cup, refused to play in Sri Lanka and suffered a humiliating defeat at the hands of Kenya. In the wake of this defeat, Lara was quoted as having made comments, racist in overtone, which did neither him nor the game of cricket any credit. Following the failures in the World Cup, Richardson announced his retirement from international cricket, and the West Indies Board swept aside the management team and replaced them with Tony Marshall and Clive Lloyd.

Lara was further involved in controversy when he engaged in an argument with the long-serving Australian-born physiotherapist Dennis Waight on a flight from Bombay after the exit from the World Cup. It was alleged that Lara again made racist remarks and that he claimed that he had got rid of Hall, Roberts and Richardson and would do the same to Waight. *The Guardian* of Trinidad later carried an apology from a contrite Lara, but the great batsman again found himself before a disciplinary committee.

Back in the Caribbean, against a young New Zealand side hit by injury and feeling its way in international cricket, West Indies were less than convincing, and once again they bowed the knee to Sri Lanka.

If it was a year best forgotten internationally, there were moments of glory and grandeur in the domestic game. In the Shell/Sandals Trophy, the one-day tournament played in October and November, Trinidad and Guyana qualified for the final. Barbados had headed Group A with Jamaica second, and Trinidad and Tobago had led Group B with Guyana second. Hooper and Chanderpaul had swept Guyana to victory over Barbados while Trinidad beat Jamaica on a faster scoring rate after they ruined their encounter in Port-of-Spain, and rain struck again to wipe out any chance of a result in the final so that Trinidad and Guyana shared the trophy.

Brian Lara became the first batsman to score two centuries in the tournament in the same season, but Carl Hooper was the leading scorer with 330 runs (average 66.00). This was a new record for the competition, beating Carlisle Best's 288 in 1987. In fairness, Best's runs came from three innings while Hooper batted on six occasions. The leading wicket-takers were Chanderpaul, 13 and the leg-spinner Robert Haynes, 12.

Red Stripe Cup

26, 27, 28 and 29 January 1996
at Guaracara Park, Pointe-à-Pierre, Trinidad
Barbados 337 (R.I.C. Holder 138, P.A. Wallace 108) and 226 (F.L. Reifer 81 not out, A. Samaroo 4 for 74)
Trinidad & Tobago 263 (B.C. Lara 77, P.V. Simmons 53, O.D. Gibson 4 for 79) and 301 for 7 (B.C. Lara 119, S. Ragoonath 85, P.I.C. Thompson 4 for 48)
Trinidad & Tobago won by 3 wickets
Trinidad & Tobago 16 pts, Barbados 5 pts

at Sabina Park, Kingston, Jamaica
Guyana 559 for 5 dec. (S. Chanderpaul 303 not out, R.A. Harper 124, A.R. Percival 78)
Jamaica 154 (N.O. Perry 56, R.A. Harper 5 for 38) and 370 for 6 (J.C. Adams 120, T.O. Powell 56, N.O. Perry 56, R.G. Samuels 52)
Match drawn
Guyana 8 pts, Jamaica 4 pts

at Ronald Webster Park, The Valley, Anguilla
Leeward Islands 320 (R.B. Richardson 82, S.C. Williams 77, R.A. Marshall 6 for 71)
Windward Islands 159 (K.C.G. Benjamin 4 for 18) and 154
Leeward Islands won by an innings and 7 runs
Leeward Islands 16 pts, Windward Islands 0 pts

The first round of matches in the Red Stripe Cup was the only round in which the leading Test players were available. Thereafter, their attention was on the World Cup. For the first time, the competition followed the format now adopted in Australia and elsewhere with the top two teams in the league meeting in a final to decide the winner of the cup.

The tournament certainly began on a high note. Philo Wallace, the Barbados opener, became the first batsman to reach a century before lunch when he hit 108 against Trinidad. Wallace was on 87 when the last over before the break began, and he reached his hundred off the fifth delivery by hitting left-arm spinner Samaroo for six. Wallace's century came off 91 balls and included five sixes and 12 fours. The eighteen-year old Avidesh Samaroo was making his first-class debut, and he recovered splendidly to bowl his side to victory. He finished the match with 7 for 154 and twice claimed Wallace. The Man of the Match was Brian Lara who, in the second innings, shared a stand of 188 with Ragoonath after two wickets had fallen for six runs.

In Kingston, Shivnarine Chanderpaul became only the 11th West Indian batsman to score a triple century. He batted for 632 minutes, faced 478 balls and hit 38 fours, reaching his triple hundred just after tea on the second day. His innings was the highest by a Guyanese and the highest recorded in the inter-island competition. He and Roger Harper shared a record fourth wicket stand of 305. Harper also bowled effectively, but a century from Jimmy Adams brought Jamaica a draw. Off-spinner Nehemiah hit 56 in each innings for Jamaica and so completed a regional double of 1,000 runs and 100 wickets. He made his debut in 1987.

Winston Benjamin announced his retirement from inter-island, and therefore from Test cricket, but even in his absence Leewards trounced Windwards in three days. Williams and Richardson shared a second wicket partnership of 143.

2, 3, 4 and 5 February 1996
at Queen's Park Oval, Port-of-Spain, Trinidad
Guyana 173 (R. Dhanraj 4 for 64) and 152 (N.A. de Groot 78, E.C. Antoine 5 for 47)
Trinidad & Tobago 238 (P.V. Simmons 80, K. Mason 67, B.S. Browne 5 for 48) and 88 for 2
Trinidad & Tobago won by 8 wickets
Trinidad & Tobago 16 pts, Guyana 0 pts

at Kensington Oval, Bridgetown, Barbados
Windward Islands 233 (K.K. Sylvester 77) and 318 (U. Pope 75, J.R. Murray 70)
Barbados 339 (A.F.G. Griffith 101, R.L. Hoyte 70, F.L. Reifer 58) and 213 for 6
Barbados won by 4 wickets
Barbados 16 pts, Windward Islands 0 pts

at Jarrett Park, Montego Bay
Jamaica 424 for 7 dec. (R.G. Samuels 125, N.O. Perry 74, D.S. Morgan 67, T.O. Powell 51, H.A.G. Anthony 4 for 84)
Leeward Islands 227 (S.C. Williams 75, R.D. Jacobs 54 not out, M.C. Gibbs 4 for 61) and 184 (M.C. Gibbs 4 for 35)
Jamaica won by an innings and 13 runs
Jamaica 16 pts, Leeward Islands 0 pts

With Lara and others departed, Phil Simmons, omitted from the World Cup squad following a run of low scores in Sharjah and Australia, led Trinidad to their second victory in as many matches. Dhanraj, another rejected by the national selectors, bowled well in the victory over a depleted Guyana side.

Tall, slim, left-handed opening batsman Adrian Griffith hit a maiden first-class century in Barbados' victory over Windward Islands, and wicket-keeper Ricky Hoyte, deputising for Courtney Browne, made the highest score of his brief career.

Jamaica's new skipper Robert Samuels played a major part in his side's commendable victory over Leeward Islands. The left-handed Samuels made the third century of his career and shared an opening partnership of 128 with Delroy Morgan. Perry was again in good form with the bat while Marlon Gibbs, on his first-class debut, had match figures of 8 for 96.

9, 10, 11 and 12 February, 1996
at Kensington Oval, Bridgetown, Barbados
Leeward Islands 446 (S.C. Williams 165, D.R.E. Joseph 78, R.D. Jacobs 70 not out, C.M. Tuckett 63, P.I.C. Thompson 4 for 115) and 84 for 4
Barbados 185 (A.F.G. Griffith 59, W.D. Phillip 5 for 37) and 342 (A.F.G. Griffith 115, S.H. Armstrong 92, V.C. Drakes 50, L.C. Weekes 4 for 34)
Leeward Islands won by 6 wickets
Leeward Islands 16 pts, Barbados 0 pts

at Guaracara Park, Pointe-à-Pierre, Trinidad
Trinidad & Tobago 408 (P.V. Simmons 156, D. Williams 102 not out, L.R. Williams 5 for 76)
Jamaica 172 (R. Dhanraj 5 for 50) and 142 (L.R. Williams 53, R. Dhanraj 6 for 48)
Trinidad & Tobago won by an innings and 94 runs
Trinidad & Tobago 16 pts, Jamaica 0 pts

at Windsor Park, Roseau, Dominica
Windward Islands 234, (D. Thomas 70, B.S. Browne 4 for 32) and 278 (D.A. Joseph 67, R.N. Lewis 51 not out)
Guyana 125 and 191 (A.R. Percival 64, R.N. Lewis 7 for 66)
Windward Islands won by 196 runs
Windward Islands 16 pts, Guyana 0 pts

Shivnarine Chanderpaul scored 303 not out for Guyana against Jamaica in Kingston. His triple century established a new record for the inter-island competition. (David Munden/Sportsline)

Adrian Griffith hit his second century in successive matches, and Sean Armstrong, in his second first-class match, hit 92, but Barbados were well beaten by Leeward Islands. Stuart Williams, another jettisoned by the national selectors, made the highest score of his career and shared stands of 138 with Tuckett and 179 with Dave Joseph to set up Leewards victory.

Trinidad made it three wins in a row. Phil Simmons led from the front in the innings victory over Jamaica, and David Williams, the veteran wicket-keeper, who had a fine season, reached the second hundred of his career. The main destroyer, however, was leg-spinner Dhanraj who had match figures of 11 for 98.

Windward Islands were surprise victors over Guyana. Another leg-break bowler, Rawl Lewis, had an excellent all-round match, and his 7 for 66 in Guyana's second innings was a career best.

16, 17, 18 and 19 February 1996
at Queen's Park, Grenada
Trinidad & Tobago 279 (M. Bodoe 59, P.V. Simmons 55) and 165 (S. Ragoonath 53, R.N. Lewis 5 for 49, R.A. Marshall 4 for 60)
Windward Islands 376 (R.A. Marshall 112, U. Pope 84, D.A. Joseph 78) and 69 for 3
Windward Islands won by 7 wickets
Windward Islands 16 pts, Trinidad & Tobago 0 pts

at Kensington Oval, Bridgetown, Barbados
Barbados 270 (R.L. Hoyte 75, A.F.G. Griffith 69, L.R. Williams 5 for 32) and 355 for 7 dec. (A.F.G. Griffith 145, A.E. Proverbs 50, B.S. Murphy 5 for 125)
Jamaica 377 (D.S. Morgan 63, S.G.B. Ford 56 not out, R.G. Samuels 53, G.R. Breese 50, P.I.C. Thompson 5 for 105) and 151 for 4 (T.O. Powell 58)
Match drawn
Jamaica 8 pts, Barbados 4 pts

at Bourda, Georgetown, Guyana
Guyana 148 (K.C.G. Benjamin 5 for 22) and 147 (W.D. Phillip 4 for 31)
Leeward Islands 210 (M.V. Nagamootoo 7 for 76) and 86 for 2
Leeward Islands won by 8 wickets
Leeward Islands 16 pts, Guyana 0 pts

Trinidad's run of success came to a surprising end when they were beaten by Windward Islands in Grenada. All-rounder Roy Marshall was the star of the game. In his 27th first-class match, the 31-year old from Dominica hit his maiden first-class century and had match figures of 8 for 91.

Adrian Griffith enhanced his reputation with his third century in successive matches for Barbados, and another to catch the eye was Patterson Thompson. Erratic but genuinely quick and hostile, he took five wickets in an innings for the first time and looked to be the brightest of fast bowling prospects.

Leeward Islands trounced Guyana in three days, but Guyana's Mahendra Nagamootoo was the Man of the Match. A left-handed batsman and leg-break and googly bowler, he had gone with West Indies Young Cricketers to Pakistan in 1995. Now established in the Guyana side, he captured 9 for 101 against Leewards, with seven of his wickets coming in a career-best first innings haul.

23, 24, 25 and 26 February 1996
at Albion, Berbice, Guyana
Barbados 216 for 6 (P.A. Wallace 81, A.F.G. Griffith 56)
v. **Guyana**
Match abandoned
Guyana 4 pts, Barbados 4 pts

at Grove Park, Nevis
Leeward Islands 295 (L.A. Harrigan 67, S.C. Williams 61, R. Dhanraj 9 for 97) and 175 (D.R.E. Joseph 62, R. Dhanraj 7 for 70)
Trinidad & Tobago 317 (P.V. Simmons 97, A. Balliram 53, K.C.G. Benjamin 5 for 82) and 156 for 1 (A. Balliram 70 not out, P.V. Simmons 64 not out)
Trinidad & Tobago won by 9 wickets
Trinidad & Tobago 16 pts, Leeward Islands 0 pts

at Sabina Park, Kingston, Jamaica
Jamaica 222 (T.O. Powell 125 not out, D. Thomas 4 for 42) and 340 (M.D. Ventura 102, T.O. Powell 69, R.A. Marshall 7 for 99)
Windward Islands 162 (J.A.R. Sylvester 52, B.S. Murphy 5 for 35) and 192 (A.J. Pierre 54, N.O. Perry 5 for 58)
Jamaica won by 208 runs
Jamaica 16 pts, Windward Islands 0 pts

No play was possible after the first day of the game in Guyana. Wallace and Griffith scored 147 for Barbados' first wicket, but the significance of the match was that it saw the debut of Ramnarseh Sarwan, a batsman and leg-spin bowler, who, at the age of 15 years, 226 days, became the youngest player to appear in first-class cricket in the West Indies. The record had previously been held by the late Roy Marshall of Barbados and Hampshire. Sarwan showed his worth with figures of ten overs, four maidens, and nine runs for the wicket of Wallace whom he caught and bowled.

For the first time in their history, Trinidad won four matches in a Red Stripe/Shell season. That they did so was due to Rajindra Dhanraj. The leg-spinner returned career best figures of 16 for 167, nine of his wickets coming in the first innings. His total of 40 wickets in five matches surpassed all previous records, and he captured eight more in the final.

Tony Powell confirmed the promise of an excellent season with a maiden first-class century in Jamaica's victory over Windward Islands. However, the win was not enough to give Jamaica a place in the final.

Red Stripe Cup – Final Table

	P	W	L	D	Pts
Trinidad & Tobago (3)	5	4	1	–	64
Leeward Islands (2)	5	3	2	–	48
Jamaica (4)	5	2	1	2	44
Windward Islands (6)	5	2	3	–	32
Barbados (1)	5	1	2	2	29
Guyana (5)	5	–	3	2	12

(1995 positions in brackets)

Red Stripe Cup Final

Trinidad & Tobago *v.* Leeward Islands

8, 9, 10, 11 and 12 March 1996
at Guaracara Park, Pointe-à-Pierre, Trinidad
Leewards Islands 400 (D.R.E. Joseph 118, R.D. Jacobs 89, H.A.G. Anthony 53, R. Dhanraj 4 for 140) and 230 (A. Samaroo 4 for 44, R. Dhanraj 4 for 67)
Trinidad & Tobago 330 (R.A.M. Smith 99, M. Bodoe 65, L.C. Weekes 5 for 83) and 227 (A. Balliram 57)
Leeward Islands won by 73 runs

The Trinidad & Tobago Cricket Board asked the West Indies Cricket Board to postpone the Red Stripe final until after the World Cup was over when the leading players would be available and interest greater. The request was refused.

The final was virtually over on the first day when, after winning the toss, Leeward Islands amassed 400. Four wickets went down for 122, but Dave Joseph, who had not enjoyed the best of seasons, and left-handed wicket-keeper Ridley Jacobs added 109 at more than a run a minute. Joseph, the Leewards skipper, was dropped three times and was aided by some untidy bowling and ragged fielding. When he was dismissed Hamesh Anthony launched a violent attack on the bowling, hitting four sixes and three fours in his 53 off 40 balls.

With Richard Smith and Mahadeo Bodoe sharing a fifth wicket partnership of 138, Trinidad were well in touch, but off-spinner Ronald Powell, on his debut, brought about a collapse. Powell finished with 3 for 68, and fast bowler Leroy Weekes enjoyed the first five-wicket haul of his career.

Leewards started their second innings early on the third day, and, with the pitch showing signs of aiding spin, they slipped to 99 for 5. Cannonier and Powell added 64 and shifted the balance in favour of Leewards, for a target of 300 looked close to impossible on a crumbling surface. Balliram held out for more than six hours and faced 233 balls for his 57, but Simmons was crucially run out for 24, and the match was over just an hour into the fifth day.

First-Class Match

10, 11 and 12 April 1996
at Sabina Park, Kingston, Jamaica
Lancashire 350 for 6 dec. (J.E.R. Gallian 97, G.D. Lloyd 61, M. Watkinson 61) and 224 for 4 dec. (M.A. Atherton 117, S. Elworthy 57 not out)
Jamaica 324 for 8 dec. (G.R. Breese 124, D. Taylor 60) and 93 for 3
Match drawn

Lancashire made a brief visit to Jamaica shortly before the start of the English season. The South African all-rounder Elworthy made his first appearance for the Red Rose county, for whom Atherton hit a welcome century. Breese celebrated his first season in the Jamaica side with a maiden first-class hundred.

The leading bowler in West Indian cricket, 1996, Rajindra Dhanraj captured 50 wickets in all first-class matches and set up a new record for the Red Stripe Cup. He took an astonishing 9 for 97 and 7 for 70 for Trinidad against Leeward Islands and regained his place in the Test side.
(David Munden/Sportsline)

One-day International

West Indies v. Sri Lanka

Less than two weeks after winning the World Cup, Sri Lanka made their first appearance in the Caribbean, such are the fruits of fame and success. In fairness, the visit had been arranged several months earlier as part of the centenary celebrations for the Queen's Park Oval. As an overture, Sri Lanka met West Indies Masters Invitational, a team of veterans which included Gordon Greenidge, Gus Logie, Joel Garner, Alvin Kallicharran and Jeff Dujon among others. Sri Lanka won by 141 runs. The official one-day international was played the following day.

Sri Lanka won the toss and batted, and Jayasuriya and Kaluwitharana began as they had done in the World Cup. Jayasuriya hit Bishop's first ball of the match to the cover boundary, and when Kaluwitharana was out after 6.2 overs the score was 67. Jayasuriya was next to go, having hit eight fours in his 46 off 33 balls. Gurusinha held one end while others pillaged freely. It was the spinner who proved most economical, but a target of 252 on a dry, turning pitch presented a stiff task. So it proved.

A brilliant piece of acrobatic wicket-keeping by Kaluwitharana brought about the run out of Chanderpaul, and Wallace quickly followed. Lara and Simmons added 116. Lara's 71 came off 93 balls, and Simmons' 45 off 63. All was going well for West Indies, until both batsmen fell to outstanding catches in successive overs. The rest crumbled, leaving Jimmy Adams high and dry, with Ian Bishop dying amid a flurry of furious shots.

A crowd of 20,000, the biggest of the season at Queen's Park Oval, saw the match. If they were disappointed at West Indies' limp batting performance, they were full of praise for the thrilling cricket played by the Sri Lankans.

One-day International – West Indies v. Sri Lanka

14 April 1996 at Queen's Park Oval, Port-of-Spain, Trinidad

Sri Lanka

S.T. Jayasuriya	c Wallace, b Walsh	46
*R.S. Kaluwitharana	c Adams, b Harper	25
A.P. Gurusinha	c Lara, b Adams	59
P.A. de Silva	c and b Williams	25
A. Ranatunga (Capt)	c Wallace, b Adams	15
H.P. Tillekeratne	c and b Chanderpaul	22
W.P.U.J.C. Vaas	b Bishop	12
R.S. Mahanama	c Chanderpaul, b Walsh	14
U. Chandana	c Adams, b Harper	7
H.P.D.K. Dharmasena	not out	3
M. Muralitharan	c Adams, b Harper	4
	lb 8, w 8, nb 3	19
	48.3 overs	251

	O	M	R	W
Bishop	5	–	49	1
Walsh	8	1	40	2
Harper	9.3	1	34	3
Williams	8	–	42	1
Adams	10	–	42	2
Chanderpaul	8	–	36	1

Fall of Wickets
1–67, 2–88, 3–137, 4–168, 5–200, 6–217, 7–219, 8–243, 9–246

West Indies

S. Chanderpaul	run out	3
P.A. Wallace	c Muralitharan, b Vaas	3
B.C. Lara	c Jayasuriya, b Dharmasena	71
P.V. Simmons	c Dharmasena, b Muralitharan	45
J.C. Adams	not out	37
R.I.C. Holder	b Dharmasena	1
R.A. Harper	c Kaluwitharana, b Chandana	0
L.R. Williams	b Muralitharan	5
*C.O. Browne	c and b Jayasuriya	9
I.R. Bishop	c Ranatunga, b Tillekeratne	22
C.A. Walsh (Capt)		
	lb 8, w 10, nb 2	20
	50 overs (for 9 wickets)	216

	O	M	R	W
Vaas	6	1	19	1
de Silva	9	1	42	–
Muralitharan	10	1	37	2
Dharmasena	9	1	33	2
Chandana	10	–	40	1
Jayasuriya	5	–	32	1
Tillekeratne	1	–	5	1

Fall of Wickets
1–8, 2–15, 3–131, 4–134, 5–140, 6–141, 7–156, 8–180, 9–216

Umpires: C.E. Cumberbatch & E. Nicholls *Man of the Match:* H.P.D.K. Dharmasena

Sri Lanka won by 35 runs

New Zealand Tour

New Zealand arrived in the Caribbean nine days after their exit in the quarter-finals of the World Cup. It was the final stage of Lee Germon's demanding seven-month period of captaincy, and he brought with him the 13 players who had been on duty in the World Cup. The manager and coach, too, were unchanged.

West Indies, in contrast, faced changes and difficult decisions. Courtney Walsh had replaced Richie Richardson as captain, and Clive Lloyd was the new coach. Many believed that the selectors should use the one-day series to blood some new players, but they opted instead to choose experience. Keith Arthurton, Sherwin Campbell, Cameron Cuffy and, initially, Courtney Browne paid the price for failure in the World Cup. Phil Simmons and Stuart Williams, dropped a few weeks earlier, were recalled as was Philo Wallace, who had last played for West Indies four years earlier. The only newcomers to be called up by West Indies were Leeward Islands' wicket-keeper Ridley Jacobs, who became the fourth man to be given the job behind the stumps for West Indies inside a year, and Laurie Williams, the Jamaican medium-pace bowler. It transpired that Jacobs was to be dropped after four matches and Williams was to be called upon to bowl only 9.5 overs in his three matches.

One-day Series

West Indies *v.* New Zealand

The series began on an excitingly high note. New Zealand, put in to bat, slumped to 113 for 6 in the 28th over. Parore and Patel then added 111. Parore managed only one six and one four in his 106-ball innings, but he batted most intelligently as he kept the score moving and helped to take his side to their highest score in 21 internationals against West Indies. Patel, who made his highest score in a one-day international, displayed an unaccustomed brutality with three sixes and five fours in an innings of 71 which occupied just 58 balls.

An opening stand of 126 in 26.4 overs seemed to set West Indies on the road to victory, but eight wickets fell for 71 runs in the next 17.2 overs. Harper remained cool, Ambrose turned the game with 17 off ten balls, but when he was bowled by Morrison 23 were still needed from 14 balls. With Harper hitting Nash for a six and a four, the penultimate over produced 16 runs. Three were needed from the final over, and Harper surprisingly took a leg-bye off the first ball to give Walsh the strike. Walsh gave Morrison a simple return catch, but umpire Barker ruled no-ball as the delivery had been above waist height. Morrison overstepped the crease on his next stride and Walsh worked the ball through mid-wicket for the winning run.

West Indies were put in to bat in the second match and lost both openers and Lara for 42. Simmons and Adams restored order, and Holder at last revealed his pedigree with his highest international score, an aggressive 65 off 48 balls. Facing a challenging target of 239, New Zealand were 71 for 4 in the 16th over. Cairns stayed with Fleming for 19.1 overs as 92 were scored, and Harris helped add 67. When he was bowled by Ambrose New Zealand needed nine runs from 13 balls. Walsh and Ambrose maintained pressure on the batsmen, and Ambrose kept Patel scoreless for the first three balls of the final over. The fourth was pushed for a single, and Fleming steered the fifth to third man for the winning two runs.

Fleming batted brilliantly, and his 106 came off 108 balls with a six and seven fours. It was his first century in international cricket, though it had been imminent for much of the New Zealand season. His innings brought New Zealand their first victory over West Indies in any kind of cricket in three tours of the Caribbean.

Twose made his first appearance of the tour in the third match and shared a second wicket stand of 94 with Astle. Sound batting from Cairns and Parore took New Zealand to a good score on a pitch, the same as had been used the previous day, that was showing signs of wear and uncertainty. This was confirmed when Stuart Williams and Chanderpaul quickly fell to the admirable Larsen. Lara took care as he and Simmons rebuilt the innings. Once assured of the pace and tricks of the pitch, Lara batted with a splendour that is his own. In front of his adoring home crowd he hit three sixes, the last of which won the match, and 12 fours, and faced just 134 balls for his 146.

The fourth match was the most remarkable of a most remarkable series. Spearman and Astle scored 55 off the first 40 balls of the match, but the visitors then collapsed miserably. Their last eight wickets went down for 68 runs, and they were bowled out with 14.1 overs of their quota unused. Ambrose bowled splendidly and effected two excellent run outs while Laurie Williams mopped up the tail in his first international spell of bowling.

Lara flicked the last ball before the lunch interval into the hands of mid-wicket and West Indies were 39 for 3 from ten overs. This dismissal had an electric effect on the match. New Zealand were inspired. Their fielding was of a standard rarely reached by any international side. Harris brought off a magnificent diving catch to his left to account for Simmons. The bowler was Vaughan, who had joined the party because of injuries to key bowlers. Holder and Ambrose seemed certain to give West Indies victory when they added 32 for the ninth wicket in 6.3 overs. When Vaughan trapped Ambrose leg before, seven runs were needed from two overs. Holder took a single off the first ball of the penultimate over. Walsh survived the next four and, unwisely, scampered a single off the last. The first ball of the final over, bowled by Cairns, knocked back Walsh's off stump. Basil Butcher named the entire New Zealand team as Man of the Match, a unique and correct judgement.

New Zealand began badly in the deciding encounter in St Vincent. Spearman and Astle were out in the first four overs, and it was Germon and Fleming who restored order

First One-day International – West Indies v. New Zealand
26 March 1996 at Sabina Park, Kingston, Jamaica

New Zealand

C.M. Spearman	c Holder, b Ambrose	11
N.J. Astle	c Adams, b Ambrose	41
*L.K. Germon (Capt)	run out	0
S.P. Fleming	b Walsh	8
C.Z. Harris	c Lara, b Walsh	2
C.L. Cairns	c and b Harper	21
A.C. Parore	c Harper, b Walsh	61
D.N. Patel	c and b Simmons	71
G.R. Larsen	b Ambrose	9
D.J. Nash	b Walsh	2
D.K. Morrison	not out	1
	lb 4, w 8, nb 4	16
	49.1 overs	243

	O	M	R	W
Ambrose	10	–	36	4
Bishop	10	–	56	–
Walsh	9.1	1	30	3
Harper	10	–	63	1
Simmons	7	–	38	1
Adams	3	–	16	–

Fall of Wickets
1–22, 2–24, 3–51, 4–70, 5–70, 6–113, 7–224, 8–238, 9–241

West Indies

S.C. Williams	b Harris	62
S. Chanderpaul	c and b Harris	61
B.C. Lara	lbw, b Harris	12
P.V. Simmons	b Larsen	28
J.C. Adams	c Fleming, b Morrison	2
R.I.C. Holder	c Germon, b Cairns	16
*R.D. Jacobs	c Spearman, b Astle	3
R.A. Harper	not out	27
I.R. Bishop	lbw, b Larsen	0
C.E.L. Ambrose	b Morrison	17
C.A. Walsh (Capt)	not out	2
	b 1, lb 6, w 4, nb 3	14
	49.1 overs (for 9 wickets)	244

	O	M	R	W
Nash	6	–	46	–
Morrison	5.1	–	36	2
Harris	10	–	45	3
Patel	5	–	28	–
Astle	6	–	28	1
Cairns	7	1	26	1
Larsen	10	3	28	2

Fall of Wickets
1–126, 2–133, 3–142, 4–147, 5–179, 6–184, 7–197, 8–197, 9–221

Umpires: S.A. Bucknor & L.H. Barker *Man of the Match:* D.N. Patel

West Indies won by one wicket

Second One-day International – West Indies v. New Zealand
29 March 1996 at Queen's Park Oval, Port-of-Spain, Trinidad

West Indies

S.C. Williams	c Cairns, b Patel	20
S. Chanderpaul	b Nash	6
B.C. Lara	c Astle, b Harris	11
P.V. Simmons	c Fleming, b Larsen	45
J.C. Adams	not out	59
R.I.C. Holder	b Astle	65
R.A. Harper	c and b Astle	2
*R.D. Jacobs	c Thomson, b Larsen	10
I.R. Bishop	not out	12
C.E.L. Ambrose		
C.A. Walsh (Capt)		
	b 1, lb 2, w 3, nb 2	8
	50 overs (for 7 wickets)	238

	O	M	R	W
Nash	6	–	29	1
Larsen	10	1	42	2
Harris	10	3	45	1
Patel	8	–	30	1
Astle	9	1	32	2
Thomson	5	–	36	–
Cairns	2	–	21	–

Fall of Wickets
1–15, 2–32, 3–42, 4–199, 5–210, 6–212, 7–225

New Zealand

C.M. Spearman	c Simmons, b Harper	37
N.J. Astle	c Harper, b Ambrose	2
*L.K. Germon (Capt)	c Simmons, b Walsh	6
S.P. Fleming	not out	106
A.C. Parore	c Adams, b Walsh	0
C.L. Cairns	b Adams	41
C.Z. Harris	b Ambrose	32
D.N. Patel	not out	4
S.A. Thomson		
G.R. Larsen		
D.J. Nash		
	lb 7, w 3, nb 1	11
	49.5 overs (for 6 wickets)	239

	O	M	R	W
Ambrose	9.5	1	42	2
Bishop	5	–	37	–
Walsh	10	–	51	2
Harper	10	2	28	1
Simmons	10	–	50	–
Adams	5	–	24	1

Fall of Wickets
1–16, 2–35, 3–71, 4–71, 5–163, 6–230

Umpires: S.A. Bucknor & L.H. Barker *Man of the Match:* S.P. Fleming

New Zealand won by 4 wickets

Third One-day International – West Indies v. New Zealand

30 March 1996 at Queen's Park Oval, Port-of-Spain, Trinidad

New Zealand

C.M. Spearman	**b** Ambrose	**7**
R.G. Twose	**c** and **b** Harper	**48**
N.J. Astle	run out	**43**
S.P. Fleming	**c** Walsh, **b** Simmons	**4**
C.L. Cairns	**st** Jacobs, **b** Harper	**38**
A.C. Parore	**c** Harper, **b** Adams	**33**
C.Z. Harris	run out	**10**
*L.K. Germon (Capt)	not out	**13**
S.A. Thomson	run out	**6**
D.N. Patel	not out	**3**
G.R. Larsen		
	b **1**, lb **6**, w **6**, nb **1**	**14**
	50 overs (for 8 wickets)	**219**

	O	M	R	W
Ambrose	10	–	33	**1**
Walsh	10	2	37	**–**
Harper	10	–	45	**2**
Simmons	10	1	35	**1**
Adams	8	–	44	**1**
L.R. Williams	2	–	18	**–**

Fall of Wickets
1–**10**, 2–**104**, 3–**105**, 4–**113**, 5–**178**, 6–**197**, 7–**205**, 8–**215**

West Indies

S.C. Williams	**c** Fleming, **b** Larsen	**4**
S. Chanderpaul	lbw, **b** Larsen	**1**
B.C. Lara	not out	**146**
P.V. Simmons	lbw, **b** Larsen	**47**
J.C. Adams	not out	**24**
R.I.C. Holder		
*R.D. Jacobs		
R.A. Harper		
L.R. Williams		
C.E.L. Ambrose		
C.A. Walsh (Capt)		
	lb **3**	**3**
	45.4 overs (for 3 wickets)	**225**

	O	M	R	W
Patel	10	–	45	**–**
Larsen	8.4	3	26	**3**
Astle	8	–	43	**–**
Harris	8	1	37	**–**
Thomson	4	–	24	**–**
Twose	3	–	19	**–**
Cairns	4	–	28	**–**

Fall of Wickets
1–**5**, 2–**6**, 3–**116**

Umpires: S.A. Bucknor & L.H. Barker *Man of the Match:* B.C.Lara

West Indies won by 7 wickets

Fourth One-day International – West Indies v. New Zealand

3 April 1996 at Bourda, Georgetown, Guyana

New Zealand

C.M. Spearman	**b** Ambrose	**40**
N.J. Astle	lbw, **b** Ambrose	**20**
*L.K. Germon (Capt)	run out	**20**
S.P. Fleming	**c** Harper, **b** Simmons	**8**
C.Z. Harris	**c** Harper, **b** Simmons	**9**
R.G. Twose	run out	**8**
C.L. Cairns	**c** and **b** L.R. Williams	**29**
S.A. Thomson	**c** Harper, **b** L.R. Williams	**6**
D.N. Patel	**c** Jacobs, **b** Walsh	**2**
J.T.C. Vaughan	not out	**4**
G.R. Larsen	hit wkt, **b** L.R. Williams	**1**
	lb **7**, w **3**, nb **1**	**11**
	35.5 overs	**158**

	O	M	R	W
Ambrose	7	1	33	**2**
Walsh	6	–	38	**1**
Simmons	10	–	42	**2**
Harper	8	1	22	**–**
L.R. Williams	4.5	–	16	**3**

Fall of Wickets
1–**55**, 2–**77**, 3–**90**, 4–**100**, 5–**112**, 6–**112**, 7–**137**, 8–**145**, 9–**154**

West Indies

S.C. Williams	lbw, **b** Larsen	**6**
S. Chanderpaul	**c** Harris, **b** Patel	**11**
B.C. Lara	**c** Astle, **b** Larsen	**17**
P.V. Simmons	**c** Harris, **b** Vaughan	**11**
J.C. Adams	run out	**23**
R.I.C. Holder	not out	**49**
*R.D. Jacobs	**c** Germon, **b** Cairns	**0**
R.A. Harper	**b** Harris	**5**
L.R. Williams	**c** Fleming, **b** Astle	**1**
C.E.L. Ambrose	lbw, **b** Vaughan	**16**
C.A. Walsh (Capt)	**b** Cairns	**1**
	b **1**, lb **8**, w **5**	**14**
	49.5 overs	**154**

	O	M	R	W
Patel	10	2	35	**1**
Larsen	10	1	18	**2**
Harris	10	1	23	**1**
Vaughan	7	–	26	**2**
Astle	7	1	26	**1**
Cairns	5.5	–	17	**2**

Fall of Wickets
1–**21**, 2–**35**, 3–**39**, 4–**68**, 5–**104**, 6–**111**, 7–**116**, 8–**120**, 9–**152**

Umpires: C. Duncan & E. Nicholls *Man of the Match:* The New Zealand Team

New Zealand won by 4 runs

Fifth One-day International – West Indies v. New Zealand

6 April 1996 at Arnos Vale, Kingstown, St Vincent

New Zealand

C.M. Spearman	c Browne, b Walsh	4
N.J. Astle	c Simmons, b Ambrose	4
*L.K. Germon (Capt)	c and b Adams	50
S.P. Fleming	c Simmons, b Adams	75
R.G. Twose	c Browne, b Chanderpaul	6
C.L. Cairns	c and b Adams	11
A.C. Parore	b L.R. Williams	23
C.Z. Harris	not out	42
D.N. Patel	run out	2
J.T.C. Vaughan	not out	13
G.R. Larsen		
	b 2, lb 2, w 6, nb 1	11
	50 overs (for 8 wickets)	241

	O	M	R	W
Ambrose	7	–	32	1
Walsh	9	–	38	1
Simmons	3	–	25	–
Harper	10	–	48	–
Adams	10	–	50	3
Chanderpaul	8	–	35	1
L.R. Williams	3	–	9	1

Fall of Wickets
1–10, 2–10, 3–131, 4–137, 5–154, 6–167, 7–189, 8–197

West Indies

P.A. Wallace	c Fleming, b Patel	0
S. Chanderpaul	c Twose, b Harris	13
B.C. Lara	c Patel, b Cairns	104
P.V. Simmons	not out	103
R.I.C. Holder	not out	13
J.C. Adams		
R.A. Harper		
*C.O. Browne		
L.R. Williams		
C.E.L. Ambrose		
C.A. Walsh (Capt)		
	lb 2, w 6, nb 1	9
	48.3 overs (for 3 wickets)	242

	O	M	R	W
Patel	10	1	46	1
Larsen	8	2	31	–
Harris	8	–	48	1
Vaughan	10	–	37	–
Cairns	8.3	–	49	1
Astle	2	–	14	–
Fleming	2	–	15	–

Fall of Wickets
1–0, 2–31, 3–217

Umpires: L.H. Barker & B. Morgan *Man of the Match:* P.V. Simmons

West Indies won by 7 wickets

with a stand of 121. Six wickets then went down for 66 runs before Harris and Vaughan added 44 from the last 46 balls of the innings.

West Indies were 31 for 2 in the 11th over and were looking far from happy when Simmons joined Lara. The pair added 186. Lara reached his ninth century in one-day internationals and hit a six and ten fours in his 103-ball innings. If he was not as sparkling as he had been in Trinidad he was still most effective, and Simmons played an outstanding knock. He hit two sixes and ten fours and faced 124 balls in what was his fifth century in one-day internationals and his first for four years. Holder gave sensible support in the closing stages as West Indies won a fascinating series with nine balls to spare.

8, 9 and 10 April 1996
at Arnos Vale, St Vincent
New Zealanders 318 for 9 dec. (S.P. Fleming 61, A.C. Parore 59, N.J. Astle 55) and 204 for 7 dec. (C.Z. Harris 55 not out)
West Indies Board XI 158 (S.L. Campbell 79, C.L. Cairns 5 for 29) and 209 (M.D. Ventura 51)
New Zealanders won by 156 runs

12, 13 and 14 April 1996
at St George's, Grenada

West Indies Board President's XI 454 (F.L. Reifer 130, R.G. Samuels 124, T.O. Powell 53, C.L. Cairns 4 for 66)
New Zealanders 113 (N.A.M. McLean 4 for 32) and 292 (C.L. Cairns 94)
West Indies Board President's XI won by an innings and 49 runs

The New Zealanders played two first-class matches in preparation for the two-Test series. Unfortunately, they lost Nash through injury after the second match, and, during net practice before the first Test, Chris Cairns broke down with a side muscle strain while bowling. He declared himself unfit and flew to England to join Nottinghamshire where his injury was not deemed serious. Cairns was prepared to play in a Benson and Hedges Cup game for his county while the Test in Bridgetown was still in progress. All this raised speculation as to Cairns' commitment and loyalty to New Zealand cricket, and it also caused debate as to the relationships between coach Glenn Turner and some of his party. Turner, a noted disciplinarian, had instituted a new regime in New Zealand cricket – it had been needed, but was not universally welcomed.

Test Series

West Indies *v.* New Zealand

New Zealand entered the first Test match at a great disadvantage. Shane Thomson had returned home injured, and Chris Cairns and Dion Nash were also unavailable through injury. West Indies gave first Test caps to Robert Samuels, a left-handed opening batsman from Jamaica, and Patterson Thompson, the quick bowler from Barbados. New Zealand's misfortune continued when they lost the toss and were asked to bat first on a grassy pitch. Within the first eight overs, they lost Spearman, Twose and Fleming for eight runs. Adam Parore and Nathan Astle revived fortunes with a partnership of 80 in 14 overs.

They were aided by some bizarre bowling from the debutant Thompson. His first two overs yielded six no-balls and a total of 25 runs. Astle was particularly severe on him, but the fast bowler did have Astle, who hit ten fours, caught behind and claimed Harris in the same over although the decision raise doubts. In eight overs, Thompson bowled 19 no-balls and a wide and finished with two for 58.

Jamaican captain Robert Samuels won a place in the West Indian Test side and scored a century in the second Test match against New Zealand.
(Patrick Eagar)

First Test Match – West Indies v. New Zealand

19, 20, 21 and 23 April 1996 at Kensington Oval, Bridgetown, Barbados

New Zealand

	First Innings		Second Innings	
C.M. Spearman	c Browne, b Ambrose	0	c Lara, b Thompson	20
R.G. Twose	c Samuels, b Walsh	2	c Lara, b Walsh	0
S.P. Fleming	c Chanderpaul, b Walsh	1	c Samuels, b Bishop	22
A.C. Parore	c Simmons, b Adams	59	(7) c Campbell, b Bishop	1
N.J. Astle	c Browne, b Thompson	54	(4) c Campbell, b Thompson	125
C.Z. Harris	c Lara, b Thompson	0	(5) c Samuels, b Bishop	0
J.T.C. Vaughan	c Bishop, b Adams	44	(6) lbw, b Bishop	24
*L.K. Germon (Capt)	c Chanderpaul, b Adams	0	lbw, b Walsh	23
G.R. Larsen	st Browne, b Adams	12	lbw, b Walsh	6
D.K. Morrison	not out	4	not out	26
R.J. Kennedy	c Browne, b Adams	0	c Adams, b Walsh	22
	lb 1, w 1, nb 17	19	lb 7, nb 29	36
		195		305

	O	M	R	W	O	M	R	W
Ambrose	13	4	33	1	18	6	41	–
Walsh	17	6	30	2	22	3	72	4
Bishop	10	3	36	–	19	1	67	4
Thompson	8	–	58	2	14	1	77	2
Simmons	3	–	11	–				
Adams	9	4	17	5	6	1	32	–
Chanderpaul	2	–	9	–	3	1	9	–

Fall of Wickets
1–2, 2–2, 3–6, 4–86, 5–87, 6–154, 7–157, 8–186, 9–193
1–14, 2–28, 3–48, 4–57, 5–201, 6–215, 7–219, 8–254, 9–260

West Indies

	First Innings		Second Innings	
S.L. Campbell	b Harris	208	not out	29
R.G. Samuels	lbw, b Larsen	12	not out	0
B.C. Lara	c Spearman, b Larsen	35		
P.V. Simmons	lbw, b Larsen	22		
J.C. Adams	c Germon, b Vaughan	21		
S. Chanderpaul	c Harris, b Morrison	82		
*C.O. Browne	c Astle, b Kennedy	20		
I.R. Bishop	c Germon, b Harris	31		
C.E.L. Ambrose	c Germon, b Vaughan	8		
C.A. Walsh (Capt)	not out	12		
P.I.C. Thompson	lbw, b Morrison	1		
	lb 8, nb 12	20		0
		472	(for no wicket)	29

	O	M	R	W	O	M	R	W
Morrison	29.3	4	120	2	2	–	8	–
Kennedy	22	3	89	1	2	–	21	–
Larsen	40	15	76	3				
Vaughan	34	10	81	2				
Harris	34	11	75	2				
Twose	4	–	20	–				
Astle	1	–	3	–				

Fall of Wickets
1–46, 2–103, 3–129, 4–182, 5–337, 6–386, 7–445, 8–458, 9–466

Umpires: S.A. Bucknor & P. Willey

West Indies won by 10 wickets

Jimmy Adams, career-best bowling and career-best batting performances in the two-Test series against New Zealand. Adams' double century in the second Test celebrated his total recovery from a year of injuries. (David Munden/Sportsline)

It was the advent of Jimmy Adams that brought about total disaster. The left-arm spinner had Parore caught off his first ball, accounted for Germon in his second over and quickly mopped up the tail, including the tenacious Vaughan, after tea. His 5 for 17 represented his best bowling performance in any form of senior cricket.

Larsen removed Samuels before the close, but, at 98 for 1, West Indies ended the day in a very strong position. The dismissal of Lara on the eighth ball of the second morning lifted New Zealand and silenced the crowd. Larsen also trapped Simmons leg before, and it was left to Campbell and Chanderpaul to revive the innings. Their stand extended into the third day and was eventually worth 155. Campbell had remained totally solid and reached his first Test century two balls before tea. It had taken him five hours 53 minutes, and he had faced 253 balls. He ended the day on 149 and West Indies were 334 for 4.

In the morning session of the third day, West Indies scored 72 runs and lost Chanderpaul, whose 82 was his highest Test score, and Browne. Campbell batted on and was at the crease for just over 11 hours before being bowled by Harris. By that time, Campbell had hit 29 fours, faced 496 balls and had become one of that rare breed whose maiden Test century was a double. It was a most impressive performance by the 25-year old Barbadian in what was his tenth Test.

West Indies were all out for 472, and New Zealand were soon sacrificing themselves as if in the last five overs of a 40-over slog. The batsmen began swinging lustfully at

Second Test Match – West Indies *v.* New Zealand

27, 28, 29 April, 1 and 2 May 1996 at Recreation Ground, St John's, Antigua

West Indies

	First Innings		Second Innings	
S.L. Campbell	run out	13	c Fleming, b Vaughan	36
R.G. Samuels	b Harris	125	lbw, b Morrison	4
B.C. Lara	c Germon, b Patel	40	c Fleming, b Morrison	74
P.V. Simmons	b Harris	59	c Vaughan, b Harris	0
J.C. Adams	not out	208	c and b Vaughan	6
S. Chanderpaul	c Astle, b Patel	41	b Morrison	8
*C.O. Browne	run out	18	lbw, b Larsen	5
I.R. Bishop	c Fleming, b Larsen	14	c Germon, b Morrison	9
C.E.L. Ambrose	not out	21	lbw, b Morrison	6
C.A. Walsh (Capt)			not out	17
R. Dhanraj			b Vaughan	9
	lb 3, nb 6	9	lb 2, nb 8	10
	(for 7 wickets, dec.)	548		184

	O	M	R	W	O	M	R	W
Morrison	26	6	124	–	20	2	61	5
Larsen	25	9	69	1	11	3	27	1
Vaughan	29	8	79	–	16.3	5	30	3
Patel	38	7	131	2				
Kennedy	13	2	59	–	10	2	30	–
Harris	35	11	83	2	4	–	34	1

Fall of Wickets
1–**35**, 2–**96**, 3–**193**, 4–**280**, 5–**445**, 6–**448**, 7–**495**
1–**5**, 2–**89**, 3–**94**, 4–**119**, 5–**128**, 6–**133**, 7–**147**, 8–**155**, 9–**158**

New Zealand

	First Innings		Second Innings	
C.M. Spearman	c Browne, b Walsh	54	c Browne, b Ambrose	24
R.G. Twose	b Ambrose	2	c Samuels, b Ambrose	2
D.K. Morrison	lbw, b Ambrose	0		
S.P. Fleming	c Browne, b Bishop	39	(3) not out	56
N.J. Astle	c Simmons, b Ambrose	103	(4) c Adams, b Simmons	8
J.T.C. Vaughan	b Dhanraj	26	(5) lbw, b Bishop	32
C.Z. Harris	c Adams, b Ambrose	40	(6) c and b Dhanraj	4
*L.K. Germon (Capt)	c Browne, b Ambrose	49	(7) not out	0
D.N. Patel	c Browne, b Bishop	78		
G.R. Larsen	not out	17		
R.J. Kennedy	c Browne, b Bishop	4		
	lb 8, nb 17	25	lb 1, w 2, nb 1	4
		437	(for 5 wickets)	130

	O	M	R	W	O	M	R	W
Ambrose	32	12	68	5	12	3	22	2
Walsh	27	5	70	1	16	5	32	–
Dhanraj	39	7	132	1	18	6	33	1
Bishop	26.3	6	90	3	7	1	25	–
Adams	19	4	59	–	2	1	5	–
Chanderpaul	2	–	10	–				
Simmons					10	6	12	1

Fall of Wickets
1–**9**, 2–**9**, 3–**98**, 4–**108**, 5–**202**, 6–**276**, 7–**281**, 8–**391**, 9–**425**
1–**19**, 2–**30**, 3–**39**, 4–**96**, 5–**126**

Umpires: L.H. Barker & C.J. Mitchley

Match drawn

everything, and the West Indian slip cordon did the rest. At 57 for 4, New Zealand were hurrying the match to an early conclusion, but Astle and Vaughan at last brought sanity. Astle, positive and determined, reached 82, and Vaughan, a most dedicated left-hander and enthusiastic cricketer, was on 10 when New Zealand closed on 151 for 4.

Nathan Astle duly reached a maiden Test hundred on the fourth morning in what was only his third Test match. It was a wonderfully aggressive and purposeful innings. He took on the West Indian pace bowlers and met fire with fire. He was out when he aimed a ferocious drive at Thompson and was taken head high at slip. He had hit two sixes and 22 fours and faced 154 balls; splendidly brave cricket. Vaughan had left earlier, falling leg before to Bishop after helping Astle to add 144. Parore, batting with a runner after pulling a muscle while fielding, was the third wicket to fall before lunch, which arrived with New Zealand still needing 33 runs to avoid an innings defeat. Germon and Larsen were both out before that task was accomplished, but, in a spirited last wicket stand, Morrison and Kennedy added 45.

West Indies needed 29 to win, and Sherwin Campbell, Man of the Match, hit all the runs required in 20 minutes to bring victory before tea on the fourth day.

Parore left the tour before the start of the second Test because of injury, and Patel replaced him in the side for the second encounter. West Indies brought in leg-spinner Dhanraj for the erratic Thompson.

Put in to bat, West Indies reacted by scoring 302 for 4 on the opening day. They were thankful for a maiden century by Robert Samuels in his second Test. He was 15 minutes on 93 and then hit Patel for four and six off successive deliveries to reach three figures. In a most attractive innings, he hit three sixes and 15 fours and faced 219 balls.

A limited New Zealand attack strove manfully, but on the second day they were savaged by Jimmy Adams. He began the day on 50, and he had not played fluently on the opening day, but now he was soon in liquid mood and produced a variety of superb shots. He reached a career-best 208 and hit a six and 31 fours in his 333-ball innings. He was at the wicket for seven and a half hours, and proved that he was now totally at ease following the blow on the cheek bone and the knee injury that had threatened his career in the past year.

In 12 overs before the close of the second day, New Zealand lost Twose, looking out of his depth in Test cricket, and night-watchman Morrison for 21 runs. Morrison collected his 24th Test 'duck', which was a record.

On the third day, New Zealand began a revival. Spearman and Fleming, two batsmen of immense promise, shared a valuable and pleasant stand that ultimately fell short of expectation, and it was Astle who once again treated the West Indian attack with disdain. Vaughan was a valiant ally for the second time and the pair added 94 for the fifth wicket, while Harris joined Astle in a stand worth 74. Astle was positivity itself, hitting a six and 12 fours in his three-and-a-half hour innings, but New Zealand were still in danger when Harris and Astle were out in successive overs. Germon and Patel carried on the fine work, however, and New Zealand closed on 346 for 7.

Their partnership became worth 110, and New Zealand finished just 111 in arrears. The game now underwent a dramatic transformation as, with Morrison in peerless form, New Zealand reduced West Indies to 147 for 7 by the close of the fourth day. With Lara in flowing mood, West Indies had been 89 for 1 before Morrison engineered the collapse, and New Zealand would have been even more in command had Fleming held on to a catch at slip that Lara offered when he had scored 13.

There seemed a possibility of a historic New Zealand victory, but Walsh and Dhanraj batted an hour for West Indies' last wicket, and the visitors' target became 296 in 73 overs. Twose again failed, and Spearman, having hit five fours, was caught behind for 24. Astle remained the hope, but he was brilliantly caught in the covers by Jimmy Adams, and New Zealand then settled for a draw.

Adams was named Man of the Match and of the series, which was a little hard on Astle. New Zealand have their problems, particularly it seems with Cairns and Parore, but they are well led and well organised, and are thinking, planning and playing positive, meaningful cricket. There is less optimism for the future of West Indian cricket after a year of turmoil and political manoeuvring.

Centuries in successive Tests for Nathan Astle of New Zealand, who accepted his debuts in international cricket in spectacular fashion. (Ross Kinnaird/Allsport)

First-Class Averages

Batting

	M	Inns	NO	Runs	HS	Av	100s	50s
S. Chanderpaul	3	4	1	434	303*	144.66	1	1
J.C. Adams	3	5	1	357	208*	89.25	2	
B.C. Lara	3	5	–	345	119	69.00	1	2
A. Balliram	2	4	1	185	70*	61.66		3
G.R. Breese	3	6	2	245	124	61.25	1	1
S.L. Campbell	4	8	1	423	208	60.42	1	1
A.F.G. Griffith	6	10	–	592	145	59.20	3	3
P.V. Simmons	8	14	1	722	156	55.53	1	6
S.C. Williams	6	10	–	548	165	54.80	1	3
T.O. Powell	6	10	1	452	125*	50.22	1	5
N.A.M. McLean	6	10	7	150	49*	50.00		
R.G. Samuels	8	14	1	629	125	48.38	3	2
F.L. Reifer	6	10	2	387	130	48.37	1	2
R.D. Jacobs	6	10	3	299	89	42.71		3
P.A. Wallace	5	9	–	373	108	41.44	1	1
R.L. Hoyte	4	7	1	244	75	40.66		2
D.R.E. Joseph	7	11	–	409	118	37.18	1	2
M. Bodoe	6	9	1	287	65	35.87		2
R.A.M. Smith	4	7	1	201	99	33.50		1
A.R. Percival	5	7	–	223	78	31.85		2
D.A. Joseph	4	7	–	220	78	31.42		2
D.S. Morgan	6	11	2	274	67	30.44		2
D. Williams	6	9	2	201	102*	28.71	1	
R.A. Marshall	5	10	–	280	112	28.00	1	
S.G.B. Ford	6	10	2	203	56*	25.37		1
M.D. Ventura	6	11	–	279	102	25.36	1	1
J.R. Murray	6	11	1	252	70	25.20		1
N.O. Perry	6	9	1	201	74	25.12		3
B.S. Murphy	6	9	3	149	47	24.83		
S.H. Armstrong	4	7	–	171	92	24.42		1
S. Ragoonath	6	11	–	267	85	24.27		2
L.A. Harrigan	6	11	–	261	67	23.72		1
D. Thomas	4	7	–	166	70	23.71		1
C.M. Tuckett	4	8	1	153	63	21.85		1
J.A.R. Sylvester	3	6	1	109	52	21.80		1
V.C. Drakes	5	9	1	171	50	21.37		1
U. Pope	6	12	–	256	84	21.33		2
A.J. Pierre	3	6	–	122	54	20.33		1
N.A. de Groot	6	9	–	182	78	20.22		1
K.A. Mason	5	7	–	140	67	20.00		1
H.A.G. Anthony	7	12	1	217	53	19.72		1
L.C. Weekes	7	12	2	194	39*	19.40		
K.K. Sylvester	5	10	–	176	77	17.60		1
C.D. Cannonier	4	7	1	104	41*	17.33		
L.R. Williams	4	7	–	119	53	17.00		1
M.V. Nagamootoo	6	9	1	132	38	16.50		
C.A. Davis	5	9	1	129	40	16.12		
R.N. Lewis	6	10	1	116	51*	12.88		1

(Qualification: 100 runs, averages 10.00)
(Played in one match: R.A. Harper 124, R.I.C. Holder 138 & 9)

Bowling

	Overs	Mds	Runs	Wks	Av	Best	10/m	5/inn
C.E.L. Ambrose	97	33	206	14	14.71	5/68		1
D. Thomas	81.5	15	203	13	15.61	4/42		
R.A. Marshall	220.5	37	516	30	17.20	7/99	1	2
L.R. Williams	140	40	351	20	17.55	5/32		2
R. Dhanraj	314.5	59	964	50	19.28	9/97	2	4
K.C.G. Benjamin	196.4	59	490	24	20.41	5/22		2
C.A. Davis	96	24	245	11	22.27	3/35		
M.V. Nagamootoo	195.5	31	544	23	23.65	7/76		1
P.I.C. Thompson	154.2	15	649	27	24.03	5/105		1
C.E.L. Stuart	78.2	9	329	13	25.30	3/43		
A. Samaroo	141.3	15	568	22	25.81	4/44		
B. St A. Browne	128	24	393	15	26.20	5/48		1
L.C. Weekes	159	28	464	17	27.29	5/83		1
R.N. Lewis	203.2	32	602	22	27.36	7/66		2
I.R. Bishop	88.3	12	316	11	28.72	4/67		
N.A.M. McLean	108.5	17	386	13	29.69	4/32		
W.D. Phillip	219.3	51	598	20	29.90	5/37		1
B.S. Murphy	200.3	30	633	21	30.14	5/35		2
H.A.G. Anthony	168	30	577	19	30.36	4/84		
W.E. Reid	139.2	43	367	12	30.58	3/32		
M.C. Gibbs	196.1	52	461	15	30.73	4/35		
N.O. Perry	206.3	54	506	16	31.62	5/58		1
M. Bodoe	104.5	18	329	10	32.90	3/65		
E.C. Antoine	127.5	17	490	14	35.00	5/47		1
N.B. Francis	98	15	367	10	36.70	3/66		

(Qualification: 10 wickets)

Leading Fielders

23 – R.D. Jacobs; 19 – S.G.B. Ford (ct 14 / st 5) and D. Williams (ct 12 / st 7); 15 – U. Pope (ct 13 / st 2); 14 – C.O. Browne (ct 13 / st 1); 13 – J.R. Murray (ct 11 / st 2); 12 – D.R.E. Joseph; 11 – P.V. Simmons; 10 – N.C. McGarrell

Sabina Park, Kingston, Jamaica. (David Munden/Sportsline)

England

Followers of English cricket have developed considerable fortitude over the past few years. Having endured the gloomiest and most humiliating of winters, the lovers of the English game still managed to approach the 1996 season with an air of anticipation. In spite of the indignities suffered in South Africa and the total failure in the World Cup, there was a feeling that English cricket was on the mend. It was difficult to find any evidence for such optimism, but it persisted.

England NCA v. Pakistan at Trowbridge. (Adrian Murrell/Allsport)

Perhaps this optimism grew as a shield against the crop of books and allegations that sought to expose only the seamier side of the game. Allan Lamb went into instant retirement because he wished to 'tell all' in a forthcoming book, and he was later involved in a court case in which he and Ian Botham took on Imran Khan. It appeared that there were several players, or past players, more intent in contesting the game off the field rather than on it.

The chairman of the England selectors could be said to be one of them. His appetite for public executions exposed the fact that a serious rift existed between Devon Malcolm and himself. This division between player and selector meant that in the immediate future England would not call upon their fasest bowler nor, as Tufnell was still, it seemed, persona non grata, their best spinner.

How refreshing it was then to attend the Cricket Writer's Club memorable 50th Anniversary dinner and to hear the words of wit and wisdom spoken by Sir Colin Cowdrey and Jim Swanton, two men who have brought only honour and dignity to the game. Cowdrey's assertion that tracksuits should be jettisoned for the only way to learn cricket is to play the game itself may not have pleased some, but it should have been digested by all.

Sir Colin's son Christopher was one of several candidates who stood for a place on the England selection panel. Like Ian Botham, Brian Bolus, Illingworth's recommendation, and Geoff Miller, he was unsuccessful, and Gooch and Graveney were elected. David Graveney had attempted to oust Illingworth from the chairmanship, a move which prompted Illingworth to state that 'life would be easier if Graveney was not on the panel.' In the end, peace broke out, and we were allowed to get on with the game, which enjoyed an uplifting tonic with the appointment of David Lloyd as England coach. He is a perpetual optimism, a witty, intelligent and inventive coach, and one whose chief philosophy of cricket is that it is a game that must be enjoyed. Long may he prosper. England hath need of him.

There were departures from the game at the end of the 1995 season, men like Larkins, Hemmings and Nicholas who had given much pleasure, and sadly, Pervaz Mirza, who looked to have much to give but who died suddenly in September 1995, at the age of 24.

There were, too, the inevitable string of 'transfers'. Yorkshire released Grayson, Milburn and Metcalfe who went to Essex, Hampshire and Nottinghamshire respectively. Sheriyar moved from Leicestershire to Worcestershire, and Davis, once of Kent, went from Warwickshire to Gloucestershire. Desperate for success in the wake of several stormy general meetings, Surrey engaged Lewis from Nottinghamshire and Pearson, once of Northamptonshire, from Essex where the presence of Such had limited his first team opportunities. The most interesting 'transfer' of all was that of John Emburey from Middlesex to Northamptonshire. Middlesex had wanted to retain the veteran off-spinner, but Northamptonshire offered a coaching appointment. It transpired that Emburey was to hold a regular place in the Northamptonshire side for the first three and a half months of the season.

Roland Lefebvre was forced to retire through injury, and Aravinda de Silva did not return as Kent's overseas player, for Carl Hooper was once again available. Overseas players were to have mixed fortunes in 1996. The Australians – Lee, Law, Bevan, Jones, brought in to captain Derbyshire, and Moody – had highly successful seasons, and it was chastening for England supporters to realise that, although the first four mentioned above figured high in the batting averages for most of the season, none of them could claim a place in the Australian side.

Shaun Pollock made a sensational start for Warwickshire in the Benson and Hedges Cup, but he did not quite strike the same fear into county batsmen as he had struck into England batsmen in South Africa.

Of the West Indians, Drakes took time to settle under Desmond Haynes' guidance at Sussex, Gibson missed the fist half of Glamorgan's season when he underwent an operation, Simmons did well at Leicestershire, often leading the side, and Hooper and Ambrose enjoyed good moments. Campbell did not find life easy in Durham, and Winston Benjamin played a handful of games for Hampshire, bowled fewer overs and was finally forced to quit through injury. Dion Nash, the New Zealander, bowled in only one match for Middlesex before returning home for treatment on a recurring injury while fellow New Zealander Chris Cairns remains an enigma as an international all-rounder. His potential is enormous; his ambition is sometimes hard to determine. For Lancashire, there was Steven Elworthy, an unpretentious South African who did honest work.

Of the new skippers, Maynard, Whitaker and Byas thrived, and at least in spirit there seemed an emphasis on youth. Spring is always a time of hope even if it does mix memory with desire.

A smiling Ray Illingworth begins his last season as chairman of selectors. (Stephen Munday/Allsport)

Oxford and Cambridge Universities

The debate as to whether cricket at the universities of Oxford and Cambridge should retain its first-class status rages more fiercely every year. The traditionalists will point to a great social occasion at Lord's in early July and to a long line of Test cricketers from Lord Harris and A.G. Steel to Mike Atherton and John Crawley, but the indisputable fact is that the well of talent is fast running dry.

Nowhere is the drought more obvious than in the lack of quality bowling to be found at the two oldest universities, and presumably in the schools from which they draw their students. Nor has that drought ever been more clearly defined than in 1996. A glance at the form charts will give sufficient evidence. While Cake, Smith, House, Singh, Khan, Kendall, Gupte, Ridley and Sutcliffe can boast batting records of which they can be proud and which are undoubtedly *first-class*, the bowlers, one feels, would rather remain anonymous.

Only two bowlers, one from either university, managed to capture ten wickets in the season, and one of those hails from Pakistan, the other from Zimbabwe. Hasnain Malik's ten wickets cost him 82.60 runs apiece; Andy Whittall's ten wickets came at 93.20 runs each. If it is not now, the time is fast approaching when realities will have to be faced, sad as that may be.

The season's first centurion, Ben Smith of Leicestershire. (Adrian Murrell/Allsport)

13, 15 and 16 April
at Oxford
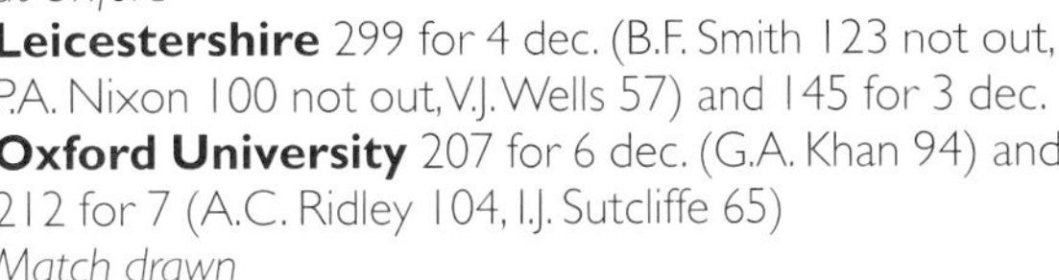
Leicestershire 299 for 4 dec. (B.F. Smith 123 not out, P.A. Nixon 100 not out, V.J. Wells 57) and 145 for 3 dec.
Oxford University 207 for 6 dec. (G.A. Khan 94) and 212 for 7 (A.C. Ridley 104, I.J. Sutcliffe 65)
Match drawn

The Parks was the venue for the beginning of the England season which, inevitably, could not begin until mid-afternoon on the Saturday because of bad weather. Under their new skipper James Whitaker, Leicestershire batted quite brightly and set a sporting target. Ben Smith hit the first century of the season, and he and Paul Nixon, on the verge of being England's wicket-keeper until troubled by injury and loss of form in 1995, added an unbeaten 176 at four runs an over for the fifth wicket.

Gul Khan, released by Essex at the end of the 1995 season, hit his first ball in first-class cricket for four and made a highly entertaining 94.

Whitaker set a target of 238, and Sutcliffe and Ridley shard a second wicket partnership of 147. Andrew Ridley hit a maiden first-class century, but six wickets, three of them run out, fell for 60 runs, and the match was drawn.

17, 18 and 19 April
at Cambridge
Glamorgan 262 for 1 dec. (H. Morris 126 not out, D.L. Hemp 103 not out) and 248 for 1 dec. (S.P. James 102 not out, M.P. Maynard 100 retired hurt)
Cambridge University 225 for 3 dec. (E.T. Smith 101, A. Singh 52 not out) and 32 for 3
Match drawn

at Oxford
Durham 334 for 0 dec. (S. Hutton 172 not out, M.A. Roseberry 145 not out) and 20 for 0
Oxford University 227 for 4 dec. (C.M. Gupte 113 not out, I.J. Sutcliffe 65)
Match drawn

There is considerable joy for county cricketers playing against the universities in early season. There is an opportunity to find form before the real battle begins and to establish a sound basis for a good average for the season. At Fenner's, James was out at 15, but Morris and Hemp then added 247 for Glamorgan's second wicket. Steve James made amends for his first innings lapse with a second innings hundred, and Maynard hit 100 off 98 balls before discovering that he had a sore back. In between these events, Edward Smith, late of Tonbridge and Kent Second XI, scored a century on his first-class debut, the first Cambridge University batsman to achieve the feat for 32 years. He batted very well, as did Anurag Singh from the Warwickshire stable.

Oxford University captain Chinmay Gupte hit 606 runs, including two centuries, during the university season.
(David Munden/Sportsline)

It was not until nine-and-a-quarter hours into the match in The Parks that a wicket fell. The first day was occupied by Stewart Hutton hitting the highest score of his career and sharing a record opening stand of 334 with his skipper Mike Roseberry. On the second day, Chinmay Gupte and Iain Sutcliffe scored 145 for Oxford's first wicket before Sutcliffe fell to Brown. Gupte, the Oxford captain, hit the fourth century of his career, but the last day brought only rain.

20, 21 and 22 April
at Cambridge
Derbyshire 287 for 4 dec. (T.A. Tweats 89 not out, D.M. Jones 71, C.J. Adams 54) and 327 for 2 dec. (A.S. Rollins 112, D.G. Cork 101 retired hurt)
Cambridge University 329 for 7 dec. (W.J. House 136, R.Q. Cake 102 not out, E.T. Smith 54)
Match drawn

20, 22 and 23 April
at Oxford
Middlesex 197 for 5 (M.W. Gatting 63)
v. **Oxford University**
Match drawn

Rain ruined the matches in both Oxford and Cambridge, but there was time for four centuries at Fenner's. Dean Jones set a pattern by declaring at teatime on Saturday, and on the Sunday, Russell Cake, who has ignored the pleas of several counties and decided to make business his career, and Will House, a left-hander from Sevenoaks, added 193 for the University's sixth wicket. Cake was of proven worth, but House caught everyone's attention with 136 off 123 balls. He hit two sixes and 20 fours and was particularly severe on Malcolm and Vandrau. Dominic Cork hit the second century of his first-class career.

Weakened by injuries, Middlesex pressed coach Ian Gould into service, but he had no opportunity to bat nor keep wicket.

2, 3 and 4 May
at Oxford
Hampshire 327 for 8 dec. (J.S. Laney 112) and 119 for 3
Oxford University 322 for 8 dec. (C.M. Gupte 75, A.C. Ridley 70, H.S. Malik 61)
Match drawn

3, 4 and 5 May
at Cambridge
Warwickshire 368 for 3 dec. (N.V. Knight 128, W.G. Khan 108, D.P. Ostler 81 not out) and 190 for 8 dec. (W.G. Khan 51)
Cambridge University 208 (R.O. Jones 61, E.T. Smith 55, N.M.K. Smith 4 for 49) and 132
Warwickshire won by 218 runs

Jason Laney made his first first-class century for Hampshire in the match at Oxford where Gupte and Ridley added 139 for the University's second wicket and wicket-keeper Batty of Combined Universities played his first first-class match.

Cambridge needed to bat only 275 minutes on a good pitch to save the game against Warwickshire, but, in spite of a brave last wicket stand by How and Janisch, they were bowled out 45 minutes after tea. This was the University's first home defeat since 1994, 13 matches. Earlier, Knight and Khan had scored 228 for Warwickshire's first wicket. Knight, who reached his hundred with a six, made 128 off 141 balls and hit 20 fours to catch the eye of the England selectors.

11 May
at Oxford
Cambridge University 321 for 6 (A. Singh 108, R.Q. Cake 74, R.T. Ragnauth 58, A.C. Ridley 4 for 68)
Oxford University 218
Cambridge University won by 103 runs

The limited-over Varsity Match resulted in an overwhelming win for Cambridge. Anurag Singh hit 108 off 86 balls as he and Ragnauth scored 137 for the second wicket. Oxford were bowled out in 42.5 overs.

16, 17 and 18 May
at Cambridge
Cambridge University 300 for 7 dec. (W.J. House 127) and 197 (E.T. Smith 76, P.C.R. Tufnell 5 for 56, P.N. Weekes 5 for 61)
Middlesex 243 for 3 dec. (J.C. Pooley 138 not out, J.P. Hewitt 72) and 211 for 6 (M.W. Gatting 77)
Match drawn

at Oxford
Northamptonshire 335 for 2 dec. (R.R. Montgomerie 126, D.J. Roberts 72, M.B. Loye 67 not out, T.C. Walton 55 not out) and 174 for 2 (A.J. Swann 76 not out, J.N. Snape 64)
Oxford University 256 for 7 dec. (G.A. Khan 96, J.N. Batty 56, M.E.D. Jarrett 50 not out)
Match drawn

Cambridge performed well against Middlesex. House hit his second hundred of the season, and Cake declared after 92 overs. Weekes was out before the close, but on the second day Jason Pooley, who had suffered a run of bad form, hit the highest score of his career as did Hewitt. Tufnell and Weekes spun out Cambridge when they batted a second time, and Middlesex faced a target of 255 in 57 overs. Weekes and Gatting both became victims of a substitute fielder who ran out Weekes with a direct hit on the stumps and caught the Middlesex skipper. The fielder was the Cambridge coach – Derek Randall.

Northamptonshire fielded three debutants at Oxford. David Roberts, a stylish opener, and Alec Swann, an all-rounder, were impressive while Gul Khan again displayed class with another fine innings for Oxford. No play was possible on the last afternoon.

23, 24 and 25 May
at Oxford
Oxford University 178 for 3 (G.A. Khan 72 not out)
v. **Nottinghamshire**
Match drawn

Oxford's wretched luck with the weather continued. There was no play on the second and third days, and only 42.3 overs were bowled on the first day.

1, 3 and 4 June
at Oxford
Glamorgan 303 for 6 dec. (G.P. Butcher 83, R.D.B. Croft 71, A.W. Evans 66 not out) and 164 for 5 dec. (A.A. Evans 71 not out, A. Dale 55)
Oxford University 196 for 6 dec. (C.M. Gupte 97, J.N. Batty 51) and 216 for 6 (W.S. Kendall 73 not out)
Match drawn

Led by Tony Cottey, Glamorgan began sketchily before Croft and Butcher added 128 in 32 overs for the third wicket. The star of the match for Glamorgan, however, was 20-year-old Alun Evans who scored 66 not out and 71 not out on the occasion of his first-class debut. Nearly two-and-a-half hours' play was lost on the Monday, and Oxford batted 25 balls into the third morning in an attempt to allow Gupte to complete his century, but not a run was scored and he was out.

6, 7 and 8 June
at Oxford
Worcestershire 403 for 4 dec. (M.J. Church 152, W.P.C. Weston 124, T.M. Moody 66 not out) and 198 for 3 dec. (K.R. Spiring 78 not out, S.R. Lampitt 70)
Oxford University 338 for 9 dec. (C.M. Gupte 132, W.S. Kendall 52, M.J. Church 4 for 50) and 195 for 9 (I.J. Sutcliffe 78, R.K. Illingworth 6 for 75)
Match drawn

An opening stand of 255 by Weston and Church was the highlight of the first day at Oxford. The runs came in 48 overs, and the occasion was particularly pleasing for Matthew Church whose previous highest first-class score was 38. Church hit 13 fours and seven sixes. He hit Wagh for three sixes in succession before being caught at deep mid-wicket off the fourth delivery. Church followed his century with the best bowling figures of his embryo career. Gupte recorded a patient century for Oxford who were eventually indebted to Thomson and du Preez, their last wicket pair, for saving the match.

Anurag Singh, who made his debut for Warwickshire in 1995, hit centuries for Cambridge University against both Hampshire and Sussex. (Ben Radford/Allsport)

The appearances of Will Kendall were restricted by examination, but he returned to play for Oxford in the last four matches. He recorded two fifties and two centuries, one of which came in the Varsity Match. (David Munden/Sportsline)

14, 15 and 16 June
at Cambridge
Hampshire 342 for 3 dec. (R.S.M. Morris 112, M. Keech 98, P.R. Whitaker 50 not out) and 210 for 6 dec. (S.D. Udal 58)
Cambridge University 286 for 7 dec. (A. Singh 101) and 152 (S.D. Udal 4 for 55)
Hampshire won by 114 runs

Returning to cricket after the three-week examination period, Cambridge found things hard against Hampshire for whom Keech hit a career-best and wicket-keeper Garaway had an impressive debut. Singh's hundred was the one bright spot for the University.

21, 22 and 23 June
at Cambridge
Essex 313 for 6 dec. (S.D. Peters 110, A.J.E. Hibbert 85) and 197 for 4 dec. (D.D.J. Robinson 97, R.J. Rollins 51)
Cambridge University 170 (R.Q. Cake 50, P.M. Such 5 for 34) and 218 (W.J. House 64, P.M. Such 4 for 55)
Essex won by 122 runs

An inexperienced Essex side inflicted the second defeat in a week upon Cambridge. Peter Such, captaining the county side, took the bowling honours, but the major heroes were two young batsmen, both of whom were born in Harold Wood. Andrew Hibbert, playing in his second first-class match, made his highest score while Stephen Peters, 17-years old, hit a century on his first-class debut.

29, 30 June and 1 July
at Canterbury
Oxford University 294 for 9 dec. (W.S. Kendall 119, I.J. Sutcliffe 83) and 216 for 4 dec. (G.A. Khan 101 not out)
Kent 200 for 0 dec. (D.P. Fulton 134 not out, C.D. Walsh 56 not out)
Match drawn

at Hove
Sussex 399 for 4 dec. (P. Moores 185, K. Newell 105 not out, M.P. Speight 50) and 243 for 2 dec. (J.W. Hall 93, M.P. Speight 64 not out, T.A. Radford 53)
Cambridge University 321 for 3 dec. (A. Singh 157, E.T. Smith 100) and 73 for 3
Match drawn

In their final games before the Varsity Match, both universities confirmed what had been evident all season, they were strong in batting and weak in bowling. Oxford could not capture a wicket at Canterbury, but they were comforted by the fact that Kendall and Khan scored centuries.

Cambridge were savaged at Hove on the Saturday where Moores, captaining Sussex but not keeping wicket, hit the highest score of his career. Cambridge responded in kind as Smith and Singh put on 240 for the second wicket.

2, 3 and 4 July
at Lord's
Oxford University 513 for 6 dec. (A.C. Ridley 155, W.S. Kendall 145 not out, C.M. Gupte 60, I.J. Sutcliffe 55) and 63 for 0 dec.
Cambridge University 164 for 3 dec. and 271 for 6 (W.J. House 54, N.J. Haste 51 not out, E.T. Smith 50)
Match drawn

Why the 151st Varsity Match was scheduled to be played from Tuesday to Thursday nobody could explain. Equally difficult to explain was why Russell Cake asked Oxford to bat when he won the toss. Gupte and Sutcliffe scored 107 for the first wicket, and Ridley, a Bradman scholar, then devastated the attack for four hours, hitting 17 fours. He and Kendall put on 149 for the fourth wicket, and Oxford closed on 390 for 4.

They scored 123 runs in 18 overs as they lost two wickets on the second morning. This took their total to 513, the highest score ever made by either side in the Varsity Match. Will Kendall remained undefeated for 145 off 166 balls. He hit a six and 16 fours. Unfortunately, three hours were lost to rain, and in spite of Cambridge declaring at their overnight score after debate between the two captains, the match was drawn. Cambridge were set to make 413 in 86 overs, but 13 of those overs were lost to rain, and neither side could force the issue.

Cambridge University First-Class Matches

Batting, 1996

	v. Glamorgan (Cambridge) 17–19 April		v. Derbyshire (Cambridge) 20–22 April		v. Warwickshire (Cambridge) 3–5 May		v. Middlesex (Cambridge) 16–18 May		v. Hampshire (Cambridge) 14–16 June		v. Essex (Cambridge) 21–23 June		v. Sussex (Hove) 29 June–1 July		Varsity Match (Lord's) 2–4 July		M	Inns	NO	Runs	HS	Av
R.T. Ragnauth	8	4	7	–	2	27*	29	0	27	2	2	13					6	11	1	121	29	12.10
E.T. Smith	101	8	54	–	55	20	15	76					100	–	40	50	6	10	–	519	101	51.90
R.Q. Cake	39	0*	102*	–	14	11	1	1	37	17	50	38	36*	5	23	33	8	15	3	407	102*	33.91
A. Singh	52*	16	13	–	26	16	42	41	101	15	0	7	157	23	36	45	8	15	1	590	157	42.14
W.J. House	14*	3*	136	–	6	0	127	11	5	1	26	64	12*	20*	47*	54	8	15	5	526	136	52.60
R.O. Jones	–	–	6	–	61	0	43	18	35	7	16	0	0	0	11*	8	8	13	1	205	61	17.08
D.R.H. Churton	–	–	0	–	0	7	3	1	–	3	20	–			–	–	7	7	–	34	20	4.85
N.J. Haste	–	–			2	5			–	34	7*	2	–	–	–	51*	6	6	2	101	51*	25.25
A.R. Whittall	–	–	–	–			–	16	22*	33	19	36	–	–	–	1	7	6	1	127	36	25.40
G.R. Moffat	–	–	1	–	27	0	1*	2	–	5*	1	8*	–	–	–	–	8	8	3	45	27	9.00
E. How	–	–			0*	7*											2	2	2	7	7*	–
P.J. Deakin			0*	–			24*	7	13	2	0	19	–	21*	–	14*	6	9	4	100	24*	20.00
A.N. Janisch			–	–	0	25	–	4*									3	3	1	29	25	14.50
J. Ratledge									30	26	19	14					2	4	–	89	30	22.25
R.W. Tennent													–	–	–	–	2	–				–
M.J. Birks													–	–			1	–				–
Byes					1	4		6	4	6	8	5		4		6						
Leg-byes	3	1	6		2	2	9	6	4	1	2	6	12		3	4						
Wides					4										4	5						
No-balls	8		4		8	8	6	8	8			6	4									
Total	225	32	329		208	132	300	197	286	152	170	218	321	73	164	271						
Wickets	3	3	7		10	9†	7	10	7	10	10	9‡	3	3	3	6						
Result	D		D		L		D		L		L		D		D							

Fielding Figures

10 – D.R.H. Churton (ct 7 / st 3)
4 – A.R. Whittall, G.R. Moffat and R.O. Jones
2 – A. Singh, W.J. House, R.Q. Cake and subs
1 – R.T. Ragnauth, M.J. Birks, E.T. Smith and N.J. Haste

† R.T. Ragnauth retired hurt
‡ D.R.H. Churton absent hurt

Bowling

	N.J. Haste	G.R. Moffat	A.R. Whittall	E. How	R.O. Jones	W.J. House	A.N. Janisch	P.J. Deakin	R.W. Tennent	A. Singh	Byes	Leg-byes	Wides	No-balls	Total	Wkts
v. Glamorgan (Cambridge)	15–0–47–1	14–6–31–0	32–16–61–0	10–3–44–0	21.4–10–36–0	7–1–35–0					4	4	1	12	262	1
17–19 April	13–1–62–0	13–2–64–0	7–0–30–0	5–1–46–0	7–1–12–1	6–0–29–0						5	2	12	248	1
v. Derbyshire (Cambridge)		14–1–73–1	27–6–92–2		10–1–53–0	3–0–7–0	13–0–45–1	2–1–9–0			5	3	1	6	287	4
20–22 April		20–3–82–0	20–4–60–0		10–4–44–0	6–0–36–0	17–3–72–0	8–0–26–1			3	4		6	327	2
v. Warwickshire (Cambridge)	17–2–74–1	16–1–50–1		11.4–1–71–0	12–1–72–0		17–3–95–0					6	1	6	368	3
3–5 May	18–3–51–3	10–3–50–2			9–1–55–1	1–0–3–0	11–4–23–2				1	7	1		190	8
v. Middlesex (Cambridge)		16–1–70–1	21–3–79–0		17–2–31–1	8–1–20–0	7–2–9–0	9–1–28–1			4	2		2	243	3
16–18 May		5–1–22–0	27.3–1–103–3		19–2–56–1		5–0–19–1				7	4	1	12	211	6
v. Hampshire (Cambridge)	12–1–39–1	16–1–64–0	23–2–101–0		16–4–51–1	11–1–37–0		11–1–38–1			7	5	1	16	342	3
14–16 June		2–0–11–0	12–0–52–1		12–0–45–2	11–0–61–1		9.4–2–35–2			6			6	210	6
v. Essex (Cambridge)	12–0–55–0	16–4–63–1	28–9–75–1		7–1–20–0	13–2–44–1		14.5–2–41–2			9	6	3	4	313	6
21–23 June	16–1–51–1	6–2–18–1	6–0–32–0		13–0–53–2	5–1–20–0		2–0–16–0			4	3	1	4	197	4
v. Sussex (Hove)	20–4–95–0	12–2–65–0	18–4–66–0		7–1–40–0	8–1–69–0		4.4–1–17–2	13–2–38–2		5	4	1	6	399	2
29 June–1 July	6–0–23–0	11–1–43–0	13–2–58–0		9–2–43–0	5–0–18–0		5–0–24–0	10–0–34–2				1		243	2
Varsity Match (Lord's)	31–4–141–1	14–0–82–1	38–8–118–3		16–3–49–0	5–1–33–0		5–1–15–0	15–3–64–0			11	6		513	5
2–4 July	5.5–0–35–0		2–1–5–0							3–0–13–0	7	3		4	63	0
	165.5–16–	185–28–	274.3–56–	26.4–5–	185.4–33–	89–8–	70–12–	71.1–9–	38–5–	3–0–						
	673–8	788–8	932–10	161–0	660–9	412–2	263–4	249–9	136–4	13–0						
Bowler's average	84.12	98.50	93.20	–	73.33	206.00	65.75	27.66	34.00	–						

Oxford University First-Class Matches

Batting, 1996

	v. Leicestershire (Oxford) 13–16 April		v. Durham (Oxford) 17–19 April		v. Middlesex (Oxford) 20–23 April		v. Hampshire (Oxford) 2–4 May		v. Northamptonshire (Oxford) 16–18 May		v. Nottinghamshire (Oxford) 23–25 May		v. Glamorgan (Oxford) 1–4 June		v. Worcestershire (Oxford) 6–8 June		v. Kent (Canterbury) 29 June–1 July		Varsity Match (Lord's) 2–4 July		M	Inns	NO	Runs	HS	Av
C.M. Gupte	29	5	113*	–	–	–	75	–	4	–	18	–	97	40	132	20	6	7	60	–	10	13	1	606	132	50.50
I.J. Sutcliffe	16	65	65	–			5	–							24	78	83	17	55	–	6	9	–	408	83	45.33
A.C. Ridley	15	104	3	–	–	–	70	–							32	14	0	24	155	–	7	9	–	417	155	46.33
G.A. Khan	94	0	33	–	–	–	37	–	96	–	72*	–	11	5			34	101*	34	–	9	11	2	517	101*	57.44
M.A. Wagh	0	13	2	–	–	–	43	–	27	–	5*	–	2*	22	33	14	0	–	8*	–	10	12	3	169	43	18.77
H.S. Malik	15	11*	1*	–	–	–	61	–	1	–	38	–	19	37	8	8	10	–	12	19*	10	13	3	240	61	24.00
M.E.D. Jarrett	8*	0	–	–	–	–	10	–	50*	–	–	–	1	13							7	6	2	82	50*	20.50
J.N. Batty	16*	1	–	–	–	–	8	–	56	–	31	–	51	8	1	48	5	20*	27	30*	10	13	3	302	56	30.20
R.B. Thomson	–	0*	–	–	–	–	7*	–	2*	–	–	–	–	–	14*	0*	11*	–	–	–	10	6	6	34	14*	–
D.P. Mather	–	–	–	–	–	–	–	–	–	–	–	–	–	–	2	0					8	2	–	2	2	1.00
S.P. du Preez	–	–	–	–	–	–	–	–	–	–	–	–	–	–	–	1*	9	–	–	–	10	2	1	10	9	10.00
G.J. Wright					–	–															1					–
C.E.R. Lightfoot									9	–	–	–	–	4*	0	2					4	4	1	15	9	5.00
J.J. Bull									4	–	–	–									2	1	–	4	4	4.00
W.S. Kendall													4	73*	52	8	119	43	145*	–	4	7	2	444	145*	88.80
A.W. Maclay																	1*	–	–	–	2	1	1	1	1*	–
Byes	4													7	8					7						
Leg-byes	10	11	8				6		9		2		3	1	13	2	4		11	3						
Wides															1				6							
No-balls		2	2								12		8	6	18		12	4		4						
Total	207	212	227				322		258		178		196	216	338	195	294	216	513	63						
Wickets	6	7	4				8		7		3		6	6	9	9	10	4	6	0						
Result	D		D		D		D		D		D		D		D		D		D							

Fielding Figures

11 – J.N. Batty (ct 9 / st 2))
7 – H.S. Malik
4 – M.E.D. Jarrett
3 – S.P. du Preez and G.A. Khan
2 – W.S. Kendall
1 – A.C. Ridley, M.A. Wagh, R.B. Thomson, I.J. Sutcliffe and C.M. Gutpe

Bowling

	S.P. du Preez	R.B. Thomson	M.A. Wagh	D.P. Mather	H.S. Malik	G.A. Khan	I.J. Sutcliffe	G.J. Wright	M.E.D. Jarrett	C.E.R. Lightfoot	W.S. Kendall	A.W. Maclay	Byes	Leg-byes	Wides	No-balls	Total	Wkts
v. Leicestershire (Oxford)	18–0–60–1	19–6–46–1	7–0–29–0	19.4–2–81–0	20–3–65–1	2–0–12–0								6	3		299	4
13–16 April	5–0–20–0		4–0–18–0	11–1–56–1	11–0–46–2	1–0–5–0									1		145	3
v. Durham (Oxford)	15–1–53–0	18–3–47–0	21–7–41–0	14–1–65–0	18–1–83–0	3–0–19–0	4–0–10–0						9	7	1		334	0
17–19 April	3–0–12–0	3–1–8–0													1		20	0
v. Middlesex (Oxford)	20–6–44–2	19.4–5–51–2		11–0–45–1	2–0–18–0			9–0–33–0						6	10		197	5
20–23 April																		
v. Hampshire (Oxford)	11–2–44–0	13–3–37–0	30–7–86–2	17–5–31–3	43–14–119–3								6	4	2		327	8
2–4 May	7–1–20–0	9–5–16–0		10–3–27–1		9–0–48–2			2–0–5–0				2	1	1	4	119	3
v. Northamptonshire (Oxford)	9–2–35–0	17–4–53–0	13–0–46–1	18–1–75–0	23–1–85–1	2–0–17–0				1–0–10–0			13	1	1		335	2
16–18 May	10–2–29–0	10–2–33–1		7–0–27–0	9–0–67–1	2–0–15–0							2	1	1		174	2
v. Nottinghamshire (Oxford)																		Ab
23–25 May																		
v. Glamorgan (Oxford)	13–2–52–0	15–2–50–0	30–5–82–3	13–3–46–2	11–0–49–2	4–0–20–1							2	3	1	18	304	6
1–4 June	7–1–19–0	7–0–23–0			13–2–57–2					13.5–3–65–2					1	8	164	5
v. Worcestershire (Oxford)	8–0–63–0	12–0–40–1	20–4–71–2	10–0–64–0	20–1–121–0		1–0–8–0			7–1–31–0			3	2		6	403	4
6–8 June	9–1–31–0	10–3–24–2	8–3–18–0	7–3–19–1	6–0–23–0					6–1–23–0	5–0–35–0		1	2			198	3A
v. Kent (Canterbury)	10–1–41–0	11–2–27–0	7.3–1–29–0		7–1–43–0						2–0–8–0	12–2–50–0		2		8	200	0
29 June–1 July																		
Varsity Match (Lord's)	13–2–78–2	1–0–4–0	2–0–12–0									11–0–67–1		3		4	164	3
2–4 July	10–3–33–0	19–0–68–2	13–0–37–1		14–0–50–0	2–0–15–0	5–1–21–2					8–1–30–0	6	4	5		271	6B
Bowler's average	168–24– 634–5 126.80	183.4–36– 527–9 58.55	155.3–27– 469–9 52.11	137.4–19– 536–9 59.55	197–23– 826–10 82.60	25–0– 151–3 50.33	10–1– 39–2 19.50	9–0– 33–0 –	2–0– 5–0 –	27.5–5– 129–2 64.50	7–0– 43–0 –	31–3– 147–1 147.00						

A. C.M. Gupte 1–0–6–0; A.C. Ridley 4–1–16–0
B. C.M. Gupte 1–0–4–0; A.C. Ridley 1–0–3–0

Benson and Hedges Cup

The longest running sponsorship in the history of English cricket was 25 years old in 1996. It was, justifiably, an occasion to celebrate for, during the quarter century of its existence, the Benson and Hedges Cup has produced some memorable cricket and given immense pleasure to millions of people, a fact which is too often overlooked.

For Leicestershire, the first winners, and for Essex, success in the Benson and Hedges Cup proved to be the catalyst which initiated a series of triumphs. Essex's victory over Surrey in the 1979 final will long be remembered for the batting of Gooch and McEwan. Gooch's innings of 120 was beaten two years later by Viv Richards who scored 132 not out as Somerset trounced Surrey, yet, arguably, neither of these innings could compare with Aravinda de Silva's 112 for Kent against Lancashire in 1995.

Gooch began the 1996 campaign with 4934 runs, average 53.63, and 14 centuries in the Benson and Hedges Cup. He scored 198 not out against Sussex at Hove in 1982, and hit 591 runs in 1979. Before the start of the 1996 season, he had played in 106 Benson and Hedges Cup matches, taken 63 catches and won 22 Gold Awards. All of the statistics mentioned above are records for the competition.

While Gooch may have dominated personal records in the Benson and Hedges Cup, the team honours have been evenly spread and, at the start of 1996, only three counties, Durham, Glamorgan and Sussex, had not won the trophy. Like other sides, their hopes were high for the jubilee year.

The Groupings for 1996 were as follows:
Group A Lancashire (holders), Warwickshire, Leicestershire, Derbyshire, Durham and Minor Counties
Group B Northamptonshire, Yorkshire, Nottinghamshire, Worcestershire and Scotland
Group C Glamorgan, Kent, Essex, Middlesex, Somerset and British Universities
Group D Surrey, Gloucestershire, Hampshire, Sussex and Ireland

---

26 April
at Oxford
Kent 250 (M.A. Ealham 75, M.V. Fleming 72)
British Universities 166 (A. Singh 72)
Kent (2 pts) won by 84 runs
(Gold Award: M.A. Ealham)

at Chesterfield
Derbyshire 266 for 4 (C.J. Adams 100 not out, D.M. Jones 67)
Durham 162
Derbyshire (2 pts) won by 104 runs
(Gold Award: C.J. Adams)

at Cardiff
Essex 151 (R.D.B. Croft 4 for 30, S.D. Thomas 4 for 51)
Glamorgan 155 for 6
Glamorgan (2 pts) won by 4 wickets
(Gold Award: S.D. Thomas)

at Bristol
Sussex 230 for 8 (N.J. Lenham 57)
Gloucestershire 232 for 5 (T.H.C. Hancock 71 not out, A. Symonds 67)
Gloucestershire (2 pts) won by 5 wickets
(Gold Award: A. Symonds)

at Southampton
Hampshire 268 for 5 (J.P. Stephenson 124 not out, W.K.M. Benjamin 58 not out)
Ireland 102
Hampshire (2 pts) won by 166 runs
(Gold Award: J.P. Stephenson)

Shaun Pollock leaves the field receiving the congratulations of his captain Dermot Reeve after taking 6 for 21 for Warwickshire against Leicestershire. Pollock became the first bowler to take four wickets in four balls in a Benson and Hedges Cup match, on 26 April. (Paul Sturgess/Sportsline)

at Old Trafford
Lancashire 232 (M. Watkinson 56)
Minor Counties 207 for 9 (S.D. Myles 56 not out)
Lancashire (2 pts) won by 25 runs
(Gold Award: M. Watkinson)

at Lord's
Somerset 322 for 4 (M.N. Lathwell 121, S.C. Ecclestone 112 not out)
Middlesex 170 (J.D. Carr 50, M.R. Ramprakash 50)
Somerset (2 pts) won by 152 runs
(Gold Award: S.C. Ecclestone)

at Edgbaston
Leicestershire 182 for 9 (B.F. Smith 61, S.M. Pollock 6 for 21)
Warwickshire 183 for 3 (D.P. Ostler 68 not out, T.L. Penney 50 not out)
Warwickshire (2 pts) won by 7 wickets
(Gold Award: S.M. Pollock)

at Worcester
Worcestershire 217 for 7 (D.A. Leatherdale 66, J.P. Taylor 4 for 32)
Northamptonshire 218 for 6 (M.B. Loye 66)
Northamptonshire (2 pts) won by 4 wickets
(Gold Award: J.P. Taylor)

at Leeds
Yorkshire 247 for 7 (D. Byas 81, C. White 57 not out)
Nottinghamshire 178 (A.A. Metcalfe 66, A.G. Wharf 4 for 29)
Yorkshire (2 pts) won by 69 runs
(Gold Award: C. White)

The Benson and Hedges Cup had a new format for its jubilee year. It became the only competition in Great Britain to adopt the rules of the World Cup. The number of overs per innings was reduced to fifty, and there was just one break, between the two innings. Fielding restrictions were those employed in the World Cup, that is that only two fieldsmen were permitted outside the circle in the first 15 overs of the innings.

The first round of matches brought much excitement. In The Parks, Ward and Fleming scored 109 in under 15 overs for Kent's first wicket, but nobody then reached double figures until Mark Ealham hit 75 off 59 balls. It was not just the Universities' bowling that suffered. Umpire Whitehead was hit on the head by Boswell's elbow as the bowler delivered the ball and was in considerable pain for some time. He and his fellow umpire White were also involved in heated debate with Kent players when they recalled Anurag Singh after Fleming had wrongly claimed a catch. The Kent side did themselves no credit, but they won with considerable ease.

Derbyshire's new skipper Dean Jones hit 67 off 65 balls, and Chris Adams made his first century in the Benson and Hedges Cup off just 93 balls. The pair added 135 in 19 overs. Durham reached 85 for 2 in 21 overs before subsiding to 162 all out in the 41st over, a worrying sign for the months ahead.

Newcomers Law and Grayson failed to spark Essex at Cardiff, but run-getting was never easy on a slow, low pitch. Croft produced his best figures in the competition, but, chasing a target of 152, Glamorgan were only 37 for 2 after 15 overs. The necessary impetus came from Thomas and Dale who shared an unbroken seventh wicket partnership of 45 in nine overs so that Glamorgan won with 14 balls to spare.

Sussex recovered from 98 for 5 to reach 230 mainly due to a sixth wicket stand of 88 between Lenham and Newell. Gloucestershire, too, were in trouble at 87 for 4 before Hancock and Symonds added 108 in 18 overs.

Hampshire's new skipper John Stephenson hit a century as his county crushed Ireland, for whom Paul McCrum bowled admirably. He finished with figures of 10–4–10–2, and one of his wickets was that of Robin Smith, who was caught first ball.

Lancashire had a less easy time against Minor Counties than Hampshire had against Ireland. At 102 for 5, there was uncertainty against a keen attack and dynamic fielding, but a pugnacious 56 from Mike Watkinson lifted the holders. Minor Counties reached 83 for 1 in the 21st over, but four wickets then fell for 22 runs and, in spite of Simon Myles' valiant innings, the momentum was never regained.

At Lord's, David Follett beat Mark Lathwell with the first ball of the match, and that was just about the last piece of joy Middlesex had all day. Somerset started slowly, but they ended with their highest score in a Benson and Hedges Cup match. Lathwell and Simon Ecclestone added 188 in 26 overs for the second wicket. Lathwell's 121 came off 135 balls with a six and 15 fours; Ecclestone needed just 96 balls for his 111. He took 20 off one over from Feltham, and his century was his first for Somerset in any competition. Turner also produced some fireworks, and once Kevin Shine, making his debut for Somerset, removed openers Weekes and Pooley, Middlesex never looked like reaching their daunting target.

The sensation of the round, and of the early part of the season as a whole, came at Edgbaston where the South African Shaun Pollock played his first game for Warwickshire. He claimed the wicket of Vince Wells with his 11th delivery, the batsman skying to cover. In his fourth over, Pollock had Macmillan taken at slip by Reeve from a delivery that rose sharply. The next ball bowled Whitaker between bat and pad, and the hat-trick was completed when Robinson was caught at short-leg off bat and pad. This was the 11th occasion on which a hat-trick had been performed in the Benson and Hedges Cup, but Pollock was not yet finished. He became the first bowler to claim four wickets in four balls in the competition when he had Maddy taken at third slip. One cannot think that any cricketer has made a more sensational debut for a county. Leicestershire were now 9 for 5. When Nixon was taken at slip, they slumped to 33 for 6. Ben Smith and Millns offered defiance, but the issue had virtually ended by the time Pollock had completed his ten overs. He was awarded his county cap to accompany the Gold Award.

Making his debut for Worcestershire, Sheriyar took 3 for 40, but Northamptonshire, who included Emburey in their side, won with an over to spare.

Metcalfe, making his Nottinghamshire debut against his old county, hit 66, but Yorkshire won comfortably. Alex Wharf, playing his first game in the competition, took four wickets for 29 in nine overs.

---

28 April
at Cambridge
British Universities 312 for 8 (G.A. Khan 147, A.C. Ridley 58)
Glamorgan 314 for 2 (S.P. James 121, M.P. Maynard 110 not out)
Glamorgan (2 pts) won by 8 wickets
(Gold Award: M.P. Maynard)

at Chelmsford
Middlesex 150 for 8 (M.R. Ramprakash 56, J.D. Carr 51, M.C. Ilott 4 for 17)
Essex 151 for 5 (N. Hussain 67 not out)
Essex (2 pts) won by 5 wickets
(Gold Award: N. Hussain)

at Maidstone
Kent 338 for 6 (C.L. Hooper 98, M.A. Ealham 72, T.R. Ward 58)
Somerset 293 for 9 (S.C. Ecclestone 92, M.A. Ealham 4 for 50)
Kent (2 pts) won by 45 runs
(Gold Award: M.A. Ealham)

at Old Trafford
Durham 214 for 9 (M.J. Foster 52)
Lancashire 217 for 3 (M.A. Atherton 121 not out)
Lancashire (2 pts) won by 7 wickets
(Gold Award: M.A. Atherton)

at Leicester
Leicestershire 282 for 9 (J.J. Whitaker 70, V.J. Wells 60, B.F. Wells 53)
Derbyshire 278 (C.J. Adams 72, C.M. Wells 56)
Leicestershire (2 pts) won by 4 runs
(Gold Award: J.J. Whitaker)

at Jesmond
Warwickshire 369 for 8 (N.V. Knight 104, D.P. Ostler 86)
Minor Counties 174 for 8 (D.A. Reeve 4 for 23)
Warwickshire (2 pts) won by 195 runs
(Gold Award: N.V. Knight)

at Trent Bridge
Scotland 172 for 9
Nottinghamshire 174 for 3 (C.M. Tolley 66, P. Johnson 54 not out)
Nottinghamshire (2 pts) won by 7 wickets
(Gold Award: J.A. Afford)

at The Oval
Surrey 333 for 6 (A.J. Stewart 160, A.D. Brown 51)
Hampshire 274 (R.A. Smith 123, A.J. Hollioake 4 for 34)
Surrey (2 pts) won by 59 runs
(Gold Award: A.J. Stewart)

at Hove
Ireland 190 for 8 (A.R. Dunlop 50, V.C. Drakes 5 for 19)
Sussex 194 for 2 (M.P. Speight 64, A.P. Wells 53 not out, K. Greenfield 51 not out)
Sussex (2 pts) won by 8 wickets
(Gold Award: M.P. Speight)

at Worcester
Worcestershire 289 for 3 (G.A. Hick 95, T.M. Moody 80 not out, T.S. Curtis 67)
Yorkshire 292 for 4 (M.G. Bevan 80 not out, M.D. Moxon 67, M.P. Vaughan 60)
Yorkshire (2 pts) won by 6 wickets
(Gold Award: M.G. Bevan)

British Universities recorded their highest score in the Benson and Hedges Cup, and Gul Khan passed Hussain's previous best score for the Universities when he hit 147 off 131 balls in a most stylish display. He gave only one chance which, sadly, caused a serious injury. On 32, he lofted a drive which Hemp caught over his shoulder before colliding with Morris and dropping the ball. It was discovered that Hemp had broken two ribs, and there were fears of damage to a lung. The injury was serious enough to bring Hemp's participation in cricket virtually to an end for the season. Glamorgan had other worries until Maynard joined James at 130 for 2 in the 27th over. The Glamorgan captain sparked a stand which brought 184 in 20 overs. Maynard's 100 came off 58 balls and was the quickest century in Glamorgan's one-day history.

A more sedate spectacle was presented at Chelmsford where a slow pitch curbed stroke-play. Hussain steered Essex to victory after Ilott had produced a fine spell of bowling. Middlesex's defeat meant that their chances of reaching the quarter-finals were very slim.

At Maidstone, Kent made their highest Benson and Hedges score and the match aggregate of 631 for 15 wickets beat the previous record by one run. Fleming began Kent's assault with 41 off 30 balls, and Hooper played a beautiful innings of 98, which included four sixes and eight fours. Ealham confirmed his growing stature as an all-rounder with an innings of 72 off 39 balls. He hit seven fours and five sixes in a thrilling display. Kent were aided by some poor fielding, and the Somerset bowlers suffered accord-

Glamorgan's new skipper Matthew Maynard led by example to take his side to the quarter-finals of the Benson and Hedges Cup. Maynard averaged 132 in the competition and hit two sparkling centuries. (Paul Sturgess/Sportsline)

ingly. Simon Ecclestone brought visions of an unlikely victory when he scored 92 off 63 balls, but he was one of three to fall to a splendid catch in the deep by Cowdrey as Somerset stumbled from 155 for 3 to 222 for 8.

The game at Old Trafford needed to go into a second day for completion. Durham made 214, and Lancashire were poised on 82 for 2 from 24 overs when rain brought a close. The second morning belonged to Mike Atherton who scored 97 out of 135 to claim his third hundred and second Gold Award in the Benson and Hedges Cup.

Leicestershire recovered from the traumatic events at Edgbaston to gain an exciting victory over Derbyshire. Macmillan was out in the first over of the day, but Wells and Smith added 107, and Whitaker hit 70 off 65 balls. Derbyshire faced a large total, but it was by no means beyond reach. Chris Adams led the way, but the late order found the task of scoring 14 from the last over too difficult. Maddy kept his head, bowled Vandrau, and the home side won by four runs.

Warwickshire made their highest score in the competition as they shattered Minor Counties. Nick Knight took the Gold Award for his century, but Dominic Ostler gave a thrilling display with six sixes in his 86. He and Knight added 159 in 23 overs for the third wicket.

Scotland, too, found county opposition too strong and Nottinghamshire won with 21.5 overs to spare.

There was a huge run feast at The Oval. Surrey hit their highest score in the competition, with Alec Stewart, 160 off 154 balls, reaching his third hundred in the Benson and Hedges Cup. The early impetus for Surrey, who were put in to bat, came from Ally Brown who reached 50 off 28 balls. After 15 overs, Surrey were 118 for 1. Stewart's last 60 runs came off 28 balls, and, in all, he hit four sixes and 15 fours. Chris Lewis, playing his first game for Surrey, produced a fine opening spell that ended Hampshire's hopes of a flying start, and Martin Bicknell dismissed Stephenson and Morris. By the 22nd over, Hampshire were 105 for 6, but Robin Smith, 123 off 114 balls, and Adrian Aymes added 119 before Lewis returned to administer the last rites.

Five wickets from Vasbert Drakes and sparkling fifties from Speight, Wells and Greenfield took Sussex to victory over Ireland with 30 overs to spare, while Yorkshire won a closer contest at Worcester. Hick scored 95 off 88 balls – he was one of six batsmen in the match to score a half century – and Worcestershire's 289 for 3 was the highest score made against Yorkshire in a Benson and Hedges Cup match. Byas was out first ball, but Vaughan and Moxon added 100 in 20 overs for Yorkshire's second wicket. Bevan, 80 off 75 balls, McGrath and White then saw the visitors to victory with five balls to spare.

30 April
at Chelmsford
Essex 331 for 5 (G.A. Gooch 100, P.J. Prichard 82, R.C. Irani 62 not out)

British Universities 224 for 9 (C.M. Gupte 54 not out, R.C. Irani 4 for 30)
Essex (2 pts) won by 107 runs
(Gold Award: R.C. Irani)

at Southampton
Hampshire 235 for 9 (P.R. Whitaker 53)
Sussex 168 (C.W.J. Athey 55)
Hampshire (2 pts) won by 67 runs
(Gold Award: P.R. Whitaker)

at Canterbury
Middlesex 219 for 6 (J.D. Carr 55)
Kent 220 for 4 (C.L. Hooper 62)
Kent (2 pts) won by 6 wickets
(Gold Award: J.B.D. Thompson)

at Trent Bridge
Worcestershire 188 (T.S. Curtis 61)
Nottinghamshire 190 for 5 (R.T. Robinson 52)
Nottinghamshire (2 pts) won by 5 wickets
(Gold Award: R.T. Bates)

at Forfar
Scotland 174 for 4 (I.L. Philip 69, J.G. Williamson 51 not out)
Northamptonshire 175 for 5 (R.J. Bailey 66)
Northamptonshire (2 pts) won by 5 wickets
(Gold Award: R.J. Bailey)

at The Oval
Gloucestershire 307 for 4 (R.J. Cunliffe 137 not out, A.J. Wright 63)
Surrey 308 for 7 (A.D. Brown 82)
Surrey (2 pts) won by 3 wickets
(Gold Award: R.J. Cunliffe)

30 April and 1 May
at Chesterfield
Derbyshire 137 (M. Watkinson 5 for 44)
Lancashire 124 for 7 (D.G. Cork 5 for 49)
Lancashire (2 pts) won on faster scoring rate
(Gold Award: D.G. Cork)

at Chester-le-Street
Durham 137 (M.A. Roseberry 55 not out)
v. **Warwickshire**
Match abandoned
Durham 1 pt, Warwickshire 1 pt

at Cardiff
Somerset 239 for 8 (R.J. Turner 70, A.N. Hayhurst 67 not out)
Glamorgan 161 for 6
Somerset (2 pts) won on faster scoring rate
(Gold Award: R.J. Turner)

at Jesmond
Minor Counties 206 for 9
Leicestershire 173 for 5
Leicestershire (2 pts) won on faster scoring rate
(Gold Award: D.L. Maddy)

The weather was unkind to the third round of matches in the Benson and Hedges Cup and four matches went into a second day. Only 34.2 overs were possible at Chester-le-Street on the Tuesday, and no play at all was possible on the Wednesday. There was also no play possible on the second day at Jesmond where Leicestershire beat Minor Counties on a faster run-rate. Darren Maddy, 1 for 25 in six overs and 33 not out, won his first Gold Award.

At Chesterfield, Dean Jones chose to bat first when he won the toss and must have regretted his decision as Derbyshire were bowled out in 33.3 overs for 137. Ian Austin took 3 for 12 in 7.3 overs while Mike Watkinson's 5 for 44 represented his best figures in the competition. These performances by the Lancashire bowlers were soon overshadowed by Dominic Cork who, having conceded 16 in his first over, produced a spell of four wickets for nine runs in 11 balls. Lancashire were trembling at 42 for 5 before Fairbrother and Watkinson added 28. There was then a break for rain and bad light, and play could not resume until six o'clock. It resumed for just one over, but in that over,

Young Gloucestershire batsman Robert Cunliffe enjoyed an outstanding competition with centuries in successive matches.
(Paul Sturgess/Sportsline)

Cork had Watkinson taken at second slip. Play could not restart until 4.20 on the Wednesday, and there was a stoppage for bad light when Lancashire had reached 107 for 7 in 25 overs. There was a restart but, in effect, the game had been decided already in anticlimactic fashion, sad after such an absorbing first day.

Put in to bat at Cardiff, Somerset descended to 69 for 5. Turner and Hayhurst brought about a revival with a partnership of 113, but when rain ended play Glamorgan, chasing a target of 240, were seemingly well placed at 108 for 2 from 27 overs. Only nine overs could be bowled on the Wednesday, a day of intermittent showers. Play resumed briefly at 2.30 pm and then again at 6.30, by which time Glamorgan's revised target meant that they needed 33 from 19 balls and, eventually, 27 from Caddick's last over. Cottey battled bravely but vainly, hitting 15.

Essex were able to complete their match against British Universities in one day. Gooch and Prichard began with a stand of 200, and Gooch reached 5000 runs in Benson and Hedges matches. Irani hit 62 off 28 balls and later took 4 for 30 to claim his first Gold Award.

Hampshire played thoughtful cricket to dispose of Sussex. Stephenson chose to bat first and hooked the second ball of the match for six, but run-getting was never easy on a pitch that increasingly offered movement off the seam. Hampshire batted with sense and good judgement against an attack which lacked necessary control. In contrast, Hampshire showed an appetite in attack which was refreshing although there were lapses in the field. The fiery Benjamin was not well served, but Hampshire still won with ease. Benjamin's 3 for 26 from eight overs was no more than he deserved.

Middlesex suffered elimination from the tournament when they were beaten for the third time in three matches. They succumbed to a Kent side eager and in form. Hooper played another majestic innings, but he was up-staged by Dr Julian Thompson, a pace bowler making his debut in the Benson and Hedges Cup. He took 3 for 29 from his ten overs. His victims were the openers Weekes and Pooley off successive balls and Gatting who was well caught behind. Kent won with 16 balls and six wickets to spare, but there was some consolation for Middlesex in the batting of 17-year-old debutant Owais Shah who hit an undefeated 42 off 38 balls. His runs included a six over long-on off McCague.

Worcestershire had another miserable day at Trent Bridge. They were 120 for 1 by the 23rd over and all out for 188 25 overs later. Bates split the Hick/Curtis partnership and bowled economically. He was one of two batsmen to fall early, but Nottinghamshire moved smoothly to victory with 44 balls not needed.

Northamptonshire made light work of beating Scotland with new skipper Bailey taking his seventh Gold Award.

Surrey had a stiffer task in overcoming Gloucestershire at The Oval which remains a batsman's paradise. Batting first, the visitors lost Dawson at 13, but Wright and Cunliffe added 161 and seized the initiative. The stand was broken when Julian took a diving catch, and the Australian compensated for some rather sloppy bowling by dismissing the dangerous Symonds caught and bowled for five. Hancock and Alleyne gave Robert Cunliffe admirable support, and Gloucestershire totalled 307, which they had every right to consider a match-winning score. Cunliffe was immensely impressive in scoring his first limited-over century. His 137 not out off 143 balls was a splendid effort for a 22-year-old whose first team experience has been restricted. To win, Surrey had to make the highest score that they had ever made batting second in the Benson and Hedges Cup. They, and coach Gilbert in particular, have learned much from the World Cup, and Sri Lanka would have been proud of David Ward and Ally Brown's opening partnership. They scored 73, and although Ward was bowled by Cawdron, Surrey were 134 for 1 by the end of the 15th over. This blistering scoring was due mostly to Brown who went from 31 to 81 off 17 balls and whose 81 came off just 57 deliveries with ten fours and four sixes. One over from Cawdron cost 25. Concentration wavered, and Surrey slipped to 185 for 4 in 29 overs before Darren Bicknell and Adam Hollioake added 69 in 12 overs to restore the prospect of victory. Julian then scored 27 off 18 balls and the target was reached with seven balls to spare.

---

7 May

at Chester-le-Street
Minor Counties 157
Durham 158 for 5
Durham (2 pts) won by 5 wickets
(Gold Award: J.I. Longley)

at Chelmsford
Essex 225 for 6 (N. Hussain 82)
Kent 226 for 9 (T.R. Ward 51)
Kent (2 pts) won by 1 wicket
(Gold Award: J.B.D. Thompson)

at Dublin (Clontarf CC)
Gloucestershire 308 for 3 (A.J. Wright 123, R.J. Cunliffe 116 not out)
Ireland 140 (D.A. Lewis 61)
Gloucestershire (2 pts) won by 168 runs
(Gold Award: A.J. Wright)

at Leicester
Leicestershire 176
Lancashire 177 for 2 (N.J. Speak 79 not out, N.H. Fairbrother 77 not out)
Lancashire (2 pts) won by 8 wickets
(Gold Award: N.J. Speak)

at Lord's
Middlesex 263 (J.C. Pooley 50, A. Dale 5 for 41)
Glamorgan 265 for 4 (M.P. Maynard 151 not out)
Glamorgan (2 pts) won by 6 wickets
(Gold Award: M.P. Maynard)

at Northampton
Nottinghamshire 232 (P.R. Pollard 79, A.A. Metcalfe 58, J.P. Taylor 5 for 45)
Northamptonshire 236 for 4 (R.J. Bailey 115 not out, K.M. Curran 50)
Northamptonshire (2 pts) won by 6 wickets
(Gold Award: R.J. Bailey)

at Taunton
British Universities 271 (A. Singh 123, A.R. Caddick 5 for 51)
Somerset 272 for 7 (M.N. Lathwell 76, S.C. Ecclestone 62)
Somerset (2 pts) won by 3 wickets
(Gold Award: A. Singh)

at Hove
Sussex 208 (A.P. Wells 69)
Surrey 209 for 1 (A.D. Brown 117 not out, A.J. Stewart 61 not out)
Surrey (2 pts) won by 9 wickets
(Gold Award: A.D. Brown)

at Edgbaston
Derbyshire 193 (D.M. Jones 64, S.M. Pollock 5 for 38)
Warwickshire 194 for 2 (N.V. Knight 91, N.M.K. Smith 80)
Warwickshire (2 pts) won by 8 wickets
(Gold Award: N.M.K. Smith)

at Leeds
Yorkshire 270 for 7 (M.G. Bevan 75, M.P. Vaughan 50)
Scotland 142 (C.E.W. Silverwood 5 for 28)
Yorkshire (2 pts) won by 128 runs
(Gold Award: C.E.W. Silverwood)

The fourth round of matches brought extinction to some counties. Durham beat Minor Counties in a rather undistinguished match at Chester-le-Street. This was Durham's first win of the season, but it could not earn them a place in the quarter-finals.

By beating Essex by one wicket with two balls to spare, Kent virtually assured themselves of a place in the last eight. Essex played some poor cricket and could only blame themselves for their defeat. Thompson struck yet again when he had Gooch caught behind for 12, and Prichard played a wretched shot across the line to be bowled by the doctor. Hussain took a long time to get going before hitting 82 off 116 balls with a six and six fours. Irani struck the ball well, but the promising Robinson, who should have opened, was too low in the order to be of real use. Kent needed only 226 to win, and Fleming hit a rapid 22. Ward and Hooper added 66, and with Cowdrey and Walker making useful contributions, Kent were strolling to victory. Essex compounded their own destruction by conceding a no-ball for having three fielders behind square on the leg side, but Grayson clawed them back into the game with his left-arm spin. The last over arrived with eight needed and the last pair at the wicket. Inexplicably, Prichard entrusted Law with the last over even though he had been the most expensive of the Essex bowlers. The captain's lapse also allowed the no-ball mentioned above, and Patel Thompson did the rest.

Cunliffe hit his second consecutive Benson and Hedges century, and he and Wright shared a second wicket stand of 222, a Gloucestershire record for the competition, and Ireland were swept aside.

Having reached 142 for 4 in 34 overs, Leicestershire collapsed to 176 all out in the next ten. Lancashire started badly, losing Gallian and Atherton with only eight runs on the board, but Speak and Fairbrother made light work of batting after that. Lancashire won with five overs to spare, and Speak won his first Gold Award.

The Middlesex misery continued. Weekes and Harrison began with 71 in 17 overs, and Pooley hit 50 off 52 balls, but from 192 for 3 they plunged to 262 all out. Glamorgan were 25 for 2 when Maynard joined Dale who had already taken five wickets in a Benson and Hedges Cup game for the first time. They added 137 in 23 overs, but when they were separated Glamorgan still needed 102 from 17 overs. Maynard was irrepressible. He hit five sixes and 11 fours as he made the highest score by a Glamorgan batsman in the competition. His 151 came off 119 balls, and he led his side to victory with seven balls to spare.

Robert Bailey was another captain to lead by example. Paul Taylor dismissed Tim Robinson in his first over and Tolley in his third. When Johnson unwisely tried to hook Ambrose, Nottinghamshire were 46 for 3. Pollard and Metcalfe added 95, but Northamptonshire contained well. Taylor finished with his first five-wicket haul in the competition. There were early setbacks for Northamptonshire before Bailey, 115 off 143 balls with two sixes and 11 fours, and Curran added 119. Victory came with two overs to spare.

Somerset had a big fright against British Universities. Anurag Singh, Cambridge University and Warwickshire, hit 123 off 133 balls, and, in spite of a late flop, the students moved to a commendable 271. The Universities' bowling is not their strength, but the attack worked hard and Somerset were reduced to 209 for 7 in the 41st over. A famous student victory seemed probable, but the unpredictable Turner and Parsons scored 63 in the next seven overs to win the match with seven balls to spare.

The blistering batting of Alistair Brown was again in evidence as Surrey roared to victory over Sussex with nine wickets and 13.5 overs to spare. Brown's first Benson and Hedges century occupied 105 balls and included five sixes and 11 fours. He and Alec Stewart shared an unbroken partnership of 151. Sussex would have succumbed even more easily had not Alan Wells batted sturdily and Paul Jarvis not hit hard for his 38 which included 20 off Pearson's last over.

Shaun Pollock struck again to help dismiss Derbyshire cheaply after Jones and Owen had added 105 for the third wicket. The first two wickets had gone down

John Emburey and Rob Bailey masterminded Northamptonshire to the final. Bailey scored 425 runs in the competition. (David Munden/Sportsline)

for 27. With Malcolm at his most wayward, conceding 54 from five overs, Knight and Neil Smith flourished and scored 162 for the first wicket in 19 overs, a Warwickshire record. After that, victory was a formality and came after 23.3 overs.

Like Warwickshire, Yorkshire confirmed a place in the last eight. Reifer and Tennant bowled well for Scotland, but Yorkshire plundered 83 off the last seven overs. Chris Silverwood, who took four wickets in his first 27 deliveries, ended with his first five-wicket haul and claimed his first Gold Award.

14 May
at Cambridge
British Universities 184
Middlesex 185 for 5 (P.N. Weekes 52)
Middlesex (2 pts) won by 5 wickets
(Gold Award: P.N. Weekes)

at Derby
Minor Counties 232 (K. Sharp 71 not out, S.D. Myles 57, C.M. Wells 4 for 36)
Derbyshire 235 for 4 (D.M. Jones 142)
Derbyshire (2 pts) won by 6 wickets
(Gold Award: D.M. Jones)

at Bristol
Gloucestershire 272 for 9 (M.W. Alleyne 75, R.J. Cunliffe 73)
Hampshire 251 (K.D. James 56)
Gloucestershire (2 pts) won by 21 runs
(Gold Award: M.W. Alleyne)

at Eglinton
Ireland 196 for 8 (N.G. Doak 84 not out)
Surrey 198 for 5 (A.J. Stewart 63)
Surrey (2 pts) won by 5 wickets
(Gold Award: N.G. Doak)

at Canterbury
Kent 208 for 9 (C.L. Hooper 62, S.L. Watkin 4 for 31)
Glamorgan 210 for 2 (H. Morris 136 not out, S.P. James 60)
Glamorgan (2 pts) won by 8 wickets
(Gold Award: S.L. Watkin)

at Old Trafford
Warwickshire 312 for 6 (S.M. Pollock 59 not out, N.M.K. Smith 51)
Lancashire 316 for 9 (G.D. Lloyd 63 not out, J.E.R. Gallian 61)
Lancashire (2 pts) won by 1 wicket
(Gold Award: G.D. Lloyd)

at Leicester
Durham 287 for 5 (J.E. Morris 145, M.A. Roseberry 57)
Leicestershire 289 for 6 (J.M. Dakin 108 not out, D.L. Maddy 61)
Leicestershire (2 pts) won by 4 wickets
(Gold Award: J.M. Dakin)

at Northampton
Yorkshire 205 for 9 (M.G. Bevan 81)
Northamptonshire 206 for 3 (D.J. Capel 82, R.J. Bailey 75 not out)
Northamptonshire (2 pts) won by 7 wickets
(Gold Award: R.J. Bailey)

at Edinburgh (Grange CC)
Scotland 159 (I.L. Philip 54, B.M.W. Patterson 50, S.R. Lampitt 4 for 29)
Worcestershire 161 for 2 (G.A. Hick 67 not out, T.S. Curtis 61)
Worcestershire (2 pts) won by 8 wickets
(Gold Award: G.A. Hick)

at Taunton
Somerset 250 for 5 (M.E. Trescothick 57 not out, M.N. Lathwell 51)
Essex 253 for 2 (S.G. Law 116, N. Hussain 68 not out)
Essex (2 pts) won by 8 wickets
(Gold Award: S.G. Law)

Middlesex and Derbyshire both had victories but could not alter the fact that they had already been eliminated from the competition. Dean Jones hit 142 off 101 balls, taking 20 in one over off Saggers and, in all, hitting 21 fours and two sixes.

The match at Bristol was more meaningful, for whichever side won would qualify for the quarter-finals. Put in to bat, Gloucestershire gradually built up momentum. Wright and Dawson scored 69, but the advent of James, one of the cricketers of the season in all forms of the game, brought an end to Wright and almost immediately Dawson mis-hit to mid-wicket. Hancock ran himself out, Symonds was taken low down at extra cover and Walsh's ploy of promoting himself in search of quick runs failed when he was caught at long-off. This left Gloucestershire at 145 for 5, but Cunliffe, enjoying an outstanding run in the competition, had stood firm and was now joined by Alleyne. In 15 overs, the pair added 113. They transformed the contest. Cunliffe provided the base; Alleyne, with 75 off 53 balls, brought the necessary vigour. Hampshire set off in brisk pursuit and scored at nearly seven an over in the early stages of their innings. Laney contributed 34 to an opening stand of 47 before falling to a catch at mid-on. James now joined Morris in a partnership worth 66, but the game changed again when Davis had Morris stumped and Smith caught in his first over. The failure of Robin Smith was a severe blow to Hampshire and worse was to come. James was brilliantly run out by Dawson, and, with the score on 186, Hancock, whose medium pace is rarely used in any form of cricket, accounted for Benjamin and Stephenson in the same over.

Jonathan Dakin drives one-handed during his match-winning century for Leicestershire against Durham, 14 May. The much-travelled Ligertwood is the wicket-keeper. (Paul Sturgess/Sportsline)

Nine runs later, he had Whitaker caught, and Hampshire were doomed.

Ireland were 17 for 5 against Surrey before Doak made the highest score recorded for them in the competition. It was brave but unavailing as Surrey maintained their one hundred per cent record.

Glamorgan clinched top spot in Group C with a remarkably easy victory over Kent. Steve Watkin took 4 for 5 in 21 balls to reduce the home county to 35 for 5, and there was no effective recovery. At least Kent lasted their 50 overs, but Morris and James scored 181 for Glamorgan's first wicket. Morris reached 100 off 68 balls, and Glamorgan won in 32.4 overs to claim top spot on nett run rate.

Glamorgan's win ousted Essex who had the best nett run rate in the group following their demolition of Somerset. Law hit his third hundred in four days and his century came off 73 balls. He and Hussain added 132 in 21 overs for the second wicket, and Essex won in 41.3 overs – but to no avail. They had needed Kent to beat Glamorgan to be sure of qualification for the last eight.

Both Lancashire and Warwickshire had qualified before the final round of matches, but they conspired to produce an outstanding game at Old Trafford. Knight and Neil Smith began the match with a partnership of 97 in 13 overs for Warwickshire, whose batting was consistent throughout the order. Warwickshire were aided by dropped catches, and Pollock's 59 off 47 balls made sure that the final overs were productive. Lancashire, too, offered consistency, but, at 292 for 9, they looked beaten. Graham Lloyd thought otherwise. He punished Pollock in the penultimate over of the innings, and his 63 came off 40 balls. Victory came with four leg-byes on the fifth ball of Reeve's final over.

In the same group, Durham hit their highest score in the competition with Morris and Roseberry scoring 167 for the second wicket. Leicestershire were 128 for 4 when Maddy joined Dakin. They were not separated until the penultimate over when Boiling dismissed both Maddy and Nixon. The Dakin/Maddy partnership was worth 153, but five were needed from the last over, a target that took just four balls. The tall, left-handed Dakin, 23 years old, seems destined to play only in limited-over matches, but this was his first century in one-day games and his first Gold Award.

The lack of composure in Yorkshire's innings at Northampton was evidenced by four run outs. They also lost Moxon with a damaged thumb although he did return to hit the last ball of the innings for four and finish with 11 not out. Northamptonshire had no trouble in reaching their target. Capel and Bailey scored 148 after Montgomerie had fallen to White at 33. Bailey took his third Gold Award in four matches.

Patterson and Philip scored 96 for Scotland's first wicket against Worcestershire, but the visitors won with 15.4 overs to spare. For both sides, there was only 1997 to dream about.

Final Group Placings

Group A	P	W	L	NR	Pts	NRR
Lancashire	5	5	–	–	10	11.57
Warwickshire	5	3	1	1	7	39.57
Leicestershire	5	3	2	–	6	-3.92
Derbyshire	5	2	3	–	4	-4.78
Durham	5	1	3	1	3	-6.83
Minor Counties	5	–	5	–	0	-26.53

Group B	P	W	L	NR	Pts	NRR
Northamptonshire	4	4	–	–	8	11.05
Yorkshire	4	3	1	–	6	15.25
Nottinghamshire	4	2	2	–	4	4.55
Worcestershire	4	1	3	–	2	2.28
Scotland	4	–	4	–	0	-36.25

Group C	P	W	L	NR	Pts	NRR
Glamorgan	5	4	1	–	8	8.73
Kent	5	4	1	–	8	4.07
Essex	5	3	2	–	6	11.24
Somerset	5	3	2	–	6	4.76
Middlesex	5	1	4	–	2	-11.46
British Universities	5	–	5	–	0	-17.94

Group D	P	W	L	NR	Pts	NRR
Surrey	4	4	–	–	8	18.97
Gloucestershire	4	3	1	–	6	17.85
Hampshire	4	2	2	–	4	12.38
Sussex	4	1	3	–	2	-1.28
Ireland	4	–	4	–	0	-49.52

Two sides in each group qualify for the quarter-finals with the top side having home advantage. Nett run rate is calculated by subtracting runs conceded per 100 balls from runs scored per 100 balls.

Quarter-Finals

28 May
at The Oval
Surrey 229
Yorkshire 230 for 1 (D. Byas 116 not out, M.G. Bevan 65 not out)
Yorkshire won by 9 wickets
(Gold Award: D. Byas)

at Cardiff
Warwickshire 239 (D.P. Ostler 85)
Glamorgan 227 (M.P. Maynard 75, O.D. Gibson 68)
Warwickshire won by 12 runs
(Gold Award: D.P. Ostler)

28 and 29 May
at Old Trafford
Gloucestershire 158 (S. Elworthy 4 for 14)
Lancashire 162 for 5 (N.H. Fairbrother 80 not out)
Lancashire won by 5 wickets
(Gold Award: N.H. Fairbrother)

at Northampton
Northamptonshire 293 for 7 (R.J. Bailey 105 not out, D.J. Capel 63)
Kent 270 (T.R. Ward 98, J.E. Emburey 4 for 24)
Northamptonshire won by 23 runs
(Gold Award: J.E. Emburey)

Having carried all before them in the zonal matches, Surrey were completely crushed by Yorkshire in the quarter-final match at The Oval. Put in to bat, Surrey began briskly enough, but both Ward and Brown offered straightforward catches, and in between their dismissals Stewart tried to cut a ball from Silverwood that was too close to him and was bowled off an inside edge. Stamp, bowling in the fashionable sunglasses, trapped Hollioake leg before with his second ball, and Surrey were disappearing quickly at 115 for 4. Thorpe and Darren Bicknell added 33, but three wickets then tumbled for 18 runs, two of them to the impressive Silverwood. Lewis and Martin Bicknell offered aggressive defiance, but no Surrey batsman played the innings of significance that was so desperately needed against a keen and well organised Yorkshire eleven. The contest became totally one-sided when the visitors raced to 94 in the 15th over before losing Vaughan to a good catch by Lewis in the gully. It was one of Surrey's better pieces of fielding, for Byas was badly dropped by Darren Bicknell when he was on 15, and the Yorkshire captain made Surrey pay for the lapse. He reached his first Benson and Hedges century off 85 balls with 16 fours and he and Bevan, a wonderfully disciplined batsman ever looking for runs, hit 136 in 22 overs to bring Yorkshire victory with 12.5 overs to spare.

Dominic Ostler of Warwickshire, Gold Award winner in the quarter-final.
(Paul-Sturgess/Sportsline)

Glamorgan's hopes were shattered by Warwickshire's unflinchable resolution at Cardiff where the pitch was less than easy. Watkin dismissed Neil Smith and Knight within five overs. The Warwickshire response was characteristically resourceful. Brown was promoted and swung the bat lustily as did Ostler whose 85 off 100 balls was the crucial innings. Butcher dismissed Brown and Penney to leave Warwickshire at 81 for 4, yet again the resource of Reeve and others conjured runs where none seemed to exist, and Warwickshire reached 239, a commendable score on this wicket. At 80 for 5, Glamorgan looked to be subsiding to a quick defeat, but Maynard and Gibson combined to add a record 136 in 22 overs for the sixth wicket. When they were separated Glamorgan were just 24 short of their target with five overs remaining. Small and Brown took charge, and the last five wickets went down in 23 balls for 11 runs.

Surrey's hopes plunge as Stewart is bowled by Silverwood in the quarter-final. (Mark Thompson/Allsport)

There was high drama at Old Trafford spread over two days. Wright and Trainor took Gloucestershire to 52 before seven wickets fell for 30 runs. The main architect of the destruction was Steven Elworthy, the South African whose profile at Lancashire had been decidedly low-key. He took 4 for 14 in his 10 overs and had seemingly won the match. Gloucestershire did not lie down so easily, and Ball and Walsh added 39 for the last wicket. Facing a target of 159, Lancashire lost Atherton, Watkinson and Austin in the six overs possible before bad light ended play. Resuming at 12 for 3, the hosts found it very difficult to score runs, and they lost Speak at 32. Gradually, the fears evaporated. Fairbrother was soon smiting the ball well, and he and Crawley added 110 in 22 overs. Crawley countered Walsh intelligently before falling to Ball, but Fairbrother scored 80 off as many balls, and Lancashire won with 10.2 overs to spare.

Asked to bat first, Northamptonshire lost Fordham for 0, but Capel played a withering innings, making 63 out of 76 off 45 balls. Capel's knock sent shock waves through the Kent attack and had bowlers in hasty retreat. Bailey, his golden streak of form continuing, maintained the assault with an unbeaten 105 from 129 balls. Loye helped him to score 87 for the fourth wicket, but, apart from a hiccup when Curran and Warren were out in quick succession, Northamptonshire scored consistently and set Kent a daunting target. Fleming batted with his customary flourish and scored 40 of the 56 made for the first wicket. By the end of 15 overs, Kent had reached 85, but it had cost them four wickets, most notably that of Carl Hooper, upon whom so much had depended. Play was abandoned for the day with Kent at 106 for 4 in 20.5 overs and Northamptonshire well on top. Ward was unbeaten on 31, having opened with Fleming, and the next morning he and Ealham extended their fifth wicket partnership to 77. Ward and Ealker then added 80 and suddenly Kent had a sniff of victory. At last, Bailey summoned Emburey to bowl. It was the 41st over. With his first ball, the veteran off-spinner trapped Ward leg before as he swept; with his fifth delivery he had Walker caught by the diving Ambrose at backward point. McCague was next to go, caught on the mid-wicket boundary, and Capel took a fine running catch to dismiss Marsh. Ambrose had Thompson caught behind, and Northamptonshire were in the semi-final.

David Byas, the Yorkshire captain, hit a century of high quality in the quarter-final against Surrey at the Oval. (Nigel French/ASP)

Australian left-hander Michael Bevan was an immense influence on Yorkshire's success in the Benson and Hedges Cup. He played an outstanding innings of 96 not out in the semi-final against Lancashire, sharing a record stand with Richard Blakey. (Graham Chadwick/Allsport)

Semi-Finals

11 and 12 June
at Old Trafford
Yorkshire 250 for 5 (M.G. Bevan 95 not out, R.J. Blakey 80 not out)
Lancashire 251 for 9 (W.K. Hegg 81, N.H. Fairbrother 59)
Lancashire won by 1 wicket
(Gold Award: W.K. Hegg)

at Northampton
Northamptonshire 220 for 7 (T.C. Walton 70 not out)
Warwickshire 193
Northamptonshire won by 27 runs
(Gold Award: T.C. Walton)

Peter Martin completes the second run which takes Lancashire into the final. Martin had to hit the last ball of the match against Yorkshire for two. (Graham Chadwick/Allsport)

There are occasions when limited-over cricket produces such excitement and drama as to leave the onlooker in a state of mental exhaustion when the final ball is bowled. The Benson and Hedges Cup semi-final between Lancashire and Yorkshire left spectators drained of emotion.

Play could not start at Old Trafford until 4.30 pm, and Yorkshire were unfortunate to lose the toss and to be asked to bat first. The pitch had sweated under the covers throughout a damp day, and Lancashire, reliant entirely upon seam, exploited the conditions well. Yorkshire reached 66 for the loss of Byas and then they lost four more wickets as 17 runs were scored. Red Rose seemed in sight of an early win. Bevan and Blakey, who was dropped on seven, set about repairing the innings. Bevan, a wonderful asset to Yorkshire, raced to 50 in 54 balls. There was a stoppage for bad light and play resumed at seven with both batsmen showing urgency as the overs remaining dwindled. Bevan ended the day on 73, and Blakey reached his 50 in the last over possible, which was the 46th. Yorkshire, 198 for 5, seemed to have little hope of securing a winning score. In the four overs available to them on the Wednesday morning, Bevan and Blakey destroyed that idea. They added an astonishing 52 runs in those overs to extend their partnership to 167, a sixth wicket record for the Benson and Hedges Cup. Bevan's 95 came from 75 balls, and Blakey, an admirable support, hit 80 off 94 balls.

A crowd of 10,000 had gathered for the second day, and just as they had thrilled to the batting of Bevan and Blakey, so now they wondered at the accuracy and variety of the Yorkshire bowling and the dynamism of the fielding. Atherton went to a good slip catch by Byas in Gough's first over, and Watkinson became the first of four Lancashire batsmen to be run out when Bevan hit the stumps from gully. Elworthy was caught at square-leg, and after 15 overs Lancashire were 48 for 3. Speak was run out and Lloyd caught behind off Silverwood to maintain Yorkshire's pressure, for Lancashire were 154 short of their target and the run rate was seven an over. There now came the first substantial partnership of the innings as Fairbrother and Hegg added 64. The stand was ended when White hit the stumps with his left-foot drive with Fairbrother short of his ground.

Lancashire were still 90 short of victory with only 10 overs of their innings remaining. Austin went cheaply, but when Stemp returned for the last of his 10 overs he was hit for straight sixes by both Yates and Hegg, and the over cost 18. White was similarly treated when Hegg hit him for sixes over long-off and cover. This violence had helped bring down Lancashire's requirement to 11 runs from 13 balls when Hegg was bowled by White. The wicket-keeper had done magnificently, his 81 off 62 balls bringing an improbable victory in sight. The penultimate over, bowled by Gough, brought three runs and saw Yates run out by McGrath's throw from third man. Eight runs were needed from White's last over with the last pair together. Chapple drove to the cover boundary, White bowled a wide and there was a single backward of square. Martin had three balls from which to score two runs. He swatted vainly at the first two, but got some bat on the third and the batsmen ran two as Vaughan covered 30 yards in a desperate attempt to prevent them doing so. Lancashire were victors off the last ball. Cricket was the winner.

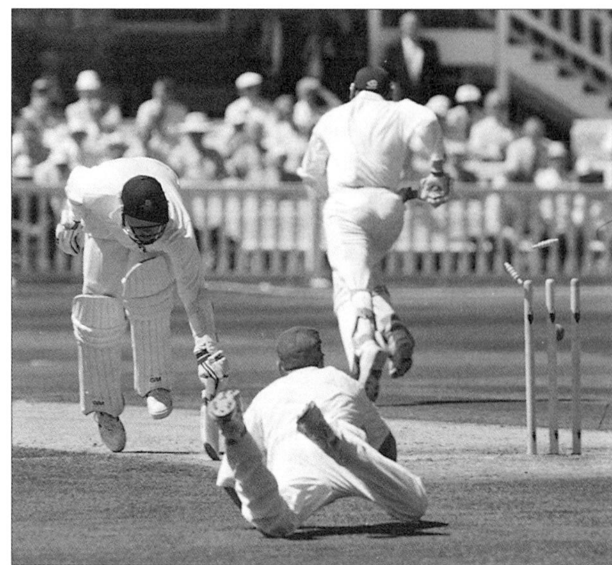

Jason Gallian is run out in the final following good fielding by Penberthy. (Adrian Murrell/Allsport)

There was not quite so much excitement at Northampton, where five interruptions for bad weather on the Tuesday took the game into a second day. Asked to bat first in overcast conditions, Northamptonshire were reduced to 88 for 6, and the contest seemed over. The front-line batsmen, of whom Montgomerie had made 49, were all gone. What hopes remained rested in Tim Walton and Tony Penberthy, and they responded to the challenge in a most positive manner. They established a county record by adding 108 for the seventh wicket before Penberthy was caught at deep mid-wicket. Walton took 12 off the first three balls of the final over and finished with a most gallant Benson and Hedges best of 70 off 73 balls. Most importantly, he had helped his side to a creditable 220 which still looked inadequate when Warwickshire finished the day on 91 for 3 from 23.2 overs.

Paul Smith and Dominic Ostler confirmed Warwickshire's superiority in the early overs of the second day, and Bailey was desperately in search of a wicket when he recalled Ambrose. The West Indian immediately yorked Ostler to leave Warwickshire 118 for 4 in the 28th over, still a comfortable position. At 147, Walton brilliantly ran out Penney with a direct hit on the stumps from deep mid-wicket, and two overs later he hit the stumps again, this time from backward point, to run out Paul Smith. This changed the complexion of the game totally. Of the last four wickets to fall, two were run out as batsmen were frustrated by the accuracy of Emburey and the pace of Ambrose. Reeve was left unbeaten among the wreckage, and Northamptonshire were in the final.

Benson and Hedges Cup Final

Lancashire *v.* Northamptonshire

The sun shone for the anniversary final, but the cricket did not quite match the weather or the occasion. It was, however, fitting that the holders should retain the cup and establish a record by winning the trophy for the fourth time.

Lancashire chose to bat first on a pitch which promised many runs. They were strengthened by the return of Crawley and Gallian, which was particularly hard on Speak who had performed well in the earlier rounds, and on Elworthy, the South African all-rounder, who had also done well and who was much hurt by his omission. Watkinson chose to open with Atherton, but he did not last long. He was out in the sixth over when he pulled Taylor to long-leg. Gallian went eight overs later, the victim of good fielding by Penberthy and the judgement of the third umpire, close but correct.

Northamptonshire had given grace to the game by taking the field, all bar Curran, wearing county caps and hats, but some of their early bowling, particularly by Taylor and Curran, was wayward. They suffered a grievous blow when Ambrose limped off after bowling five overs. He had a hamstring injury, and although he returned to complete his quota and batted with a runner, he was a weakened force.

Crawley batted with engaging elegance for 47 minutes and hit 34 off 40 balls. His injection of life was necessary, for Lancashire reached the 15-over mark with only 59 runs on the board for the loss of two wickets. Crawley's brief interlude ended in the 26th over when he leg-glanced Penberthy to the wicket-keeper with the score at 105. Atherton remained, and he had seemingly done all the hard ground work when he clouted Emburey to mid-wicket. This was in the 31st over, and Atherton had faced 93 balls. His dismissal was symptomatic of the match itself. Every time a batsman or a partnership looked like prospering a wicket fell, and we had to begin again.

Inevitably, it was Neil Fairbrother who brought real purpose to the Lancashire innings. He drove, pulled, pushed and ran, and gave further evidence that he was really made for the one-day game as he hit 63 off 70 balls. He is an infectious cricketer and a delight to watch. Lloyd helped him to add 49 in nine overs, and Hegg and Austin made sure that the momentum did not flag. Fairbrother and Yates fell to successive balls in the 49th over, and, more than anything, Lancashire's 245 was the product of overall team effort rather than of any individual brilliance. It should not have been a big enough score to win them the game.

The beginning of Northamptonshire's decline: Alan Fordham is bowled by Ian Auston for four. (Clive Mason/Allsport)

The score grew to immense proportions after 6.4 overs of the Northamptonshire innings. Capel edged Austin to Hegg in the third over, and, in the seventh, the same bowler found a way past Fordham's defence. Bailey and Montgomerie seemed unperturbed by the apparent seriousness of the situation and batted with charm and correctness. At 97 for 2 in the 27th over, the game was within Northamptonshire's grasp, but Bailey had begun to fret unnecessarily and he cut at Chapple and was caught behind. Three overs later, Montgomerie tickled Yates down the leg side, and Hegg, who did not have one of his best days, took the catch.

Curran was unable to accept the responsibility thrust upon him, unable to decide between attack and defence. Warren was positive. He swung Watkinson high to mid-wicket where Crawley ran to take the catch before tumbling

Neil Fairbrother's exciting innings comes to an end when he is bowled by Capel. (Adrian Murrell/Allsport)

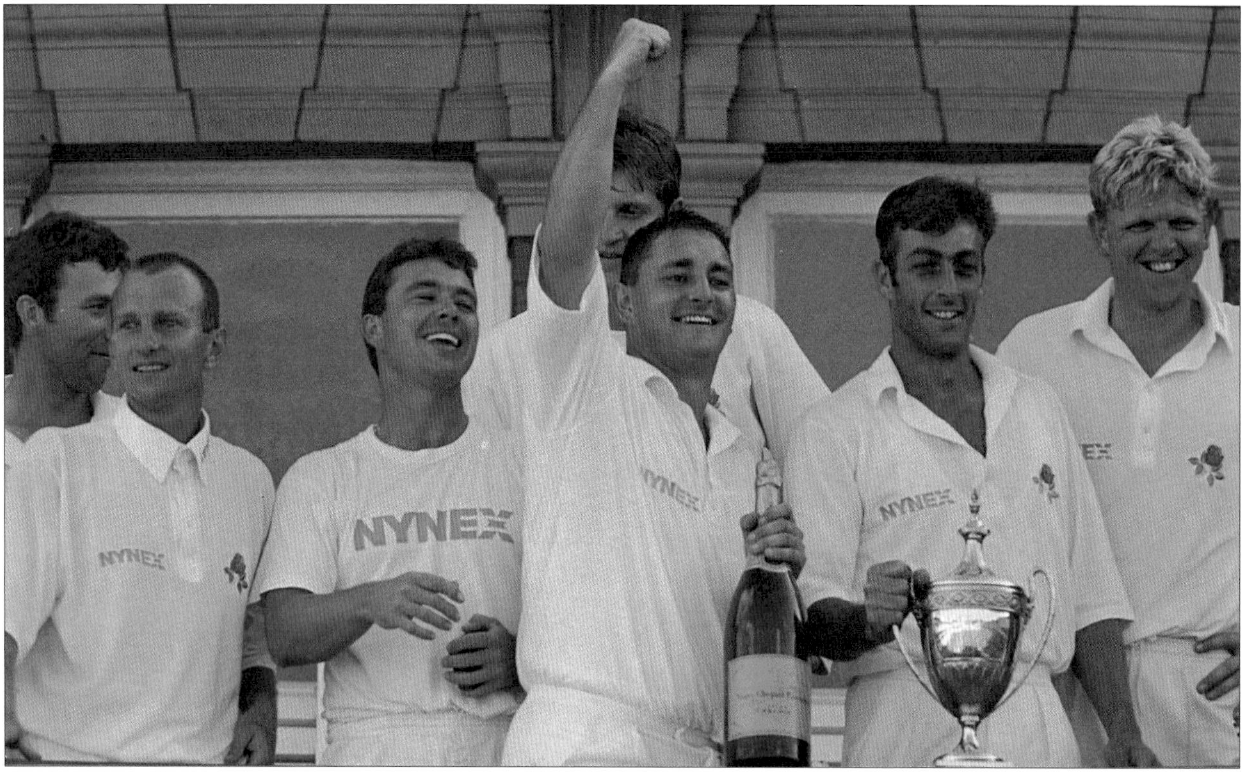

Above: Having fallen over the boundary to give Warren six for a shot off Watkinson, Crawley falls forward when the batsman attempts to repeat the shot to take a splendid catch. (Paul Sturgess/Sportsline)

Top: Lancashire retain the Benson and Hedges Cup. Skipper Mike Watkinson holds the cup. Gold Award winner Ian Austin is content with champagne. (Adrian Murrell/Allsport)

Richard Montgomerie raises Northamptonshire's hopes as he sweeps during his innings of 42. (Clive Mason/Allsport)

over the rope to concede six. Warren repeated the stroke, and this time Crawley fell forward and claimed the catch. Walton, who might well have been better used at number five, scored 28 off 26 balls before being stumped. Curran was out in the following over and the cause was lost.

Ian Austin returned to stifle any remaining ambitions and to take two more wickets. He bowled straight with some late movement off the seam and deceptive pace. He was well worthy of the Gold Award.

The presentation ceremony was marred by annoying interviews for the sake of Sky Television and by the raucous behaviour of some Lancashire supporters. Such an important game of cricket and such a delightful occasion deserves better.

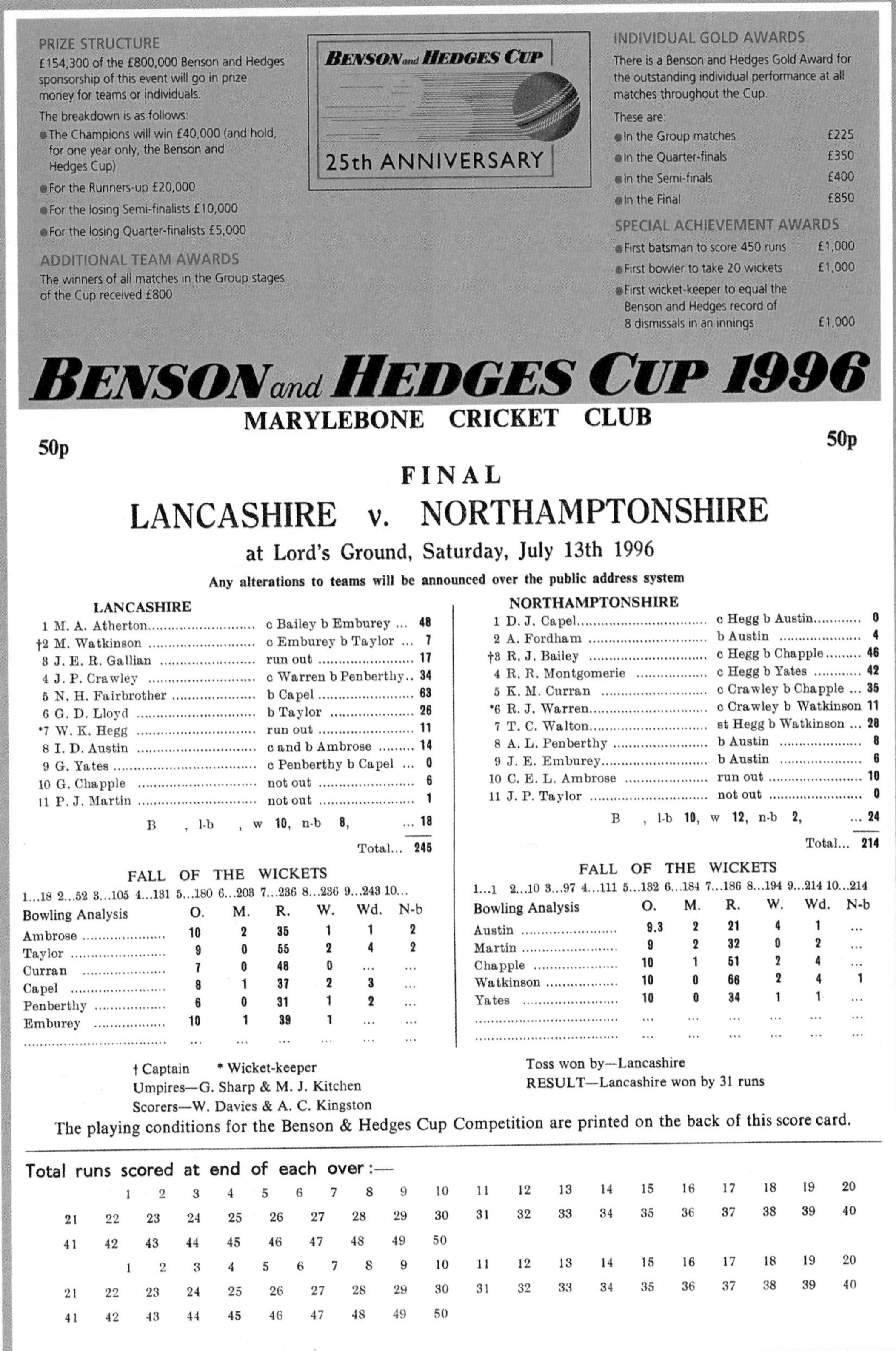

PRIZE STRUCTURE

£154,300 of the £800,000 Benson and Hedges sponsorship of this event will go in prize money for teams or individuals.

The breakdown is as follows:

- The Champions will win £40,000 (and hold, for one year only, the Benson and Hedges Cup)
- For the Runners-up £20,000
- For the losing Semi-finalists £10,000
- For the losing Quarter-finalists £5,000

ADDITIONAL TEAM AWARDS

The winners of all matches in the Group stages of the Cup received £800.

BENSON and HEDGES CUP

25th ANNIVERSARY

INDIVIDUAL GOLD AWARDS

There is a Benson and Hedges Gold Award for the outstanding individual performance at all matches throughout the Cup.

These are:

- In the Group matches £225
- In the Quarter-finals £350
- In the Semi-finals £400
- In the Final £850

SPECIAL ACHIEVEMENT AWARDS

- First batsman to score 450 runs £1,000
- First bowler to take 20 wickets £1,000
- First wicket-keeper to equal the Benson and Hedges record of 8 dismissals in an innings £1,000

BENSON and HEDGES CUP 1996

MARYLEBONE CRICKET CLUB

50p 50p

FINAL

LANCASHIRE v. NORTHAMPTONSHIRE

at Lord's Ground, Saturday, July 13th 1996

Any alterations to teams will be announced over the public address system

LANCASHIRE

1	M. A. Atherton	c Bailey b Emburey	48
†2	M. Watkinson	c Emburey b Taylor	7
3	J. E. R. Gallian	run out	17
4	J. P. Crawley	c Warren b Penberthy	34
5	N. H. Fairbrother	b Capel	63
6	G. D. Lloyd	b Taylor	26
*7	W. K. Hegg	run out	11
8	I. D. Austin	c and b Ambrose	14
9	G. Yates	c Penberthy b Capel	0
10	G. Chapple	not out	6
11	P. J. Martin	not out	1
	B , l-b , w 10, n-b 8,		18
		Total...	245

FALL OF THE WICKETS

1...18 2...52 3...105 4...131 5...180 6...203 7...236 8...236 9...243 10...

Bowling Analysis	O.	M.	R.	W.	Wd.	N-b
Ambrose	10	2	35	1	1	2
Taylor	9	0	55	2	4	2
Curran	7	0	48	0	...	...
Capel	8	1	37	2	3	...
Penberthy	6	0	31	1	2	...
Emburey	10	1	39	1	...	...
...	...	...	...	...	...	...

NORTHAMPTONSHIRE

1	D. J. Capel	c Hegg b Austin	0
2	A. Fordham	b Austin	4
†3	R. J. Bailey	c Hegg b Chapple	46
4	R. R. Montgomerie	c Hegg b Yates	42
5	K. M. Curran	c Crawley b Chapple	35
*6	R. J. Warren	c Crawley b Watkinson	11
7	T. C. Walton	st Hegg b Watkinson	28
8	A. L. Penberthy	b Austin	8
9	J. E. Emburey	b Austin	6
10	C. E. L. Ambrose	run out	10
11	J. P. Taylor	not out	0
	B , l-b 10, w 12, n-b 2,		24
		Total...	214

FALL OF THE WICKETS

1...1 2...10 3...97 4...111 5...132 6...184 7...186 8...194 9...214 10...214

Bowling Analysis	O.	M.	R.	W.	Wd.	N-b
Austin	9.3	2	21	4	1	...
Martin	9	2	32	0	2	...
Chapple	10	1	51	2	4	...
Watkinson	10	0	66	2	4	1
Yates	10	0	34	1	1	...
...	...	...	...	...	...	...
...	...	...	...	...	...	...

† Captain * Wicket-keeper

Umpires—G. Sharp & M. J. Kitchen

Scorers—W. Davies & A. C. Kingston

Toss won by—Lancashire

RESULT—Lancashire won by 31 runs

The playing conditions for the Benson & Hedges Cup Competition are printed on the back of this score card.

Total runs scored at end of each over:—

1 2 3 4 5 6 7 8 9 10 11 12 13 14 15 16 17 18 19 20
21 22 23 24 25 26 27 28 29 30 31 32 33 34 35 36 37 38 39 40
41 42 43 44 45 46 47 48 49 50
1 2 3 4 5 6 7 8 9 10 11 12 13 14 15 16 17 18 19 20
21 22 23 24 25 26 27 28 29 30 31 32 33 34 35 36 37 38 39 40
41 42 43 44 45 46 47 48 49 50

Reproduced by kind permission of MCC.

Benson and Hedges Cup Averages

British Universities

Batting	M	Inns	NO	Runs	HS	Av	100s	50s	ct/st
A. Singh	5	5	–	260	123	52.00	1	1	1
G.A. Khan	5	5	–	232	147	46.40	1		1
C.M. Gupte	3	3	1	76	54*	38.00		1	
A.C. Ridley	4	4	–	152	58	38.00		1	2
U.B.A. Rashid	4	4	1	81	29	27.00			1
R.Q. Cake	5	5	–	111	28	22.20			2
M.R. Evans	4	4	2	34	16*	17.00			2
M.A. Wagh	2	2	–	29	23	14.50			
R.S.C. Martin-Jenkins	3	3	–	16	12	5.33			
S.A.J. Boswell	5	5	1	21	14	5.25			1
K. Marc	4	4	–	19	13	4.75			1
M.E. Harvey	2	2	–	6	5	3.00			1
J. Bahl	5	4	2	1	1*	0.50			2
A.R. Whittall	2	2	–	0	0	0.00			

Played in one match: S.W.K. Ellis 4; W.J. House 22 (ct 1)

Bowling	Overs	Mds	Runs	Wks	Av	Best	4/inn
R.S.C. Martin–Jenkins	27.4	–	136	4	34.00	3/46	
A.R. Whittall	17.4	1	112	3	37.33	2/52	
M.A. Wagh	20	2	80	2	40.00	1/39	
M.R. Evans	35	1	245	6	40.83	3/64	
U.B.A. Rashid	34.3	3	146	3	48.66	2/57	
S.W.K. Ellis	9	–	50	1	50.00	1/50	
K. Marc	34	–	214	4	53.50	2/30	
S.A.J. Boswell	49.5	2	302	2	151.00	1/61	
A.C. Ridley	7	–	49	–	–		

Derbyshire

Batting	M	Inns	NO	Runs	HS	Av	100s	50s	ct/st
C.J. Adams	5	4	1	202	100*	67.33	1	1	1
D.M. Jones	5	5	–	302	142	60.40	1	2	4
J.E. Owen	2	2	–	70	49	35.00			
A.S. Rollins	2	2	–	61	42	30.50			
C.M. Wells	5	4	1	62	56	20.66		1	
K.J. Barnett	5	5	–	97	48	19.40			1
P.A.J. DeFreitas	5	4	–	68	23	17.00			
D.G. Cork	4	4	1	44	16	14.66			2
D.E. Malcolm	5	3	2	14	12	14.00			2
K.M. Krikken	5	4	1	35	27	11.66			3/1
M.J. Vandrau	3	3	1	23	12*	11.50			1
F.A. Griffith	4	3	–	33	24	11.00			

Played in two matches: T.A. Tweats 10; P. Aldred 7
Played in one match: A.J. Harris did not bat (ct 1)

Bowling	Overs	Mds	Runs	Wks	Av	Best	4/inn
C.M. Wells	20	2	93	6	15.50	4/36	1
D.G. Cork	33	8	123	6	20.50	5/49	1
K.J. Barnett	5	–	23	1	23.00	1/1	
P. Aldred	9	–	53	2	26.50	2/35	
P.A.J. DeFreitas	30	3	135	5	27.00	2/20	
A.J. Harris	7	–	34	1	34.00	1/34	
F.A. Griffith	21	–	144	4	36.00	3/63	
D.E. Malcolm	41	1	233	5	46.60	3/36	
M.J. Vandrau	20	1	112	2	56.00	1/53	
D.M. Jones	2	–	18	–	–		

Durham

Batting	M	Inns	NO	Runs	HS	Av	100s	50s	ct/st
J.E. Morris	5	5	–	235	145	47.00	1		3
J.I. Longley	4	4	1	119	38*	39.66			
P. Bainbridge	2	2	1	39	39	39.00			
C.W. Scott	4	2	1	36	27*	36.00			3
M.J. Foster	5	5	2	105	52	35.00		1	
M.A. Roseberry	5	5	1	130	57	32.50		2	2
J. Boiling	4	2	1	22	15	22.00			1
P.D. Collingwood	5	4	1	42	17	14.00			1
J.A. Daley	4	4	–	55	33	13.75			
S.L. Campbell	2	2	–	27	27	13.50			1
P.D. Birbeck	2	2	–	9	5	4.50			
N. Killeen	4	2	–	4	4	2.00			1
S.J.E. Brown	5	2	1	2	2*	2.00			1

Played in two matches: M.M. Betts did not bat (ct 1)
Played in one match: S. Hutton 36; D.G.C. Ligertwood did not bat (ct 1 / st 1)
One catch was taken by a substitute

Durham (cont.)

Bowling	Overs	Mds	Runs	Wks	Av	Best	4/inn
P. Bainbridge	2	–	15	1	15.00	1/15	
M.M. Betts	9	2	36	2	18.00	2/36	
J. Boiling	29	–	100	5	20.00	2/22	
P.D. Collingwood	30.1	1	160	5	32.00	3/28	
S.J.E. Brown	40	6	147	4	36.75	2/28	
M.J. Foster	39.2	1	183	4	45.75	2/52	
N. Killeen	28.4	3	153	2	76.50	1/46	
J.A. Daley	2	–	19	–	–		
S.D. Birbeck	15	–	86	–	–		

Essex

Batting	M	Inns	NO	Runs	HS	Av	100s	50s	ct/st
N. Hussain	5	5	2	238	82	79.33		3	3
S.G. Law	5	5	–	225	116	45.00	1		
R.C. Irani	5	4	1	134	62*	44.66		1	1
G.A. Gooch	5	5	1	172	100	43.00	1		5
P.J. Prichard	5	4	–	119	82	29.75		1	1
D.D.J. Robinson	5	5	1	93	36	23.25			1
A.P. Grayson	5	4	2	35	12*	17.50			2
R.J. Rollins	5	2	1	3	3	3.00			4

Played in five matches: M.C. Ilott 12 (ct 2); P.M. Such 10*
Played in two matches: D.M. Cousins 10; A.P. Cowan did not bat
Played in one match: N.F. Williams

Bowling	Overs	Mds	Runs	Wks	Av	Best	4/inn
M.C. Ilott	46	8	151	9	16.77	4/17	1
R.C. Irani	40	3	156	9	17.33	4/30	1
A.P. Grayson	40	4	156	5	31.20	3/30	
N.F. Williams	10	–	67	2	33.50	2/67	
P.M. Such	46	5	141	4	35.25	2/32	
D.M. Cousins	14.4	4	41	1	41.00	1/33	
S.G. Law	31.4	1	183	4	45.75	2/57	
A.P. Cowan	19	2	66	1	66.00	1/38	

Glamorgan

Batting	M	Inns	NO	Runs	HS	Av	100s	50s	ct/st
M.P. Maynard	6	6	3	396	151*	132.00	2	1	3
H. Morris	6	6	1	285	136*	57.00	1		2
S.P. James	6	6	1	208	121*	41.60	1	1	4
A. Dale	5	5	1	130	46	32.50			2
P.A. Cottey	6	4	1	55	29	18.33			3
S.D. Thomas	6	3	1	27	27*	13.50			4
G.P. Butcher	2	2	1	12	9	12.00			
R.D.B. Croft	6	4	1	24	12	8.00			

Played in six matches: C.P. Metson 4 (ct 10 / st 1); S.L. Watkin 2* (ct 1); S.R. Barwick 0 (ct 1)
Played in three matches: O.D. Gibson 68
Played in two matches: D.L. Hemp 33

Bowling	Overs	Mds	Runs	Wks	Av	Best	4/inn
A. Dale	30	3	130	7	18.57	5/41	1
R.D.B. Croft	57.1	4	240	12	20.00	4/30	1
S.L. Watkin	58	12	246	12	20.50	4/31	1
G.P. Butcher	12	–	48	2	24.00	2/21	
S.D. Thomas	46	1	244	7	34.85	4/41	1
P.A. Cottey	10	–	49	1	49.00	1/49	
S.R. Barwick	57.3	3	276	5	55.20	2/49	
O.D. Gibson	25	3	126	1	126.00	1/33	

Gloucestershire

Batting	M	Inns	NO	Runs	HS	Av	100s	50s	ct/st
R.J. Cunliffe	5	5	2	353	137*	117.66	2	1	1
M.W. Alleyne	5	4	2	111	75	55.50		1	3
A.J. Wright	5	5	–	258	123	51.60	1	1	2
T.H.C. Hancock	5	5	2	150	71*	50.00		1	
C.A. Walsh	2	2	1	27	21*	27.00			1
A. Symonds	5	5	–	111	67	22.20		1	
R.I. Dawson	4	4	–	73	33	18.25			
R.C. Russell	5	2	–	32	24	16.00			3/2
M.C.J. Ball	2	2	–	25	25	12.50			2
A.M. Smith	5	2	1	7	7	7.00			3
R.P. Davis	5	2	–	12	10	6.00			2

Played in four matches: K.E. Cooper did not bat
Played in one match: N.J. Trainor 25; M.J. Cawdron and J. Lewis did not bat

Benson and Hedges Cup Averages (continued)

Gloucestershire (cont.)

Bowling	Overs	Mds	Runs	Wks	Av	Best	4/inn
J. Lewis	10	1	31	3	10.33	3/31	
T.H.C. Hancock	13	1	51	4	12.75	3/13	
M.J. Cawdron	6	–	48	2	24.00	2/48	
A.M. Smith	47.1	7	213	8	26.62	3/23	
R.P. Davis	41.1	1	193	7	27.57	2/25	
C.A. Walsh	18.4	2	74	2	37.00	1/33	
M.W. Alleyne	36	–	168	4	42.00	2/47	
K.E. Cooper	37	2	183	4	45.75	2/48	
M.C.J. Ball	16	1	71	1	71.00	1/17	
A. Symonds	4	–	23	–	–		

Hampshire

Batting	M	Inns	NO	Runs	HS	Av	100s	50s	ct/st
J.P. Stephenson	4	4	1	185	124*	61.66	1		1
R.A. Smith	4	4	–	165	123	41.25	1		2
W.K.M. Benjamin	4	4	1	119	58*	39.66		1	3
J.S. Laney	4	4	–	109	41	27.25			
A.N. Aymes	4	3	–	73	38	24.33			5
R.S.M. Morris	3	3	–	71	39	23.66			3
S.D. Udal	2	2	–	42	32	21.00			
M.J. Thursfield	3	2	1	20	19	20.00			1
P.R. Whitaker	4	4	–	74	53	18.50		1	
G.W. White	3	3	–	32	30	10.66			
C.A. Connor	4	3	2	5	4*	5.00			

Played in two matches: S.M. Milburn 2 (ct 1)
Played in one match: M. Keech 0 (ct 3); K.D. James 56 (ct 1); R.J. Maru 6*

Bowling	Overs	Mds	Runs	Wks	Av	Best	4/inn
J.P. Stephenson	17.1	2	71	5	14.20	3/33	
W.K.M. Benjamin	34	6	165	8	20.62	3/26	
R.J. Maru	10	–	43	2	21.50	2/43	
P.R. Whitaker	27	1	92	4	23.00	2/33	
K.D. James	4	–	24	1	24.00	1/24	
S.M. Milburn	14.1	6	61	2	30.50	2/7	
M.J. Thursfield	28	2	123	4	30.75	2/33	
C.A. Connor	30	–	171	4	42.75	2/22	
S.D. Udal	20	–	101	–	–		

Ireland

Batting	M	Inns	NO	Runs	HS	Av	100s	50s	ct/st
N.G. Doak	2	2	1	85	84*	85.00		1	1
A.T. Rutherford	4	4	2	60	26	30.00			3
D.A. Lewis	4	4	–	81	61	21.00			1
S.G. Smyth	2	2	–	36	32	18.00			
A.R. Dunlop	3	3	–	51	50	17.00		1	
J.D.R. Benson	4	4	–	64	35	16.00			3
U. Graham	2	2	–	31	18	15.50			
M.W. Patterson	4	2	1	11	8*	11.00			
R.L. Eagleson	3	3	–	31	13	10.33			1
G.D. Harrison	4	4	–	26	12	6.50			
P. McCrum	4	3	1	11	9	5.50			2
D.A. Moore	2	2	–	10	10	5.00			
S.J.S. Warke	3	3	–	7	4	2.33			

Played in one match: M.P. Rea 0; P.G. Gillespie 0; D. Heasley 36

Bowling	Overs	Mds	Runs	Wks	Av	Best	4/inn
D. Heasley	7	–	32	1	32.00	1/32	
G.D. Harrison	30	–	135	4	33.75	2/30	
M.W. Patterson	30	2	208	5	41.60	2/55	
P. McCrum	30	4	134	2	67.00	2/10	
J.D.R. Benson	15	–	88	1	88.00	1/41	
R.L. Eagleson	15.5	–	159	1	159.00	1/51	
D.A. Moore	2	–	11	–	–		
P.G. Gillespie	5	–	17	–	–		
N.G. Doak	6	1	33	–	–		
D.A. Lewis	6	–	58	–	–		
U. Graham	11	–	65	–	–		

Kent

Batting	M	Inns	NO	Runs	HS	Av	100s	50s	ct/st
T.R. Ward	6	6	–	300	98	50.00		3	1
C.L. Hooper	6	6	–	277	98	46.16		3	1
M.A. Ealham	6	6	1	211	75	42.20		2	
M.V. Fleming	6	6	–	203	72	33.83		1	2

Kent (cont.)

Batting (cont.)	M	Inns	NO	Runs	HS	Av	100s	50s	ct/st
M.J. Walker	6	6	1	139	41	27.80			2
S.A. Marsh	6	5	1	81	29	20.25			10/1
J.B.D. Thompson	4	3	2	17	12*	17.00			
N.J. Llong	6	5	1	48	31	12.00			
G.R. Cowdrey	6	6	–	67	31	11.16			4
M.J. McCague	6	4	–	22	17	5.50			1

Played in six matches: M.M. Patel 6*, 6*, 18* & 8* (ct 2)
Played in two matches: T.N. Wren 0 (ct 1)

Bowling	Overs	Mds	Runs	Wks	Av	Best	4/inn
J.B.D. Thompson	30	4	114	6	19.00	3/29	
N.J. Llong	10	–	38	2	19.00	2/38	
M.A. Ealham	51	–	236	10	23.60	4/50	1
M.V. Fleming	47.4	3	234	5	46.80	2/53	
M.M. Patel	36	2	198	4	49.50	2/74	
T.N. Wren	5	–	53	1	53.00	1/21	
C.L. Hooper	43	–	197	3	65.66	2/36	
M.J. McCague	50.4	4	267	4	66.75	2/30	
G.R. Cowdrey	8	–	45	–	–		

Lancashire

Batting	M	Inns	NO	Runs	HS	Av	100s	50s	ct/st
N.H. Fairbrother	8	8	3	360	80*	72.00		4	4
N.J. Speak	4	4	1	147	79*	49.00		1	
W.K. Hegg	7	4	1	130	81	43.33		1	16/3
J.P. Crawley	6	6	–	208	48	34.66		2	
M.A. Atherton	8	8	1	221	121*	31.57	1		7
G.D. Lloyd	8	6	2	119	63*	29.75		1	1
M. Watkinson	8	6	–	120	56	20.00		1	6
G. Chapple	6	4	3	20	8	20.00			
J.E.R. Gallian	6	6	–	115	61	19.16		1	2
I.D. Austin	8	6	1	84	39	16.80			1
G. Yates	8	5	–	46	26	9.20			
S. Elworthy	5	3	–	26	13	8.66			

Played in six matches: P.J. Martin 5*, 2* & 1*

Bowling	Overs	Mds	Runs	Wks	Av	Best	4/inn
J.E.R. Gallian	14	2	61	4	15.25	3/30	
I.D. Austin	75	12	266	14	19.00	4/21	1
M. Watkinson	71.5	3	329	17	19.35	5/44	1
S. Elworthy	47	4	204	10	20.40	4/14	1
G. Yates	55	4	222	7	31.71	3/65	
G. Chapple	55	2	256	8	32.00	3/31	
P.J. Martin	55	5	273	6	45.50	3/43	

Leicestershire

Batting	M	Inns	NO	Runs	HS	Av	100s	50s	ct/st
J.M. Dakin	2	2	1	128	108*	128.00	1		
D.L. Maddy	5	5	1	163	61	40.75		1	
D.J. Millns	2	2	1	40	39*	40.00			
B.F. Smith	5	5	–	161	61	32.20		2	3
J.J. Whitaker	5	5	–	143	70	28.60		1	2
V.J. Wells	5	5	–	135	60	27.00			2
T.J. Mason	3	2	1	26	19	26.00			1
P.A. Nixon	5	5	1	67	26*	16.75			3/1
P.E. Robinson	3	3	–	45	40	15.00			
G.I. Macmillan	3	3	–	44	40	14.66			2
G.J. Parsons	5	3	–	32	19	10.66			
P.V. Simmons	2	2	–	15	11	7.50			1
A.D. Mullally	5	2	1	7	6	7.00			

Played in two matches: D. Williamson 6
Played in one match: A.R.K. Pierson 2*; C.C. Remy 1*; M.T. Brimson did not bat

Bowling	Overs	Mds	Runs	Wks	Av	Best	4/inn
D.L. Maddy	13	2	81	4	20.25	3/32	
A.D. Mullally	50	4	186	6	31.00	2/44	
G.J. Parsons	46	3	187	6	31.16	2/33	
T.J. Mason	23	–	97	3	32.33	2/35	
V.J. Wells	33	2	168	3	56.00	2/39	
M.T. Brimson	10	–	56	1	56.00	1/56	
D.J. Millns	16.2	2	71	1	71.00	1/26	
D. Williamson	14	–	91	1	91.00	1/64	
C.C. Remy	3	–	29	–	–		
A.R.K. Pierson	9	–	57	–	–		
P.V. Simmons	12	–	63	–	–		

Benson and Hedges Cup Averages (continued)

Middlesex

Batting	M	Inns	NO	Runs	HS	Av	100s	50s	ct/st
J.D. Carr	5	5	1	219	55	54.75		3	2
M.R. Ramprakash	4	4	–	143	56	35.75		2	1
O.A. Shah	3	3	1	52	46*	26.00			
A.R.C. Fraser	5	4	1	23	10*	23.00			
P.N. Weekes	5	5	–	113	52	22.60		1	1
K.R. Brown	5	5	1	82	43	20.50			2/2
M.W. Gatting	5	5	–	83	45	16.60			4
J.C. Pooley	5	5	–	77	50	15.40		1	2
R.L. Johnson	3	3	–	18	9	6.00			1
R.A. Fay	4	2	–	1	1	0.50			

Played in four matches: D. Follett 0
Played in three matches: P.C.R. Tufnell 3* (ct 1)
Played in one match: M.A. Feltham 12 (ct 2); J.C. Harrison 24; K.P. Dutch 13; P.E. Wellings 14* (ct 1)
One catch was taken by a substitute

Bowling	Overs	Mds	Runs	Wks	Av	Best	4/inn
M.R. Ramprakash	15	1	65	3	21.66	3/35	
P.C.R. Tufnell	22.5	2	90	4	22.50	2/31	
A.R.C. Fraser	43	11	149	4	37.25	2/27	
P.N. Weekes	38.2	–	205	5	41.00	2/39	
R.A. Fay	34	4	123	3	41.00	1/13	
P.E. Wellings	5.5	–	45	1	45.00	1/45	
M.A. Feltham	10	–	63	1	63.00	1/63	
D. Follett	29	3	133	2	66.50	1/11	
R.L. Johnson	27	2	164	1	164.00	1/66	
J.D. Carr	9	1	31	–	–		
K.P. Dutch	5	–	33	–	–		

Minor Counties

Batting	M	Inns	NO	Runs	HS	Av	100s	50s	ct/st
S.D. Myles	4	4	–	155	57	38.75		2	2
L. Potter	3	3	–	93	47	31.00			4
M.J. Saggers	5	5	3	58	34*	29.00			2
K. Sharp	5	5	–	140	71	28.00		1	1
S.J. Dean	5	5	–	135	40	27.00			4
R.J. Evans	2	2	–	46	34	23.00			1
J.P.J. Sylvester	2	2	–	41	30	20.50			
S.V. Laudat	3	3	–	46	17	15.33			
K.G. Hignett	2	2	–	25	19	12.50			1
M.J. Marvell	2	2	–	24	14	12.00			
J.N. Batty	5	5	1	43	26*	10.75			4
M.A. Sharp	5	5	3	15	10*	7.50			2
I. Cockbain	2	2	–	15	9	7.50			1
G.T.J. Townsend	2	2	–	12	10	6.00			
M.G. Powell	2	2	–	11	11	5.50			
M.F.D. Robinson	3	3	–	14	7	4.66			1

Played in two matches: M.A. Fell 0
Played in one match: Z.A. Sher 14
One catch was taken by a substitute

Bowling	Overs	Mds	Runs	Wks	Av	Best	4/inn
Z.A. Sher	4.5	1	20	3	6.66	3/20	
K.G. Hignett	7.1	1	62	4	15.50	3/25	
M.F.D. Robinson	22	–	133	5	26.60	3/75	
M.J. Marvell	11	–	59	1	29.50	1/21	
S.V. Laudat	22	1	106	3	35.33	2/40	
L. Potter	25.3	2	120	3	40.00	2/72	
M.J. Saggers	41	2	247	5	49.40	2/49	
S.D. Myles	20	–	152	3	50.66	2/54	
M.A. Sharp	45	6	177	2	88.50	1/36	
M.G. Powell	13.3	–	68	–	–		

Northamptonshire

Batting	M	Inns	NO	Runs	HS	Av	100s	50s	ct/st
R.J. Bailey	7	7	3	425	115*	106.25	2	2	3
T.C. Walton	3	3	1	98	70*	98.00		1	
R.R. Montgomerie	7	6	2	159	49	39.75			2
D.J. Capel	7	7	–	255	82	36.42		2	2
M.B. Loye	6	6	1	168	66	33.60		1	4
A.L. Penberthy	7	4	1	91	41	30.33			3
K.M. Curran	7	7	1	143	50	23.83		1	1
J.E. Emburey	6	3	2	17	9*	17.00			3
K.J. Warren	7	6	1	38	14*	7.60			4
A. Fordham	5	5	–	29	14	5.80			2

Played in seven matches: J.P. Taylor 0*
Played in five matches: C.E.L. Ambrose 10 (ct 4)
Played in two matches: N.A. Mallender did not bat
Played in one match: J.N. Snape did not bat

Northamptonshire (cont.)

Bowling	Overs	Mds	Runs	Wks	Av	Best	4/inn
J.P. Taylor	64	6	279	15	18.60	5/45	2
J.E. Emburey	53.5	3	203	8	25.37	4/24	1
A.L. Penberthy	54	4	259	10	25.90	3/38	
C.E.L. Ambrose	48.2	4	176	5	35.20	2/40	
D.J. Capel	30	1	137	3	45.66	2/37	
N.A. Mallender	17	1	63	1	63.00	1/30	
K.M. Curran	58	4	261	4	65.25	1/20	
J.N. Snape	9	–	38	–	–		
R.J. Bailey	11	–	63	–	–		

Nottinghamshire

Batting	M	Inns	NO	Runs	HS	Av	100s	50s	ct/st
P. Johnson	4	4	2	114	54*	57.00		1	1
A.A. Metcalfe	4	4	–	161	66	40.25		2	3
P.R. Pollard	4	4	1	112	79	37.33		1	1
M.P. Dowman	3	2	1	33	19*	33.00			1
C.M. Tolley	4	4	–	90	66	22.50			
R.T. Robinson	4	4	–	88	52	22.00		1	
R.T. Bates	4	3	–	45	27	15.00			4
W.M. Noon	4	2	–	11	10	5.50			2/2
D.B. Pennett	4	2	1	5	4*	5.00			3

Played in three matches: K.P. Evans; J.A. Afford 1*
Played in one match: C.L. Cairns 21; R.A. Pick 7; G.W. Mike 1*

Bowling	Overs	Mds	Runs	Wks	Av	Best	4/inn
R.A. Pick	9	1	29	2	14.50	2/29	
M.P. Dowman	19.2	1	86	5	17.20	3/21	
J.A. Afford	28	5	73	4	18.25	3/18	
R.T. Bates	37	3	128	7	18.28	3/21	
G.W. Mike	8	3	33	1	33.00	1/33	
K.P. Evans	27	2	97	2	48.50	1/29	
C.M. Tolley	28	–	132	2	66.00	1/29	
D.B. Pennett	30	1	175	2	87.50	2/57	

Scotland

Batting	M	Inns	NO	Runs	HS	Av	100s	50s	ct/st
I.L. Philip	4	4	–	173	69	43.25		2	
B.M.W. Patterson	3	3	–	91	50	30.33		1	
J.G. Williamson	4	4	1	73	51*	24.33		1	
S. Gourlay	3	2	1	20	18	20.00			1
M.J.D. Allingham	3	3	1	37	30	18.50			1
K. Thompson	3	2	1	17	16*	17.00			
J.A.R. Blain	2	2	1	14	10*	14.00			
M.J. Smith	4	4	–	55	33	13.75			
G. Salmond	4	4	–	44	26	11.00			1
I.M. Stanger	2	2	–	22	13	11.00			
I.R. Beven	3	2	–	12	12	6.00			2
A.G. Davies	4	3	–	16	15	5.33			5
G.N. Reifer	4	3	–	15	11	5.00			1

Played in one match: A.M. Tennant 2* (ct 2)
One catch was taken by a substitute

Bowling	Overs	Mds	Runs	Wks	Av	Best	4/inn
A.M. Tennant	10	1	29	2	14.50	2/29	
K. Thompson	22.5	3	100	4	25.00	2/24	
G.N. Reifer	24	2	109	4	27.25	2/20	
I.R. Beven	21	2	118	3	39.33	3/34	
J.A.R. Blain	9	–	58	1	58.00	1/37	
J.G. Williamson	22	3	121	2	60.50	2/54	
S. Gourlay	17.2	2	73	1	73.00	1/21	
M.J.D. Allingham	8	–	60	–	–		
I.M. Stanger	10	–	96	–	–		

Somerset

Batting	M	Inns	NO	Runs	HS	Av	100s	50s	ct/st
A.N. Hayhurst	4	3	2	116	67*	116.00		1	1
S.C. Ecclestone	4	4	1	270	112*	90.00	1	2	1
R.J. Turner	5	5	2	224	70	74.66		1	3
M.N. Lathwell	5	5	–	278	121	55.60	1	2	1
K.A. Parsons	3	2	1	36	33*	36.00			2
S. Lee	5	5	1	63	23	15.75			2
P.D. Bowler	5	5	–	74	26	14.80			1
R.J. Harden	5	4	–	57	38	14.25			
G.D. Rose	5	5	–	50	27	10.00			2

Played in five matches: H.R.J. Trump 10 (ct 5)
Played in three matches: K.J. Shine 38*; A.R. Caddick 7*
Played in one match: J.D. Batty 14; M.E. Trescothick 57*; M. Dimond did not bat

Benson and Hedges Cup Averages (continued)

Somerset (cont.)

Bowling	Overs	Mds	Runs	Wks	Av	Best	4/inn
A.R. Caddick	27	6	124	7	17.71	5/51	1
A.N. Hayhurst	24	4	96	5	19.20	3/29	
G.D. Rose	44	6	183	5	36.60	2/42	
S. Lee	40.2	2	245	6	40.83	3/60	
H.R.J. Trump	40	1	191	4	47.75	3/28	
K.A. Parsons	13	–	97	2	48.50	2/60	
K.J. Shine	19	2	162	2	81.00	2/57	
P.D. Bowler	0.3	–	4	–	–		
M. Dimond	3	–	26	–	–		
S.C. Ecclestone	8	–	31	–	–		

Surrey

Batting	M	Inns	NO	Runs	HS	Av	100s	50s	ct/st
A.D. Brown	5	5	1	314	117*	78.50	1	2	2
A.J. Stewart	5	5	1	297	160	74.25	1	2	5
C.C. Lewis	5	4	3	72	30*	72.00			2
G.P. Thorpe	5	4	–	130	41	32.50			3
D.J. Bicknell	5	4	1	108	46	27.00			3
D.M. Ward	5	5	–	105	32	21.00			1
A.J. Hollioake	5	4	–	61	45	15.25			
B.P. Julian	5	2	–	29	27	14.50			

Played in five matches: M.P. Bicknell 22; R.M. Pearson 12*
Played in three matches: M.A. Butcher 42* & 6* (ct 1)
Played in one match: J.E. Benjamin 3; B.C. Hollioake did not bat

Bowling	Overs	Mds	Runs	Wks	Av	Best	4/inn
C.C. Lewis	47	6	195	9	21.66	3/29	
B.C. Hollioake	7	1	25	1	25.00	1/25	
M.P. Bicknell	42	6	198	6	33.00	3/19	
B.P. Julian	46.1	3	232	7	33.14	3/28	
A.J. Hollioake	29	2	162	4	40.50	4/34	1
J.E. Benjamin	10	2	53	1	53.00	1/53	
R.M. Pearson	41.5	1	232	4	58.00	3/60	
M.A. Butcher	12	–	74	–	–		

Sussex

Batting	M	Inns	NO	Runs	HS	Av	100s	50s	ct/st
A.P. Wells	4	4	1	146	69	48.66		2	1
N.J. Lenham	3	2	–	71	57	35.50		1	
K. Greenfield	4	4	1	89	51*	29.66		1	1
V.C. Drakes	4	3	1	55	26	27.50			
P.W. Jarvis	4	3	1	51	38	25.50			
C.W.J. Athey	4	4	–	98	55	24.50		1	1
K. Newell	3	2	–	46	26	23.00			
M.P. Speight	4	4	–	88	64	22.00		1	
I.D.K. Salisbury	3	2	–	26	19	13.00			4
P. Moores	4	3	–	37	17	12.33			3/1
D.R.C. Law	2	2	–	8	8	4.00			

Played in three matches: E.S.H. Giddins 0* (ct 1)
Played in one match: J.D. Lewry 8*; N.C. Phillips 10

Bowling	Overs	Mds	Runs	Wks	Av	Best	4/inn
V.C. Drakes	35	6	142	7	20.42	5/19	1
P.W. Jarvis	37	2	158	6	26.33	3/48	
I.D.K. Salisbury	30	1	152	5	30.40	2/50	
K. Newell	13.1	1	57	1	57.00	1/25	
D.R.C. Law	16	–	76	1	76.00	1/44	
E.S.H. Giddins	29.4	2	122	1	122.00	1/42	
N.J. Lenham	1	–	12	–	–		
J.D. Lewry	6	–	22	–	–		
K. Greenfield	8	–	48	–	–		
N.C. Phillips	5	–	49	–	–		

Warwickshire

Batting	M	Inns	NO	Runs	HS	Av	100s	50s	ct/st
D.P. Ostler	6	5	1	293	86	73.25		3	5
N.V. Knight	6	5	–	252	104	50.40	1	1	
S.M. Pollock	7	4	2	98	59*	49.00		1	1
T.L. Penney	7	5	1	136	50*	34.00			
P.A. Smith	6	5	1	134	45	33.50			1
N.M.K. Smith	7	6	–	196	80	32.66		2	1

Warwickshire (cont.)

Batting (cont.)	M	Inns	NO	Runs	HS	Av	100s	50s	ct/st
D.A. Reeve	7	4	1	96	27	32.00			7
D.R. Brown	7	4	1	85	44	28.33			3
G. Welch	4	2	–	25	24	12.50			
A.F. Giles	4	2	–	17	9	8.50			2
K.J. Piper	7	3	1	12	7	6.00			12/1

Played in four matches: T.A. Munton 6*
Played in two matches: A.J. Moles 33 (ct 2) G.C. Small 1
Played in one match 0* (ct 1)
One catch was taken by a substitute

Bowling	Overs	Mds	Runs	Wks	Av	Best	4/inn
G.C. Small	9	–	25	3	8.33	3/25	
D.A. Reeve	63.5	7	218	13	16.76	4/23	1
S.M. Pollock	64	10	277	15	18.46	6/21	2
N.M.K. Smith	32	1	167	6	27.83	2/37	
G. Welch	27	1	126	4	31.50	2/13	
D.R. Brown	59.3	10	210	6	35.00	2/26	
T.A. Munton	32	3	125	3	41.66	2/31	
P.A. Smith	25	–	153	3	51.00	2/56	
A.F. Giles	19	1	105	1	105.00	1/49	

Worcestershire

Batting	M	Inns	NO	Runs	HS	Av	100s	50s	ct/st
G.A. Hick	4	4	1	206	95	68.66		2	2
T.S. Curtis	4	4	–	238	67	59.50		3	2
D.A. Leatherdale	4	4	2	99	66	49.50		1	2
S.R. Lampitt	4	2	1	44	25*	44.00			1
T.M. Moody	4	4	1	99	80*	33.00		1	2
W.P.C. Weston	4	3	–	50	20	16.66			2
R.K. Illingworth	4	2	1	10	8	10.00			
S.J. Rhodes	4	2	–	12	8	6.00			3

Played in three matches: K.R. Spiring 33 (ct 2); A. Sheriyar 1*; J.E. Brinkley did not bat
Played in two matches: P.A. Thomas
Played in one match: P.J. Newport 15

Bowling	Overs	Mds	Runs	Wks	Av	Best	4/inn
S.R. Lampitt	37.2	1	140	7	20.00	4/29	
A. Sheriyar	25.1	3	108	5	21.60	3/40	
J.E. Brinkley	25	6	136	4	34.00	2/44	
T.M. Moody	21	6	90	2	45.00	1/22	
R.K. Illingworth	39	3	158	3	52.66	1/18	
P.A. Thomas	18.4	2	85	1	85.00	1/34	
D.A. Leatherdale	5	–	23	–	–		
P.J. Newport	10	–	39	–	–		
G.A. Hick	8	–	61	–	–		

Yorkshire

Batting	M	Inns	NO	Runs	HS	Av	100s	50s	ct/st
M.G. Bevan	6	6	3	397	95*	132.33		5	
D. Byas	6	6	1	267	116*	53.40	1	1	3
R.J. Blakey	6	4	1	121	80*	40.33		1	4/1
M.P. Vaughan	6	6	–	211	60	35.16		2	3
C. White	6	5	2	94	57*	31.33		1	
M.D. Moxon	5	5	1	123	67	30.75		1	2
D. Gough	6	3	1	53	48*	26.50			4
A. McGrath	6	5	–	106	43	21.20			

Played in six matches: P.J. Hartley 17* & 8* (ct 2); R.D. Stemp 1
Played in four matches: C.E.W. Silverwood 1 (ct 2)
Played in two matches: A.G. Wharf did not bat
Played in one match: A.C. Morris (ct 1)

Bowling	Overs	Mds	Runs	Wks	Av	Best	4/inn
A. McGrath	2	–	10	2	5.00	2/10	
C.E.W. Silverwood	37.4	5	158	11	14.36	5/28	1
A.G. Wharf	19	–	89	5	17.80	4/29	1
M.G. Bevan	5.1	–	25	1	25.00	1/25	
M.P. Vaughan	8	1	34	1	34.00	1/22	
D. Gough	51	6	190	5	38.00	2/39	
C. White	49	1	284	7	40.57	2/56	
R.D. Stemp	57	3	248	6	41.33	2/33	
P.J. Hartley	50	7	200	3	66.66	1/27	
A.C. Morris	1	–	4	–	–		

India Tour of England

Texaco and Test Series

India's exit from the World Cup was accompanied by riots, suicides and demands for the replacement of Azharuddin as captain. The elimination of England had brought calls for another enquiry.

India had not enjoyed the best of fortune since the World Cup, either in Singapore or Sharjah, and it was not surprising that the party selected to tour England included some new names. The most notable omission from the chosen 16 was Vinod Kambli. The 24-year-old left-hander, who has more than a thousand Test runs to his credit at an average of more than 54, was not considered for the tour for disciplinary reasons, and with Prabhakar now retired, the batting suddenly appeared weaker than expected.

Three batsmen, Rathore, Dravid and Ganguly, would be vying for Kambli's place. Rathore, an elegant and forceful opener, was the man expected to win a first Test cap, and Dravid was to act as reserve wicket-keeper to Mongia.

The bowling had a strange appearance. With Prabhakar absent, Mhambrey or Venkatesh Prasad would share the new ball with the admirable Srinath, but this hardly suggested the most potent strike force. The spin attack, so long the most lethal of India's weapons, suddenly had an unbalanced look. Neither Kapoor nor Chauhan was chosen, and the party contained two left-arm spinners, the experienced and successful Venkatapathy Raju and the uncapped Joshi who had done well in the Ranji Trophy. There were also two leg-spinners, Kumble and Hirwani, but no off-spinner. It seemed from the outset that Azharuddin, Tendulkar, Sidhu and Manjrekar would carry a heavy burden, and England – incredibly, in view of their recent record – started the series as favourites.

5 May

at Arundel

Duke of Norfolk's XI 168 for 9 (R.A. Smith 60)
Indians 173 for 1 (S.R. Tendulkar 108 not out)
Indians won by 9 wickets

The problem with the opening match of the Indian tour was finding opposition. Counties were engaged in the first round of matches in the Sunday League and needed their top players. This meant that the Duke of Norfolk's XI consisted of six Hampshire players, John Childs, not required by Essex, and Tony Dodemaide, in England following his brilliant form at the end of the Australian season, with Rao, Randall and Kirtley making up the number. The beauties of Arundel were marred by cold and rain, and the match was reduced to 48 overs. The tourists needed only 35 to reach their target, Tendulkar hitting a thrilling hundred off 97 balls.

6 May

at Uxbridge

Indians 290 for 4 (M. Azharuddin 119, V. Rathore 103)
England NCA 176 for 8
Indians won by 114 runs

Another cold day awaited a 50-over encounter in which Azharuddin excelled with 119 off 113 balls. Rathore was equally impressive in a second wicket stand that realised 167.

8, 9 and 10 May

at Worcester

Indians 349 for 5 dec. (V. Rathore 165, M. Azharuddin 68, S.R. Tendulkar 52) and 240 for 2 (A.D. Jadeja 105 not out, V. Rathore 72)
Worcestershire 476 for 6 dec. (G.A. Hick 215, W.P.C. Weston 98, S.J. Rhodes 53)
Match drawn

The Indians showed an urgency that the county side lacked, and there were criticisms of Moody's decision to bat into the last day and condemn the match to a draw. With the weather still cold, Rathore hit a splendid century on the first day, 165 in five hours with 26 boundaries. He was elegant and assured in all he did. The declaration came before the end of the day, and the second day belonged to Hick. He plundered a sub-standard attack on a slow wicket in cold weather that was a hindrance to the spinners and reached the tenth double century of his career. There were 30 fours, and six sixes off the leg-spinner Hirwani in his innings, but, in context, it was no true pointer of what would happen in the Test series to come. On the third day, Jadeja reached his century in four hours and shared an opening stand of 146 with Rathore.

11, 12 and 13 May

at Bristol

Indians 406 (N.S. Sidhu 115, R.S. Dravid 86 not out, V. Rathore 63, S.V. Manjrekar 55, M.W. Alleyne 5 for 81) and 144 for 6 dec. (S.C. Ganguly 64 not out)
Gloucestershire 251 for 4 dec. (A. Symonds 120 not out, D.R. Hewson 53) and 158 for 8
Match drawn

Gloucestershire and the tourists did their best to beat the weather and bring about a positive result. Gloucestershire ultimately had to fight a stern rearguard action to avoid defeat. Another sparkling innings by Rathore and a more sedate hundred by Sidhu dominated the first part of the match. Symonds dominated the second. He had had a miserable season with Queensland, and it seemed he was now reconsidering his earlier decision to be recognised as Australian rather than English. Symonds hit two sixes and 16 fours in an innings of 120 which occupied 138 balls. He and Dominic Hewson, making his first-class debut, added 140 after three wickets had gone for 38. Alleyne declared at the end of the second day in an attempt to keep the game alive, and the Indians went for quick runs, which was not an easy task. Gloucestershire were given a target of 300 in 65 overs, but the first three wickets went for six runs, and thereafter they were on the defensive on a pitch growing ever more difficult.

16, 17 and 18 May
at Hove
Sussex 247 for 4 dec. (C.W.J. Athey 80, K. Greenfield 65) and 234 for 2 dec. (K. Greenfield 141 not out)
Indians 185 for 3 dec. (S.R. Tendulkar 85, S.V. Manjrekar 66 not out) and 184 for 4 (S.R. Tendulkar 67)
Match drawn

Still the sun refused to shine, and with only 66 overs possible on the first day at Hove, declarations were needed to bring any chance of a result. Even so, the cruel north wind, the cold and the rain made cricket far from pleasurable. Greenfield hit the highest score of his career, the sixth century by the still uncapped all-rounder, and the Indians were asked to make 297 in 46 overs. There was a second brilliant miniature innings by Tendulkar, and then all retired to the warmth of the pavilion – thankfully.

19 May
at Lord's
Indians 232 for 8 (M. Azharuddin 73)
Middlesex 192 for 7 (P.N. Weekes 81)
Indians won on faster scoring rate

Even India's one-day preparations for the Texaco Trophy were hampered by the weather. Rain interrupted the 50-over match at Lord's, and the game was eventually abandoned with four overs of the Middlesex quota unbowled. The tourists scored 136 from the last 20 overs of their innings, and the batting was generally pleasing, but the bowling still looked below par.

21 May
at Luton
Indians 228 for 9 (S.R. Tendulkar 88, A.L. Penberthy 4 for 42)
Northamptonshire 195 for 5 (M.B. Loye 83)
Northamptonshire won on faster scoring rate

In their last match before the Texaco Trophy, the Indians surrendered their unbeaten record. Rain was again the real winner. Tendulkar played majestically for 108 balls, being particularly severe on Emburey. The home side's target was reduced to 192 from 42 overs, and that they won with eight balls to spare was mainly due to the rejuvenated Loye who hit 83 from 95 balls.

Texaco Trophy

England v. India

The Texaco Trophy was upon us as quickly and as unexpectedly as Magwitch in the graveyard. The season had hardly started, and the Indians, suffering in the cold, looked far from prepared.

The England selectors, with Ray Illingworth still in command and still surrounded by volumes of criticism regarding the serialisation in a daily newspaper of a forthcoming book attributed to him, selected a party which, if controversial in content, showed a refreshingly positive and new approach. With coach David Lloyd unquestionably the main influence, the selectors chose cricketers with a proficiency in the limited-over game. Stewart was named as wicket-keeper, and his county colleagues Lewis and Brown were also in the squad. Lewis, after a handful of games for Surrey, could consider himself very lucky to have earned forgiveness and recall. Whether this very talented cricketer could maintain form and interest for the four and a half months of the season remained to be seen. Alistair Brown, whose inclusion had been strongly advocated in the press, is a product of the modern age of English cricket, a one-day batsman capable of hitting hard and often. He is not a player of Test potential, for his technical limitations are patently obvious, and countries more successful than England do not select cricketers for limited-over competitions who do not have the ability to go on to Test cricket.

The tour was not a great success for India. They returned home without a first-class win to their credit, but they unearthed two outstanding Test cricketers: Saurav Ganguly and Rahul Dravid. (David Munden/Sportsline)

Neil Smith, Mark Ealham and Matthew Maynard are three other cricketers who were selected simply as one-day players. Ealham, a dynamic, enthusiastic all-rounder was new to international cricket, as was Ronnie Irani of Essex. Irani has Test potential as he proved with the England 'A' side in Pakistan and with his match-winning efforts for Essex, but his medium-pace bowling is, as yet, not of international standard.

Gough and Maynard were omitted from the final eleven at The Oval where Ealham, Brown and Irani made their international debuts. Atherton won the toss, and England batted.

The blistering opening that was part of the plan did not materialise. The first delivery that Brown received, from Venkatesh Prasad, went right through him. The second was edged to second slip where Rathore dropped the easiest of chances. Atherton was looking an international player; Brown was not, and he had another escape when he skied a ball over slip. Running back, Tendulkar failed to reach the catch. In spite of Brown's uncertainties, it was Atherton who was the first to go, edging Venkatesh Prasad to the wicket-keeper in the tenth over.

Smith was promoted to pep up the scoring, and he hit Mhambrey for two fours in the pace bowler's first over in international cricket only to be well caught at slip off the fifth delivery.

Kumble posed Brown considerable problems, but the Surrey batsman survived until, with one ball of the 19th over remaining, he hoiked at Mhambrey and was bowled. Hick and Thorpe now joined in a partnership that was urgent and sensible. They added 56 before Thorpe sliced a ball from Jadeja to Mongia who took the catch wide to his left. Stewart ran himself out when he pushed the ball back to the bowler Jadeja and essayed a run. Jadeja picked the ball up in his left hand, turned and threw with his right all in one movement, and Stewart was stranded.

Irani batted with boldness, hitting 11 off 13 balls before hooking Kumble to long-leg where Venkatesh Prasad took a catch high above his head. Had he not intercepted the ball, it would have gone for six.

Now came the stand that turned the match firmly in England's favour. From 34 balls, Mark Ealham hit 40 runs, including two sixes and three fours, and he and Hick added 76 in one ball under ten overs. Ealham had some fortune in that an appeal for run out was referred to the third umpire. The television replay suggested that Ealham was clearly out, but umpire Balderstone showed the green light. Reprieved, Ealham played magnificently. There was one glorious square-cut off Srinath, and his two sixes were mighty affairs to long-on.

Hick had batted with the sense and authority that was needed, and he was within nine runs of his century when he fell to a splendid running catch on the cover boundary. He had faced 102 balls and hit a six and four fours. Always he had kept the score moving. Lewis plundered at the death, and India, who had taken some good catches but who had generally fielded poorly, faced a big target.

Mark Ealham in lavish form on the occasion of his international debut. He hits Tendulkar for six during his innings of 40 in the first Texaco Trophy match at The Oval. Mongia is the wicket-keeper. (David Munden/Sportsline)

It seemed that they would make light work of it as Tendulkar and Rathore dismissed Cork from the attack after two overs. When Martin began the fifth over the score was 37. At the end of the over it was 52.

The Indians were batting as we read that men used to bat in that golden age which is always just out of reach, but then, suddenly, it all fell apart. Rathore played over a ball from Lewis and was leg before. Kumble, incomprehensibly promoted to number three, was caught at slip second ball. Five balls later, Tendulkar suffered a wretched decision, given out leg before to a ball that appeared to be missing leg stump by a considerable margin.

As the afternoon became more and more grey, Sidhu played outside a ball from Lewis, and Manjrekar became the Surrey all-rounder's fourth victim when he pushed forward lamely and was bowled. Jadeja hit his first ball through mid-off for four, but the grey had now turned black. The drizzle turned to rain, and the Friday offered no respite. England could feel aggrieved that they were denied victory.

For the second match, England brought in Maynard and Gough for Irani and Smith. India were unchanged. Atherton again won the toss, but this time he asked India to bat first. Rain restricted the match to 42 overs per side.

Disaster began early for India. In miserable conditions on a green wicket, neither Rathore nor Tendulkar could find the freedom that they had found at The Oval. Frustrated, Rathore drove Cork to mid-on and called for a run. Realising his folly, he sent Tendulkar back, but the great man was stranded as Ealham's throw hit the stumps.

Rathore's unhappy stay ended ten minutes later when he was taken low at slip. Azharuddin and Sidhu suggested crisper form, but Cork's direct hit on the stumps from mid-off brought a red-light verdict from the third umpire and the end of Sidhu. Azharuddin began to find it increasingly difficult to reach the boundary. The England fielding was

Tendulkar is run out by Ealham as the Indian innings begins to disintegrate in the second Texaco Trophy match at Leeds. (David Munden/Sportsline)

good and had an air of confidence rather than of the desperation that had long been its trade mark. The Indian captain clouted Martin over mid-wicket for six, but he was caught when he attempted to repeat the shot.

India suffered their third run out when Maynard's throw from the square-leg boundary beat Manjrekar's valid attempt at a second run. Jadeja was successfully aggressive, but he gained little support against accurate bowling and keen fielding. India failed to complete their 42 overs, and England faced a moderate target of 160.

This suddenly took on huge proportions. Srinath and Venkatesh Prasad made admirable use of the new ball. Brown was caught in no-man's land second ball and was leg before. Hick lasted only one ball. England were now pressured by attacking field-placings, and Atherton, having been dropped at slip, was taken at first slip when he slashed at Venkatesh Prasad. Thorpe had been most uncertain, and Maynard survived a concerted appeal for a catch behind second ball. The sun hinted it might try to appear, and Thorpe and Maynard settled to add a reassuring 45. They had negotiated the difficult period, and even though Maynard ran himself out, Stewart overcame a nervous beginning to help Thorpe take England to what was, ultimately, a comfortable victory.

England brought back Smith for Ealham for the final match. This meant that only Irani had not played in two matches, which was unwise and unnecessary. India brought in Ganguly for Sidhu, Venkatapathy Raju for Mhambrey, and Dravid for Manjrekar. These all seemed sound enough changes in the context of the tour and of the three Tests to come. Sidhu saw it otherwise. Believing he had been badly treated, he announced his immediate retirement from international cricket, could not be dissuaded and returned to India. One is no longer surprised at the petulance and immaturity of cricketers for whom the title *first-class* seems inappropriate.

Miserable weather took the game at Old Trafford into a second day. India won the toss, batted first and soon lost Tendulkar caught at slip off a fine outswinger. The left-handed Ganguly settled into a useful partnership with Rathore which minimised the early loss of Tendulkar. The

Ganguly is stumped by Stewart off Thorpe in the match at Old Trafford. (Patrick Eagar)

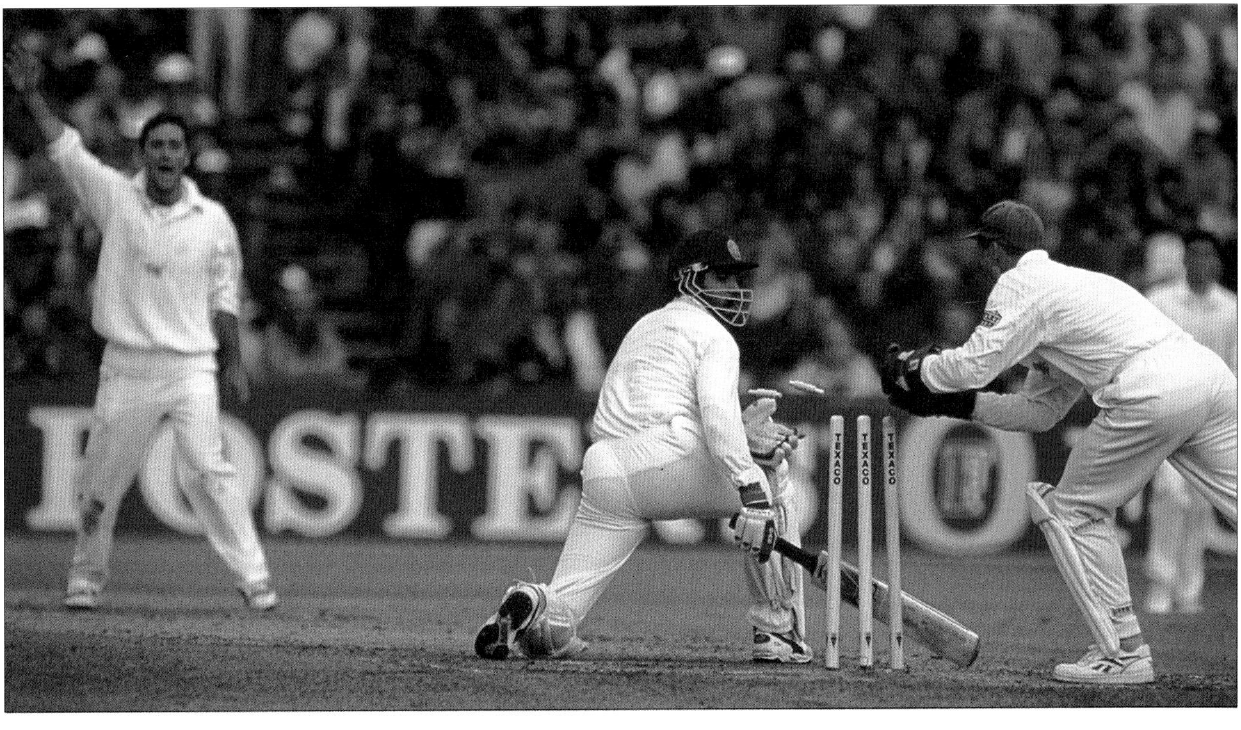

First Texaco Trophy International – England v. India

23 May 1996 at The Oval, Kennington

England

M.A. Atherton (Capt)	c Mongia, b Venkatesh Prasad	13
A.D. Brown	b Mhambrey	37
N.M.K. Smith	c Tendulkar, b Mhambrey	17
G.A. Hick	c Manjrekar, b Srinath	91
G.P. Thorpe	c Mongia, b Jadeja	26
*A.J. Stewart	run out	3
R.C. Irani	c Venkatesh Prasad, b Kumble	11
M.A. Ealham	b Kumble	40
C.C. Lewis	not out	29
D.G. Cork	not out	0
P.J. Martin		
	b 1, lb 11, w 11, nb 1	24
	50 overs (for 8 wickets)	291

	O	M	R	W
Srinath	10	1	45	1
Venkatesh Prasad	10	1	63	1
Mhambrey	9	–	69	2
Kumble	10	1	29	2
Tendulkar	6	–	44	–
Jadeja	5	–	29	1

Fall of Wickets
1–**31**, 2–**57**, 3–**85**, 4–**141**, 5–**147**, 6–**176**, 7–**252**, 8–**276**

India

V. Rathore	lbw, b Lewis	23
S.R. Tendulkar	lbw, b Martin	30
A.R. Kumble	c Hick, b Lewis	0
N.S. Sidhu	b Lewis	3
M. Azharuddin (Capt)	not out	15
S.V. Manjrekar	b Lewis	3
A.D. Jadeja	not out	11
*N.R. Mongia		
J. Srinath		
P.L. Mhambrey		
Venkatesh Prasad		
	b 4, lb 2, w 4, nb 1	11
	17.1 overs (for 5 wickets)	96

	O	M	R	W
Cork	3	–	21	–
Lewis	8.1	–	40	4
Martin	6	–	29	1

Fall of Wickets
1–**54**, 2–**54**, 3–**56**, 4–**62**, 5–**68**

Umpires: R. Julian & P. Willey *Man of the Match:* C.C. Lewis

Match abandoned

Second Texaco Trophy International – England v. India

25 May 1996 at Headingley, Leeds

India

V. Rathore	c Thorpe, b Cork	7
S.R. Tendulkar	run out	6
N.S. Sidhu	run out	20
M. Azharuddin (Capt)	c Brown, b Martin	40
S.V. Manjrekar	run out	24
A.D. Jadeja	c Martin, b Cork	33
*N.R. Mongia	c Atherton, b Cork	9
A.R. Kumble	c Stewart, b Martin	0
J. Srinath	c Cork, b Gough	5
P.L. Mhambrey	not out	7
Venkatesh Prasad	c Stewart, b Martin	1
	lb 1, w 5	6
	40.2 overs	158

	O	M	R	W
Cork	9	1	46	3
Lewis	9	1	30	–
Martin	8.2	1	34	3
Gough	8	1	24	1
Ealham	6	–	23	–

Fall of Wickets
1–**16**, 2–**17**, 3–**58**, 4–**94**, 5–**113**, 6–**145**, 7–**145**, 8–**149**, 9–**155**

England

M.A. Atherton (Capt)	c Tendulkar, b Venkatesh Prasad	7
A.D. Brown	lbw, b Srinath	0
G.A. Hick	lbw, b Venkatesh Prasad	0
G.P. Thorpe	not out	79
M.P. Maynard	run out	14
*A.J. Stewart	not out	47
M.A. Ealham		
C.C. Lewis		
D. Gough		
D.G. Cork		
P.J. Martin		
	lb 5, w 8, nb 2	15
	39.3 overs (for 4 wickets)	162

	O	M	R	W
Srinath	9	4	18	1
Venkatesh Prasad	9	2	33	2
Kumble	9	–	36	–
Mhambrey	6	–	29	–
Tendulkar	3	–	15	–
Manjrekar	0.3	–	4	–

Fall of Wickets
1–**1**, 2–**17**, 3–**23**, 4–**68**

Umpires: M.J. Kitchen & A.G.T. Whitehead *Man of the Match:* G.P. Thorpe

England won by 6 wickets

conditions were not easy, for the ball was moving appreciably at first, but, having reached the 25th over with only 77 scored, Rathore and Ganguly began to accelerate. An over by Lewis produced ten runs, and Smith's first spell of three overs cost 18 runs. Atherton took the novel approach of bringing Thorpe into the attack. The Surrey man recalled his days as a medium-pacer by claiming his first two wickets in international cricket. Rathore was caught at long-off in the 30th over, and four overs later, Ganguly overbalanced and Stewart pulled off a smart leg side stumping. Stewart also took a spectacular right-handed catch to dismiss Jadeja who had 29 off 32 balls, including an incredible six over long-off off Lewis.

Azharuddin was at his best. His unbeaten 73 came off 64 deliveries. His two sixes came in one over from Smith, and although he hit only three fours, his supple wrists were ever steering the ball through gaps in the field. He led India to a total of 236, and when Atherton fell second ball and rain ended play with England 2 for 1 from one over, India's chances of drawing the series looked bright.

Early on the Bank Holiday Monday, Smith mis-hit a ball from Venkatesh Prasad and was caught and bowled. Brown showed fine temperament in curbing his natural aggression to be more watchful. With first Hick and then Thorpe playing increasingly forceful support roles, Brown began to attack more and more. He and Hick added 85 in 15 overs; he and Thorpe 69 in 13. When Thorpe was run out Brown had 102 out of 186 to his credit, and when he was fifth out at 217 he had scored 118 off 137 balls with two sixes and ten fours. It was an effort worthy of the highest praise, and it was a performance that won England the match and the series.

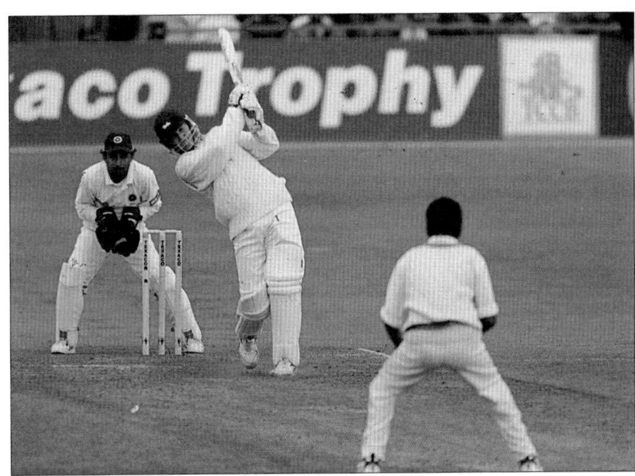

Brown hits Venkatapathy Raju to the boundary during his century in the third Texaco match at Old Trafford. The Surrey batsman made his international debut during the series. (Adrian Murrell/Allsport)

Sandeep Patil named Lewis as England's Man of the Series, and David Lloyd cited Azharuddin for India. The weather had made this a far from satisfactory few days, but the Tests beckoned, and there was something close to enjoyment back in English cricket.

Third Texaco Trophy International – England v. India

26 and 27 May 1996 at Old Trafford, Manchester

India

Batsman	Dismissal	Runs
V. Rathore	c Cork, b Thorpe	54
S.R. Tendulkar	c Hick, b Cork	1
S.C. Ganguly	st Stewart, b Thorpe	46
M. Azharuddin (Capt)	not out	73
A.D. Jadeja	c Stewart, b Cork	29
R.S. Dravid	not out	22
A.R. Kumble		
*N.R. Mongia		
J. Srinath		
Venkatapathy Raju		
Venkatesh Prasad		
	b 1, lb 4, w 6	11
	50 overs (for 4 wickets)	236

	O	M	R	W
Cork	10	3	35	2
Lewis	10	1	49	–
Gough	10	1	43	–
Martin	10	–	50	–
Smith	6	–	39	–
Thorpe	4	–	15	2

Fall of Wickets
1–11, 2–103, 3–118, 4–190

England

Batsman	Dismissal	Runs
M.A. Atherton (Capt)	lbw, b Srinath	0
A.D. Brown	c Dravid, b Srinath	118
N.M.K. Smith	c and b Venkatesh Prasad	11
G.A. Hick	c Dravid, b Venkatesh Prasad	32
G.P. Thorpe	run out	29
M.P. Maynard	lbw, b Kumble	14
A.J. Stewart	not out	13
C.C. Lewis	not out	4
D.G. Cork		
D.Gough		
P.J. Martin		
	lb 10, w 8	18
	48.5 overs (for 6 wickets)	239

	O	M	R	W
Srinath	10	1	35	2
Venkatesh Prasad	10	1	26	2
Kumble	10	–	52	1
Venkatapathy Raju	9.5	1	50	–
Ganguly	2	–	14	–
Tendulkar	2	–	22	–
Jadeja	5	–	30	–

Fall of Wickets
1–2, 2–32, 3–117, 4–186, 5–217, 6–226

Umpires: D.J. Constant & A.A. Jones *Man of the Match:* A.D. Brown

England won by 4 wickets

The decisive moment in the first Test match. Srinath celebrates the dismissal of Hussain, caught behind, but the umpire rules not out. Hussain went on to complete a maiden Test century.
(David Munden/Sportsline)

28, 29 and 30 May
at Chelmsford
Indians 320 for 8 dec. (V. Rathore 95, S.R. Tendulkar 74, S.C. Ganguly 51, R.C. Irani 4 for 37) and 223 for 6 dec. (A.D. Jadeja 87, J.H. Childs 4 for 99)
Essex 269 for 5 dec. (S.G. Law 153, P.J. Prichard 53) and 207 for 6 (N. Hussain 85)
Match drawn

Navjot Singh Sidhu ignored the entreaties of Sandeep Patil, packed his bags and returned to India. The Indian batting did not look greatly weakened by his absence in the match at Chelmsford where Rathore and Tendulkar thrived. The bowling, on the other hand, looked frighteningly brittle without Kumble and Srinath and was severely punished by Law who, with every match, gave further evidence that he was the outstanding overseas acquisition of the season. Essex recognised this by awarding him his county cap. Hussain brightened the last afternoon with nine fours in his 89 off 105 balls.

1, 2 and 3 June
at Leicester
Indians 305 for 3 dec. (M. Azharuddin 111 not out, V. Rathore 71, R.S. Dravid 58 not out) and 273 for 3 dec. (V. Rathore 91, M. Azharuddin 72 retired hurt, S.V. Manjrekar 65 not out)
Leicestershire 318 for 5 dec. (A. Habib 90, D.L. Maddy 61, P.V. Simmons 58, V.J. Wells 52)
Match drawn

Ankola, the replacement for Sidhu, played his first match, but this was not a game for bowlers as the batsmen thrived. Shrugging off criticism, Azharuddin reached 100 off 86 balls on the Saturday, his second fifty occupying only 27 balls. In all, he hit six sixes and ten fours. Leicestershire, too, batted vigorously, and Habib, still benefiting from his transfer from Middlesex, and Simmons added 103 in 15 overs for the fourth wicket. There was more sparkle from Rathore and Azharuddin before rain ended the match early.

First Test Match

England *v.* India *at Edgbaston*

From the 13 chosen for the first Test, England omitted Crawley and Martin. Knight had been recalled to open the innings with Atherton, and Hussain, too long in the shade, was given the number three spot. There was a return to Test cricket for Lewis, and there were three new caps in Irani, the Essex all-rounder, Patel, the Kent slow left-arm bowler, and Mullally, enjoying a successful time for Leicestershire with his fast medium left-arm bowling. The England side had a brighter, fresher look, reflecting the sunny disposition of the new coach, David Lloyd. Unfortunately, the chairman of the England selectors had been involved in politics and recrimination in the days before the Test, and it was pleasing to be able to concentrate on the playing of the game on the field rather than within the pages of the tabloids or ghosted books.

India entered the Test without a first-class win to their credit, but they did win the toss and chose to bat. It was evident from the outset that the pitch would not be a batsman's paradise and that application was needed. It was a quality that India seemed to lack. Hussain, surprisingly, dropped Rathore at point in Cork's first over, but Jadeja had no reprieve when he sliced Lewis to gully.

Manjrekar and Rathore saw the shine off the new ball, but Manjrekar was forced to retire with a twisted ankle with the score at 40. Only one run had been added when Rathore steered a lifting ball to third slip. This brought Azharuddin and Tendulkar together, but, although Azharuddin hit three fours, he did not look at ease as the ball bounced unevenly. Irani came on as second change, and his fifth ball in Test cricket was flicked to leg by Azharuddin for Knight to take a spectacular catch. Both Gooch and Botham himself have compared Irani to the young Botham, and he certainly has the capacity for taking wickets with innocuous deliveries.

The vital wicket came when Tendulkar drove loosely at Cork and was bowled. On the evidence of 11 Tests, Cork is an outstanding bowler, the best opening bowler England have possessed since Botham's glory days, so that it is the greatest of pities that he accompanies his successes with gestures that are both arrogant and ill-mannered.

Mullally, who bowled steadily, claimed his first Test victim when he bowled Mongia who flailed wildly. Manjrekar returned and added 13 to his earlier score before cutting hard into the hands of Atherton in the gully. Kumble parried the aggressive and demanding Cork to slip, and it was left to Srinath and debutant Mhambrey to show the first real application and positivity in a ninth wicket stand of 53. Srinath, in particular, shamed his colleagues with nine fours in an innings that occupied only 65 balls and 92 minutes.

India had thrown away the advantage of winning the toss, and with Knight and Atherton hitting 60 in 19 overs before the close, England ended the first day in complete control.

Their control was weakened by the second ball of the second morning which kept low and deceived Knight whose technique looks suspect at Test level. Atherton twice edged Venkatesh Prasad short of slip and was caught when he drove at Mhambrey. Rathore juggled nervously with the ball at second slip before holding on to give Mhambrey his first Test wicket.

Edgbaston is the best appointed ground in England, but the pitch is not on a par with the facilities and for the second year in succession, batsmen found the Edgbaston wicket untrustworthy. Thorpe came to the crease with all guns blazing. He hit a six and two fours, lived dangerously and made 21 off 30 balls before being bowled off bat and pad. England lunched at 114 for 3, and Hussain had displayed the application, technique and temperament that the conditions demanded. In two hours, he had made 19.

His care and control were qualities much admired and much needed, especially when Hick pulled wastefully to long-leg. Srinath and Venkatesh Prasad had bowled beautifully, and they deserved whatever luck came their way. So did Irani. He announced his Test debut with an innings of freshness and enthusiasm. He hit the ball cleanly and claimed seven fours in his 34 which came off 34 deliveries. He and Hussain added 46 in ten overs, and it seemed that England were regaining control until Irani fell to a lifting ball from Srinath.

Irani's wicket was the first of four to fall for 20 runs. The remaining three went down in eight balls bowled by Venkatesh Prasad. Russell was yorked after a painfully embarrassing innings lasting 23 minutes while Lewis was out first ball, caught at slip, and Cork, too, paid the penalty for nibbling outside the off stump.

When Cork was out Hussain was on 64, but for the next 52 minutes he received sensible support from Patel. The Kent spinner was finally trapped leg before by Kumble who was well below his best, and Hussain was now on 93 while England had a lead of 50. In the next 47 minutes, that lead was increased to 99 and Nasser Hussain reached a splendid century, emphasising the folly of his omission from

A disaster for India in the first Test. Tendulkar is bowled by Dominic Cork for 24, and the innings is in ruins. (Patrick Eagar)

Chris Lewis had a highly successful return to international cricket and took five wickets in the second innings of the first Test. His first victim was Jadeja, caught behind. Russell throws the ball in the air. Thorpe and Hick run to congratulate the bowler. (Patrick Eagar)

the side in the past three years. He was finally caught when he swung too merrily, but by then he had made 128 off 227 balls with a six and 18 fours. It was a most impressive innings. England had found a number three.

Much credit should be given to Patel and Mullally. They stayed with Hussain as 98 runs were added for the last two wickets, and India, having been right back in the game, were now deflated. They were thankful that bad light ended play early with Rathore having scored five.

He added only two on the third morning before edging to second slip. Jadeja, not an opening batsman, followed when he touched Lewis to the wicket-keeper. Mongia, promoted because of the injury to Manjrekar, looked sound for a while before driving at Cork to be brilliantly caught low in the gully by Hussain. When, third ball, Azharuddin attempted to turn Mullally to leg and left his leg stump unguarded India were 36 for 4, and an early finish looked inevitable.

Joshi, unable to bowl because of a broken finger, looked a useful batsman for 20 minutes and then he offered Russell a high catch off a lifting delivery. India were 89 for 5 at lunch. Tendulkar was on 50.

Between lunch and tea, England captured only one wicket, that of Manjrekar, who had batted with a runner and played his shots off one leg. Bravely, he stayed with Tendulkar for 98 minutes and scored 18 invaluable runs.

For Tendulkar, no praise can be too high. Here was majesty on a difficult pitch by, arguably, the greatest batsman in the world at the present time. He destroyed Irani

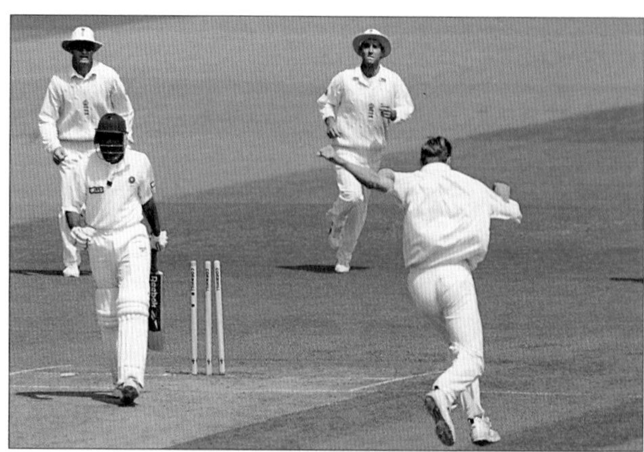

The Indian captain Azharuddin is bowled round his legs by Mullally for 0. The Indian skipper had a miserable Test series. (Adrian Murrell/Allsport)

with a two-over cascade of shots, and he went to his hundred by driving Patel straight for six. In all, he hit 19 fours as well as that six and faced 176 balls. He was ninth out, having scored his 122 out of 191 runs made while he was at the wicket. Manjrekar's 18 was the next highest score in another feeble Indian batting display.

Lewis confirmed his rejuvenation with five wickets, and England needed 121 to win; 80 or 90 more, and it would have been a very difficult task. Knight was leg before to Venkatesh Prasad and Atherton should have been leg

First Cornhill Test Match – England v. India

6, 7, 8 and 9 June 1996 at Edgbaston, Birmingham

India

	First Innings		Second Innings	
V. Rathore	c Knight, b Cork	20	c Hick, b Cork	7
A.D. Jadeja	c Atherton, b Lewis	0	c Russell, b Lewis	6
S.V. Manjrekar	c Atherton, b Lewis	23	(7) c Knight, b Lewis	18
S.R. Tendulkar	b Cork	24	c Thorpe, b Lewis	122
M. Azharuddin (Capt)	c Knight, b Irani	13	b Mullally	0
*N.R. Mongia	b Mullally	20	(3) c Hussain, b Cork	9
S.B. Joshi	c Thorpe, b Mullally	12	c Russell, b Mullally	12
A.R. Kumble	c Knight, b Cork	5	run out	15
J. Srinath	c Russell, b Mullally	52	lbw, b Lewis	1
P.L. Mhambrey	c Thorpe, b Cork	28	b Lewis	15
Venkatesh Prasad	not out	0	not out	0
	b 3, lb 10, lb 4	17	b 4, lb 9, nb 1	14
		214		219

	O	M	R	W	O	M	R	W
Lewis	18	2	44	2	22.4	6	72	5
Cork	20.1	5	61	4	19	5	40	2
Mullally	22	7	60	3	15	4	43	2
Irani	7	4	22	1	2	–	21	–
Patel	2	–	14	–	8	3	18	–
Hick					4	1	12	–

Fall of Wickets
1–8, 2–41, 3–64, 4–93, 5–103, 6–118, 7–127, 8–150, 9–203
1–15, 2–17, 3–35, 4–36, 5–68, 6–127, 7–185, 8–193, 9–208

England

	First Innings		Second Innings	
N.V. Knight	c Mongia, b Srinath	27	lbw, b Prasad	14
M.A. Atherton (Capt)	c Rathore, b Mhambrey	33	not out	53
N. Hussain	c sub (Dravid), b Srinath	128	c Srinath, b Prasad	19
G.P. Thorpe	b Srinath	21	not out	17
G.A. Hick	c Mhambrey, b Prasad	8		
R.C. Irani	c Mongia, b Srinath	34		
*R.C. Russell	b Prasad	0		
C.C. Lewis	c Rathore, b Prasad	0		
D.G. Cork	c Jadeja, b Prasad	4		
M.M. Patel	lbw, b Kumble	18		
A.D. Mullally	not out	14		
	b 16, lb 3, nb 7	26	b 8, lb 7, w 1, nb 2	18
		313	(for 2 wickets)	121

	O	M	R	W	O	M	R	W
Srinath	28.2	5	103	4	14.5	3	47	–
Venkatesh Prasad	28	9	71	4	14	–	50	2
Kumble	24	4	77	1	5	3	9	–
Mhambrey	10	–	43	1				

Fall of Wickets
1–60, 2–72, 3–109, 4–149, 5–195, 6–205, 7–205, 8–215, 9–264
1–37, 2–77

Umpires: D.B. Hair & D.R. Shepherd

England won by 8 wickets

The fifth ball of the second Test match at Lord's, and umpire Bird raises his finger in response to Srinath's appeal. Atherton is gone for 0. Bird was standing in a Test match for the last time. (Patrick Eagar)

before, but umpire Hair thought otherwise. He did not have a good match. Some thought Hussain had gloved to the 'keeper when 14, others were convinced that Rathore's second innings edge did not carry to Hick. Certainly that looked the case on the television replay, but only Hick knows the real truth.

England scored 73 for 1 before the close of the third day, and the match ended just after noon on the fourth. Hussain, named Man of the Match, was caught hooking.

India had chosen Mhambrey as third seamer, but he bowled only ten overs in the first innings and not at all in the second – a gross misjudgment by Azharuddin who was nobly served by two fine opening bowlers, Srinath and Venkatesh Prasad. India disappointed bitterly, but Tendulkar left a lasting memory of splendour.

13, 14 and 15 June
at Derby
Indians 229 (N.R. Mongia 74 not out, D.E. Malcolm 4 for 60) and 192 (S.C. Ganguly 64, D.E. Malcolm 4 for 50)
Derbyshire 409 (D.M. Jones 93, K.M. Krikken 70, A.R. Kumble 4 for 111) and 13 for 0
Derbyshire won by 10 wickets

Put in to bat, India were embarrassed at 87 for 7 before Mongia shared stands of 58 with Ankola and 61 with Venkatapathy Raju for the ninth and tenth wickets. The tourists' bowling and fielding was even worse than their batting. They conceded 72 extras, were dreadful in the field and saw Derbyshire build a lead of 180. The most notable incident came with Krikken, who batted well, wafted away a ball from Srinath with his hand much as Gooch had done in the Old Trafford Test of 1993 and was given out handled ball. The Indians surrendered lamely for a second time, and Derbyshire won massively inside three days. Unquestionably, this was the lowest point of India's tour.

Second Test Match

England *v.* India *at Lord's*

Knight was unable to play because of injury and Stewart was brought in to open the innings with Atherton. Martin replaced Patel, and India chose Ganguly and Dravid, neither of whom had played Test cricket before, instead of Manjrekar and Joshi, both of whom were injured. Indeed, Joshi's part in the tour was over following the broken finger sustained at Edgbaston. Azharuddin won the toss, and India bowled first on an overcast morning that gave the bowlers considerable assistance.

This was umpire Bird's last Test, an emotional occasion for him, but he was soon in action with the tears wiped away as he lifted his finger in response to Srinath's appeal on the fifth ball of the match. Atherton was quite comfortably leg before.

There now ensued a period in which Stewart and Hussain suffered and survived. There were several optimistic appeals which were rejected, and the ball consistently beat the bat. The first runs did not come until the last ball of the fourth over when Stewart turned Venkatesh Prasad square for three. A single past gully off the last ball of the seventh over was the next scoring shot. The first boundary did not come until the last ball of the 14th over when Stewart edged Mhambrey through the slips. This brought England to 17 for 1 in an hour.

The luck was not with the Indian seamers. Srinath's first spell brought him 1 for 5 from seven overs; Venkatesh Prasad had 0 for 4 from five overs. Mhambrey too bowled well, but he, in particular, offered far too many deliveries which the batsmen did not have to play. At lunch, England were 39 for 1 from 21 overs.

England's application was a model for what India's batting should have been in the first Test. The runs had just begun to come when Stewart, adopting a stance with legs wide apart, went across his stumps to an inswinger and was bowled. He had batted for over two hours, and the dismissal seemed to waste that period of vigilance.

Thorpe began with a flourish, but Hussain had now become becalmed and was caught at second slip when he drove at Ganguly with his bat far from his body. This, too, was a waste of 170 minutes of dedication. Having captured his first wicket in Test cricket, Ganguly added a second when Hick drove lazily to mid-off. Two wickets in his first 15 balls in Test cricket was a commendable achievement by Ganguly, and Venkatesh Prasad compounded England's discomfort when he bowled Irani who moved too far across his wicket and left his leg stump unguarded. Three wickets had fallen for nine runs, and England were 107 for 5.

Salvation came in the form of Thorpe and Russell. One has never been totally convinced about Thorpe. In spite of his several successes, he has never assured one that he was a permanent fixture in Test cricket, but now he came of age. At tea, England were 144 for 5 from 53 overs; by the close, they were 238 from 80 overs with Thorpe on 85 and

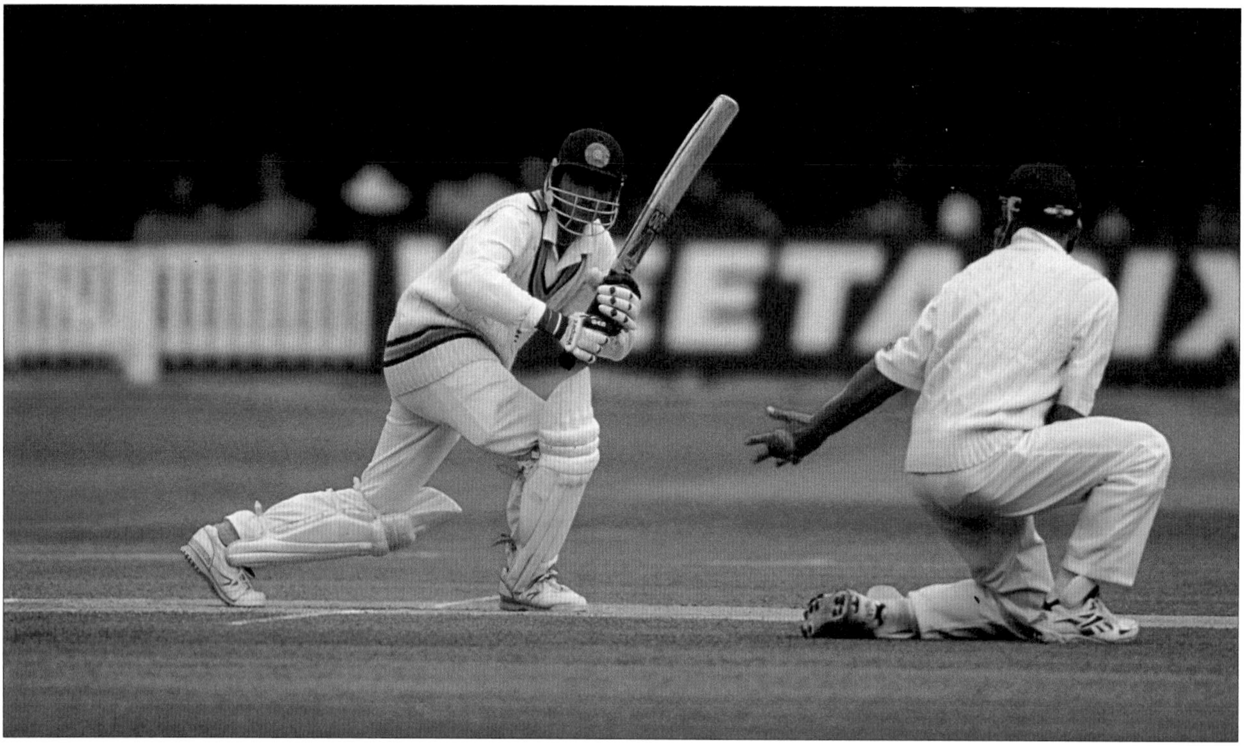

Saurav Ganguly turns the ball to leg on his way to a magnificent 131 in his first Test match.
(David Munden/Sportsline)

Russell on 69. Thorpe was commanding, giving confidence to colleagues and supporters and delighting the crowd with some exquisite shots, and Russell was Russell; deflecting and scampering and effective.

The second day began badly for England. Thorpe almost ran himself out, hit a boundary and, in the next over, played on to the admirable Srinath. Thorpe had batted with such composure and intelligence that his failure to reach his hundred could only be recognised as a bitter disappointment.

Russell was not a disappointment. He gives no aesthetic pleasure when batting, but he has character and he can be mightily, frustratingly effective. He and Lewis added 83, and India must have wondered if they would ever take another wicket even though Russell's batting subsided in a perverse manner once he had reached his second Test century. He was to be last out, the fourth of Venkatesh Prasad's four wickets in 32 balls which brought the England innings to an abrupt end. Russell's 124 occupied 372 minutes during which he faced 261 deliveries and hit 13 fours. Venkatesh Prasad's final spell of 4 for 8 in 33 balls gave him five wickets in the innings, a most impressive performance in what was his second Test.

Rathore was brilliantly caught at third slip by Hussain off Cork, and one suspected that the Indian innings might decline rapidly, but Ganguly exuded confidence and elegance, and Mongia, promoted to open, looked durable until receiving a leg before decision from Dickie Bird at which he had every right to weep as much in anger as the umpire had done in emotional farewell on the first day. Tendulkar calmed nerves, and India were 83 for 2 at the close.

The Saturday of the Lord's Test is one of the social events of the summer, and a capacity crowd settled back to enjoy the splendour of Tendulkar. It seemed that this would be the case when the great man offered a simple catch to Hick at second slip in the first over of the day and the chance was spurned by the Zimbabwean. Tendulkar immediately square cut the unlucky Lewis for four, but Lewis came back to produce a splendid ball that hit the top of Tendulkar's off

Jack Russell pushes the ball to the off during his defiant century.
(David Munden/Sportsline)

stump. Azharuddin should now have taken responsibility as Ganguly confidently and elegantly found his way into Test cricket, but the Indian captain waved his bat meaninglessly at a ball from Mullally which was slanted across him, and Russell moved in front of first slip to take the catch. At lunch, India were 166 for 4 with Ganguly on 63. The young left-hander had moved purposefully to fifty before becoming becalmed, but his concentration never wavered.

Only one wicket fell in the afternoon, that of Jadeja who was comprehensively bowled by Irani's full length inswinger. After 340 minutes at the crease, Ganguly drove Cork through the covers, a regal stroke, and raised his bat to acknowledge the plaudits of the crowd. He had become only the third batsman to score a century at Lord's on his Test debut. He was now accompanied by another making his Test debut, Rahul Dravid, who began to play with equal style and assurance.

Only in his hooking did Ganguly suggest fallibility, but once he was past three figures he displayed an array of majestic strokes, and it was a surprise when, after 439 minutes and 301 balls, he played over a full-length delivery from Mullally and was bowled. He had 20 fours, but, above all, he had shown the beauty of batsmanship which is at the very heart and joy of the game. We were in the presence of greatness, not yet perhaps fully flowered but surely to be the source of much pleasure in the years to come.

India finished the third day on 326 for 6 with Dravid on 56. It took England more than three hours on the fourth day to capture the last four Indian wickets, and their attack, lacking in variety, looked far inferior to Srinath and Venkatesh Prasad. Dravid dominated the play with batting that was selective, thoughtful, positive and ever graceful. It seemed certain that history would be made and that two debutants would score centuries in a Lord's Test, but Dravid was on 95 when he touched a ball from Lewis to Russell who

Ronnie Irani bowls Jadeja for 10. The young Essex all-rounder made an impressive entry into international cricket.
(Adrian Murrell/Allsport)

Second Cornhill Test Match – England v. India

20, 21, 22, 23 and 24 June 1996 at Lord's

England

	First Innings		Second Innings	
M.A. Atherton (Capt)	lbw, **b** Srinath	**0**	**b** Kumble	**17**
A.J. Stewart	**b** Srinath	**20**	**b** Srinath	**66**
N. Hussain	**c** Rathore, **b** Ganguly	**36**	**c** Dravid, **b** Srinath	**28**
G.P. Thorpe	**b** Srinath	**89**	(5) **c** Rathore, **b** Kumble	**21**
G.A. Hick	**c** Srinath, **b** Ganguly	**1**	(6) **c** Mongia, **b** Prasad	**6**
R.C. Irani	**b** Venkatesh Prasad	**1**	(7) **b** Mhambrey	**41**
*R.C. Russell	**c** Tendulkar, **b** Prasad	**124**	(8) lbw, **b** Ganguly	**38**
C.C. Lewis	**c** Mongia, **b** Prasad	**31**	(9) not out	**26**
D.G. Cork	**c** Mongia, **b** Prasad	**0**	(10) **c** Azharuddin, **b** Kumble	**1**
P.J. Martin	**c** Tendulkar, **b** Prasad	**4**	(4) **c** Rathore, **b** Prasad	**23**
A.D. Mullally	not out	**0**	not out	**0**
	b **13**, lb **11**, nb **14**	**38**	b **1**, lb **5**, nb **5**	**11**
		344	(for 9 wickets, dec.)	**278**

	O	M	R	W	O	M	R	W
Srinath	33	9	76	**3**	29	8	76	**2**
Venkatesh Prasad	33.3	10	76	**5**	24	8	54	**2**
Mhambrey	19	3	58	**–**	14	3	47	**1**
Kumble	28	9	60	**–**	51	14	90	**3**
Ganguly	15	2	49	**2**	3	–	5	**1**
Tendulkar	2	1	1	**–**				

Fall of Wickets
1–**0**, 2–**67**, 3–**98**, 4–**102**, 5–**107**, 6–**243**, 7–**326**, 8–**337**, 9–**343**
1–**49**, 2–**109**, 3–**114**, 4–**154**, 5–**167**, 6–**168**, 7–**228**, 8–**274**, 9–**275**

India

	First Innings	
V. Rathore	**c** Hussain, **b** Cork	**15**
*N.R. Mongia	lbw, **b** Lewis	**24**
S.C. Ganguly	**b** Mullally	**131**
S.R. Tendulkar	**b** Lewis	**31**
M. Azharuddin (Capt)	**c** Russell, **b** Mullally	**16**
A.D. Jadeja	**b** Irani	**10**
R.S. Dravid	**c** Russell, **b** Lewis	**95**
A.R. Kumble	lbw, **b** Martin	**14**
J. Srinath	**b** Mullally	**19**
P.L. Mhambrey	not out	**15**
Venkatesh Prasad	**c** Stewart, **b** Cork	**4**
	b **11**, lb **25**, w **10**, nb **9**	**55**
		429

	O	M	R	W
Lewis	40	11	101	**3**
Cork	42.3	10	112	**2**
Mullally	39	14	71	**3**
Martin	34	10	70	**1**
Irani	12	3	31	**1**
Hick	2	–	8	**–**

Fall of Wickets
1–**25**, 2–**59**, 3–**123**, 4–**154**, 5–**202**, 6–**296**, 7–**351**, 8–**388**, 9–**419**

Umpires: H.D. Bird & D.B. Hair

Match drawn

Graham Thorpe batted well in the second Test match. In the second innings, he fell to spectacular catch at short-leg by Rathore off the bowling of Kumble. (Adrian Murrell/Allsport)

had not looked very tidy behind the stumps. Dravid departed without waiting for the umpire's finger to be raised. He had not matched Ganguly's elegance, but his tenacity and temperament were second to none.

Srinath and Mhambrey gave sensible assistance and India led by 85 on the first innings.

If Srinath is one of the best new-ball bowlers in the world at the present time, which he is, he is also one of the unluckiest. He gave Atherton a most torrid time. The England skipper survived appeals for leg before and balls that leapt and fell just short of the fielders' clutching hands. Shortly after tea he was bowled by a massive leg-break from Kumble. The ball pitched on middle stump and hit off, and Atherton's poor run continued. Stewart was dropped by Mongia off Kumble, a difficult leg side chance, but Hussain was caught at cover as he tried to withdraw his bat from an intended hook. Martin helped Stewart see out the last four overs of the day, and with England at 113 for 2, a draw looked inevitable.

Stewart must have begun the last day looking for a century, but he dragged the fourth ball he faced into his stumps. Night-watchman Martin stood firm in contrast to Thorpe who was acrobatically caught at short-leg off a ball that spun and bounced and Hick who spent 25 minutes on nought before square-cutting a four and being caught behind off a ball that lifted sharply. Martin had batted for over two hours before dabbing a ball to slip so that England lunched at an uncomfortable 170 for 6. They led by 85 and suddenly India looked likely to square the series.

Irani lived dangerously against Srinath until he settled to play some majestic shots as he was the leading partner in a stand of 60 with Russell. The partnership took the game further and further away from India, and England's salvation was completed by Lewis and Russell, who took the Man of the Match award, which was a little hard on Ganguly.

At least India had revived their spirits, and interest in the final game at Trent Bridge was sharpened.

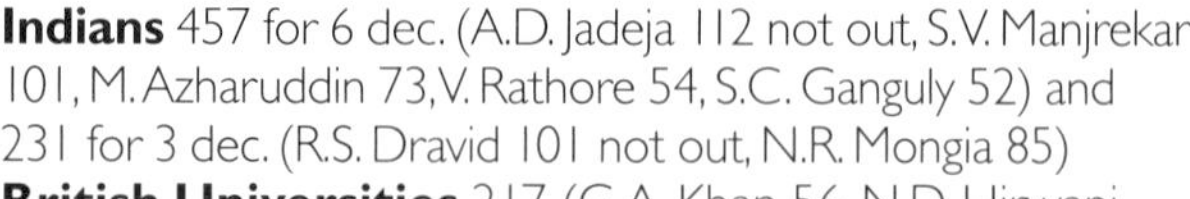

26, 27 and 28 June
at Cambridge
Indians 457 for 6 dec. (A.D. Jadeja 112 not out, S.V. Manjrekar 101, M. Azharuddin 73, V. Rathore 54, S.C. Ganguly 52) and 231 for 3 dec. (R.S. Dravid 101 not out, N.R. Mongia 85)
British Universities 217 (G.A. Khan 56, N.D. Hirwani 6 for 60)
Match drawn

There are events in first-class cricket that even the closest students of the game fail to comprehend. At Fenner's, the Indians occupied the first day compiling 391 for 5 with Manjrekar, fit again, hitting a century. Azharuddin did not declare, but batted into the second day and allowed Jadeja to complete his hundred. With leg-spinner Hirwani producing his best form of the tour, India bowled out the Universities for 217, the last six wickets falling for 41 runs. Azharuddin did not enforce the follow-on. Rathore and Mongia scored two runs in six overs before the close, and the rate did not reach above one an over in the early part of the final day. Eventually Dravid scored his first century of the tour as the Indians, without a first-class win on the tour, batted out the last day. The meaning of all this escaped those who love and follow the game.

29, 30 June and 1 July
at Southampton
Indians 362 for 5 dec. (S.C. Ganguly 100 not out, V. Rathore 95, A.D. Jadeja 91, A.R. Kumble 59 not out, K.D. James 5 for 74)
Hampshire 458 for 9 (K.D. James 103, J.S. Laney 100, S.M. Milburn 54 not out, S.A. Ankola 4 for 120)
Match drawn

India's final match against a county was a remarkable affair. Jadeja followed his century at Fenner's with 95 in an opening partnership of 192 with Rathore. It failed to allow him to keep his place in the Test side. Kevan James took the first wicket, and, at 207, he had Rathore stumped down the leg side by Adrian Aymes. Next ball, he had Tendulkar taken at short-leg and completed the hat-trick when he trapped Dravid leg before. When he had Manjrekar caught at second slip he became the first Englishman to take four wickets in four balls for 24 years and only the 31st bowler in the history of the game to achieve the feat. He had Ganguly dropped four balls later, and the left-hander responded by going on to reach a century. Tendulkar declared, and Hampshire were 49 for 2 at the close with James 2 not out. On the Sunday, James and Laney made their partnership worth 175. Both batsmen reached centuries so that the left-handed James became the first cricketer to take four wickets in four balls and score a hundred in the same match. His hundred took three-and-a-half hours and included three straight sixes off Hirwani and 10 fours. Hampshire ended the day on 383 for 9, and during what play was possible on the final morning they scored another 75 with Stuart Milburn hitting the first fifty of his career.

Third Test Match

England v. India at Trent Bridge

England brought back Patel for Martin and gave Ealham a first Test cap in place of Irani, which was as surprising as it was harsh. Salisbury was also named in the original party but was released in time to play for Sussex at Arundel on the Wednesday. India won the toss and batted. They had brought in Venkatapathy Raju for Mhambrey in whom Azharuddin appeared to have little faith, and Manjrekar returned in place of Jadeja who had just run into form.

At the start, all went well for England. Within 38 minutes, both openers, Rathore and Mongia, were back in the pavilion with 33 scored, and Cork and Lewis had each claimed a wicket. That was the end of England's joy for the day. By the close, India had reached 287 for 2 from 90 overs. Ganguly had made 136, and Tendulkar 123. In making centuries in his first two Test innings, Ganguly became the first batsman since Kallicharran 24 years earlier to achieve such a feat. The pitch was one of those that bowlers 'watered with their tears', and Ganguly, having proved himself at Lord's, batted with a fluency that made him a worthy and admirable partner for Tendulkar who, having been dropped by Atherton in the gully before he had scored, gave a masterly display of batting and was the first to reach three figures.

Only one run had been added to the overnight score when, in the third over on Friday morning, Ganguly was out. He was hit on the fingers by Mullally and required treatment. The next delivery he sliced to Hussain in the gully. It was a disappointing end to a fine innings which had seen the young left-hander hit 17 fours and two sixes from the 268 balls he faced.

Manjrekar came in at number five, and neither he nor Tendulkar could recapture the brisk run rate of the previous day. Soon, however, Tendulkar was asserting himself, and it seemed that he would register his first double century in Test cricket. However, he had hit 26 fours and batted for 462 minutes when he tried to pull the 360th ball he faced from outside the off stump. He succeeded only in lofting a catch to mid-on to give Ealham his first Test wicket.

Azharuddin came and went in 11 balls, well caught at short-leg when he jabbed at a rising ball from Lewis. Dravid and Manjrekar added 61 before England captured three wickets for seven runs. Dravid then farmed the bowling in a mature manner and appeared likely to claim the century that had eluded him at Lord's, but he was last out, having made 84 off 149 balls with 12 fours. If India now have worries concerning their bowling, they should have none with regard to their batting since the arrival of Ganguly and Dravid on this tour.

India's 521 was the second highest score that they have made in a Test match in England and the stand of 255 between Ganguly and Tendulkar was the highest for any wicket for India against England.

England considered themselves a little unfortunate in that umpire Francis from Sri Lanka refused requests for lbw on numerous occasions. Dominic Cork felt particularly hard done by, but he is his own worst enemy with his constant appeals when the ball is clearly missing leg stump, and each demand accompanied by a theatricality reminiscent of Sir Donald Wolfit on a bad day.

In the last 11 overs of the second day, England enjoyed much fortune. Srinath and Venkatesh Prasad once more posed problems, but Atherton was put down at third slip by Dravid off Srinath before he had scored. Atherton and Stewart made an uneasy 32 and lived to fight another day.

In fact, they lived to fight until after lunch on Saturday when Stewart was given out caught behind by umpire Francis when he was clearly nowhere near the ball with bat or glove. That was the only wicket to fall during the day by the end of which England were 322 for 1, Atherton was 145, Hussain 107 and the match and the series were effectively dead.

The third Test match at Trent Bridge. India's two centurions Sachin Tendulkar and Saurav Ganguly congratulate each other. The pair added 255, the highest partnership by Indian batsmen against England. (Stuart Franklin/ASP)

Third Cornhill Test Match – England v. India

4, 5, 6, 8 and 9 July 1996 at Trent Bridge, Nottingham

India

	First Innings		Second Innings	
V. Rathore	c Russell, b Cork	4	absent hurt	–
*N.R. Mongia	c Russell, b Lewis	9	(1) c Lewis, b Mullally	45
S.C. Ganguly	c Hussain, b Mullally	136	b Cork	48
S.R. Tendulkar	c Patel, b Ealham	177	c Stewart, b Lewis	74
S.V. Manjrekar	c Hick, b Patel	53	(2) c Stewart, b Lewis	11
M. Azharuddin (Capt)	c Patel, b Lewis	5	c Cork, b Ealham	8
R.S. Dravid	c Russell, b Ealham	84	(5) c Thorpe, b Mullally	8
A.R. Kumble	lbw, b Mullally	0	(7) lbw, b Ealham	2
J. Srinath	c Cork, b Lewis	1	(8) c Thorpe, b Ealham	3
Venkatesh Prasad	run out	13	(9) not out	0
Venkatapathy Raju	not out	1	(10) c sub (Gie), b Ealham	0
	b 6, lb 12, w 7, nb 13	38	b 1, lb 1, w 1, nb 9	12
		521		211

	O	M	R	W	O	M	R	W
Lewis	37	10	89	3	14	4	50	2
Cork	32	6	124	1	7	–	32	1
Mullally	40	12	88	2	13	3	36	2
Ealham	29	9	90	2	14	5	21	4
Patel	24	2	101	1	12	3	47	–
Hick	4	1	8	–	9	4	23	–
Thorpe	1	–	3	–				

Fall of Wickets
1–7, 2–33, 3–288, 4–377, 5–385, 6–446, 7–447, 8–453, 9–513
1–17, 2–103, 3–140, 4–160, 5–204, 6–208, 7–208, 8–211, 9–211

England

	First Innings	
M.A. Atherton (Capt)	c Manjrekar, b Prasad	160
A.J. Stewart	c Mongia, b Srinath	50
N. Hussain	retired hurt	107
G.P. Thorpe	lbw, b Ganguly	45
G.A. Hick	c Srinath, b Venkatapathy Raju	20
M.A. Ealham	c sub (Jadeja), b Srinath	51
*R.C. Russell	c Mongia, b Venkatesh Prasad	0
C.C. Lewis	lbw, b Kumble	21
D.G. Cork	not out	32
M.M. Patel	c Manjrekar, b Ganguly	27
A.D. Mullally	c Mongia, b Ganguly	1
	b 18, lb 18, nb 14	50
		564

	O	M	R	W
Srinath	47	12	131	2
Venkatesh Prasad	43	12	124	2
Kumble	39	6	98	1
Venkatapathy Raju	43	12	76	1
Ganguly	19.5	2	71	3
Tendulkar	7	–	28	–

Fall of Wickets
1–130, 2–360, 3–396, 4–444, 5–444, 6–491, 7–497, 8–558, 9–564
N. Hussain retired hurt at 322 for 1

Umpires: K.T. Francis & G. Sharp

Match drawn

Test Match Averages
England v. India

England Batting

	M	Inns	NO	Runs	HS	Av	100s	50s
N. Hussain	3	5	1	318	128	79.50	2	
M.A. Atherton	3	5	1	263	160	65.75	1	
G.P. Thorpe	3	5	1	193	89	48.25		1
A.J. Stewart	2	3	–	136	66	45.33		2
R.C. Russell	3	4	–	162	124	40.50	1	
C.C. Lewis	3	4	1	78	31	26.00		
R.C. Irani	2	3	–	76	41	25.33		
M.M. Patel	2	2	–	45	27	22.50		
A.D. Mullally	3	4	3	15	14*	15.00		
D.G. Cork	3	4	1	37	32*	12.33		
G.A. Hick	3	4	–	35	20	8.75		

(Played in one Test: M.A. Ealham 51; N.V. Knight 27 & 14; P.J. Martin 23 & 4)

India Batting

	M	Inns	NO	Runs	HS	Av	100s	50s
S.C. Ganguly	2	3	–	315	136	105.00	2	
S.R. Tendulkar	3	5	–	428	177	85.60	2	1
R.S. Dravid	2	3	–	187	95	62.33		2
P.L. Mhambrey	2	3	1	58	28	29.00		
S.V. Manjrekar	2	4	–	105	53	26.25		1
N.R. Mongia	3	5	–	107	45	21.40		
J. Srinath	3	5	–	76	52	15.20		1
V. Rathore	3	4	–	46	20	11.50		
Venkatesh Prasad	3	5	3	17	13	8.50		
M. Azharuddin	3	5	–	42	16	8.40		
A.R. Kumble	3	5	–	36	15	7.20		
A.D. Jadeja	2	3	–	16	10	5.33		

(Played in one Test: S.B. Joshi 12 & 12; Venkatapathy Raju 1* & 0)

England Bowling

	Overs	Mds	Runs	Wks	Av	Best	10/m	5/inn
M.A. Ealham	43	14	111	6	18.50	4/21		
C.C. Lewis	131.4	33	356	15	23.73	5/72		1
A.D. Mullally	129	40	298	12	24.83	3/60		
D.G. Cork	120.4	26	369	10	36.90	4/61		
R.C. Irani	21	7	74	2	37.00	1/22		
M.M. Patel	46	8	180	1	180.00	1/10		
G.A. Hick	19	6	51	–	–			

(Bowled in one innings: P.J. Martin 34–10–70–1; G.P. Thorpe 1–0–3–0)

India Bowling

	Overs	Mds	Runs	Wks	Av	Best	10/m	5/inn
S.C. Ganguly	37.5	4	125	6	20.83	3/71		
Venkatesh Prasad	142.3	39	375	15	25.00	5/76		1
J. Srinath	152.1	37	433	11	39.36	4/103		
A.R. Kumble	147	36	334	5	66.80	3/90		
P.L. Mhambrey	43	6	148	2	74.00	1/43		
S.R. Tendulkar	9	1	29	–	–			

(Bowled in one innings: Venkatapathy Raju 43–12–76–1)

England Fielding Figures

8 – R.C. Russell; 5 – G.P. Thorpe; 4 – N.V. Knight; 3 – N. Hussain and A.J. Stewart;
2 – M.A. Atherton, D.G. Cork, M.M. Patel and G.A. Hick; 1 – C.C. Lewis and sub (N.A. Gie)

India Fielding Figures

8 – N.R. Mongia; 5 – V. Rathore; 3 – J. Srinath; 2 – S.V. Manjrekar and S.R. Tendulkar;
1 – R.S. Dravid (plus one as sub), A.D. Jadeja (plus one as sub), P.L. Mhambrey and M. Azharuddin

England's centurions in the third Test, Mike Atherton and Nasser Hussain. Hussain was named as England's Man of the Series for his two centuries in three Tests. Ganguly took India's award. Watching Atherton and Hussain leave the field is Srinath who bowled magnificently throughout the series with no luck whatsoever.
(Ross Kinnaird/Allsport)

Atherton did not bat well, but he showed immense determination and emerged from his barren spell. He was aided by umpire Francis' reluctance to give anyone out leg before. Hussain did bat well and simply added to the sense of bewilderment one has that he was ever exiled from Test cricket for so long.

Hussain did not resume on the Monday, for it was discovered that he had sustained a broken finger during his innings on the Saturday. This was a pity, for he might have enlivened what was a meaningless, desultory day. Atherton was dropped at slip by Rathore who then joined Azharuddin in the injury room: Azharuddin had been hit on the ankle while fielding; Rathore dislocated his shoulder throwing. Atherton, having batted just under eight hours, was caught at third slip, and Thorpe was out immediately after lunch. Hick went into a period of inertia before hitting lazily to mid-on, and Russell was caught behind fifth ball. Ealham reached a pleasant fifty in his first Test, and by the end of the day, England were 29 runs ahead and had lost seven wickets. With one day to go, one side was still engaged in its first innings. Is this really the type of pitch on which the TCCB wants Test cricket to be played? We had suffered similar boredom at The Oval in 1995.

For reasons not readily apparent, a handful of spectators arrived for the last day's play. Ganguly took the last two wickets to confirm his standing as the find of the tour, and he then hit 48 off 86 balls with eight fours before playing on to Cork, who is in great danger of being burned out for so much is demanded of him.

Tendulkar batted with great panache, hit a six and 11 fours and made 74 off 97 balls before falling to a careless shot, but nothing can dim his splendour. Sadly, Azharuddin's brightness was almost totally extinguished on this tour, and he perished yet again as Ealham enjoyed a spell of four wickets in 17 balls to complete a satisfactory Test debut. His Kent colleague Patel had no reason to rejoice. The last day had found him wanting.

England won the series, and David Lloyd had marshalled the side well, but certain questions remained unanswered: Hick? an opener? a place for Irani? and, above all, a spinner of quality? The second half of the summer, one felt, would provide more testing opposition.

India in England, 1996 First-Class Matches

Batting

Batting	v. Worcestershire (Worcester) 8–10 May		v. Gloucestershire (Bristol) 11–13 May		v. Sussex (Hove) 16–18 May		v. Essex (Chelmsford) 28–30 May		v. Leicestershire (Leicester) 1–3 June		First Test Match (Edgbaston) 6–10 June		v. Derbyshire (Derby) 13–16 June		Second Test Match (Lord's) 20–24 June		v. British Universities (Cambridge) 26–28 June		v. Hampshire (Southampton) 29 June–1 July		Third Test Match (Trent Bridge) 4–9 July		M	Inns	NO	Runs	HS	Av
V. Rathore	165	72	63	1			95	18	71	91	20	7	2	16	15	–	54	16	95	–	4	–	10	17	–	805	165	47.35
A.D. Jadeja	22	105*			6	0	7	87			0	6	17	26	10	–	112*	–	91	–			8	13	2	489	112*	44.45
S.V. Manjrekar	0	27	55	–	66*	1	32	48	40	65*	23	18					101	–	0	–	53	11	9	15	2	540	101	41.53
S.R. Tendulkar	52	–			85	67	74	1			24	122			31	–			0	–	177	74	7	11	–	707	177	64.27
M. Azharuddin	68	–	13	10					111*	72*	13	0	21	29	16	–	73	–			5	8	8	13	2	439	111*	39.90
S.C. Ganguly	19*	14*	0	64*	–	35*	51	34*					14	64	131	–	52	–	100*	–	136	48	9	14	6	762	136	95.25
N.R. Mongia	11*	–							22	24	20	9	74*	20	24	–	21	85			9	45	7	12	2	364	85	36.40
A.R. Kumble	–	–	6	1					–	–	5	15	5	5	14	–			59*	–	0	2	8	10	1	112	59*	12.44
P.L. Mhambrey	–	–			–	–	1	24*	–	–	28	15	4	1	15*	–	15*	8*					8	9	4	111	28	22.20
Venkatesh Prasad	–	–	2	–			6*	–			0*	0*			4	–			–	–	13	0*	7	7	4	25	13	8.33
N.D. Hirwani	–	–			–	–	–	–									–	–	–	–			5					–
N.S. Sidhu			115	16	14	26																	2	4	–	171	115	42.75
R.S. Dravid			86*	28	7*	44*	17	6	58*	12			0	7	95	–	0	101*	0	–	84	8	9	16	5	553	101*	50.27
S.B. Joshi			15	2	–	–	22	0	–	4*	12	12											5	7	1	67	22	11.16
J. Srinath			29	21*	–	–			–	–	52	1	1	1	19	–					1	3	7	9	1	128	52	16.00
Venkatapathy Raju			0*	–	–	–	1*	–	–	–			31	0*			–	–	–	–	1*	0	8	6	3	33	31	11.00
S.A. Ankola									–	–			45	0			–	8	–	–			4	3	–	53	45	17.66
Byes		4	2							4	3	4	1	4	11		12	7	2		6	1						
Leg-byes	3	7	12		2	3	5	1		1	10	9	4	9	25		12		6		12	1						
Wides	1	1	8	1	5		3		1				2		10		3	6	1		7	1						
No-balls	8	10				8	6	4	2		4	1	8	10	9		2		8		13	9						
Total	349	240	406	144	185	184	320	223	305	273	214	219	229	192	429		457	231	362		521	211						
Wickets	5	2	10	6	3	4	8	6	3	3	10	10	10	10	10		10	3	5		10	9						
Result	D		D		D		D		D		L		L		D		D		D		D							

Fielding Figures

14 – N.R. Mongia (ct 13 / st 1)
9 – V. Rathore
7 – R.S. Dravid (ct 6 / st 1)
6 – A.D. Jadeja
5 – S.R. Tendulkar
4 – Venkatesh Prasad and S.V. Manjrekar
3 – J. Srinath and M. Azharuddin
2 – P.L. Mhambrey and subs
1 – S.C. Ganguly, N.D. Hirwani and A.R. Kumble

Bowling

Bowling	Venkatesh Prasad	P.L. Mhambrey	A.R. Kumble	N.D. Hirwani	S.C. Ganguly	A.D. Jadeja	J. Srinath	Venkatapathy Raju	S.B. Joshi	S.R. Tendulkar	S.A. Ankola	Byes	Leg-byes	Wides	No-balls	Total	Wkts
v. Worcestershire (Worcester)	29–5–93–2	23–5–103–1	32–4–123–2	21–3–116–0	7–2–13–1	5–1–18–0						5	5		8	476	6
8–10 May																	
v. Gloucestershire (Bristol)	14–2–40–0		18–2–59–1				16–5–58–3	8–1–35–0	8–2–47–0			5	7			251	4
11–13 May	17–3–38–3		10–5–16–0		6–0–37–1		19–8–27–3	10–4–10–1	3–1–8–0			21	1		6	138	8
v. Sussex (Hove)		7–1–34–0		10.4–4–21–2	12–1–70–1	3–0–10–0	12–7–26–0	13–3–19–0	13–2–33–0	9–1–28–1		1	5	1	40	247	4
16–18 May		13–3–27–0		9–1–28–0	1–0–8–0	1–0–2–0	4–3–4–0	11–3–58–0	14–1–84–2	3–0–20–0			3		6	234	2
v. Essex (Chelmsford)	11–2–57–1	10–5–23–2		16–3–53–1	4–0–19–0			19–6–62–1	14–3–50–0	1–1–0–0		5			4	269	5
28–30 May	14–1–63–2	8–1–24–0		9–4–24–2	3–0–12–0			7–2–27–0	8–0–41–2	2–1–7–0		8	1			207	6
v. Leicestershire (Leicester)		7–0–57–0	18–4–55–1				15–4–44–2	16–5–52–0	7.3–0–54–1		10–2–37–0	5	14		12	318	5
1–3 June																	
First Test Match (Edgbaston)	28–9–71–4	1–0–43–1	24–4–77–1				28.2–5–103–4					16	3		7	313	10
6–10 June	14–0–50–2		5–3–9–0				14.5–3–47–0					8	7			121	2
v. Derbyshire (Derby)		25–3–118–2	39–15–111–4		6–0–20–0		15.2–4–36–1	1–0–5–0			24–2–91–2	3	25	3	41	409	10
13–16 June					1.5–0–12–0	2–1–1–0										13	0
Second Test Match (Lord's)	33.3–10–76–5	19–3–58–0	28–9–60–0		15–2–49–2		33–9–76–3			2–1–1–0		13	11		14	344	10
20–24 June	24–8–54–2	14–3–47–1	51–4–90–3		3–0–5–1		29–8–76–2					1	5		5	278	9
v. British Universities (Cambridge)		10–1–38–1		29.5–8–60–6	2–0–19–0			21–8–45–1			12–2–37–2	12	6	1	6	217	10
26–28 June																	
v. Hampshire (Southampton)	25–7–68–2		17–7–41–0	20–1–73–1	5–3–5–1			23–3–75–1		4–1–25–0	30–3–120–4	23	28	2	4	458	9
29 June–1 July																	
Third Test Match (Trent Bridge)	43–12–124–2		39–6–98–1		19.5–2–71–3		43–12–131–2	43–12–76–1		7–0–28–0		18	18		14	564	9
4–9 July																	
Bowler's average	252.3–59– 734–25 29.36	146–25– 572–8 71.50	281–73– 739–13 56.84	115.3–24– 375–12 31.25	85.4–10– 340–10 34.00	11–2– 31–0 –	233.3–68– 628–20 31.40	172–47– 464–5 92.80	67.3–9– 317–5 63.40	28–5– 109–1 109.00	76–9– 285–8 35.62						

Pakistan Tour of England

Test and Texaco Series

For Pakistan, the cricket year had not started well. Defeat at the hands of Sri Lanka had been followed by defeat in Australia. In Sydney, and later in New Zealand, there had been a resurgence – only to be dampened by the disappointment of the World Cup.

This disappointment had tended to strengthen resolve. Majid Khan had become Chief Executive of the Pakistan Cricket Board and had made an immediate impact. He pledged to improve the standard of domestic cricket, and the party chosen to tour England brought little criticism. It seemed that the factions and disagreements of the past had disappeared. The party was chosen on merit, and, refreshingly, it was united under the leadership of Wasim Akram, who had Aamir Sohail as his vice-captain. The middle-order batting, for so long an Achilles heel, looked more solid, and the attack was balanced. It had pace second to none in the world, and the spin of Mushtaq Ahmed and the young Saqlain Mushtaq would pose problems for any international batsmen. It was apparent that England would find Pakistan stiffer opposition than India had provided.

27 June
at Trowbridge
England NCA 182 for 6 (D.R. Clarke 65 not out)
Pakistanis 183 for 2 (Aamir Sohail 104)
Pakistanis won by 8 wickets

The Pakistan tourists began their tour with victory over a team of club and Minor County cricketers. A fifth wicket partnership of 68 in 13 overs between Clarke and Laudat helped towards a respectable total after NCA had elected to bat first on winning the toss, but Pakistan needed only 30.2 of their 50 overs to reach their target. Aamir Sohail and Saeed Anwar made 131 in 18 overs for the first wicket, and Aamir's 104 came off 77 balls.

29, 30 June and 1 July
at Pontypridd
Glamorgan 304 (S.P. James 79, Ata-ur-Rehman 4 for 82) and 60 for 2
Pakistanis 461 for 2 dec. (Saeed Anwar 219 not out, Inzamam-ul-Haq 169 not out)
Match drawn

A lively looking Pakistan attack bowled out Glamorgan in 79 overs. The tourists themselves were 99 for 2 with Ijaz Ahmed going first ball. Saaed Anwar, in astonishing form, and Inzamam-ul-Haq joined in an unbroken third wicket partnership of 362 in five hours. This is the highest partnership by any Pakistani pair in England and equals the highest for any wicket against Glamorgan. Saeed hit a six and 31 fours, and his form and fitness was of great importance to Pakistan, for he had been forced to miss the tour of Australia with a stomach complaint. Inzamam-ul-Haq, too, was in devastating form and reached 100 off 132 balls. Rain ruined the last day's play in this splendidly entertaining, sportingly competitive and very well organised match.

The Pakistan touring side in England, 1996: (back row) Mushtaq Ahmed, Saeed Anwar, Rashid Latif, Saqlain Mushtaq, Inzamam-ul-Haq, Shahid Anwar, Mohammad Akram, Ata-ur-Rehman, Shahid Nazir, Moin Khan, Shadab Kabir, Dr Dan Kiesel (physiotherapist); (front row) Ijaz Ahmed, Waqar Younis, Aamir Sohail, Yawar Saeed (manager), Wasim Akram (captain), Nasin-ul-Ghani (cricket manager), Salim Malik, Asif Mujtaba. (Patrick Eagar).

3, 4 and 5 July

at Taunton
Pakistanis 300 for 7 dec. (Saeed Anwar 130, Asif Mujtaba 54, S. Lee 4 for 65) and 174 for 1 dec. (Saeed Anwar 60, Inzamam-ul-Haq 51 not out)
Somerset 159 (P.D. Bowler 68, Mushtaq Ahmed 5 for 36) and 210 (S.C. Ecclestone 57, P.D. Bowler 52, Mushtaq Ahmed 5 for 72)
Pakistanis won by 105 runs

Saeed Anwar produced another sparkling innings and shared a third wicket stand of 157 with Asif Mujtaba. Saeed hit 21 fours in his 130. Shane Lee took three wickets in 18 balls, and Pakistan closed on 263 for 5. Somerset struggled on the second day with only Bowler offering resistance to Mushtaq Ahmed and Waqar Younis. There was a sense of purpose about the Pakistani cricket, and they cracked 107 for 1 in 25 overs before the end of the day with Saeed again hitting sweetly. The declaration came after ten overs on the last morning, and Somerset were asked to make 316 in 78 overs. Waqar was withdrawn from the attack as a precaution after a slight hamstring injury, but Mushtaq Ahmed was too much for his county colleagues and finished with match figures of 10 for 108. The game was over at 4.25pm. There was consolation for Somerset in that Mushtaq signed a new contract and will return to the county in 1997.

6, 7 and 8 July

at Northampton
Northamptonshire 152 (Wasim Akram 5 for 58, Shahid Nazir 4 for 43) and 396 for 4 dec. (R.R. Montgomerie 168, A. Fordham 144 retired hurt)
Pakistanis 323 (Shadab Kabir 99, Saqlain Mushtaq 78, D.J. Capel 4 for 60) and 205 for 8 (Shadab Kabir 52)
Match drawn

Northamptonshire reached 89 before the fall of their first wicket and saw all ten go down for 63 runs. Shahid Nazir bowled commendably, but the Northamptonshire demise was really brought about by Wasim Akram who bowled very quickly in taking 5 for 14 in 40 deliveries. On the second day, the 19-year-old Shadab Kabir batted quite beautifully, and he and Saqlain Mushtaq added 171 for the eighth wicket, a record against Northamptonshire. The game was transformed when the county batted again. Montgomerie and Fordham scored 255 for the first wicket, and the partnership only ended when Fordham retired. He later endorsed his retirement with 'hurt' when he discovered a spot of eye trouble. The stand was aided by some friendly bowling, but there was nothing friendly about a declaration which asked the tourists to score 226 in 33 overs. It was a measure of Wasim's determination to attempt to win every match that his side came heroically close to the target.

11 July

at Stone
Pakistanis 310 for 7 (Aamir Sohail 133)
Minor Counties 140 for 8
Pakistanis won by 170 runs

The tourists showed no mercy in the 50-over match against Minor Counties. Aamir Sohail hit 133 off 102 balls, and his innings included two sixes and 21 fours. He hit Saggers for five fours in one over.

14 July

at Shenley
Pakistanis 230 for 7 (Wasim Akram 74)
MCC 63 for 8
Pakistanis won on faster run rate

Rain ruined the 50-over match on the beautiful Compton Ground at Shenley. Wasim Akram and Moin Khan added 112 for Pakistan's sixth wicket.

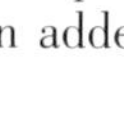

17, 18 and 19 July

at Edgbaston
Pakistanis 297 (Saeed Anwar 131, Inzamam-ul-Haq 51) and 158 (Ijaz Ahmed 52)
Warwickshire 310 (D.R. Brown 76, T.L. Penney 66, Mushtaq Ahmed 7 for 91) and 148 for 3 (N.V. Knight 90 not out)
Warwickshire won by 7 wickets

The Pakistanis suffered their first defeat of the tour, but they again won friends. Saeed Anwar's brilliance continued with a century before lunch on the first day. He hit three sixes and 20 fours. Pakistan made 187 for 2 from the first 36 overs of their innings, but the next 37.4 overs produced only 110 runs as eight wickets fell. Brown and Penney scored 142 in 34 overs for the sixth wicket to give Warwickshire's innings substance. There was again some top quality leg-spin bowling from Mushtaq Ahmed, but Waqar Younis was absent from the Pakistani attack. The visitors collapsed in their second innings, and Warwickshire were steered to victory by Nick Knight who thereby enhanced his chances of a recall to the Test side.

20, 21 and 22 July

at Canterbury
Kent 262 (D.P. Fulton 58, T.R. Ward 58, M.A. Ealham 57, Wasim Akram 4 for 74) and 200 (Saqlain Mushtaq 4 for 43)
Pakistanis 194 (Rashid Latif 61, M.A. Ealham 4 for 48) and 269 for 2 (Ijaz Ahmed 136 not out, Shadab Kabir 84)
Pakistanis won by 8 wickets

The Pakistanis won a brilliant victory at Canterbury after trailing Kent by 68 runs on the first innings. Kent's first knock on the Saturday was something of a stop/start affair, but by the end of the day the county were well on top. Ealham grabbed three wickets to follow his 57, and the tourists closed on 74 for 5. Rashid Latif effected something of a recovery on the Sunday, and the Pakistan bowlers then took control. Wasim Akram and Ata-ur-Rehman made early inroads while Shahid Nazir and Saqlain Mushtaq kept the middle order on a tight rein. The outcome was that the tourists were left the last day in which to score 269 to win. They needed just over two sessions. Ijaz Ahmed was at his most dominant, hitting 136 off 163 balls. He hit four sixes, one of which was the winning hit, and 19 fours. The precocious Shadab Kabir gave further evidence of his talent with 84 off 177 balls, an innings which included 12 fours.

The Kent supporters were less than happy to learn that Ray Illingworth had been quoted as saying that Patel was not a Test match bowler. Yet another opportunity to remain silent had been lost.

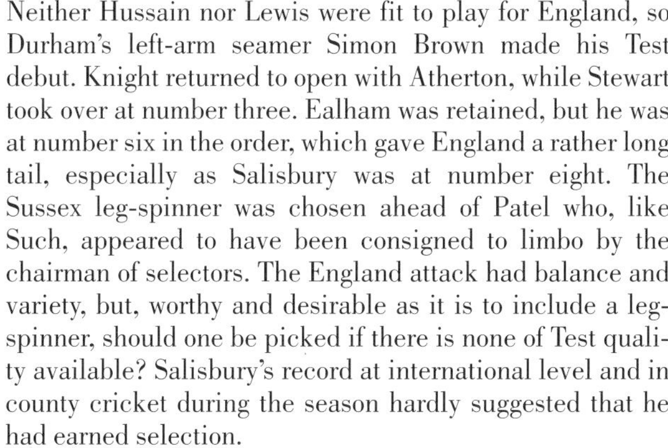

First Test Match

England *v.* Pakistan *at Lord's*

Neither Hussain nor Lewis were fit to play for England, so Durham's left-arm seamer Simon Brown made his Test debut. Knight returned to open with Atherton, while Stewart took over at number three. Ealham was retained, but he was at number six in the order, which gave England a rather long tail, especially as Salisbury was at number eight. The Sussex leg-spinner was chosen ahead of Patel who, like Such, appeared to have been consigned to limbo by the chairman of selectors. The England attack had balance and variety, but, worthy and desirable as it is to include a leg-spinner, should one be picked if there is none of Test quality available? Salisbury's record at international level and in county cricket during the season hardly suggested that he had earned selection.

Pakistan gave a Test debut to Shadab Kabir in preference to the left-handed Asif Mujtaba and chose Ata-ur-Rehman as third seamer in a four-man attack that would be

Atherton's defiant innings is brought to an end when he is caught at slip by Asif Mujtaba off Mushtaq Ahmed for 64. After Atherton's dismissal came the deluge. (David Munden/Sportsline)

supplemented by the left-arm spin of Aamir Sohail. Wasim Akram won the toss, and Pakistan batted on a dry, slow, true pitch which always looked as if it would produce a result.

Saeed Anwar steered the first ball of the third over to third man for four, but swung lavishly at the next delivery and was fortunate to escape. Aamir Sohail was less lucky. He offered no shot to Brown's tenth ball in Test cricket and was adjudged leg before although he was hit rather high. Further disaster followed for Pakistan when Ijaz Ahmed was bowled by Cork. It was an astonishing dismissal. The batsman moved right across his wicket to turn the ball to leg and was bowled middle stump behind his legs.

Ijaz was out on the third ball of the seventh over of the innings. The next wicket to fall was that of Saeed Anwar on the fourth ball of the 40th over, by which time the score had progressed from 12 to 142. Uninhibited by the loss of Ijaz, Saeed and Inzamam-ul-Haq played some glorious attacking cricket. Twice in one over, Saeed flicked Brown off his legs for four, and Inzamam was truly regal as he drove through the covers and then hit Cork square for four on either side of the wicket. When Salisbury joined the attack in the 17th over, Inzamam drove him straight for four and flicked him nonchalantly through mid-wicket to the boundary. The hundred came up on the first ball of the last over before lunch. Saeed's fifty followed next ball, and Pakistan were 112 for 2 from 30 overs at the interval. Saeed had scored 59, Inzamam-ul-Haq 48.

Inzamam's fifty came two overs after the break with a wonderful off-drive off Brown. He repeated the shot in the same over, and all he did was with an economy of movement. This was batting that touched the heart with its beauty. There was no brutality as the ball was caressed to all parts of the field.

Ealham was steady but ineffective. He rarely looked like conceding many runs, but he never looked like taking a

Inzamam-ul-Haq on his way to a majestic 148 drives Salisbury through the covers. (Adrian Murrell/Allsport)

Mark Ealham is bowled round his legs by Mushtaq Ahmed, whose five wickets were a match-winning contribution for Pakistan. (Adrian Murrell/Allsport)

wicket. Mullally strayed too often down the leg side. Hick was brought on from the Pavilion End, and Saeed Anwar cut at his fourth ball to offer a catch to Russell, which was accepted at the second attempt.

Salim Malik offered a difficult chance to Ealham at short mid-off before he scored, and was then needlessly run out by the length of the pitch when he unwisely suggested a second run. Salisbury's throw to Russell left him stranded. The afternoon became generally passive, punctuated by some majestic shots from Inzamam. Atherton manipulated his bowlers thoughtfully, and at tea Pakistan were 193 for 4 from 59 overs.

Shadab Kabir batted soundly in his first Test innings, but Inzamam was too often denied the strike. He seized the initiative after tea as he went down the pitch and hit Hick to long-on to bring up the 200, and two balls later hit a six in the same position to reach a glorious hundred.

Shadab Kabir did not add to his tea-time score and was leg before when he played across the line to Cork, who was grossly overworked. Wasim was lucky to escape the same fate, but he was not so lucky a second time when Ealham trapped him leg before. Mullally had now discovered a better line, and, at 267, he bowled Inzamam-ul-Haq off an inside edge. Inzamam had hit a six and 19 fours in his 218-ball innings. His 148 was his highest Test score, and for a minute under five hours he had batted with composure and majesty. This was a knock of the highest quality.

Pakistan now lost their way as Mullally had Mushtaq caught behind and dismissed Waqar in the last over of the day to complete a spell of 3 for 14. Pakistan ended on 290 for 9, and England could claim to have won the first round.

Optimism began to evaporate at the start of the second day. For 75 minutes, Rashid Latif and Ata-ur-Rehman not only held England at bay but batted with style and purpose. Rashid is a good player whose batting has yet to realise its full potential, but he showed good sense and good technique as well as some attractive shots as he dominated a last wicket stand that was worth 50. Ata-ur-Rehman is a sensible and correct cricketer, and he played his part admirably in this vital stand, which was ended when Salisbury pitched a leg-break in the right spot and had Rashid taken at slip.

England lost Atherton in the fifth over of their innings, leg before to Wasim. At lunch, the score was 32 for 1. Knight does not suggest that he has the technical competence to thrive at international level, but he does have confidence and a good temperament which could serve him well for a while. He hit seven fours and seemingly reached 50 when he edged a Mushtaq googly through the slips just past Aamir Sohail's clutching hand. He had begun to acknowledge applause when umpire Willey signalled leg-byes. Three overs later, he was palpably leg before to Waqar without having added to his score, and he trudged off sulking. Later he was credited with the two 'leg-byes' and awarded his 50, but what if Aamir had caught the ball? The third umpire would then have had no power to intervene. The position of the third official is, at present, a confused one.

The fall of Knight heralded an England collapse. Stewart, who does not read the leg-spinner well, offered no stroke to Mushtaq's googly and was emphatically leg before. Hick was out shortly after tea, the victim of a magnificent yorker from Waqar, and England had lost three wickets for nine. Ealham is a calm and sensible cricketer, and he stayed with Thorpe for 80 minutes, helping to add 64 and to ease the tension. A lapse in concentration saw him flash at a wide ball from Ata-ur-Rehman and give Rashid a catch. Russell battled out the last half hour of the day, and England closed on 200 for 5, Thorpe 43, Russell 4.

The beginning of the third day offered little comfort to England. Russell was beaten five times in one over by Waqar, who must have wondered what he had to do to earn the wicket. Russell survived, and so did Thorpe, who batted with that serene technical assurance that makes one wonder why he does not score a hundred every time he goes to the wicket. England's hopes rested heavily upon him, and he was responding coolly when, having batted for four hours, he was bowled off the inside edge by Ata-ur-Rehman. Once

Russell caught by Rashid Latif off the bowling of Man of the Match Waqar Younis. For England the end is nigh. (Patrick Eagar)

again Thorpe had failed to deliver the complete product after promising so much.

Pakistan had exposed the England tail, and Cork chased a wide delivery to be caught at second slip. Salisbury soon fell to Waqar's yorker, and Mullally's bails were sent flying by a high inswinging full toss. Sixteen valuable runs came after lunch before Brown's stumps were wrecked by Ata-ur-Rehman, who deserved his four wickets.

Aamir Sohail had damaged his wrist while fielding, and Shadab Kabir was promoted to open with Saeed Anwar. Where batting had looked painfully difficult it now looked easy. In the 22 overs available to them before tea, Saeed, 51, and Shadab, 14, hit 78. Eighteen years old and playing in his first Test, Shadab showed fine powers of concentration and was the perfect foil for Saeed, who hit a six and eight fours as he raced to 88 before touching Mullally to the 'keeper. Shadab immediately followed suit, but, although Pakistan lost night-watchman Mushtaq before the close, they finished on 162 for 3, the game very much in their grasp.

In spite of limping because of a leg injury sustained when he was struck while fielding, Inzamam-ul-Haq again batted with consummate authority and added 118 with Ijaz Ahmed, who atoned for his first innings lapse with an innings of grace, style and aggression. Predictably, Wasim's declaration allowed his bowlers four sessions in which to account for England, who were set the unlikely target of 408.

In the sixth over of the England innings, Knight went back to Waqar and was clearly leg before. Stewart and Atherton did well to keep out yorkers from Waqar, and their confidence increased as they reached 74 by the close to give England every chance of saving the game.

That England would save the game appeared increasingly likely when Atherton and Stewart negotiated the prelunch session of the final day with few alarms and 78 runs. They began the afternoon with something of a flourish, but Mushtaq Ahmed, having bowled over the wicket, changed to round and attempted to pitch into the leg-stump rough. At two o'clock, Mushtaq turned a ball from outside Atherton's leg-stump that drifted across the batsman's body, clipped the outside edge and was taken at slip. Atherton had been at the crease for 279 minutes, and he and Stewart had added 154. It was a partnership of both skill and character, but once it was broken it was if the floodgates were open.

Wasim had instilled discipline and patience into his side, and, for once, England was seeing a Pakistan team that was in harmony. There was great spirit in the side, and that spirit found expression in a dynamic desire to win. Having dismissed Atherton in his 25th over, Mushtaq accounted for Stewart in his 26th, the batsman being caught off his glove as he played no shot at a ball that lifted sharply out of the rough. Hick was most fortunate to survive an appeal for a catch two balls later, but his fortune did not last long. Waqar's second ball to him scattered his stumps as he offered only limp resistance. It was apparent that Hick's Test career, at least in the short term, was at an end.

First Cornhill Test Match – England v. Pakistan

25, 26, 27, 28 and 29 July 1996 at Lord's

Pakistan

	First Innings		Second Innings	
Aamir Sohail	lbw, **b** Brown	**2**		
Saeed Anwar	**c** Russell, **b** Hick	**74**	(1) **c** Russell, **b** Mullally	**88**
Ijaz Ahmed	**b** Cork	**1**	lbw, **b** Cork	**76**
Inzamam-ul-Haq	**b** Mullally	**148**	(5) **c** Ealham, **b** Cork	**70**
Salim Malik	run out	**7**	(6) not out	**27**
Shadab Kabir	lbw, **b** Cork	**17**	(2) **c** Russell, **b** Cork	**33**
Wasim Akram (Capt)	lbw, **b** Ealham	**10**	not out	**34**
*Rashid Latif	**c** Hick, **b** Salisbury	**45**		
Mushtaq Ahmed	**c** Russell, **b** Mullally	**11**	(4) **c** Thorpe, **b** Brown	**5**
Waqar Younis	**c** Brown, **b** Mullally	**4**		
Ata-ur-Rehman	not out	**10**		
	b **3**, lb **5**, nb **3**	**11**	b **4**, lb **14**, nb **1**	**19**
		340	(for 5 wickets, dec.)	**352**

	O	M	R	W	O	M	R	W
Cork	28	6	100	**2**	24	4	86	**3**
Brown	17	2	78	**1**	16	2	60	**1**
Mullally	24	8	44	**3**	30.2	9	70	**1**
Salisbury	12.2	1	42	**1**	20	4	63	**–**
Ealham	21	4	42	**1**	16	4	39	**–**
Hick	6	–	26	**1**	7	2	16	**–**

Fall of Wickets
1–**7**, 2–**12**, 3–**142**, 4–**153**, 5–**209**, 6–**257**, 7–**267**, 8–**280**, 9–**290**
1–**136**, 2–**136**, 3–**161**, 4–**279**, 5–**308**

England

	First Innings		Second Innings	
N.V. Knight	lbw, **b** Waqar Younis	**51**	lbw, **b** Waqar Younis	**1**
M.A. Atherton (Capt)	lbw, **b** Wasim Akram	**12**	**c** sub (Asif Mujtaba), **b** Mushtaq	**64**
A.J. Stewart	lbw, **b** Mushtaq Ahmed	**39**	**c** sub (Moin Khan), **b** Mushtaq	**89**
G.P. Thorpe	**b** Ata-ur Rehman	**77**	lbw, **b** Mushtaq Ahmed	**3**
G.A. Hick	**b** Waqar Younis	**4**	**b** Waqar Younis	**4**
M.A. Ealham	**c** Rashid, **b** Ata-ur-Rehman	**25**	**b** Mushtaq Ahmed	**5**
*R.C. Russell	not out	**41**	**c** Rashid, **b** Waqar Younis	**1**
D.G. Cork	**c** Saeed, **b** Ata-ur-Rehman	**3**	**b** Waqar Younis	**3**
I.D.K. Salisbury	lbw, **b** Waqar Younis	**5**	**c** Rashid, **b** Wasim Akram	**40**
A.D. Mullally	**b** Waqar Younis	**0**	**c** sub (Moin Khan), **b** Mushtaq	**6**
S.J.E. Brown	**b** Ata-ur-Rehman	**1**	not out	**10**
	b **9**, lb **13**, w **1**, nb **4**	**27**	b **6**, lb **7**, nb **4**	**17**
		285		**243**

	O	M	R	W	O	M	R	W
Wasim Akram	22	4	49	**1**	21.1	5	45	**1**
Waqar Younis	24	6	69	**4**	25	3	85	**4**
Mushtaq Ahmed	38	5	92	**1**	38	15	57	**5**
Ata-ur-Rehman	15.4	3	50	**4**	11	2	33	**–**
Aamir Sohail	3	1	3	**–**				
Salim Malik					1	–	1	**–**
Shadab Kabir					1	–	9	**–**

Fall of Wickets
1–**27**, 2–**107**, 3–**107**, 4–**116**, 5–**180**, 6–**260**, 7–**264**, 8–**269**, 9–**269**
1–**14**, 2–**168**, 3–**171**, 4–**176**, 5–**181**, 6–**182**, 7–**186**, 8–**186**, 9–**208**

Umpires: P. Willey & S.A. Bucknor

Pakistan won by 164 runs

Ealham, two places too high at number six, was bowled round his legs by a ball that Mushtaq turned considerably. Waqar struck twice to have Russell caught off an unworthy shot and, inevitably, Cork yorked. Thorpe had watched the carnage without ever seeming willing or able to assert himself, and he had batted more than an hour for 3 when he fell leg before to Mushtaq. Seven wickets had gone down for 18 runs.

Mullally swatted, and Salisbury and Brown delayed the inevitable until eight minutes past four when Wasim had Salisbury caught behind off a steepler.

That the England batting following Atherton and Stewart was inept is undeniable, but this must not take credit away from outstanding bowling by Mushtaq and Waqar. Waqar is quickly reclaiming his place as the world's greatest fast bowler, and he was named Man of the Match, but the award could just as well have gone to Mushtaq or Inzamam-ul-Haq or two or three others in this fervent Pakistan team.

1 August

at Grange CC, Edinburgh
Pakistanis 286 for 5 (Shadab Kabir 135, Asif Mujtaba 63 not out)
Scotland 178 (I.L. Philip 50, Shahid Nazir 4 for 31, Saqlain Mushtaq 4 for 35)
Pakistanis won by 108 runs

A scintillating century from Shadab Kabir and four wickets in as many overs from Saqlain Mushtaq set up Pakistan's victory in the 50-over match at The Grange. Scotland were bowled out in 45.3 overs.

3, 4 and 5 August

at Chester-le-Street
Durham 307 (M.A. Roseberry 93 not out) and 135 (Wasim Akram 4 for 19)
Pakistanis 309 (Wasim Akram 68, Rashid Latif 55, S.J.E. Brown 5 for 88) and 134 for 3
Pakistanis won by 7 wickets

Durham's problems continued, as did Pakistan's success. The county side batted with customary inconsistency on the Saturday. Skipper Roseberry, suffering a miserable season, retired hurt when hit on the hand with his score at 41. He returned to add 52 more, but was left unbeaten seven runs short of a much-needed century. The tourists were 157 for 6, undone by the left-arm pace of Simon Brown, whose reward for taking five good wickets was to be dropped from the Test side. Wasim Akram, highly competitive throughout, and Rashid Latif added 129, and Pakistan took a two-run first innings lead. This took on huge proportions when Wasim and Ata-ur-Rehman sent back the first four Durham batsmen for 15 runs. Roseberry hit 48 before being bowled by the impressive Saqlain Mushtaq, a young off-spinner of high quality. Needing 134 to win, the Pakistanis reached their target in under 26 overs.

Second Test Match

England v. Pakistan *at Leeds*

As predicted, Hick was dropped from the England side. His place went to John Crawley, whose county form hardly warranted his inclusion. Lewis and Hussain returned at the expense of Ealham, who was injured, and Brown, while Caddick was surprisingly recalled and Salisbury, in the original party of 13, was excluded to make room for him. Irani, also in the original selection, was not used, so England went into the match with no spinner and a totally unbalanced side. Selection, it seemed, had gone full circle, and there never seemed any prospect that the eleven that took the field were capable of winning a Test match. Knight moved down to number six, and Stewart opened. If Knight was not considered competent enough to open then Irani should have batted at number six and a spinner should have replaced one of the four seamers.

With Aamir Sohail still unfit, Pakistan brought in Asif Mujtaba, and Moin Khan came in as wicket-keeper in place of Rashid Latif who had a back injury.

Atherton won the toss and asked Pakistan to bat first. His ploy, not appreciated by all, had instant reward when

Ijaz Ahmed pulls the ball for four during his brilliant innings of 141 on the opening day of the second Test.
(David Munden/Sportsline)

Moin Khan hits Dominic Cork for six as he moves closer to his century in the Headingley Test. (Adrian Murrell/Allsport)

Saeed Anwar drove lavishly at Mullally and was well taken in the gully by Atherton himself. Caddick and Mullally bowled tightly and troubled both Shadab and Ijaz, but when they were replaced by Lewis and Cork runs began to flow. Lewis was especially profligate. He consistently bowled short and three long-hops in one over were sent crashing to the boundary by Ijaz Ahmed.

Caddick was recalled and, on the stroke of lunch, he trapped Shadab Kabir leg before. Inzamam-ul-Haq wildly sliced Mullally to gully in the third over of the afternoon, and England had regained some control. The joy was premature. Ijaz played with considerable skill, great character and undoubted panache. His hundred came off only 128 balls. He had already hit Caddick for six, and he now took three fours in one over from Mullally and then pulled him for six. When one considers that conditions on this first day were never in favour of the batsman, Ijaz's innings was an outstanding display of batting. After 279 minutes his brilliance ended in an anti-climax. He flashed at a very wide ball from Cork, a dreadful shot, and edged to the 'keeper. He had faced 201 deliveries, hit two sixes and 20 fours.

The most consistent England batsman of the summer Alec Stewart pulls another boundary and takes England to an impregnable position with his innings of 170. (Graham Chadwick/Allsport)

Salim, a patient and reliable partner, was bowled by a good ball from Cork, and there were not too many of those during the day, and Wasim was soon undone by Caddick, but Moin hit the last ball of the day for four, and Pakistan were happy to rest on 281 for 6. A sparse crowd had seen some fine batting.

Whatever hopes England had of winning the match disappeared early on the second morning when Moin Khan hit Caddick high to long-leg where Mullally spilled a simple catch. At lunch, Moin and Asif were still together, and Pakistan had 360 on the board.

Asif Mujtaba had offered unwavering defence for 267 minutes when he cut at Cork and was held at slip by Thorpe, who juggled with the ball before clasping it at the third attempt. This was England's only success in the afternoon session, and Moin Khan, who had enjoyed some fortune, scampered a single off the last ball before tea to reach his century. On a pitch now docile, and against bowling lacking in variety and content to defend, he had offered a cheerful inventiveness, and when, after the break, he was caught behind off Cork he had faced 191 balls and hit a six and ten fours.

It was later than 4.30 when the Pakistan innings finally ended. Cork finished with five wickets, although this was not a bowling performance of which he will be particularly proud.

In the third over of their innings, England lost Atherton, caught off an inside edge. They could well have lost Hussain leg before to Mushtaq when he swept and missed, but umpire Bucknor showed mercy. Stewart raced to 52 off 68 balls, and England ended on 104 for 1.

Only one wicket fell before lunch on the third day. Hussain was completely bamboozled by a slower ball from Waqar and offered a simple return catch. In the afternoon, Thorpe was caught bat and pad at short-leg, but by then Stewart was well past his hundred. The start had been delayed by an hour through overnight rain, but the pitch became slower and all demons had long since disappeared. Stewart responded by taking total control, and with Waqar unable to find rhythm from either end, he flourished.

Nick Knight flicks the ball to leg on his way to a maiden Test hundred. (Graham Chadwick/Allsport)

There was, too, a delightful little innings from Crawley, who suggested that he had worked to overcome technical weaknesses and was now confident in his choice and range of stroke. He fell unworthily, flashing at Ata-ur-Rehman. At 356, in the 106th over, Stewart was caught and bowled by Mushtaq. His 170 was his eighth Test century, and he was at the crease for 437 minutes. He faced 315 balls and hit 24 fours. His winter failures have had something of a chastening effect upon him, and it must be recalled that he had not been part of England's plans at the start of the season. These and other events have made him a more mature batsman, less flamboyant perhaps, and certainly with a greater sense of seriousness and responsibility. He banished all thoughts of England following on in this match, and no one offered more consistency throughout the summer.

Nick Knight enjoyed the closing stages of the day and raced to 51 as England reached 373 for 5. He continued to enjoy himself on the fourth day and hit 16 fours in his 176-ball innings of 113, his maiden Test hundred. It was full of some most pleasing and attractive shots, and he is undoubtedly a cricketer of character, but he has yet to convince that he has the technical ability to survive long at this level. All but 15 minutes of the morning's play was lost, and the day was cut short by two hours just when Pakistan were about to begin their innings.

Shadab Kabir was out in the sixth over of the last morning, but Saeed and Inzamam blasted away while Ijaz was more sedate. Salim reached 5000 runs in Test cricket, but the batting, like much of the match, had little meaning. Poor attendances on three days; crowd disturbances on the Saturday; a pitch accompanied by uncertain weather, which gave the match an inevitably drawn outcome from the second day: this was not a game to lift the spectator or to stay in the memory.

Second Cornhill Test Match – England v. Pakistan

8, 9, 10, 11 and 12 August 1996 at Headingley, Leeds

Pakistan

	First Innings		Second Innings	
Saeed Anwar	c Atherton, b Mullally	1	c Russell, b Cork	22
Shadab Kabir	lbw, b Caddick	35	c and b Lewis	2
Ijaz Ahmed	c Russell, b Cork	141	c Russell, b Caddick	52
Inzamam-ul-Haq	c Atherton, b Mullally	2	c Stewart, b Caddick	65
Salim Malik	b Cork	55	c Cork, b Caddick	6
Asif Mujtaba	c Thorpe, b Cork	51	run out	26
Wasim Akram (Capt)	c Russell, b Caddick	7	lbw, b Atherton	7
*Moin Khan	c Russell, b Cork	105	not out	30
Mushtaq Ahmed	c Atherton, b Caddick	20	not out	6
Waqar Younis	c and b Cork	7		
Ata-ur-Rehman	not out	0		
	b 4, lb 10, nb 10	24	b 4, lb 12, nb 10	26
		448	(for 7 wickets, dec.)	242

	O	M	R	W	O	M	R	W
Caddick	40.2	6	113	3	17	4	52	3
Mullally	41	10	99	2	15	2	43	–
Lewis	32	4	100	–	16	3	52	1
Cork	37	6	113	5	16	2	49	1
Thorpe	3	1	9	–	10	3	10	–
Atherton					7	1	20	1

Fall of Wickets
1–1, 2–98, 3–103, 4–233, 5–252, 6–266, 7–378, 8–434, 9–444
1–16, 2–34, 3–132, 4–142, 5–188, 6–201, 7–221

England

	First Innings	
M.A. Atherton (Capt)	c Moin, b Wasim	12
A.J. Stewart	c and b Mushtaq Ahmed	170
N. Hussain	c and b Waqar Younis	48
G.P. Thorpe	c Shadab, b Mushtaq	16
J.P. Crawley	c Moin, b Ata-ur-Rehman	53
N.V. Knight	c Mushtaq, b Waqar	113
*R.C. Russell	b Wasim Akram	9
C.C. Lewis	b Mushtaq Ahmed	9
D.G. Cork	c Shadab, b Wasim	26
A.R. Caddick	b Waqar Younis	4
A.D. Mullally	not out	9
	b 7, lb 23, nb 2	32
		501

	O	M	R	W
Wasim Akram	39.5	10	106	3
Waqar Younis	33	7	127	3
Ata-ur-Rehman	22	1	90	1
Mushtaq Ahmed	55	17	142	3
Asif Mujtaba	7	5	6	–

Fall of Wickets
1–14, 2–121, 3–168, 4–257, 5–365, 6–402, 7–441, 8–465

Umpires: D.R. Shepherd & S.A. Bucknor

Match drawn

Stewart was named Man of the Match, and, indeed, it was he and Ijaz Ahmed who had most cause to draw pleasure from this contest.

14, 15 and 16 August
at Leicester
Pakistanis 221 (M.T. Brimson 4 for 39) and 262 for 6 dec. (Shahid Anwar 89, Saeed Anwar 69)
Leicestershire 199 (Mohammad Akram 7 for 51) and 183 (Saqlain Mushtaq 6 for 52)
Pakistanis won by 101 runs

The tourists endured a hard opening day at Leicester where their batsmen struggled uncharacteristically to score runs against the spinners. In contrast, the county side succumbed to the pace of Mohammad Akram, who gave an outstanding display of speed, movement and control and furthered his claims to be included in the Test side at The Oval. Batting a second time, the Pakistanis rediscovered their stroke-play with Shahid Anwar and Saeed Anwar adding 118 for the third wicket. Facing a target of 285 in 72 overs, Leicestershire lost two wickets to Mohammad Akram, who finished with match figures of 9 for 99. The star of the second innings, however, was Saqlain Mushtaq whose off-breaks totally perplexed the opposition and suggested that he was more than worthy of a Test place.

17, 18 and 19 August
at Chelmsford
Pakistanis 303 for 9 dec. (Inzamam-ul-Haq 106, Asif Mujtaba 100 not out, R.C. Irani 4 for 67) and 277 for 2 dec. (Salim Malik 104 not out, Saeed Anwar 102)
Essex 191 (D.D.J. Robinson 57, Waqar Younis 5 for 42, Saqlain Mushtaq 4 for 47) and 118 (D.D.J. Robinson 55, Saqlain Mushtaq 5 for 34, Waqar Younis 4 for 26)
Pakistanis won by 271 runs

Pakistan tumbled to 63 for 4 in the 18th over on the first day and had Inzamam-ul-Haq retired hurt with a knee injury. At 172 for 7, Inzamam returned, and he and Asif Mujtaba added 120. Both batsmen reached centuries, and Aamir Sohail declared. Essex finished the day on 29 for 3, and there was no recovery on the Sunday as the pace of Waqar and the spin of Saqlain brought havoc. Batting a second time, Pakistan gave a thrilling display. Saeed Anwar hit 102 off 96 balls with 14 fours and two sixes; and Salim Malik hit 15 fours in his 113-ball innings. Runs came at more than five an over. Essex collapsed for a second time against Waqar and Saqlain, and once more it was only Robinson who offered serious resistance.

Third Test Match

England *v.* Pakistan *at The Oval*

In the past few years within these pages we have consistently sung the praises of Robert Croft, the Glamorgan off-spinner, and it was gratifying that his talent should at last be recognised by the selectors. He was included in the side for the third Test, and Ian Salisbury was also included, giving England two spinners where none had been before. Russell's wicket-keeping was sacrificed to accommodate the pair, and Stewart donned the gloves. This was a little hard on Russell, who had scored a Test century during the summer and had performed competently for the most part, although he had not reached the standard he had achieved in the winter. Most surprisingly, Lewis was retained and Caddick omitted from the final eleven. Lewis had bowled poorly at Leeds and quite dreadfully for Surrey against Essex in the NatWest semi-final, and his retention was hard to understand.

For Pakistan, Aamir Sohail returned in place of Shadab Kabir, and Mohammad Akram replaced Ata-ur-Rehman, but no place could be found for Saqlain Mushtaq, a young off-spinner of immense talent. Having scored a century at Headingley, Moin Khan retained the wicket-keeping spot although Rashid Latif, an excellent 'keeper, was fit again.

Atherton won the toss, and England batted. Wasim Akram opened the bowling from the Vauxhall End and showed immediate hostility. Stewart was composed against Waqar and steered the fourth ball of his former team-mate's first over through the slips for four. The first ball of Wasim's second over was a vicious delivery which struck Atherton on the shoulder and went for four leg-byes. The blow left the England captain in obvious discomfort, and he flashed wildly at Waqar, who was beginning to trouble and beat both batsmen, although he was a little wayward.

The bowling was very hostile, but Stewart adopted a positive approach and hit Waqar for three fours in one over with pulls of varying violence. Mohammad Akram replaced Wasim at the Vauxhall End and he was twice driven straight

John Crawley provided one of the brightest spots of England's summer with a maiden Test century of the highest quality at The Oval. (Clive Mason/Allsport)

The power and the glory – Saeed Anwar on his way to 176 at The Oval. (Clive Mason/ Allsport)

into an unoccupied outfield. The second shot brought an all-run four and a more defensive field-setting.

Wasim brought himself on at the Pavilion end and subjected Atherton to a leg-stump attack. He employed a forward and backward short-leg, and, in spite of some brisk scoring, a wicket never looked to be far away, for there was menace in the Pakistani bowling. Stewart pulled anything short and consistently found the leg side boundary, but Atherton struggled and, in one torrid over from Wasim, he was dropped at short-leg by Asif Mujtaba.

The next over, the 17th, Wasim introduced Mushtaq, and he totally bemused and bowled Stewart with his second delivery. As bowler and fielders celebrated, Stewart stood his ground wondering what all the excitement was about only to turn and see his wicket broken. He had been beaten by a leg-break which turned and lifted as he attempted to play the ball to leg.

Hussain was far from happy against Mushtaq, and Atherton was still subjected to the leg stump attack until Wasim tired and brought Waqar on from the Pavilion End. The change brought immediate results. A magnificent delivery from Waqar turned Hussain almost front on, took a thick edge and was comfortably taken at second slip. Thorpe began confidently enough, and a fascinating morning's cricket ended with England 100 for 2 from 27 overs, Atherton 27, Thorpe 12.

The restart was so bright and positive it gave no indication of any gloom to come. The first two overs after lunch saw four boundaries, one of them leg-byes, but the first ball of the third over accounted for Atherton as another magnificent Waqar delivery hit the England captain's leg stump.

If there was joy in this match for England it came in the shape of John Crawley. He had given indication at Headingley that he had worked to eradicate the technical limitations that were obvious when he first played at international level, particularly the tendency to drag his shots to leg. Now he gave proof not only that he had eradicated problems, but that he had built upon his strengths. He offered assurance, power and beauty. In grace and charm and positivity he matched Pakistan's batsmen, and that is very high praise. He began with a fine on-drive off Waqar which brought three runs, and although Mushtaq Ahmed perplexed both him and Thorpe, Crawley countered by hitting the leg-spinner for three glorious off-side fours in one over. He was equally effective off his legs, and there was one memorable straight drive off Wasim Akram.

Thorpe was less commanding, but he batted well and reached 50 when he square cut Aamir Sohail for four. Two balls later, Crawley reached his half-century. The next over saw the end of Thorpe, who misjudged a straight ball from Mohammad Akram. Tea came with England 218 for 4 from 56 overs, an excellent platform for a big score.

Mushtaq Ahmed operated from the Vauxhall End straight after tea, and Knight swiped him rashly for six with the spin in his second over after the break. Crawley looked totally composed and there was delight in all he did. Knight, in contrast, increasingly exposed his technical deficiencies, and England began to lose momentum. It was no surprise when, thrusting at Mushtaq and offering no shot, he dropped the ball onto his own stumps via glove and arm. It was the dismissal of a technically careless batsman.

If Knight had batted poorly, Lewis was even worse. He struggled to put bat on ball for 45 minutes during which time he faced 40 deliveries. When Wasim bowled him it was a merciful release. So becalmed had England become that even the crowd could not manage the Mexican wave. At the close, they were 278 for 6 with the so impressive Crawley six runs short of a maiden Test century. In spite of his splendid innings, England had lost the initiative, and the last 31 overs of the day had produced only 58 runs. There was also the fact that Wasim had chosen the 90th over to call upon the second new ball, and he and Waqar would have it afresh on the Friday.

Nasser Hussain is adjudged leg before as he offers no shot to Mushtaq Ahmed's googly. (Clive Mason/Allsport)

Alec Stewart stands bemused, dismissed by Mushtaq Ahmed. (Adrian Murrell/Allsport)

Twenty-three overs were lost to rain at the start of the second day, and play did not begin until 2.15, by which time sunshine had replaced the darkness at noon. In the second over, Salisbury pulled unconvincingly at Wasim and the ball looped to slip off bat and shoulder as the batsman stood wondering where his shot had gone. In the next over, Cork carved at Waqar and was gone. Thankfully, Crawley reached his well deserved hundred with an all-run four off Waqar. He responded to the crowd's ovation with a pleasing dignity and humility. He then hit Waqar for another four and a two, but the last ball of the over was a delivery of considerable pace that knocked back his off stump. Only a ball of such quality deserved to end an innings of such quality. Crawley faced 217 balls and hit 12 fours and provided England with their most satisfying innings of the summer.

Mullally hit five fours in a rustic innings of 24 off 12 balls. He was badly dropped by Ijaz off Waqar, but Wasim hit his leg stump next over, and England were all out ten overs into the day for a bitterly disappointing 326. There was also the mystery as to why the all-rounder Croft was batting below Salisbury and Cork.

If there had been disappointment in the England batting, there was shame and embarrassment in the bowling. Lewis, with the new ball and a breeze at his back, was dreadful. Cork conceded 15 runs in a two-over spell, and after 11 overs of quick bowling, Atherton turned to his two spinners. Croft immediately found length and aggression, attacking the batsmen in a refreshingly dynamic manner. Salisbury, alas, had neither length nor direction as often before and was as profligate as Lewis. By the time the spinners were in action, 59 runs were on the board, and only Croft offered threat or containment. He earned his wicket, which came when Aamir Sohail hit low to cover in the 23rd over. This was, however, only a temporary respite. By the end of the day, Pakistan had moved to 229 for 1 from 56 overs, and Saeed Anwar, 116, had completed a century of liquid power and supple wrists. What joy to see such aggression and beauty in the Test arena. For England, it had been a day of total misery and abject poverty.

The third day was ruined by rain, with only 38.3 overs possible. While Croft was again reliable, Salisbury was awful. His first ball, a leg side full toss, was sent singing to the boundary by Saaed Anwar, and by the end of the day his 17 overs in the innings had cost 91 runs. Ijaz had fallen early to Mullally, but Saaed and Inzamam continued the blistering attack upon the England bowling. They took the score to 334 before falling in the 90th and 91st overs. Inzamam had a narrow escape in hooking, but, undeterred, he repeated the shot and fell into Mullally's trap, caught at square-leg. Saeed had reached his highest score in Test cricket before he hooked at Cork in the next over. He was through his shot too soon and skied to Croft at mid-on. Saaed had faced 264 balls and hit 26 fours in his 378-minute innings. It was batting of the highest quality and wonderfully entertaining.

The Pakistan innings had lost its impetus, but it was soon ended by rain at 339 for 4.

Sunday was another soggy day, and it was the day on which the England selectors announced their squad for the Texaco Trophy matches. There were some strange decisions. There was no place for Hussain and Crawley, probably because their places on the winter tour were certain and because they had proved their worth. Others were on trial. Cork, too, was 'rested' while Lewis, originally chosen, was then dropped for disciplinary reasons. He arrived late at The Oval on the Sunday morning and offered no excuse that the selectors could find acceptable. His season had begun with customary optimism and was ending with customary controversy and anger at a waste of talent.

Lewis did contribute to the day's play by running out Asif Mujtaba with a fine, fast, flat throw from the boundary. Wasim raised the tempo with some fierce hitting until he was stumped off the persevering Croft who, it seemed, was less willing to give the ball as much air as he gives it in county cricket. Nevertheless, he had a good Test debut. Salisbury had a better day and claimed a wicket when Moin cut at him unwisely, but Salim Malik accelerated and Wasim declared as soon as Salim had reached a determined and admirable hundred. The past 18 months could not have been the easiest of periods for him, and his important innings was a triumph for his character as well as for his temperament and technique.

England trailed by 195 runs and Atherton and Stewart had 23 overs to negotiate on a pitch that was showing little sign of deterioration. There should have been no trouble in saving the match except that one remembered Lord's. Wasim, in particular, and Waqar bowled at a furious pace, but the England openers batted with discipline and courage and had 74 runs on the board by the close.

Mushtaq Ahmed occupied the Vauxhall End on the final day for the remainder of the England innings. The three pace bowlers rotated at the Pavilion End. Atherton and Stewart gave no cause for concern in the initial stages although Stewart's fifty came with a drive at Mushtaq which flew past where gully is often posted. Shortly after, in the 11th over of the day, he was caught at short-leg off pad and a thick inside edge. Hussain was subjected to a withering attack by Wasim, but he responded with bravery and determination as well as skill. He was less happy against Mushtaq, but he remained firm. The leg-spinner was posing all sorts of threats and he claimed the vital wicket of Atherton, who pushed forward and was very well taken low at silly mid-off. The England skipper turned quickly on his heel unable to disguise his anger with himself. He must have anticipated what was to follow.

At lunch, England were 158 for 2, still 47 runs adrift but with wickets in hand. In the fourth over of the afternoon, Thorpe was caught at slip. Thorpe's position in the England side seems impregnable, and he is high in computer rankings, yet, in the heat of battle, he remains a great under-achiever.

Hussain batted with great character, but suddenly he offered no stroke to a Mushtaq googly and umpire Cooray adjudged him leg before. Some criticised this decision, but Cooray had a very good game, which was refreshing as one had almost come to believe that every Test match should be umpired by Shepherd and Venkataraghavan.

Crawley was facing some very hostile bowling with the same courage that Hussain had shown, but Knight looked woeful against Mushtaq. Twice the left-hander square cut wide deliveries for four, but he gave a simple return catch to the leg-spinner when it became increasingly obvious that he was unable to fathom which way the ball would turn.

Third Cornhill Test Match – England v. Pakistan

22, 23, 24, 25 and 26 August 1996 at The Oval, Kennington

England

	First Innings		Second Innings	
M.A. Atherton (Capt)	b Waqar Younis	31	c Inzamam, b Mushtaq	43
*A.J. Stewart	b Mushtaq Ahmed	44	c Asif, b Mushtaq	54
N. Hussain	c Saeed, b Waqar	12	lbw, b Mushtaq Ahmed	51
G.P. Thorpe	lbw, b Mohammad Akram	54	c Wasim, b Mushtaq	9
J.P. Crawley	b Waqar Younis	106	c Aamir, b Wasim Akram	19
N.V. Knight	b Mushtaq Ahmed	17	c and b Mushtaq Ahmed	8
C.C. Lewis	b Wasim Akram	5	lbw, b Waqar Younis	4
I.D.K. Salisbury	c Inzamam, b Wasim	5	(10) not out	0
D.G. Cork	c Moin Khan, b Waqar	0	(8) b Mushtaq Ahmed	26
R.D.B. Croft	not out	5	(9) c Ijaz, b Wasim	6
A.D. Mullally	b Wasim Akram	24	b Wasim Akram	0
	lb 12, w 1, nb 10	23	b 6, lb 2, w 1, nb 13	22
		326		242

	O	M	R	W	O	M	R	W
Wasim Akram	29.2	9	83	3	15.4	1	67	3
Waqar Younis	25	6	95	4	18	3	55	1
Mohammad Akram	12	1	41	1	10	3	30	–
Mushtaq Ahmed	27	5	78	2	37	10	78	6
Aamir Sohail	6	1	17	–	2	1	4	–

Fall of Wickets
1–**64**, 2–**85**, 3–**116**, 4–**205**, 5–**248**, 6–**273**, 7–**283**, 8–**284**, 9–**295**
1–**96**, 2–**136**, 3–**166**, 4–**179**, 5–**187**, 6–**205**, 7–**220**, 8–**238**, 9–**242**

Pakistan

	First Innings		Second Innings	
Saeed Anwar	c Croft, b Cork	176	c Knight, b Mullally	1
Aamir Sohail	c Cork, b Croft	46	not out	29
Ijaz Ahmed	c Stewart, b Mullally	61	not out	13
Inzamam-ul-Haq	c Hussain, b Mullally	35		
Salim Malik	not out	100		
Asif Mujtaba	run out	13		
Wasim Akram (Capt)	st Stewart, b Croft	40		
*Moin Khan	b Salisbury	23		
Mushtaq Ahmed	c Crawley, b Mullally	2		
Waqar Younis	not out	0		
Mohammad Akram				
	b 4, lb 5, nb 16	25	nb 5	5
	(for 8 wickets, dec.)	521	(for one wicket)	48

	O	M	R	W	O	M	R	W
Lewis	23	3	112	–				
Mullally	37.1	7	97	3	3	–	24	1
Croft	47	10	116	2	0.4	–	9	–
Cork	23	5	71	1	3	–	15	–
Salisbury	29	3	116	1				

Fall of Wickets
1–**106**, 2–**239**, 3–**334**, 4–**334**, 5–**365**, 6–**440**, 7–**502**, 8–**519**
1–**7**

Umpires: M.J. Kitchen & B.C. Cooray

Pakistan won by 9 wickets

The first five wickets had fallen to Mushtaq Ahmed, but now the sequence was broken as Waqar's yorker trapped Lewis leg before. The Surrey man mouthed his disagreement with the decision – Chris Broad was once disciplined for doing the same and, like Lewis, being caught on television. Only umpire Kitchen knows why Cork was not leg before first ball, but it was Crawley who was the next to go. A ball from Wasim was on him before he knew where he was and Aamir dived to take the catch.

Croft suffered a similar fate. Wasim, bowling as fast as one can remember seeing him and often pitching short, made a ball rise in a violent manner and Croft lost it completely as it looped off his bat to Ijaz running in at square-leg. Cork had gone on the last ball of the previous over, bowled by a Mushtaq 'grounder', so that only Mullally and Salisbury were the last pair. Wasim shattered Mullally's stumps first ball and fell to his knees in joy and thanks. He had become only the 11th bowler and only the second Pakistani to capture 300 Test wickets.

Needing 48 to win, Pakistan lost Saeed Anwar when he swotted at Mullally and skied over slip. There was to be no miracle. Cork overstepped the crease four times in his eagerness to succeed. Aamir Sohail clipped five fours, the last two in an over from Croft in which victory was achieved. As with everything else they had done in the match,

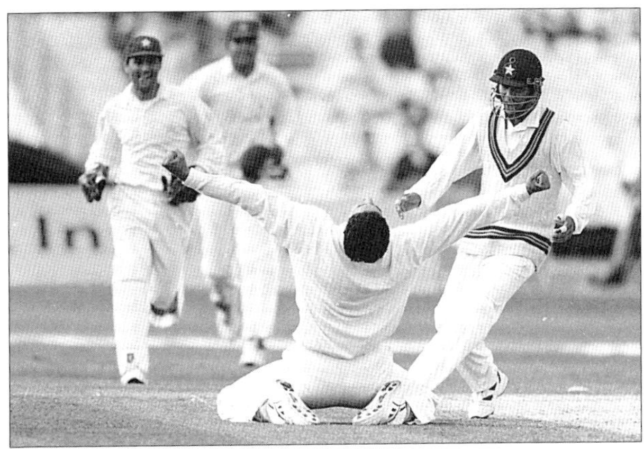

Wasim Akram falls to his knees after wrecking Mullally's stumps and claiming his 300th Test wicket. (Clive Mason/Allsport)

Pakistan won with style and passion, and with 23 overs to spare, even though nearly a day's play had been lost to rain. While there was the customary post-mortem on England's inadequacies, there was no denying that a team of great skill, intense commitment, total dedication and fervent enthusiasm were not flattered by their two-nil win in the series. They had a formula which brought success to them and joy to all who watched them.

Test Match Averages
England v. Pakistan

England Batting

	M	Inns	NO	Runs	HS	Av	100s	50s
A.J. Stewart	3	5	–	396	170	79.20	1	2
J.P. Crawley	2	3	–	178	106	59.33	1	1
N.V. Knight	3	5	–	190	113	38.00	1	1
N. Hussain	2	3	–	111	51	37.00		1
M.A. Atherton	3	5	–	162	64	32.40		1
G.P. Thorpe	3	5	–	159	77	31.80		2
R.C. Russell	2	3	1	51	41*	25.50		
I.D.K. Salisbury	2	4	1	50	40	16.66		
D.G. Cork	3	5	–	58	26	11.60		
A.D. Mullally	3	5	1	39	24	9.75		
C.C. Lewis	2	3	–	18	9	6.00		

Played in one Test: R.D.B. Croft 6 & 5*; G.A. Hick 4 & 4; S.J.E. Brown 1 & 10*; M.A. Ealham 25 & 5; A.R. Caddick 4

Pakistan Batting

	M	Inns	NO	Runs	HS	Av	100s	50s
Moin Khan	2	3	1	158	105	79.00	1	
Ijaz Ahmed	3	6	1	344	141	68.80	1	3
Salim Malik	3	5	2	195	100*	65.00	1	1
Inzamam-ul-Haq	3	5	–	320	148	64.00	1	2
Saeed Anwar	3	6	–	362	176	60.33	1	2
Aamir Sohail	2	3	1	77	46	38.50		
Asif Mujtaba	2	3	–	90	51	30.00		1
Wasim Akram	3	5	1	98	40	24.50		
Shadab Kabir	2	4	–	87	35	21.75		
Mushtaq Ahmed	3	5	1	44	20	11.00		
Waqar Younis	3	3	1	11	7	5.50		

Played in two Tests: Ata-ur-Rehman 0* & 10*
Played in one Test: Rashid Latif 45; Mohammad Akram did not bat

England Bowling

	Overs	Mds	Runs	Wks	Av	Best	10/m	5/inn
A.R. Caddick	57.2	10	165	6	27.50	3/52		
D.G. Cork	131	23	434	12	36.16	5/113		1
A.D. Mullally	150.3	36	377	10	37.70	3/44		
G.A. Hick	13	2	43	1	43.00	1/26		
R.D.B. Croft	47.4	10	125	2	62.50	2/116		
S.J.E. Brown	33	4	138	2	69.00	1/60		
M.A. Ealham	37	8	81	1	81.00	1/42		
I.D.K. Salisbury	61.2	8	221	2	110.50	1/42		
C.C. Lewis	71	10	264	1	264.00	1/52		
G.P. Thorpe	13	4	19	–	–			

Bowled in one innings: M.A. Atherton 7–1–20–1

Pakistan Bowling

	Overs	Mds	Runs	Wks	Av	Best	10/m	5/inn
Mushtaq Ahmed	195	52	447	17	26.29	6/78		2
Waqar Younis	125	25	431	16	26.93	4/69		
Wasim Akram	128	29	350	11	31.81	3/67		
Ata-ur-Rehman	48.4	6	173	5	34.60	4/50		
Mohammad Akram	22	4	71	1	71.00	1/41		
Aamir Sohail	11	3	24	–	–			

Bowled in one innings: Asif Mujtaba 7–5–6–0; Salim Malik 1–0–1–0; Shadab Kabir 1–0–9–0

England Fielding Figures

9 – R.C. Russell; 3 – M.A. Atherton, A.J. Stewart (ct 2 / st 1) and D.G. Cork; 2 – G.P. Thorpe; 1 – N. Hussain, J.P. Crawley, N.V. Knight, R.D.B. Croft, G.A. Hick, M.A. Ealham and S.J.E. Brown

Pakistan Fielding Figures

3 – Moin Khan (plus 2 as sub), Mushtaq Ahmed and Rashid Latif; 2 – Saeed Anwar, Inzamam-ul-Haq and Shadab Kabir; 1 – Asif Mujtaba (plus 1 as sub), Aamir Sohail, Ijaz Ahmed, Wasim Akram and Waqar Younis

Adam Hollioake enjoyed a highly successful international debut in the Texaco Trophy. He and Alec Stewart leave the field with victor's spoils at Edgbaston. (Clive Mason/Allsport)

Texaco Trophy

Three one-day internationals after a Test series can only mean anti-climax, but at least they gave England a chance for some measure of revenge. It was not easy to comprehend England's selection policy. As we have stated, Hussain and Crawley were omitted, presumably on the grounds that their places in the England side were secure and that to omit them would give the selectors an opportunity to look at others. Cork was left out of the party on the grounds that he needed a rest, and Gough returned. In the opinion of many he should have returned much earlier. Lewis was dropped for disciplinary reasons, and his place went to Headley who had bowled well on the 'A' tour of Pakistan but who had missed the early part of the season through injury. Caddick, who took six wickets in the second Test and was in the twelve for the third Test, was not selected. Martin was brought back in place of Salisbury, who had not enjoyed a happy summer, and Irani was included. Maynard, a one-day expert, was brought in, and there were newcomers in Hollioake and Graham Lloyd. Both of these choices were hard to explain. England were said to be looking for an all-rounder whose principal skill was bowling. Hollioake had batted well all summer, but he was bowling less and less and had taken just 11 first-class wickets in the season. Lloyd was a good one-day cricketer who had never fulfilled the promise he had shown when he first came into the game, and why he was chosen ahead of Adams of Derbyshire and other batsmen who had scored heavily in all forms of cricket was a mystery.

England omitted Hollioake and Martin from the chosen 13 when they took the field for the first game. The Old Trafford pitch looked absolutely dreadful, but it was to play better than it looked. Pakistan chose to bat first, but the England bowlers held a good line and runs were hard to come by. Aamir Sohail was unable to find his touch and after the first 15 overs, a period of expected productivity, he had only three singles to his credit and Pakistan were 38. Saeed was his usual aggressive self, and he hit seven fours in his 57, which came off 75 balls.

Well as Gough and Mullally had bowled, it was Irani who broke the opening partnership when Saeed mishit to long-on in the 24th over. Aamir was now batting with more freedom, but he was one of two batsmen to fall to Croft, who bowled a very tidy 10-over spell. His second victim was Wasim, who had promoted himself to try to get some life into the innings.

Ijaz scored 48 off 56 balls, and Inzamam at last gave the Pakistan knock some impetus with 37 off 28 balls. Moin, too, scored two fours in his 10 off deliveries, but the Pakistan score looked far from daunting.

It became increasingly insignificant as Knight and Stewart hit 57 in ten overs before Knight was out. Stewart continued in pugnacious mood until he was leg before to Waqar at 98. Atherton was supremely confident as he nursed England towards their target. Thorpe fell to a rush of blood, and Maynard lived perilously before chopping on to Wasim with six runs needed. Irani strode to the wicket exuding confidence and hit the first ball he received through the off side for four and turned the second to leg for two to give England victory with 20 balls to spare.

Hollioake made his international debut in place of Lloyd in the second match. If Knight and Stewart had been positive in the first match, they were blistering in the second. Knight, suited to the gambling expression that the first 15 overs of an international match now offer, was bludgeoning from the start, and, in 13 overs, England were 103. Stewart, who hit two sixes, and Atherton were out in the same over.

Thorpe gave Knight brisk and sensible support before falling leg before, and Maynard ran himself out insanely when he lost a sight of a ball that was in the hands of Inzamam at short third man. Knight reached his hundred in the 34th over and by the time he was well stumped off Saqlain he had hit 11 fours and faced 132 balls. He has the important quality of self-belief, and it paid dividends here.

Hollioake and Gough, first ball, were both run out, but Irani, like Knight, is a supremely confident young man and drove Aamir for six in his 63-ball innings. Croft also did well, and England reached a commendable 292.

The game was virtually decided when Aamir pulled rashly and skied to mid-on and Moin was leg before with only six scored. Saeed, 33 off 25 balls, hit a six and a four but was brilliantly caught by the diving Stewart. Ijaz savaged Irani and hit ten fours in his 80-ball innings, but Pakistan fell apart as slogging became the order of the day. The main beneficiary was Adam Hollioake, who gave credence to the old adage that it is not how you bowl but when you bowl that matters. He kept the ball up to the bat, and the Pakistani batsmen did the rest.

First Texaco Trophy International – England v. Pakistan

29 August 1996 at Old Trafford, Manchester

Pakistan

Saeed Anwar	c Mullally, b Irani	57
Aamir Sohail	b Croft	48
Ijaz Ahmed	c Irani, b Mullally	48
Wasim Akram (Capt)	b Croft	6
Inzamam-ul-Haq	not out	37
*Moin Khan	b Gough	10
Salim Malik	not out	6
Mushtaq Ahmed		
Saqlain Mushtaq		
Waqar Younis		
Ata-ur-Rehman		
	b 2, lb 4, w 7	13
	50 overs (for 5 wickets)	225

	O	M	R	W
Gough	10	–	44	1
Mullally	10	3	31	1
Headley	10	–	52	–
Irani	10	–	56	1
Croft	10	1	36	2

Fall of Wickets
1–82, 2–141, 3–160, 4–174, 5–203

England

N.V. Knight	c Moin Khan, b Wasim Akram	26
*A.J. Stewart	lbw, b Waqar Younis	48
M.A. Atherton (Capt)	b Wasim Akram	65
G.P. Thorpe	st Moin Khan, b Aamir Sohail	23
M.P. Maynard	b Wasim Akram	41
G.D. Lloyd	not out	2
R.C. Irani	not out	6
R.D.B. Croft		
D. Gough		
D.W. Headley		
A.D. Mullally		
	lb 4, w 7, nb 4	15
	46.4 overs (for 5 wickets)	226

	O	M	R	W
Wasim Akram	9.4	1	45	3
Waqar Younis	7	–	28	1
Saqlain Mushtaq	10	1	54	–
Ata-ur-Rehman	3	–	14	–
Mushtaq Ahmed	10	–	52	–
Aamir Sohail	7	1	29	1

Fall of Wickets
1–57, 2–98, 3–146, 4–200, 5–220

Umpires: N.T. Plews & G. Sharp *Man of the Match:* M.A. Atherton

England won by 5 wickets

Martin replaced Headley and Lloyd came in for Thorpe in the third match, which was overhung by an end-of-term feeling. England batted first, quickly lost Stewart and Atherton, who was forced to retire hurt with an injured thumb but returned at the fall of the fifth wicket. Generally, the England innings stuttered along, with Knight hitting his second century of the weekend. He faced 145 balls and batted throughout the 50 overs. He was dropped in the 12th over, a simple chance at square-leg, but the Pakistan fielding in all three matches was dreadful. Knight's innings was less risky than his innings at Edgbaston, but support was so lacking that it needed to be.

Pakistan raced away and were 92 for 0 after 15 overs. At 177 for 2, victory was assured it seemed, but they contrived to lose five wickets in ten overs for 42 runs. The wickets were suicidal, and where once an easy victory looked certain, it came eventually with just two balls to spare. Hollioake, bowling straight and varying pace, again benefited. Croft once more suggested that he is a bowler of international class.

So ended the tour. Pakistan were on the verge of greatness, and England recorded rays of hope.

Nick Knight hit two centuries in the Texaco Trophy series against Pakistan. He pulls a ball to the boundary on his way to his hundred at Old Trafford. (Clive Mason/Allsport)

Second Texaco Tropy International – England v. Pakistan
31 August 1996 at Edgbaston, Birmingham

England

N.V. Knight	**st** Moin Khan, **b** Saqlain	**113**
*A.J. Stewart	**b** Mushtaq Ahmed	**46**
M.A. Atherton (Capt)	lbw, **b** Mushtaq Ahmed	**1**
G.P. Thorpe	lbw, **b** Ata-ur-Rehman	**21**
M.P. Maynard	run out	**1**
R.C. Irani	not out	**45**
A.J. Hollioake	run out	**15**
D. Gough	run out	**0**
R.D.B. Croft	**b** Waqar Younis	**15**
D.W. Headley	not out	**3**
A.D. Mullally		
	lb **25**, w **4**, nb **3**	**32**
	50 overs (for 8 wickets)	**292**

	O	M	R	W
Wasim Akram	10	–	50	**–**
Waqar Younis	9	–	54	**1**
Ata-ur-Rehman	6	–	40	**1**
Saqlain Mushtaq	10	–	59	**1**
Mushtaq Ahmed	10	–	33	**2**
Aamir Sohail	5	–	31	**–**

Fall of Wickets
1–**103**, 2–**105**, 3–**163**, 4–**168**, 5–**221**, 6–**257**, 7–**257**, 8–**286**

Pakistan

Saeed Anwar	**c** Stewart, **b** Gough	**33**
Aamir Sohail	**c** Croft, **b** Gough	**0**
*Moin Khan	lbw, **b** Mullally	**0**
Ijaz Ahmed	**b** Croft	**79**
Inzamam-ul-Haq	**c** Thorpe, **b** Croft	**6**
Salim Malik	**c** Stewart, **b** Hollioake	**23**
Wasim Akram (Capt)	**c** Knight, **b** Hollioake	**21**
Mushtaq Ahmed	not out	**14**
Saqlain Mushtaq	**b** Hollioake	**0**
Waqar Younis	lbw, **b** Gough	**4**
Ata-ur-Rehman	**c** Knight, **b** Hollioake	**2**
	lb **2**, nb **1**	**3**
	37.5 overs	**185**

	O	M	R	W
Gough	8	–	39	**3**
Mullally	6	–	30	**1**
Headley	7	–	32	**–**
Irani	2	–	22	**–**
Croft	8	–	37	**2**
Hollioake	6.5	1	23	**4**

Fall of Wickets
1–**1**, 2–**6**, 3–**54**, 4–**104**, 5–**137**, 6–**164**, 7–**164**, 8–**168**, 9–**177**

Umpires: M.J. Kitchen & P. Willey *Man of the Match:* N.V. Knight

England won by 107 runs

Third Texaco Trophy International – England v. Pakistan
1 September 1996 at Trent Bridge, Nottingham

England

N.V. Knight	not out	**125**
*A.J. Stewart	**c** and **b** Wasim Akram	**3**
M.A. Atherton (Capt)	**c** Shahid Nazir, **b** Wasim	**30**
M.P. Maynard	**b** Shahid Nazir	**24**
G.D. Lloyd	**c** Shadab Kabir, **b** Saqlain	**15**
R.C. Irani	**b** Shahid Nazir	**0**
A.J. Hollioake	**c** Ijaz Ahmed, **b** Saqlain	**13**
D. Gough	**b** Wasim Akram	**5**
R.D.B. Croft	**b** Waqar Younis	**0**
P.J. Martin	run out	**6**
A.D. Mullally	**b** Waqar Younis	**2**
	b **2**, lb **8**, w **9**, nb **4**	**23**
	50 overs	**246**

	O	M	R	W
Wasim Akram	10	1	45	**3**
Waqar Younis	10	1	49	**2**
Shahid Nazir	10	–	47	**2**
Asif Mujtaba	5	–	27	**–**
Saqlain Mushtaq	10	–	35	**2**
Aamir Sohail	5	–	33	**–**

Fall of Wickets
1–**10**, 2–**108**, 3–**137**, 4–**139**, 5–**178**, 6–**216**, 7–**226**, 8–**231**, 9–**240**

Pakistan

Saeed Anwar	**b** Martin	**61**
Shahid Anwar	lbw, **b** Martin	**37**
Ijaz Ahmed	**c** Lloyd, **b** Gough	**59**
Aamir Sohail	**b** Croft	**29**
Shadab Kabir	**c** Irani, **b** Hollioake	**0**
Asif Mujtaba	**b** Hollioake	**2**
Wasim Akram (Capt)	lbw, **b** Hollioake	**5**
*Rashid Latif	not out	**31**
Saqlain Mushtaq	**c** Maynard, **b** Hollioake	**12**
Waqar Younis	not out	**0**
Shahid Nazir		
	lb **5**, w **6**	**11**
	49.4 overs (for 8 wickets)	**247**

	O	M	R	W
Gough	10	1	43	**1**
Mullally	9	–	66	**–**
Martin	10	–	38	**2**
Croft	10	–	38	**1**
Irani	2	–	12	**–**
Hollioake	8.4	–	45	**4**

Fall of Wickets
1–**93**, 2–**114**, 3–**177**, 4–**182**, 5–**187**, 6–**199**, 7–**219**, 8–**240**

Umpires: J.W. Holder & D.R. Shepherd *Man of the Match:* The Pakistan Team

Pakistan won by 2 wickets

Pakistan in England, 1996 First-Class Matches

Batting

	v. Glamorgan (Pontypridd) 29 June–1 July		v. Somerset (Taunton) 3–5 July		v. Northamptonshire (Northampton) 6–8 July		v. Warwickshire (Edgbaston) 17–19 July		v. Kent (Canterbury) 20–22 July		First Test Match (Lord's) 25–29 July		v. Durham (Chester-le-Street) 3–5 August		Second Test Match (Leeds) 8–12 August		v. Leicestershire (Leicester) 14–16 August		v. Essex (Chelmsford) 17–19 August		Third Test Match (The Oval) 22–26 August		M	Inns	NO	Runs	HS	Av
Aamir Sohail	49	–	0	28*			30	4	12	30	2	–					30	34	0	40	46	29*	8	14	2	334	49	27.83
Saeed Anwar	219*	–	130	60	20	8	131	23			74	88	20	36	1	22	22	69	22	102	176	1	10	19	1	1224	219*	68.00
Ijaz Ahmed	0	–			29	39	10	52	19	136*	1	76	17	12	141	52			6	–	61	13*	9	16	2	664	141	47.42
Inzamam-ul-Haq	169*	–	4	51*			51	4	9	–	148	70	44	34	2	65			106	–	35	–	9	14	2	792	169*	66.00
Asif Mujtaba	–	–	54	–	15	31*	38	34	6	5*			0	19*	51	26	14	12*	100*	27*	13	–	10	16	6	445	100*	44.50
Rashid Latif	–	–	38	–	3	0			61	–	45	–	55	–					30	–			7	7	–	232	61	33.14
Wasim Akram	–	–			21	12			12	–	10	34*	68	–	7	7					40	–	7	9	1	211	40	26.37
Mushtaq Ahmed	–	–	12	–			18	6			11	5			20	6*	38	–			2	–	7	9	1	118	38	14.75
Waqar Younis	–	–	0*	–			0	8			4	–			7	–			0	–	0*	–	7	7	2	19	8	3.80
Ata-ur-Rehman	–	–	–	–			0	1	4	–	10*	–	15	–	0*	–	30	–	1	–			9	8	2	61	30	10.16
Salim Malik	–	–					0	9	37	–	7	27*	30	17*	55	6	32	22	4	104*	100*	–	9	14	4	450	104*	45.00
Shahid Anwar			21	17*	26	12											1	89					3	6	1	166	89	33.20
Shadab Kabir			21*	–	99	52			3	84	17	33	18	–	35	2	25	1					7	12	1	390	99	35.45
Mohammad Akram			–	–	2*	–	0*	4*									0*	–	1*	–	–	–	6	5	5	7	4*	–
Moin Khan					1	39	0	4							105	30*	2	11			23	–	5	9	1	215	105	26.87
Saqlain Mushtaq					78	2			14*	–			0	–			4	11*	21	–			5	7	2	130	78	26.00
Shahid Nazir					3	–			13	–			5*	–									3	3	1	21	13	10.50
Byes	8		4			4		5	1	10	3	4	1		4	4	5	10	8	2	4							
Leg-byes	6			1	8	3	3		1	2	5	14	5		10	12	13	1	4	1	5							
Wides	3		4	1		1							3				1	2		1								
No-balls	7		12	16	18	2	16	4	2	2	3	1	28	16	10	10	4				16	5						
Total	461		300	174	323	205	297	158	194	269	340	352	309	134	448	242	221	262	303	277	521	48						
Wickets	2		7	1	10	8	10	10	10	2	10	5	10	3	10	7	10	6	9	2	8	1						
Result	D		W		D		L		W		W		W		D		W		W		W							

Fielding Figures

21 – Rashid Latif (ct 17 / st 4)
12 – Aamir Sohail
8 – Asif Mujtaba
7 – Moin Khan (ct 5 / st 2) and subs
6 – Shadab Kabir and Saeed Anwar
5 – Inzamam-ul-Haq and Ata-ur-Rehamn
4 – Mushtaq Ahmed, Wasim Akram and Mohammad Akram
3 – Saqlain Mushtaq
2 – Waqar Younis and Ijaz Ahmed
1 – Salim Malik

Bowling

	Wasim Akram	Waqar Younis	Ata-ur-Rehman	Mushtaq Ahmed	Mohammad Akram	Asif Mujtaba	Aamir Sohail	Shahid Nazir	Saqlain Mushtaq	Salim Malik	Shahid Anwar	Moin Khan	Ijaz Ahmed	Rashid Latif	Inzamam-ul-Haq	Shadab Kabir	Byes	Leg-byes	Wides	No-balls	Total	Wkts
v. Glamorgan (Pontypridd)	16.5–1–64–1	18–4–70–2	20–3–82–4	25–5–76–3													4	8	2	30	304	10
29 June–1 July	10–1–34–1	4–1–8–0	3.1–0–17–1	2–1–1–0															1	7	60	2
v. Somerset (Taunton)		15.1–0–59–3	6–1–24–0	13–5–36–5	6–0–31–0												8	1		2	159	9A
3–5 July		3–1–10–0	7.5–1–29–2	23–6–72–5	6–0–34–1	4–0–12–1	15–2–41–1										6	6		2	210	10
v. Northamptonshire (Northampton)	20–5–58–5				15–4–39–1			16.4–5–43–4									5	7	3	8	152	10
6–8 July	15–4–46–0				13–2–49–0	9–0–52–0		7–1–27–0	13–1–45–0		7.3–2–46–2	9–0–78–2	2–0–13–0	5–1–26–0			3	11		16	396	4
v. Warwickshire (Edgbaston)		3–1–8–0	16–3–63–2	28–6–91–7	14–2–64–1		15–3–73–0										6	5		4	310	10
17–19 July			3–0–9–0	10–1–47–1	4–0–21–0		7–2–29–1			3–1–9–1					4–0–24–0		8	1		6	148	3
v. Kent (Canterbury)	23–5–74–4		13–1–74–0				2–0–9–0	7.1–1–32–3	26–8–59–3								8	6		14	262	10
20–22 July	17–6–56–3		7–0–32–1					10–0–42–2	17.3–4–63–4								4	3	6	5	200	10
First Test Match (Lord's)	22–4–49–1	24–6–69–4	15.4–3–50–4	38–5–92–1			3–1–3–0										9	13	1	4	285	10
25–29 July	21.1–5–45–1	25–3–85–4	11–2–33–0	38–15–57–5						1–0–1–0						1–0–9–0	6	7		4	243	10
v. Durham (Chester-le-Street)	23.2–6–86–3		16–0–67–0			7–1–22–1		6.1–1–20–3	34–6–89–3				2.5–0–14–0				7	2		33	307	10
3–5 August	18.4–10–19–4		18–3–59–2			3–0–8–1			16–7–37–3	1–0–1–0							3	8		6	135	10
Second Test Match (Leeds)	39.5–0–106–3	33–7–127–3	22–1–90–1	55–17–142–3		7–5–6–0											7	23		2	501	10
8–12 August																						
v. Leicestershire (Leicester)			10–2–30–0	13–4–44–2	19.2–4–51–7				12–2–48–1								21	5	4	10	199	10
14–16 August			4–1–12–0	16–5–47–1	13–2–48–2	2–1–4–0	6.4–2–4–1		25–7–52–6								7	9		2	183	10
v. Essex (Chelmsford)		16–5–42–5	8–3–18–0		12–2–51–1		4–0–8–0		14–3–47–4	2–0–13–0							1	11	1	4	191	10
17–19 August		11–5–26–4	4–0–21–0		4–1–14–0		5–2–17–0		13.2–5–34–5									6		2	118	9B
Third Test Match (The Oval)	29.2–9–83–3	25–6–95–4		27–5–78–2	12–1–41–1		6–1–17–0											12	1	10	326	10
22–26 August	15.4–1–67–3	18–3–55–1		37–10–78–6	10–3–30–0		2–1–4–0										6	2	1	13	242	10
	271.5–67–787–32	195.1–42–654–30	184.4–24–710–17	325–85–861–41	128.2–21–473–14	32–7–104–3	65.4–14–205–3	47–8–164–12	170.5–43–474–29	7–1–24–1	7.3–2–46–2	9–0–78–2	4.5–0–27–0	5–1–26–0	4–0–24–0	1–0–9–0						
Bowler's average	24.59	21.80	41.76	21.00	33.78	34.66	68.33	13.66	16.34	24.00	23.00	39.00	–	–	–	–						

A. S. Lee retired hurt
B. P.J. Prichard absent

South Africa 'A' Tour

England should take note of the composition of the South Africa 'A' party which began a short tour at the beginning of July. Managed by Goolam Rajah and guided by coach Duncan Fletcher, the 15 players had an average age of under 24, and yet eight of them, including Kallis and Adams, had had experience at international level. The team was captained by John Commins of Western Province, who had led the 'A' side against England in South Africa and had appeared in three Test matches.

3, 4 and 5 July
at Leeds
Yorkshire 331 (C. White 77, R.J. Blakey 64, B. Parker 59, P.R. Adams 4 for 116) and 90 for 0 dec. (A. McGrath 50 not out)
South Africa 'A' 226 (R.D. Stemp 5 for 69)
Match drawn

Captain of South Africa 'A' John Commins. (Mark Thompson/Allsport)

A chilly wind, a slow pitch and rain which wiped out play on the first day greeted the South Africans at Headingley. Yorkshire gave a first-class debut to medium-pacer Matthew Hoggard and included another medium-pacer of limited experience, Gavin Hamilton. White and Blakey added 123 for the county's third wicket, and Parker hit a breezy 59. The tourists ended the second day on 21 for 3. They continued to struggle, but a ninth wicket stand of 58 between Adams and Klusener enabled the game to be drawn.

6, 7 and 8 July
at Chesterfield
South Africa 'A' 322 for 4 dec. (J.H. Kallis 92, H.D. Ackerman 79) and 335 for 5 dec. (G.F.J. Liebenberg 123, H.H. Gibbs 68, J.B. Commins 59 not out)
Derbyshire 316 for 5 dec. (C.J. Adams 66, M.R. May 63 not out, C.M. Wells 61) and 175 for 3 (T.J.G. O'Gorman 68 not out, A.S. Rollins 50)
Match drawn

Chris Adams captained Derbyshire for the first time, and Khan, who had done well for Oxford University, made his debut for the county. The wicket was unhelpfully slow, but Kallis and Ackerman added 135 in 33 overs for the third wicket. Michael May hit a maiden first-class fifty, and Adams declared six runs in arrears. South Africa 'A' scored 128 in 31 overs before the close of the second day, and Gerhadus Liebenberg went on to reach 123 off 150 balls with a six and 18 fours. A target of 342 in 56 overs was beyond Derbyshire's ambitions, and coach Les Stillman accused the tourists of over-caution. The principal concern for South Africa was the wayward and expensive bowling of Brett Schultz.

10, 11 and 12 July
at Shenley
MCC 391 for 7 dec. (G.W. Flower 98, K.L.T. Arthurton 82, A. Flower 70, A.I.C. Dodemaide 62 not out, R. Telemachus 4 for 99)
South Africa 'A' 204 (H.H. Gibbs 57, N. Francis 4 for 34) and 490 for 4 dec. (H.H. Gibbs 183, J.B. Commins 114 not out, G.F.J. Liebenberg 73, N. Pothas 62)
Match drawn

Shenley Park in Hertfordshire is one of the most beautiful grounds in England and staged its first first-class fixture when MCC played South Africa 'A'. During the match, the ground was officially renamed the Denis Compton Ground, although it had originally been constructed by the father of John Raphael, the Surrey cricketer and multi-talented sportsman who was killed in the First World War. Under the guidance of Eric Russell, the former England and Middlesex opener, the ground has been regenerated, and, if cricketing politics allow, it should play a major part in the future of English cricket, hopefully as an academy of excellence.

With the match against South Africa 'A' scheduled to coincide with the second round of the NatWest Trophy, the MCC side consisted of Morris and Croft of Glamorgan and nine overseas cricketers. Arthurton hit six sixes in his 82 off 78 balls as MCC raced to 391 for 7. South Africa 'A' began badly and never totally recovered, Francis, a fast bowler from Trinidad, taking four wickets. In the circumstances, it was unwise for MCC to enforce the follow-on. Gibbs and Commins added 239 at five an over for the fourth wicket. Herschelle Gibbs, a 22-year-old right-hander, hit five sixes and 25 fours in a masterly display of aggression which brought him his highest score in first-class cricket.

14 July
at Swansea
South Africa 'A' 277 for 5 (J.H. Kallis 105, S. Koenig 66, H.H. Gibbs 57 not out)
Wales 152 for 7
South Africa 'A' won by 125 runs

17, 18 and 19 July
at Cardiff
South Africa 'A' 346 (D.N. Crookes 105, H.D. Ackerman 99, N. Pothas 64)
Glamorgan 165 (J.H. Kallis 4 for 31, L. Klusener 4 for 39) and 137
South Africa 'A' won by an innings and 44 runs

The South Africans enjoyed themselves in Wales. They trounced the national side in a 50-over match and beat Glamorgan by an innings inside two days. Derek Crookes hit the season's second fastest century, 100 off 77 balls, and he and Ackerman added 180 in 32 overs for the fifth wicket. Bowled out by Kallis and Klusener in the first innings, Glamorgan were tantalised by Adams in the second.

20, 21 and 22 July
at Taunton
Somerset 301 (M.N. Lathwell 108, K.A. Parsons 62, L. Klusener 5 for 74) and 309 for 8 (G.D. Rose 64, J.I.D. Kerr 56, M.E. Trescothick 55)
South Africa 'A' 509 for 7 dec. (D.N. Crookes 155 not out, N. Boje 89, J.B. Commins 73, S.J. Palframan 55)
Match drawn

This was a game of mixed fortune for the South Africans. Crookes pulled the first ball he received for six and went on to reach his second century in five days off just 107 deliveries. He and Palframan added 130 for the seventh wicket. Earlier, Parsons and Lathwell scored 125 for Somerset's second wicket. Lathwell hit 17 fours and a six. Somerset faced an innings defeat when they slipped to 163 for 6 in their second innings, but Rose and Kerr saved the match with a stand of 123.

South Africa 'A' lost both Telemachus and Kallis with injuries during the game, and the pair flew back to South Africa after a few days.

24 July
at Cheltenham
South Africa 'A' 297 for 8 (D.N. Crookes 66, J.H. Kallis 60, H.H. Gibbs 55)
Gloucestershire 269 (A. Symonds 84, M.A. Lynch 52)
South Africa 'A' won by 28 runs

An innings of 84 off 74 balls by Andrew Symonds could not save Gloucestershire from defeat in the 50-over game. South Africa 'A' scored at six an over in the early part of their innings, and Crookes and Ackerman added 99 in 14 overs for the fifth wicket.

Outstanding batsman of the tour for South Africa 'A' – Herschelle Gibbs. (Mark Thompson/Allsport)

26, 27, 28 and 29 July
at Trent Bridge
South Africa 'A' 455 (H.H. Gibbs 95, N. Pothas 90, L. Klusener 79, H.D. Ackerman 66, D.N. Crookes 59, R.J. Champan 4 for 109) and 180 for 6 dec. (H.H. Gibbs 85)
Nottinghamshire 340 (G.F. Archer 87) and 144 for 2 (P.R. Pollard 72 not out)
Match drawn

After losing both openers for 50, South Africa 'A' scored briskly and consistently. Nottinghamshire responded solidly, but South Africa 'A' pressed for victory by scoring at more than four an over in their second innings and declaring at their end of third day score. Rain restricted play on the last day.

Wicket-keeper Walker, who had displaced Noon in the Nottinghamshire side, was injured and Noon kept wicket as substitute in the second innings. He stumped Gibbs and caught Koenig.

1, 2, 3 and 4 August
at The Oval
South Africa 'A' 379 (D.N. Crookes 70, N. Boje 58 not out, H.H. Gibbs 58, J.B. Commins 55, M.W. Patterson 6 for 80) and 339 for 6 dec. (H.H. Gibbs 178, H.D. Ackerman 57)
Surrey 286 (J.D. Ratcliffe 69, A.D. Brown 69, C.C. Lewis 52) and 275 (N. Boje 5 for 58)
South Africa 'A' won by 157 runs

It is difficult to understand why Surrey agree to play matches against 'A' touring teams. In 1995, they fielded six cricketers against Australia 'A' who had never appeared in the Surrey first eleven before. In 1996, they turned out seven players making their first appearances of the season, two who did not claim a regular place in the side and Lewis and Brown, both in need of practice, against South Africa 'A'. The tourists were far from pleased. Patterson, the Irish medium-pacer who was making his debut for Surrey, recorded the best figures for a Surrey bowler on his first-class debut and was contracted for the rest of the season. Like Kallis, Schultz had returned home to South Africa and replacements Gilder and Pringle appeared in this match. Klusener, who had enjoyed considerable all-round success, did not endear himself to the umpires with his antics, and both umpires reported that they were unhappy with the South Africans' behaviour in the field. Gibbs produced another blistering innings, 178 off 209 balls, but skipper Commins voiced the general disappointment of facing weak opposition on flat tracks.

6 August
at Chelmsford
South Africa 'A' 287 for 6 (G.F.J. Liebenberg 73)
Essex 276 for 6 (D.G. Wilson 52 not out)
South Africa 'A' won by 11 runs

A second wicket stand of 103 in 17 overs between Gibbs and Liebenberg gave basis to the South African innings, and a weakened Essex side was never really in touch with the required rate. All-rounder Danny Wilson, making his Essex debut, shared an unbroken seventh wicket stand of 80 with Ilott and took two wickets for 40.

9, 10, 11 and 12 August
at Worcester
South Africa 'A' 202 (J.B. Commins 61, P.A. Thomas 4 for 33, B.E.A. Preece 4 for 79) and 325 (M.W. Pringle 105, D.N. Crookes 62, D.A. Leatherdale 4 for 75)
Worcestershire 77 (G. Gilder 8 for 22) and 278 (D.A. Leatherdale 73, S.J. Rhodes 51, G.J. Smith 4 for 70, M.W. Pringle 4 for 90)
South Africa 'A' won by 172 runs

On a blameless pitch at Worcester, 26 wickets fell on the first day. The star of the day was Gary Gilder, who bowled his left-arm at a lively pace and achieved not only a career best 8 for 22, but the best performance by a tourist at New Road. Gilder had come to England as replacement for the injured Telemachus. Worcestershire, who gave debuts to Ralph and Amjad, also suffered a maiden first-class century from Meyrick Pringle, whose 105 came off 116 balls.

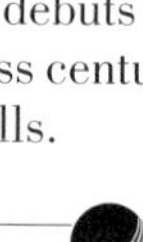

15, 16, 17 and 18 August
at Chester-le-Street
South Africa 'A' 302 (N. Boje 65, G.F.J. Liebenberg 54, M.W. Pringle 52, I.D.K. Salisbury 52) and 192 (J.B. Commins 85, R.J. Kirtley 5 for 51)
TCCB XI 338 (A.D. Brown 79, J.A. Daley 76, M.W. Pringle 4 for 123) and 158 for 2 (A.P. Wells 58 not out)
TCCB XI won by 8 wickets

While England have gained much advantage from 'A' tours to India, Pakistan, South Africa and Zimbabwe 'A' visitors to this country are offered less encouragement. They are generally opposed by weakened sides and even the concluding match, against a select eleven, sees them facing not a truly representative England reserve side, but a side selected from counties not otherwise engaged. So the TCCB XI chosen for the final match of the South Africa 'A' tour was drawn from five counties, and, of the original selection, Brown of Durham and Lewry of Sussex withdrew. The replacement for Brown was Robert Kirtley of Sussex, whose fifth first-class match this was. Only two of the side, Wells and Salisbury, had played Test cricket while Surrey's Alistair Brown had barely scored a run since appearing in the Texaco Trophy matches early in the season.

As it transpired, Kirtley had a fine match. He bowled at a lively pace and helped reduce the tourists to 232 for 7.

South Africa 'A' First-Class Averages

Batting

	M	Inns	NO	Runs	HS	Av	100s	50s
H.H. Gibbs	8	14	1	867	183	66.69	2	5
D.N. Crookes	7	11	1	566	155*	56.60	2	3
J.B. Commins	9	15	3	597	114*	49.75	1	5
N. Pothas	6	9	2	309	90	44.14		3
N. Boje	7	9	2	289	89	41.28		3
H.D. Ackerman	7	11	–	447	99	40.63		4
L. Klusener	8	8	3	171	79	34.20		1
G.F.J. Liebenberg	8	14	–	453	123	32.35	1	2
J.H. Kallis	4	4	–	128	92	32.00		1
P.R. Adams	4	5	3	63	37	31.50		
M.W. Pringle	4	6	–	170	105	28.33	1	1
S.G. Koenig	7	11	–	221	46	20.09		
S.J. Palframan	5	7	1	104	55	17.33		1
G.M. Gilder	4	6	–	43	22	7.16		
B.N. Schultz	3	2	–	12	9	6.00		
R. Telemachus	3	2	–	8	4	4.00		
G.J. Smith	5	5	3	7	5	3.50		

Bowling

	Overs	Mds	Runs	Wks	Av	Best	10/m	5/inn
H.H. Gibbs	12	2	43	3	14.33	2/14		
G.M. Gilder	95.1	29	243	13	18.69	8/22	1	1
J.H. Kallis	56.3	19	145	6	24.16	4/31		
L. Klusener	232.2	44	783	31	25.25	5/74		1
G.J. Smith	125.2	24	402	15	26.80	4/70		
R. Telemachus	40	5	188	7	26.85	4/99		
P.R. Adams	108.4	19	390	10	39.00	4/116		
M.W. Pringle	173.4	41	579	14	41.35	4/90		
N. Boje	160.4	30	562	12	46.83	5/58		1
B.N. Schultz	67	6	297	6	49.50	2/45		
D.N. Crookes	84	15	259	3	86.33	1/7		
G.F.J. Liebenberg	3	2	1	–	–			
S.G. Koenig	3	2	5	–	–			
N. Pothas	1	–	5	–	–			
H.D. Ackerman	5	1	10	–	–			

Fielding Figures

15 – N. Pothas; 11 – S.J. Palframan (ct 10 / st 1); 9 – H.H. Gibbs; 8 – G.F.J. Liebenberg and D.N. Crookes; 6 – subs; 5 – N. Boje; 4 – L. Klusener; 3 – H.D. Ackerman and S.G. Koenig; 2 – J.B. Commins and R. Telemachus; 1 – P.R. Adams, G.M. Gilder, J.H. Kallis, B.N. Schultz and G.J. Smith

They were revitalised by Pringle, who hit 52 off 56 balls, but a total of 302 was a disappointment. TCCB XI reached 81 for 1 by the close. They took a 36-run lead on the second day, helped considerably by 52 extras which included 36 no-balls. Kirtley then made decisive inroads, and South Africa 'A' closed on 150 for 6. There was no recovery, and they tumbled to their only defeat of the tour inside three days. Kirtley enjoyed the best haul of his short career.

This was a disappointing end for the South Africans who were still left speculating as to what use the tour had been to them.

MCC v. South Africa 'A' at Shenley. This beautiful ground has been named after Denis Compton, and surely it is destined to play an important part in the development of English cricket.
(Mark Thompson)

NatWest Bank Trophy

The sixty-over knock-out competition is the longest running of the limited-over tournaments, and it has given much joy and produced memorable moments over the past 33 years. It is organised with warmth and generosity, and the goodwill generated by Lord Alexander through Steve Austin, Barbara Quin and the rest of the NatWest team is immeasurable. It is such a pity then that the TCCB have chosen this competition as a means of extracting more revenue from the paying public.

In the past few years, country members have been offered less and less cricket for their annual subscription, yet, even though in some cases they may be paying more than £200 for executive membership for the season, they are still asked to pay a levy of £8 if they wants to see a NatWest cup tie, even if that cup tie is between Somerset and Suffolk or Essex and Devon. This cannot be right, and the sooner the problem is addressed, the better. The patience of county members is being tested to the full, and there is a breaking point.

Season ticket holders of major Premier League clubs in soccer are offered a better deal. The price of the season ticket includes several cup ties, and if the club makes an early exit from a cup competition, the vouchers for those matches carry over to the next season. Cricket stands accused of greed.

First Round

25 June

at March
Kent 275 for 6 (N.J. Llong 115 not out, M.A. Ealham 51)
Cambridgeshire 182 (G.W. Ecclestone 92)
Kent won by 93 runs
(Man of the Match: N.J. Llong)

at St Austell
Warwickshire 311 for 9 (T.L. Penney 90, D.R. Brown 67, D.J. Angove 4 for 65)
Cornwall 168
Warwickshire won by 133 runs
(Man of the Match: D.J. Angove)

at Carlisle
Middlesex 270 for 8 (M.W. Gatting 71, J.D. Carr 62)
Cumberland 164
Middlesex won by 102 runs
(Man of the Match: M.W. Gatting)

at Chester-le-Street
Durham 300 for 7 (J.E. Morris 109)
Scotland 202 for 6 (G.N. Reifer 103 not out, G. Salmond 52)
Durham won by 98 runs
(Man of the Match: J.E. Morris)

at Chelmsford
Essex 312 for 5 (N. Hussain 105, G.A. Gooch 50, R.C. Irani 50)
Devon 193 (N.A. Folland 64)
Essex won by 119 runs
(Man of the Match: N. Hussain)

at Cardiff
Worcestershire 253 for 9 (T.M. Moody 123, V.S. Solanki 50)
Glamorgan 210
Worcestershire won by 43 runs
(Man of the Match: T.M. Moody)

at Southampton
Hampshire 322 for 6 (J.S. Laney 153, J.P. Stephenson 107, S.C. Goldsmith 4 for 64)
Norfolk 223 (N. Fox 68)
Hampshire won by 99 runs
(Man of the Match: J.S. Laney)

at Leicester
Leicestershire 406 for 5 (V.J. Wells 201, P.V. Simmons 82)
Berkshire 300 for 6 (H.M. Hall 108, S.D. Myles 81)
Leicestershire won by 106 runs
(Man of the Match: V.J. Wells)

Shane Lee, Somerset's Australian all-rounder, hit a century on his debut in the NatWest Trophy, 104 v. Suffolk at Taunton.
(Nigel French/ASP)

Australian batsman Stuart Law was a pillar of strength for Essex in all competitions. He hit centuries for Essex against Hampshire and Durham in the NatWest Trophy and a blazing fifty in the semi-final of the competition. International duty with Australia kept him out of the final.
(Clive Mason/Allsport)

at Sleaford
Gloucestershire 222 (A. Symonds 87, N.S. Gill 4 for 44)
Lincolnshire 135
Gloucestershire won by 87 runs
(Man of the Match: A. Symonds)

at Northampton
Cheshire 135 (R.G. Hignett 52)
Northamptonshire 139 for 1 (R.R. Montgomerie 69 not out)
Northamptonshire won by 9 wickets
(Man of the Match: R.G. Hignett)

at Aston Rowant
Lancashire 310 for 6 (N.J. Speak 83, M.A. Atherton 79, M. Watkinson 62)
Oxfordshire 201 (C.S. Knightley 61 not out, S.V. Laudat 57)
Lancashire won by 109 runs
(Man of the Match: M.A. Atherton)

at Taunton
Somerset 333 for 6 (S. Lee 104, K.A. Parsons 51)
Suffolk 271 for 6 (P.J. Caley 88 not out, A. Jones 62)
Somerset won by 62 runs
(Man of the Match: S. Lee)

at Stone
Staffordshire 175
Derbyshire 180 for 2 (C.J. Adams 68 not out, T.J.G. O'Gorman 62 not out)
Derbyshire won by 8 wickets
(Man of the Match: P.A.J. DeFreitas)

at The Oval
Surrey 346 (A.D. Brown 72, M.A. Butcher 60, A.J. Stewart 50, S. van Dijk 4 for 57)
Holland 187
Surrey won by 159 runs
(Man of the Match: S. van Dijk)

at Leeds
Yorkshire 345 for 5 (M.D. Moxon, M.G. Bevan 69, M.P. Vaughan 64)
Nottinghamshire 140 (R.D. Stemp 4 for 45)
Yorkshire won by 205 runs
(Man of the Match: M.D. Moxon)

25 and 26 June
at Belfast
Sussex 384 for 9 (A.P. Wells 113, C.W.J. Athey 57, D. Heasley 4 for 66)
Ireland 80
Sussex won by 304 runs
(Man of the Match: A.P. Wells)

There were no surprises in the first round of the NatWest Trophy, with all the first-class counties victorious over Minor County opposition.

The left-handed Nigel Llong hit his first century in limited-over cricket as Kent beat Cambridgeshire, and Penney hit his highest NatWest score in the match at St Austell. It was here that Lovell of Cornwall took 2 for 107, the most expensive analysis in the competition's history.

The West Indian Reifer hit a century for Scotland, who conceded 29 wides, against Durham, and Devon batted two short against Essex because of injuries in the field.

Tom Moody scored 123 off 129 balls to lead Worcestershire's recovery against Glamorgan. They were 35 for 3 and finished with 253 for 9. In the other match which pitted first-class counties against each other, Yorkshire overwhelmed Nottinghamshire, and Stemp's best one-day analysis brought him the award of his county cap.

Laney scored a century before lunch for Hampshire against Norfolk, and he and Stephenson put on 269 for the first wicket, a record for the competition.

Andrew Caddick has Symonds caught behind first ball as Somerset beat Gloucestershire in the second round of the NatWest Trophy. Symonds was the second victim in Caddick's hat-trick. (Clive Mason/Allsport)

At Leicester, Vince Wells became only the second batsman to score a double century in the competition, while Leicestershire's 406 for 5 was the second highest score ever recorded. Wells and Simmons added 202 for Leicestershire's third wicket. Berkshire responded bravely with the second highest score by a Minor County and with Hall becoming the twelfth Minor County batsman to hit a century in the competition.

John Emburey rounded off the Cheshire innings with a hat-trick, while Somerset ran into an old adversary in Derek Randall, who opened the innings for Suffolk. Shane Lee hit a six and 10 fours in his 104, which came off 103 balls.

Another Australian, Dean Jones, took the last two Staffordshire wickets with the only two balls he bowled.

The New Zealand Test bowler Chris Pringle played for Holland against Surrey at The Oval, and Sussex's 304-run victory over Ireland was second only to Somerset's 346-run victory over Devon in 1990.

Second Round

10 July
at Derby
Kent 251 for 8 (M.J. Walker 51)
Derbyshire 254 for 8 (D.G. Cork 61, K.M. Krikken 55)
Derbyshire won by 2 wickets
(Man of the Match: P.A.J. DeFreitas)

at Chelmsford
Essex 361 for 7 (R.C. Irani 124, S.G. Law 100, R.J. Rollins 54 not out)
Durham 294 (M.A. Roseberry 100)
Essex won by 67 runs
(Man of the Match: S.G. Law)

at Old Trafford
Northamptonshire 223 (A.L. Penberthy 79, P.J. Martin 4 for 36, S. Elworthy 4 for 40)
Lancashire 225 for 9
Lancashire won by 1 wicket
(Man of the Match: P.J. Martin)

at Leicester
Sussex 220
Leicestershire 188 (J.J. Whitaker 54)
Sussex won by 32 runs
(Man of the Match: I.D.K. Salisbury)

at Taunton
Gloucestershire 118 (A.R. Caddick 4 for 39)
Somerset 122 for 5
Somerset won by 5 wickets
(Man of the Match: H.R.J. Trump)

at Edgbaston
Surrey 291 for 7 (G.P. Thorpe 96, A.J. Hollioake 57, S.M. Pollock 4 for 37)
Warwickshire 203 (N.V. Knight 68)
Surrey won by 88 runs
(Man of the Match: G.P. Thorpe)

at Worcester
Hampshire 328 for 6 (R.A. Smith 158, J.S. Laney 82)
Worcestershire 203 (K.D. James 4 for 42)
Hampshire won by 125 runs
(Man of the Match: R.A. Smith)

at Leeds
Middlesex 199 for 9 (P.N. Weekes 104)
Yorkshire 200 for 3 (D. Byas 73 not out)
Yorkshire won by 7 wickets
(Man of the Match: P.N. Weekes)

Derbyshire lost Dean Jones with a sprained ankle before the match against Kent. DeFreitas took over the captaincy and Cork was promoted to open. Both performed admirably. DeFreitas bowled a miserly spell of 1 for 28 from his 12 overs and helped restrict Kent to 251 for 8. Barnett ran himself out going for a third run, but Cork stayed firm to take Derbyshire to 210 for 4. The vision of victory then became blurred as McCague took three wickets in 10 balls to reduce them to 217 for 7. DeFreitas steadied the side, and he and Harris scored the last 26 runs needed to bring victory with four balls to spare.

Essex were without Hussain, who was injured, and they looked decidedly wobbly when they lost their first three wickets, including Gooch for 0, for 43 runs. Law and Prichard added 64, but the real substance to the innings came when Irani joined Law in a stand worth 121 in 18 overs. Law's 100 came off 114 balls with two sixes and 10 fours, and it was he who took the individual award, for he had checked the collapse which threatened disaster. Irani's 124 was a wonderfully violent affair with two sixes, eight fours and energetic running. His hundred came off only 85 balls, and there was a joyful contribution from Rollins, who hit 54 in 43 balls.

To their credit, Durham faced a daunting target with vigour. Roseberry reached 100 off 103 balls, and at 208 for 5 there was a glimmer of hope. Such's second spell ended all speculation, for he dismissed Ligertwood and Brown in the same over.

Northamptonshire and Lancashire, due to meet in the Benson and Hedges Cup Final a few days later, played out a tense drama at Old Trafford. Put in to bat, the visitors slumped to 29 for 4 and went to lunch at 105 for 7. They had been mostly undermined by Martin, who revelled on a pitch containing early moisture in an atmosphere heavy with cloud. Fordham and Curran offered temporary salvation with a fifth wicket stand of 43, but both fell to Elworthy in the same over.

The not out batsmen at lunch were Penberthy and Emburey, and it was they who staged the Northamptonshire recovery, adding 112 for the eighth wicket. Emburey batted with his customary resilience and was never found wanting when a loose ball was delivered. Penberthy made his highest one-day score, 79 off 84 balls, and was the prime reason for Lancashire facing a target as high as 224.

There seemed no problems for Atherton and Gallian as they kept Ambrose at bay and took the score to 68 at tea. Without addition, both fell in the space of five balls on the resumption, and Crawley went cheaply, sweeping at the admirable Emburey.

Fairbrother, Lloyd and Watkinson adopted a positive approach, but, with six wickets down and 12 overs remaining, Lancashire still needed 42 to win. Hegg and Austin scored 16 of them, and Elworthy and Hegg 19. Hegg looked likely to win the match, but, with three required in the 59th over, he was caught at mid-off. Martin strode to the crease and immediately hit Capel through mid-wicket for the winning boundary.

Sussex chose to bat first at Leicester and were struggling at 129 for 6. Salisbury batted with the composure that the situation required, and he and Drakes put on 43. The Sussex innings was also boosted by 42 extras. This was top score ahead of Lenham's 36, Speight's 33, and Salisbury's 30.

Leicestershire lost Wells to the second ball of their innings. Smith quickly followed, and the home side plummeted to 78 for 5. Whitaker and Nixon added 60, but Lewry dismissed Whitaker, and Salisbury, who took 2 for 23 in his 12 overs, bowled Millns as Sussex gained a surprisingly easy win.

Gloucestershire's dreams were shattered at Taunton by Rose, Caddick and Trump. They lost two wickets to Rose for 17 before Lynch and Cunliffe hit 57 in seven overs. At this point, Caddick performed the first hat-trick of his career, having Lynch and Symonds caught behind and Cunliffe taken low in the gully by Trump. Shattered at suddenly finding themselves of 75 for 5, Gloucestershire became strokeless, and with Trump taking 3 for 15 in 11 overs, they were bowled out in 32.4 overs.

Gloucestershire performed better in the field than they had done with the bat, but Somerset won with 27.4 overs to spare.

Warwickshire, the holders, fell to the strength of the Surrey batting. Surrey had been asked to bat first, and they

Tony Penberthy during his valiant 79, his highest one-day score, for Northamptonshire against Lancashire in the second round the NatWest Trophy.
(Graham Chadwick/Allsport)

responded with valuable contributions from all after Stewart had gone at 20. The substance of the innings was provided by Thorpe, who batted superbly for three hours and faced 139 balls for his 96. It was a beautifully judged innings, full of good running and perfectly suited to the occasion. Adam Hollioake gave the necessary spice with a 46-ball half century, and Surrey set an imposing target.

They matched their batting with aggressive bowling and fielding, and Warwickshire's last seven wickets went down for 45 runs.

Hampshire totally outplayed Worcestershire at New Road. The home county had a nightmare. They asked Hampshire to bat when they won the toss and then found that Sheriyar, their main strike bowler, could not find the right line. He conceded 35 runs in five overs, 13 of the runs being wides. In all, Worcestershire conceded 22 wides among the 43 extras that contributed to Hampshire's score. Stephenson fell to Newport at 34, but Robin Smith joined Laney, 82 off 129 balls, in a stand that realised 179 in 33 overs.

Smith was magnificent, striking the ball with great power and placing his shots with skill and intelligence. He hit 21 fours and two sixes and faced 151 balls for his 158, his highest one-day score. He was out in the final over of the innings, but even then he had taken 10 runs off the first two balls of that over.

No side in the competition had ever scored 329 to win a match, and Worcestershire did not suggest for one moment that they would set a record. They fell apart as soon as Kevan James came on to bowl. He had Curtis caught behind, bowled Church and beat Hick with a straight ball which had the batsman leg before for 0. James' three wickets came in the space of 14 balls, and in spite of Moody and Spiring adding 54, the rest was silence.

Middlesex could manage only 45 runs for the loss of Ramprakash in the first 20 overs at Leeds. Gatting was run out at 50 and the only substance to the innings came in a fifth wicket stand of 53 between Weekes and Brown. Weekes batted until the final over, and extras at 34 were second highest scorer to his 104.

Vaughan and Moxon were out with 36 scored, but Yorkshire took complete control as Byas and Bevan added 91 in 17 overs. Bevan was caught off Fraser, and McGrath joined Byas for the last 73 runs as Yorkshire won with 16 overs to spare.

Quarter-Finals

30 July
at Southampton
Essex 286 (S.G. Law 107, R.J. Rollins 53)
Hampshire 186
Essex won by 100 runs
(Man of the Match: S.G. Law)

at Old Trafford
Lancashire 289 for 9 (M.A. Atherton 115, G.D. Lloyd 61, K.J. Barnett 5 for 32)
Derbyshire 287 for 9 (D.M. Jones 100 not out, D.G. Cork 59)
Lancashire won by 2 runs
(Man of the Match: M.A. Atherton)

at Hove
Sussex 212 for 9 (C.W.J. Athey 54)
Yorkshire 215 for 5 (M.D. Moxon 76, D. Byas 52)
Yorkshire won by 5 wickets
(Man of the Match: D. Gough)

30 and 31 July
at The Oval
Somerset 225 (P.D. Bowler 52, S.C. Ecclestone 52)
Surrey 226 for 5 (M.A. Butcher 91)
Surrey won by 5 wickets
(Man of the Match: M.A. Butcher)

Electing to bat first at Southampton, Essex had some early trouble against a swinging ball under an overcast sky. Gooch and Robinson laid a useful foundation with 56 for the first wickets, but Gooch was caught off a violent pull, and Hussain and Robinson were out in successive overs. James captured two of these wickets and was by far the best of the Hampshire bowlers.

Stephenson, erratic and heavily punished at first, removed Prichard and Irani in quick succession, and Essex were 127 for 5 in the 37th over. Even so, there seemed little threat to Essex, for Law was at the crease and already exuding an authority. In the next 18 overs, he and Rollins doubled the score. Law hit three sixes and nine fours, and his 107 came off 81 balls. While he was batting it looked a different game.

Rollins' half century came off 59 balls, and his rapidly improving batting allied to his outstanding wicket-keeping make him a fine prospect as an England 'keeper in the near future.

Hampshire were soon struggling. Ilott trapped Smith leg before for 7, and tidy bowling and fine fielding – three men were run out – quickly reduced the home county to 127 for 7, and the contest was over. The question as to who would be Man of the Match had been settled in the early afternoon.

Lancashire's penchant for close finishes continued with a two-run victory over Derbyshire at the impregnable fortress of Old Trafford. The Red Rose innings was built around Mike Atherton's 115, which took him to the 58th over. His principal ally was Graham Lloyd, who hit 61 off 59 balls in a fourth wicket stand of 101. The 59th over of the Lancashire innings was somewhat bizarre, with Kim Barnett taking three wickets, but the final over was even more bizarre. Kevin Dean, the very promising young left-arm fast bowler, had both Yates and Martin caught on the boundary by DeFreitas, but each time umpire Sharp called no-ball, judging the deliveries to be above waist height full tosses. The over produced 13 runs.

Barnett and Cork gave the Derbyshire innings a sound foundation with 92 for the first wicket. None of the middle-order stayed long enough to make telling contributions, but Dean Jones continued a valiant battle. From the last five overs, 51 runs were needed, and Fairbrother made a vital stop when he knocked down a Jones drive off Austin which was going for six in the penultimate over. This meant that Derbyshire needed 10 from the final over, and, ultimately, four from the final ball bowled by Chapple. Jones drove along the ground to long-off, a shot which completed his century but did not win the match.

Sussex reached 130 for 3 against Yorkshire before Gough, bowling fast and swinging the ball late, took two wickets in four balls and set in motion a collapse that saw five wickets fall for nine runs. Jarvis and Drakes scored 56 in 11 overs, but the damage had been done.

For Yorkshire, Vaughan went early, but the hundred came up in 20 overs as Moxon and Byas added 99. With the power of Bevan still to come, victory was a formality, and White and Blakey scored the last 39 runs as the target was reached with 12.3 overs unused.

Dark and drizzle took the match at The Oval into a second day, but Surrey, 126 for 4 for 35 overs, with their batting in depth appeared to have the upper hand. Somerset had flattered to deceive. Bowler and Ecclestone scored 97 for the second wicket, but, from 117 for 1, Somerset descended to 225 all out as batsmen perished to rash shots and the last 10 overs produced a meagre 45 runs.

Caddick took three wickets at the start of the Surrey innings, but when play ended on the Tuesday he had only two overs of his quota remaining, and Mark Butcher was unbeaten on 52. By the time Butcher was stumped off Parsons on the Wednesday morning, he and Adam Hollioake had added 87 and the match was virtually won. Julian joined the elder Hollioake to apply the last rites with 43 balls remaining.

Semi-Finals

13 August
at Old Trafford
Lancashire 293 for 9 (G.D. Lloyd 81, J.P. Crawley 62)
Yorkshire 274 for 8 (M.G. Bevan 85)
Lancashire won by 19 runs
(Man of the Match: I.D. Austin)

at The Oval
Surrey 275 for 5 (A.J. Stewart 125 not out)
Essex 278 for 6 (S.G. Law 53, R.C. Irani 52 not out, G.A. Gooch 50)
Essex won by 4 wickets
(Man of the Match: A.J. Stewart)

Drawn to meet Lancashire in a semi-final at Old Trafford for the second time in the season, Yorkshire once more failed to bring down the fortress, nor this time did they really dent the walls. There are some who might argue with this last statement, for Lancashire were 52 for 3 after 20 overs. Atherton had been caught behind cutting at Stemp after facing 60 balls for his 18, and Fairbrother had insanely slogged the second ball he received to long-on. Gallian had been run out after scoring 19 out of 26 for the first wicket.

Mark Butcher is run out, the first Surrey wicket to fall, and his side tumbles to a semi-final defeat against Essex.
(Clive Mason/Allsport)

In spite of these successes, the Yorkshire cricket looked tense. There was an air of desperation, four dropped catches and some rather ragged fielding. Nor was the bowling too intelligent as Crawley and Lloyd composed a stand of 125 from 27 overs which put Lancashire firmly on top. Lloyd's 81 came from 90 balls, but he and Crawley were out in quick succession.

Watkinson maintained the momentum with 35 off 28 balls, and Hegg, as ever, was lively and inventive. Only three wickets in the last over by Gough prevented Lancashire from topping 300.

The Yorkshire response never touched the right note. Moxon and Vaughan could not catch the tempo, and Byas was taken at mid-wicket when he suggested he might lead a serious challenge. What challenge there was came from Bevan, who shared a fourth wicket stand of 80 with McGrath, but this good work was undone when Austin captured three wickets in nine balls. Gough hit 42 off 33 balls, but Lancashire moved comfortably into their second final of the season.

At The Oval, Essex won the toss and asked Surrey to bat in conditions which gave the bowlers slight advantage. The ball moved about early on and, after early morning rain, the outfield was not fast. Ilott began by conceding four wides from a prodigious out-swinger, but soon the bowling settled and the bat was passed on numerous occasions. Butcher seemed totally out of touch, failing to punish what few half-volleys were on offer, and it was not until the 14th over when Stewart turned a ball off his legs that the first boundary was registered since the wides of the opening over. In the 18th, Butcher hooked Irani for four to bring up 50, but there was a certain desperation in the running which suggested the batsmen were not at ease.

Stewart drove Law for six in the 24th over to indicate an increase in tempo, but eight balls later, a terrible mix-up left Butcher dithering and run out by a combination involving Law, Rollins and Such.

Surprisingly, Shahid came in ahead of Thorpe, which meant that Surrey's leading batsman did not get to the crease until after 44 overs. At lunch, Surrey were 130 for 1 from 38 overs with Stewart, not really convincing, on 68.

Shahid's 25 occupied 18 overs, and when he was caught off Williams this allowed Thorpe to the wicket. Stewart should have gone in the same over as Shahid, but Ilott dropped a simple offering at mid-off. Thorpe was under too much pressure to score quickly and sliced to extra cover, while Brown showed why he had not been scoring runs of late when he charged down the wicket at Grayson and was stumped. It was the last thing that Surrey needed, and one had to question why, since he was completely out of touch, Brown was in the side ahead of David Ward. Adam Hollioake, too, disappointed, hitting Grayson to mid-wicket where Law ran in to take a fine low catch. To the consternation of the Essex players, Hollioake stood his ground until Gooch persuaded him to leave.

At 214 for 5, Surrey were great under-achievers, but Lewis arrived to strike three sixes and assemble 45 off 29 balls. With Stewart holding steady to the end, Surrey reached 275, less than hoped, better than expected. Stewart finished with two sixes and nine fours to his credit.

Essex lost Grayson leg before to Martin Bicknell at 10, and Hussain slashed a wide long hop from Lewis into the hands of gully. Gooch scored only five in the first 10 overs, but he was offering a solid base, and he and Law added 96 in 17 overs. Law gave the Essex innings the increase in tempo that it needed with 53 off 44 balls, a blistering innings. Prichard, too, played well for 33, and when Gooch was out for 50 in the 38th over, Essex were 175 for 4.

The over in which Gooch was out epitomised much of Surrey's cricket. Lewis started with four wides, bowled Gooch with a fine delivery, was struck for two boundaries by the new batsman Irani and then conceded another wide. In the main, Lewis' bowling was awful. His 12 overs cost 71 runs, and Essex were presented with 47 extras of which 23 were wides and 15 were no-balls. This was a total lack of discipline, confirmed by an over-rate that was so slow as to lose them nearly half of their £10,500 reward for being defeated semi-finalists.

Julian had conceded 22 runs in his first two overs, but, unlike Lewis, he returned to better effect and accounted for Prichard and Robinson in the same over. This was shortly after Prichard had declined the offer to leave the field because of bad light.

The aggressive batting of Graham Lloyd was a vital factor in Lancashire's semi-final victory over Yorkshire at Old Trafford. (Graham Chadwick/Allsport)

If his decision troubled him, his worries did not last long, for Irani and Rollins scored the final 65 runs in 13 overs to take Essex to victory with 20 balls to spare. Irani's 52 came off 61 balls, and, like Rollins, he had every right to leave the field exultant.

NatWest Trophy Final

Essex v. Lancashire

Essex did not have the comfort of Law for the final. He was on duty in Sri Lanka with Australia, while Lancashire again chose to omit Elworthy from a Lord's final.

Prichard won the toss and decided to field. He must have been swayed by the fact that pre-match publicity had emphasised the fact that the side batting second invariably won the NatWest final and that Essex had chased Surrey's 275 in the semi-final most successfully. Mike Watkinson later confirmed that he would have chosen to bat if he had won the toss, for the pitch looked doubtful, which proved to be an understatement.

For Essex, all went as planned – initially. Ilott and Williams bowled well, runs were hard to come by, and Ilott bowled Atherton with his first ball of the seventh over. Crucially, Crawley survived an appeal for leg before first ball, and only umpire Shepherd can tell why the appeal was not upheld. It seemed to matter little when Irani joined the attack from the Nursery End and immediately had Gallian leg before with the first ball of the 18th over.

What followed should have given us some indication of what we were to suffer in the afternoon. For 53 minutes, 38 balls, Neil Fairbrother, arguably the most accomplished hitter in the one-day game, was unable to hit the ball off the

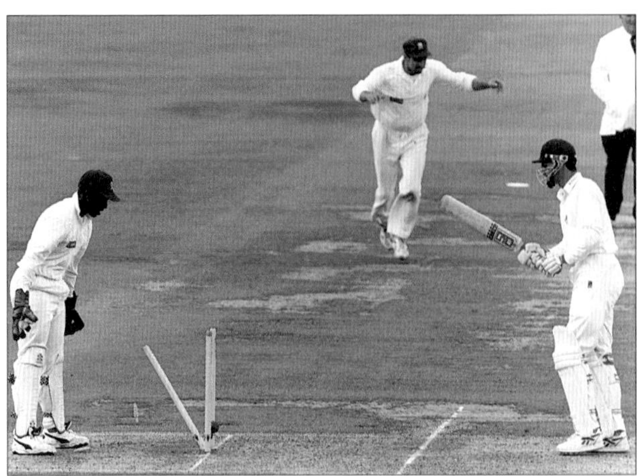

Top: Watkinson looks back in dismay, bowled by Such for 18. (David Munden/Sportsline)

Above: Warren Hegg dives low to his right to catch Nasser Hussain, and the Essex decline begins. (Adrian Murrell/Allsport)

Below: First blood to Essex as Atherton is bowled by Ilott. Gooch is at slip. (Clive Mason/Allsport)

square. He scored nine runs before dragging his bat across the line to Irani and being bowled. Irani claimed his third wicket in his next over, having Lloyd splendidly taken at slip by Gooch. At lunch, Lancashire were 90 for 4 from 35 overs with Crawley on 42 and Watkinson on 1.

The pitch was offering extravagant sideways movement, but what we should have noted was that Crawley had survived and Fairbrother, however uncomfortably, had survived for nearly an hour, through their determination to play forward and smother the ball. It was a lesson the Essex batsmen did not heed.

Glen Chapple completes the best analysis in a NatWest Final when he bowls Peter Such first ball. The match is over, and Man of the Match Chapple has figures of 6 for 18.
(David Munden/Sportsline)

Watkinson struck two boundaries and added 34 in 10 overs with Crawley before being bowled by Such. Crawley's 129-ball innings ended when he got an inside edge as he went down the pitch to Such and was stumped. Crawley had hit seven boundaries and confirmed that he is an intelligent batsman, sound of temperament, elegant of style.

Hegg busied for half and hour, and Austin hit Grayson for six, only to be caught next ball when he tried to repeat the shot. Grayson claimed a third wicket and ran out Yates on the last ball of the innings. Lancashire were out for 186, and Essex, in bowling and fielding, had done all that could have been asked of them, particularly when one considers that Williams had broken down with an injury in the middle of his eighth over.

The sun shone only temporarily, and the pitch began to decline rapidly. Grayson was very well caught low down

The end of a lonely vigil. Gooch walks away as Gallian raises his arms in triumph having trapped the former England captain leg before with his first delivery. Skipper Mike Watkinson joins the celebrations. (David Munden/Sportsline)

NatWest Bank Trophy Final – Essex v. Lancashire

7 September 1996 at Lord's

Lancashire

J.E.R. Gallian	lbw, **b** Irani	**21**
M.A. Atherton	**b** Ilott	**4**
J.P. Crawley	**st** Rollins, **b** Such	**66**
N.H. Fairbrother	**b** Irani	**9**
G.D. Lloyd	**c** Gooch, **b** Irani	**1**
M. Watkinson (Capt)	**b** Such	**18**
*W.K. Hegg	**b** Grayson	**15**
I.D. Austin	**c** Cowan, **b** Grayson	**18**
G. Chapple	**c** Cowan, **b** Grayson	**4**
G. Yates	run out	**9**
P.J. Martin	not out	**5**
	b **4**, lb **3**, w **5**, nb **4**	**16**
	60 overs	**186**

	O	M	R	W
Ilott	12	2	29	**1**
Williams	7.4	–	39	**–**
Irani	12	5	25	**3**
Cowan	12	2	33	**–**
Such	12	1	29	**2**
Grayson	4.2	–	24	**3**

Fall of Wickets
1–**16**, 2–**48**, 3–**86**, 4–**88**, 5–**122**, 6–**139**, 7–**157**, 8–**168**, 9–**175**

Essex

G.A. Gooch	lbw, **b** Gallian	**10**
A.P. Grayson	**c** Hegg, **b** Martin	**6**
N. Hussain	**c** Hegg, **b** Martin	**2**
P.J. Prichard (Capt)	**c** Fairbrother, **b** Martin	**6**
R.C. Irani	**b** Chapple	**5**
D.D.J. Robinson	**c** Fairbrother, **b** Chapple	**2**
*R.J. Rollins	**b** Chapple	**0**
M.C. Ilott	lbw, **b** Chapple	**0**
N.F. Williams	not out	**11**
A.P. Cowan	**b** Chapple	**11**
P.M. Such	**b** Chapple	**0**
	lb **1**, w **3**	**4**
	27.2 overs	**57**

	O	M	R	W
Martin	10	2	17	**3**
Austin	7	3	10	**–**
Chapple	6.2	1	18	**6**
Gallian	4	–	11	**1**

Fall of Wickets
1–**13**, 2–**17**, 3–**25**, 4–**31**, 5–**33**, 6–**33**, 7–**33**, 8–**34**, 9–**57**

Umpires: D.R. Shepherd & P. Willey *Man of the Match:* G. Chapple

Lancashire won by 129 runs

in the seventh over, and two overs later Hussain was out in a similar manner as Martin again moved the ball late. Prichard became Martin's third victim when he was very well caught at slip by Fairbrother, and when Chapple took over at the Nursery End he bowled Irani with a ball that barely left the ground. This was an ominous sign for Essex and for a crowd who had hoped to see a fair game of cricket.

Chapple has been a most promising quick bowler for two or three seasons now, and at last he was able to show a large audience why he is so highly rated. He had Robinson caught at slip, the first Essex batsman to be out playing an attacking shot, and he bowled Rollins first ball with an unplayable delivery. Gallian replaced Martin at the Pavilion End, and his first ball kept very low and had Gooch leg before. Essex were 33 for 7 in 20.1 overs. They were 34 for 8 when Ilott was out in the next over.

Williams, batting with a runner, and Cowan played a couple of extravagant shots, and at tea, Williams 2, Cowan 10, the score was 46 for 8.

Cowan and Such fell to successive balls in the 28th over, and Essex were out for the lowest total in a NatWest Final to give Lancashire a remarkable victory and a magnificent double in the two cup competitions.

Chapple took the individual award for a wonderfully successful piece of bowling, but there were many who were far from satisfied. Brian Luckhurst, the former Kent and England opener, described the pitch as a disgrace, with the ball moving anywhere and everywhere as if by whim. The bounce was inconsistent to an incredible degree, and this pitch was totally unfit for any one-day game let alone a show-piece final.

Some years ago, Essex were deprived of the championship by having 25 points deducted for a sub-standard pitch at Southend which was far superior to this track at Lord's. In 1996, 25,000 people, most of whom had paid £42 for their seats, were deprived of a fair day's cricket. Lancashire were worthy winners and are a fine one-day side, but the public and the sponsors were cheated, and as with so much else concerning the paying spectator, attention must be paid.

AXA Equity and Law League

and minor limited-over competitions

Friendly match

21 April
at Old Trafford
Yorkshire 152 for 9
Lancashire 154 for 5 (A. Flintoff 50 not out)
Lancashire won by 5 wickets

Lancashire won with 22 balls to spare.

5 May
at Derby
Leicestershire 225 (J.J. Whitaker 60, P. Aldred 4 for 41)
Derbyshire 229 for 6 (D.M. Jones 103 not out)
Derbyshire (4 pts) won by 4 wickets

at Chester-le-Street
Durham 141 for 9 (P.D. Collingwood 54 not out)
Northamptonshire 142 for 2 (R.J. Bailey 62 not out)
Northamptonshire (4 pts) won by 8 wickets

at Cardiff
Yorkshire 167 for 7
Glamorgan 168 for 6 (A. Dale 53 not out)
Glamorgan (4 pts) won by 4 wickets

at Lord's
Middlesex 255 for 6 (J.D. Carr 106)
Gloucestershire 224 (R.C. Russell 59, R.J. Cunliffe 52, P.N. Weekes 4 for 29)
Middlesex (4 pts) won by 31 runs

at Trent Bridge
Nottinghamshire 292 for 2 (P.R. Pollard 118, P. Johnson 97 not out)
Sussex 163
Nottinghamshire (4 pts) won by 129 runs

at Canterbury
Kent 184 for 9 (M.A. Ealham 53)
Lancashire 185 for 1 (J.E.R. Gallian 85, M. Atherton 79 not out)
Lancashire (4 pts) won by 9 wickets

at Taunton
Somerset 285 for 4 (S.C. Ecclestone 130, P.D. Bowler 66)
Surrey 232 (A.J. Stewart 101)
Somerset (4 pts) won by 53 runs

at Worcester
Essex 159
Worcestershire 161 for 6
Worcestershire (4 pts) won by 4 wickets

The first round of matches in the Sunday League faced no weather problems but the cold. On his Sunday League debut as Derbyshire captain, Dean Jones hit 103 from 108 balls and won his side the match with four balls to spare. He and Barnett hit 117 in 22 overs for the first wicket, and Paul Aldred returned his best bowling figures in limited-over cricket.

Paul Collingwood continued his success of the previous day in the championship match and hit his highest one-day score, but Northamptonshire beat Durham with ease.

Glamorgan needed seven from the last over to beat Yorkshire and got the winning run on the last ball, while

Derbyshire's Australian skipper Dean Jones excelled in the Sunday League and hit a century against Leicestershire in the opening match of the season.
(Paul Sturgess/Sportsline)

Middlesex swamped Gloucestershire, who had beaten them in three days in the championship match. John Carr made his highest score in one-day cricket and Weekes returned his best bowling figures.

Pollard, 118 off 108 balls with two sixes and nine fours, added 165 with new skipper Johnson as Nottinghamshire overwhelmed Sussex, and Atherton and Gallian scored 159 for Lancashire's first wicket as Kent were beaten with five overs to spare.

Simon Ecclestone hit 11 fours and five sixes in his highest one-day score, and he and Bowler added 183 for Somerset's second wicket to give them victory over Surrey in spite of Alec Stewart's hundred.

Worcestershire beat Essex with 10 balls to spare in a rather drab encounter at New Road.

12 May

at Southampton
Hampshire 187 for 5 (J.P. Stephenson 110 not out)
Essex 190 for 0 (S.G. Law 108 not out, D.D.J. Robinson 76 not out)
Essex (4 pts) won by 10 wickets

at Old Trafford
Leicestershire 252 for 7 (P.V. Simmons 91)
Lancashire 251 for 6 (N.H. Fairbrother 93, G.D. Lloyd 51)
Leicestershire (4 pts) won by 1 run

at Lord's
Middlesex 208 for 5 (P.N. Weekes 57)
Durham 191
Middlesex (4 pts) won by 17 runs

at Northampton
Glamorgan 199 for 6 (R.D.B. Croft 68)
Northamptonshire 200 for 6 (M.B. Loye 58, S.R. Barwick 4 for 34)
Northamptonshire (4 pts) won by 4 wickets

at Taunton
Somerset 232 for 8 (S. Lee 68, R.J. Harden 66)
Nottinghamshire 234 for 4
Nottinghamshire (4 pts) won by 6 wickets

at The Oval
Surrey 307 for 5 (D.M. Ward 112, A.D. Brown 84)
Kent 157 (A.J. Hollioake 4 for 34)
Surrey (4 pts) won by 150 runs

at Hove
Sussex 241 for 6 (K. Greenfield 72)
Warwickshire 245 for 2 (N.M.K. Smith 111 not out, D.P. Ostler 91 not out)
Warwickshire (4 pts) won by 8 wickets

at Sheffield
Yorkshire 210 for 9
Derbyshire 165 (K.J. Barnett 52)
Yorkshire (4 pts) won by 45 runs

Skipper John Stephenson's highest Sunday League score was not enough to save Hampshire from being routed by his old county Essex. Robinson and Law, the Essex openers, hit off the runs required for victory in 32.2 overs.

There was greater tension at Old Trafford, where Simmons and Wells scored 107 for Leicestershire's first wicket. Neil Fairbrother, who hit 93 off 77 balls and added 107 for the fourth wicket with Lloyd, was involved in an incident with Pierson. Fairbrother survived a united appeal for a catch behind, and later Pierson ran him out while backing out. Following discussion between Whitaker and Fairbrother, the Leicestershire captain withdrew the appeal. Lancashire arrived at the last over, bowled by Mullally, needing 12 to win, but Hegg's last ball, hit towards the boundary, was stopped by Maddy's dive, and Leicestershire won by one run.

Chasing 209, Durham were 116 for 7. The last three wickets realised 75 runs, but off-spinner Dutch took three wickets in 13 balls at a personal cost of 10 runs to win the match for Middlesex.

Warwickshire's Neil Smith hit a century against Sussex at Hove, and his aggressive opening batting won him a place in England's Texaco Trophy side against India.
(Paul Sturgess/Sportsline)

Northamptonshire recovered from 79 for 4 to beat Glamorgan with two balls to spare, and consistent batting took Nottinghamshire to victory over Somerset with 3.3 overs to spare.

David Ward and Alistair Brown hit 127 in 18 overs for Surrey's first wicket against Kent. Ward, one of the most entertaining batsmen in the game, made his highest Sunday League score, hitting seven fours and five sixes. Kent batted as if shell-shocked.

Sussex gave a quite dreadful display of out cricket to be massacred by Warwickshire. The Midlanders, chasing a target of 242, lost two wickets for 31 runs before Dominic Ostler and Neil Smith added a record 214. Smith reached his first Sunday League century off 88 balls with 13 fours and two sixes. Ostler hit 10 fours, but it must be said that much of the bowling was both unintelligent and uncontrolled.

Yorkshire easily defended a moderate total against Derbyshire where the main talking point was the home side's failure to provide white balls. They had been left elsewhere.

19 May

at Chester-le-Street
Yorkshire 199 for 5 (R.J. Blakey 61 not out)
Durham 136 (C.E.W. Silverwood 4 for 26)
Yorkshire (4 pts) won by 63 runs

at Ilford
Kent 272 for 6 (M.V. Fleming 112, C.L. Hooper 73)
Essex 267 for 9 (R.C. Irani 80, D.D.J. Robinson 54)
Kent (4 pts) won by 5 runs

at Cardiff
Glamorgan *v.* **Derbyshire**
Match abandoned
Glamorgan 2 pts, Derbyshire 2 pts

at Bristol
Gloucestershire *v.* **Somerset**
Match abandoned
Gloucestershire 2 pts, Somerset 2 pts

at Leicester
Leicestershire *v.* **Worcestershire**
Match abandoned
Leicestershire 2 pts, Worcestershire 2 pts

at Trent Bridge
Nottinghamshire 209 for 7 (C.L. Cairns 53)
Lancashire 212 for 3 (M. Watkinson 121)
Lancashire (4 pts) won by 7 wickets

at Edgbaston
Warwickshire 263 for 4 (N.V. Knight 134, D.P. Ostler 53)
Hampshire 145 (D.R. Brown 4 for 47)
Warwickshire (4 pts) won on faster scoring rate

Rain hit the Sunday League with three games being abandoned without a ball being bowled, and the match at Edgbaston being reduced to 35 overs and later to 30. Nick Knight's 134 was the highest score made for Warwickshire in the Sunday League.

Durham incurred penalties for failing to bowl their 40 overs in the required time. They reduced Yorkshire to 106 for 5 after 29 overs, but Blakey and Morris then added 93.

Kent destroyed Essex at Ilford. Fleming hit 11 fours and five sixes in his 91-ball innings. Hooper made 73 off 57 balls, and Law conceded 81 runs in his eight overs and took the wickets of Ward and Fleming. No Essex bowler had conceded more in the Sunday League. To their credit, Essex made a wonderful effort to reach a target of 273. Irani hit 80 off 63 balls, and nine were needed from the last over. In the scramble three wickets fell, and Kent won by five runs.

At Trent Bridge, Mike Watkinson opened the Lancashire innings and he and Atherton put on 145. Watkinson went on to record his first century in a one-day match. His 121 came off 75 balls and included seven sixes and 11 fours. In a match reduced to 38 overs, Lancashire won with 6.5 overs to spare

26 May

at Derby
Essex 207 for 7
Derbyshire 17 for 1
Match abandoned
Derbyshire 2 pts, Essex 2 pts

at Ebbw Vale
Glamorgan 114 for 5
Worcestershire 34 for 0
Match abandoned
Glamorgan 2 pts, Worcestershire 2 pts

at Gloucester
Surrey 138 for 5 (D.J. Bicknell 51)
Gloucestershire 66
Surrey (4 pts) won by 72 runs

at Portsmouth
Hampshire *v.* **Durham**
Match abandoned
Hampshire 2 pts, Durham 2 pts

at Canterbury
Yorkshire 87 for 5 (M.V. Fleming 4 for 13)
Kent 90 for 0 (M.V. Fleming 63 not out)
Kent (4 pts) won by 10 wickets

at Taunton
Somerset 141 for 6 (A.N. Hayhurst 60 not out)
Northamptonshire 145 for 9 (K.J. Shine 4 for 31)
Northamptonshire (4 pts) won by 1 wicket

A Sunday League master – Matthew Fleming of Kent. He hit 63 off 20 balls against Yorkshire. (David Munden/Sportsline)

at Horsham
Sussex *v.* **Middlesex**
Match abandoned
Sussex 2 pts, Middlesex 2 pts

at Edgbaston
Leicestershire 148 (D.L. Maddy 55)
Warwickshire 96 (A.D. Mullally 5 for 15)
Leicestershire (4 pts) won on faster scoring rate

No match escaped the rain. At Gloucester, the contest was reduced to 15 overs, and Courtney Walsh conceded 51 runs in his three overs. Only Wright and Russell reached double figures when Gloucestershire batted. Julian had 3 for 5 off eight balls.

There was a 10-over slog at Canterbury, and it was dominated by Matthew Fleming. He took 4 for 13 in two overs and then hit 63 off 20 balls. He hit seven sixes and three fours as Kent scored 90 off 5.5 overs.

The game at Taunton was reduced to 28 overs. Somerset slipped to 40 for 5 before Hayhurst and Turner put on 86 in 12 overs. Northamptonshire looked beaten at 127 for 9, but Ambrose and Taylor scored 18 off eight balls with Ambrose hitting the winning boundary off the penultimate ball of the match.

Leicestershire were bowled out for 148 in 37.1 overs, and Warwickshire's target was reduced to 134 from 36 overs after another brief stoppage for rain. This proved beyond them. Nixon held five catches behind the stumps and Mullally returned his best bowling figures in the Sunday League. Warwickshire were all out in 26.3 overs. The fortress was no longer impregnable.

2 June
at Tunbridge Wells
Kent 221 for 9 (N.J. Llong 70)
Sussex 186 (D.R. Law 79 not out, M.V. Fleming 4 for 33)
Kent (4 pts) won by 35 runs

at Old Trafford
Lancashire 187 for 9 (M. Watkinson 79)
Gloucestershire 180 for 8
Lancashire (4 pts) won by 7 runs

at Lord's
Yorkshire 167 for 8
Middlesex 170 for 4 (P.N. Weekes 50)
Middlesex (4 pts) won by 6 wickets

at Northampton
Warwickshire 184 for 8 (G. Welch 54)
Northamptonshire 188 for 7 (D.J. Capel 81)
Northamptonshire (4 pts) won by 3 wickets

at Trent Bridge
Nottinghamshire 267 for 5 (P. Johnson 99 not out)
Durham 228 (S.L. Campbell 56)
Nottinghamshire (4 pts) won by 39 runs

at The Oval
Surrey 221 for 6 (A.J. Stewart 112 not out)
Derbyshire 171 (B.C. Hollioake 5 for 10)
Surrey (4 pts) won by 50 runs

at Worcester
Worcestershire 220 for 6 (G.A. Hick 61)
Hampshire 184 for 9 (S.R. Lampitt 4 for 40)
Worcestershire (4 pts) won by 36 runs

From the last 20 overs, Kent scored 145 of their 221 runs, with Llong making his highest Sunday League score. As in the championship match, Sussex offered little resistance.

At Old Trafford, Watkinson hit 79 off as many deliveries after Atherton and Speak had failed to score. On a sluggish pitch, Gloucestershire could never manage the required run rate against some excellent fielding.

Middlesex beat Yorkshire with 25 balls to spare, and Northamptonshire made four wins in four matches when they beat Warwickshire with two balls to spare. Capel hit 81 off 82 balls, and Ambrose hit the winning boundary.

Paul Johnson, the Nottinghamshire skipper, hit a spectacular 99 not out off 68 balls, but lost the strike in the final over and was left one short of his century. Sherwin

Ben Hollioake made a significant impression with his all-round work for England Under-19 and for Surrey on his occasional appearances in the Sunday League. He took 5 for 10 against Derbyshire at The Oval. (Paul Sturgess/Sportsline)

Campbell scored his first Sunday League fifty, but Nottinghamshire were always on top.

Surrey were 6 for 3 against Derbyshire and the fourth wicket went down at 16. Alec Stewart and Nadeem Shahid added 118 for the fifth wicket, and Stewart made 112 off 121 balls with 12 fours. Surrey then found another hero in 18-year old Ben Hollioake who took 5 for 10 in his eight overs. Derbyshire went from 88 for 2 to 111 for 9. Malcolm then hit three sixes and three fours in his 42.

Hick and Spiring put on 106 for the third wicket as Worcestershire beat Hampshire with considerable ease.

9 June
at Chelmsford
Essex 249 for 6 (G.A. Gooch 87, P.J. Prichard 50)
Lancashire 232 (M. Watkinson 88, A.P. Grayson 4 for 46)
Essex (4 pts) won by 17 runs

at Southampton
Derbyshire 226 for 7 (D.M. Jones 101 not out)
Hampshire 227 for 5 (R.A. Smith 91)
Hampshire (4 pts) won by 5 wickets

at Leicester
Leicestershire 311 for 4 (P.V. Simmons 139, V.J. Wells 84)
Kent 314 for 6 (C.L. Hooper 145, M.A. Ealham 56)
Kent (4 pts) won by 4 wickets

at Lord's
Glamorgan 221 for 6 (H. Morris 55)
Middlesex 222 for 2 (P.N. Weekes 119 not out, M.W. Gatting 90)
Middlesex (4 pts) won by 8 wickets

at Trent Bridge
Nottinghamshire 157 for 8
Northamptonshire 158 for 5 (R.R. Montgomerie 77)
Northamptonshire (4 pts) won by 5 wickets

at Taunton
Somerset 249 (M.N. Lathwell 93, S. Lee 71)
Warwickshire 223 (N.M.K. Smith 89)
Somerset (4 pts) won by 26 runs

at Hove
Sussex 217 for 7
Durham 211 for 7 (M.A. Roseberry 65)
Sussex (4 pts) won by 6 runs

at Leeds
Surrey 90
Yorkshire 93 for 2
Yorkshire (4 pts) won by 8 wickets

Gooch and Prichard hit 123 in 16 overs for Essex's fourth wicket, a stand which proved decisive in the home side's win over Lancashire. Dean Jones made 101 off 128 balls, but Derbyshire lost to Hampshire, for whom Robin Smith scored 91 off 92 balls. Victory came with five balls to spare.

The outstanding game of the day was at Leicester where the home county hit their highest score in the Sunday League and lost. They began with an opening stand of 228 between Simmons and Wells. Simmons' 139 came off 105 balls and included five sixes and 16 fours. It looked like the innings of the season until Hooper went in. A beautifully judged innings saw him score 145 off 109 balls with 12 fours and three sixes. He and Ealham added 104 in 13 overs, and Kent won with 10 balls to spare.

Middlesex won with 27 balls to spare, and Weekes completed a wonderful weekend against Glamorgan with 119 not out off 111 balls. He and the equally impressive Gatting won the match with a second wicket stand of 203 in 30 overs.

Northamptonshire stood two points ahead of Kent and Middlesex at the head of the table when they won their fifth game in a row. There were also victories for Somerset and Sussex, while Yorkshire bowled out Surrey in 32.4 overs and completed a happy weekend.

16 June
at Chester-le-Street
Durham 173 for 8
Lancashire 174 for 2 (M.A. Atherton 91 not out)
Lancashire (4 pts) won by 8 wickets

at Chelmsford
Essex 178 (N. Hussain 70)
Northamptonshire 179 for 2 (K.M. Curran 70 not out, R.J. Bailey 70)
Northamptonshire (4 pts) won by 8 wickets

at Swansea
Somerset 217 for 5 (S. Lee 71 not out)
Glamorgan 193 for 9 (H. Morris 59)
Somerset (4 pts) won by 24 runs

at Bristol
Sussex 236 for 7 (K.A. Rao 91)
Gloucestershire 222 for 8 (A.J. Wright 96)
Sussex (4 pts) won by 14 runs

at Canterbury
Kent 303 for 5 (M.A. Ealham 89 not out, G.R. Cowdrey 68, T.R. Ward 65)
Middlesex 211 (K.R. Brown 74)
Kent (4 pts) won by 92 runs

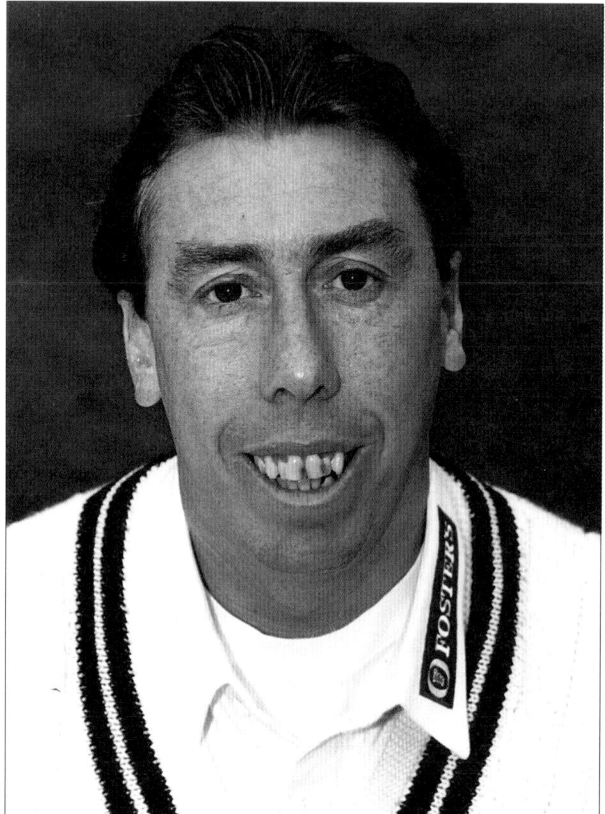

at The Oval
Leicestershire 48
Surrey 50 for 0
Surrey (4 pts) won by 10 wickets

at Worcester
Worcestershire 213 (G.A. Hick 63 not out)
Nottinghamshire 216 for 4 (A.A. Metcalfe 65, P. Johnson 58)
Nottinghamshire (4 pts) won by 6 wickets

at Leeds
Warwickshire 205 for 9 (D.P. Ostler 86)
Yorkshire 200 for 8 (M.G. Bevan 89, D. Byas 77)
Warwickshire (4 pts) won by 5 runs

An unbroken third wicket partnership of 126 between Atherton and Speak saw Lancashire to victory over Durham with 27 balls to spare, while at Chelmsford Northamptonshire strolled to their 12th win in 12 one-day matches in the season. They beat Essex by eight wickets and with seven overs to spare.

Somerset won comfortably at Swansea, and Rao hit a maiden fifty as Sussex beat Gloucestershire. This was hard on Wright who made his highest Sunday League score but received inadequate support.

Kent scored 300 for the second week in succession. In all, they hit 11 sixes and 21 fours with Ealham in the starring role. His 89 came off 51 balls and included four sixes and six fours. He took 20 off Fay's last over. In contrast, at The Oval, Leicestershire were bowled out in 22 overs with only extras reaching double figures. It took Surrey just 29 balls to reach their target. Brown hit five fours and a six in making 30 off 15 balls. The game was over in five minutes under two hours, the shortest ever duration of a Sunday League match.

Nottinghamshire beat Worcestershire with five balls to spare. This was the first Sunday League defeat suffered by Worcestershire for nearly a year.

Yorkshire suffered a traumatic defeat against Warwickshire. Byas and Bevan shared a second wicket stand of 140, and, chasing a target of 206, Yorkshire were 190 for 3. They lost five wickets for 10 runs and the match by five runs. Their last six wickets went down in 20 balls.

23 June
at Derby
Middlesex 278 for 4 (M.R. Ramprakash 122, P.N. Weekes 52)
Derbyshire 270 for 6 (D.M. Jones 118, K.J. Barnett 64)
Middlesex (4 pts) won by 8 runs

A Surrey hero – David Ward. He hit two blistering centuries in the early weeks of the competition, but, incomprehensibly, he played no part in Surrey's final surge on the title.
(Paul Sturgess/Sportsline)

at Stockton
Surrey 268 for 8 (D.M. Ward 108)
Durham 209
Surrey (4 pts) won by 59 runs

at Basingstoke
Northamptonshire 169 (C.A. Connor 5 for 25)
Hampshire 170 for 3 (W.K.M. Benjamin 104 not out)
Hampshire (4 pts) won by 7 wickets

at Trent Bridge
Gloucestershire 220 for 8 (A. Symonds 76, R.I. Dawson 61)
Nottinghamshire 101
Gloucestershire (4 pts) won by 119 runs

at Bath
Somerset 150
Worcestershire 152 for 3 (T.M. Moody 50)
Worcestershire (4 pts) won by 7 wickets

at Hove
Glamorgan 183 for 8 (M.P. Maynard 52)
Sussex 59 (O.T. Parkin 5 for 25)
Glamorgan (4 pts) won by 124 runs

at Edgbaston
Warwickshire 222 for 6 (S.M. Pollock 57)
Kent 214 for 8 (M.A. Ealham 56)
Warwickshire (4 pts) won by 8 runs

at Bradford
Yorkshire 181
Leicestershire 145 (D.L. Maddy 54)
Yorkshire (4 pts) won by 36 runs

An opening stand of 136 between Ramprakash and Weekes set Middlesex on the way to victory over Derbyshire. Ramprakash's 122 came off 113 balls with a six and 11 fours, and Middlesex plundered 115 from the last 10 overs. Jones and Barnett responded in kind, but the task of reaching 279 was just too great.

Another scintillating hundred from David Ward was the basis of Surrey's win over Durham. Ward's 100 came off 55 balls and included eight sixes in 14 balls, four of them off consecutive deliveries from Phil Bainbridge. Ward's second 50 came off only 13 balls.

Northamptonshire suffered their first one-day defeat of the season. Cardigan Connor had his first five-wicket haul in the Sunday League, and Northamptonshire were restricted to a moderate 169. It took on greater proportions when Hampshire were 6 for 2, but Winston Benjamin, playing solely as a batsman, hit four sixes and 13 fours in his first Sunday League century. He hit Ambrose for a straight six off the third ball of the 33rd over to win the match and to reach his hundred off 71 balls.

Gloucestershire bowled out Nottinghamshire in 26.5 overs to claim their first Sunday League win of the season, and Worcestershire won by seven wickets with six overs remaining. Only Athey reached double figures for Sussex, who were bowled out for 59 in 26 overs. Their main destroyer was medium-pacer Owen Parkin who took 5 for 25 on his Sunday League debut.

Warwickshire dented Kent's title hopes when they beat the hop county for the seventh consecutive time in a limited-over match at Edgbaston. Pollock hit his first Sunday League 50, and he bowled the last over when Kent needed 15 to win. He restricted them to six.

Leicestershire had another bad Sunday, with only Simmons and Maddy reaching double figures and the side being bowled out in 34.3 overs.

30 June
at Chester-le-Street
Gloucestershire 180 for 7 (R.I. Dawson 67)
Durham 176 (D.L. Campbell 57)
Gloucestershire (4 pts) won by 4 runs

at Southend
Essex 278 for 8 (S.G. Law 110, D.D.J. Robinson 80)
Surrey 251 for 7
Essex (4 pts) won by 27 runs

at Old Trafford
Somerset 175 for 7
Lancashire 174 for 8
Somerset (4 pts) won by 1 run

at Lord's
Middlesex 241 (P.N. Weekes 52, A.F. Giles 4 for 34)
Warwickshire 184 (R.A. Fay 4 for 33)
Middlesex (4 pts) won by 57 runs

at Northampton
Derbyshire 222 for 6 (P.A.J. DeFreitas 61 not out)
Northamptonshire 132
Derbyshire (4 pts) won by 90 runs

at Worcester
Worcestershire 175 for 9 (V.S. Solanki 55)
Yorkshire 177 for 5 (M.P. Vaughan 53)
Yorkshire (4 pts) won by 5 wickets

Dawson bettered his highest League score of the previous Sunday as Gloucestershire gained a narrow victory over Durham, who were still seeking a win of some kind against another first-class county.

Darren Robinson made his highest limited-over score and shared a first wicket partnership of 203, the last 102 coming off 10 overs. Law hit his eighth century of the season in all competitions off 95 balls, and Essex's 278 was always just out of reach for Surrey.

Lancashire established themselves as the supreme close-finishers. Chapple's 2 for 6 in six overs, and Yates' 3 for 18 in four helped restrict Somerset to 175 in their 40 overs, but Lancashire could never get the run-rate correct and arrived at Lee's last over of the match needing 21 to win. Yates and Chapple, who had come together at 132 for 8, made a valiant effort. They took 18 off the first five balls, but Yates missed the last delivery and a bye to the wicket-keeper still left them losers by one run.

Weekes and Ramprakash scored 101 for Middlesex's first wicket before falling to consecutive balls. Pooley and Gatting then scored 94 in 71 balls, and the Middlesex total proved well beyond Warwickshire's capabilities.

The win put Middlesex top of the table, two points ahead of Northamptonshire, who had a wretched match against Derbyshire. The visitors were 146 for 6 until DeFreitas scored 61 off 33 balls and put on 76 in 43 balls with Cork. The slow pitch was offering help to the off-spinners, and DeFreitas turned to this form of bowling to supplement Jones and Vandrau, with the result that Northamptonshire were bowled out in 31.4 overs.

In spite of Solanki's maiden Sunday League fifty, Yorkshire beat Worcestershire with seven balls to spare. Gough opened the batting for Yorkshire and scored 22.

---

7 July

at Bristol
Glamorgan 196 for 7 (A.W. Evans 50 not out)
Gloucestershire 102 (G.P. Butcher 4 for 32)
Glamorgan (4 pts) won by 94 runs

at Maidstone
Durham 207 for 8 (P.D. Collingwood 61 not out, S. Hutton 58)
Kent 211 for 4 (C.L. Hooper 76 not out, G.R. Cowdrey 59)
Kent (4 pts) won by 6 wickets

at Old Trafford
Worcestershire 261 for 3 (T.M. Moody 104)
Lancashire 257 (T.M. Moody 4 for 46)
Worcestershire (4 pts) won by 4 runs

at Leicester
Leicestershire 260 for 8 (P.V. Simmons 71)
Essex 251 for 5 (R.C. Irani 60, J.J.B. Lewis 53 not out)
Leicestershire (4 pts) won by 9 runs

at The Oval
Middlesex 131
Surrey 132 for 2 (D.J. Bicknell 52 not out)
Surrey (4 pts) won by 8 wickets

at Arundel
Hampshire 208 for 7
Sussex 168
Hampshire (4 pts) won by 40 runs

at Edgbaston
Warwickshire 197 for 6 (T.L. Penney 62 not out)
Nottinghamshire 179 for 6 (R.T. Robinson 52)
Warwickshire (4 pts) won by 18 runs

Glamorgan were 56 for 6 before Evans, making his Sunday League debut, and Gibson added 91. This was followed by Gary Butcher's best bowling performance in a one-day match and a comfortable win for the visitors.

Kent crushed Durham with 29 balls to spare. Hooper, who had earlier taken three wickets, and Cowdrey scored 120 in 19 overs for the third wicket to make victory a formality.

There was another astonishing finish at Old Trafford. Moody and Curtis began the match with 136 for Worcestershire's first wicket. Moody hit six sixes, four of them in one Yates' over which yielded 28 runs. Lancashire were 175 for 9 and looking well beaten before Chapple and Martin added 82 and brought them within five runs of their target.

Essex died bravely at Leicester. They needed 30 off the last over, bowled by Maddy, to win. They managed 20 with Jonathan Lewis hitting three consecutive sixes.

In spite of Julian conceding six wides in his first over and Surrey conceding 21 wides in all, the South Londoners trounced Middlesex in David Ward's benefit match. Victory came with 11.2 overs to spare. Ward made 22 not out.

Sussex recovered from 58 for 7 to 168 all out but still lost to Hampshire by 40 runs, while Nottinghamshire found a target of 198 too much for them at Edgbaston.

---

14 July

at Derby
Derbyshire 240 for 7 (K.J. Barnett 69)
Durham 180 for 7
Derbyshire (4 pts) won by 60 runs

at Chelmsford
Glamorgan 255 for 5 (H. Morris 101, M.P. Maynard 87)
Essex 251 for 7 (P.J. Prichard 102, P.A. Cottey 4 for 56)
Glamorgan (4 pts) won by 4 runs

at Moreton-in-Marsh
Gloucestershire 165 for 7 (M.W. Alleyne 67 not out)
Kent 143
Gloucestershire (4 pts) won by 22 runs

at Southampton
Nottinghamshire 209 (R.T. Robinson 76, P.R. Pollard 58, K.D. James 6 for 35)
Hampshire 127 (C.M. Tolley 5 for 16)
Nottinghamshire (4 pts) won by 82 runs

at Leicester
Middlesex 180 for 8 (P.V. Simmons 5 for 37)
Leicestershire 181 for 3 (P.V. Simmons 92 not out)
Leicestershire (4 pts) won by 7 wickets

at The Oval
Worcestershire 175
Surrey 162 for 4 (A.D. Brown 55)
Surrey (4 pts) won on faster scoring rate

at Hove
Sussex 263 (M.P Speight 62, A.P. Wells 56, S. Lee 4 for 40)
Somerset 251 for 9 (R.J. Harden 90, K.A. Parsons 56)
Sussex (4 pts) won by 12 runs

16 July
at Northampton
Northamptonshire 236 for 4 (K.M. Curran 92 not out, R.R. Montgomerie 69)
Yorkshire 240 for 8 (M.D. Moxon 72, A. McGrath 69)
Yorkshire (4 pts) won by 2 wickets

at Edgbaston
Warwickshire 212 for 6 (N.M.K. Smith 76)
Lancashire 199 for 9 (J.P. Crawley 52)
Warwickshire (4 pts) won by 13 runs

Durham's despair continued, and Essex lost narrowly for the second week running. Morris and Maynard established a Glamorgan second wicket record for the Sunday League with a partnership of 174. Again Essex responded positively. Prichard hit 102 off 95 balls and added 104 in 13 overs for the third wicket with Irani. The last over arrived with 18 needed for victory. Ilott and Grayson could manage only 13. Cottey returned his best bowling figures in the competition.

Kent had a surprising setback against Gloucestershire who were 54 for 5 but rallied when Ball and Alleyne added 83. Robinson and Pollard put on 135 for Nottinghamshire's third wicket, but saw the last eight wickets go down for 55 runs. Hampshire suffered even more badly, collapsing from 108 for 3 to 127 all out as Tolley returned his best one-day bowling figures. Earlier, Kevan James, enjoying a wonderful season in all forms of cricket, completed his best bowling figures in any one-day competition.

Phil Simmons opened the bowling for Leicestershire and had his best Sunday League figures. He then hit 92 off 92 balls to give Middlesex's title hopes another setback.

Middlesex were replaced at the top of the table by Surrey who, because of rain, chased a target of 157 in 34 overs and won with 10 overs to spare.

Sussex won a high-scoring match at Hove while both of the finalists in the Benson and Hedges Cup, Northamptonshire and Lancashire, lost their matches which were rescheduled to the Tuesday. Blakey hit the last ball of the match at Northampton for four to give Yorkshire victory, and Lancashire were never quite in contention at Edgbaston.

21 July
at Chelmsford
Essex 219 for 9 (J.J.B. Lewis 61)
Nottinghamshire 222 for 5 (C.L. Cairns 66 not out)
Nottinghamshire (4 pts) won by 5 wickets

at Cheltenham
Gloucestershire 284 for 4 (M.W. Alleyne 100 not out, A. Symonds 60)
Leicestershire 286 for 4 (A. Habib 99 not out, G.I. Macmillan 58, P.V. Simmons 51)
Leicestershire (4 pts) won by 6 wickets

at Old Trafford
Lancashire 188 (C.M. Wells 4 for 20)
Derbyshire 191 for 5 (P.A.J. DeFreitas 50 not out)
Derbyshire (4 pts) won by 5 wickets

at Northampton
Middlesex 181 for 8 (P.N. Weekes 54)
Northamptonshire 182 for 4 (R.R. Montgomerie 69)
Northamptonshire (4 pts) won by 6 wickets

at Guildford
Sussex 281 (M.P. Speight 117, A.J. Hollioake 5 for 44)
Surrey 206 (A.J. Hollioake 74, V.C. Drakes 4 for 50)
Sussex (4 pts) won by 75 runs

After missing the 1995 season through illness Martin Speight returned to play some spectacular innings for Sussex. He hit 117 off 96 balls as Sussex inflicted a rare defeat upon Surrey. (George Herringshaw/ASP)

Tom Moody, powerful all-round cricket for Worcestershire. (George Herringshaw/ASP)

at Worcester
Durham 172 for 8 (A. Sheriyar 4 for 27)
Worcestershire 175 for 1 (W.P.C. Weston 80 not out, G.A. Hick 54 not out)
Worcestershire (4 pts) won by 9 wickets

at Leeds
Hampshire 211 for 8 (W.K.M. Benjamin 62)
Yorkshire 213 for 3 (M.G. Bevan 98 not out)
Yorkshire (4 pts) won by 7 wickets

Lewis hit a one-day best for Essex, but Nottinghamshire won with three balls to spare. They needed 22 from the last two overs, and Cairns hit 17 off the penultimate over, bowled by Ilott.

Alleyne scored 100 off 95 balls and Symonds hit 60 off 27 balls, but Gloucestershire still lost to Leicestershire with 16 balls remaining. Simmons and Wells, who had conceded 81 in his eight overs, hit 90 in 13 overs for the first wicket, and Habib and Macmillan put on 143 for the fourth. Habib was on 99 and facing Walsh with one run needed to win, but Walsh bowled a no-ball to settle the issue.

Derbyshire beat Lancashire with ease, O'Gorman and DeFreitas concluding with a 64-run stand, and Northamptonshire drew level at the top with Surrey and Yorkshire when they beat Middlesex with equal ease.

Surrey lapsed at Guildford. They were penalised an over for bowling their quota too slowly and they suffered a 96-ball innings by Speight who hit five sixes and 10 fours. Adam Hollioake's best Sunday League bowling performance and 74 off 50 balls proved in vain.

Worcestershire trounced Durham with nine wickets and 27 balls to spare, and Michael Bevan passed a thousand runs in Sunday League cricket when he hit 98 off 96 balls and took Yorkshire to victory with two overs to spare.

28 July
at Derby
Derbyshire 183 for 6 (P.A.J. DeFreitas 72 not out)
Kent 183 for 8 (M.V. Fleming 65)
Match tied
Derbyshire 2 pts, Kent 2 pts

at Hartlepool
Essex 165
Durham 169 for 2 (S.L. Campbell 77)
Durham (4 pts) won by 8 wickets

at Swansea
Lancashire 219 for 5 (G.D. Lloyd 116)
Glamorgan 185 for 7
Lancashire (4 pts) won on faster scoring rate

at Cheltenham
Warwickshire 235 for 8 (T.L. Penney 75 not out)
Gloucestershire 38 for 1
Match abandoned
Gloucestershire 2 pts, Warwickshire 2 pts

at Southampton
Surrey 222 for 9 (M.A. Butcher 57, A.D. Brown 51)
Hampshire 199 (A.J. Hollioake 4 for 38)
Surrey (4 pts) won by 23 runs

at Leicester
Leicestershire 199 for 8 (P.V. Simmons 83)
Sussex 16 for 0
Match abandoned
Leicestershire 2 pts, Sussex 2 pts

at Worcester
Worcestershire 80 for 1
v. **Northamptonshire**
Match abandoned
Worcestershire 2 pts, Northamptonshire 2 pts

at Scarborough
Somerset 232 for 5 (R.J. Harden 57, P.D. Bowler 53, S. Lee 52)
Yorkshire 230 for 8
Somerset (4 pts) won by 2 runs

Paul Johnson had some troubled times in his first season as captain of Nottinghamshire, but he led by example in the Sunday League and took his county to within a fraction of winning the title. (Nigel French/ASP)

Four of the eight matches fell foul of the weather, but Durham gave themselves something to celebrate with victory over Essex with 27 balls to spare. This was Durham's first win of the season against a first-class county in any of the four major competitions, although they had won the Costcutter Cup at Harrogate.

Rain at Swansea reduced Glamorgan's target to 198 in 28 overs, but they failed to reach it by 13 runs. Surrey's convincing win at Southampton took them two points clear at the top of the table, and once again they were indebted to a fine bowling performance by Adam Hollioake. Yorkshire slipped to third place when they just failed to reach a target of 233 set by Somerset, who owed much to the controlled bowling of Andrew Caddick at the death.

---

4 August
at Derby
Gloucestershire 208 for 9 (R.I. Dawson 68, K.J. Dean 5 for 32)
Derbyshire 212 for 2 (D.M. Jones 101 not out)
Derbyshire (4 pts) won by 8 wickets

at Canterbury
Kent 135
Worcestershire 139 for 0 (W.P.C. Weston 78 not out, T.M. Moody 53 not out)
Worcestershire (4 pts) won by 10 wickets

at Leicester
Leicestershire 133
Northamptonshire 136 for 4 (K.M. Curran 57 not out)
Northamptonshire (4 pts) won by 6 wickets

at Lord's
Middlesex 220 for 6 (J.C. Pooley 68, S.G. Law 4 for 40)
Essex 215 for 9 (N. Hussain 77, P.N. Weekes 4 for 29)
Middlesex (4 pts) won by 5 runs

at Trent Bridge
Glamorgan 157 for 9
Nottinghamshire 158 for 1 (M.P. Dowman 74 not out, R.T. Robinson 55)
Nottinghamshire (4 pts) won by 9 wickets

at Taunton
Hampshire 229 for 5 (R.A. Smith 122 not out)
Somerset 185
Hampshire (4 pts) won by 44 runs

at Eastbourne
Sussex 206 (R.K. Rao 64, M.G. Bevan 4 for 29)
Yorkshire 207 for 2 (M.P. Vaughan 71 not out, D. Byas 61)
Yorkshire (4 pts) won by 8 wickets

Dawson and Lynch took Gloucestershire from 5 for 2 to 110 at which point six wickets fell for 27 runs. Cawdron and Walsh arrested the slide, but Dean finished with his best bowling figures in the Sunday League, and Jones hit his fourth century in the competition to take Derbyshire to victory with 19 balls to spare.

Kent had a bad weekend. With extras their top scorer, they were crushed by 10 wickets by Worcestershire, who took only 17.1 overs to reach a target of 136. Northamptonshire had an equally impressive victory at Leicester. They bowled out the home county in 34.1 overs and hit 136 in 28.1 overs to go top of the table two points ahead of Surrey.

Middlesex stayed in the hunt with a narrow victory over Essex whose Sunday form had collapsed, and Nottinghamshire moved to within six points of Northamptonshire with a game in hand when they overwhelmed Glamorgan. Robinson and Dowman scored 111 for the first wicket and victory came with 7.4 overs to spare.

Robin Smith hit two sixes and 18 fours in his 102-ball innings as Hampshire beat Somerset. Somerset were 108 for 3 before losing five wickets for 14 runs in six overs.

Supreme with the bat, Michael Bevan took five wickets in a senior match for the first time, the first five to fall after Rao and Greenfield had scored 108 for the first wicket. Yorkshire won with 26 balls to spare. Sussex awarded county caps to Drakes, Law and Lewry.

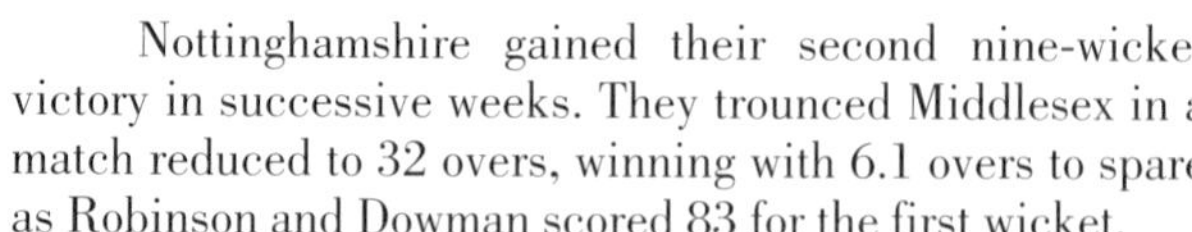

11 August
at Swansea
Leicestershire 218 for 7 (B.F. Smith 80, D.L. Maddy 51)
Glamorgan 158
Leicestershire (4 pts) won by 60 runs

at Southampton
Hampshire v. **Gloucestershire**
Match abandoned
Hampshire 2 pts, Gloucestershire 2 pts

at Old Trafford
Surrey 202 for 7 (N. Shahid 58)
Lancashire 128
Surrey (4 pts) won on faster scoring rate

at Northampton
Northamptonshire 235 for 7 (A.L. Penberthy 70, R.R. Montgomerie 66)
Kent 236 for 6 (M.V. Fleming 72, G.R. Cowdrey 52 not out, D.J. Capel 4 for 44)
Kent (4 pts) won by 4 wickets

at Trent Bridge
Middlesex 137 (C.L. Cairns 4 for 22)
Nottinghamshire 139 for 1 (R.T. Robinson 66 not out)
Nottinghamshire (4 pts) won by 9 wickets

at Taunton
Essex 148 for 8 (R.C. Irani 58)
Somerset 152 for 2 (P.D. Bowler 68 not out, M.N. Lathwell 51)
Somerset (4 pts) won by 8 wickets

at Hove
Derbyshire 232 for 5 (C.J. Adams 88 not out)
Sussex 200 for 5 (K. Greenfield 65)
Sussex (4 pts) won on faster scoring rate

at Edgbaston
Warwickshire 187 for 8 (S.M. Pollock 56)
Durham 99 (G.C. Small 4 for 14)
Warwickshire (4 pts) won by 88 runs

The match at Swansea was restricted to 35 overs although Brimson, with his best Sunday League spell of 3 for 23, helped bowl Glamorgan out in 33.5 overs. Rain also affected the game at Old Trafford, and Lancashire's target was reduced to 182 in 36 overs. They only lasted 31.3 overs. Surrey's victory took them back to the top of the table as Northamptonshire lost at home to Kent. A stand of 88 for the fifth wicket between Walton and Penberthy, whose 70 came off 55 balls, seemed to have put Northamptonshire in a strong position, but Fleming played a customary violent innings and, with 95 needed off the last 11 overs, Cowdrey hit 55 off 36 balls and Kent won with eight balls to spare.

Nottinghamshire gained their second nine-wicket victory in successive weeks. They trounced Middlesex in a match reduced to 32 overs, winning with 6.1 overs to spare as Robinson and Dowman scored 83 for the first wicket.

The matches at Taunton and Hove were both rain-affected, and Warwickshire kept alive their slender hopes of regaining the title when they dismissed Durham in 32.4 overs.

18 August
at Derby
Derbyshire 229 for 6 (K.J. Barnett 99)
Nottinghamshire 232 for 2 (R.T. Robinson 90, P. Johnson 71 not out)
Nottinghamshire (4 pts) won by 8 wickets

at Bristol
Yorkshire 262 for 7 (D. Byas 56, P.J. Hartley 52)
Gloucestershire 129 (R.D. Stemp 4 for 25)
Yorkshire (4 pts) won by 133 runs

at Canterbury
Kent 206 for 9 (T.R. Ward 52, C.L. Hooper 50)
Somerset 210 for 7 (S. Lee 62 not out, R.J. Harden 56)
Somerset (4 pts) won by 3 wickets

at Old Trafford
Lancashire 223 for 8 (N.H. Fairbrother 55, M.A. Atherton 53)
Hampshire 222 for 9 (R.A. Smith 77)
Lancashire (4 pts) won by 1 run

at Lord's
Worcestershire 173 for 7 (D.A. Leatherdale 50)
Middlesex 171 (D.A. Leatherdale 4 for 31)
Worcestershire (4 pts) won by 2 runs

at Edgbaston
Glamorgan 128
Warwickshire 131 for 3 (N.V. Knight 73 not out)
Warwickshire (4 pts) won by 7 wickets

With Surrey idle, Nottinghamshire and Yorkshire claimed victories that brought the three counties level at the top of the table, although Yorkshire had three matches remaining to the other two teams' four. Nottinghamshire's Sunday League form remained in sharp contrast to their championship form, which was often drab and spiritless. At Derby, another fine opening stand between Robinson and Dowman, this time of 87, set them on the way to victory with 19 balls to spare. Johnson and Robinson doubled the score in their second wicket stand and nullified Barnett's fine 99 for Derbyshire.

Yorkshire won with 10.5 overs to spare, but Kent and Middlesex saw their hopes fade with narrow defeats. Lee stroked Somerset to victory over Kent with a ball to spare. Lee's 62 came from 46 deliveries. Leatherdale returned his best bowling figures in the Sunday League as Worcester-

shire beat Middlesex on a pitch that was ill-suited to the one-day game.

Hampshire needed four off the last ball at Old Trafford but could only manage two while Warwickshire bowled out Glamorgan in 39.2 overs and reached their target in 37.5.

25 August

at Colchester
Essex 176
Gloucestershire 178 for 6 (A. Symonds 70)
Gloucestershire (4 pts) won by 4 wickets

at Cardiff
Kent 147
Glamorgan 149 for 2 (A. Dale 65 not out, S.P. James 50)
Glamorgan (4 pts) won by 8 wickets

at Leicester
Hampshire 199 for 9 (P.R. Whitaker 54)
Leicestershire 38 for 3
Match abandoned
Leicestershire 2 pts, Hampshire 2 pts

at Northampton
Sussex 229 for 8 (M. Newell 69)
Northamptonshire 127 for 5
Northamptonshire (4 pts) won on faster scoring rate

at Trent Bridge
Nottinghamshire *v.* **Surrey**
Match abandoned
Nottinghamshire 2 pts, Surrey 2 pts

at Weston-super-Mare
Durham 183 for 5 (M.A. Roseberry 63)
Somerset 187 for 3 (S.C. Ecclestone 75, P.D. Bowler 62)
Somerset (4 pts) won by 7 wickets

at Edgbaston
Worcestershire 154 (A.F. Giles 5 for 36)
Warwickshire 109 for 3 (N.M.K Smith 62 not out)
Warwickshire (4 pts) won on faster scoring rate

at Leeds
Lancashire 205 for 9
Yorkshire 206 for 4 (D. Byas 111 not out)
Yorkshire (4 pts) won by 6 wickets

Rain in the Midlands affected four matches, one of which, sadly, was the game at Trent Bridge where Nottinghamshire were due to play Surrey in the most crucial encounter of the season. The abandonment left Yorkshire free to go top. Lancashire scored 55 in the first five overs at Headingley, but White produced a containing spell of 2 for 18 in eight overs, and Yorkshire fought back splendidly. Skipper Byas hit a 95-ball century to set up victory with 6.5 overs to spare.

Northamptonshire and Warwickshire had wins which took them level with Surrey and Nottinghamshire on 38 points, but Kent surrendered their title when they were crushed by Glamorgan. Parkin took three wickets in his third over to spark a Kent collapse, and James and Dale hit 85 for Glamorgan's first wicket.

1 September

at Chesterfield
Worcestershire 158
Derbyshire 159 for 4 (K.J. Barnett 51)
Derbyshire (4 pts) won by 6 wickets

at Chester-le-Street
Durham 173 for 7
Glamorgan 112 for 2
Glamorgan (4 pts) won on faster scoring rate

at Bristol
Gloucestershire 175 for 9
Northamptonshire 179 for 5
Northamptonshire (4 pts) won by 5 wickets

at Portsmouth
Hampshire 184 (S.D. Udal 54)
Middlesex 185 for 3 (M.W. Gatting 55 not out, M.R. Ramprakash 54 not out)
Middlesex (4 pts) won by 7 wickets

at Tunbridge Wells
Kent 99 (C.L. Cairns 4 for 26)
Nottinghamshire 103 for 3
Nottinghamshire (4 pts) won by 7 wickets

at Leicester
Leicester 194 for 8 (D.L. Maddy 57)
Somerset 195 for 3 (P.D. Bowler 76, M.N. Lathwell 63)
Somerset (4 pts) won by 7 wickets

at The Oval
Warwickshire 185 (D.R. Brown 66)
Surrey 186 for 8
Surrey (4 pts) won by 2 wickets

at Hove
Sussex 204 for 8
Lancashire 207 for 6 (N.H. Fairbrother 93)
Lancashire (4 pts) won by 4 wickets

at Leeds
Essex 108 (C. White 4 for 21)
Yorkshire 109 for 4
Yorkshire (4 pts) won by 6 wickets

Within an hour of the start at Tunbridge Wells, Kent were 34 for 6 and Nottinghamshire were virtually certain of maintaining their challenge for the title. The early damage was done by Evans and Bowen, and Cairns finished the demolition of Kent. Yorkshire, too, had an easy task in disposing of Essex, whose minds were on other things. White again bowled splendidly, and Essex were indebted to a last wicket stand of 35 between Andrew and Such to take them past the hundred mark. Yorkshire won with 15.4 overs to spare.

Surrey, not for the first time, were fined and penalised for a slow over-rate against Warwickshire and had to score 186 from 37 rather than 40 overs. They were losing their way until Lewis, skippering the side, hit 26 off 24 balls, and in the end victory came with just two balls to spare.

Northamptonshire and Somerset gained victories in contention, for, with all bar Yorkshire in the top six having two matches to play, only six points separated Yorkshire in first place and Somerset in sixth.

8 September
at Southampton
Hampshire 220 for 7 (G.W. White 55)
Glamorgan 224 for 3 (S.P. James 91, D.L. Hemp 64 not out)
Glamorgan (4 pts) won by 7 wickets

at Trent Bridge
Leicestershire 194 for 7
Nottinghamshire 198 for 4 (P. Johnson 85 not out)
Nottinghamshire (4 pts) won by 6 wickets

at Taunton
Somerset 221 for 5 (M.E. Trescothick 61 not out)
Derbyshire 209 for 8 (D.M. Jones 81)
Somerset (4 pts) won by 12 runs

at The Oval
Northamptonshire 234 for 9 (D.J. Capel 112, M.B. Loye 53, A.J. Hollioake 5 for 58)
Surrey 237 for 8 (C.C. Lewis 63)
Surrey (4 pts) won by 2 wickets

at Worcester
Sussex 216 for 9 (R.K. Rao 59, P. Moores 51 not out)
Worcestershire 187 for 9
Sussex (4 pts) won by 29 runs

10 September
at Old Trafford
Middlesex 165 for 7 (M.R. Ramprakash 74)
Lancashire 166 for 4 (G.D. Lloyd 58)
Lancashire (4 pts) won by 6 wickets

at Edgbaston
Essex 138 for 7
Warwickshire 142 for 4
Warwickshire (4 pts) won by 6 wickets

Often inspiring as a captain, a record breaker as a bowler – with more league wickets in a season than anyone in the competition's history – and a splendidly effective batsman, Adam Hollioake of Surrey. (David Munden/Sportsline)

Nottinghamshire enjoyed an emphatic win at Leicester with skipper Paul Johnson hitting three sixes and six fours in his 85 off 61 balls. The match was reduced to 33 overs, and Nottinghamshire won with 2.4 overs to spare. This win left them at the top of the table in company with Surrey who had the powerful advantage of commanding the better run-rate.

Surrey's victory at The Oval ended Northamptonshire's hopes, but it was a very close contest. Northamptonshire, put in to bat, made only 26 for 2 off the first 10 overs. Thereafter Surrey lost their way in both bowling and fielding. Julian was wayward, Lewis retired hurt and Hollioake, in spite of his five wickets, was below his best, four of his victims being suicides in the closing overs. This should not detract from the fact that Hollioake's bowling had been a major factor in Surrey's success in the competition, and, with one match remaining, he had established a new record for the competition, surpassing the previous record of 34 wickets in a season held jointly by Bob Clapp and Clive Rice.

Northamptonshire's revival was due to David Capel who played superbly for his 112 off 88 balls. He hit two sixes and 11 fours and was responsible for his side setting Surrey a challenging target. At 100 for 5 after 22 overs, the target looked beyond Surrey, but Lewis and Shahid scored 59 off 44 balls. When the eighth wicket went down 45 were needed from six overs. This became 26 off three at which point Curran conceded 13 runs in his penultimate over. When he bowled the last over seven were needed. He dismissed Lewis with his second ball, and the last ball arrived with two still wanted. In poor light, Martin Bicknell clumped it for four, and The Oval witnessed jubilation it had not seen for many years.

15 September
at Derby
Warwickshire 156 for 9
Derbyshire 160 for 2 (K.J. Barnett 57 not out)
Derbyshire (4 pts) won by 8 wickets

at Chester-le-Street
Leicestershire 344 for 4 (P.V. Simmons 115, D.L. Maddy 106 not out, A. Habib 50 not out)
Durham 214 for 3 (S. Hutton 81, D.G.C. Ligertwood 54)
Leicestershire (4 pts) won by 130 runs

at Chelmsford
Sussex 215 for 8 (P. Moores 55)
Essex 217 for 3 (S.G. Law 120, N. Hussain 71)
Essex (4 pts) won by 7 wickets

at Cardiff
Glamorgan 159 for 9
Surrey 161 for 3
Surrey (4 pts) won by 7 wickets

at Canterbury
Kent 172 (C.L. Hopper 70, T.R. Ward 51)
Hampshire 171 for 4 (J.S. Laney 57, G.W. White 56)
Kent (4 pts) won by 1 run

at Uxbridge
Somerset 194 (G.D. Rose 54)
Middlesex 195 for 6 (M.R. Ramprakash 80 not out)
Middlesex (4 pts) won by 4 wickets

at Northampton
Northamptonshire 202 for 5 (A.L. Penberthy 80, R.J. Bailey 57 not out)
Lancashire 203 for 3 (J.E.R. Gallian 70, P.C. McKeown 69)
Lancashire (4 pts) won by 7 wickets

at Worcester
Worcestershire 257 for 2 (T.M. Moody 102, T.S. Curtis 77, G.A. Hick 57 not out)
Gloucestershire 243 for 7 (R.I. Dawson 85)
Worcestershire (4 pts) won by 14 runs

at Scarborough
Nottinghamshire 251 for 5 (P. Johnson 52, R.T. Robinson 51)
Yorkshire 227 (C.L. Cairns 5 for 41)
Nottinghamshire (4 pts) won by 24 runs

The race for the AXA Equity and Law Sunday League title had involved six counties until the penultimate week of the season, but on the final Sunday there were just two main

Graham Thorpe putting Surrey on the way to victory over Glamorgan and clinching the Sunday League title.
(Mike Hewitt/Allsport)

contenders, Surrey and Nottinghamshire. Surrey were the firm favourites, not only because they seemed to have the easier final fixture, but because they had a vastly superior run-rate to the nearest rivals. As is so often the case, the favourites won.

Nottinghamshire did all that could be expected of them. They travelled to Scarborough, batted consistently and bowled out Yorkshire, who had had an outside chance of taking the title themselves. Robinson and Dowman, who had performed well in the closing weeks of the season, once more gave Nottinghamshire a good start, and Paul Johnson hit 52 off 47 balls. The last 10 overs of the Nottinghamshire innings produced a vital 93 runs, thanks mainly to an aggressive knock by Cairns, who had an excellent all-round match. He broke Yorkshire's resistance when he dismissed Moxon and White in successive overs and then accounted for McGrath.

Alas, Nottinghamshire's fine effort did not win them the title. At Cardiff, Surrey restricted Glamorgan to 159 in their 40 overs, with Adam Hollioake taking 3 for 28 to complete his outstanding season in the League. Mark Butcher and Alistair Brown began the Surrey innings at a brisk rate. When Brown was second out Surrey were 90 for 2 in 16 overs so that all pressure had been taken off the later batsmen. Stewart and Thorpe added 67 to take Surrey to within three runs of victory, and although Thorpe was caught off Cottey, Shahid came in to clout the winning boundary.

So Surrey won the Sunday League title for the first time and their first trophy of any nature since 1982. It was cause for justified celebration.

AXA Equity and Law League – Final Table

	P	W	L	Ab	Pts
Surrey (9)	17	12	4	1	50
Nottinghamshire (11)	17	12	4	1	50
Yorkshire (12)	17	11	6	–	44
Warwickshire (2)	17	10	6	1	42
Somerset (14)	17	10	6	1	42
Northamptonshire (13)	17	10	6	1	42
Middlesex (17)	17	9	7	1	38
Worcestershire (3)	17	8	6	3	38
Lancashire (4)	17	9	8	–	36
Kent (1)	17	8	8	1*	34
Derbyshire (8)	17	7	7	3*	34
Leicestershire (7)	17	7	7	3	34
Glamorgan (6)	17	7	8	2	32
Sussex (10)	17	6	9	2	28
Hampshire (18)	17	4	10	3	22
Gloucestershire (15)	17	4	10	3	22
Essex (5)	17	4	12	1	18
Durham (16)	17	1	15	1	6

(1995 positions in brackets)
* indicates includes one match tied

Costcutter Cup

at Harrogate

15 July
Gloucestershire 297 for 6 (M.A. Lynch 68, T.H.C. Hancock 56)
Yorkshire 208 (M.G. Bevan 51, J. Lewis 4 for 24)
Gloucestershire won by 89 runs

16 July
Leicestershire 211 for 9 (B.F. Smith 65)
Durham 215 for 3 (S.L. Campbell 99, S. Hutton 87)
Durham won by 7 wickets

Final

17 July
Gloucestershire 249 for 7 (M.G.N. Windows 72, M.A. Lynch 63 not out)
Durham 252 for 6 (S. Hutton 105 not out, S.L. Campbell 56)
Durham won by 5 wickets

Few counties have ever endured a more wretched season than Durham did in 1996, so victory in the Costcutter Cup at Harrogate was some small consolation. They were, perhaps, fortunate in that Gloucestershire disposed of Yorkshire in the first semi-final, bowling them out in 46.1 overs of the 55-over contest. Durham's win over Leicestershire came with nine overs to spare. Sherwin Campbell and Stewart Hutton scored 196 for the first wicket, but three wickets then fell for two runs before Durham regained their nerve. Hutton and Campbell scored 95 for the first wicket in the final, and Hutton, man of the tournament, steered them to victory with 10 balls to spare.

Scarborough Festival

6 September
Tesco International XI 249 for 6 (C.Z. Harris 89 not out)
Yorkshire 253 for 7 (A. McGrath 79, M.D. Moxon 71, C.Z. Harris 4 for 39)
Yorkshire won by 3 wickets

Yorkshire won with 10 balls to spare and owed much to Darren Gough's hard hitting at the end.

Northern Electric Trophy

7 September
Yorkshire 337 for 9 (M.P. Vaughan 85, A. McGrath 54)
Durham 292 for 7 (J.E. Morris 92, J.A. Daley 54)
Yorkshire won by 45 runs

McCain Challenge

8 September
Yorkshire 204
Holland 206 for 7
Holland won by 3 wickets

Yorkshire won the Northern Electric trophy with ease, but Holland proved stiffer opposition. Yorkshire were bowled out in 48.4 overs, and Holland won with 13 balls to spare.

Impressive as captain of Holland and for the International XI in the Scarborough Festival, Tim de Leede.
(Ben Radford/Allsport)

The Scarborough Festival.
(Ben Radford/Allsport)

Tetley Bitter Trophy

9 September
Yorkshire 366 for 9 (M.P. Vaughan 118, D. Byas 113, J. Wood 4 for 92)
Durham 243 (M.A. Roseberry 66, G.M. Hamilton 4 for 63)
Yorkshire won by 123 runs

10 September
Worcestershire 202 for 9 (T.S. Curtis 91)
Nottinghamshire 189 (P.R. Pollard 82 not out)
Worcestershire won by 13 runs

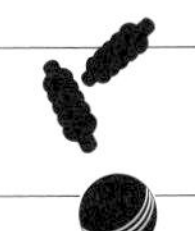

Final

Worcestershire 196
Yorkshire 198 for 5 (D. Byas 106 not out)
Yorkshire won by 5 wickets

The Yorkshire skipper David Byas was unquestionably the man of the Tetley Bitter Trophy with centuries in both matches as his side took the trophy for the fifth time in seven years. The Durham bowlers took a terrible pounding in the first match with Wood's 4 for 92 coming from nine overs and Betts having figures of 2 for 88 in 10 overs.

Axa Equity and Law League Averages

Derbyshire

Batting	M	Inns	NO	Runs	HS	Av	100s	50s	ct/st
D.M. Jones	15	15	3	749	118	62.41	4	1	8
K.J. Barnett	16	16	2	649	99	46.35		6	6
P.A.J. DeFreitas	14	12	4	342	72*	42.75		3	4
D.E. Malcolm	2	1	–	42	42	42.00			
T.J.G. O'Gorman	10	9	3	201	43*	33.50			4
C.J. Adams	14	13	2	295	88*	26.81		1	7
C.M. Wells	9	7	2	94	39*	18.80			4
G.A. Khan	7	6	1	81	27	16.20			2
P. Aldred	9	2	1	16	9	16.00			3
J.E. Owen	7	6	–	95	40	15.83			2
D.G. Cork	9	7	2	74	35	14.80			5
K.M. Krikken	16	13	3	127	27*	12.70			12/5
F.A. Griffith	3	2	1	6	6*	6.00			
A.S. Rollins	5	3	–	6	4	2.00			1
A.J. Harris	11	3	1	1	1	0.50			4
T.A. Tweats	1	1	–	0	0	0.00			

M.J. Vandrau 21* (7 matches, ct 3); K.J. Dean 8* (12 matches, ct 4); G.M. Roberts 2* & 4* (5 matches, ct 2); S.J. Base (3 matches, ct 2); D.R. Womble (1 match)

Bowling	Overs	Mds	Runs	Wks	Av	Best	4/inn
M.J. Vandrau	40	1	225	10	22.50	3/30	
K.J. Barnett	47.2	–	301	13	23.15	3/26	
A.J. Harris	76	4	358	15	23.86	3/41	
C.M. Wells	56.3	1	252	10	25.20	4/20	1
D.G. Cork	64	2	257	10	25.70	3/41	
K.J. Dean	77	2	359	13	27.61	5/32	1
G.M. Roberts	38	1	198	6	33.00	2/28	
S.J. Base	20	–	106	3	35.33	2/34	
F.A. Griffith	22	–	111	3	37.00	2/36	
P. Aldred	48.5	2	299	8	37.37	4/41	1
D.M. Jones	27.1	–	160	4	40.00	2/15	
P.A.J. DeFreitas	71.4	5	406	9	45.11	3/38	
D.E. Malcolm	8	–	64	1	64.00	1/64	
D.R. Womble	3	–	29	–	–		

Durham

Batting	M	Inns	NO	Runs	HS	Av	100s	50s	ct/st
M.A. Roseberry	11	10	3	272	65	38.85		2	5
J.A. Daley	5	5	2	104	47	34.66			2
S. Hutton	13	13	1	369	81	30.75		2	4
J. Wood	6	5	3	61	21	30.50			
S.L. Campbell	15	15	–	455	77	30.33		3	4
M.J. Foster	4	4	–	96	44	24.00			
P.D. Collingwood	14	14	2	268	61*	22.33		2	8
D.G.C. Ligertwood	13	12	2	205	54	20.50		1	11/3
S.J.E. Brown	10	8	4	76	18	19.00			
J.E. Morris	9	9	–	154	46	17.11			2
P. Bainbridge	7	7	–	111	34	15.85			
J. Boiling	12	6	2	62	27	15.50			1
S.D. Birbeck	2	2	–	31	24	15.50			
D.A. Vlenkiron	9	8	1	107	34	15.28			1
J.I. Longley	3	3	–	44	21	14.66			1
M.M. Betts	8	7	5	28	11	14.00			1
M.J. Swaggers	3	1	–	13	13	13.00			
R.M.S. Weston	1	1	–	13	13	13.00			
C.W. Scott	3	3	–	26	17	8.66			2/1
N. Killeen	14	11	2	56	32	6.22			4
D.M. Cox	3	2	–	7	7	3.50			1
A. Walker	9	2	–	4	3	2.00			1
C.L. Campbell	2	1	–	0	0	0.00			

Bowling	Overs	Mds	Runs	Wks	Av	Best	4/inn
M.J. Saggers	20	–	59	3	19.66	2/24	
C.L. Campbell	16	–	89	3	29.66	2/45	
S.J.E. Brown	73	5	367	11	33.36	3/50	
J. Boiling	92.2	3	445	13	34.23	3/65	
A. Walker	59.3	–	317	9	35.22	3/31	
S.D. Birbeck	11	–	71	2	35.50	1/21	
N. Killeen	103.3	1	570	16	35.62	3/45	
M.J. Foster	28	1	146	3	48.66	2/57	
J. Wood	48	2	294	6	49.00	2/36	
M.M. Betts	54	–	316	6	52.66	3/26	
D.M. Cox	24	–	106	2	53.00	2/34	
P.D. Collingwood	12	–	53	1	53.00	1/37	
P. Bainbridge	44.1	1	237	4	59.25	2/26	
J.A. Daley	0.1	–	4	–	–		
S.L. Campbell	5.3	–	34	–	–		
D.A. Blenkiron	8	–	56	–	–		

Essex

Batting	M	Inns	NO	Runs	HS	Av	100s	50s	ct/st
N. Hussain	10	9	–	389	77	43.22		3	4
S.G. Law	13	13	1	501	120	41.73	3		4
J.J.B. Lewis	14	11	3	270	61	33.75		2	2
D.D.J. Robinson	14	14	1	432	80	33.23		3	1
R.C. Irani	12	11	1	311	80	31.10		3	4
G.A. Gooch	7	6	–	186	87	31.00		1	4
P.J. Prichard	14	14	–	374	102	26.71	1	1	2
P.M. Such	16	8	7	26	9*	26.00			4
R.J. Rollins	16	15	2	204	32	15.69			9/2
S.J.W. Andrew	14	7	3	60	32	15.00			1
A.P. Grayson	17	15	3	178	34	14.83			7
N.F. Williams	2	1	–	12	12	12.00			
A.P. Cowan	9	6	2	48	22*	12.00			3
A.J.E. Hibbert	6	6	2	45	25	11.25			1
T.P. Hodgson	4	3	–	27	21	9.00			
D.G. Wilson	2	1	–	7	7	7.00			1
M.C. Ilott	14	13	3	62	24*	6.20			5
S.D. Peters	1	1	–	1	1	1.00			
B.J. Hyam	1	1	–	0	0	0.00			

(J.C. Powell 1 match)

Bowling	Overs	Mds	Runs	Wks	Av	Best	4/inn
D.G. Wilson	8	–	40	3	13.33	3/40	
J.C. Powell	8	–	62	2	31.00	2/62	
A.P. Grayson	96.2	1	601	19	31.63	4/46	1
N.F. Williams	11	–	71	2	35.50	2/56	
R.C. Irani	74	2	417	11	37.90	2/23	
M.C. Ilott	93	6	402	10	40.20	2/37	
S.G. Law	66.5	3	362	9	40.22	4/40	1
S.J.W. Andrew	87.2	6	423	10	42.30	2/27	
P.M. Such	97.1	3	494	10	49.40	3/53	
A.P. Cowan	47.2	4	217	4	54.25	2/17	
J.J.B. Lewis	0.2	–	4	–	–		

Glamorgan

Batting	M	Inns	NO	Runs	HS	Av	100s	50s	ct/st
S.R. Barwick	15	5	5	7	3*	–			1
R.D.B. Croft	12	11	3	302	68	39.75		1	2
H. Morris	12	11	1	372	101	37.20	1	2	3
A. Dale	14	14	3	358	65*	32.54		2	1
S.D. Thomas	5	4	3	30	20*	30.00			
M.P. Maynard	14	13	–	363	87	27.92		2	10
A.D. Shaw	10	7	3	105	36*	26.25			3/4
A.W. Evans	6	6	2	99	50*	24.75		1	2
S.P. James	14	14	1	295	91	22.69		1	4
P.A. Cottey	16	15	3	243	44*	20.25			6
O.D. Gibson	12	9	1	156	47*	19.50			4
D.L. Hemp	8	7	1	108	64*	18.00		1	4
A.J. Dalton	2	2	–	25	19	12.50			
G.P. Butcher	9	7	2	59	20*	11.80			1
S.L. Watkin	15	6	2	25	9*	6.25			2
D.A. Cosker	1	1	–	4	4	4.00			
C.P. Metson	6	2	–	0	0	0.00			4/1

(O.T. Parkin 5 matches)

Bowling	Overs	Mds	Runs	Wks	Av	Best	4/inn
D.A. Cosker	8	–	38	2	19.00	2/38	
O.T. Parkin	38	5	173	9	19.22	5/28	1
G.P. Butcher	25.2	1	142	6	23.66	4/32	1
P.A. Cottey	20.5	1	144	6	24.00	4/56	1
S.R. Barwick	101.5	6	437	15	29.13	4/34	1
R.D.B. Croft	77	4	350	11	31.81	3/21	
S.L. Watkin	108	10	430	13	33.07	2/9	
O.D. Gibson	76.4	5	339	10	33.90	2/18	
A. Dale	64	–	348	9	38.66	2/32	
D.L. Hemp	6	–	42	1	42.00	1/14	
M.P. Maynard	0.2	–	2	–	–		
S.D. Thomas	18.4	–	136	–	–		

Gloucestershire

Batting	M	Inns	NO	Runs	HS	Av	100s	50s	ct/st
M.J. Cawdron	3	3	1	76	37	38.00			1
R.I. Dawson	15	15	1	458	85	32.71		4	
A. Symonds	14	13	–	365	76	28.07		3	12
M.A. Lynch	11	10	1	242	47	26.88			1

Axa Equity and Law League Averages (continued)

Gloucestershire (continued)

Batting (continued)	M	Inns	NO	Runs	HS	Av	100s	50s	ct/st
J. Lewis	14	8	7	26	9*	26.00			3
M.W. Alleyne	15	15	3	295	100*	24.58	1	1	3
R.J. Cunliffe	3	3	–	71	52	23.66		1	2
A.J. Wright	10	10	–	229	96	22.90		1	5
N.J. Trainor	1	1	–	20	20	20.00			
A.M. Smith	14	8	4	79	26*	19.75			2
R.C. Russell	11	11	2	158	59	17.55		1	5/1
M.G.N. Windows	10	9	1	138	37*	17.25			1
T.H.C. Hancock	10	9	–	95	31	10.55			3
C.A. Walsh	10	6	1	52	38	10.40			3
M.C.J. Ball	14	12	3	79	24*	8.77			6
R.C.J. Williams	3	2	–	13	11	6.50			4/2
D.R. Hewson	1	1	–	3	3	3.00			
R.P. Davis	4	3	1	2	2*	1.00			

J.M.M. Averis 1* (matches)

Bowling	Overs	Mds	Runs	Wks	Av	Best	4/inn
J.M.M. Averis	14	–	78	4	19.50	2/35	
T.H.C. Hancock	14.5	–	92	4	23.00	2/6	
A. Symonds	38	1	217	9	24.11	3/34	
A.M. Smith	96	7	446	18	24.77	3/16	
M.C.J. Ball	92	2	513	16	32.06	2/16	
C.A. Walsh	65.4	8	297	9	33.00	2/17	
R.P. Davis	28	–	179	5	35.80	3/42	
M.W. Alleyne	99.1	3	533	12	44.41	3/52	
J. Lewis	90	2	496	11	45.09	2/28	
M.J. Cawdron	13	–	91	2	45.50	1/28	
R.I. Dawson	1	–	8	–	–		

Hampshire

Batting	M	Inns	NO	Runs	HS	Av	100s	50s	ct/st
W.K.M. Benjamin	8	8	2	304	104*	50.66	1	1	2
R.A. Smith	14	14	2	551	122*	45.91	1	2	3
G.W. White	9	7	–	207	56	29.57		2	2
J.P. Stephenson	11	11	1	279	110*	27.90	1		10
S.D. Udal	14	9	5	100	54	25.00		1	3
J.S. Laney	12	12	–	288	57	24.00		1	4
M. Keech	10	10	–	201	37	20.10			4
P.R. Whitaker	13	12	1	218	54	19.81		1	1
R.S.M. Morris	2	2	–	39	21	19.50			
W.S. Kendall	8	8	1	130	38*	18.57			4
R.J. Maru	7	4	3	18	11	18.00			3
K.D. James	11	9	2	120	37	17.14			5
A.N. Aymes	15	13	3	148	31	14.80			12/6
S.M. Milburn	5	2	1	9	8	9.00			2
C.A. Connor	8	3	1	14	14*	7.00			2
D.A, Masceranhas	3	2	1	7	7*	7.00			1
M.J. Thursfield	5	2	–	3	3	1.50			1
L.J. Botham	1	1	–	1	1	1.00			

S.J. Renshaw 1* & 6* (5 matches); J.N.B. Bovill 6* (4 matches)

Bowling	Overs	Mds	Runs	Wks	Av	Best	4/inn
J.P. Stephenson	83	3	349	20	17.45	3/22	
K.D. James	77	1	404	21	19.23	6/35	1
D.A. Masceranhas	21.2	–	124	5	24.80	2/34	
J.N.B. Bovill	17.2	–	100	4	25.00	3/45	
P.R. Whitaker	31.2	–	182	6	30.33	3/44	
C.A. Connor	59	2	320	10	32.00	5/25	1
M. Keech	5.4	–	34	1	34.00	1/26	
S.J. Renshaw	23	–	109	3	36.33	2/18	
S.D. Udal	88.5	1	476	13	36.61	3/36	
S.M. Milburn	40	1	199	5	39.80	2/18	
R.J. Maru	43	2	223	2	111.50	2/25	
M.J. Thursfield	27	–	174	1	174.00	1/38	
L.J. Botham	4	–	33	–	–		
W.K.M. Benjamin	13	–	68	–	–		

Kent

Batting	M	Inns	NO	Runs	HS	Av	100s	50s	ct/st
D.W. Headley	6	4	3	50	29*	50.00			2
C.L. Hooper	17	16	1	579	145	38.60	1	4	9
M.A. Ealham	11	11	2	303	89*	33.66		4	1
M.V. Fleming	17	17	1	496	112	31.00	1	3	1
S.A. March	13	10	5	155	32*	31.00			5/2

Kent (continued)

Batting (continued)	M	Inns	NO	Runs	HS	Av	100s	50s	ct/st
S.C. Willis	4	4	2	55	31*	27.50			5
T.R. Ward	17	17	1	424	65	26.50		3	3
G.R. Cowdrey	16	15	1	360	68	25.71		3	6
W.J. House	4	4	1	46	19*	15.33			1
N.J. Llong	17	16	–	231	70	14.43		1	3
M.J. Walker	16	15	3	169	27	14.08			4
B.J. Phillips	4	4	1	33	29	11.00			3
N.W. Preston	5	2	1	11	7*	11.00			
D.P. Fulton	2	2	–	18	18	9.00			1
J.B.D. Thompson	12	8	3	44	30	8.80			1
T.N. Wren	13	6	3	19	7*	6.33			1
M.J. McCague	13	7	–	37	16	5.28			3

Bowling	Overs	Mds	Runs	Wks	Av	Best	4/inn
M.V. Fleming	104	–	650	29	21.72	4/13	2
N.J. Llong	23.1	–	166	5	33.20	2/35	
D.W. Headley	39	2	213	6	35.50	2/31	
J.B.D. Thompson	51	2	250	7	35.71	3/26	
B.J. Phillips	20.5	–	112	3	37.33	2/42	
G.R. Cowdrey	6	–	44	1	44.00	1/44	
C.L. Hooper	97	3	467	10	46.79	3/21	
M.J. McCague	71	–	457	9	50.77	2/34	
T.N. Wren	83	3	429	6	71.50	2/32	
M.A. Ealham	72	3	363	5	72.60	3/21	
N.W. Preston	13	–	83	–	–		

Lancashire

Batting	M	Inns	NO	Runs	HS	Av	100s	50s	ct/st
M.A. Atherton	8	8	2	335	91*	55.83		3	4
N.H. Fairbrother	15	14	4	408	93	40.80		3	8
G.D. Lloyd	16	13	1	434	116	36.16	1	2	3
M. Watkinson	16	15	1	486	121	34.71	1	2	6
J.E.R. Gallian	13	13	1	333	85	27.75		2	7
W.K. Hegg	16	12	3	246	47*	27.33			8/2
N.J. Speak	8	7	1	158	39*	26.33			3
P.C. McKeown	5	5	–	117	69	23.40		1	3
S.P. Titchard	2	2	–	41	40	20.50			
J.P. Crawley	10	10	–	186	52	18.60		1	3
G. Chapple	12	8	3	90	43	18.00			3
I.D. Austin	14	10	3	120	31	17.14			3
G. Yates	17	9	3	92	38	15.33			3
S. Elworthy	14	9	2	59	15	8.42			4
A. Flintoff	1	1	–	2	2	2.00			
P.J. Martin	14	5	5	53	35*	–			1

R.J. Green 0* (5 matches); J.J. Haynes (1 match, ct 1)

Bowling	Overs	Mds	Runs	Wks	Av	Best	4/inn
R.J. Green	38	1	193	8	24.12	2/23	
G. Yates	99	–	492	18	27.33	3/18	
M. Watkinson	104	1	592	21	28.19	3/40	
G. Chapple	77	6	387	13	29.76	3/29	
P.J. Martin	100	8	502	16	31.37	3/29	
J.E.R. Gallian	29.1	1	187	5	37.40	2/34	
S. Elworthy	94	5	477	11	43.36	2/33	
I.D. Austin	110.5	4	496	10	49.60	3/39	
G.D. Lloyd	2	–	18	–	–		

Liecestershire

Batting	M	Inns	NO	Runs	HS	Av	100s	50s	ct/st
P.V. Simmons	16	16	1	815	139	54.33	2	5	8
A. Habib	9	7	3	183	99*	45.75		2	3
D.L. Maddy	16	13	2	486	106*	44.18	1	4	2
V.J. Wells	16	16	–	382	84	23.87		1	1
G.I. Macmillan	11	10	2	186	58	23.25		1	3
B.F. Smith	15	15	1	320	80	22.85		1	5
J.J. Whitaker	12	11	2	192	60	21.33		1	5
P.A. Nixon	16	13	3	177	32*	17.70			11/5
G.J. Parsons	9	7	4	39	23*	13.00			1
D. Williamson	12	7	4	23	9	7.66			3
C.C. Remy	13	10	1	67	17*	7.44			3
T.J. Mason	1	1	–	7	7	7.00			
A.R.K. Pierson	7	3	–	20	11	6.66			2
J.M. Dakin	4	4	–	15	8	3.75			1
V.P. Clarke	2	2	–	2	1	1.00			

M.T. Brimson 5* (5 matches); A.D. Mullally 0*, 0* & 2* (6 matches); J. Ormond 2* (3 matches); D.J. Millns (2 matches, ct 1); C.D. Crowe (1 match)

Axa Equity and Law League Averages (continued)

Liecestershire (continued)

Bowling	Overs	Mds	Runs	Wks	Av	Best	4/inn
D.J. Millns	14	1	84	4	21.00	2/37	
A.D. Mullally	39	5	168	8	21.00	5/15	1
G.I. Macmillan	16	1	76	3	25.33	2/37	
C.C. Remy	63	2	331	11	30.09	2/9	
M.T. Brimson	33	–	154	5	30.80	3/23	
P.V. Simmons	34.1	–	480	14	34.28	5/37	1
V.P. Clarke	6	–	36	1	36.00	1/36	
A.R.K. Pierson	30	1	188	5	37.60	3/21	
G.J. Parsons	62	–	316	8	39.50	3/37	
D. Williamson	55.5	1	295	7	42.14	3/29	
V.J. Wells	75.5	1	458	10	45.80	3/19	
J. Ormond	11	–	63	1	63.00	1/32	
A. Habib	0.1	–	4	–	–		
T.J. Mason	4	–	29	–	–		
J.M. Dakin	2.3	–	32	–	–		
D.L. Maddy	14.2	–	120	–	–		

Middlesex

Batting	M	Inns	NO	Runs	HS	Av	100s	50s	ct/st
M.R. Ramprakash	14	14	1	515	122	39.61	1	3	4
J.D. Carr	13	13	3	368	106	36.80	1		
P.N. Weekes	16	16	1	535	119*	35.66	1	5	9
M.W. Gatting	12	12	1	375	90	34.09		2	2
K.R. Brown	16	14	4	295	74	29.50		1	12/5
O.A. Shah	11	8	2	161	38	26.83			4
J.C. Pooley	15	14	1	283	68	21.76		1	6
R.L. Johnson	11	7	3	64	29	16.00			3
P.E. Wellings	8	7	1	70	42	11.66			3
J.F. Hewitt	11	5	1	46	16*	11.50			5
A.R.C. Fraser	16	7	2	54	16*	10.80			2
M.A. Feltham	4	4	–	32	12	8.00			
K.P. Dutch	9	8	1	34	12	4.85			4
R.A. Fay	14	4	3	2	1*	2.00			2
U.B.A. Rashid	3	1	–	0	0	0.00			

P.C.R. Tufnell (1 match); D. Follett (2 matches, ct 1)

Bowling	Overs	Mds	Runs	Wks	Av	Best	4/inn
O.A. Shah	1.1	–	4	1	4.00	1/4	
K.P. Dutch	26.1	–	149	7	21.28	3/10	
M.A. Feltham	27	4	138	6	23.00	3/30	
P.N. Weekes	94.1	1	497	21	23.66	4/29	2
J.P. Hewitt	54.3	5	249	10	24.90	3/26	
R.A. Fay	98	8	451	16	28.17	4/33	1
J.D. Carr	38	3	184	6	30.66	2/25	
D. Follett	16	–	95	3	31.66	2/47	
P.E. Wellings	7	–	72	2	36.00	1/22	
M.R. Ramprakash	8.5	–	76	2	38.00	1/21	
U.B.A. Rashid	14	–	117	3	39.00	2/57	
A.R.C. Fraser	126	9	569	14	40.64	2/20	
R.L. Johnson	75.5	1	369	9	44.13	2/24	
P.C.R. Tufnell	5	–	28	–	–		

Northamptonshire

Batting	M	Inns	NO	Runs	HS	Av	100s	50s	ct/st
A.L. Penberthy	15	11	4	343	80	49.00		2	1
K.M. Curran	17	16	4	456	92*	38.00		3	5
D.J. Capel	16	13	1	442	112	36.83	1	1	5
R.J. Bailey	14	14	4	337	70	33.70		3	10
R.R. Montgomerie	13	13	–	371	77	28.53		4	1
M.B. Loye	14	13	1	265	58	22.08		2	2
T.C. Walton	14	11	3	163	40	20.37			1
A. Fordham	6	5	–	71	43	14.20			4
J.P. Taylor	16	14	3	14	9*	14.00			4
C.E.L. Ambrose	14	5	3	26	11*	13.00			6
R.J. Warren	10	7	2	56	17	11.20			11/2
J.E. Emburey	16	6	3	23	8*	7.66			5
D.G.J. Sales	3	2	1	6	6	6.00			1
N.A. Mallender	5	1	–	5	5	5.00			
J.N. Snape	6	2	–	6	6	3.00			3

D. Ripley 0* (7 matches, ct 8); K.J. Innes (1 match)

Bowling	Overs	Mds	Runs	Wks	Av	Best	4/inn
C.E.L. Ambrose	102.2	17	347	17	20.41	3/14	
J.P. Taylor	116.5	10	599	24	24.95	3/22	
K.M. Curran	66	1	381	15	25.40	3/16	
J.E. Emburey	107	7	439	17	25.82	2/15	
D.J. Capel	91	3	431	16	26.93	4/44	1
J.N. Snape	24	2	108	4	27.00	2/18	

Northamptonshire (continued)

Bowling (continued)	Overs	Mds	Runs	Wks	Av	Best	4/inn
N.A. Mallender	37	4	158	5	31.60	2/20	
A.L. Penberthy	62	1	387	10	38.70	3/44	
K.J. Innes	6.4	–	57	1	57.00	1/57	
R.J. Bailey	13	1	87	1	87.00	1/17	

Nottinghamshire

Batting	M	Inns	NO	Runs	HS	Av	100s	50s	ct/st
C.L. Cairns	15	12	6	414	66*	69.00		2	
P. Johnson	16	15	5	635	99*	63.50		6	3
R.A. Pick	8	3	2	54	32*	54.00			4
R.T. Robinson	14	14	2	602	90	50.16		6	2
M.N. Bowen	13	3	2	45	23*	45.00			4
A.A. Metcalfe	12	9	3	225	65	37.50		1	4
P.R. Pollard	14	12	1	384	118	34.90	1	1	8
M.P. Dowman	11	11	1	254	74*	25.40		1	3
C.M. Tolley	15	8	3	112	20*	22.40			8
G.F. Archer	7	6	1	97	47	19.40			
R.T. Bates	16	6	2	58	16	14.50			9
W.M. Noon	16	5	2	27	12	9.00			14/2
K.P. Evans	14	4	1	14	5	4.66			6

D.B. Pennett (5 matches, ct 1)

Bowling	Overs	Mds	Runs	Wks	Av	Best	4/inn
C.L. Cairns	90.5	6	409	25	16.36	5/41	3
D.B. Pennet	37	–	210	9	23.33	3/49	
C.M. Tolley	92	1	476	19	25.05	5/16	1
R.A. Pick	56	1	283	11	25.72	3/31	
R.T. Bates	86	1	452	17	26.58	3/30	
K.P. Evans	100.5	7	419	15	27.93	3/38	
M.P. Dowman	27	1	172	5	34.40	2/34	
M.N. Bowen	88	1	471	13	36.23	3/28	
G.F. Archer	5	–	19	–	–		

Somerset

Batting	M	Inns	NO	Runs	HS	Av	100s	50s	ct/st
A.N. Hayhurst	7	5	4	122	60*	122.00		1	
R.J. Harden	11	11	4	442	90	63.14		4	3
S. Lee	16	15	4	442	71*	40.18		5	7
P.D. Bowler	15	15	1	497	76	35.50		5	4
M.N. Lathwell	15	15	–	414	93	27.60		3	3
S.C. Ecclestone	13	13	–	347	130	26.69	1	1	4
A.R. Caddick	15	4	1	68	39	22.66			7
G.D. Rose	15	13	4	183	54	20.33		1	6
M.E. Trescothick	13	10	1	171	61*	19.00			4
K.A. Parsons	14	7	2	92	56	18.40		1	8
R.J. Turner	16	12	2	172	39	17.20			14/3
H.R.J. Trump	16	4	2	30	14*	15.00			7
J.I.D. Kerr	5	2	1	12	8	12.00			1
J.D. Batty	1	1	–	6	6	6.00			

P.C.L. Holloway 3* (1 match, ct 1); K.J. Shine 1* (3 matches, ct 1)

Bowling	Overs	Mds	Runs	Wks	Av	Best	4/inn
A.N. Hayhurst	41.3	–	198	10	19.80	3/21	
K.J. Shine	19	–	103	5	20.60	4/31	1
A.R. Caddick	111.3	5	530	23	23.04	3/21	
J.I.D. Kerr	28	–	144	6	24.00	3/27	
S. Lee	115.5	2	618	25	24.72	4/40	1
M.E. Trescothick	9	–	55	2	27.50	1/13	
H.R.J. Trump	123	4	634	23	27.56	3/28	
K.A. Parsons	38	1	218	7	31.14	3/36	
G.D. Rose	111	4	535	11	48.63	3/33	
S.C. Ecclestone	8	1	49	1	49.00	1/49	

Surrey

Batting	M	Inns	NO	Runs	HS	Av	100s	50s	ct/st
J.D. Ratcliffe	2	2	1	60	42	60.00			1
A.J. Stewart	9	7	2	296	112*	59.20	2		11
C.C. Lewis	8	5	1	168	63	42.00		1	4
A.D. Brown	15	15	1	471	84	33.64		3	3
D.M. Ward	11	10	1	301	112	33.44	2		9
N. Shahid	12	11	1	327	58	32.70		1	4
D.J. Bicknell	12	12	3	280	52*	31.11		2	3
G.P. Thorpe	7	5	1	122	36*	30.50			8
A.J. Hollioake	15	12	1	291	74	26.45		1	3
M.A. Butcher	6	6	–	145	57	24.16		1	4
B.P. Julian	15	11	1	167	41	16.70			5
M.P. Bicknell	16	8	5	47	19*	15.66			3

Axa Equity and Law League Averages (continued)

Surrey (continued)

Batting (continued)	M	Inns	NO	Runs	HS	Av	100s	50s	ct/st
R.M. Pearson	14	5	4	12	9*	12.00			2
B.C. Hollioake	11	8	2	70	22*	11.66			5
G.J. Kersey	7	5	1	41	22*	10.25			8
I.J. Ward	3	2	1	2	1*	2.00			1
J.E. Benjamin	13	3	1	0	0*	0.00			3

P.C.R. Tufnell (1 match); D. Follet (2 matches ct 1)

Bowling	Overs	Mds	Runs	Wks	Av	Best	4/inn
A.J. Hollioake	91.1	1	474	39	12.15	5/44	4
C.C. Lewis	46.1	2	163	11	14.81	3/13	
J.E. Benjamin	82	3	322	17	18.94	3/33	
B.C. Hollioake	58.4	4	268	13	20.61	5/10	1
M.P. Bicknell	115	8	535	21	25.47	3/16	
B.P. Julian	77	1	449	15	29.93	3/5	
R.M. Pearson	67.5	–	389	12	32.41	3/33	
M.A. Butcher	0.4	–	0	–	–		
N. Shahid	1	–	18	–	–		
I.J. Ward	3.5	–	41	–	–		

Sussex

Batting	M	Inns	NO	Runs	HS	Av	100s	50s	ct/st
N.C. Phillips	5	4	3	55	38*	55.00			2
M. Newell	5	5	1	165	69	41.25		1	3
M.P. Speight	10	9	–	309	117	34.33	1	1	4
D.R. Law	16	15	3	370	79*	30.83		1	2
R.K. Rao	11	11	1	293	91	29.30		3	4
P. Moores	15	13	2	268	55	24.36		2	9/1
A.P. Wells	15	14	–	325	56	23.21		1	3
K. Greenfield	16	16	1	343	72	22.86		2	5
P.W. Jarvis	9	6	2	90	43	22.50			2
J.W. Hall	4	4	–	69	33	17.25			
V.C. Drakes	14	12	2	165	37	16.50			2
N.J. Lenham	7	5	–	78	43	15.60			
I.D.K. Salisbury	12	11	2	138	42	15.33			4
C.W.J. Athey	3	3	–	38	18	12.66			
K. Newell	9	8	1	80	32	11.42			2
J.J. Bates	1	1	–	8	8	8.00			1
G.R. Haywood	1	1	–	4	4	4.00			
M.R. Strong	2	2	1	3	2*	3.00			
E.S.H. Giddins	6	3	1	3	2	1.50			1
J.D. Lewry	8	4	1	4	4	1.33			
R.S.C. Martin-Jenkins	1	1	–	0	0	0.00			

R.J. Kirtley 1* & 0* (6 matches)

Bowling	Overs	Mds	Runs	Wks	Av	Best	4/inn
R.K. Rao	9	–	48	3	16.00	3/31	
J.D. Lewry	50	1	245	11	22.27	3/22	
P.W. Jarvis	63	2	340	15	22.66	3/29	
K. Greenfield	21	–	119	5	23.80	2/42	
N.J. Lenham	10	1	49	2	24.50	2/32	
D.R. Law	98.5	3	566	20	28.30	3/34	
V.C. Drakes	103.2	3	580	17	34.11	4/50	1
R.J. Kirtley	36	–	185	4	46.25	1/19	
I.D.K. Salisbury	92	2	468	8	58.50	2/37	
E.S.H. Giddins	43	2	268	4	67.00	1/23	
K. Newell	7	–	69	1	69.00	1/12	
N.C. Phillips	21.5	–	162	1	162.00	1/55	
R.S.C. Martin-Jenkins	1	–	6	–	–		
J.J. Bates	3	–	46	–	–		
M.R. Strong	12.2	2	74	–	–		

Warwickshire

Batting	M	Inns	NO	Runs	HS	Av	100s	50s	ct/st
N.M.K. Smith	15	15	2	533	111*	41.00	1	3	2
N.V. Knight	10	9	1	322	134	40.25	1	1	3
G. Welch	10	6	3	116	54	38.66		1	1
D.P. Ostler	15	15	1	462	91*	33.00		3	3
S.M. Pollock	14	11	2	273	57	30.33		2	3
T.L. Penney	17	16	5	329	75*	29.90		2	9
D.R. Brown	17	15	2	314	66	24.15		1	6
M. Burns	12	10	2	179	37	22.37			8/1
A.F. Giles	16	8	2	110	36	18.33			7
A.J. Moles	8	8	1	110	36	15.71			1
G.C. Small	12	6	3	37	15*	12.33			2
P.A. Smith	8	7	1	72	25	12.00			1
M. Edmond	3	2	1	9	5*	9.00			1
K.J. Piper	10	6	2	32	12	8.00			10/4
T.A. Munton	9	2	1	6	3*	6.00			1

Warwickshire (continued)

Batting (continued)	M	Inns	NO	Runs	HS	Av	100s	50s	ct/st
W.G. Khan	5	5	–	24	9	4.80			1
D.A. Reeve	5	4	1	10	5	3.33			2
A. Singh	1	1	–	2	2	2.00			

Bowling	Overs	Mds	Runs	Wks	Av	Best	4/inn
S.M. Pollock	104.3	6	387	25	15.48	3/27	
A.F. Giles	79	4	353	22	16.04	5/36	2
D.A. Reeve	34.4	2	138	8	17.25	3/22	
G.C. Small	78	6	312	15	20.80	4/14	1
D.R. Brown	76.3	5	401	15	26.73	4/47	1
T.A. Munton	62	8	259	9	28.77	3/17	
M. Edmond	21	2	87	3	29.00	1/26	
P.A. Smith	23.4	–	163	4	40.75	3/27	
N.M.K. Smith	72	2	338	7	48.28	1/19	
G. Welch	56.5	–	340	6	56.66	3/37	

Worcestershire

Batting	M	Inns	NO	Runs	HS	Av	100s	50s	ct/st
T.M. Moody	16	16	3	680	104	48.57	2	2	5
G.A. Hick	12	11	3	368	63*	46.00		5	7
W.P.C. Weston	15	14	4	416	80*	41.60		2	2
A. Sheriyar	14	5	4	35	19	35.00			2
K.R. Spiring	15	12	4	276	48	34.50			4
T.S. Curtis	7	7	1	197	77	32.83		1	2
R.K. Illingworth	15	5	3	50	27*	25.00			3
V.S. Solanki	14	8	2	124	55	20.66		1	5
S.R. Lampitt	16	8	1	129	30	18.42			5
D.A. Leatherdale	14	8	1	122	50	17.42		1	6
S.J. Rhodes	16	8	3	75	27*	15.00			14/5
M.J. Church	3	1	–	11	11	11.00			
M.J. Rawnsley	3	3	–	11	7	3.66			
S.W.K. Ellis	6	1	–	1	1	1.00			2
J.E. Brinkley	2	1	–	0	0	0.00			

B.E.A. Preece 1* (1 match); P.J. Newport (6 matches); P.A. Thomas (1 match)

Bowling	Overs	Mds	Runs	Wks	Av	Best	4/inn
B.E.A. Preece	2	–	10	1	10.00	1/10	
D.A. Leatherdale	21.5	–	95	7	13.57	4/31	1
J.E. Brinkley	12	1	56	3	18.66	2/26	
G.A. Hick	24	–	101	5	20.20	2/13	
R.K. Illingworth	102.2	3	446	19	23.47	3/34	
T.M. Moody	108	5	496	20	24.80	4/46	1
S.R. Lampitt	101.4	4	500	19	26.31	4/40	1
P.J. Newport	35	2	132	5	26.40	3/21	
V.S. Solanki	15	–	91	3	30.33	1/19	
S.W.K. Ellis	26	1	141	4	35.25	2/35	
A. Sheriyar	65	3	373	9	41.44	4/27	1
M.J. Church	1	–	12	–	–		
P.A. Thomas	6	–	30	–	–		
M.J. Rawnsley	12.5	1	69	–	–		

Yorkshire

Batting	M	Inns	NO	Runs	HS	Av	100s	50s	ct/st
M.G. Bevan	12	11	2	404	98*	44.88		2	4
D. Byas	17	16	4	523	111*	43.88	1	3	6
R.J. Blakey	17	12	4	293	61*	36.62		1	13/2
P.J. Hartley	17	11	5	188	52	31.33		1	1
M.P. Vaughan	17	17	2	439	71*	29.26		2	4
M.D. Moxon	10	10	–	271	72	27.10		1	3
A. McGrath	16	15	3	255	69	21.25		1	3
A.C. Morris	9	6	1	99	48*	19.80			2
C. White	17	15	1	249	45	17.78			3
C.E.W. Silverwood	16	7	5	35	14*	17.50			
D. Gough	15	11	1	152	30	15.20			1
R.D. Stemp	16	2	–	18	11	9.00			9

R.A. Kettleborough 12* & 11* (4 matches, ct 4); A.G. Wharf 2* (2 matches); G.M. Hamilton (2 matches)

Bowling	Overs	Mds	Runs	Wks	Av	Best	4/inn
M.G. Bevan	31	1	165	11	15.00	5/29	1
A.C. Morris	14	–	81	4	20.25	2/19	
P.J. Hartley	119	6	533	25	21.32	3/27	
C. White	101.1	6	443	20	22.15	4/21	1
D. Gough	109.5	6	501	20	25.05	3/31	
R.D. Stemp	107.3	5	484	19	25.47	4/25	1
C.E.W. Silverwood	108	9	485	17	28.52	4/26	1
G.M. Hamilton	10	2	59	1	59.00	1/26	
M.P. Vaughan	1	–	13	–	–		
A.G. Wharf	3	1	14	–	–		

Britannic Assurance County Championship
and other county matches

There was a change in the point-scoring system in the Britannic Assurance County Championship in 1996. It was decided to award three points for a draw to try to encourage sides to battle to the end and gain some reward for doing so. It was also decided that the curtain-raiser to the season would not involve the Champion County, but would see England 'A' play The Rest at Chelmsford.

18, 19 and 20 April
at Old Trafford
Lancashire 212 (S. Elworthy 88, A.G. Wharf 4 for 29) and 24 for 1
Yorkshire 237 for 9 dec. (R.A. Kettleborough 85, A.C. Morris 60, R.J. Green 6 for 41)
Match drawn

Since the championship has been restructured so that counties meet each other only once a season Lancashire and Yorkshire have played a friendly match to ensure that there are two Roses' games each season. The weather was not kind to this encounter, which saw both sides bereft of leading players because of the demands of the game at Chelmsford. In his first game for Lancashire, Elworthy, the South African, hit a career-best 88 and Richard Green took a career-best 6 for 41.

20, 21, 22 and 23 April
at Chelmsford
The Rest 123 (T.A. Munton 4 for 41) and 253 (G.P. Thorpe 141 not out, E.S.H. Giddins 4 for 60)
England 'A' 317 (T.A. Munton 54, G. Chapple 5 for 99) and 60 for 2
England 'A' won by 8 wickets

The Rest side included seven players who had been with England in South Africa, but they were no match for Hussain's 'A' side, which had Rollins as wicket-keeper instead of Piper. Russell, captaining The Rest, chose to bat first, but his side was bowled out by Munton, Giddins and Irani inside 49 overs. Consistent batting took England 'A' to a commanding lead after Knight had gone for 0. The redeeming feature for The Rest was the bowling of Glen Chapple, who has long been seen as an England prospect but whose career faltered in 1995. The Rest slipped to 128 for 5 when they batted a second time, but Thorpe and Watkinson added 95, only for the last five wickets to fall for 30 runs and for England 'A' to win in three days.

Giddins bowled with pace and aggression, and the enigmatic Thorpe batted well. The main honours, however, went to Hussain, who led his side well, and his eager team.

2, 3, 4 and 6 May
at Derby
Derbyshire 362 for 8 dec. (K.J. Barnett 200 not out, A.D. Mullally 5 for 83) and 89 (A.D. Mullally 6 for 47, D.J. Millns 4 for 34)
Leicestershire 315 (J.J. Whitaker 110, D.G. Cork 4 for 96) and 137 for 4
Leicestershire won by 6 wickets
Leicestershire 22 pts, Derbyshire 8 pts

at Chester-le-Street
Northamptonshire 320 (K.M. Curran 68, M.M. Betts 4 for 120) and 122 for 4 dec. (R.R. Montgomerie 55 not out)
Durham 221 for 7 dec. (P.D. Collingwood 91, M.A. Roseberry 59) and 168 for 7
Match drawn
Northamptonshire 9 pts, Durham 8 pts

Mike Smith of Gloucestershire wrecked Middlesex at Lord's in May by taking 8 for 73.
(Paul Sturgess/Sportsline)

The curtain raiser to the season. England 'A' v. The Rest at Chelmsford. Ed Giddins of Sussex bowls Mark Ramprakash. Giddins had an impressive match and began the season on the verge of the England side. He ended it in disgrace, banned from first-class cricket for a year.
(Clive Mason/Allsport)

at Cardiff
Yorkshire 536 for 8 dec. (M.D. Moxon 213, M.P. Vaughan 183, R.D.B. Croft 5 for 133) and 205 for 7 dec. (M.G. Bevan 77, A.G. Wharf 62)
Glamorgan 482 for 7 dec. (H. Morris 202 not out, M.P. Maynard 136) and 216 (S.P. James 62, H. Morris 51, C. White 4 for 33)
Yorkshire won by 43 runs
Yorkshire 22 pts, Glamorgan 5 pts

at Canterbury
Kent 320 (T.R. Ward 106, C.L. Hooper 54, G.R. Cowdrey 52) and 66 for 3 dec.
Lancashire 47 for 1 dec. and 275 (M.A. Atherton 98, N.H. Fairbrother 85, M.M. Patel 5 for 65)
Kent won by 64 runs
Kent 19 pts, Lancashire 4 pts

at Lord's
Middlesex 200 (K.E. Cooper 4 for 54) and 247 (J.C. Pooley 73, M.W. Gatting 54, P.N. Weekes 50, A.M. Smith 8 for 73)
Gloucestershire 218 (D. Follett 5 for 94) and 231 for 5 (A.J. Wright 106, R.J. Cunliffe 51)
Gloucestershire won by 5 wickets
Gloucestershire 21 pts, Middlesex 5 pts

at Trent Bridge
Sussex 303 for 8 dec. (N.J. Lenham 100 not out) and 278 for 9 dec. (C.L. Cairns 4 for 70)
Nottinghamshire 255 for 5 dec. (P. Johnson 90, P.R. Pollard 63) and 68 for 2
Match drawn
Nottinghamshire 8 pts, Sussex 8 pts

at Taunton
Surrey 367 (A.J. Hollioake 128, G.P. Thorpe 52, B.P. Julian 50, K.J. Shine 6 for 95) and 410 for 4 (A.J. Hollioake 117 not out, G.P. Thorpe 100 not out, D.J. Bicknell 58, M.A. Butcher 52)
Somerset 558 (P.D. Bowler 207, S. Lee 87 not out, A.N. Hayhurst 69, P.C.L. Holloway 54)
Match drawn
Somerset 11 pts, Surrey 9 pts

Michael Vaughan hit a career-best 183 for Yorkshire against Glamorgan and shared a record opening partnership with Martyn Moxon.
(David Munden/Sportsline)

at Worcester
Worcestershire 201 (D.A. Leatherdale 50, N.F. Williams 5 for 57) and 415 (D.A. Leatherdale 69, P.J. Newport 68, R.K. Illingworth 66 not out, M.C. Ilott 5 for 105)
Essex 430 (S.G. Law 93, G.A. Gooch 85, D.D.J. Robinson 61, M.C. Ilott 58, S.R. Lampitt 5 for 116) and 190 for 5 (R.C. Irani 110 not out)
Essex won by 5 wickets
Essex 24 pts, Worcestershire 5 pts

The first round of matches was plagued by bad weather, and, in some instances, captains had to resort to challenging declarations to keep games alive.

There were remarkable events at Derby where no play was possible on the first day. Put in to bat, Derbyshire thrived on the second day when Kim Barnett hit the third double century of his career, the second against Leicestershire. Conditions were far from ideal for batting, but Barnett reached his double century off 307 balls and shared a fifth wicket stand of 101 with Wells and an eighth wicket stand of 104 with Krikken.

Barnett had relinquished the Derbyshire captaincy, while Whitaker had just taken on the captaincy at Leicester, and he celebrated by hitting a century off 114 balls. There was little other substance to the Leicestershire innings, however, and Barnett continued to flourish by taking the last three wickets with his leg-spin, so giving his side a first innings lead of 47. It would have been more but for a last wicket stand of 49 between Pierson and Parsons.

The complexion of the game changed completely when Derbyshire batted again. In 25 overs before the end of the second day, Millns and Mullally tore them apart and left them stranded on 68 for 6. There was no reprieve on the Monday, and Leicestershire reached a target of 137 with 36 overs to spare.

There was also no play on the first day at the Riverside Stadium, and on the second Northamptonshire ground to 273 for 7 in 105 overs. There were two rays of light for Durham in that Betts returned the best bowling figures of his career and Paul Collingwood, on his first-class debut, yorked Capel with his first ball in first-class cricket. He also hit a six and eight fours in an innings of 91, but Durham found the task of scoring 222 in 44 overs to win the match beyond their capabilities.

John Emburey appeared in his 500th first-class match, his first for Northamptonshire.

The first day at Cardiff produced 316 runs in 94 overs without a wicket falling. On the second day, Moxon and Vaughan took their opening stand to 362 before Vaughan fell to Gary Butcher for 183, his highest first-class score. Moxon reached the fifth double century of his career, and his partnership with Vaughan was a record for any Yorkshire wicket against Glamorgan and the highest first wicket stand for the White Rose county since the Second World War.

Glamorgan responded positively. Hugh Morris reached his fourth century in succession, and he and Maynard, who had succeeded him as captain, scored 228 for the third wicket. Morris' 202 not out was the first double century of his career and the highest score by a Glamorgan batsman against Yorkshire. Maynard's declaration gave Yorkshire a lead of 54 on the first innings, but Glamorgan then reduced Yorkshire to 32 for 4 on the Saturday evening and seemed in charge of the game.

The last day saw another dramatic change. Bevan and night-watchman Wharf, who hit a maiden first-class fifty, added 133 for the fifth wicket, and Byas' declaration left Glamorgan a target of 260 in 50 overs. They reached 202 for 3 needing 58 from nine overs, but their last seven wickets went down for 14 runs in 45 balls.

No play was possible after noon on the first day at Canterbury and none at all was possible on the second day. Ward and Hooper added 127 for Kent's third wicket, and Lancashire were left the last day in which to score 340 to win. Atherton and Fairbrother scored 140 in 101 minutes for the third wicket, but Patel then took over, taking five of the last eight wickets, which went down for 85 runs.

At Lord's, Gloucestershire enjoyed a resounding victory over Middlesex inside three days. Fourteen wickets fell on the opening day, four of them going to Kevin Cooper, the 38-year old medium-pacer, who was playing because Walsh had not yet arrived from the Caribbean. Starting the second day at 94 for 4, Gloucestershire immediately lost Symonds, who was caught off Hewitt's first ball of the day. Hewitt had already created an impression by dismissing Dawson with his first ball in first-class cricket on the opening day.

Gloucestershire took a first innings lead of 18, but Pooley and Weekes began Middlesex's second innings with a partnership of 124, and the home side ended the second day on a comfortable 207 for 4.

The Saturday brought a remarkable transition. Mike Smith produced a devastating spell of 5 for 16 in 10 overs to give him career-best bowling figures of 8 for 73, and the last six Middlesex wickets went down for only 25 runs. Needing 230 to win, Gloucestershire now found themselves in a winning position. Dawson fell to Fraser at 19, but Cunliffe, out first ball in the first innings, helped Wright to add 108 for the second wicket. Wright went on to hit 106 off 178 balls with a six and 15 fours. Symonds made a valuable contribution, and Gloucestershire claimed their first win at Lord's for 21 years.

There was no play on the first day at Trent Bridge, and the Sussex innings was not completed until the third morning when Lenham reached his century. Nottinghamshire went for brisk runs, and new skipper Johnson hit 90 off 77 balls as he attempted to keep the game alive. Sussex had other ideas, and number nine Nicholas Phillips batted two hours for his 45 in the second innings. Wells then left Nottinghamshire a target of 327 in 31 overs.

Only 68 balls were bowled on the first day at Taunton from which Surrey made 34 for 2. They descended to 55 for 4 before Hollioake and Thorpe put on 99. Hollioake hit 22 fours in his 141-ball innings, and he dominated a sixth wicket stand of 127 with Lewis. Kevin Shine, once of Hampshire and Middlesex, took 6 for 95 on his debut for Somerset.

Somerset lost Lathwell for 0, but Bowler hit his first double century for the county. He faced 349 balls, hit 29 fours and added 248 for the second wicket with skipper Hayhurst. Lee, Somerset's Australian newcomer, also batted impressively.

Surrey batted out the last day with Adam Hollioake hitting his second century of the match and becoming the first Surrey batsman to score a century in each innings for 12 years. Surrey needed to reflect that there were 79 extras in Somerset's innings, 54 runs coming from no-balls.

Mark Ilott took three wickets on a restricted first day at Worcester which ended with the home county 78 for 4 in chilly and gloomy weather. Essex took command on the second day. Williams returned his best bowling figures for the county, capturing the last three wickets in nine balls. Gooch and Robinson began the Essex innings with 158 in 25 overs, and Law ended the day in impressively aggressive fashion. Surprisingly, he fell short of his century, but Ilott and Williams scored 76 in 10 overs for the ninth wicket, and Essex led by 229 on the first innings.

By the end of the third day, Worcestershire were just 17 runs ahead with five wickets down, and they lost Leatherdale early on the last morning. When Lampitt went to Ilott they were 256 for 7, just 27 runs on. Newport and Illingworth now fashioned a stand of 100 to frustrate the Essex attack. When Worcestershire were finally bowled out Essex found themselves facing a target of 187 off 43 overs, a far sterner task than they had anticipated.

Five overs after tea, Essex were 32 for 5 and an historic Worcestershire victory seemed likely. Irani and Grayson, imported from Yorkshire, had other ideas and shared an unbroken stand of 158 in 29 overs to win the match with 16 balls to spare. Irani reached a magnificent century off 84 balls, and he finished the match by hitting Newport for six. It was his fifth six, and he also hit 12 fours. Grayson batted with good sense for his 46 and played a major part in a thrilling victory.

9, 10, 11 and 13 May

at Southampton

Hampshire 539 (W.K.M. Benjamin 117, A.N. Aymes 113, P.R. Whitaker 55, J.P. Stephenson 50, R.A. Smith 50) and 221 (P.R. Whitaker 67 not out, P.M. Such 5 for 74, A.P. Grayson 4 for 82)
Essex 432 (S.G. Law 143, G.A. Gooch 130, W.K.M. Benjamin 4 for 96) and 331 for 6 (R.C. Irani 81 not out, P.J. Prichard 69, N. Hussain 60)
Essex won by 4 wickets
Essex 23 pts, Hampshire 8 pts

at Old Trafford

Lancashire 495 (W.K. Hegg 134, M.A. Atherton 87, G.D. Lloyd 65, N.J. Speak 55, A.R.K. Pierson 4 for 100) and 191 for 3 dec. (J.E.R. Gallian 63, J.P. Crawley 61)
Leicestershire 377 (P.A. Nixon 106, B.F. Smith 81, D.J. Millns 73, M. Watkinson 4 for 71)
Match drawn
Lancashire 9 pts, Leicestershire 8 pts

at Lord's

Middlesex 191 (M.W. Gatting 74, M.J. Foster 4 for 21) and 391 (M.W. Gatting 171, P.N. Weekes 73, M.M. Betts 4 for 101)
Durham 209 (C.W. Scott 59) and 67 (D. Follett 8 for 22)
Middlesex won by 306 runs
Middlesex 20 pts, Durham 5 pts

at Northampton

Northamptonshire 451 for 6 dec. (R.J. Warren 201 not out, D.J. Capel 83, A. Fordham 52, R.R. Montgomerie 51) and 178 for 5 dec. (R.R. Montgomerie 53)
Glamorgan 351 for 7 dec. (G.P. Butcher 89, S.P. James 76, M.P. Maynard 52) and 279 for 5 (A. Dale 120, P.A. Cottey 65 not out)
Glamorgan won by 5 wickets
Glamorgan 22 pts, Northamptonshire 7 pts

David Follett promised so much in his second season in first-class cricket with five wickets in the opening match and an astonishing 8 for 22 against Durham in the second. The promise was cut short by injury. (Paul Sturgess/Sportsline)

at Taunton
Nottinghamshire 200 (G.F. Archer 83, G.D. Rose 6 for 41) and 238 (G.D. Rose 7 for 47)
Somerset 309 (S. Lee 82, P.C.L. Holloway 50, D.B. Pennett 4 for 116) and 130 for 0 (M.N. Lathwell 66 not out, P.D. Bowler 57 not out)
Somerset won by 10 wickets
Somerset 23 pts, Nottinghamshire 5 pts

at The Oval
Kent 225 (M.A. Ealham 51) and 361 (M.J. McCague 63, D.P. Fulton 59, M.V. Fleming 56)
Surrey 360 (M.A. Butcher 94, B.P. Julian 74, C.C. Lewis 61, J.B.D. Thompson 5 for 72) and 160 for 6 (M.J. McCague 4 for 33)
Match drawn
Surrey 11 pts, Kent 8 pts

at Hove
Warwickshire 645 for 7 dec. (D.A. Reeve 168 not out, T.L. Penney 134, N.V. Knight 132, D.P. Ostler 90)
Sussex 222 (D.R. Law 53, G. Welch 4 for 50) and 284 (J.W. Hall 57, A.P. Wells 51)
Warwickshire won by an innings and 139 runs
Warwickshire 24 pts, Sussex 2 pts

at Sheffield
Yorkshire 561 (M.G. Bevan 136, A. McGrath 91, D. Byas 79, C. White 61, M.D. Moxon 59, D.E. Malcolm 4 for 109) and 138 for 3 dec. (M.D. Moxon 74 not out)
Derbyshire 412 for 4 dec. (D.M. Jones 214 not out, J.E. Owen 101) and 248 for 8 (C.J. Adams 66, K.J. Barnett 51, C. White 4 for 15)
Match drawn
Derbyshire 10 pts, Yorkshire 8 pts

Essex claimed their second victory in as many matches when they staged an astonishing recovery to beat Hampshire. Prichard asked Hampshire to bat first when he won the toss, which initially seemed the correct decision. At 225 for 6, Winston Benjamin joined Adrian Aymes, and by the end of the day they had added 156 in 32 overs and Benjamin had scored a hundred between tea and the close. Eventually, the partnership was worth 178 with both batsmen reaching career-best scores. Udal and Aymes hit 98 in 21 overs for the eighth wicket, and Hampshire made their highest score against Essex. Four Essex bowlers conceded more than 100 runs.

Essex responded positively, with Gooch reaching the 121st century of his career off 161 balls. Law, too, took up the challenge, and he and Gooch added 132 for the third wicket. Law was to hit centuries on successive days against Hampshire, for he followed his Saturday with a hundred in the Sunday League. Essex lost their last six wickets for 57 runs, but Hampshire floundered against Such's off-spin on the Saturday evening.

Whitaker stood firm, and on the Monday morning another 91 runs were realised from the last three wickets, so that Essex were left with the daunting task of scoring 329 off 68 overs.

Robinson was run out before lunch, and Gooch went early in the afternoon, but Hussain, Law and Prichard all hustled runs. With Prichard and Irani together, 162 were needed from 27 overs and the pair put on 102 in 16 overs. Prichard and Grayson left in quick succession, but Rollins stayed with Irani until the job was completed with an over to spare. Once again Irani had proved to be a match-winner, his 81 coming off 77 balls with four sixes and four fours.

There was less excitement at Old Trafford where Lancashire failed to collect three batting points on the opening day, although they lost only five wickets. Hegg made a career-best 134 off 199 balls and shared a ninth wicket stand of 106 with Martin. Leicestershire ended the second day in disarray on 98 for 5, but they recovered on the Saturday, when overs were lost to bad weather, when Nixon and Millns began a record eighth wicket partnership of 172.

Middlesex shrugged off a bad start to the season with victory over Durham. The Lord's wicket again proved unpredictable and 16 wickets fell on the first day when Middlesex lost their last six wickets for 35 runs and Durham closed on 114 for 6.

Graham Rose had match figures of 13 for 88, the best of his career, to take Somerset to victory over Nottinghamshire at Taunton. Sadly, Rose's season was shortened by injury.
(Nigel French/ASP)

Durham took a first innings lead of 18 before Middlesex set about reparation. They ended the second day on 167 for 3 and batted throughout the Saturday, when Gatting scored his 90th first-class century and brought his record to a hundred against each first-class county.

What happened on the Monday was totally unexpected as David Follett, playing his third first-class match, took 8 for 22 in 12.2 overs and Durham were bowled out for 67 half an hour after lunch.

There was another exceptional bowling performance at Taunton where Somerset won in three days. Fourteen wickets fell on the first day, with Nottinghamshire losing their last six wickets for 30 runs. Somerset trailed by only 13 at the end of the day thanks to Lee's blistering 80 off 77 balls. Batty, Rose and Shine all made valuable contributions to help Somerset to a lead of 109, and Rose then tore Nottinghamshire apart. His 7 for 47 was the best bowling performance of his career and he captured ten or more wickets in a match for the first time. Somerset won before lunch on the third morning.

Russell Warren hit the first double century of his career but finished on the losing side at Northampton. Warren's 201 came off 307 balls and he hit two sixes and 27 fours. He and Capel added 239 for the fifth wicket.

Glamorgan scored with consistent rapidity, and Gary Butcher made his highest first-class score. Maynard declared as soon as the fourth batting point was claimed.

Northamptonshire, too, scored quickly, and Bailey set Glamorgan a target of 279 in 64 overs. A fourth wicket stand of 117 in 22 overs between Dale and Cottey gave the innings the necessary impetus, and the target was reached with one ball to spare.

At The Oval, Kent lost two wickets to Martin Bicknell in the first over of the match, and there was no total recovery. Surrey stuttered at 88 for 3 at the close, but Mark Butcher, Lewis and Julian all showed determination on the Friday to take Surrey to a substantial lead of 135. Dr Julian Thompson took five wickets in an innings for the first time.

Play was limited to 73 overs on the Saturday, and Kent scored 241 for 6. They seemed to be facing defeat, but McCague, who hit seven fours, and Patel added 89 for the ninth wicket, and Surrey were set a target of 227 in 50 overs. McCague continued to plague them, taking the first three wickets for three runs in 11 balls. At 81 for 6, hope of a Surrey victory had gone, and Butcher and Julian batted out time.

Reigning champions Warwickshire entered the campaign in fearsome style. At Hove, Nick Knight hit a century before lunch on the first day, his 132 coming off 113 balls. He and Ostler added 141 for the second wicket, and Penney and Reeve took the champions to 494 for 3 off 108 overs by the close.

The Penney/Reeve partnership was eventually worth 220. Reeve's innings lasted five hours and he hit 11 fours and a six in what was only his seventh first-class hundred. Facing a frightening 645 for 7, Sussex scored 136 for 5 by the end of the second day, and by the close on Saturday evening they were 187 for 6 in their second innings.

In 65 minutes on the fourth morning, Sussex scored 97 bright runs but lost their last four wickets, three of them to Neil Smith, who had savaged them the day before when they had suffered another humiliating defeat at the hands of Warwickshire.

For the second successive match, Yorkshire scored massively. They made 486 for 5 from 106 overs on the opening day with Bevan, a powerful force in the side, hitting 136 off 160 balls. The Australian left-hander hit three sixes and 16 fours and put on 164 for the fourth wicket with McGrath.

Half of the second day was lost to rain after Yorkshire's last five wickets realised 75 runs in as many minutes and Derbyshire began the third day on 128 for 3. The third day belonged to Derbyshire. Dean Jones and John Owen scored 278 for their fourth wicket, a record for any Derbyshire

Warwickshire, the reigning champions, began the season in magnificent fashion, totally destroying Sussex at Hove. Ashley Giles catches Neil Lenham off his own bowling as Ostler, Reeve and Piper celebrate. Giles had an outstanding season with bat as well as ball and recorded a maiden first-class hundred. (Phillip Wilcox)

wicket against Yorkshire, and while Jones announced his presence as Derbyshire's new captain with a commanding double century, Owen reached a maiden first-class hundred. He hit 14 fours and two sixes in his 183-ball innings.

Brisk hitting on the last morning brought the conclusion that Derbyshire would have to score 288 in what became 50 overs if they were to win the match. The visitors appeared to be cruising to victory at 201 for 2, but White took 4 for 3 in 11 balls and eventually Derbyshire were thankful for Wells and Aldred standing firm in an unbroken ninth wicket stand which occupied seven overs.

16, 17, 18 and 20 May
at Chester-le-Street
Yorkshire 335 (M.G. Bevan 90, R.D. Stemp 65, S.J.E. Brown 4 for 93) and 210 (M.G. Bevan 51, S.J.E. Brown 5 for 54, M.M. Betts 5 for 87)
Durham 215 (J.E. Morris 83, P.J. Hartley 4 for 67) and 186 (P.J. Hartley 4 for 32)
Yorkshire won by 144 runs
Yorkshire 23 pts, Durham 5 pts

at Ilford
Kent 590 (C.L. Hooper 155, S.A. Marsh 127, G.R. Cowdrey 111, P.M. Such 5 for 145)
Essex 306 (G.A. Gooch 74, R.C. Irani 50, M.M. Patel 4 for 128, C.L. Hooper 4 for 151) and 218 (S.G. Law 115, D.D.J. Robinson 75, M.M. Patel 6 for 97)
Kent won by an innings and 66 runs
Kent 24 pts, Essex 5 pts

at Cardiff
Derbyshire 464 (C.M. Wells 165, J.E. Owen 105, A.S. Rollins 73, K.M. Krikken 51, G.P. Butcher 4 for 28, R.D.B. Croft 4 for 122) and 132 (S.L. Watkin 4 for 61)
Glamorgan 379 for 5 dec. (P.A. Cottey 135 not out, H. Morris 90, G.P. Butcher 61 not out) and 107 (D.E. Malcolm 6 for 52, A.J. Harris 4 for 55)
Derbyshire won by 110 runs
Derbyshire 22 pts, Glamorgan 6 pts

at Bristol
Gloucestershire 263 (T.H.C. Hancock 89, R.C. Russell 63, S. Lee 4 for 55) and 245
Somerset 259 (S. Lee 65, R.J. Harden 54, R.J. Turner 50) and 171 for 8 (C.A. Walsh 5 for 69)
Match drawn
Gloucestershire 9 pts, Somerset 9 pts

John Owen suddenly found form and scored hundreds in successive matches for Derbyshire, his first in county cricket.
(Paul Sturgess/Sportsline)

at Leicester
Leicestershire 638 for 8 dec. (A. Habib 215, J.J. Whitaker 168, D.L. Maddy 63, P.V. Simmons 51)
Worcestershire 155 (D.J. Millns 4 for 37) and 353 (T.M. Moody 104, W.P.C. Weston 69, K.R. Spiring 51)
Leicestershire won by an innings and 130 runs
Leicestershire 24 pts, Worcestershire 2 pts

at Trent Bridge
Nottinghamshire 452 (R.T. Robinson 122, C.L. Cairns 64, P. Johnson 63, S. Elworthy 4 for 91) and 238 (P. Johnson 88, P.J. Martin 7 for 50)
Lancashire 397 for 9 dec. (J.E.R. Gallian 94, N.H. Fairbrother 80, J.P. Crawley 77, W.K. Hegg 54 not out) and 225 for 9 (N.J. Speak 74 not out, N.H. Fairbrother 59, J.A. Afford 6 for 51)
Match drawn
Nottinghamshire 11 pts, Lancashire 9 pts

at Edgbaston
Hampshire 274 (J.S. Laney 73) and 276 for 5 dec. (K.D. James 118 not out)
Warwickshire 192 (C.A. Connor 5 for 57) and 236 (T.L. Penney 73, N.V. Knight 60)
Hampshire won by 122 runs
Hampshire 22 pts, Warwickshire 4 pts

Yorkshire beat Durham with more than a day to spare, yet, on the first day, in spite of Bevan's fine innings and Gough's hitting, they were trembling on 225 for 9. Stemp joined Silverwood, and the last wicket pair added 110 with Stemp reaching a maiden fifty. Shattered, Durham then lost 3 for 19 before the close. The bright part of the day for the home side was that wicket-keeper Chris Scott held seven catches, and he was to take three more when Yorkshire batted a second time.

Morris made his highest score of the season on the second day, but Durham trailed by 120 runs. On a pitch now giving help to the bowler, Yorkshire slipped to 149 for 7 by the close, and Melvyn Betts was to finish with his best bowling figures. This only served to warn Durham of the fate that they were to suffer on the third afternoon.

At Ilford, Essex were brought down to earth with a crash. Kent hit 323 for 4 from 85.1 overs. Hooper dominated the day with an innings of power and beauty, and he and Cowdrey added 224 for the fourth wicket. Cowdrey reached his hundred on the second morning, and this was followed by Marsh and Thompson putting on 170 for the seventh wicket. Marsh, the Kent skipper, hit the highest score of his career.

McCague and Thompson bowled an over each, after which the spinners took over and bowled for the next 102 overs of the Essex innings. McCague returned for 3.5 overs to take the last two wickets, and Essex followed on 284 runs in arrears. They immediately lost Gooch and Hussain on the Saturday evening, but Robinson and Law batted comfortably in adding 157. Once they were separated, Patel took over and the last seven wickets went down for 21 runs in 83 balls.

The game at Cardiff was one of fluctuating fortunes. Derbyshire finished the first day on 334 for 5 from 111 overs. They had lost Barnett at 0 and Adams at 9. Jones was out at 51 before Rollins and Owen put on 101. Owen and Wells then combined in a partnership worth 151. Both batsmen reached centuries. For Owen, it was his second in consecutive matches; and Wells made his highest score for Derbyshire. He was dismissed by Gary Butcher, who finished with a career-best bowling performance.

Butcher also aided Cottey in a sixth wicket stand of 154 which was ended only when Maynard declared 85 runs in arrears on the Saturday evening.

Derbyshire began the last day on 34 for 1, but their innings was wrecked by Butcher and Watkin, who were aided by some good slip catching and the fine wicket-keeping of Metson. The last nine Derbyshire wickets went down for 76, and Glamorgan faced a target of 218 in 62 overs.

Bowling unchanged, Malcolm and Harris bowled Glamorgan out in 21.4 overs. At one time, the home side were 3 for 4, and then 48 for 6. Malcolm returned his best bowling figures for Derbyshire, and Harris the best of his career.

A contributor to the Leicestershire triumph, Aftab Habib, a double century against Worcestershire. (Paul Sturgess/Sportsline)

Lee showed his best bowling form for Somerset as Gloucestershire were bowled out on the first day at Bristol. Rain and gloom restricted the second day to two hours' play. Lee shone again on the third day, adding 92 with Turner as Somerset struggled. The last five wickets fell for 28 runs, two of them to Ball who was awarded his county cap.

With the pitch growing more uncertain, Somerset faced a target of 250 in 47 overs. Walsh was quick and menacing, and both Turner and Bowler were forced to retire hurt. Turner returned, but Somerset were reduced to 122 for 8. Batty and Shine batted out the last 12 overs to secure the draw, although Bowler had returned from hospital ready to bat again if necessary.

Leicestershire crushed Worcestershire in three days to go top of the embryo table, although three points separated them from Kent in fourth place. The outstanding feature of the match was an innings of 215 by Aftab Habib, formerly of Middlesex, who turned a maiden championship century into a double century and shared a record fifth wicket stand of 320 with skipper Whitaker. Leicestershire scored 481 for 4 in 106 overs on the first day. By the end of the second, Worcestershire were 8 for 1 in their second innings.

Habib faced 322 balls and hit two sixes and 32 fours; Whitaker hit a six and 25 fours.

Moody and Weston put on 121 after three wickets had gone for 36 on the third day, but Leicestershire were still victors with more than a day to spare.

Tim Robinson shared two century stands as he moved to his 59th first-class hundred on the opening day at Trent Bridge which ended with Nottinghamshire on 320 for 4 from 106 overs. Johnson and Cairns provided substance in the middle order, and the fourth batting point was obtained with ease, but with Gallian and Crawley sharing a second wicket partnership of 142, and Lancashire ending the second day on 237 for 3, a draw began to look an inevitable result.

Lancashire had a collapse on the Saturday morning as four wickets fell for 47 runs before Hegg and Elworthy stopped the rot.

When Nottinghamshire batted a second time their last seven wickets went down for 56 runs. Martin took six of the last seven, and finished with a career-best 7 for 50. Lancashire were left 72 overs in which to score 294, and, at 172 for 3, they seemed set for victory, for 23 overs still remained. Fairbrother was then caught at the wicket sweeping at Afford, who now took control. Pitching into the rough, he accounted for Elworthy, Chapple, Martin and Keedy in quick succession, and his 6 for 51 was the best bowling performance of his career. Keedy had lasted 27 balls as he and Speak scored 24 runs in 10 overs, and it was that ninth wicket partnership that thwarted Nottinghamshire.

Keedy was out to the second ball of the last over, and this brought in Gallian, who had broken an index finger when dropping a catch earlier in the day. His right arm was in plaster, and he batted one-handed, keeping out the last four balls of the match as nine men crouched around him.

At the start of the season, there seemed to be no place in the Hampshire line-up for Kevan James, the 35-year-old all-rounder, but injuries brought him into the side for the game at Edgbaston. Hampshire struggled on the first day, reaching 242 for 7 at two-and-a-half an over.

When Warwickshire batted on the second day they quickly lost Knight and Ostler to Connor. There was no effective recovery as James took 3 for 17 in 13.5 overs to give Connor fine support and bowl Hampshire to a first innings lead of 82, substantial on a pitch that was showing signs of wear.

On the Saturday, James, batting at number three, played an innings of great character in chilling and difficult conditions. He batted for five hours and hit two sixes and 12 fours to hold together the Hampshire innings and make possible a declaration which left three overs and a day in which Warwickshire were asked to make 359 to win.

This was going to be a difficult task, in spite of the fact that Winston Benjamin was forced to retire from the Hampshire attack with a shoulder injury. It was not realised at the time, but this injury heralded the end of his career. Benjamin had taken two wickets when he left the field, but the rest of the Hampshire bowlers worked their way patiently through the Warwickshire batting.

The home county reached 173 for 4 with Reeve controversially throwing his bat away as he padded up to the

Omitted from the Hampshire side at the start of the season, Kevan James returned with a century and wickets in a surprise win over Warwickshire. His success continued and, against the Indian tourists, he had an astonishing achievement when he took four wickets in four balls and scored a century in the same match. (David Munden/Sportsline)

left-arm spin of Maru when the bowler pitched outside leg stump. It was estimated that Reeve threw his bat away 15 times, an act for which he received a reprimand from Lord's, before being caught behind off James.

Warwickshire slipped to 215 for 9 with 13 overs left. Brown and Giles lasted until with nine balls remaining Brown was caught by Aymes off Connor, and Warwickshire had suffered their first home defeat in any competition since July 1995.

22, 23, 24 and 25 May
at Horsham
Sussex 319 for 7 dec. (A.P. Wells 92, C.W.J. Athey 77) and 0 for 0 dec.
Middlesex 0 for 0 dec. and 85
Sussex won by 234 runs
Sussex 19 pts, Middlesex 3 pts

23, 24, 25 and 27 May
at Derby
Essex 353 for 7 dec. (N. Hussain 81, D.D.J. Robinson 74) and 44 for 1
Derbyshire 315 (J.E. Owen 78, C.J. Adams 58)
Match drawn
Essex 11 pts, Derbyshire 9 pts

at Abergavenny
Glamorgan 328 (R.D.B. Croft 73 not out, G.P. Butcher 73, O.D. Gibson 51, P.J. Newport 6 for 100) and 194 for 5 dec. (S.P. James 89)
Worcestershire 200 for 0 dec. (W.P.C. Weston 121 not out, T.S. Curtis 62 not out) and 172 for 5 (S.J. Rhodes 53 not out)
Match drawn
Worcestershire 8 pts, Glamorgan 6 pts

at Gloucester
Gloucestershire 373 (T.H.C. Hancock 116, N.J. Trainor 67, A.J. Wright 51, B.P. Julian 5 for 97) and 163 for 2 dec. (N.J. Trainor 57)
Surrey 228 for 6 dec. (D.M. Ward 64 not out) and 174 for 8 (M.A. Butcher 58, A.J. Hollioake 52)
Match drawn
Gloucestershire 9 pts, Surrey 8 pts

at Portsmouth
Hampshire 206 (S.J.E. Brown 4 for 55, J. Wood 4 for 60) and 97 for 5
Durham 303 for 8 dec. (D.A. Blenkiron 102 not out, P.D. Collingwood 80)
Match drawn
Durham 10 pts, Hampshire 7 pts

at Canterbury
Yorkshire 350 for 8 dec. (M.G. Bevan 80, R.J. Blakey 60 not out, N.W. Preston 4 for 68) and 223 for 4 (A. McGrath 101, D. Byas 79)
Kent 299 (T.R. Ward 161, C. White 4 for 42)
Match drawn
Yorkshire 11 pts, Kent 8 pts

at Taunton
Northamptonshire 383 for 9 dec. (M.B. Loye 114, D.J. Capel 68) and 34 for 0 dec.
Somerset 88 for 0 dec. and 330 for 6 (S. Lee 113 not out, M.E. Trescothick 83, P.D. Bowler 66)
Somerset won by 4 wickets
Somerset 20 pts, Northamptonshire 4 pts

at Edgbaston
Warwickshire 164 (A.D. Mullally 4 for 53) and 241 for 8 (D.R. Brown 55, A.R.K. Pierson 5 for 68)
Leicestershire 353 for 8 dec. (P.V. Simmons 143 not out, G. Welch 4 for 83)
Match drawn
Leicestershire 11 pts, Warwickshire 6 pts

The fourth round of matches in the Britannic Assurance County Championship was badly hit by the weather, and only two games produced a definite result, and in both of those captains had to come to an agreement.

At Horsham, there was no play on the first or third days and only 62.3 overs on the second. Each side forfeited an innings, and Middlesex faced a target of 320 in 72 overs. Only two men reached double figures, and they lost their last four wickets in 14 balls for four runs. Jarvis, Law and Giddins each took three wickets.

There were 73 overs bowled on the first day at Derby, during which Essex scored 225 for 3. Robinson and Hussain added 158 for the second wicket. No play was possible on the second day, and play could not begin before lunch on the fourth.

The match at Abergavenny followed a similar pattern. Glamorgan made 148 for 5 from 54.4 overs on the first day, and there was no play on the second. On the third day, Glamorgan's last four wickets realised 171 runs. Weston raced to his highest first-class score, and Worcestershire declared after making 200 in 48.4 overs.

On the last day, Worcestershire, facing a target of 323 in 60 overs, were 11 for 3 and 97 for 5 before Rhodes and Lampitt dropped anchor.

Gloucestershire gave a first-class debut to Trainor, who hit 67 on the opening day, sharing a first wicket stand of 111 with Wright. His side made 223 for 4 from 61.1 overs, and they advanced to 303 for 5 from 86 overs by Friday evening.

There was more action on the Saturday when Hancock reached his century off 64 balls. At 137 for 6, Surrey were in danger of having to follow on, but David Ward, typically pugnacious, and Kersey added 91 for the seventh wicket.

Hollioake, captaining Surrey for the first time, declared at the Saturday evening score, and eventually the South Londoners faced a target of 309 in 65 overs. This proved to be far beyond them, and they were thankful to draw.

At Portsmouth, Hampshire made 192 for 9 from 54.3 overs on the Thursday, and there was no play on the second day. On the fourth morning, after a long wait through the nervous nineties, Blenkiron hit the second century of his career.

Yorkshire fared better than most in scoring 261 for 5 from 86 overs on the first day at Canterbury, but their innings limped into a third day. Preston finished with the best bowling figures of his brief career.

Trevor Ward faced 222 balls and hit 28 fours, and White had a spell of 3 for 0 in 11 balls, but thereafter farce took over, with all 11 Kent players bowling in Yorkshire's second innings, which spanned 105 overs.

There was more enterprise at Taunton where only 21.1 overs were possible on the first day and none at all on the second. Northamptonshire's 383 came off 99 overs with Loye hitting a six and 20 fours in his 175-ball innings. Penberthy and Capel added 108 for the seventh wicket.

Somerset declared at their Saturday evening score, and Northamptonshire scored 34 in 5.2 overs to leave the home county a target of 33Q in 89 overs. They lost Lathwell at 0 and were 114 for 4. Lee, who hit his first hundred for Somerset, and Trescothick then added 152. Lee continued to dominate, and his 135-ball innings contained 11 fours and two sixes and brought Somerset victory with nine balls to spare.

Edgbaston was another sodden place, with just 15 overs on the first day and 40 on the second. Warwickshire's innings finally ended on the Saturday after 67.3 overs, and Leicestershire took a first innings lead of 189 on the Monday morning, thanks mainly to the exuberance of Simmons. It nearly proved sufficient for victory. Pierson took five wickets as Warwickshire were reduced 196 for 8 with 13 overs remaining, but Giles and Piper held the Leicestershire attack at bay to earn a draw.

30, 31 May, 1 and 3 June

at Tunbridge Wells
Sussex 142 and 164 (A.P. Ealham 5 for 55)
Kent 280 (C.L. Hooper 72, T.R. Ward 52, D.R. Law 5 for 62) and 30 for 0
Kent won by 10 wickets
Kent 22 pts, Sussex 4 pts

at Old Trafford
Gloucestershire 270 (M.W. Alleyne 96, R.C. Russell 60, S. Elworthy 4 for 80)
Lancashire 335 for 9 (M.A. Atherton 80, J.P. Crawley 70, R.P. Davis 4 for 93)
Match drawn
Lancashire 10 pts, Gloucestershire 9 pts

at Lord's
Middlesex 447 (M.R. Ramprakash 134, J.D. Carr 94) and 171 for 4 dec. (M.R. Ramprakash 60 not out, K.R. Brown 60 not out)
Yorkshire 275 (P.J. Hartley 88 not out, D. Follett 5 for 99) and 322 (M.G. Bevan 107, M.P. Vaughan 67, P.C.R. Tufnell 4 for 106)
Middlesex won by 21 runs
Middlesex 24 pts, Yorkshire 4 pts

at Northampton
Northamptonshire 314 (R.J. Warren 76, D.J. Capel 57, K.M. Curran 55, D.A. Reeve 5 for 37) and 174
Warwickshire 447 (A.J. Moles 164, S.M. Pollock 107, C.E.L. Ambrose 5 for 62) and 44 for 1
Warwickshire won by 9 wickets
Warwickshire 24 pts, Northamptonshire 5 pts

at Trent Bridge
Durham 455 (D.A. Blenkiron 130, S.L. Campbell 118, K.P. Evans 4 for 68)
Nottinghamshire 269 (S.J.E. Brown 5 for 70) and 408 for 3 (R.T. Robinson 184, G.F. Archer 85 not out, P.R. Pollard 64)
Match drawn
Durham 11 pts, Nottinghamshire 7 pts

at The Oval
Surrey 477 (G.P. Thorpe 185, A.J. Hollioake 72, A.J. Stewart 53, M.A. Butcher 52) and 345 for 4 dec. (A.J. Hollioake 71 not out, G.P. Thorpe 68, M.A. Butcher 57, A.D. Brown 56 not out)
Derbyshire 469 (K.J. Barnett 94, C.M. Wells 82, D.M. Jones 76, J.E. Owen 54) and 246 for 9 (D.G. Cork 82 not out, M.P. Bicknell 4 for 17)
Match drawn
Surrey 10 pts, Derbyshire 10 pts

at Worcester
Worcestershire 431 (K.R. Spiring 144, G.A. Hick 123) and 288 for 4 dec. (T.M. Moody 138 not out, K.R. Spiring 82)
Hampshire 393 for 7 dec. (A.N. Aymes 100 not out, J.P. Stephenson 74, G.W. White 66, S.D. Udal 50 not out)
Match drawn
Worcestershire 9 pts, Hampshire 9 pts

At the Nevill Ground, surely one of the most beautiful cricket grounds in the world, 16 wickets fell on the first day, which ended with Kent leading Sussex by 58 runs. The home side had seemed totally in control as Hooper and Ward shared a third wicket stand of 127 in 20 overs, but Kent lost four wickets in the last five overs of the day, and Sussex had salvaged something from the mess their batting had put them into.

The salvation was short-lived. Marsh fell without addition on the second morning, but Ealham and McCague then added 54. Ealham's 31 not out was a beginning to what was a good day for him, for he then claimed 5 for 55 as Sussex disintegrated for a second time. Another to draw comfort from Kent's victory in two days was Ben Phillips, a tall medium-pacer, who took 3 for 34 in Sussex's second innings on the occasion of his first-class debut.

The match at Old Trafford was badly hit by the weather, with no play before lunch on the first day, no play after lunch on the fourth and restricted play on the second. Gloucestershire were 35 for 4, but Alleyne and Russell shared a sixth wicket stand of 138. Both fell to catches by Hegg, who had five in the innings.

Lancashire batted throughout the Saturday before the game faded into obscurity.

There was more substance and excitement at Lord's where Middlesex indicated that they were throwing off the traumatic start that they had had to the season. Ramprakash hit his first century of the summer as Middlesex hit 322 for 5 on the opening day. There was commendably sound batting throughout the order, not least from Fraser and Tufnell, who made 45 in 49 balls for the last wicket. This so incensed Darren Gough that he bowled three consecutive bouncers to Fraser for which he was warned by umpire Jones and no-balled.

The most successful uncapped batsman in the country, Mark Butcher was the rock on which many Surrey victories were founded. (Paul Sturgess/Sportsline)

Follett again bowled splendidly, and Yorkshire were reduced to 162 for 9. Hartley and Stemp put on 113 in 20 overs, Yorkshire's second last wicket century stand of the season. Stemp then combined with Silverwood to shoot out the first four Middlesex batsmen for 54, but Ramprakash and Brown added 117, and Gatting declared at the Saturday evening score.

Yorkshire went in search of a target of 344 in 101 overs, and with Bevan batting majestically and hitting 12 fours in his 183-ball innings, they reached 294 for 4. The last six wickets went down for 28 runs in 34 balls. Middlesex won with 10 balls to spare when Ramprakash ran out Stemp with a direct hit on the stumps from cover.

The sleeping giant of Warwickshire re-awoke at Northampton, although the first day's play gave no hint as to the final outcome. Consistent batting took Northamptonshire to 314, and Warwickshire lost Khan and Ostler for 34. The day was marked by an altercation between Capel on the one side and Reeve and Piper, a debate which was cooled only by the intervention of the umpires.

The game continued to go in favour of the home county as Warwickshire slipped to 118 for 5. Shaun Pollock joined Andy Moles, who remains one of the soundest openers in the country, and the pair added 194. Pollock reached a maiden first-class century, and Moles batted throughout the day to claim 160 out of 360 for 6. He was out early on the third morning, but Warwickshire took a lead of 133. Northamptonshire fell apart. They descended to 89 for 7 before Penberthy and Ripley at last offered some resistance and took the score to 148 by the close. Their stand was finally worth 70, but it only delayed the inevitable as Warwickshire won before lunch on the last day.

Like Northamptonshire, neither Durham nor Nottinghamshire had a championship victory to their credit, and their encounter at Trent Bridge ended in stalemate, although Durham did well on the first day after being put in. Roseberry and Morris were out quickly, but Sherwin Campbell raced to a century before lunch, and he and Blenkiron, who hit his second consecutive century, scored 142 for the third wicket. Collingwood and Betts made valuable contributions, and Durham batted into the second day to reach 455. They then reduced Nottinghamshire to 194 for 7 by the close.

Evans and Pick added 63 for the ninth wicket, but they could not save the follow-on. Until the afternoon of the third day, all had gone Durham's way, but then things changed. Pollard and Robinson made 211 from 66 overs by the close, and although they were soon separated on the final morning, the bat continued to dominate and a draw looked certain even before rain ended the match at tea time.

Like Trent Bridge, The Oval usually offers little help to the bowler, and Derbyshire found this as Surrey hit 382 for 7 on the opening day. Thorpe and Adam Hollioake put on 151 for the fifth wicket.

By the end of the second day, Derbyshire were 286 for 3, and Kim Barnett had become the highest run-scorer in the county's history. The final difference between the two sides on the first innings was eight, and it needed some friendly bowling on the Monday morning to give Stewart the opportunity to declare and set Derbyshire a target of 354 in 71 overs. They reached 81 for 2, but Martin Bicknell took four wickets in 10 balls before being forced to retire with a groin strain, and Derbyshire collapsed to 124 for 8. Cork batted with care for 142 minutes and with Wells put on 58. Wells was batting with a runner because of a foot injury, but his brave innings helped save the match.

Hick scored an uncharacteristically slow hundred against Hampshire, but Worcestershire had been 6 for 2 and needed rescuing. Hick and Spiring added 152 for the fourth wicket, and on the second day, Spiring reached his maiden first-class century. He hit 15 fours and shared a sixth wicket stand of 108 with Rhodes.

Beginning the third day on 152 for 4, Hampshire slipped to 168 for 6 and were in danger of having to follow on. They were saved by Adrian Aymes, who hit his second century of the season and shared an unbroken eighth wicket stand of 120 with Udal.

Moody, Spiring and Hick all batted with enterprise on the last morning, but rain prevented any chance of a declaration and a result.

5, 6, 7 and 8 June
at Leicester
Kent 324 (T.R. Ward 90, G.R. Cowdrey 71, S.A. March 51) and 351 for 8 dec. (M.V. Fleming 114, D.P. Fulton 88, M.T. Brimson 5 for 97)
Leicestershire 431 (B.F. Smith 174 not out, P.V. Simmons 82) and 173 for 6 (B.F. Smith 60, V.J. Wells 57)
Match drawn
Leicestershire 11 pts, Kent 9 pts

6, 7, 8 and 9 June
at Chelmsford
Essex 509 (S.G. Law 144, A.P. Grayson 129, G.A. Gooch 101, J.J.B. Lewis 69, I.D. Austin 5 for 116) and 229 for 6 (J.J.B. Lewis 54 not out, D.D.J. Robinson 50)
Lancashire 686 (G.D. Lloyd 241, S.P. Titchard 163, I.D. Austin 89 not out, P.M. Such 4 for 178)
Match drawn
Essex 9 pts, Lancashire 9 pts

at Southampton
Derbyshire 472 (C.J. Adams 239, A.S. Rollins 131, S.D. Udal 4 for 127) and 192 (S.D. Udal 4 for 44, C.A. Connor 4 for 64)
Hampshire 494 (R.A. Smith 141, J.P. Stephenson 85, A.N. Aymes 55 not out, D.M. Jones 5 for 112) and 116 (M.J. Vandrau 6 for 34, A.J. Harris 4 for 48)
Derbyshire won by 54 runs
Derbyshire 24 pts, Hampshire 6 pts

at Lord's
Glamorgan 238 (G.P. Butcher 63, R.A. Fay 4 for 53) and 141 (P.N. Weekes 8 for 39)
Middlesex 335 (M.R. Ramprakash 97, R.D.B. Croft 6 for 88) and 45 for 1
Middlesex won by 9 wickets
Middlesex 23 pts, Glamorgan 5 pts

at Trent Bridge
Northamptonshire 601 for 9 dec. (R.J. Bailey 163, M.B. Loye 98, J.E. Emburey 67 not out, J.P. Taylor 57, A.L. Penberthy 54, C.M. Tolley 4 for 107)
Nottinghamshire 359 (P. Johnson 103, C.L. Cairns 62, P.R. Pollard 58, C.E.L. Ambrose 6 for 91) and 176 for 4
Match drawn
Northamptonshire 10 pts, Nottinghamshire 8 pts

at Taunton
Warwickshire 255 (T.L. Penney 75) A.R. Caddick 5 for 76) and 325 (A.J. Moles 75, D.P. Ostler 66, T.L. Penney 52, A.R. Caddick 5 for 85)

Somerset 242 (S. Lee 65) and 239 (S. Lee 61, A.F. Giles 4 for 69)
Warwickshire won by 99 runs
Warwickshire 22 pts, Somerset 5 pts

at Hove
Sussex 552 for 8 dec. (K. Greenfield 124 not out, A.P. Wells 113, C.W.J. Athey 102, V.C. Drakes 56)
Durham 159 (I.D.K. Salisbury 6 for 15) and 326 (S.L. Campbell 87, D.M. Cox 67, M.M. Betts 57 not out, C.W. Scott 52, D.R. Law 5 for 33)
Sussex won by an innings and 67 runs
Sussex 24 pts, Durham 1 pt

at Middlesborough
Yorkshire 305 (M.P. Vaughan 135, B.C. Hollioake 4 for 74) and 387 (M.G. Bevan 160 not out, M.P. Vaughan 91)
Surrey 197 (D.J. Bicknell 52, R.D. Stemp 4 for 44, M.P. Vaughan 4 for 62) and 274 (MA. Butcher 112, D. Gough 5 for 36)
Yorkshire won by 221 runs
Yorkshire 23 pts, Surrey 4 pts

A full day's play at Leicester saw Kent finish comfortably on 318 for 8, but, in effect, this was something of a disappointment after being 107 for 2 at lunch. The early initiative which Ward's 90 off 139 balls had given them was lost. Ward had hit 15 fours when he was brilliantly caught by Maddy, and only Marsh's 51 off 67 balls helped keep the momentum going.

The Kent innings lasted just four overs into the second day, and a third wicket stand of 101 between Simmons, who hit 82 off 75 balls, and Smith tilted the game in Leicestershire's favour. This was confirmed on the third day when Smith and Pierson added 89 for the ninth wicket. Ben Smith's 174 was an innings of great patience occupying 520 minutes and it gave the Leicestershire innings substance. Leading by 107, the home county frittered away their advantage with some wayward bowling. At the close, Kent were 185 for 0 from 48 overs, Fleming having run to a hundred off 128 balls with three sixes and 12 fours.

The partnership was broken for the addition of 10 more runs the following morning, and Marsh's declaration left Leicestershire 48 overs in which to score 245 to win. They reached 120 for 1, but five wickets fell for 50 runs and the chase ended.

There were three centuries on the opening day at Chelmsford after Robinson had gone for 0. Gooch and Grayson scored 175 for the second wicket, and Grayson and the mighty Law added 205 in 44 overs for the third wicket. Grayson's first century for Essex was the highest score of his career, and he hit 17 fours in his 237-ball innings. Essex ended the day on 448 for 6.

The second day belonged to Lancashire. Speak, Wood (son of Barry Wood and making his first-class debut) and Crawley were out for 55, but by the close, Lancashire were 387 for 3. When Titchard and Lloyd were finally parted they had added 358, a record for Lancashire's fourth wicket. Titchard made the highest score of his career, facing 367 balls and hitting 18 fours. Graham Lloyd reached a hundred off 70 balls, the fastest century of the season, and his first double century came off 141 balls. In all, he faced 187 balls and hit 12 sixes and 25 fours. Essex survived the last day to draw the match.

There was another double centurion at Southampton where Chris Adams hit the highest score of his career. Rollins and Adams put on 298 in 77 overs for the second wicket. Rollins batted for five hours and hit a six and 18 fours, but Adams, the principal slaughterer, batted into the second day. He scored another 26 on the second morning, but by the end of the day Robin Smith was two runs short of his century, having added 105 for the third wicket with Stephenson, and Hampshire were 291 for 5.

The most remarkable event of the third day was Dean Jones completing the first five-wicket haul of his career. In his years in Australia, Jones had never taken more than one wicket in an innings. His performance could not stop Hampshire taking a first innings lead of 22, and with Derbyshire finishing on 145 for 5, the home county seemed well on top.

It transpired that Hampshire had 73 overs in which to score 171 to win the match on the final day, but they had already received warning signals in that Udal and Connor had taken only 14 overs to dismiss the last five Derbyshire batsmen, who managed just 27 runs. Hampshire lost both openers to Andrew Harris in successive overs before lunch, and the rest of the wickets fell in the afternoon, with Harris and Vandrau both recording career-best bowling performances.

The match at Lord's was over in three days. Fay was the principal architect in reducing Glamorgan to 143 for 6 before Shaw and Thomas added 86. Defending a small total, Glamorgan's spirits were lifted by dismissing both Middlesex openers for 25 before the close.

The following day, Ramprakash, again in fine form, and Carr put on 129 for Middlesex's sixth wicket, and on the third morning, Fraser and Tufnell scored an invaluable 47 for the last wicket. None of this prepared spectators for what was coming as Paul Weekes ran through Glamorgan to take a career-best 8 for 39 in 20 overs. He then celebrated by scoring 40 of the 45 runs that Middlesex needed for victory, finishing the match with a six off Kendrick.

In spite of scoring 601 for 9 off 184 overs, Northamptonshire remained without a victory after five matches, as did their opponents Nottinghamshire. The Northamptonshire innings was held together by Rob Bailey, who made 163 in nearly eight hours. He and Loye added 191 for the third wicket.

Nottinghamshire, who brought in Walker as wicket-keeper in place of Noon, finished the second day on 95 for 3 and were forced to follow on on the third day in spite of a fighting 103 off 175 balls with 17 fours by Johnson, a determined defensive innings from Pollard and some belligerence from Cairns. They began the last day at 29 for 0, but with only four balls bowled before lunch, a draw became inevitable.

Warwickshire reasserted their determination to retain their title with victory at Taunton. With Munton and Reeve injured, Moles led the side, lost the toss and saw Warwickshire bundled out for 255. Most of the damage was done by Andrew Caddick who was to finish the match with figures of 10 for 161.

Somerset began the second day on 106 for 4 and seemed set for a good lead, but they fell apart and lost their last five wickets for 49 runs. A second wicket stand of 101 between Moles and Ostler took Warwickshire to a strong position, but, at one time in their second innings, they lost four wickets for 16 runs as Caddick took 4 for 3 in 26 balls. Neil Smith and Graeme Welch stopped the rot with a stand of 69, and Somerset had more than a day to score the 339 they needed to win the match. Lathwell was out on the Saturday evening, and five wickets were down for 79 on the Monday morning. Holloway and Lee added 96 for the sixth wicket. Holloway continued to defy Warwickshire, but shortly after tea the left-hander was bowled behind his legs by Giles and the reigning champions had won. Holloway had resisted for 56 overs and scored 42.

Sussex batted into the second day against Durham. Athey and Wells put on 196 for the second wicket, but the real honours went to Keith Greenfield, who hit his highest championship score and after nine years on the staff and seven first-class hundreds was at last awarded his county cap.

Durham were bowled out on the second day. They were 132 for 3, at which point Ian Salisbury took 5 for 0 in three overs and they collapsed to 139 for 8. Following on on the Saturday, they were 50 for 5 before Campbell and Scott added 129. More significantly, they were 223 for 9, and the game seemed certain to end in three days, but Betts and Cox hit maiden first-class fifties and took the match to the fourth morning with a record stand of 103.

Yorkshire moved a point ahead of Kent at the top of the table with a victory over Surrey. Two young cricketers starred on the opening day. Vaughan hit 135 off 217 with 23 fours, and Ben Hollioake, on his championship debut, took 4 for 74 with his medium pace. Surrey lost Butcher and Kersey before the close and fell apart against the off-breaks of Vaughan and the slow left-arm of Stemp on the second day.

Yorkshire moved into an impregnable position as Vaughan, who again batted splendidly, and Bevan shared a third wicket stand of 170. Bevan also shared a sixth wicket stand of 104 with Blakey and was left unbeaten on 160, which included 17 fours. It was his highest score for Yorkshire and another impressive display of power and authority.

Really all that Surrey could hope for was survival, but five wickets went down for 230 on the Saturday, and the late order collapsed before Gough on the Monday.

13, 14, 15 and 17 June

at Chester-le-Street
Lancashire 264 (I.D. Austin 95 not out) and 441 for 8 dec. (I.D. Austin 91, W.K. Hegg 89, S.P. Titchard 60)
Durham 181 (J.E. Morris 52, G. Chapple 5 for 64) and 179 (P. Bainbridge 53, I.D. Austin 4 for 33)
Lancashire won by 345 runs
Lancashire 22 pts, Durham 4 pts

at Chelmsford
Northamptonshire 214 and 482 for 9 dec. (R.R. Montgomerie 120, D.J. Roberts 73, A.L. Penberthy 66 not out)
Essex 308 (G.A. Gooch 128, N. Hussain 53, J.P Taylor 7 for 88) and 204 for 8 (J.E. Emburey 4 for 48)
Match drawn
Essex 10 pts, Northamptonshire 8 pts

at Swansea
Glamorgan 310 (P.A. Cottey 112, H. Morris 54, G.D. Rose 4 for 45) and 354 for 7 dec. (S.P. James 110, A. Dale 62, P.A. Cottey 61)
Somerset 338 (A.N. Hayhurst 96, P.D. Bowler 73, M.N. Lathwell 68, S.L. Watkin 4 for 47, N.M. Kendrick 4 for 89) and 153 (R.D.B. Croft 6 for 78)
Glamorgan won by 173 runs
Glamorgan 22 pts, Somerset 7 pts

at Bristol
Sussex 157 (N.J. Lenham 70, M.W. Alleyne 5 for 32) and 231 (D.R. Law 97, C.A. Walsh 6 for 57)
Gloucestershire 151 (E.S.H. Giddins 5 for 53) and 234 (M.W. Alleyne 71, A.J. Wright 51)
Sussex won by 3 runs
Sussex 20 pts, Gloucestershire 4 pts

at Canterbury
Middlesex 441 (P.N. Weekes 108, J.C. Pooley 67, M.R. Ramprakash 66) and 247 (N.J. Llong 5 for 21)
Kent 390 for 8 dec. (N.J. Llong 63 not out, M.A. Ealham 59, G.R. Cowdrey 51) and 205 for 6 (M.V. Fleming 59)
Match drawn
Middlesex 10 pts, Kent 9 pts

at The Oval
Surrey 452 (G.P. Thorpe 154, M.A. Butcher 120, A.R.K. Pierson 6 for 158) and 242 for 6 dec. (M.A. Butcher 66, G.J. Kersey 59 not out, P.V. Simmons 4 for 56)
Leicestershire 411 (A. Habib 79, A.D. Mullally 68, P.A. Nixon 66, G.J. Parsons 51, J.E. Benjamin 4 for 74) and 175 (C.C. Lewis 5 for 25)
Surrey won by 128 runs
Surrey 24 pts, Leicestershire 5 pts

at Worcester
Worcestershire 493 for 9 dec. (T.M. Moody 212,

K.R. Spiring 64, S.R. Lampitt 59, K.P. Evans 5 for 116) and 196 for 4 dec. (G.A. Hick 85, W.P.C. Weston 54)
Nottinghamshire 392 (R.T. Robinson 83, A.A. Metcalfe 80 not out, G.F. Archer 70) and 159 for 4 (R.T. Robinson 111 not out)
Match drawn
Worcestershire 10 pts, Nottinghamshire 10 pts

at Leeds
Warwickshire 306 (T.L. Penney 125, D.P. Ostler 85, D. Gough 4 for 66) and 229
Yorkshire 508 (M.D. Moxon 131, D. Gough 121, A. McGrath 65, N.M.K. Smith 5 for 127) and 28 for 0
Yorkshire won by 10 wickets
Yorkshire 22 pts, Warwickshire 5 pts

The pitch at Chester-le-Street was reported to Lord's by the umpires after 18 wickets fell on the first day. Ian Austin, as ever, adopted attack as the best form of defence and hit 17 fours in his 95 off 89 balls. He and Hegg added 77 in 13 overs for the seventh wicket. Betts was at his most profligate and there were 32 no-balls in Lancashire's first innings total. Betts had 2 for 65 from *six* overs.

When Lancashire batted a second time with a lead of 83, Austin and Hegg were again the principal scorers with a stand of 175 in 31 overs for the seventh wicket. Facing a target of 525, Durham were 0 for 2. Demoralised, they were bowled out in 49.3 overs as Lancashire won with more than a day to spare.

Essex had a good first day against Northamptonshire when only a last wicket partnership of 51 between Taylor and Mallender really disturbed them. Gooch hit a six and 20 fours in his 123rd first-class hundred, but Taylor's spell of 5 for 16 in 48 balls restricted the Essex lead.

David Roberts, on his championship debut, and Montgomerie scored 185 for Northamptonshire's first wicket when they batted a second time, and Essex toiled throughout the Saturday. On the Monday, they were happy to draw a game which they had once looked like winning.

Glamorgan gained their first championship victory at Swansea for four years, disposing of the inconsistent Somerset side in a highly competent fashion. In spite of Cottey's 178-ball innings, they trailed by 28 runs on the first innings, but James hit 17 fours in his 110, Cottey again batted well, Dale gave good support, and Somerset were set a target of 327 in 90 overs. They lost three wickets at 59 to slump to 59 for 4, and with Croft spinning the ball to good effect, Somerset were all out in under 76 overs.

The match at Bristol was over in three days, and, as at Chester-le-Street, 18 wickets went down on the first day. Sussex, electing to bat, found themselves at 37 for 5 and were saved from total humiliation by Lenham and Moores, who added 86.

Gloucestershire were in a similar position, but, at 72 for 8, Smith joined Ball, and the pair took the innings into the second day with stand worth 73. It was the late order batsmen who starred, for Sussex were 82 for 5 in their second innings, but the last five wickets realised 159 runs. This was thanks mainly to Danny Law, who hit his highest championship score.

Gloucestershire had more than two days in which to score 238 to win. They began badly and were 81 for 4. Wright and Alleyne then added 79, and Gloucestershire reached the stage where, with three wickets standing, they needed only 12 to win. Unfortunately, those last three wickets fell for eight runs, and Sussex won an exciting victory.

Weekes was again in outstanding form for Middlesex, and he and Harrison scored 110 for the first wicket. Pooley later hit 67 off 81 balls with 12 fours, and there was an impressive debut innings of 48 from Wellings.

The Kent batting was less enterprising, but there was a fifth wicket stand of 116 between Cowdrey and Ealham which gave the innings some substance. Llong also batted well and had a spell of 4 for 10 in 21 balls when Middlesex batted again. His final analysis, 5 for 21, was his best in first-class cricket.

Kent's target was 299 in 56 overs, and Fleming suggested a challenge with a six and 11 fours before Tufnell took 3 for 6 in 22 balls. Sadly, Tufnell was also at the centre of controversy again when he threw down his cap in disgust on umpire Plews rejecting an appeal for a bat and pad catch.

Mark Butcher, who was awarded his county cap, hit his third century of the season and shared a second wicket stand of 115 with Stewart. Thorpe continued his excellent run of form, and Surrey reached 452 from 135.3 overs on the second day. They quickly had Leicestershire in trouble at 65 for 5, but Habib and Nixon added 157 for the sixth wicket. Millns, Parsons and Mullally all made valuable contributions to take Leicestershire within 41 of Surrey's score. Mullally's 68 was double his previous highest score, which had been made in his days with Western Australia.

Simmons appeared to have bowled Leicestershire to a good position when Surrey slipped to 139 for 6, but wicket-keeper Kersey and Adam Hollioake shared an unbroken stand of 103, and Leicestershire faced a target of 284 in 56 overs. They were never in touch, and Lewis took the last three wickets in 11 balls to give Surrey victory with less than six overs remaining.

In an acrimonious match at Worcester, Moody hit a hundred between lunch and tea on the first day and shared a fourth wicket stand of 199 with the ever-improving Spiring which spanned the first two days. Five wickets fell in the first 45 minutes of the second day before Lampitt and Illingworth added 116 for the ninth wicket. Moody's 212 was his highest championship score.

Nottinghamshire finished 101 runs behind the home county, but the captains, Moody and Johnson, had exchanged words when Johnson was given not out after Moody claimed a low slip catch. There was more bad feeling when Nottinghamshire made no attempt to chase a target of 296 in 69 overs. Moody was sharply critical of their attitude, while Johnson claimed the Worcestershire declaration had been too long delayed.

Yorkshire gave credibility to their championship challenge and moved 14 points clear at the top of the table when they crushed Warwickshire at Headingley. Warwickshire were 10 for 2 before Ostler and Penney added 116. Craig White took the last three wickets in 14 balls, but Warwickshire's 306 did not seem a bad score. It was soon put in perspective by Moxon, who hit a six and 17 fours in his 316-ball innings, during which he passed 20,000 runs in first-class cricket.

There was greater excitement on the third day when Darren Gough hit a maiden first-class hundred. He hit 11 fours and four sixes and shared stands of 72 and 90 with Stemp and Silverwood for the ninth and tenth wickets. Batting a second time, Warwickshire capitulated, and Yorkshire raced to victory.

19, 20, 21 and 22 June
at Basingstoke
Hampshire 394 (R.A. Smith 179, J.S. Laney 81, A.L. Penberthy 4 for 54)
Northamptonshire 147 (K.M. Curran 53, J.P. Stephenson 5 for 27) and 175
Hampshire won by an innings and 72 runs
Hampshire 24 pts, Northamptonshire 4 pts

at Bath
Somerset 263 (P.D. Bowler 112, R.K. Illingworth 5 for 40) and 376 for 6 dec. (S. Lee 167 not out, R.J. Turner 100 not out)
Worcestershire 194 (A.R. Caddick 7 for 83) and 449 for 9 (S.J. Rhodes 92 not out, T.S. Curtis 85, V.S. Solanki 71, T.M. Moody 54, A.R. Caddick 4 for 151)
Worcestershire won by 1 wicket
Worcestershire 20 pts, Somerset 6 pts

20, 21, 22 and 24 June
at Derby
Derbyshire 321 (C.J. Adams 125, K.J. Barnett 53, P.C.R. Tufnell 5 for 72) and 383 for 2 dec. (C.J. Adams 136 not out, D.M. Jones 100 not out, A.S. Rollins 79, K.J. Barnett 55)
Middlesex 165 (A.J. Harris 6 for 43) and 176 (P.N. Weekes 58, A.J. Harris 6 for 40)
Derbyshire won by 363 runs
Derbyshire 23 pts, Middlesex 4 pts)

at Stockton
Durham 377 (S.L. Campbell 69, S.J.E. Brown 60, D.G.C. Ligertwood 56, J.E. Benjamin 4 for 69) and 203
Surrey 440 (M.A. Butcher 160, D.J. Bicknell 106, J.D. Ratcliffe 51) and 142 for 2 (J.D. Ratcliffe 68 not out, N. Shahid 52 not out)
Surrey won by 8 wickets
Surrey 24 pts, Durham 7 pts

Andy Harris, the Derbyshire pace bowler, took 12 for 83 to bowl his side to victory over Middlesex in late June. He was later capped and chosen to tour Australia with the England 'A' side.
(Paul Sturgess/Sportsline)

at Trent Bridge
Nottinghamshire 460 (C.L. Cairns 114, R.T. Robinson 84, A.A. Metcalfe 78)
Gloucestershire 190 (A. Symonds 57, A.M. Smith 55 not out) and 267 (A. Symonds 117, K.P. Evans 5 for 30)
Nottinghamshire won by an innings and 3 runs
Nottinghamshire 24 pts, Gloucestershire 3 pts

at Hove
Glamorgan 133 (J.D. Lewry 6 for 44) and 266 (M.P. Maynard 112, P.A. Cottey 57, E.S.H. Giddins 4 for 65)
Sussex 406 (K. Greenfield 154 not out, I.D.K. Salisbury 83, A.P. Wells 78, S.D. Thomas 5 for 121)
Sussex won by an innings and 7 runs
Sussex 24 pts, Glamorgan 3 pts

at Edgbaston
Kent 258 (M.V. Fleming 61, D.R. Brown 5 for 68, S.M. Pollock 4 for 60) and 164 (N.J. Llong 53, D.R. Brown 6 for 62)
Warwickshire 137 (M.A. Ealham 8 for 36) and 253 (A.J. Moles 76, A.F. Giles 65, M.J. McCague 5 for 101)
Kent won by 32 runs
Kent 22 pts, Warwickshire 4 pts

at Bradford
Leicestershire 681 for 7 dec. (J.J. Whitaker 218, V.J. Wells 200, P.A. Nixon 77 not out, P.V. Simmons 69)
Yorkshire 342 (M.G. Bevan 82, R.D. Stemp 51 not out, D. Gough 50, G.J. Parsons 4 for 83) and 188 (M.G. Bevan 65 not out, M.P. Vaughan 54, D.J. Millns 4 for 67)
Leicestershire won by an innings and 151 runs
Leicestershire 24 pts, Yorkshire 4 pts

Hampshire took under three days to beat Northamptonshire who were struggling in the championship. Robin Smith and Laney gave substance to the Hampshire innings with a third wicket stand of 144, and, by the end of the second day, Northamptonshire were in total disarray at 58 for 6. Curran offered some respectability, but the only setback Hampshire suffered was injury to Laney, who was hit in the larynx while fielding at short-leg.

Worcestershire gained a remarkable victory over Somerset at Bath. Andrew Caddick proved his full fitness with a long spell of bowling which brought him seven wickets and Somerset a first innings lead of 69. On top of this, Worcestershire's Leatherdale suffered a broken finger.

Somerset's strong position began to seem eroded when they tumbled to 98 for 6 in their second innings, but, at this point, Turner joined Lee and the pair added a county record of 278 without being parted. Lee hit 25 fours and a six and faced 227 balls for his career-best 167 while Turner hit a six and 14 fours in his 211-ball innings.

Worcestershire faced a target of 449 in 109 overs. Curtis provided a base with 85 off 129 balls and Moody hit a brisk 54. There was a fine effort from Solanki, whose 71 came off 83 balls and was his highest first-class score. The true hero, however, was Rhodes who nursed the later balls closer to the target, which was reached when Sheriyar hit the third ball of the final over for four.

Chris Adams hit a century in each innings for the first time in his career as Derbyshire crushed Middlesex. Adams and Barnett scored 158 for the second wicket in Derbyshire's first innings, and Adams and Jones shared an unbroken partnership of 208 for the third wicket in the second. Andrew Harris gave further indication of his growing stature as a medium pace bowler with career-best figures for both innings and match as Derbyshire swept to victory inside half an hour on the fourth morning.

Sherwin Campbell and Stewart Hutton put on 130 for Durham's first wicket, the county's first century opening stand of the season. They then slipped 244 for 8 before Ligertwood and Brown scored a record 127 for the ninth wicket. The Surrey wicket-keeper Graham Kersey held six catches.

Darren Bicknell and Mark Butcher began Surrey's innings with a stand of 245. The last nine wickets fell for 95 runs, but Surrey had total control of the match and moved to a comfortable win on the fourth day.

Nottinghamshire completed their first win in the season's championship with a day to spare. Robinson and Metcalfe began with a partnership of 155, and Cairns scored a typically pugnacious century with three sixes and 11 fours. Walker claimed six dismissals in Gloucestershire's first innings, four catches and two stumpings, and Nottinghamshire moved to an innings victory.

There was no play on the first day at Hove where Sussex, a model of inconsistency, gained an innings victory. Greenfield hit 15 fours in the highest score of his career after 15 wickets had fallen on the second day, six of them to the left-arm medium pace of Lewry. Greenfield and Salisbury added 172 for Sussex's seventh wicket, and the home county clinched victory before lunch on the fourth day. This was Sussex's fourth championship win in their last five matches.

Kent, too, took only three days to beat Warwickshire in spite of Douglas Brown's first ten-wicket haul for the Midlanders. Kent were all out in 78.1 overs, but they had a grip on the game by the end of the first day, which saw Warwickshire reduced to 42 for 4, Ealham having taken 3 for 5 in six overs. He was to take five more wickets on the second day when 18 wickets fell to finish with a career-best 8 for 36. His two second innings wickets also meant that he had the first ten-wicket match return of his career, 10 for 74.

Needing 286 to win, Warwickshire lost eight wickets for 139 runs. Moles had retired hurt earlier with a damaged thumb, and he now returned to share a ninth wicket stand of 92 in 10 overs with Giles. Moles' 76 came off 45 balls, and he took 24 off one over from Headley, but he could not prevent Kent winning with more than a day to spare.

A Leicestershire hero in phenomenal form – Vince Wells, two double centuries within a fortnight. (Paul Sturgess/Sportsline)

There was a feast of runs at Bradford. Vince Wells hit the first double century of his career. He hit two sixes and 33 fours and faced 301 balls. He shared stands of 153 for the third wicket with Simmons and 218 for the fourth with Whitaker, who reached the highest score of his career. Leicestershire's 681 was the highest total ever conceded by Yorkshire who battled bravely but in vain and were beaten early on the fourth day.

Yorkshire's one consolation was that Bevan became the season's first batsman to score a thousand first-class runs.

27, 28, 29 June and 1 July

at Chester-le-Street
Durham 175 (A.M. Smith 4 for 39) and 385 for 8 dec. (S. Hutton 143 not out, P. Bainbridge 83, J.E. Morris 68)
Gloucestershire 166 (T.H.C. Hancock 65 not out, M.M. Betts 5 for 68) and 150 for 2 (T.H.C. Hancock 59 not out, A.J. Wright 58)
Match drawn
Durham 7 pts, Gloucestershire 7 pts

at Southend
Surrey 476 for 8 dec. (G.P. Thorpe 143, A.J. Hollioake 128, M.A. Butcher 53) and 167 for 2 (M.A. Butcher 85 not out)
Essex 425 for 9 dec. (G.A. Gooch 149, S.G. Law 125, A.P. Grayson 62, R.M. Pearson 5 for 142)
Match drawn
Surrey 10 pts, Essex 8 pts

at Old Trafford
Lancashire 380 for 5 dec. (S.P. Titchard 121 not out) and 45 for 0 dec.
Somerset 75 for 3 dec.
Match drawn
Lancashire 8 pts, Somerset 5 pts

at Lord's
Middlesex 413 (M.R. Ramprakash 169, K.R. Brown 79, S.M. Pollock 6 for 56) and 122 for 3
Warwickshire 445 for 9 dec. (A.J. Moles 176, T.L. Penney 101, P.C.R. Tufnell 5 for 71)
Match drawn
Warwickshire 10 pts, Middlesex 8 pts

at Northampton
Derbyshire 98 (C.E.L. Ambrose 5 for 15) and 239 (C.J. Adams 68, C.E.L. Ambrose 6 for 55)
Northamptonshire 210 (R.J. Bailey 68, D.E. Malcolm 4 for 59, D.G. Cork 4 for 63) and 130 for 6
Northamptonshire won by 4 wickets
Northamptonshire 21 pts, Derbyshire 4 pts

at Worcester
Yorkshire 321 (M.G. Bevan 61, A. McGrath 60, C. White 53, S.R. Lampitt 5 for 58) and 266 for 7 dec. (C. White 65, M.P. Vaughan 60, M.G. Bevan 57)
Worcestershire 355 for 9 dec. (K.R. Spiring 109, T.S. Curtis 72, C.E.W. Silverwood 5 for 72) and 121 (D. Gough 4 for 27)
Yorkshire won by 111 runs
Yorkshire 23 pts, Worcestershire 8 pts

Bowlers enjoyed Chester-le-Street once again with 15 wickets falling on the first day. Durham had been put in to bat, and the highest stand in their innings was between Brown and Lugsden for the last wicket. It was worth 44. Gloucestershire ended the day on 90 for 5, and with Betts again bettering his career-best bowling, Durham took a narrow first innings lead which was expanded to 103 for the loss of Sherwin Campbell by close of play on Friday.

On the Saturday, Stewart Hutton reached his second championship century. The left-handed opener hit eight fours, faced 331 balls and was at the crease for eight hours, enabling Durham to declare and set Gloucestershire a target of 395 off a minimum of 104 overs. Durham seemed set for their first victory of the season, but rain obliterated most of the post-lunch play on the Monday.

A few years ago, Essex beat Yorkshire in an exciting match at Southend but were deducted 25 points for a substandard wicket. The 'perfect' wicket of 1996 produced the dullest of draws. Surrey scored 345 for 3 from 105 overs on the first day, with Thorpe and Adam Hollioake, who were separated early next morning, scoring 201 for the fourth wicket. Thorpe became the second batsman to reach 1000 first-class runs for the season with his fifth century, while Adam Hollioake's run of success continued with 128 off 260 balls.

Gooch and Grayson began Essex's innings with a partnership of 131, and Gooch, in one of his more circumspect moods, reached his 124th first-class century on the third day. Law was altogether more dazzling, hitting 15 fours and a six and facing 187 balls for his 125. He and Gooch put on 232 for the fourth wicket.

The match extended meaninglessly into the last day. No run was scored, and Prichard declared when Such was out second ball. Rain at tea time ended the match. Pearson, the former Essex off-spinner, returned his best bowling figures for Surrey.

Following a prolific run in the second eleven, McKeown made his first-class debut for Lancashire, but was out for nine. Titchard and Fairbrother added 203 for the third wicket. Fairbrother hit six sixes and 16 fours in his 162-ball innings, and Lancashire romped to 373 for 5 by the end of the day. That was virtually the end of proceedings. Only two overs could be bowled on the second day. Somerset declared after 30.1 overs on the third day, and Lancashire after another 15.3. The last day was lost to rain.

There was high scoring at Lord's, but the game started uneasily for Middlesex who were 138 for 5. Ramprakash, in top form but never mentioned now as an England possible, and Brown reversed their side's fortunes by adding 184. Ramprakash hit a six and 17 fours and batted for more than six-and-a-half hours. By the end of the second day, in which only 58 overs were possible, Warwickshire were 76 for 1.

Moles and Penney shared a fourth wicket stand of 235, and both batsmen reached their centuries off 225 balls, but the Warwickshire innings lasted until the fourth day, which was shortened by rain, and the match was drawn.

Northamptonshire gained their first championship win of the season, and it came against the strong challenging Derbyshire side inside three days. Derbyshire chose to bat first but were shot out in 35.3 overs for 98, the damage being done by Ambrose, Capel and Taylor. The formidable Derbyshire pace trio could not emulate the Northamptonshire bowlers, and the home county ended the day strongly, all out 210, a lead of 112 which Barnett and Rollins reduced by seven.

It seemed Derbyshire would stage a major recovery on the second day when, with Adams in full flow, they reached 136 for 2. Four wickets then fell for eight runs, but Krikken offered stern resistance, and the game was back in the balance with Derbyshire ending a rain-curtailed day on 210 for 7.

Krikken was out for 44, no addition to his overnight score, on the third morning, and Northamptonshire had the best part of two days in which to score 128. They took only 45.2 overs, but not without some frights. They were 77 for 5 before Curran adopted the positive approach and hit 29 not out, the top score, to bring victory by four wickets.

Yorkshire beat Worcestershire at Worcester to begin July top of the Championship, 19 points ahead of Kent and 30 ahead of Derbyshire, both of whom had a game in hand.

Bevan, McGrath and White gave substantial middle order contributions to take Yorkshire to 312 for 7 on the opening day. The innings ended quickly on the second morning, and Worcestershire reached 147 for 3 in 47 overs. Rain reduced play to 54 overs for the day, but the greatest consternation during the match was from the Worcestershire supporters, who were grieved by the fact that Graeme Hick had chosen to miss the game to become more mentally prepared to play for England. He had obviously not heard Sir Colin Cowdrey's advice that the best preparation for batting is to play cricket. Cowdrey was quite a good player.

The third day was graced by a century from Spiring, a most impressive young cricketer. He and Curtis added 176 for the fourth wicket, and Worcestershire took a first innings lead of 34.

Ignoring a collapse which saw them go from 106 for 0 to 130 for 4, Yorkshire pressed for quick runs, and Byas set Worcestershire a target of 233 at not more than four an over. It was positive thinking. Illingworth had turned the ball appreciably until a split finger had forced his retirement, and the pitch was aiding the bowlers more and more with its uneven bounce.

Gough soon sent back Church, victim of a grounder, and Curtis, caught behind. Stemp's second ball had Moody leg before offering no stroke, and the increasingly effective Silverwood accounted for Weston and Spiring to reduce Worcestershire to 28 for 5. Rhodes and Solanki added 54, but once they were separated Gough and Stemp finished the job, and victory came with 10 minutes to spare. This was championship-winning form.

3, 4, 5 and 6 July
at Arundel
Hampshire 270 (M. Keech 104, V.P. Terry 52) and 238 for 5 dec. (J.S. Laney 83, K.D. James 72, J.D. Lewry 5 for 73)
Sussex 193 (J.P. Stephenson 6 for 48, C.A. Connor 4 for 57) and 128 for 5 (N.J. Lenham 55 not out)
Match drawn
Hampshire 9 pts, Sussex 7 pts

4, 5, 6 and 8 July
at Bristol
Glamorgan 509 for 3 dec. (M.P. Maynard 145 not out, S.P. James 118, H. Morris 108, P.A. Cottey 101 not out)
Gloucestershire 181 (G.P. Butcher 7 for 77) and 224 for 8 (R.J. Cunliffe 82, R.D.B. Croft 4 for 39)
Match drawn
Glamorgan 11 pts, Gloucestershire 4 pts

at Maidstone
Kent 363 (C.L. Hooper 66, N.J. Llong 64, D.P. Fulton 64, T.R. Ward 50, S.J.E. Brown 5 for 76) and 244 (C.L. Hooper 105, T.R. Ward 60, S.J.E. Brown 4 for 58)
Durham 269 (P. Bainbridge 71, M.A. Roseberry 60, M.J. McCague 4 for 69) and 255 (S.L. Campbell 85)
Kent won by 83 runs
Kent 24 pts, Durham 6 pts

at Old Trafford
Lancashire 392 (J.E.R. Gallian 140, G.D. Lloyd 59, V.S. Solanki 5 for 116) and 256 for 7 dec. (G.D. Lloyd 72, N.H. Fairbrother 5 for 140)
Worcestershire 350 for 3 dec. (W.P.C. Weston 171 not out, T.M. Moody 108) and 171 for 4 (T.M. Moody 67 not out, V.S. Solanki 62 not out)
Match drawn
Worcestershire 11 pts, Lancashire 8 pts

at Leicester
Essex 163 (G.J. Parsons 4 for 21, D.J. Millns 4 for 74) and 247 (G.A. Gooch 72, D.J. Millns 6 for 54)
Leicestershire 454 for 9 dec. (V.J. Wells 197, D.J. Millns 103)
Leicestershire won by an innings and 44 runs
Leicestershire 24 pts, Essex 3 pts

at The Oval
Middlesex 232 (M.R. Ramprakash 80, M.W. Gatting 52, M.P. Bicknell 5 for 54, B.P. Julian 4 for 63) and 194 (M.W. Gatting 53, M.P. Bicknell 4 for 57)
Surrey 366 (A.J. Hollioake 84, A.D. Brown 57, P.C.R. Tufnell 5 for 56) and 61 for 3
Surrey won by 7 wickets
Surrey 24 pts, Middlesex 5 pts

David Millns receives the congratulations of Ben Smith. Millns had an outstanding season. Against Essex at the beginning of July, he took 10 for 128 and hit a maiden first-class century.
(Paul Sturgess/Sportsline)

at Edgbaston
Warwickshire 350 for 8 dec. (M. Burns 81, T.L. Penney 60, N.M.K. Smith 54) and 158 for 2 dec. (M. Burns 65 not out)
Nottinghamshire 212 for 4 dec. (A.A. Metcalfe 91, C.L. Cairns 66 not out) and 211 (K.P. Evans 60, P.R. Pollard 57, A.F. Giles 5 for 70)
Warwickshire won by 85 runs
Warwickshire 21 pts, Nottinghamshire 4 pts

The weather has not been kind to the lovely ground at Arundel, and the ration for the first day in 1996 was 37 overs after tea during which Hampshire, put in to bat, made 82 for 4. The stand between Keech and Terry, which had begun on the Wednesday, lasted well into the second day and realised 136. Keech, who has never lived up to the promise he first showed when with Middlesex, hit a maiden first-class century, a most worthy innings. Sussex slipped to 82 for 3, and Stephenson put Hampshire well on top as five wickets fell for 32 runs on the third morning.

Stephenson's declaration on the last day left Sussex 62 overs in which to score 316 runs. They lost 5 for 81, and Hampshire scented victory before being thwarted by the rain.

Glamorgan did not lose a wicket on the first day at Bristol. James and Morris completed centuries and scored 233 runs in 72 overs. They were separated at 240, and the score was 258 when Maynard and Cottey came together. They added an unbroken 251 in 200 minutes. Both completed hundreds so that Glamorgan had four centurions in the same innings for the first time.

On a restricted third day, Gloucestershire were bowled out for 181, with Gary Butcher returning the best bowling figures of his young career. Following on, Gloucestershire were 220 for 5, but three wickets fell to Watkin with the second new ball as three runs were scored. Ball and Lewis survived the last four overs to gain a draw.

The match at Maidstone went as expected. Kent raced to 363 in 95.3 overs on the first day, with Simon Brown manfully trying to stem the flow of runs and take wickets as he had been doing all season.

Bouts of food poisoning struck several players on the second day, and Durham suffered a customary plague when they toppled to 59 for 4. Bainbridge and Roseberry added 89, and the rain-shortened day ended with Durham recovering to 217 for 6.

The tail wagged well to cut the arrears to under 100, and Brown quickly sent back Fleming and Llong to give Durham a further boost. Alas, Carl Hooper, who favours The Mote, hit five sixes and nine fours to race to a hundred off 78 balls. He and Ward put on 154. Kent were bowled out in the day, and Simon Brown became the first bowler in the country to take 50 wickets in the season.

Durham had more than a day in which to score 339. At 139 for 2, with Sherwin Campbell going strongly, they had a chance of victory, but the last eight wickets fell for 116 runs and they suffered their sixth defeat in 10 championship matches.

Less than six overs were possible on the first day at Old Trafford, but, on the second, Lancashire scored freely with 199 runs coming from their last four wickets. Worcestershire's innings began on the third day. Weston, who made the highest score of his career, and Moody shared a third wicket stand of 224. They raced their side to maximum batting points in under 96 overs.

Gallian and Speak were out before the close, but with Lloyd and Fairbrother in sparkling form, Watkinson was able to set a target of 299 in 54 overs. The chase ended when four wickets fell for 53. Solanki and Moody dropped anchor. Solanki had a fine all-round match. His off-breaks had brought him three wickets before the start of the season, and he had increased that total to seven before this match. His 10 for 256 was an outstanding performance.

Essex received a terrible thrashing at the hands of Leicestershire. They were put in to bat and bowled out for 163 on the opening day. By the end of the second day, Leicestershire were 304 for 6 from 86 overs with Wells, 150, and Millns, 51, at the wicket. These two had come together after a spate in which five wickets had fallen for 27 runs.

Things did not improve for Essex on the Saturday, as Wells and Millns extended their partnership to 187. Vince Wells just escaped making history when he was bowled by Steve Andrew three runs short of what would have been his third double century in four innings. David Millns did make history with a maiden first-class century which included 13 fours and came off 190 balls.

Trailing by 291 runs, Essex were 193 for 4 at the close, but this was to be Millns' match. He won the game on the last morning by taking the last six wickets for 20 runs. He took three wickets in six balls.

Australian coach David Gilbert had a marked effect on Surrey's cricket in 1996. A side of constant under-achievers, at times lacking spirit and purpose, played with a refreshingly new resolve and challenged strongly in all competitions. The victory over Middlesex at The Oval was their first win against their closest rivals for nine years and was a triumph of teamwork. They bowled well, with Martin Bicknell performing better than ever, fielded keenly and scored their runs quickly with a strength in depth down the order which was the envy of all. They demolished Middlesex on the last day, but they also revealed a weakness. They conceded 98 extras in the match, 76 of them coming from no-balls.

Play was limited to 52 overs on the first day at Edgbaston, and Warwickshire scored 148 for 3. This advanced to 251 for 6 from the further 38 overs the weather allowed on the second day. Reserve keeper Burns made the highest score of his career.

With Neil Smith hitting briskly, four points were duly gained on the Saturday, and Johnson kept the game alive by declaring Nottinghamshire's innings closed as soon as the 140-run partnership between Metcalfe and Cairns was broken.

Eventually, the visitors were set a target of 297 in 81 overs, but the left-arm spin of Ashley Giles, a bowler of immense potential, proved too much for them, and Warwickshire won with ample time to spare.

17, 18, 19 and 20 July
at Guildford
Surrey 411 (A.J. Stewart 74, G.J. Kersey 68 not out, G.P. Thorpe 66, M.A. Butcher 57, P.W. Jarvis 4 for 82) and 304 for 6 dec. (G.P. Thorpe 130, A.J. Stewart 80, P.W. Jarvis 4 for 60)
Sussex 265 (A.P. Wells 81, I.D.K. Salisbury 62, N.J. Lenham 51, B.P. Julian 4 for 41) and 315 (P. Moores 119 not out, C.W.J. Athey 91)
Surrey won by 135 runs
Surrey 24 pts, Sussex 6 pts

18, 19, 20 and 22 July
at Chelmsford
Nottinghamshire 97 (R.C. Irani 5 for 27, M.C. Ilott 4 for 31) and 415 (P.R. Pollard 86, P. Johnson 61, K.P. Evans 56, C.L. Cairns 51, R.T. Robinson 51)
Essex 368 (G.A. Gooch 91, P.J. Prichard 80, M.N. Bowen 5 for 119) and 145 for 4 (R.J. Rollins 74 not out, P.M. Such 54)
Essex won by 6 wickets
Essex 24 pts, Nottinghamshire 4 pts

at Cheltenham
Leicestershire 159 (B.F. Smith 68 not out, A.M. Smith 6 for 55) and 150 (C.A. Walsh 4 for 40)
Gloucestershire 71 and 136 (A.D. Mullally 4 for 22)
Leicestershire won by 102 runs
Leicestershire 20 pts, Gloucestershire 4 pts

at Old Trafford
Lancashire 587 for 9 dec. (J.E.R. Gallian 312, S.P. Titchard 96, J.P. Crawley 54) and 174 for 3 dec. (J.P. Crawley 97 not out)
Derbyshire 473 for 8 dec. (C.J. Adams 119, K.M. Krikken 106, D.G. Cork 83 not out, G. Chapple 4 for 83) and 289 for 8 (D.M. Jones 107, K.J. Barnett 92)
Derbyshire won by 2 wickets
Derbyshire 21 pts, Lancashire 7 pts

Jason Gallian, 312 for Lancashire against Derbyshire at Old Trafford in mid-July, yet still on the losing side. (David Munden/Sportsline)

at Northampton
Middlesex 157 (K.R. Brown 54, J.P. Taylor 5 for 36) and 302 (P.N. Weekes 140, J.D. Carr 57, J.P. Taylor 6 for 68)
Northamptonshire 172 (K.M. Curran 55 not out, A.R.C. Fraser 4 for 28) and 261 (D.J. Capel 95, K.M. Curran 62, P.N. Weekes 4 for 61)
Middlesex won by 26 runs
Middlesex 20 pts, Northamptonshire 4 pts

at Worcester
Durham 240 (P. Bainbridge 67, S.R. Lampitt 4 for 57) and 152 (A. Sheriyar 4 for 46)
Worcestershire 302 (G.A. Hick 150, S.J.E. Brown 6 for 77) and 93 for 1
Worcestershire won by 9 wickets
Worcestershire 23 pts, Durham 5 pts

at Harrogate
Hampshire 266 (K.D. James 71, M. Keech 63) and 249 (M. Keech 87, P.J. Hartley 5 for 57)
Yorkshire 427 (D. Byas 138, A. McGrath 137, J.N.B. Bovill 5 for 58, C.A. Connor 4 for 97) and 89 for 0 (M.P. Vaughan 61 not out)
Yorkshire won by 10 wickets
Yorkshire 24 pts, Hampshire 6 pts

Surrey seemed to have wasted the fine base given them by their top order batsmen with a middle order collapse. Darren Bicknell and Mark Butcher scored 99 for the first wicket, and Stewart and Thorpe 128 for the third, but from 251 for 2 they subsided to 320 for 9 on the second morning. Kersey and Pearson then added a spirited 91 for the last wicket.

Sussex lost Athey at 1, but Lenham and Wells added only 123 for six wickets to fall for 51 runs. Salisbury and Jarvis produced another salvation act with a stand of 83, but two wickets fell quickly before the close, both of them to the left-arm spin of Darren Bicknell who dismissed Salisbury on the third morning to finish with 3 for 7.

A delightful century on the third day from Thorpe, his sixth of the season, occupied 190 balls and contained 14 fours. He and Stewart again combined to advantage, putting on 163 for the third wicket. This brought a declaration which left Sussex more than a day in which to score 451.

They were 60 for 1 on the Friday evening and slipped to 95 for 5 on the final morning. Athey and Moores stopped the slide with a stand of 164. Moores was the more aggressive of the two, and his 119 came in 113 balls. Athey was bowled padding up to Darren Bicknell who helped mop up the tail to finish with 3 for 41.

There was an astonishing start to the game at Chelmsford where Nottinghamshire reached 40 without loss but were bowled out for 97 in 36.3 overs. Well as Ilott and Irani bowled, the Nottinghamshire batting was awful, suffering as much from lack of will as deficiencies in technique. Gooch and Darren Robinson quickly put the Nottinghamshire batting effort into perspective with an opening stand of 104, and by the end of the day, Essex had a lead of 137 with six wickets standing.

Prichard played a pleasing innings on the Friday, and Williams struck some lusty blows which claimed the fourth batting point. Nottinghamshire showed much more resilience when they batted a second time, and the Essex attack looked far from lethal. Robinson and Pollard made 133 for the first wicket before Robinson was out towards the end of the day.

Six batsmen passed 40, and the Nottinghamshire score crept to 415, meaning that Essex, once seeming easy victors, faced a target of 145. When Grayson and Robinson fell in the last 13 overs of the day and Essex closed on 26 for 2, it seemed the visitors might pull off a remarkable victory.

Night-watchman Such had other ideas, and he and Rollins put on 110 for the third wicket. Such equalled his highest score with the second fifty of his career. Gooch went for 0, but Essex claimed their first victory since the second match of the season.

The match at Cheltenham was over before 5.00pm on the second day. Twenty-five wickets fell on the Thursday, but there seemed no indication of what was to come as Ben Smith and Maddy put on 71 for Leicestershire's second wicket. Indeed, Smith batted for more than three hours with no hint of trouble. The rest were undone by the swing of Mike Smith. Gloucestershire fared even worse against a four-pronged seam attack and were all out in 27 overs.

Batting a second time, the visitors lost Simmons for his second 'duck' of the day and batted on 80 for 5. Night-watchman Pierson stood firm with Whitaker to add 47 for the sixth wicket. Needing 239 to win, Gloucestershire crumbled again before the four seamers, and Leicestershire maintained their title challenge, winning by 102 runs although they themselves had managed only 309 runs in the match.

Mike Atherton was out for 0 at Old Trafford, but Lancashire ended the day on 334 for 2. Gallian and Titchard were separated 10 runs into the second morning having added 244 for the third wicket. Gallian batted on, and when he was finally caught, by Rollins, bowled Vandrau, he had batted for 11 hours 10 minutes, a championship record, faced 583 balls, hit four sixes and 33 fours and scored 312, the highest score ever made at Old Trafford.

Derbyshire were 78 for 2 at the end of the second day, and, in spite of another fine century from Chris Adams, they slumped to 253 for 7, still 185 runs short of avoiding the follow-on. Dominic Cork then joined Karl Krikken in a record partnership of 198. Krikken hit the first century of his career with 14 fours and three sixes.

Jones declared at the Saturday night score, and Lancashire went for quick runs, leaving Derbyshire a target of 287 in two sessions. Rollins and Adams went cheaply, but Barnett and Jones scored a rollicking 198 for the third wicket. Five wickets fell for 20 runs when Derbyshire needed 69 in 13 overs. Three of these wickets went to the left-arm spinner Keedy, but, with two overs remaining and 19 wanted, Cork hit Keedy for 17 in an over, and Derbyshire cantered home with three balls to spare.

History had repeated itself. In 1904, 'Percy' Perrin hit 343 not out for Essex against Derbyshire, but Derbyshire won the match. Ninety-two years on, Gallian had made the second highest score against Derbyshire and suffered the same fate.

The pitch at Northampton was reported after 15 wickets had fallen on the first day. Middlesex were 28 for 5 before Brown and Hewitt added 67. Emburey arrived from court (the omnipresent Lamb, Botham, Imran saga) to claim the last two Middlesex wickets and was then out for 11 as Northamptonshire slipped to 92 for 5. They recovered enough to take a lead of 15, but Warren had sustained a broken thumb and Fordham took over the wicket-keeping duties. He was one of four culprits who dropped catches offered by Weekes as he moved to 133 on the second day. He was caught by Fordham seven runs into the third day, but Middlesex were able to set Northamptonshire a target of 288.

The home county finished the Saturday on 211 for 4 with Curran and Capel well set. Curran was out without addition on the Monday as the last five wickets went down for 23 runs. Weekes and Tufnell did the damage.

Durham were bowled out on the first day at Worcester, but they reduced the home county to 39 for 4. Their luck changed on the second day when Hick hit his first century against them, so giving him a century against each of the other 17 first-class counties. The match was over in three days as Durhams's woe continued.

Keech again batted well for Hampshire, but they were bowled out on the first day at Harrogate. Moxon and Vaughan hit 76 off the last 13 overs of the day, and on the second, Byas and McGrath put on 272 for the fourth wicket. McGrath's highest score included 20 fours and two sixes. Yorkshire lost their last seven wickets for 34 runs in nine overs, but they led by 161 runs. Hampshire lost five wickets in clearing the arrears, and Yorkshire romped to victory in three days.

The Warwickshire captain Dermot Reeve, a major figure in English cricket for the past three years, announced that he had been forced to retire through injury. He will be missed. He has had no superior as a leader in the one-day game.

24, 25, 26 and 27 July
at Kidderminster
Northamptonshire 328 (D. Ripley 88 not out, R.K. Illingworth 4 for 89) and 446 for 3 dec. (D.J. Sales 210 not out, D.J. Capel 103)
Worcestershire 350 for 7 dec. (T.M. Moody 106, V.S. Solanki 68, W.P.C. Weston 68, T.S. Curtis 65) and 388 for 7 (T.M. Moody 169, T.S. Curtis 107, S.J. Rhodes 53 not out)
Match drawn
Worcestershire 11 pts, Northamptonshire 9 pts

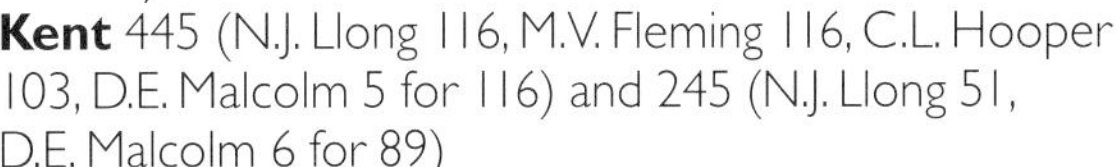

25, 26, 27 and 28 July
at Derby
Kent 445 (N.J. Llong 116, M.V. Fleming 116, C.L. Hooper 103, D.E. Malcolm 5 for 116) and 245 (N.J. Llong 51, D.E. Malcolm 6 for 89)
Derbyshire 292 (T.J.G. O'Gorman 62, C.M. Wells 62, D.W. Headley 8 for 98) and 162 for 5 (K.J. Barnett 54)
Match drawn
Kent 11 pts, Derbyshire 8 pts

at Hartlepool
Essex 334 (A.P. Grayson 74, S.G. Law 73, R.C. Irani 56, N. Killeen 4 for 57) and 370 for 8 dec. (S.G. Law 172, A.P. Grayson 85)
Durham 188 (S.L. Campbell 56, M.C. Ilott 5 for 53) and 224 (S.L. Campbell 72, D.M. Cox 52, P.M. Such 4 for 49)
Essex won by 292 runs
Essex 23 pts, Durham 4 pts

at Cardiff
Glamorgan 505 (M.P. Maynard 214, P.A. Cottey 74, H. Morris 71) and 259 for 3 dec. (M.P. Maynard 68 not out, H. Morris 61, P.A. Cottey 55 not out)
Lancashire 478 for 5 dec. (G.D. Lloyd 142, N.J. Speak 138 not out, S.P. Titchard 67) and 238 (R.D.B. Croft 5 for 47, D.A. Cosker 4 for 60)
Glamorgan won by 48 runs
Glamorgan 22 pts, Lancashire 7 pts

at Cheltenham
Gloucestershire 569 (M.G.N. Windows 184, A. Symonds 127, M.A. Lynch 69, T.H.C. Hancock 57, G.C. Small 4 for 99)
Warwickshire 216 (D.P. Ostler 73, C.A. Walsh 6 for 26) and 237 (D.P. Ostler 90, S.M. Pollock 53, C.A. Walsh 5 for 91)
Gloucestershire won by an innings and 116 runs
Gloucestershire 24 pts, Warwickshire 3 pts

at Southampton
Hampshire 359 (J.P. Stephenson 61, V.P. Terry 57, R.A. Smith 54, M.P. Bicknell 4 for 64) and 301 for 4 dec. (V.P. Terry 87 not out, R.A. Smith 70 not out, J.P. Stephenson 62)
Surrey 331 (A.J. Hollioake 83, M.A. Butcher 58) and 333 for 5 (A.J. Hollioake 104 not out, N. Shahid 101, M.A. Butcher 53)
Surrey won by 5 wickets
Surrey 23 pts, Hampshire 8 pts

at Leicester
Leicestershire 266 (P.A. Nixon 74, J.J. Whitaker 58 not out, J.D. Lewry 5 for 74) and 240 (D.L. Maddy 68, J.D. Lewry 6 for 73)
Sussex 294 (K. Greenfield 69, M.P. Speight 68, P.V. Simmons 5 for 58) and 154 (J.W. Hall 52, M.T. Brimson 5 for 12, P.V. Simmons 4 for 70)
Leicestershire won by 58 runs
Leicestershire 22 pts, Sussex 6 pts

at Scarborough
Somerset 309 (K.A. Parsons 62, R.J. Harden 54, C.E.W. Silverwood 4 for 53) and 395 (S. Lee 134, M.N. Lathwell 80)
Yorkshire 292 (D. Byas 88, D. Gough 51) and 215 (P.J. Hartley 57 not out, K.J. Shine 5 for 48)
Somerset won by 197 runs
Somerset 23 pts, Yorkshire 6 pts

The main feature of the game at Kidderminster, not forgetting Tome Moody's fine feat of a century in each innings, was David Sales' achievement of hitting a double century on his first-class debut. Sales was out third ball in the first innings, but, with Montgomerie having retired hurt, he joined David Capel in a stand worth 243 for the third wicket. Sales, 128 days short of his 19th birthday, was 191 not out on the Friday evening and moved to 210 within four overs on the last morning. He hit 28 fours and three sixes, faced 226 balls in his 260-minute innings and became the first batsman to score a double century on his debut in the championship. The match aggregate of 1512 runs suggested that this was a good pitch to bat on.

Matthew Windows came down from university at the end of July and hit a career-best 184 for Gloucestershire against Warwickshire at Cheltenham. (David Munden/Sportsline)

Kent and Derbyshire, both title aspirants, were thwarted by rain at Derby and had to settle for a draw. There were three Kent centurions on the opening day, but Derbyshire dropped straightforward chances offered by both Llong and Fleming. The most enterprising of the three centurions was Fleming, who hit 20 fours and reached three figures off 88 balls. Closing at 381 for 5, Kent were in a commanding position, and they did not loosen their grip on the second day, although their last five wickets fell for the addition of 64 runs. Marsh suffered a broken finger, and Fulton took over behind the stumps where he held four catches.

The outstanding performance on the second day, however, came from Dean Headley, recently returned to the side after injury. In his first over, Headley conceded two boundaries to Barnett and also sent down two no-balls so that the over cost 12 runs, but he also completed one of the most formidable hat-tricks one could imagine by dismissing Barnett, Adams and Jones with successive deliveries. He finished the day with a career best 8 for 98, and Kent led by 153.

They did not enforce the follow-on and closed on 30 for 2, Fulton being out for 0 for the second time in the match. Malcolm bowled with fire to help dismiss them for 245. Needing 399 to win, Derbyshire were 121 for 5 at the close, and rain allowed only 11 overs on the Monday.

Essex gained their fourth win of the season and moved up to fifth place in the championship, and Durham suffered another miserable defeat in three days. Essex batted unevenly and were disappointed to miss a fourth batting point on the opening day, but by the end of the second day they were in charge. Ilott, Such and Irani bowled Durham out in 66.3 overs, the last nine wickets going down for 83 runs, and the tenth wicket stand between Wood and Saggers producing 31 of them. Saggers from Norfolk, a medium pace bowler, was making his first-class debut, and the last wicket stand saved the follow-on.

Essex, 121 for 2 at the close, powered to victory on the third day. Law and Grayson hit 134 runs off 37 overs before lunch, and their third wicket stand was worth 165. Law hit seven sixes and 22 fours in another mighty innings which brought him 172 off 170 balls.

Sherwin Campbell and Stewart Hutton gave Durham a good start as they went in search of an impossible target of 517, but the inevitable collapse followed, and Essex claimed the extra half hour to win the match in three days.

Maynard and Cottey put on 193 for Glamorgan's fourth wicket before Cottey was out without addition on the second morning. Maynard went on to complete the third double century of his career, hitting three sixes and 22 fours in the process. Lancashire made a spirited reply and were 280 for 3 on the Friday evening.

The game lost a charismatic character and an inventive and highly-successful one-day captain when Dermot Reeve announced his retirement through injury. His influence on Warwickshire cricket had been enormous and the dividends great.
(Ross Kinnaird/Allsport)

Speak and Lloyd, enjoying a good season, scored centuries and added 251 for the fourth wicket. Watkinson declared 27 runs behind, and Glamorgan rushed to 259 for 3 at nearly five an over on the Saturday evening.

Rain delayed the start on the Monday until 2.15pm, and Maynard declared immediately. Needing 287 from 57 overs, Lancashire reached 128 for 2, but five wickets fell for 22 runs in 29 balls to the spinners Croft and Cosker, who was making his first-class debut. Chapple and Martin offered resistance, but the end came with 15 minutes remaining.

Cheltenham was at its most capricious as it followed the two-day defeat for Gloucestershire with a three-day win for the home county. Matthew Windows, available after the term at Durham University, hit 19 fours in the highest score of his career, sharing stands of 148 with Hancock and 140 with Lynch. Symonds hit three sixes and 14 fours and raced to 127 off 103 balls to put Gloucestershire in a very strong position on the second morning.

Warwickshire, 206 for 7 on Friday evening, lost their remaining 13 wickets on the Saturday with Walsh taking five wickets in an innings for the 50th time for Gloucestershire.

Surrey moved equal with Leicestershire at the top of the table after a brilliant win at Southampton. They were set a daunting task of scoring 330 in 54 overs, and they were 119 for 4. Adam Hollioake, who led Surrey splendidly in the absence of Stewart, joined Shahid, not a regular in the side, to put on 195 in 28 overs. Shahid faced 92 balls and Hollioake 93. From the last five overs, 34 were needed, but 14 came from the penultimate over, bowled by Milburn, and Surrey won with five balls to spare.

The young left-arm pace bowler Jason Lewry enjoyed an outstanding match at Leicester with match figures of 11 for 147, but Leicestershire overcame a first innings deficit of 28 and considerable adversity to win by 58 runs and go top of the table with Surrey. They struggled to 258 for 9 in 104 overs on the first days, and saw Sussex take the lead on the second in spite of more fine bowling from Simmons.

Whitaker was injured and batted at number nine in the second innings, and Sussex faced a target of 213 which, even though they closed on 76 for 4 on the Saturday evening, seemed well within their reach.

Leicestershire were without Whitaker, Millns and Pierson on the Monday, but Brimson, slow left-arm, returned the best bowling figures of his career as the last six Sussex wickets fell for 27 runs.

Yorkshire's championship hopes were badly dented when they lost to Somerset. Nothing went right for them McGrath was twice out first ball, Lee hit 139 off 104 balls with two sixes and 22 fours after his side had slipped to 121 for 5, and Shine took three wickets in seven balls to leave Yorkshire at 46 for 5 when they were chasing a target of 413.

1, 2, 3 and 5 August

at Derby
Gloucestershire 217 (M.G.N. Windows 76, P.A.J. DeFreitas 5 for 72) and 201 (M.W. Alleyne 50 not out, D.G. Cork 4 for 53)
Derbyshire 335 (D.G. Cork 71, D.M. Jones 69, K.J. Barnett 65, C.A. Walsh 4 for 110) and 87 for 3
Derbyshire won by 7 wickets
Derbyshire 23 pts, Gloucestershire 5 pts

at Canterbury
Worcestershire 459 for 9 dec. (G.A. Hick 148, S.R. Lampitt 88, K.R. Spiring 71, S.J. Rhodes 68) and 207 for 6 dec. (G.A. Hick 86, D.W. Headley 4 for 81)
Kent 366 (C.L. Hooper 76, M.J. Walker 57, S.R. Lampitt 4 for 92) and 108 (A. Sheriyar 4 for 58)
Worcestershire won by 192 runs
Worcestershire 24 pts, Kent 6 pts

at Leicester
Leicestershire 422 (V.J. Wells 204, P.V. Simmons 75, J.N. Snape 4 for 42) and 298 for 7 dec. (D.L. Maddy 101 not out, P.V. Simmons 72)
Northamptonshire 425 (K.M. Curran 150, A.L. Penberthy 87, T.C. Walton 51, A.D. Mullally 4 for 112) and 212 for 5 (M.B. Loye 69, K.M. Curran 62 not out, A.R.K. Pierson 4 for 49)
Match drawn
Northamptonshire 11 pts, Leicestershire 9 pts

at Lord's
Middlesex 264 (J.D. Carr 66, K.R. Brown 64 not out, J.C. Pooley 50, M.C. Ilott 4 for 47, A.P. Cowan 4 for 76) and 121 (A.P. Cowan 4 for 35)
Essex 436 (A.P. Grayson 140, G.A. Gooch 92, P.J. Prichard 67, A.R.C. Fraser 4 for 122)
Essex won by an innings and 51 runs
Essex 24 pts, Middlesex 5 pts

at Worksop
Nottinghamshire 371 (A.A. Metcalfe 128) and 241 (C.L. Cairns 70, R.T. Robinson 61)
Glamorgan 489 (S.P. James 235, H. Morris 69, R.D.B. Croft 56) and 126 for 2 (H. Morris 71)
Glamorgan won by 8 wickets
Glamorgan 23 pts, Nottinghamshire 6 pts

at Taunton
Somerset 541 (M.E. Trescothick 178, G.D. Rose 93 not out, R.J. Turner 57, R.J. Harden 54, J.N.B. Bovill 4 for 140)
Hampshire 159 (J.S. Laney 50, A.R. Caddick 5 for 46) and 231 (M. Keech 61, J.D. Batty 5 for 85)
Somerset won by an innings and 151 runs
Somerset 24 pts, Hampshire 3 pts

at Eastbourne
Yorkshire 345 (P.J. Hartley 89, R.J. Blakey 80 not out, V.C. Drakes 5 for 99) and 133 (D. Byas 72 not out, E.S.H. Giddins 6 for 47)
Sussex 253 (C.W.J. Athey 100, P.J. Hartley 6 for 67) and 226 for 8 (V.C. Drakes 59, P.J. Hartley 4 for 86)
Sussex won by 2 wickets
Sussex 22 pts, Yorkshire 7 pts

Derbyshire beat Gloucestershire in three days to maintain their title challenge. DeFreitas took five wickets on the opening day, four of them with the aid of Krikken who took four catches standing up to the medium-pacer. They ended the first day on 166 for 4, and reached 293 for the loss of one more wicket on the second day, but the last five wickets fell for 42 runs. It cost them a point, but did nothing to slow their march to victory.

Kent suffered their first championship defeat of the season and, to make matters worse, lost Ealham with a muscle strain. The Jekyll and Hyde of Hick continued. Suffering at Test level, he moved inevitably to a century in the championship match and shared a fourth wicket stand of 160 with Spiring, a young batsman who continues to impress. Rhodes and Lampitt took Worcestershire into the second day with a seventh wicket stand of 159.

The home county batted purposefully to reach 213 for 3 at the close on Friday, and, in spite of Ealham limping at number 11, they came within 93 of Worcestershire's score on the Saturday. When the visitors batted again, Headley seized the initiative by performing his second hat-trick in successive matches. His victims this time were Moody, Spiring and Solanki. Rhodes and Lampitt effected a recovery, and Kent were asked to make 301 in 84 overs. Batting a man short, they collapsed before Sheriyar and Lampitt, who finished the match by bowling Headley and Patel with successive deliveries.

Acting captain Fordham asked Leicestershire to bat first when he won the toss. The home side responded by scoring 364 for 7 on the first day, with Vince Wells completing his second double century of the season. Northamptonshire were equally prolific, scoring 301 for 4 from 89 overs on the second day after the Leicestershire tail had proved rather vigorous. Curran and Penberthy added 226 for the fifth wicket as runs continued to flow on the Saturday. The visitors were eventually set a target of 296 in 59 overs, but this match always looked as if it was destined to be drawn.

With Surrey otherwise engaged, Leicestershire moved three points clear of Yorkshire at the top of the table and had a game in hand of their nearest rivals. Ominously, Essex moved into fourth place with their third victory on the trot. They crushed Middlesex in three days, and Middlesex never truly recovered from losing Weekes and Ramprakash for 0 in the first three overs. Gooch and Grayson scored 171 for Essex's first wicket. Gooch became Essex's highest run-scorer while Grayson made his second century for his adopted county. Weekes and Ramprakash collected 'pairs' on the Saturday as Middlesex went limply to defeat.

Metcalfe hit his first hundred for Nottinghamshire in the match at Worksop, but he was upstaged by Stephen James who made the highest score of his career, 235 off 397 balls with 32 fours. For a batsman who was considered a mere slogger, James has matured into a reliable opening batsman, and his partnership with Morris is one of the most successful in the country. They put on 152 in this match.

Nottinghamshire reached 232 for 5 in their second innings, but lost their last five wickets for nine runs. Gibson claimed three of them, and Glamorgan won with ease.

Andy Hayhurst, the Somerset captain, arrived at Taunton to be told that he had been dropped and that Bowler was to captain the side. A few weeks later, Hayhurst was informed he was not being engaged. The past three years had been uneasy ones for Somerset. Trescothick, who replaced Hayhurst in the side, made the highest score of his career with 32 fours. In spite of being without Shine, injured in the warm-up, Somerset beat Hampshire in three days. Caddick had his fourth five-wicket haul of the season, and Batty returned his best bowling figures for Somerset.

Yorkshire suffered a further setback at Eastbourne. They made 345 on the first day and captured two Sussex wickets for 33. Again they owed much to their lower order with Blakey and Hartley scoring 151 in 24 overs for the eighth wicket.

Sussex fought back well on the second day when 18 wickets fell. Athey made 100 off 183 balls, but Yorkshire took a lead of 92 runs thanks to Peter Hartley. Giddins retaliated with the best bowling performance of his career which, sadly, was to end a few weeks later when he was banned by the TCCB for using an illegal substance and, consequently, not re-engaged by Sussex.

Needing 226 to win, Sussex were 47 for 4, but Athey and Law added 64. Three wickets fell for three runs until Drakes joined Moores in a stand of 104, and Lewry joined Moores for the winning runs. The game was over on the Saturday evening.

7, 8, 9 and 10 August
at Southport
Surrey 211 (I.D. Austin 4 for 46, P.J. Martin 4 for 49) and 442 (B.P. Julian 119, M.A. Butcher 66, N. Shahid 66, J.E.R. Gallian 6 for 115)
Lancashire 145 (M.P. Bicknell 5 for 48, J.E. Benjamin 4 for 38) and 368 (J.E.R. Gallian 57, S.P. Titchard 54, M. Watkinson 53, B.P. Julian 5 for 99)
Surrey won by 140 runs
Surrey 21 pts, Lancashire 4 pts

8, 9, 10 and 12 August
at Swansea
Leicestershire 538 (B.F. Smith 190, P.V. Simmons 92, P.A. Cottey 4 for 49) and 231 for 7 dec. (F.D.B. Croft 4 for 47)
Glamorgan 433 (P.A. Cottey 203, O.D. Gibson 97, P.V. Simmons 5 for 62) and 299 for 9 (H. Morris 106)
Match drawn
Leicestershire 11 pts, Glamorgan 9 pts

at Southampton
Hampshire 186 (M. Keech 55, C.A. Walsh 5 for 34) and 356 (R.A. Smith 77, W.S. Kendall 63, M. Keech 61, K.D. James 50, M.W. Alleyne 4 for 86)
Gloucestershire 164 (D.R. Hewson 87, C.A. Connor 9 for 38) and 315 (A. Symonds 90, D.R. Hewson 58, S.D. Udal 5 for 82)
Hampshire won by 63 runs
Hampshire 20 pts, Gloucestershire 4 pts

at Northampton
Kent 316 (S.C. Willis 78) and 17 for 0
Northamptonshire 133 (A. Fordham 53, M.J. McCague 5 for 21) and 196 (R.R. Montgomerie 57, T.N. Wren 5 for 49, C.L. Hooper 4 for 7)
Kent won by 10 wickets
Kent 23 pts, Northamptonshire 4 pts

at Trent Bridge
Nottinghamshire 257 (U. Afzaal 51, P.C.R. Tufnell 4 for 41) and 163 (R.L. Johnson 5 for 29)
Middlesex 427 (M.R. Ramprakash 71, K.R. Brown 70, P.N. Weekes 58, O.A. Shah 53)
Middlesex won by an innings and 7 runs
Middlesex 24 pts, Nottinghamshire 6 pts

at Taunton
Essex 465 (G.A. Gooch 201, R.C. Irani 87, S.G. Law 63, A.P. van Troost 4 for 90)
Somerset 246 (P.D. Bowler 88, P.M. Such 6 for 63) and 208 (P.M. Such 6 for 72)
Essex won by an innings and 11 runs
Essex 24 pts, Somerset 5 pts

at Hove
Derbyshire 320 (K.J. Barnett 55, T.J.G. O'Gorman 54) and 220 (A.S. Rollins 78 not out, V.C. Drakes 5 for 47)
Sussex 265 (M.P. Speight 122, D.E. Malcolm 5 for 119) and 228 (P. Moores 56, K. Greenfield 51, D.E. Malcolm 5 for 96)
Derbyshire won by 47 runs
Derbyshire 23 pts, Sussex 6 pts

at Edgbaston
Warwickshire 306 (D.P. Ostler 86, N.M.K. Smith 64, D.M. Cox 5 for 97) and 361 for 9 dec. (W.G. Khan 130, A.J. Moles 74, D.R. Brown 51, D.M. Cox 5 for 139)
Durham 255 (S.L. Campbell 64, P. Bainbridge 54, N.M.K. Smith 5 for 75) and 130 (A.F. Giles 6 for 45)
Warwickshire won by 282 runs
Warwickshire 23 pts, Durham 6 pts

Victory in three days at Southport took Surrey one point clear at the top of the table ahead of Leicestershire. Play began an hour late and Lancashire put Surrey in to bat when they won the toss. The decision seemed justified when the visitors were bowled out in 55.4 overs for 211, the seamers doing all the damage. Martin Bicknell, bowling better than ever before in his career and keeping fit, was mainly responsible for Lancashire closing on 128 for 5.

Harry Brind arrived on the second day to inspect the pitch that had aided the hasty fall of 15 wickets. He saw the last five Lancashire wickets fall for 13 runs in under 10 overs, and then he saw the pitch as benign as he could wish while Surrey reached 366 for 6 at five runs an over. Darren Bicknell and Mark Butcher scored 96 for the first wicket, but the highlight of the day was a maiden first-class century from Brendon Julian who hit five sixes and 13 fours. He was out without addition on the third morning, but he was, in fact, 'out' when he had made 66. He hit Chapple high to the boundary where Speak, running fast from square-leg, took the catch, but, realising his momentum could take him over the boundary, tossed the ball to Titchard. Umpire Holder ruled 'not out' and awarded Julian a single. This decision was as strange as it was wrong, for Law 32, section 3 (b) states, 'If a fieldsman releases the ball before he crosses the boundary, the ball will be considered to be still in play and it may be caught by another fieldsman.'

The decision did not have a great influence on the outcome of the match, for, although they offered consistency, Lancashire had little chance of reaching a target of 509 with Julian enjoying a very good all-round match.

Leicestershire were thwarted by Glamorgan's last wicket pair at Swansea. On a restricted first day,

Cardigan Connor, 9 for 38 for Hampshire against Gloucestershire at Southampton, and then an abrupt end to the season through injury. (David Munden/Sportsline)

Leicestershire scored 298 for 3 from 73 overs. The following day, Ben Smith and Phil Simmons extended their fourth wicket partnership to 200, with Smith, who had hit the season's first century, making the highest score of his career. In spite of the abundance of runs, Tony Cottey, pressed into action because Kendrick injured a hand, returned the best bowling figures of his career. At the end of the second day, Glamorgan were in trouble at 133 for 6, but the next day, Cottey and Gibson were not separated until the score reached 338. They had added 211, a record for Glamorgan's seventh wicket. Cottey faced 333 balls and hit a six and 32 fours in the first double century of his career, and Glamorgan trailed by 105 having avoided the follow-on.

Leicestershire pressed for quick runs and set a target of 335 in 86 overs. Morris hit his fourth century of the summer, and Glamorgan reached 228 for 4 with 16 overs remaining. Five wickets fell for 71 runs, and Metson and the injured Kendrick survived the last eight balls to save the match.

Hampshire chose to bat first when they won the toss at Southampton, but 14 wickets fell on the first day, which ended with Gloucestershire only 48 runs behind with six wickets standing. The hero of the day was Hewson who, on his championship debut, stood firm while others surrendered to seam. He was out four runs into the second day without addition to his overnight score, the first of six Hampshire wickets to fall for 22 runs. Cardigan Connor finished with 9 for 38, a career-best bowling performance, and the best bowling performance at Southampton. It was a just reward for an honest, hard-working cricketer.

With an unexpected lead, Hampshire built upon their position in a third wicket stand of 112 between Smith and James, and a fifth wicket stand of 185 between Keech and Kendall. Gloucestershire needed 379 to win in more than a day's play, and with Hewson and Symonds scoring 102 for the second wicket and Bovill unable to bowl and Connor at half pace through injury, an injury which was to shorten his season, they reached 248 for 4. Udal then struck, and the last six wickets fell for 67 runs. Davis and Lewis, the last pair, survived for 10 overs before Lewis was taken at short-leg.

Willis and Fleming added 65 for the sixth wicket to rescue Kent at Northampton, and on the second day, the fragile Northamptonshire batting collapsed before McCague. Following-on, they were 91 for 3 at the close, and on the Saturday, they lost their last seven wickets for 53 runs. Wren, in one his rare outings, took five wickets, and Hooper finished the innings with four wickets in 26 balls. Kent, led by Ward, their fourth captain of the season, won with more than a day to spare.

So, too, did Middlesex who were captained by Ramprakash, who was to succeed Carr as vice-captain in 1997. Nottinghamshire succumbed to a varied attack on the opening day, and with a most even batting display, Middlesex took a lead of 150 on the second. Owais Shah was most impressive on his first-class debut.

Brown and Tufnell, the last pair, frustrated the home county as 20 more runs were scored on the Saturday, after which Nottinghamshire surrendered lamely, their last six wickets falling for 57 runs.

Essex moved into third place in the table with a resounding three-day win over Somerset. They pounded the home county on the first day, with Gooch and Law hitting 101 in 19 overs for the third wicket, and Gooch and Irani adding 170 for the sixth. Gooch completed his double century on the second morning, his tenth for Essex, and by the end of the day, Somerset were batting a second day. They lost their last six wickets for 25 runs to Such and Irani. At 105 for 6, they looked set for total humiliation, but Turner and Lee added 81 to bring some dignity but not to avoid defeat. Such's off-spin was the decisive factor, and he had match figures of 12 for 135.

It was all action at Hove where 15 wickets fell on the first day as 408 runs were scored. Ian Salisbury, not required by England, arrived at the ground in time to take the last three Derbyshire wickets. Sussex lost three wickets for three runs in the closing overs of the day, and, on a restricted second day, they crawled to 212 for 7. Speight completed his first hundred for two seasons on the Saturday, hitting three sixes and 13 fours. Drakes, with his best figures for Sussex, then led a fightback which saw Derbyshire bowled out for 220. Rollins carried his bat throughout the innings and shared last wicket stand of 55 with Malcolm.

Sussex needed 276 to win and closed at 91 for 2 on the Saturday. They lost three wickets for five runs in the first

Matthew Walker hit the highest score ever made at Canterbury, 275 not out for Kent against Somerset. (John Gichigi/Allsport)

three overs of the fourth day, and, in spite of Law, Keith Newell and Moores offering some hope, they never totally recovered. They lost their last four wickets for 20 runs.

Warwickshire were bowled out on the first day at Edgbaston, with Durham's left-arm spinner David Cox taking five wickets in an innings for the first time. Cox also batted well, hitting 45 off 52 balls after six wickets had fallen for 197. He helped keep Durham's hopes alive, but they vanished on the third day when Khan hit a six and 14 fours in his hundred off 143 balls. Cox was again to the fore, bowling 44 consecutive overs to take 10 wickets in a match for the first time. His effort was in vain as Durham lost two for 24 before the close and fell to Ashley Giles' best bowling performance on the Monday. The Warwickshire spinner was rewarded with his county cap.

15, 16, 17 and 19 August
at Derby
Derbyshire 341 (D.M. Jones 105, D.G. Cork 97, M.N. Bowen 5 for 53) and 377 for 8 dec. (C.J. Adams 106, K.J. Barnett 103, T.J.G. O'Gorman 58, J.A. Afford 6 for 87)
Nottinghamshire 317 (P. Johnson 82, C.L. Cairns 75, R.T. Robinson 53, P.A.J. DeFreitas 5 for 54) and 98 (D.E. Malcolm 5 for 43, P.A.J. DeFreitas 4 for 53)
Derbyshire won by 303 runs
Derbyshire 23 pts, Nottinghamshire 7 pts

at Bristol
Yorkshire 166 (C. White 74, C.A. Walsh 6 for 22) and 179 (R.J. Blakey 52 not out)
Gloucestershire 329 (A. Symonds 75, C.E.W. Silverwood 5 for 78) and 17 for 0
Gloucestershire won by 10 wickets
Gloucestershire 23 pts, Yorkshire 4 pts

at Canterbury
Kent 616 for 7 dec. (M.J. Walker 275 not out, C.L. Hooper 76, D.W. Headley 63 not out, T.R. Ward 57) and 92 for 2 dec.
Somerset 389 for 8 dec. (R.J. Harden 136, S.C. Ecclestone 94) and 257 (M.N. Lathwell 81, S.C. Ecclestone 56, M.J. McCague 4 for 21)
Kent won by 62 runs
Kent 21 pts, Somerset 5 pts

at Old Trafford
Lancashire 342 (M.A. Atherton 63, N.H. Fairbrother 54) and 306 for 5 dec. (J.P. Crawley 100 not out, M.A. Atherton 50)
Hampshire 234 (M. Keech 60 not out, G. White 58, W.S. Kendall 53, G. Chapple 4 for 43) and 304 for 6 (R.A. Smith 77, W.S. Kendall 75)
Match drawn
Lancashire 10 pts, Hampshire 8 pts

A richly deserved cap for Keith Greenfield of Sussex after nine years on the staff and six centuries. (Graham Chadwick/Allsport)

at Lord's
Worcestershire 369 (T.M. Moody 124, V.S. Solanki 69, W.P.C. Weston 59) and 233 for 8 dec. (T.S. Curtis 118, P.C.R. Tufnell 4 for 72)
Middlesex 352 for 9 dec. (P.C.R. Tufnell 67 not out, J.D. Carr 66 not out, M.R. Ramprakash 64, R.K. Illingworth 5 for 85) and 242 for 9 (J.C. Pooley 87, V.S. Solanki 5 for 69)
Match drawn
Worcestershire 11 pts, Middlesex 9 pts

at Edgbaston
Warwickshire 498 (S.M. Pollock 150 not out, K.J. Piper 82, D.P. Ostler 65, N.V. Knight 63) and 136 for 8
Glamorgan 214 (S.P. James 90, M.P. Maynard 69, A.F. Giles 6 for 63) and 419 (S.P. James 148, M.P. Maynard 95, R.D.B. Croft 78, N.M.K. Smith 5 for 166)
Warwickshire won by 2 wickets
Warwickshire 24 pts, Glamorgan 5 pts

17, 18 and 19 August
at Linlithgow
Scotland 380 for 5 dec. (G. Salmond 181, J.G. Williamson 55, M.D. Allingham 50 not out) and 261 for 7 dec. (I.L. Philip 110)
Ireland 323 for 6 dec. (A.R. Dunlop 57, K.C. McCallam 51, D.M.P. Moore 51, I.L. Eagleson 50 not out) and 301 for 6 (D.A. Lewis 71, P.G. Gillespie 53)
Match drawn

Karl Ruben Spiring scored 1084 runs in his first full season in first-class cricket for Worcestershire. (Clive Brunskill/Allsport)

Derbyshire leap-frogged over Surrey and other counties to take top spot in the table with a convincing win over Nottinghamshire. Derbyshire recovered from the loss of two early wickets through Jones' century and later through Cork's aggressive 97. It was he who was mainly responsible for Derbyshire's last three wickets conjuring 146 runs. Nottinghamshire, first through the careful Robinson and then through the more adventurous and expansive Johnson and Cairns, seized the initiative when they reached 281 for 5, but their last five wickets fell for 36 runs to give Derbyshire a lead of 24 which they extended to 73 without loss by the close.

On the third day, Chris Adams, always so attractive to watch, joined with the admirably consistent Kim Barnett in a second wicket stand of 177 so that Jones was able to declare in the final session and set Nottinghamshire a target of 402. By the end of the day, they were 72 for 4 and had lost Pollard who retired hurt after being hit on the helmet. The match was soon over on the Monday morning with Malcolm, enjoying his best season in county cricket and having the most fruitful period of his career, and DeFreitas bowling unchanged.

Derbyshire's lead over Kent was a tenuous one in that they now faced ten days without cricket as other counties made up the game in hand, but, of their rivals, Yorkshire were virtually eliminated when they lost in two days to the unpredictable Gloucestershire. At Bristol, 16 wickets tumbled on the first day. Yorkshire were routed by Walsh and were 15 for 5 before White and Blakey put on 98. Walsh returned to claim three of the last five wickets, and there was a feeling that Yorkshire might find life after Bevan rather hard. A typically belligerent innings from Symonds took Gloucestershire into the lead, and the later batsmen plundered 118 on the second day. Walsh, Smith and Davis then demolished Yorkshire for a second time. The one bright spark for the visitors was the bowling of Silverwood, a most promising quick bowling prospect.

Some contrivance was needed for Kent to beat Somerset and climb to second place. They scored 413 for 4 from 104 overs on the first day, and on the second they reached 616 for 7 before declaring. The highest of several high partnerships were the unbroken eighth wicket stand of 137 between Walker and Headley, and the third wicket stand of 155 between Walker and Hooper. The match on the first two days undoubtedly belonged to the chunky, left-handed Matthew Walker, playing only his third championship game of the season, whose unbeaten 275 occupied nine-and-a-half hours and was the highest score made by a Kent batsman at Canterbury. He hit 41 fours and showed powers of concentration and the ability to hit the ball hard in what transpired to be the highest score of the season. At 22 years old, he is a batsman of immense promise.

Somerset had to score 467 to save the follow-on, and there seemed little hope of that when they were 119 for 3 on

Vikram Solanki, another young Worcestershire player to make his mark in 1996, an all-rounder of immense potential.
(Clive Brunskill/Allsport)

the Friday evening. They dug in on the Saturday with Harden and Ecclestone added 172 in 72 overs. The left-handed Ecclestone made his highest championship score as Kent toiled. They were rewarded for their toil with four wickets in the evening, and Somerset ended the day on 389 for 8, still 78 short of salvation point.

Ward agreed not to enforce the follow-on if Somerset declared, and his declaration left the visitors a target of 320 in 81 overs. Trescothick went quickly before Lathwell and Bowler put on 84. A draw looked the most likely result until Headley dismissed Lathwell and Lee with consecutive deliveries just before tea. Parsons and Ecclestone scored 75 in 16 overs before McCague took four of the last five wickets to bring Kent victory.

Consistency rather than flair took Lancashire to 342 against Hampshire, who responded in similar fashion. Delightfully, Crawley scored his first century of the season, and Watkinson's declaration left his bowlers more than a day to bowl out the visitors. Chapple had White leg before on the Saturday evening, and two wickets fell on the Monday morning, one of them when Whitaker was run out in a mix-up. Robin Smith batted for more than three hours and William Kendall hit his highest county score to give Hampshire a hard-earned draw.

Middlesex and Worcestershire, too, settled for a draw. Worcestershire batted into the second day by the end of which Middlesex, perplexed by Illingworth's spin, were struggling at 167 for 6. Salvation came from a most unexpected quarter as Tufnell joined Carr in an unbroken last wicket stand of 101. Tufnell dominated the stand and hit 15 fours in the highest score of his career which was rapturously received by the crowd. He then took two wickets before the close, but Curtis' well-judged century allowed Moody to set a target of 251 in 49 overs. At 131 for 1 after 30 overs, Middlesex were winning, but Solanki turned the game with his off-breaks claiming a career best 5 for 69. Johnson hit hard for his 28, and Pooley's 87 off 105 balls was a masterly effort. Ultimately, Middlesex finished nine short of their target as the last pair played out the last two balls.

Warwickshire were in command from the start against Glamorgan with Pollock hitting the highest score of his career and Giles bowling out the visitors on the second day so that they followed on 284 runs in arrears. Morris was out before the close of the second day, and a Warwickshire victory seemed a formality. James defied them, and he and Maynard added 195. Croft gave the late order a boost as he totally dominated a last wicket stand with Parkin which realised 77 in 18 overs. Parkin made 4 not out.

Warwickshire needed 136 to win and scored 11 on the Saturday evening. The climate of the match changed on the Monday when six middle order wickets fell for 51 runs. Giles joined Brown with 23 wanted and only two wickets standing, and they batted with admirable composure to secure victory.

21, 22, 23 and 24 August
at Weston-super-Mare
Durham 326 (D.M. Cox 95 not out, S.L. Campbell 69, G.D. Rose 7 for 73)
Somerset 298 for 6 (M.N. Lathwell 85, R.J. Harden 65)
Match drawn
Somerset 9 pts, Durham 8 pts

22, 23, 24 and 26 August
at Colchester
Gloucestershire 280 (R.C. Russell 63, A. Symonds 52, A.P. Cowan 5 for 68) and 188 (R.C. Russell, M.A. Lynch 50, N.F. Williams 5 for 43)
Essex 532 for 8 dec. (G.A. Gooch 111, R.C. Irani 91, P.J. Prichard 88, D.D.J. Robinson 72 retired hurt, M.W. Alleyne 4 for 80)
Essex won by an innings and 64 runs
Essex 24 pts, Gloucestershire 3 pts

at Cardiff
Kent 323 for 5 dec. (C.L. Hooper 77, D.P. Fulton 64, N.J. Llong 63, M.J. Walker 59) and 0 for 0 dec.
Glamorgan 0 for 0 dec. and 273 for 5 (H. Morris 118, P.A. Cottey 70)
Match drawn
Kent 6 pts, Glamorgan 5 pts

Chris Silverwood, the Yorkshire pace bowler, voted Young Cricketer of the Year. (Nigel French/ASP)

at Leicester
Leicestershire 353 (P.V. Simmons 108, P.A. Nixon 67, S.J. Renshaw 4 for 56, J.N.B. Bovill 4 for 102)
Hampshire 137 (G.J. Parsons 4 for 36) and 135 for 9
Match drawn
Leicestershire 11 pts, Hampshire 7 pts

at Northampton
Sussex 389 (N.J. Lenham 145, V.C. Drakes 59, A.P. Wells 51, A.L. Penberthy 4 for 36) and 112 (C.E.L. Ambrose 6 for 26)
Northamptonshire 361 (K.M. Curran 117, D. Ripley 66 not out) and 142 for 4
Northamptonshire won by 6 wickets
Northamptonshire 24 pts, Sussex 8 pts

at Trent Bridge
Nottinghamshire 446 for 9 dec. (G.F. Archer 143, M.P. Dowman 107, W.M. Noon 57, B.P. Julian 4 for 104) and 0 for 0 dec.
Surrey 128 for 4 dec. (A.D. Brown 56 not out) and 53 for 0
Match drawn
Nottinghamshire 8 pts, Surrey 7 pts

at Worcester
Warwickshire 310 (A.F. Giles 83, T.A. Munton 54 not out, W.G. Khan 52, R.K. Illingworth 4 for 54, S.R. Lampitt 4 for 90) and 162 for 4 dec.
Worcestershire 205 for 9 dec. (K.R. Spiring 52) and 164 for 4 (W.P.C. Weston 52)
Match drawn
Warwickshire 10 pts, Worcestershire 8 pts

at Leeds
Yorkshire 529 for 8 dec. (C. White 181, R.J. Blakey 109 not out, M.D. Moxon 66, M.P. Vaughan 57)
Lancashire 323 (N.H. Fairbrother 86, M. Watkinson 64, D. Gough 4 for 53) and 231 for 7 (N.J. Speak 77, N.H. Fairbrother 55, D. Gough 4 for 48)
Match drawn
Yorkshire 11 pts, Lancashire 8 pts

The weather was cruel. At Weston, only 54 overs were possible on the second day, 22 on the third and none on the fourth. The first day was significant for a spell of bowling by Rose which reduced Durham from 145 for 1 to 170 for 6, and for a violent career-best unbeaten innings of 95 by David Cox, Durham's left-arm spinner.

Limited play on the first two days, none on the third and forfeitures of innings brought no result at Cardiff. Leicestershire lost the whole of the Friday in their match against Hampshire. They lost their last two wickets on the Saturday but claimed the fourth batting point and then reduced Hampshire to 81 for 7 on a rain-restricted day. The Hampshire innings lasted another 17 overs on the Monday, but they duly followed on. Whitaker fell to Millns in the first over of Hampshire's second innings, and wickets fell regularly until Leicestershire were on the verge of victory with the visitors 105 for 9, but showers and the determination of Bovill and Renshaw brought a draw which Hampshire hardly deserved and which left Leicestershire frustrated in fourth place in the table.

Arch and Dowman scored centuries and shared a third wicket stand of 187 for Nottinghamshire against Surrey, but there was no play on the second day and very little on the last so that a draw was inevitable.

A last wicket stand of 141 between Giles and Munton, a Warwickshire record, could not compensate for the loss of much of the second and third day's play at Worcester. Giles hit the highest score of his career and furthered his reputation to be considered an all-rounder.

Sussex seemed to hold the upper hand against Northamptonshire when they hit 368 for 7 in 107 overs on the opening day at Northampton. Lenham, returning after a three-week break because of a finger injury, hit 145 and shared a third wicket stand of 149 with Wells. The home side ended the second day on 160 for 4 but effected a recovery on the Saturday through Curran, Ripley, Emburey and Ambrose. The last two wickets realised 125 runs. Sussex than had one of their all too common second innings collapses. They disintegrated before Ambrose and Taylor, and

A record three hat-tricks in the season for Dean Headley, the Kent pace bowler. What might he have achieved had he not missed the first half of the season through injury?
(John Gichigi/Allsport)

their last six wickets fell for 32 runs. Northamptonshire were 42 for 3 on the Saturday evening, but lost only the wicket of Ripley on the Monday as they completed their second championship win of the season.

Yorkshire batted into the second day to reach 529 for 8 against Lancashire. Moxon and Vaughan had started with a stand worth 110, but the highlight of the innings came in a sixth wicket stand of 252 between White and Blakey. This was the second highest partnership for this wicket in Yorkshire's history, and White's 181 was by far the best score of his career. Lancashire finished in some disarray at 162 for 4, and, in spite of stern resistance from the late order, they followed on the Saturday. Only 13 overs were possible on the last day during which Speak and Chapple were out, but rain was the only winner.

The real winner of the round of matches was Essex. Gloucestershire were bowled out on the first day by an attack that was, to say the least, variable. The main performer for the home county was Ashley Cowan who took five wickets in an innings for the first time and completed the hat-trick when he had Davis caught at slip and Ball taken at short-leg before yorking Smith. Only 34 overs could be bowled on the second day, but Gooch had completed a century by the end of it and Essex were 194 for 0. Robinson could not resume his innings on the Saturday, having suffered damage on a finger when hit on the hand by Walsh. There were two ferocious innings by Prichard and Irani, and Prichard was able to declare with a lead of 252. His bowlers responded by reducing Gloucestershire to 27 for 4 by the close.

On the Monday, Essex duly completed their fifth championship victory in succession and went level at the top of the table with Kent, who had only three games left as opposed to Essex's two. Russell and Lynch offered resistance for Gloucestershire, but Neil Williams returned his best figures for Essex and the title beckoned.

28, 29, 30 and 31 August
at Chester-le-Street
Glamorgan 259 (P.A. Cottey 81, M.J. Saggers 6 for 65) and 207 (H. Morris 69, A. Dale 69, D.A. Blenkiron 4 for 43)
Durham 114 (S.L. Watkin 4 for 28) and 211
Glamorgan won by 141 runs
Glamorgan 22 pts, Durham 4 pts

at Portsmouth
Middlesex 199 (K.R. Brown 57, L.J. Botham 5 for 67) and 426 (J.C. Pooley 111, M.R. Ramprakash 108, M.W. Gatting 83)
Hampshire 232 (A.R.C. Fraser 5 for 55, R.A. Fay 4 for 77) and 205 (A.R.C. Fraser 5 for 79, P.C.R. Tufnell 4 for 39)
Middlesex won by 188 runs
Middlesex 20 pts, Hampshire 5 pts

29, 30, 31 August and 2 September
at Chesterfield
Worcestershire 238 (W.P.C. Weston 100 not out, V.S. Solanki 58, A.J. Harris 4 for 31) and 303 (K.R. Spiring 130 not out, S.J. Rhodes 57, P.A.J. DeFreitas 4 for 70)
Derbyshire 471 (C.J. Adams 123, T.J.G. O'Gorman 109 not out, K.J. Barnett 87, T.M. Moody 6 for 82) and 71 for 1
Derbyshire won by 9 wickets
Derbyshire 24 pts, Worcestershire 5 pts

at Bristol
Gloucestershire 183 (R.C. Russell 50) and 249 (R.C. Russell 75)
Northamptonshire 190 (K.M. Curran 52, A.M. Smith 5 for 68) and 227
Gloucestershire won by 15 runs
Gloucestershire 20 pts, Northamptonshire 4 pts

at Tunbridge Wells
Nottinghamshire 214 (P. Johnson 84, M.J. McCague 4 for 54) and 242 (C.M. Tolley 67, K.P. Evans 54, M.A. Ealham 5 for 52, M.J. McCague 4 for 80)
Kent 244 (C.L. Hooper 58, C.M. Tolley 4 for 68, K.P. Evans 4 for 71) and 215 for 3 (C.L. Hooper 86, T.R. Ward 54 not out)
Kent won by 7 wickets
Kent 21 pts, Nottinghamshire 5 pts

at Leicester
Somerset 83 (D.J. Millns 4 for 35) and 174 (P.V. Simmons 4 for 38)
Leicestershire 296
Leicestershire won by an innings and 39 runs
Leicestershire 20 pts, Somerset 4 pts

at The Oval
Warwickshire 195 (A.F. Giles 50, C.C. Lewis 4 for 45, B.P. Julian 4 for 66) and 109 (J.E. Benjamin 4 for 17, M.P. Bicknell 4 for 38)
Surrey 468 (C.C. Lewis 94, M.A. Butcher 70, J.D. Ratcliffe 63, G.J. Kersey 63, D.J. Bicknell 55)
Surrey won by an innings and 164 runs
Surrey 24 pts, Warwickshire 2 pts

at Hove
Sussex 363 (C.W.J. Athey 111, V.C. Drakes 52, I.D. Austin 4 for 37) and 144
Lancashire 218 (W.K. Hegg 54) and 290 for 5 (J.P. Crawley 112 not out, N.H. Fairbrother 79, I.D.K. Salisbury 4 for 100)
Lancashire won by 5 wickets
Lancashire 21 pts, Sussex 8 pts

at Leeds
Yorkshire 290 (C. White 76, M.D. Moxon 59, R.J. Blakey 57) and 329 (R.A. Kettleborough 108, G.M. Hamilton 61, P.M. Such 118)
Essex 372 (N. Hussain 158, P.J. Prichard 71) and 149 (R.D. Stemp 5 for 38)
Yorkshire won by 98 runs
Yorkshire 22 pts, Essex 8 pts

Simon Brown worked his heart out for lowly Durham and was asked to add the responsibility of captain to his burden as the season drew to its close.
(David Munden/Sportsline)

In 1996, life at the top of the Britannic Assurance County Championship was brief, as Essex discovered, and, with three rounds of matches remaining in September, only 13 points separated the first five counties. Kent moved one point clear at the head of the table by beating Nottinghamshire. Just 10 overs were possible on the first day at Tunbridge Wells. Kent found runs as hard to get as the visitors, but they drew level with only five wickets down before losing their last five wickets for 30 runs. Nottinghamshire slipped to 105 for 6 on the Saturday before Tolley and Evans added 65. They were separated early on the last morning. McCague, enjoying a fine season, sent back both of them, but Kent faced a difficult target of 213 on a pitch that was not easy. Ward dropped anchor after two wickets had gone for 47, and Hooper played a scintillating knock, dominating a partnership of 116 of which he scored all of the last 45 runs. When he was caught behind off Bowen, Llong came in to help Ward finish the job.

Derbyshire moved into second place by crushing Worcestershire in three days. Weston carried his bat through the 51.5 overs of the Worcestershire innings on the opening day, but the second belonged to Chris Adams. He played another blinding innings, hitting four sixes and 17 fours as he faced 188 balls for his 123. He and Tim O'Gorman, who, having started the season with a future uncertain, reached his first century in two years, added 130 for the fourth wicket and took Derbyshire to a commanding position.

Worcestershire closed on 133 for 5 but made a fine recovery on the Saturday. Ruben Spiring and Vikram Solanki, two exciting young cricketers, added 146, but their work was wasted when the last five wickets fell for 28 runs and Derbyshire cantered to their fourth victory in a row.

Leicestershire, playing some good, emphatic cricket and very much a team, beat Somerset in two days to go third. Parsons, Millns, Simmons and Wells bowled the visitors out in 41.2 overs on the first day, by the end of which Leicestershire, with five wickets standing, led by 119 runs. Lee and Batty robbed them of a third batting point on the second morning, but they romped to victory as Somerset crumbled again before bowling that was aggressive and fielding that was tigerish. Phil Simmons took four wickets and his commitment to the Leicestershire cause was a joy to behold.

Surrey had been asked by the TCCB to omit Chris Lewis from the side to play Warwickshire. Rightly, Surrey refused. Lewis had been dropped from the England squad

Chris Adams hit 1742 runs in the season – only Gooch scored more – yet the Derbyshire batsman found no place in either of the England parties, one of the season's great mysteries. (Paul Sturgess/Sportsline)

for arriving late at The Oval Test. It was not his first offence, and the punishment was immediate and correct. He was to receive more severe treatment a fortnight later when his name was not to be found among those invited to tour Zimbabwe and New Zealand. He had offended at national level and was punished at the level. For Surrey to have agreed to the TCCB's request would have been wrong. He would have been trebly punished. Ironically, Lewis captained Surrey against Warwickshire, hit his highest score of the season and played a major part in his county's innings victory in three days.

Surrey moved to fourth place, but Essex's defeat at Headingley left the former leaders in fifth place. For two days, Essex appeared to be heading for certain victory, a victory which would have given them a firm grip on the title. On the first day, they bowled Yorkshire out for 290. The Yorkshire innings was boosted by a sixth wicket stand of 115 between White and Blakey, two batsmen very much in form, and the Essex bowlers must have been disappointed to have let their opponents get so many, for the pitch gave every indication that it would present a far from easy surface in the fourth innings. Essex lost Gooch and Grayson for 79 before the close, but on the second day, Hussain and Prichard extended their third wicket stand until it was worth 135. Prichard followed his breezy innings at Colchester with another bright knock, 71 off 83 balls. Hussain, missed off the simplest of chances on 98, hit two sixes and 17 fours in his first championship hundred of the season. It came when most needed.

Essex led by 82 runs, and by the close, Yorkshire were in dire straits at 119 for 5. It was on the Saturday that the match was transformed. Kettleborough could have been stumped early on, but Rollins missed the chance, and the Yorkshire sixth wicket pair were not parted until Blakey was caught behind off Ilott at 193. The stand had realised 102, but the Yorkshire lead was still only 111 with just four wickets standing. Those wickets proved costly for Essex. Hamilton, playing in place of Gough, who was on international duty, hit 61 off 80 balls and added 93 in 22 overs for the eighth wicket with Kettleborough.

The left-handed Kettleborough, deputising for the departed Bevan, played a wonderfully gritty innings. His maiden first-class hundred occupied 288 balls and included 10 fours. It was a most brave and intelligent innings on a pitch which was increasingly offering more to the spinners, as Such demonstrated in taking eight wickets.

Essex faced a target of 248, a mountain on this pitch, and Gooch, Grayson, Hussain, to a rash clout, Prichard, to an unplayable ball from Stemp, and Lewis, run out, were all back in the pavilion with only 100 on the board by the close. Stemp duly mopped up on the last morning, and Essex's championship aspirations dived. Yorkshire, in sixth place, retained only a remote interest, for their form before this match had been poor since Bevan's departure.

For the rest, Glamorgan predictably beat Durham, who did little to improve their form with poor team selection. The decision to play an all seam attack to the exclusion of Cox, their best player with bat and ball in recent weeks, was nonsense. There was a beam of light in the performance of Martin Saggers, a recent arrival from King's Lynn, who took 6 for 65 on the second day after a rain-restricted first day. His analysis was the best by a Durham bowler in the season, but the batsmen, inevitably, undermined his work and defeat followed.

The match which dominated the news was that at Portsmouth where Liam Botham, 19-year-old son of the great 'Beefy', came into the Hampshire side as a late replacement for the injured John Stephenson. Botham junior responded to the call by establishing himself in his own right. He claimed Gatting as his first victim and finished with 5 for 67. The pitch did give help to the bowlers, and Hampshire struggled to 105 for 4 by the Wednesday evening.

They did take a first innings lead of the second day, with Botham contributing 30, but Jason Pooley emerged from a miserable season with an innings of 111. He and Ramprakash, who hit his third championship hundred of the season, added 187 for the second wicket. Gatting punched as well as ever, and, needing 394 to win, Hampshire were 109 for 5 by the close. Aymes and Maru offered defiance, but Fraser accounted for them both before Tufnell spun Middlesex to victory.

Frail batting brought 14 wickets on the first day at Bristol, and it was Russell's determination in both innings which brought Gloucestershire to the point of victory on the Saturday evening. Needing 243 to win, Northamptonshire descended to 201 for 9, but Snape and Taylor refused to surrender and scored 17 runs before stumps were finally drawn. Dreams were shattered nine runs into Monday morning when Smith trapped Snape leg before for 33.

A sensational entry into first-class cricket for Liam Botham who took 5 for 67 for Hampshire against Middlesex. He takes a catch off his own bowling to dismiss Richard Johnson. Following in father's footsteps? (Allsport)

Sussex performed one of their customary second innings collapses to lose to Lancashire. Athey faced 217 balls and batted for 268 minutes for his 111 on the first day, and a varied attack gave Sussex a first innings advantage of 145. This was frittered away on the Saturday when Sussex were bowled out for 144, the last two wickets providing 45 of those runs. Crawley's excellent hundred and a third wicket partnership of 150 with Fairbrother took Lancashire to their second championship win of the season on the Monday.

3, 4, 5 and 6 September
at Southampton
Glamorgan 401 (S.P. James 103, H. Morris 80, R.D.B. Croft 67, A.D. Shaw 53, D.A. Mascarenhas 6 for 88) and 281 for 6 dec. (M.P. Maynard 69, O.D. Gibson 62 not out)
Hampshire 352 for 4 dec. (J.S. Laney 102, G.W. White 70, R.J. Maru 55 not out, R.A. Smith 54) and 261 for 8 (R.A. Smith 91, W.S. Kendall 71)
Match drawn
Hampshire 11 pts, Glamorgan 8 pts

at Old Trafford
Middlesex 160 (M. Watkinson 5 for 15, P.J. Martin 4 for 31) and 231 (K.R. Brown 83, M.W. Gatting 50, M. Watkinson 4 for 104)
Lancashire 262 (S.P. Titchard 67, P.C.R. Tufnell 6 for 74) and 106 (P.C.R. Tufnell 7 for 49)
Middlesex won by 23 runs
Middlesex 20 pts, Lancashire 6 pts

at Trent Bridge
Nottinghamshire 324 (K.P. Evans 71) and 196 (R.T. Robinson 50, D.J. Millns 5 for 31)
Leicestershire 439 (J.J. Whitaker 129, V.J. Wells 119, G.J. Parsons 53) and 82 for 4
Leicestershire won by 6 wickets
Leicestershire 24 pts, Nottinghamshire 6 pts

at Taunton
Derbyshire 524 (A.S. Rollins 127, K.M. Krikken 89, D.G. Cork 77, P.A.J. DeFreitas 60, G.M. Roberts 52) and 322 for 6 dec. (K.J. Barnett 141, D.M. Jones 74)
Somerset 464 (S. Lee 110, M.N. Lathwell 109, A.J. Harris 4 for 95) and 296 for 8 (J.I.D. Kerr 68 not out, P.D. Bowler 60, M.N. Lathwell 54, D.G. Cork 4 for 55)
Match drawn
Somerset 10 pts, Derbyshire 10 pts

at The Oval
Surrey 395 (A.J. Hollioake 129, B.P. Julian 117, J.P. Taylor 4 for 87) and 298 (A.J. Hollioake 98, C.E.L. Ambrose 4 for 55)
Northamptonshire 235 (D. Ripley 55, B.P. Julian 6 for 37) and 233
Surrey won by 225 runs
Surrey 24 pts, Northamptonshire 5 pts

at Edgbaston
Essex 238 (R.C. Irani 69, G.C. Small 4 for 41) and 450 for 6 dec. (G.A. Gooch 147, P.J. Prichard 108, R.C. Irani 82 not out)
Warwickshire 253 (W.G. Khan 126) and 265 (D.R. Brown 70, N.F. Williams 4 for 57, P.M. Such 4 for 114)
Essex won by 170 runs
Essex 21 pts, Warwickshire 6 pts

at Worcester
Sussex 219 (V.C. Drakes 103) and 180 (D.R. Law 75, A. Sheriyar 6 for 99)
Worcestershire 413 for 9 dec. (D.A. Leatherdale 122, S.J. Rhodes 110, T.S. Curtis 61)
Worcestershire won by an innings and 14 runs
Worcestershire 24 pts, Sussex 4 pts

Having introduced Liam Botham to first-class cricket with a bang, Hampshire unveiled another discovery in medium-pacer Dmitri Mascarenhas who, on the occasion of his debut, returned figures of 6 for 88. Three of his victims were the first three batsmen in the Glamorgan order. Rain limited

Still the leading batsman in England, Graham Gooch. (Allsport)

the first day, but there was time for James and Morris to score 177 for the first wicket. Shaw and Croft boosted the tail on the second morning as Glamorgan's runs came at four an over. Hampshire could not quite match that rate, but Laney and White gave them a substantial start with an opening partnership of 153. Laney's improvement throughout the season had been marked and that he reached his first championship hundred off 163 balls with 19 fours seemed the logical conclusion to what had gone before. Smith declared as soon as Hampshire had claimed their fourth batting point, and Maynard's declaration left the home county the last day in which to score 331. Three wickets went down for 39 runs before Robin Smith and Will Kendall added 156 in 51 overs. The rate of scoring always looked like leaving Hampshire short of their target. Eventually, Hampshire were indebted to Keech and Maru earning them a draw.

Lancashire had been anxious to have a rest before the NatWest Trophy and Middlesex obliged by beating them in three days. The first day at Old Trafford saw 17 wickets fall, but Lancashire took a first innings lead of 102. On a pitch increasingly encouraging spin, Middlesex were indebted to Brown and Gatting who battled well so that the home side faced a target of 130. In four overs before the end of the second day, Lancashire scored two runs and lost Titchard, Gallian and Crawley. They crashed to 72 for 8 on the third morning before Haynes and Martin added 31. Tufnell claimed them both to finish with 7 for 49 and bring about a sensational victory.

Leicestershire went top of the table with maximum points against Nottinghamshire, whose innings just crept into the second day. Leicestershire immediately showed their strength as Wells and Whitaker combined to score 167 for their second wicket. With Cairns resting and Evans unable to bowl after mid-afternoon because of an injury, the Nottinghamshire attack looked thinner than ever. Leicestershire claimed their fourth batting point early on the third morning, and some late runs were plundered to give them a substantial first innings lead. By the end of the day, a mixture of pace and spin had reduced Nottinghamshire to 189 for 8, and Leicestershire completed victory before lunch on the fourth day.

Mullally did not play in this game, but Millns took five second innings wickets. A few years ago he was deprived of an England cap by injury, yet he now looks a better bowler than ever, and Leicestershire owe much of their success to him.

Taunton offered a pitch that threatened to break the hearts of bowlers. Derbyshire, with Rollins patiently accumulating a century and sharing a fifth wicket partnership of 135 with Cork, scored 389 for 7 on the first day. Krikken and Roberts extended their eighth wicket stand until it was worth 118. Roberts, a left-arm spinner, was making his first-class debut and celebrated with a lively 52.

Roberts took his first wicket when he had Ecclestone leg before, but a Lathwell century kept Somerset in touch. On the third day, Lee hit a six and 16 fours as he nursed the late order to such good effect that the last four wickets added 135 runs and the Derbyshire lead was restricted to 60. Kim Barnett romped to the third century of the match, and he and Jones added 187. The dilemma that confronted Jones was when to declare, and eventually he set Somerset a target of 383 in 78 overs. Arguably, Jones was too cautious, and he was certainly reluctant to use spin. Cork and DeFreitas, in particular, bowled manfully, and at 177 for 6, Somerset looked beaten. Turner and Kerr disputed that scenario by adding 75, and Derbyshire were frustrated.

Surrey emphatically asserted their championship potential with a four-day victory over Northamptonshire. They were 147 for 6 on the first afternoon when Julian joined Adam Hollioake in a stand of 181 in 40 overs. Hollioake's exceptional season continued, and he was only two runs short of a century in each innings. His 129 was his fifth championship century in 14 matches. Julian had proved to be a most worthy acquisition as an overseas player and he followed his bubbling century with a career-best 6 for 37.

Northamptonshire's misery continued into the last day when they lost the match and Ripley with a damaged hand.

Essex kept their championship hopes alive with victory at Edgbaston. They struggled early on a green pitch of variable bounce. Irani batted in a typically positive manner, and there was a useful 40 from Ilott as the last three wickets added 78. Ilott then trapped night-watchman leg before after Williams had dismissed both openers. Such should also have caught Khan off the last ball of the day, and this proved a costly miss as Khan batted admirably on the second day to score a fine century to take his side to a first innings lead. This was an excellent recovery, for they had lost Ostler to the first ball of the day to decline to 14 for 4.

Essex did not catch well, but they batted with great determination and considerable panache in their second innings. Gooch was at his best, remaining supreme among English batsmen at the age of 43. He hit the 127th century of his first-class career, so moving ahead of W.G. Grace in the elite band of those who had scored a hundred hundreds. The pitch had eased and Warwickshire emulated Essex in not accepting the chances that were offered, but Gooch batted with majestic authority. Prichard hit a six and 11 fours in a most welcome century, for his form had been miserable for much of the summer, and Irani played a typically ebullient innings which enabled Prichard to declare and set his bowlers the task of dismissing Warwickshire in 17 overs and a day. They did not fail him. They captured three wickets before the close, and the game was over just after lunch on the fourth day with Williams and Such in starring roles.

Vasbert Drakes rescued Sussex from the depths of 93 for 6 with a gloriously attacking maiden first-class century. His 103 came off 134 balls. Law captured the wickets of Weston and Hick before the end of the first day, but Worcestershire raced to 109. On the second day, Leatherdale and Rhodes put the home side in total command with a sixth wicket stand of 219. Both batsmen reached centuries. For Leatherdale, it was the first in two years; for Rhodes, the first in three. The third day saw Sussex plunge to their eighth defeat in a strife-ridden summer. They faced total humiliation when spiritless batting on a blameless pitch took them to 72 for 8. Law hit 75 off 45 balls before he was caught off Sheriyar, who finished with his best bowling figures in the championship.

So, with each county having two matches to play, Leicestershire had 248 points, Surrey 247, Derbyshire 242, Essex 241 and Kent 233. The finish promised to be one of the tightest in the history of the championship, but Leicestershire had the edge and looked the most competent and best equipped side.

12, 13, 14 and 16 September

at Derby

Derbyshire 242 (C.J. Adams 80) and 255 (T.J.G. O'Gorman 66)
Warwickshire 231 (N.V. Knight 54, P.A.J. DeFreitas 7 for 101) and 270 for 6 (T.L. Penney 83 not out, A.F. Giles 67 not out)
Warwickshire won by 4 wickets
Warwickshire 21 pts, Derbyshire 5 pts

at Chester-le-Street

Durham 126 (P.V. Simmons 6 for 14) and 139 (A.D. Mullally 5 for 27, V.J. Wells 4 for 44)
Leicestershire 516 for 6 dec. (P.V. Simmons 171, P.A. Nixon 103 not out, D.L. Maddy 82, B.F. Smith 70)
Leicestershire won by an innings and 251 runs
Leicestershire 24 pts, Durham 2 pts

at Chelmsford
Sussex 363 (A.P. Wells 122, I.D.K. Salisbury 70, N.J. Lenham 55) and 417 for 8 dec. (V.C. Drakes 145 not out, C.W.J. Athey 74, P.M. Such 4 for 149)
Essex 360 (G.A. Gooch 82, S.G. Law 64, R.J. Kirtley 4 for 94) and 283 (R.J. Rollins 59, I.D.K. Salisbury 8 for 75)
Sussex won by 137 runs
Sussex 24 pts, Essex 8 pts

at Cardiff
Glamorgan 364 (A. Dale 90, M.P. Maynard 82) and 442 for 9 dec. (S.P. James 131, P.A. Cottey 83, A.D. Shaw 74)
Surrey 471 (N. Shahid 79, G.P. Thorpe 77, M.P. Bicknell 59 not out, C.C. Lewis 57, A.J. Hollioake 51, D.A. Cosker 4 for 142) and 205 for 7 (A.J. Hollioake 85)
Match drawn
Surrey 11 pts, Glamorgan 9 pts

at Canterbury
Kent 445 (N.J. Llong, C.L. Hooper 84, T.R. Ward 79, M.A. Ealham 74, J.P. Stephenson 5 for 104) and 211 (S.A. Marsh 55, S.J. Renshaw 4 for 75)
Hampshire 358 (J.S. Laney 105, R.A. Smith 60, A.N. Aymes 52, D.W. Headley 5 for 83, M.A. Ealham 4 for 73) and 150 (G.W. White 66, P.R. Whitaker 53, M.J. McCague 6 for 51)
Kent won by 148 runs
Kent 24 pts, Hampshire 5 pts

at Uxbridge
Somerset 485 (P.C.L. Holloway 168, R.J. Turner 75, K.A. Parsons 72) and 258 for 3 dec. (P.C.L. Holloway 90 not out, K.A. Parsons 83 not out)
Middlesex 350 for 3 dec. (P.N. Weekes 171 not out, O.A. Shah 75, K.R. Brown 56 not out) and 357 for 8 (P.N. Weekes 160, M.R. Ramprakash 110)
Match drawn
Middlesex 9 pts, Somerset 7 pts

at Northampton
Lancashire 356 (J.E.R. Gallian 113, K.J. Innes 4 for 61, J.P. Taylor 4 for 73) and 275 (G.D. Lloyd 70, J.P. Crawley 58, J.P. Taylor 4 for 72, J.N. Snape 4 for 102)
Northamptonshire 471 (K.M. Curran 93, M.B. Loye 90, K.J. Innes 63, T.C. Walton 52, R.J. Green 4 for 78) and 163 for 1 (R.J. Bailey 92 not out, M.B. Loye 67 not out)
Northamptonshire won by 9 wickets
Northamptonshire 24 pts, Lancashire 7 pts

at Worcester
Gloucestershire 334 (M.W. Alleyne 149, M.A. Lynch 70, T.M. Moody 6 for 67) and 292 (M.A. Lynch 72, R.C. Russell 50 not out, T.M. Moody 7 for 92)
Worcestershire 319 (D.A. Leatherdale 70, G.A. Hick 54, C.A. Walsh 5 for 64) and 311 for 5 (G.A. Hick 106, W.P.C. Weston 89)
Worcestershire won by 5 wickets
Worcestershire 23 pts, Gloucestershire 7 pts

at Scarborough
Nottinghamshire 187 and 117 (D.A. Gough 6 for 36)
Yorkshire 310 (A. McGrath 63, D. Byas 56, C.L. Cairns 6 for 110)
Yorkshire won by an innings and 6 runs
Yorkshire 23 pts, Nottinghamshire 4 pts

Derbyshire's last hopes of championship glory disappeared when they were beaten inside three days by Warwickshire. Andy Harris, the pace bowler who had enjoyed such a successful season and who had earned a place in the England 'A' party, was awarded his county cap before the start of the match. He celebrated with the wicket of Moles, but that was after Derbyshire had been put in and bowled out in 69.5 overs. The only batsman to show form was Chris Adams, but he had been doing that all season, a fact which the selectors overlooked. He is a wonderfully talented and entertaining batsman and a fine fielder, and it would be criminal to ignore what he could offer in England.

Dismissed for 242, Derbyshire fought back to take five Warwickshire wickets for 131 before the close. A last wicket stand of 62 between Welch and Munton thwarted the home side on the second day, but they had a narrow first innings lead thanks to Phil DeFreitas returning his best figures for the county. The pitch was growing no easier, however, and Derbyshire finished the day with six wickets down and a lead of exactly 200.

As with Warwickshire, Derbyshire were boosted by the later batsmen, DeFreitas, Cork, bravely scoring 23 although batting with a broken bone in his left arm which prevented him from bowling, and Krikken, a rapidly improving and most valuable number seven or eight. Warwickshire needed 267 to win, but, at 141 for 6, they looked beaten. Giles then joined Penney. In the closing weeks of the season, Giles had shown that he was a most capable batsman as well as a left-arm spinner pressing for international recognition. He displayed his talent yet again, and he and Penney, admirably composed and stylish, added 129 and took Warwickshire to victory.

Derbyshire need not feel too despondent. Under Dean Jones they had become a formidable side, and the emergence of a quality spinner would make them real championship contenders.

There seemed little doubt as to which side was best equipped to win the 1996. With a potent attack of pace and spin well supported in the field, batting that brought runs quickly and surely, total team commitment and enthusiastic leadership, Leicestershire put one hand on the pennant when they crushed Durham in two days. Roseberry had relinquished the Durham captaincy and, with vice-captain Morris totally out of form, Simon Brown had been persuaded to lead the side until the end of the season. David Boon, the former Australian Test player and captain of Tasmania, had been recruited for 1997. Perhaps one of the first things Boon will do will be to bring some sanity and stability into selection. Cox was again omitted, and another seamer, 17-year-old Harmison, was rushed into the side.

Captain supreme – James Whitaker led Leicestershire to the Britannic Assurance County Championship. Whitaker led by example with the bat and intelligently in the field.
(Paul Sturgess/Sportsline)

Durham collapse against weak bowling, so it was no surprise when they disintegrated against the Leicestershire attack. Ten wickets fell for 76 runs, and Simmons, a genuine all-rounder now, took 6 for 14 in 9.3 overs. He tore out the middle order as Durham went from 91 for 2 to 101 for 9.

A second wicket stand of 148 between Maddy and Smith, two fine young players, took Leicestershire to 209 before they lost their second wicket. Four wickets fell for 23 runs, and then Simmons arrived. He was unbeaten on 28 at the start of the second day, and Leicestershire were 253 for 5. He and Nixon extended their partnership to a record 284. The pair battered the Durham bowling, and their runs came in 53 overs, 199 came in the morning session. Simmons hit 23 fours and two sixes and faced 170 balls; Nixon faced 168 balls. Leicestershire's 516 came from less than 100 overs. Nixon, who should surely have been chosen for the England 'A' tour, took catches as Durham drowned again, with Wells and Mullally their principal executioners.

Essex followed their traumatic experience in the NatWest Final with defeat at home to Sussex and an end to their title hopes. They lost the toss and laboured to dismiss Sussex. Wells hit his highest score of the season, and Salisbury and Phillips took Sussex into the second day. On a wicket that was showing signs of wear and offering help to the spinners, Essex went for quick runs and took a small lead as they claimed their four batting points, but Gooch and Law fell to poor shots after threatening to dominate the bowling, and it was Cowan and Such in a ninth wicket stand of 52 who made the last two points possible.

The Saturday was not a happy day for Essex. They toiled but suddenly captured three wickets as Sussex went from 154 for 1 to 169 for 4. Drakes then joined Wells in a stand which brought 106 runs in 38 overs, but it was shot with controversy. When he had scored 10, Drakes appeared to have been caught bat and pad by Cowan off Law, who was bowling leg spin. Cowan was fielding in the gully. Drakes stood his ground, and umpire Whitehead did not raise his finger. Law and Prichard reacted angrily, and heated words were exchanged. Thereafter Essex's hopes died. Drakes, his second forceful century in successive matches, and Phillips took their ninth wicket partnership into the last morning, and when the declaration came it was worth 90.

Essex faced a target of 421 in 86 overs. They had to attempt to win and raced off at seven an over, but, at 167, Law, Prichard and Irani were all dismissed. Salisbury went on to take a career-best 8 for 75, and Essex were out of the running for the championship. In truth, they never looked to be a side good enough to lift the title. Their attack so often seemed incapable of finishing off opponents when they had them down, and they had played some gruesome cricket in mid-season. The tail was woefully long, and one questioned why Andrew was chosen and bowled so little instead of the batting being strengthened and Irani trusted as third seamer.

Surrey's flame, too, was virtually extinguished. They, too, lost the toss and saw Matthew Maynard, who had a good first year as captain, lead Glamorgan to 361 for 9 on the opening day. His own contribution was 82 off 120 balls with 13 boundaries, and there was an excellent innings from Dale who hit 10 fours and batted for three hours. He was regaining his best form late in the season.

Surrey lost both openers before lunch on the second day and Stewart was run out. Shahid and Thorpe repaired the innings, but runs came slowly. Starting the third day at 273 for 3, Surrey pressed for quick runs and the essential fourth point. They had only 19 overs in which to make the necessary 77 runs, and they launched an attack on the bowling which brought 198 off 37 overs. Chris Lewis hit 59 off 44 balls, and Surrey's star was ascending.

Glamorgan lost three wickets in clearing the first innings arrears, but on Saturday evening, with James and Cottey well set, they were 218 for 3, 111 runs ahead.

Alan Mullally bowls Peter Wellings and Leicestershire are on their way to victory over Middlesex and to winning the championship. (David Munden/Sportsline)

The home county batsmen continued to dominate on the last day, and Stewart erred in offering 'friendly' bowling in an attempt to buy a declaration. He was unlikely to be given a reachable target by Maynard in view of the context of the match and of Surrey's decision to extend their first innings. So it proved. Glamorgan asked Surrey to score 336 in 37 overs. There were some bizarre adjustments to the batting order, and ultimately Surrey were thankful to draw.

Kent continued to live in hope with a remarkable victory over Hampshire at Canterbury. Hooper and Llong pounded the visiting attack on the opening day with Llong hitting his second century of the summer. Hampshire had dropped catches on the first day; Kent spilled them on the second. Laney, rapidly maturing into a fine opening batsman, hit his second century in successive championship matches, and Hampshire reached 249 for 5. The drama began on the Saturday. Desperate for maximum bowling points, Kent reached the 119th over still two short of their target. Dean Headley then had Stephenson caught at third man and with his next two deliveries he had both Bovill and Renshaw leg before. This gave him his third hat-track of the summer and an equal share in a world record of three in a season.

Pressing for quick runs, Kent were undermined by the bowling of Renshaw, Stephenson and Mascarenhas, as impressive in his second match as he had been in his first. Hampshire had the last day in which to score 299 to win. At 143 for 1 shortly after lunch, Hampshire were strolling to victory. At this point, McCague, who had bowled very quickly and very well for much of the season, knocked back Whitaker's off stump. Almost immediately, McCague had Smith caught behind. The crunch came when the fast bowler dismissed Kendall, Aymes and Mascarenhas with successive deliveries to complete the second hat-trick of the match. With Fleming also bowling admirably to take 3 for 6 from 4.3 overs, the last eight Hampshire wickets went down in 44 balls for seven runs. Stephenson was unable to bat because of injury.

Uxbridge is renowned as a bowler's graveyard, and it lived up to its reputation. The match between Middlesex and Somerset produced 1450 runs for 24 wickets. There were four centuries. Piran Holloway hit the highest score of this career, as did Paul Weekes, who hit a century in each innings for the first time in his career. Set 411 to win, Middlesex began well with Weekes and Pooley scoring a hundred. Weekes and Ramprakash then added 197, but a clatter of wickets followed in the stampede for runs, and the match was drawn.

At the foot of the table, Northamptonshire showed commendable zeal in beating Lancashire. Gallian grafted a century on the opening day. Northamptonshire displayed consistency and commitment in taking the lead on the second. Lancashire showed little stomach for the fight with Watkinson's place as captain under ever-increasing pressure. On the last afternoon, Rob Bailey hit 92 off 99 balls to take his side to victory before tea.

At New Road, Mark Alleyne hit his first century of the season and Monte Lynch his highest score as Gloucestershire recovered from 37 for 4. Worcestershire, inevitably tormented by Walsh, showed consistency on the second day, and only 15 runs separated the sides on the first innings. Skipper Tom Moody had returned his best bowling figures for Worcestershire in the first innings, and he now bettered those figures in the second. Needing 308 in 81 overs to win, Worcestershire were indebted to Hick and Weston who shared a second wicket stand of 201. Hick hit 18 fours to sign off with a century in a season he would rather forget.

Nottinghamshire offered threadbare opposition to Yorkshire and were beaten in two days. Yorkshire ended the first day just 24 runs short of the visitors with eight wickets standing. Cairns bowled well, and Yorkshire did not bat particularly well but still took a first innings lead of 123 on the Friday. The Yorkshire batting, though, was vintage stuff as opposed to the dross that Nottinghamshire produced at their second attempt. Their last nine wickets went down for 56 runs with Gough showing fire and determination as he claimed six wickets.

19, 20, 21 and 22 September

at Derby
Durham 142 (P.A.J. DeFreitas 5 for 60) and 332 (D.M. Cox 91, S. Hutton 86, P.A.J. DeFreitas 4 for 54)
Derbyshire 256 (C.J. Adams 81, D.M. Jones 77, M.M. Betts 4 for 69) and 220 for 2 (D.M. Jones 71 not out, A.S. Rollins 69 not out, C.J. Adams 64)
Derbyshire won by 8 wickets
Derbyshire 22 pts, Durham 4 pts

at Chelmsford
Essex 367 (G.A. Gooch 170 retired not out, N. Hussain 68, S.G. Law 66, A. Dale 4 for 52, S.L. Watkin 4 for 64) and 259 for 9 dec. (N. Hussain 64, D.A. Cosker 4 for 66)
Glamorgan 353 for 6 dec. (M.P. Maynard 122, D.L. Hemp 95, P.A. Cottey 69 not out) and 284 for 3 (H. Morris 149, S.P. James 78)
Glamorgan won by 7 wickets
Glamorgan 24 pts, Essex 6 pts

at Bristol
Kent 154 (T.R. Ward 86, C.A. Walsh 4 for 50) and 117 (C.A. Walsh 4 for 21)
Gloucestershire 241 (M.A. Lynch 54, D.W. Headley 4 for 65) and 33 for 0
Gloucestershire won by 10 wickets
Gloucestershire 21 pts, Kent 4 pts

at Southampton
Hampshire 513 for 4 dec. (R.A. Smith 161, W.S. Kendall 103 not out, J.S. Laney 97, G.W. White 73) and 181 for 5 dec. (G.W. White 53)
Nottinghamshire 391 for 4 dec. (G.F. Archer 120, P. Johnson 109, U. Afzaal 67 not out) and 152 for 5 (G.F. Archer 63)
Match drawn
Hampshire 8 pts, Nottinghamshire 8 pts

at Leicester
Middlesex 190 (M.R. Ramprakash 71, A.D. Mullally 4 for 53) and 248 (M.R. Ramprakash 78, D.J. Millns 4 for 48)
Leicestershire 512 (P.V. Simmons 142 not out, J.J. Whitaker 89, A.D. Mullally 75, R.A. Fay 4 for 140)
Leicestershire won by an innings and 74 runs
Leicestershire 24 pts, Middlesex 4 pts

at Northampton
Yorkshire 478 (M.P. Vaughan 183, C. White 66, M.D. Moxon 57, A.L. Penberthy 5 for 92)
Northamptonshire 222 and 531 for 4 (M.B. Loye 205, R.R. Montgomerie 127, R.J. Bailey 61 not out, T.C. Walton 58)
Match drawn
Yorkshire 11 pts, Northamptonshire 6 pts

at The Oval
Worcestershire 362 (V.S. Solanki 90, K.R. Spiring 63, T.M. Moody 60) and 61 for 1 dec.
Surrey 0 for 0 dec. and 299 (D.J. Bicknell 129 not out, B.P. Julian 80)
Worcestershire won by 124 runs
Worcestershire 20 pts, Surrey 4 pts

at Hove
Sussex 141 (A.R. Caddick 5 for 58, S. Lee 4 for 52) and 270 (N.J. Lenham 64, C.W.J. Athey 57, A.R. Caddick 5 for 122)
Somerset 354 (S. Lee 126, R.J. Harden 78, M.N. Lathwell 56, I.D.K. Salisbury 5 for 91) and 60 for 2
Somerset won by 8 wickets
Somerset 24 pts, Sussex 4 pts

at Edgbaston
Warwickshire 386 (A.F. Giles 106 not out, N.M.K. Smith 74, M. Burns 61, G. Chapple 4 for 85) and 359 for 6 (N.V. Knight 103, T.L. Penney 70 not out, A.J. Mole 59)
Lancashire 597 (N.H. Fairbrother 204, G.D. Lloyd 113, J.P. Crawley 73, P.C. McKeown 64, A.F. Giles 4 for 165)
Match drawn
Lancashire 11 pts, Warwickshire 9 pts

Leicestershire duly won the county championship for the second time in their history. At first there was a sense of anti-climax about their success, but in the end it was an emphatic triumph for a joyous team who play their cricket with infectious enthusiasm and commitment and who are ever supportive of each other. They bowled out Middlesex for 190 on a shortened first day after the visitors had elected to bat first.

Phil Simmons drinks deep from the cup he did so much to win. (David Munden/Sportsline)

Gatting began the second day keeping wicket and, when Brown took over after receiving treatment, the Middlesex captain was involved in controversy when he sanctioned Tufnell bowling left-arm over the wicket and pitching outside leg stump with wicket-keeper Brown positioning himself some two feet outside the leg stump to take the ball. It could be no more than a minor irritant, although it was not an action within the spirit of the game. With Whitaker and Habib sharing a fourth wicket stand of 138 and Simmons and Millns adding a spirited 90 for the seventh wicket, Leicestershire accomplished the first part of their mission in taking maximum bonus points.

Middlesex suffered the ultimate indignity on the Saturday when Simmons and Mullally, an old-fashioned number eleven, scored 112 in 13 overs for the last wicket. Mullally's rustic batting brought him a career-best 75 from 47 balls. Simmons, 95 overnight, reached his fourth century of the summer and his contribution to Leicestershire with bat and ball over the last testing weeks of the campaign was immeasurable. It was he who broke a threatening second wicket stand of 105 between Wellings and Ramprakash, and by Saturday afternoon Leicestershire knew they were champions, for Surrey had forfeited their first innings against Worcestershire at The Oval. On the Sunday, Leicestershire completed their innings victory over Middlesex and claimed the championship by their own might. The title had gone to the county who had played the best cricket throughout the season, and that is as it should be.

Surrey never had a realistic chance of catching Leicestershire, and all hope went when there was no play on the first day and little on the second at The Oval. Worcestershire's young batsmen gave further evidence of good things to come. Stewart's decision to forfeit the first innings was an acceptance that the best that could be hoped for was runners-up place, but the Saturday evening was incomprehensible as Worcestershire scored 61 in 31 overs of mostly 'friendly' bowling before setting a target of 424. Surrey never looked like getting the runs, and the comfort came in the fact that Darren Bicknell carried his bat through the innings and Julian hit 80 off 86 in an eighth wicket stand of 141. David Gilbert has done an excellent job at The Oval, but the jigsaw is not yet complete, and he and the new chief executive, Mr Sheldon, are surely putting the club on the right basis after some trouble years.

Derbyshire took second place, deservedly, beating the hapless Durham in three days. Stewart Hutton played another useful innings, and there were more fireworks from David Cox, but Durham must have looked at what Dean Jones had achieved at Derby and wondered why he was not still in the north-east.

Somerset, too, won in three days with Shane Lee signing off with another blazing century. The chastening thought is that he is unlikely to make the Australian party that tours England next summer. Caddick had 10 wickets in the match, and Sussex could point to the fact that they have some very promising bowlers. If they could find some batting stability, their problems would be fewer.

Gloucestershire, spearheaded as ever by Walsh, demolished Kent in three days, but Kent, having risen from 18th to fourth, could be well satisfied with their season. The same could be said of Yorkshire who have young players who could well bring back the glory days. They were thwarted on the last at Northampton by Mal Loye and Richard Montgomerie, whose 372 in 101 overs was the highest opening stand of the season and a record for Northamptonshire. Loye's double hundred was the first of his career and came off 296 balls.

Edgbaston produced one of those matches in which there was a double century, three centuries and six fifties as well as 67 extras in Lancashire's innings. In all, there were 1342 runs for 26 wickets. The most noteworthy performance in the match was probably Ashley Giles' maiden century. It came off 133 balls and included a six and 16 fours, and Giles had been threatening it for some weeks. His advance as batsman and bowler has been so rapid that it is hard to believe he is only 23.

Another young player to confirm his continued development was Laney, who put on 147 for Hampshire's first wicket with White and 156 for the third wicket with Robin Smith, who was in dominant form. Smith hit 28 fours in his innings, and Will Kendall 21 in his first championship hundred. Hampshire's innings occupied the first two days, and on the third, Nottinghamshire made 391 for 34 in 100 overs with Archer and Johnson sharing a fourth wicket stand of 157. The last day on which neither side seemed to aim for victory is best forgotten. Hampshire are building, but it is difficult to see where Nottinghamshire cricket is going.

Graham Gooch remained the leading batsman in the country, hitting 170 on the second day at Chelmsford before temporarily retiring to take his father to hospital. Unfortunately, when he returned he found his side had been dismissed, six wickets falling for 21 runs. Maynard asserted Glamorgan's position with his sixth hundred of the summer which included 17 fours. He faced 150 balls for his 122 and was as entertaining as ever. He and Hemp, restored to fitness, added 222 for the third wicket, and Glamorgan claimed four batting points in 88 overs. To keep hopes alive of earning £30,000 for finishing in second place, Essex had to score quickly and set the visitors a target, which turned out to be 284 in two sessions. James and Morris scored 199 for the first wicket and virtually settled the issue. The Essex bowling needs more fire and the batting more depth. Glamorgan have recruited Waqar Younis for 1997. They have a balanced and keen side, and one would not bet against them winning the championship.

Britannic Assurance County Championship – Final table

	P	W	L	D	Bat	Bo	Pts
Leicestershire (7)	17	10	1	6	57	61	296
Derbyshire (14)	17	9	3	5	52	58	269
Surrey (12)	17	8	2	7	49	64	262
Kent (18)	17	9	2	6	47	52	261
Essex (5)	17	8	5	4	58	57	255
Yorkshire (8)	17	8	5	4	50	58	248
Worcestershire (10)	17	6	4	7	45	60	222
Warwickshire (1)	17	7	6	4	39	55	218
Middlesex (2)	17	7	6	4	30	59	213
Glamorgan (16)	17	6	5	6	50	43	207
Somerset (9)	17	5	6	6	36	61	197
Sussex (15)	17	6	9	2	36	58	196
Gloucestershire (6)	17	5	7	5	23	59	177
Hampshire (13)	17	3	7	7	41	56	166
Lancashire (4)	17	2	6	9	49	52	160
Northamptonshire (3)	17	3	8	6	36	57	159
Nottinghamshire (11)	17	1	9	7	42	52	131
Durham (17)	17	–	12	5	22	60	97

(1995 positions in brackets)

Grace Road, the home of the champions, Leicestershire v. Middlesex. (David Munden/Sportsline)

First-Class Averages

Batting

	M	Inns	NO	Runs	HS	Av	100s	50s
M.R. May	3	4	2	160	63*	80.00		1
G.A. Gooch	17	30	1	1944	201	67.03	8	6
A.J Hollioake	17	29	5	1522	129	66.17	5	8
M.G. Bevan	12	22	3	1225	160*	64.47	3	8
G.P. Thorpe	16	29	4	1569	185	62.76	6	7
M.P. Maynard	17	30	4	1610	214	61.92	6	6
S. Lee	17	25	4	1300	167*	61.90	5	5
S.G. Law	15	26	1	1545	172	61.80	6	5
M.J. Walker	8	13	3	606	275*	60.60	1	2
K.M. Curran	15	28	7	1242	150	59.14	2	8
P.V. Simmons	17	24	2	1244	171	56.54	4	7
H. Morris	18	32	2	1666	202*	55.53	6	9
W.S. Kendall	12	23	4	1045	145*	55.00	3	6
J.J. Whitaker	16	23	3	1093	218	54.65	4	2
N.H. Fairbrother	12	20	–	1068	204	53.40	2	8
C.J. Adams	20	36	3	1742	239	52.78	6	8
W.J. House	8	15	5	526	136	52.60	2	2
D.M. Jones	19	34	5	1502	214*	51.79	4	7
M.A. Butcher	18	34	3	1604	160	51.74	3	13
P.A. Cottey	20	36	6	1543	203	51.43	4	9
T.M. Moody	19	31	3	1427	212	50.96	7	4
D.A. Reeve	5	8	1	351	168*	50.14	1	
J.P. Crawley	15	25	3	1102	112*	50.09	3	8
D. Ripley	11	16	7	448	88*	49.77		3
G.D. Lloyd	15	25	1	1194	241	49.75	3	4
M.R. Ramprakash	17	31	2	1441	169	49.68	4	8
I.D. Austin	10	12	3	437	95*	48.55		3
D.M. Cox	7	13	4	434	95*	48.22		4
R.A. Smith	17	31	2	1396	179	48.13	3	8
E.T. Smith	7	12	–	576	101	48.00	2	4
N.V. Knight	15	28	3	1196	132	47.84	4	5
B.F. Smith	20	29	3	1243	190	47.80	3	4
S.P. James	20	38	1	1766	235	47.72	7	6
C.L. Hooper	17	29	2	1287	155	47.66	3	9
C.M. Gupte	11	14	1	606	132	46.61	2	3
A.C. Ridley	7	9	–	417	155	46.33	2	1
N. Hussain	18	31	1	1386	158	46.20	3	7
M.B. Loye	14	25	2	1048	205	45.56	2	5
K.J. Barnett	18	34	2	1456	200*	45.50	3	9
R.T. Robinson	17	31	2	1302	184	44.89	3	6
S.P. Titchard	13	23	2	939	163	44.71	2	5
N.C. Phillips	8	12	7	223	45	44.60		
G.A. Hick	17	29	1	1245	215	44.46	5	3
J.E.R. Gallian	15	29	3	1156	312	44.46	3	3
V.J. Wells	20	30	–	1331	204	44.36	4	3
M. Keech	12	21	3	793	104	44.05	1	7
M.N. Lathwell	18	32	4	1224	109	43.71	2	7
G.F. Archer	13	24	3	918	143	43.71	2	5
M.D. Moxon	14	25	3	961	213	43.68	2	5
W.P.C. Weston	20	37	5	1389	171*	43.40	4	7
T.L. Penney	19	34	4	1295	134	43.16	3	8
A.J. Stewart	14	24	1	966	170	42.00	1	7
T.R. Ward	18	31	1	1252	161	41.73	2	9
K.R. Spiring	18	32	6	1084	144	41.69	3	7
K. Greenfield	14	26	4	916	154*	41.63	3	3
P.D. Bowler	19	34	4	1228	207	40.93	2	7
A.G. Wharf	4	4	1	121	62	40.33		1
K.M. Krikken	19	29	7	882	104	40.09	1	3
A.N. Aymes	19	32	12	801	113	40.05	2	2
D.J. Sales	4	8	1	280	210*	40.00	1	
P.A. Nixon	20	27	5	880	106	40.00	3	4
V.S. Solanki	14	24	3	828	90	39.42		6
C.L. Cairns	16	29	5	946	114	39.41	1	6
S.J. Rhodes	19	29	5	939	110	39.12	1	8
J.S. Laney	17	30	–	1163	112	38.76	4	5
M.P. Vaughan	18	32	2	1161	183	38.70	3	6
M.A. Atherton	15	26	1	963	160	38.52	1	7
R.C. Irani	19	31	4	1039	110*	38.48	1	7
N.J. Llong	14	22	2	763	130	38.15	2	5
C.M. Wells	12	19	3	609	165	38.06	1	3
R.R. Montgomerie	18	34	3	1178	168	38.00	4	4
G.A. Khan	13	18	2	608	101*	38.00	1	4
V.P. Terry	7	12	2	379	87*	37.90		3
A. Symonds	18	30	1	1097	127	37.82	3	4
A.W. Evans	7	13	3	376	71*	37.60		2
W.K. Hegg	17	25	6	713	134	37.52	1	3
T.J.G. O'Gorman	11	20	3	636	109*	37.41	1	6
O.D. Gibson	9	15	3	449	97	37.41		3
I.J. Sutcliffe	8	12	–	443	83	36.91		5

Batting

	M	Inns	NO	Runs	HS	Av	100s	50s
P.N. Weekes	19	35	2	1218	171*	36.90	4	4
D.L. Hemp	8	13	2	405	103*	36.81	1	1
A.P. Wells	19	35	2	1206	122	36.54	2	6
D.J. Roberts	4	7	–	254	73	36.28		2
B.P. Julian	16	23	2	759	119	36.14	2	3
A.J. Moles	13	25	–	903	176	36.12	2	4
N.J. Lenham	16	28	3	903	145	36.12	2	5
R.J. Bailey	12	22	2	722	163	36.10	1	3
M.W. Gatting	16	25	–	901	171	36.04	1	8
A. Habib	16	24	2	792	215	36.00	1	2
A. Singh	12	22	2	718	157	35.90	2	1
S.L. Campbell	16	29	–	1041	118	35.89	1	7
P.C.L. Holloway	10	16	1	535	168	35.66	1	3
R.J. Harden	12	20	1	676	136	35.57	1	5
A.S. Rollins	19	36	5	1101	131	35.51	3	5
K.R. Brown	18	31	5	917	83	35.26		8
D.D.J. Robinson	12	23	2	738	97	35.14		8
A.A. Metcalfe	12	22	–	771	128	35.04	1	3
W.K.M. Benjamin	2	4	–	140	117	35.00	1	
R.J. Blakey	19	30	6	839	109*	34.95	1	5
A.P. Grayson	17	30	3	939	140	34.77	2	3
D.J. Bicknell	17	31	3	969	129*	34.60	2	3
A.J.E. Hibbert	2	4	1	103	85	34.33		1
R.C. Russell	19	30	5	858	124	34.32	1	7
P. Bainbridge	11	19	1	617	83	34.27		5
D.L. Maddy	20	30	2	958	101*	34.21	1	4
R.A. Kettleborough	7	9	–	307	108	34.11	1	1
N.J. Speak	12	21	4	579	138*	34.05	1	3
G.P. Butcher	14	24	4	679	89	33.95		5
D.G. Cork	18	29	6	779	101*	33.86	1	5
P.E. Wellings	4	8	1	237	48	33.85		
S. Hutton	14	26	2	812	172*	33.83	2	1
D.A. Leatherdale	11	18	2	539	122	33.68	1	4
T.C. Walton	6	10	1	302	58	33.55		4
K.D. James	13	23	1	738	118*	33.54	2	3
A. Fordham	10	18	3	502	144*	33.46	1	2
N. Shahid	11	19	3	535	101	33.43	1	4
A.F. Giles	17	27	9	600	106*	33.33	1	4
J.E. Owen	9	15	–	499	105	33.26	2	2
C.W.J. Athey	18	33	–	1091	111	33.06	3	5
J.D. Ratcliffe	9	16	1	494	69	32.93		4
M.W. Alleyne	18	30	3	887	149	32.85	1	3
T.S. Curtis	17	31	2	952	118	32.82	2	5
C. White	19	30	1	949	181	32.72	1	7
R.Q. Cake	9	16	3	425	102*	32.69	1	1
M.A. Ealham	14	23	4	618	74	32.52		5
R.K. Illingworth	19	23	10	420	66*	32.30		1
A. McGrath	19	33	2	999	137	32.22	2	5
K.P. Evans	14	18	3	482	71	32.13		4
P.R. Pollard	13	25	2	737	86	32.04		6
C.C. Lewis	14	22	2	639	94	31.95		4
R.J. Turner	18	27	6	668	100*	31.80	1	3
P. Johnson	19	33	2	980	109	31.61	2	6
D.P. Fulton	17	30	3	852	134*	31.55	1	5
G.R. Cowdrey	11	17	–	529	111	31.11	1	3
D. Byas	19	32	2	933	138	31.10	1	5
G.W. White	13	24	3	652	73	31.04		6
P.J. Prichard	19	31	–	959	108	30.93	1	6
M.A. Lynch	11	19	1	553	72	30.72		5
M.V. Fleming	18	30	2	855	116	30.53	2	3
S.M. Pollock	13	21	1	606	150*	30.30	2	1
J.N. Batty	10	13	3	302	56	30.20		2
S.R. Lampitt	19	27	5	658	88	29.90		3
D.P. Ostler	18	32	3	863	90	29.75		8
T.H.C. Hancock	15	27	3	709	116	29.54	1	4
M.G.N. Windows	9	17	2	443	184	29.53	1	1
T.A. Munton	12	15	9	177	54*	29.50		2
J.I.D. Kerr	6	9	3	176	68*	29.33		2
U. Afzaal	6	10	1	264	67*	29.33		2
K. Newell	5	9	1	234	105*	29.25	1	
K.A. Parsons	8	15	1	408	83*	29.14		4
D.J. Capel	16	30	2	814	103	29.07	1	4
J.D. Carr	17	28	1	783	94	29.00		4
A. Dale	15	25	1	690	120	28.75	1	4
R.J. Warren	11	18	1	486	201*	28.58	1	1
R.M. Pearson	14	14	9	142	37	28.40		
J.P. Hewitt	10	15	4	312	72	28.36		1
S.C. Willis	5	6	1	141	78	28.20		1
P.R. Whitaker	12	22	3	535	67*	28.15		4

First-Class Averages (continued)

Batting

	M	Inns	NO	Runs	HS	Av	100s	50s
P. Moores	19	32	4	782	185	27.92	2	1
S.C. Ecclestone	8	13	1	334	94	27.83		3
M.E. Trescothick	15	26	–	720	178	27.69	1	2
J.C. Pooley	18	34	2	881	138*	27.53	2	4
W.G. Khan	18	28	1	738	130	27.33	3	2
N.M.K. Smith	16	27	4	626	74	27.21		3
M.P. Speight	11	21	2	514	122*	27.05	1	3
V.C. Drakes	15	27	3	649	145*	27.04	2	4
R.D.B. Croft	20	30	6	647	78	26.95		5
M.A. Roseberry	17	30	2	744	145*	26.57	1	3
J.P. Stephenson	15	25	2	611	85	26.56		5
O.A. Shah	5	9	1	212	75	26.50		2
J.A. Daley	12	21	3	477	76	26.50		1
J.J.B. Lewis	6	11	2	238	69	26.44		2
T.A. Tweats	4	7	2	130	89*	26.00		1
M.P. Bicknell	16	18	5	333	59*	25.61		1
C.M. Tolley	9	14	2	306	67	25.50		1
G.D. Rose	15	21	5	408	93*	25.50		2
M.J. Church	6	11	–	280	152	25.45	1	
A.R. Whittall	7	6	1	127	36	25.40		
A.L. Penberthy	18	29	4	635	87	25.40		3
J.W. Hall	7	13	–	330	93	25.38		3
R.J. Maru	11	17	5	303	55*	25.25		1
N.J. Haste	6	6	2	101	51*	25.25		1
G.J. Kersey	15	20	4	402	68*	25.12		3
A.J. Swann	3	5	1	100	76*	25.00		1
M. Burns	8	15	1	345	81	24.64		3
A.J. Wright	9	17	–	415	106	24.41	1	3
A.D. Brown	16	26	3	555	79	24.13		5
M.P. Dowman	9	14	–	337	107	24.07	1	
H.S. Malik	10	13	3	240	61	24.00		1
R.J. Rollins	21	34	4	719	74*	23.96		
M. Watkinson	17	28	1	645	64	23.88		2
D.R. Hewson	6	12	1	261	87	23.72		3
S.D. Peters	4	7	1	142	110	23.66	1	
P.J. Newport	6	6	–	142	68	23.66		1
P.W. Jarvis	8	11	4	164	35	23.42		
D.A. Blenkiron	9	16	2	328	130	23.42	2	
P.D. Collingwood	11	20	–	464	91	23.20		2
C.W. Scott	7	10	1	208	59	23.11		2
R.J. Cunliffe	6	11	–	252	82	22.90		2
D. Gough	16	25	3	501	121	22.77	1	2
M.J. Powell	4	8	–	182	39	22.75		
P.J. Hartley	16	24	3	476	89	22.66		3
D.R. Brown	19	32	2	671	76	22.36		3
D.J. Millns	19	20	1	424	103	22.31	1	1
J.E. Emburey	11	13	4	200	67*	22.22		1
D.R. Law	17	28	–	619	97	22.10		3
R.S.M. Morris	5	9	–	195	112	21.66	1	
K.J. Innes	4	5	–	108	63	21.50		1
K.J. Piper	13	22	2	429	82	21.45		1
J.N. Snape	10	16	3	277	64	21.30		1
S.D. Udal	17	25	4	447	58	21.28		2
A.C. Morris	6	9	–	189	60	21.00		1
I.D.K. Salisbury	18	30	3	562	83	20.81		3
S.A. Marsh	15	24	1	478	127	20.78	1	2
A.D. Mullally	17	17	5	249	75	20.75		2
S. Elworthy	12	16	2	288	88	20.57		1
D.G.C. Ligertwood	12	23	5	367	56	20.38		1
A.R.K. Pierson	20	23	10	263	44	20.23		
N.J. Trainor	8	14	1	261	67	20.07		2
P.J. Deakin	6	9	4	100	24*	20.00		
P.J. Martin	13	18	4	278	42	19.85		
M.A. Wagh	11	13	3	198	43	19.80		
D.W. Headley	12	16	3	253	63*	19.46		1
G. Chapple	16	23	6	329	37*	19.35		
M.J. McCague	18	26	7	357	63*	18.78		1
A.N. Hayhurst	9	13	1	224	96	18.66		2
W.M. Noon	13	21	3	332	57	18.44		1
G.I. Macmillan	7	12	1	201	41	18.27		
P.C.R. Tufnell	18	26	10	290	67*	18.12		1
J.C. Harrison	7	13	2	199	40	18.09		
S.M. Milburn	10	12	2	180	54*	18.00		1
P.A.J. DeFreitas	14	22	–	394	60	17.90		1
J.E. Benjamin	13	14	6	141	38*	17.62		
A.R. Roberts	6	8	–	141	39	17.62		
M.J. Vandrau	10	16	6	175	34*	17.50		
R.D. Stemp	19	24	9	260	65	17.33		2
J.P. Taylor	17	23	9	242	57	17.28		1

Batting

	M	Inns	NO	Runs	HS	Av	100s	50s
M.M. Betts	14	21	3	308	57*	17.11		1
R.O. Jones	8	13	1	205	61	17.08		1
N.F. Williams	12	16	3	221	39	17.00		
R.C.J. Williams	5	8	–	133	44	16.62		
A.M. Smith	16	25	3	364	55*	16.54		1
A.D. Shaw	13	18	1	281	74	16.52		2
R.T. Bates	11	15	1	229	34	16.35		
G.J. Parsons	18	23	5	290	53	16.11		2
J.D. Batty	16	24	4	321	44	16.05		
P.M. Such	19	22	11	176	54	16.00		1
M.C. Ilott	17	24	2	343	58	15.59		1
C.A. Connor	10	12	3	140	42	15.55		
S.J.E. Brown	19	31	5	404	60	15.53		1
M.M. Patel	18	23	5	278	33	15.44		
R.P. Davis	15	22	2	308	43	15.40		
S.D. Thomas	11	16	3	199	48	15.30		
J.E. Morris	17	31	1	429	83	14.30		
C.A. Walsh	15	24	13	154	25	14.00		
M.C.J. Ball	13	21	4	236	46	13.88		
A.P. Cowan	15	20	6	188	34	13.42		
A.R. Caddick	15	20	5	199	38	13.26		
G. Welch	13	17	1	210	45	13.12		
R.L. Johnson	11	20	1	243	37*	12.78		
R.T. Ragnauth	6	11	1	121	29	12.10		
R.I. Dawson	7	13	1	141	21	11.75		
J.D. Lewry	10	15	3	138	28*	11.50		
C.E.W. Silverwood	16	24	6	198	45*	11.00		
K.J. Shine	12	15	4	121	40	11.00		
S.L. Watkin	18	20	6	153	34	10.92		
A.R.C. Fraser	18	28	6	238	33	10.81		
M.N. Bowen	13	18	2	173	22	10.81		
C.E.L. Ambrose	9	13	2	116	25*	10.54		

(Qualification: 100 runs, average 10.00)
(G. Salmond 0 & 181; I.L. Philip 2 & 110; J.G. Williamson 49 & 55)

Bowling

	Overs	Mds	Runs	Wks	Av	Best	10/m	5/inn
C.E.L. Ambrose	284.4	80	717	43	16.67	6/26	1	5
C.A. Walsh	526.3	145	1432	85	16.84	6/22	1	7
P.V. Simmons	364.4	87	1021	56	18.23	6/14		3
D.A. Mascarenhas	52	21	297	16	18.56	6/88		1
M.A. Ealham	401.4	130	995	47	21.17	8/36	1	3
C.A. Connor	362.4	99	1071	49	21.85	9/38		2
P.C.R. Tufnell	839.1	273	1712	78	21.94	7/49	1	6
N.J. Llong	80.5	23	249	11	22.63	5/21		1
D. Gough	573.3	142	1535	67	22.91	6/36		2
J.D. Lewry	302	59	942	41	22.97	6/44	1	4
D.J. Bicknell	124.2	21	368	16	23.00	3/7		
D.J. Millns	538.1	133	1659	72	23.04	6/54	1	2
S. Lugsden	70.3	9	262	11	23.81	3/45		
G.D. Rose	393.2	98	1218	50	24.36	7/47	1	3
M.W. Alleyne	458.1	123	1316	54	24.37	5/32		2
M.P. Bicknell	568.1	146	1633	66	24.74	5/17		3
M.J. McCague	590	120	1897	76	24.96	6/51		3
E.S.H. Giddins	367.4	66	1204	48	25.08	6/47		2
B.C. Hollioake	65	12	252	10	25.20	4/74		
A.F. Giles	633.3	191	1615	64	25.23	6/45		3
A.D. Mullally	628.5	166	1774	70	25.34	6/47	1	3
D. Follett	147.2	26	589	23	25.60	8/22	1	3
T.M. Moody	319.5	86	956	37	25.83	7/92	1	3
A.J. Harris	379.1	78	1380	53	26.03	6/40	1	2
P.A.J. DeFreitas	545.2	107	1687	64	26.35	7/101		4
P.J. Martin	427.4	106	1161	44	26.38	7/50		1
P.M. Such	771.4	190	2164	82	26.39	8/118	1	6
S.L. Watkin	616.4	159	1797	67	26.82	4/28		
M.V. Fleming	168.3	29	484	18	26.88	3/5		
A.M. Smith	487.3	114	1615	60	26.91	8/73	1	3
S.J.E. Brown	642.1	105	2130	79	26.96	6/77		5
D.W. Headley	423	69	1387	51	27.19	8/98	1	2
R.J. Green	187.4	37	599	22	27.22	6/41		1
J.P. Taylor	549.2	116	1766	64	27.59	7/88	1	3
A.R. Caddick	604.1	133	2029	73	27.79	7/83	3	6
R.J. Kirtley	193.3	32	756	27	28.00	5/51		1
R.C. Irani	395	74	1320	47	28.08	5/27		1
S.M. Pollock	446.4	112	1183	42	28.16	6/56		1

First-Class Averages (continued)

Bowling

	Overs	Mds	Runs	Wks	Av	Best	10/m	5/inn
G.C. Small	164	35	536	19	28.21	4/41		
J.P. Hewitt	179.3	38	681	24	28.37	3/27		
J.A. Afford	579.5	164	1471	51	28.84	6/51		2
B.P. Julian	447.4	83	1762	61	28.88	6/37		3
I.D.K Salisbury	505	109	1506	52	28.96	8/75	1	3
D.R. Law	320.4	45	1221	42	29.07	5/33		2
I.D. Austin	223.4	64	645	22	29.31	5/116		1
K.D. James	301.1	57	882	30	29.40	5/74		1
V.J. Wells	255.1	70	765	26	29.42	4/44		
K.J. Dean	144.1	32	471	16	29.43	3/47		
P.J. Hartley	459.2	96	1602	54	29.66	6/67	1	2
C. White	299.2	51	1100	37	29.72	4/15		
C.L. Hooper	231.3	83	789	26	30.34	4/7		
G. Welch	275.5	42	1035	34	30.44	4/50		
J.P. Stephenson	336.4	73	1098	36	30.50	6/48		3
C.E.W Silverwood	404.3	79	1442	47	30.68	5/72		2
P.W. Jarvis	168	27	592	19	31.15	4/60		
A. Symonds	118.3	25	374	12	31.16	2/21		
T.A. Munton	404	116	1092	35	31.20	4/41		
J.E. Benjamin	375.3	83	1217	39	31.20	4/17		
M.T. Brimson	360.2	76	1106	35	31.60	5/12		2
A.L. Penberthy	352.2	68	1077	34	31.67	5/92		1
D.E. Malcolm	639.1	99	2597	82	31.67	6/52	2	6
V.S. Solanki	215.2	37	863	27	31.96	5/69	1	3
N.W. Preston	130.5	27	352	11	32.00	4/68		
G.J. Parsons	553	171	1536	47	32.68	4/21		
R.D.B. Croft	955.4	236	2486	76	32.71	6/78		4
N.M.K. Smith	486.4	116	1417	43	32.95	5/76		3
N.F. Williams	331.4	59	1160	35	33.14	5/43		2
D.G. Cork	589	121	1891	57	33.17	5/113		1
M.C. Ilott	550.2	118	1666	50	33.32	5/53		2
A.R.C. Fraser	592.4	138	1636	49	33.38	5/55	1	2
G. Chapple	477.1	94	1671	50	33.42	5/64		2
V.C. Drakes	454.3	79	1675	50	33.50	5/47		2
R.K. Illingworth	708.1	204	1721	51	33.74	6/75		3
D.J. Capel	348.1	57	1181	35	33.74	4/60		
P.N. Weekes	371	75	1082	32	33.81	8/39		2
D.M. Cox	306	87	883	26	33.96	5/97	1	2
M.J. Saggers	101	12	443	13	34.07	6/65		1
K.J. Shine	276.3	44	1209	35	34.54	6/95		2
D.A. Leatherdale	106	21	384	11	34.90	4/75		
R.L. Johnson	242.5	36	878	25	35.12	5/29		1
D.R. Brown	407.2	81	1410	40	35.25	6/52	1	2
P.J. Newport	187.3	44	670	19	35.26	6/100		1
J.N.B. Bovill	328	62	1199	34	35.26	5/58		1
C.C. Lewis	488.2	98	1597	45	35.48	5/25		2
S.R. Lampitt	520.5	103	1919	54	35.53	5/58		2
A.R.K. Pierson	544.2	107	1710	48	35.62	6/158		2
J.E.R. Gallian	150.4	28	574	16	35.87	6/115		1
R.A. Fay	360	84	1121	31	36.16	4/53		
N. Killeen	114.5	22	434	12	36.16	4/57		
R.D. Stemp	566	165	1537	42	36.59	5/38		2
S.P. Cowan	409.1	66	1464	40	36.60	5/68		1
J.E. Emburey	396.2	94	1042	27	38.59	4/48		
M.N. Bowen	366.2	64	1281	33	38.81	5/53		2
D.A. Cosker	155.4	38	622	16	38.87	4/60		
A. Dale	141.1	36	470	12	39.16	4/52		
G.P. Butcher	199.1	30	826	21	39.33	7/77		1
C.L. Cairns	427.3	73	1461	37	39.48	6/110		1
M.M. Betts	389.5	48	1753	44	39.84	5/68		2
J.H. Childs	222.4	56	765	19	40.26	4/99		
K.P. Evans	412.4	99	1217	30	40.56	5/30		2
M. Watkinson	433	78	1501	37	40.56	5/15		1
R.J. Maru	306.2	101	734	18	40.77	3/50		
N.M. Kendrick	236	74	706	17	41.52	4/89		
S. Elworthy	308.1	43	1165	28	41.60	4/80		
A.P. Grayson	264.3	58	759	18	42.16	4/82		
K.J. Barnett	139.2	15	507	12	42.25	3/26		
P.R. Whitaker	118.2	28	423	10	42.30	3/36		
S.J.W. Andrew	198.4	47	641	15	42.73	3/67		
M.P. Vaughan	187.3	28	728	17	42.82	4/62		
O.T. Parkin	224.4	47	744	17	43.76	3/22		
J.N. Snape	313.3	62	1013	23	44.04	4/42		
S. Lee	418.3	66	1770	40	44.25	4/52		
A. Sheriyar	460	78	1661	37	44.89	6/99		1
R.P. Davis	314.2	70	1053	23	45.78	4/93		
R.T. Bates	278.2	46	969	21	46.14	3/42		
S.D. Udal	497.4	101	1582	34	46.52	5/82		1
J. Lewis	276	61	846	18	47.00	3/74		

Bowling

	Overs	Mds	Runs	Wks	Av	Best	10/m	5/inn
M.M. Patel	586	176	1554	33	47.09	6/97	1	2
P.A. Thomas	121	14	575	12	47.91	4/33		
R.M. Pearson	475	101	1509	31	48.67	5/142		1
J. Wood	291.3	46	1266	26	48.69	4/60		
S.W.K. Ellis	170	27	686	14	49.00	3/29		
J.D. Batty	486.4	99	1572	32	49.12	5/85		1
M.C.J. Ball	225	61	639	13	49.15	3/40		
M.J. Vandrau	226	30	789	16	49.31	6/34		1
S.J. Renshaw	206.5	51	743	15	49.53	4/56		
O.D. Gibson	254	41	1040	20	52.00	3/43		
A.R. Roberts	172.5	44	527	10	52.70	3/57		
G. Keedy	475.1	131	1215	23	52.82	3/45		
J.I.D. Kerr	131	16	586	11	53.27	3/108		
S.G. Law	208.4	46	760	14	54.28	3/100		
S.M. Milburn	257	49	939	17	55.23	3/47		
C.M. Tolley	216	37	804	14	57.42	4/68		
K.M. Curran	180	34	641	11	58.27	3/75		
S.D. Thomas	297	33	1175	20	58.75	5/121		1
N.C. Phillips	224	50	778	13	59.84	2/54		
M.A. Wagh	187.3	31	632	10	63.20	3/82		
A.J. Hollioake	237	45	793	12	66.08	3/80		
H.S. Malik	197	23	826	10	82.60	3/119		
A.R. Whittall	274.3	56	932	10	93.20	3/103		

(Qualification: 10 wickets)

Leading Fielders

67 – K.M. Krikken (ct 64 / st 3) and R.J. Turner (ct 64 / st 3); 62 – P.A. Nixon (ct 56 / st 6) and R.J. Rollins (ct 56 / st 6); 61 – K.R. Brown (ct 60 / st 1); 55 – W.K. Hegg (ct 50 / st 5); 52 – P. Moores (ct 50 / st 2); 51 – R.C. Russell (ct 48 / st 3); 48 – S.J. Rhodes (ct 40 / st 8); 46 – G.J. Kersey (ct 45 / st 1) and A.N. Aymes (ct 43 / st 3); 44 – R.J. Blakey (ct 40 / st 4); 36 – D.G.C. Ligertwood (ct 31 / st 5); 35 – P.V. Simmons and D.P. Ostler; 34 – S.A. Marsh (ct 28 / st 6); 33 – C.J. Adams, C.L. Hooper, A.D. Shaw (ct 28 / sp 5) and W.M. Noon (ct 30 / st 3); 32 – D. Byas; 28 – J.D. Carr; 27 – K.J. Piper (ct 24 / st 3); 25 – S.G. Law and D.P. Fulton; 23 – J.C. Pooley and D. Ripley; 22 – G.J. Parsons; 21 – M.A. Butcher; 20 – C.W. Scott, M.P. Maynard, V.J.Wells, R.J. Warren (ct 19 / st 1) and W.P.C. Weston.

Derbyshire CCC First-Class Matches Batting

	v. Cambridge University (Cambridge) 20–22 April	v. Leicestershire (Derby) 2–6 May	v. Yorkshire (Sheffield) 9–13 May	v. Glamorgan (Cardiff) 16–20 May	v. Essex (Derby) 23–27 May	v. Surrey (The Oval) 30 May–3 June	v. Hampshire (Southampton) 6–10 June	v. Indians (Derby) 13–16 June	v. Middlesex (Derby) 20–24 June	v. Northamptonshire (Northampton) 27 June–1 July	v. South Africa 'A' (Chesterfield) 6–8 July	M	Inns	NO	Runs	HS	Av
K.J. Barnett	20 –	200* 8	11 51	0 22	39 –	94 0	7 49		53 55	5 27		18	34	2	1456	200*	45.50
A.S. Rollins	2 112	4 18	20 36	73 2	27 –	28 21	131 7	25 –	14 79	0 7	7* 50	19	36	5	1101	131	35.51
C.J. Adams	54 31*	31 1	37 66	7 37	58 –	24 42	239 5	1 –	125 136*	3 68	66 –	20	36	3	1742	239	52.78
D.M. Jones	71 –	27 14	214* 10	22 12	43 –	76 10	19 19	93 –	10 100*	6 17		19	34	5	1502	214*	51.79
T.A. Tweats	89* –	3 4					0 26	7 1*				4	7	2	130	89*	26.00
C.M. Wells	36* –	40 4	12* 19*	165 3	5 –	82 28					61 –	12	19	3	609	165	38.06
K.M. Krikken	– 36	43 1*	– 47	51 26*	22 –	20 9	6 1	70 –	46* –	9 44		19	29	7	882	104	40.09
D.G. Cork	– 101*	0 8	– 0	10 12		10 82*				0 21		12	20	5	684	101*	45.60
M.J. Vandrau	– 34*		– 0	2 0			8* 1			16* 9*	– –	10	16	6	175	34*	17.50
A.E. Warner	– –											1					–
D.E. Malcolm	– –	– 0	– –	2* 1	7* –	4 4	4 0	9* 12*	11 –	5 0		18	23	7	119	21	7.43
P.A.J. DeFreitas		0 19					11 29	38 –	18 –	14 22		14	22	–	394	60	17.90
P. Aldred		– 4	– 5*		1 –	33 7*					– –	5	5	2	50	33	16.66
J.E. Owen			101 6	105 0	78 –	54 11	20 33	41 –	9 –	17 0	23 1	9	15	–	499	105	33.26
A.J. Harris				1 17	9 –	3* 0	11 8*	0 –	0 –			12	16	3	102	17	7.84
S.J. Base					1 –							1	1	–	1	1	1.00
M.R. May								49 –	16 –		63* 32*	3	4	2	160	63*	80.00
K.J. Dean								4 –	7 –		– –	8	8	1	33	12	4.71
T.J.G. O'Gorman										7 3	53 68*	11	20	3	636	109*	37.41
G.A. Khan											10 15	3	6	–	35	15	5.83
F.A. Griffith											– –	1					–
G.M. Roberts												1	1	–	52	52	52.00
Byes	5 3	2 3	2	1	5	2	1	3	6	8 6	4						
Leg-byes	3 4	7 5	5 6	8	11	10 5	15 10	25	12 7	7 9	15 1						
Wides	1	3		1	1	3 1	2	3		1							
No-balls	6 6	2	12	16	8	26 26	2	41		6	14 8						
Total	287 327	362 89	412 248	464 132	315	469 246	472 192	409 13	321 383	98 239	316 175						
Wickets	4 2	8 10	4 8	10 10	10	10 9	10 10	10 0	10 2	10 10	5 3						
Result	D	L	D	W	D	D	W	W	W	L	D						
Points	–	8	10	22	9	10	24	–	23	4	–						

Fielding Figures

67 – K.M. Krikken (ct 64 / st 3)
33 – C.J. Adams
16 – D.M. Jones
12 – P.A.J. DeFreitas
11 – A.S. Rollins
7 – D.G. Cork
6 – T.J.G. O'Gorman
5 – K.J. Barnett
4 – M.J. Vandrau, C.M. Wells, T.A. Tweats and G.A. Khan
3 – A.J. Harris and J.E. Owen
2 – subs
1 – M.R. May, D.E. Malcolm, K.J. Dean and G.M. Roberts

Batting

	v. Lancashire (Old Trafford) 18–22 July	v. Kent (Derby) 25–29 July	v. Gloucestershire (Derby) 1–5 August	v. Sussex (Hove) 8–12 August	v. Nottinghamshire (Derby) 15–19 August	v. Worcestershire (Chesterfield) 29 August–2 September	v. Somerset (Taunton) 3–6 September	v. Warwickshire (Derby) 12–16 September	v. Durham (Derby) 19–22 September	M	Inns	NO	Runs	HS	Av
K.J. Barnett	12 92	11 54	65 31	55 17	32 103	87 27*	27 141	27 14	16 4	18	34	2	1456	200*	45.50
A.S. Rollins	7 4		0 31*	1 78*	4 1*	39 41	127 0	27 5	4 69*	19	36	5	1101	131	35.51
C.J. Adams	119 1	0 13	15 –	43 1	1 106	123 1*	7 32	80 24	81 64	20	36	3	1742	239	52.78
D.M. Jones	28 107	0 43*	69 14*	17 30	105 36	9 –	11 74	9 39	77 71*	19	34	5	1502	214*	51.79
T.A. Tweats										4	7	2	130	89*	26.00
C.M. Wells	35 1	52 –	22 1	11 13					19 –	12	19	3	609	165	38.06
K.M. Krikken	104 12	45* –	17 –	48 1	22 10	0 –	89 12	32* 30*	29* –	19	29	7	882	104	40.09
D.G. Cork	83* 34*		71 –		97 4	10 –	77 12*	29 23		12	20	5	684	101*	45.60
M.J. Vandrau	10* 1*	26 10		29 0	7 22					10	16	6	175	34*	17.50
A.E. Warner										1					–
D.E. Malcolm		6 –	4* –	4* 21	1 –	0 –	6* –	13 4	1 –	18	23	7	119	21	7.43
P.A.J. DeFreitas	1 4	47 –	13 –	14 7	0 15	38 –	60 11	0 23	10 –	14	22	–	394	60	17.90
P. Aldred										5	5	2	50	33	16.66
J.E. Owen										9	15	–	499	105	33.26
A.J. Harris	– –	11 15*				6 –	15 –	2 3	1 –	12	16	3	102	17	7.84
S.J. Base										1	1	–	1	1	1.00
M.R. May										3	4	2	160	63*	80.00
K.J. Dean			3 –	3 1	3* –	12 –			0 –	8	8	1	33	12	4.71
T.J.G. O'Gorman	28 6	62 2	21 0	54 22	34 58	109* –	10 18*	4 66	11 –	11	20	3	636	109*	37.41
G.A. Khan		2 4						0 4		3	6	–	35	15	5.83
F.A. Griffith										1					–
G.M. Roberts							52 –			1	1	–	52	52	52.00
Byes	20 11	5 10	8	2 4	10 9	3	4	2	4						
Leg-byes	14 12	6 3	11 9	18 6	9 13	4 1	15 7	11 10	3 6						
Wides	2 2	1	1	1 3		1 1	1	4	4						
No-balls	10 2	18 8	16	20 16	16	30	24 14	2 10	2						
Total	473 289	292 162	335 87	320 220	341 377	471 71	524 322	242 255	256 220						
Wickets	8 8	10 5	10 3	10 10	10 8	10 2	10 6	10 10	10 2						
Result	W	D	W	W	W	W	D	L	W						
Points	21	8	23	23	23	24	10	5	22						

Bowling

	D.E. Malcolm	D.G. Cork	A.E. Warner	M.J. Vandrau	K.J. Barnett	T.W. Tweats	P. Aldred	P.A.J. DeFreitas	D.M. Jones	C.M. Wells	A.J. Harris	S.J. Base	F.A. Griffith	C.J. Adams	K.J. Dean	A.S. Rollins	Byes	Leg-byes	Wides	No-balls	Total	Wkts
v. Cambridge University	16–1–80–1	14–2–49–0	8–0–41–1	24–3–90–3	13–4–49–2	3–0–14–0												6		4	329	7
(Cambridge) 20–22 April																						
v. Leicestershire (Derby)	22–2–82–1	26–5–96–4			10.2–1–26–3		16–4–65–2	9–1–41–0									2	3	1	6	315	10
2–6 May	13–1–42–1	16–1–49–1			1–0–5–0		11.1–5–16–1	7–1–17–1	1–0–7–0									1		4	137	4
v. Yorkshire (Sheffield)	25–5–109–4	37–7–148–3		25–1–108–0	8–0–45–0		18.5–1–79–1			10–1–53–2							5	14	2	12	561	10
9–13 May	9–0–30–2			9–2–29–0			13–3–50–1			7–2–24–0								5	1	2	138	3
v. Glamorgan (Cardiff)	20–4–91–2	17.1–4–40–2		13–2–64–0	6–2–21–0				1–1–0–0	12–3–49–0	23–5–104–1						4	6	7	6	379	5
16–20 May	11–3–52–6										10.4–1–55–4										107	10
v. Essex (Derby)	23–3–87–1						8–1–37–0		8–2–24–2	10–2–12–0	30–9–87–3	23.2–4–105–1						1		12	353	7
23–27 May	4–0–18–1						8–1–17–0		6–2–8–0									1	1		44	1
v. Surrey (The Oval)	31–4–121–1	30–7–94–3					18.1–2–81–1		6–0–27–0	20–3–65–2	21–5–79–2							10	3	12	477	10
30 May–3 June	11–2–39–0	10–1–40–1			17–0–99–2		4.4–0–43–0		6.5–0–23–0		14–2–68–0			1–0–3–0		2–0–25–0	4	1		2	345	3
v. Hampshire (Southampton)	19–1–93–1			23–3–73–1	12–1–43–0			28–1–103–2	23.5–2–112–5		12–3–59–1						6	5	1	14	494	10
6–10 June	9–2–32–0			19–4–34–6							15.5–2–48–4							2	2	6	116	10
v. Indians (Derby)	21–6–60–4							13–1–40–1	1–0–8–0		17–3–67–3			1–0–4–0	13–2–45–2		1	4	2	8	229	10
13–16 June	16.1–5–50–4							10–1–37–1			11–4–31–2				15–1–61–2		4	9		10	192	10
v. Middlesex (Derby)	12–5–31–0							14–3–50–3	2–1–1–0		14.3–4–43–6				11–4–33–1		4	3	1	4	165	10
20–24 June	18.1–4–60–1				4–0–17–1			10–3–20–0			16–4–40–6				7–2–30–1		4	5	3	8	176	10
v. Northamptonshire (Northampton)	19.2–5–59–4	18–2–63–4		2–0–17–0				21–3–64–2									4	3		14	210	10
27 June–1 July	11–3–28–2	14–1–49–2						20.2–9–39–2										14		6	130	6
v. South Africa 'A' (Chesterfield)				24–4–82–2			22–2–63–1			3–0–12–0			20–1–70–1		20–3–69–0			6			322	4A
6–8 July				16–0–71–1			20–2–86–1			7–3–17–0			7–0–67–0	3–0–8–0	11–3–32–1	3–0–25–0		10		4	335	3B
v. Lancashire (Old Trafford)		26–11–62–1		42–5–134–2	23–0–73–2			30–4–120–0	5–1–26–0	34–7–67–2	29–4–91–1						8	6	2	8	587	9
18–22 July					2–0–17–0			11–1–41–1	16–2–79–1		2–0–3–0			9–1–29–0			4	1			174	3
v. Kent (Derby)	37.2–3–116–5			15–3–43–0	7–0–22–0			29–6–123–2	1–0–6–1	17–3–47–1	20–4–78–1						5	5		2	445	10
25–29 July	25.1–5–89–6			5–1–16–0	6–3–7–1			26.1–9–52–1		12–4–34–0	12.5–1–42–2							5		8	245	10
v. Gloucestershire (Derby)	13–3–38–2	17–2–72–1						26–10–72–5							10–2–29–2			6		12	217	10
1–5 August	14–6–25–2	26–9–53–4						27.4–5–93–4							6–2–24–0			6		14	201	10
v. Sussex (Hove)	21–2–119–5							38–10–87–2		17–7–20–2					8–2–22–1			17		6	265	10
8–12 August	25–6–96–5			8–2–11–1				17–1–59–3							15–3–57–1		4	1		6	228	10
v. Nottinghamshire (Derby)	19–1–108–2	14–2–53–0		1–0–17–0	7–2–20–0			20.5–4–54–5							17–4–47–3		15	3	2	20	317	10
15–19 August	16–2–43–5							15.3–3–53–4										2	5	10	98	9C
v. Worcestershire (Chesterfield)	14–2–95–2	17–4–57–1						10–1–44–2			8.5–1–31–4				2–0–5–0			6	1	10	238	10
29 August–2 September	20–1–102–2	22.1–6–60–3			1.3–0–14–0			25.3–5–70–4			13–4–54–0						2	1	1	8	303	9D
v. Somerset (Taunton)	34–5–146–3	14–5–48–1			9–0–18–0			22–3–90–0			23.4–5–95–4						5	7		14	464	10E
3–6 September	18–1–108–1	19–3–55–4						20–3–60–3			10–1–48–0							7		10	296	8
v. Warwickshire (Derby)	8–0–62–0							32–7–101–7			24.5–4–63–3							5		8	231	10
12–16 September	24–2–104–2				12.3–2–31–1			21–7–43–1			15–1–82–2							10	1	8	270	6
v. Durham (Derby)	11–2–41–1							21–2–60–5			12–4–32–3				1.1–0–4–1		1	4	1		142	10
19–22 September	29–2–141–3							20.2–3–54–4		15–5–40–0	23–7–80–1				8–4–13–1			4	2		332	10
	639.1–99–	337.2–72–	8–0–	226–30–	139.2–15–	3–0–	139.5–21–	545.2–107–	77.4–11–	164–40–	379.1–78–	28.2–4–	27–1–	14–1–	144.1–32–	5–0–						
	2597–82	1088–35	41–1	789–16	507–12	14–0	537–8	1687–64	321–9	440–9	1380–53	105–1	137–1	44–0	471–16	50–0						
Bowler's average	31.67	31.08	41.00	49.31	42.25	–	67.12	26.35	35.66	48.88	26.03	105.00	137.00	–	29.43	–						

A G.A. Khan 2–0–20–0
B M.R. May 3–0–19–0
C P.R. Pollard retired hurt
D R.K. Illingworth absent
E G.M. Roberts 25–11–55–1, 11–7–18–0

Durham CCC First-Class Matches

Batting

Batting	v. Oxford University (Oxford) 17–19 April		v. Northamptonshire (Chester-le-Street) 2–6 May		v. Middlesex (Lord's) 9–13 May		v. Yorkshire (Chester-le-Street) 16–20 May		v. Hampshire (Portsmouth) 23–27 May		v. Nottinghamshire (Trent Bridge) 30 May–3 June	
S. Hutton	172*	–	0	16	0	7						
M.A. Roseberry	145*	–	59	33	43	5	3	37	10	–	9	–
J.A. Daley	–	12*	13	20*	34	3	28	6*				
J.E. Morris	–	7*	7	35	0	3	83	5	35	–	1	–
J.I. Longley	–	–					2	4				
S.D. Birbeck	–	–										
C.W. Scott	–	–	5	4	59	9	15*	42	10	–	12	–
N. Killeen	–	–										
J. Boiling	–	–	–	2*	14	6	4	5	0*	–	31*	–
S.J.E. Brown	–	–	–	–	15	0*	28	6	3	–	19	–
M.M. Betts	–	–	–	–	8*	1	2	0*	–	–	46	–
P.D. Collingwood			91	16	7	0	6	48	80	–	46	–
M.J. Foster			6	12	9	3	25	12				
P. Bainbridge			25*	19					16	–	8	–
S.L. Campbell					13	23	0	6	9	–	118	–
D.A. Blenkiron									102*	–	130	–
J. Wood									14	–	2	–
D.M. Cox												
D.G.C. Ligertwood												
S. Lugsden												
C.L. Campbell												
M.J. Saggers												
R.M.S. Weston												
A. Walker												
S.J. Harmison												
Byes	9		5					1	8			
Leg-byes	7		6	5	5	5	5	10	12		27	
Wides	1	1							2			
No-balls			4	6	2	2	14	4	2		6	
Total	334	20	221	168	209	67	215	186	303		455	
Wickets	0	0	7	7	10	10	10	9†	8		10	
Result	D		D		L		L		D		D	
Points	–		8		5		5		10		11	

Batting	v. Sussex (Hove) 6–10 June		v. Lancashire (Chester-le-Street) 13–17 June		v. Surrey (Stockton) 20–24 June		v. Gloucestershire (Chester-le-Street) 27 June–1 July		v. Kent (Maidstone) 4–8 July		M	Inns	NO	Runs	HS	Av
S. Hutton					47	6	4	143*	8	35	14	26	2	812	172*	33.83
M.A. Roseberry	34	11	2	0					60	17	17	30	2	744	145*	26.57
J.A. Daley											11	20	3	401	36	23.58
J.E. Morris	12	0	52	0	23	4	12	68	4	18	17	31	1	429	83	14.30
J.I. Longley											2	2	–	6	4	3.00
S.D. Birbeck	0	8									2	2	–	8	8	4.00
C.W. Scott	0	52									7	10	1	208	59	23.11
N. Killeen											5	7	1	40	32	6.66
J. Boiling	4	1			0	12*					8	11	4	79	31*	11.28
S.J.E. Brown	12	16	17	10*	60	18	39*	2	13	8	18	29	4	393	60	15.72
M.M. Betts	0	57*	0	4			16	8	32	0	14	21	3	308	57*	17.11
P.D. Collingwood	16	5	4	21	25	21	2	28			11	20	–	464	91	23.20
M.J. Foster											3	6	–	67	25	11.16
P. Bainbridge			41	53	35	18	34	83	71	47	11	19	1	617	83	34.27
S.L. Campbell	45	87	7	39	69	34	8	14	31	85	16	29	–	1041	118	35.89
D.A. Blenkiron	22	3	2	10	3	1	11	4	3	5	9	16	2	328	130	23.42
J. Wood			5	0	0	2			0	0*	9	16	2	97	35*	6.92
D.M. Cox	4*	67							15*	3	7	13	4	434	95*	48.22
D.G.C. Ligertwood			31*	10	56	44	23	8	11	8	12	23	5	367	56	20.38
S. Lugsden			1	7	1*	1	9	–			3	5	1	19	9	4.75
C.L. Campbell							7	–			1	1	–	7	7	7.00
M.J. Saggers											5	9	1	89	18	11.12
R.M.S. Weston											3	5	–	29	15	5.80
A. Walker											3	6	3	25	20	8.33
S.J. Harmison											1	2	–	10	6	5.00
Byes	2	1		6	9	1	1	4	1	5						
Leg-byes	2	6	11	7	12	5	3	13	4	8						
Wides		1	2	4	1	4										
No-balls	6	11	6	8	36	32	6	10	16	16						
Total	159	326	181	179	377	203	175	385	269	255						
Wickets	10	10	10	10	10	10	10	8	10	10						
Result	L		L		L		L		L							
Points	1		4		7		7		6							

†J.A. Daley retired hurt

Batting

Batting	v. Worcestershire (Worcester) 18–22 July		v. Essex (Hartlepool) 25–29 July		v. Pakistanis (Chester-le-Street) 3–5 August		v. Warwickshire (Edgbaston) 8–12 August		v. Somerset (Weston-super-Mare) 21–24 August		v. Glamorgan (Chester-le-Street) 28–31 August		v. Leicestershire (Chester-le-Street) 12–16 September		v. Derbyshire (Derby) 19–22 September	
S. Hutton	24	0	31	23	34	7	27	16	37	–	4	19	30	17	19	86
M.A. Roseberry	7	1	1	19	93*	48	18	16	0	–	23	20	0	27	2	1
J.A. Daley			5	21	27	5	23	2	22	–	36	33	14	29	35	33
J.E. Morris	10	0	13	6	12	0					10	3	1	0	5	0
J.I. Longley																
S.D. Birbeck																
C.W. Scott																
N. Killeen			0	0	32	0*	6	0	2	–						
J. Boiling																
S.J.E. Brown	1	1			1	3	0	22	18	–	2	6	18*	8	3	44
M.M. Betts	31	26									6	5	1	7	32	26
P.D. Collingwood	1	8													5	34
M.J. Foster																
P. Bainbridge	67	9	16	3			54	7	11	–						
S.L. Campbell	43	32	56	72	22	0	64	15	69	–	22	23	35	0		
D.A. Blenkiron											0	6	3	23*		
J. Wood	3	9	35*	0	21	0	1	5								
D.M. Cox	16*	9	5	52			45	10	95*	–					22	91
D.G.C. Ligertwood	10	35*	1	1	16	27	3*	22*	14	–	4	33*	1	9	0	0
S. Lugsden																
C.L. Campbell																
M.J. Saggers			11	10*	7	13			18	–	0	11			12	7
R.M.S. Weston					0	15	3	9	2	–						
A. Walker											0*	20	0	0	1*	4*
S.J. Harmison													6	4		
Byes					7	3	4	1	1		4	3		1	1	
Leg-byes	3	3	8	13	2	8	5	1	7		1	16	4	8	4	4
Wides	2	1	1						6			1	3		1	2
No-balls	22	18	5	4	33	6	2	4	24		2	12	10	6		
Total	240	152	188	224	307	135	255	130	326		114	211	126	139	142	332
Wickets	10	10	10	10	10	10	10	10	10		10	10	10	10	10	10
Result	L		L		L		L		D		L		L		L	
Points	5		4		–		6		8		4		2		4	

Batting	M	Inns	NO	Runs	HS	Av
S. Hutton	14	26	2	812	172*	33.83
M.A. Roseberry	17	30	2	744	145*	26.57
J.A. Daley	11	20	3	401	36	23.58
J.E. Morris	17	31	1	429	83	14.30
J.I. Longley	2	2	–	6	4	3.00
S.D. Birbeck	2	2	–	8	8	4.00
C.W. Scott	7	10	1	208	59	23.11
N. Killeen	5	7	1	40	32	6.66
J. Boiling	8	11	4	79	31*	11.28
S.J.E. Brown	18	29	4	393	60	15.72
M.M. Betts	14	21	3	308	57*	17.11
P.D. Collingwood	11	20	–	464	91	23.20
M.J. Foster	3	6	–	67	25	11.16
P. Bainbridge	11	19	1	617	83	34.27
S.L. Campbell	16	29	–	1041	118	35.89
D.A. Blenkiron	9	16	2	328	130	23.42
J. Wood	9	16	2	97	35*	6.92
D.M. Cox	7	13	4	434	95*	48.22
D.G.C. Ligertwood	12	23	5	367	56	20.38
S. Lugsden	3	5	1	19	9	4.75
C.L. Campbell	1	1	–	7	7	7.00
M.J. Saggers	5	9	1	89	18	11.12
R.M.S. Weston	3	5	–	29	15	5.80
A. Walker	3	6	3	25	20	8.33
S.J. Harmison	1	2	–	10	6	5.00

Fielding Figures

36 – D.G.C. Ligertwood (ct 31 / st 5)
20 – C.W. Scott
15 – S.L. Campbell
10 – P. Bainbridge
9 – J.E. Morris
8 – J. Boiling
7 – J.A. Daley
6 – P.D. Collingwood, M.A. Roseberry and S. Hutton
4 – S.J.E. Brown, M.M. Betts, J. Wood and D.A. Blenkiron
2 – D.M. Cox
1 – R.M.S. Weston, S. Lugsden, N. Killeen and sub

Bowling

Bowling	S.J.E. Brown	M.M. Betts	S.D. Birbeck	J.A. Boiling	N. Killeen	M.J. Foster	P. Bainbridge	P.D. Collingwood	J. Wood	D.M. Cox	D.A. Blenkiron	S. Lugsden	C.L. Campbell	S.L. Campbell	A. Walker	M.J. Saggers	Byes	Leg-byes	Wides	No-balls	Total	Wkts
v. Oxford University (Oxford) 17–19 April	15–5–26–1	14–0–45–0	11–0–56–1	26–8–50–1	13–1–42–1													8		2	227	4
v. Northamptonshire (Chester-le-Street) 2–6 May	29.4–5–78–3	29–5–120–4		21–10–30–1		22–4–59–1	9–4–14–0	7–2–13–1										6	1	20	320	10
	8–1–36–2	6–0–21–1		5–0–22–0		4–0–28–0		2.2–0–14–1										1			122	4
v. Middlesex (Lord's) 9–13 May	14–2–53–2	20–5–78–3		8–2–20–0		10.3–4–21–4		3–1–9–0										10		12	191	10
	42–8–115–2	28.1–5–101–4		11–3–23–0		30–5–117–2		10–1–22–1									6	7	3	4	391	10
v. Yorkshire (Chester-le-Street) 16–20 May	26–3–93–4	16.2–3–96–3		34–15–69–2		16–1–49–1		3–0–22–0									1	5	1	16	335	10
	20–6–54–5	23.4–4–87–5		12–7–27–0		11–1–37–0											4	1	1	4	210	10
v. Hampshire (Portsmouth) 23–27 May	20–2–55–4	19–1–83–2						3–0–7–0	17.4–3–60–4									1	5	20	206	10
	15–6–19–2	8–0–27–1		11–6–7–0					9.2–5–34–2								2	8		12	97	5
v. Nottinghamshire (Trent Bridge) 30 May–3 June	19.2–4–70–5	14–2–70–1		21–7–44–1				3–0–16–0	21–3–66–3									3		18	269	10
	24–4–71–1	15–0–79–0		33–6–81–2			4–0–18–0	23–3–76–0	21–4–67–0								3	13		18	408	3
v. Sussex (Hove) 6–10 June	35–10–96–2	22–1–148–0	31–9–88–3	34–10–74–0						40–10–116–2	1.5–0–14–0						1	15	3	38	552	8
v. Lancashire (Chester-le-Street) 13–17 June	19–3–75–3	6–0–65–2					7–1–16–1		16–1–61–1			11.3–2–45–3						2	5	32	264	10
	20–1–100–1	14–4–72–0					14–0–52–1		23–0–96–3		3–0–14–0	23–1–91–3					2	14	17	4	441	8
v. Surrey (Stockton) 20–24 June	23–3–78–0			35.1–7–90–2			14.4–2–44–2		28–5–113–2			28.2–5–96–3					8	11	10	10	440	10
				12–4–45–0			6.5–0–26–0		5–0–30–0			7–1–28–2						3	2	4	142	2A
v. Gloucestershire (Chester-le-Street) 27 June–1 July	20–4–59–3	18.1–0–68–5					4–1–4–0					0.4–0–2–0	9.2–1–29–1					4	1	4	166	10
	17–1–52–1	15–2–76–0					4–2–2–0	1–0–2–0					6–2–15–0					3	1	8	150	2
v. Kent (Maidstone) 4–8 July	23–1–76–5	20–6–58–0					18–3–54–2		19.3–5–78–3	15–1–83–0								14	1	4	363	10
	18–1–58–4						14–2–52–0		17–2–78–1	22.4–8–53–3							2	1			244	10
v. Worcestershire (Worcester) 18–22 July	27–9–77–6	19.3–4–85–3					3–0–14–0		18–3–73–0	14–5–38–1							3	12		16	302	10
		6–2–16–0							6–0–43–0	10–5–17–1				6.2–1–16–0				1		4	93	1
v. Essex (Hartlepool) 25–29 July					21–6–57–4		7–3–25–0		21–4–89–3	39.4–14–83–3						12–0–69–0	4	7		8	334	10
					19.3–4–72–3		10–0–50–1		13–1–77–0	28–5–103–3				1–0–4–0		12–0–53–1	4	7		6	370	8
v. Pakistanis (Chester-le-Street) 3–5 August	20–1–88–5				12–3–56–0				20–4–105–2							10.1–2–54–3	1	5	3	28	309	10
	7–1–19–2				6.3–0–43–1				8–1–49–0							3–1–17–0				16	134	3B
v. Warwickshire (Edgbaston) 8–12 August	22–1–71–3				18–4–52–1				13–0–83–1	42.1–14–97–5								3	1	18	306	10
	18–0–70–1				14.5–2–78–1				15–5–64–1	44–11–139–5								10		14	361	9C
v. Somerset (Weston-super-Mare) 21–24 August	27–9–91–2				10–2–34–1		8–5–11–0			30–11–76–1						21.4–3–67–1	1	18	1		298	6
v. Glamorgan (Chester-le-Street) 28–31 September	21–3–62–1	17–1–71–2									2–1–1–0				21–2–50–1	16.1–2–65–6	5	5	6	4	259	10
	10.1–0–38–3	15–1–47–2									18–5–43–4			3–1–2–0	11–1–33–0	12–3–39–0		5	5	4	207	10
v. Leicestershire (Chester-le-Street) 12–16 September	26–4–106–1	18–0–117–2									13–3–51–1			6.2–1–38–1	27–4–117–1			10	5	44	516	6D
v. Derbyshire (Derby) 19–22 September	14–3–55–2	17–1–69–4								6–1–23–1					11–4–46–0	9–0–60–2		3	4		256	10
	9–1–51–1	9–1–54–0								14.3–2–55–1					9–2–31–0	5–1–19–0	4	6		2	220	2
	609.1–102–1992–77	389.5–48–1753–44	42–9–144–4	263.1–85–582–9	114.5–22–434–12	93.3–15–311–8	123.3–23–382–7	55.2–7–181–3	291.3–46–1266–26	306–87–883–26	37.5–9–123–5	70.3–9–262–11	15.2–3–44–1	16.4–3–60–1	79–13–277–2	101–12–443–13						
Bowler's average	25.87	39.84	36.00	64.66	36.16	38.87	54.57	60.33	48.69	33.96	24.60	23.81	44.00	60.00	138.50	34.07						

A J.E. Morris 1–0–10–0
B R.M.S. Weston 1–0–6–0
C R.M.S. Weston 1–1–0–0
D S.J. Harmison 9–1–77–0

Essex CCC First-Class Matches

Batting

Batting	v. Worcestershire (Worcester) 2–6 May		v. Hampshire (Southampton) 9–13 May		v. Kent (Ilford) 16–20 May		v. Derbyshire (Derby) 23–27 May		v. Indians (Chelmsford) 28–30 May		v. Lancashire (Chelmsford) 6–10 June	
G.A. Gooch	85	10	130	21	74	1	17	0			101	21
D.D.J. Robinson	61	0	18	18	17	75	74	18*	1	2	0	50
N. Hussain	2	1	22	60	36	3	81	–	7	85		
S.G. Law	93	1	143	44	9	115	30	–	153	13	144	3
P.J. Prichard	20	9	23	69	41	1	44	–	53	13	2	31
R.C. Irani	14	110*	25	81*	50	0			29*	29		
R.J. Rollins	2	–	7	25*	34	5	46*	–	15*	33	9	22
M.C. Ilott	58	–	13	–	23	1	6	–			22	0*
A.P. Grayson	6	46*	17	8			27	24*	2	1*	129	27
A.P. Cowan	3*	–	–				–	–	–	22*	0	12*
N.F. Williams	39	–	15	–	14	0	15	–				
P.M. Such			1*	–	3	4	–	–	–	–	4	–
J.H. Childs					1*	0*			–	–		
S.J.W. Andrew									–	–	8*	–
J.J.B. Lewis											69	54*
A.J.E. Hibbert												
S.D. Peters												
B.J. Hyam												
N.A. Derbyshire												
Byes	11	1				5			5	8		
Leg-byes	14	6	16	5	4	4	1	1		1	7	5
Wides	2		2					1				
No-balls	20	6				4	12		4		14	4
Total	430	190	432	331	306	218	353	44	269	207	509	229
Wickets	10	5	10	6	10	10	7	1	5	6	10	6
Result	W		W		L		D		D		D	
Points	24		23		5		11		–		9	

Batting	v. Northamptonshire (Chelmsford) 13–17 June		v. Cambridge University (Cambridge) 21–23 June		v. Surrey (Southend) 27 June–1 July		v. Leicestershire (Leicester) 4–8 July		v. Nottinghamshire (Chelmsford) 18–22 July		M	Inns	NO	Runs	HS	Av
G.A. Gooch	128	40			149	–	30	72	91	0	17	30	1	1944	201	67.03
D.D.J. Robinson			11	97			13	15	29	8	12	23	2	738	97	35.14
N. Hussain	53	46			0	–					12	21	–	903	158	43.00
S.G. Law	40	23			125	–	21	41	45	1*	15	26	1	1545	172	61.80
P.J. Prichard	0	45			7	–	1	28	30	–	19	31	–	959	108	30.93
R.C. Irani	2	2			17	–	0	0	36	–	16	27	4	923	110*	40.13
R.J. Rollins	4	14	48	51	12	–	38	0	0	74*	19	32	4	688	74*	24.57
M.C. Ilott			–	–	9*	–			2	–	17	24	2	343	58	15.59
A.P. Grayson	30	17			62	–	11	35	17	0	17	30	3	939	140	34.77
A.P. Cowan	0	5*			0	–	25	4			14	19	6	177	34	13.61
N.F. Williams							8	17	34*	–	12	16	3	221	39	17.00
P.M. Such	31*	0	–	–	0	–	0*	13	2	54	19	22	11	176	54	16.00
J.H. Childs	0	–	–	–	–	–					6	5	3	1	1*	0.50
S.J.W. Andrew	13	4*	3*	–			6	4*	12	–	10	14	6	61	13	7.62
J.J.B. Lewis			29	5							6	11	2	238	69	26.44
A.J.E. Hibbert			85	9*							2	4	1	103	85	34.33
S.D. Peters			110	12*							4	7	1	142	110	23.66
B.J. Hyam			5	11							2	4	–	73	49	18.25
N.A. Derbyshire			–	–							1					–
Byes	5	1	9	4	9		1	5								
Leg-byes	1	3	6	3	11		5	7	3	2						
Wides	1		3	1												
No-balls		4	4	4	24		4	6	17	6						
Total	308	204	313	197	425		165	247	368	145						
Wickets	10	8	6	4	9		10	10	10	4						
Result	D		W		D		L		W							
Points	10		–		8		3		24							

Fielding Figures

56 – R.J. Rollins (ct 50 / st 6)
25 – S.G. Law
19 – A.P. Grayson
18 – G.A. Gooch
12 – P.J. Prichard, N. Hussain and P.M. Such
11 – J.J.B. Lewis
8 – R.C. Irani
6 – D.D.J. Robinson
5 – B.J. Hyam (ct 4 / st 1), S.P. Peters and A.P. Cowan
4 – M.C. Ilott and subs
2 – N.A. Derbyshire, N.F. Williams and S.J.W. Andrew
1 – J.H. Childs

Batting

Batting	v. Durham (Hartlepool) 25–29 July		v. Middlesex (Lord's) 1–5 August		v. Somerset (Taunton) 8–12 August		v. Pakistanis (Chelmsford) 17–19 August		v. Gloucestershire (Colchester) 22–26 August		v. Yorkshire (Leeds) 29 August–2 September	
G.A. Gooch	22	33	92	–	201	–			111	–	15	30
D.D.J. Robinson	38	9					57	55	72*	–		
N. Hussain			35	–							158	38
S.G. Law	73	172	9	–	63	–						
P.J. Prichard	0	23	67	–	23	–	16	–	88	–	71	2
R.C. Irani	56	12	9	–	87	–	32	17	91	–		
R.J. Rollins	1	0	10	–	10	–			33	–	18	23
M.C. Ilott	17	13	1	–	13	–	0	0	33	–	26	6
A.P. Grayson	74	85	140	–	14	–			45	–	9	15
A.P. Cowan			24	–	4	–			10*	–	0	0*
N.F. Williams	23	6*	13	–	11	–			1	–	15	1
P.M. Such	10*	–	1*	–	5*	–	5*	3	–	–	0*	0
J.H. Childs							0	0*				
S.J.W. Andrew	1	–					3	2				
J.J.B. Lewis							2	21	15	–	33	2
A.J.E. Hibbert							5	4				
S.D. Peters					4	–	5	0			0	11
B.J. Hyam							49	8				
N.A. Derbyshire												
Byes	4	4					1		16		8	9
Leg-byes	7	7	20		10		11	6	5		5	4
Wides		6	1				1					
No-balls	8		14		20		4	2	12		14	8
Total	334	370	436		465		191	118	532		372	149
Wickets	10	8	10		10		10	9†	8		10	10
Result	W		W		W		L		W		L	
Points	23		24		24		–		24		8	

Batting	v. Warwickshire (Edgbaston) 3–6 September		v. Sussex (Chelmsford) 12–16 September		v. Glamorgan (Chelmsford) 19–22 September		M	Inns	NO	Runs	HS	Av
G.A. Gooch	5	147	82	41	170*	25	17	30	1	1944	201	67.03
D.D.J. Robinson							12	23	2	738	97	35.14
N. Hussain	26	39	44	35	68	64	12	21	–	903	158	43.00
S.G. Law			64	28	66	26	15	26	1	1545	172	61.80
P.J. Prichard	26	108	2	14	14	38	19	31	–	959	108	30.93
R.C. Irani	69	82*	43	0	10	20	16	27	4	923	110*	40.13
R.J. Rollins	20	2	27	59	0	46	19	32	4	688	74*	24.57
M.C. Ilott	43	4	2	16	5	30	17	24	2	343	58	15.59
A.P. Grayson	4	30	16	29	12	7	17	30	3	939	140	34.77
A.P. Cowan	2	–	34	21	5	6	14	19	6	177	34	13.61
N.F. Williams	9	–					12	16	3	221	39	17.00
P.M. Such	11*	–	19	9*	1*	–	19	22	11	176	54	16.00
J.H. Childs							6	5	3	1	1*	0.50
S.J.W. Andrew			4*	0	0	1*	10	14	6	61	13	7.62
J.J.B. Lewis	0	8*					6	11	2	238	69	26.44
A.J.E. Hibbert							2	4	1	103	85	34.33
S.D. Peters							4	7	1	142	110	23.66
B.J. Hyam							2	4	–	73	49	18.25
N.A. Derbyshire							1					–
Byes	9	14	2	13		2						
Leg-byes	10	10	14	1	6	2						
Wides	2	2	1	1								
No-balls	2	4	6	16	10	2						
Total	238	450	360	283	367							
Wickets	10	6	10	10	10	9						
Result	W		L		L							
Points	21		8		6							

† P.J. Prichard absent

Bowling	M.C. Ilott	N.F. Williams	A.P. Cowan	R.C. Irani	S.G. Law	A.P. Grayson	P.M. Such	J.H. Childs	G.A. Gooch	S.J.W. Andrew	N.A. Derbyshire	D.D.J. Robinson	J.J.B. Lewis	Byes	Leg-byes	Wides	No-balls	Total	Wkts
v. Worcestershire (Worcester)	32–7–82–3	22.2–6–57–5	17–9–32–1	8–3–16–1										2	12	2	8	201	10
2–6 May	43–9–105–5	30–6–107–1	15.5–0–64–2	26–7–93–1	11–5–30–1	1–1–0–0								5	11		30	415	10
v. Hampshire (Southampton)	37–8–111–1	28.2–3–106–2		21–1–103–2	9–0–39–0	13–2–52–1	35–10–108–3							6	14	1	26	539	10
9–13 May	14–0–20–0	3–0–27–0		3–1–12–0		28.3–5–82.4	32–7–74–5							4	2		2	221	10
v. Kent (Ilford)	33–9–107–1	16–1–89–0		20–2–75–1	6–1–33–0		50.5–8–145–5	26–5–108–2	6–1–25–1						8		10	590	10
16–20 May																			
v. Derbyshire (Derby)	29–7–87–3	16–2–69–2	28.3–3–105–2			6–2–14–0	11–4–24–2							5	11	1	8	315	10
23–27 May																			
v. Indians (Chelmsford)			17–3–57–0	15–3–37–4	9–2–26–1	4–0–33–0	17–1–75–0	16–3–72–2		7–1–15–1					5	3	6	320	8
28–30 May			14–4–45–0	4–0–9–0			5–0–25–1	22–3–99–4		17–5–44–1					1		4	223	6
v. Lancashire (Chelmsford)	32–5–124–1		32–3–135–3		6–0–30–0	22–2–106–1	42–12–178–4			22.4–2–91–1				3	19		14	686	10
6–10 June																			
v. Northamptonshire (Chelmsford)			22–6–66–3	16.2–4–42–2	10–4–27–0		5–0–12–0	15–5–31–3		20–7–35–2				1			6	214	10
13–17 June			18–1–74–0	12–2–44–0	9–0–41–0	22–9–33–2	46–13–110–2	39.4–10–102–2		21–5–50–2				19	9		12	482	9
v. Cambridge University (Cambridge)	11–3–26–2						11–2–34–5	14–6–38–1		9–1–42–2	6–0–20–0			8	2			170	10
21–23 June	12–4–30–1						24.4–6–55–4	25–9–54–3		5–4–1–0	14–2–67–1			5	6		6	218	9A
v. Surrey (Southend)	27.4–3–78–2		17–3–63–1	13–1–47–2	2–0–11–0	12–1–35–0	38–11–102–2	42–13–116–1						3	21	5	4	476	8
27 June–1 July	3–1–4–0		2–0–8–0		11–3–39–1	15–2–42–0	24–5–66–1							3	5			167	2
v. Leicestershire (Leicester)		30–6–79–1	16–2–82–0	25–4–100–3	14–4–38–0	13–2–34–2	13–3–31–0			22–5–67–3				1	22	3	34	454	9
4–8 July																			
v. Nottinghamshire (Chelmsford)	13–5–31–4	6–2–18–1		11.3–3–27–5						6–2–20–0					1		4	97	10
18–22 July	22.5–2–62–3	25–9–51–1		7–2–23–0	27–8–100–3	21–8–55–0	34–12–80–2			8–1–27–1				8	9	5	10	415	10
v. Durham (Hartlepool)	21–4–53–5	6–0–20–0		12.3–2–33–2			22–4–52–3			5–1–22–0					8	1	5	188	10
25–29 July	19–2–81–1	10–3–33–3		12–5–31–1	3.1–0–9–1		22–9–49–4			2–1–8–0					13		4	224	10
v. Middlesex (Lord's)	22.4–11–47–4	20–4–78–1	21–2–76–4	15–5–34–1	14–9–14–0		2–0–9–0								6		16	264	10
1–5 August	7–2–16–2	6–1–39–1	12.3–2–35–4	13–4–29–3											2		6	121	10
v. Somerset (Taunton)	17–5–59–0	13–3–59–1	10–5–31–1	8–1–15–2	4–2–4–0	4–1–8–0	31.2–10–63–6							5	2	1	8	246	10
8–12 August	5–1–19–0			4–0–4–0	12–2–39–0	30–12–56–3	42.3–17–72–6							5	3	1		208	10
v. Pakistanis (Chelmsford)	12–5–45–2			14.5–0–67–4			26–13–35–2	14–2–82–0		18–3–62–1				8	4			303	9
17–19 August	10–1–39–0			6–2–27–1			8–0–26–0	9–0–63–1		10–0–79–0		5–0–24–0	4–0–16–0	2	1	1		277	2
v. Gloucestershire (Colchester)	16–1–47–2	16–2–62–1	16–3–68–5	11–0–53–1		3–0–14–0	15–7–25–1							2	9		20	280	10
22–26 August	15–6–35–2	17–3–43–5	17–0–76–2	7–1–25–1			1–0–1–0							4	4		4	188	10
v. Yorkshire (Leeds)	15.1–0–63–3	15–3–52–3	13–1–74–0			9–4–21–2	19–6–47–1		13–5–20–1					4	9		4	290	10
29 August–2 September	13–3–43–1	19–2–44–0	11–1–39–0			22–1–62–1	46.2–7–118–8							7	16		6	329	10
v. Warwickshire (Edgbaston)	19–5–42–1	20–1–70–3	16.4–4–37–3	17–4–36–1			16–4–43–2		2–1–12–0					1	12		14	253	10
3–6 September	8–1–35–0	13–2–57–4	8.4–1–34–2			3–0–8–0	24–2–114–4							5	12		12	265	10
v. Sussex (Chelmsford)	12–1–52–0		16.1–2–58–2	19–3–62–2	5–0–17–1	8–1–19–1	28–6–95–3			14–5–45–0					15			363	10
12–16 September	13–1–38–0		13.5–2–30–0	15–2–47–0	25–4–113–3	8–3–12–0	49–11–149–4			5–2–14–1				4	10		8	417	8
v. Glamorgan (Chelmsford)	19–4–68–1		20–4–56–2	7–0–47–0	18–2–69–1	6–1–21–1	11–0–60–1			7–2–19–0				2	11			353	6
19–22 September	7–2–17–0		4–1–19–0	5–0–21–0	13.3–0–81–2	14–1–52–0	20–0–87–1							2	5		2	284	3
	550.2–118–	331.4–59–	379.1–62–	348.1–62–	208.4–46–	264.3–58–	771.4–190–	222.4–56–	21–7–	198.4–47–	20–2–	5–0–	4–0–						
	1666–50	1160–35	1364–37	1169–40	760–14	759–18	2164–82	765–19	57–2	641–15	87–1	24–0	16–0						
Bowler's average	33.32	33.14	36.86	29.22	54.28	42.16	26.39	40.26	28.50	42.73	87.00	–	–						

A D.R.H. Churton absent hurt

Glamorgan CCC First-Class Matches Batting

Batting	v. Cambridge University (Cambridge) 17–19 April		v. Yorkshire (Cardiff) 2–6 May		v. Northamptonshire (Northampton) 9–13 May		v. Derbyshire (Cardiff) 16–20 May		v. Worcestershire (Abergxxemy) 23–27 May		v. Oxford University (Oxford) 1–4 June		v. Middlesex (Lord's) 6–10 June		v. Somerset (Swansea) 13–17 June		v. Sussex (Hove) 20–24 June		v. Pakistanis (Pontypool) 29 June–1 July		v. Gloucestershire (Bristol) 4–8 July		M	Inns	NO	Runs	HS	Av
S.P. James	12	102*	40	62	76	9	7	0	20	89			16	33	0	110	9	8	79	9	118	–	20	38	1	1766	235	47.72
H. Morris	126*	–	202*	51	20	38	90	0	4	4					54	31	7	19			108	–	17	31	2	1656	202*	57.10
D.L. Hemp	103*	–																	4	–			8	13	2	405	103*	36.81
A. Dale	–	–	5	23	5	120	26	3	29	–	0	55			35	62	4	5					15	25	1	690	120	28.75
M.P. Maynard	–	100*	136	27	52	27	35	0					11	2	1	13	7	112	40	–	145*	–	17	30	4	1610	214	61.92
P.A. Cottey	–	21	1	21	48	65*	135*	45	2	3	27	0	7	22	112	61	23	57			101*	–	20	36	6	1543	203	51.43
R.D.B. Croft	–	6*	12	0	25	0	–	8	73*	9*	71	–	28	19	37	7	0	4	14	–	–	–	18	27	5	634	78	28.81
S.D. Thomas	–	–	18	4	2*	–	–	28	23	–	9*	6	48	4	12	1*	12	6	9	–			11	16	3	199	48	15.30
C.P. Metson	–	–	12*	2*	–	–	2	0									18*	6					8	11	4	53	18*	7.57
S.L. Watkin	–	–	–	0	–	–	–	16*	17	0			3*	0	0*	–	16	5			–	–	18	20	6	153	34	10.92
S.R. Barwick	–	–	–	4					1	–			1	6									7	7	1	34	20*	5.66
G.P. Butcher			25	0	89	8*	61*	7	73	42	83	–	63	8	15	33*	15	20	35	14*	–	–	14	24	4	679	89	33.95
N.M. Kendrick					16*	–	–	0			–	1*	0	0	2	–					–	–	10	11	6	35	16*	7.00
A.D. Shaw									8	–	7	7	38	9*	15	3			22	–	–	–	13	18	1	281	74	16.52
O.D. Gibson									51	34*													9	15	3	449	97	37.41
A.W. Evans											66*	71*	12	27					39	18	4	–	7	13	3	376	71*	37.60
A.J. Dalton											17	15							5	–			2	3	–	37	17	12.33
A.P. Davies											–	–							8	11*			2	2	1	19	11*	19.00
O.T. Parkin											–	–					0	0*	5*	–	–	–	10	12	7	65	14	13.00
D.A. Cosker																							5	6	1	45	24	9.00
Byes	4		13	8		1	4		2		2			2	2	4	1	4	4		5							
Leg-byes	4	5	8	14	4	4	6		7	9	3		6	9	13	8	6	11	8		5							
Wides	1	2	2		4	1	7				1	1	1		4	1	1	1	2	1	1							
No-balls	12	12	8		10	6	6		18	4	18	8	4		8	20	14	8	30	7	22							
Total	262	248	482	216	351	279	379	107	328	194	304	164	238	141	310	354	133	266	304	60	509							
Wickets	1	1	7	10	7	5	5	10	10	5	6	5	10	10	10	7	10	10	10	2	3							
Result	D		L		W		L		D		D		L		W		L		D		D							
Points	–		5		22		6		6		–		5		22		3		–		11							

Batting

Batting	v. South Africa 'A' (Cardiff) 17–19 July		v. Lancashire (Cardiff) 25–29 July		v. Nottinghamshire (Worksop) 1–5 August		v. Leicestershire (Swansea) 8–12 August		v. Warwickshire (Edgbarton) 15–19 August		v. Kent (Cardiff) 22–26 August		v. Durham (Chester-le-Street) 28–31 August		v. Hampshire (Southampton) 3–6 September		v. Surrey (Cardiff) 12–16 September		v. Essex (Chelmsford) 19–22 September		M	Inns	NO	Runs	HS	Av
S.P. James	14	18	18	49	235	0	5	29	90	148	–	3	4	2	103	24	4	131	12	78	20	38	1	1766	235	47.72
H. Morris			71	61	69	71	8	106	7	0	–	118	25	69	80	35	6	17	10	149	17	31	2	1656	202*	57.10
D.L. Hemp	12	19							11	29	–	4	28	12			47	8	95	33*	8	13	2	405	103*	36.81
A. Dale	37	13							4	20	–	11*	29	69	0	11	90	11	23	–	15	25	1	690	120	28.75
M.P. Maynard			214	68*	38	4*	21	33	69	95	–	47			15	69	82	16	122	9	17	30	4	1610	214	61.92
P.A. Cottey	4	15	74	55*	11	–	203	10	1	22	–	70	81	14	8	41	25	83	69*	6*	20	36	6	1543	203	51.43
R.D.B. Croft			0	–	56	–	29	0	0	78					67	23*	25	38	5*	–	18	27	5	634	78	28.81
S.D. Thomas							4	13													11	16	3	199	48	15.30
C.P. Metson					11	–	1	1*	0	0											8	11	4	53	18*	7.57
S.L. Watkin	7	22*	11	–	0	–			5*	0	–	–	0	9	34	–	8*	0	–	–	18	20	6	153	34	10.92
S.R. Barwick	1	1	20*	–							–	–									7	7	1	34	20*	5.66
G.P. Butcher			35	3	1	–	3	15					19	12							14	24	4	679	89	33.95
N.M. Kendrick	5*	10			1*	–	0*	0*			–	–									10	11	6	35	16*	7.00
A.D. Shaw	11	0	0	–							–	–	0	0	53	11	19	74	4	–	13	18	1	281	74	16.52
O.D. Gibson	30	11	19	–	30	–	97	42	4	0	–	12*	41	2	14	62*					9	15	3	449	97	37.41
A.W. Evans	21	13			21	48*	13	23													7	13	3	376	71*	37.60
A.J. Dalton																					2	3	–	37	17	12.33
A.P. Davies																					2	2	1	19	11*	19.00
O.T. Parkin	0	0							14	4*			9*	0*	13*	–	12	8*	–	–	10	12	7	65	14	13.00
D.A. Cosker			24	–									3	4	6	–	0	8*	–	–	5	6	1	45	24	9.00
Byes		4	1	14	6		6	13	4	5		2	5					5	2	2						
Leg-byes	12	7	16	7	4	3	11	14	3	2		3	5	5	4	3	9	20	11	5						
Wides	1	2					1					1	6	5		2	5	5								
No-balls	10	2	2	2	6		31		2	16		2	4	4	4		32	18		2						
Total	165	137	505	259	489	126	433	299	214	419	0	273	259	207	401	281	364	442	353	284						
Wickets	10	10	10	3	10	3	10	9	10	10	0	5	10	10	10	6	10	9	6	3						
Result	L		W		W		D		L		D		W		D		D		W							
Points	–		22		23		9		5		5		22		8		9		24							

Fielding Figures

33 – A.D. Shaw (ct 28 / st 5)
20 – M.P. Maynard
16 – S.P. James, P.A. Cottey and C.P. Metson (ct 14 / st 2)
14 – H. Morris
13 – R.D.B. Croft
9 – S.L. Watkin
8 – G.P. Butcher
7 – A. Dale
6 – O.D. Gibson
5 – N.M. Kendrick and A.W. Evans
4 – O.T. Parkin and subs
3 – S.R. Barwick and D.L. Hemp
2 – S.D. Thomas and D.A. Cosker

Bowling

	S.L. Watkin	S.D. Thomas	R.D.B. Croft	S.R. Barwick	A. Dale	D.L. Hemp	G.P. Butcher	P.A. Cottey	N.M. Kendrick	D.A. Cosker	O.D. Gibson	O.T. Parkin	Byes	Leg-byes	Wides	No-balls	Total	Wkts
v. Cambridge University (Cambridge)	17–6–43–1	18–4–73–1	17–3–54–0	22–11–24–1	2–1–1–0	3–0–27–0								3		8	225	3
17–19 April	4–1–10–1	3–0–16–1	4–2–2–0			3–1–3–1								1			32	3
v. Yorkshire (Cardiff)	28.5–6–101–2	26–3–89–0	45–11–133–5	29–12–70–0	7–0–44–0		12–1–62–1	3–0–15–0						22		2	536	8
2–6 May	17–4–64–2	13–0–47–2	24–7–47–1	5–1–19–0			2–0–21–0						2	5	1	6	205	7
v. Northamptonshire (Northampton)	35–6–110–3	27–3–118–0	21–2–69–0		21–4–68–3		2–0–19–0		16–6–55–0				4	8	1	8	451	6
9–13 May	5–2–8–0	8–0–34–0	12–2–52–3				7–0–26–0		11–0–49–2				3	6			178	5
v. Derbyshire (Cardiff)	25–8–55–1	27–3–129–1	55–12–122–4		11–0–43–0		17.4–5–28–4		28–8–78–0				1	8	1	16	464	10A
16–20 May	18–2–61–4	7–2–12–2	6–2–14–1		4–2–5–0		9–3–30–3		5–1–10–0								132	10
v. Worcestershire (Abergavenny)	7–3–24–0	11.4–2–62–0	11–4–25–0	7–3–13–0	5–1–24–0		5–0–30–0				2–0–13–0		5	4		8	200	0
23–27 May	14–3–41–3	11–0–43–1	19–1–57–0	11–8–4–0			5–1–19–1						2	6		6	172	5
v. Oxford University (Oxford)		20–2–49–0	17.1–7–32–3		2–0–3–0		5–1–16–1		18–7–45–2			8–1–30–0		3		8	196	6B
1–4 June		3–1–3–0	19–4–48–2				4–1–20–0		20–3–79–2			6–0–33–1	7	1		6	216	6
v. Middlesex (Lord's)	33–9–89–2	21–4–43–1	31.2–5–88–6	20–5–47–0			12–6–27–1		8–1–29–0					12	1	2	335	10
6–10 June		3–0–16–0	5–2–8–1						2.3–0–20–0					1	1		45	1
v. Somerset (Swansea)	27.5–13–47–4	10–2–53–0	51–11–113–2				5–0–16–0	4–1–9–0	33–8–89–4				7	4	1	2	338	10
13–17 June	9–1–28–1	5–1–9–1	33.2–12–78–6						28–16–34–2				4				153	10
v. Sussex (Hove)	31–7–78–2	28.2–4–121–5	32–4–75–1				9–1–41–0					29–8–84–2		7	3	4	406	10
20–24 June																		
v. Pakistanis (Pontypool)		23–110–2	27–3–129–0				10–1–74–0					22–4–59–0	8	6	3	7	461	2C
29 June–1 July																		
v. Gloucestershire (Bristol)	24–8–64–3		6–4–7–0				23.3–4–77–7		2–2–0–0			16–4–26–0		7		12	181	10
4–8 July	24.5–10–37–3		36–20–39–4				15–2–54–1		12–7–25–0			17–6–58–0	7	4		4	224	8D
v. South Africa 'A' (Cardiff)	15–3–52–2			26.4–4–81–2		6–1–23–3			10–1–66–0		11–0–49–0	14–1–69–3	5	1	1	4	346	10
17–19 July																		
v. Lancashire (Cardiff)	20–3–82–2		33–6–97–1	12–0–48–0			4–0–25–0			25–6–90–2	17.4–0–112–0		15	9	1	22	478	5
25–29 July	11–0–54–1		17.1–6–47–5				3–0–13–0			16–4–60–4	7–0–54–0		7	3		6	238	10
v. Nottinghamshire (Worksop)	33–16–74–3		36–19–66–2				17–2–74–0		23–8–59–2		30.1–8–83–3			15	1	13	371	10
1–5 August	11–3–23–1		35–8–92–3				3–0–18–0		13–5–31–3		28.3–7–67–3		6	4	1	4	241	10
v. Leicestershire (Swansea)		21–1–97–1	52–8–137–3				26–2–112–2	17–2–49–4	1.3–1–0–0		24–4–131–0		2	8	10	30	536	10E
8–12 August		9–0–51–2	17–2–47–4				2–0–16–0	7–0–22–0			11–0–78–0		4	7	1	2	231	7
v. Warwickshire (Edgbarton)	34–7–136–3		36–7–110–3		11–2–39–0	2–0–11–0					26.4–2–122–3	15–3–56–1	10	13	1	16	498	10F
15–19 August	16–4–38–3		16–5–47–2								8–0–43–3		4	4			136	8
v. Kent (Cardiff)	19–3–56–1			30.3–10–85–2	15–2–70–1	5–0–21–0		1–0–4–0	5–0–37–0		16–3–40–1		8	2	1	12	323	5
22–26 August																	0	0
v. Durham (Chester-le-Street)	15–6–28–4				11–6–19–1						12–4–40–1	9.4–3–22–3	4	1		2	114	10
28–31 August	23.5–7–71–2				11–6–15–2		1–0–8–0	1–0–4–0		2–0–3–0	20–4–59–3	15–5–32–3	3	16	1	12	211	10
v. Hampshire (Southampton)	14–0–60–1		31–11–51–3		4.1–1–17–0					20–4–98–0	15–3–75–0	17–4–38–0	5	8	1	2	352	4
3–6 September	21.5–6–49–3		23–9–41–0		3–1–7–0					9–4–27–0	25–6–74–3	17–3–51–2	4	8	1		261	8
v. Surrey (Cardiff)	26–4–85–3		56–11–158–1		8–4–12–0					34–10–142–4		14–3–55–0	11	8		4	471	9
12–16 September	3.4–0–26–1		22–6–49–3					1–0–4–0		20–6–80–2		3–0–42–1	1	3		2	205	7G
v. Essex (Chelmsford)	22.5–6–64–4		23–3–102–0		16–4–52–4					10–0–56–0		19–2–59–1		6		10	367	9
19–22 September	10–2–39–1		23–5–79–3		10–2–51–1					19.4–4–66–4		3–0–30–0	2	2		2	269	9
	616.4–159–	295–33–	892–224–	163.1–54–	141.1–36–	21–2–	199.1–30–	34–3–	236–74–	155.4–38–	254–41–	224.4–47–						
	1797–67	1175–20	2315–72	391–5	470–12	113–4	826–21	107–4	706–17	622–16	1040–20	744–17						
Bowler's average	26.82	58.75	32.15	78.20	39.16	28.25	39.33	26.75	41.52	38.87	52.00	43.76						

A M.P. Maynard 1–1–0–0
B A.P. Davis 6–3–18–0; 5–0–25–1
C A.P. Davis 15–2–75–0
D M.P. Maynard 2–2–0–0
E M.P. Maynard 0.3–0–0; 2–0–6–0
F M.P. Maynard 1–0–1–0
G M.P. Maynard 1–1–0–0

Gloucestershire CCC First-Class Matches Batting

Batting	v. Middlesex (Lord's) 2–6 May		v. Indians (Bristol) 11–13 May		v. Somerset (Bristol) 16–20 May		v. Surrey (Gloucester) 23–27 May		v. Lancashire (Old Trafford) 30 May–3 June		v. Sussex (Bristol) 13–17 June		v. Nottinghamshire (Trent Bridge) 20–24 June		v. Durham (Chester-le-Street) 27 June–1 July		v. Glamorgan (Birstol) 4–8 July		v. Leicestershire (Cheltenham) 18–22 July		v. Warwickshire (Cheltenham) 25–29 July		M	Inns	NO	Runs	HS	Av
A.J. Wright	0	106			11	17	51	32	1	–	12	51	0	19	5	58	15	30	0	7			9	17	–	415	106	24.41
R.I. Dawson	7	11	15	3											0	14*	11	18					7	13	1	141	21	11.75
R.J. Cunliffe	0	51			3	25			10	–	10	6	40	7			18	82					6	11	–	252	82	22.90
T.H.C. Hancock	27	13	4	33	89	9	116	19*	13	–	3	17	11	36	65*	59*	5	6	4	18	57	–	15	27	3	709	116	29.54
A. Symonds	42	31	120*	28	18	47	32	–	38	–	11	9	57	117	15	–	8	30	3	2	127	–	18	30	1	1097	127	37.82
M.W. Alleyne	39	6*	43*	13	1	27	11	–	96	–	6	71	0	0	8	–	27	29	20	14	30	–	18	30	3	887	149	32.85
R.C. Russell	26	3*			63	1	42	–	60	–	14	13			20	–			0	19*			13	21	4	634	75	37.29
R.P. Davis	27*	–	–	16	19	31	0	–	0	–	5	13	–	0							23	–	15	22	2	308	43	15.40
K.E. Cooper	5	–																					1	1	–	5	5	5.00
A.M. Smith	32	–			16	25	0	–	2	–	48	2	55*	4	13	–	18*	0	0	0	15	–	16	25	3	364	55*	16.54
J. Lewis	6	–	–	22*	0	20							17	9	1	–	8	1*	6	4			10	16	2	119	22*	8.50
D.R. Hewson			53	2																			6	12	1	261	87	23.72
M.A. Lynch			4	1			0	46*											18	38	69	–	11	19	1	553	72	30.72
R.C.J. Williams			–	9									0	40			44	13			10	–	5	8	–	133	44	16.62
D.J.P. Boden			–	–											1	–							2	1	–	1	1	1.00
K.P. Sheeraz			–	3*																			1	1	1	3	3*	–
M.J.C. Ball					19	22	7*	–	11	–	26*	9			17	–	6	0*	4	11	12	–	13	21	4	236	46	13.88
C.A. Walsh					38	11*	8	–	15*	–	2	1*	1	2*			2	–	1*	4	12*	–	15	24	13	154	25	14.00
N.J. Trainor							67	57	9	–	4	6	3	20	12	7					6	–	8	14	1	261	67	20.07
M.G.N. Windows																			0	4	184	–	9	17	2	443	184	29.53
Byes			5	21	8	1			3		1	8		4				7			5							
Leg-byes	3	7	7	1		3	7	1	10		5	11	2	5	4	3	7	4	2	5	19							
Wides		1			3	2	2	2				2			1	1			5									
No-balls	4	2		6	10	4	30	6	2		4	15	4	4	4	8	12	4	8	10								
Total	218	231	251	158	263	245	373	163	270		151	234	190	267	166	150	181	224	71	136	569							
Wickets	10	5	4	8	10	10	10	2	10		10	10	9†	10	10	2	10	8	10	10	10							
Result	W		D		D		D		D		L		L		D		D		L		W							
Points	21		–		9		9		9		4		3		7		4		4		24							

†R.P. Davis, absent

Batting

Batting	v. Derbyshire (Derby) 1–5 August		v. Hampshire (Southampton) 8–12 August		v. Yorkshire (Bristol) 15–19 August		v. Essex (Colchester) 22–26 August		v. Northamptonshire (Bristol) 29 August–2 September		v. Worcestershire (Worcester) 12–16 September		v. Kent (Bristol) 19–22 September		M	Inns	NO	Runs	HS	Av
A.J. Wright															9	17	–	415	106	24.41
R.I. Dawson									21	20	0	16	5	1	7	13	1	141	21	11.75
R.J. Cunliffe															6	11	–	252	82	22.90
T.H.C. Hancock	27	14	3	9	29	–	15	8							15	27	3	709	116	29.54
A. Symonds	10	19	26	90	75	–	52	0	38	21	11	6	14	–	18	30	1	1097	127	37.82
M.W. Alleyne	25	50*	17	45	25	–	22	23	0	23	149	44	23	–	18	30	3	887	149	32.85
R.C. Russell	15	0			26*	–	63	57	50	75	29	50*	8	–	13	21	4	634	75	37.29
R.P. Davis	16	5	6	37*	19	–	5	7	7	43	7	16	6	–	15	22	2	308	43	15.40
K.E. Cooper															1	1	–	5	5	5.00
A.M. Smith	1	10			19	–	0	7	15	19*	30	5	28	–	16	25	3	364	55*	16.54
J. Lewis	11	8	0	6	0	–									10	16	2	119	22*	8.50
D.R. Hewson			87	58	0	6*	37	1	0	3	5	9			6	12	1	261	87	23.72
M.A. Lynch	1	48	0	13	36	–	18	50	6	9	70	72	54	–	11	19	1	553	72	30.72
R.C.J. Williams			16	1											5	8	–	133	44	16.62
D.J.P. Boden															2	1	–	1	1	1.00
K.P. Sheeraz															1	1	1	3	3*	–
M.J.C. Ball			0	0			1	9	7	4	5*	46	20	–	13	21	4	236	46	13.88
C.A. Walsh	17*	0	0*	0	25	–	3*	13*	10*	12	0	0	12*	–	15	24	13	154	25	14.00
N.J. Trainor	0	2											48	20*	8	14	1	261	67	20.07
M.G.N. Windows	76	25	0	38	40	10*	33	1	6	4	0	6	8	8*	9	17	2	443	184	29.53
Byes				7	13		2	4	1	4	4	6	8							
Leg-byes	6	6	4	4	4		9	4	7	8	6	9	5							
Wides			1	1		1			1			1		5						
No-balls	12	14	4	6	18		20	4	14	4	18	6	2							
Total	217	201	164	315	329	17	280	188	183	249	334	292	241	33						
Wickets	10	10	10	10	10	0	10	10	10	10	10	10	10	0						
Result	L		L		W		L		W		L		W							
Points	5		4		23		3		20		7		21							

Fielding Figures

33 – R.C. Russell (ct 31 / st 2)
17 – R.P. Davis
16 – M.C.J. Ball
15 – M.W. Alleyne
13 – R.C.J. Williams (ct 12 / st 1)
11 – T.H.C. Hancock and A.J. Wright
10 – M.A. Lynch
9 – A.J. Symonds
7 – C.A. Walsh
5 – N.J. Trainor and subs
4 – J. Lewis and M.G.N. Windows
2 – A.M. Smith and D.R. Hewson
1 – R.J. Cunliffe and D.J.P. Boden

Bowling

Bowling	A.M.Smith	K.E. Cooper	M.W. Alleyne	J. Lewis	R.P. Davis	T.H.C. Hancock	A. Symonds	K.P. Sheezaz	D.J.P. Boden	R.I. Dawson	C.A. Walsh	M.C.J. Ball	Byes	Leg-byes	Wides	No-balls	Total	Wkts
v. Middlesex (Lord's)	16.4–1–45–2	22–5–54–4	17–3–46–2	11–0–53–2										2	2	2	200	10
2–6 May	32–10–78–8	17–7–28–1	10–3–21–0	25–4–74–1	7–0–39–0	2–1–2–0	2–0–5–0						1	4	1	4	247	10
v. Indians (Bristol)			29.1–5–81–5	34–4–86–1	26–2–88–2	5–0–14–0		32–5–101–0	6–0–19–0	2–0–3–1			2	12	8		406	10
11–13 May			7–3–26–2	8–4–17–1	8–0–60–2			7–1–41–1							1		144	6
v. Somerset (Bristol)	21.3–6–55–3		5–1–15–0	19–7–46–0	9–0–44–0						24–6–73–3	7–0–24–2		2	1	6	259	10
16–20 May	7–3–18–0			6–1–21–1	1–0–9–0						21–3–69–5	12–2–38–2	4	12	1	4	171	8
v. Surrey (Gloucester)	13–2–31–2		14–5–40–1		13–4–37–0	2–0–10–0	1.4–0–20–0				19–7–43–1	17–5–41–1		6	1		228	6
23–27 May	10–2–33–1		7–2–23–1		7–1–19–0						18–3–52–3	23–12–40–3	4	3		4	174	8
v. Lancashire (Old Trafford)	26–7–93–1		14–6–24–1		35–12–93–4						31–10–59–2	19–5–54–1	5	3		6	335	9A
30 May–3 June																		
v. Sussex (Bristol)	18.2–5–58–1		17–6–32–5		5–1–13–1	3–2–3–0					15.4–7–48–3			3		14	157	10
13–17 June	22.1–4–73–1		17–5–48–2		16–5–31–0						27–9–57–6	7–3–10–0	8	4	2	6	231	10
v. Nottinghamshire (Trent Bridge)	26–4–110–2		21–3–62–1	23–3–90–1	24–6–58–1		14–2–47–2				28.3–9–80–3		5	8	1	12	460	10
20–24 June																		
v. Durham (Chester-le-Street)	20–8–39–4		21–8–40–3	16.4–5–42–2					13–4–50–1				1	3		6	175	10
27 June–1 July	31.3–9–81–3		26–5–83–2	21–7–48–0		2–0–17–0	17–5–40–2		18–1–71–0			13–5–28–1	4	13		10	385	8
v. Glamorgan (Bristol)	26–3–113–3		20–3–78–0	26–6–88–0		4–1–14–0	12.3–1–62–0				15–5–33–0	33–7–111–0	5	5	1	22	509	3
4–8 July																		
v. Leicestershire (Cheltenham)	18–3–55–6		11–3–23–1	9–5–19–2							16–3–42–1	4–2–5–0	5	10	1	16	159	10
18–22 July	14–2–60–2		8.3–5–12–3	5–0–21–0							18–6–40–4	2–0–8–0	8	1	1	20	150	10
v. Warwickshire (Cheltenham)	9–2–66–0		9–3–31–1		20–8–63–2						14.5–6–26–6	6–2–20–1	1	9		17	216	10
25–29 July	15–3–59–2		6–2–10–0		18.4–5–46–2						21–2–91–5	9–2–30–1		1		6	237	10
v. Derbyshire (Derby)	7–0–33–0		19–5–60–1	21.1–6–74–3	10–2–28–0		2–0–11–1				28–6–110–4		8	11		16	335	10
1–5 August			5–1–8–1	11.1–2–37–2							7–0–33–0			9	1		87	3
v. Hampshire (Southampton)			12–4–49–1	10–2–40–1	13.2–3–54–3						17–7–34–5	5–1–8–0		1		2	186	10
8–12 August			22.2–5–86–4	17–3–52–1	27–8–79–1						29–9–55–3	18–1–72–0	6	6		2	356	10
v. Yorkshire (Bristol)	10–1–46–2		7–1–31–0	6–0–21–0	6–0–42–2						14.2–8–22–6			4		12	166	10
15–19 August	13–2–56–3		12–5–29–1	17–2–17–0	8.2–1–31–3		1–0–5–0				12–2–37–3			4		12	179	10
v. Essex (Colchester)	27–4–118–0		30–8–80–4		26–2–129–0		4–0–10–0				28.1–3–102–1	24–5–72–1	16	5		12	532	8
22–26 August																		
v. Northamptonshire (Bristol)	24–11–68–5		16–4–69–3								21–8–44–2	1–0–1–0	4	4		12	190	10
29 August–2 September	18.4–6–40–2		23–9–49–3				10–4–21–2				28–9–62–3	11–3–34–0	12	9	2	16	227	10
v. Worcestershire (Worcester)	12–4–32–1		27.1–6–73–3		20–7–47–0		17–3–47–0				24–6–64–5	11–4–40–0	2	14	1	16	319	10
12–16 September	20–5–81–1		7–1–38–0		14–3–43–0		13–2–44–1			0.2–0–4–0	19–2–85–3		12	4		10	311	5
v. Kent (Bristol)	14.4–5–36–2		10–1–30–2				17–6–31–2				15–3–50–4	3–2–3–0		4	1	8	154	10
19–22 September	15–2–43–3		8–2–19–1				7.2–2–31–2				15–6–21–4		1	2	2	8	117	10
	487.3–114–	39–12–	458.1–123–	276–61–	314.2–70–	18–4–	118.3–25–	39–6–	37–5–	2.2–0–	526.3–145–	225–61–						
	1615–60	82–5	1316–54	846–18	1053–23	60–0	374–12	142–1	140–1	7–1	1432–85	639–13						
Bowler's average	26.91	16.40	24.37	47.00	45.78	–	31.16	142.00	140.00	7.00	16.84	49.15						

A N.J. Trainor 1–0–4–0

Hampshire CCC First-Class Matches Batting

Batting	v. Oxford University (Oxford) 2–4 May		v. Essex (Southampton) 9–13 May		v. Warwickshire (Edgbaston) 16–20 May		v. Durham (Portsmouth) 23–27 May		v. Worcestershire (Worcester) 30 May–3 June		v. Derbyshire (Southampton) 6–10 June		v. Cambridge University (Cambridge) 14–16 June		v. Northamptonshire (Basingstoke) 19–22 June		v. Indians (Southampton) 29 June–1 July		v. Sussex (Arundel) 3–6 July		v. Yorkshire (Harrogate) 18–22 July		M	Inns	NO	Runs	HS	Av
J.P. Stephenson	47	–	50	36			0	6	74	–	85	5			16	–	14	–	5	9*	39	5	15	25	2	611	85	26.56
J.S. Laney	112	–	31	28	73	40	0	0	39	–	21	7	4	15	81	–	100	–	8	83	5	37	17	30	–	1163	112	38.76
R.S.M. Morris	28	11	0	11	7	9	8	9					112	–									5	9	–	195	112	21.66
R.A. Smith	2	46	50	9	20	–			8	–	141	17			179	–			21	28	0	44	17	31	2	1396	179	48.13
G.W. White	10	29*	0	1	21	24	19	16*	66	–	7	8*	–	34									13	24	3	652	73	31.04
P.R. Whitaker	38	20	55	67*	21	37	8	10	22	–	27	0	50*	23*			19	–					12	22	3	535	67*	28.15
S.N. Udal	1	5*	38	16			5	–	50*	–	42	17	–	58	8	–	9	–	18	–	6	0	17	25	4	447	58	21.28
A.N. Aymes	30	–	113	4	28	22*	48*	21*	100*	–	55*	0			37*	–	1	–	29	11*	9*	4	19	32	12	801	113	40.05
M.J. Thursfield	30*	–											–	0			37*	–					5	5	2	89	37*	29.66
C.A. Connor	–	–	25*	14	0	–	42	–	–	–	8	15			0	–			8	–	0	4*	10	12	3	140	42	15.55
S.M. Milburn	17*	–	13	22	9	–	19	–	–	–							54*	–	0	–	2	25	10	12	2	180	54*	18.00
W.K.M. Benjamin			117	5	16	2																	2	4	–	140	117	35.00
K.D. James					28	118*	23	13	7	–	28	25			9	–	103	–	3	72	71	6	13	23	1	738	118*	33.54
R.J. Maru					28*	–	8	–			34	4			8	–							11	17	5	303	55*	25.25
J.N.B. Bovill									10	–	20	8	–	–	29	–	8	–	1*	–	5	0	14	19	2	131	29	7.70
M. Keech													98	15*	1	–	36	–	104	19	63	87	12	21	3	793	104	44.05
V.P. Terry													49*	9	19	–	20	–	52	4	23	26	7	12	2	379	87*	37.90
M. Garaway													–	44									1	1	–	44	44	44.00
S.J. Renshaw													–	–									7	7	5	10	9*	5.00
W.S. Kendall																							8	16	2	601	103*	42.92
L.J. Botham																							3	3	–	31	30	10.33
D.A. Mascarenhas																							2	3	–	24	14	8.00
Byes	6	2	6	4	9	7		2			6		7	6			23		12		7	4						
Leg-byes	4	1	14	2	8	17	1	8	7		5	2	5		7		28		8	11	9	2						
Wides	2	1	1				5				1	2	1				2		1	1	9	3						
No-balls		4	26	2	6		20	12	10		14	6	16	6			4				18	2						
Total	327	119	539	221	274	276	206	97	393		494	116	342	210	394		458		270	238	266	249						
Wickets	8	3	10	10	10	5	10	5	7		10	10	3	6	10		9		10	5	10	10						
Result	D		L		W		D		D		L		W		W		D		D		L							
Points	–		8		22		7		9		6		–		24		–		9		6							

Batting	v. Surrey (Southampton) 25–29 July		v. Somerset (Taunton) 1–5 August		v. Gloucestershire (Southampton) 8–12 August		v. Lancashire (Old Trafford) 15–19 August		v. Leicestershire (Leicester) 22–26 August		v. Middlesex (Portsmouth) 28–31 August		v. Glamorgan (Southampton) 3–6 September		v. Kent (Canterbury) 12–16 September		v. Nottinghamshire (Southampton) 19–22 September		M	Inns	NO	Runs	HS	Av
J.P. Stephenson	61	62	5	21	0	0	7	25*	0	11					28	–			15	25	2	611	85	26.56
J.S. Laney	8	8	50	32	0	27							102	11	105	14	97	25	17	30	–	1163	112	38.76
R.S.M. Morris																			5	9	–	195	112	21.66
R.A. Smith	54	70*	8	3	26	77	17	77	17	14	42	28	54	91	60	1	161	31*	17	31	2	1396	179	48.13
G.W. White							58	4	8	13	32	20	70	14	6	66	73	53	13	24	3	652	73	31.04
P.R. Whitaker							10	37	14	0					18	53	0	6	12	22	3	535	67*	28.15
S.N. Udal	31	–	0	25*	8	28*	10	–	43	0	9	18					–	2	17	25	4	447	58	21.28
A.N. Aymes	27	–	24*	12	0	7	0	7*	21	4	27	41	–	0	52	0	38*	29*	19	32	12	801	113	40.05
M.J. Thursfield							4	–					–	18					5	5	2	89	37*	29.66
C.A. Connor					0*	24													10	12	3	140	42	15.55
S.M. Milburn	8	–	7	4															10	12	2	180	54*	18.00
W.K.M. Benjamin																			2	4	–	140	117	35.00
K.D. James	49	27	12	19	42	50			5	23	1	4							13	23	1	738	118*	33.54
R.J. Maru	14*	27			9	5	1	21			33	38	55*	7*	10*	1	–	–	11	17	5	303	55*	25.25
J.N.B. Bovill	0	–	17	1	1	0			0	17*	5	9			0	0	–	–	14	19	2	131	29	7.70
M. Keech	15	–	0	61	55	61	60*	42	0	13	13	12	12	26*					12	21	3	793	104	44.05
V.P. Terry	57	87*	13	20															7	12	2	379	87*	37.90
M. Garaway																			1	1	–	44	44	44.00
S.J. Renshaw							1	–	0*	9*	0*	0*	–	–	0	0*	–	–	7	7	5	10	9*	5.00
W.S. Kendall			6	19	42	63	53	75	14	11	24	18	43*	71	34	3	103*	22	8	16	2	601	103*	42.92
L.J. Botham											30	1	–	0			–	–	3	3	–	31	30	10.33
D.A. Mascarenhas													–	10	14	0			2	3	–	24	14	8.00
Byes	1	2				6	2		4	10		10	5	4		6								
Leg-byes	4	3	12	6	1	6	9	7	3	6	4	6	8	8	29	6	18	6						
Wides		1	1					5	2	4			1	1			1	1						
No-balls	30	14	4	8	2	2	2	4	6		12		2		2		22	6						
Total	359	301	159	231	186	356	234	304	137	135	232	205	352	261	358	150	513	181						
Wickets	10	4	10	10	10	10	10	6	10	9	10	10	4	8	10	9†	4	5						
Result	L		L		W		D		D		L		D		L		D							
Points	8		3		20		8		7		5		11		5		8							

†J.P. Stephenson absent

Fielding Figures

46 – A.N. Aymes (ct 43 / st 3)
17 – R.J. Maru
13 – J.S. Laney
12 – G.W. White, S.D. Udal and V.P. Terry
10 – M. Keech
8 – W.S. Kendall and subs
6 – K.D. James and J.P. Stephenson
5 – M. Garaway (ct 4 / st 1) and R.S.M. Morris
4 – P.R. Whitaker
3 – W.K.M. Benjamin and S.J. Renshaw
2 – L.J. Botham
1 – R.A. Smith

Bowling	S.M. Milburn	C.A. Connor	S.N. Udal	J.P. Stephenson	M.J. Thursfield	P.R. Whitaker	L.J. Botham	R.J. Maru	K.D. James	J.N.B. Bovill	D.A. Mascarenhas	S.J. Renshaw	Byes	Leg-byes	Wides	No-balls	Total	Wkts
v. Oxford University (Oxford)	23–3–76–0	20–8–38–1	28.4–5–80–1	18–5–41–0	19.3–6–45–3	20.2–8–36–3								6			322	8
2–4 May																		
v. Essex (Southampton)	27–6–104–3	23–8–73–1	14–2–56–1	11–2–63–0		8–3–24–1								16	2		432	10A
9–13 May	15–0–81–2	16–2–73–3	14–0–86–0			6–0–23–0								5			331	6
v. Warwickshire (Edgbaston)	8–0–28–0	24–6–57–5				6–3–12–0		25–8–49–2	13.5–3–17–3					4			192	10B
16–20 May	19.4–9–47–3	23.3–9–56–3				4–0–13–0		23–9–37–1	20–3–51–1				10	5			236	10
v. Durham (Portsmouth)	32–8–79–3	27.5–7–82–1	18–5–37–1	9–0–22–1				13–3–29–0	13–3–34–1				8	12	2	2	303	8
23–27 May																		
v. Worcestershire (Worcester)	23–11–41–1	35–11–84–3	26–2–106–1	20–5–53–0		4–0–13–0			29–8–55–2	22.3–4–68–3				11	2		431	10
30 May–3 June		16–3–48–3	23–5–67–0	11–4–35–0		15–2–48–0			5–0–21–0	15–2–59–0			6	4	2	2	288	4
v. Derbyshire (Southampton)		22–5–70–3	40–11–127–4	8–1–32–0		3–0–20–0		22.3–5–56–1	22–2–53–2	15–4–64–0			1	15			472	10C
6–10 June		19.3–3–64–4	27–10–44–4						9–2–31–1	9–2–43–1				10	2	2	192	10
v. Cambridge University (Cambridge)			25.5–7–80–3		22–6–59–1	4–0–25–1				17–5–60–1		14–3–54–1	4	4		8	286	7
14–16 June			20.2–4–55–4		9–5–13–1	13–6–51–3				8–2–26–2			6	1			152	10
v. Northamptonshire (Basingstoke)		17–8–38–2		14.2–4–27–5					10–3–30–2	12–3–45–1			5	2	1	2	147	10
19–22 June		16–7–34–2	6–1–17–1	9.1–1–48–2					11–3–27–3	11–3–35–2			4	10		2	175	10
v. Indians (Southampton)	18.2–2–72–0		6–0–34–0	4–0–22–0	18–0–86–0				25–4–74–5	15–3–66–0			2	6	1	8	362	5
29 June–1 July																		
v. Sussex (Arundel)	15–3–43–0	20.5–5–57–4		20–7–48–6					7–2–24–0	6–2–17–0				4	2		183	10
3–6 July	10–2–29–1	11–2–33–1		16–7–30–2					7–3–23–1				4	9			128	5
v. Yorkshire (Harrogate)	9–0–56–0	23.5–4–97–4	26–8–77–0	18–3–58–1					16–2–67–0	17–4–58–5			7	7	1	10	427	10
18–22 July		5–0–33–0	7–1–27–0							8.3–2–27–0				2			89	0
v. Surrey (Southampton)	21–4–85–3		15–1–47–0	18–2–64–3				12–2–29–1	9–1–35–1	16.3–3–63–2			1	7		16	331	10
25–29 July	9–0–71–0		14–0–83–1	10.1–0–59–2				12–2–69–1	3–0–12–0	5–1–23–0			2	13	1	2	332	5
v. Somerset (Taunton)	27–1–127–1		23–6–63–1	23–2–97–2					23–2–101–1	32.3–5–140–4			2	8	3	18	541	9D
1–5 August																		
v. Gloucestershire (Southampton)		18.1–8–38–9	8–2–18–0	10–3–30–0				6–3–17–0	11–5–18–0	5–0–21–1				4	1	4	164	10E
8–12 August		24–3–96–0	30.5–7–82–5	12–1–43–0				33–17–50–3	15–5–33–1				7	4	1	6	315	10
v. Lancashire (Old Trafford)			41–8–105–3	23–8–64–3	11–1–45–0	9–3–18–0		24–10–61–1				19–5–42–3		7	1	4	342	10
15–19 August			18–1–69–1	13–2–56–1	4–0–18–0	11–0–64–2		27–7–49–1				9–2–36–0	5	9		4	306	5
v. Leicestershire (Leicester)			10–2–33–0	17–6–53–1					24–1–89–1	29–3–102–4		24–9–56–4	9	3	1	8	353	10F
22–26 August																		
v. Middlesex (Portsmouth)			5–1–27–0				15–1–67–5	2–0–9–0	13–4–23–2	14–1–40–2		11–2–33–1			2	6	199	10
28–31 August			8–2–19–0				15–3–83–1	23–8–50–2	15.2–1–64–3	23–2–91–3		26–5–103–1	9	6	3	6	426	10G
v. Glamorgan (Southampton)					18–3–75–0		14–2–59–1	19.5–9–45–1			32–8–88–6	30–7–110–1		4		4	401	10H
3–6 September					7–1–20–0		6–2–33–1	12–1–71–1			16–2–62–3	9–1–46–0		3	2		281	6I
v. Kent (Canterbury)				36–8–104–5		4–1–21–0		12–3–29–1		24–7–91–0	28–7–101–4	26–7–94–0		5	1	6	445	10
12–16 September				16–2–49–2						11–0–33–1	16–4–46–3	14.5–0–75–4	1	7		6	211	10
v. Nottinghamshire (Southampton)			13–2–50–0			11–2–55–0	5–1–26–0	20–6–46–0		9–2–25–2		17–6–78–0	4	8			391	4J
19–22 September			30–8–93–3					20–8–38–2		3–2–2–0		7–4–16–0		3	1		152	5
	257–49– 939–17	362.4–99– 1071–49	497.4–101– 1582–34	336.4–73– 1098–36	108–22– 361–5	118.2–28– 423–10	55–9– 268–8	306.2–101– 734–18	301.1–57– 882–30	328–62– 1199–34	92–21– 297–16	206.5–51– 743–15						
Bowler's average	55.23	21.85	46.52	30.50	72.20	42.30	33.50	40.77	29.40	35.26	18.56	49.53						

A W.K.M. Benjamin 33–9–96–4, 16–2–63–0
B W.K.M. Benjamin 12–2–25–0, 8.2–0–17–2
C G.W. White 6–0–34–0
D J.S. Laney 2–0–3–0
E M. Keech 6–0–18–0
F M. Keech 5–1–8–0
G W.S. Kendall 1–0–1–0
H G.W. White 7–2–20–0
I G.W. White 9–1–37–0; J.S. Laney 2–0–9–0
J W.S. Kendall 13–1–46–2; G.W. White 2–1–4–0; J.S. Laney 10–2–49–0

Kent CCC First-Class Matches

Batting

Batting	v. Lancashire (Canterbury) 2–6 May		v. Surrey (The Oval) 9–13 May		v. Essex (Ilford) 16–20 May		v. Yorkshire (Canterbury) 23–27 May		v. Sussex (Tunbridge Wells) 30 May–3 June		v. Leicestershire (Leicester) 5–8 June		v. Middlesex (Canterbury) 13–17 June		v. Warwickshire (Edgbaston) 20–24 June		v. Oxford University (Canterbury) 29 June–1 July		v. Durham (Maidstone) 4–8 July		v. Pakistanis (Canterbury) 20–22 July		M	Inns	NO	Runs	HS	Av
D.P. Fulton	5	1	28	59	34	–	34	–	6	17*	34	88	32	11			134*	–	64	5	58	17	17	30	3	852	134*	31.55
M.V. Fleming	8	18	0	56	19	–	17	–	41	8*	5	114	31	59	61	5			0	12	26	15	18	30	2	855	116	30.53
T.R. Ward	106	25	0	14	12	–	161	–	51	–	90	44	41	45	0	25			50	60	58	3	18	31	1	1252	161	41.73
C.L. Hooper	54	17*	7	23	155	–	0	–	72	–	26	22	33	25	12	20			66	105			17	29	2	1287	155	47.66
G.R. Cowdrey	52	–	45	41	111	–	7	–	0	–	71	28	51	–	26	11			9	15	1	22	11	17	–	529	111	31.11
M.A. Ealham	48*	5*	51	0	37	–			31*	–	14	6	59	23*	24	5					57	28	12	20	4	537	74	33.56
S.A. Marsh	10	–	29	26	127	–	4	–	0	–	51	2	20	0	14	6			42	10	1	28	15	24	1	478	127	20.78
M.J. McCague	0	–	14	63*	28	–	4	–	32	–	0	24*	34	24*	36	8*			0	1	1	9	18	26	7	357	63*	18.78
M.M. Patel	5	–	13	26	12*	–	0	–	6	–			0*	–	15	2	–	–			4*	5*	16	21	5	233	33	14.56
J.B.D. Thompson	0	–	16	8	37	–	28	–									–	–					5	5	–	89	37	17.80
T.N. Wren	8	–	1*	6													–	–					7	5	2	15	8	5.00
N.W. Preston					0	–	4*	–	5	–	12	3			6*	2	–	–	2	10			8	11	4	63	17*	9.00
N.J. Llong							10	–					63*	0	20	53	–	–	64	0	15	29	14	22	2	763	130	38.15
B.J. Phillips									2	–	1	–											3	3	–	5	2	1.66
E.J. Stanford											0*	–							10*	2*			2	3	3	12	10*	–
D.W. Headley													–	–	15	4	–	–	37	21	13	14	12	16	3	253	63*	19.46
C.D. Walsh																	56*	–					1	1	1	56	56*	–
M.J. Walker																	–	–					8	13	3	606	275*	60.60
J.A. Ford																	–	–					1					–
S.C. Willis																	–	–			0	12	5	6	1	141	78	28.20
E.T. Smith																							1	2	–	57	31	28.50
Byes	1			5			1				2	11	10		4	6				2	8	4						
Leg-byes	8		4	12	8		7		9		6	3	8	10	5	8	2		14	1	6	3						
Wides	3		1	6					1	1	4	4			4	1			1			6						
No-balls	12		16	16	10		22		24	4	8	2	8	8	16	8	8		4		14	15						
Total	320	66	225	361	590		299		280	30	324	351	390	205	258	164	200		363	244	262	200						
Wickets	10	3	10	10	10		10		10	0	10	8	8	6	10	10	0		10	10	10	10						
Result	W		D		W		D		W		D		D		W		D		W		L							
Points	19		8		24		8		22		9		9		22		–		24		–							

Batting

Batting	v. Derbyshire (Derby) 25–29 July		v. Worcestershire (Canterbury) 1–5 August		v. Northamptonshire (Northampton) 8–12 August		v. Somerset (Canterbury) 15–19 August		v. Glamorgan (Cardiff) 22–26 August		v. Nottinghamshire (Tunbridge Wells) 29 August–2 September		v. Hampshire (Canterbury) 12–16 September		v. Gloucestershire (Bristol) 19–22 September		M	Inns	NO	Runs	HS	Av
D.P. Fulton	0	0	28	1	39	6*	29	9	64	–	0	26	15	8			17	30	3	852	134*	31.55
M.V. Fleming	116	27	37	31	40	–	26	–	9*	–	39	–	7	7	21	0	18	30	2	855	116	30.53
T.R. Ward	9	16	41	16	0	–	57	24	25	–	10	54*	79	44	86	6	18	31	1	1252	161	41.73
C.L. Hooper	103	5	76	8	41	–	76	16*	77	–	58	86	84	14	6	0	17	29	2	1287	155	47.66
G.R. Cowdrey															4	35	11	17	–	529	111	31.11
M.A. Ealham			0	–							25	–	74	22	11	17	12	20	4	537	74	33.56
S.A. Marsh	7	15							3*	–	23	–	1	55	0	4	15	24	1	478	127	20.78
M.J. McCague	27	4	0	4	1*	–	–	–	–	–	0	–	4*	5	12*	22	18	26	7	357	63*	18.78
M.M. Patel	10	33	15*	0	31	–	14	–	–	–			9	32	0	1	16	21	5	233	33	14.56
J.B.D. Thompson																	5	5	–	89	37	17.80
T.N. Wren					0	–	–	–	–	–	0*	–					7	5	2	15	8	5.00
N.W. Preston	2*	17*															8	11	4	63	17*	9.00
N.J. Llong	116	51	49	0	7	–	26	–	63	–	22	34*	130	3	0	8	14	22	2	763	130	38.15
B.J. Phillips											2	–					3	3	–	5	2	1.66
E.J. Stanford																	2	3	3	12	10*	–
D.W. Headley	12	38	10	5	19	–	63*	–	–	–			0	1*	1	0*	12	16	3	253	63*	19.46
C.D. Walsh																	1	1	1	56	56*	–
M.J. Walker			57	15	40	11*	275*	43*	59	–	49	10	30	6	0	11	8	13	3	606	275*	60.60
J.A. Ford																	1					–
S.C. Willis			29	21*	78	–	1	–									5	6	1	141	78	28.20
E.T. Smith	31	26															1	2	–	57	31	28.50
Byes	5		6		4		9		8		1	4		1		1						
Leg-byes	5	5	2	3	12		14		2		6	1	5	7	4	2						
Wides			2	2					1		1		1		1	2						
No-balls	2	8	14	2	4		26		12		8		6	6	8	8						
Total	445	245	366	108	316	17	616	92	323	0	244	215	445	211	154	117						
Wickets	10	10	10	9†	10	0	7	2	5	0	10	3	10	10	10	10						
Result	D		L		W		W		D		W		W		L							
Points	11		6		23		21		6		21		24		4							

†M.A. Ealham absent injured

Fielding Figures

34 – S.A. Marsh (ct 28 / st 6)
33 – C.L. Hooper
25 – D.P. Fulton
12 – N.J. Llong and T.R. Ward
11 – S.C. Willis
10 – M.J. McCague
9 – M.V. Fleming
6 – M.M. Patel and M.A. Ealham
5 – G.R. Cowdrey and subs
4 – D.W. Headley
3 – T.N. Wren and N.W. Preston
2 – C.D. Walsh and M.J. Walker
1 – B.J. Phillips, J.A. Ford and E.J. Stanford

Bowling	M.J. McCague	J.D.B. Thompson	T.N. Wren	M.V. Fleming	M.M. Patel	C.L. Hooper	M.A. Ealham	T.R. Ward	N.W. Preston	N.J. Llong	B.J. Phillips	D.W. Headley	Byes	Leg-byes	Wides	No-balls	Total	Wkts
v. Lancashire (Canterbury)	3–1–11–0	5.1–0–28–1	3–1–8–0														47	1
2–6 May	23–3–75–2	16–4–44–1	12–3–44–1	7–0–37–1	28.2–13–65–5	1–0–5–0							1	4		6	275	10
v. Surrey (The Oval)	28–9–76–2	24.1–2–72–5	7–0–44–0	9–3–22–0	11–1–34–0	13–4–27–1	17–1–64–2						4	17	1	2	360	10
9–13 May	10–2–33–4	5–1–18–0			15–5–36–1	15–3–45–1	5–0–23–0						3	2			160	6
v. Essex (Ilford)	4.5–0–16–2	1–0–7–0			51–17–128–4	54–10–151–4								4			306	10
16–20 May	6–2–28–0				37.3–8–97–6	35–9–67–3	5–3–5–1	1–0–5–0	2–1–7–0				5	4		4	218	10
v. Yorkshire (Canterbury)	33–7–97–3	15–4–66–0		11–3–30–0	29.1–7–84–1				25–5–68–4				2	3	1	10	350	8
23–27 May	10–2–43–1	9–3–33–0		3–0–12–1	30–15–28–0	13–7–22–0		6–3–10–2	5–0–11–0	12–8–9–0			12	6		2	223	4A
v. Sussex (Tunbridge Wells)	12.2–3–36–2			6–1–13–1	3–0–5–0		16–12–16–3		14–2–46–3		12–3–22–1			4		10	142	10
30 May–3 June	14–4–43–1			6–2–10–1	1–0–6–0	1–0–4–0	18.2–4–55–5		7–3–9–0		14–5–34–3		1	2			164	10
v. Leicestershire (Leicester)	25–5–79–3			11–3–26–2		33–8–68–2	29–10–82–0		8–1–27–0		14–4–53–0		8	4		2	431	10B
5–8 June	9–0–53–2					19–3–56–2	3–1–13–0						7	2	1		173	6
v. Middlesex (Canterbury)	30–6–84–3			16–1–43–1	27–6–104–2	11–1–53–1	16.1–4–46–2					28–5–101–1	5	5	1	14	441	10
13–17 June	15–4–47–1				37–14–77–3	4–0–19–0	10–4–15–0			8.5–2–21–5		8–1–34–0	24	10		4	247	10
v. Warwickshire (Edgbaston)	9–3–22–0						20–8–36–8		13–3–29–0			12–1–43–2	1	6	1	8	137	10
20–24 June	21–3–101–5			0.4–0–0–1			15–6–38–2		10–3–29–0			19–3–73–2	10	2	1	4	253	10
v. Oxford University (Canterbury)		16–2–68–2	13–3–47–0		28–8–63–1				11–2–26–1	13–4–38–1		20–3–48–3		4		12	294	9
29 June–1 July			7–2–15–1							8–2–33–1		7–2–13–0				4	216	4C
v. Durham (Maidstone)	26–7–69–4			14–3–37–1		9–2–24–1			16.1–4–42–2			27–4–86–2	1	4		16	269	10D
4–8 July	21.1–7–60–3					23–8–46–1			6–2–15–0	8–1–18–2		26.2–5–77–3	5	8		16	255	10
v. Pakistanis (Canterbury)	16–2–42–1			0.2–0–0–1	26–13–59–2		16–4–48–4					17–3–43–2	1	1		2	194	10
20–22 July	10–1–40–0			5–1–12–0	18–5–66–0		10–3–29–0			7–0–43–0		15–2–48–1	10	2		2	269	2E
v. Derbyshire (Derby)	16–1–85–1			5–1–22–0	5–0–36–0				11–1–40–1			18.3–1–98–8	5	6	1	18	292	10
25–29 July	19–1–79–2								2.4–0–3–0			16–2–67–3	10	3		8	162	5
v. Worcestershire (Canterbury)	27–3–93–1			18–2–53–2	39–9–82–1	8–1–28–0	23–10–39–2			1–0–8–0		35.1–3–139–2	9	8		20	459	9
1–5 August	11–1–49–2				22–7–49–0	4–1–6–0						17.3–1–81–4	12	10		4	207	6
v. Northamptonshire (Northampton)	13–5–21–5		3–1–20–1		13.4–2–46–3	1–1–0–0						13–1–41–1		5			133	10
8–12 August	15–2–44–1		16–3–49–5	3–0–14–0	13–4–26–0	6.2–2–7–4						14–2–37–0	10	9		10	196	10
v. Somerset (Canterbury)	23–6–69–1		20–7–53–1	4–1–12–0	43–18–94–0	31–10–49–2				15–5–32–1		29–10–60–3	12	8	11	8	389	8
15–19 August	10.3–3–21–4		7–1–29–0		29–8–81–1	15–7–38–1				6–1–37–1		13–4–39–3	4	8		2	257	10
v. Glamorgan (Cardiff)																	0	0
22–26 August	14–4–46–2		6–0–30–0	2–0–5–0	7–0–38–0	10.1–4–29–1						18–1–82–2	2	3	1	2	273	5F
v. Nottinghamshire (Tunbridge Wells)	20–4–55–4		8–0–44–0	14–0–34–3		5–0–11–1	20.1–7–58–2						5	7	1	2	214	10
29 August–2 September	26.4–4–80–4		10–1–26–0	15–3–46–0		6–1–17–1	28–11–52–5						8	13	7	2	242	10
v. Hampshire (Canterbury)	32–6–99–1			7–0–36–0	11–1–22–0	3–1–16–0	33–11–73–4					32.3–6–83–5		29		2	358	10
12–16 September	17–4–51–6			4.3–2–6–3	4–0–10–0	1–0–1–0	11–1–41–0					10–1–29–0	6	6			150	9G
v. Gloucestershire (Bristol)	19.3–5–50–3			6–3–10–0	11–4–33–2		26–8–70–0					27–8–65–4	8	5		2	241	10
19–22 September				1–0–4–0	1.2–1–5–0			2–0–14–0		2–0–10–0					5		33	0
	590–120–1897–76	91.2–16–336–9	112–22–409–9	168.3–29–484–18	540–166–1374–32	321.3–83–789–26	321.4–108–803–40	9–3–29–2	130.5–27–352–11	80.5–23–249–11	40–12–109–4	423–69–1387–51						
Bowler's average	24.96	37.33	45.44	26.88	42.93	30.34	20.07	14.50	32.00	22.63	27.25	27.19						

A S.A. Marsh 6–4–5–0; G.R. Cowdrey 8–3–23–0; D.P. Fulton 3–1–9–0
B E.J. Stanford 38–12–84–3, 16.3–4–42–1
C D.P. Fulton 2–0–37–1; J.A. Ford 11.1–1–54–0; C.D. Walsh 12–0–64–0
D E.J. Stanford 3–1–6–0, 10–5–26–1
E G.R. Cowdrey 3.3–0–19–1
F D.P. Fulton 1–0–19–0; M.J. Walker 1–0–19–0
G J.P. Stephenson absent

Lancashire CCC First-Class Matches Batting

	v. Yorkshire (Old Trafford) 18–20 April		v. Kent (Canterbury) 2–6 May		v. Leicestershire (Old Trafford) 9–13 May		v. Nottinghamshire (Trent Bridge) 16–20 May		v. Gloucestershire (Old Trafford) 30 May–3 June		v. Essex (Chelmsford) 6–10 June	
S.P. Titchard	4	–									163	–
M.A. Atherton	3	16	11	98	87	29	11	13	80	–		
N.J. Speak	12	8*	–	4	55	17*	1	74*	44	–	29	–
G.D. Lloyd	33	–			65	12*			43	–	241	–
A. Flintoff	2	–										
W.K. Hegg	27	–	–	2	134	–	65*	9	5	–	37	–
I.D. Austin	4	–	–	0	16	–					89*	–
S. Elworthy	88	–	–	10	18	–	20	0	21*	–	19	–
G. Yates	5	0*										
R.J. Green	14	–										
G. Keedy	8*	–			4	–	17*	0	6*	–	26*	–
J.E.R. Gallian			18*	12	24	63	94	0*				
J.P. Crawley			–	5	27	61	77	11	70	–	1	–
G. Chapple			18*	7*			2	1	9	–	10	–
M. Watkinson			–	21	1	–	6	39	15	–	34	–
P.J. Martin			–	20	34*	–	0	0	22	–		
N.H. Fairbrother			–	85			80	59	6	–		
N.T. Wood											1	–
P.C. McKeown												
J.J. Haynes												
Byes	1			1	2	1	5	4	5		3	
Leg-byes	7			4	20	3	9	7	3		19	
Wides					4	1						
No-balls	4			6	4	4	10	8	6		14	
Total	212	24	47	275	495	191	397	225	335		686	
Wickets	10	0	1	10	10	3	9	9	9		10	
Result	D		L		D		D		D		D	
Points	–		4		9		9		10		9	

	v. Durham (Chester-le-Street) 13–17 June		v. Somerset (Old Trafford) 27 June–1 July		v. Worcestershire (Old Trafford) 4–8 July		v. Derbyshire (Old Trafford) 18–22 July		v. Glamorgan (Cardiff) 25–29 July		M	Inns	NO	Runs	HS	Av
S.P. Titchard	12	60	121*	21*	8	20	96	15	67	42	13	23	2	939	163	44.71
M.A. Atherton	16	37					0	–			9	16	–	538	98	33.62
N.J. Speak	12	8			5	11			138*	6	12	21	4	579	138*	34.05
G.D. Lloyd	12	29	11	–	59	72	7	46	142	15	15	25	1	1194	241	49.75
A. Flintoff											1	1	–	2	2	2.00
W.K. Hegg	37	89	–	–	1	30*	2	–	24*	28	17	25	6	713	134	37.52
I.D. Austin	95*	91	–	–	47	37*			–	0	10	12	3	437	95*	18.55
S. Elworthy	3	17*	13		45	–	13	–			12	16	2	288	88	20.57
G. Yates											3	5	1	21	16	5.25
R.J. Green											7	10	3	91	25*	13.00
G. Keedy			–	–	0*	–	–	–	–	0	14	14	8	73	26	12.16
J.E.R. Gallian			14	22*	140	0	312	11	13	29	14	27	3	1136	312	47.33
J.P. Crawley							54	97*	46	25	12	20	3	904	112*	53.17
G. Chapple	12	30*	–	–	18	19	32	–	–	21*	15	21	6	313	37*	20.86
M. Watkinson	5	25	49*	–	2	9	46	–	1	22	16	26	1	610	64	24.40
P.J. Martin	0	–					1*	–	–	34	12	16	4	251	42	20.91
N.H. Fairbrother	21	18	144	–	46	53					12	20	–	1068	204	53.40
N.T. Wood											1	1	–	1	1	1.00
P.C. McKeown			9	–							2	2	–	73	64	36.50
J.J. Haynes											1	2	–	26	16	13.00
Byes		2	4	1	4	4	8	4	15	7						
Leg-byes	2	14	5	1	3	1	6	1	9	3						
Wides	5	17			2		2		1							
No-balls	32	4	10		12		8		22	6						
Total	264	441	380	45	392	256	587	174	478	238						
Wickets	10	8	5	0	10	7	9	3	5	10						
Result	W		D		D		L		L							
Points	22		8		8		7		7							

Batting

	v. Surrey (Southport) 7–10 August		v. Hampshire (Old Trafford) 15–19 August		v. Yorkshire (Leeds) 22–26 August		v. Sussex (Hove) 29 August–2 September		v. Middlesex (Old Trafford) 3–6 September		v. Northamptonshire (Northampton) 12–16 September		v. Warwickshire (Edgbaston) 19–22 September		M	Inns	NO	Runs	HS	Av
S.P. Titchard	17	54			9	18	41	30	67	0	0	26	48	–	13	23	2	939	163	44.71
M.A. Atherton			63	50					14	10					9	16	–	538	98	33.62
N.J. Speak	34	39			4	77	0	1							12	21	4	579	138*	34.05
G.D. Lloyd	19	46	21	19	36	19			5	42	17	70	113	–	15	25	1	1194	241	49.75
A. Flintoff															1	1	–	2	2	2.00
W.K. Hegg	32	0	48	6*	0	24*	54	10*			28	7	14	–	17	25	6	713	134	37.52
I.D. Austin	0	40					18	–							10	12	3	437	95*	18.55
S. Elworthy	0	17							3	1					12	16	2	288	88	20.57
G. Yates											16	0	0	–	3	5	1	21	16	5.25
R.J. Green			9	–	6	1*	9	–	20	2	25*	5*	0	–	7	10	3	91	25*	13.00
G. Keedy			8*	–	0	–	0	–	1*	2*			1*	–	14	14	8	73	26	12.16
J.E.R. Gallian	3	57	41	44	27	12	20	37	26	0	113	1	3	–	14	27	3	1136	312	47.33
J.P. Crawley			4	100*			1	112*	36	0	46	58	73	–	12	20	3	904	112*	53.17
G. Chapple	1	12*	1	–	23	0	37*	–			30	20	10	–	15	21	6	313	37*	20.86
M. Watkinson	27	53	44	33	64	6	9	1	0	13	46	39			16	26	1	610	64	24.40
P.J. Martin	1*	0	37	–	19*	–			42	21	2	18			12	16	4	251	42	20.91
N.H. Fairbrother	0	1	54	36	86	55	15	79			9	17	204	–	12	20	–	1068	204	53.40
N.T. Wood															1	1	–	1	1	1.00
P.C. McKeown													64	–	2	2	–	73	64	36.50
J.J. Haynes									16	10					1	2	–	26	16	13.00
Byes		10		5	4	4	1	4	19		9	2	34							
Leg-byes	1	4	7	9	19	1	5	9	5	3	9	5	15							
Wides	2	4	1				2	1			2		2							
No-balls	8	31	4	4	26	14	6	6	8	2	4	7	16							
Total	145	368	342	306	323	231	218	290	262	106	356	275	597							
Wickets	10	10	10	5	10	7	10	5	10	10	10	10	10							
Result	L		D		D		W		L		L		D							
Points	4		10		8		21		6		7		11							

Fielding Figures

55 – W.K. Hegg (ct 50 / st 5)
11 – S.P. Titchard and M. Watkinson
10 – N.H. Fairbrother and N.J. Speak
9 – J.E.R. Gallian
7 – G. Keedy
6 – S. Elworthy
5 – G.D. Lloyd
3 – I.D. Austin, J.P. Crawley and M.A. Atherton
2 – G. Yates and R.J. Green
1 – A. Flintoff, G. Chapple, P.C. McKeown, P.J. Martin, J.J. Haynes (ct 0 / st 1) and sub

Bowling

	S. Elworthy	I.D. Austin	R.J. Green	G. Keedy	G. Yates	S.P. Titchard	P.J. Martin	G. Chapple	M. Watkinson	J.E.R. Gallian	N.J. Speak	M.A. Atherton	Byes	Leg-byes	Wides	No-balls	Total	Wkts
v. Yorkshire (Old Trafford)	24–3–89–2	23–13–43–1	16.5–5–41–6	18–8–32–0	10–4–12–0	2–0–14–0							1	5		2	237	9
18–20 April																		
v. Kent (Canterbury)	23–3–78–1	18.1–3–79–3					20–6–55–0	20–5–57–2	8–1–25–3	9–3–17–1			1	8	3	12	320	10
2–6 May							6–0–19–1		5.3–0–47–2								66	3
v. Leicestershire (Old Trafford)	24.4–0–133–3	22–6–35–0		29–10–59–2			28–7–57–1		34–12–71–4	3–0–6–0			10	6		20	377	10
9–13 May																		
v. Nottinghamshire (Trent Bridge)	30.5–8–91–4			23–4–71–0			25–5–83–2	24–2–88–1	18–2–46–0	14–2–60–2			6	7	2	8	452	10
16–20 May	20–3–52–2			13–2–47–0			20–5–50–7	5–0–19–0	11–3–43–0	4–2–20–1				7	2	4	238	10
v. Gloucestershire (Old Trafford)	26–6–80–4			22–9–33–0			26–8–45–3	25–8–55–3	18–3–44–0				3	10		2	270	10
30 May–3 June																		
v. Essex (Chelmsford)	21–3–78–0	31–5–116–5		34–11–75–2				20.1–1–110–2	28–6–105–1		5–0–18–0			7		14	509	10
6–10 June	9–0–38–0	5–3–9–0		29–13–45–3				9–1–32–1	28–4–91–2		1–0–9–0			5		4	229	6
v. Durham (Chester-le-Street)	9–1–37–2	6–1–25–0					21–6–44–3	22–6–64–5						11	2	6	181	10
13–17 June	11–1–54–1	10.3–4–33–4					14–6–33–2	14–4–46–3					6	7	4	8	179	10
v. Somerset (Old Trafford)	5–1–18–1	7–1–20–0		2.1–0–10–1				6–3–14–0	10–5–12–1					1		6	75	3
27 June–1 July																		
v. Worcestershire (Old Trafford)	10.2–2–42–0	17–5–52–0		27–7–67–1				12–1–61–0	23–4–82–1	6–0–35–0			11		1	2	350	3
4–8 July	11–1–38–1	3–0–13–0		10–3–27–0				7–1–19–2	11–2–62–1	3–1–6–0				6			171	4
v. Derbyshire (Old Trafford)	21–4–92–1			21–6–67–0		6–2–8–0	22–3–69–1	23–7–83–4	28–1–108–2	5–0–12–0			20	14	2	10	473	8
18–22 July	8–0–35–0			21–1–91–3			8–1–15–1	15–0–55–3	12.3–0–70–0				11	12	2	2	289	8
v. Glamorgan (Cardiff)		23–6–57–1		28–5–70–0			32–8–115–3	33–8–122–3	22.2–3–73–3	14–5–51–0			1	16		2	505	10
25–29 July		7–0–36–0		16–4–50–1			14–2–47–2	8–1–46–0	12–0–59–0				14	7		2	259	3
v. Surrey (Southport)	11–0–59–1	16–4–46–4					16.4–2–59–4	12–3–37–1						10		19	211	10
7–10 August	24.1–4–88–2	8–1–44–0				5–0–24–0	3–1–27–0	15–2–93–2	10–2–39–0	24–4–115–6			4	8		8	442	10
v. Hampshire (Old Trafford)			11–1–22–0	21–6–44–0			19–0–26–3	18–7–43–4	18–2–71–2	4–1–10–1		2–0–7–0	2	9		2	234	10
15–19 August			11–0–54–1	27–10–49–2			25–8–64–0	19–7–48–1	20–5–62–1	2–0–12–0		3–1–8–0		7	5	4	304	6
v. Yorkshire (Leeds)			27–5–88–2	44–10–122–2			26–6–98–1	16–2–81–0	19–4–73–2	13–2–55–1			7	5		8	529	8
22–26 August																		
v. Sussex (Hove)		27–12–37–4	25–6–101–2	8–2–20–0				29.3–2–118–2	20–6–55–1	8–3–17–1			7	8	1	2	363	10
29 August–2 September			14–7–20–3	13–2–34–2				16–5–38–1	9–5–22–1	4.4–0–20–2			4	6		2	144	10
v. Middlesex (Old Trafford)	10–1–48–1		15–3–42–0	2–1–4–0			14–5–31–4		9.4–1–15–5	3–0–9–0			8	3		2	160	10
3–6 September	9.1–2–15–2		4–0–14–0	27–6–55–2			15–2–37–2		25–2–104–4					6	1	4	231	10
v. Northamptonshire (Northampton)			25.5–7–78–4		31–10–91–3		30–4–92–2	26–6–94–0	18–2–63–1	11–3–33–0			4	16			471	10
12–16 September			4–0–20–0		8.2–0–53–0		8–1–25–1	4–0–14–0	10–0–47–0				1	3			163	1
v. Warwickshire (Edgbaston)			18–1–67–2	15–4–50–1	16–0–65–1	15–3–51–1		28.3–6–85–4		14–2–56–1			5	7	2	18	386	10
19–22 September			16–2–52–2	28–7–93–1	28–6–104–1	9–2–27–0		21–2–50–1		2–0–18–0				11	1	4	359	6A
	308.1–43–	223.4–64–	187.4–37–	475.1–131–	93.2–20–	37–7–	392.4–86–	448.1–90–	428–75–	143.4–28–	6–0–	5–1–						
	1165–28	645–22	599–22	1215–23	325–5	124–1	1091–43	1572–45	1489–37	552–16	27–0	15–0						
Bowler's average	41.60	29.31	27.22	52.82	65.00	124.00	25.37	34.93	40.24	34.50	–	–						

A G.D. Lloyd 2–0–4–1

Leicestershire CCC First-Class Matches Batting

Batting	v. Oxford University (Oxford) 13–16 April		v. Derbyshire (Derby) 2–6 May		v. Lancashire (Old Trafford) 9–13 May		v. Worcestershire (Leicester) 16–20 May		v. Warwickshire (Edgbaston) 23–27 May		v. Indians (Leicester) 1–3 June		v. Kent (Leicester) 5–8 June		v. Surrey (The Oval) 13–17 June		v. Yorkshire (Bradford) 20–24 June		v. Essex (Leicester) 4–8 July		v. Gloucestershire (Cheltenham) 18–22 July		M	Inns	NO	Runs	HS	Av
G.I. Macmillan	8	17	41	0																			7	12	1	201	41	18.27
V.J. Wells	57	33	0	24	4	–	35	–	21	–	52	–	44	57	41	0	200	–	197	–	5	13	20	30	–	1331	204	44.36
B.F. Smith	123*	–	0	3	81	–	25	–	45	–	2	–	174*	60	7	17	23	–	18	–	68*	7	20	29	3	1243	190	47.80
D.L. Maddy	2	33*	43	39	10	–	63	–	36	–	61	–	16	2	7	43	18	–	35	–	31	14	20	30	2	958	101*	34.12
J.J. Whitaker	0	47	110	24*	18	–	168	–	15	–			15	6	7	32	218	–	4	–	5	31	16	23	3	1093	218	54.65
P.A. Nixon	100*	–	31	–	106	–	0	–	1	–	24*	–	8	7	66	5	77*	–	0	–	4	3	20	27	5	880	106	40.00
C.C. Remy	–	–																					1					–
A.D. Mullally	–	–	1	–	7*	–	–	–	–	–	–	–			68	13					1	1	11	8	1	195	75	27.85
G.J. Parsons	–	14*	21	–			46*	–	1	–			14	–	51	0	0*	–	8	–	13	10*	18	23	5	290	53	16.11
A.R.K. Pierson	–	–	20*	–	0	–	8*	–	2*	–	–	–	44	0*	33*	0	14	–	11*	–	0	16	20	23	10	263	44	20.23
D.J. Millns	–	–	9	–	73	–	4	–	28	–	–	–	0	–	23	26*	–	–	103	–	0	21	19	20	1	424	103	22.31
A. Habib			27	42*	17	–	215	–	24	–	90	–	20	9*	79	16	17	–	1	–	0	4	16	24	2	792	215	36.00
P.V. Simmons					25	–	51	–	143*	–	58	–	82	22	0	9	69	–	4	–	0	0	17	24	2	1244	171	56.54
M.T. Brimson					0	–					–	–	0	–			–	–	13*	–			12	12	6	51	13*	8.50
D. Williamson											–	–											1					–
I.J. Sutcliffe																							1	2	–	16	15	8.00
V.P. Clark																							1	2	–	43	43	21.50
Byes			2		10				8		5		8	7	3	4	10		1		5	8						
Leg-byes	6		3	1	6		6		13		14		4	2	5	1	15		22		10	1						
Wides	3	1	1				1							1	5	3			3		1	1						
No-balls			6	4	20		16		16		12		2		16	6	20		34		16	20						
Total	299	145	315	137	377		638		353		318		431	173	411	175	681		454		159	150						
Wickets	4	3	10	4	10		8		8		5		10	6	10	10	7		9		10	10						
Result	D		W		D		W		D		D		D		L		W		W		W							
Points	–		22		9		24		11		–		11		5		24		24		20							

Batting

Batting	v. Sussex (Leicester) 25–29 July		v. Northamptonshire (Leicester) 1–5 August		v. Glamorgan (Swansea) 8–12 August		v. Pakistanis (Leicester) 14–16 August		v. Hampshire (Leicester) 22–26 August		v. Somerset (Leicester) 29 August–2 September		v. Nottinghamshire (Trent Bridge) 3–6 September		v. Durham (Chester-le-Street) 12–16 September		v. Middlesex (Leicester) 19–22 September		M	Inns	NO	Runs	HS	Av
G.I. Macmillan			2	12	18	31					37	–	28	7*	0	–			7	12	1	201	41	18.27
V.J. Wells	7	28	204	4	44	46	17	0	24	–	9	–	119	13	28	–	5	–	20	30	–	1331	204	44.36
B.F. Smith	22	45	9	41	190	32	7	43	34	–	48	–	24	11	70	–	14	–	20	29	3	1243	190	47.80
D.L. Maddy	18	68	23	101*	43	2	31	16	11	–	47	–	28	5	82	–	30	–	20	30	2	958	101*	34.12
J.J. Whitaker	58*	3							48	–	33	–	129	30*	3	–	89	–	16	23	3	1093	218	54.65
P.A. Nixon	74	14	18	33	42	27*	6	21	67	–	23	–	18	–	103*	–	2	–	20	27	5	880	106	40.00
C.C. Remy																			1					–
A.D. Mullally			29	–											–	–	75	–	11	8	1	195	75	27.85
G.J. Parsons	2	17	5	8	0	6*	0	10	0	–	5	–	53	–	–	–	6	–	18	23	5	290	53	16.11
A.R.K. Pierson	9	1*	16	8*	13*	–	4	11	9*	–	29	–	12	–	–	–	3	–	20	23	10	263	44	20.23
D.J. Millns	23	0			6	11	9	26	17	–	5	–	0	–	–	–	40	–	19	20	1	424	103	22.31
A. Habib	30	16	19	1	34	28	23	27	4	–							49	–	16	24	2	792	215	36.00
P.V. Simmons	13	36	75	72	92	34			108	–	27	–	0	11	171	–	142*	–	17	24	2	1244	171	56.54
M.T. Brimson	3	0	2*	–	4	–	4*	10*	10	–	1*	–	4*	–					12	12	6	51	13*	8.50
D. Williamson																			1					–
I.J. Sutclifee							15	1											1	2	–	16	15	8.00
V.P. Clark							43	0											1	2	–	43	43	21.50
Byes		9	1	1	2	4	21	7	9		1		8				16							
Leg-byes	4	1	14	12	8	7	5	9	3		7		4	1	10		25							
Wides	1		1	1	10	1	4		1						5		2							
No-balls	2	2	4	4	30	2	10	2	8		24		12	4	44		14							
Total	266	240	422	298	536	231	199	183	353		296		439	82	516		512							
Wickets	10	10	10	7	10	7	10	10	10		10		10	4	6		10							
Result	W		D		D		L		D		W		W		W		W							
Points	22		9		11		–		11		22		24		24		24							

Fielding Figures

62 – P.A. Nixon (ct 56 / st 6)
35 – P.V. Simmons
22 – G.J. Parsons
20 – V.J. Wells
18 – D.L. Maddy
16 – A.R.K. Pierson
10 – A. Habib
6 – D.J. Millns
5 – B.F. Smith
2 – G.J. Whitaker and M.T. Brimson
1 – A.D. Mullally, V.P. Clarke and sub

Bowling	D.J. Millns	A.D. Mullally	G.J. Parsons	A.R.K. Pierson	V.J. Wells	D.L. Maddy	G.I. Macmillan	P.V. Simmons	M.T. Brimson	D. Williamson	V.P. Clarke	Byes	Leg-byes	Wides	No-balls	Total	Wkts
v. Oxford University (Oxford)	18–6–59–2	15–2–53–1	13–3–37–1	13–2–33–1	4–0–9–1	2–1–1–0	2–1–1–0					4	10			207	6
13–16 April	6–1–21–1	9.4–2–31–0	10–2–43–1	9–0–58–0	2–0–20–0	5–0–28–2							11		2	212	7
v. Derbyshire (Derby)	19–0–97–0	24–3–83–5	16.4–1–59–2	16–4–63–1	14–2–41–0	7–3–10–0						2	7	3	2	362	8
2–6 May	17.5–5–34–4	17–4–47–6										3	5			89	10
v. Lancashire (Old Trafford)	24–9–62–2	32–9–94–0		34.5–7–100–4	11–2–53–0	11–4–21–2		17–2–48–1	31–4–95–1			2	20	4	4	495	10
9–13 May		7–2–7–0		20–3–72–0	4–0–16–0	7–2–29–0		7–4–8–0	25.2–8–55–3			1	3	1	4	191	3
v. Worcestershire (Leicester)	14.1–4–37–4	9–3–35–3	12–3–35–1	5–2–7–0	5–2–21–1			7–1–16–1					4	1		155	10
16–20 May	22–4–67–2	22.5–4–101–3	14–3–47–1	10–1–32–0	16–1–64–2			7–2–18–2				11	13	2	2	353	10
v. Warwickshire (Edgbaston)	20–6–51–2	22.3–8–53–4	20–4–37–2		5–1–8–1							9	6	1		164	10
22–27 May	14–3–48–1	16–2–56–1	13–2–41–1	30.5–12–68–5	1–0–10–0			6–4–7–0				6	5	1	2	241	8
v. Indians (Leicester)	18–4–57–1	8–0–28–0		20–0–103–0	6–1–21–1				10–2–64–0	12–4–32–1				1	2	305	3
1–3 June	7–0–20–0			22–3–81–1	4–1–9–0	4–1–15–0			22–3–80–2	17–4–63–0		4	1			273	3
v. Kent (Leicester)	21–9–43–3		21–5–56–3	22–5–70–1	8–1–22–0			18–3–43–3	24–5–82–0			2	6	4	8	324	10
5–8 June	8–2–21–0		20–8–57–0	35.4–5–133–3				9–1–29–0	26–5–97–5			11	3	4	2	351	8
v. Surrey (The Oval)	18–5–58–0	24–6–61–0	23.3–4–81–3	46–7–158–6	17–2–67–1			7–2–16–0				5	6	4	2	452	10
13–17 June	17–6–36–1	10–2–48–0	9–3–36–1	15–2–52–0	4–2–2–0			18–2–56–4				6	6	2	19	242	6
v. Yorkshire (Bradford)	20–4–95–2		21–7–83–4		16–9–27–1			15–2–73–0	14.3–2–57–3			4	3		20	342	10
20–24 June	20–4–67–4		21–13–40–3	18–6–30–2	8–2–26–0				4–0–20–1			3	2	3	2	188	10
v. Essex (Leicester)	20–3–74–4		16–8–21–4	8–2–29–0	7–3–19–1			13–4–14–1				1	5		4	163	10
4–8 July	13.4–2–54–6		20–5–40–1	19–6–44–0	4–1–16–0			15–2–65–2	7–1–16–1			5	7		6	247	10
v. Gloucestershire (Cheltenham)	8–3–14–2	8–4–16–3	6–1–20–2					5–0–19–2					2	5	8	71	10
18–22 July	11.3–3–41–3	12–5–22–4	10–4–27–1					9–2–41–2					5		10	136	10
v. Sussex (Leicester)	13.5–5–30–3		29–6–85–1	10–2–36–0	10.1–4–28–1			20.4–6–58–5	23–5–48–0			2	7			294	10
25–29 July	3–0–10–0		15–5–45–1		6–4–9–0			24–8–70–4	10.3–3–12–5			2	6		8	154	10
v. Northamptonshire (Leicester)		38.2–10–112–4	19–5–49–0	32–4–85–1	10–3–37–1		1–0–5–0	14–2–50–2	19–5–65–2			13	9	2	9	425	10
1–5 August		14–4–85–1	21–8–56–0	18–5–49–4			1–0–9–0		5–1–11–0			1	1		8	212	5
v. Glamorgan (Swansea)	20–1–115–1		17–5–55–0	15–1–44–1	13–1–42–1			22.3–4–62–5	30–6–98–1			6	11	1	31	433	10
8–12 August	5–1–19–0		6–1–15–0	20–4–75–2	6–4–3–0		12–4–44–2	10–4–30–1	27–6–86–3			13	14			299	8
v. Pakistanis (Leicester)	18–3–50–1		23–9–42–2	20–8–44–3	5–2–18–0				21–9–39–4		4–1–10–0	5	13	1	4	221	10
14–16 August	5–0–15–0		21–8–62–3	16–2–58–1					19–0–74–0		7–0–42–1	10	1	2		262	6
v. Hampshire (Leicester)	17–10–28–2		16–9–36–4	1–1–0–0	10–2–34–2			10.2–3–32–2				4	3	2	6	137	10
22–26 August	12–2–28–1		9–4–15–1	6–2–9–2	9–2–23–3			13–3–26–0	8–2–18–2			10	6	4		135	9
v. Somerset (Leicester)	12.2–3–35–4		16–8–22–2		5–3–5–2			8–2–19–2					2			83	10
29 August–2 September	12.3–1–43–2		14–7–22–0	6–0–18–2	8–3–17–1			18–6–38–4	16–5–31–1				5		8	174	10
v. Nottinghamshire (Trent Bridge)	20–4–69–1		24.3–6–78–1	14–2–31–3	10–4–23–0			26–7–64–3	15–3–52–1			1	6	1	16	324	10
3–6 September	18.1–6–31–5		16–5–54–0	15–3–43–3				18–4–46–2	3–1–6–0			6	10	2	8	196	10
v. Durham (Chester-le-Street)	5–1–16–1	13–4–47–1	11–3–36–0	4–2–2–0	4–2–7–1			9.3–3–14–6					4	3	10	126	10
12–16 September	8–2–24–1	15–5–27–5	8–0–35–0		14–3–44–4							1	8		6	139	10
v. Middlesex (Leicester)	12.4–5–42–2	18–6–53–4	13.2–3–54–1		7–2–17–2			5.4–2–14–1					10		22	190	10
19–22 September	18.3–6–48–4	14–5–40–3	8–3–15–0	23–4–83–2	2–1–7–0			12–2–45–1				4	6		30	248	10
	538.1–133–	349.2–90–	553–171–	544.2–107–	255.1–70–	36–11–	16–5–	364.4–87–	360.2–76–	29–8–	11–1–						
	1659–72	1099–48	1536–47	1710–48	765–26	104–4	59–2	1021–56	1106–35	95–1	52–1						
Bowler's average	23.04	22.89	32.68	35.62	29.42	26.00	29.50	18.23	31.60	95.00	52.00						

Middlesex CCC First-Class Matches Batting

Batting	v. Oxford University (Oxford) 20–23 April		v. Gloucestershire (Lord's) 2–6 May		v. Durham (Lord's) 9–13 May		v. Cambridge University (Cambridge) 16–18 May		v. Sussex (Horsham) 22–25 May		v. Yorkshire (Lord's) 30 May–3 June		v. Glamorgan (Lord's) 6–10 June		v. Kent (Canterbury) 13–17 June		v. Derbyshire (Derby) 20–24 June		v. Warwickshire (Lord's) 27 June–1 July		v. Surrey (The Oval) 4–8 July		M	Inns	NO	Runs	HS	Av
P.N. Weekes	8	–	34	50	19	73	14	5	–	1	1	15	15	40*	108	14	1	58	42	42	5	3	19	35	2	1218	171*	36.90
J.C. Harrison	38	–					3	7*			37	17	35	3*	40	10	4	0	5	0			7	13	1	199	40	18.09
M.W. Gatting	63	–	23	54	74	171	–	77	–	1	17	–	19	–			29	24	1	–	52	53	16	25	–	901	171	36.04
J.D. Carr	43	–	48	14	16	23	–	34	–	1	94	0	49	–	6	49	36	9	2	–	20	0	17	28	1	783	94	29.00
S.P. Moffat	0	–																					1	1	–	0	0	0.00
M.A. Feltham	13*	–													0	0	0	1					3	5	1	14	13*	3.50
J.P. Hewitt	16*	–	15	4			72	15*	–	4			4	–							19	29*	10	15	4	312	72	28.36
I.J. Gould	–	–																					1					–
A.R.C. Fraser	–	–	7	1	10	2			–	2	15	–	33	–	31	9	24*	2	17	–	1	2	18	28	6	238	33	10.81
D. Follett	–	–	0*	0*	0*	5*	–	–	–	0*	17	–											6	6	5	22	17	22.00
P.C.R. Tufnell	–	–			2	11	–	–	–	0	30*	–	16*	–	17*	6	17	7	8	–	0*	3	18	26	10	290	67*	18.12
J.C. Pooley			3	73	1	23	138*	10	–	5	28	9	1	0	67	20	35	10	5	12	2	3	17	32	1	843	138*	27.19
M.R. Ramprakash			7	34	6	9			–	24	134	60*	97	–	66	30	6	16	169	22*	80	28	16	29	2	1406	169	52.07
K.R. Brown			44	1	32	1	–	33	–	28	49	60*	25	–	21	30	1	29*	79	–	4	5	18	31	5	917	83	35.26
D.J. Goodchild			4	0																			1	2	–	4	4	2.00
U.B.A. Rashid			9	6																			1	2	–	15	9	7.50
R.L. Johnson					9	35													15	37*	0	3	11	20	1	243	37*	12.78
R.A. Fay					0	18	–	–			1	–	26	–	12	0	0	0	25*	–	2	14	15	24	2	163	26	7.40
D.J. Nash							8*	6	–	1													2	3	1	15	8*	7.50
P.E. Wellings															48	41*							4	8	1	237	48	33.85
O.A. Shah																							5	9	1	212	75	26.50
K.P. Dutch																							3	4	–	39	27	9.75
Byes				1		6	4	7				5			5	24	4	4	5	5	1	8						
Leg-byes	6		2	4	10	7	2	4		3	8	3	12	1	5	10	3	5	24	1	2	3						
Wides	10		2	1		3		1		1			1	1	1		1	3	4	1	2	6						
No-balls			2	4	12	4	2	12		14	16	2	2		14	4	4	8	12	2	42	34						
Total	197		200	247	191	391	243	211	0	85	447	171	335	45	441	247	165	176	413	122	232	194						
Wickets	5		10	10	10	10	3	6	0	10	10	4	10	1	10	10	10	10	10	3	10	10						
Result	D		L		W		D		L		W		W		D		L		D		L							
Points	–		5		20		–		3		24		23		10		4		5		5							

Batting

Batting	v. Northamptonshire (Northampton) 18–22 July		v. Essex (Lord's) 1–5 August		v. Nottinghamshire (Trent Bridge) 8–12 August		v. Worcestershire (Lord's) 15–19 August		v. Hampshire (Portsmouth) 28–31 August		v. Lancashire (Old Trafford) 3–6 September		v. Somerset (Uxbridge) 12–16 September		v. Leicestershire (Leicester) 19–22 September		M	Inns	NO	Runs	HS	Av
P.N. Weekes	8	140	0	0	58	–	0	37	28	24	26	12	171*	160	5	1	19	35	2	1218	171*	36.90
J.C. Harrison																	7	13	1	199	40	18.09
M.W. Gatting	0	1					25	0	8	83	40	50	–	5	7	24	16	25	–	901	171	36.04
J.D. Carr	6	57	66	17	49	–	66*	14	10	4	37	13					17	28	1	783	94	29.00
S.P. Moffat																	1	1	–	0	0	0.00
M.A. Feltham																	3	5	1	14	13*	3.50
J.P. Hewitt	45	11	27	27			10	14*					–	–			10	15	4	312	72	28.36
I.J. Gould																	1					–
A.R.C. Fraser	8*	0	3	4	9	–	29	3	2*	7	2	2*	–	4*	8*	1	18	28	6	238	33	10.81
D. Follett																	6	6	5	22	17	22.00
P.C.R. Tufnell	0	8	6	16*	13*	–	67*	1*	17	7	0*	22	–	0*	16	0	18	26	10	290	67*	18.12
J.C. Pooley	8	3	50	15	21	–	45	87	1	111	12	4	0	41			17	32	1	843	138*	27.19
M.R. Ramprakash			0	0	71	–	64	10	46	108	24	10	26	110	71	78	16	29	2	1406	169	52.07
K.R. Brown	54	18*	64*	6	70	–	0	30	57	0	1	83	56*	11	4	21	18	31	5	917	83	35.26
D.J. Goodchild																	1	2	–	4	4	2.00
U.B.A. Rashid																	1	2	–	15	9	7.50
R.L. Johnson	6	6	5	5	15	–	9	28	1	15	0	9	–	2	27	16	11	20	1	243	37*	12.78
R.A. Fay	11	0	2	0	14	–	14	3	4	5	0	2			0	10*	15	24	2	163	26	7.40
D.J. Nash																	2	3	1	15	8*	7.50
P.E. Wellings	4	42	19	23											18	42	4	8	1	237	48	33.85
O.A. Shah					53	–			17	38*	5	13	75	2	2	7	5	9	1	212	75	26.50
K.P. Dutch					27	–							–	4	0	8	3	4	–	39	27	9.75
Byes	5	5			4		2	5		9	8		2	1		4						
Leg-byes	2	2	6	2	6		14	2		6	3	6	9	14	10	6						
Wides		1			1		5	2	2	3		1	1	1								
No-balls		8	16	6	16		2	6	6	6	2	4	10	2	22	30						
Total	157	302	264	121	427		352	242	199	426	160	231	350	357	190	248						
Wickets	10	10	10	10	10		9	9	10	10	10	10	3	8	10	10						
Result	W		L		W		D		W		W		D		L							
Points	20		5		24		9		20		20		9		4							

Fielding Figures

61 – K.R. Brown (ct 60 / st 1)
28 – J.D. Carr
23 – J.C. Pooley
11 – P.N. Weekes
10 – M.W. Gatting and J.C. Harrison
7 – P.C.J. Tufnell and M.R. Ramprakash
5 – R.A. Fay and J.P. Hewitt
3 – A.R.C. Fraser and subs
2 – D. Follett and K.P. Dutch
1 – D.J. Nash, P.E. Wellings, R.L. Johnson and O.H. Shah

Bowling

Bowling	A.R.C. Fraser	D. Follett	J.P. Hewitt	D.J. Goodchild	U.B.A. Rashid	P.N. Weekes	R.L. Johnson	R.A. Fay	P.C.R. Tufnell	K.P. Dutch	M.R. Ramprakash	M.A. Feltham	Byes	Leg-byes	Wides	No-balls	Total	Wkts
v. Oxford University (Oxford)																		Ab
20–23 April																		
v. Gloucestershire (Lord's)	17–7–33–3	18–3–94–5	17–4–77–2	2–0–11–0										3		4	218	10
2–6 May	22–4–73–1	11–1–47–1	13–0–53–2	2.5–0–15–0	6–1–17–0	6–0–19–1								7	1	2	231	5
v. Durham (Lord's)	23.2–5–47–3	14–2–65–2				6–4–10–0	11–3–47–2	16–4–33–3	4–3–2–0					5		2	209	10
9–13 May	10–3–20–1	12.2–3–22–8						8–2–12–0	6–1–8–1					5		2	67	10
v. Cambridge University (Cambridge)		21–4–77–0	12–3–34–3			25–6–73–2		4–1–19–1	30–3–88–1					9		6	300	7
16–18 May		11–1–54–0				24–6–61–5		6–1–14–0	28.3–11–56–5				6	6		8	197	10
v. Sussex (Horsham)	24–6–56–1	24–6–99–1	11–3–43–1			1–0–2–0			11–2–42–0		4–0–26–2			7	1	22	319	7A
22–25 May																	0	0
v. Yorkshire (Lord's)	20–6–50–0	26–4–99–5						16–1–40–2	29–9–73–3				2	11	1	16	275	10
30 May–3 June	29.2–7–92–3	10–2–32–1				6–2–25–0		11–2–51–1	43–13–106–4				3	13		4	322	10
v. Glamorgan (Lord's)	24–9–60–3		11.1–0–56–3			10–5–14–0		18–5–53–4	28–9–49–0					6	1	4	238	10
6–10 June	11–4–26–0		2–0–11–0			20–5–39–8		4–1–15–0	25.2–7–39–2				2	9			141	10
v. Kent (Canterbury)	31–8–72–1					13–2–39–0		24–5–73–1	50–17–126–3			24–10–62–3	10	8		8	390	8
13–17 June	12–0–41–1					17–5–63–0		4–1–19–1	27.3–9–60–3		7–4–12–0			10		8	205	6
v. Derbyshire (Derby)	27–6–78–1					10–2–40–0		17–1–71–3	40.3–14–72–5			14–3–48–1		12			321	10
20–24 June	13–1–55–1					12–2–42–0		25–8–84–1	30–6–85–0		1–0–4–0	19–1–75–0	6	7			383	2B
v. Warwickshire (Lord's)	30.2–6–109–2					11–2–43–0	23–2–109–1	29–8–86–1	46–17–71–5		1–0–2–0		1	24		12	445	9
27 June–1 July																		
v. Surrey (The Oval)	22–5–59–1		12–4–44–2			11–4–29–1	17–0–70–1	29–9–95–0	25.3–6–56–5				2	11	4	16	366	10
4–8 July	5–2–19–0		1.2–0–7–0				6–1–18–2		12–5–17–1							2	61	3
v. Northamptonshire (Northampton)	17–6–28–4		9–3–20–2			11–4–18–0	6–0–20–1	15–4–45–2	8–1–36–1					5	1	4	172	10
18–22 July	14–1–41–0		10–1–27–3			20–1–61–4		10–1–47–0	36.4–9–79–3				1	5	1	10	261	10
v. Essex (Lord's)	40–6–122–4		17–3–101–0			8–0–44–1	23–3–96–2		39.4–21–53–3					20	1	14	436	10
1–5 August																		
v. Nottinghamshire (Trent Bridge)	23–7–73–3					12–1–28–1	19–2–66–2	11–3–31–0	38–15–41–4				8	10		6	257	10
8–12 August	12–3–18–0					14–4–31–2	19.5–6–29–5	12–3–22–1	33–13–45–2				11	7			163	10
v. Worcestershire (Lord's)	33.5–8–69–3		23–5–73–3			6–0–28–0	11–0–70–0	27–7–70–2	26–11–48–2					11		4	369	10
15–19 August	8–3–11–0		8–4–17–1			29–2–103–3	5–2–12–0	3–0–9–0	47–17–72–4				2	7		8	233	8
v. Hampshire (Portsmouth)	28–8–55–5					2–0–4–0	26–5–87–1	28–9–77–4	3–1–5–0					4		12	232	10
28–31 August	22–5–79–5					25–6–62–1		6–3–9–0	24.1–10–39–4				10	6			205	10
v. Lancashire (Old Trafford)	6–1–17–0					36–7–119–2	2–0–7–0	3–0–6–0	38.1–11–74–6		7–0–15–1		19	5		8	262	10
3–6 September	3–0–7–0					3–0–10–0	15–3–37–3		20.1–4–49–7					3		2	106	10
v. Somerset (Uxbridge)	29–4–96–1		33–8–118–2			28–4–65–0	30–5–89–3		45–19–86–1	7–2–25–3			2	4			485	10
12–16 September	4–2–11–0						3–1–8–0		18–5–46–2	16–2–60–0	11–0–62–0			5		2	258	3C
v. Leicestershire (Leicester)	31.5–5–119–2					5–1–10–1	26–3–113–2	34–5–140–4	26–4–89–1				16	25	2	14	512	10
19–22 September																		
	592.4–138–	147.2–26–	179.3–38–	4.5–0–	6–1–	371–75–	242.5–36–	360–84–	839.1–273–	23–4–	31–4–	57–14–						
	1636–49	589–23	681–24	26–0	17–0	1082–32	878–25	1121–31	1712–78	85–3	121–3	185–4						
Bowler's average	33.38	25.60	28.37	–	–	33.81	35.12	36.16	21.94	28.33	40.33	46.25						

A D.J. Nash 10–1–44–1
B M.W. Gatting 4–0–25–0
C J.C. Pooley 4–0–42–0; O.A. Shah 5–0–24–1

Northamptonshire CCC First-Class Matches Batting

	v. Durham (Chester-le-Street) 2–6 May		v. Glamorgan (Northampton) 9–13 May		v. Oxford University (Oxford) 16–18 May		v. Somerset (Taunton) 23–27 May		v. Warwickshire (Northampton) 30 May–3 June		v. Nottinghamshire (Trent Bridge) 6–10 June		v. Essex (Chelmsford) 13–17 June		v. Hampshire (Basingstoke) 19–22 June		v. Derbyshire (Northampton) 27 June–1 July		v. Pakistanis (Northampton) 6–8 July		v. Middlesex (Northampton) 18–22 July		M	Inns	NO	Runs	HS	Av
R.R. Montgomerie	22	55*	51	53	126	–	5	19*	7	12	31	–	4	120	0	0	7	18	43	168	4	26	17	32	3	1111	168	38.31
A. Fordham	40	–	52	29*			4	14*			2	–							37	144*	2	29	10	18	3	502	144*	33.46
R.J. Bailey	45	3	0	34			34	–	25	16	163	–	16	10	11	11	68	13	7	29	6	9	12	22	2	722	163	36.10
M.B. Loye	4	11	36	28	67*	–	114	–	39	7	98	–	42	40	1	0	23	13	1	6			14	25	2	1048	205	45.56
R.J. Warren	34	2	201*	–			28	–	76	0	22	–	0	45	0	8	4	17	1	–	6	11	11	18	1	486	201*	28.58
D.J. Capel	14	40	83	10			68	–	57	0	3	–	6	37	9	18	9	0	2	9*	19	95	16	30	2	814	103	29.07
K.M. Curran	68	10*	0	5*			5	–	55	16					53	49	47	29*			55*	62	15	28	7	1242	150	59.14
A.L. Penberthy	31	–	7*	5	–	7	45	–	10	43	54	–	8	66*	20	30	17	7*			25	0	18	29	4	635	87	25.40
D. Ripley	34	–	–	5*	–	23*			20	35*									13	–			11	16	7	448	88*	49.77
J.E. Emburey	1	–	–	–			12	–			67*	–	2	40	0*	11*	5	–			11	0	11	13	4	200	67*	22.22
J.P. Taylor	0*	–	–	–			18*	–	1*	3	57	–	38*	–	10	1	3*	–			4	2	17	23	9	242	57	17.28
D.J. Roberts					72	–							41	73	23	29	3	13					4	7	–	254	73	36.28
T.C. Walton					55*	–																	6	10	1	302	58	33.55
A.J. Swann					–	76*																	3	5	1	100	76*	25.00
J.N. Snape					–	64													8	4*	29	8	10	16	3	277	64	21.30
A.R. Roberts					–	–			0	19	34	–	37	0	10	2							6	8	–	141	39	17.62
N.A. Mallender					–	–							13	11					7	–			3	3	–	31	13	10.33
R. Wild					–	–																	1					–
C.E.L. Ambrose							21*	–	6	3	25*	–					3	–					9	13	2	116	25*	10.54
J.G. Hughes																			8	6			2	3	–	22	8	7.33
S.A.J. Boswell																			2*	–	1	2*	2	3	2	5	2*	5.00
D.J.Sales																							4	8	1	280	210*	40.00
K.J. Innes																							4	5	–	108	63	21.60
T.M.B. Bailey																							2	2	1	33	31*	33.00
J.F. Brown																							1	1	1	0	0*	–
Byes			4	3	13	2	5		4	5	14		1	19	5	4	4		5	3		1						
Leg-byes	6	1	8	6	1	1	10		4	1	17			9	2	10	3	14	7	11	5	5						
Wides	1		1		1	1	6	1							1				3		1	1						
No-balls	20		8				8		10	14	14		6	12	2	2	14	6	8	16	4	10						
Total	320	122	451	178	335	174	383	34	314	174	601		214	482	147	175	210	130	152	396	172	261						
Wickets	10	4	6	5	2	2	9	0	10	10	9		10	9	10	10	10	6	10	4	10	10						
Result	D		L		D		L		L		D		D		L		W		D		L							
Points	9		7		–		4		5		8		8		4		21		–		4							

Batting

	v. Worcestershire (Kidderminster) 24–27 July		v. Leicestershire (Leicester) 1–5 August		v. Kent (Northampton) 8–12 August		v. Sussex (Northampton) 22–26 August		v. Gloucestershire (Bristol) 29 August–2 September		v. Surrey (The Oval) 3–6 September		v. Lancashire (Northampton) 12–16 September		v. Yorkshire (Northampton) 19–22 September		M	Inns	NO	Runs	HS	Av
R.R. Montgomerie	34	17*			8	57	6	14	20	5	4	38			10	127	17	32	3	1111	168	38.31
A. Fordham	29	31	9	19	53	1	4	3									10	18	3	502	144*	33.46
R.J. Bailey													41	92*	28	61*	12	22	2	722	163	36.10
M.B. Loye			4	69							9	45	90	67*	29	205	14	25	2	1048	205	45.56
R.J. Warren													31	0			11	18	1	486	201*	28.58
D.J. Capel	32	103	29	14	1	0	0	39*	18	39	12	48					16	30	2	814	103	29.07
K.M. Curran	40	42*	150	62*	45	49	117	30*	52	13	17	1	93	–	48	29	15	28	7	1242	150	59.14
A.L. Penberthy	2	–	87	0	14	3	42	–	19	2	28	26	29	–	6	2*	18	29	4	635	87	25.40
D. Ripley	88*	–	9	–	5	0	66*	30	20*	36	55	9*					11	16	7	448	88*	49.77
J.E. Emburey			6*	–			30	–							15	–	11	13	4	200	67*	22.22
J.P. Taylor	36	–	5	–	0*	0*	7	1	6	13*	0	0*	1	–	36	–	17	23	9	242	57	17.28
D.J. Roberts																	4	7	–	254	73	36.28
T.C. Walton	0	27	51	38	0	15							52	–	6	58	6	10	1	302	58	33.55
A.J. Swann									2	14	6	2					3	5	1	100	76*	25.00
J.N. Snape	1	–	37	0*	0	16	0	–	9	33	36*	20	12	–			10	16	3	277	64	21.30
A.R. Roberts	39	–															6	8	–	141	39	17.62
N.A. Mallender																	3	3	–	31	13	10.33
R. Wild																	1					–
C.E.L. Ambrose			5	–	2	1	23	–	11	11	3	2					9	13	2	116	25*	10.54
J.G. Hughes													8	–			2	3	–	22	8	7.33
S.A.J. Boswell																	2	3	2	5	2*	5.00
D.J.Sales	0	210*			0	25			10	2	33	0					4	8	1	280	210*	40.00
K.J. Innes							20	–	3	20			63	–	2	–	4	5	–	108	63	21.60
T.M.B. Bailey													31*	–	2	–	2	2	1	33	31*	33.00
J.F. Brown															0*	–	1	1	1	0	0*	–
Byes		4	13	1		10	1	8	4	12		12	4	1	9	5						
Leg-byes	16	3	9	1	5	9	8	4	4	9	10	11	16	3	7	11						
Wides	3	1	2				3	1		2		5										
No-balls	8	8	9	8		10	34	12	12	16	22	14			24	33						
Total	328	446	425	212	133	196	361	142	190	227	235	233	471	163	222	531						
Wickets	10	3	10	5	10	10	10	4	10	10	10	9†	10	1	10	4						
Result	D		D		L		W		L		L		W		D							
Points	9		11		4		24		4		5		24		6							

†D. Ripley retired hurt

Fielding Figures

23 – D. Ripley
20 – R.J. Warren (ct 19 / st 1)
16 – K.M. Curran
13 – D.J. Capel and R.R. Montgomerie
11 – C.E.L. Ambrose
9 – A.L. Penberthy
8 – R.J. Bailey and A. Fordham
6 – J.E. Emburey
5 – M.B. Loye
4 – D.J. Sales and T.M.B. Bailey
3 – J.P. Taylor, J.N. Snape and K.J. Innes
2 – T.C. Walton
1 – J.G. Hughes, A.R. Roberts, N.A. Mallender, A.J. Swann, J.F. Brown and sub

Bowling

	J.P. Taylor	D.J. Capel	K.M. Curran	J.E. Emburey	A.L. Penberthy	R.J. Bailey	N.A. Mallender	S.A.J. Boswell	A.R. Roberts	T.C. Walton	J.N. Snape	C.E.L. Ambrose	Byes	Leg-byes	Wides	No-balls	Total	Wkts
v. Durham (Chester-le-Street)	20–4–47–2	17–0–46–0	14–3–34–2	25–8–53–1	12.4–3–30–2								5	6		4	221	7
2–6 May	11–2–29–3	7–0–32–0	4–1–9–0	14–1–54–1	7–0–37–3	0.4–0–2–0								5		6	168	7
v. Glamorgan (Northampton)	15–4–46–1	20.2–4–74–2	20–5–77–1	29–5–76–2	17–1–59–1	5–2–15–0								4	4	10	351	7
9–13 May	16–3–45–2	5–0–40–0	10–1–39–1	19.5–2–85–2	9–0–50–0	4–0–15–0							1	4	1	6	279	5
v. Oxford University (Oxford)							15–7–27–1		30–11–57–3	10–1–42–0	24.2–5–46–0			9			258	7A
16–18 May																		
v. Somerset (Taunton)	7–2–31–0	5–2–7–0	7–1–26–0	3–1–6–0								6–1–12–0		6		4	88	0
23–27 May	15–2–67–1	7–1–23–1	6–1–34–0	19.3–0–70–0	15–0–52–1	4–0–14–0						21–2–61–2	5	4	1	14	330	6
v. Warwickshire (Northampton)	26–1–106–1	24–4–66–1	14–4–35–0		23–2–70–1	11–0–32–0			24.5–3–64–2			28–6–62–5	5	7		12	447	10
30 May–3 June	2–0–8–0					1.5–0–10–1			2–0–19–0			1–0–6–0	1				44	1
v. Nottinghamshire (Trent Bridge)	27–6–84–2	8–1–18–0		24–6–69–2	10–2–26–0				22–7–58–0			22.5–6–91–6	7	6		16	359	10
6–10 June	11–6–15–0	11–3–17–0		26–7–43–3	8–3–13–0	5–3–5–0			24–8–61–1			7–5–5–0	8	9		6	176	4
v. Essex (Chelmsford)	22.2–2–88–7	16–2–52–1		8–1–32–0	16–4–57–2		17–3–73–0						5	1	1		308	10
13–17 June	12–3–31–0	7–1–19–1		32–16–48–4	6–3–9–0	2–0–6–0	7–2–17–0		29–10–70–3				1	3		4	204	8
v. Hampshire (Basingstoke)	28–3–117–2	17.4–4–64–2	11–4–30–0	38–9–81–2	27–8–54–4	1–0–3–0			8–2–38–0					7			394	10
19–22 June																		
v. Derbyshire (Northampton)	8.3–3–19–2	8–2–31–3		1–0–2–0	7–1–16–0							11–4–15–5	8	7	1		98	10
27 June–1 July	19–3–68–1	10–1–34–1	3–0–26–0	18–7–29–2	5–1–12–0							18.4–3–55–6	6	9		6	239	10
v. Pakistanis (Northampton)		17.1–1–60–4				6–3–13–0	2–0–20–0	23–3–77–2			23–7–63–1			8		18	323	10B
6–8 July		7–1–34–1				0.5–0–3–1		9–0–52–2			9–0–63–3		4	3	1	2	205	8
v. Middlesex (Northampton)	22–9–36–5	12–1–30–2	8–1–25–0	4.1–2–7–2	7–1–8–1			14–2–44–0					5	2			157	10
18–22 July	26–7–68–6	11–4–34–1	5–1–16–0	20–3–59–1	15–5–27–1	8–0–31–0		9.4–2–23–1			13–4–37–0		5	2	1	8	302	10
v. Worcestershire (Kidderminster)	22–3–67–0	12–5–46–1	19–5–58–1		7–1–35–0				10–1–41–1		32–8–98–3			5		8	350	7
24–27 July	15–4–53–3	15–3–48–2	11–0–41–1						23–2–119–0		26.4–2–123–1			4		2	388	7
v. Leicestershire (Leicester)	15–1–66–0	16–3–58–1	16–2–75–3	24–5–58–1	14–3–33–0					3–0–16–0	12.1–0–42–4	22–6–59–1	1	14	1	4	422	10
1–5 August	11–0–36–1			33.5–6–99–1	8–2–23–0						38–13–93–1	13–1–34–2	1	12	1	4	298	7
v. Kent (Northampton)	17.4–4–68–3	13–1–40–2	11–1–30–1		10–1–28–1					7–0–26–1	16–2–63–1	17–6–45–1	4	12		4	316	10
8–12 August					1–0–7–0						1.5–0–10–0						17	0
v. Sussex (Northampton)	21.1–2–104–3	15–1–58–0		31–8–77–3	15–4–36–4						15–2–49–0	20–7–46–0	6	13	1	10	389	10
22–26 August	5–1–21–2	6–1–38–1	4–0–19–0									10.5–2–26–6	1	7	2	4	112	10
v. Gloucestershire (Bristol)	18.5–9–38–1	13–2–34–3	6–2–19–1		16–1–50–3							16–4–34–2	1	7	1	14	183	10
29 August–2 September	21–5–61–2	13–1–37–2	6–2–21–0		17–5–43–1						14–5–23–2	22.2–9–35–2	4	8		4	249	10C
v. Surrey (The Oval)	23.5–5–87–4	19–4–74–2	5–0–27–0		17–4–57–2						14–1–59–0	23–6–76–1	2	13		16	395	10
3–6 September	15–7–19–1	16–4–67–1			18–2–71–1						17.3–2–67–2	25–12–55–4	4	15	2	14	298	9
v. Lancashire (Northampton)	27.1–6–73–4				14–4–49–1	3–0–8–0					26–6–75–1		9	9	2	4	356	10D
12–16 September	21.5–6–72–4				7–1–33–0	3–1–4–0					31–5–102–4		2	5		7	275	10
v. Yorkshire (Northampton)	27–3–96–1			26–7–94–0	23.4–6–92–5					9–1–29–1			9	15	1	4	478	10E
19–22 September																		
	549.2–116–	348.1–57–	180–34–	396.2–94–	352.2–68–	55.2–9–	41–12–	55.4–7–	172.5–44–	29–2–	313.3–62–	284.4–80–						
	1766–64	1181–35	641–11	1042–27	1077–34	161–2	137–1	196–5	527–10	113–2	1013–23	717–43						
Bowler's average	27.59	33.74	58.27	38.59	31.67	80.50	137.00	39.20	52.70	56.50	44.04	16.67						

A A.J. Swann 5–1–15–0; R. Wild 14–4–62–1
B J.G. Hughes 22–5–82–1, 7–2–46–0
C K.J. Innes 5–0–17–1
D J.G. Hughes 18–3–72–0, 6–1–21–2; K.J. Innes 22–3–61–4, 7–1–36–0
E K.J. Innes 25–3–79–3; J.F. Brown 22–6–44–0

Nottinghamshire CCC First-Class Matches Batting	*v.* Sussex (Trent Bridge) 2–6 May		*v.* Somerset (Taunton) 9–13 May		*v.* Lancashire (Trent Bridge) 16–20 May		*v.* Oxford University (Oxford) 23–25 May		*v.* Durham (Trent Bridge) 30 May–3 June		*v.* Northamptonshire (Trent Bridge) 6–10 June		*v.* Worcestershire (Worcester) 13–17 June		*v.* Gloucestershire (Trent Bridge) 20–24 June		*v.* Warwickshire (Edgbaston) 4–8 July		*v.* Essex (Chelmsford) 18–22 July		*v.* South Africa 'A' (Trent Bridge) 26–29 July		M	Inns	NO	Runs	HS	Av
P.R. Pollard	63	24			47	2			30	64	58	40	4	–			0	57	14	86	34	72*	13	25	2	737	86	32.04
R.T. Robinson	22	14*	34	37	122	31			14	184	9	44	83	111*	84	–	5	0	38	51			17	31	2	1302	184	44.89
A.A. Metcalfe	1	16	9	47	31	41							80	1	78	–	91	44	7	43			12	22	–	771	128	35.04
P. Johnson	90	6*	0	0	63	88	–	–	34	7	103	24	22	15	36	–	6	2	1	61	26	–	19	33	2	980	109	31.61
C.L. Cairns	33	–	15	48	65	8			42	34*	62	22*	18	1*	114	–	66*	24	3	51			16	29	5	946	114	39.41
C.M. Tolley	13*	–	9	12					31	–	4	–									43	0*	9	14	2	306	67	25.50
R.T. Bates	–	–			18	25*					0	–	34	–	28	–			0	17	15	–	11	15	1	229	34	16.35
K.P. Evans	–	–					–	–	40*	–	46	–	18*	–	33	–	–	60	21*	56			14	18	3	482	71	32.13
W.M. Noon	–	–	6	18	20	7			17	–									0	2			13	21	3	332	57	18.44
D.B. Pennett	–	–	8	7	10	2																	3	4	–	27	10	6.75
J.A. Afford	–	–	0*	2*	0*	4			1	–	1*	–	2	–	5*	–	–	0*	1	0	0	–	18	24	14	34	11*	3.40
G.F. Archer			83	36	48	14			2	85*	7	6	70	3	5	–	35*	1			87	12*	13	24	3	918	143	43.71
M.P. Dowman			22	6			–	–							9	–					27	22	9	14	–	337	107	24.07
R.A. Pick			0	10	5	3			32	–	4	–	10	–			–	2					6	8	–	66	32	8.25
J.R. Wileman							–	–															1					–
N.A. Gie							–	–															1					–
J.E. Hindson							–	–															1					–
L.N.P. Walker							–	–			36	17*	14	5	20	–	–	1			–	–	6	6	1	93	36	18.60
U. Afzaal							–	–											3	5	47	26	6	10	1	264	67*	29.33
M.N. Bowen							–	–	5	–					22	–	–	2	4	11*			13	18	2	173	22	10.81
R.J. Chapman							–	–													0	–	2	1	–	0	0	0.00
M. Broadhurst							–	–															1					–
G.W. Mike																					13*	–	3	5	1	25	13*	6.25
J.P. Hart																							1	2	2	18	18*	–
P.J. Franks																							1					–
Byes					6					3	7	8	5	12	5		4	10		8	18							
Leg-byes	12		6	10	7	7			3	13	6	9	8	1	8			8	1	9	10	10						
Wides	5		3	1	2	2							2		1		1			5								
No-balls	16	8	5	4	8	4			18	18	16	6	22	10	12		4		4	10	20	2						
Total	255	68	200	238	452	238			269	408	359	176	392	159	460		212	211	97	415	340	144						
Wickets	5	2	10	10	10	10			10	3	10	4	10	4	10		4	10	10	10	9†	2						
Result	D		L		D		D		D		D		D		W		L		L		D							
Points	8		5		11		–		7		8		10		24		4		4		–							

†L.N.P. Walker absent hurt

Batting	*v.* Glamorgan (Worksop) 1–5 August		*v.* Middlesex (Trent Bridge) 8–12 August		*v.* Derbyshire (Derby) 15–19 August		*v.* Surrey (Trent Bridge) 22–26 August		*v.* Kent (Tunbridge Wells) 29 August–2 September		*v.* Leicestershire (Trent Bridge) 3–6 September		*v.* Yorkshire (Scarborough) 12–16 September		*v.* Hampshire (Southampton) 19–22 September		M	Inns	NO	Runs	HS	Av
P.R. Pollard	34	24	0	2	2	14*					5	5	26	30			13	25	2	737	86	32.04
R.T. Robinson	43	61	23	11	53	15	34	–	10	12	18	50	23	27	39	–	17	31	2	1302	184	44.89
A.A. Metcalfe	128	41	17	37	16	3	21	–	9	10							12	22	–	771	128	35.04
P. Johnson	7	4	18	0	82	0	13	–	84	5	27	10	16	14	109	7*	19	33	2	980	109	31.61
C.L. Cairns	38	70	46	32	75	20	4	–	11	9			5	4	23*	3	16	29	5	946	114	39.41
C.M. Tolley					27	0			3	67	40	46			–	11	9	14	2	306	67	25.50
R.T. Bates	21	0					13	–			31	8	11	8			11	15	1	229	34	16.35
K.P. Evans	15	24	23	0	9	1	6	–	4	54	71	1					14	18	3	482	71	32.13
W.M. Noon	26	0	43*	21	9*	7	57	–	19	2	42	1	6	4	–	25	13	21	3	332	57	18.44
D.B. Pennett																	3	4	–	27	10	6.75
J.A. Afford	11*	1*	4	1*	0	0*	–	–	0*	0*	1*	0*	0	0	–	–	18	24	14	34	11*	3.40
G.F. Archer							143	–	0	34	32	31	0	1	120	63	13	24	3	918	143	43.71
M.P. Dowman							107	–	37	0	19	3	44	0	21	20	9	14	–	337	107	24.07
R.A. Pick																	6	8	–	66	32	8.25
J.R. Wileman																	1					–
N.A. Gie																	1					–
J.E. Hindson																	1					–
L.N.P. Walker																	6	6	1	93	36	18.60
U. Afzaal			51	39	0	7									67*	19	6	10	1	264	67*	29.33
M.N. Bowen	12	1	3	2	4	14	1*	–	22	19	14	15	15	7	–	–	13	18	2	173	22	10.81
R.J. Chapman																	2	1	–	0	0	0.00
M. Broadhurst																	1					–
G.W. Mike	7	0	5	0													3	5	1	25	13*	6.25
J.P. Hart													18*	0*			1	2	2	18	18*	–
P.J. Franks															–	–	1					–
Byes		6	8	11	15		8		5	8	1	6	3	4	4							
Leg-byes	15	4	10	7	3	2	11		7	13	6	10	8	10	8	3						
Wides	1	1			2	5	6		1	7	1	2				1						
No-balls	13	4	6		20	10	22		2	2	16	8	12	8								
Total	371	241	257	163	317	98	446	0	214	242	324	196	187	117	391	152						
Wickets	10	10	10	10	10	9‡	9	0	10	10	10	10	10	10	4	5						
Result	L		L		L		D		L		L		L		D							
Points	6		6		7		8		5		6		4		8							

‡P.R. Pollard retired hurt

Fielding Figures

33 – W.M. Noon (ct 30 / st 3)
18 – L.N.P. Walker (ct 16 / st 2)
17 – G.F. Archer
11 – P.R. Pollard
10 – P. Johnson and C.L. Cairns
8 – R.T. Robinson and R.T. Bates
5 – subs (ct 4 / st 1)
4 – A.A. Metcalfe and M.P. Dowman
3 – K.P. Evans, M.N. Bowen and U. Azaal
2 – G.W. Mike and C.M. Tolley
1 – D.B. Pennett, M. Broadhurst, R.A. Pick and R.J. Chapman

Bowling

	C.L. Cairns	D.B. Pennett	K.P. Evans	C.M. Tolley	R.T. Bates	J.A. Afford	U. Afzaal	R.A. Pick	M.P. Dowman	M.N. Bowen	R.J. Chapman	G.W. Mike	Byes	Leg-byes	Wides	No-balls	Total	Wkts
v. Sussex (Trent Bridge)	19–5–56–0	22–5–61–3	23.3–7–67–1	13–3–36–2	14–1–40–0	20–9–29–2								14	1	12	303	8
2–6 May	22.4–4–70–4	19–5–57–0	14–3–38–0	9–3–25–0	14–4–42–3	25–15–22–2							4	16	2	14	278	9A
v. Somerset (Taunton)	18.3–2–81–2	20–2–116–4		5–0–27–0		13–4–26–3		11–2–41–0	3–1–12–0				1	5	2	14	309	10
9–13 May	7–1–26–0	6–1–45–0		4–0–19–0				5–0–37–0						3		4	130	0
v. Lancashire (Trent Bridge)	30–7–95–2	20–2–76–0			17–5–55–1	44–15–83–3		20.4–4–74–3					5	9		10	397	9
16–20 May	19–2–77–1	4–0–21–0			17–3–42–2	25–8–51–6		7–1–23–0					4	7		8	225	9
v. Oxford University (Oxford)			8.3–0–38–1				1–0–3–0			10–4–18–1	13–1–50–1			2		12	178	3B
23–25 May																		
v. Durham (Trent Bridge)	26–2–88–1		29–9–68–4	20–5–60–0		30–8–68–1		23.1–2–71–2		23–5–67–1				27		6	455	10C
30 May–3 June																		
v. Northamptonshire (Trent Bridge)	27–4–75–1		35–12–71–2	26–3–107–4	30–5–140–0	38–9–106–2		28–7–71–0					14	17		14	601	9
6–10 June																		
v. Worcestershire (Worcester)	39–8–124–2		47–12–116–5		20–2–77–0	22–6–55–1		25.2–6–69–1					11	20		2	493	9D
13–17 June	7–1–33–1		8–1–40–0		2–0–7–0	18–5–55–1		15–2–58–0						1		6	194	4
v. Gloucestershire (Trent Bridge)	17–3–56–2		9–1–48–0		13–5–45–2	5–3–8–2				9.1–2–31–3				2		4	190	9E
20–24 June	20–1–62–2		18.4–8–30–5		16–2–63–0	19–4–62–1				13–5–41–2			4	5		4	267	10
v. Warwickshire (Edgbaston)	26–4–84–3		33–5–101–0			13–4–43–1		16–4–35–1		22.5–5–80–3			2	5	2	18	350	8
4–8 July			5–0–34–1			4–0–27–1		4–3–4–0		9–1–54–0			4	3		10	158	2F
v. Essex (Chelmsford)	8–3–13–0		26–5–83–2		21–1–88–1	32–14–62–2	1–1–0–0			31.5–3–119–5				3		17	368	10
18–22 July			7–3–10–0		13–1–36–2	15–3–45–1	3–0–21–0			8–1–31–1				2		6	145	4
v. South Africa 'A' (Trent Bridge)				12–2–50–0	23–5–74–2	28–9–66–4	7–2–27–0		4–1–14–0		23.5–3–109–4	23–7–106–0	7	2	2		455	10
26–29 July				11–1–45–1		8–1–23–0	12–0–52–1				4–0–24–1	11.5–1–34–2		2	1	4	180	6
v. Glamorgan (Worksop)	15–2–60–2		25–4–89–1		23.5–4–72–3	35–9–90–2				20–7–64–0		23–4–104–2	6	4		6	489	10
1–5 August	7–3–14–0		3–1–10–0		10.3–0–39–1	15–6–39–0				4–0–21–1				3			126	2
v. Middlesex (Trent Bridge)	21.4–2–79–3		17–3–68–2			30–1–87–3	12–0–55–1			16–0–60–0		16–1–68–0	4	6	1	16	427	10
8–12 August																		
v. Derbyshire (Derby)	29–8–105–2		22–3–74–1	21–2–67–0		9–2–23–2				30.2–10–53–5			10	9		16	341	10
15–19 August	12–2–42–1		20–3–57–0	7–0–59–0		33.5–8–87–6	2–0–1–0			24–2–100–0			9	13			377	8
v. Surrey (Trent Bridge)	7–0–25–1		11–3–33–1		2–1–7–0	5.3–1–32–1				11–3–29–1				2	1	2	128	4
22–26 August	4–1–7–0		3–1–12–0							5.5–0–31–0				3		6	53	0
v. Kent (Tunbridge Wells)	4–3–9–1		24–8–71–4	25–6–68–4		2–0–14–0				21–3–75–1			1	6	1	8	244	10
29 August–2 September			12–3–36–0	7–1–36–1		20–6–60–0				14.5–2–78–2			4	1			215	3
v. Leicestershire (Trent Bridge)			12–4–23–0	25–6–93–2	25–2–88–2	33–7–83–2			14–3–43–2	32.3–5–97–2			8	4		12	439	10
3–6 September				2–0–10–0	5–0–21–1	1.3–0–13–0			2–0–8–0	8–0–29–3				1		4	82	4
v. Yorkshire (Scarborough)	22.4–2–110–6				12–5–33–1	11–1–33–2			2–1–8–0	17–2–66–1			3	6		32	310	10G
12–16 September																		
v. Hampshire (Southampton)	19–3–70–0			25–5–80–0		25–6–79–0	6–0–31–1		4–0–29–0	31–4–120–1				18	1	22	513	4H
19–22 September				4–0–22–0					7–4–8–0	4–0–17–0				6	1	6	181	5
Bowler's average	427.3–73– 1461–37 39.48	91–15– 376–7 53.71	412.4–99– 1217–30 40.56	216–37– 804–14 57.42	278.2–46– 69–21 46.14	579.5–164– 1471–51 28.84	44–3– 199–3 66.33	155.1–31– 483–7 69.00	36–10– 122–2 61.00	366.2–64– 1281–33 38.81	40.5–4– 183–6 30.50	73.5–13– 312–4 78.00						

A R.T. Robinson 1–0–4–0
B M. Broadhurst 7–0–60–0; J.E. Hindson 3–1–7–0
C G.F. Archer 2–0–6–0
D G.F. Archer 7–1–21–0
E R.P. Davis absent
F G.F. Archer 3–0–32–0
G J.P. Hart 18–7–51–0
H G.F. Archer 4–1–21–0, 11–3–18–3; P.J. Franks 28–9–65–2, 13–5–37–1; W.M. Noon 4–1–22–0; P. Johnson 12–2–51–1

Somerset CCC First-Class Matches Batting

Batting	v. Surrey (Taunton) 2–6 May		v. Nottinghamshire (Taunton) 9–13 May		v. Gloucestershire (Bristol) 16–20 May		v. Northamptonshire (Taunton) 23–27 May		v. Warwickshire (Taunton) 6–10 June		v. Glamorgan (Swansea) 13–17 June		v. Worcestershire (Bath) 19–22 June		v. Lancashire (Old Trafford) 27 June–1 July		v. Pakistanis (Taunton) 3–5 July		v. South Africa 'A' (Taunton) 20–22 July		v. Yorkshire (Scarborough) 25–29 July		M	Inns	NO	Runs	HS	Av
M.N. Lathwell	0	–	40	66*	49	29	44*	0	18	1	68	10	37	18	37*	–	0	25	108	32	43	80	18	32	4	1224	109	43.71
P.D. Bowler	207	–	7	57*	1	12*	34*	66	30	16	73	25	112	22	6	–	68	52	1	32	30	6	19	34	4	1228	207	40.93
S.C. Ecclestone	6	–													16	–	18	57	7	15			8	13	1	334	94	27.83
R.J. Harden	3	–	0	–	54	7															54	8	12	20	1	676	136	35.57
A.N. Hayhurst	69	–	5*	–	6	1	–	15	11	5	96	0	4	10	–	–					0	2	9	13	1	224	96	18.66
S. Lee	87*	–	82	–	65	35	–	113*	65	61			4	167*	–	–	0*	0			22	134	17	25	4	1300	167*	61.90
R.J. Turner	6	–	4	–	50	4	–	15	24*	14	31	21	12	100*	–	–	14	9			13	42	18	27	6	668	100*	31.80
G.D. Rose	1	–	29	–	7	5	–	9*	0	13*	18	23	6	–	–	–			6	64*	34*	29	15	21	5	408	93*	25.50
P.C.L. Holloway	54	–	50	–	14	14	–	5	0	42	3	20	11	11					45	8			10	16	1	535	168	35.66
K.J. Shine	40	–	19	–	0	5*	–	–	9	0	6	1					19*	6	5*	–	7	3*	12	15	4	121	40	11.00
A.P. van Troost	6	–															0	5*					6	8	2	27	11	4.50
J.D. Batty			44	–	4	36*	–	–	8	21	2	19*	5	0	–	–	0	27	18	0	4	26	16	24	4	321	44	16.05
A.R. Caddick			7	–	0*	2	–	–	10	11	16*	1	4	–	–	–			0	8*	0	23	14	19	5	195	38	13.92
M.E. Trescothick							–	83	34	20	9	11	27	16	9	–	27	4	6	55			15	26	–	720	178	27.69
K.A. Parsons											2	18					0	9	62	5	62	4	8	15	1	408	83*	29.14
H.R.J. Trump													0*	–	–	–							3	2	1	0	0*	0.00
I.E. Bishop																	2	2					1	2	–	4	2	2.00
J.I.D. Kerr																			4	56			6	9	3	176	68*	29.33
A.C. Cottam																							2	2	–	15	12	7.50
Byes	5		1			4		5	6	5	7	4	8		1		8	6	2	8	4	12						
Leg-byes	16		5	3	2	12	6	4	8	13	4		1	16			1	6	8	11	6	12						
Wides	4		2		1	1		1	11	1	1			2					1	1								
No-balls	54		14	4	6	4	4	14	8	16	2		32	14	6		2	2	28	14	30	14						
Total	558		309	130	259	171	88	330	242	239	338	153	263	376	75		159	210	301	309	309	395						
Wickets	10		10	0	10	8	0	6	10	10	10	10	10	6	3		9†	10	10	8	10	10						
Result	D		W		D		W		L		L		L		D		L		D		W							
Points	11		23		9		20		5		7		6		5		–		–		23							

†S. Lee retired hurt

Fielding Figures

67 – R.J. Turner (ct 64 / st 3)
14 – S. Lee
13 – M.N. Lathwell
11 – R.J. Harden and M.E. Trescothick
7 – P.C.L. Holloway, G.D. Rose and A.R. Caddick
5 – P.D. Bowler
4 – J.D. Batty
3 – H.R.J. Trump, K.J. Shine and subs
2 – A.N. Hayhurst, S.C. Ecclestone and K.A. Parsons
1 – I.E. Bishop

Batting

Batting	v. Hampshire (Taunton) 1–5 August		v. Essex (Taunton) 8–12 August		v. Kent (Canterbury) 15–19 August		v. Durham (Weston-super-Mare) 21–24 August		v. Leicestershire (Leicester) 29 August–2 September		v. Derbyshire (Taunton) 3–6 September		v. Middlesex (Uxbridge) 12–16 September		v. Sussex (Hove) 19–22 September		M	Inns	NO	Runs	HS	Av
M.N. Lathwell	13	–	12	15	43	81	85	–	0	13	109	54			56	38*	18	32	4	1224	109	43.71
P.D. Bowler	0	–	88	16	48*	32	9	–	13	14	37	60	12	22	20	0	19	34	4	1228	207	40.93
S.C. Ecclestone					94	56	34*	–	5	5	13	8					8	13	1	334	94	27.83
R.J. Harden	54	–	41	18	136	29	65	–	5	30	43	3	20	12	78	16*	12	20	1	676	136	35.57
A.N. Hayhurst																	9	13	1	224	96	18.66
S. Lee	26	–	18	36	1	0	40	–	7	43	110	14	44	–	126	–	17	25	4	1300	167*	61.90
R.J. Turner	57	–	0	44*	11	1	4*	–	20*	0	21	49	75	–	27*	–	18	27	6	668	100*	31.80
G.D. Rose	93*	–	12	46	6	7	–	–	0	0							15	21	5	408	93*	25.50
P.C.L. Holloway													168	90*	0	–	10	16	1	535	168	35.66
K.J. Shine	–	–											0	–	1	–	12	15	4	121	40	11.00
A.P. van Troost			4	0			–	–	11	1	0*	–					6	8	2	27	11	4.50
J.D. Batty	21	–	0*	10	–	7*	8	–	7	13	27	14					16	24	4	321	44	16.05
A.R. Caddick	38	–							9	8*	21	1*	26	–	10	–	14	19	5	195	38	13.92
M.E. Trescothick	178	–	3!	9	8	0	33	–	4	34	42	8	27	44	1	0	15	26	–	720	178	27.69
K.A. Parsons	30	–	24	5	2	30							72	83*			8	15	1	408	83*	29.14
H.R.J. Trump															0	–	3	2	1	0	0*	0.00
I.E. Bishop																	1	2	–	4	2	2.00
J.I.D. Kerr			0	0	1*	0	–	–			15	68*	32	–			6	9	3	176	68*	29.33
A.C. Cottam													3	–	12	–	2	2	–	15	12	7.50
Byes	2		5	5	12	4	1				5		2		4	5						
Leg-byes	8		2	3	8	8	18		2	5	7	7	4	5	10	1						
Wides	3		1	1	11		1								1							
No-balls	18		8		8	2				8	14	10		2	8							
Total	541		246	208	389	257	298		83	174	464	296	485	258	354	60						
Wickets	9‡		10	10	8	10	6		10	10	10	8	10	3	10	2						
Result	W		L		L		D		L		D		D		W							
Points	24		5		5		9		4		10		7		24							

‡K.J. Shine absent hurt

Bowling

	K.J. Shine	A.P. van Troost	S. Lee	G.D. Rose	A.N. Hayhurst	P.D. Bowler	P.C.L. Holloway	A.R. Caddick	J.D. Batty	J.I.D. Kerr	K.A. Parsons	H.R.J. Trump	Byes	Leg-byes	Wides	No-balls	Total	Wkts
v. Surrey (Taunton)	24–5–95–6	22–2–109–2	19.2–1–88–2	15–3–68–0										7	3	10	367	10
2–6 May	22–6–101–1	15–2–86–1	16–2–95–1	18–4–79–1	5–1–29–0	2–0–4–0	2–1–5–0						4	7	1	18	410	4
v. Nottinghamshire (Taunton)	15–3–50–1		15–2–68–2	19–9–41–6				14–4–35–1						6	3	5	200	10
9–13 May	11–2–53–1		10–2–30–1	20.2–8–47–7				21–8–70–1	11–3–28–0					10	1	4	238	10
v. Gloucestershire (Bristol)	11–0–63–2		14–4–55–4	13–2–44–2				18–6–43–2	20–5–50–0				8		3	10	263	10
16–20 May	14.4–0–50–3		15–3–59–2	5–1–20–0				22–4–83–2	13–3–29–3				1	3	2	4	245	10
v. Northamptonshire (Taunton)	22–4–95–3		11–2–78–0	22–7–47–3	3–0–20–0			23–5–56–1	18–0–72–2				5	10	6	8	383	9
23–27 May					2–0–8–0		0.2–0–8–0								1		34	0A
v. Warwickshire (Taunton)	11–1–33–0		19–5–85–2	13.1–4–37–2				23–6–76–5	7–3–19–0				2	3	6	10	255	10
6–10 June	13–1–52–0		15–2–42–1	19–5–58–2				25–7–85–5	24.2–6–72–2				4	12	1	10	325	10
v. Glamorgan (Swansea)	14–5–50–1			23–4–45–4	4–1–17–0			28–8–92–3	29–9–80–2		3–1–11–0		2	13	4	8	310	10
13–17 June	22–3–123–2			15–3–40–1				24–4–70–1	37–13–107–3		3–2–2–0		4	8	1	20	354	7
v. Worcestershire (Bath)			19–3–75–2	8–2–20–1				27.4–10–83–7						16		2	194	10
19–22 June			11–0–65–1	25–6–80–1	2–0–3–0			36.3–5–151–4	26–5–79–1			12–1–55–0	8	8	1	4	449	9
v. Lancashire (Old Trafford)			18–1–74–1	18–5–53–0	5–2–8–1			18–7–28–0	38–5–127–2			18–3–81–1	4	5		10	380	5
27 June–1 July					4–1–6–0	3.3–0–15–0			7–0–19–0				1	1			45	0B
v. Pakistanis (Taunton)	15–0–77–2	10–1–41–0	21.4–4–65–4						26–7–60–0		5–1–24–1		4		4	12	300	7C
3–5 July	11–0–64–0	5–0–35–0							12.5–1–61–1					1	1	16	174	1D
v. South Africa 'A' (Taunton)	12–1–61–1			11–2–47–0				22–1–121–2	36–3–153–2	15–2–74–1	4–0–28–0		5	6	4	26	509	7E
20–22 July																		
v. Yorkshire (Scarborough)	7.3–1–55–3		17–4–49–1	15–5–53–2				24–5–81–2	15–2–53–2					1	6	21	292	10
25–29 July	11–1–48–5		7–0–54–1	6–0–29–1				19–3–72–3	1–0–1–0				6	5	1	12	215	10
v. Hampshire (Taunton)			9–2–36–1	13–3–49–3				14–1–46–5	3.4–0–16–1					12	1	4	159	10
1–5 August			2–0–25–0	16–6–46–1				20–8–44–2	24.4–4–85–5		7–2–25–1			6		8	231	10
v. Essex (Taunton)		20–2–90–4	20–2–74–0	26–5–100–2					23–2–115–2	17–3–64–2	2–0–12–0			10		20	465	10
8–12 August																		
v. Kent (Canterbury)			35–3–159–1	27–5–92–2					41.3–11–122–2	27–3–143–2	12–2–40–0		9	14		26	616	7F
15–19 August						6–0–53–1											92	2G
v. Durham (Weston-super-Mare)		17–6–45–0	24–2–101–3	26.5–6–73–7		2–0–7–0			3–0–19–0	13–1–73–0			1	7	6	24	326	10
21–24 August																		
v. Leicestershire (Leicester)		10–0–39–0	21–5–78–3	19–3–50–2				31–8–83–3	14.4–3–38–2				1	7		24	296	10
29 August–2 September																		
v. Derbyshire (Taunton)		8.3–0–40–2	24–5–121–2			4–2–2–0		37.4–5–140–3	34–11–94–0	25–2–108–3			4	15		24	524	10
3–6 September			4–1–20–0			8–0–54–2		20–1–104–3	21–3–73–0	8–1–42–1				7	1	14	322	6H
v. Middlesex (Uxbridge)	16–8–36–2		12–1–35–1			6–0–42–0	2.2–0–21–0	18–3–72–0		11–2–37–0	2–0–12–0		2	9	1	10	350	3I
12–16 September	11–0–59–0		14–1–62–0					15–4–49–2		15–2–45–2			1	14	1	2	357	8
v. Sussex (Hove)	10–3–28–1		18.1–5–52–4					15–2–58–5						3		7	141	10
19–22 September	3.2–0–16–1		8–4–25–0					31–8–122–5				13–6–43–3		4	4	22	270	10J
	276.3–44–	107.3–13–	418.3–66–	393.2–98–	25–5–	31.3–2–	4.4–1–	546.5–123–	486.4–99–	131–16–	38–8–	43–10–						
	1209–35	485–9	1770–40	1218–50	91–1	177–3	4–0	1864–67	1572–32	586–11	154–2	179–4						
Bowler's average	34.54	53.88	44.25	24.36	91.00	59.00	–	27.82	49.12	53.27	77.00	44.75						

A M.E. Trescothick 3–0–18–0
B R.J. Turner 1–0–3–0
C I.E. Bishop 7–0–29–0
D M.N. Lathwell 6–0–13–1
E M.N. Lathwell 1.4–0–14–1
F M.E. Trescothick 9–1–37–0
G R.J. Harden 7–0–39–1
H M.E. Trescothick 6–0–22–0
I A.C. Cottan 27–10–61–0, 29–1–127–2; M.E. Trescothick 5–0–20–0; R.J. Harden 1–0–3–0
J A.C. Cottan 33–11–60–1

Surrey CCC First-Class Matches

Batting

Batting	v. Somerset (Taunton) 2–6 May		v. Kent (The Oval) 9–13 May		v. Gloucestershire (Gloucester) 23–27 May		v. Derbyshire (The Oval) 30 May–3 June		v. Yorkshire (Middlesbrough) 6–10 June		v. Leicestershire (The Oval) 13–17 June		v. Durham (Stockton) 20–24 June		v. Essex (Southend) 27 June–1 July		v. Middlesex (The Oval) 4–8 July		v. Sussex (Guildford) 17–20 July		v. Hampshire (Southampton) 25–29 July		M	Inns	NO	Runs	HS	Av
D.J. Bicknell	4	58	8	3	30	0	3	39	52	20	34	6	106	4	30	30	48	–	48	2	48	26	17	31	3	969	129*	34.60
M.A. Butcher	13	52	94	35*	38	58	52	57	29	112	120	66	160	9	53	85*	42	26	57	0	58	53	17	32	3	1540	160	53.10
A.J. Stewart	21	33	6	22			53	47*			33	3			2	33			74	80			9	16	1	434	80	28.93
G.P. Thorpe	52	100*	8	0			185	68			154	2			143	11*			66	130			9	17	2	1044	185	69.60
A.D. Brown	7	20	27	2			3	56*	10	31	7	0	28	–	31	–	57	2	0	–	20	0	15	24	2	462	69	21.00
A.J. Hollioake	128	117*	40	42	17	52	72	71*	11	30	7	37*	19	–	128	–	84	6*	20	27	83	104*	16	28	6	1521	129	69.13
C.C. Lewis	42	–	61	10			5	–			20	36							7	29*			9	15	1	543	94	38.78
B.P. Julian	50	–	74	41*	9	32	7	–	0	20			31	–	36	–	9	–	5	0	12	4*	16	23	2	759	119	36.14
G.J. Kersey	3	–	5	–	34*	6	37	–	1	10	28	59*	0	–	8	–	3	–	68*	18*	0	–	15	20	4	402	68*	25.12
M.P. Bicknell	19	–	13	–	–	6*	28	–			15	–	5	–	10*	–	25	–	13	–	15*	–	16	17	5	331	59*	27.58
R.M. Pearson	8*	–	0*	–	–	1*	7*	–	16*	8	8*	–	1	–	–	–	14*	–	37	–	6	–	14	14	9	142	37	28.40
J.D. Ratcliffe					29	1			20	26			51	68*			37	8			23	26	9	16	1	494	69	32.93
N. Shahid					0	7							0	52*			13	17*			14	101	11	19	3	535	101	33.43
D.M. Ward					64*	0			15	2													2	4	1	81	64*	27.00
J.E. Benjamin					–	–			23	2*	9	–	0*	–	2*	–	1	–			28	–	13	15	6	143	38*	14.30
B.C. Hollioake									8	2													3	4	–	63	46	15.75
G.J. Kennis																							1	2	1	3	2*	3.00
A.W. Smith																							1	2	–	23	16	11.50
I.J. Ward																							1	2	–	19	15	9.50
J.A. Knott																							1	2	1	52	49*	52.00
R.W. Nowell																							1	2	1	28	28*	28.00
S.G. Kenlock																							1	2	–	5	5	2.50
M.W. Patterson																							1	2	–	6	4	3.00
Byes		4	4	3		4		4			5	6	8		3	3	2		4	1	1	2						
Leg-byes	7	7	17	2	6	3	10	1	3	1	6	6	11	3	21	5	11		6	14	7	13						
Wides	3	1	1		1		3		1		4	2	10	2	5		4		2	1		1						
No-balls	10	8	2			4	12	2	8	10	2	19	10	4	4		16	2	4	2	16	2						
Total	367	410	360	160	228	174	477	345	197	274	452	242	440	142	476	167	366	61	411	304	331	332						
Wickets	10	4	10	6	6	8	10	3	10	10	10	6	10	2	8	2	10	3	10	6	10	5						
Result	D		D		D		D		L		W		W		D		W		W		W							
Points	9		11		8		10		4		24		24		10		24		24		23							

Batting

Batting	v. South Africa 'A' (The Oval) 1–4 August		v. Lancashire (Southport) 7–10 August		v. Nottinghamshire (Trent Bridge) 22–26 August		v. Warwickshire (The Oval) 29 August–2 September		v. Northamptonshire (The Oval) 3–6 September		v. Glamorgan (Cardiff) 12–16 September		v. Worcestershire (The Oval) 19–22 September		M	Inns	NO	Runs	HS	Av
D.J. Bicknell			12	42	11	30*	55	–	5	29	30	27*	–	129*	17	31	3	969	129*	34.60
M.A. Butcher			10	66	6	14*	70	–	26	37	31	9	–	2	17	32	3	1540	160	53.10
A.J. Stewart									15	–	10	2	–	0	9	16	1	434	80	28.93
G.P. Thorpe									25	2	77	10	–	11	9	17	2	1044	185	69.60
A.D. Brown	69	32	0	1	56*	–	3	–					–	0	15	24	2	462	69	21.00
A.J. Hollioake			20	22	7*	–			129	98	51	85	–	14	16	28	6	1521	129	69.13
C.C. Lewis	52	49					94	–	10	31	57	40			9	15	1	543	94	38.78
B.P. Julian			41	119	–	–	11	–	117	20	41	0	–	80	16	23	2	759	119	36.14
G.J. Kersey			3	24	–	–	63	–	11	21					15	20	4	402	68*	25.12
M.P. Bicknell			23	23	–	–	17	–	18*	19	59*	2	–	23	16	18	5	333	59*	25.61
R.M. Pearson			15*	13	–	–					8*	–			14	14	9	142	37	28.40
J.D. Ratcliffe	69	22	20	8	23	–	63	–							9	16	1	494	69	32.93
N. Shahid	3	84	32	66	20	–	18	–	1	2	79	24*	–	2	11	19	3	535	101	33.43
D.M. Ward															2	4	1	81	64*	27.00
J.E. Benjamin			6	38*	–	–	2*	–	7	4*	5	–	–	14	13	14	6	141	38*	17.62
B.C. Hollioake							46	–					–	7	3	4	–	63	46	15.75
G.J. Kennis	2*	1													1	2	1	3	2*	3.00
A.W. Smith	7	16													1	2	–	23	16	11.50
I.J. Ward	15	4													1	2	–	19	15	9.50
J.A. Knott	3	49*													1	2	1	52	49*	52.00
R.W. Nowell	28*	0													1	2	1	28	28*	28.00
S.G. Kenlock	0	5													1	2	–	5	5	2.50
M.W. Patterson	4	2													1	2	–	6	4	3.00
Byes	9	2		4			12		2	4	11	1								
Leg-byes	10	2	10	8	2	3	9		13	15	8	3		7						
Wides	1	1			1		1			2				10						
No-balls	14	6	19	8	2	6	4		16	14	4	2								
Total	286	275	211	442	128	53	468		395	298	471	205	0	299						
Wickets	9†	10	10	10	4	0	10		10	9	9	7	0	10						
Result	L		W		D		W		W		D		L							
Points	–		21		7		24		24		11		4							

†G.J. Kennis retired hurt

Fielding Figures

46 – G.J. Kersey (ct 45 / st 1)
21 – M.A. Butcher
18 – A.D. Brown
17 – A.J. Hollioake
13 – C.C. Lewis
10 – G.P. Thorpe and A.J. Stewart
9 – B.P. Julian and D.J. Bicknell
6 – N. Shahid
5 – J.D. Ratcliffe
4 – B.C. Hollioake
3 – R.M. Pearson
2 – D.M. Ward, M.P. Bicknell and subs
1 – J.E. Benjamin and G.J. Kennis

Bowling

	M.P. Bicknell	C.C. Lewis	B.P. Julian	A.J. Hollioake	R.M. Pearson	M.A. Butcher	G.A. Thorpe	J.E. Benjamin	J.D. Ratcliffe	D.J. Bicknell	B.C. Hollioake	N. Shahid	Byes	Leg-byes	Wides	No-balls	Total	Wkts
v. Somerset (Taunton)	32–5–105–3	28–3–125–3	24–2–98–1	17–1–80–3	12–0–53–0	16–3–50–0	8–2–26–0						5	16	4	54	558	10
2–6 May																		
v. Kent (The Oval)	17–6–52–2	20–4–57–2	14.4–3–36–2		13–5–35–3	13–3–41–1								4	1	16	225	10
9–13 May	35–12–79–3	27–3–81–3	22–5–82–1	6–1–18–0	32.1–8–84–3								5	12	6	16	361	10
v. Gloucestershire (Gloucester)	29–6–98–3		30.5–7–97–5	8–1–25–0	18–2–62–0			21–4–77–0	2–1–7–1					7	2	30	373	10
23–27 May	6–0–31–0		5–1–22–0	2–0–14–0	11–0–58–0			8–0–37–2						1	2	6	163	2
v. Derbyshire (The Oval)	31–9–101–1	28–6–98–2	23–5–100–2	17–2–70–0	26.5–6–75–2		6–2–13–2						2	10	3	26	469	10
30 May–3 June	9–3–17–5	15–3–61–0	18–5–93–3	6–0–25–0	15–5–41–1		1–1–0–0			1–0–4–0				5	1	26	246	9
v. Yorkshire (Middlesborough)			17–2–60–1	6–2–24–1	15–3–68–1			18.3–4–75–3			21–5–74–4			4	2	18	305	10
6–10 June			9–1–44–1	7–2–25–0	24–3–80–1	11–1–49–3		12–2–67–0	6–0–26–2	10.5–1–29–2	13–1–48–1		4	15	3	22	387	10
v. Leicestershire (The Oval)	24–6–92–2	28–6–77–1		15–5–25–0	34–13–60–0	1–0–12–0	6–3–13–0	21–4–74–4		19.4–5–50–3			3	5	5	16	411	10
13–17 June	12–0–58–3	11.2–4–25–5		3–2–4–0	9–2–50–1			7–2–15–0		8–2–18–1			4	1	3	6	175	10
v. Durham (Stockton)	20–3–73–2		15.1–1–72–1	11–1–39–0	31–7–103–3			19–3–69–4					9	12	1	36	377	10
20–24 June	18–5–40–3		12.5–3–38–3	10–4–26–2	15–4–42–1	1–0–6–0		19–3–33–1	2–0–12–0			1–1–0–0	1	5	4	32	203	10
v. Essex (Southend)	25–7–63–1		22.2–5–84–2	4–1–9–0	46–11–142–5			16–6–65–0		12–2–42–1			9	11		24	425	9
27 June–1 July																		
v. Middlesex (Lord's)	24–6–54–5		15.2–4–63–4	15–6–30–1	1–0–13–0			20–5–69–0					1	2	2	42	232	10
4–8 July	25–5–57–4		21–6–54–3	5–0–22–1				22–10–50–2					8	3	6	34	194	10
v. Sussex (Guildford)	17–4–45–2	17–4–57–0	13–0–41–4	15–1–48–1	9–1–52–0					3–1–7–3			5	10		12	265	10
17–20 July	17–9–22–1		18–4–81–1	10–3–30–1	31–10–73–2	5–0–52–0				18.5–5–41–3			13	3	6	12	315	10
v. Hampshire (Southampton)	22.4–3–64–4		15–1–71–0	19–5–44–1	29–3–80–2			21–3–73–2		4–1–18–0		2–0–4–0	1	4		30	359	10
25–29 July	21–6–66–1		15–4–49–2	9–0–43–0	10–0–60–0			18–5–38–1		2–0–8–0		5–0–32–0	2	3	1	14	301	4
v. South Africa 'A' (The Oval)		16–5–46–1							13–4–54–1			4–0–22–0	5	3	2	16	379	10[A]
1–4 August		9–0–42–1							10–0–37–1			29.1–2–93–3	8	1			339	6
v. Lancashire (Southport)	17–2–48–5		8–0–42–1	2–0–16–0				15.3–4–38–4						1	2	8	145	10
7–10 August	23–7–83–2		20.3–3–99–5	2–0–18–0	9–1–44–1			21–5–80–2	9–2–30–0				10	4	4	31	368	10
v. Nottinghamshire (Trent Bridge)	17–2–56–0		21–2–104–4	12–3–43–0	29–4–87–2			16–2–59–1		15–0–51–2		4–0–27–0	8	11	6	22	446	9
22–26 August																	0	0
v. Warwickshire (The Oval)	12–4–29–1	14–3–45–4	12–1–66–4					9–4–22–1		1–0–6–0	2–0–19–0			8	1	20	195	10
29 August–2 September	15.3–3–38–4	5–2–6–0	10–4–20–0					8–2–17–4			8–2–22–2		2	4		8	109	10
v. Northamptonshire (The Oval)	14–2–58–2	15–1–60–2	13–5–37–6	5–0–22–0				14–1–48–0		1–1–0–0				10		22	235	10
3–6 September	22–11–38–2	22–5–65–3	11–3–43–2					13.3–3–57–2		2–1–7–0			12	11	5	14	233	9B
v. Glamorgan (Cardiff)	19–8–49–2	21.2–2–86–2	15–3–54–1		21–6–59–2			20–4–53–2		15–0–54–1				9	5	32	364	10
12–16 September	12–2–37–0	14–4–46–0	8–1–40–1	5–1–12–0	34–7–88–1	5–0–23–3		10–2–25–1		5–0–26–0		29–5–96–3	5	20	5	18	442	9C
v. Worcestershire (The Oval)	29–9–75–2		18–2–72–1	15–3–52–1				26–5–76–3			18–3–78–3			9		26	362	10
19–22 September	3–1–5–1						2–0–12–0			6–2–7–0	3–1–11–0	11–5–11–0	1	6		4	61	1D
	568.1–146–	285.4–55–	447.4–83–	226–44–	475–101–	52–7–	23–8–	375.3–83–	42–7–	124.2–21–	65–12–	85.1–13–						
	1633–66	977–29	1762–61	764–12	1509–31	233–7	64–2	1217–39	166–5	368–16	252–10	285–6						
Bowler's average	24.74	33.68	28.86	63.66	48.67	33.28	32.00	31.20	33.20	23.00	25.20	47.50						

A Bowling *v.* South Africa 'A': A.W. Smith 4–0–32–0, 3–0–29–0; I.J. Ward 7–2–21–0, 2–0–28–0; R.W. Nowell 18–2–76–2, 13–3–57–0; M.W. Patterson 17.3–4–80–6, 10–3–44–1; S.G. Kenlock 12–2–40–0

B D. Ripley retired hurt

C A.J. Stewart 2–0–24–0

D A.D. Brown 6–2–8–0

Sussex CCC First-Class Matches

Batting

	v. Nottinghamshire (Trent Bridge) 2–6 May		*v.* Warwickshire (Hove) 9–13 May		*v.* Indians (Hove) 16–18 May		*v.* Middlesex (Horsham) 22–25 May		*v.* Kent (Tunbridge Wells) 30 May–3 June		*v.* Durham (Hove) 6–10 June		*v.* Gloucestershire (Bristol) 13–17 June		*v.* Glamorgan (Hove) 20–24 June		*v.* Cambridge University (Hove) 29 June–1 July		*v.* Hampshire (Arundel) 3–6 July		*v.* Surrey (Guildford) 17–20 July		M	Inns	NO	Runs	HS	Av
C.W.J. Athey	43	27	6	14	80	31	77	–	16	34	102	–	0	4	11	–			39	24	1	91	18	33	–	1091	111	33.06
J.W. Hall	34	0	3	57			4	–	10	23							29	93					7	13	–	330	93	25.38
M.P. Speight	16	29	11	13	46	5	24	–	10	5							50	64*			8	0	11	21	2	514	122*	27.05
A.P. Wells	24	38	8	51	1	48*	92	–	5	45	113	–	1	36	78	–			43	8	81	27	18	33	1	1121	122	35.03
N.J. Lenham	100*	43	41	13	8*	–	40	–	9	10	10	–	70	6	0	–			14	55*	51	9	16	28	3	903	145	36.12
P. Moores	2	18	39	13	–	–	36	–	13	2	4	–	28	8	23	–	185	–	8	7*	2	119*	19	32	4	782	185	27.92
I.D.K. Salisbury	14	2					10*	–	18	1	22	–	4	24	83	–			19*	–	62	12	14	24	2	473	83	21.50
V.C. Drakes	4	14	21	41			3*	–	23	3	56	–	0	6	9	–							15	27	3	649	145*	27.04
N.C. Phillips	20	45	6*	29*	–	–											–	–					8	12	7	223	45	44.60
P.W. Jarvis	19*	26*	5	23	–	–	–	–	5	1*									35	–	21	1	8	11	4	164	35	23.42
E.S.H. Giddins	–	–	0	0	–	–	–	–	2*	4	–	–	6*	4*	5	–			11	–	1*	0	13	15	5	46	11	4.60
D.R. Law			53	18	–	–	3	–	17	33	35	–	0	97	0	–			17	13	0	1	16	27	–	609	97	22.55
K. Greenfield					65	141*					124*	–	10	2	154*	–			0	6	11	5	14	26	4	916	154*	41.63
J.D. Lewry					–	–					28*	–	10	10	28	–			0	–	0	16	9	13	3	138	28*	13.80
T.A. Radford											1	–	11	14	1	–	14	53	1	2			5	8	–	97	53	12.12
K. Newell																	105*	–					5	9	1	234	105*	29.25
R.K. Rao																	–	32*					2	3	1	87	38	43.50
S. Humphries																	–	–					1					–
R.S.C. Martin-Jenkins																	–	–					1					–
A.D. Edwards																	–	–					1					–
R.J. Kirtley																	–	–					7	11	3	15	7	1.87
M.Newell																							1	2	–	0	0	0.00
Byes		4	4	4	1					1	1			8			5			4	5	13						
Leg-byes	14	16	2	2	5	3	7		4	2	15		3	4	7		4		4	9	10	3						
Wides	1	2	1		1		1				3			2	3		1	1	2			6						
No-balls	12	14	22	6	40	6	22		10		38		14	6	4		6				12	12						
Total	303	278	222	284	247	234	319	0	142	164	552		157	231	406		399	243	193	128	265	315						
Wickets	8	9	10	10	4	2	7	0	10	10	8		10	10	10		4	2	10	5	10	10						
Result	D		L		D		W		L		W		W		W		D		D		L							
Points	8		2		–		19		4		24		20		24		–		7		6							

Batting

	v. Leicestershire (Leicester) 25–29 July		*v.* Yorkshire (Eastbourne) 1–5 August		*v.* Derbyshire (Hove) 8–12 August		*v.* Northamptonshire (Northampton) 22–26 August		*v.* Lancashire (Hove) 29 August–2 September		*v.* Worcestershire (Worcester) 3–6 September		*v.* Essex (Chelmsford) 12–16 September		*v.* Somerset (Hove) 19–22 September		M	Inns	NO	Runs	HS	Av
C.W.J. Athey	0	35	100	47	6	19	13	2	111	8	0	6	6	74	7	57	18	33	–	1091	111	33.06
J.W. Hall	16	52	6	3													7	13	–	330	93	25.38
M.P. Speight	68	2	22	0	122*	1	12	6									11	21	2	514	122*	27.05
A.P. Wells	7	15	31	0	35	2	51	40	21	29	16	5	122	46	1	1	18	33	1	1121	122	35.03
N.J. Lenham	27	2					45	0	37	17	1	14	55	44	18	64	16	28	3	903	145	36.12
P. Moores	47	14*	0	39*	8	56	2	8	22	8	11	6	13	4	33	4	19	32	4	782	185	27.92
I.D.K. Salisbury			2	0	20	13			40	27	4	9	70	5	6	6	14	24	2	473	83	21.50
V.C. Drakes	16	5	0*	59	0	2	59	6	52	0	103	1	19	145*	2	0	15	27	3	649	145*	27.04
N.C. Phillips							30*	0	4	24			15*	40*	1*	9*	8	12	7	223	45	44.60
P.W. Jarvis	28*	0															8	11	4	164	35	23.42
E.S.H. Giddins	7	2	0	–	1	3*											13	15	5	46	11	4.60
D.R. Law			39	43	8	32	11	13	3	9	18	75	0	0	32	39	16	27	–	609	97	22.55
K. Greenfield	69	9	15	12	12	51	22	9	24	7	26	36*	36	37	11	22	14	26	4	916	154*	41.63
J.D. Lewry	0	2	13	6*			14	11*									9	13	3	138	28*	13.80
T.A. Radford																	5	8	–	97	53	12.12
K. Newell					30	31			31	2	22	2	11	0			5	9	1	234	105*	29.25
R.K. Rao															17	38	2	3	1	87	38	43.50
S. Humphries																	1					–
R.S.C. Martin-Jenkins																	1					–
A.D. Edwards																	1					–
R.J. Kirtley					0	7	0	3	0*	1*	0*	0	1	–	3	0	7	11	3	15	7	1.87
M.Newell											0	0					1	2	–	0	0	0.00
Byes	2	2	4	2		4	6	1	7	4	1	8		4								
Leg-byes	7	6	3	5	17	1	13	7	8	6	8	6	15	10	3	4						
Wides			2				1	2	1		1	4				4						
No-balls		8	16	10	6	6	10	4	2	2	8	8		8	7	22						
Total	294	154	253	226	265	228	389	112	363	144	219	180	363	417	141	270						
Wickets	10	10	10	8	10	10	10	10	10	10	10	10	10	8	10	10						
Result	L		W		L		L		L		L		W		L							
Points	6		22		6		8		8		4		24		4							

Fielding Figures

52 – P. Moores (ct 50 / st 2)
15 – C.W.J. Athey
12 – A.P. Wells and K. Greenfield
9 – M.P. Speight
7 – I.D.K. Salisbury
6 – J.W. Hall and D.R. Law
4 – R.J. Kirtley and N.C. Phillips
3 – P.W. Jarvis and N.J. Lenham
2 – T.A. Radford and subs
1 – V.C. Drakes, S. Humphries, M. Newell and K. Newell

Bowling	V.C. Drakes	E.S.H. Giddins	P.W. Jarvis	I.D.K. Salisbury	N.C. Phillips	D.R. Law	J.D. Lewry	K. Greenfield	R.J. Kirtley	N.J. Lenham	R.S.C. Martin-Jenkins	K. Newell	Byes	Leg-byes	Wides	No-balls	Total	Wkts
v. Nottinghamshire (Trent Bridge)	12.1–0–52–1	11–1–44–1	16–4–47–1	14–2–60–2	4–0–40–0									12	5	16	255	5
2–6 May	7–2–24–0	5–2–5–1	6–1–29–1		6–3–10–0											8	68	2
v. Warwickshire (Hove)	28–4–143–1	29–3–113–1	23–2–102–1		33–2–145–2	29.4–2–132–2							1	9	1	29	645	7
9–13 May																		
v. Indians (Hove)		9–0–52–0	12–2–31–1		5–1–38–1	9–1–45–0	4–1–17–1							2	5		185	3
16–18 May		8–1–28–1	9–0–51–0		9–3–44–1	8–0–27–1	8–2–31–1							3		8	184	4
v. Middlesex (Horsham)																	0	0
22–25 May	9–0–36–1	3.2–1–6–3	8–4–26–3			4–0–14–3								3	1	14	85	10
v. Kent (Tunbridge Wells)	17–4–65–3	14–4–46–1	15–1–59–1	5–0–39–0		18.5–3–62–5								9	1	24	280	10
30 May–3 June	2–0–16–0		1.3–0–14–0												1	4	30	0
v. Durham (Hove)	11.1–3–46–2	10–1–36–2		11–6–15–6		4–0–30–0	8–0–28–0						2	2		6	159	10
6–10 June	15–2–84–2	12.1–2–56–1		26–5–84–2		12–4–33–5	10–0–57–0	3–2–5–0					1	6	1	11	326	10
v. Gloucestershire (Bristol)	9–2–27–2	15.2–3–53–5		2–0–4–0		13–4–35–3	9–1–26–0						1	5		4	151	10
13–17 June	23.4–4–66–3	20–5–45–3		14–1–27–0		12–1–36–2	15–1–41–2						8	11	2	15	234	10
v. Glamorgan (Hove)	7.3–1–25–1	12–2–29–0				8–2–28–3	16–4–44–6						1	6	1	14	133	10
20–24 June	16–3–63–1	19.3–1–65–4		24–4–49–2		3–0–18–0	16–4–56–2						4	11	1	8	266	10
v. Cambridge University (Hove)					28–11–70–1				17–3–91–1		8–0–39–0	14–4–38–1		12		4	321	3A
29 June–1 July									8–1–31–2		9–1–26–1	2–0–12–0	4				73	3
v. Hampshire (Arundel)		26–5–56–3	23–5–58–2	14–2–33–0		13.3–3–39–2	17–3–46–2			13–1–18–1			12	8	1		270	10
3–6 July		16–2–49–0	4–0–10–0	16–2–56–0		13–2–28–0	19–4–73–5			5–1–11–0				11	1		238	5
v. Surrey (Guildford)		14–2–55–0	28–7–82–4	32.2–10–85–2		26–5–85–2	22–3–64–2	6–2–13–0		4–1–17–0			4	6	2	4	411	10
17–20 July		4–1–9–0	14.3–0–60–4	20–1–89–1		10–2–37–1	23–2–79–0	5–0–15–0					1	14	1	2	304	6
v. Leicestershire (Leicester)	30–9–79–0	24.5–9–60–3	8–1–23–1				30.2–6–74–5	3–1–4–0		11.1–3–22–1				4	1	2	266	10
25–29 July	32–9–108–3	7–1–16–1					27.4–6–73–6	1–0–4–0		7–0–29–0			9	1		2	240	10
v. Yorkshire (Eastbourne)	27–5–99–5	19–2–76–2		17–11–42–1		9–0–61–0	17–4–54–2						1	12	1	21	345	10
1–5 August	14–1–36–3	16.3–4–47–6				5–1–19–0	11–3–28–1							3		4	133	10
v. Derbyshire (Hove)	19–5–73–2	17–1–78–1		8–5–10–3		17–2–78–2			16–2–61–2				2	18	1	20	320	10
8–12 August	21–5–47–5	17–3–68–2		11–2–33–1		5–0–29–1			7.5–0–33–1				4	6	3	16	220	10
v. Northamptonshire (Northampton)	24–1–103–3				22–2–76–2	14.4–0–47–2	17–5–53–1		17–5–63–2	3–0–10–0			1	8	3	34	361	10
22–26 August	13–2–56–2					7–0–35–0	6–0–20–2		5.2–2–19–0				8	4	1	12	142	4
v. Lancashire (Hove)	20–3–45–2			33–12–67–2	31–13–49–1	7–1–18–1			14.5–0–30–3	3–2–3–1			1	5	2	6	218	10
29 August–2 September	18–2–58–0			26–6–100–4	10–1–44–0	9–3–25–1			6.3–0–33–0	3–0–17–0			4	9	1	6	290	5
v. Worcestershire (Worcester)	37–9–123–3			24.1–6–60–2		21–4–67–2		5–1–11–0	30–7–112–2	4–0–13–0		3–0–16–0	2	9	4	16	413	9
3–6 September																		
v. Essex (Chelmsford)	14–2–57–1			28.2–3–94–3	21–4–54-2	11–3–39–0			23–3–94–4	2–0–6–0			2	14	1	6	360	10
12–16 September	10–1–56–1			29.4–9–75–8	34–8–116–1				3–0–22–0				13	1	1	16	283	10
v. Somerset (Hove)	18–0–88–3			31.–6–91–5	21–2–92–2	9–0–32–0			9–1–37–0	1–1–0–0			4	10	1	8	354	10
19–22 September				4.4–0–23–0					5–2–31–2				5	1			60	2
	454.3–79–	329.4–56–	168–27–	391.93–93–	224-50–	298.4–43–	276–49–	23–6–	162.3–26–	56.1–9–	17–1–	19–4-						
	1675–50	1092–41	592–19	1136–44	778–13	1099–38	864–38	52–0	657–19	146–3	65–1	66–1						
Bowler's average	33.50	26.63	31.15	25.81	59.84	28.92	22.73	–	34.57	48.66	65.00	66.00						

A A.D. Edwards 13–2–64–0; R.K. Rao 5–3–7–0

Warwickshire CCC First-Class Matches Batting

	v. Cambridge University (Cambridge) 9–13 May		v. Sussex (Hove) 9–13 May		v. Hampshire (Edgbaston) 16–20 May		v. Leicestershire (Edgbaston) 23–27 May		v. Northamptonshire (Northampton) 30 May–3 June		v. Somerset (Taunton) 13–17 June		v. Yorkshire (Leeds) 13–17 June		v. Kent (Edgbaston) 20–24 June		v. Middlesex (Lord's) 27 June–1 July		v. Nottinghamshire (Edgbaston) 4–8 July		v. Pakistanis (Edgbaston) 17–19 July		M	Inns	NO	Runs	HS	Av
N.V. Knight	128	1*	132	–	5	60	34	23											33	46	45	90*	10	19	2	929	132	54.64
W.G. Khan	108	51	19	–	13	3			0	32*	1	15	6	35	13	4	17	–					15	28	1	738	130	27.33
D.P. Ostler	81*	31*	90	–	0	3	9	25	15	6*	2	66	85	7	8	17	17	–	9	–	3	23	17	31	3	850	90	30.35
T.L. Penney	0	1	134	–	48	73	6	3	20	–	77	52	125	18	33	20	101	–	60	–	66	7*	19	34	4	1295	134	43.16
D.R. Brown	38*	17	0	–	11	33	1	55	8	–	34	11	32	31	6	0	14	–	4	–	76	–	19	32	2	671	76	22.36
A.F. Giles	–	17	–	–	1*	2*	0	21*			5	3	0*	2	0	65			31*	–	28	–	17	27	9	600	106*	33.33
P.A. Smith	–	2															21	–					2	2	–	23	21	11.50
N.M.K. Smith	–	20	28	–	2	0			34	–	28	37	9	22*	9*	15	31	–	54	5*	23	–	16	27	4	626	74	27.21
K.J. Piper	–	6	11*	–	13	19	15	28*	8	–	18	8	6	14									13	22	2	429	82	21.45
G. Welch	–	35	–	–	9	0	4	0	19	–	9	31	5	13	6	12			–	–	9	–	13	17	1	210	45	13.12
T.A. Munton	–	–													3	0*					5*	–	11	14	9	123	54*	24.60
D.A. Reeve			168*	–	41	22	26	29	36	–			24	5									5	8	1	351	168*	50.14
S.M. Pollock			24	–	45	6	8	22	107	–	43	0	0	34	14	6	10	–	1	–			13	21	1	606	150*	30.30
A.J. Moles							45	21	164	5	17	75	0	7	2	76	176	–	27	25			13	25	–	903	176	36.12
G.C. Small							0*	–	12*	–							2*	–	23*	–			7	9	5	55	23*	13.75
D.A. Altree											0*	0*									0	–	3	5	2	0	0*	0.00
M. Burns															27	21	11	–	81	65*	36	4	8	15	1	345	81	24.64
M. Edmond																	8*	–					1	1	1	8	8*	–
A. Singh																					4	9	3	6	1	79	23*	15.80
M.J. Powell																							4	8	–	182	39	22.75
Byes		1	1			10	9	6	5	1	2	4	1	13	1	10	1		2	4	6	8						
Leg-byes	6	7	9		4	5	6	5	7		3	12	11	10	6	2	24		5	3	5	1						
Wides	1	1	1				1	1			6	1			1	1			2									
No-balls	6		28					2	12		10	10	2	18	8	4	12		18	10	4	6						
Total	368	190	645		192	236	164	241	447	44	255	325	306	229	137	253	445		350	158	310	148						
Wickets	3	8	7		10	10	10	8	10	1	10	10	10	10	10	10	9		8	2	10	3						
Result	W		W		L		D		W		W		L		L		D		W		W							
Points	–		24		4		6		24		22		5		4		7		21		–							

Fielding Figures

35 – D.P. Ostler
27 – K.J. Piper (ct 21 / st 6)
18 – M. Burns (ct 16 / st 2)
14 – T.L. Penney and D.R. Brown
11 – A.F. Giles and W.G. Khan
10 – N.V. Knight and N.M.K. Smith
9 – G. Welch
7 – D.A. Reeve and A.J. Moles
5 – S.M. Pollock
3 – A. Singh
2 – G. C. Small, T.A. Munton and M.J. Powell
1 – P.A. Smith and D.A. Altree

Batting

	v. Gloucestershire (Cheltenham) 25–29 July		v. Durham (Edgbaston) 8–12 August		v. Glamorgan (Edgbaston) 15–19 August		v. Worcestershire (Worcester) 22–26 August		v. Surrey (The Oval) 29 August–2 September		v. Essex (Edgbaston) 3–6 Septembr		v. Derbyshire (Derby) 12–16 September		v. Lancashire (Edgbaston) 19–22 September		M	Inns	NO	Runs	HS	Av
N.V. Knight					63	12					2	24	54	41	33	103	10	19	2	929	132	54.64
W.G. Khan			0	130	0	8	52	44	0	14	126	0	1	8	6	32	15	28	1	738	130	27.33
D.P. Ostler	73	90	86	6	65	2	0	10	7	2	1	11					17	31	3	850	90	30.35
T.L. Penney	26	0	3	2	37	0	14	31*	38	27	15	70	12	83*	23	70*	19	34	4	1295	134	43.16
D.R. Brown	6	39	31	51	20	26*	0	–	11	11	31	4	27	4	14	25	19	32	2	671	76	22.36
A.F. Giles	6	18	13	6*	1	10	83	–	50	7	0	49	9	67*	106*	–	17	27	9	600	106*	33.33
P.A. Smith																	2	2	–	23	21	11.50
N.M.K. Smith	41	14	64	0	26	6	9	12			15	46			74	2*	16	27	4	626	74	27.21
K.J. Piper					82	17	6	–	45	0	27	13	16	32	17	28	13	22	2	429	82	21.45
G. Welch									4	5*			45	–	4	–	13	17	1	210	45	13.12
T.A. Munton	0	6*	3*	–	14	–	54*	–	2	4*	1*	0*	26*	–	5	–	11	14	9	123	54*	24.60
D.A. Reeve																	5	8	1	351	168*	50.14
S.M. Pollock	4	53	26	30	150*	8	15	–									13	21	1	606	150*	30.30
A.J. Moles	16	0	26	74					0	23	2	9	28	15	11	59	13	25	–	903	176	36.12
G.C. Small	2*	0									6	10	0	–			7	9	5	55	23*	13.75
D.A. Altree									0	0							3	5	2	0	0*	0.00
M. Burns	2	0	6	6									0	1	61	24	8	15	1	345	81	24.64
M. Edmond																	1	1	1	8	8*	–
A. Singh	13	10					20	23*									3	6	1	79	23*	15.80
M.J. Powell			26	32	0	39	36	38	9	2							4	8	–	182	39	22.75
Byes	1				10	4				2	1	5			5							
Leg-byes	9	1	3	10	13	4	5	4	8	4	12	12	5	10	7	11						
Wides			1		1		4		1					1	2	1						
No-balls	17	6	18	14	16		12		20	8	14	12	8	8	18	4						
Total	216	237	306	361	498	136	310	162	195	109	253	265	231	270	386	359						
Wickets	10	10	10	9	10	8	10	4	10	10	10	10	10	6	10	6						
Result	L		W		W		D		L		L		W		D							
Points	3		23		24		8		2		6		21		9							

Bowling

	T.A. Munton	D.R. Brown	A.F. Giles	G. Welch	N.M.K. Smith	P.A. Smith	S.M. Pollock	D.A. Reeve	G.C. Small	D.A. Altree	W.G. Khan	M. Edmond	M.J. Powell	M. Burns	Byes	Leg-byes	Wides	No-balls	Total	Wkts
v. Cambridge University (Cambridge)	13–6–18–1	10–3–31–1	10.4–5–34–2	7.3–0–61–0	22–7–49–4	6.2–2–12–1									1	2	4	8	208	10
3–5 May	11–6–19–2	11–3–36–2	8.2–2–10–2	8–0–29–3	5–1–14–0	6–2–18–0									4	2		8	132	9A
v. Sussex (Hove)		9–1–32–0	21–10–40–2	16.3–4–50–4	11–3–31–0		20–5–56–2	7–2–7–2							4	2	1	22	222	10
9–13 May		17–5–46–2	39–14–86–3	6–2–23–0	8.1–1–39–3		26–4–76–2	4–2–8–0							4	2		6	284	10
v. Hampshire (Edgbaston)		12–4–39–0	31–14–49–3	16–5–39–1	11–5–32–1		31–9–78–3	18–8–20–2							9	8		6	274	10
16–20 May		9.2–1–36–0	25–8–62–2	11–2–29–1	19–4–41–1		16–5–42–0	21–7–42–0							7	17			276	5
v. Leicestershire (Edgbaston)		10.5–0–49–1	15–4–38–0	19–3–83–4			21–3–64–0	23–6–43–0	12–0–55–2						8	13		16	353	8
23–27 May																				
v. Northamptonshire (Northampton)		10–1–34–0		15–1–78–1	16–5–57–1		20–3–78–3	19–4–37–5	8–2–22–0						4	4		10	314	10
30 May–3 June		8–2–29–1		15–4–46–2	12–4–20–2		22.1–4–49–3	7–2–21–0	2–0–3–1						5	1		14	174	10
v. Somerset (Taunton)		20–6–61–3		15–1–64–3	1–1–0–0		21–8–35–2			13–2–68–1					6	8	11	8	242	10
6–10 June		9–5–15–0	28.2–10–69–4	8–1–31–0	29–10–57–2		22–8–37–3			3–0–12–0					5	13	1	16	239	10
v. Yorkshire (Leeds)		23–6–47–2	68.3–18–174–2	7–0–38–0	49–11–127–5		29–9–89–1	4–1–17–0							7	9	1	10	508	10
13–17 June			2–0–12–0		2–0–15–0						0.1–0–1–0								28	0
v. Kent (Edgbaston)	19.1–17–35–1	20–3–68–5		14–0–79–0	2–0–7–0		23–6–60–4								4	5	4	16	258	10
20–24 June		21.3–5–52–6	3–1–10–0	13–2–31–2			18–3–57–2								6	8	1	8	164	10
v. Middlesex (Lord's)		33–7–93–3			8–1–32–0	20–3–58–1	28.4–9–56–6		26–6–72–0			16–1–73–0			5	24	4	12	413	10
27 June–1 July		10–2–26–0			7.1–3–33–0		8–2–13–0		7–0–37–2		2–1–1–0	0.5–0–6–1			5	1	1	2	122	3
v. Nottinghamshire (Edgbaston)		9–1–53–0	12–0–48–0		16.2–4–52–1		10–1–31–3		11–4–24–0						4		1	4	212	4
4–8 July		5–0–16–0	26–7–70–5	5–2–7–0	7–0–29–0		10.5–4–19–3		13–2–52–2						10	8			211	10
v. Pakistanis (Edgbaston)	16–5–46–0	21–4–86–3	4–3–2–2	14.4–2–58–3	3–0–30–0					15–0–72–2						3		16	297	10
17–19 July	7–2–17–0		26–13–39–3		20–5–56–3					12–1–41–3					5			4	158	10
v. Gloucestershire (Cheltenham)	33–13–85–2	22.4–4–97–2	31–4–131–1		16–2–62–0		29–7–71–1		24–3–99–4						5	19			569	10
25–29 July																				
v. Durham (Edgbaston)	16–4–54–3		29–7–53–2		41–14–76–5		19–3–64–0								4	5		2	255	10
8–12 August	10–2–29–3		18–4–45–6		18–4–25–1		9–3–29–0								1	1		4	130	10
v. Glamorgan (Edgbaston)	12–2–54–1		28.2–8–63–6		18–3–52–3		10–3–38–0								4	3		2	214	10
15–19 August	17.5–2–62–2	1–0–9–0	34–4–118–3		49–13–166–5		20–4–57–0								5	2		16	419	10
v. Worcestershire (Worcester)	24–8–58–3	10–3–24–0	8–4–12–3		15–1–42–0		23–6–58–3								8	3	1	4	205	9
22–26 August	10–3–45–0		13–5–32–1		13–1–50–2		10–3–26–1								8	3		2	164	4
v. Surrey (The Oval)	36–8–100–2	21–4–98–1	36–14–82–3	31.3–7–75–3						24–6–74–0			4–0–18–1		12	9	1	4	468	10
29 August–2 September																				
v. Essex (Chelmsford)	34–14–70–1	18–2–62–3	12.4–4–32–1		9–2–14–1				20–8–41–4						9	10	2	2	238	10
3–6 September	24–2–78–1	15–2–50–1	41–9–119–3		27–1–117–0				11–1–62–0						14	10	2	4	450	6
v. Derbyshire (Derby)	19–5–57–1	15–5–69–3		17.5–2–62–3					18–6–41–3						2	11	4	2	242	10
12–16 September	33–8–79–3	16–2–46–1	14–6–20–1	18.5–2–59–2					12–3–28–1					3–0–13–0		10		10	255	10
v. Lancashire (Edgbaston)	29–6–92–2	20–0–106–0	48.4–13–165–4	17–2–93–1	32–10–92–3										34	15	2	16	597	10
19–22 September																				
	362–103–	407.2–81–	633.3–191–	275.5–42–	486.4–116–	32.2–7–	446.4–112–	103–32–	164–35–	67–9–	2.1–1–	16.5–1–	4–0–	3–0–						
	997–28	1410–40	1615–64	1035–34	1417–43	88–2	1183–42	195–9	536–19	267–6	2–0	79–1	18–1	13–0						
Bowler's average	35.60	35.25	25.23	30.44	32.95	44.00	28.16	21.66	28.21	44.50	–	79.00	18.00	–						

A R.T. Ragnauth retired hurt

Worcestershire CCC First-Class Matches Batting

Batting	v. Essex (Worcester) 2–6 May	v. Indians (Worcester) 8–10 May	v. Leicestershire (Leicester) 16–20 May	v. Glamorgan (Abergavenny) 23–27 May	v. Hampshire (Worcester) 30 May–3 June	v. Oxford University (Oxford) 6–8 June	v. Nottinghamshire (Worcester) 13–17 June	v. Somerset (Bath) 19–22 June	v. Yorkshire (Worcester) 27 June–1 July	v. Lancashire (Old Trafford) 4–8 July	v. Durham (Worcester) 18–22 July	M	Inns	NO	Runs	HS	Av
T.S. Curtis	2 32	19 –	9 5	62* 42	4 6		46 –	7 85	72 0	29 0		17	31	2	952	118	32.82
W.P.C. Weston	13 7	98 –	15 69	121* 1	0 1	124 –	21 54	15 34	18 12	171* 11	6 40*	20	37	5	1389	171	43.40
G.A. Hick	18 36	215 –	1 4		123 44		17 85				150 25*	13	23	1	1202	215	54.63
T.M. Moody	20 33	– –	8 104	– 1	33 138*	66* –	212 17	20 54	0 3	108 67*	3 –	19	31	3	1427	212	50.96
D.A. Leatherdale	50 69	28 –	27 27	– 30	0 3*		0 7*	12 0				11	18	2	539	122	33.68
S.J. Rhodes	9 2	53 –	23 36	– 53*	47 –		0 4	47 92*	51 16	– –	29 –	19	29	5	939	110	39.12
S.R. Lanpitt	46 45	0* –	23 2	– 31*	14 –	16* 70	59 –	30 32	0 17	– –	24 –	19	27	5	658	88	29.09
P.J. Newport	0 68			– –	33 –	– –	0 –	18 23				6	6	–	142	68	23.66
R.K. Illingworth	17 66*	– –	31 4	– –	20* –	– 17*	41* –	0 32	18 4*	– –	23 –	18	21	9	405	66*	33.75
P.A. Thomas	1 11	– –	5 11									5	7	–	46	11	6.57
A. Sheriyar	1* 0	– –	0* 12*	– –	0 –			0* 4*	0* 0	– –	4 –	16	15	9	38	13	6.33
K.R. Spiring		45 –	8 51	– 0	144 82	12 78*	64 20*	14 1	109 6	0* 21	0 –	18	32	6	1084	144	41.69
M. Rawnsley				– –		– –	– –					4	1	1	4	4*	–
M.J. Church						152 –			29 5	28 4	2 23	6	11	–	280	152	25.45
V.S. Solanki						22 29		13 71	32 40	– 62*	16 –	14	24	3	828	90	39.42
I. Dawood						– 1						1	1	–	1	1	1.00
B.E.A. Preece						– –						3	4	2	5	3*	2.50
S.W.K. Ellis									0* 0	– –	14* –	9	10	4	63	15	10.50
J.T. Ralph												1	2	–	0	0	0.00
M. Amjad												1	2	–	8	7	4.00
Byes	2 5	5	11	5 2	6	3 1	11	8	4 6	11	3						
Leg-byes	12 11	5	4 13	4 6	11 4	2 2	20 1	16 8	6 5	6	12 1						
Wides	2		1 2		2 2			1	1	1							
No-balls	8 30	8	2	8 6	2	6	2 6	2 4	16 6	2	16 4						
Total	201 415	476	155 353	200 172	431 288	403 198	493 194	194 449	355 121	350 171	302 93						
Wickets	10 10	6	10 10	0 5	10 4	4 3	9 4	10 9	9 10	3 4	10 1						
Result	L	D	L	D	D	D	D	W	L	D	W						
Points	5	–	2	8	9	–	10	20	8	11	23						

Batting

Batting	v. Northamptonshire (Kidderminster) 24–27 July	v. Kent (Canterbury) 1–5 August	v. South Africa 'A' (Worcester) 9–12 August	v. Middlesex (Lord's) 15–19 August	v. Warwickshire (Worcester) 22–26 August	v. Derbyshire (Chesterfield) 29 August–2 September	v. Sussex (Worcester) 3–6 September	v. Gloucestershire (Worcester) 12–16 September	v. Surrey (The Oval) 19–22 September	M	Inns	NO	Runs	HS	Av
T.S. Curtis	65 107	6 19		14 118	16 44	0 8	61 –	20 10	16 28*	17	31	2	952	118	32.82
W.P.C. Weston	68 7	19 0	3 17	59 12	20 52	100* 18	42 –	28 89	2 22*	20	37	5	1389	171	43.40
G.A. Hick		148 86		0 7	15 15	9 30	1 –	54 106	13 –	13	23	1	1202	215	54.63
T.M. Moody	106 169	11 2		124 1	3 7	4 12	30 –	0 11	60 –	19	31	3	1427	212	50.96
D.A. Leatherdale			2 73				122 –	70 19	0 –	11	18	2	539	122	33.68
S.J. Rhodes	12* 53*	68 41*	0 51	15 1	27 –	24 57	110 –	12 –	6 –	19	29	5	939	110	39.12
S.R. Lanpitt	0 28	88 33*		30 22*	7 –	1 1	5 –	5 –	29 –	19	27	5	658	88	29.09
P.J. Newport										6	6	–	142	68	23.66
R.K. Illingworth	16* 5*	10 –		12 2*	4 –	0 –		44 –	39* –	18	21	9	405	66*	33.75
P.A. Thomas			8 1						9 –	5	7	–	46	11	6.57
A. Sheriyar	– –	– –		2* –	0* –	13 2	– –	0* –		16	15	9	38	13	6.33
K.R. Spiring	0 9	71 0	33 4	19 12	52 8*	12 130*		12 4*	63 –	18	32	6	1084	144	41.69
M. Rawnsley							4* –			4	1	1	4	4*	–
M.J. Church	2 4		0 31							6	11	–	280	152	25.45
V.S. Solanki	68 0	1 0	14 29	69 26	45 25*	58 31	0 –	41 46*	90 –	14	24	3	828	90	39.42
I. Dawood										1	1	–	1	1	1.00
B.E.A. Preece			0* 3*			0 2				3	4	2	5	3*	2.50
S.W.K. Ellis	– –	0* –	4 13	10 15	0* –		7 –			9	10	4	63	15	10.50
J.T. Ralph			0 0							1	2	–	0	0	0.00
M. Amjad			1 7							1	2	–	8	7	4.00
Byes		9 12	18	2	8 8	2	2	2 12	1						
Leg-byes	5 4	8 10	1 7	11 7	3 3	6 1	9	14 4	9 6						
Wides			3 2		1	1 1	4	1							
No-balls	8 2	20 4	8 22	4 8	4 2	10 8	16	16 10	26 4						
Total	350 388	459 207	77 278	369 233	205 164	238 303	413	319 311	362 61						
Wickets	7 7	9 6	10 10	10 8	9 4	10 9†	9	10 5	10 1						
Result	D	W	L	D	D	L	W	W	W						
Points	11	24	–	11	8	5	24	23	20						

†R.K Illingworth absent

Fielding Figures

48 – S.J. Rhodes (ct 40 / st 8)
20 – W.P.C. Weston
16 – G.A. Hick
14 – S.R. Lampitt
12 – T.M. Moody
10 – T.S. Curtis and R.K. Illingworth
9 – K.R. Spiring and V.S. Solanki
8 – D.A. Leatherdale
6 – S.W.K. Ellis
4 – A. Sheriyar and M.J. Church
3 – I. Dawood
1 – P.J. Newport, M. Rawnsley, B.E.A. Preece, J.T. Ralph and sub

Bowling

	P.J. Newport	A. Sheriyar	S.R. Lampitt	P.A. Thomas	R.K. Illingworth	D.A. Leatherdale	M.J. Church	T.M. Moody	G.A. Hick	M. Rawnsley	S.W.K. Ellis	V.S. Solanki	Byes	Leg-byes	Wides	No-balls	Total	Wkts
v. Essex (Worcester)	18–4–87–1	14–1–86–1	24–3–116–5	11–0–84–1	11.3–3–23–2	2–0–9–0							11	14	2	20	430	10
2–6 May	11.2–4–49–2	9–3–32–2	10–1–57–0	6–0–26–0	4–0–19–0								1	6		6	190	5
v. Indians (Worcester)		22–3–64–3	18–4–70–0	23–6–89–1	15–2–52–0	7–0–34–1			7–0–37–0					3	1	8	349	5
8–10 May		6–1–21–0	12–5–30–1	14–1–48–0	12–3–37–0	12–3–53–0		6–2–5–1					4	7	1	10	240	2A
v. Leicestershire (Leicester) 16–20 May		32–5–110–0	20–3–105–2	20–1–119–2	38–4–129–0	6–0–40–0		27–4–112–3	8–1–17–0					6	1	16	638	8
v. Glamorgan (Abergavenny)	28–7–100–6	14–1–56–1	15.1–4–62–0		30–11–46–1					14–3–55–1			2	7		18	328	10
23–27 May	9–4–41–0	12–2–57–2	9–1–43–2		8–0–34–1					2–0–10–0				9		4	194	5
v. Hampshire (Worcester) 30 May–3 June	25.2–5–120–2	24–5–71–0	28–6–103–2		17–4–49–0			2–2–0–0	20–6–43–2					7		10	393	7
v. Oxford University (Oxford)	11–5–13–0		5–1–18–1		15–0–55–0		11–1–50–4	8.1–1–25–1		19–3–44–1		11–3–35–0	8	13	1	18	338	9B
6–8 June	6–0–14–0				24–4–75–6			10–0–34–1		16–3–43–1		3–1–6–1		2			195	9B
v. Nottinghamshire (Worcester)	24–5–98–3		23–6–97–2		34–12–64–1	1.5–1–2–2		5–3–5–1	19–3–60–0	17–5–52–1			5	8	2	22	392	10C
13–17 June	15–2–41–1		11–2–30–1		14–4–14–1			4–1–13–0	12–4–37–1	7–4–11–0			12	1		10	159	4
v. Somerset (Bath)	20.5–5–54–2	13–2–62–1	23–6–70–1		29–10–40–5	14–5–28–1							8	1		32	263	10
19–22 June	19–3–53–2	25.1–1–107–2	14–2–70–0		31–7–69–2			4–1–14–0				11–2–47–0		16	2	14	376	6
v. Yorkshire (Worcester)		23–4–77–1	23–6–58–5		24–12–33–0			16–6–41–1			19–1–80–3	6–1–27–0	4	1	3	4	321	10
27 June–1 July		9–2–27–0	4–0–10–0		28–10–41–2		6–0–27–2	3–0–18–0			6–2–20–0	25.5–2–111–3	5	7	1		266	7
v. Lancashire (Old Trafford)		18–4–47–1	14–4–43–1		35–12–86–2		4–0–16–0	5–0–19–0			14–1–58–1	25.2–3–116–5	4	3	2	12	392	10
4–8 July		4–0–11–0			28–9–93–1						5–3–7–1	27–3–140–5	4	1			256	7
v. Durham (Worcester)		11–3–46–0	18.2–1–57–4		16–5–39–2		6–3–16–1	20–6–39–3			12–0–38–0	1–0–2–0		3	2	22	240	10
18–22 July		14.3–4–46–4	8–0–45–2					10–4–29–0			12–2–29–3			3	1	18	152	10
v. Northamptonshire (Kidderminster)		27–4–81–1	25–6–47–3		43–12–89–4		2.1–0–6–1	4–0–17–0			15–3–51–0	6–1–21–1		16	3	8	328	10
24–27 July		10–1–39–0	18–4–84–2		16–4–57–0		6–0–33–0	10–0–50–0			13–0–73–0	22–1–103–1	4	3	1	8	446	3
v. Kent (Canterbury)		20–3–83–0	28–7–92–4		33.3–10–61–3			24–8–67–2			9–0–55–1		6	2	2	14	366	10
1–5 August		16–6–58–4	8.4–3–25–3					7–2–22–1						3	2	2	108	9D
v. South Africa 'A' (Worcester)				12–3–33–4		8–0–37–0	4–1–11–1				6–0–34–0	4–1–7–0		1	6	18	202	10E
9–12 August				20–0–109–3		16–2–75–4					5–1–22–1			14	3	18	325	10E
v. Middlesex (Lord's)		24–5–53–1	31.4–7–87–2		47–15–85–5			12–0–52–0			11–1–39–1	11–4–20–0	2	14	5	2	352	9
15–19 August		6–0–19–0	8–0–42–0		14–0–57–1				7–1–31–1		3–0–17–0	11–1–69–5	5	2	2	6	242	9
v. Warwickshire (Worcester)		15.2–3–61–2	30–7–90–4		38–17–54–4			9–1–34–0	4–2–15–0		10–2–51–0			5	4	12	310	10
22–26 August		7–0–29–0			4–0–31–1						7–1–40–0	8–0–41–2		4		1	162	4F
v. Derbyshire (Chesterfield)		29–5–95–1	18–2–105–1		24–10–71–1			16.5–3–82–6				9–3–27–0	3	4	1	30	471	10G
29 August–2 September		5–0–22–0												1	1		71	1G
v. Sussex (Worcester)		13–3–50–2	16–2–57–1			3–1–5–1		17–5–36–2		1–0–4–1	17–6–58–3		1	8	1	8	219	10
3–6 September		24–7–99–6	10–2–23–2			1.1–01–0		7–2–27–0			6–4–14–0	1–0–2–0	8	6	4	8	180	10
v. Gloucestershire (Worcester)		13–1–52–2	22–4–83–0		19–6–52–0	12–3–47–1		35–16–67–6				12–7–23–1	4	6		18	334	10
12–16 September			12–3–40–1		23–5–57–1	23–6–53–1		36.5–13–92–7				14–4–35–0	6	9	1	6	292	10
v. Surrey (The Oval)																	0	0
19–22 September			14–1–60–2	15–3–67–1	27–9–78–2			21–6–56–2				7.1–0–31–3		7		10	299	10
	187.3–44–670–19	460–78–1661–37	520.5–103–1919–54	121–14–575–12	693–200–1690–48	106–21–384–11	39.1–5–159–9	319.5–86–956–37	77–17–240–4	76–18–219–5	170–27–686–14	215.2–37863–27						
Bowler's average	35.26	44.89	35.53	47.91	35.20	34.90	17.66	25.83	60.00	43.80	49.00	31.96						

A W.P.C. Weston 6–0–35–0
B B.E.A. Preece 19–1–77–1, 6–1–21–0
C W.P.C. Weston 1–0–1–0
D M.A. Ealham absent injured
E B.E.A. Preece 15.2–0–79–4, 16–1–80–2; M. Amjad 4–0–25–0
F T.S. Curtis 4–0–17–1
G B.E.A. Preece 15–0–84–1, 5–0–47–0; T.S. Curtis 0.3–0–1–1

Yorkshire CCC First-Class Matches Batting

	v. Lancashire (Old Trafford) 18–20 April		v. Glamorgan (Cardiff) 2–6 May		v. Derbyshire (Sheffield) 9–13 May		v. Durham (Chester-le-Street) 16–20 May		v. Kent (Canterbury) 23–27 May		v. Middlesex (Lord's) 30 May–3 June		v. Surrey (Middlesbrough) 6–10 June		v. Warwickshire (Leeds) 13–17 June		v. Leicestershire (Bradford) 20–24 June		v. Worcestershire (Worcester) 27 June–1 July		v. South Africa 'A' (Leeds) 3–5 July		M	Inns	NO	Runs	HS	Av
C.J. Schofield	25	–																					1	1	–	25	25	25.00
M.P. Vaughan	5	–	183	3	41	0	1	0	24	1	0	67	135	91	18	6*	0	54	9	60			18	32	2	1161	183	38.70
D. Byas	32	–	12	2	79	0	22	7	44	79	30	33	8	5	13	–	42	0	14	0	16	27*	19	32	2	933	138	31.10
C. White	0	–	1	14*	61	–	5	15	13	7	29	39	0	0	12	–	15	5	53	65	77	–	19	30	1	949	181	32.72
R.A. Kettleborough	85	–																			0	–	7	9	–	307	108	34.11
R.J. Blakey	7	–	38	2	32*	–	27	7	60*	0*	8	19	3	45	9	–	4	0	14	22	64	–	19	30	6	839	109*	34.95
A.C. Morris	60	–					0	40	27	–	0	3	21	5							33	–	6	9	–	189	60	21.00
D. Gough	7	–	31*	19*	4	–	43	0			9	10	28	16	121	–	50	0	26	1*			16	25	3	501	121	22.77
G.M. Hamilton	0	–																			1	–	4	5	1	71	61	17.75
I.D. Fisher	0*	–																					1	1	1	0	0*	–
A.G. Wharf	8*	–	–	62					41	–											10	–	4	4	1	121	62	40.33
M.D. Moxon			213	10	59	74*									131	22*	0	18	36	42			13	23	3	961	213	48.05
M.G. Bevan			15	77	136	26	90	51	80	15*	31	107	38	160*	43	–	82	65*	61	57			12	22	3	1225	160*	64.47
A. McGrath			9	2	91	30*	0	27	40	101	27	12	41	13	65	–	24	32	60	6	3	50*	18	31	2	962	137	33.17
P.J. Hartley			10	–	5	–	14	38	5	–	88*	12	3	5	5	–	3	4	28*	–			16	24	3	476	89	22.66
R.D. Stemp			–	–	20	–	65	14	–	–	22	0	4*	3	27*	–	51*	0	0	–	22*	–	18	23	9	252	65	18.00
C.E.W. Silverwood					0	–	45*	1*	0*	–	1	0*	0	0	37	–	44	0	8	–			16	24	6	198	45*	11.00
B. Parker																					59	–	1	1	–	59	59	59.00
M.J. Hoggard																					10	–	1	1	–	10	10	10.00
Byes	1			2	5		1	4	2	12	2	3		4	7		4	3	4	5								
Leg-byes	5		22	5	14	5	5	1	3	6	11	13	4	15	9		3	2	1	7	6	5						
Wides				1	2	1	1	1	1		1		2	3	1			3	3	1	4							
No-balls	2		2	6	12	2	16	4	10	2	16	4	18	22	10		20	2	4		26	8						
Total	237		536	205	561	138	335	210	350	223	275	322	305	387	508	28	342	188	321	266	331	90						
Wickets	9		8	7	10	3	10	10	8	4	10	10	10	10	10	0	10	10	10	7	10	0						
Result	D		W		D		W		D		L		W		W		L		W		D							
Points	–		22		8		23		11		4		23		22		4		23		–							

Batting

	v. Hampshire (Harrogate) 18–22 July		v. Somerset (Scarborough) 25–29 July		v. Sussex (Eastbourne) 1–5 August		v. Gloucestershire (Bristol) 15–19 August		v. Lancashire (Leeds) 22–26 August		v. Essex (Leeds) 29 August–2 September		v. Nottinghamshire (Scarborough) 12–16 September		v. Northamptonshire (Northampton) 19–22 September		M	Inns	NO	Runs	HS	Av
C.J. Schofield																	1	1	–	25	25	25.00
M.P. Vaughan	49	61*	8	12	1	6	1	35	57	–	3	10	37	–	183	–	18	32	2	1161	183	38.70
D. Byas	138	–	88	4	5	72*	9	3	45	–	23	4	56	–	21	–	19	32	2	933	138	31.10
C. White	5	–	28	1	47	7	74	20	181	–	76	10	23	–	66	–	19	30	1	949	181	32.72
R.A. Kettleborough							2	7	34	–	28	108	11	–	32	–	7	9	–	307	108	34.11
R.J. Blakey	2	–	21	25	80*	2	38	52*	109*	–	57	44	15	–	33	–	19	30	6	839	109*	34.95
A.C. Morris																	6	9	–	189	60	21.00
D. Gough	0	–	51	47	4	5	3	4	0	–			4	–	18	–	16	25	3	501	121	22.77
G.M. Hamilton											9*	61			0	–	4	5	1	71	61	17.75
I.D. Fisher																	1	1	1	0	0*	–
A.G. Wharf																	4	4	1	121	62	40.33
M.D. Moxon	38	26*	24	7	2	10	1	1	66	–	59	23	42	–	57	–	13	23	3	961	213	48.05
M.G. Bevan	18	–	19	29	24	1											12	22	3	1225	160*	64.47
A. McGrath	137	–	0	0	41	9	0	3	15	–	16	18	63	–	27	–	18	31	2	962	137	33.17
P.J. Hartley	1	–	10	57*	89	4	20	38	1	–	2	20	14	–			16	24	3	476	89	22.66
R.D. Stemp	0*	–	0*	2	5	10	2*	0	–	–	0	1*	4	–	0*	–	18	23	9	252	65	18.00
C.E.W. Silverwood	14	–	15	7	12	0	0	0	1*	–	0	1	0*	–	12	–	16	24	6	198	45*	11.00
B. Parker																	1	1	–	59	59	59.00
M.J. Hoggard																	1	1	–	10	10	10.00
Byes	7			6	1				7		4	7	3		9							
Leg-byes	7	2	1	5	12	3	4	4	5		9	16	6		15							
Wides	1		6	1	1										1							
No-balls	10		21	12	21	4	12	12	8		4	6	32		4							
Total	427	89	292	215	345	133	166	179	529		290	329	310		478							
Wickets	10	0	10	10	10	10	10	10	8		10	10	10		10							
Result	W		L		L		L		D		W		W		D							
Points	24		6		7		4		11		22		23		11							

Fielding Figures

44 – R.J. Blakey (ct 40 / st 4)
32 – D. Byas
14 – C. White
11 – A. McGrath
8 – R.D. Stemp
6 – D. Gough, M.G. Bevan, P.J. Hartley, A.C. Morris and R.A. Kettleborough
5 – C.E.W. Silverwood and M.D. Moxon
4 – M.P. Vaughan
2 – G.M. Hamilton
1 – A.G. Wharf

Bowling

	D. Gough	A.G. Wharf	G.M. Hamilton	I.D. Fisher	C. White	A.C. Morris	M.P. Vaughan	P.J. Hartley	R.D. Stemp	M.G. Bevan	C.E.W. Silverwood	R.A. Kettleborough	Byes	Leg-byes	Wides	No-balls	Total	Wkts
v. Lancashire (Old Trafford)	18–7–37–1	19–10–29–4	15–0–53–1	9–2–29–1	13–3–43–1	5–1–11–1	1–0–2–1						1	7		4	212	10
18–20 April		2.4–0–13–0	3–0–11–1														24	1
v. Glamorgan (Cardiff)	26–5–66–1	18–1–121–1			20–6–44–2		11–3–30–0	26–6–104–3	29–10–68–0	4–0–28–0			13	8	2	8	482	7
2–6 May	14–5–34–2				8.3–2–33–4			10–1–56–1	16–2–71–2				8	14			216	10
v. Derbyshire (Sheffield)	23–2–82–1				13–2–60–1		7–1–38–0	17–3–78–0	15–3–50–0		25.1–5–99–2			5		12	412	4
9–13 May	12–2–51–1				7–2–15–4		8–1–52–0	5–2–17–0	11–1–42–1	3–0–37–0	4–0–26–0		2	6			248	8
v. Durham (Chester-le-Street)	20–3–57–3				5–1–11–0	5–0–28–1		18–2–67–4	4.4–0–27–1		9–3–20–1			5		14	215	10
16–20 May	16–6–36–2				5–1–12–0		1–0–8–0	22–7–32–4	7–2–23–0	6–2–24–0	13.5–3–40–2		1	10		4	186	9A
v. Kent (Canterbury)		13–4–45–0			12.2–3–42–4	8–2–23–1		14–5–46–1	15–5–50–2		17–3–85–2		1	7		22	299	10
23–27 May																		
v. Middlesex (Lord's)	32–7–81–1				25–3–111–3	8–2–30–0		26–9–63–3	21–6–53–0	2–0–10–0	25.4–7–91–3			8		16	447	10
30 May–3 June	12–5–11–0				4–0–14–0			10–0–36–0	25.1–6–68–2		12–1–34–2		5	3		2	171	4
v. Surrey (Middlesbrough)	14–4–37–1						17–3–62–4	3–0–13–0	25.5–11–44–4	1–0–8–0	6–1–30–0			3	1	8	197	10
6–10 June	24–9–36–5						17.3–6–39–2	12–3–34–2	27–7–83–0	9–2–35–0	6–1–34–1			1		10	274	10B
v. Warwickshire (Leeds)	23–5–66–4				18.3–9–31–3			11–1–45–1	23–8–65–1	15–1–47–0	11–3–40–1		1	11		2	306	10
13–17 June	22–4–60–2				4–1–7–0			18–5–51–3	23.4–10–44–2	10–2–36–3	5–2–8–0		13	10		18	229	10
v. Leicestershire (Bradford)	26–5–96–1				26–2–111–1		23–2–88–0	27–4–113–1	43–12–123–2	2–0–15–0	25–4–110–2		10	15		20	681	7
20–24 June																		
v. Worcestershire (Worcester)	29–7–68–1				3–0–25–0		16–4–51–1	19–6–52–1	25–11–59–1	6–1–18–0	23–5–72–5		4	6		16	355	9
27 June–1 July	14–9–27–4						7–1–19–1	2–0–12–0	21–7–32–3	1–0–4–0	13–7–16–2		6	5	1	6	121	10
v. South Africa 'A' (Leeds)		7–3–13–1	15–3–46–2		4–1–22–0	5–1–24–1			25.2–7–69–5				7	4		10	226	10C
3–5 July																		
v. Hampshire (Harrogate)	20.3–8–50–2				10–2–20–1			19–4–66–2	11–4–27–1	9–0–25–0	20–3–62–3		7	9	9	18	266	10
18–22 July	18–5–39–2				8–1–41–0		9–1–33–0	19.5–5–57–5	12–5–21–1	4–0–16–0	11–3–36–1		4	2	3	2	249	10
v. Somerset (Scarborough)	21–3–74–3				13–1–52–0		3–0–7–0	19.4–7–66–3	7–2–24–0	5–0–23–0	21–5–53–4		4	6		30	309	10
25–29 July	25–6–71–2				7–0–44–1			26–3–100–3	11–0–50–1	6.3–0–29–1	20–6–77–2		12	12		14	395	10
v. Sussex (Eastbourne)	15–3–51–1				12–2–50–3			16.5–2–67–6	6–2–14–0		15–2–64–0		4	3	2	16	253	10
1–5 August	19–6–59–3				4–2–11–0			22–4–86–4	9–6–17–0	3–0–14–0	8–0–32–1		2	5		10	226	8
v. Gloucestershire (Bristol)	24–3–72–2				14–0–59–1			20–2–76–2	7–0–27–0		24.5–5–78–5		13	4		18	329	10
15–19 August	2.1–0–7–0										2–0–10–0				1		17	0
v. Lancashire (Leeds)	21.3–6–53–4				5–0–32–1		9–3–45–4	8–1–52–0	26–10–85–2		8–1–33–1		4	19		26	323	10
22–26 August	19–3–48–4				5–2–14–0		10–1–37–1	15–5–40–1	14–3–50–0		13–4–37–1		4	1		14	231	7
v. Essex (Leeds)			19.4–1–65–3		15–0–45–3		8–0–56–1	19–2–73–1	13–1–60–1		12–1–60–1		8	5		14	372	10
29 August–2 September			6–0–14–0		9–0–33–1		8–1–14–2	8–1–20–1	24–7–38–5		5–0–17–0		9	4		8	149	10
v. Nottinghamshire (Scarborough)	11.5–3–26–3							17–3–65–2	1–0–4–0		13–1–55–3	10–1–26–2	3	8		12	187	10
12–16 September	16.3–4–36–6				6–1–15–2			9–3–15–0	16–5–23–2		7–1–14–0		4	10		8	117	10
v. Northamptonshire (Northampton)	22–5–62–3		17–4–33–1		3–2–1–1				16.2–3–49–3		17–1–61–2		9	7		24	222	10
19–22 September	13–2–42–2		26–4–82–0		20–2–102–0		32–1–147–2		25–7–51–0		12–1–48–0	2–0–14–0	5	11		33	531	4D
Bowler's average	573.3–142– 1535–67 22.91	59.4–18– 221–6 36.83	101.4–12– 304–8 38.00	9–2– 29–1 29.00	299.2–51– 1100–37 29.72	31–6– 116–4 29.00	187.3–28– 728–17 42.82	459.2–96– 1602–54 29.66	556–163– 1511–42 35.97	86.3–8– 369–4 92.25	404.3–79– 1442–47 30.68	12–1– 40–2 20.00						

A J.A. Daley retired hurt
B A. McGrath 1–0–12–0
C M.J. Hoggard 15–3–41–1
D A. McGrath 6–0–29–0